PATENT LAW AND POLICY

CONTEMPORARY
LEGAL EDUCATION SERIES

Patent Law and Policy

CASES AND MATERIALS

Second Edition

ROBERT PATRICK MERGES
Professor of Law
University of California at Berkeley

MICHIE
Law Publishers
CHARLOTTESVILLE, VIRGINIA

1230511

For Jo and Robbie

Remember these our favorite times ...

Preface to the Second Edition

I waited as long as I could to prepare a second edition of this casebook. Patent law, it seemed to me, was in the midst of sweeping changes; I wanted to ride out the storm, if possible, and then survey the new landscape.

In many ways this was the right decision. Many changes, large and small, have worked their way through patent law in recent years. Thus the book takes into full account the major overhaul to the priority system brought on by the GATT amendments of 1994. Likewise, the recent cases on software patents are canvassed and assessed, as are the many other changes in the law since the first edition in 1992.

One thing I have not changed about the book is the extensive notes and analysis interspersed throughout the text. I have retained these for two reasons. First, the book has turned out, somewhat surprisingly, to be of use not only to law students, but also to other scholars interested in learning about the patent system. Thus for a graduate student in economics, for example, a note on § 102 and search theory may prove very helpful in establishing a conceptual grounding for the subject. In some cases, notes such as these connect the doctrines of patent law to theoretical concepts tightly enough to spur some new theoretical thinking. This has been one of the most gratifying applications of the ideas in this book.

The second reason I have kept the detailed analytical sections is more selfish: These are the sections I enjoy writing the most. One motivation for the first edition was to use it as a vehicle for presenting brief and, it is hoped, provocative scholarly perspectives on the doctrines. Many readers have found these interesting. For those who have not, I can only hope that the case selection, description of inventions, and other doctrinal exegesis prove satisfactory. Note that the electronic media version of the casebook, offered in the Lexis-Nexis Electronic Authors Program (LEAP), enhances these features considerably by providing "hyperlinks" to copies of all important patents at issue in the cases.

Anyone who teaches knows that the minds of a steady stream of students provide a constant source of new angles, new ideas, and new objections to all that is conventional. If there is any "value added" in the new edition, it is largely the reflected wisdom of those students — first at Boston University and now at Berkeley — who have engaged and tested the material in this book during the past four years. In addition, my colleagues on both coasts have helped me immensely.

Even on the home front, things have changed since the first edition. Not even a Harvard dissertation committee could keep my wife from finishing graduate school and beginning her own teaching career. And the little baby whose cries sent me rushing from the manuscript of the first edition keeps me rushing still — up the mountain, for example, on hikes in the Sierras. Indeed, I sometimes

vii

think that my family and patent law have a great deal in common: I am always struggling to keep up with them both. Fortunately for me, the effort is pure joy.

ROBERT PATRICK MERGES
Berkeley, California
October, 1996

Preface to the First Edition

My goals in writing this book were: (1) to open up patent law, in all its intriguing detail, to a wider audience of law students and teachers; (2) to stimulate discussion of the vital policy issues lying beneath the surface of many patent doctrines; and (3) to highlight decisions of the Court of Appeals for the Federal Circuit, the court that since its inception in 1982 has revolutionized and revitalized patent law.

In pursuing these goals, I have applied a few simple lessons learned while teaching patent law. First, choose cases involving simple inventions, and explain the inventions as thoroughly and clearly as possible. I have found that it is easy for students to get lost in the details of the invention — either because they don't understand it, or because they do and are interested in exactly how it works. Either way, the overall *legal* point of the case is often lost. In writing this book, I have labored to find cases concerning straightforward inventions, and to provide descriptions and drawings that will allow anyone with a modicum of interest to get the gist of the invention and get on to what is important — the legal point. To further this goal I have edited the cases significantly, often without indicating omissions.

The second lesson I have tried to apply is not to fight the material. When learning most subjects, it is advisable to "start with the basics" and build your way up. While I have tried to keep to that principle, several features of patent law make it impossible to follow that approach strictly. Most significantly, patent law, even more than most legal subjects, is a densely intertwined whole. It can be very difficult to separate one doctrine or issue from the whole and discuss it in isolation; in many cases, other issues intrude, and it becomes clear that a thorough understanding of Topic *A* simply demands some discussion of Topics *B* and *C*.* In a book whose design is necessarily linear, this requires some repetition, some "previewing" of later material, and a good deal of cross-referencing. I have used all three techniques liberally.

A further word about case selection is in order. Although, in general, inventive simplicity and legal clarity have been my guides, some inventions are too

---

*I have found that in this respect the intricate structure of patent law is reminiscent of a ditty by Swift, in *On Poetry* (1733), at 1.337:

> So naturalists observe, a flea
> Hath smaller fleas that on him prey;
> And these have smaller fleas to bite 'em,
> And so proceed *ad infinitum*.

I have tried to keep the fleas discussed in this book from becoming too small, on the theory that students and other readers can only take so many bites.

important to be left out. After all, patent law is ultimately about momentous inventions and their economic impact (an impact that surpasses, I can't help noting, most kings, many wars, and most Supreme Court decisions). So you will find here cases on some of the significant inventions that have found their way into the patent system: the light bulb, the train brake, the semiconductor, the laser, and the products of recombinant gene technology, among others. If my book communicates some of the grandeur of these creations, even indirectly, I would consider that an extra reward for having written it.

But, of course, I would not have written it at all if not for the help of my colleagues and research assistants. Among the latter I must thank Evan Ackiron, Beth Boyer, Rob Cobert, Joe Kirk, Janine McGrath, Tony Pelligrini, Brent Sokol, John Stout, and Valerie Weiner (who drew many of the illustrations in the book on her trusty Apple computer). My colleagues at Boston University, a group which includes our Dean, Ron Cass, deserve kudos for general support. Among others, Hal Wegner of Washington, D.C. stands out. Finally, although the contributions of my friends are in general too subtle and numerous to mention, I must thank one person — my wife Jo.

ROBERT PATRICK MERGES
South Natick, Mass.
April, 1992

Summary Table of Contents

Table of Contents

Chapter 1

INTRODUCTION

This chapter has two goals: to situate the law of patents in its legal and historical landscape, and to introduce matters at the heart of the patent system — inventions and the drafting of patent claims. Claims and related topics are so important that they are best introduced by means of several simple examples. Experience has shown that only when one understands what a patent *is* can one properly begin to assimilate the principles, doctrines and rules that comprise the body of patent law. But even longer experience suggests that it is helpful to get a grip on where patent law came from before delving into the joys of drafting claims to protect particular inventions. And so we begin at the beginning, with an historical overview.

A. HISTORICAL OVERVIEW OF PATENT LAW

This brief introductory essay surveys the beginnings of patent law. While its purpose is primarily to set patents in their proper historical perspective, it is also intended to trace the development of the conceptual origins of patents, that is, to explore where the *idea* of a patent system came from and how it has evolved.

The first recorded reference to patents seems to be in Aristotle's *Politics*, composed in the fourth century B.C. In the course of a discussion of rival descriptions of a good constitution, Aristotle mentions a proposal by one Hippodamus. According to Aristotle, Hippodamus of Miletos calls for a system of rewards to those who discover things useful to the state. Aristotle condemns this proposal in the following passage:

> Concerning the matter of those who discover something advantageous for the city, to legislate that they receive some honor is not safe, though it sounds appealing; it would involve harassments and, it might well happen, changes of regime.[1]

---

[1] ARISTOTLE, POLITICS, Book II, Chap. 8, lines 23-26, at 72 (C. Lord trans., University of Chicago Press 1984) (footnote omitted). The translator mentions in a footnote that by harassment (sykophantia) Aristotle meant blackmail, and that he was concerned that citizens might pretend to "discover" various types of malfeasance on the part of officials and prominent public figures. *Id.*, at 250 n.56. Other translators translate sykophantia as encouragement to inform (B. Jowett trans., Modern Library Edition, at 105) or sedition (Personal Letter from Professor James Doull, Classics Department, Dalhousie University). A third century A.D. reference to protective grants covering novel recipes by the luxury-loving Sybarites of the sixth century B.C. is said to be "apocryphal." *See* B. BUGBEE, THE GENESIS OF AMERICAN PATENT AND COPYRIGHT LAW 166 n.5 (1967). For speculation on the Roman origins of intellectual property, see Vukmir, *The Roots of Anglo-*

Aristotle here shows a concern for the general tenor of Hippodamus' proposal, which appears to encourage innovations in all fields, for example law. In the section of the *Politics* that refers to Hippodamus, Aristotle asserts that unlike "the other sciences," law should not change too quickly. This is because too rapid change will weaken the habit of obedience to law that is so valuable to a state.[2]

Hippodamus' proposal introduces several themes that characterize patent laws right down to the present day. First is the obvious fact that Hippodamus was himself a technically trained person: he was an architect of some renown. Quite clearly this training gave him what might be called a "problem-solving" outlook on all issues, including the design of the optimal state, or utopia. This mode of thinking has been very significant in the development of patent law; this field of law bears the distinct imprint of the background of those who have shaped it. It is thus only appropriate that the very *idea* of a patent law came from a person who worked in a technical field.

The belief in innovation that made Hippodamus a celebrated architect led him to propose a legal instrument to encourage innovation. And this proposal contains the seeds of a practical utilitarianism: honor the creator of a useful thing, and society will get more useful things. This proposal, this mode of thought, is the core of all patent systems, ancient as well as modern.

Another important theme in the history of patents is anticipated in Aristotle's response as well. Aristotle's main point is that rewards to *individuals* can cause problems for the state; in honoring one who discovers something new, the state may actually weaken itself. Why might this be so? The answer, for Aristotle, would likely center around the notion of the good. If citizens seek only individual honors, rather than the health of the community, then the community might suffer; this is true even in cases where Hippodamus' proposal leads to real, not spurious, discoveries. Apparently one threat Aristotle sees is the danger of introducing the notion of "utility" into judgments about what is desirable. For if any citizen can propose a legal innovation that is "useful to the state," this might imply that the current legal regime is less useful, or even illegitimate; thus the idea that encouraging new proposals might weaken the state. The better state, according to Aristotle, is one where citizens obey the law not because it is in their interest, but because it is good to do so.

What is important here is the juxtaposition of individual interest and the good of the community. These opposing forces have often exerted a strong pull on the development of patent law. What is interesting about Aristotle's comments is that they foreshadow the essential tension — it might even be called a paradox — inherent in a system where *social* benefits via technological progress are achieved by means of *private* rewards. One need only think of a number of contemporary

---

American Intellectual Property Law in Roman Law, 32 IDEA 123 (1992).

[2] ARISTOTLE, POLITICS, *supra* note 1, at 73.

With the accession of James I in England in the early seventeenth century, [pat]ents became less an incentive for the introduction of new arts and more a royal [fav]or to be dispensed to well-placed courtiers. Under this rubric, "patents" were [gra]nted on such enterprises as running ale-houses. Parliament, whose members [rep]resented many trades injured by these special privileges, was displeased. Thus [aro]se the Statute of Monopolies of 1623, which forbade all grants of exclusive [pri]vileges except those described in the famous Section 6:

> [B]e it declared and enacted that any declaration before mentioned shall not extend to any letters patent and grants of privilege for the term of fourteen years or under, hereafter to be made, of the sole working or making of any manner of new manufactures within this realm, to the true and first inventor and inventors of such manufacture, which others at the time of making such letters patent shall not use, so as also they be not contrary to law, nor mischievous to the State, by raising prices of commodities at home, or hurt of trade, or generally inconvenient; the said fourteen years to be accounted from the date of the first letters patents, or grant of such privilege hereafter to be made ....[14]

This statute called on the common law courts to review all privileges granted [by] the crown and outlawed all but those based on true inventions.[15]

Even with the Statute of Monopolies in effect, the British patent system [rem]ained a largely informal administrative apparatus. After the vicissitudes of the [Ci]vil War period, during which the Cromwell government "called in" all extant [pat]ents and privileges, the *status quo ante* was for the most part restored. [Inf]luence in the royal court was still helpful until the latter part of the eighteenth [cen]tury. Patent applications were registered rather than examined. And, most [tell]ingly, very few patents were granted.

But as the Industrial Revolution picked up steam (so to speak), attention began [to] focus on patents once again. An important change at this time was the increas[ing]ly stringent requirement that the applicant for a patent describe his or her [inv]ention clearly and completely, a development most often associated with the [17]78 opinion of the well-respected Judge Mansfield in *Liardet v. Johnson*.[16] The

---

[...]en people could simply memorize the necessary information).

[1]4 Great Britain, Statutes at Large, 21 Jam. 1, ch. 3, § 6 (1623). *See generally* E. Wyndham [Hul]me, *The History of the Patent System Under the Prerogative and at Common Law*, 12 L.Q.R. [...]1 (1896).

[1]5 C. MacLeod, *supra* note 10, at 15. *See also* Douglass C. North & Robert Paul Thomas, [Th]e Rise of the Western World: A New Economic History 152-55 (1973) (arguing that [pat]ent system evidenced well-functioning economic institutions, and paved the way for other "[gro]wth" property rights in Great Britain).

[1]6 *See* Adams & Averly, *The Patent Specification: The Role of* Liardet v. Johnson, 7 J. Leg. [His]t. 156 (1986) (arguing in opposition to earlier writers that *Liardet* represented the culmination [of] eighteenth century trends rather than a sharp break with past practice). For much detail on the

---

debates involving patents, such as the pricing of patented pharmaceuticals, for instance, to realize how strong this tension remains today.

After this isolated classical reference, the history of patents skips over several historical epochs. Although in recent years scholars have begun to revise the orthodox view of the Middle Ages as a period devoid of innovation, this era does not appear to have been conducive to the idea of patents, at least in the West.[3] Perhaps this is because of the prevalence of rigid social hierarchies, which discouraged the recognition of an individual inventor's genius.[4] Perhaps it is because recent historians are wrong, and not much in the way of innovation was occurring. Whatever the reason, one must skip ahead to the early Renaissance to find the first references to a real patent system.

Historians recognize the key intellectual change of the Renaissance as the renewed emphasis on the individual. It is no surprise that in this environment patent systems — with their recognition of discrete inventions attributable to identifiable individuals — began to appear and flourish.

The first regular administrative apparatus for granting patents — the first real patent "system" — arose in Venice in the late fifteenth century. Isolated grants in Venice and elsewhere were made earlier: in Venice in the early fourteenth

---

[3] One historian, however, claims that the modern patent system has its origins in the Byzantine Empire:

> It is likely that the modern monopoly originated in Byzantium, and became the invention patent at the Renaissance when numbers of inventions appeared. A traveller of the twelfth century, Benjamin of Tudela, mentions an exclusive privilege for dyeing cloth in the semi-Byzantine kingdom of Jerusalem.

Frumkin, *Early History of Patents for Invention*, 26 Trans. Newcomen Soc. 47 (1947). Frumkin notes several other isolated instances of protective grants: in Bordeaux, in 1236, a fifteen year monopoly for the manufacture of cloth; and in 1331, by King Edward III of Great Britain, a nonexclusive grant to export woollen cloth. *Id.*, at 48. This is not to say that there were no technical achievements to admire during this period, especially in the Arabic world. *See* D. Hill, A History of Engineering in Classical and Medieval Times 2, 5 (1984).

[4] The uneasy relationship between the craft guilds and early Renaissance patents suggests that the guilds, either directly or indirectly, may have had a hand in the suppression of innovation, if not patents themselves. *See* C. MacLeod, Inventing the Industrial Revolution: The English Patent System, 1660-1800, at 13 (1989) (describing successful efforts by cutler's guild to block issuance of a patent for a new knife handle design). There is some evidence that early exclusive privileges were granted in various German principalities. *See* Pohlmann, *The Inventor's Right in Early German Law: Materials of the Time from 1531-1700*, 43 J. Pat. Off. Soc'y 121, 122 (1961) ("proto-patents were issued as early as 1378"). Some have gone so far as to argue that exclusive grants to German mining operations were the first quasi-patents, *see* E. Kaufer, The Economics of the Patent System at 2 (1989), but Venice is still the consensus choice as the cradle of patent law. Nevertheless, beginning in 1484, patents began to issue in Germany as well. *See* Edward C. Walterscheid, *The Early Evolution of the United States Patent Law: Antecedents (Part 1)*, 76 J. Pat. & Trademark Off. Soc'y 697, 711 (1994). France was not far behind, issuing patents beginning in 1551. *Id.*, at 711. *Cf.* L. Hilaire-Perez, *Invention and the State in 18th-Century France*, 32 Tech. & Cult. 911 (1991).

century, for corn mill designs, and in Florence to the celebrated architect Brunelleschi, for his invention in 1421 of a barge with hoist for transporting marble.[5] The term patent — from the Latin *patere* (to be open) and referring to an open letter of privilege from the sovereign — originated in this period.[6] But not until the Venetian Senate's 1474 Act was the practice of granting patents regularized:

> Be it enacted that, by the authority of this Council, every person who shall build any new and ingenious device in this City, not previously made in this Commonwealth, shall give notice of it to the office of our General Welfare Board when it has been reduced to perfection so that it can be used and operated. It being forbidden to every other person in any of our territories and towns to make any further device conforming with and similar to said one, without the consent and license of the author, for the term of 10 years. And if anybody builds it in violation hereof, the aforesaid author and inventor shall be entitled to have him summoned before any Magistrate of this City, by which Magistrate the said infringer shall be constrained to pay him one hundred ducats; and the device shall be destroyed at once.[7]

The Venetian Act lays out all the essential features of a modern patent statute. It covers "devices"; states that they must be registered with a specific administrative agency; says that they must be "new and useful," "reduced to perfection," and "not previously made in this Commonwealth"; provides a fixed term of ten years; and sets forth a procedure to determine infringement, as well as a remedy. Interestingly, the Venetian Act reserved to the Republic the right to use any invention without compensating the inventor.[8] This is an early attempt to reconcile individual interest with the good of the community, a problem identified in Aristotle's critique of Hippodamus' proposal. It implies that the inventor's protection, provided by the grace of the state, ought naturally to be subject to the needs of the state.

The opening of trade in Europe insured that the new Venetian co spread. As Italian craftsmen — particularly glass workers — fanne Europe, they brought with them the idea of legal protection for invent according to one scholar of the British patent system,

> [S]ix of the first nine patents in the Archives of Brussels, for ex: issued to Italians. It is no coincidence that the first recorde several countries at this time were for glassmaking, a skill i Venetians excelled. German merchants trading with Venice a with the idea, and the petty German states were among the fir: to grant patents.[10]

Patents came to Great Britain by this route, sometime in the m sixteenth century. The chief minister under Elizabeth I, William Burghley), used patent grants as an inducement for foreign artisans continental technologies into England. Thus, what later became American patent system was ushered in as a mercantilist instrument – would be called a "strategic international trade" policy. The idea emigrants with desirable skills and know-how with the promise of privilege. Faint glimmers of this early policy survive in certain od today's patent laws, mostly by way of favorable treatment for domes activities.[11] Note that this policy reflects another attempt to balance the community against the individual interests of inventors. By l artisans with the reward of exclusive rights, it was thought, the gained the fruits of this skilled labor.[12] Ironically, by the mid-eightee Britain began to show a concern with the reverse problem — le technical prowess to its overseas rivals, including the American co

---

[5] *See* Frumkin, *Early History of Patents for Invention*, 26 TRANS. NEWCOMEN SOC. 47 (1947); Prager, *A History of Intellectual Property from 1545 to 1787*, 26 J. PAT. & TRADEMARK OFF. SOC'Y 714 (1944). On Brunelleschi, see L. SPRAGUE DE KAMP, THE ANCIENT ENGINEERS (1963).

[6] *Cf.* WILLIAM BLACKSTONE, 2 COMMENTARIES ON THE LAWS OF ENGLAND *316-17 (1768):

> The king's grants are also matter[s] of public record.... These grants, whether of lands, honors, liberties, franchises, or aught besides, are contained in charters, or letters patent, that is, open letters, literae patentes: so called, because they are not sealed up, but exposed to open view, with the great seal pendant at the bottom; and are usually directed or addressed by the king to all his subjects at large.

[7] Mandich, *Venetian Patents (1450-1550)*, 30 J. PAT. OFF. SOC'Y 166, 177 (1948). For a very thorough review of the literature on early patents, see Edward C. Walterscheid, *The Early Evolution of the United States Patent Law: Antecedents (Part 1)*, 76 J. PAT. & TRADEMARK OFF. SOC'Y 697 (1994).

[8] *Id.*

---

[9] J. Phillips, *The English Patent as a Reward for Invention: The Importation o* LEG. HIST. 71, 75 (1982).

[10] C. MACLEOD, INVENTING THE INDUSTRIAL REVOLUTION: THE ENG SYSTEM, 1660-1800, at 11 (1989). On glassmaking, see E. GODFREY, THE DEV ENGLISH GLASSMAKING 1560-1640 (1975). *See also* the works of E. Wyndhan which are cited in Edward C. Walterscheid, *The Early Evolution of the United Sta Antecedents (Part 2)*, 76 J. PAT. & TRADEMARK OFF. SOC'Y 849, 849 (1994), e. *History of the Patent System Under the Prerogative and at Common Law*, 12 L.Q.

[11] *See* Chisum, *Foreign Activity: Its Effect on Patentability Under United States* REV. OF IND. PROP. & COPYRIGHT L. 26 (1980). *See* Chapter 4, Section K.4, *Ove and U.S. Interferences: Section 104 of the Act.*

[12] Thus the first patents were described as "passports" which allowed their holder freely and practice their trade. W. HAMILTON, THE POLITICS OF INDUSTRY 68 (1!

[13] *See, e.g.*, D. Jeremy, Penetrating British Barriers to Technology Transfer in t trial Period, 1790s-1840s: Some Recent Research, Paper presented at the Society of Technology, Annual Meeting, Sacramento, Cal., Oct. 1989, at 6 (describing immigrants in transfer of technology to the colonies, and the ineffectiveness of export laws due to the fact that it was not necessary to transfer physical embodiment

importance of the specification requirement is that it reflected a changed perception about what the inventor was contributing to society in exchange for the patent grant. Under the original patent systems, society's benefit was the introduction of a new art or technology into the country. By the late eighteenth century, the primary benefit was seen as the technological know-how behind the inventor's patent. The beneficiaries on this view were not just the public at large, but instead others skilled in the technical arts who could learn something from the patentee's invention. This was a major change in the economic role of patents, for it shifted the emphasis from the introduction of finished products into commerce to the introduction of new and useful *information* to the technical arts. While it is difficult to speculate on the significance of this transition, it does seem to address a complaint voiced by Lord Burghley over the original patent system — its dismal success rate in introducing new industries to the country. Perhaps, paradoxically, the emphasis on technical specifications, while recognizing that not every invention will lead to a new industry, may have more efficiently fostered the growth of industry as a whole by ensuring that up-to-date technical information was disseminated rapidly after its creation.

Although the overall contribution of the patent system to the Industrial Revolution has been a matter of debate in historical circles, it seems no coincidence that the patent system matured alongside the early industrial technologies. One historian, H.I. Dutton, noted that the British patent system of this period was less than water-tight from the inventor's point of view. But Dutton argues that this actually redounded to the benefit of the economy as a whole since "leaks" in the grant to one inventor benefitted other inventors.[17]

---

context of the *Liardet* case, see Edward C. Walterscheid, *The Early Evolution of the United States Patent Law: Antecedents (Part 3)*, 77 J. PAT. & TRADEMARK OFF. SOC'Y 771 (1995).

[17] In his thorough review of the role of the patent system in the "first" Industrial Revolution in Great Britain, *The Patent System and Inventive Activity During the Industrial Revolution, 1750-1852* (1984), Dutton concludes that the system was instrumental in fostering almost all of the key technologies of the era. In addition, in chapters on "Trade in Invention" and "Investment in Patents," he documents the historical connections between patents and the financing of invention, thus illustrating that the early patent system did not reward innovation directly but instead played much the same role it does today, i.e., fostering *invention* (creation of new technology) and thus indirectly encouraging innovation (introduction of new products embodying that technology on the market). H. DUTTON, *supra*, at 103-48. And in his conclusion Dutton argues that the patent system's inefficiencies actually made it close to an ideal system since it encouraged invention but did not protect new technology too much from those who would try to improve it. *Id.* at 204-05. *See also* MacLeod, *Accident or Design? George Ravenscroft's Patent and the Invention of Lead-Crystal Glass*, 28 TECH. & CULTURE 776-80 (1987) (describing the long time-lag between the invention of lead crystal glass and introduction of the final product with "bugs" all worked out); Scherer, *Invention and Innovation in the Watt-Boulton Steam-Engine Venture*, 6 TECH. & CULTURE 184 (1965) (role of the patent system in Watt's seminal steam engine invention). *But cf.* J. Mokyr, *The Industrial Revolution and the New Economic History*, in THE ECONOMICS OF THE INDUSTRIAL REVOLUTION 1, 28 (J. Mokyr ed., 1989) (arguing that "[p]roperty rights in new techniques were protected, albeit imperfectly by British patent law," yet "[t]he cumulative effect of small improve-

Patents were among the many British legal concepts introduced to the American colonies between 1640 and 1776. State patents were granted in most of the original thirteen colonies, beginning with a Massachusetts patent in 1641.[18] Even after the Revolution, during the Articles of Confederation, the new states continued to issue patents.

Perhaps inevitably, however, conflicts began to arise between the states — most notably over steamboat patents, which were issued to two different inventors during this period. This led to a great deal of confusion over who was actually the inventor of the steamboat creating an obstacle to the successful operation of interstate steam lines.[19] With this problem (among others) in mind, the Constitutional Convention of 1789 resolved to create a national patent system rooted in the Constitution itself,[20] thus the famous provision of Article I, Section 8, authorizing Congress to reward exclusive rights for a limited time to authors and inventors "for their respective writings and discoveries." One historical footnote is worth mentioning in this connection: an early draft of this provision, set out in James Madison's notes to the Convention, called for both exclusive rights *and* outright subsidies for new inventions. But, reflecting the somewhat "minimalist" view of government involvement in the economy enshrined in the Constitution, this was rejected in favor of exclusive rights only.[21] In any event, the first U.S.

---

ments made by mostly anonymous workers and technicians was often more important than most of the great inventions.").

[18] *See* V. CLARK, HISTORY OF MANUFACTURES IN THE UNITED STATES I: 1607-1860, at 50 (1929). *See generally* B. BUGBEE, THE GENESIS OF AMERICAN PATENT AND COPYRIGHT LAW 57-103 (1967) (good description of colonial patent scene).

[19] *See* J. FLEXNER, INVENTORS IN ACTION: THE STORY OF THE STEAMBOAT 133, 172, 175 (1962).

[20] The expressly national patent law was one of several *national* solutions to interstate conflicts envisioned by the Constitution, most famously the Commerce Clause. For a description of the economic dislocations caused by interstate rivalries prior to the Constitution, see R. MORRIS, THE FORGING OF THE UNION 1781-1789, at 148-52 (1987). *Cf.* Edward C. Walterscheid, *To Promote the Progress of Science and the Useful Arts: The Background and Origin of the Intellectual Property Clause of the United States Constitution*, 2 J. INTELL. PROP. L. 1 (1994).

[21] B. BUGBEE, THE GENESIS OF THE AMERICAN PATENT AND COPYRIGHT LAW 126, 143 (1967) (describing Madison and Pinckney proposals, both of which included some form of subsidies; and noting that the Senate proposed a compulsory licensing provision in the first Patent Act of 1790, modelled on similar provisions in state copyright acts, but it was rejected by the House). At least one contemporary of the Framers saw things the same way; Adam Smith argued that

> Some [monopolies] are harmless enough. Thus the inventor of a new machine or any other invention for the space of 14 yrs by the law of this country, as a reward for his ingenuity, and it is probable that this is an equal an one as could be fallen upon. For if the legislature should appoint pecuniary rewards for the inventors of new machines, etc., they would hardly ever be so precisely proportioned to the merit of the invention as this is. For here, if the invention be good and such as is profitable to mankind, he will probably make a fortune by it; but if it be of no value he will also reap no benefit.

ADAM SMITH, LECTURES ON JURISPRUDENCE 83 (Liberty Classics ed. 1978).

patent statute was passed in May, 1790,[22] the very early days of the first Congress (reflecting the importance of this matter), and the first patent was issued shortly thereafter — to Samuel Hopkins of Pittsford, Vermont, for a process for making potash from wood ashes.[23]

The story of Thomas Jefferson's involvement in the early national patent system has often been told. He was chiefly responsible for implementing the first Patent Act (1790) in his role as Secretary of State, and his views on the subject — expressed in a series of letters — have proven influential, especially in the Supreme Court.[24] But while the patent system got on its feet under Jefferson,[25]

---

[22] Patent Act of 1790, Ch. 7, 1 Stat. 109-12 (Apr. 10, 1790).

[23] Paynter, *The First U.S. Patent*, AM. HERITAGE OF INVENTION AND TECH., Fall 1990, at 18. Although historians such as Paynter uniformly identify Hopkins' home state as Vermont, I am informed in a letter from Judge Alan Lourie of the Federal Circuit that Hopkins' patent lists a Philadelphia address. At least until Judge Lourie's opinion in the matter is overruled, Hopkins is from Philadelphia.

Hopkins was not the only early inventor to avail himself of the new Patent Act; evidently, the 1790 statute took hold quite rapidly. *See* Kenneth L. Sokoloff, *Inventive Activity in Early Industrial America: Evidence From Patent Records, 1790-1846*, 48 J. ECON. HIST. 813, 846 (1988) ("early industrialization [in the U.S.] was characterized by a dramatic upswing in inventive activity").

[24] *See* Edward C. Walterscheid, *Patents and the Jeffersonian Mythology*, 29 J. MARSHALL L. REV. 269 (1995).

[25] Earlier histories giving Jefferson credit for almost single-handedly drafting the Patent Acts of 1790 and 1793 have been discredited by recent historical work. *See* Walterscheid, *Patents and the Jeffersonian Mythology*, *supra*. Indeed, Jefferson's antipathy toward government-created monopolies, and his general distaste for centralized economic power, would seem to make him an unlikely candidate for the role of intellectual godfather to the patent system. Why then are courts, commentators, and even inventors themselves so drawn to the image of Jefferson? Several reasons might be given, including that the award of discrete property rights to individual inventors spread throughout the country is consistent with certain Jeffersonian themes. Nevertheless, the true explanation may lie on the level of collective mythology: the historical Jefferson embodies those values that the patent system, at its best, seeks to reward and encourage, particularly intellectual curiosity and independence. Besides, who wouldn't claim as their own someone who can write like this:

> It has been pretended by some, (and in England especially,) that inventors have a natural and exclusive right to their inventions, and not merely for their own lives, but inheritable to their heirs. But while it is a moot question whether the origin of any kind of property is derived from nature at all, it would be singular to admit a natural and even an hereditary right to inventors. It is agreed by those who have seriously considered the subject, that no individual has, of natural right, a separate property in an acre of land, for instance. By a universal law, indeed, whatever, whether fixed or movable, belongs to all men equally and in common, is the property for the moment of him who occupies it, but when he relinquishes the occupation, the property goes with it. Stable ownership is the gift of social law, and is given late in the progress of society. It would be curious then, if an idea, the fugitive fermentation of an individual brain, could, of natural right, be claimed in exclusive and stable property. If nature has made any one thing less susceptible than all others of exclusive property, it is the action of the thinking power called an idea, which an individual may exclusively possess as long as he keeps it to himself; but the moment it is divulged, it forces

it did not grow to its full stature until the 1836 revision, when a formal system of examination, with professional examiners, was substituted for the pro forma registration system of the 1793 Act, a system which had itself been substituted for the original (1790) procedure under which patentability was determined by three high-level government officials (including Jefferson as Secretary of State).[26]

Since 1836 the patent system has grown dramatically by any standard — number of patents issued, number of cases litigated, number of significant inventions patented, etc. As greater demands were placed on it, the patent system developed new rules. For example, the requirement that an invention be more than novel, that it reveal true "invention" — what is now called nonobviousness — developed in the mid-nineteenth century to limit the number of patents that were being issued.[27] Late in the nineteenth century, the bureaucratic structure of the Patent Office as we know it began to take shape as well.[28]

In Europe, the nineteenth century was a time when a new generation of analytical economists questioned the economic foundations of the patent system.[29]

---

itself into the possession of every one, and the receiver cannot dispossess himself of it. Its peculiar character, too, is that no one possesses the less, because every other possesses the whole of it. He who receives an idea from me, receives instruction himself without lessening mine; as he who lights his taper at mine, receives light without darkening me. That ideas should freely spread from one to another over the globe, for the moral and mutual instruction of man, and improvement of his condition, seems to have been peculiarly and benevolently designed by nature, when she made them, like fire, expansible over all space, without lessening their density in any point, and like the air in which we breathe, move, and have our physical being, incapable of confinement or exclusive appropriation. Inventions then cannot, in nature, be a subject of property. Society may give an exclusive right to the profits arising from them, as an encouragement to men to pursue ideas which may produce utility, but this may or may not be done, according to the will and convenience of society, without claim or complaint from anybody.

Letter to Isaac McPherson (Aug. 13, 1813), reprinted in 13 THE WRITINGS OF THOMAS JEFFERSON (Andrew A. Lipscomb et al. eds., 1903), at 333-34.

[26] There is some evidence that the early patent acts were a significant stimulus to invention in the new nation. *See, e.g.*, Folsom & Lubar, *Introduction*, in THE PHILOSOPHY OF MANUFACTURES at xxvii-xxviii (M. Folsom & S. Lubar eds., 1982) ("Given the fact that the primary inducement and reward for industrial development was money, new industrial interests exerted pressure to establish safeguards for the investment of time and capital in technological innovation. The first great American industrial corporation, the Boston Manufacturing Company, made a significant early profit selling other textile companies rights to the machine patents it held."). A patent bar was quick to form to help inventors deal with the new act. The first patent treatise, by the eminent Fessenden, appeared in Boston very early in the nineteenth century. *See* I.G. FESSENDEN, AN ESSAY ON THE LAW OF PATENTS FOR INVENTIONS (1st ed. 1810).

[27] *See* Kitch, Graham v. John Deere: *New Standards for Patents*, 1966 SUP. CT. REV. 293 (1966).

[28] *See* D. NOBLE, AMERICA BY DESIGN (1977); Lubar, *The Transformation of Antebellum Patent Law*, 32 TECH. & CULT. 932 (1991).

[29] *See* Machlup & Penrose, *The Patent Controversy in The Nineteenth Century*, 10 J. ECON. HIST. 1 (1950); F. Machlup, *Patents*, in 2 INT'L ENCYCLOPEDIA OF THE SOCIAL SCIENCES 461 (1968).

Indeed, Switzerland and the Netherlands had no patent systems for more than fifty years during this period.[30]

Despite the period of transition and questioning, the patent system was a well-accepted feature of the economic landscape by the beginning of the twentieth century. Key patents on the light bulb, the basic design of the automobile, and the first airplanes symbolized the technical virtuosity and dynamism of the age. As the scale of industry grew, research and development departments began to appear in the large firms.[31] Patents were not only a valuable output of these departments, they helped measure their productivity and served to justify their importance.

Unfortunately for the patent system, the identification of patents with big business meant that when big business lost favor, so too would patents. This is precisely what happened in the trust-busting era of the 1920s and '30s. The growth of the antitrust movement led to an increasing focus on patents, which were viewed as important weapons in the suffocating arsenal of big business. The exclusive nature of the patent grant, coupled with the actual market power that some patents conferred on their holders, seemed closely related to many of the monopolists' oppressive practices. Expert consultants to Congress criticized the role of patents and called for radical reforms such as the compulsory licensing of all patents to anyone who wanted to use them. The central idea behind the anti-patent movement was that the rights of powerful corporations had come to dominate the interests of the community. The tension at the heart of patent law, identified since the time of Aristotle, had become too great.[32]

Perhaps predictably, the attacks on the patent system ended when the attack on Pearl Harbor began. As the nation threw all available resources at the war effort, the armed forces called on engineers and scientists to perfect a vast array of new technologies in short order. Even independent inventors were invited to submit ideas. By the time the war was over, many of the most strident anti-patent voices in Congress were silenced. In fact, the 1952 Patent Act, the first major revision

---

[30] E. SCHIFF, INDUSTRIALIZATION WITHOUT NATIONAL PATENTS: THE NETHERLANDS 1869-1912; SWITZERLAND 1850-1907 (1971). Schiff's book is rather inconclusive on the effect of this non-patent era on the economic development of the two countries. He states in regards to the Netherlands, for instance, that "it seems unlikely that the overall rate of progress in industry would have been markedly different if a patent system ... had been in operation." *Id.*, at 40. On the other hand, he notes the statistical evidence which shows "that the reintroduction of a patent system in 1912 has given an extra spur to Dutch inventive activity." *Id.* The evidence cries out for close reexamination by some future scholar.

[31] *See* T. HUGHES, AMERICAN GENESIS 150-80 (1989). It has been argued that the patent system was twisted to serve the aims of large-scale capital during this period. *See* D. NOBLE, AMERICA BY DESIGN (1977).

[32] *See* F. VAUGHAN, THE UNITED STATES PATENT SYSTEM: LEGAL AND ECONOMIC CONFLICTS IN AMERICAN PATENT HISTORY (1956). A recent article clearly explains the ideological tenor of the anti-patent period. *See* Owens, *Patents, the "Frontiers" of American Invention, and the Monopoly Committee of 1939: Anatomy of a Discourse*, 32 TECH. & CULTURE 1076 (1991).

of the patent statute since the nineteenth century, restated many of the fundamental principles on which American patent law had been based since 1790.

Nevertheless, even after the 1952 Act much of the anti-patent sentiment of the 1930s could still be found in the courts and among many commentators. This sentiment was fed in part by the generally anti-technology tenor of much thinking in the 1960s and early 1970s. The patent system by general consensus reached a low water mark during this period. It was difficult to get a patent upheld in many federal circuit courts, and the circuits diverged widely both as to doctrine and basic attitudes toward patents. As a consequence, industry downplayed the significance of patents. It was at this time that an old idea, which had originally surfaced in the late nineteenth century, was proposed as a way to return patents to a more central position in the commercial world — a single, unified court of appeals for patent cases.

Throughout much of the 1970s this idea was studied, debated and modified. Finally in 1982 Congress passed the Federal Courts Improvement Act, creating the new Court of Appeals for the Federal Circuit (or CAFC, as it is now widely known).[33] The CAFC handles several important types of cases, but from the beginning one of its primary functions has been to hear all appeals from the federal district courts involving patents. While the CAFC was ostensibly formed strictly to unify patent doctrine, it was no doubt hoped by some (and expected by others) that the new court would make subtle alterations in the doctrinal fabric, with an eye toward enhancing the stature of the patent system.

To judge by results, that is exactly what happened. Patents are more likely to be held valid now than in the anti-patent era of the 30s to the 70s.[34] It is much easier to get an injunction against an infringer. And money damages have soared, both on average and in the highest-visibility cases. Whether intentional or not, the creation of the CAFC will surely be seen as a watershed event by future historians of the patent system.

At the same time, the environment in which the CAFC operates has been changing as well. Exports have grown considerably as a source of national wealth. As a result, policymakers in the government now pay much closer attention to the legal and economic features of our major trading partners. This naturally includes much closer scrutiny of the intellectual property systems in these other countries. At the same time, it has become clear that other countries have identified technology-intensive industries as keys to economic growth in the future. This has led to a new focus on the economic policy instruments that can be used to foster these industries — including intellectual property. Finally, because intellectual property legislation has no direct, immediate cost to the

---

[33] *See* Dreyfuss, *The Federal Circuit: A Case Study in Specialized Courts,* 64 N.Y.U. L. REV. 1, 25-26 (1989); Jordan, *Specialized Courts: A Choice?*, 76 Nw. U.L. REV. 745 (1981) (describing competing arguments over specialized courts).

[34] *See* Merges, *Commercial Success and Patent Standards: Economic Perspectives on Innovation,* 76 CAL. L. REV. 803, 820-21 (1988) (comparing pre- and post-Federal Circuit era statistics).

government, it seems to many to be a relatively cheap aid to industry. Whether this is true, and indeed the entire question of what contribution intellectual property can make to future economic growth, are as yet unresolved. These are the major questions that will shape the next chapter in the history of the patent system.

No matter what answers history provides, however, the patent system is likely to remain a fixture of American economic life. What is more, its impact will likely continue to be felt even beyond the world of commerce. As one commentator put it,[35]

> The significance of patents is not that they offer strong and indisputable incentives for invention. The most that can be said is that at some times and under certain circumstances patents have probably been beneficial in promoting economic growth and inventiveness. In fact, the effectiveness of the patent system is less important than the fact that every industrialized country in the West has made patenting a national institution, complete with supporting bureaucracy, legislation, and state funding. When combined with the zealous pursuit of patents by industry, the existence of professional careers in patent law practice, the transformation of the patent in Communist countries, the popular enthusiasm for the idea of the patent, and the economist's and historian's interest in probing the meaning of patents, the result is an obsession with technological novelty that is without precedent. No other cultures have been as preoccupied with the cultivation, production, diffusion, and legal control of new machines, tools, devices and processes as Western culture has been since the eighteenth century.

Even if, as the present author firmly believes, there are compelling economic reasons to have patents, this "obsession with technological novelty" by itself makes the patent system a fascinating field to work in and to study. At the heart of this system, now as in much of the past, is the claim. So we turn now to a discussion of patent claims.

B. PATENT DRAFTING EXERCISES

You will see as you go through this book that claims are the essence of the legal right granted by a patent; they define the boundaries of the property right that the patent confers. (Innumerable patent cases therefore analogize claims to the "metes and bounds" of a real property deed.) But our focus on claims should not mislead you into believing that the claims are the only important part of a patent. Quite the opposite: they are only one of the key elements. Claims must always be accompanied by a specification, and in addition most patents also have one or more drawings.

---

[35] GEORGE BASALLA, THE EVOLUTION OF TECHNOLOGY 124 (1988).

The specification describes the invention. It names all the parts or components of the invention; describes how they work; and illustrates how they work together to perform the invention's function.

1. DRAFTING CLAIMS

The purpose of this section is to introduce the essence of the patent system: the claim. On the theory that the best way to see how claims work is to draft a few yourself, this chapter will lead you through a few simple exercises designed to communicate some of the rudiments of the art.

But before you sit down to do the exercises, you need to know some basic points about claim drafting. Here is a brief summary.

The overall goal when drafting claims is to make them as broad as the Patent Office will allow. There are essentially two constraints on the breadth of the claims you can draft: (a) the mass of publicly available information on your problem — what patent practitioners call "the prior art"; and (b) the actual work the inventor has done, in the sense that you may not claim anything beyond what the inventor has discovered, i.e., beyond the limits of the principle of the invention. To use a famous example: the inventor of the telegraph, Samuel Morse, was not permitted to claim "all forms of communicating at a distance" using electromagnetic waves, since he had only discovered one — the telegraph. It would be unfair to permit Morse to claim, e.g., microwave communications, since he did not actually discover this.

In patent parlance, these "embodiments" were not "enabled" by Morse, and so he may not claim them. You will grow accustomed to the notion of an invention and its embodiments throughout the course, but an introductory word is in order. An invention, strictly speaking, is only a concept, though it must take on a tangible form. The many particular physical instances of this concept are called embodiments. Some inventions are capable of being manifested in a very wide array of embodiments; think of the Velcro fastener, for instance, present on everything from shoes to spacesuits to huge industrial storage sacks. The point to keep in mind is that all these embodiments share the same inventive principle, i.e., are instances of the same underlying invention.

But the inventive principle, as we were discussing, is expressed in the claim. To understand claims, we need to identify their main parts. In general, a claim has three parts: (a) preamble; (b) transition; (c) body. We discuss each in turn.

a. Preamble

The preamble introduces and identifies the basic nature of the invention. For example, an invention of a new type of car might begin "An automobile ..."; a new device for holding pages together might read "A device for attaching pages together ..."; etc. The preamble identifies *what **kind** of invention* you will be claiming, in a general sense. Sometimes it is important in interpreting what comes after it, but usually it just introduces the claim. One point to note: be as broad as possible in the general definition; don't limit yourself to a specific *type* of the general thing claimed. If you do, it may be used to narrow the scope of your claim in those cases where it is found relevant to the claim's meaning. Finally, the preamble should not sing the praises of the invention; in fact, this is inappropriate anywhere in the claims (though not necessarily in the specification). Just state what the invention is, not its advantages.

b. Transition

The transition is a formal part of the claim that serves a vital role in defining claim breadth. There are three basic types of transitions, each with a specific phrase that is usually used:

(1) "Open" Claims: "Comprising"

If you claim "An invention comprising elements *A*, *B* and *C*," long tradition in the patent field dictates that this claim covers the same invention having additional elements. Thus, if someone begins selling a product with elements *A*, *B*, *C and D*, this will be held to infringe the claim. This is obviously very powerful; it brings many more potentially infringing embodiments of the invention within the scope of one's claims. For example, an invention claimed as "comprising" a fishing pole and line is infringed by the combination of a fishing pole, line and a reel to take up the line. Quite clearly, "comprising" is the preferred transition — when the prior art allows it.

(2) "Closed" Claims: "Consisting of"

If you claim "An invention consisting of elements *A*, *B* and *C*," someone selling a variant that also incorporates element *D does not infringe* your claim. This is obviously therefore a much narrower claim than the "open" claim just described. One will of course prefer not to limit the claims in this manner, but sometimes, especially where the invention is in a field jammed with many earlier inventions and other prior art — a so-called "crowded art" — the prior art dictates that a claim be drafted in this closed format.

(3) An In-between Format: "Consisting Essentially of"

There is a third type of claim, which occupies a position somewhere between an open and a closed claim. A claim for the invention we have been discussing, if drafted in this format, would read: "An invention consisting essentially of elements *A*, *B* , and *C*." This claim would cover a variant on the invention having element *D only if* element *D* did not make the variant essentially different from the claimed invention. That is, variants having basic and fundamental additions would fall outside the scope of the claim, but those with less significant additions would fall within it.[36] Other phrases have been found equivalent to "consisting essentially of," and thereby also occupy a "middle ground" between completely open and completely closed claims.[37]

c. The Body

The body of a claim is all the rest, which is obviously the most important part. In general, the function of the body is to do two things: (a) list all the elements; and (b) describe how they interact. In drafting this section of the claim, the goal of breadth within the constraints mentioned above must be kept in mind. The drafter makes critically important decisions that affect the breadth of the resulting claim in choosing which elements will be considered essential enough to list, how each element will be described, and how the elements' interaction will be presented.

Since the art of drafting patent claims (at least in their present form) is over one hundred years old, a wide array of specialized words has developed. These words are important for two reasons. First, they have been selected over time to most succinctly and yet *most generally* describe elements and their interaction. And second, because many of them appear in claims that have been challenged and litigated, they have withstood "trial by fire." Patent attorneys are of course most anxious about the prospects for the claims they nurture and then send into the world; and it is comforting to know that one has used descriptions and words to which courts have in the past given their blessing. Thus the demand for in-house "exemplar" files and other sources, such as Appendix A to R. FABER, LANDIS ON MECHANICS OF PATENT CLAIM DRAFTING (3d ed. 1990), which list words that have appeared in prior U.S. patents. Naturally, simply using a tried-and-tested word in a patent does not guarantee the patent will be upheld (after all, one is always working with a *new* invention). But it is better in many cases than resorting to entirely new words. And of course it saves a great deal of time. However, where the inventor has opened a new field, and the vocabulary of technology has yet to catch up, the inventor is perfectly justified in coining new terminology to describe her invention. Like any claim language, of course, such new terminology must be thoroughly described and defined in the patent's specification.

The Patent Office requires the body of a claim to meet several formal requirements. First, the entire claim must be stated in the form of a single sentence. This sometimes leads to very long sentences, which can be confusing; but the Patent Office follows this convention, so the drafter must. Secondly, as mentioned, the claim must set forth how each element interacts with at least one other element; the claim must be more than a list of elements. It must describe what

---

[36] *Dow Chem. Co. v. American Cyanamid Co.*, 229 U.S.P.Q. (BNA) 171, 180 (E.D. La. 1985).

[37] *See, e.g., Ziegler v. Phillips Petrol Co.*, 177 U.S.P.Q. (BNA) 481 (5th Cir. 1973); R. FABER, LANDIS ON MECHANICS OF PATENT CLAIM DRAFTING 13-14 (3d ed. 1990).

they do when they act together. For example, to claim a windmill to be used for pumping water, one must do more than list "blades or a fan for catching wind; shaft; gears; pump; water pipes." Something like the following would be appropriate:

I claim —

1. A windmill comprising a wind-catching device, which turns a shaft, which acts on gears or another device to change the direction of the force, so as to operate a pump that pumps water.

The third important point to keep in mind about the body of a claim is that any internal references must be clear. The examples used so far involve claims that are short enough so that this would not be a problem, but for many inventions requiring long and complex claims, the problem does arise. As an illustration, consider the following fragment from an imaginary claim:

3. A windmill according to claim 1 wherein the force-changing device is a set of gears the first of which is attached to the end of the shaft of claim 1 and the second of which contacts *the gear* ....

It is not clear what the italicized phrase "the gear" means. This claim would be rejected by an examiner because the phrase "the gear" has no *antecedent basis*; which gear is meant? The way to fix the problem is to clarify the initial phrase — "set of gears" — by specifying how many, and then enumerating them as follows:

3. A windmill according to claim 1 wherein the force-changing device is a set of two or more gears wherein a first gear is attached to the end of the shaft of claim 1 and a second gear contacts *said first gear* ....

A special problem involves "means-plus-function" claims. These claims find their basis in § 112 ¶ 6 of the Patent Act, 35 U.S.C. § 112. This provision explicitly authorizes claims in the form "means for doing X," where "doing X" is the *function*. Take, for example, the claim element "means for fastening," which would include nails, scotch tape, screws, glue, Velcro, and any other "means for" attaching one thing to another. In this claim, the "function" is fastening, and the "means for fastening" element of the claim therefore includes many means for doing this task. Does it include *all* means? The patent statute states that such claims "shall be construed to cover the corresponding structure, material, or acts described in the specification *and equivalents thereof*" (emphasis added). As we shall see in Chapter 8, this allows many means indeed, but not *all* means. For present purposes, just remember when you see a means plus function claim (i.e., "means for doing X") that this is a very broad claiming format.

Independent and Dependent Claims

The claim just described is an example of an *independent claim*; it does not refer to any other claim or claims. This is in contrast to a dependent claim, an example of which is given above (the second windmill claim). Another example follows:

> 2. The windmill of claim 1 wherein the wind-catching device is a set of blades, such as those in an electric fan.

The preamble of this claim — "the windmill of claim 1" — identifies it as a dependent claim; several other similar phrases can also be used (e.g., "the windmill according to claim 1"). A dependent claim specifies some feature of the general invention claimed in the independent claim to which the dependent claim refers. The "dependency" then means that the second claim is narrower than the first, in at least one respect. In the example above, claim 2 narrows the range of "wind-catching" devices to those that are like a fan, i.e., those with blades that turn in a circle.

Thus, a wind-catching device made of a series of sails on a frame would not infringe this claim; they are not "blades."[38] Note, however, that a windmill along these lines *would* infringe the independent claim, claim 1. So why would anyone ever draft a narrower claim? Because often the Patent Office rejects claims, or courts declare them invalid, for a myriad of reasons that we will learn about in this book. Thus, the use of a dependent claim is really a form of insurance: an attempt to draft a claim that will survive because it is narrower than the independent claim on which it depends.[39] In this connection, note that even if claim 1 is declared invalid by a court, claim 2 does not also fail, at least not automatically; even though it is dependent, its validity must be separately determined.

Often the claims section of a patent begins with the broadest claim which is then "qualified" in a series of dependent claims. This is followed perhaps by a narrower independent claim, again qualified by a series of dependent claims. In this way, the general structure of a patent often resembles an inverted pyramid: the broadest claims are first, the narrowest last, and the scope of the claims generally "tapers" from the first to the last.

Thus, the use of independent and subsequent dependent claims makes sense from the drafter's point of view. As it turns out, it also makes the patent examiner's job much easier. By identifying the fact that "this claim is a modification of

---

[38] Windmills made of sails have been used for centuries in China. *See* S. STRANDH, THE HISTORY OF THE MACHINE 108 (1979). *See also* RICHARD HILLS, POWER FROM WIND: A HISTORY OF WINDMILL TECHNOLOGY (1994).

[39] I have to confess that although "on which it depends" is perfectly proper English, it is *im*proper Patent English; patent practitioners almost always say "*from* which" the claim depends. In the past, I considered "depends from" an abomination concocted by the patent bar — until I saw this usage in the introduction to the OXFORD DICTIONARY OF QUOTATIONS at xx (3d ed. 1979) ("Each quotation without a full source depends from its immediate predecessor.") Though chastened, I still prefer "depends on."

another claim," a dependent claim indicates that if the claim on which it depends is valid, then it must be also. And it relates one claim to another; since there are often a series of dependent claims following an independent claim, the examiner can deal with entire groups of claims together, in a logical way. This too simplifies his or her job. In fact, the Patent Office likes these claims so much it encourages their use by adjusting the fees charged to patent applicants. Although the fee structure is complicated, in general it encourages the use of dependent claims by charging higher fees for applications with a greater number of independent claims.[40] The Patent Act, at § 112 ¶ 2, explicitly authorizes both dependent and multiple dependent claims, i.e., claims that refer back to more than one preceding claims (e.g., "a widget as in claim 3 or 4, wherein ...").

2. DRAFTING A SET OF CLAIMS FOR THE PENCIL

Now that we have reviewed the rudiments of claim drafting, it is time to draft a real claim. For help, we turn to the pencil (as the subject of our patent application, not as a drafting aid).

What could be simpler than a pencil — an everyday object so familiar it hardly seems like an "invention" at all? But of course, like all human-made objects, it was once new; someone really did invent every essential element of the pencil we now take for granted. *See* H. PETROSKY, THE PENCIL (1990).

Your task is to put yourself into the past. Imagine you inhabit a pre-pencil world, at least one where the modern pencil does not exist. You are sitting at your desk, drafting patent specifications and claims with a quill pen and ink-well; your hands are black with smudges, and every time you make a mistake you have to either start again or blot the page with an ugly smear.

In walks an inventor.

"I've invented a revolutionary new writing instrument," he says. (Happens to be a he.) "It makes a mark that is dark but doesn't tear the paper; it doesn't blot like pens; and, best of all, if you make a mistake, you can *rub it out completely* with this other thing I've invented, made out of rubber. Look, I'll show you." At that he pulls out a primitive-looking pencil, a long rectangular chunk of wood with a narrow, flat piece of soft mineral stuck in the top.

"That looks like a bit of rock stuck in a piece of wood. How can you write with *that*?" you ask, incredulously. You've seen inventors before — lots of them — and you are wary of his claims.

"It's all in the *kind* of 'rock' you use," he says. With that he grabs a piece of paper and draws a nice, long dark line. You notice that indeed the paper does not tear and that the line laid down is dry the moment it is drawn.

"You might have something there," you say. "Tell me about it."

---

[40] *See* PATENT AND TRADEMARK OFFICE, MANUAL OF PATENT EXAMINING PROCEDURES § 608.01(n) (5th ed. 1983 & Supp. 1989). .

a. The Invention Disclosure

At this point the inventor gives you a preliminary description of the invention: what it is, what it does, and a rough sketch of what came before. This is similar to a more formal disclosure statement — actually a written form — often used in large, organized research and development departments. He also gives you a sketch of his invention, shown in Figure 1-1. He lists the following facts:

(1) In the Classical world, the Greeks and Romans had used a thin metal stylus made of hard lead to make very *light* marks on paper. This was apparently used primarily for sketching and drawing. This was a refinement of primitive techniques whereby burnt charcoal was used to make marks.

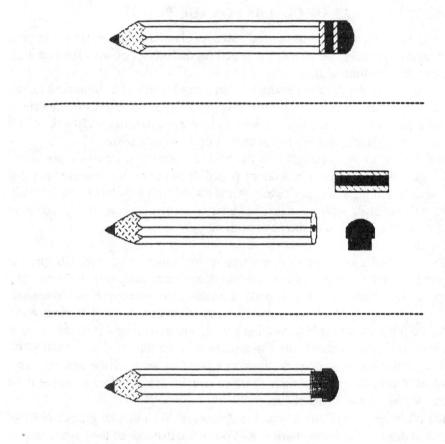

Figure 1-1

(2) Also in antiquity, the Romans used a very thin ink brush known as a peniculum. It was really a paintbrush or inkbrush, but painted a very thin line.

(3) Your inventor discovered that two materials work in his writing instrument: lead (which works less well), and graphite (which works better). Moreover, graphite from certain locations made a much darker line than the type of lead used in antiquity. Specifically, he had discovered that graphite taken from deposits in the vicinity of Cumberland, England, worked best. He had noticed that this graphite was "softer" than other types of graphite, as well as lead. Although graphite was preferred, the inventor insisted on referring to the writing part of his instrument as a "lead."

(4) Your inventor also discovered that most leads were difficult to work with when used in their "pure" form. So he experimented with mixtures of graphite and clay, which he found made the composition more stable. He combined them as follows:

- (a) 90% graphite, 10% clay, which he found worked better than graphite alone, but not much better.
- (b) 60% graphite, 40% clay, which he found worked very well.
- (c) 30% graphite, 70% clay, which he found worked better than (a) but not as well as (b), and which tended to crumble if you put too much pressure on it.

(5) The inventor has found that for the "lead-holder" part of his instrument, many woods worked well, but that softer woods like cedar were easier on the hand than harder woods like oak.

(6) The inventor has found that gobs of rubber can be used to partly erase pencil markings. He has even thought of attaching rubber or some other material to the end of his pencils, but presently they are not connected.

b. The Prior Art

At this point you tell the inventor you would be glad to draft a patent application in exchange for a lifetime supply of pencils. But, of course, before you do so, you must check the prior art to be sure you aren't wasting your time. (Someone may have just recently patented the very thing your inventor is describing.) You do and discover that the inventor has knowledge of what seems to be all the relevant prior art. You find nothing he hasn't mentioned.

Recall from above that you are constrained not only by the prior art but also by the fact that the inventor in your office has not actually discovered *all* writing instruments. You will therefore not be able to claim **all writing instruments**, only some kinds of writing instruments.

Now for the exercise: Based on the inventor's disclosure, draft at least three claims: one as broad as possible; another to an intermediate range; and the third, your "fallback" claim, to the precise invention he has so far produced. In the broadest claim, try to use at least one "means-plus-function" phrase; recall that this gives very broad coverage. Try to include the "pencil-plus-eraser" combination in at least one claim. The claims should take up less than half a page, but don't just dash them off; think about them first.

Two points to ponder: can you claim the Cumberland graphite as a separate invention? Or are such "products of nature" off-limits to inventors? (See Chapter 2.) Second, what if you claim both the pencil and the eraser as two separate inventions; could another inventor come along later and claim the *combination* of pencil and eraser? Are such combinations always unpatentable? (See Chapter 5.)

3. A SECOND EXAMPLE: AN IMPROVEMENT TO THE CANDY DISPENSER

Now let us move on to another example of how claims are crafted. Consider the following claim:

> 1. A receptacle having a housing for receiving and sequentially dispensing individual shaped bodies from a stack of like ... bodies received in the housing, the housing having two side wall extensions at a dispensing end thereof, a cover pivotally mounted on the sidewall extensions at the dispensing end about a transverse pivoting axis, the cover having an abutment adjacent the pivot for pushing an uppermost of the shaped bodies and dispensing it from the receptacle housing when the cover is pivoted..., and spring means in the housing for pressing the stack of shaped bodies towards the dispensing end to place sequential uppermost ones of the shaped bodies of the stack into a dispensing position ....

You probably would not have guessed that the title of this patent is "candy dispenser"; it describes the basic invention behind what is now commonly known as the Pez (Registered Trademark) brand candy dispenser. *See* Haas, U.S. Patent 1,736,078 (1929).

If you have ever used one of these candy dispensers, you know the basic idea behind it: a stack of brick-shaped candies is held in a vertical dispenser, which is topped by a plastic head in the image of a famous cartoon character or the like. When you tilt the head back, a candy is pushed off the stack, out of an opening, where it can easily be taken. The basic principle behind the design can be seen in Figure 1-2, taken from a subsequent patent to Haas (discussed below).

The exercise we will consider here is based on an improvement in the way these dispensers are manufactured. In the original design, two springs were used: one to push up the bottom of the vertical tube holding the candy, thus pushing the candy toward the top; and one to hold the head on top of the tube, and allow the head to be tilted backward to get the candy. As you can imagine, given the size of the candy dispenser (less than four inches long, usually), it was a difficult task to assemble the head on top of the dispenser. The looped end of a tiny spring had to be hooked onto 'a small plastic hook inside the head. Over time, it became apparent that there had to be a better way.

U.S. Patent   March 9, 1976   **3,942,683**

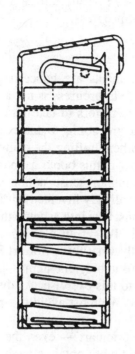
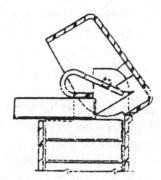

Figure 1-2

A patent issued to the original candy dispenser inventor in 1971 describes the solution to the problem. Instead of using a spring to hold the head on, it uses a plastic hinge coupled with a bar inside the head. As the head is tilted back, two pins push on the plastic hinge, which is simply a flat piece of plastic that folds back on itself at about a 30-45 degree angle. As the head is tilted back, the pins push down on the top piece of plastic; the plastic flexes, reducing the angle between the two pieces of plastic that form the hinge. Once you are finished taking your candy, the head swings back down into place on top of the stack of candy. You can see how this works in Figure 1-2.

The exercise at hand is to draft a claim to the new hinge on the candy dispenser. This is an example of a very common type of patent claim: a claim to a so-called improvement invention. Step-by-step improvements to a basic design are often critical to the overall development of a particular technology. *See, e.g.*, S. HOLLANDER, THE SOURCES OF INCREASED EFFICIENCY: A STUDY OF DUPONT RAYON PLANTS 203-04 (1965) (classic study which concluded that "minor" improvements "accounted for over two-thirds of the unit-cost reductions attributable to technical change at most of the plants considered"); Enos, *A Measure of the Rate of Technological Progress in the Petroleum Refining Industry*, 6 J. INDUS. ECON. 180, 187 (1958) (emphasizing the cumulative quantitative importance of small improvements in petroleum refining processes). So in drafting this claim, you are participating in the long, steady march of progress.

a. The Prior Art

However, as is often the case where improvements are concerned, other inventors have been active in the field. (The march to progress is not a particularly solitary one.) This means that there are more factors to take into account when drafting your claims. To be precise, you are going to have to "skirt around" the work of other inventors in the field when drafting the claims to the improved hinge. We will delve into this idea deeply in this book, as many cases turn on this issue; for now, just consider the common-sense notion that you cannot claim in your patent what someone else has already invented or described to the public. In patent parlance, this means you must take into account the "prior art" in drafting your claims to the improvement. To get an idea of what this involves, we must first see a description of exactly what this prior art is.

Fortunately, in this case the "prior art" is limited to only one item — the basic dispenser patent quoted from in the introduction to this exercise. As discussed, this is described in a 1929 patent to Eduard Haas. We must avoid this prior art when drafting our claims.

Incidentally, everyone must draft around this prior art — even the original inventor, Eduard Haas. That is, if he were attempting to obtain a patent for the plastic hinge improvement (as he in fact did), he would still have to craft his claims so as to avoid the basic dispenser design patent of 1929. An original inventor who goes on to make improvements has all the constraints of any other inventor after his original patent issues; the original design is off limits in his claims as well. Put another way, there are no "breaks" for an inventor when she later files for an improvement patent on some feature of her already-patented original design; the same prior art must be drafted around, even though she *created* that prior art. (This does not mean she cannot add improved features to a patent application before it issues.) In short, the patent system awards inven*tions*, not invent*ors*. We will have occasion to dwell on this principle many times in this book.

To summarize: the basic two-spring dispenser design is in the prior art. We must draft the claims to our improvement so that they do not cover this design.

b. Drafting Around the Prior Art

The goal of the exercise is to draft claims that cover our improvement as broadly as possible, yet that do *not* cover any ground properly within the original 1929 patent. This means you will have to emphasize what is new about the improvement we wish to patent.

Well, what is new? Certainly not the basic idea of the long dispenser of candies, nor the basic idea of a spring-loaded top to the device which pushes the candy out and closes shut when the candy removal is complete. In the end, only the hinge is new. So that is what the claims must reflect.

But how best to draft these claims? Consider the following possibility:

> **Alternative 1**. In a standard candy-dispensing mechanism having a bottom spring to push the candy toward the top of the dispenser, and a top spring to hold the cover of the dispenser in place, and bias the cover in the downward position, the improvement of a plastic leaf spring as the top spring.

Obviously Alternative 1 serves the major purpose we have identified; it separates what is truly new (the new "leaf spring" design for the top spring) from what is well-known (the "standard" candy dispenser). Even so, there are some potential problems with this claim. First, the specification would have to define what the inventor means by "leaf spring." This is a common enough phrase, to be sure; but it might be somewhat ambiguous. At a minimum, one familiar with the C-shaped leaf springs on the underside of an automobile would not immediately be apprised of the candy dispenser spring, which has a sort of sideways V shape, when the phrase "leaf spring" was mentioned. As mentioned earlier, the specification is the place to define such terms. To be proper, the specification would have to contain a sentence such as: "The claimed invention uses a 'leaf spring,' preferably but not necessarily V-shaped, to bias the dispensing head in the closed position."

Secondly, Alternative 1 might appear to be a bit narrow. It is, after all, limited to a *"plastic"* leaf spring. Isn't it possible to implement the same design with a metal spring, or a very flexible spring made of wood? If we go with the phrase *plastic* leaf spring, we are leaving a wide hole through which imitators may pass unscathed, since a candy dispenser with a metal spring would not infringe a claim drafted in the form of Alternative 1. Note that inserting a sentence such as "The leaf spring may be made of plastic or any material suitable for this purpose" would *not* solve the problem so long as the *claim* was limited to a plastic spring; it is what is in the claims that count, in general.

Before we get to Alternative 2, it might be useful to take a step back for a moment and consider this issue of plastic springs versus springs made of other materials. If Alternative 1 were the language contained in an actual patent, we would refer to the requirement that the spring be plastic as a **limitation** on the claim, or as an **element** of the claim. Adding the word "plastic" makes the claim narrower than it would otherwise be, since without this word springs made from any material would be covered by the claim. Candy dispensers sold with metal or wooden leaf springs would infringe the claim, which means that the patentee could have the competing products removed from the market and sue for damages. With the word "plastic" in the claim, however, as in Alternative 1, these same competitors could keep right on selling their products.

What if the *specification* said "I use a leaf spring made of plastic in my device"; would that mean that competing devices with wooden or metal leaf springs did not infringe? No; as the courts are wont to repeat, a limitation cannot be read into a claim from the specification. Again, it's the claims that count.

The basic lesson of Alternative 1 is simple: the more limitations or elements in a claim, the fewer the competing products that will infringe that claim. We say that such a claim has a narrow **scope**. It is very important to keep in mind when drafting claims what is really at stake: the number of competing products that can be forced off the market or prevented from entering it. And, since added limitations come from added words (like "plastic" in a claim), the basic lesson may be restated: shorter claims are broader. (An extreme example is discussed in *In re Seaborg*, 328 F.2d 996, 140 U.S.P.Q. (BNA) 662 (C.C.P.A. 1964), concerning a patent filed by the Nobel prize-winning physicist Glenn Seaborg; claim 1 reads simply "Element 95" — a two-word tour de force of claim drafts-manship.)

So we have seen the problems inherent in Alternative 1. Let's take a look at another alternative.

Since the basic advantage of the improvement we have before us is that it makes the manufacture of candy dispensers cheaper, we might think of drafting a claim that tries to capture this advantage. Consider the following example.

> **Alternative 2**. In a standard candy-dispensing mechanism having a bottom spring to push the candy toward the top of the dispenser, and a top spring to hold the cover of the dispenser in place, and bias the cover in the down-ward position, the improvement of a top spring which is cheap to manu-facture.

This has the major advantage of capturing the major feature of our improve-ment — the inexpensive spring. But it is clearly ambiguous. In the language of the claim, how would "cheap" be defined? One factor of course would be the total assembly cost for the original design. And we would need some sort of definition of how much the improvement saved. Even assuming we knew that, it would be difficult for a competitor to know whether she had infringed the improvement patent. If the competitor came up with a design that saved some money, but not an astounding amount, she would want to know whether she was infringing the improvement patent. The language of the claim in Alternative 2 gives very little guidance on this point.

Moreover, the language of Alternative 2 covers more than the inventor has actually conceived and executed. If, for instance, someone were to devise an ingenious, new (and cheap) mechanism to replace the spring in the original dispenser design, this new mechanism would infringe the claim — no matter how original the mechanism was. Imagine, for instance, a design featuring a rubber band in place of the original spring, or, an entirely radical solution to the problem, using two oppositely charged magnets, for instance. Either invention would infringe Alternative 2, *despite* the fact that the inventor of the plastic hinge design never even imagined these possibilities.

To allow the inventor to exclude competing products whose designs are so very different might strike you as unfair. Yet this would be the result if the patent system permitted the inventor to use the language of Alternative 2 in a patent claim.

To summarize, the language of Alternative 2 has two major problems. First, it is simply too "loose" to define a clear verbal boundary around the essence of the improvement invention we are faced with. And second, it is so broad it encompasses many designs very far removed from the basic plastic hinge idea.

You might try drafting a claim to this invention that avoids these problems, and the others discussed above. *After* you have done so, compare it with the following claim, which is adapted from the actual patent used in this example.

What is claimed is:

> 1. In a receptacle [for dispensing candies, as described above], the improvement of an elastically deformable transverse ledge extending between the side wall extensions of the housing in a horizontal plane and integral with the side wall extensions, the uppermost candy being pressed by the spring means toward the top of the dispenser, and a bent over leaf spring projecting upward from the ledge, one edge of the spring engaging the top or head of the dispenser and biasing it into the closed position, the same edge also engaging means for pushing the topmost candy out of the dispenser.

Note several factors of this claim. First, it specifies "an improvement" in a basic design — and is therefore an example of a so-called "Jepson claim." *See* R. ELLIS, PATENT CLAIMS 197 (1949). Second, it uses general language to describe the features of the invention: "elastically deformable," for instance. Third, it takes advantage of "means plus function" claim language: "spring means" and "means for pushing the topmost candy out of the dispenser."

4. A THIRD EXAMPLE: AN ANTI-TANGLING DEVICE FOR SAILBOATS

In this third example of what patent claims are all about, we will consider another simple invention. The basic idea behind it is to prevent the ropes on a sailboat from becoming tangled in the cables that support the main mast, which is usually quite tall. As you may know, these cables typically connect the deck of the boat with the top part of the mast. They keep the mast from bending under the heavy load of a sail filled with wind. On many boats, there is a smaller sail in front of the main sail, called the jib sail. Unlike the main sail, the jib is not attached to a mast; it is attached instead to a cable running from the very front of the boat to a point at or near the top of the main mast. Also unlike the main sail, the jib has no boom; that is, it has no metal pole running along its bottom

side. Instead, the jib is controlled by two ropes, tied to a corner of the jib. When
the sailboat is turned onto a new course at an opposite angle to the wind, it is
said to "tack." It is during the tacking maneuver that the boom of the mainsail
swings across to the other side of the boat, sometimes knocking unaware sailors
in the head. The top drawing in Figure 1-3 shows a jib sail.

Since there is no boom on the jib, it must be handled differently during
tacking. When a boat is sailing, the jib is on either one side of the boat or the
other. Whichever side it is on, one of the ropes on the bottom of the jib is tied
down to the boat to hold the jib in place. When the boat tacks, this rope is let
loose. Just as the mainsail swings to the other side of the boat, so does the jib,
once this rope is let loose. (Actually there is often quite a bit of flapping about
as the jib first "collapses" and then fills with wind on the side of the boat that it
has just moved to.) When the jib has caught the wind on the other side of the
boat, the second rope is tied down. Then the captain sets a new course, the crew
moves to the other side of the boat, and everyone takes another swig of rum.
(Tacking isn't *all* business.)

Since a boat tacks many times when it is taken out to sail, the ropes that are
connected to the bottom of the jib experience a good deal of wear and tear. Much
of this is caused by friction with the metal cables that hold the mast up. As the
ropes swing from side to side, they rub across the vertical cables; in time they
become frayed. Figure 1-3, top drawing, shows a jib sail rope running over the
two stays on the right side of the boat.

A number of ingenious solutions have been devised to overcome the problem
of this fraying rope. The one we are concerned with is particularly simple. It
involves simply placing a plastic cylinder around the part of the metal cables
where the jib lines (that's what salty types call the ropes) routinely cross the
cables. The bottom right drawing in Figure 1-3 shows how this works.

While this is a fairly straightforward solution to the basic problem, a further
problem emerges that might not be so simple: how to get the plastic cylinders
onto the metal cables (which sailing aficionados call "stays" or "shrouds"). The
solution to *this* problem is to manufacture the plastic cylinders in two halves,
which can be snapped or slid together without having to detach the stays from the
deck of the boat. (This is a very desirable feature, since it is a royal pain to
remove the stays; asking a boat owner to remove them just to put in a jib line
guard would be like asking a car owner to remove her engine just to put in
antifreeze.) The bottom left drawing in Figure 1-3 shows how the cylinder halves
fit together.

At this point, before we check the prior art, it would be instructive to draft a
claim, worded as broadly as possible, to the invention as we have described it.
Consider the following possibility:

    1. An anti-fraying device comprising a rope, cable or other item to be
covered and means for covering the item causing the fraying with a material
that reduces fraying or friction.

U.S. Patent   Sep. 25, 1984   4,473,024

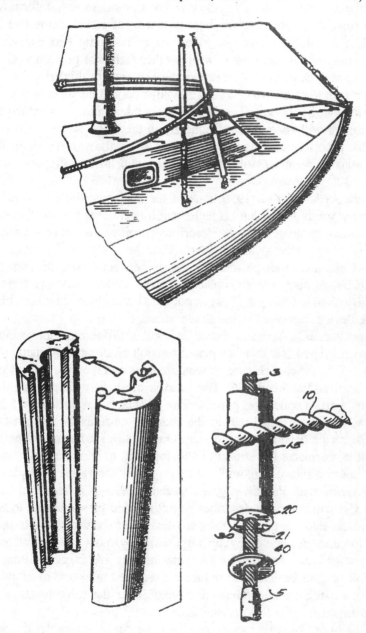

Figure 1-3

a. The Prior Art

While this claim would be nice from the inventor's point of view, unfortunately other ways to solve the problem of fraying lines have suggested themselves over the years. Also, as one might suspect, the idea of fastening two interlocking plastic pieces together has been used to solve other technical problems. Consequently, the claims to be drafted must reflect the existence of this prior art, since to permit a patentee to claim what is already known would be socially wasteful. (This basic principle, by the way, is called the Principle of Nonremoval from the Public Domain; we will encounter it frequently in this book.)

To determine precisely what is already known about the various elements of the invention at hand, we must consult all the relevant prior art. Suppose we did, and encountered the following items:

1. **The Smith Article.**[41] In a 1956 issue of the magazine *Sailing World*, we find an article by Smith describing his technique for reducing jib line chafing. It involves several components. First he describes slipping a series of metal disks over the stays, spaced several inches apart. Then he describes inserting some foam pieces of cylindrical shape into the spaces between disks, to keep them separated. Finally, a plastic sheath is placed over the entire assembly. Note that the stay must be removed from the boat to put the plastic sheath in place. Figure 1-4 shows the device described in the Smith article.

2. **The Pope Patent.**[42] A patent issued in 1952 to Pope describes a plastic "lock seal device." The basic idea is a plastic version of the familiar metal clothing snap, which is found as a closure on windbreakers and the like. The snap has two parts, a head and a receptacle. The head is mushroom-shaped, so that a narrow neck supports a wider end portion. The receptacle has a ridge or "shoulder"; when the head is inserted into it, the shoulder engages the bottom of the head, which keeps the head from falling out. One significant feature of the Pope design is that the receptacle has slits cut in the top of it, to let it expand when the wide head is inserted into it. Figure 1-5 (see page 32) shows the Pope device.

3. **The Toussaint et al. Patent.** A patent issued in 1975 to Toussaint et al. and assigned to a German company describes a wing-shaped plastic sheath to cover underwater cables. Because certain cables are designed to be dragged through the water, e.g., for underwater surveying purposes, they must be very strong to withstand the severe force exerted by the water as they are dragged through it. This invention has as its basic aim to reduce the required thickness of cables and "drag lines," by placing a hydrodynamic "wing" over the cable to allow it to slice through the water with less resistance.

To permit the hydrodynamic cable covering to be put on the cable, the patent describes making the covering in two halves, which can then be snapped together.

---

[41] The description of this fictional article is based loosely on Palm, U.S. Patent 3,318,277 (May 9, 1969).

[42] This is based on an actual patent to Pope, U.S. Patent 2,610,879 (Sept. 16, 1962).

May 9, 1967   J. A. PALM   3,318,277

SHROUD GUARD
Filed March 15, 1965

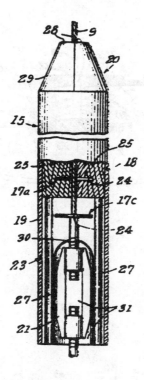

Figure 1-4

The snapping mechanism concerns us most, since this is the element that is common to this invention and our stay cover. The snap is described simply as a "snap-action ridge and groove" in the two halves of the cable cover assembly. The only details of the snap are contained in a drawing, which shows a series of snap-like protrusions, with matching receptacles, on either side of the cable covering. See Figure 1-6; the snap is element 3 in the drawing. The patent states merely that "[t]he fastening means may have construction of plastic zippers established by snap-action grooves and mating ridges for coaction with the ridges and grooves in the respective other strip part."

b. Summary of the Prior Art

When comparing an invention with its prior art, it is sometimes useful to construct a table. The table should list the major features or elements of the

Sept. 16, 1952   P. M. POPE   2,610,879

LOCK SEAL SUITABLE FOR MANUFACTURE IN PLASTICS
Filed Aug. 23, 1946

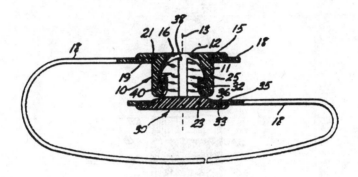

Figure 1-5

U.S. Patent   Jan. 14, 1975   3,859,949

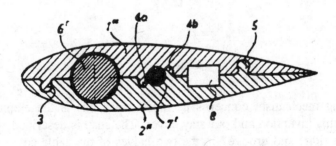

Figure 1-6

invention and show which of the features the invention shares with each item in
the prior art. Table 1-1 is an example of such a table, drawn from the stay cover
invention described in this section.

	[1] 2 Halves	[2] Tongue	[2b] Narrow Entrance in Channel	[2c] Expansion Slit
Stay Cover Invention:	X	X	X	X
Prior Art: Smith Article	X	—	—	—
Pope Snap	X	X	X	—
Toussaint et al. Pat.	X	X	—	—

Table 1-1

Tables such as this are useful for several reasons. First, they force us to identify the key elements in an invention. Second, they provide an instant summary of the prior art. Finally, they allow a quick comparison of the invention with the prior art. For all these reasons, they help clarify issues concerning the patentability of an invention. By the same token, similar tables can be constructed to compare a patented invention with a competing product accused of infringing the patent.

From the table, we can begin to see what elements of the stay guard are new; this will help us draft our claims to this invention. Although we would like to have drafted our claims to include the very broad concept of a smooth covering on rough cables or ropes to reduce fraying, we can see that this is not possible in light of the prior art. In addition, we can see that even the basic concept of a sheath formed from two interlocking halves is old; we cannot claim this concept either — likewise for the general notion of a two-piece closure where one piece (the "head") is broader than the other (the receptacle).

The table makes clear that what is really new about the way our stay cover works is the slit that runs the length of the receptacle or channel. Recall that this slit allows the channel to open up to receive the broad protrusion from the other half of the stay cover. None of the items in the prior art has this element. So our claims must include it if they are to cover new ground.

Here is a sample claim whose elements are drawn from the comparison table above. The numbering of the elements follows the numbering used in the comparison table.[43]

---

[43] This way of writing a claim is called a schematic or outline claim. This is a useful way to represent the claim, since it makes it much easier to refer to elements in the claim in a subsequent discussion. Although the use of bracketed numbers or letters in the body of a claim is not officially frowned upon, it appears to be extremely rare. The use of indentations and blank spaces between elements, however, is more common, and is permitted in the "bible" of claim drafting, the Manual of Patent Examination and Practice (or "MPEP"). *See* PATENT AND TRADEMARK OFFICE, MANUAL OF PATENT EXAMINING PROCEDURES § 608.01(m) (5th ed. 1983 & Supp. 1989). An example of the schematic form of a claim is presented below; it is drawn from the case of *Barret v. United States*, 405 F.2d 502, 505, 186 Ct. Cl. 210, 160 U.S.P.Q. 224 (Ct. Cl. 1968):

> (a) The method of modifying the absolute coefficients of lift and drag of an aerodynamic section while in motion, said section possessing
> (b) in the vicinity of its leading edge a normal atmospheric pressure zone,
> (c) above its upper cambered surface a subatmospheric pressure zone,
> (d) below its lower cambered surface a superatmospheric pressure zone at a higher pressure than the subatmospheric pressure zone and
> (e) adjacent its trailing edge a resultant atmospheric pressure zone created by the convergence of the airflows passing from the section and of a higher pressure than the normal pressure zone,
> (f) the steps of removing the boundary layer volume of air substantially over the entire span of said section from and at a point adjacent the normal atmospheric pressure zone,
> (g) compressing said boundary layer volume of air and
> (h) discharging said volume at a point adjacent the resultant atmospheric pressure zone in rear of trailing edge of the said aerodynamical section.

Another example is given in Hildreth, *Preparation of Patent Claims: Review of the Basics*, in ADVANCED CLAIM DRAFTING AND AMENDMENT WRITING WORKSHOP 7, 12-13 (Practicing Law Institute, Patents, Copyrights, Trademarks and Literary Property Course Handbook Series, No. 327, 1991):

> 1. A composition comprising
>   (a) a solid selected from the group consisting of
>   (1) sodium chloride,
>   (2) potassium chloride and
>   (3) lithium chloride;
>   (b) a liquid selected from the group consisting of
>   (1) sulfuric acid,
>   (2) nitric acid ....

Here is an example of the outline form of a claim, drawn from the case of *Gardner v. TEC Sys., Inc.*, 725 F.2d 1338, 1340, 220 U.S.P.Q. 777 (Fed. Cir. 1984):

> 1. Means for positioning a moving web by subjecting a transverse zone spanning the web to uniform static pressure,
>   said positioning means comprising
>   a suppression plate
>
>   extending transversely across said web and spaced therefrom as closely as is mechanically practicable,
>
>   nozzle means no closer to the web than said plate and having slots which extend

1. A self-locking stay roller, consisting of

[1][a] At least two interlocking parts that
    [b] snap together,

[2] Tongues and grooves that hold the parts together,

    [a] each tongue having a neck portion and a head portion, said neck portion being wider than said head portion,

    [b] each groove having an entrance narrower than the width of the head portion of the tongue, and

    [c] a slit running the length of each groove that allows the groove to expand to receive the head.

C. OVERVIEW OF THE PATENT SYSTEM

Although claims are the heart of patent law, to understand the cases and commentary in this book you must be familiar with some other introductory concepts.

First is the nature of the patent itself. A patent gives an inventor the right to exclude others from making, using or selling his or her patented invention. After an applicant has established all the necessary requirements, the patent is granted by the U.S. Patent and Trademark Office in Washington, D.C. (often referred to as "the PTO"); it grants exclusive rights for seventeen years beginning the date the patent issues. *See* 35 U.S.C. § 154 (1988). (Throughout this book, 35 U.S.C. is referred to as "the Patent Act.") This type of patent is sometimes referred to as a "utility patent," to distinguish it from such special types of patents as **plant patents** or **design patents**. Also, don't confuse a utility **patent** with a **utility model**, a kind of "junior patent" given in some foreign systems which has less stringent conditions on patentability and (usually) a shorter term.

The process of obtaining a patent from the Patent Office is known as "**prosecution**."[44] The time and effort required to prosecute a patent varies immensely from case to case. A few applications are reviewed quickly and are issued within a year of the date of application. Others languish in the PTO for years and some even decades, especially when several inventors claim they were the first to produce a particular invention.

---

substantially continuously across said web and are spaced at opposite sides of said plate, ...

A variation on this latter format is to intersperse part numbers taken from a diagram or patent drawing to illustrate the parts referred to in the text of the claim. *See, e.g.*, *Dresser Indus. v. United States*, 432 F.2d 787, 796, 193 Ct. Cl. 140, 167 U.S.P.Q. 473 (Ct. Cl. 1970).

[44] The *Oxford English Dictionary*'s first definition of "prosecute" is: "To follow up, pursue; to persevere or persist in; follow out, go on with (some action, undertaking, or purpose) with a view to completing or attaining it." Compact ed., vol. 2. at 2332 col. 1 (1971 & Supp. 1988). Patent lawyers sometimes confuse this term with "persecute," which, though not a formal part of the law, is not surprising, given the great deal of discretion placed in the hands of the individual examiner.

But the "average" prosecution takes approximately two to three years. During this time the examiner and the inventor or inventor's attorney[45] engage in a series of negotiations. First the examiner may reject the application as deficient under a number of sections of the Patent Act. Then the examiner will normally attempt to narrow the wording of the claims. The process is helped immensely by the fact that examiners are specialists; they concentrate only on particular technologies, or commonly even a precise corner of a particular technology.

A patent specification describes the problem the inventor faced and the steps she took to solve it. It also provides a precise characterization of the "best mode" of solving the problem, in accordance with the first paragraph of section 112 of the patent statute, which reads:

> "[t]he specification shall contain a written description of the invention, and of the manner and process of making and using it, in such full, clear, concise, and exact terms as to enable any person skilled in the art to which it pertains ... to make and use the same, and shall set forth the best mode contemplated by the inventor of carrying out his invention."

The battle over the precise verbal boundary to the patentee's invention — i.e., the claims — is at the heart of patent prosecution, but the specification must *support* the claims.

Prosecution is a give and take affair. In the course of responding to an examiner's objections, an applicant will often amend her specification and claims. She can then file a **continuation** of the original application, changing only the claims; she can change her specification, and re-file her patent application as a so-called **continuation-in-part** or "C-I-P" application. The original filing date is preserved so long as no "new matter" is added. In either case, the original application is referred to as the **parent** application. If two continuations are filed, the original is the **grandparent**, and so on.

An application that the examiner believes contains more than one invention will be subject to a **restriction** requirement. The applicant must then decide which of the multiple "inventions" in the application she wishes to pursue; the others will have to be placed in a new and separate application. The claims corresponding to the invention she decides to pursue in the original applications are called the **elected** claims. Non-elected claims must be filed separately, along with an appropriate specification, in a **divisional application**.

Prosecution ends when one of two things happens: either the patent is granted, or it is the subject of a Final Rejection by the examiner. In the former case, the application — which will have been kept secret during prosecution — will mature into a full-fledged patent, which is then summarized in the Patent Gazette and made available for the public to copy it.

---

[45] Non-lawyer "Patent Agents" are permitted to practice before the PTO, but most who prosecute patent applications are patent lawyers.

Prosecution can in a sense continue after a patent has issued. A patentee who comes to believe that her patent claims are either too broad or too narrow can seek a **reissue** of the patent, so long as the deficiency in the original patent is the result of a bona fide error or omission. Reissues to broaden the scope of claims must be initiated within two years of the original issuance, however.

In a related proceeding, *anyone* (including the patentee) can seek a **reexamination** of a patent if a substantial new basis for questioning the patentability of the invention arises after issuance.

Often a patent applicant or patentee must show that she invented or filed her patent application before another person invented or disclosed the same or a similar invention. Proving first invention is known as establishing **priority**. The **Paris Convention** helps inventors establish priority by giving them one year from initial filing in a Convention Country to file in other Convention Countries. Another international treaty allows a patent applicant to wait even longer to "designate" which countries she wants to file patents in—the **Patent Cooperation Treaty** or **PCT**. These matters are discussed in Chapter 4 Section K.

For priority and other matters, U.S. patent lawyers need to be aware of the major foreign patent systems, primarily Japan and Europe. Both Japan and Europe base priority on the date a patent application is filed; like almost the entire world, they are **first to file** patent systems. The U.S., as we shall see, awards priority to the **first to invent,** though that may eventually change due to international negotiations and calls for domestic reform. The European countries have joined together in the **European Patent Convention** or **EPC** which provides for centralized patent prosecution in the **European Patent Office (EPO).** After prosecution, a European application issues as a "bundle" of national patents in those European countries the applicant "designates." After a brief **opposition** period, when rivals can challenge the validity of the patent in the EPO, the patent is enforced in the national courts of the designated countries. Europe is moving toward a system of European-wide patents, with centralized enforcement, via the **Community Patent Convention (CPC).**

1. PATENT COURTS AND CASES

A patent case can arise in two ways: either as an appeal from a decision by a patent examiner to reject a patent application, or as an action by a patentee against an accused infringer. An appeal of a rejected application follows a procedure not unlike that of many other administrative agency appeals. There is an internal Board of Appeals within the Patent Office which hears cases where an application has been the subject of a "final rejection." If an applicant is dissatisfied with the opinion of the Board of Appeals, he or she may appeal to the Court of Appeals for the Federal Circuit (described below).

Cases also arise when a patentee, whose patent has been issued by the Patent Office, brings a lawsuit against someone accused of infringing the patent. There are typically two defenses to such a suit: First, the accused infringer will argue that the patentee's patent is invalid for any number of reasons; an invalid patent, of course, cannot be infringed. Second, the accused infringer will usually argue that even if the patent is valid, the products being made or sold by the accused do not infringe the patentee's patent. Because invalidity is often argued as a defense in an infringement case, all the issues of patent validity dealt with by the Patent Office may also be considered by a court. As we shall see, the standard of review of the Patent Office's decision to issue a patent is a contentious question. But there is no doubt that a patent is "born valid": the Patent Act contains a provision stating that there is a "presumption of validity" that accompanies any issued patent. 35 U.S.C. § 282.

Nevertheless, one important function of judicial review of issued patents is to make sure that invalid patents are weeded out. In fact, this policy figured into an important recent case in the Supreme Court. In *Cardinal Chem. Co. v. Morton Int'l, Inc.*, 508 U.S. 83, 113 S. Ct. 1967 (1993), the Court reviewed the Federal Circuit's practice of vacating as moot trial court findings of patent invalidity in cases where the Federal Circuit reversed a finding that a patent had been infringed. The Federal Circuit had thought it prudent to reinstate the validity of a patent when the invalidity defense of an accused infringer had been rendered moot by a finding that the patent was not infringed. The Supreme Court ended this practice. In *Cardinal Chemical*, the Court emphasized the important judicial role in reviewing issued patents. In addition, the Court pointed out that great uncertainty surrounds a patent once found invalid, even if that finding is later vacated.

A unique form of patent dispute is a priority dispute between two or more inventors, all of whom claim to have been the first inventor of a particular invention. These are known as **interference** proceedings. They are an outgrowth of the fact that the U.S. awards a patent to the first inventor, unlike almost every other country, which awards the patent to the **first to file**. The United States is likely to adopt a first to file system at some point in the future, which will eliminate the need for most interference proceedings. Also, with the advent of the new **provisional patent application** procedure of § 111(b) of the Act (described in Section C.2.b, below), many inventors may adopt the practice of filing very early in the inventive process. This would effectively reduce the number of interferences, and make the U.S. something close to a de facto "first to file" country.

Finally, two types of "post-issuance" procedures are available in the U.S. First, anyone, including the patentee, can ask for a **reexamination** of the patent by the Patent Office. This requires new prior art, not considered during the original prosecution, which raises a substantial new issue of patentability. Accused infringers use reexamination to isolate the validity issue and put it before an expert tribunal, the Patent Office, which may be a cheaper and more reliable way to resolve these issues. See Chapter 10.

The second procedure is known as a **reissue**. Only the patentee can seek a reissue, and only if an error in the claims or disclosure was made "without deceptive intent" during the original prosecution. When a patentee seeks to broaden claims via reissue, she must do so within two years; third parties sometimes acquire "intervening rights" after issuance of the original patent and before the reissue. See Chapter 10.

2. HARMONIZATION

Given its mercantilist roots, it is not surprising that patent law is basically a domestic, territorial legal regime. In other words, a patent is valid and effective only in the country that issued it.

Patents may be territorial, but trade is global. This basic fact of economic life has long been true; it led to the adoption of the Paris Convention (discussed in detail in Chapter 4) in the late 19th century. Although the Paris Convention was primarily procedural, especially with respect to the uniform, world-wide priority date it made possible, it did contain some minimum substantive standards of protection (also described in Chapter 4). Even so, further efforts at harmonizing worldwide standards of patentability, patentees' rights, and infringement bore little fruit for most of the twentieth century.

This was in part due to the fact that the international business community seemed little interested in investing time in the esoteric issues of detailed harmonization. Although it was cumbersome to deal with the divergent standards held by the world's many individual domestic patent jurisdictions, some level of effective protection was available in most of the commercially important countries. Furthermore, patent law harmonization was the domain of a highly specialized affiliate of the United Nations, the World Intellectual Property Organization, a forum not thought to be particularly friendly to Western business interests.

Things were changing by the mid-1980s, however. For one thing, the perceived value of intellectual property was increasing; it was beginning to take on a more central role in business planning and strategy. (The establishment of the Federal Circuit in 1982 was both a consequence of this trend, and a partial cause of its continuation.) Of special concern was the increasing importance of overseas markets in developing countries — countries that had traditionally disfavored strong intellectual property protection. Businesses in the U.S. and Europe, aware both of the increasing importance of intellectual property and of WIPO's slow progress in harmonization, were thus on the lookout for an alternative forum in which to pursue harmonization. The search ended with the announcement of the Uruguay Round of negotiations to revise the main international trade agreement/organization, the General Agreement on Tariffs and Trade (GATT).

In addition to proposed reforms to the core function and structure of the GATT, the early Uruguay Round agenda soon grew to encompass negotiations on the "Trade Related Aspects of Intellectual Property," or TRIPs, as it soon became known. The reference in the title to "Trade Related" issues was a concession to those who doubted the relevance of intellectual property to the basic GATT mission. It soon became clear, however, that most of the basic elements of intellectual property protection would be up for discussion, and potential harmonization, in the TRIPs negotiations. And, by the time the GATT round ended in a flurry of brinkmanship in late 1993, TRIPs had become one of the principal components in the overall package of changes.

Although the post-TRIPs amendments in domestic U.S. law are important, they pale in contrast to the revolutionary changes the agreement makes to the intellectual property regimes of many developing countries. To summarize the highlights, all signatories of the Uruguay Round treaty (which, under the agreement, become members of the newly-created World Trade Organization (WTO)) must now:

- Include virtually all important commercial fields within the ambit of patentable subject matter, a major change for countries that, for example, have traditionally refused to enforce pharmaceutical patents on public health/access grounds;
- Test patent applications for the presence of an inventive step, which is defined as precisely synonymous with nonobviousness under § 103 of the U.S. Patent Act, as well as for "industrial application," similarly defined as coextensive with the U.S. utility requirement;
- Include in the patentees' bundle of exclusive rights the right to supply the market with imports of the patented products; and
- Curtail the practice of granting compulsory licenses for patented technology, by (1) requiring a good faith attempt to license voluntarily, (2) limiting duration, (3) requiring termination if conditions change, and (3) requiring compensation, subject to judicial review (Article 31).

See Final Act Embodying the Results of the Uruguay Round of Multilateral Trade Negotiations, April 15, 1994, at 2-3 (GATT Secretariat 1994); Annex 1C: Agreement on Trade-Related Aspects of Intellectual Property Rights, *id.* at 6-19, 365-403, reproduced at 33 I.L.M. 81 (1994).

The civil and administrative procedures outlined in the Agreement include provisions on evidence, injunctions, damages, and other remedies. (*See* Articles 45-48). It authorizes border measures, and provides for criminal penalties in at least the case of counterfeited copyrighted goods. There is in addition a provision authorizing courts to act promptly to order seizure of evidence that might be destroyed (Article 50).

Each of these provisions — along with all the other components of the new GATT agreement — are given teeth by the inclusion of detailed dispute resolution procedures. Any WTO member nation that feels aggrieved by the failure of another member to live up to its obligations under the Agreement can, after appropriate attempts at consultation, convene a dispute resolution panel. Unlike older GATT procedures, the panel's findings, which must be made quickly, are appealable to a special appellate body. *See* Understanding on Rules and Procedures Governing the Settlement of Disputes, GATT Document MTN/F-II-A2, Provision 17.

Changes to U.S. law brought on by the TRIPs Agreement are found in the Uruguay Round Agreements Act, Pub. L. No. 103-465 (H.R. 5110), Dec. 8, 1994. *See also* J.H. Reichman, *Universal Minimum Standards of Intellectual Property Protection Under the TRIPs Component of the WTO Agreement*, 29 INT'L LAW. 345 (1995) (able summary of provisions and open questions).

GATT-related changes to U.S. law are described in detail throughout this book. By way of summary, the most important provisions are:

- Changed the U.S. patent term to 20 years, measured from the date the patent application is filed, rather than 17 years, measured from the date the patent was issued by the Patent Office. 35 U.S.C. § 154. (Under certain circumstances, such as interferences and appealed rejections, this term may be extended for up to five years. *Id.*)
- Opened up the U.S. "first to invent" system by allowing members of the WTO to introduce evidence of pre-patent filing inventive acts in their home country for purposes of establishing priority. *See* 35 U.S.C. § 104.
- Expanded the definition of infringement to include the acts of unauthorized offering for sale and importing. 35 U.S.C. § 271.
- Added a new procedure for filing "provisional applications," 35 U.S.C. § 111, which must satisfy § 112, but need not include claims. Such an application does not begin the 20-year clock for the applicant's patent term, however.

a. A Note on the Patent Term

For a long time, the patent term was fixed at seventeen years, measured from the date of grant. Congress made an exception for pharmaceutical patents in 1984, providing extended patent terms to offset the lengthy review process of the Food and Drug Administration. The elaborate provisions on term extensions are found at 35 U.S.C. § 155 et seq. *Cf.* Grabowski & Vernon, *Longer Patents for Lower Imitation Barriers*, 76 AM. ECON. REV. 195 (Papers & Procs.) (1986) (economic analysis of tradeoff in Patent Term Restoration and Drug Price Competition Act of 1984, between term extensions and provisions allowing generic pharmaceutical firms to begin FDA testing prior to expiration of patent).

Patent terms are one of the areas of U.S. patent law most heavily affected by the TRIPs Agreement of the Uruguay Round. Patents will now be valid for a term of twenty years *measured from the filing date*, rather than the issue date. This change was made primarily for the sake of international uniformity. In addition, however, it creates a disincentive for patent applicants to stretch out prosecution for long periods of time, a practice that has led to such outrageous results as the 1994 issuance of a patent whose original counterpart was filed in *1954! See* Jerome Lemelson, U.S. Patent 5,351,078, issued September 27, 1994 on an application originally filed December 24, 1954. *See* Teresa Riordan, *A Submarine Patent Surfaces 40 Years After the Inventor Filed His Application*, N.Y. TIMES, Apr. 4, 1994. Such "submarine patents" will be eliminated now that long pendency times come at the expense of the applicant. For an excellent study on the benefits of the new twenty-year term, see Mark Lemley, *An Empirical Study of the Twenty-Year Patent Term*, 22 AM. INTELL. PROP. L. ASS'N Q.J. 369, 391 (1995) (thirty-one patents out of over two thousand studied would have lost four or more years of protection under the new term; of these, fifteen (48%) qualify as submarine patents as defined in the study).

The statute setting forth the patent term does list several circumstances under which applicants can apply for an extension of the basic twenty-year term. These are set forth in the following excerpt from 35 U.S.C. § 154.

§ 154. Contents and term of patent

(a) In general. —

(1) Contents. — Every patent shall contain a short title of the invention and a grant to the patentee, his heirs or assigns, of the right to exclude others ....

(2) Term. — Subject to the payment of fees under this title, such grant shall be for a term beginning on the date on which the patent issues and ending 20 years from the date on which the application for the patent was filed in the United States or, if the application contains a specific reference to an earlier filed application or applications under section 120, 121, or 365(c) of this title, from the date on which the earliest such application was filed.

(3) Priority. — Priority under section 119, 365(a), or 365(b) of this title shall not be taken into account in determining the term of a patent.

(4) Specification and drawing. — A copy of the specification and drawing shall be annexed to the patent and be a part of such patent.

(b) Term extension. —

(1) Interference delay or secrecy orders. — If the issue of an original patent is delayed due to a proceeding under section 135(a) of this title, or because the application for patent is placed under an order pursuant to section 181 of this title, the term of the patent shall be extended for the period of delay, but in no case more than 5 years.

(2) Extension for appellate review. — If the issue of a patent is delayed due to appellate review by the Board of Patent Appeals and Interferences or by a Federal court and the patent is issued pursuant to a decision in the review reversing an adverse determination of patentability, the term of the patent shall be extended for a period of time but in no case more than 5 years. A patent shall not be eligible for extension under this paragraph if it is subject to a terminal disclaimer due to the issue of another patent claiming subject matter that is not patentably distinct from that under appellate review.

(3) Limitations. — The period of extension referred to in paragraph (2) —

(A) shall include any period beginning on the date on which an appeal is filed under section 134 or 141 of this title, or on which an action is commenced under section 145 of this title, and ending on the date of a final decision in favor of the applicant;

(B) shall be reduced by any time attributable to appellate review before the expiration of 3 years from the filing date of the application for patent; and

(C) shall be reduced for the period of time during which the applicant for patent did not act with due diligence, as determined by the Commissioner.

(4) Length of extension. — The total duration of all extensions of a patent under this subsection shall not exceed 5 years.

(c) Continuation. —

(1) Determination. — The term of a patent that is in force on or that results from an application filed before the date that is 6 months after the date of the enactment of the Uruguay Round Agreements Act shall be the greater of the 20-year term as provided in subsection (a), or 17 years from grant, subject to any terminal disclaimers.

(2) Remedies. — The remedies of sections 283, 284, and 285 of this title shall not apply to acts which —

(A) were commenced or for which substantial investment was made before the date that is 6 months after the date of the enactment of the Uruguay Round Agreements Act; and

(B) became infringing by reason of paragraph (1).

(3) Remuneration. — The acts referred to in paragraph (2) may be continued only upon the payment of an equitable remuneration to the patentee that is determined in an action brought under chapter 28 and chapter 29 (other than those provisions excluded by paragraph (2)) of this title.

A careful reading of § 154 reveals some statutory changes that will greatly impact standard patent practice. First, the term of a patent that issues from a divisional or a continuation application will run from the filing date of the parent U.S. application, not from the filing date of the divisional or continuation application. This simple provision ends the longstanding practice — common especially in the pharmaceutical industry — of "serial prosecution." A single application is filed claiming a number of distinct variants on the invention: a therapeutic molecule, for instance, together with a claim to the molecule in a mixture of other constituents, and a claim to a method of making the molecule. The assumption is that the examiner will order a restriction. After the restriction, the invention is divided into its several components. The molecule, for instance is "elected" for initial prosecution. Meanwhile, the other claims are left in limbo, to be taken up only when the initial elected invention has completed its path through prosecution. In this way, the same (early) priority date is secured for each of the three components of the invention, and yet the applicant can let a stream of related patents issue over a long period of time. This enhances the ability of the applicant to exclude competition in the market for the invention, or at least limit it along various dimensions, often for a period much longer than the initial seventeen-year term of the molecule patent. *See* Kenneth J. Burchfiel, *U.S. GATT Legislation Changes Patent Term*, 77 J. PAT. & TRADEMARK OFF. SOC'Y 222, 224-25 (1995).

Second, the new statute makes appeals more appealing, so to speak. This is because any appeal from an adverse determination of patentability has the potential to add time back onto the patent term. In essence, the appeal provisions allow patent applicants to offset somewhat the limiting effects of the new patent term. Under the new statute, time will be added back onto the term due to an appeal when (1) the appeal is successful (obviously!), and (2) when at least part of the appeal period comes more than three years after the original filing date for the application. (Do you see why this limitation is necessary? What if all appeals, no matter when filed, added time to the patent term — what incentives would applicants have, and what kind of workload would the Board of Appeals and the Federal Circuit have?) *Cf.* Comment, Patricia Montalvo, *How Will the New Twenty-Year Patent Term Affect You? A Look at the TRIPS Agreement and the Adoption of a Twenty-Year Patent Term*, 12 SANTA CLARA COMPUTER & HIGH TECH. L.J. 139 (1996).

The ability to add patent term due to an appeal will change patent strategy in profound ways. Instead of arguing with an examiner over the patentability of broad claims, the savvy applicant might choose instead to appeal an examiner's rejection as soon as it becomes apparent that prosecution will extend beyond three years. The strategic use of appeals is one of the few ways that patent term can be saved under the new version of § 154.

Third, § 154 sets the patent term clock running when a U.S. patent application is filed. Under § 154(a)(3), patent applications claiming the benefit of earlier foreign filing dates (under the Paris Convention or under the Patent Cooperation Treaty (PCT); see Chapter 4) have terms measured only when their U.S. counterpart applications are filed. While this provides somewhat of an advantage to those who file abroad first, the new provisional patent application procedure — described in the next section — gives U.S. applicants some of the same advantages vis-à-vis the measurement of patent term.

Section 154 also sets out transitional provisions that will apply to certain applications "in the pipeline" at the time the URAA was passed and took effect (generally, June 8, 1995). Two features of the transition period are especially important: (1) All patents still valid on June 8, 1995 automatically receive the longer of the original seventeen-year term *or* the new twenty year from filing term, which automatically extends all patents that had been issued with less than three years of prosecution; and (2) Third parties who had relied on the expiration of these extant patents will be subject to the special remedial provisions of § 154, which provides for "equitable remuneration" in place of the normal remedies of compensatory damages, injunctions, and punitive damages (for willful infringement). *See* Chapter 9.

b. Provisional Applications

It is ironic that one of the most important post-GATT additions to U.S. patent law merely rode the coattails of the Uruguay Round. Strictly speaking, the addition of provisional patent applications was not essential to the Uruguay Round of amendments to U.S. patent law, since there is no such requirement in the GATT TRIPs Agreement.

Nevertheless, provisional patent applications were considered an important component in the overall attractiveness of the GATT package, especially because the pendency of provisional applications is *excluded* from the twenty-year patent term now in effect.

Provisional applications are the subject of 35 U.S.C. § 111 and § 119(e), reproduced below.

§ 111. Application

(a) In general. —

(1) Written application. — An application for patent shall be made, or authorized to be made, by the inventor, except as otherwise provided in this title, in writing to the Commissioner.

(2) Contents. — Such application shall include —

(A) a specification as prescribed by section 112 of this title;

(B) a drawing as prescribed by section 113 of this title; and

(C) an oath by the applicant as prescribed by section 115 of this title.

(3) Fee and oath. — The application must be accompanied by the fee required by law. The fee and oath may be submitted after the specification and any required drawing are submitted, within such period and under such conditions, including the payment of a surcharge, as may be prescribed by the Commissioner.

(4) Failure to submit. — Upon failure to submit the fee and oath within such prescribed period, the application shall be regarded as abandoned, unless it is shown to the satisfaction of the Commissioner that the delay in submitting the fee and oath was unavoidable or unintentional. The filing date of an application shall be the date on which the specification and any required drawing are received in the Patent and Trademark Office.

(b) Provisional application. —

(1) Authorization. — A provisional application for patent shall be made or authorized to be made by the inventor, except as otherwise provided in this title, in writing to the Commissioner. Such application shall include —

(A) a specification as prescribed by the first paragraph of section 112 of this title; and

(B) a drawing as prescribed by section 113 of this title.

(2) Claim. — A claim, as required by the second through fifth paragraphs of section 112, shall not be required in a provisional application.

(3) Fee. — (A) The application must be accompanied by the fee required by law.

(B) The fee may be submitted after the specification and any required drawing are submitted, within such period and under such conditions, including the payment of a surcharge, as may be prescribed by the Commissioner.

(C) Upon failure to submit the fee within such prescribed period, the application shall be regarded as abandoned, unless it is shown to the satisfaction of the Commissioner that the delay in submitting the fee was unavoidable or unintentional.

(4) Filing date. — The filing date of a provisional application shall be the date on which the specification and any required drawing are received in the Patent and Trademark Office.

(5) Abandonment. — The provisional application shall be regarded as abandoned 12 months after the filing date of such application and shall not be subject to revival thereafter.

(6) Other basis for provisional application. — Subject to all the conditions in this subsection and section 119(e) of this title, and as prescribed by the Commissioner, an application for patent filed under subsection (a) may be treated as a provisional application for patent.

(7) No right of priority or benefit of earliest filing date. — A provisional application shall not be entitled to the right of priority of any other application under section 119 or 365(a) of this title or to the benefit of an earlier filing date in the United States under section 120, 121, or 365(c) of this title.

(8) Applicable provisions. — The provisions of this title relating to applications for patent shall apply to provisional applications for patent, except as otherwise provided, and except that provisional applications for patent shall not be subject to sections 115, 131, 135, and 157 of this title.

§ 119. Benefit of earlier filing date; right of priority

....

(e)(1) An application for patent filed under section 111(a) or section 363 of this title for an invention disclosed in the manner provided by the first paragraph of section 112 of this title in a provisional application filed under section 111(b) of this title, by an inventor or inventors named in the provisional application, shall have the same effect, as to such invention, as though filed on the date of the provisional application filed under section 111(b) of this title, if the application for patent filed under section 111(a) or section 363 of this title is filed not later than 12 months after the date on which the provisional application was filed and if it contains or is amended to contain a specific reference to the provisional application.

(2) A provisional application filed under section 111(b) of this title may not be relied upon in any proceeding in the Patent and Trademark Office unless the fee set forth in subparagraph (A) or (C) of section 41(a)(1) of this title has

been paid and the provisional application was pending on the filing date of the application for patent under section 111(a) or section 363 of this title.

Section 111(b) merely allows provisional applications. But § 119 provides that a provisional application can establish priority for a "normal" application filed within one year of the provisional.[46] This means that the provisional — simpler and cheaper than a regular application — can serve as a "placeholder" for a regular application. The only requirement in this regard is that a provisional application must be converted to a regular application within a year. Indeed, this is essential if a patent is ever to issue; provisional applications are not examined. They simply preserve the applicant's priority date until converted into regular applications.

Most importantly from the applicant's point of view, the time in which a provisional application is pending *does not count* toward the new 20-year patent term. The patent term is triggered only by the filing of a *regular* (§ 111(a)) patent application. Thus the pendency of a provisional application provides a kind of "patent term grace period" that applicants will surely learn to take advantage of. (There is a similar grace period built into the new § 154 for inventors who file abroad first; their U.S. term is measured from the date of their first U.S. application, as opposed to their first application abroad; see preceding section.)

Provisional applications create, in effect, a system of "internal priority" for applications filed in the U.S. Patent Office. An application can be filed with minimal formalities; it is then held for up to one year. During that year, the application will not be examined by the Patent Office, unless the applicant converts the *provisional* application into a regular, or nonprovisional, one. For a minimal filing fee — a key advantage of a provisional over a normal application — the applicant preserves an early filing date while still gaining time to perfect the invention and seek financing to implement it. The fee is set at $150 for 1996, for instance, which compares quite favorably with the nonprovisional fee, which starts at $500 and quickly mounts. *See* 35 U.S.C. § 41 (1996). Of course, the provisional application must be converted to a nonprovisional one within one

---

[46]This is by virtue of § 119(e)(1), which reads in part:

> An application for patent filed under section 111(a) [i.e., a "regular," nonprovisional application] or section 363 [the equivalent for certain international applications; see Chapter 4] of this title for an invention disclosed in the manner provided by the first paragraph of section 112 of this title in a provisional application filed under section 111(b) of this title, by an inventor or inventors named in the provisional application, shall have the same effect, as to such invention, as though filed on the date of the provisional application filed under section 111(b) of this title, if the application for patent filed under section 111(a) or section 363 of this title is filed not later than 12 months after the date on which the provisional application was filed and if it contains or is amended to contain a specific reference to the provisional application.

35 U.S.C. § 119 (1996).

year, but that year is very valuable for someone trying to perfect an invention, or trying to raise money to commercialize it.

On its face, section 111 seems to contain a minor bit of favoritism for those who file first in the U.S. Section 111(b)(7) says that an applicant "shall not be entitled to the right of priority of any other application under section 119 or 365(a) of this title ...," which effectively eliminates the possibility of using a foreign application to establish an earlier priority date for a U.S. provisional application. There is more to the story, however. In many countries, something like an internal priority system already exists. *Cf.* Yoshikazu Tani, *Preparation and Prosecution of Electronic and Computer Related Patent Application in Japan*, PRACTISING LAW INSTITUTE PATENTS, COPYRIGHTS, TRADEMARKS, AND LITERARY PROPERTY COURSE HANDBOOK SERIES, PLI/PAT. 371 (1990) (describing system of internal priority in Japan). Hence some of the benefits of provisional filings may well be available to foreign applicants, in their home country. Section 111 merely levels the playing field. Section 111(b)(7) is also necessary to prevent a windfall to foreign applicants. Since neither foreign pendency nor provisional application pendency counts against the new U.S. patent term, and since both these periods can be up to one year long, without § 111(b)(7) foreign applicants could have up to two years of "free" application pendency. This would be most unfair, since domestic U.S. inventors who file provisional applications have at most one year of pendency that is not counted against the twenty-year patent term. *Cf.* 35 U.S.C. § 154(a)(3).

On the other hand, it is fairly clear that a provisional application can preserve international priority under the Paris Convention. *See* "Provisional Applications for Patent Meet Paris Convention Requirements," 1180 OFFICIAL GAZETTE 131 (Nov. 28, 1995). This is of course essential. If they did not preserve international priority for up to one year under the Convention, provisional applications would have to be supplemented immediately with at least one other "regular" application in a Paris Convention country, making provisional applications much less attractive. On the details of using provisional applications as the basis of international priority, see Charles E. Van Horne, *Practicalities and Potential Pitfalls When Using Provisional Patent Applications*, 22 AM. INTELL. PROP. L. ASS'N Q.J. 259 (1994). In addition, a provisional application preserves some rights not normally available to foreign applicants, such as the right to claim the patent application as effective prior art under § 102(e) as of its U.S. filing date. (Section 102(e) establishes that disclosed but unclaimed material in a patent application operates as prior art against later claims to the same material, but only for applications filed "in this country"; see Chapter 4.)

The simplicity and low cost of filing a provisional application makes this an important addition to the applicant's arsenal of strategic tools. It has even been suggested that, in a pinch, one can file documents already on hand — e.g., a draft of a scientific article or even copies of lab notebooks — in the form of a provisional application:

The disclosure of a provisional application need not follow any particular form and can contain a diversity of documentary materials. For reasons of necessity (i.e., an imminent statutory bar [see Chapter 4]), convenience or cost, one might be inclined to provide part or even all of the disclosure of the application in the form of one or more documents that are already on hand. Certainly, there is no intrinsic objection to doing so. However, there is the danger that one or more of the documents may include subject matter that is not needed to satisfy § 112 [see Chapter 6] but embodies valuable proprietary information not intended for disclosure. Review of the documents with a view to their judicious editing prior to inclusion in the provisional application will usually prevent an unintentional disclosure of such information. One must be mindful not to over-edit and delete disclosure required to satisfy best mode [see Chapter 6]. This presupposes a good understanding of the decisional law relating to best mode and sound judgement in applying that law to a particular situation.

Peter G. Dilworth, *Some Suggestions for Maximizing the Benefits of Provisional Applications*, 78 J. PAT. & TRADEMARK OFF. SOC'Y 233, 238-39 (1996).

3. THE NEXT WAVE?

Many expect a wave of follow-on amendments to U.S. law. Typical candidates include:

- Publication of all U.S. patent applications 18 months after filing, as is now the case in Europe and Japan;
- "Prior user rights" for independent inventors using an invention later claimed in a U.S. patent by another inventor; and
- A first to file priority rule, in line with the rest of the world.
- Redesignation of the Patent Office as an independent, government-affiliated corporation, so as to give the Office greater flexibility in hiring, etc., and to increase control over financial affairs.

All of these provisions — except the last one — are in place in many foreign countries. These are primarily discussed in Chapter 4, on Novelty and Priority.

Chapter 2

PATENTABLE SUBJECT MATTER

A. INTRODUCTION TO THE PATENT ACT

This chapter deals with what is known as patentable subject matter under § 101 of the Patent Act: that is, the issue of which *types* of inventions will be considered for patent protection. We will be concerned with the general classes into which inventions fit, rather than their particular characteristics. We ask, for instance, whether living things can be patented, or whether mathematical algorithms are proper patent subject matter. We are not concerned here whether any *particular* plant or algorithm meets the technical requirements of patentability (novelty, utility, nonobviousness, etc.) — these requirements are the subject of Chapters 3 through 6.

The statutory provision on patentable subject matter is quite brief, and has changed very little from the first version, penned by Thomas Jefferson:

§ 101. Inventions Patentable

Whoever invents or discovers any new and useful process, machine, manufacture, or composition of matter, or any new and useful improvement thereof, may obtain a patent therefor, subject to the conditions and requirements of this title.

At first glance, applying this statute might seem quite straightforward: simply ask whether an invention fits one of these categories, and if it does, consider § 101 satisfied. For various reasons, however, the approach taken by the courts over the years has not always been so simple. To take one example (developed at length later in this chapter), many a researcher who "discovers ... [a] new and useful ... composition of matter" — a pine needle with medicinal properties, for example — has been denied a patent. As it turns out, in this and many other examples, the language of the Patent Act must be read in light of the many cases over the past two hundred or so years that have interpreted it and its predecessors in now defunct versions of the statute. (In this way, certain provisions of the Patent Act have a distinctly common law feel.) And as we will see, in at least some cases these accumulated interpretations are driven by common sense judgments about the economics of patents.

The best way to see these principles at work is to start with the following opinion. It introduces us to the issue of patents for living subject matter, and "biotechnology" in general; we deal with this in depth later in this chapter, in Section D.

DIAMOND v. CHAKRABARTY

447 U.S. 303, 206 U.S.P.Q. (BNA) 193 (1980)

BURGER, C.J.

We granted certiorari to determine whether a live, human-made micro-organism is patentable subject matter under 35 U.S.C. § 101.

I

In 1972, respondent Chakrabarty, a microbiologist, filed a patent application, assigned to the General Electric Co. The application asserted 36 claims related to Chakrabarty's invention of "a bacterium from the genus *Pseudomonas* containing therein at least two stable energy-generating plasmids, each of said plasmids providing a separate hydrocarbon degradative pathway." [1] This human-made, genetically engineered bacterium is capable of breaking down multiple components of crude oil. Because of this property, which is possessed by no naturally occurring bacteria, Chakrabarty's invention is believed to have significant value for the treatment of oil spills.

Chakrabarty's patent claims were of three types: first, process claims for the method of producing the bacteria; second, claims for an inoculum comprised of a carrier material floating on water, such as straw, and the new bacteria; and third, claims to the bacteria themselves. The patent examiner allowed the claims falling into the first two categories, but rejected claims for the bacteria. His decision rested on two grounds: (1) that micro-organisms are "products of nature," and (2) that as living things they are not patentable subject matter under 35 U.S.C. § 101.

Chakrabarty appealed the rejection of these claims to the Patent Office Board of Appeals, and the Board affirmed the examiner on the second ground. [2] Relying on the legislative history of the 1930 Plant Patent Act, in which Congress extended patent protection to certain asexually reproduced plants, the Board concluded that § 101 was not intended to cover living things such as these laboratory created micro-organisms. [After the Supreme Court vacated its original opinion,] [t]he Court of Customs and Patent Appeals vacated its judgment in *Chakrabarty* and consolidated the case with *Bergy* for reconsideration. After re-

---

[1] Plasmids are hereditary units physically separate from the chromosomes of the cell. In prior research, Chakrabarty and an associate discovered that plasmids control the oil degradation abilities of certain bacteria. In particular, the two researchers discovered plasmids capable of degrading camphor and octane, two components of crude oil. In the work represented by the patent application at issue here, Chakrabarty discovered a process by which four different plasmids, capable of degrading four different oil components, could be transferred to and maintained stably in a single *Pseudomonas* bacterium, which itself has no capacity for degrading oil.

[2] The Board concluded that the new bacteria were not "products of nature," because *Pseudomonas* bacteria containing two or more different energy-generating plasmids are not naturally occurring.

examining both cases in the light of our holding in [*Parker v.*] *Flook*, [437 U.S. 584 (1978)], that court reaffirmed its earlier judgments.

The Commissioner of Patents and Trademarks again sought certiorari, and we granted the writ as to both *Bergy* and *Chakrabarty*. Since then, *Bergy* has been dismissed as moot, leaving only *Chakrabarty* for decision.

II

The Constitution grants Congress broad power to legislate to "promote the Progress of Science and useful Arts,..." The patent laws promote this progress by offering inventors exclusive rights for a limited period as an incentive for their inventiveness and research efforts. The authority of Congress is exercised in the hope that "[t]he productive effort thereby fostered will have a positive effect on society through the introduction of new products and processes of manufacture into the economy, and the emanations by way of increased employment and better lives for our citizens."

The question before us in this case is a narrow one of statutory interpretation requiring us to construe 35 U.S.C. § 101. Specifically, we must determine whether respondent's micro-organism constitutes a "manufacture" or "composition of matter" within the meaning of the statute.

III

[T]his Court has read the term "manufacture" in § 101 in accordance with its dictionary definition to mean "the production of articles for use from raw or prepared materials by giving to these materials new forms, qualities, properties, or combinations, whether by hand-labor or by machinery." *American Fruit Growers, Inc. v. Brogdex Co.*, 283 U.S. 1, 11 (1931). Similarly, "composition of matter" has been construed consistent with its common usage to include "all compositions of two or more substances and ... all composite articles, whether they be the results of chemical union, or of mechanical mixture, or whether they be gases, fluids, powders or solids." *Shell Development Co. v. Watson*, 149 F. Supp. 279, 280 (D.D.C. 1957). In choosing such expansive terms as "manufacture" and "composition of matter," modified by the comprehensive "any," Congress plainly contemplated that the patent laws would be given wide scope.

The relevant legislative history also supports a broad construction. The Patent Act of 1793, authored by Thomas Jefferson, defined statutory subject matter as "any new and useful art, machine, manufacture, or composition of matter, or any new or useful improvement [thereof]." Act of Feb. 21, 1793, § 1, 1 Stat. 319. The Act embodied Jefferson's philosophy that "ingenuity should receive a liberal encouragement." 5 Writings of Thomas Jefferson 75-76 (Washington ed. 1871). Subsequent patent statutes in 1836, 1870, and 1874 employed this same broad language. In 1952, when the patent laws were recodified, Congress replaced the word "art" with "process," but otherwise left Jefferson's language intact. The Committee Reports accompanying the 1952 Act inform us that Congress intended statutory subject matter to "include anything under the sun that is made by man." S. Rep. No. 1979, 82d Cong., 2d Sess., 5 (1952); H.R. Rep. No. 1923, 82d Cong., 2d Sess., 6 (1952).

This is not to suggest that § 101 has no limits or that it embraces every discovery. The laws of nature, physical phenomena, and abstract ideas have been held not patentable. Thus, a new mineral discovered in the earth or a new plant found in the wild is not patentable subject matter. Likewise, Einstein could not patent his celebrated law that $E = mc^2$; nor could Newton have patented the law of gravity. Such discoveries are "manifestations of ... nature, free to all men and reserved exclusively to none."

Judged in this light, respondent's micro-organism plainly qualifies as patentable subject matter. His claim is not to a hitherto unknown natural phenomenon, but to a nonnaturally occurring manufacture or composition of matter — a product of human ingenuity "having a distinctive name, character [and] use." The point is underscored dramatically by comparison of the invention here with that in *Funk [Bros. Seed Co. v. Kalo Inoculant Co.,* 333 U.S. 127 (1948)]. There, the patentee had discovered that there existed in nature certain species of root-nodule bacteria which did not exert a mutually inhibitive effect on each other. He used that discovery to produce a mixed culture capable of inoculating the seeds of leguminous plants. Concluding that the patentee had discovered "only some of the handiwork of nature," the Court ruled the product nonpatentable:

> Each of the species of root-nodule bacteria contained in the package infects the same group of leguminous plants which it always infected. No species acquires a different use. The combination of species produces no new bacteria, no change in the six species of bacteria, and no enlargement of the range of their utility. Each species has the same effect it always had. The bacteria perform in their natural way. Their use in combination does not improve in any way their natural functioning. They serve the ends nature originally provided and act quite independently of any effort of the patentee.

333 U.S., at 131.

Here, by contrast, the patentee has produced a new bacterium with markedly different characteristics from any found in nature and one having the potential for significant utility. His discovery is not nature's handiwork, but his own; accordingly it is patentable subject matter under § 101.

IV

Two contrary arguments are advanced, neither of which we find persuasive.

The petitioner's first argument rests on the enactment of the 1930 Plant Patent Act, which afforded patent protection to certain asexually reproduced plants, and the 1970 Plant Variety Protection Act, which authorized protection for certain sexually reproduced plants but excluded bacteria from its protection.[3] In the petitioner's view, the passage of these Acts evidences congressional understanding that the terms "manufacture" or "composition of matter" do not include living things; if they did, the petitioner argues, neither Act would have been necessary.

We reject this argument. Prior to 1930, two factors were thought to remove plants from patent protection. The first was the belief that plants, even those artificially bred, were products of nature for purposes of the patent law. This position appears to have derived from the decision of the Patent Office in *Ex parte Latimer*, 1889 Dec. Com. Pat. 123, in which a patent claim for fiber found in the needle of the *Pinus australis* was rejected. The Commissioner reasoned that a contrary result would permit "patents [to] be obtained upon the trees of the forest and the plants of the earth, which of course would be unreasonable and impossible." *Id.*, at 126. The *Latimer* case, it seems, came to "se[t] forth the general stand taken in these matters" that plants were natural products not subject to patent protection. Thorne, Relation of Patent Law to Natural Products, 6 J. Pat. Off. Soc. 23, 24 (1923).[4] The second obstacle to patent protection for plants was the fact that plants were thought not amenable to the "written description" requirement of the patent law. See 35 U.S.C. § 112. Because new plants may differ from old only in color or perfume, differentiation by written description was often impossible.

In enacting the Plant Patent Act, Congress addressed both of these concerns. It explained at length its belief that the work of the plant breeder "in aid of nature" was patentable invention. S. Rep. No. 315, 71st Cong., 2d Sess., 6-8 (1930); H.R. Rep. No. 1129, 71st Cong., 2d Sess., 7-9 (1930). And it relaxed the written description requirement in favor of "a description ... as complete as is reasonably possible." 35 U.S.C. § 162. No committee or Member of Congress, however, expressed the broader view, now urged by the petitioner, that the

---

[3] The Plant Patent Act of 1930, 35 U.S.C. § 161, provides in relevant part:

Whoever invents or discovers and asexually reproduces any distinct and new variety of plant, including cultivated sports, mutants, hybrids, and newly found seedlings, other than a tuber propagated plant or a plant found in an uncultivated state, may obtain a patent therefor....

The Plant Variety Protection Act of 1970, provides in relevant part:

The breeder of any novel variety of sexually reproduced plant (other than fungi, bacteria, or first generation hybrids) who has so reproduced the variety, or his successor in interest, shall be entitled to plant variety protection therefor....

84 Stat. 1547, 7 U.S.C. § 2402(a). See generally, 3 A. Deller, Walker on Patents, ch. IX (2d ed. 1964); R. Allyn, The First Plant Patents (1934).

[4] Writing three years after the passage of the 1930 Act, R. Cook, Editor of the Journal of Heredity, commented: "It is a little hard for plant men to understand why [Art. I, § 8] of the Constitution should not have been earlier construed to include the promotion of the art of plant breeding. The reason for this is probably to be found in the principle that natural products are not patentable." Florists Exchange and Horticultural Trade World, July 15, 1933, p. 9.

terms "manufacture" or "composition of matter" exclude living things. The sole support for that position in the legislative history of the 1930 Act is found in the conclusory statement of Secretary of Agriculture Hyde, in a letter to the Chairmen of the House and Senate Committees considering the 1930 Act, that "the patent laws ... at the present time are understood to cover only inventions or discoveries in the field of inanimate nature." See S. Rep. No. 315, *supra*, at Appendix A; H.R. Rep. No. 1129, *supra*, at Appendix A. Secretary Hyde's opinion, however, is not entitled to controlling weight. His views were solicited on the administration of the new law and not on the scope of patentable subject matter — an area beyond his competence. Moreover, there is language in the House and Senate Committee Reports suggesting that to the extent Congress considered the matter it found the Secretary's dichotomy unpersuasive. The Reports observe:

> There is a clear and logical distinction *between the discovery of a new variety of plant and of certain inanimate things*, such, for example, as a new and useful natural mineral. The mineral is created wholly by nature unassisted by man.... On the other hand, a plant discovery resulting from cultivation is unique, isolated, and is not repeated by nature, nor can it be reproduced by nature unaided by man....

S. Rep. No. 315, *supra*, at 6; H.R. Rep. No. 1129, *supra*, at 7 (emphasis added). Congress thus recognized that the relevant distinction was not between living and inanimate things, but between products of nature, whether living or not, and human-made inventions. Here, respondent's micro-organism is the result of human ingenuity and research. Hence, the passage of the Plant Patent Act affords the Government no support.

Nor does the passage of the 1970 Plant Variety Protection Act support the Government's position. As the Government acknowledges, sexually reproduced plants were not included under the 1930 Act because new varieties could not be reproduced true-to-type through seedlings. By 1970, however, it was generally recognized that true-to-type reproduction was possible and that plant patent protection was therefore appropriate. The 1970 Act extended that protection. There is nothing in its language or history to suggest that it was enacted because § 101 did not include living things.

In particular, we find nothing in the exclusion of bacteria from plant variety protection to support the petitioner's position. The legislative history gives no reason for this exclusion. As the Court of Customs and Patent Appeals suggested, it may simply reflect congressional agreement with the result reached by that court in deciding *In re Arzberger*, 27 C.C.P.A. (Pat.) 1315, 112 F.2d 834 (1940), which held that bacteria were not plants for the purposes of the 1930 Act. Or it may reflect the fact that prior to 1970 the Patent Office had issued patents for bacteria under § 101. In any event, absent some clear indication that Congress "focused on [the] issues ... directly related to the one presently before the

Court," there is no basis for reading into its actions an intent to modify the plain meaning of the words found in § 101.

The petitioner's second argument is that micro-organisms cannot qualify as patentable subject matter until Congress expressly authorizes such protection. His position rests on the fact that genetic technology was unforeseen when Congress enacted § 101. From this it is argued that resolution of the patentability of inventions such as respondent's should be left to Congress. The legislative process, the petitioner argues, is best equipped to weigh the competing economic, social, and scientific considerations involved, and to determine whether living organisms produced by genetic engineering should receive patent protection. In support of this position, the petitioner relies on our recent holding in *Parker v. Flook*, 437 U.S. 584 (1978), and the statement that the judiciary "must proceed cautiously when ... asked to extend patent rights into areas wholly unforeseen by Congress." *Id.*, at 596.

It is, of course, correct that Congress, not the courts, must define the limits of patentability; but it is equally true that once Congress has spoken it is "the province and duty of the judicial department to say what the law is." *Marbury v. Madison*, 1 Cranch 137, 177 (1803). Congress has performed its constitutional role in defining patentable subject matter in § 101; we perform ours in construing the language Congress has employed. In so doing, our obligation is to take statutes as we find them, guided, if ambiguity appears, by the legislative history and statutory purpose. Here, we perceive no ambiguity. The subject-matter provisions of the patent law have been cast in broad terms to fulfill the constitutional and statutory goal of promoting "the Progress of Science and the useful Arts" with all that means for the social and economic benefits envisioned by Jefferson. Broad general language is not necessarily ambiguous when congressional objectives require broad terms.

Nothing in *Flook* is to the contrary. The Court carefully scrutinized the claim at issue to determine whether it was precluded from patent protection under "the principles underlying the prohibition against patents for 'ideas' or phenomena of nature." *Id.*, at 593. We have done that here. *Flook* did not announce a new principle that inventions in areas not contemplated by Congress when the patent laws were enacted are unpatentable *per se*.

To read that concept into *Flook* would frustrate the purposes of the patent law. This is especially true in the field of patent law. A rule that unanticipated inventions are without protection would conflict with the core concept of the patent law that anticipation undermines patentability. Mr. Justice Douglas reminded that the inventions most benefiting mankind are those that "push back the frontiers of chemistry, physics, and the like." *Great A.&P. Tea Co. v. Supermarket Corp.*, 340 U.S. 147, 154 (1950) (concurring opinion). Congress employed broad general language in drafting § 101 precisely because such inventions are often unforeseeable.[5]

---

[5] Even an abbreviated list of patented inventions underscores the point: telegraph (Morse, No.

To buttress his argument, the petitioner, with the support of *amicus*, points to grave risks that may be generated by research endeavors such as respondent's. The briefs present a gruesome parade of horribles. Scientists, among them Nobel laureates, are quoted suggesting that genetic research may pose a serious threat to the human race, or, at the very least, that the dangers are far too substantial to permit such research to proceed apace at this time. We are told that genetic research and related technological developments may spread pollution and disease, that it may result in a loss of genetic diversity, and that its practice may tend to depreciate the value of human life. These arguments are forcefully, even passionately, presented; they remind us that, at times, human ingenuity seems unable to control fully the forces it creates — that, with Hamlet, it is sometimes better "to bear those ills we have than fly to others that we know not of."

It is argued that this Court should weigh these potential hazards in considering whether respondent's invention is patentable subject matter under § 101. We disagree. The grant or denial of patents on micro-organisms is not likely to put an end to genetic research or to its attendant risks. The large amount of research that has already occurred when no researcher had sure knowledge that patent protection would be available suggests that legislative or judicial fiat as to patentability will not deter the scientific mind from probing into the unknown any more than Canute could command the tides. Whether respondent's claims are patentable may determine whether research efforts are accelerated by the hope of reward or slowed by want of incentives, but that is all.

What is more important is that we are without competence to entertain these arguments — either to brush them aside as fantasies generated by fear of the unknown, or to act on them. The choice we are urged to make is a matter of high policy for resolution within the legislative process after the kind of investigation, examination, and study that legislative bodies can provide and courts cannot. That process involves the balancing of competing values and interests, which in our democratic system is the business of elected representatives. Whatever their validity, the contentions now pressed on us should be addressed to the political branches of the Government, the Congress and the Executive, and not to the courts.[6]

1,647); telephone (Bell, No. 174,465); electric lamp (Edison, No. 223,898); airplane (the Wrights, No. 821,393); transistor (Bardeen & Brattain, No. 2,524,035); neutronic reactor (Fermi & Szilard, No. 2,708,656); laser (Schawlow & Townes, No. 2,929,922). See generally Revolutionary Ideas, Patents & Progress in America, United States Patent and Trademark Office (1976).

[6] We are not to be understood as suggesting that the political branches have been laggard in the consideration of the problems related to genetic research and technology. They have already taken action. In 1976, for example, the National Institutes of Health released guidelines for NIH-sponsored genetic research which established conditions under which such research could be performed. 41 Fed. Reg. 27902. In 1978 those guidelines were revised and relaxed. 43 Fed. Reg. 60080, 60108, 60134. And Committees of the Congress have held extensive hearings on these matters. See, *e.g.*, Hearings on Genetic Engineering before the Subcommittee on Health of the Senate Committee on Labor and Public Welfare, 94th Cong.; 1st Sess. (1975); Hearings before the Subcommittee on Science, Technology, and Space of the Senate Committee on Commerce, Science,

Accordingly, the judgment of the Court of Customs and Patent Appeals is [a]ffirmed.

MR. JUSTICE BRENNAN, with whom MR. JUSTICE WHITE, MR. JUSTICE MARSHALL, and MR. JUSTICE POWELL join, dissenting.

I agree with the Court that the question before us is a narrow one. Neither the future of scientific research, nor even the ability of respondent Chakrabarty to reap some monopoly profits from his pioneering work, is at stake. Patents on the processes by which he has produced and employed the new living organism are not contested. The only question we need decide is whether Congress intended that he be able to secure a monopoly on the living organism itself, no matter how produced or how used. Because I believe the Court has misread the applicable legislation, I dissent.

The patent laws attempt to reconcile this Nation's deep-seated antipathy to monopolies with the need to encourage progress. Given the complexity and legislative nature of this delicate task, we must be careful to extend patent protection no further than Congress has provided. In particular, were there an absence of legislative direction, the courts should leave to Congress the decisions whether and how far to extend the patent privilege into areas where the common understanding has been that patents are not available.

In this case, however, we do not confront a complete legislative vacuum. The sweeping language of the Patent Act of 1793, as re-enacted in 1952, is not the last pronouncement Congress has made in this area. In 1930 Congress enacted the Plant Patent Act affording patent protection to developers of certain asexually reproduced plants. In 1970 Congress enacted the Plant Variety Protection Act to extend protection to certain new plant varieties capable of sexual reproduction. Thus, we are not dealing — as the Court would have it — with the routine problem of "unanticipated inventions." In these two Acts Congress has addressed the general problem of patenting animate inventions and has chosen carefully limited language granting protection to some kinds of discoveries, but specifically excluding others. These Acts strongly evidence a congressional limitation that excludes bacteria from patentability.[7]

---

and Transportation, 95th Cong., 1st Sess. (1977); Hearings on H.R. 4759 et al. before the Subcommittee on Health and the Environment of the House Committee on Interstate and Foreign Commerce, 95th Cong., 1st Sess. (1977).

[7] But even if I agreed with the Court that the 1930 and 1970 Acts were not dispositive, I would dissent. This case presents cogent reasons not to extend the patent monopoly in the face of uncertainty. At the very least, these Acts are signs of legislative attention to the problems of patenting living organisms, but they give no affirmative indication of congressional intent that bacteria be patentable. The caveat of *Parker v. Flook*, 437 U.S. 584, 596 (1978), an admonition to "proceed cautiously when we are asked to extend patent rights into areas wholly unforeseen by Congress," therefore becomes pertinent. I should think the necessity for caution is that much greater when we are asked to extend patent rights into areas Congress has foreseen and considered but has not resolved.

First, the Acts evidence Congress' understanding, at least since 1930, that § 101 does not include living organisms. If newly developed living organisms not naturally occurring had been patentable under § 101, the plants included in the scope of the 1930 and 1970 Acts could have been patented without new legislation. Those plants, like the bacteria involved in this case, were new varieties not naturally occurring.[8] Although the Court rejects this line of argument, it does not explain why the Acts were necessary unless to correct a pre-existing situation. I cannot share the Court's implicit assumption that Congress was engaged in either idle exercises or more correction of the public record when it enacted the 1930 and 1970 Acts. And Congress certainly thought it was doing something significant. The Committee Reports contain expansive prose about the previously unavailable benefits to be derived from extending patent protection to plants.[9] H.R. Rep. No. 91-1605, pp. 1-3 (1970); S. Rep. No. 315, 71st Cong., 2d Sess., 1-3 (1930). Because Congress thought it had to legislate in order to make agricultural "human-made inventions" patentable and because the legislation Congress enacted is limited, it follows that Congress never meant to make items outside the scope of the legislation patentable.

Second, the 1970 Act clearly indicates that Congress has included bacteria within the focus of its legislative concern, but not within the scope of patent protection. Congress specifically excluded bacteria from the coverage of the 1970 Act. 7 U.S.C. § 2402(a). The Court's attempts to supply explanations for this explicit exclusion ring hollow. It is true that there is no mention in the legislative history of the exclusion, but that does not give us license to invent reasons. The fact is that Congress, assuming that animate objects as to which it had not

---

[8] The Court refers to the logic employed by Congress in choosing not to perpetuate the "dichotomy" suggested by Secretary Hyde. But by this logic the bacteria at issue here are distinguishable from a "mineral ... created wholly by nature" in exactly the same way as were the new varieties of plants. If a new Act was needed to provide patent protection for the plants, it was equally necessary for bacteria. Yet Congress provided for patents on plants but not on these bacteria. In short, Congress decided to make only a subset of animate "human-made inventions" patentable.

[9] Secretary Hyde's letter was not the only explicit indication in the legislative history of these Acts that Congress was acting on the assumption that legislation was necessary to make living organisms patentable. The Senate Judiciary Committee Report on the 1970 Act states the Committee's understanding that patent protection extended no further than the explicit provisions of these Acts:

> "Under the patent law, patent protection is limited to those varieties of plants which reproduce asexually, that is, by such methods as grafting or budding. No protection is available to those varieties of plants which reproduce sexually, that is, generally by seeds."
> S. Rep. No. 91-1246, p. 3 (1970).

Similarly, Representative Poage, speaking for the 1970 Act, after noting the protection accorded asexually developed plants, stated that "for plants produced from seed, there has been no such protection." 116 Cong. Rec. 40295 (1970).

specifically legislated could not be patented, excluded bacteria from the set of patentable organisms.

The Court protests that its holding today is dictated by the broad language of § 101, which cannot "be confined to the 'particular application[s] ... contemplated by the legislators.'" But as I have shown, the Court's decision does not follow the unavoidable implications of the statute. Rather, it extends the patent system to cover living material even though Congress plainly has legislated in the belief that § 101 does not encompass living organisms. It is the role of Congress, not this Court, to broaden or narrow the reach of the patent laws. This is especially true where, as here, the composition sought to be patented uniquely implicates matters of public concern.

NOTES

1. Justice Burger in his opinion notes that Chakrabarty's "discovery is not nature's handiwork, but his own." Do you agree? What do you make of the category of human-produced discoveries? Would it be more accurate to distinguish between *discovery* and *invention*?

Recall, however, that § 101 calls for protection of discoveries *and* inventions. Does the language of § 101 distinguish between human-made discoveries and inventions, and discoveries of ready-made items in nature?

To begin to see how this all works, consider the following hypothetical problems. These are designed to lead us to ask whether, and under what conditions, patents are necessary or beneficial.

1. WHY *CAN'T* YOU PATENT THAT?

If an invention is new, useful, and nonobvious — if in short it represents some significant advance over what was known before — why ask the further question of whether it fits into one of the statutory categories? In other words, why distinguish among significant inventions, patenting some (because they "fit" in one of the categories) but not others (because they do not)? To be more concrete, consider the following examples; ask yourself if you believe they should be patentable.

a. **A new tennis stroke, baseball pitch, or basketball move**, e.g., the two-handed backhand or the knuckleball. (Note that sports commentators often refer to an athlete's characteristic technique or move as "her *patented*" shot, maneuver, etc.) According to a recent article, "Some lawyers ... are pushing the idea that athletes actually can obtain patents on the sports moves they develop." Richard B. Schmitt, *Effort Is Under Way to Put New Meaning on Moves in Sports*, WALL ST. J., May 10, 1996, at A5, col. 1. It is clear that in some cases a single individual can be identified as the originator of a certain sports maneuver. For example, a baseball player named Candy Cummings is thought to have introduced the curveball to baseball games in the 1860s. *See* ROBERT G. WATTS & A. TERRY BAHILL, KEEP YOUR EYE ON THE BALL: THE SCIENCE AND

FOLKLORE OF BASEBALL 7-8 (1990). Likewise, a high-jump specialist named Dick Fosbury is widely credited with creating the back-first high-jump technique now known as the "Fosbury Flop."

b. **A new chess move.** Chess moves — especially openings — are widely studied. A characteristic move may even prove decisive in particular matches. Why not permit a patent on them?

By the same token, why not allow patents on other sports-related tactics and practices? Someone, for example, was the first to hang back in a track race, saving speed for the end of the race. Likewise, in baseball, the famous "Boudreau shift" was invented by manager Lou Boudreau of the Cleveland Indians in an attempt to stop the great Red Sox hitter Ted Williams. The shift involved playing almost all the infielders on the right side of the infield, where Williams (a lefthanded batter) preferred to hit. Others soon adopted the strategy. Similar innovations can be discovered in basketball (zone defenses), volleyball (various setting/spiking tactics), and so on. Finally, how about the idea of the minor league system, developed by baseball pioneer Branch Rickey? Note that this verges on a business concept, discussed next.

c. **Overnight package delivery, or any other idea for a new type of business.** A good account of the origins of Federal Express — the first integrated, overnight package delivery company — can be found in JOHN DIEBOLD, THE INNOVATORS ch. 2, at 25 et seq. (1990). If the description is accurate, there was certainly no lack of risk involved in starting up this venture; indeed, the story includes a few close brushes with bankruptcy early on. In light of the high risk, why not allow patents in exchange for a detailed description of such a business concept?

d. **A recipe.** (One often hears the expression, "his patented chili," or chicken stir-fry, or whatever.)

e. **A newly discovered Amazonian flower, or other plant.** More on this below.

f. **A "social innovation," such as the concept of the "designated driver."** It can take a certain amount of time and effort to improve some aspect of social life, and it no doubt takes a great deal of effort — and sometimes money — to diffuse a new idea sufficiently to reach acceptance. Occasionally, these ideas are very valuable indeed, as the example of the designated driver demonstrates. (Imagine the lives saved, and economic devastation avoided, by this simple idea — which really was the brainchild of a single individual.) Why not provide a special form of protection for them?

NOTE

Assume that each of these inventions is considered significant in its field, even revolutionary. Should its patentability turn on which category of invention it falls into? Why distinguish between categories in the first place? Does it matter that the Constitution speaks in terms of promoting the "useful arts"? Are sports, new businesses, recipes, and plants "useful arts"? Are categories of inventions just historical artifacts, rooted in the early industrial era, which have grown out of date? Or are they indicative of a Congressional belief that some types of new human creations are more socially and economically beneficial? Or do patentable categories represent a judgment about which types of inventions will not be created without the special lure of a patent?

2. NOTE ON PATENTING SCIENTIFIC PRINCIPLES AND DISCOVERIES

It is axiomatic that the following may not be patented:

> principles, laws of nature, mental processes, intellectual concepts, ideas, natural phenomena, mathematical formulae, methods of calculation, fundamental truths, original causes, motives, [and] the Pythagorean theorem ....

In re Bergy, 596 F.2d 952, 201 U.S.P.Q. (BNA) 352 (C.C.P.A. 1979). *See also* 1 D. CHISUM, PATENTS § 1.03[2] (1995). Some have proposed that it is a mistake to exclude such things, however.

One such proposal was introduced into the French Chamber of Deputies in 1922 by Professor J. Barthelemy.[1] Professor Barthelemy's proposal would have overturned a provision of the French Patent Law of 1844 which declared null and void all patents concerning "principles, methods, systems, discoveries and theoretical or purely scientific conceptions of which no industrial applications are indicated."[2] Barthelemy's proposal contained two essential provisions. First, it stipulated that a scientist who has made a discovery may take no action so long as no one tries to apply the discovery. But as soon as a practical application of the theoretical discovery is made, the scientist may present a claim for a part of the profits. Second, a scientist may obtain a "patent of principle." This would not confer on the patentee an exclusive right to make or use the discovery, but only the right to grant licenses for those working the practical applications of the discovery. Anyone would be free to work the invention or discovery, so long as he or she paid royalties to the scientist who had discovered it. The duration of protection would have been more akin to copyright: the life of the discoverer plus 50 years. As Stephen Ladas points out, the Barthelemy proposal was part of a larger post-World War I movement in France in favor of a "Droit de Suite" or set of "moral rights" for authors and creators.

Also in 1922, the Committee on Intellectual Cooperation of the League of Nations took up the question of scientific property at the insistence of its Chairman, Professor Bergson. The Committee eventually approved a plan drafted by Senator Ruffini of Italy. Ruffini's proposal began by dismissing the theoretical

---

[1] No. 233, Chambre des D/Aeput/Aes, Session de 1922.

[2] Quoted in 3 S. LADAS, PATENTS, TRADEMARKS, AND RELATED RIGHTS: NATIONAL AND INTERNATIONAL PROTECTION 1850-1851 (1975).

objections to the patenting of scientific discoveries. After reciting the various objections to protecting "discoveries" rather than inventions, Ruffini concludes: "The whole question is dominated by crudest utilitarianism, empiricism unhappily disguised in scientific nebulosity, and, finally, the most disconcerting arbitrariness."[3] Ruffini also pointed out that one objection to the proposal of Barthelemy in France was that French industry would be handicapped by being forced to recognize an intellectual property right not recognized throughout the world. Ruffini's solution was to propose an international treaty which would create such a right in all signatory nations, thus eliminating the possibility that companies in one country would carry the extra financial burden of paying royalties to scientists.

Ruffini's substantive proposals were straightforward. He proposed a term of protection identical to that of Barthelemy's plan: life plus 50 years. He called for the exclusion of discoveries which merely presented a scientific explanation of obvious facts or practices of human life. (This point was made in response to a memorandum from Dean Wigmore of Northwestern Law School, who objected to the proposal on this basis.) In addition, the plan provided for four possible means of establishing priority in an idea, including publication, self-authentication, "patents of principle," and ordinary patents.

While these proposals drew criticism, there were also defenders. One view had it that the industries that used a scientific discovery in particular applications had a "quasi-contractual obligation" to remunerate the discoverer of the principle.[4] In fact, the plan went so far as to be made the subject of a Draft Convention prepared by a committee of experts at the League of Nations.[5] However, the project lost momentum in 1930 and was never revitalized, except in France. There the government adopted a decree creating a Medal of Scientific Research with prizes, which took the place of the discovery patent. This, together with certain legislated principles in the socialist countries, are the only actual legislative products of the scientific discovery patent movement.[6]

Stephen Ladas has pointed out several of the flaws in these proposals. First, it is very often difficult to trace the scientific origins of a particular industrial application. Second, there is a significant lag time between the disclosure of a scientific discovery and the development of the first application; it seems unfair to require royalties when the discovery precedes the application by a long period.

---

[3] F. Ruffini, *Report on Scientific Property, Committee on Intellectual Cooperation*, League of Nations Doc. A.38 (1923), XII, 10, quoted in 3 S. LADAS, *supra* note 2, § 1012 at 1856.

[4] *See* S. LADAS, *supra* note 2, § 1017 at 862. *See also* Gordon, *On Owning Information: Intellectual Property and the Restitutionary Impulse*, 78 VA. L. REV. 149 (1992).

[5] LADAS, *supra* note 2, § 1020 at 1866.

[6] *See* S. LADAS, *supra* note 2, §§ 1021-1026 at 1868-75. It should be noted that Article 2(viii) of the Convention establishing the World Intellectual Property Organization (WIPO) includes in the definition of "intellectual property" rights relating to "scientific discoveries" and "all other rights resulting from intellectual activity in the ... scientific ... fields."

Third, very often it can be assumed that a scientific disclosure will be missed by industrialists; they will thus end up paying royalties for a scientific discovery which in fact was not relied upon in creating their industrial application. And finally, the very significant burdens on scientific communication that a system of property rights would create represent perhaps the most severe problem. In a world where an increasing number of products of intellectual work come with a price tag, the traditionally "open" branches of intellectual work should be guarded with care.[7]

An additional objection to patents in scientific discoveries is that they are unnecessary. As Judge Jerome Frank put it:

> Epoch-making "discoveries" or "mere" general scientific "laws," without more, cannot be patented .... So the great "discoveries" of Newton or Faraday could not have been rewarded with such a grant of monopoly. Interestingly enough, apparently many scientists like Faraday care little for monetary rewards; generally the motives of such outstanding geniuses are not pecuniary.... Perhaps (although no one really knows) the same cannot be said of those lesser geniuses who put such discoveries to practical uses.

Katz v. Horni Signal Mfg. Corp., 145 F.2d 961, 63 U.S.P.Q. (BNA) 190 (2d Cir. 1944). On this view, granting patents for discoveries that scientists *would have made anyway* would be socially wasteful. For an explanation and critique of this rationale as a standard of patentability, see Chapter 5.

Notice the differences in these arguments. The "lag time" and "fairness" arguments center on the strength of a scientist's claims to property rights in his or her discovery. These are rights-based arguments, which turn on the inherent fairness of the scientist's claims. The other arguments are more pragmatic; they focus on the consequences of granting or denying these rights. As we shall see, both strands of argument appear frequently in discussions of patent law.

NOTES

1. Before becoming familiar with the details of the patent law, you might ask yourself how you view the question of patents for scientific discoveries. If you are opposed, which arguments appeal to you? If in favor, how could such a system be implemented?

2. Proposals to grant property rights for the findings of basic scientific researchers are described in Robert P. Merges, *Property Rights Theory and the Commons: The Case of Scientific Research*, 13 J. SOC. PHIL. & POL'Y 145 (1996). This article describes some "informal norms" commonly practiced by scientific researchers, and points out that these norms serve to define quasi-prop-

---

[7] *See* Eisenberg, *Patents and the Progress of Science: Exclusive Rights and Experimental Use*, 56 U. CHI. L. REV. 1017 (1989) (describing interaction between scientific research ethos and intellectual property rules).

erty rights to basic scientific research. The article then argues that good reasons still remain for refusing patents for the results of such research.

3. Some intellectual property scholars claim that the law's emphasis on individual creations — which they call the "search for an author" — has little coherence in itself, but instead reflects socially determined judgments about which creations are meritorious and therefore should be rewarded. *See* Jaszi, *Toward a Theory of Copyright: The Metamorphosis of "Authorship,"* 1991 DUKE L.J. 455 (1991). On this view, the only barrier to patents for basic science is a social convention that they are inappropriate. *But cf.* Michael Polanyi, *Patent Reform,* 1 REV. ECON. STUDIES 61, 70 (1944) ("Invention, and particularly modern invention which relies more and more on a systematic process of trial and error, is a drama enacted on a crowded stage. It may be possible to analyze its various scenes and acts, and to ascribe different degrees of merit to the participants; but it is not possible, in general, to attribute to any one of them one decisive self-contained mental operation which can be formulated in a definite claim."). Polanyi, a famous economist, argues that patents are necessary anyway to overcome uncertainty, generate new, socially useful knowledge, and attract "speculative capital." *Id.,* at 61. Since most basic research is still funded by the federal government, it might be argued on this basis that patents are not necessary. For a thorough, enlightened treatment of these issues, see Rebecca Eisenberg, *Technology Transfer and the Genome Project: Problems with Patenting Research Tools,* 5 RISK: HEALTH, SAFETY & ENV'T 163 (1994).

B. SOFTWARE AND MATHEMATICAL ALGORITHMS

In the previous section, we were introduced to the problems that living things presented to the basic concepts of patentability embodied in § 101 of the Patent Act. Section C of this chapter takes up this issue in more detail. We turn our attention now to another problem area — computer software.

Although the first electronic computers, assembled sometime in the 1930s, were built on mathematical ideas that originated in the nineteenth century, the programs they ran were quite primitive. Not until the general purpose computer reached the stage where it could run a wide variety of programs did the field of computer science begin to blossom. Only slowly did the designers of programs (software) separate themselves from the designers of the machines they ran on (hardware). At this early stage, not many people really understood the nature of software.

With the growth of the field came an early crop of patent applications. In the 1950s and early 1960s, the Patent Office met these with a uniform response: whatever software is, it is definitely *not* patentable subject matter. Some programmers persisted in their efforts to have software recognized with the traditional badge of technical achievement — an issued patent. Some did obtain patents, but not for software *per se.* On several notable occasions, early programmer/applicants brought their fight to the Supreme Court. We begin with the first Supreme Court opinion on the patentability of computer software, *Gottschalk v. Benson*.

GOTTSCHALK v. BENSON
409 U.S. 63, 175 U.S.P.Q. (BNA) 673 (1972)

MR. JUSTICE DOUGLAS delivered the opinion of the Court.

Respondents filed in the Patent Office an application for an invention which was described as being related "to the processing of data by program and more particularly to the programmed conversion of numerical information" in general-purpose digital computers. They claimed a method for converting binary-coded decimal (BCD) numerals into pure binary numerals. The claims were not limited to any particular art or technology, to any particular apparatus or machinery, or to any particular end use. They purported to cover any use of the claimed method in a general-purpose digital computer of any type. Claims 8 and 13 were rejected by the Patent Office but sustained by the Court of Customs and Patent Appeals.

The question is whether the method described and claimed is a "process" within the meaning of the Patent Act.[1]

A digital computer, as distinguished from an analog computer, operates on data expressed in digits, solving a problem by doing arithmetic as a person would do it by head and hand. Some of the digits are stored as components of the computer. Others are introduced into the computer in a form which it is designed to recognize. The computer operates then upon both new and previously stored data. The general-purpose computer is designed to perform operations under many different programs.

The representation of numbers may be in the form of a time series of electrical impulses, magnetized spots on the surface of tapes, drums, or discs, charged spots on cathode-ray tube screens, the presence or absence of punched holes on paper cards, or other devices. The method or program is a sequence of coded instructions for a digital computer.

The patent sought is on a method of programming a general-purpose digital computer to convert signals from binary-coded decimal form into pure binary form. A procedure for solving a given type of mathematical problem is known as an "algorithm." The procedures set forth in the present claims are of that kind; that is to say, they are a generalized formulation for programs to solve mathemat-

---

[1] Title 35 U.S.C. § 100(b) provides:

> The term "process" means process, art or method, and includes a new use of a known process, machine, manufacture, composition of matter, or material.

Title 35 U.S.C. § 101 provides:

> Whoever invents or discovers any new and useful process, machine, manufacture, or composition of matter, or any new and useful improvement thereof, may obtain a patent therefor, subject to the conditions and requirements of this title.

ical problems of converting one form of numerical representation to another. From the generic formulation, programs may be developed as specific applications.

The decimal system uses as digits the 10 symbols 0, 1, 2, 3, 4, 5, 6, 7, 8, and 9. The value represented by any digit depends, as it does in any positional system of notation, both on its individual value and on its relative position in the numeral. Decimal numerals are written by placing digits in the appropriate positions or columns of the numerical sequence, *i.e.*, "unit" (10^0), "tens" (10^1), "hundreds" (10^2), "thousands" (10^3), etc. Accordingly, the numeral 1492 signifies $(1\times10^3)+(4\times10^2)+(9\times10^1)+(2\times10^0)$.

The pure binary system of positional notation uses two symbols as digits — 0 and 1, placed in a numerical sequence with values based on consecutively ascending powers of 2. In pure binary notation, what would be the tens position is the twos position; what would be hundreds position is the fours position; what would be the thousands position is the eights. Any decimal number from 0 to 10 can be represented in the binary system with four digits or positions as indicated in the following table.

Shown as the sum of powers of 2

Decimal	2^3 (8)		2^2 (4)		2^1 (2)		2^0 (1)	Pure Binary
0 =	0	+	0	+	0	+	0	= 0000
1 =	0	+	0	+	0	+	2^0	= 0001
2 =	0	+	0	+	2^1	+	0	= 0010
3 =	0	+	0	+	2^1	+	2^0	= 0011
4 =	0	+	2^2	+	0	+	0	= 0100
5 =	0	+	2^2	+	0	+	2^2	= 0101
6 =	0	+	2^2	+	2^1	+	0	= 0110
7 =	0	+	2^2	+	2^1	+	2^0	= 0111
8 =	2^3	+	0	+	0	+	0	= 1000
9 =	2^3	+	0	+	0	+	2^0	= 1001
10 =	2^3	+	0	+	2^1	+	2	= 1010

The BCD System using decimal numerals replaces the character for each component decimal digit in the decimal numeral with the corresponding four-digit binary numeral, shown in the righthand column of the table. Thus decimal 53 is represented as 0101 0011 in BCD, because decimal 5 is equal to binary 0101 and decimal 3 is equivalent to binary 0011. In pure binary notation, however, decimal 53 equals binary 110101. The conversion of BCD numerals to pure binary numerals can be done mentally through use of the foregoing table. The method sought to be patented varies the ordinary arithmetic steps a human would use by changing the order of the steps, changing the symbolism for writing the multiplier used in some steps, and by taking subtotals after each successive operation. The mathematical procedures can be carried out in existing computers long in use, no new machinery being necessary. And, as noted, they can also be performed without a computer.

The Court stated in *Mackay Co. v. Radio Corp.*, 306 U.S. 86, 94 [1939], that "[w]hile a scientific truth, or the mathematical expression of it, is not a patentable invention, a novel and useful structure created with the aid of knowledge of scientific truth may be." That statement followed the longstanding rule that "[a]n idea of itself is not patentable." "A principle, in the abstract, is a fundamental truth; an original cause; a motive; these cannot be patented, as no one can claim in either of them an exclusive right." *Le Roy v. Tatham*, 14 How. [55 U.S.] 156, 175 [1853]. Phenomena of nature, though just discovered, mental processes, and abstract intellectual concepts are not patentable, as they are the basic tools of scientific and technological work. As we stated in *Funk Bros. Seed Co. v. Kalo Co.*, 333 U.S. 127, 130 [1948], "He who discovers a hitherto unknown phenomenon of nature has no claim to a monopoly of it which the law recognizes. If there is to be invention from such a discovery, it must come from the application of the law of nature to a new and useful end." We dealt there with a "product" claim, while the present case deals with a "process" claim. But we think the same principle applies.

Here the "process" claim is so abstract and sweeping as to cover both known and unknown uses of the BCD to pure binary conversion. The end use may (1) vary from the operation of a train to verification of drivers' licenses to researching the law books for precedents and (2) be performed through any existing machinery or future-devised machinery or without any apparatus.

In *O'Reilly v. Morse*, 15 How. [56 U.S.] 62 [1853], Morse was allowed a patent for a process of using electromagnetism to produce distinguishable signs for telegraphy. *Id.*, at 111. But the Court denied the eighth claim in which Morse claimed the use of "electromagnetism, however developed for marking or printing intelligible characters, signs, or letters, at any distances." *Id.*, at 112. The Court in disallowing that claim said, "If this claim can be maintained, it matters not by what process or machinery the result is accomplished. For aught that we now know, some future inventor, in the onward march of science, may discover a mode of writing or printing at a distance by means of the electric or galvanic current, without using any part of the process or combination set forth in the plaintiff's specification. His invention may be less complicated — less liable to get out of order — less expensive in construction, and in its operation. But yet, if it is covered by this patent, the inventor could not use it, nor the public have the benefit of it, without the permission of this patentee." *Id.*, at 113.

In *The Telephone Cases*, 126 U.S. 1, 534 [1887], the Court explained the *Morse* case as follows: "The effect of that decision was, therefore, that the use of magnetism as a motive power, without regard to the particular process with which it was connected in the patent, could not be claimed, but that its use in that connection could." Bell's invention was the use of electric current to transmit vocal or other sounds. The claim was not "for the use of a current of electricity in its natural state as it comes from the battery, but for putting a continuous current in a closed circuit into a certain specified condition suited to the transmission of vocal and other sounds, and using it in that condition for that purpose." *Ibid*. The claim, in other words, was not "one for the use of electricity distinct from the particular process with which it is connected in his patent." *Id.*, at 535. The patent was for that use of electricity "both for the magneto and variable resistance *methods.*" *Id.*, at 538. Bell's claim, in other words, was not one for all telephonic use of electricity.

In *Corning v. Burden*, 15 How. [56 U.S.] 252, 267-268 [1853], the Court said, "One may discover a new and useful improvement in the process of tanning, dyeing, etc., irrespective of any particular form of machinery or mechanical device." The examples given were the "arts of tanning, dyeing, making waterproof cloth, vulcanizing India rubber, smelting ores." *Id.*, at 267. Those are instances, however, where the use of chemical substances or physical acts, such as temperature control, changes articles or materials. The chemical process or the physical acts which transform the raw material are, however, sufficiently definite to confine the patent monopoly within rather definite bounds.

Cochrane v. Deener, 94 U.S. 780 [1876], involved a process for manufacturing flour so as to improve its quality. The process first separated the superfine flour and then removed impurities from the middlings by blasts of air, reground the middlings, and then combined the product with the superfine. *Id.*, at 785. The claim was not limited to any special arrangement of machinery. *Ibid*. The Court said,

> That a process may be patentable, irrespective of the particular form of the instrumentalities used, cannot be disputed. If one of the steps of a process be that a certain substance is to be reduced to a powder, it may not be at all material what instrument or machinery is used to effect that object, whether a hammer, a pestle and mortar, or a mill. Either may be pointed out; but if the patent is not confined to that particular tool or machine, the use of the others would be an infringement, the general process being the same. A process is a mode of treatment of certain materials to produce a given result. It is an act, or a series of acts, performed upon the subject-matter to be transformed and reduced to a different state or thing.

Id., at 787-88.

It is argued that a process patent must either be tied to a particular machine or apparatus or must operate to change articles or materials to a "different state or thing." We do not hold that no process patent could ever qualify if it did not meet the requirements of our prior precedents. It is said that the decision precludes a patent for any program servicing a computer. We do not so hold. It is said that we have before us a program for a digital computer but extend our holding to programs for analog computers. We have, however, made clear from the start that we deal with a program only for digital computers. It is said we freeze process patents to old technologies, leaving no room for the revelations of the new, onrushing technology. Such is not our purpose. What we come down to in a nutshell is the following.

It is conceded that one may not patent an idea. But in practical effect that would be the result if the formula for converting BCD numerals to pure binary numerals were patented in this case. The mathematical formula involved here has no substantial practical application except in connection with a digital computer, which means that if the judgment below is affirmed, the patent would wholly preempt the mathematical formula and in practical effect would be a patent on the algorithm itself.

It may be that the patent laws should be extended to cover these programs, a policy matter to which we are not competent to speak. The President's Commission on the Patent System[2] rejected the proposal that these programs be patentable:[3]

> Uncertainty now exists as to whether the statute permits a valid patent to be granted on programs. Direct attempts to patent programs have been rejected on the ground of nonstatutory subject matter. Indirect attempts to obtain patents and avoid the rejection, by drafting claims as a process, or a machine or components thereof programmed in a given manner, rather than as a program itself, have confused the issue further and should not be permitted. The Patent Office now cannot examine applications for programs because of a lack of a classification technique and the requisite search files. Even if these were available, reliable searches would not be feasible or economic because of the tremendous volume of prior art being generated. Without this search, the patenting of programs would be tantamount to mere registration and the presumption of validity would be all but nonexistent.
>
> It is noted that the creation of programs has undergone substantial and satisfactory growth in the absence of patent protection and that copyright protection for programs is presently available.

If these programs are to be patentable, considerable problems are raised which only committees of Congress can manage, for broad powers of investigation are needed, including hearings which canvass the wide variety of views which those operating in this field entertain. The technological problems tendered in the many briefs before us indicate to us that considered action by the Congress is needed.

Reversed.

---

[2] "To Promote the Progress of ... Useful Arts," Report of the President's Commission on the Patent System (1966).

[3] *Id.*, at 13.

APPENDIX TO OPINION OF THE COURT

Claim 8 reads:

"The method of converting signals from binary coded decimal form into binary which comprises the steps of

"(1) storing the binary coded decimal signals in a re-entrant shift register,

"(2) shifting the signals to the right by at least three places, until there is a binary 1 in the second position of said register,

"(3) masking out said binary 1 in said second position of said register,

"(4) adding a binary 1 to the first position of said register,

"(5) shifting the signals to the left by two positions,

"(6) adding a 1 to said first position, and

"(7) shifting the signals to the right by at least three positions in preparation for a succeeding binary 1 in the second position of said register."

NOTES

1. Prior to the *Benson* case, the Court of Customs and Patent Appeals (CCPA) had heard eight appeals from applicants claiming computer program-related inventions. According to a recent in-depth analysis of these cases and other matters pertaining to *Benson*,

> A curious thing about these eight pre-*Benson* cases is that none of them, not even the CCPA's decision in the *Benson* case, makes any more than an incidental use of the word "algorithm" in discussing the patentability issue. Hence, none of the analysis contained in these lower court decisions focused on the patentability of "algorithms." It was the Supreme Court's decision in *Benson* that shifted the focus of attention to "algorithms."

Samuelson, *Benson Revisited: The Case Against Patent Protection for Algorithms and Other Computer Program-Related Inventions*, 39 EMORY L.J. 1025, 1042-43 (1990).* After *Benson*, Samuelson states, the case law "is focused almost exclusively on algorithms." *Id.*, at 1059.

2. The author of the authoritative patent law treatise, Donald Chisum, has criticized the *Benson* decision and called for it to be overruled. The result in the case, he argues, "stemmed from an antipatent judicial bias that cannot be reconciled with the basic elements of the patent system established by Congress." Chisum, *The Future of Software Protection: The Patentability of Algorithms*, 47 U. PITT. L. REV. 959, 961 (1986). Chisum states that the "awkward distinctions and seemingly irreconcilable results of the case law since *Benson* ... are the product of the analytical and normative weakness of *Benson* itself." *Id.*, at 961-62. Professor Chisum believes there are strong policy reasons to favor the

---

*Excerpts from Professor Samuelson's article in this chapter are reprinted with permission of the author and Emory Law Journal. Copyright © 1990 by Emory Law Journal.

patentability of computer algorithms. See the note on "Legislative Proposals" below in this chapter.

3. Of what value would a patent be if the inventor were limited in her claims to *existing* technology? On the other hand, what about the objection stated in the *Morse* case, that allowing Morse to patent *"any method"* of communicating via electric signals at a distance would preempt much future inventive work? Would this claim have covered microwave communication, space satellites, fiber optics? This issue is discussed in Chapter 6.

4. Justice Douglas writes: "Transformation and reduction of an article 'to a different state or thing' is the clue to the patentability of a process claim that does not include particular machines." What argument would you make to show that Benson's invention did this? The quoted phrase comes from *Cochrane v. Deener*, a nineteenth century case. This attempt to tie software patentability to some tangible (rather than abstract) transformation presages the direction of the caselaw after *Diamond v. Diehr*, excerpted below.

5. Recall this statement from Justice Douglas' opinion:

> Here the "process" claim is so abstract and sweeping as to cover both known and unknown uses of the BCD to pure binary conversion. The end use may (1) vary from the operation of a train to verification of drivers' licenses to researching the law books for precedents and (2) be performed through any existing machinery or future-devised machinery or without any apparatus.

Is this truly a § 101 objection, or is it an objection to the *scope* of the claims sought by the patentee? How are the two related? Is § 101 designed to exclude from patentability discoveries and inventions so basic and fundamental to future advances that patenting them would unduly burden future inventors? Recall the *Bergy* case with which we began this section. How does Judge Rich in that case resolve these issues? Recall also the statement by Douglas in *Benson* that "mental processes" (which he holds includes algorithms) represent "the basic tools of scientific and technological work." 409 U.S. at 67. Again, the thought seems to be that these inventions are so basic — have so many applications — that they are not an appropriate subject for patents. Indeed, this very objection has been made with respect to software patents; see below the excerpt from the League for Programming Freedom, "Software Patents: Is This the Future of Programming?." However, if this is true, then *any* invention which has a very wide range of applications might be thought to be unpatentable. Yet these are perhaps the most valuable types of inventions! Ultimately, resistance to the patentability of software inventions under the current § 101 of the Patent Act cannot be logically based on the breadth of potential applications. This is not to say, however, that special legislation dealing with the problem is not warranted or wise. See below, Section B.5.a, "If it ain't broke ...".

1. THE "MENTAL STEPS" DOCTRINE

The *Benson* Court's invocation of what had been known as the "mental steps" doctrine followed the lead of several software-related cases that had been decided by the CCPA prior to the 1972 decision in *Benson*. *See, e.g., In re Prater*, 415 F.2d 1378 (C.C.P.A. 1968), *modified on rehearing*, 415 F.2d 1393 (C.C.P.A. 1969). Indeed, the pre-*Benson* cases were primarily concerned with the application of the "mental process" or "mental steps" doctrine, and only tangentially referred to the concept of an algorithm. The mental steps doctrine was eventually repudiated by the CCPA in *In re Musgrave*, 431 F.2d 882 (C.C.P.A. 1970), but the Supreme Court's reference to "mental processes" in the passage above makes it unclear whether the doctrine has been entirely eliminated from current law.

In its 1968 *Prater* decision the CCPA affirmed the Patent Office's rejection of process claims for identifying the optimal set of equations for determining the gaseous composition of materials subjected to spectrographic analysis, i.e., analysis based on radiation reflected off a sample. The CCPA noted that the applicant in *Prater I* had failed to limit his claims to machine implementations of his method. If the claims were allowed, said the court, then merely working through the claimed procedure by hand or in one's head would constitute infringement. This would run afoul of the "mental steps" doctrine developed in earlier cases. *See, e.g., In re Shao Wen Yuan*, 188 F.2d 377 (C.C.P.A. 1951) (finding mathematical means to determine optimal profile of airfoil exhibiting desired aerodynamic characteristics not patentable); *Don Lee, Inc. v. Walker*, 61 F.2d 58 (9th Cir. 1932) (finding formula for computing the centrifugal force of engine shafts to determine the appropriate mass and positions of counterbalances not patentable).

The earlier mental steps cases are aptly summarized by Professor Samuelson in her article, Benson *Revisited: The Case Against Patent Protection for Algorithms and Other Computer Program-Related Inventions*, 39 EMORY L.J. 1025, 1034-35 (1990):

> These decisions involved claims for patenting processes in which human beings took measurements about something, and after making calculations with data derived from these measurements, learned useful information about how to solve a problem in a technological field. The measurements, calculations, and interpretations of data are the "mental processes" or "mental steps" to which the cases refer.
>
> One of these cases, *In re Abrams*, endorsed a set of "rules" by which to judge processes involving mental steps. [*Abrams*, 188 F.2d at 166.] The first rule is that if a process is "purely mental," it is not patentable. The second is that if a process contains both mental and physical steps, but the advance over the prior art is found in the mental steps, it too is not patentable. The third is that if both mental and physical steps have been claimed and there is some novelty in the physical as well as the mental steps, then the process is patentable. The courts deciding Abrams and the other "mental process"

cases, although they spoke frequently about "mental processes" and "mental steps," largely seemed to be concerned not with the "mental" character of the invention (all inventions, after all, are mental conceptions). Instead, these courts concentrated on not granting patent protection to data collection and analysis, just as the courts deciding the "printed matter" cases concentrated on not granting patent protection to data representation or presentation.

Although, as mentioned, the mental steps doctrine has faded into obscurity since the *Benson* case, it contains the kernel of an objection to software patents that many observers feel is very important: the sacrosanct legal status of human thinking. To claim a thought process, the objection goes, is to assert ownership over something that should simply not be owned. (Note the similarity to the "gut-level" objection to animal patents discussed in the first section of this chapter.) Indeed, First Amendment objections were raised in some of the earliest software patent cases — the thought being that these patents might infringe a person's right to think certain thoughts. *See* Samuelson, *supra*, at 1044, n.60 (discussing Patent Office brief in the first *Prater* case, discussed above).

A prominent computer scientist and pioneer in the field of machine or "artificial" intelligence, Professor Alan Newell, voiced this objection in a response to the article by Professor Chisum cited earlier.

> Next consider algorithms and mental steps. The main line of progress in psychology for the last thirty years (called cognitive psychology) has been to describe human behavior as computational. We model what is going on inside the thinking human brain, as the carrying out of computational steps. Therefore, humans think by means of algorithms. Sequences of mental steps and algorithms are the same thing. Any attempt in the law to make distinctions that depend upon contrasting mental steps versus algorithms is doomed to eventual confusion. It is not important whether you accept this computational view of human thinking. There can be controversy about whether such an approach is the correct one for psychology. What is important is that such a view is a major one in the study of the human mind — that many psychologists see the mind this way and that thousands of technical papers are written from within this view, covering large expanses of psychological phenomena. Any attempt to erect a patent system for algorithms that tries to distinguish algorithms as one sort of thing and mental steps as another, will ultimately end up in a quagmire.

> Just avoiding the use of this distinction is only half the story. *An identity between algorithms and mental steps leads to such questions as whether you can keep people from thinking patented thoughts.* You might attempt to avoid such an untenable position by invoking a doctrine of fair use. Indeed, I found the comments by Professor Chisum on the problem of fair use interesting. But the implications of this identity go much further. We are talking about people who engage in those patented thoughts daily and hourly

— even every few seconds — in the pursuit of their business and who make their money and their livelihood by so doing. I expect that any doctrine of fair use would experience substantial strain under such challenges.

Alan Newell, *The Models Are Broken, The Models Are Broken!*, 47 U. PITT L. REV. 1023, 1025 (1986) (emphasis added).

Later in the same article, Professor Newell considers a series of problems with the legal status of software patents, and comments on the problems that would attend the use of a basic algorithm that had been patented:

> [C]ertainly one might contemplate patenting addition.... [I]f you want actually to do addition — that requires doing a sequence of things, not to the integers, which are abstract (so you cannot do things to them anyhow), but to some representation of the integers. Doing addition is accomplished by carrying out an algorithm. If algorithms are patentable, then I can keep you from doing addition with the algorithms invented for it. There would be ever so many things that the poor would not be able to do, such as add up their grocery bill.

Id. at 1027.

NOTES

1. For examples of the "printed matter" rule referred to in the preceding excerpt, see *In re Rice*, 132 F.2d 140 (C.C.P.A. 1942) (holding pictorial method of writing sheet music not patentable); *In re Russell*, 48 F.2d 668 (C.C.P.A. 1931) (holding method of arranging directories in a phonetic order not patentable); *Guthrie v. Curlett*, 10 F.2d 725 (2d Cir. 1926) (holding consolidated tariff index not patentable). In *Boggs v. Robertson*, 13 U.S.P.Q. (BNA) 214 (D.C. Cir. 1931), which involved a patent for a map projection system, the court regarded printed matter as unpatentable when it merely reduces an abstract idea to written form. *See* Note, *The Patentability of Printed Matter: Critique and Proposal*, 18 GEO. WASH. L. REV. 475 (1950). *But cf. In re Beauregard*, 53 F.3d 1583, 1584 (Fed. Cir. 1995) (reciting "concession" by Commissioner of Patents that printed matter rule is "not applicable" to claims covering software residing on a floppy disk, vacating Board opinion and remanding for reconsideration in light of Commissioner's concessions).

2. Authors of at least two early law review articles have argued that the "mental steps" rule should be rejected. *See* McClaskey, *The Mental Process Doctrine: Its Origin, Legal Basis, and Scope*, 55 IOWA L. REV. 1148 (1970); Comment, *The Mental Steps Doctrine*, 48 TENN. L. REV. 903 (1981).

3. In footnote 15 of *Benson*, the court states: "The underlying notion is that a scientific principle, such as that expressed in respondent's algorithm, reveals a relationship that has always existed." This idea is explored in the section below entitled "Is Mathematics Discovered or Invented?"

2. *ALAPPAT* AND ITS AFTERMATH

Benson introduced a set of issues that have occupied — some would say plagued — the software patent field ever since. The core problem with software, or at least "algorithms," is its abstract, mathematical nature. The implicit contrast is to concrete, tangible inventions — the stuff of traditional "machines and manufactures" under § 101. The holding in *Benson* was an open invitation to courts and patent lawyers to argue for patentability by tying software-related inventions to something tangible. This they did in two ways: (1) by focusing on the fact that the numerical values manipulated by software represent real things in the real world, and (2) by emphasizing that software operates on computer hardware, and thus (though in a very limited sense) each computer program creates a "different computer" each time it runs. Be aware of these themes as you read the following case.

In re ALAPPAT

33 F.3d 1526, 31 U.S.P.Q.2d 1545
(Fed. Cir. 1994) (en banc)

RICH, J., with whom ... as to Part II (Merits): NEWMAN, LOURIE, MICHEL, PLAGER, and RADER, JJ., join; ARCHER, C.J., and NIES, J., dissent ....

Kuriappan P. Alappat [et al.] ... (collectively Alappat) appeal the April 22, 1992, reconsideration decision of the Board of Patent Appeals and Interferences (Board) of the United States Patent and Trademark Office (PTO), *Ex parte Alappat*, 23 U.S.P.Q.2d 1340 (BPAI, 1992), which sustained the Examiner's rejection of claims 15-19 of application Serial No. 07/149,792 ('792 application) as being unpatentable under 35 U.S.C. Section 101 (1988)....

[In Part I, the Federal Circuit held that the "reconsideration decision" was rendered by a legally constituted panel of the Board of Appeals and Interferences, and therefore the Federal Circuit could properly move to a consideration of the merits.]

....

II
The Merits

Our conclusion is that the appealed decision should be reversed because the appealed claims are directed to a "machine" which is one of the categories named in 35 U.S.C. Section 101, as the first panel of the Board held.

A. *Alappat's Invention*

Alappat's invention relates generally to a means for creating a smooth waveform display in a digital oscilloscope. The screen of an oscilloscope is the front of a cathode-ray tube (CRT), which is like a TV picture tube, whose screen, when in operation, presents an array (or raster) of pixels arranged at intersections of vertical columns and horizontal rows, a pixel being a spot on the screen which may be illuminated by directing an electron beam to that spot, as in TV. Each column in the array represents a different time period, and each row represents a different magnitude. An input signal to the oscilloscope is sampled and digitized to provide a waveform data sequence (vector list), wherein each successive element of the sequence represents the magnitude of the waveform at a successively later time. The waveform data sequence is then processed to provide a bit map, which is a stored data array indicating which pixels are to be illuminated. The waveform ultimately displayed is formed by a group of vectors, wherein each vector has a straight line trajectory between two points on the screen at elevations representing the magnitudes of two successive input signal samples and at horizontal positions representing the timing of the two samples.

Because a CRT screen contains a finite number of pixels, rapidly rising and falling portions of a waveform can appear discontinuous or jagged due to differences in the elevation of horizontally contiguous pixels included in the waveform. In addition, the presence of "noise" in an input signal can cause portions of the waveform to oscillate between contiguous pixel rows when the magnitude of the input signal lies between values represented by the elevations of the two rows. Moreover, the vertical resolution of the display may be limited by the number of rows of pixels on the screen. The noticeability and appearance of these effects is known as aliasing.

To overcome these effects, Alappat's invention employs an anti-aliasing system wherein each vector making up the waveform is represented by modulating the illumination intensity of pixels having center points bounding the trajectory of the vector. The intensity at which each of the pixels is illuminated depends upon the distance of the center point of each pixel from the trajectory of the vector. Pixels lying squarely on the waveform trace receive maximum illumination, whereas pixels lying along an edge of the trace receive illumination decreasing in intensity proportional to the increase in the distance of the center point of the pixel from the vector trajectory. Employing this anti-aliasing technique eliminates any apparent discontinuity, jaggedness, or oscillation in the waveform, thus giving the visual appearance of a smooth continuous waveform. In short, and in lay terms, the invention is an improvement in an oscilloscope comparable to a TV having a clearer picture.

Reference to Fig. 5A of the '792 application, reproduced below [as the drawing in the upper left corner of Figure 2-1], better illustrates the manner in which a smooth appearing waveform is created.

Each square in this figure represents a pixel, and the intensity level at which each pixel is illuminated is indicated in hexadecimal notation by the number or letter found in each square. Hexadecimal notation has sixteen characters, the numbers 0-9 and the letters A-F, wherein A represents 10, B represents 11, C represents 12, D represents 13, E represents 14, and F represents 15. The intensity at which each pixel is illuminated increases from 0 to F. Accordingly, a square with a 0 (zero) in it represents a pixel having no illumination, and a

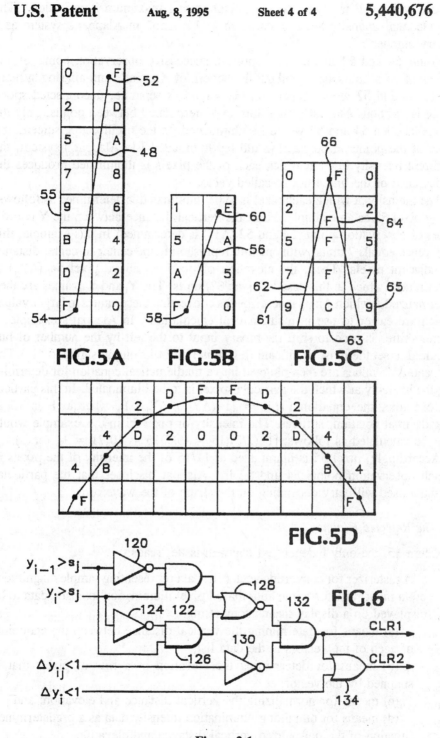

FIG.5A   FIG.5B   FIG.5C

FIG.5D

FIG.6

Figure 2-1

square with an F in it represents a pixel having maximum illumination. [The hexadecimal intensity level is stored in a "bit map" in Alappat's system as a binary number.]...

Points 54 and 52 in Fig. 5A represent successive observation points on the screen of an oscilloscope. Without the benefit of Alappat's anti-aliasing system, points 54 and 52 would appear on the screen as separate, unconnected spots. [That is, without Alappat's algorithm to "interpolate" between points, only the pixels labelled 54 and 52 would be illuminated on the oscilloscope screen, and none of the points in between would be illuminated.] In Alappat's system, the different intensity level at which each of the pixels is illuminated produces the appearance of the line 48, a so-called vector.

The intensity at which each pixel is to be illuminated is determined as follows, using pixel 55 as an example. First, the vertical distance between the Y coordinates of observation points 54 and 52 (ΔY_i) is determined. In this example, this difference equals 7 units, with one unit representing the center-to-center distance of adjacent pixels. Then, the elevation of pixel 55 above pixel 54 (ΔY_{ij}) is determined, which in this case is 2 [*sic*: 3?] units. The Y_i and Y_{ij} values are then "normalized," which Alappat describes as converting these values to larger values which are easier to use in mathematical calculations. In Alappat's example, a barrel shifter is used to shift the binary input to the left by the number of bits required to set the most significant (left-most) bit of its output signal to "1." The ΔY_i and ΔY_{ij} values are then plugged into a mathematical equation for determining the intensity at which the particular pixel is to be illuminated. In this particular example, the equation $I'(i,j) = [1-(\Delta Y_{ij} / \Delta Y_i)]$ F, wherein F is 15 in hexadecimal notation, suffices. The intensity of pixel 55 in this example would thus be calculated as follows: $[1-(2/7)]15 = (5/7)15 = 10.71 = 11$ (or B).

Accordingly, pixel 55 is illuminated at 11/15 of the intensity of the pixels in which observation points 54 and 52 lie. Alappat discloses that the particular formula used will vary depending on the shape of the waveform.

B. *The Rejected Claims*

Claim 15, the only independent claim in issue, reads:

A rasterizer for converting vector list data representing sample magnitudes of an input waveform into anti-aliased pixel illumination intensity data to be displayed on a display means comprising:
(a) means for determining the vertical distance between the endpoints of each of the vectors in the data list;
(b) means for determining the elevation of a row of pixels that is spanned by the vector;
(c) means for normalizing the vertical distance and elevation; and
(d) means for outputting illumination intensity data as a predetermined function of the normalized vertical distance and elevation.

Each of claims 16-19 depends directly from claim 15 and more specifically defines an element of the rasterizer claimed therein. Claim 16 recites that means (a) for determining the vertical distance between the endpoints of each of the vectors in the data list, described above, comprises an arithmetic logic circuit configured to perform an absolute value function. Claim 17 recites that means (b) for determining the elevation of a row of pixels that is spanned by the vector, j described above, comprises an arithmetic logic circuit configured to perform an absolute value function. Claim 18 recites that means (c) for normalizing the vertical distance and elevation comprises a pair of barrel shifters. Finally, claim 19 recites that means (d) for outputting comprises a read only memory (ROM) containing illumination intensity data. As the first Board panel found, each of (a)-(d) was a device known in the electronics arts before Alappat made his invention.

C. *The Examiner's Rejection and Board Reviews*

The Examiner's final rejection of claims 15-19 was under 35 U.S.C. Section 101 "because the claimed invention is non statutory subject matter," and the original three-member Board panel reversed this rejection. That Board panel held that, although claim 15 recites a mathematical algorithm, the claim as a whole is directed to a machine and thus to statutory subject matter named in Section 101. In reaching this decision, the original panel construed the means clauses in claim 15 pursuant to 35 U.S.C. Section 112, paragraph six (Section 112 Para. 6), as corresponding to the respective structures disclosed in the specification of Alappat's application, and equivalents thereof.

In its reconsideration decision, the five member majority of the expanded, eight-member Board panel "modified" the decision of the original panel and affirmed the Examiner's Section 101 rejection. The majority held that the PTO need not apply Section 112 Para. 6 in rendering patentability determinations, characterizing this court's statements to the contrary in *In re Iwahashi*, 888 F.2d 1370, 1375, 12 U.S.P.Q.2d 1908, 1912 (Fed. Cir. 1989), "as dicta," and dismissing this court's discussion of Section 112 Para. 6 in *Arrhythmia Research Technology, Inc. v. Corazonix Corp.*, 958 F.2d 1053, 1060, 22 U.S.P.Q.2d 1033, 1038 (Fed. Cir. 1992) on the basis that the rules of claim construction in infringement actions differ from the rules for claim interpretation during prosecution in the PTO. The majority stated that, during examination, the PTO gives means-plus-function clauses in claims their broadest interpretation and does not impute limitations from the specification into the claims. See Applicability of the Last Paragraph of 35 U.S.C. Section 112 to Patentability Determinations Before the Patent and Trademark Office, 1134 [Off. Gazz. Pat. Off.] 633 (1992); Notice Interpreting *In re Iwahashi* (Fed. Cir. 1989), 1112 [Off. Gazz. Pat. Off.] 16 (1990). Accordingly, the majority held that each of the means recited in claim 15 reads on any and every means for performing the particular function recited.

The majority further held that, because claim 15 is written completely in "means for" language and because these means clauses are read broadly in the

PTO to encompass each and every means for performing the recited functions, claim 15 amounts to nothing more than a process claim wherein each means clause represents only a step in that process. The majority stated that each of the steps in this postulated process claim recites a mathematical operation, which steps combine to form a "mathematical algorithm for computing pixel information," *Alappat*, 23 U.S.P.Q.2d at 1345, and that, "when the claim is viewed without the steps of this mathematical algorithm, no other elements or steps are found." *Alappat*, 23 U.S.P.Q.2d at 1346. The majority thus concluded that the claim was directed to nonstatutory subject matter.

In its analysis, the majority further stated:

> It is further significant that claim 15, as drafted, reads on a digital computer "means" to perform the various steps under program control. In such a case, it is proper to treat the claim as if drawn to a method. We will not presume that a stored program digital computer is not within the Section 112 Para. 6 range of equivalents of the structure disclosed in the specification. The disclosed ALU, ROM and shift registers are all common elements of stored program digital computers. Even if appellants were willing to admit that a stored program digital computer were not within the range of equivalents, Section 112 Para. 2 requires that this be clearly apparent from the claims based upon limitations recited in the claims.

Alappat, 23 U.S.P.Q.2d at 1345. The Board majority also stated that dependent claims 16-19 were not before them for consideration because they had not been argued by Alappat and thus not addressed by the Examiner or the original three-member Board panel. *Alappat*, 23 U.S.P.Q.2d at 1341 n.1.

D. *Analysis*

(1) *Section 112, Paragraph Six*

As recently explained in *In re Donaldson*, 16 F.3d 1189, 1193, 29 U.S.P.Q.2d 1845, [1850] (Fed. Cir. 1994), the PTO *is not exempt* from following the statutory mandate of Section 112 Para. 6, which reads:

> An element in a claim for a combination may be expressed as *a means* or step for performing a specified function without the recital of structure, material, or acts in support thereof, and such claim *shall be construed* to cover the corresponding structure, material, or acts described in the specification and equivalents thereof.

35 U.S.C. Section 112, paragraph 6 (1988) (emphasis added). The Board majority therefore erred as a matter of law in refusing to apply Section 112 Para. 6 in rendering its Section 101 patentable subject matter determination.

Given Alappat's disclosure, it was error for the Board majority to interpret each of the means clauses in claim 15 so broadly as to "read on any and every means for performing the functions" recited, as it said it was doing, and then to conclude that claim 15 is nothing more than a process claim wherein each means clause represents a step in that process. Contrary to suggestions by the Commissioner, this court's precedents do not support the Board's view that the particular apparatus claims at issue in this case may be viewed as nothing more than process claims....

When independent claim 15 is construed in accordance with Section 112 Para. 6, claim 15 reads as follows, the subject matter in brackets representing the structure which Alappat discloses in his specification as corresponding to the respective means language recited in the claims:

A rasterizer [a "machine"] for converting vector list data representing sample magnitudes of an input waveform into anti-aliased pixel illumination intensity data to be displayed on a display means comprising:

(a) [an arithmetic logic circuit configured to perform an absolute value function, or an equivalent thereof] for determining the vertical distance between the endpoints of each of the vectors in the data list;

(b) [an arithmetic logic circuit configured to perform an absolute value function, or an equivalent thereof] for determining the elevation of a row of pixels that is spanned by the vector;

(c) [a pair of barrel shifters, or equivalents thereof] for normalizing the vertical distance and elevation; and

(d) [a read only memory (ROM) containing illumination intensity data, or an equivalent thereof] for outputting illumination intensity data as a predetermined function of the normalized vertical distance and elevation.

As is evident, claim 15 unquestionably recites a machine, or apparatus, made up of a combination of known electronic circuitry elements.

Despite suggestions by the Commissioner to the contrary, each of dependent claims 16-19 serves to further limit claim 15. Section 112 Para. 6 requires that each of the means recited in independent claim 15 be construed to cover at least the structure disclosed in the specification corresponding to the "means." Each of dependent claims 16-19 is in fact limited to one of the structures disclosed in the specification.

(2) *Section 101*

The reconsideration Board majority affirmed the Examiner's rejection of claims 15-19 on the basis that these claims are not directed to statutory subject matter as defined in Section 101 .... As discussed ... *supra*, claim 15, properly construed, claims a machine, namely, a rasterizer "for converting vector list data representing sample magnitudes of an input waveform into anti-aliased pixel illumination intensity data to be displayed on a display means," which machine is made up of, at the very least, the specific structures disclosed in Alappat's specification corresponding to the means-plus-function elements (a)-(d) recited in the claim. According to Alappat, the claimed rasterizer performs the same overall function as prior art rasterizers, but does so in a different way, which is represented by the combination of four elements claimed in means-plus-function terminology. Because claim 15 is directed to a "machine," which is one of the four categories of patentable subject matter enumerated in Section 101, claim 15 appears on its face to be directed to Section 101 subject matter.

This does not quite end the analysis, however, because the Board majority argues that the claimed subject matter falls within a judicially created exception to Section 101 which the majority refers to as the "mathematical algorithm" exception. Although the PTO has failed to support the premise that the "mathematical algorithm" exception applies to true apparatus claims, we recognize that our own precedent suggests that this may be the case.... Even if the mathematical subject matter exception to Section 101 does apply to true apparatus claims, the claimed subject matter in this case does not fall within that exception.

(a)

The plain and unambiguous meaning of Section 101 is that any new and useful process, machine, manufacture, or composition of matter, or any new and useful improvement thereof, may be patented if it meets the requirements for patentability set forth in Title 35, such as those found in Sections 102, 103, and 112. The use of the expansive term "any" in Section 101 represents Congress's intent not to place any restrictions on the subject matter for which a patent may be obtained beyond those specifically recited in Section 101 and the other parts of Title 35. Indeed, the Supreme Court has acknowledged that Congress intended Section 101 to extend to "anything under the sun that is made by man." *Diamond v. Chakrabarty*, 447 U.S. 303, 309 (1980) .... Thus, it is improper to read into Section 101 limitations as to the subject matter that may be patented where the legislative history does not indicate that Congress clearly intended such limitations....

Despite the apparent sweep of Section 101, the Supreme Court has held that certain categories of subject matter are not entitled to patent protection. In *Diehr*, its most recent case addressing Section 101, the Supreme Court explained that there are three categories of subject matter for which one may not obtain patent protection, namely "laws of nature, natural phenomena, and abstract ideas." *Diehr*, 450 U.S. at 185. Of relevance to this case, the Supreme Court also has held that certain mathematical subject matter is not, standing alone, entitled to patent protection.... A close analysis of *Diehr*, *Flook*, and *Benson* reveals that the Supreme Court never intended to create an overly broad, fourth category of subject matter excluded from Section 101. Rather, at the core of the Court's analysis in each of these cases lies an attempt by the Court to explain a rather straightforward concept, namely, that certain types of mathematical subject matter, standing alone, represent nothing more than abstract ideas until reduced to some type of practical application, and thus that subject matter is not, in and of itself, entitled to patent protection....

(b)

Given the foregoing, the proper inquiry in dealing with the so called mathematical subject matter exception to Section 101 alleged herein is to see whether the claimed subject matter as a whole is a disembodied mathematical concept, whether categorized as a mathematical formula, mathematical equation, mathematical algorithm, or the like, which in essence represents nothing more than a "law of nature," "natural phenomenon," or "abstract idea." If so, *Diehr* precludes the patenting of that subject matter. That is not the case here.

Although many, or arguably even all, of the means elements recited in claim 15 represent circuitry elements that perform mathematical calculations, which is essentially true of all digital electrical circuits, the claimed invention as a whole is directed to a combination of interrelated elements which combine to form a machine for converting discrete waveform data samples into anti-aliased pixel illumination intensity data to be displayed on a display means. This is not a disembodied mathematical concept which may be characterized as an "abstract idea," but rather a specific machine to produce a useful, concrete, and tangible result.

The fact that the four claimed means elements function to transform one set of data to another through what may be viewed as a series of mathematical calculations does not alone justify a holding that the claim as a whole is directed to nonstatutory subject matter. See *In re Iwahashi*, 888 F.2d at 1375, 12 U.S.P.Q.2d at 1911. Indeed, claim 15 as written is not "so abstract and sweeping" that it would "wholly pre-empt" the use of any apparatus employing the combination of mathematical calculations recited therein. See *Benson*, 409 U.S. at 68-72 (1972). Rather, claim 15 is limited to the use of a particularly claimed combination of elements performing the particularly claimed combination of calculations to transform, i.e., rasterize, digitized waveforms (data) into anti-aliased, pixel illumination data to produce a smooth waveform.

Furthermore, the claim preamble's recitation that the subject matter for which Alappat seeks patent protection is a rasterizer for creating a smooth waveform is not a mere field-of-use label having no significance. Indeed, the preamble specifically recites that the claimed rasterizer converts waveform data into output illumination data for a display, and the means elements recited in the body of the claim make reference not only to the inputted waveform data recited in the preamble but also to the output illumination data also recited in the preamble. Claim 15 thus defines a combination of elements constituting a machine for producing an anti-aliased waveform.

The reconsideration Board majority also erred in its reasoning that claim 15 is unpatentable merely because it "reads on a general purpose digital computer 'means' to perform the various steps under program control." *Alappat*, 23 U.S.P.Q.2d at 1345. The Board majority stated that it would "not presume that a stored program digital computer is not within the Section 112 Para. 6 range of equivalents of the structure disclosed in the specification." *Alappat*, 23

U.S.P.Q.2d at 1345. Alappat admits that claim 15 would read on a general purpose computer programmed to carry out the claimed invention, but argues that this alone also does not justify holding claim 15 unpatentable as directed to non-statutory subject matter. We agree. We have held that such programming creates a new machine, because a general purpose computer in effect becomes a special purpose computer once it is programmed to perform particular functions pursuant to instructions from program software. *In re Freeman*, 573 F.2d 1237, 1247 n.11, 197 U.S.P.Q. 464, 472 n.11 (C.C.P.A. 1978); *In re Noll*, 545 F.2d 141, 148, 191 U.S.P.Q. 721, 726 (C.C.P.A. 1976); *In re Prater*, 415 F.2d at 1403 n.29, 162 U.S.P.Q. at 549-50 n.29.

Under the Board majority's reasoning, a programmed general purpose computer could never be viewed as patentable subject matter under Section 101. This reasoning is without basis in the law. The Supreme Court has never held that a programmed computer may never be entitled to patent protection. Indeed, the *Benson* court specifically stated that its decision therein did not preclude "a patent for any program servicing a computer." *Benson*, 409 U.S. at 71. Consequently, a computer operating pursuant to software may represent patentable subject matter, provided, of course, that the claimed subject matter meets all of the other requirements of Title 35. In any case, a computer, like a rasterizer, is apparatus not mathematics.

CONCLUSION

For the foregoing reasons, the appealed decision of the Board affirming the examiner's rejection is

Reversed.

ARCHER, C.J., with whom NIES, J., joins, concurring in part and dissenting in part.

....

I disagree with the majority's conclusion that Alappat's "rasterizer," which is all that is claimed in the claims at issue, constitutes an invention or discovery within 35 U.S.C. Section 101. I would affirm the board's decision sustaining the examiner's rejection of claims 15-19 to the rasterizer under 35 U.S.C. Section 101 because Alappat has not shown that he invented or discovered a machine within Section 101.

In 1873, George Curtis made certain general observations about patent law, the scope of patentable subject matter being at its heart. He stated them with such force and eloquence, and in my view they have such relevance to the issue we face today, that I repeat them as follows:

> It is necessary ... to have clear and correct notions of the true scope of a patent right ... which may be found to assist, in particular cases, the solution

of the question, whether a particular invention or discovery is by law a patentable subject.

In this inquiry it is necessary to commence with the process of exclusion; for although, in their widest acceptation, the terms "invention" and "discovery" include the whole vast variety of objects on which the human intellect may be exercised, so that in poetry, in painting, in music, in astronomy, in metaphysics, and in every department of human thought, men constantly invent or discover, in the highest and the strictest sense, their inventions and discoveries in these departments are not the subjects of the patent law.... The patent law relates to a great and comprehensive class of discoveries and inventions of some new and useful effect or result in matter, not referable to the department of the fine arts. The matter of which our globe is composed is the material upon which the creative and inventive faculties of man are exercised, in the production of whatever ministers to his convenience or his wants. Over the existence of matter itself he has no control....

The direct control of man over matter consists, therefore, in placing its particles in new relations. This is all that is actually done, or that can be done, namely, to cause the particles of matter existing in the universe to change their former places, by moving them, by muscular power or some other force. But as soon as they are brought into new relations, it is at once perceived that there are vast latent forces in nature, which come to the aid of man, and enable him to produce effects and results of a wholly new character, far beyond the mere fact of placing the particles in new positions. He moves certain particles of matter into a new juxtaposition, and the chemical agencies and affinities called into action by this new contact produce a substance possessed of new properties and powers, to which has been given the name of gunpowder. He takes a stalk of flax from the ground, splits it into a great number of filaments, twists them together, and laying numbers of the threads thus formed across each other, forms a cloth, which is held together by the tenacity or force of cohesion in the particles, which nature brings to his aid. He moves into new positions and relations certain particles of wood and iron, in various forms, and produces a complicated machine, by which he is able to accomplish a certain purpose, only because the properties of cohesion and the force of gravitation cause it to adhere together and enable the different parts to operate upon each other and to transmit the forces applied to them, according to the laws of motion. It is evident, therefore, that the whole of the act of invention, in the department of useful arts, embraces more than the new arrangement of particles of matter in new relations. The purpose of such new arrangements is to produce some new effect or result, by calling into activity some latent law, or force, or property, by means of which, in a new application, the new effect or result may be accomplished. In every form in which matter is used, in every production of the ingenuity of man, he relies upon the laws of nature and the properties of matter, and seeks for new effects and results through their agency and aid. Merely inert matter alone is not the sole material with which he works. Nature supplies powers, and forces, and active properties, as well as the particles of matter, and these powers, forces, and properties are constantly the subjects of study, inquiry, and experiment, with a view to the production of some new effect or result in matter.

Any definition or description, therefore, of the act of invention, which excludes the application of the natural law, or power, or property of matter, on which the inventor has relied for the production of a new effect, and the object of such application, and confines it to the precise arrangement of the particles of matter which he may have brought together, must be erroneous.

G. Curtis, A Treatise on the Law of Patents for Useful Inventions at xxiii-xxv (4th ed. 1873) ....

Alappat has arranged known circuit elements to accomplish nothing other than the solving of a particular mathematical equation represented in the mind of the reader of his patent application. Losing sight of the forest for the structure of the trees, the majority today holds that any claim reciting a precise arrangement of structure satisfies 35 U.S.C. Section 101. As I shall demonstrate, the rationale that leads to this conclusion and the majority's holding that Alappat's rasterizer represents the invention of a machine are illogical, inconsistent with precedent and with sound principles of patent law, and will have untold consequences.

B

... The terms used in Section 101 have been used for over two hundred years — since the beginnings of American patent law — to define the extent of the subject matter of patentable invention.... Coexistent with the usage of these terms has been the rule that a person cannot obtain a patent for the discovery of an abstract idea, principle or force, law of nature, or natural phenomenon, but rather must invent or discover a practical "application" to a useful end. *Diamond v. Diehr* ....

Thus patent law rewards persons for inventing technologically useful applications, instead of for philosophizing unapplied research and theory....

Additionally, unapplied research, abstract ideas, and theory continue to be the "basic tools of scientific and technological work," which persons are free to trade in and to build upon in the pursuit of among other things useful inventions. *Flook*, 437 U.S. at 589, 198 U.S.P.Q. at 197 (quotations omitted). Even after a patent has been awarded for a new, useful, and nonobvious practical application of an idea, others may learn from the underlying ideas, theories, and principles to legitimately "design around" the patentee's useful application. See *Slimfold Mfg. Co. v. Kinkead Indus., Inc.*, 932 F.2d 1453, 1457, 18 U.S.P.Q.2d 1842, 1845-46 (Fed. Cir. 1991)....

In addition to the basic principles embodied in the language of Section 101, the section has a pragmatic aspect. That subject matter must be new (Section 102) and nonobvious (Section 103) in order to be patentable is of course a separate requirement for patentability, and does not determine whether the applicant's purported invention or discovery is within Section 101.... Section 101 must be satisfied before any of the other provisions apply, and in this way Section 101 lays the predicate for the other provisions of the patent law.... When considering that the patent law does not allow patents merely for the discovery of ideas, principles, and laws of nature, ask whether, were it not so, the other provisions of the patent law could be applied at all. If Einstein could have obtained a patent for his discovery that the energy of an object at rest equals its mass times the speed of light squared, how would his discovery be meaningfully judged for nonobviousness, the sine qua non of patentable invention? 35 U.S.C. Section 103. When is the abstract idea "reduced to practice" as opposed to being "conceived"? See *id*. Section 102(g). What conduct amounts to the "infringement" of another's idea? See *id*. Section 271.

....

Consider for example the discovery or creation of music, a new song. Music of course is not patentable subject matter; a composer cannot obtain exclusive patent rights for the original creation of a musical composition. But now suppose the new melody is recorded on a compact disc. In such case, the particular musical composition will define an arrangement of minute pits in the surface of the compact disc material, and therefore will define its specific structure. See D. Macaulay, The Way Things Work 248-49 (Houghton Mifflin 1988). Alternatively suppose the music is recorded on the rolls of a player piano or a music box.

Through the expedient of putting his music on known structure, can a composer now claim as his invention the structure of a compact disc or player piano roll containing the melody he discovered and obtain a patent therefor? The answer must be no. The composer admittedly has invented or discovered nothing but music. The discovery of music does not become patentable subject matter simply because there is an arbitrary claim to some structure.

And if a claim to a compact disc or piano roll containing a newly discovered song were regarded as a "manufacture" and within Section 101 simply because of the specific physical structure of the compact disc, the "practical effect" would be the granting of a patent for a discovery in music. Where the music is new, the precise structure of the disc or roll would be novel under Section 102. Because the patent law cannot examine music for "nonobviousness," the Patent and Trademark Office could not make a showing of obviousness under Section 103. The result would well be the award of a patent for the discovery of music. The majority's simplistic approach of looking only to whether the claim reads on structure and ignoring the claimed invention or discovery for which a patent is sought will result in the awarding of patents for discoveries well beyond the scope of the patent law.

....

So what did Alappat invent or discover? Alappat's specification clearly distinguishes between an "oscilloscope" and a "rasterizer," and Alappat claims his invention in claims 15-19 to be only the "rasterizer."

The "rasterizer" as claimed is an arrangement of circuitry elements for converting data into other data according to a particular mathematical operation. The rasterizer begins with vector "data" — two numbers. "[I]t does not matter how they are ascertained." Brief for Alappat at 39. The two numbers, as they might to any algebra student, "represent" endpoints of a line.

The claimed "rasterizer" ends with other specific "data" — an array of numbers, as the original and reconsideration panels of the board both expressly agreed....

Alappat admits that each of the circuitry elements of the claimed "rasterizer" is old. He says they are merely "form." Thus, they are only a convenient and basic way of electrically representing the mathematical operations to be performed, that is, converting vector data into matrix or raster data. In Alappat's view, it is the new mathematic operation that is the "substance" of the claimed invention or discovery. Claim 15 as a whole thus claims old circuitry elements in an arrangement defined by a mathematical operation, which only performs the very mathematical operation that defines it. Rather than claiming the mathematics itself, which of course Alappat cannot do, Alappat claims the mathematically defined structure. But as a whole, there is no "application" apart from the mathematical operation that is asserted to be the invention or discovery. What is going on here is a charade.

NOTES

1. Does Alappat's invention — essentially, interpolating between points to display a line on an oscilloscope's screen — seem straightforward? Does the Federal Circuit say that this invention deserves a patent? What is the precise legal holding of the opinion?

2. In one portion of one of the many omitted opinions, Judge Pauline Newman, concurring on the merits, states: "Mathematics is not a monster to be struck down or out of the patent system, but simply another resource whereby technological advance is achieved." *Ex parte Alappat*, 31 U.S.P.Q.2d 1545, 1579 (Newman, J., concurring). Is this sentiment inconsistent with the view taken in *Benson*? How about *Diehr*? What is the difference between (1) pure mathematics; (2) applied mathematics, as that term is used in mathematics department course catalogues; and (3) mathematics applied to solve a problem in the real world?

3. *Critique of the Nominal Hardware Limitation.* One commentator has criticized the reasoning in *Iwahashi*, a case in many ways similar to *Alappat*. In a perceptive series of articles, Richard Stern argues that the court's approval of means-plus-function claims will, despite its intentions, lead patent attorneys to draft all software-related claims in this form in the future. Richard Stern, *Patenting Algorithms in America: Part I — Benson to Iwahashi, It's Deja vu All Over*

Again, 8 EUR. INTELL. PROP. REV. 292 (1990), and Richard Stern, *Patenting Algorithms in America: Part II — Back from* Iwahashi, 9 EUR. INTELL. PROP. REV. 321 (1990) (arguing against the sort of nominal hardware limitation present in *Iwahashi*, and pointing out that "means plus function" language is capable of converting any process claim into a claim for a very broad class of "structures").

4. *Alappat* is by no means the last word on software patents from the Federal Circuit. For example, in the first post-*Alappat* case decided by the court, a three-judge panel invalidated method (process) and means-plus-function claims to a technique in "graph theory" for determining the shortest (or cheapest) path between two points. *In re Trovato*, 42 F.3d 1376, 33 U.S.P.Q.2d 1194 (Fed. Cir. 1994), *vacated & remanded*, 60 F.3d 807, 33 U.S.P.Q.2d 1194 (Fed. Cir. 1995) (en banc). In the view of the original panel,

> [u]nlike the invention claimed in *Diehr*, the specifications involved here provide no grasp of any underlying physical process. Although cursory references to such diverse apparatus as robots, dynamic emergency exit routes and electronic maps are present, no computer architecture is provided, no circuit diagram is revealed, and no hardware at all receives more than a brief mention. Indeed, the specifications note the inventions' "general applicability to numerical methods" and seek to describe them "[f]rom a mathematical point of view." When questioned during oral argument before this Court, counsel for Trovato admitted that neither specification includes a hardware enablement of the claimed invention. Instead, the entire disclosure consists of flow charts and program code computing the least cost path from starting to goal states based upon the data in the configuration space. We therefore conclude that Trovato claims nothing more than the process of performing a numerical calculation. Simply stated, viewing the claims absent the algorithm, and as a whole, no statutory subject matter is present....
>
> Although some of Trovato's claims describe an electronic readout of the computed data, it is well established that mere post-solution display does not render patentable a mathematical algorithm. As our predecessor court noted in *Walter*, "[i]f Section 101 could be satisfied by the mere recordation of the results of a nonstatutory process on some record medium, even the most unskilled patent draftsman could provide for such a step." ... Nor do Trovato's applications describe inventions which manipulate physical qualities, as with the inventions held to fall within statutory subject matter in cases such as *Arrhythmia* [*Research Technology Inc. v. Corazonix Corp.*, 958 F.2d 1053, 22 U.S.P.Q.2d 1033 (Fed. Cir. 1992)] .... Indeed, the claimed invention does not even take the actual step of gathering the data from the "physical task space" that is arranged into the recited "configuration space data structure," a procedure which in itself cannot render an otherwise nonstatutory subject matter patentable....

Trovato's applications fail even to explain how the claimed inventions actually employ the numbers derived to control movement. Although the inventions likely employ techniques known to the art to move an object along the lowest cost path it calculates, the absence of even a cursory description of how the computed values are implemented further indicates that the claimed methods comprise only numerical manipulation.

42 F.3d 1376, 1380-83. Does the *Trovato* panel succeed in distinguishing this case from *Alappat*? A majority of the Federal Circuit apparently thought not: in July 1995, the court sitting en banc vacated the panel opinion in *Trovato*, remanding the case to the PTO for further proceedings consistent with *Alappat*. *In re Trovato*, 60 F.3d 807, 33 U.S.P.Q.2d 1194 (Fed. Cir. 1995) (en banc) (remanding for reconsideration in light of new patent guidelines).

While this rather unusual step might suggest an emerging consensus in support of *Alappat*'s broad reading of section 101, other cases leave the outcome in doubt. Two cases decided just after *Alappat* differed over the patentability of data structures, an issue not directly presented in *Alappat* but certainly related to it. *Compare In re Lowry*, 32 F.3d 1579, 32 U.S.P.Q.2d 1031 (Fed. Cir. 1994) (upholding as patentable abstract claims to a type of software data structure wherein data "objects" are arranged in complex relationships) *with In re Warmerdam*, 33 F.3d 1354, 31 U.S.P.Q.2d 1754 (Fed. Cir. 1994) (affirming rejection of process claims to data structure for representing proximity and shape of objects in the immediate environment, e.g., for use by a mobile machine with robot vision, and based on idea of representing objects in computer memory as increasingly fine-grained "bubbles"). *But cf.* Shtayer et al., U.S. Patent 5,414,701, "Method and *Data Structure* for Performing Address Compression in an Asynchronous Transfer Mode (ATM) System," issued May 9, 1995 (emphasis added); Kurosawa et al., U.S Patent 5,504,895, "Method of Managing *Data Structure* Containing Both Consistent Data and Transient Data," issued April 2, 1996 (emphasis added).

Yet another post-*Alappat* case, *In re Schraeder*, 22 F.3d 290, 30 U.S.P.Q.2d 1455 (Fed. Cir. 1994), found unpatentable claims to a method for competitively bidding on a plurality of related items, such as contiguous tracts of land. The court held (1) that a mathematical algorithm is implicit in the claim; (2) the algorithm is not applied to or limited by physical elements or process steps, in that grouping or regrouping of bids is not physical change, effect, or result; and (3) the mere entering of bids in a "record" is insufficient to impart patentability under the cases.

For discussions of these cases, see Ronald S. Laurie & Joseph K. Siino, *A Bridge Over Troubled Waters? The PTO's Proposed Guidelines*, 12 COMP. L. 6, 18 (1995) (Parts I and II) (Federal Circuit cases dealing with software patentability defy attempts at full reconciliation, although important factors can be identified); John A. Burtis, *Towards a Rational Jurisprudence of Computer-Related Patentability in Light of* In re Alappat, 79 MINN. L. REV. 1129 (1995).

See also State Street Bank & Trust Co. v. Signature Financial Group, Inc., 38 U.S.P.Q.2d 1530 (D. Mass. 1996) (excerpted and discussed below in Section C) (distinguishing *Alappat*, holding financial service software patent invalid, and finding continuing vitality in test drawn from *Freeman* and *Diehr*).

5. The *Alappat* approach was foreshadowed by early attempts to characterize software inventions as hardware claims. *See In re Bernhart*, 417 F.2d 1395 (C.C.P.A. 1969) (upholding the patentability of apparatus and method claims for improved way to depict three-dimensional objects in two-dimensional form). In *Bernhart* the CCPA accepted the argument that "if a machine is programmed in a certain new and unobvious way, it is physically different from the machine without that program.... The fact that these physical changes are invisible to the eye should not tempt us to conclude that the machine has not been changed." *Id.* at 1400. This theory lay dormant for a long while, however; very few subsequent cases made serious use of it — until *Alappat* and the PTO Guidelines that followed.

a. The 1996 PTO Guidelines

In 1995, IBM appealed the PTO's rejection of a claim to "software contained on a floppy disk." *See In re Beauregard*, 53 F.3d 1583 (Fed. Cir. 1995). While the appeal was pending, the PTO decided not to oppose the claim, and promised the court that it would shortly issue new examining guidelines for software patents. *Id.* at 1584 ("[T]he Board rejected Beauregard's computer program product claims on the basis of the printed matter doctrine. Beauregard appealed. The Commissioner now states 'that computer programs embodied in a tangible medium, such as floppy diskettes, are patentable subject matter under 35 U.S.C. § 101 and must be examined under 35 U.S.C. §§ 102 and 103.' The Commissioner states that he agrees with Beauregard's position on appeal that the printed matter doctrine is not applicable."). The court vacated the Board decision and remanded "for further proceedings in accordance with the Commissioner's concessions." *Id.* In early 1996 the PTO did indeed issue final Examination Guidelines for Computer-Implemented Inventions. *See* U.S. Patent and Trademark Office, Examination Guidelines for Computer-Related Inventions, 61 Fed. Reg. 7478 (Feb. 28, 1996) ("Guidelines").

To begin, the Guidelines define the following claimed inventions as "non-statutory":

- "natural phenomena such as magnetism, and abstract ideas or laws of nature, which constitute 'descriptive material'" (p. 7481);
- "data structures and computer programs which impart functionality when encoded on a computer-readable medium .... when claimed as descriptive material per se." (*Id.*);
- "music, literary works and a compilation or mere arrangement of data." (*Id.*);

- "A process that merely manipulates an abstract idea or performs a purely mathematical algorithm ... despite the fact that it might inherently have some usefulness." (*Id.*).

On the other hand, the Guidelines provide:

> When functional descriptive material is recorded on some computer-readable medium it becomes structurally and functionally interrelated to the medium and will be statutory in most cases....
>
> (a) Functional Descriptive Material: "Data Structures" Representing Descriptive Material Per Se or Computer Programs Representing Computer Listings Per Se. Data structures not claimed as embodied in computer-readable media are descriptive material per se and are not statutory because they are neither physical "things" nor statutory processes. Such claimed data structures do not define any structural and functional interrelationships between the data structure and other claimed aspects of the invention which permit the data structure's functionality to be realized. In contrast, a claimed computer-readable medium encoded with a data structure defines structural and functional interrelationships between the data structure and the medium which permit the data structure's functionality to be realized, and is thus statutory.
>
> Similarly, computer programs claimed as computer listings per se, i.e., the descriptions or expressions of the programs, are not physical "things," nor are they statutory processes, as they are not "acts" being performed. Such claimed computer programs do not define any structural and functional interrelationships between the computer program and other claimed aspects of the invention which permit the computer program's functionality to be realized. In contrast, a claimed computer-readable medium encoded with a computer program defines structural and functional interrelationships between the computer program and the medium which permit the computer program's functionality to be realized, and is thus statutory. Accordingly, it is important to distinguish claims that define descriptive material per se from claims that define statutory inventions.

Id. at 7481-82.

Examples of this type of claimed statutory process include the following:

> ....

- A method of making a word processor by storing an executable word processing application program in a general purpose digital computer's memory, and executing the stored program to impart word processing functionality to the general purpose digital computer by changing the state of the computer's arithmetic logic unit when program instructions of the word processing program are executed.

Id. at 7484.

In addition, the Guidelines contain some very informative examples of acceptable and non-acceptable claim language. For example:

A claim limited to a specific machine or manufacture, which has a practical application in the technological arts, is statutory. In most cases, a claim to a specific machine or manufacture will have a practical application in the technological arts.

(iii) Hypothetical Machine Claims ....

Two applicants present a claim to the following process:

A process for determining and displaying the structure of a chemical compound comprising:

(a) Solving the wavefunction parameters for the compound to determine the structure of a compound; and
(b) Displaying the structure of the compound determined in step (a).

Each applicant also presents a claim to the following apparatus:

A computer system for determining the three dimensional structure of a chemical compound comprising:

(a) Means for determining the three dimensional structure of a compound; and
(b) Means for creating and displaying an image representing a three-dimensional perspective of the compound.

In addition, each applicant provides the noted disclosures to support the claims:

Applicant A	Applicant B
Disclosure:	
The disclosure describes specific software, i.e., specific program code segments, that are to be employed to configure a general purpose microprocessor to create specific logic circuits. These circuits are indicated to be the "means" corresponding to the claimed means limitations	The disclosure states that it would be a matter of routine skill to select an appropriate conventional computer system and implement the claimed process on that computer system. The disclosure does not have specific disclosure that corresponds to the two "means" limitations recited in the claim (i.e., no specific software or logic circuit). The disclosure does have an explanation of how to solve the wave function equations of a chemical compound, and indicates that the solutions of those wave function equations can be employed to determine the physical structure of the corresponding compound.

Applicant A	Applicant B
Result:	
Claim defines specific computer, patentability stands independently from process claim	Claim encompasses any computer embodiment of process claim; patentability stands or falls with process claim.
Explanation:	
Disclosure identifies the specific machine capable of performing the indicated functions	Disclosure does not provide any information to distinguish the "implementation" of the process on a computer from the factors that will govern the patentability determination of the process per se. As such, the patentability of this apparatus claim will stand or fall with that of the process claim.

To be statutory, a claimed computer-related process must either: (1) Result in a physical transformation outside the computer for which a practical application in the technological arts is either disclosed in the specification or would have been known to a skilled artisan ... or (2) be limited by the language in the claim to be practical application within the technological arts ....

Id. at 7483.

NOTES

1. What exactly do the new Guidelines define as patentable subject matter? Do they really allow IBM to patent "software on a floppy disk"? Or does the rule against patenting "creative or artistic expression" (apparently including the literal code of programs) bar the application in *Beauregard*?

2. The preceding excerpts accentuate two aspects of *Alappat, supra*: (1) the ascendancy of "means plus function" claims in the software arts; and (2) the importance of claim language tying software to hardware. While the overall effect is surely to strengthen the hand of software patent applicants (and patentees), the reliance on hardware as the grounding for section 101 patentability also carries some risks. Chief among these is that hardware limitations narrow the class of direct infringers to those not simply in possession of a copy of the software, but also operating the software on the hardware included in the claim. See Section 4 below, on Infringement.

3. While the PTO Guidelines for examiners are obviously important to the continued development of the law in this area, they cannot substitute for the judgment of the courts. If the Federal Circuit decides, for example, that "software on a floppy disk" is not within the ambit of 35 U.S.C. § 101, the PTO does not have the power to issue such patents regardless of the Court decision. Similarly, the PTO cannot reject an application under section 101 if the courts

have decided that it is patentable subject matter. Thus, while important, the Guidelines do not represent the final word on the section 101 issue.

4. Despite the ongoing struggle to define the contours of algorithm patentability in the United States, the world trade community in 1994 adopted an expansive patent subject matter provision as part of the Trade-Related Aspects of Intellectual Property (TRIPs) accord in the "Uruguay Round" of agreements under the General Agreement on Tariffs and Trade (GATT). *See* General Agreement on Tariffs and Trade: Multilateral Trade Negotiations Final Act Embodying the Results of the Uruguay Round of Trade Negotiations, Done at Marrakech, April 15, 1994, 33 I.L.M. 1125 (1994), at Art. 27, ¶ 1:

> Subject to the provisions of paragraphs 2 and 3 [which do not deal with software], patents shall be available for any inventions, whether products or processes, in all fields of technology, provided that they are new, involve an inventive step and are capable of industrial application.... [P]atents shall be available and patent rights enjoyable without discrimination as to the place of invention, the field of technology and whether products are imported or locally produced.

This language suggests agreement upon a more or less uniform rule world-wide favoring patents for at least some types of software, although there is no evidence that this was intended by the drafters of Article 27. For a more detailed discussion of the treatment of software under GATT, see Chapter 8.

5. *Internationalizing the Issue.* Despite the ongoing struggle to define the contours of algorithm patentability in the United States, the world trade community in 1994 adopted an expansive patent subject matter provision as part of the Trade-Related Aspects of Intellectual Property (TRIPs) accord in the "Uruguay Round" of agreements under the General Agreement on Tariffs and Trade (GATT). *See* General Agreement on Tariffs and Trade: Multilateral Trade Negotiations Final Act Embodying the Results of the Uruguay Round of Trade Negotiations, Done at Marrakech, April 15, 1994, 33 I.L.M. 1125 (1994), at Art. 27, ¶ 1:

> Subject to the provisions of paragraphs 2 and 3, patents shall be available for any inventions, whether products or processes, in all fields of technology, provided that they are new, involve an inventive step and are capable of industrial application.... [P]atents shall be available and patent rights enjoyable without discrimination as to the place of invention, the field of technology and whether products are imported or locally produced.

This is expected to lead (eventually) to a more or less uniform rule world-wide favoring patents for at least some types of software.

b. Note on Metaphysics and New Machines

Legal doctrine regarding software patents was shaped from the outset by the murky metaphysics of the majority opinion in *Benson*. Nowhere is this more clear than in the concept of "software as hardware," so forcefully rediscovered in *Alappat* and the 1996 PTO Guidelines described earlier.

In response to the *Benson* Court's emphasis on the intangible, abstract nature of software, *Alappat* and its predecessors (and now, progeny) stress that each computer program

> creates a new machine, because a general purpose computer in effect becomes a special purpose computer once it is programmed to perform particular functions pursuant to instructions from program software.

Alappat, supra, at 1545.

With due regard to the difficult constraints that *Benson* places on courts who see no principled difference between software and other fields of technology, this line of reasoning has some glaring weaknesses. At the conceptual level, it is akin to arguing that every time a person's brain holds a new thought, it is a new brain. Does this sound plausible? Is it correct to say that your brain somehow differs when it is thinking "red" and when it is thinking "blue"? Isn't it much more natural, and hence more plausible, to say that it is the *thought* that differs, and not the brain, in the two cases? Only someone resolutely opposed to focusing attention on the thought itself would even conceive of the "different brain" line of reasoning. *Benson*, sadly, creates just such an impetus; in this and other ways, it directs attention away from the important issues (see, e.g., Section 5 below, "Impact of Patents on the Software Industry").

The different thought/different brain concept is so anomalous it does not even find its way into the writings of hardcore "philosophical materialists," those who believe that, roughly, physical matter is all there is in the universe. Even these philosophers, apparently, would distinguish between reconfiguring the brain and making a new brain. *See, e.g.,* RICHARD RORTY, PHILOSOPHY AND THE MIRROR OF NATURE (1979) Ch. 2, at 70 et seq. (quoting various materialists' statements about "mental states" [of a static brain], in chapter critiquing different forms of materialism).

It is easy to see why philosophers do not focus their attention on the reconfigured brain. It would distract attention from the central problem they are grappling with: the nature of the mental phenomena going on inside the brain. *See, e.g.,* JOHN SEARLE, MINDS, BRAINS AND SCIENCE (1984). By the same token, the discussion of computer programs as merely so many reconfigured computers will inevitably deflect attention from the main issues at hand: which software increases productivity the most, costs the most to create and disseminate, needs the greatest degree of legal protection, and so on. As one scholar puts it in a related context:

> The principle of the subroutine operation [in a computer program] is not itself to be understood and explained just by examining the hardware, in just the same way that the point of multiplication tables could not be grasped by examining the brain. Similarly, an understanding of how the subroutines themselves work does not explain the principle of solving problems in terms of a sequence of steps.... For that, one must look at the executive process, which in the machine embodies the overall organization and goal of the program, and in the human being a less clearly understood "goal directedness."

P.C. Dodwell, *Is a Theory of Conceptual Development Necessary?*, in COGNITIVE DEVELOPMENT AND EPISTEMOLOGY 370 (Theodore Mischel ed., 1971).

In other words, if the goal is to keep our eye on the ball, we will not make progress by pretending that it is only part of the bat.

NOTE

The analogy between minds/brains and computers is the subject of lively debate among philosophers and cognitive scientists. *Compare* JOHN SEARLE, *supra*, at 32-41 (defending the special status of thinking, as distinct from the operation of a computer program, through his famous "Chinese translation procedure" example, where he contrasts a person translating Chinese with a person or computer merely carrying out detailed instructions that, when done properly, results in a correct translation), *with* Marvin L. Minsky, *Matter, Mind, and Models*, in SEMANTIC INFORMATION PROCESSING (MARVIN L. MINSKY ED., 1968) (arguing against such a distinction, in favor of "artificial" intelligence) and HERBERT A. SIMON, THE SCIENCES OF THE ARTIFICIAL (1969) (same).

3. FROM *BENSON* TO *ALAPPAT*

a. *Musgrave, Flook, Diehr*, and the "Technological Arts"

Consider the following passage from *Parker v. Flook*, 437 U.S. 584, 198 U.S.P.Q. (BNA) 193 (1978), which held unpatentable a process claim to a program for updating an "alarm limit" and performing some token "post-solution activity":

> The rule that the discovery of a law of nature cannot be patented rests, not on the notion that natural phenomena are not processes, but rather on the more fundamental understanding that they are not the kind of "discoveries" that the statute was enacted to protect.

437 U.S. at 593.

This passage states the idea that computer programs, or at least some aspects of them, are not within the class of human inventions patents were meant to protect. An early version of this argument was made in the 1966 Presidential

Commission Report on the patent system, entitled "To Promote the Progress of Science and the Useful Arts ...," and in the first set of Patent Office "Guidelines" on patenting computer programs, 829 Off. Gaz. Pat. Office, Aug. 16, 1966, at 865. (The Guidelines became effective in 1968. *See* 33 Fed. Reg. 15,609 (1968)). In one sense it is simply a restatement of the core of the "mental steps" doctrine as applied to software. But in *In re Musgrave*, 431 F.2d 882 (C.C.P.A. 1970), the CCPA had attempted to make it the cornerstone of patentability in this area. Near the end of the *Musgrave* opinion, which reversed the Patent Office Board of Appeals and upheld the patentability of a process for determining subsurface geological characteristics with computer assistance, the CCPA made the following statement:

> We cannot agree with the board that these claims (all the steps of which can be carried out by the disclosed apparatus) are directed to non-statutory processes merely because some or all the steps therein can also be carried out in or with the aid of the human mind or because it may be necessary for one performing the processes to think. All that is necessary, in our view, to make a sequence of operational steps a statutory "process" within 35 U.S.C. 101 is that it be in the technological arts so as to be in consonance with the Constitutional purpose to promote the progress of "useful arts." Const. Art. 1, sec. 8.

The effort to define software patentability according to whether a particular set of claims falls within the "technological arts" has its supporters, most notably Professor Donald Chisum, who wrote that *Musgrave* was "the highwater mark of rationality" in the software patent debate. Chisum, *The Future of Software Protection: The Patentability of Algorithms*, 47 U. PITT. L. REV. 959, 961 (1986). Even so, the "technological arts" argument was met with immediate skepticism in a concurring opinion by Judge Baldwin in *Musgrave*:

> It seems that whenever a court decides to go beyond what is necessary to decide the case before it, more problems are generated than are solved. I foresee quite a few with the majority's new holding.
>
> First and foremost will be the problem of interpreting the meaning of "technological arts."...
>
> Justifying the decision finding claims drawn entirely to purely mental processes to be statutory, the majority states that "[a] step requiring the exercise of subjective judgment without restriction might be objectionable as rendering a claim indefinite." It should not require much imagination to see the many problems sure to be involved in trying to decide whether a step requiring certain human judgment evaluations is definite or not.
>
> As one more example, suppose a claim happens to contain a sequence of operational steps which can reasonably be read to cover a process performable both within and without the technological arts? This is not too far

fetched. Would such a claim be statutory? Would it comply with section 112 [on enablement]? We will have to face these problems some day.

415 F.2d at 893-94.

The problems identified by Judge Baldwin are largely the result of the ever-expanding applications of computer programs. One case which illustrates this well is *In re Toma*, 575 F.2d 872, 877 (C.C.P.A. 1978). Toma's claim was for an algorithm for a computerized natural language translation process. The Patent Office rejected the claim because it was for an algorithm under *Benson* and for a mental process, and because it made a contribution to the liberal, not the technological, arts. Toma's claim, however, was eventually ruled patentable by the CCPA. Yet it is obvious that this decision would have been more difficult, and might even have gone the other way, if the "technological arts" theory of *Musgrave* had been scrupulously applied.

DIAMOND v. DIEHR
450 U.S. 175, 209 U.S.P.Q. (BNA) 1 (1981)

REHNQUIST, J. We granted certiorari to determine whether a process for curing synthetic rubber which includes in several of its steps the use of a mathematical formula and a programmed digital computer is patentable subject matter under 35 U.S.C. § 101.

I

The patent application at issue was filed by the respondents on August 6, 1975. The claimed invention is a process for molding raw, uncured synthetic rubber into cured precision products. The process uses a mold for precisely shaping the uncured material under heat and pressure and then curing the synthetic rubber in the mold so that the product will retain its shape and be functionally operative after the molding is completed.[1]

Respondents claim that their process ensures the production of molded articles which are properly cured. Achieving the perfect cure depends upon several factors including the thickness of the article to be molded, the temperature of the molding process, and the amount of time that the article is allowed to remain in the press. It is possible using well-known time, temperature, and cure relationships to calculate by means of the Arrhenius equation[2] when to open the press

---

[1] A "cure" is obtained by mixing curing agents into the uncured polymer in advance of molding, and then applying heat over a period of time. If the synthetic rubber is cured for the right length of time at the right temperature, it becomes a usable product.

[2] The equation is named after its discoverer Svante Arrhenius and has long been used to calculate the cure time in rubber-molding presses. The equation can be expressed as follows:

$$\ln v = CZ + x$$

and remove the cured product. Nonetheless, according to the respondents, the industry has not been able to obtain uniformly accurate cures because the temperature of the molding press could not be precisely measured, thus making it difficult to do the necessary computations to determine cure time. Because the temperature inside the press has heretofore been viewed as an uncontrollable variable, the conventional industry practice has been to calculate the cure time as the shortest time in which all parts of the product will definitely be cured, assuming a reasonable amount of mold-opening time during loading and unloading. But the shortcoming of this practice is that operating with an uncontrollable variable inevitably led in some instances to overestimating the mold-opening time and overcuring the rubber, and in other instances to underestimating that time and undercuring the product.

Respondents characterize their contribution to the art to reside in the process of constantly measuring the actual temperature inside the mold. These temperature measurements are then automatically fed into a computer which repeatedly recalculates the cure time by use of the Arrhenius equation. When the recalculated time equals the actual time that has elapsed since the press was closed, the computer signals a device to open the press. According to the respondents, the continuous measuring of the temperature inside the mold cavity, the feeding of this information to a digital computer which constantly recalculates the cure time, and the signaling by the computer to open the press, are all new in the art. [Figure 2-2 is a block diagram of the invention.]

The patent examiner rejected the respondents' claims on the sole ground that they were drawn to nonstatutory subject matter under 35 U.S.C. § 101.[3] He

---

wherein ln v is the natural logarithm of v, the total required cure time; C is the activation constant, a unique figure for each batch of each compound being molded, determined in accordance with rheometer measurements of each batch; Z is the temperature in the mold; and x is a constant dependent on the geometry of the particular mold in the press. A rheometer is an instrument to measure flow of viscous substances.

[3] Respondents' application contained 11 different claims. [Two] examples are claims 1 [and] 2 which provide:

"1. A method of operating a rubber-molding press for precision molded compounds with the aid of a digital computer, comprising:

"providing said computer with a data base for said press including at least,

"natural logarithm conversion data (ln),

"the activation energy constant (C) unique to each batch of said compound being molded, and

"a constant (x) dependent upon the geometry of the particular mold of the press,

"initiating an interval timer in said computer upon the closure of the press for monitoring the elapsed time of said closure,

"constantly determining the temperature (Z) of the mold at a location closely adjacent to the mold cavity in the press during molding,

"constantly providing the computer with the temperature (Z),

"repetitively calculating in the computer, at frequent intervals during each cure, the Arrhenius equation for reaction time during the cure, which is

determined that those steps in respondents' claims that are carried out by computer under control of a stored program constituted nonstatutory subject matter under this Court's decision in *Gottschalk v. Benson*. The remaining steps — installing rubber in the press and the subsequent closing of the press — were "conventional and necessary to the process and cannot be the basis of patentability." The examiner concluded that respondents' claims defined and sought protection of a computer program for operating a rubber-molding press.

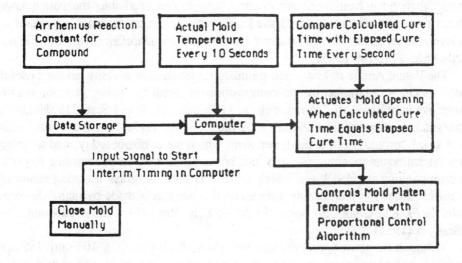

Figure 2-2

The Patent and Trademark Office Board of Appeals agreed with the examiner, but the Court of Customs and Patent Appeals reversed. The court noted that a claim drawn to subject matter otherwise statutory does not become nonstatutory because a computer is involved. The respondents' claims were not directed to a mathematical algorithm or an improved method of calculation but rather recited an improved process for molding rubber articles by solving a practical problem which had arisen in the molding of rubber products.

"ln v = CZ + x

"where v is the total required cure time,

"repetitively comparing in the computer at said frequent intervals during the cure each said calculation of the total required cure time calculated with the Arrhenius equation and said elapsed time, and

"opening the press automatically when a said comparison indicates equivalence.

"2. The method of claim 1 including measuring the activation energy constant for the compound being molded in the press with a rheometer and automatically updating said data base within the computer in the event of changes in the compound being molded in said press as measured by said rheometer.

II

Last Term in *Diamond v. Chakrabarty*, 447 U.S. 303 (1980), this Court discussed the historical purposes of the patent laws and in particular 35 U.S.C. § 101. As in *Chakrabarty*, we must here construe 35 U.S.C. § 101.

In cases of statutory construction, we begin with the language of the statute. Unless otherwise defined, "words will be interpreted as taking their ordinary, contemporary, common meaning," and, in dealing with the patent laws, we have more than once cautioned that "courts 'should not read into the patent laws limitations and conditions which the legislature has not expressed.'" *Diamond v. Chakrabarty, supra*, at 308, quoting *United States v. Dubilier Condenser Corp.*, 289 U.S. 178, 199 (1933).

The Patent Act of 1793 defined statutory subject matter as "any new and useful art, machine, manufacture or composition of matter, or any new or useful improvement [thereof]." Act of Feb. 21, 1793, ch. 11, § 1, 1 Stat. 318. Not until the patent laws were recodified in 1952 did Congress replace the word "art" with the word "process." It is that latter word which we confront today, and in order to determine its meaning we may not be unmindful of the Committee Reports accompanying the 1952 Act which inform us that Congress intended statutory subject matter to "include anything under the sun that is made by man." S. Rep. No. 1979, 82d Cong., 2d Sess., 5 (1952); H.R. Rep. No. 1923, 82d Cong., 2d Sess., 6 (1952).

Although the term "process" was not added to 35 U.S.C. § 101 until 1952, a process has historically enjoyed patent protection because it was considered a form of "art" as that term was used in the 1793 Act.

[W]e think that a physical and chemical process for molding precision synthetic rubber products falls within the § 101 categories of possibly patentable subject matter. That respondents' claims involve the transformation of an article, in this case raw, uncured synthetic rubber, into a different state or thing cannot be disputed. The respondents' claims describe in detail a step-by-step method for accomplishing such, beginning with the loading of a mold with raw, uncured rubber and ending with the eventual opening of the press at the conclusion of the cure. Industrial processes such as this are the types which have historically been eligible to receive the protection of our patent laws.

III

Our conclusion regarding respondents' claims is not altered by the fact that in several steps of the process a mathematical equation and a programmed digital computer are used. This Court has undoubtedly recognized limits to § 101 and every discovery is not embraced within the statutory terms. Excluded from such patent protection are laws of nature, natural phenomena, and abstract ideas. Only last Term, we explained:

[A] new mineral discovered in the earth or a new plant found in the wild is not patentable subject matter. Likewise, Einstein could not patent his celebrated law that $E = mc^2$; nor could Newton have patented the law of gravity. Such discoveries are "manifestations of ... nature, free to all men and reserved exclusively to none."

Diamond v. Chakrabarty, 447 U.S., at 309, quoting *Funk Bros. Seed Co. v. Kalo Inoculant Co., supra*, at 130.

Our recent holdings in *Gottschalk v. Benson, supra*, and *Parker v. Flook, supra*, both of which are computer-related, stand for no more than these long-established principles. In *Benson*, we held unpatentable claims for an algorithm used to convert binary code decimal numbers to equivalent pure binary numbers. The sole practical application of the algorithm was in connection with the programming of a general purpose digital computer. We defined "algorithm" as a "procedure for solving a given type of mathematical problem," and we concluded that such an algorithm, or mathematical formula, is like a law of nature, which cannot be the subject of a patent.

Parker v. Flook presented a similar situation. The claims were drawn to a method for computing an "alarm limit." An "alarm limit" is simply a number and the Court concluded that the application sought to protect a formula for computing this number. Using this formula, the updated alarm limit could be calculated if several other variables were known. The application, however, did not purport to explain how these other variables were to be determined, nor did it purport "to contain any disclosure relating to the chemical processes at work, the monitoring of process variables, or the means of setting off an alarm or adjusting an alarm system. All that it provides is a formula for computing an updated alarm limit." 437 U.S., at 586.

In contrast, the respondents here do not seek to patent a mathematical formula. Instead, they seek patent protection for a process of curing synthetic rubber. Their process admittedly employs a well-known mathematical equation, but they do not seek to pre-empt the use of that equation. Rather, they seek only to foreclose from others the use of that equation in conjunction with all of the other steps in their claimed process. These include installing rubber in a press, closing the mold, constantly determining the temperature of the mold, constantly recalculating the appropriate cure time through the use of the formula and a digital computer, and automatically opening the press at the proper time. Obviously, one does not need a "computer" to cure natural or synthetic rubber, but if the computer use incorporated in the process patent significantly lessens the possibility of "overcuring" or "undercuring," the process as a whole does not thereby become unpatentable subject matter.

Our earlier opinions lend support to our present conclusion that a claim drawn to subject matter otherwise statutory does not become nonstatutory simply because it uses a mathematical formula, computer program, or digital computer. In *Gottschalk v. Benson* we noted: "It is said that the decision precludes a patent for any program servicing a computer. We do not so hold." 409 U.S., at 71. Similarly, in *Parker v. Flook* we stated that "a process is not unpatentable simply because it contains a law of nature or a mathematical algorithm." 437 U.S., at 590. It is now commonplace that an *application* of a law of nature or mathematical formula to a known structure or process may well be deserving of patent protection. As Justice Stone explained four decades ago:

> While a scientific truth, or the mathematical expression of it, is not a patentable invention, a novel and useful structure created with the aid of knowledge of scientific truth may be.

Mackay Radio & Telegraph Co. v. Radio Corp. of America, 306 U.S. 86, 94 (1939).

We think this statement in *Mackay* takes us a long way toward the correct answer in this case. Arrhenius' equation is not patentable in isolation, but when a process for curing rubber is devised which incorporates in it a more efficient solution of the equation, that process is at the very least not barred at the threshold by § 101.

In determining the eligibility of respondents' claimed process for patent protection under § 101, their claims must be considered as a whole. It is inappropriate to dissect the claims into old and new elements and then to ignore the presence of the old elements in the analysis. This is particularly true in a process claim because a new combination of steps in a process may be patentable even though all the constituents of the combination were well known and in common use before the combination was made. The "novelty" of any element or steps in a process, or even of the process itself, is of no relevance in determining whether the subject matter of a claim falls within the § 101 categories of possibly patentable subject matter.

IV

We have before us today only the question of whether respondents' claims fall within the § 101 categories of possibly patentable subject matter. We view respondents' claims as nothing more than a process for molding rubber products and not as an attempt to patent a mathematical formula. We recognize, of course, that when a claim recites a mathematical formula (or scientific principle or phenomenon of nature), an inquiry must be made into whether the claim is seeking patent protection for that formula in the abstract. A mathematical formula as such is not accorded the protection of our patent laws, *Gottschalk v. Benson*, and this principle cannot be circumvented by attempting to limit the use of the formula to a particular technological environment. Similarly, insignificant post-solution activity will not transform an unpatentable principle into a patentable process. To hold otherwise would allow a competent draftsman to evade the recognized limitations on the type of subject matter eligible for patent protection. On the other hand, when a claim containing a mathematical formula implements or applies that formula in a structure or process which, when considered as a whole, is performing a function which the patent laws were designed to protect (*e.g.*, transforming or reducing an article to a different state or thing), then the claim satisfies the requirements of § 101. Because we do not view respondents' claims as an attempt to patent a mathematical formula, but rather to be drawn to an industrial process for the molding of rubber products, we affirm the judgment of the Court of Customs and Patent Appeals.

NOTES

1. According to Professor Samuelson, after *Diehr*, "Increasingly, the [CCPA] emphasized the 'industrial' or 'transformative' character of program-related process claims under review." She goes on to state:

> [Among the] CCPA decisions typical of this new emphasis [was] the *Bradley* case[]. [In *In re Bradley*, 600 F.2d 807 (C.C.P.A. 1979)], Bradley's microcode-related invention was characterized as a new combination of tangible hardware elements, even though Bradley's claims seemed to be for a new data structure for a microprogram function. Such characterizations, which gave the claims the flavor of traditional industrial processes and hardware, enhanced the likelihood of getting positive review from the Supreme Court. Even unsuccessful claimants tended to pick up on this theme and made efforts to characterize their inventions as "transformative" or technological in nature. One claimant tried to make his claim appear more technological by drafting his claims in apparatus form. [Citing *In re Maucorps*, 609 F.2d 481, 203 U.S.P.Q. (BNA) 812 (C.C.P.A. 1979)].

Samuelson, *Benson Revisited*, at 1089-90.

b. The Signal Versus Data Controversy

As mentioned in the introduction to Section 2, before the *Alappat* case, one of the strategies open to the patent community after *Benson* was to focus on the fact that the numerical values manipulated by software represent real things in the real world. The cases discussed here took this tack in embracing patents for software, though like other approaches it has not always been effective. (See the Notes following.)

In *Arrythmia Research Tech., Inc. v. Corazonix Corp.*, 958 F.2d 1053, 22 U.S.P.Q.2d (BNA) 1033 (Fed. Cir. 1992), the Federal Circuit addressed the "signal versus data" controversy. The case concerned an invention by Simson in the art of analyzing electrocardiographic signals of heart attack victims. Simson perfected a technique for detecting which heart attack victims were most at risk for suffering severe subsequent heart arrhythmia, which centered on measuring telltale electrical signals known as "late potentials." His technique involved converting the signals from analog to digital form, and then manipulating the signal and analyzing it against stored baseline values. The Federal Circuit reversed a district court's decision to uphold final rejection of both process and apparatus claims in the application, finding that although they recited a mathematical algorithm, "[w]hen mathematical formulae are the standard way of expressing certain functions or apparatus, it is appropriate that mathematical terms be used." 958 F.2d 1053, 1060. Moreover, the court focused on the fact that "the number obtained [from the algorithm] is not just an abstraction; it is a measure in microvolts of a specified heart activity." Finally, the court hearkened back to the "number versus signal" distinction, holding that "the claimed steps of 'converting,' 'applying,' 'determining,' and 'comparing' are physical process steps that transform one physical, electrical signal into another."

Despite strong evidence to the contrary, courts have often stated that the "label" of signal versus data is not determinative of patentability. *See, e.g., In re Grams*, 888 F.2d 835, 12 U.S.P.Q.2d (BNA) 1824 (Fed. Cir. 1989) ("It is manifest that the statutory nature of the subject matter does not depend on the labels 'signals' or 'data.'"). What then is determinative? Refer to the *Iwahashi* case, above; of what significance is the ROM limitation added to the claim in that case except to convert the claim from one describing an algorithm that operates on numbers to one describing an algorithm running on a piece of hardware that therefore operates on electronic signals? *See also Alappat, supra*; does the same point hold true?

NOTES

1. *Drafting Around the Cases.* Courts have been aware for some time that patent applicants often see the rules regarding software patents as an invitation to re-characterize their inventions via carefully crafted claims, or at least to add "field of use" limitations. *See, e.g., In re Waldbaum*, 559 F.2d 611, 617 (C.C.P.A. 1977) (rejecting the argument that because Waldbaum had limited the scope of his claims — some to data processing applications, and some to telephone service applications — the claims did not fail the test enunciated in *Benson*; a patent on these claims "would, in practical effect, be a patent on the algorithm itself — albeit in its limited, specific application to calculating the number of busy and idle lines in a telephone system"). Professor Samuelson comments on these attempts to "draft around" the rules on software patents:

> In view of *Iwahashi*, it is worth recalling that the CCPA had upheld one of Benson's claims because it made reference to "signals" and "reentrant shift registers." ... The Supreme Court, however, ruled that both of Benson's claims were for unpatentable subject matter. In *Iwahashi*, the Federal Circuit characterized *Benson* as making unpatentable only claims for "abstract" mathematical formulae and algorithms. *Iwahashi*, 888 F.2d at 1374.

Samuelson, *Benson Revisited*, at 1102.

2. *International Comparisons*. The patent systems of Europe have been grappling with the same issues, as the following excerpt demonstrates.

*T 208/84, 15 July 1986, Computer related Invention/*VICOM

In the case in question the patent application related to an image-processing method and apparatus designed to improve image contrast by means of a digital filtering process.

Having decided that a method for obtaining and/or reproducing an image of a physical or simulated object or a method for enhancing or restoring such an image was susceptible of industrial application within the meaning of Art[icle] 57 EPC [European Patent Convention], the Board examined whether or not such a method is excluded from patentability under Art. 52(2) and (3) EPC. On this question the decision states:

> There can be little doubt that any processing operation on an electric signal can be described in mathematical terms.... A basic difference between a mathematical method and a technical process [i.e., one that affects some tangible article] can be seen, however, in the fact that a mathematical method or a mathematical algorithm is carried out on numbers (whatever these numbers may represent) and provides a result also in numerical form, the mathematical method or algorithm being only an abstract concept prescribing how to operate on the numbers. No direct technical result is produced by the method as such. In contrast thereto, if a mathematical method is used in a technical process, that process is carried out on a physical entity (which may be a material object but equally an image stored as an electric signal) by some technical means implementing the method and provides as its result a certain change in that entity. The technical means might include a computer comprising suitable hardware or an appropriately programmed general computer.

> Generally speaking, an invention which would be patentable in accordance with conventional patentability criteria should not be excluded from protection by the mere fact that for its implementation modern technical means in the form of a computer program are used. Decisive is what technical contribution the invention as defined in the claim when considered as a whole makes to the known art.

Clément Payraudeau, *Recent Decisions of the EPO Technical Boards of Appeal*, 20 INT'L REV. IND. PROP. & COPYRIGHT L. 362 (1989). *See also In re IBM Corp.* (*"Data Processor Network"*), Case No. T 6/83, *reprinted in* 21 INT'L REV. OF IND. PROP. & COPYRIGHT L. 358 (1990) (software control function which does not cause a change in configuration of hardware elements, is nonetheless patentable). *See generally*, Meijboom, *Software Protection in "Europe 1992,"* 16 RUTGERS COMPUTER & TECH. L.J. 407, 409-20 (1990) (skillfully summarizing the law of the European Patent Convention's European Patent Office, as well as national courts, in the area of computer software-related inventions). *See generally* EEC Directive for Legal Protection of Software, Directive 91/250, January 1, 1993 (setting forth harmonized, European-wide standards for protecting software).

The situation in Japan was similarly restrictive until recently. *Compare* Jack M. Haynes, *Computer Software: Intellectual Property Protection in the United States and Japan*, 13 J. MARSHALL J. COMPUTER & INFO. L. 245, 261 (1996): ("[M]any of the computer programs which would be patentable under *Diehr* would be patentable in Japan. However, under Japanese patent law, the guidelines are rather stringent, and many computer programs would not be protected under patent law.") *with Japan Said Considering Awarding Separate Patents on Computer Software*, 13 INT'L TRADE REP. 602 (April 10, 1996) ("Japan has begun exploring the viability of awarding patents to computer software separately from hardware, an official of the Japan Patent Office said April 5.") [Rieko cites]. On the software industry in Japan, see Robert P. Merges, *A Comparative View of Property Rights in Software*, in THE INTERNATIONAL COMPUTER SOFTWARE INDUSTRY: A COMPARATIVE STUDY OF INDUSTRY EVOLUTION AND STRUCTURE 272 (1996) (David Mowery ed.).

Despite these individual differences in domestic law, all signatories to the agreement implementing the Uruguay Round of the General Agreement on Tariffs and Trade (GATT) have now agreed on a provision regarding patentable subject matter, Article 27, which provides that, subject to some exceptions not relevant here,

> patents shall be available for any inventions, whether products or processes, in all fields of technology, provided that they are new, involve an inventive step and are capable of industrial application.

Agreement on Trade-Related Aspects of Intellectual Property Rights (TRIPs), Dec. 15, 1993, reprinted in 33 I.L.M. 81, 93-94 (1994). (The entire text of Article 27 appears below in Section D, *Natural Substances and Living Things*.

c. Limiting the Category of "Mathematical Algorithm": The *"Freeman"* Test

In re FREEMAN
573 F.2d 1237, 197 U.S.P.Q. (BNA) 464 (C.C.P.A. 1978)

The subject matter of Freeman's invention is a system for typesetting alphanumeric information, using a computer-based control system in conjunction with a phototypesetter of conventional design. Freeman's overall scheme is represented by Figure 1 of his application. [See Figure 2-3.]

Input device 140 provides the identities of symbols and alphanumeric characters to be composed and the positional commands for placement of such symbols and characters in the final composition. Although shown in [Figure 2-3] as a key-

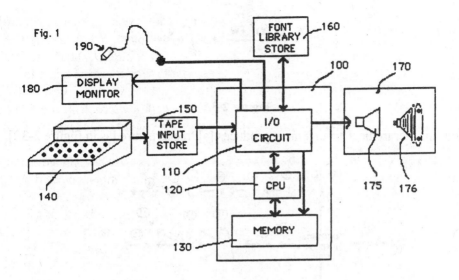

Figure 2-3

board, input device 140 may be a card reader, a magnetic or paper tape reader, or other known input device. Memory 160 stores character specifications and provides computer 100 with detailed information about the exact nature of the characters which may be selected by coded input signals from input device 140. Memory 160 may be part of computer memory 130. Computer 100 represents a broad category of data processors, including general purpose digital computers.

Output unit 170 receives character position signals from computer 100 and generates a permanent record of the desired positional relationship of the characters. As shown in [Figure 2-3], output unit 170 may include a display device, such as cathode ray tube (CRT) 175, and a photographic system, such as camera 176. Output unit 170 may also be a computer microfilm printer, or other means of producing a permanent record.

Freeman's system is especially useful in printing mathematical formulae. Its particular advantage over prior computer-aided printing systems is its positioning of mathematical symbols in an expression in accordance with their appearance, while maintaining the mathematical integrity of the expression.

The functioning of appellant's invention is best understood in appellant's example, wherein the objective is the photocomposing of the mathematical expression [shown in Figure 2-3A].

One embodiment of appellant's invention employs a hierarchical "tree structure" computer storage arrangement. Applied to the above mathematical expres-

$$Z = \frac{(T+X)^4 + W}{Y+4} + \int^7 h^\vee dv$$

Figure 2-3A

sion, the hierarchical arrangement produces [a] tree structure [as in Figure 2-3B].

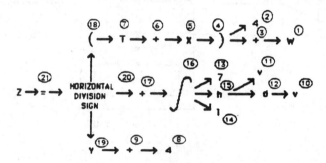

Figure 2-3B

Each particular tree structure depends on spatial relationships of the symbols, not on their mathematical meaning, *i.e.*, all symbols, whether characters or operators, are treated in the same way. As in Figure [2-3B] above, the "head" of the tree structure is the symbol at the extreme left of the main line of the formula. New "branches" of the tree are started by those symbols which begin new lines, above, on, or below the main line of the formula, *e.g.*, exponents and initial symbols of numerators and denominators.

The tree structure storage arrangement is used to determine the sequence, indicated by the circled numbers in Figure [2-3B], in which the symbols of the formula are processed by the "local positioning algorithm" disclosed by appellant. Symbols attached by arrows leading out from a given symbol are called "subordinates" of the given symbol. In Figure [2-3B], for example, the "1," the "7," and the "h" are subordinates of the integral sign.

Another basic feature of appellant's invention is the use of a set of "concatenation points" for each character. Prior art devices, like the typical Linotype machine, employed a rectangular, edge-to-edge concatenation system. Appellant's sets of concatenation points correspond roughly to the eight major compass directions, as shown in [Figure 2-4].

To form the expression "2†" from the above characters, the West concatenation point of the "†" is specified to coincide with the East concatenation point of the "2." A particular advantage of appellant's concatenation point positioning technique is its applicability to both straight linear text and to subscripts, superscripts, division signs, and integral signs. To form the expression "†^{2}," the

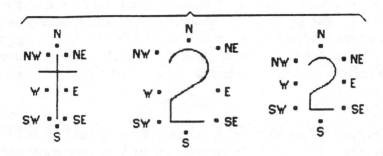

Figure 2-4

Southwest concatenation point of the "small 2" is specified to coincide with the Northeast concatenation point of the "†." ...

We have indicated the inappropriateness of the "point of novelty" approach in determining whether a claimed invention is statutory subject matter under 35 U.S.C. § 101. See *In re de Castelet*, 562 F.2d 1236, 1240, 195 U.S.P.Q. 439, 443 (C.C.P.A. 1977). Though the solicitor refers to language appearing in *In re Christensen*, 478 F.2d 1392, 178 U.S.P.Q. 35 (C.C.P.A. 1973), we clarified that language in *In re Chatfield, supra,* 545 F.2d [152] at 158, 191 U.S.P.Q. [730] at 736 [(C.C.P.A. 1976)]:

> Our reference in *Christensen* to the mathematical equation as being "at the point of novelty" does not equate to a holding that a claim may be dissected, the claim components searched in the prior art and, if the only component found novel is outside the statutory classes of invention, the claim may be rejected under 35 U.S.C. § 101. That procedure is neither correct nor within the intent of Congress, for the reasons we stated in [*In re Bernhart*, 417 F.2d 1395, 57 C.C.P.A. 737, 163 U.S.P.Q. (BNA) 611 (1969)].

Determination of whether a claim preempts nonstatutory subject matter as a whole, in the light of *Benson*, requires a two-step analysis. First, it must be determined whether the claim directly or indirectly recites an "algorithm" in the *Benson* sense of that term, for a claim which fails even to recite an algorithm clearly cannot wholly preempt an algorithm. Second, the claim must be further analyzed to ascertain whether in its entirety it wholly preempts that algorithm. We do not reach the second step in this case because method claims 8-10 do not recite an algorithm in the *Benson* sense....

Because every process may be characterized as "a step-by-step procedure ... for accomplishing some end," a refusal to recognize that *Benson* was concerned only with *mathematical* algorithms leads to the absurd view that the Court was reading the word "process" out of the statute....

The apparatus claims [drafted in means-plus-function format] do not directly or indirectly recite any mathematical equation, formula, or calculation and thus do not preempt the use of any mathematical problem-solving algorithm. It is unnecessary, therefore, to consider the effect of specific apparatus limitations in some of the apparatus claims. Accordingly, the decision of the board is *reversed*.

NOTES

1. The "point of novelty" rule discussed in the case was a major issue in the cases decided after *Benson*. To clarify the point of novelty issue, consider an application for a computer-related invention with elements A, B, and C, where C is the actual program code and A and B are hardware elements or process steps. If only C is new, i.e., if the elements A and B are well-known in the art, no patent will issue because the only novel element is, when taken by itself, unpatentable. If either A or B are new, however, a patent will issue, since the new material — the "point of novelty" — in this case includes something outside the suspect category of pure software. Professor Samuelson describes the history of the rule. Samuelson, *Benson Revisited, supra*, at 1064, 1067.

2. In another important CCPA case, *In re Walter*, 618 F.2d 758, 205 U.S.P.Q. (BNA) 397 (C.C.P.A. 1980), the test of patentability was stated as follows:

> Once a mathematical algorithm has been found, the claim as a whole must be further analyzed. If it appears that the mathematical algorithm is implemented in a specific manner to define structural relationships between the physical elements of the claim (in apparatus claims) or to refine or limit claim steps (in process claims), the claim being otherwise statutory; the claim passes muster under § 101.

618 F.2d at 767, 205 U.S.P.Q. (BNA) at 407. This is often cited as part of what is called the *Freeman-Walter* test. The *Walter* decision went on to say that if the claim presented an algorithm and solved it, but did not apply it to physical elements or process steps, then no amount of post-solution activity, and no field of use limitation would save it. *Id.* In *In re Abele*, 684 F.2d 902, 906-07 (C.C.P.A. 1982), the patent applicant complained that *Walter*, even with this proviso, did not provide very clear guidance about what would satisfy this second step.

3. *Section 101 and "Nature's Library."* The Court in *Parker v. Flook, supra*, states that "Whether the algorithm was in fact known or unknown … it is treated as though it were a familiar part of the prior art." This posits an interesting rationale for § 101: that all naturally existing plants, scientific principles, laws of nature, and mathematical algorithms are unpatentable because they pre-exist in "nature's library." Nature, in other words, is a huge source of prior art that defeats the novelty of any invention drawn from it. What do you think of this justification? Should it matter that it takes brilliance to discover a natural fact —

that in effect it takes real inventive effort to find a particular "book" on "nature's shelves"? Why discriminate against expensive and difficult research that happens to take place in this "library"?

4. Professor Samuelson argues that

> The *Freeman* case is one of a number of CCPA cases that misconstrues the nature of the invention being claimed. Freeman's invention did involve a mathematical problem, not because the items to be typeset were mathematical equations, but because the concatenation points, the hierarchical tree for noting positions, and the positioning algorithm were mathematical in character. However, the only thing the CCPA focused on in the *Freeman* claim was a typesetting process.

Samuelson, Benson Revisited, at 1076. Other cases also illustrate this point. *See, e.g., In re Chatfield*, 545 F.2d 152, 158 (C.C.P.A. 1976) (stating that the only patentability problems presented in program-related cases concerned efforts to patent mathematics); *In re Toma*, 575 F.2d 872, 877 (C.C.P.A. 1978) ("Translating between natural languages is not a mathematical problem as we understand the term to have been used in *Benson*. Nor are any of the recited steps in the claims mere procedures for solving mathematical problems"); *In re Bradley*, 600 F.2d 807 (C.C.P.A. 1979) (rejecting the Patent Office's argument that because digital computers operate through use of a numerical radix, methods of operating them were inherently mathematical in character and, hence, unpatentable under *Benson* and *Flook*), *aff'd by an equally divided court sub nom. Diamond v. Bradley*, 450 U.S. 381 (1981).

It might be supposed that the troublesome attempt to distinguish "mathematical" from "non-mathematical" algorithms stems from the Supreme Court's original categorization of computer programs along with scientific principles and products of nature. Whatever the logic of this distinction, it has provided an important framework for the analysis of software-related claims since *Freeman*. And yet other distinctions have also played a role, most notably that between "pure" algorithms and algorithms that form part of "industrial processes." The story of the birth and growth of this distinction begins with *Diamond v. Diehr*.

d. *In re Iwahashi*: Precursor to *Alappat*

Alappat bears some similarity — as to both facts and holding — to the prior case of *In re Iwahashi*, 888 F.2d 1370; 12 U.S.P.Q.2d (BNA) 1908 (Fed. Cir. 1989). *Iwahashi* centered around an invention in the field of computer pattern recognition, with special application to the recognition of human speech. The invention involves a new technique for what amounts to indexing or cataloguing discrete parts of a pattern. As it applies to speech, for instance, the invention takes as its "input" some snippet of human speech. The speech is first converted into its electronic equivalent, a waveform, which can be represented on an oscilloscope (a television-like monitor for displaying visual representations of waves). The aim of the invention is to catalogue or classify the segments of speech. In the speech recognition art, the first step in doing this is to assess certain key features of the electronic version of the speech fragment. The invention at issue assigns some of these features by means of a mathematical operation known as *autocorrelation*, which essentially involves comparing snippets of speech with other snippets from the same input. The output of this mathematical operation is a series of numerical "tags" called *autocorrelation coefficients*; these are numerical values which reflect key characteristics or features of the various speech segments. By taking the speech input, breaking it up into segments, and assigning coefficients to the segments, a computer can "understand" the meaning of the speech. The specific advance of the invention is its improved method for calculating autocorrelation coefficients. In the prior art, these coefficients were calculated using a lengthy and time-consuming digital electronic circuit, which involved bulky multiplication operations. The invention at issue in the case represented a new technique — one that is much faster — for calculating these coefficients. The new technique involves looking up the square of a number in a table, rather than multiplying the number by itself to get the square. This saves a good deal of calculating time, which is important in pattern recognition applications that must respond quickly to actual human inquiries or commands — i.e., ones that operate in "real time."

The applicant in *Iwahashi* claimed the invention in "means-plus-function" format. The key claim in the case recited

> An auto-correlation unit … comprising … means for extracting N pieces of sampled input values … means for calculating the sum of the sample values … a read only memory associated with said means for calculating … means for storing in said read only memory the squared value of each sum ….

The diagram in Figure 2-5 represents a block diagram of one embodiment of the invention, but the claims (reproduced in schematic form below) make it clear that this is only one embodiment out of the many they embrace.

The claims are described in the case as follows:

Claim		Drawings
[a]	An auto-correlation unit for providing auto-correlation coefficients for use as feature parameters in pattern recognition for N pieces of sampled input values X_n (n = 0 to N-1), said unit comprising:	
[b]	means for extracting N pieces of sample input values X_n from a series of sample values in an input pattern expressed with an accuracy of optional multi-bits;	Not shown in Figure [2-5]
[c]	means for calculating the sum of the sample values X_n and X_n-Z (t = 0–P, P < N);	Adder 1.

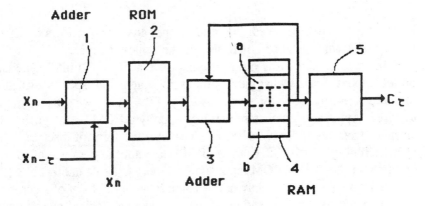

Figure 2-5

[d]	a read only memory associated with said means for calculating;	ROM 2.
[e]	means for feeding to said read only memory the sum of the sampled input values as an address signal;	Signal path connecting adder 1 to ROM 2.
[f]	means for storing in said read only memory the squared value of each sum, $(X_n + X_n\text{-}Z)^2$;	Internal structure of ROM after being programmed to store squared values.
[g]	means for fetching and outputting squared values of each such sum of the sample input values from said read only memory when said memory is addressed by the sum of the sample input values; and	Read pulse (not shown) is applied to ROM 2.
[h]	means responsive to the output $(X_n + X_n\text{-}Z)^2$ of said read only memory for providing an auto-correlation coefficient for use as a feature parameter according to the following formula:	Calculating circuit 5.

$$\frac{\displaystyle\sum_{n=0}^{N-1} (X_n + X_n - Z)2}{2 \cdot \displaystyle\sum_{n=0}^{N-1} X_n^2} - 1$$

The court held:

> Element [d], it will be noted, is not in means-plus-function form but specifies a "read only memory" or ROM, as the Solicitor says....
>
> Though the claim starts out by saying ... that it is a "unit," appellants prefer to characterize what they claim as apparatus with specific structural limitations. By the Solicitor's own analysis of the claim, we are constrained to agree. Appellants emphasize that they specify a ROM ... to which is fed an input from an adder .... Next are means in the form of disclosed electronic circuitry which take from the ROM its output in the form of squares of numbers supplied as ROM input and feed them to a calculating circuit .... The claim as a whole certainly defines apparatus in the form of a combination of interrelated means and we cannot discern any logical reason why it should not be deemed statutory subject matter as either a machine or a manufacture as specified in § 101. The fact that the apparatus operates according to an algorithm does not make it nonstatutory. We therefore hold that the claim is directed to statutory subject matter.

4. INFRINGEMENT

We now have the first decided case where a software patent has been successfully enforced. In 1994, a jury ruled that Microsoft had infringed data compression software patents held by Stac Electronics, and awarded damages of $120 million to Stac. *See Stac Electronics v. Microsoft Corp.*, No. C-93-0413-ER (C.D. Cal. 1994); J. Burgess, *Microsoft Found Guilty of Patent Infringement: Software Giant Ordered to Pay $120 Million*, WASH. POST 2/24/94, at D11. (Although two software patents were asserted, the jury failed to specify whether one or both of the patents were infringed.) According to reports in the press, Microsoft tried to license Stac but the parties failed to reach agreement. Microsoft temporarily excised the infringing code from its MS-DOS operating system software, then settled. The case clearly shows the potential impact of software patents in that Stac was able to force Microsoft to temporarily pull a multi-million-dollar product from the market. To some, this case serves as an example of why patents for software are so problematical. *See, e.g.*, L.M. Fisher, *The Executive Computer: Will Users Be the Big Losers in Software Patent Battles?*, N.Y. TIMES 5/6/94, sec. 3, at 7.

The jury also ruled that Stac had misappropriated Microsoft trade secrets embodied in limited-distribution "Beta" software, and awarded Microsoft $13.6 million in damages. *See* Ronald L. Johnston & Allen R. Grogan, *Trade Secret Protection for Mass Distributed Software*, 11 COMP. L. 1 (1994).

Judging from the volume of patent applications, as well as reports of threatened litigation and licensing activity, there will soon be many more infringement cases involving software patents. *See, e.g.*, Paul Heckel, *Epilogue: The Wright Brothers and Software Innovation* in THE ELEMENTS OF FRIENDLY SOFTWARE DESIGN 223 (1991) (description of enforcement and licensing activity by inventor and patentee of "Zoomracks" database and organizer software product); Gregory Aharonian, *ACM Forum* (letter to editor), 36 COMM. OF THE ACM 17 (1993) (reporting an apparent rumor that "Microsoft just paid $20,000,000 to license IBM's software patents"). A good "cyberspace" location for following licensing and enforcement activities and controversies is the Internet Patent News Service, E-mail address: patents@world.std.com.

Hardware Limitations and Infringement

Means-plus-function claims in software are not new, as the preceding sections of this chapter make clear. Nor, indeed, are software claims couched in terms of hardware. As the prevalence of software patents increases, however, the latter practice has given rise to a new concern. Due to the inclusion of hardware elements in these claims, patentees and their lawyers have begun to worry about precisely who would infringe such claims. The basic worry is that someone who merely copies a computer program from one medium (e.g., diskette) to another — or someone merely found in possession of such a diskette — cannot be said to infringe a claim that includes hardware elements. (For the law on infringement, see Chapter 8.) Under the widely accepted theories of "contributory infringement" and "inducement," however, a cause of action will lie against this class of infringers in most cases. *See* 35 U.S.C. § 271. Proving "direct" infringement does carry some subtle advantages, however — which means that the "safe harbor" of *Alappat* and the post-*Alappat* Guidelines might be fraught with rough water for some patentees. On the other hand, "program on diskette" claims of the type approved in *In re Beauregard* might be a solution to the problem. Do you see why? *See generally* Steven W. Lundberg & Russell D. Slifer, *"Program Product" Patents: Savior or Blunder*, 12 COMPUTER LAW. 1 (1995).

5. IMPACT OF PATENTS ON THE SOFTWARE INDUSTRY

The spectre of software patents has been hanging over the head of the software industry since at least the late 1980s. And, in general, the arguments for and against these patents have not changed much since then.

The following is excerpted from the statement of Daniel Bricklin, President of Software Garden, Inc., recorded in the Seminar Notes of an MIT Communications Forum on March 23, 1989, entitled "Software Patents: a Horrible Mistake?" Mr. Bricklin is best known as one of the two creators of VisiCalc, the first electronic spreadsheet program. His views are quite representative of those of many — but by no means all — professional software developers.

Bricklin emphasized that a sophisticated applications program may involve 10-10,000 patentable processes. He noted that if companies began spending money to obtain software patents for these processes then the current royalty structure would have to change in order for companies to remain profitable.

Bricklin noted that there is an important distinction to be made [between] ... most patents [and] ... software patents. He explained that there is usually one patent that covers the whole product in the case of plant or chemical products. In contrast, a software product can easily involve hundreds of patents for a single product.

Bricklin characterized the software industry as inherently cottage-based. He explained how most of the major advances in the PC industry seem to come out of small shops or out of small development teams. Some examples include WordPerfect Corp., Lotus Corp., and Software Arts. Bricklin noted that with even better tools today one programmer can do even more than he accomplished in the past. He believes that some products should be written by individuals or small groups to achieve better cohesiveness while there is still demand for large companies to handle the larger scale projects. In some cases, Bricklin notes that it is cheaper for a company to go outside and buy a software product rather than develop [it] themselves. He believes that if the industry had the copyright protection just on the source code, it would be cheaper to buy than to make.

Bricklin commented that many people feel software must be "protectable" because it is a product of someone's hard work. In his opinion, "craftsman-ship" is not protectable and he does not feel that just because you work hard on something, e.g., software, that it should be protectable. He believes we should have patents because patents advance technology, not because patents are inherently good.

Bricklin also cited the problem of "mine fields" in that a software devel-oper often finds out about a related patent after the product has been shipped. He also questions the motives of many lawyers who are getting patents and copyrights to be expanded to apply to a broader range of things since it is self-serving. As a developer of software he is also uneasy about patents since he admits having limited knowledge about intellectual property. In reaction to the increase in software patents, Bricklin noted he has been working on lower tech products which involve using information in the public domain.

... Bricklin thinks that it is going to take ten years to work things out and that there will be a change in the industry while some of the protection comes in. Bricklin believes that the software industry has "done very well and has moved ahead very quickly because it is satisfying the demands of customers." He believes that given the software industry's working well, there is not room for the expanding role of patents and copyrights to fix anything.

(pp. 15-16 of the Seminar Notes.)

At the same Forum, the Senior Counsel for Digital Equipment Corporation (DEC), Lindsey Kiang, provided counter-arguments.

Companies like DEC believe that patent protection is necessary to protect their investment in software R&D, especially when they're spending more than $1 billion a year on such work. He believes that R&D costs will only rise as software development becomes more advanced and complex to meet the needs of customers. Kiang believes that companies like DEC will continue to feel an obligation to its investors to protect its R&D investment with patents. He believes that patent protection for software will continue to stimulate innovation and creativity.

Kiang does not believe the issue of patents is a "big versus little company" issue. He would argue that a small company needs the power of patent protection even more than the big company. In his opinion, small companies are usually putting everything at stake on one product. Kiang made two additional points: (1) Very few patent cases are actually litigated in the courts, which implies that most conflicts are settled by licensing; and (2) since there have been more than 1,000 software patents issued in the U.S. since 1981, most in the last 4 or 5 years, he stated that it is hard to argue that patents have stifled creativity in this industry. His basic position was that patents can only increase the fund of software inventions, not decrease it.

See also Pamela Samuelson, Randall Davis, Mitchell D. Kepor & J.H. Reichman, *A Manifesto Concerning the Legal Protection of Computer Programs*, in *Symposium: Toward a Third Intellectual Property Paradigm*, 94 COLUM. L. REV. 2308 (1994) (calling for a "sui generis" system of software protection, partly because "the incremental nature of innovation in software largely precludes patent protection"); Mitch Kapor, *Testimony at Hearings before U.S. House of Representatives, Subcommittee on Courts, Intellectual Property and the Administration of Justice, of the Committee on the Judiciary* (Mar. 5, 1990) (testimony of another software entrepreneur, the founder of Lotus Development Corporation, who also opposes software patents); *Software Patents: Law of the Jungle*, ECONOMIST, Aug. 18, 1990, at 59; *Will Software Patents Cramp Creativity?*, WALL ST. J., Mar. 14, 1989, at B1, col. 3.

Another concern is that patents are issued several years after being applied for, which could upset plans and disturb existing product markets:

> [P]atents on pieces of computer programs "have become an enormous problem for our industry," says Kenneth Wasch, executive director of the Software Publisher's Association. A flood of newly issued patents has raised the concern that many programs on the market may soon be found to be in violation of patents held by others. The impact of these patents and others, some say, may stifle innovation and put an end to the freewheeling creativity that has been a hallmark of the nation's $2.6 billion software industry.

S. Garfinkel, *Software Makers Row Over Patents*, CHRISTIAN SCI. MONITOR, Sept. 12, 1989, at 8. *Compare* Gibbons, *Patents Throw Obstacles in the Way*, PC

WEEK, Sept. 18, 1989, at 77 (opinion piece by president of medium-sized software publishing house decrying growing importance of patents in industry) *with* Lastova & Hoffman, *Patent Protection for Software Gives Businesses Extra Leverage*, NAT'L L.J., June 26, 1989, at 38, cols. 2-4 (use of method, apparatus, and means-plus-function claim formats to claim software inventions will permit industry to protect more of its R&D investment). *Cf.* Bender, *The Renaissance of the "Software Patent,"* 13 HAMLINE L. REV. 205, 220 (1990) (whereas the 1970s was the decade of trade secret litigation in the software industry, and the 1980s was the decade of copyright, the 1990s will be the decade of patents).

NOTES

1. *Patent Concentration*. Should it be relevant to the Patent Office, courts, or Congress *who* is getting software patents — large companies or small? Is it possible to use the patent system to "control" the structure or development of an industry? If so, is § 101 the proper place to make these determinations? There is a large literature in economics inquiring into the optimal industry structure for fostering innovations. *See, e.g.*, M. KAMIEN & N. SCHWARTZ, MARKET STRUC-TURE AND INNOVATION (1982) (stating case that modest levels of industry con-centration bring best innovation results). Note that in some cases, stronger property rights can lead to a more *dis*-integrated industry structure, because these rights lower the transaction costs associated with transferring information and certain products across firm boundaries. *See* Robert P. Merges, *A Comparative View of Property Rights in Software*, in THE INTERNATIONAL COMPUTER SOFT-WARE INDUSTRY: A COMPARATIVE STUDY OF INDUSTRY EVOLUTION AND STRUCTURE 272 (David Mowery ed., 1996) (arguing that weak property rights may have contributed to the slow emergence of independent firms selling pre-packaged (versus custom) software in Japan); Robert P. Merges, *Intellectual Property and the Costs of Commercial Exchange: A Review Essay (Book Review)*, 93 MICH. L. REV. 1570 (1995) (arguing the general point that strong and well-defined property rights can lower transaction costs and thus indirectly affect industry structure).

2. *Floodgates Open*. Even before *Iwahashi*, the number of software patents issued by the Patent Office was on the increase. Patent lawyers had begun to conclude that obtaining a patent for a program-related invention was merely a matter of proper claim drafting. *See, e.g.*, Smith, Yoches & Anzalone, *Computer Program Patents*, COMPUTER LAW., Apr. 1988, at 1, 3 (arguing that one must simply be careful in drafting the claims to obtain a patent on an algorithm). Soma & Smith, *Software Trends: Who's Getting How Many of What? 1978 to 1987*, 71 J. PAT. & TRADEMARK OFF. SOC'Y 415 (1989) (Between Jan. 1, 1978 and Dec. 31, 1987, 262 software patents issued, of which 26% were issued to IBM).

These figures were only the prelude, however. By one estimate, there were 4,569 software patents issued in 1994 alone! *See* Jeffrey J. Blatt, *Software Patents: Myth Versus Virtual Reality*, 17 HASTINGS COMM. & ENT. L.J. 795, 815

(1995). As had been the case earlier, a preponderance of these patents were issued to large firms, e.g., IBM. *Id.*

a. "If it ain't broke ..."

The President's Commission of 1966, cited in the *Benson* case, made the following statement:

> It is noted that the creation of programs has undergone substantial and satisfactory growth in the absence of patent protection and that copyright protection for programs is presently available.

Should it matter — to Congress or the courts — that patents have different impacts on different industries? That patents are part of a larger landscape of techniques and mechanisms whereby firms can recoup the costs of expensive R&D?

The software industry, for example, is composed of some large firms and many small ones. *See* David C. Mowery, *Introduction*, in THE INTERNATIONAL COMPUTER SOFTWARE INDUSTRY: A COMPARATIVE STUDY OF INDUSTRY EVOLUTION AND STRUCTURE 3 (David Mowery ed., 1996); MASSACHUSETTS COMPUTER SOFTWARE COUNCIL, INC., SOFTWARE INDUSTRY BUSINESS PRACTICES SURVEY 8, 9 (Joyce L. Plotkin, Exec. Dir., 1991) (showing survey responses which indicate that at least 75% of software firms have fewer than 100 employees, with 49% having fewer than 30; and showing that 29% have revenues of less than $500,000 and 51% have revenues of less than $2 million per year). Slightly more than half of the survey respondents said they spent less than $100,000 before making their first sale, and 52 percent shipped product within 12 months of launching a business.

Patents are thought by some to pose a threat to this small-firm-dominated industry structure. Small firms generally fear patents because of the cost involved. There is some evidence that these concerns are legitimate, given the experience of other industries. *See* Vandenberg, *The Truth About Patent Litigation for Patent Owners Contemplating Suit*, 73 J. PAT. & TRADEMARK OFF. SOC'Y 301 (1991) (average cost of patent litigation is $350,000, with range from $100,000 to $1 million). *Cf.* Mueller & Tilton, *Research and Development Costs as a Barrier to Entry*, 2 CAN. J. ECON. 570, 579 (1969) ("The second major factor contributing to barriers is the accumulation of patents and know-how on the part of incumbent firms. Even if there were no economies of scale in R&D, a late entrant would have to undertake more R&D than an average firm of its size in order to acquire information about the technology and to invent around existing patents.").

Many of these fears are expressed in the following article, written by a group of software engineers and designers opposed to software patents.

LEAGUE FOR PROGRAMMING FREEDOM, SOFTWARE PATENTS: IS THIS THE FUTURE OF PROGRAMMING?, Dr. Dobb's Journal, Nov. 1990, at 56*

Software patents threaten to devastate America's computer industry. Newly granted software patents are being used to attack companies such as Lotus and Microsoft for selling programs that they have independently developed. Soon new companies will be barred from the software arena — most major programs will require licenses for dozens of patents, and this will make them infeasible. This problem has only one solution: Software patents must be eliminated.

[The article goes on to criticize the fact that the Patent Office has not hired professional programmers with computer science degrees to examine computer science-related patent applications.]

Licensing may be prohibitively expensive, as in the case when the patent is held by a competitor. Even 'reasonable' license fees for several patents can add up to make a project infeasible. Alternatively, the developer may wish to avoid using the patent altogether; but there may be no way around it.

A programmer reading a patent may not believe that his program violates the patent, but a federal court may rule otherwise. It is thus now necessary to involve patent attorneys at every phase of program development.... However, for the inexpensive programming project, the same extra cost [for dealing with the patent system] is prohibitive. Individuals and small companies especially cannot afford these costs. Software patents will put an end to software entrepreneurs.

For example, the implementors of the widely used public domain data compression program *Compress* followed an algorithm obtained from *IEEE Computer* Magazine. They and the user community were surprised to learn later that [U.S.] Patent #4,558,302 had been issued to one of the authors of the article. Now [the] Unisys [Co.] is demanding royalties for using this algorithm. [U]sing [this program] means risking a law suit.

Most large software companies are trying to solve the problem of patents by getting patents of their own. Then they hope to cross-license with the other large companies that own most of the patents, so they will be free to go on as before.

While this approach will allow companies such as Microsoft, Apple, and IBM to continue in business, it will shut new companies out of the field. A future start-up, with no patents of its own, will be forced to pay whatever price the giants choose to impose. That price might be high: Established companies have an interest in excluding future competitors.

There will be little benefit to society from software patents because invention in software was already flourishing before software patents, and inventions were normally published in journals for everyone to use. Invention flourished so strongly, in fact, that the same inventions were often found again and again.

---

*Reprinted with permission from *Dr. Dobb's Journal*, © 1990.

By reducing the number of people engage [sic] in software development, software patents will actually impede innovation ... when patents make development more difficult, and cut down on development projects, they will also cut down on the byproducts of development — new techniques.

We recommend the passage of a law to exclude software from the domain of patents.

Overturning patents in a court requires *prior art*, which may not be easy to find. The League for Programming Freedom will try to serve as a clearing house for this information, to assist the defendants in software patent suits. This depends on your help. If you know about *prior art* for any software patent, please send the information to the League....

To picture the effects [of patents], imagine that each square of pavement on the sidewalk has an owner and that pedestrians must obtain individual licenses to step on particular squares. Think of the negotiations necessary to walk an entire block under this system. That is what writing a program will be like in the future if software patents continue.

NOTES

1. One point mentioned in the preceding excerpt deserves mention: the idea that so many individual algorithms may be patented that it will be very difficult and expensive to obtain the necessary licenses to incorporate them all in a new software product. According to conventional economic theory, which pays little attention to the costs of engaging in such transactions, this should really be no problem. Since patentees and those writing programs which incorporate patentees' algorithms would both gain from a licensing transaction, it is thought that the appropriate licenses would be easily arranged. Implicit in the foregoing excerpt is a doubt that this would be so. And there is some support for such a doubt; some research shows that technology licensing transactions are expensive to arrange and administer, due to such factors as the difficulty of placing an "objective" value on technology. *See, e.g.*, F. CONTRACTOR, INTERNATIONAL TECHNOLOGY LICENSING: COMPENSATION, COSTS, AND NEGOTIATION 104-05 (1981) (transaction costs averaged over $100,000 for licensing deals studied); D. TEECE, THE MULTINATIONAL CORPORATION AND THE RESOURCE COST OF INTERNATIONAL TECHNOLOGY TRANSFER 44 (1976) (transfer costs constituted over 19% of total project costs in international projects studied); E. VON HIPPEL, THE SOURCES OF INNOVATION 48 (1988) (summarizing empirical studies finding generally low net returns from licensing). More subtle transaction costs, such as possible opportunistic behavior, are described in F. BIDAULT, TECHNOLOGY PRICING: FROM PRINCIPLES TO STRATEGY 126-27 (B. Page & P. Sherwood trans., 1989), and Teece, *Profiting from Technological Innovation: Implications for Integration, Collaboration, Licensing and Public Policy*, 15 RES. POL'Y 285, 294 (1986). It has even been suggested that high transaction costs are a good rationale for the exclusion of certain subject matter from intellectual property protection. *See* Robert P. Merges, *Property Rights Theory and the Commons: The Case of Scientific Research*, 13 J. SOC. PHIL. & POL'Y 145 (1996); Besen & Raskind, *An Introduction to the Law and Economics of Intellectual Property*, 5 J. ECON. PERSP. 3, 10 (1991).

On the other hand, in certain cases businesses have been fairly creative in solving the problem of excessive patent licensing costs; one interpretation of industry-wide "patent pools" is that they lower the transaction costs of exchanging patented new technology. *See, e.g.*, Robert P. Merges, *Contracting Into Liability Rules: Intellectual Property Rights and Collective Rights Organizations*, 84 CAL. L. REV. __ (1996) (Hereinafter Merges, *Contracting Into Liability Rules*); Bittlingmayer, *Property Rights, Progress, and the Aircraft Patent Agreement*, 31 J.L. & ECON. 227, 232 (1988) (describing operation and efficiency of long-lived and industry-wide patent pool in aircraft industry). *But cf.* Dykman, *Patent Licensing Within the Manufacturer's Aircraft Association (MAA)*, 46 J. PAT. OFF. SOC'Y 646, 647 (1964) (describing formation of industry licensing pool at behest of government because, "[n]o one would license the other under anything like a reasonable basis"). In another context, artists' rights groups have been formed to issue "blanket licenses" of all members' works to media outlets. These groups are widely believed to be the only effective way for individual artists to make their works available for licensing. *See* Merges, *Contracting Into Liability Rules, supra*; Besen, Kirby & Salop, *An Economic Analysis of Copyright Collectives*, 78 VA. L. REV. 383 (1992). To some extent, then, the debate over software patents may be viewed as a debate about how well the market for licenses of patented algorithms can be expected to work.

Some have called for a statutory compulsory license to lower the transaction costs that software patents will bring. *See, e.g.*, *Patent and Trademark Office: Improved Patents for Software Urged at Second Round of Hearings*, 47 PAT. TRADEMARK & COPYRIGHT J. 357 (1994) (describing testimony of Paul Robinson of Tansin A. Darcos & Co., calling for a compulsory licensing scheme for software patents, in hearings on this issue before the Commissioner of Patents). But I have cautioned against this tempting *ex ante* solution, arguing instead that private organizations are likely to arise, at least among "repeat play" transactors, and that these private organizations can be expected to be superior to legislative solutions. *See* Merges, *Contracting Into Liability Rules, supra*. For a description of possible judicial responses to bargaining breakdown between patent holders in non-repeat play situations, see Robert P. Merges, *Intellectual Property Rights and Bargaining Breakdown: The Case of Improvement Patents*, 62 TENN. L. REV. 75 (1994).

2. Given the record of success in the software industry, should we worry about permitting extensive patenting of software and algorithms? Is this a relevant concern when interpreting § 101 of the Patent Act?

Many of the issues that vex the software industry in relation to patents are *transitional* issues; they are problems that are occurring, or are feared, due to the fact that the industry was born in an era when software was generally viewed as unpatentable subject matter. Should Congress worry about who would win and who would lose during the transition from a pre-patent to a post-patent industry? Should we become alarmed over the obvious cases where patents have issued on simple programming techniques long known to the field, or should we expect the normal court invalidation procedure to work if they are ever asserted? (Note that an organization called the Software Patent Institute, an independent not-for-profit entity administered by University of Michigan computer science professor Bernard Galler, has set up a data base to collect prior art to help in these cases; see their World Wide Web site, www.spi.org, for details.)

In countries in which a software industry was slow to develop, copyright protection has been credited with helping to create conditions that permitted a domestic industry to take root. *See* INTELLECTUAL PROPERTY RIGHTS IN SCIENCE, TECHNOLOGY AND ECONOMIC PERFORMANCE (F. Rushing & C. Brown eds., 1990), where the authors point to the case of India.

b. The Case for Software Patents

The case *against* proposals to limit software patents is argued persuasively by Donald Chisum in his article *The Future of Software Protection: The Patentability of Algorithms*, 47 U. PITT. L. REV. 959, 1014-15 (1986)*:

1. The continuing trend is for hardware technology, including semiconductor technology (e.g., processor and memory chips) and peripheral devices (e.g., mass storage and interfacing devices), to become more powerful and cheaper.

2. While the powerful new hardware has tremendous potential for satisfying human needs, that potential can only be realized by production of suitable programming (software).

3. The continuing trend is for software technology to become more complex and more expensive to produce, the primary reason being that such production continues to use intensively highly skilled labor.

4. The production of software entails at least two stages. One is the conceptualization of the basic method for solving the problems at hand (i.e., the generation of algorithms). The other is the preparation of detailed instructions to implement the method on a computer (i.e., the preparation of computer programs and detailed code based on the algorithms).

5. Algorithm generation is qualitative in nature and may entail either the application of known techniques or the formulation of distinctly new and superior techniques. Better algorithms enable computers to be used more efficiently and effectively.

---

*Copyright © 1986 by University of Pittsburgh Law Review. Reprinted with permission.

6. Program preparation is quantitative in nature and entails a large amount of intellectual work that follows known techniques.

7. Both algorithm generation and program preparation are expensive, but in different ways and for different reasons. In the qualitative, algorithm-generation stage, much time is likely to be devoted to efforts that turn out to be nonproductive. There is no guarantee that superior techniques will in fact be produced. In the implementation, program preparation stage, the results are more predictable; the expense factor is simply a function of the amount of time that must be devoted to achieving those results.

8. Once software in the form of a computer program is produced and publicly distributed, it may be copied and utilized easily by others in a number of ways.... The algorithms may be used without any close copying of the detailed instructions of the source program and indeed can be used to prepare entirely new programs that achieve different results in different ways.

Assuming that these are the facts (and I strongly suspect that these "hypothetical" findings closely track reality), then the "expert opinion" must be that exclusion from the patent system of algorithms useful in computer programming cannot be justified. The pattern of production of algorithms and computer programs is the same as the production of other products and services. The lure of patent protection attracts greater investment in the research stage, whether it be in the exploration for a new chemical process or compound or in the generation of algorithms. Since patents may properly be granted only for new innovations, the result will be the disclosure through the publication of patents of new and superior technology. The trend in hardware technology seems to guarantee an almost perpetual shortage of needed software. Hence incentives to increase the general level of investment in software generation are perfectly appropriate.

NOTE

On Professor Chisum's prediction that software is increasingly complex and expensive to produce, see Jim Erickson, *Software, Jets Drive Seattle; New Products from Microsoft, Boeing Add Luster to Local Economy*, SEATTLE POST-INTELLIGENCER, Aug. 10, 1995, at 1D (Windows 95 "reportedly cost about $300 million" to develop).

On the other hand, what assumption lies behind the notion that more expensive R&D projects require "stronger" intellectual property rights? Are there alternatives means of appropriating returns for R&D investments in the software industry? Again, should the law take the availability and sufficiency of these alternative means into account in setting patent policy?

c. Of Defensive Patenting and the Prisoners' Dilemma

Despite the arguments in favor of software patents, many patentees in the software industry can only be described as reluctant. They are obtaining patents for purely defensive purposes, motivated by a fear of exclusion from markets at the hands of other patentees. *See, e.g.*, Mark Walsh, *Bowing to Reality, Software Maker Begins Building a Patent Portfolio*, THE RECORDER, Aug. 17, 1995, at 1 ("while [Oracle Corporation, a $3 billion software firm] says it still [opposes software patents], it has ... embarked on an aggressive program to secure patents for its software products — primarily to protect itself against potential infringement claims, in the face of a sharp increase in recent years in the number of software patents issued by the PTO."). Notice the irony: money that would be spent on R&D is diverted to patent activities, as industry members reluctantly pursue the "incentive" of patents; see *id*. ("[M]any in the software industry see the legal fees spent on prosecuting patents as an unnecessary drain on capital that could go into developing new software.").

It is of course perfectly rational for Oracle and firms like it to pursue patents under these circumstances, even though they would prefer not to. This predicament, indeed, is so common it has been modeled by game theorists, who call it the "Prisoners' Dilemma." The name stems from one version of the game in which two prisoners are captured and threatened with several forms of punishment depending on their actions. Each prisoner is told that if she refuses to confess the guilt of both prisoners, she will be let free — but only if the other prisoner does not confess either. If the other confesses and the first one does not, a very severe punishment will result for the first (non-confessing) prisoner, but only a mild punishment will be assessed on the other (confessing) prisoner. The same mild punishment will be handed out to the first if she confesses and the other does not, while the other will receive the very stiff punishment in this case. Finally, if both confess, a mild punishment will be meted out to each.

The famous outcome of this game, played once, is that both prisoners will confess. This despite the fact that their best mutual outcome occurs when neither confesses. The reason they confess, however, is the terrible outcome that results when one does not confess but the other does. The fear of this "worst case," in other words, drives them to an act (or "strategy") that is less good than their optimum. Of course, this only happens because they cannot coordinate their actions. If they could confer before their jailer asked for confessions, they would agree not to confess. Assuming the agreement was plausible and/or enforceable, they would then achieve their best outcome.

Notice how closely the situation of firms such as Oracle fits this description. They would prefer (best outcome) not to patent. But they fear being caught without patents — and being in the position of the prisoner who, having not confessed, is confessed upon by her counterpart. So they acquire patents, reluctantly. In the lingo of game theory, their "equilibrium strategy" is to "defect," rather than "cooperate"; they have been "driven to quadrant IV." *See, e.g.*, DAVID KREPS, GAME THEORY AND ECONOMIC MODELING (1990).

The table below summarizes the "payoffs" to each of two software firms deciding whether or not to obtain patents; payoffs are listed in the order Firm 1, Firm 2.

		Firm 2	
		No Patent	Patent
Firm 1	No Patent	3,3	1,4
	Patent	4,1	2,2

This table is read as follows. If Firm 1 decides not to patent, it will make either 3 or 1 (the figures are in dollars, and you can multiply them by hundreds of millions to make the scenario more realistic). On the other hand, if Firm 1 decides to patent, it will make either 4 or 2. Given these payoffs, Firm 1 will always patent. Why? Because it is better off if it patents, regardless of what Firm 2 does. Patenting, in other words, is Firm 1's "dominant strategy." This also holds true for Firm 2, and for the same reasons. The effect is that the two firms will always wind up in the lower right-hand quadrant of the table, which is therefore the equilibrium in this game. In the original prisoner's dilemma game, this is the quadrant where both prisoners confess, or "defect" from the strategy of cooperating in mutual non-confession.

Are these payoffs realistic? People in the software industry say yes. The gist of the story by Walsh, cited above, is often repeated in industry circles. Many people seem to believe that the industry is better off without patents, given its history of aggressive R&D spending in the absence of patents, and the very real added costs associated with "patent overhead" (prosecution, recordkeeping, litigation, licensing).

However, given the payoff structure and the other assumptions behind the prisoners' dilemma game, there does not appear to be any way out. Note, however, that two of these assumptions are at least possibly open to doubt in the software industry context: the assumption of no communication between the players prior to the time when each selects his or her strategy; and the assumption that the game is a "one shot" affair. Relax either assumption, and the outcome can change dramatically.

The assumption that the players can't communicate, or more generally, *coordinate*, prior to choosing strategy is subject to doubt in the real-world setting of industry. Firms could agree, after all, not to seek patents. And, given the payoffs outlined above, it would be in their interest to do so, since this would place them in Quadrant 1, whose outcome of "3,3" yields the highest *total* gain for both players combined. The one dollar difference between this total of 6 and the next-highest total of 5 (in either the 1,4 or 4,1 situation) is the "cooperative surplus," the net gain from making the deal. The problem with this outcome, however, is that to achieve it one has to have a binding agreement with the other party. If the other party can *purport* to agree to the "no patent, no patent" strategy, and then *secretly* pursue patents, it will be better off, since its payoff from this duplicitous strategy will be 4 as opposed to the 3 it would get from remaining true to its word. Indeed, it is apparent to both players that this is an attractive strategy — so much so that each will expect the other to pursue it. That is why the cooperative strategy is not an equilibrium.

Note that the patent system enables the "promise no patent, then obtain patent" strategy to work. Because patent applications are kept secret until issued, it is difficult to detect whether someone is cheating on an agreement not to seek patents. And because it may be too late for the foolishly trusting firm to retaliate, the risks associated with the "no patent" strategy are great indeed. And, of course, there is nothing preventing a third party, who has not signed the "no patent" pact, from undermining the whole deal by getting patents of its own and asserting them against Firm 1 and Firm 2.

The no-coordination assumption, therefore, while not literally accurate, would seem to capture an important truth about the real world of industry.

The "one shot" assumption, on the other hand, is not as accurate. In reality, there will be many rounds to the game. Firms will have many patents, and many opportunities to patent; they will frequently be on both sides of patent litigation This much seems clear already, as several large firms have begun to offer portions of their patent portfolio for licensing to their competitors. *See* Gregory Aharonian, *ACM Forum* (letter to editor), 36 COMM. OF THE ACM 17 (1993) (reporting an apparent rumor that "Microsoft just paid $20,000,000 to license IBM's software patents"; Mark Walsh, *Bowing to Reality, Software Maker Begins Building a Patent Portfolio*, THE RECORDER, Aug. 17, 1995, at 1 (reporting that Microsoft is filing patent applications also).

What difference does it make that the game will have many rounds? A great deal, if economic theory is correct. A famous study of repeated prisoners' dilemma games found that the strategy of initial cooperation, and subsequent retaliation, won out in many cases over competing strategies. *See* ROBERT AXELROD, THE EVOLUTION OF COOPERATION (1984). And economists have verified the prediction of this model in studies of actual institutions, which often show that in "repeat-play" situations, institutions evolve to move people from defection borne of self-interest to cooperation that leaves everyone better off. *See, e.g.*, ELEANOR OSTROM, GOVERNING THE COMMONS (1990). These insights are applied to the evolution of collective rights organizations, institutions designed to foster intellectual property rights transactions, in Robert P. Merges, *Contracting Into Liability Rules: Intellectual Property Rights and Collective Rights Organizations*, 84 CAL. L. REV. __ (1996).

Of course, in order for firms to move from Quadrant IV to Quadrant I, they must be able to coordinate. They will have to gather together to figure out an institutional mechanism for dealing with patent issues. Such an institution could take many forms: a patent pool, with an arbitration arm, is certainly one.

The only problem with such an arrangement, from the point of view of legal policy, is that it may provide an occasion for anticompetitive horizontal arrangements. In general, it appears that the gains from allowing cooperation are great enough to justify relatively liberal antitrust policy in this setting. These issues are discussed in Chapter 11; see especially the section on Patent Pools.

6. IS MATHEMATICS DISCOVERED OR INVENTED?

In the early 1990s the Patent Office issued several patents that reawakened interest in the patentability of "pure" algorithms. The first, U.S. Patent No. 4,744,028, issued to one Dr. Karmarkar and was assigned to AT&T Bell Labs. This patent covers a new linear algebra technique for allocating scarce resources in a large system such as a telephone network (AT&T's obvious application of the invention). The Karmarkar algorithm describes an improvement on the well-known (to mathematicians) "simplex method" for solving a very large series of equations, which is how these resource allocation problems are set up mathematically.

The second patent issued on a "pure algorithm" covers a mathematical technique known as the Discrete Bracewell Transform in the field of signal processing. Bracewell's advance was to create an algorithm that handles sophisticated signal processing without using what are known as "complex" numbers. (These are numbers which are based on the square root of negative one.)

These patents, which are expected to lead to applications by other mathematicians, raise anew the problems hinted at in the *Benson* and *Diehr* cases: what is the nature of mathematics? How do algorithms relate to laws of nature and natural products? Should patents be allowed on "this type" of subject matter?

In comparing computer algorithms to natural products and laws of nature, Justice Douglas states:

> Phenomena of nature, though just discovered, mental processes, and abstract intellectual concepts are not patentable, as they are the basic tools of scientific and technological work.

Benson, 409 U.S. at 67. What view of algorithms, and mathematics as a whole, is implicit in this statement?

The debate amongst mathematicians on the exact nature of what they do has taken many forms. However, it is possible to simplify the various positions by marshalling them into two main groups. First are the Platonists, who believe that mathematics is a real phenomenon which is discovered by mathematicians in the course of their research. On this view, mathematicians simply discover the ordered relationships that nature has laid down. The alternative view is that mathematics is simply a formal game, which mathematicians "make up" in accordance with strict rules. According to this "formalist" theory, mathematics does not describe any underlying reality. One must simply be careful to state mathematical assertions according to the accepted "rules of the game." This view comes closer to a theory that math is "invented" by mathematicians.

One overview of the field states:

> Most writers on the subject seem to agree that the typical working mathematician is a Platonist on weekdays and a formalist on Sundays. That is, when he is doing mathematics he is convinced that he is dealing with an objective reality whose properties he is attempting to determine. But then, when challenged to give a philosophical account of this reality, he finds it easiest to pretend that he does not believe in it after all.

P. DAVIS & R. HERSH, THE MATHEMATICAL EXPERIENCE 321 (1981).*

But the view that math is invented is more starkly stated in the philosophy of Imre Lakatos. Lakatos, whose *Proofs and Refutations* was published in 1976, sets out a theory of mathematics which places it more properly within modern traditions of the history of science. That is, Lakatos believed that mathematics grows by the criticism and corrections of theories which are never entirely free of ambiguity or the possibility of error. According to Davis and Hersh:

> Starting from a problem or a conjecture, there is a simultaneous search for proofs and counterexamples. New proofs explain old counterexamples, new counterexamples undermine old proofs. To Lakatos, "proof" in this context of informal mathematics does not mean a mechanical procedure which carries truth in an unbreakable chain from assumptions to conclusions. Rather, it means explanations, justifications, elaborations which make the conjecture more plausible, more convincing, while it is being made more detailed and accurate under the pressure of counterexamples.

DAVIS & HERSH, THE MATHEMATICAL EXPERIENCE, *supra*, at 347. Note that in this passage, the authors are discussing Lakatos' view of that part of mathematics which is in the process of growth and discovery, rather than "settled" mathematics. However, the authors point out that "informal" or unsettled mathematics "is of course mathematics as it is known to mathematicians and students of mathematics" — i.e., the most significant part of the field.

These two authors conclude that neither the Platonist nor the "Formalist" philosophy of mathematics is ultimately satisfying. They propose instead a view of mathematics that combines the objectivity of the Platonist view with the reliance on social consensus of the Formalist view:

> Mathematics is not the study of an ideal, preexisting nontemporal reality. Neither is it a chess-like game with made-up symbols and formulas. Rather, it is the part of human studies which is capable of achieving a science-like

consensus, capable of establishing *reproducible* results. The existence of the subject called mathematics is a fact, not a question. This fact means no more and no less than the existence of modes of reasoning and argument about ideas which are compelling and conclusive, "noncontroversial" when once understood.

DAVIS & HERSH, *supra*, at 410.

Mathematics, the authors conclude, has "conclusions [which] are compelling, like the conclusions of natural science. They are not simply products of opinion, and not subject to permanent disagreement like the ideas of literary criticism." That is, while admitting that at any given time certain propositions at the frontiers of mathematics may be fallible or correctable, they deny that this makes mathematics a meaningless battle of symbols.

What does all this mean for the patent system? First of all, it sheds some light on the naive Platonism of the early Supreme Court opinions on algorithms. As Davis and Hersh point out, there is no consensus among mathematicians that they are in fact discovering a preexisting reality. Thus, the Supreme Court's treatment of algorithms — as akin to other "found" natural objects, such as products of nature — conflicts with the views that many sophisticated mathematicians seem to have of their field. Of course, these views are normally expressed only when "frontier" or pioneer mathematics is at issue; much of the applied mathematics which is the subject matter of algorithm claims would probably be considered outside the discussion of mathematical philosophy anyway. However, even these applied algorithms raise the same philosophical problems. It must be noted that since applied mathematics strives to emulate underlying physical relationships, there is a much stronger pull toward the Platonist position when this branch of mathematics is under investigation.

Perhaps this explains some of the cases we have examined. For instance, the use of the Arrhenius Equation in the rubber-curing process at issue in the *Diehr* case is well within the realm of applied mathematics. That is, this equation tries to capture a physical relationship and state it as a "law." For the variables stated in this equation, the relationship which it sets forth will always hold. On the other hand, consider the algorithm at issue in the *Benson* case. This was a "pure" mathematical algorithm which converts binary coded decimal numerals into their binary equivalents. Since numbers of a given base (e.g., base 2 or base 10, the decimal system) do not really correspond to any physical objects, this is an algorithm which states only an abstract relationship. (Compare this to the variables in the Arrhenius equation, which stand for physical properties — pressure, heat and so on.) Perhaps the differences between the Arrhenius equation in the *Diehr* case and the "pure" number conversion algorithm in the *Benson* case go a long way toward explaining the different outcomes of the two cases. In any event, the statements made in *Benson* about the nature of mathematics surely conflict both with the offhand treatment of the mathematical aspects of the *Diehr* process and the way in which mathematicians themselves view their field, or at least that part of it which deals with purely abstract matters.

The underlying view of mathematics contained in the *Benson* case may one day be tested when the new generation of mathematical algorithm patents — such as the Karmarkar patent discussed above — come under review.

In the meantime, the debate over the nature of mathematical algorithms is very much alive. Consider some recent comments on the Bracewell and Karmarkar patents, discussed above:

> Unlike an industrial technology, an algorithm, the step-by-step recipe for carrying out a mathematical calculation, might seem more like something that is discovered than invented. But in the last few years, corporations have been patenting these abstract procedures, leading many mathematicians to complain that the free flow of ideas is in danger of being interrupted.
>
> "The tradition in algorithms has been that they should be free," said Ronald Rivest, a mathematician at the Massachusetts Institute of Technology, who said he had mixed feelings on the subject. "Research generally has proceeded on that basis."
>
> Michael Ian Shamos, a mathematician and computer scientist at Carnegie-Mellon University in Pittsburgh and a lawyer in private practice, said that the patenting of important algorithms is contrary to the best interests of science.
>
> "Mathematical facts are the building blocks of research," he said. "I'm an intellectual property attorney. I like patents. But the patent law was never designed to apply to algorithms. The argument that you spent lots of money developing an algorithm and therefore you should be able to protect it is nonsense."

G. Kolata, *Mathematicians Are Troubled by Claims on Their Recipes*, N.Y. TIMES, Mar. 12, 1989, sec. 4, at 26.

For an argument that the entire software patent issue should turn on the invention/discovery distinction, see John A. Burtis, Comment, *Towards a Rational Jurisprudence of Computer-related Patentability in Light of* In re Alappat, 79 MINN. L. REV. 1129, 1153, 1157 (1995). Burtis observes that "Mathematical expressions may be used to describe both discovered and invented subject matter and are therefore imperfect proxies for mathematical truths and other laws of nature." He concludes by arguing that a "tightly-defined test built on a robust discovery and invention distinction" would improve on *Alappat*. He then tries to enunciate a test to identify whether an algorithm claim essentially encompasses a "natural truth," in which case it is an unpatentable discovery, or whether it contains "an implicit, but real, use limitation," i.e., is tied to a specific application or field of use. *Id.*, at 1165. In the end, the analysis is helpful because it focuses on the scope of software claims. Recall that in many ways this was the underlying concern in *Benson* — the case that caused most of the headaches that now plague the law in this area. This approach can be seen as implicitly arguing that software patent doctrine went awry when it rejected "field of use" limitations as a way of preserving patentability in the face of § 101. *See, e.g., In re Waldbaum*, 559 F.2d 611, 617 (C.C.P.A. 1977) (rejecting the argument that because Waldbaum had limited the scope of his claims — some to data processing applications, and some to telephone service applications — the claims did not fail the test enunciated in *Benson*; a patent on these claims "would, in practical effect, be a patent on the algorithm itself — albeit in its limited, specific application to calculating the number of busy and idle lines in a telephone system").

7. DESIGN PATENTS FOR SOFTWARE

While the most common form of patent is a "utility" patent, described in 35 U.S.C. § 101, patents are also available for certain industrial designs. 35 U.S.C. § 171 et seq. Relatively recently, some software designers have attempted to protect elements of their user interface as design patents.

Ex parte DONALDSON

26 U.S.P.Q.2d 1250 (Bd. Pat. App. & Int. 1992)

MANBECK, COMMISSIONER.

This is an appeal from the examiner's decision finally rejecting the sole claim in the application.

The subject matter on appeal is a design for an icon. The sole claim on appeal states:

> The ornamental design for a softkey display or the like, as shown and described.

....

The sole claim stands rejected as unpatentable under 35 U.S.C. § 171. After careful consideration of appellant's arguments presented in the briefs and at oral hearing, we affirm the examiner's rejection.

Section 171 of Title 35 provides:

> Whoever invents any new, original and ornamental design for an article of manufacture may obtain a patent therefor, subject to the conditions and requirements of this title.

The examiner concluded that the claimed design was nonstatutory, finding that the design was not an "ornamental design for an article of manufacture...." While the examiner set forth her reasoning in great detail, the thrust of her position is that the design, as claimed, is merely a picture or surface ornamentation per se rather than a design applied to an article. The examiner notes that the specification does not describe, claim or show the claimed design applied to any article of manufacture. Appellant argues that the

> claimed invention is an ornamental design for the display screen of a programmed computer system. A programmed computer system, comprising a processor, a display device and a program executing on the processor is an article of manufacture. The claimed design is surface ornamentation for a particular region of the display screen, and thus qualifies as statutory subject matter.

The examiner responded stating:

> The fact that a programmed computer system running the necessary software may be an article of manufacture does not help appellant here. No programmed computer system is either depicted or described. Section 1.152 [of 37 CFR] is explicit in requiring that the article of manufacture be shown in the drawings.

The respective positions of the examiner and appellant require us to consider the meaning of "ornamental design for an article of manufacture" as used in § 171.

The phrase "design for an article of manufacture" has long appeared in the design statutes. The language appears in Revised Statutes § 4929, May 9, 1902, ch. 783, 32 Stat. 209, was reenacted in 35 U.S.C. § 73 (1946) and again reenacted in 35 U.S.C. § 171 (1952). The CCPA construed the phrase in *In re Schnell*, 46 F.2d 203, 8 U.S.P.Q. 19 (C.C.P.A. 1931). The court noted that the language "new, original and ornamental design for an article of manufacture encompassed at least three kinds of designs: 1) a design for an ornament, impression, print or picture to be applied to an article of manufacture (surface ornamentation); 2) a design for the shape or configuration of an article of manufacture; and 3) a combination of the first two categories. 46 F.2d at 209, 8 U.S.P.Q. at 26. With respect to the first category the court indicated the design statute required more than a mere picture.

> We think that Assistant Commissioner Clay was right in saying [in *Ex parte Cady*, 1916 Dec. Com'r. Pat. 57, 58] that the design must be shown not to be the mere invention of a picture, irrespective of its manner of use, but that the applicant should be required to show by an appropriate drawing the manner of its application.

46 F.2d at 209, 8 U.S.P.Q. at 26. The Court went on to state:

> It is the application of the design to an article of manufacture that Congress wishes to promote, and an applicant has not reduced his invention to practice and has been of little help to the art if he does not teach the manner of applying his design.

46 F.2d at 209, 8 U.S.P.Q. at 26.

The CCPA again interpreted the phrase in *In re Zahn*, 617 F.2d 261, 204 U.S.P.Q. 988 (C.C.P.A. 1980). The issue in *Zahn* was whether or not § 171 permitted claiming a design for a portion of an article of manufacture, a drill tool. The court noted that under § 171 a design must be "embodied" in an article:

> Section 171 authorizes patents on ornamental designs *for* articles of manufacture. While the design must be *embodied* in some article, the statute is not limited to designs for complete articles, or "discrete" articles, and certainly not to articles separately sold.... Here the design is embodied in the shank portion of a drill and a drill is unquestionably an article of manufacture. It is applied design as distinguished from abstract design. (Emphasis original.)

617 F.2d at 268, 204 U.S.P.Q. at 995.

These decisions indicate that a picture standing alone is not protectable by a design patent. The factor which distinguishes statutory design subject matter from mere pictures or surface ornamentation per se (i.e., abstract designs) is the embodiment of the design in an article of manufacture. In order to meet this threshold requirement of an applied design, we conclude that an applicant's specification must expressly disclose some article of manufacture ornamented by the design.

We find that appellant's claimed design, as disclosed in the application before us, is merely a picture. Appellant's specification does not show, describe or claim the design embodied in any article of manufacture. Only pictures of the icon are shown or described. The claimed subject matter, therefore, does not meet the requirements of 35 U.S.C. § 171.

Appellant asserts that the design should be considered surface ornamentation upon the display screen of a computer system. We have no doubt that the claimed design, like all surface ornamentation-type designs, could be used to ornament a wide variety of articles, including computers. However, the phrase "design for an article of manufacture" in § 171 requires more than a depiction of the surface ornamentation alone. It requires disclosure of the ornamentation applied to or embodied in an article of manufacture. More than an applicant's generalized intent to ornament some article is required. It is the application of the design to an article which separates mere pictures from a design protectable by a patent. Without express disclosure of an article, the design is not an applied design contemplated for protection under § 171.

Consistent with § 171, PTO regulations expressly require such disclosure. Thus, 37 CFR § 1.153(a) states:

> (a) The title of the design must designate the particular article. No description, other than a reference to the drawing, is ordinarily required. The claim shall be in formal terms to the ornamental design for the article (specifying name) as shown, or as shown and described....

37 CFR § 1.152 states:

> The design must be represented by a drawing made in conformity with the rules laid down for drawings of mechanical inventions and must contain a sufficient number of views to constitute a *complete disclosure of the appearance of the article*. Appropriate surface shading must be used to show the character or contour of the surfaces represented. Broken lines may be used to show visible environmental structure, but may not be used to show hidden planes and surfaces which cannot be seen through opaque materials. (Emphasis added [by court].)

Appellant has not described, shown or claimed the design as surface ornamentation for a computer system. The word "icon" does not limit the design to use with a display screen of a computer or any other article of manufacture. Icons are and have been used with a variety of articles. As we stated above, appellant's design, as shown and described, is merely a picture which has not been disclosed applied to any article.

NOTES

1. In a companion case to *Donaldson*, the BPAI held that an applicant was not entitled to claim an icon on a computer screen as a design patent, for essentially the same reasons. *Ex parte Strijland*, 26 U.S.P.Q.2d 1259 (Bd. Pat. App. & Int. 1992). However, the Board suggested that if the patentee had claimed an "information icon for display screen of a programmed computer system," and submitted a drawing *of the entire computer system* showing the icon on the screen, the Board would have held the claim to be patentable subject matter.

Why does it matter how the design is described in the drawings?

2. Design patents are not available for designs which are "dictated by functional considerations." *See Power Controls Corp. v. Hybrinetics, Inc.*, 806 F.2d 234, 238 (Fed. Cir. 1986). To what extent does this limit the availability of design patent protection for the screen displays in *Donaldson*? For the icon in *Strijland*?

C. METHODS OF DOING BUSINESS

PAINE, WEBBER, JACKSON & CURTIS, INC. v. MERRILL LYNCH, PIERCE, FENNER & SMITH, INC.

564 F. Supp. 1358, 218 U.S.P.Q. (BNA) 212 (D. Del. 1983)

Plaintiff, Paine, Webber, Jackson and Curtis, Inc. ("Paine Webber"), seek[s] a declaratory judgment of noninfringement, invalidity and unenforceability of United States Patent No. 4,346,442 ("the '442 patent"), and ancillary injunctive relief against defendant Merrill Lynch, Pierce, Fenner & Smith, Inc. ("Merrill Lynch"), from initiating infringement litigation. Merrill Lynch has counterclaimed seeking injunctive relief against Paine Webber for infringing or contributing to infringe the '442 patent, and monetary damages for Paine Webber's infringing activities.

I
The Cash Management Account

In 1977 Merrill Lynch offered to the public the Cash Management Account program ("CMA") which combined three financial services commonly offered by financial institutions and brokerage houses and included a brokerage security account (the "Securities Account"), several money market funds (the "Money Market Fund"), and a charge/checking account (the "Visa Account"). The Securities Account, the primary component of the CMA program, is a conventional Merrill Lynch margin account which may be used to purchase and sell securities and options on margin or on a fully-paid basis. As is the case with [a] conventional margin account, the customer of the CMA pays normal brokerage fees for securities transactions in the Securities Account.

The Money Market Fund is a conventional money market fund which provides the customer of the CMA with a choice of three CMA money market funds: the CMA Money Fund, the CMA Government Securities Funds, or the CMA Tax-Exempt Fund. Each of these funds is a no-load, diversified, open-end management investment company. Dividends are declared daily and automatically reinvested in the Money Market Fund similar to the method by which the dividends are distributed, and reinvested in other money market funds.

The Visa Account is the third component of the CMA and is managed by Bank One of Columbus, N.A. ("Bank One"). Bank One issues a Visa card and checks to each person who is a CMA customer. The card may be used to make purchases of merchandise or services at Visa-participating establishments or to obtain cash advances from any Visa-participating bank or branch.

No question exists that the three major components of the CMA were offered to the public prior to the marketing of the CMA by financial institutions and/or brokerage houses: one could have placed securities into a brokerage account, purchased shares in a money market fund, or obtained a Visa charge account. Merrill Lynch, however, argues that by combining the three components of the CMA, the customer receives synergistic benefits. According to Merrill Lynch, one of the advantages of the CMA is that all money generated in the Securities Account is automatically invested within a week into the Money Market Fund. This differs from a conventional brokerage account, which might not invest money generated from activity in the brokerage account and thus some money might remain in an account without yielding any financial return. These proceeds, referred to as "idle cash" do not enhance the customer's portfolio and [this] usually is not compatible with the customer's overall financial objectives. By investing any idle cash generated in the Securities Account, into the Money

Market Fund, the customer apparently receives a greater return on his initial investment and [this] therefore is consistent with the customer's overall objectives.

Another advantage of having an integrated financial service, as provided by the CMA, is that the cash balances in the Securities Account, shares in the Money Market Fund, and available margin loan value of the securities in the Securities Account are calculated when determining the amount of credit available in the Visa Account. Also, payments made by Merrill Lynch to Bank One in payment of Visa balances, on behalf of the CMA customers, are made in the following order of priority: (1) from the cash balances, if any held in the Securities Account; (2) from the proceeds of redemption of Money Fund shares in CMA accounts; and (3) from margin loans to the customer by Merrill Lynch within the available margin loan value of the securities in the Securities Account. This system of priority arguably provides for an efficient use of funds because the customer will not incur the cost of a margin loan until all free credit cash balances and funds invested in Money Market Fund shares are fully utilized.

Another advantage of the CMA, according to Merrill Lynch, is that those customers who subscribe to the CMA receive a monthly transaction statement from Merrill Lynch which details all CMA transactions during the preceding month. [The basic features of the CMA are illustrated in Figure 2-6.]

II
The Invention

A. *The Patent Office*

The '442 patent application assert[ed] twelve claims for a "Securities Brokerage-Cash Management System." [T]he Examiner rejected all twelve claims on the grounds that all the claims were obvious under Section 103, and that Claims 1-6 and 12 were not adequately described under Section 112.

[T]he '442 patent application was amended. It cancelled claims 7-12 inclusive, thus leaving claims 1-6. Further it substituted certain terminology in each of the remaining claims in an attempt to overcome the Section 112 rejection. Further in response to the Section 103 objection, Merrill Lynch maintained that the claims in the '442 application were more complex than the prior art and that it would be virtually impossible for one skilled in the art to duplicate the CMA System by using only the information in the [prior art] Prospectus and Brochure without resorting to the use of a large staff, personal innovation and problem-solving by members of that staff, and a major program of experimentation and testing. Furthermore, Merrill Lynch represented to the Examiner that even given all of the above, it would be uncertain that the results called for in the claims could be achieved.

B. *The '442 Patent*

[T]he United States Patent and Trademark Office ("PTO") issued the '442 patent for a Securities Brokerage-Cash Management System on the six remaining

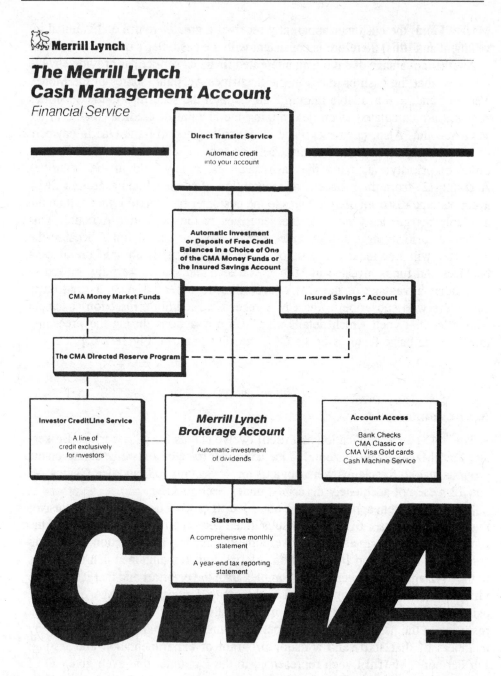

Figure 2-6

claims. Merrill Lynch is the assignee of the patent. The '442 patent relates to the CMA, and more specifically, to the data processing methodology and apparatus for effecting the CMA. The specifications of the '442 patent primarily teach the schematic flow chart for the CMA, but do not include any descriptions of any apparatus to effectuate the CMA.

Claim[] 1 [is] illustrative of the six claims set forth in the '442 patent:

1. In combination in a system for processing and supervising a plurality of composite subscriber accounts each comprising a margin brokerage account, a charge card and checks administered by a first institution, and participation in at least one short term investment, administered by a second institution, said system including brokerage account data file means for storing current information characterizing each subscriber margin brokerage account of the second institution, manual entry means for entering short term investment orders in the second institution, data receiving and verifying means for receiving and verifying charge card and check transactions from said first institution and short term investment orders from said manual entry means, means responsive to said brokerage account data file means and said data receiving and verifying means for generating an updated credit limit for each account, short term investment updating means responsive to said brokerage account data file means and said data receiving and verifying means for selectively generating short term investment transactions as required to generate and invest proceeds for subscribers' accounts, wherein said system includes plural such short term investments, said system further comprising means responsive to said short term updating means for allocating said short term investment transactions among said plural short term investments, communicating means to communicate said updated credit limit for each account to said first institution.

As [this] claim demonstrate[s], the claims of the '442 patent are directed to the CMA system described in the specifications. Unlike the specifications, and for the purpose of the present motions, the various elements of the claims are cast in terms of apparatus, that is, "means for" performing certain tasks or steps, rather than in terms of the method steps themselves.

III
Paine Webber Contentions

Paine Webber contends that the '442 patent is invalid under 35 U.S.C. § 101 because it does not claim a "process, machine, manufacture or composition of matter" as required by Section 101. It argues that the '442 patent is unpatentable because the claims "define nothing more than the combination of familiar business systems, that is, a margin brokerage account, one or more money market funds, and a checking/charge account, which have been connected together so that financial information can be exchanged among them." It argues that business methods and systems cannot form the subject matter of a valid patent monopoly and that courts do not hesitate to invalidate patents on the grounds that they merely describe business systems.

According to Paine Webber, in an attempt to obscure the fact that the invention is merely a business system, the claims were drafted to recite a combination of various "means" for performing certain functions. Paine Webber argues that the specifications do not refer to any apparatus, but merely describe a method, and thus the claims of the '442 patent are limited to the method described in the specifications. According to Paine Webber, the "means" portions of the claims thereby refer only to the functional steps rather than to specific apparatus or structure and that the method claimed merely describes a series of manipulative steps that can be performed by hand with the aid of paper, pencil and telephone. Therefore Paine Webber maintains that the claims and the specifications of the '442 patent reveal that the invention fits squarely into the business system category and has nothing to do with machinery, technology, process, manufacture, or composition of matter.

The Court need not determine, at this time, whether the '442 patent claims an apparatus or a process because labels are not determinative in a Section 101 analysis. [W]hether the '442 patent claims a process or an apparatus, is not relevant in a Section 101 analysis; the Court must determine as a threshold matter whether the claims include statutory matter, regardless of the label of the claims.

IV
Section 101

A. *Algorithm*

Section 101 enumerates the categories into which inventions must fall to qualify for patent protection. An invention not falling within one of these four classes is deemed nonstatutory subject matter and is not eligible for patent protection. The phrase "whoever invents" requires that the claimed invention be man-made and lays the foundation for the doctrine that phenomena of nature, mental process and abstract intellectual concepts are not patentable because they are not the basic tools of technology. *Gottschalk v. Benson*, 409 U.S. 63, 67 (1972). Thus if a computer program is viewed as a series of thought processes, then it merely consists of mental steps which is nonstatutory subject matter and not patentable. This view has not been accepted and computer programs are recognized as being patentable.

Although a computer program is recognized to be patentable, it must nevertheless meet the same requirements as other inventions in order to qualify for patent protection. For example, the Pythagorean theorem (a geometric theorem which states that the square of the length of the hypotenuse of a right triangle equals the sum of the squares of the lengths of the two sides — also expressed $A^2 + B^2 = C^2$) is not patentable because it defines a mathematical formula. Likewise a computer program which does no more than apply the theorem to a set of numbers is not patentable. The Supreme Court and the CCPA have clearly stated that a mathematical algorithmic formula is merely an idea and not patentable unless there is a new application of the idea to a new and useful end. *See Gottschalk v. Benson.*

Unfortunately, the term "algorithm" has been a source of confusion which stems from different uses of the term in the related, but distinct fields of mathematics and computer science. In mathematics, the word algorithm has attained the meaning of recursive computational procedure and appears in notational language, defining a computational course of events which is self contained, for example, $A^2 + B^2 = C^2$. In contrast, the computer algorithm is a procedure consisting of operations to combine data, mathematical principles and equipment for the purpose of interpreting and/or acting upon a certain data input. In comparison to the mathematical algorithm, which is self-contained, the computer algorithm must be applied to the solution of a specific problem. *See* J. Goodman, *An Economic Analysis of the Policy Implications of Granting Patent Protection for Computer Programs* ([37] Vand. L. Rev. [147] ([1984])). Although one may devise a computer algorithm for the Pythagorean theorem, it is the step-by-step process which instructs the computer to solve the theorem which is the algorithm, rather than the theorem itself.

[U]nder [its decisions] the CCPA has held that the Supreme Court in *Benson* used the term "algorithm" in a specific sense, "a procedure for solving a given type of mathematical problem." 409 U.S. at 65. Using this definition, this Court has carefully examined the claims in this case and is unable to find any direct or indirect recitation of a procedure for solving a mathematical problem. Rather, the patent allegedly claims a methodology to effectuate a highly efficient business system and does not restate a mathematical formula as defined by *Benson*. Nor are any of the recited steps in the claims mere procedure[s] for solving mathematical problems. Accordingly, the claims do not recite or preempt an algorithm.

B. *Method of Doing Business*

Paine Webber contends that the '442 patent is unpatentable for another reason. It claims that the patent defines "nothing more than familiar business systems, that is, the financial management of individual brokerage accounts." It urges the Court to focus on the product of the '442 patent claims, that is, the services the CMA provides to the customers of Merrill Lynch rather than to focus on the method by which the CMA operates.

[The court compares this case with *In re Toma*, 575 F.2d 872, 877 (C.C.P.A. 1978).] In *Toma*, the Examiner first noted that all statutory subject matter "must be in the 'technical' or 'useful' arts, and that, as far as computer-related inventions are concerned, *only* those inventions which 'enhance the internal operation of the digital computer' are in the 'technological' or 'useful' arts." The Examiner thereafter found that natural language translation was merely a "liberal art" and that the translation by a computer does not "transform the activity into a technological art." Thus, the Examiner held the patent was unpatentable under Section 101. 575 F.2d at 877.

The CCPA disagreed with the Examiner and looked to the method by which the computer translated the natural languages. It held that the focus of analysis should be on the operation of the computer program and not on the product of the computer program (i.e. the translation). It stressed that the operation of the computer is within the "technological arts" and a computer which effects the operation of the computer is also patentable. *See also Application of Phillips*, 608 F.2d 879 (C.C.P.A. 1979) (computer program designed to prepare architectural specification eliminating handwritten specification constitute[s] proper statutory subject matter); *In re Johnston*, 502 F.2d 765 (C.C.P.A. 1974), *rev'd on other grounds sub nom. Dann v. Johnston*, 425 U.S. 219 (1976) (computer program for an automatic financial record-keeping system within the technological arts; the Supreme Court expressly declined to discuss the Section 101 arguments because it held that the patent was invalid and unenforceable under Section 103).

The subject matter of the '442 patent claims are [sic] similar to the claims of the patents in *Toma*, *Phillips*, and *Johnston*. The product of the claims of the '442 patent effectuates a highly useful business method and would be unpatentable if done by hand. The CCPA, however, has made clear that if no *Benson* algorithm exists, the product of a computer program is irrelevant, and the focus of analysis should be on the operation of the program on the computer. The Court finds that the '442 patent claims statutory subject matter because the claims allegedly teach a method of operation on a computer to effectuate a business activity. Accordingly, the '442 patent passes the threshold requirement of Section 101.

Motion denied.

NOTES

1. *Open Door Policy?* The court says the patentee claimed "a method of operation on a computer to effectuate a business activity." Is this an open invitation to other applicants to frame method-of-business claims as computer program claims? What problems might this bring? Would you expect it to change the way businesses conduct research on new products such as Merrill Lynch's CMA, or do you believe that most activity in the financial services industry is already computer-based anyway? *But cf. Ex parte Murray*, 9 U.S.P.Q.2d (BNA) 1819 (Bd. Pat. App. Int. 1988) (affirming rejection of claimed method that involved creating special documents containing preprinted account numbers, which made it easy to keep track of expenses and compile expense reports).

2. *Related Cases.* In *Hotel Security Checking Co. v. Lorraine Co.*, 160 F. 467 (2d Cir. 1908), one Hicks had patented a "method of and means for cash-registering and account-checking" designed to prevent theft by waiters and cashiers in hotels and restaurants. The invention was to keep "accounts" for cashiers or waiters. Each of these employees were given slips of paper with a unique code on them. An overseer kept track of the food delivered by each waiter, and then compared this with what was recorded on the slips. This prevented waiters from

overcharging customers or misreporting orders and pocketing the difference. At the end of the day, total orders were compared with the cash in the register, as a way to check up on cashiers. The court declared the patent invalid because it lacked novelty and invention, and suggested in dictum that such a method of doing business might be invalid even if the other requirements for patentability had been met.

3. *A "CD" Patent.* From the following story, based on a settled suit concerning U.S. Patent No. 4,839,804, "Method and Apparatus for Insuring the Funding of a Future Liability of Uncertain Cost," what can you tell about the financial services industry's view of the distinction between a computer program and a method of doing business?

> A New Jersey bank's out-of-court victory in a patent infringement case has added weight to the argument that financial products can be protected under patent law, according to legal experts.
>
> Under a settlement announced last week by College Savings Bank, Princeton, CenTrust Savings Bank of Miami agreed to pay license fees for certain features of the CollegeSure certificate of deposit. The CD, which has attracted considerable publicity nationwide, is designed to appreciate to meet future education costs.
>
> The CD is one of the few financial instruments to obtain patent protection, which has historically been reserved for industrial inventions. If other financial products can be patented and are marketed successfully, their inventors stand to profit by collecting licensing fees from competitors.

R. Cox, *License for CollegeSure CD Expected to Bolster Case for Financial Patents*, AM. BANKER, Nov. 14, 1989, at 1. *See also* Becker, *Drafting Patent Applications on Computer-Implemented Inventions*, 4 HARV. J.L. & TECH. 237, 246 (1991) (noting that the only distinction between *Paine Webber* and *Murray* appears to be the form of the claims).

4. *Critique.* For criticism of the *Merrill Lynch* case, which the author says allowed the preemption of a broad program idea, see Comment, *A Plea for Due Process: Defining the Proper Scope of Patent Protection for Computer Software*, 85 Nw. U. L. REV. 1103 (1991).

STATE STREET BANK & TRUST CO. v. SIGNATURE FINANCIAL GROUP, INC.

38 U.S.P.Q.2d 1530 (D. Mass. 1996)

SARIS, J.

I

Introduction

Plaintiff, State Street Bank and Trust Company ("State Street") brings this action against Defendant, Signature Financial Group, Inc. ("Signature"), seeking a declaratory judgment that Signature's patent for a computerized accounting system for managing a mutual fund investment structure is invalid and unenforceable. After hearing, the Court ALLOWS Plaintiff's motion for partial summary judgment ....

State Street and Signature are companies, which, among other things, act as administrators and accounting agents of mutual funds. Signature owns U.S. Patent No. 5,193,056 (" '056 Patent"), entitled "Data Processing System for Hub and Spoke Financial Services Configuration," issued on March 9, 1993, by assignment of the inventor, R. Todd Boes. As the patent summary states, the claimed invention "provides a data processing system and method for monitoring and recording the information flow and data, and making all calculations, necessary for maintaining a partnership portfolio and partner fund (Hub and Spoke) financial services configuration." In order to assess the scope and nature of the claimed invention, it is first necessary to discuss briefly the financial configuration which the data processing system is designed to service.

A. *Hub And Spoke Configuration*

The invention relates to a newly-developed financial investment vehicle, which State Street terms a "multi-tiered fund complex" and Signature calls by its own proprietary mark, a "Hub and Spoke" configuration. In essence, a Hub and Spoke arrangement is an investment structure whereby mutual funds ("Spokes") pool their assets in an investment portfolio ("Hub") organized as a partnership. "This financial services configuration involves an entity that is treated as a partnership for federal income tax purposes and that holds the investment portfolio ... and funds that invest as partners in the partnership portfolio." '056 Patent, col. 1. Enabling mutual funds to pool their assets in this manner provides for economies of scale with regard to the costs of fund administration and has beneficial tax consequences.

This complex financial structure, however, creates its own set of administrative challenges. As a partnership, the Hub portfolio assesses all economic gains and losses with respect to the Spoke funds on a pro rata basis. Because each of the Spokes are themselves investment vehicles, which are subject to constant changes in assets as individual investors add or withdraw funds and market prices fluctuate, the partnership interest of the Spokes in the Hub constantly varies. Administering this structure requires a daily allocation of income, capital gains, and expenses or investment losses. The daily allocations are made on the basis of the Spoke funds' percentage share in the total assets of the Hub portfolio.

B. *The Claimed Invention*

Signature's invention is directed to a data processing system for administering this Hub and Spoke configuration. The disclosure provides extensive flowcharts and a detailed description of the invention's preferred embodiment. The system is operated by means of a personal computer, software capable of performing the various functions described in the claims and detailed in the preferred embodiment and flowcharts, data storage means such as a floppy disk, and display means such as printed output and a computer screen.

Specifically, the invention calculates and stores data representing: the percentage share that each Spoke fund holds in the Hub portfolio; any daily activity affecting the portfolio's assets; allocations of gains, losses and expenses to each of the Spoke member funds; and tracking and updating data that are used to determine aggregate year-end income, gains, losses, and expenses for accounting and tax purposes.

The invention is claimed in means-plus-function language as an apparatus. Of the six claims, only the first is independent:

[1.] A data processing system for managing a financial services configuration of a portfolio established as a partnership, each partner being one of a plurality of funds, comprising:

(a) computer processor means for processing data:

(b) storage means for storing data on a storage medium;

(c) first means for initializing the storage medium;

(d) second means for processing data regarding assets in the portfolio and each of the funds from a previous day and data regarding increases or decreases in each of the funds' assets and for allocating the percentage share that each fund holds in the portfolio;

(e) third means for processing data regarding daily incremental income, expenses, and net realized gain or loss for the portfolio and for allocating such data among each fund;

(f) fourth means for processing data regarding daily net unrealized gain or loss for the portfolio and for allocating such data among each fund; and

(g) fifth means for processing data regarding aggregate year-end income, expenses, and capital gain or loss for the portfolio and each of the funds.

....

Signature admits that it informed State Street that any data processing system designed to perform book accounting for a multi-tiered fund arranged in a Hub and Spoke configuration likely would infringe the '056 Patent. Answer Para. 12. State Street serves as the custodian and accounting agent for several multi-tiered fund complexes and had negotiated with Signature for a license for its patented data processing system. When negotiations broke down, State Street brought the present declaratory judgment action seeking to invalidate Signature's patent.

III

Analysis

The core issue on summary judgment is whether computer software that essentially performs mathematical accounting functions and is configured to run on a general purpose (i.e., personal) computer is patentable under 35 U.S.C. Section 101.

As repeated thrice by the Supreme Court and echoed by the Federal Circuit and the CCPA, the best clue to patentability remains the mathematical algorithm/physical transformation test.... Although the Federal Circuit's developing precedent is not crystal clear on this point, this test remains the best guidepost for determining the patentability of computer software.

....

Although the '056 Patent claims do not directly recite a mathematical formula, the data processing system is an apparatus specifically designed to solve a mathematical problem. Indeed, the specification is quite clear in this regard: "The present invention provides a data processing system and method for monitoring and recording the information flow and data, and *making all calculations*, necessary for maintaining a partnership portfolio and partner fund (Hub and Spoke) financial services configuration." '056 Patent col. 4 (emphasis added). The specification also is replete with flow charts that describe the numerous data processing steps. Most importantly, the claims themselves recite calculating data as a function of the machine. *Id.* at col. 13-15 (claims 3-6).

....

The invention claimed by the '056 Patent is unlike the computer-implemented inventions that the Federal Circuit has deemed statutory in the past. *Alappat* held patentable a device for transforming numerical values to display smooth waveform data on an oscilloscope. Through mathematical operations that could be performed on a computer, the "rasterizer" permitted an oscilloscope to operate in a manner theretofore not possible and thus was "a specific machine to produce a useful, concrete, and tangible result." 33 F.3d at 1544.... Similarly, *Arrhythmia* [*Research Technology, Inc. v. Corazonix Corp.*, 958 F.2d 1053 (Fed. Cir. 1992), discussed earlier this chapter] involved an invention that enabled a certain type of human heart activity to be measured, processed, and displayed electronically. Although mathematical calculations were part of the process, the invention "was properly viewed as a method of analyzing electrocardiograph signals in order to determine a specified heart activity." 958 F.2d at 1059.

Signature's invention does not involve this type of transformation. Rather, like other accounting methods, it is designed to manipulate and record numbers. Unlike the electrocardiograph in *Arrhythmia* ..., Signature's data processing system does not "involve [ ] the transformation or conversion of subject matter representative of or constituting physical activity or objects." *Schrader* [also discussed earlier], 22 F.3d at 294. And, unlike the rasterizer in *Alappat*, the invention does not physically convert the data upon which it operates into a new and totally different form. A change of one set of numbers into another, without more, is insufficient to confer patent protection.

....

G. *The Business Methods Exception*

The Court's decision comports with another doctrinal exclusion from subject matter patentability known as the "business methods exception." Numerous patent treatises recite the long-established principle that "business 'plans' and 'systems' are not patentable, even though they may not be dependent upon the aesthetic, emotional, or judgmental reactions of a human." 1 DONALD S. CHISUM, PATENTS: A TREATISE ON THE LAW OF PATENTABILITY, VALIDITY AND INFRINGEMENT § 1.03[5], at 1-75 (1990) ....

As established by a series of older cases, business methods are unpatentable abstract ideas. *See Loew's Drive-In Theatres, Inc. v. Park-In Theatres, Inc.*, 174 F.2d 547, 552 (1st Cir.) (equating methods of doing business with abstract idea doctrine), *cert. denied*, 338 U.S. 822 (1949); *Hotel Security Checking Co. v. Lorraine Co.*, 160 F. 467, 469 (2d Cir. 1908) (same). Recent decisions, while not holding explicitly on these grounds, recognize the continued validity of that rule. *See Alappat*, 33 F.3d at 1541 (suggesting that "business methodology" is not Section 101 subject matter); *Grams*, 888 F.3d at 837 (listing "methods of doing business" as among categories of non-patentable subject matter); *Ex parte Murray*, 9 U.S.P.Q.2d 1819, 1820 (PTO Bd. of Patent App. & Int. 1988) (declaring non-statutory bank accounting system). *But see Paine, Webber, Jackson & Curtis, Inc. v. Merrill Lynch, Pierce, Fenner & Smith, Inc.*, 564 F. Supp. 1358, 1369 [218 U.S.P.Q. 212] (D. Del. 1983) (holding patentable computerized system of combining package of popular financial services because invention did not recite *Benson* algorithm); *Schrader*, 22 F.3d at 297 (Newman, J. dissenting) (urging that the method of doing business exception be "described as error-prone, redundant and obsolete.")

If Signature's invention were patentable, any financial institution desirous of implementing a multi-tiered funding complex modelled on a Hub and Spoke configuration would be required to seek Signature's permission before embarking on such a project. This is so because the '056 Patent is claimed sufficiently broadly to foreclose virtually any computer-implemented accounting method necessary to manage this type of financial structure. Indeed, during licensing negotiations, Signature informed State Street that any data processing system designed to perform book accounting for a multi-tiered fund based on a partnership portfolio configuration would infringe the '056 Patent....

In effect, the '056 Patent grants Signature a monopoly on its idea of a multi-tiered partnership portfolio investment structure; patenting an accounting system necessary to carry on a certain type of business is tantamount to a patent on the business itself. Because such abstract ideas are not patentable, either as methods of doing business or as mathematical algorithms, the '056 Patent must fail. [Partial summary judgment granted.]

NOTES

1. Attorneys for State Street Bank indicate that a notice of appeal has been filed for this case; stay tuned for Federal Circuit resolution.

2. Is the subject matter of the patent at issue in this case any more or less abstract than other patents on specific applications of computer technology, such as distributed computer processing, client/server communications, and the like? Would Judge Saris's reasoning imply that patents on these applications violate § 101 also? Why might business methods patents be more suspect under § 101 than other patents on computer applications? See the next section of discussion.

1. POTENTIAL IMPACT OF PATENTS ON THE FINANCIAL SERVICES INDUSTRY

The *Merrill Lynch* case (discussed earlier in this chapter) demonstrates the confluence of two key trends. The first is that patents for computer software are now being granted much more freely by the Patent Office. The second, which is closely related, is that since today new financial instruments and techniques are almost universally implemented in software on computer systems, these instruments and techniques are now being characterized as essentially *computer*-related inventions, with a predictable result: the Patent Office is issuing patents on them. Thus it is the very computer-dependence of these financial "inventions" that makes them patentable.

This is clear from the way these patents are drafted. Their claims describe them as "systems" or "apparatus." Merrill Lynch's patent, for example, is for a "Securities Brokerage-Cash Management System." Other patents in this line include U.S. Patent No. 4,642,767, a "Bookkeeping and Accounting System" patent granted to one M. Lerner; U.S. Patent No. 4,648,038, a "Method and Apparatus for Restructuring Debt Obligations," issued to P. Roberts et al. and assigned to Lazard Freres & Co.; U.S. Patent No. 4,839,804, a "Method and Apparatus for Insuring the Funding of a Future Liability of Uncertain Cost," issued to P. Roberts et al. and assigned to College Savings Bank of Princeton, N.J. (discussed in the news story in Note 3 following the *Paine Webber* case above). U.S. Patent No. 4,736,294, entitled "Data Processing Methods and Apparatus for Managing Vehicle Financing" (Apr. 5, 1988), and U.S. Patent No. 4,694,397, entitled "Banking/Brokerage Computer Interface System," (granted Sept. 15, 1987), are also examples of business method/software patents. The computer interface patent "uses a computer and associated program as an interface between a conventional bank account and a securities brokerage account." This is very similar to the inter-account communication function of the patent at issue in the *Paine Webber* case. The second patent, on Vehicle Financing, processes vehicle financing data and provides information to assist the lender in granting a loan.

In each case the patent describes the invention as relating to "data processing," while in fact the real contribution of the inventor involves a new financial instrument or technique.

In the past, courts have declined to uphold patents on a new bookkeeping system employing novel checkbooks,[8] and a system for conducting commodities trades at a distance without using brokers.[9] In each case, the courts distinguished between the *method* of doing business, or the new business concept, and the *physical apparatus* or tools needed to carry out the new method.[10] If the tools meet all the tests of patentability, they are patentable, the courts said; but never the business concept itself.

It is now possible to implement many business concepts on computers. In fact, in the area of sophisticated financial instruments and services, just about every new concept is carried out with computers. Once a new product is dreamed up, according to an industry executive, "software is written to support the new [financial] instrument within months."[11] And the sophisticated, round-the-clock handling of millions of transactions per day in the stock market and inter-bank funds transfer systems would of course be impossible without computers, so innovations in these areas must necessarily be computer-based. Thus from the standpoint of the financial services industries, the liberalization of patent rules regarding software inventions came at an opportune time — just when these industries are themselves becoming totally dependent on advanced data processing technology.

2. WHY NOT PATENT BUSINESS METHODS?

The computer tie-in allowed the financial services industry to overcome the traditional objection to patenting business methods. But the question still remains: why not allow patents for financial instruments and techniques, or business methods in general?

---

[8] *In re Sterling*, 70 F.2d 910 (C.C.P.A. 1934). Although conceding that Sterling's checkbook, which included both regular checks and checks designed to transfer funds to a savings account, was "an ingenious and convenient arrangement," the court refused patent protection because the physical structure presented no novelty.

[9] *In re Wait*, 73 F.2d 982 (C.C.P.A. 1934). The patent applicant claimed a process which involved three functions: transmitting offers to buy or sell to distant locations where interested parties could see the offers posted, transmitting acceptances, and recording each transaction. The court ruled it was not patentable.

[10] Patents have always been granted on the *tools* of business. *See, e.g.*, JOANNE YATES, CONTROL THROUGH COMMUNICATION: THE RISE OF SYSTEM IN AMERICAN MANAGEMENT (1989), which describes the Wootan Patent Desk, Edison's patented "Electric Pen," the patented Underwood typewriter, and other major office equipment innovations.

[11] R. Glasser, *The Intersection of Technology and Financial Services*, in INNOVATION AND TECHNOLOGY IN THE MARKETS 13, 18 (D. Siegel ed., 1990).

a. The Traditional Rationale

Although the older cases do not articulate their reasoning very clearly, they seem to center around one idea: that the patent system was meant to protect *technology* — actual machines, devices, and new chemical compositions — rather than pure concepts. Since business methods were not tied to particular machinery or devices, they were mere concepts, and hence not patentable.

b. Economic Rationales

Even if courts no longer rely on the distinction between concepts and machines, the rule against business methods might be justified on other — primarily economic — grounds.

Are These Patents Necessary?

First one might argue that such patents are simply not necessary. After all, there seemed to be no shortage of new accounting methods, financial instruments, or financial services techniques throughout the history of the American economy, when business methods were not patentable. Even into the mid-1980s, when these patents were just beginning to appear, the U.S. was considered the world leader in this service industry. Thus on this view, the proper question is: why fix it if it ain't broke?

Three responses suggest themselves. First, one can point out the rising cost of creating an innovative financial service or instrument. The old rules, that is, might no longer provide enough of an incentive to innovate in this field. This argument is frequently made with respect to computer program patents — which also suffer from the "it ain't broke" critique. But this argument requires empirical support, which so far has been lacking.

A second response to the opponents of business method patents might be that it is unfair to exclude these innovations from the umbrella of patent protection. After all, it is argued, entrepreneurs work just as hard in this field as in biotechnology, organic chemistry, diesel engine design, and all the other fields where patents are routinely handed out. Why discriminate on the basis of subject matter;[12] why not simply reward hard work and innovative results in whatever form they take?

A third argument is perhaps more speculative. This would concede that the financial services sector has performed admirably in the U.S. but argue that it would have done — and will do, in light of new patent rules — *even better* in the brave new world of financial services patents. Investments that were not made

---

[12] For a proposal to create a system of patent-like rights to protect *all* innovations, whether technological, "business method," or otherwise, see W. KINGSTON, ED., DIRECT PROTECTION OF INNOVATION (1987). Kingston proposes a system of property rights to come into effect only when a new product is actually introduced on the market. *See id.*, at 1-34.

because of a fear of piracy, will be made, now that companies know their innovations will be protected.

These last two points are both correct, in a sense, but they do not resolve the matter. The first assumes that the patent system has adopted the property theory associated with John Locke: namely, that when a person expends labor on an object, he or she then deserves to enjoy property rights in the fruits of his or her labor. *See* J. LOCKE, TWO TREATISES OF GOVERNMENT 129-132 (Everyman ed. 1924). But this ignores an important point: a system of property rights must consider the effect of an award of rights *on others*. The claims of the laborer — the innovator, in our case — are not the only ones that count; competitors, users, and the public at large matter too.

This point answers the second objection as well. Consider, for example, that many "innovations" are in fact improvements on, applications of, and refinements of prior innovations. Only if the original innovator will develop these follow-on innovations, or license others to do so, will social welfare be unaffected by the award of a patent. If there is reason to believe that the innovator would not in fact push the field as far forward, or as quickly, as it and its competitors together, those competitors have a strong claim to be allowed access to the innovation at issue. *See* Merges & Nelson, *On the Complex Economics of Patent Scope*, 90 COLUM. L. REV. 839 (1990).

Alternatives to Patents

In deciding whether financial instrument patents are really necessary, it is important to consider alternative means by which companies can reap returns on innovative financial instruments and services. Recent empirical research has revealed that in many industries, patents are not necessary for firms to secure an adequate return on research and development investment.[13] In many industries, trade secrets or a "head start" on the competition allow firms to capture enough of the value of their research to continue doing it. In other industries, according to recent studies, firms use strategies such as ownership of complementary assets intimately tied to an innovation — such as service networks — to capture the value of that innovation. *See* Teece, *Profiting from Technological Innovation: Implications for Integration, Collaboration, and Public Policy*, 15 RES. POL'Y 285 (1986).

Regardless of specific strategies, the point is the same: firms can capture the value of innovations many ways. The question for policymakers is whether patents should be permitted, in light of the other "appropriability mechanisms" available. Again, the relatively frequent innovations in the financial services industry prior to the era of patentability suggest that firms had adequate means to appropriate the value of their new financial innovations.

---

[13] *See* Levin, Klevorick, Nelson & Winter, *Appropriating the Returns from Industrial Research and Development*, 1987 BROOKINGS PAPERS ECON. ACTIVITY 783 (1987).

What alternative, non-patent means have companies traditionally used to capture the value of their financial innovations? Three come to mind (there may be more): head start, trade secrets, and promotional value. The head start advantage is obvious; if a particular firm were recognized as the originator of a novel financial instrument — an interest rate swap, for example — it could expect to garner clients and make money before competitors figured out how to put the instrument together. Trade secrets have traditionally been used to protect a host of financial techniques; even now, the internal financial dealings of large firms are only made public to the extent SEC and IRS oversight make necessary. On a more general level, many "methods of doing business" such as vertical integration and just-in-time inventory practices can be kept secret or at least quiet; it is only *after* such practices have shown good results that they become widely known. And as to promotional value, it has surely been common to tout one's firm as "the originator of debt-for-equity swaps," or "the company that invented unbundled stock units." The prestige this brings helps firms recover the costs of creating these instruments.

What Is the Cost?

To say that patents are not necessary to call forth innovations implies a further point: that granting patents will cost too much. There are so many ways a new business method or financial instrument might be adapted to particular business situations, it might be deemed inefficient to give one patentee exclusive rights to the method or technique. The losses — in the form of foregone applications and modifications — may simply outweigh the gain of a greater incentive to innovate.

NOTES

1. What rationale(s) can you think of for the rule prohibiting patents for "methods of doing business"? If one spends a great deal of money developing a new method of doing business — e.g., delivering packages overnight to a large area, such as Federal Express pioneered in the 1980s — why shouldn't the law protect this investment? For a proposal to supplement the patent system with a new system of "Innovation Warrants," which *would* protect methods of doing business (among other innovations), *see* W. KINGSTON, ED., DIRECT PROTECTION OF INNOVATION (1987). Kingston proposes a system of property rights to come into effect only when a new product is actually introduced on the market. *See id.* at 1-34. These proposals contain some useful suggestions, as indicated by the commentators assembled to critique them. *See* G. Tullock, *Intellectual Property*, in *id.* at 171; B. Wright, *On the Design of a System to Improve the Production of Innovations*, in *id.* at 227.

2. As with computer software patents, those who oppose patents for "business methods" must confront the very broad language of § 101 of the Patent Act; surely business methods can be "processes" and "improvements thereon." Is legislation the only way to deal with this problem, or is it possible to interpret the § 101 categories in light of the potential impact of patents on the particular field in question?

D. NATURAL SUBSTANCES AND LIVING THINGS

1. INTRODUCTION

The foundational case on patents for living subject matter is *Diamond v. Chakrabarty*, the first case in this chapter.

A very significant development since *Chakrabarty* is the adoption of the Uruguay Round of amendments to the General Agreement on Tariffs and Trade (GATT), which included an agreement on Trade-Related Aspects of Intellectual Property Rights (TRIPs). *See* 33 I.L.M. 81 (1994). Article 27 of the TRIPs agreement covers patentable subject matter.

Article 27
Patentable Subject Matter

1. Subject to the provisions of paragraphs 2 and 3 below, patents shall be available for any inventions, whether products or processes, in all fields of technology, provided that they are new, involve an inventive step and are capable of industrial application.[5] Subject to paragraph 4 of Article 65, paragraph 8 of Article 70 and paragraph 3 of this Article, patents shall be available and patent rights enjoyable without discrimination as to the place of invention, the field of technology and whether products are imported or locally produced.

2. Members may exclude from patentability inventions, the prevention within their territory of the commercial exploitation of which is necessary to protect *ordre public* or morality, including to protect human, animal or plant life or health or to avoid serious prejudice to the environment, provided that such exclusion is not made merely because the exploitation is prohibited by domestic law.

3. Members may also exclude from patentability: (a) diagnostic, therapeutic and surgical methods for the treatment of humans or animals; (b) plants and animals other than microorganisms, and essentially biological processes for the production of plants or animals other than non-biological and microbiological processes. However, Members shall provide for the protection of plant varieties either by patents or by an effective *sui generis* system or by any combination thereof. The provisions of this sub-paragraph shall be

---

[5] For the purposes of this Article, the terms "inventive step" and "capable of industrial application" may be deemed by a Member to be synonymous with the terms "non-obvious" and "useful" respectively.

reviewed four years after the entry into force of the Agreement Establishing the [World Trade Organization, or WTO].

33 I.L.M. 81, 93-94 (1994).

PARKE-DAVIS & CO. v. H.K. MULFORD & CO.
189 F. 95 (S.D.N.Y. 1911) (L. Hand, J.)
[aff'd, 196 F. 496 (2d Cir. 1912)]

[Inventor Jokichi Takamine had invented a purified form of adrenaline, isolated and purified from the natural adrenal gland. He obtained two patents, patent No. 730,176, dated June 2, 1903, for glandular extractive product, and patent No. 753,177, dated February 23, 1904, for glandular extractive compound (consisting of the former isolated product of the '176 patent in a solution with salt and a preservative), and assigned them to Mulford. Takamine's primary contribution was to isolate adrenaline in the form of a chemical base, as opposed to an acid, thereby overcoming any of the problems associated with prior art acid-based compounds. The following two claims are illustrative:

['176 patent] 1. A substance possessing the herein-described physiological characteristics and reactions of the suprarenal glands in a stable and concentrate form, and practically free from inert and associated gland-tissue.

['177 patent] 1. As an article of manufacture, a substance consisting of the blood pressure raising principle of the suprarenal glands chemically combined with a nonsuprarenal substance whereby the stability of a water solution of said blood pressure raising principle is maintained.

[Parke-Davis defended an infringement suit against its sale of a similar product on several grounds, including that the Takamine patents were unpatentable natural products.

[The first part of the opinion deals with infringement. Judge Hand found that although defendant's method of preparing the adrenaline differed from plaintiff's (in that different compounds were added to the raw grandular isolate to precipitate the end product), the resulting product still fell within the claims of the '176 patent, i.e., it was adrenaline, "free from inert and associated gland-tissue." Judge Hand concludes: "[C]onsidering the similarity of the processes, the use of each substance practically, and the approximation of result physiologically, the two are near enough to be an infringement one of the other." He then turns to the invalidity defense.]

The question next arises of the validity of [the] claims [in the '176 patent]. This is attacked, first, because they are anticipated in the art; and, second, for a number of technical grounds .... The anticipations I will deal with first, because, in the view which I have taken of the two patents, that is the simpler consideration. The patentee originally attempted to claim the active principle itself. This was in his first application where he claimed process and product; but the examiner would not allow these claims, basing his rejection upon his interpretation of *American Wood Paper Co. v. Fibre Disintegrating Co.*, [90 U.S.] 23

Wall. 566, 23 L. Ed. 31 [(1874)], that no product is patentable, however it be of the process, which is merely separated by the patentee from its surrounding materials and remains unchanged....

[A]ll of [the] four alleged anticipating products never existed except in the form of a salt.... [T]he only necessary question here is: Since they were not actually themselves bases, whether pure or impure, whether it involved invention to produce the base of Takamine. This question does not deserve any extended consideration. The difficulties of the old products were so great as made any substantial advance from them important. It is enough that Takamine was the first to isolate any base whatever, all other products existing in the form of a salt, because prior investigators were all trying to reduce the principle down as purely as possible. The invention was therefore novel.

Nor is the patent only for a degree of purity, and therefore not for a new "composition of matter." As I have already shown, it does not include a salt, and no one had ever isolated a substance which was not in salt form, and which was anything like Takamine's. Indeed, [defendant's expert witness] supposes it to exist as a natural salt, and that the base was an original production of Takamine's. That was a distinction not in degree, but in kind. But, even if it were merely an extracted product without change, there is no rule that such products are not patentable. Takamine was the first to make it available for any use by removing it from the other gland-tissue in which it was found, and, while it is of course possible logically to call this a purification of the principle, it became for every practical purpose a new thing commercially and therapeutically. That was a good ground for a patent. That the change here resulted in ample practical differences is fully proved. Everyone, not already saturated with scholastic distinctions, would recognize that Takamine's crystals were not merely the old dried glands in a purer state, nor would his opinion change if he learned that the crystals were obtained from the glands by a process of eliminating the inactive organic substances. The line between different substances and degrees of the same substance is to be drawn rather from the common usages of men than from nice considerations of dialectic....

Whatever confusion the intricacy of the subject-matter causes, one fact stands out, which no one ought fairly to forget. Before Takamine's discovery the best experts were trying to get a practicable form of the active principle. The uses of the gland were so great that it became part of the usual therapy in the best form which was accessible. As soon as Takamine put out his discovery, other uses practically disappeared; by that I do not mean absolutely, but that the enormous proportion of use now is of Takamine's products. There has been no successful dispute as to that; hardly indeed any dispute at all. What use remains is, so far as the evidence shows, of the old dried glands, which every one concedes to have been dangerous, at least for intravenous use. All this ought to count greatly for the validity of the patent, and Takamine has a great start, so to speak, from such facts. It is true that he overstates the degree of stability of his acid solution without any preservative. Strictly it is not in that form fit for sale about in drug stores where it may be kept for long even in a stoppered bottle; but commercial or practical stability is a somewhat elastic term, and this is a case where he should be entitled to a lenient construction, for he has been author of a valuable invention and has succeeded where the most expert have failed.

NOTE

Inventor *A* discovers a technique for purifying a certain hormone from human tissue and applies for a patent on the purified form of the hormone. Inventor *B* discovers the gene coding for the hormone, clones it, and obtains expression in a mammalian cell culture environment. Are any of these inventions/discoveries patentable? Under the *Mulford* rationale, the answer is yes. *See, e.g.*, U.S. Patent 4,751,084, "Tissue Plasminogen Activator From Normal Human Colon Cells," to Feder et al., June 14, 1988; U.S. Patent 4,713,332, "T Cell Specific cDNA Clone," to Mak, Dec. 15, 1987, claim 3:

> An isolated [cDNA] sequence encoding a polypeptide which is at least part of the beta chain of a human T cell antigen receptor comprising at least 936 nucleotides.

U.S. Patent 4,666,837, "DNA Sequences, Recombinant DNA Molecules and Processes for Producing the A and B Subunits of Cholera Toxin and Preparations Containing So-obtained Subunit or Subunits," to Harford et al., May 19, 1987, claim 1:

> A recombinant DNA molecule comprising at least a portion coding for subunits A and B of cholera toxin or a fragment or derivative of said portion wherein the fragment or derivative codes for a polypeptide having an activity which (a) can induce an immune response to subunit A; ... (c) can bind to the membrane receptor for the B subunit of cholera toxin; ... (e) can induce an immune response to subunit B and bind to said membrane receptor ....

U.S. Patent 4,713,332, *supra*, claim 13:

> A method of preparing the cDNA of claim 3 [*supra*] which comprises obtaining mRNA from a human T cell, preparing cDNA complementary to the mRNA, inserting the cDNA into an appropriate cloning vehicle, introducing the cloning vehicle into an appropriate host, culturing the resulting host under appropriate conditions permitting production of multiple copies of the cDNA, recovering the cDNA so produced and screening the cDNA to determine whether said cDNA is expressed only in T cells.

Should these patents have issued? Does your answer depend on the degree of human intervention they required? What other issues, besides those associated with § 101, do they raise? *Cf. Pending Patent on Cystic Fibrosis Gene Triggers Research Worries*, PAT. WORLD, Mar. 1993, at 18 (patent for gene on chromosome 7 worries scientific researchers who may have to pay royalties to continue work on cystic fibrosis treatments).

FUNK BROS. SEED CO. v. KALO INOCULANT CO.
333 U.S. 127, 76 U.S.P.Q. (BNA) 280 (1948)

This is a patent infringement suit brought by respondent. The charge of infringement is limited to certain product claims[1] of Patent No. 2,200,532 issued to Bond on May 14, 1940. Petitioner filed a counterclaim asking for a declaratory judgment that the entire patent be adjudged invalid. The District Court held the product claims invalid for want of invention and dismissed the complaint. It also dismissed the counterclaim. Both parties appealed. The Circuit Court of Appeals reversed, holding that the product claims were valid and infringed and that the counterclaim should not have been dismissed. The question of validity is the only question presented by this petition for certiorari.

Through some mysterious process leguminous plants are able to take nitrogen from the air and fix it in the plant for conversion to organic nitrogenous compounds. The ability of these plants to fix nitrogen from the air depends on the presence of bacteria of the genus Rhizobium which infect the roots of the plant and form nodules on them. These root-nodule bacteria of the genus Rhizobium fall into at least six species. No one species will infect the roots of all species of leguminous plants. But each will infect well-defined groups of those plants. Each species of root-nodule bacteria is made up of distinct strains which vary in efficiency. Methods of selecting the strong strains and of producing a bacterial culture from them have long been known. The bacteria produced by the laboratory methods of culture are placed in a powder or liquid base and packaged for sale to and use by agriculturists in the inoculation of the seeds of leguminous plants. This also has long been well known.

It was the general practice, prior to the Bond patent, to manufacture and sell inoculants containing only one species of root-nodule bacteria. The inoculant could therefore be used successfully only in plants of the particular cross-inoculation group corresponding to this species. Thus if a farmer had crops of clover, alfalfa, and soy beans he would have to use three separate inoculants. There had been a few mixed cultures for field legumes. But they had proved generally unsatisfactory because the different species of the Rhizobia bacteria produced an inhibitory effect on each other when mixed in a common base, with the result that their efficiency was reduced. Hence it had been assumed that the

---

[1] The product claims in suit are 1, 3, 4, 5, 6, 7, 8, 13, and 14. Claim 4 is illustrative of the invention which is challenged. It reads as follows:

"An inoculant for leguminous plants comprising a plurality of selected mutually non-inhibitive strains of different species of bacteria of the genus Rhizobium, said strains being unaffected by each other in respect to their ability to fix nitrogen in the leguminous plant for which they are specific."

different species were mutually inhibitive. Bond discovered that there are strains of each species of root-nodule bacteria which do not exert a mutually inhibitive effect on each other. He also ascertained that those mutually non-inhibitive strains can, by certain methods of selection and testing, be isolated and used in mixed cultures. Thus he provided a mixed culture of Rhizobia capable of inoculating the seeds of plants belonging to several cross-inoculation groups. It is the product claims which disclose that mixed culture that the Circuit Court of Appeals has held valid.

We do not have presented the question whether the methods of selecting and testing the non-inhibitive strains are patentable. We have here only product claims. Bond does not create a state of inhibition or of non-inhibition in the bacteria. Their qualities are the work of nature. Those qualities are of course not patentable. For patents cannot issue for the discovery of the phenomena of nature. The qualities of these bacteria, like the heat of the sun, electricity, or the qualities of metals, are part of the storehouse of knowledge of all men. They are manifestations of laws of nature, free to all men and reserved exclusively to none. He who discovers a hitherto unknown phenomenon of nature has no claim to a monopoly of it which the law recognizes. If there is to be invention from such a discovery, it must come from the application of the law of nature to a new and useful end. The Circuit Court of Appeals thought that Bond did much more than discover a law of nature, since he made a new and different composition of non-inhibitive strains which contributed utility and economy to the manufacture and distribution of commercial inoculants. But we think that that aggregation of species fell short of invention within the meaning of the patent statutes.

Discovery of the fact that certain strains of each species of these bacteria can be mixed without harmful effect to the properties of either is a discovery of their qualities of non-inhibition. It is no more than the discovery of some of the handiwork of nature and hence is not patentable. The aggregation of select strains of the several species into one product is an application of that newly-discovered natural principle. But however ingenious the discovery of that natural principle may have been, the application of it is hardly more than an advance in the packaging of the inoculants. Each of the species of root-nodule bacteria contained in the package infects the same group of leguminous plants which it always infected. No species acquires a different use. The combination of species produces no new bacteria, no change in the six species of bacteria, and no enlargement of the range of their utility. Each species has the same effect it always had. The bacteria perform in their natural way. Their use in combination does not improve in any way their natural functioning. They serve the ends nature originally provided and act quite independently of any effort of the patentee.

[T]here is no invention here unless the discovery that certain strains of the several species of these bacteria are non-inhibitive and may thus be safely mixed is invention. But we cannot so hold without allowing a patent to issue on one of the ancient secrets of nature now disclosed.

Reversed.

MR. JUSTICE FRANKFURTER, concurring.

[Under my view of] Bond's endeavors, two different claims of originality are involved: (1) the idea that there are compatible strains, and (2) the experimental demonstration that there were in fact some compatible strains. Insofar as the court below concluded that the packaging of a particular mixture of compatible strains is an invention and as such patentable, I agree, provided not only that a new and useful property results from their combination, but also that the particular strains are identifiable and adequately identified. I do not find that Bond's combination of strains satisfies these requirements. The strains by which Bond secured compatibility are not identified and are identifiable only by their compatibility.

[Bond] appears to claim that since he was the originator of the idea that there might be mutually compatible strains and had practically demonstrated that some such strains exist, everyone else is forbidden to use a combination of strains whether they are or are not identical with the combinations that Bond selected and packaged together.

The consequences of such a conclusion call for its rejection. Its acceptance would require, for instance in the field of alloys, that if one discovered a particular mixture of metals, which when alloyed had some particular desirable properties, he could patent not merely this particular mixture but the idea of alloying metals for this purpose, and thus exclude everyone else from contriving some other combination of metals which, when alloyed, had the same desirable properties. In patenting an alloy, I assume that both the qualities of the product and its specific composition would need to be specified. It only confuses the issue, however, to introduce such terms as "the work of nature" and the "laws of nature." For these are vague and malleable terms infected with too much ambiguity and equivocation. In finding Bond's patent invalid I have tried to avoid a formulation which, while it would in fact justify Bond's patent, would lay the basis for denying patentability to a large area within existing patent legislation.

NOTE

Degree of Human Intervention. In *Chakrabarty*, the Court emphasizes the transformations that the inventor makes on the admittedly natural raw materials of the invention. But in *Funk Bros.*, the Court emphasizes that the bacteria, though combined in a novel way, still perform their same old natural function. Can the cases be reconciled? Should human intervention be the touchstone for patentability in this area?

2. PLANTS

The Supreme Court in *Diamond v. Chakrabarty* stated:

> [A] new mineral discovered in the earth or *a new plant found in the wild is not patentable subject matter*. Likewise, Einstein could not patent his celebrated law that $E = mc^2$; nor could Newton have patented the law of gravity. Such discoveries are "manifestations of ... nature, free to all men and reserved exclusively to none."

Diamond v. Chakrabarty, 447 U.S., at 309, quoting *Funk Bros. Seed Co. v. Kalo Inoculant Co.*, at 130 (emphasis added).

No doubt plants have something in common with minerals and laws of nature — they are all "discovered," as opposed to *invented*. The presumption is that discoveries are already "out there" waiting to be found. In accordance with this logic, the Constitution's patent and copyright clause speaks of granting to "inventors" exclusive rights over their "inventions."

But putting aside the language of the Constitution for a moment, it might be asked whether this distinction makes sense. Consider the following passage written by the noted libertarian philosopher Robert Nozick, in which he sets forth the reasons why one who discovers a new plant is entitled to assert property rights over it:[14]

> He does not worsen the situation of others; if he did not stumble upon the substance no one else would have, and the others would remain without it. However, as time passes, the likelihood increases that others would have come across the substance; upon this fact might be based a limit to his

---

[14] The passage comes in the midst of a section discussing John Locke's theory of property; thus the emphasis on not worsening anyone else's position, one of the "Lockean provisos" that must be met under this theory for property rights to be defensible. *See* J. LOCKE, TWO TREATISES OF GOVERNMENT 129, 131 (Everyman ed. 1924):

> [T]hough all the fruits [the earth] naturally produces, and beasts it feeds, belong to mankind in common, as they are produced by the spontaneous hand of Nature, and nobody has originally a private dominion exclusive of the rest of mankind in any of them, as they are thus in their natural state, yet being given for the use of men, there must of necessity be a means to appropriate them some way or other before they can be of any use, or at all beneficial, to any particular men....

> Nor was this appropriation of any parcel of land, by improving it, any prejudice to any other man, since there was still enough and as good left, and more than the as yet unprovided could use. So that, in effect, there was never the less left for others because of his enclosure for himself. For he that leaves as much as another can make use of does as good as take nothing at all.

See generally Hettinger, *Justifying Intellectual Property*, 18 PHIL. & PUB. AFF. 31 (1989) (discussing Lockean property rights theory and intellectual property).

property right in the substance so that others are not below their baseline position; for example, its bequest might be limited.

R. NOZICK, ANARCHY, STATE AND UTOPIA 181 (1974).

Ex parte HIBBERD

227 U.S.P.Q.2d (BNA) 443 (Pat. Off. Bd. App. 1985)

This is an appeal from the examiner's decision finally rejecting claims 239 through 243, 249 through 255 and 260 through 265 as unpatentable under 35 U.S.C. 101. Claims 1 through 238 have been cancelled, and claims 244 through 248, 256 through 259, and 266 through 270 have been allowed.

The subject matter on appeal relates to maize plant technologies, including seeds (claims 239 through 243), plants (claims 249 through 255) and tissue cultures (claims 260 through 265) which have increased free tryptophan levels, or which are capable of producing plants or seeds having increased tryptophan content. Claim[] 239 [is] representative of the rejected claims:

> 239. A maize seed having an endogenous free tryptophan content of at least about one-tenth milligram per gram dry seed weight and capable of germinating into a plant capable of producing seed having an endogenous free tryptophan content of at least about one-tenth milligram per gram dry seed weight.

There are no rejections based on prior art; rather, [the] claims are rejected solely under 35 U.S.C. 101. It is the examiner's position that the claims drawn to seeds and plants respectively, comprise subject matter which is inappropriate for protection under 35 U.S.C. 101 because the subject matter of plants and seeds is within the purview of the Plant Variety Protection Act of 1970 administered by the U.S. Department of Agriculture, 7 U.S.C. 2321 *et seq.* The examiner's position with respect to claims 260 through 265 drawn to tissue cultures is that such subject matter is inappropriate for protection under 35 U.S.C. 101 because it is within the purview of the Plant Patent Act of 1930, 35 U.S.C. 161. The examiner asserts that, to the extent that the claimed subject matter can be protected under the Plant Variety Protection Act (PVPA) or the Plant Patent Act (PPA), protection under 35 U.S.C. 101 is not available.[1]

We shall not sustain this rejection. Preliminarily, we note that the Supreme Court has interpreted the scope of 35 U.S.C. 101 in the recent case of *Diamond v. Chakrabarty*. The Court noted that the use of the expansive terms "manufacture" and "composition of matter" modified by the comprehensive "any"

---

[1]Claims directed to hybrid seeds, claims 244 through 248, and to hybrid plants, claims 256 through 259, have been allowed because the PVPA and the PPA exclude such subject matter. 35 U.S.C. 161 and 7 U.S.C. 2402(a). The examiner also allowed claim 266 drawn to a method for producing a tryptophan overproducing maize plant and claims 267 through 270 drawn to methods for producing hybrid seeds.

indicated that Congress "plainly contemplated that the patent laws would be given wide scope."

The examiner acknowledges in his answer that, in view of the decision in *Diamond v. Chakrabarty, supra*, it appears clear that Section 101 includes man-made life forms, including plant life. Moreover, the examiner's allowance of claims drawn to hybrid seeds and hybrid plants is a further indication that the examiner considers the scope of Section 101 to include man-made plant life. The examiner asserts in his answer, however, that by enacting the PPA in 1930 and the PVPA in 1970 "Congress has specifically set forth how and under what conditions plant life covered by these Acts should be protected." The examiner contends that the only reasonable statutory interpretation is that the PPA and PVPA, which were later in time and more specific than Section 101, each carved out from Section 101, for specific treatment, the subject matter covered by each. Thus, it is the position of the examiner that the plant-specific Acts (PPA and PVPA) are the *exclusive* forms of protection for plant life covered by those acts.

We disagree with these contentions that the scope of patentable subject matter under Section 101 has been narrowed or restricted by the passage of the PPA and the PVPA and that these plant-specific Acts represent the exclusive forms of protection for plant life covered by those acts. The position taken by the examiner presents a question of statutory construction concerning the scope of patentable subject matter under 35 U.S.C. 101, i.e., has the scope of Section 101 been narrowed or restricted by reason of the enactment of the plant-specific Acts.

In cases of statutory construction we begin, as did the Court in *Diamond v. Chakrabarty, supra*, with the language of the statutes. The language of Section 101 has been interpreted by the Supreme Court to include everything under the sun that is made by man. The examiner does not point to any specific language in the plant-specific Acts to support his position that the plant-specific Acts restrict the scope of patentable subject matter under Section 101. We have examined the provisions of the PPA and the PVPA and we find, as did appellants, that neither the PPA nor the PVPA expressly excludes any plant subject matter from protection under Section 101. Accordingly, we look next to the legislative histories of the plant-specific Acts to determine whether there is any clear indication of congressional intent that protection under the plant-specific Acts be exclusive.

The examiner does not refer to the legislative histories of the plant-specific Acts to support his position as to the intent of Congress. Rather, he merely asserts that "... it is clear that Congress intended a 'distinct and new variety of plant' covered by the Plant Patent Act to be something apart from the statutory categories of invention embraced by Section 101" and "the only reasonable statutory interpretation is that each [PPA and PVPA] carved out from Section 101, for specific treatment, the subject matter covered by each." However, as noted by appellants, there is nothing in the legislative histories of the plant-specific Acts from which one could conclude that Congress intended to remove from protection under Section 101 any subject matter already within the scope of that section. Rather, the Senate Committee on the Judiciary concluded on September 29, 1970 in its Report on Senate bill S.3070 in which it recommended passage of the Plant Variety Protection Act that "... it does not alter protection currently available within the patent system."

The examiner tacitly admits such lack of explicit support for his notion of legislative intent by his failure to refer to the legislative history and by the following statement in his Supplemental Examiner's Answer:

> When Congress carved out and established distinct forms of protection for certain plants, they *implicitly excluded* protection of these plants under Section 101. (Emphasis added).

Thus, the examiner's rejection in the final analysis is based on an *implied* narrowing of Section 101, i.e., an implied partial repeal of Section 101 based on the passage of the plant-specific Acts.

The examiner's contention that Section 101 has been "implicitly" narrowed or partially repealed by implication is not persuasive. The overwhelming weight of authority is to the effect that repeals by implication are not favored and that when there are two acts on the same subject the rule is to give effect to both unless there is such a "positive repugnancy" or "irreconcilable conflict" that the statutes cannot co-exist. This "cardinal rule" of statutory construction was set forth by the Supreme Court in *United States v. Borden Co.*, 308 U.S. 189 at 198-99 (1939).

In the absence of such "positive repugnancy" or "irreconcilable conflict" [indicating] that the statutes cannot co-exist, both statutes, i.e., Section 101 and the plant-specific Acts must be given full effect. Indeed, it is our duty to regard each as effective.

These principles of statutory construction were followed in a recent decision of the Court of Appeals, Federal Circuit, *Roche Products, Inc. v. Bolar Pharmaceutical Co.*, 733 F.2d 858, 221 U.S.P.Q. 937 (Fed. Cir. 1984), *cert. denied*, 225 U.S.P.Q. 792 (1984). In *Roche* the Court stated as follows:

> Simply because a later enacted statute affects in some way an earlier enacted statute is poor reason to ask us to rewrite the earlier statute. Repeals by implication are not favored. Thus, "courts are not at liberty to pick and choose among congressional enactments, and when two statutes are capable of coexistence it is the duty of the courts, absent a clearly expressed congressional intention to the contrary, to regard each as effective."

The examiner in his answer cited *Bulova Watch Co. v. United States*, 365 U.S. 753 (1961) for the proposition that a specific statute controls over a general statute where there is a conflict. We find no application of this principle to the facts involved here because before a specific statute can be found to control over a general statute, there must first be an irreconcilable conflict between them. As noted, *supra*, since we find no such irreconcilable conflict, it is our duty to give effect to both Section 101 and the plant-specific Acts.

In an attempt to show a conflict, the examiner points in his answer to provisions of the plant-specific Acts which differ from Section 101. He notes, for example, that (1) the PVPA contains both research (experimental use) and farmer's crop exemptions, while Section 101 does not explicitly contain such exemptions; (2) the PVPA spells out infringement in great detail and includes a compulsory licensing provision, while no such congressional guidance exists under Section 101 protection; (3) the PVPA limits protection to a single variety, whereas the opportunity for greater and broader exclusionary rights exists under Section 101 protection; (4) under 35 U.S.C. 162 (PPA), the applicant is limited to one claim in formal terms to the plant described, whereas there is no such limitation on coverage under Section 101; and (5) under 35 U.S.C. 163 (PPA), the plant patent conveys the right to exclude others from asexually reproducing the plant, or selling or using the plant so produced. However, this analysis by the Examiner merely serves to indicate that there are differences in the scope of protection offered by Section 101 and the plant-specific Acts. In our view, such differences fall far short of what would be required to find an irreconcilable conflict or positive repugnancy that would mandate a partial repeal of Section 101 by implication.

Nor does the fact that subject matter patentable under Section 101 overlaps with subject matter protectable under the plant-specific Acts provide a basis for concluding that there is irreconcilable conflict between the statutes. There is ample precedent that the availability of one form of statutory protection does not preclude (or irreconcilably conflict with) the availability of protection under another form. For example, in *In re Yardley*, 493 F.2d 1389, 181 U.S.P.Q. 331 (C.C.P.A. 1974) the Court held that there was an overlap between statutory subject matter under the copyright statute and statutory subject matter under the design patent statute. Such overlap was not found to be an irreconcilable conflict by the Court; rather, the overlap was viewed as an indication that Congress intended the availability of both modes of protection.

The examiner urges that protection under 35 U.S.C. 101 under the circumstances of this case would be a violation of Article 2 of the International Union for the Protection of New Plant Varieties (UPOV). As pointed out by appellants, however, UPOV is an Executive Agreement that has not been ratified by the Senate. Such agreements are not treaties within the Constitution, and are not the Supreme Law of the Land. Valid enactments of Congress, such as Section 101, override conflicting provisions of international executive agreements, irrespective of which came first in point of time. *United States v. Capps, Inc.*, 204 F.2d 655 (4th Cir. 1953), *aff'd on other grounds*, 348 U.S. 296 (1955); Restatement (Second) of the Foreign Relations Law of the United States, § 144(1) (1965).

The examiner acknowledges that an executive agreement cannot modify a federal statute, but urges, nevertheless, that the agreement can and should be considered "in interpreting a statute on which it bears." This argument overlooks the fact that the Supreme Court in *Diamond v. Chakrabarty*, *supra*, has already interpreted this scope of Section 101 to cover everything under the sun made by man. In our view, the examiner is asking for an implied partial repeal of Section 101 on the basis of an executive agreement. To do so would, in our opinion, elevate the agreement to a status superior to an Act of Congress, i.e., Section 101, and we decline to do so.

In his rejection of claims 260 through 265 drawn to tissue cultures, the examiner contends that the claims to tissue cultures are drawn to "asexual propagating material" and may, therefore, be protected under the PPA under Section 161. We disagree, and the rejection of claims 260 through 265 is, therefore, *reversed* for the additional reason that tissue cultures are not "plants" within the purview of 35 U.S.C. 161. The Court of Customs and Patent Appeals in its decision in *In re Bergy*, 596 F.2d 952, 201 U.S.P.Q. 352 (C.C.P.A. 1979), *vacated as moot sub nom. Diamond v. Chakrabarty, supra*, interpreted the meaning and scope of the term "plant" in the PPA as having its common, ordinary meaning which is limited to those things having roots, stems, leaves and flowers or fruits. In our view, tissue cultures manifestly do not come within the noted "common, ordinary meaning" of the term "plants" and are, therefore, not within the scope of the PPA (35 U.S.C. 161).

NOTE

The court states that "the examiner's rejection in the final analysis is based on an *implied* narrowing of § 101, i.e., an implied partial repeal of Section 101 based on the passage of the plant-specific Acts." The opinion then goes on to discuss the cases holding that such "partial repeals" are disfavored.

One problem with this analysis is that it *assumes* that § 101 extended to plant subject matter prior to enactment of the plant-specific statutes (the PPA and PVPA). Only if § 101 already included this subject matter could these statutes be characterized as "partial repeals." Check the precise language of the Patent Office's brief cited in the case; does it make this assumption as well? Is the argument that these acts "implicitly excluded" plant subject matter tantamount to an argument that they "implicitly repealed" a portion of § 101's preexisting coverage?

The Board's opinion might be analyzed as follows. First, it assumes that § 101 included plant subject matter prior to the enactment of the plant-specific statutes. Second, it notes that to repeal a statute, in whole or part, Congress must be very clear about its purpose. Third, it states that no such clear statement of purpose can be found in connection with the plant-specific statutes. And fourth, it concludes that because plants were patentable before the plant-specific acts, and those acts did not explicitly make them unpatentable, plants must still be patentable — above and beyond the fact that they are also covered by the plant-specific acts. On this analysis, the Board has engaged in a form of argumentation known as begging the question (*petitio principii*). One source, describing this argumentative fallacy, states: "In an inquiry, the premises must be better established or known than the conclusion to be proved. Otherwise, the inquiry makes no progress." D. WALTON, INFORMAL LOGIC 54 (1989). One key premise of the Board's opinion is that § 101 already included plants prior to the enactment of the plant-specific statutes. Is this the conclusion towards which the Board is arguing? If this is in fact a premise of the Board's opinion, is it supportable? What sources would you consult to determine whether Congress in fact considered plants already patentable prior to the enactment of the plant-specific acts? Even if Congress made this assumption, is this dispositive of the question whether § 101 included plant subject matter at that time? Is the dictum from the Supreme Court in the 1980 *Chakrabarty* case ("anything under the sun that is made by man") dispositive of this issue?

a. The UPOV Treaty and the United States

> In 1961, the International Union for the Protection of New Varieties of Plants (UPOV) ... was instituted by a number of countries, principally European ones, to provide protection to seed plant varieties. The technology of plant breeding had developed sufficiently between 1930 and 1970 that there was a generalized perception that new sexually reproduced varieties could be replicated true-to-type in a way that was not thought possible in 1930. Sexually reproduced varieties are non-hybrid varieties or cultivars of plants that, for practical purposes, breed true-to-form when self-pollinated.

Seay, *Protecting the Seeds of Innovation: Patenting Plants*, 16 AM. INTELL. PROP. L. ASS'N Q.J. 418 (1989).

The U.S. version of the Union for the Protection of Plant Varieties (UPOV) contains its basic features: limited protection for sexually reproduced plants; a scaled-down "enablement" or description requirement; a "farmer's exemption," permitting farmers to save seed from a protected variety and plant it; and an exemption from infringement liability for experimentation using a protected variety. *See* International Convention for the Protection of New Varieties of Plants of 2 Dec. 1961, 815 U.N.T.S. 89; codified in U.S. as Plant Variety Protection Act of 1970, 7 U.S.C. §§ 2421 et seq. (1988). The U.S., however, joined the UPOV Convention (i.e., acceded to the Treaty) under a reservation made possible by a 1978 amendment to the Convention. The reservation stated that the U.S. would not adhere to Article 2(1) of the Convention, which makes breeder's rights the exclusive form of protection for any single "genus or species."

An important point under the U.S. PVPA was settled by the Supreme Court in *Asgrow Seed Co. v. Winterboer*, __ U.S. __, 115 S. Ct. 788 (1995). Under 7 U.S.C. § 2541(1), it is a violation for anyone other than the PVPA certificate holder to sell or offer to sell the seed, and, under § 2541(3), to "sexually multiply the novel varieties as a step in marketing [them] (for growing purposes)." A certificate holder brought suit against an alleged infringer, who defended on the ground of the statutory exemption from liability under § 2543, which provides in relevant part that "[e]xcept to the extent that such action may constitute an infringement under [§ 2541(3)]," a farmer may "save seed ... and use such saved seed in the production of a crop for use on his farm, or for sale as provided in this section," subject to the proviso that such saved seed can be sold for reproductive purposes only where both buyer and seller are farmers "whose primary farming occupation is the growing of crops for sale for other than reproductive purposes." The Court held that a farmer who meets the requirements set forth in § 2543's proviso may sell for reproductive purposes only such seed as he has saved for the purpose of replanting his own acreage. This ended a practice known as "brown bagging," which had been approved by prior interpretations of § 2543, under which farmers could sell as seed up to half of every crop produced from PVPA-protected seed, so long as they sold the other half for food or feed.

b. The UPOV Treaty in Europe

In Europe, an extra prohibition on "double protection" is in place: Article 53(b) of the European Patent Convention (EPC), which states that "European patents shall not be granted in respect of plant or animal varieties or essentially biological processes." There is an explicit reservation, however, for "microbiological processes or the products thereof." Likewise, until very recently the European countries had not taken advantage of the UPOV provision making it possible for a country to grant "double protection" for plant varieties.

Largely out of a concern that UPOV-type protection is not enough of an incentive to propel investment in plant biotechnology (because of the limited nature of the protection; see above), European commentators argued strenuously that Article 53(b) and the UPOV Convention itself should not prevent the issuance of utility patents (i.e., regular patents, as opposed to special plant protection) in this area. *See, e.g.*, Straus, *AIPPI and the Protection of Inventions in Plants — Past Developments, Future Perspectives*, 20 INT'L REV. IND. PROP. & COPYRIGHT L. 600, 614 (1989) (UPOV not enough protection to encourage biotech-related R&D in plants); Straus, *Patent Protection for New Varieties of Plants: Should "Double Patenting" Be Prohibited?*, 17 INT'L REV. IND. PROP. & COPYRIGHT L. 195 (1986). *But see* Greengrass, *UPOV and the Protection of Inventions in Plants — Past Developments, Future Perspectives*, 20 INT'L REV. IND. PROP. & COPYRIGHT L. 622 (1989) (written by UPOV official, arguing that "double protection" is unnecessary and will undermine UPOV). These arguments culminated in the recent adoption of a revised UPOV in Europe, which now explicitly permits "double protection" for plant varieties. See Nott, *Patent Protection for Plants and Animals,* [1992] EUR. INTELL. PROP. REV. 79.

NOTES

1. Plants have always been an important medical and economic resource. Consider the following:

There are about 121 clinically useful prescription drugs worldwide that are derived from higher plants. About 74% of them came to the attention of pharmaceutical houses because of their use in traditional medicine. Among the drugs derived from plants are the anticancer agents vinblastine and vincristine. Morphine, codeine, quinine, atropine, and digitalis come from plants.... In 1985, worldwide, a total of 3500 new chemical structures were discovered. Some 2619 of the chemicals were isolated from higher plants.

Philip Abelson, *Medicine From Plants (Editorial)*, 247 SCI. 513 (2 Feb. 1990). *See also* Constance Holden, *Entomologists Wane as Insects Wax*, 246 SCI. 754 (10 Nov. 1989) (Thomas Eisner of Cornell, an entomologist, notes that "many medically and economically important substances are derived from plants and microorganisms, the traditional sources of antibiotics and other drugs," and that " 'biological impoverishment is tantamount to chemical impoverishment,' [and] has been pressing for an activity he calls 'chemical prospecting,' " primarily in the tropics). Indeed, much of the diplomatic wrangling surrounding the 1992 Ecological Summit in Rio de Janeiro centered on whether some form of property rights should be granted for tropical plants found to have medical or other uses. *See* Merges, Patents and the Rainforest: Preservation Through Property Rights (working paper 1993).

2. There is no question that intellectual property rights have affected the growth and structure of the seed industry. One recent article observes:

[Since *Chakrabarty*,] "[n]umerous companies have ... filed patent applications that cover the genes, the processes of isolating the genes, and making the genetically modified plants and seeds themselves.. ... Although no one disputes that companies that have invested heavily in R&D to isolate, test, and commercialize genes are entitled to protection for their inventions, there is considerable debate within the seed industry concerning how much protection is deserved and what impact patents will have on the cooperative nature of the seed industry itself."

C.S. Gasser & R.T. Fraley, *Genetically Engineering Plants for Crop Improvement*, 244 SCI. 1293 (16 June 1989). The authors note that before the passage of the Plant Variety Protection Act in 1970, three companies sold commercial soybean seeds; now there are "more than 40." *Id. See also* W. LESSER & R. MASSON, AN ECONOMIC ANALYSIS OF THE PLANT VARIETY PROTECTION ACT 123 (1985) (summarizing positive stimulus to industry from PVPA); Evenson, *Intellectual Property Rights and Agribusiness Research and Development: Implications for the Public Agricultural Research System*, 65 AM. J. AGRIC. ECON. 967 (1983) (same). A good case can be made that the expanded coverage of the conventional patent act (as opposed to the American version of the UPOV convention, the PVPA), will further spur plant-related research in this country. *See* Lesser, *Patenting Seeds in the United States of America: What to Expect*, INDUS. PROP., Sept. 1986, at 360. There is an inevitable cost, however: more

litigation. *See, e.g.*, A. Hagedorn, *Suits Sprout Over Rights to Seeds*, WALL ST.
J., Mar. 5, 1990, at B1 col. 3, B8 cols. 1-2 (describing suit under U.S. Plant
Variety Protection Act (PVPA) over "Napolean" celery variety: "With companies
spending millions of dollars yearly on biotechnology to create novel seed
varieties, the costs of losing the seeds to competitors are greater than ever."). For
an example of a recent patent (not PVPA certificate) in a plant-related technology, see Edmund L. Andrews, *Patents: Creating New Tomatoes in Test Tube
Procedure*, N.Y. TIMES, Oct. 2, 1989, at 32, cols. 2-3 (description of U.S.
patent 4,863,863, issued to researchers from DNA Plant Technologies, Inc. on
tomatoes produced by protoplast fusion, a form of test-tube "mating" that creates
hybrid plants in the laboratory). *See generally* Barton, *The International Breeders
Rights System and Crop Plant Improvement*, 216 SCI. 1071 (4 June 1982).

3. Critics of intellectual property rights in the agriculture sector contend that
they help accelerate undesirable trends such as centralization and the loss of
economic power by small farmers. *See, e.g.*, J. KLOPPENBURG, FIRST THE
SEED: THE POLITICAL ECONOMY OF PLANT BIOTECHNOLOGY (1988). Kloppenburg notes that there was a great controversy in the agriculture world when
in 1956 a researcher received a patent for hybrid plant breeding techniques. *Id.*,
at 113. He uses this as an example of a long-standing rift between the open and
public-minded nature of federally-funded agriculture research and the orientation
toward private gain of private commercial researchers in this sector, whose growing prominence he says contributes to "the commodification of the seed." *Id.*, at
282-84. His general thrust, echoed by others, is that agriculture is a special
industry which is not always well-served by competition among private interests.

4. Recall the excerpts from the *Chakrabarty* case and the book by Robert
Nozick at the beginning of this chapter. What is the difference between what is
protected by patents (and by the UPOV) and the protection of "discovered" plants
alluded to in the excerpts? What arguments could you make that no special
incentives are needed to discover plants, as opposed to the creation of plant-
related "inventions" protectible under the Patent Act and the UPOV? Even if
"discovered" plants were given some sort of protection, does that mean that all
work on plant-related inventions would cease? *See* J. Brodovsky, *The Mexican
Pharmochemical and Pharmaceutical Industries*, in THE UNITED STATES AND
MEXICO: FACE TO FACE WITH NEW TECHNOLOGY 198 (C. Thorup ed. 1987)
(Mexican monopoly on barbasco, a plant which was a good source for making
steroids, ended when purchasers developed alternative supply sources after Mexican government imposed higher price for barbasco).

5. Some countries have asserted that they "own" the genetic material from
plants that grow inside their borders. Many are poor countries from tropical
regions where a great variety of plant species grow. These countries insist that
companies from developed countries pay "royalties" for the right to remove
genetic material for research or the development of new products. *See* M.
Simons, *Poor Nations Seeking Rewards for Contributions to Plant Species*, N.Y.

TIMES, May 16, 1989, at 4, col. 4. Is this a form of intellectual property? Could the U.S. government make such a claim?

Some have contended that for humans to assert any "ownership" over inventions derived essentially from nature is sheer hubris. *See* Kass, *Patenting Life*, 63 J. PAT. OFF. SOC'Y 571, 599 (1981). The standard reply is to point out that incentives are needed to induce people to perform research in this socially valuable field. *Cf.* Comment, *In His Image: On Patenting Human-Based Bioproducts*, 25 U.S.F. L. REV. 583 (1991). *Cf.* DAVID F. CHANNELL, THE VITAL MACHINE: A STUDY OF TECHNOLOGY AND ORGANIC LIFE (1992) (describing breakdown of the distinction between artificial and natural, alive and inert). An interesting middle ground is suggested in the following excerpt, which, like the excerpt from Nozick above, is drawn from a longer discussion of the extent to which property rights ought to be based on how hard someone works to create something — i.e., on a "labor" theory of intellectual property.

> [A]ssuming that labor's fruits are valuable, and that laboring gives the laborer a property right in this value, this would entitle the laborer only to the value she added, and not to the *total* value of the resulting product. Though exceedingly difficult to measure, these two components of value (that attributable to the object labored on and that attributable to the labor) need to be distinguished.

Hettinger, *Justifying Intellectual Property*, 18 PHIL. & PUB. AFF. 31, 37 (1989). Imagine that a company from a developed country "prospects" for genetic material in a poor tropical country, takes some plant specimens back to the lab, and inserts a gene from the "prospected" material into an ordinary domestic plant, thereby producing a very valuable new plant. According to the approach taken in the excerpt, how should the rights be allocated between (1) the poor country's government, which claims ownership of the raw genetic material, and (2) the company that developed the new plant? How would one determine the "value added" by the company's researchers as opposed to the value contributed by the original genetic material? In some ways, this problem is similar to certain issues that arise in determining damages for patent infringement. See Chapter 11.

6. The notion of granting intellectual property rights over the genetic material in native species may seem strange to some, but it might actually serve two purposes. In addition to more fairly distributing the gains from recombinant genetic products based on those species, it would also give developing countries an incentive to protect rainforests and other genetically rich areas. In general, the granting of property rights over a resource can be expected to lead to more efficient use of the resource; at the very least, it will prevent over-exploitation of the resource due to its free (or "public good") quality. *See, e.g.*, H. Demsetz, *Toward a Theory of Property Rights*, in OWNERSHIP, CONTROL, AND THE FIRM 104 (1988); Charles, *Fishery Socioeconomics: A Survey*, 64 LAND ECON. 276, 279-80 (1988) (describing allocation of fish catches via property rights). *See generally* MERGES, PATENTS AND THE RAINFOREST, *supra*.

3. ANIMALS

Ex parte ALLEN

2 U.S.P.Q.2d (BNA) 1425 (Bd. Pat. App. & Int. 1987)

This is an appeal from the rejection of claims 8, 12, 13 and 14. Claims 1 through 7 and 9 through 11 have been allowed.

The subject matter on appeal relates to polyploid oysters. The four rejected claims are product-by-process claims. They read as follows:

8. Polyploid Pacific oysters produced by the method of claim 1.

12. Polyploid Pacific oysters produced by the method of claim 9.

13. The Pacific oysters of claim 8 belonging to the species *Crassostrea gigas*.

14. The Pacific oysters of claim 12 belonging to the species *Crassostrea gigas*.

The rejected claims are dependent on allowed claims drawn to a method of inducing polyploidy in oysters utilizing hydrostatic pressure which read as follows [bracketed elements inserted]:

1. A method of inducing polyploidy in oysters, comprising: [a] separating oysters from one another such that male oysters are isolated from female oysters; [b] inducing said oysters to spawn; [c] controlling the temperature of eggs from said oysters; [d] fertilizing said eggs with sperm to form zygotes; [e] applying hydrostatic pressure to said zygotes at a predetermined intensity for a predetermined duration after a predetermined time following formation of said zygotes to induce polyploidy; and [f] cultivating said polyploid zygotes.

....

9. A method of inducing polyploidy in oysters, comprising: [a] separating oysters from one another such that male oysters are isolated from female oysters; [b] inducing said oysters to spawn; [c] controlling the temperature of eggs from said oysters at approximately 25° C; [d] fertilizing said eggs with sperm to form zygotes; [e] applying hydrostatic pressure of approximately 6000 to 10,000 psi for a predetermined duration approximately 15 minutes after fertilization to said zygotes to induce polyploidy; and [f] cultivating said polyploid zygotes.

The reference of record relied on by the examiner is: Stanley et al., "Growth of American Oysters Increased by Polyploidy Induced by Blocking Meiosis I But Not Meiosis II," *Aquaculture*, 37 (1984), pages 147-155.

Claims 8 and 12 through 14 are rejected for obviousness under 35 U.S.C. 103 in view of Stanley et al. and are also rejected under 35 U.S.C. 101 on the ground that the claimed invention is directed to nonstatutory subject matter.

In support of his rejection under 35 U.S.C. 101, the examiner states that polyploid oysters are held to be living entities and do not fall within the statutory subject matter of 35 U.S.C. 101. The examiner adds that the animal produced by the method claimed is "controlled by laws of nature and not a manufacture by man that is patentable." The examiner also relies on *In re Merat*, 519 F.2d 1390, 186 U.S.P.Q. 471 (C.C.P.A. 1975) and *In re Bergy*, 563 F.2d 1031, 195 U.S.P.Q. 344 (C.C.P.A. 1977) in support of his position. In its 1975 decision in *Merat* the Court affirmed a rejection under 35 U.S.C. 112 and did not reach the 35 U.S.C. 101 rejection made by the examiner and affirmed by the Board of Appeals. Although the Court reversed a 35 U.S.C. 101 rejection in *Bergy* and held that living microorganisms were within the terms "manufacture" and "composition of matter" in § 101, the examiner notes that the Court in its opinion categorized the claimed microorganisms as "more akin to inanimate chemical compositions such as reactants, reagents, and catalysts than they are to horses and honeybees or raspberries and roses."

We shall not sustain this rejection.

The examiner's position that the claimed polyploid oysters are "held to be living entities" is not controlling on the question of whether the claims are drawn to patentable subject matter under 35 U.S.C. 101 because the Supreme Court made it clear in its decision in *Diamond v. Chakrabarty, supra*, that Section 101 includes man-made life forms. The issue, in our view, in determining whether the claimed subject matter is patentable under Section 101 is simply whether that subject matter is made by man. If the claimed subject matter occurs naturally, it is not patentable subject matter under Section 101. The fact, as urged by the examiner, that the oysters produced by the claimed method are "controlled by the laws of nature" does not address the issue of whether the subject matter is a non-naturally occurring manufacture or composition of matter. The examiner has presented no evidence that the claimed polyploid oysters occur naturally without the intervention of man, nor has the examiner urged that polyploid oysters occur naturally. The record before us leads to no conclusion other than that the claimed polyploid oysters are non-naturally occurring manufactures or compositions of matter within the confines of patentable subject matter under 35 U.S.C. 101. Accordingly, the rejection under Section 101 must be reversed.

[T]he examiner's position [does not] find any support in the *Bergy* decision. The holding in *Bergy* that the fact that the claimed culture was alive did not remove it from the categories of invention enumerated in § 101 is consistent with *Chakrabarty*. The Court in *Bergy* made clear that it was only deciding the case before it and was not "deciding whether living things in general, or, at most, whether any living things other than microorganisms, are within § 101." More-over, the decision by the Supreme Court in *Chakrabarty* is controlling authority that Congress intended statutory subject matter to "include anything under the sun that is made by man."

With respect to the rejection under 35 U.S.C. 103 we have carefully consid-ered the respective positions of the examiner and the appellants and the declara-tion of co-inventor Allen, who is also a co-author of the Stanley et al. reference relied on by the examiner in support of the rejection. We have decided that we will affirm this rejection.

We agree with the examiner that in view of the express recommendation by Stanley et al., experts in the art who have successfully induced polyploidy in one species of oysters, it would have been obvious to one of ordinary skill in the art to induce polyploidy in Pacific *Crassostrea gigas* oysters. Moreover, one of ordinary skill in the art would have a reasonable expectation that the Stanley et al. method would be successful in inducing polyploidy in *Crassostrea gigas* oysters based on the success by Stanley et al. with *Crassostrea virginica* oysters and the recommendation by Stanley et al. to utilize the method with cultured oysters. [T]he examiner has correctly adduced a prima facie case of obviousness for the claimed polyploid oysters, and the burden shifted to appellants to rebut the prima facie obviousness. In our view appellants have not done so. The decision of the examiner is affirmed.

NOTES

From *Louis Pasteur's Patents*, SCI., Oct. 8, 1937:

> Pasteur's inventions relating to the production of beer were patented in at least France, England, Italy and the U.S. In the U.S., two patents were obtained, No. 135,245 for "improvements in the process of making beer," granted on January 28, 1873, and No. 141,072 for "improvements in the manufacture and in the treatment of yeast and wort, together with apparatus for the same," granted on July 22, 1873. The '245 patent recites a method for eliminating air from the vessel containing the malt in beer making, and cooling the malt by cooling the entire vessel with water.
>
> The second patent is directed to the production of pure yeast, free from "organic germs of disease." The patent also describes a method and an apparatus for brewing beer with the pure yeast.... The second claim, which reads, "Yeast, free from organic germs of disease, as an article of manufacture," is unique in patents, in respect to its subject-matter. A claim of this type would now probably be refused by the examiner, since it is doubted that the subject matter is capable of being patented.

a. The Ethical Debate Over Animal Patents

Animal Legal Defense Fund v. Quigg, 932 F.2d 920, 18 U.S.P.Q.2d (BNA) 1677 (Fed. Cir. 1991). This is an appeal from the order of the District Court for the Northern District of California (Smith, J.) granting defendants' motion to dismiss the complaint ... for failure to state a claim under the Administrative Procedure Act (APA). Various plaintiffs, individual farmers and groups of animal husbanders or nonprofit organizations whose goal is the protection of animals, filed suit in district court under the APA challenging, on procedural and substantive grounds, a Notice issued by the Department of Commerce Patent and

Trademark Office (PTO) which stated, inter alia, that the PTO "now considers non-naturally occurring, non-human multicellular organisms, including animals, to be patentable subject matter within the scope of 35 U.S.C. § 101."

[The court reviews the requirements for standing.]

Here appellants assert no adverse effect on any individual's rights to benefits under the patent statute. Rather, they assert that the general public has an interest in the statutory limitations to patentability. Essentially, appellants assert a right, as members of the public particularly interested in animals, to sue for what they perceive to be an unwarranted interference with the discretionary judgment of an examiner. However, it must be noted that whether patents are allowable for animal life forms is not a matter of discretion but of law....

As previously indicated, the farmers' alleged injuries are (1) having to pay increased costs in the form of royalties on patented animals and (2) suffering decreased profits because of competition from more productive non-naturally occurring animals. With respect to the alleged "royalties" injury, farmers cannot be forced to purchase improved animals and pay the premium (i.e., "royalty") which the farmers say is likely to be asked. Indeed, their allegation that their costs of operation will increase by reason of "royalties" is at best speculative. The motivation to purchase normally arises from the prospect of an economic advantage. Further, the ability of a market participant to affect price, i.e., exert market power, depends on whether competitive patented or non-patented animals are available. This in turn depends on the speculative activities of third party competitors whose market actions would determine the existence and extent of acceptable, noninfringing substitutes in the relevant product market.... Such speculation as to market actors and their activities further beclouds the issue of causation as it concerns the farmers' alleged economic injury. [Affirmed.]

NOTES

1. Questions regarding the impact of patents on a particular industry, the economy, or even society as a whole are not generally dealt with when "patentability" under 35 U.S.C. § 101 is the issue. *See, e.g.,* Markey, *Patentability of Animals in the United States,* 20 INT'L REV. INDUS. PROP. & COPYRIGHT L. 372 (1989). Advocates of "technology assessment," however, would like to change what they view as the overly "narrow" approach to such issues. *See, e.g.,* H. HAZEL, CREATING ALTERNATIVE FUTURES (1978); T. ROSZAK, THE CULT OF INFORMATION (1986); L. WINNER, AUTONOMOUS TECHNOLOGY (1977).

Patent law is not wholly devoid of any discussion of the impact of the technologies it aims to foster. The best example will be seen in Chapter 3, on the requirement of Utility. This has been interpreted in some cases as calling for an assessment of whether the "useful" properties of a technology outweigh its potential for harmful effects. *See, e.g.,* Merges, *Intellectual Property in Higher*

Life Forms: The Patent System and Controversial Technologies, 47 MD. L. REV. 1051, 1062-68 (1988).

2. On attempts to curb animal patents via legislation, see *New Bill Would Impose Five Year Ban on Animal Patenting*, 39 PAT. TRADEMARK & COPYRIGHT J. (BNA) 339 (1990).

3. For an example of a recent patent on animal-related technology, see Edmund L. Andrews, *Patents: Producing Hormones in Farm Animals*, N.Y. TIMES, Sept. 30, 1989, at 32, cols. 2-3 (describing U.S. patent 4,870,009, a method of producing human hormones by inserting human genes into animals and inducing the animals to express the hormones in collectible form).

b. Animal Patents in Europe

Article 53 of the European Patent Convention (EPC) prohibits the patenting of plant or animal "varieties." Many have argued in recent years for a narrow interpretation of the term "varieties" to encourage utility patents for plant- and animal-related subject matter. *See* Waite & Jones, *Biotechnological Patents in Europe — The Draft Directive*, 5 EUR. INTELL. PROP. REV. 145 (1989) (summarizing Draft Directive of European Community concluding that Article 53 means only breeding-related "biological" inventions; microbiology products are therefore patentable); Moufang, *Patentability of Genetic Engineering in Animals*, 20 INT'L REV. INDUS. PROP. & COPYRIGHT L. 823, 834 (1989) ("varieties" in Article 53 should be narrowly construed; for example, where a gene can be transferred to a large number of animals, it should be patentable, since this is not a "variety").

The policy behind EPC Article 53 was put to the test recently in a celebrated case. Doctors Phillip Leder and Timothy Stewart of the Harvard Medical School received a U.S. patent for their successful work involving transgenic mice. They isolated a gene which is associated with cancer in mammals (including humans) and then injected the gene into a fertilized mouse egg, which yielded transgenic mice that are extremely sensitive to carcinogens. *See* U.S. Patent No. 4,736,866, issued April 12, 1988. This makes the mice excellent animal "models" for studying cancer drugs. Leder and Stewart claimed not only the technique they had used, or the particular transgenic mice variety they had created, but rather all "non-human transgenic mammals" produced by their technique.

The European Patent Office cited both the animal variety provision of the EPC and the provision requiring full enablement of claims (see Chapter 6) when it rejected those claims in the Leder and Stuart patent that went beyond mice and rodents. *See* European Patent Office, *In re President and Fellows of Harvard College, "Onco-Mouse" case*, July 14, 1989, *reported in* 20 INT'L REV. INDUS. PROP. & COPYRIGHT L. 889, 895-96 (1989). This aspect of the decision was reversed in the European Patent Office's Technical Board of Appeal, but the Board remanded for specific findings on the patentability of animals, including the problems of environmental risk and animal suffering. *In re President and*

Fellows of Harvard College (Eur. Pat. Off. Tech. Bd. of App., Case No. T19/90), rep. at 22 INT'L REV. INDUS. PROP. & COPYRIGHT L. 74, 84 (1991). On remand, the European Patent Office found that the Harvard Mouse was patentable. *See* decision of the European Patent Office, reported in *Harvard Mouse Patent to Be Issued*, 22 INT'L REV. INDUS. PROP. & COPYRIGHT L. 839 (1991). Several oppositions followed, but the patent is expected to issue eventually. Professor Leder, incidentally, has invented an even better mouse, and the world is no doubt beating a path to his door. *See* U.S. Patent 5,175,383, "Animal Model for Benign Prostatic Disease."

4. MEDICAL PROCEDURES

In a legislative development that surprised almost everyone, Congress in 1996 passed — and the President signed — a late-night amendment to the Patent Act that was tucked into a complex appropriations bill. *See Bill With PTO Funding and Patent Reform on Medical Procedures Is Signed into Law*, 52 PAT. TRADEMARK & COPYRIGHT J. (BNA) 597 (Oct. 3, 1996). The new legislation takes away essentially all remedies from owners of medical procedure patents granted after September 30, 1996, in suits these owners bring against "medical practitioners." The text of new section 287(c) of 35 U.S.C. is as follows:

(c)(1) With respect to a medical practitioner's performance of a medical activity that constitutes an infringement under section 271 (a) or (b) of this title, the provisions of sections 281, 283, 284, and 285 of this title shall not apply against the medical practitioner or against a related health care entity with respect to such medical activity.

(2) This subsection does not apply to the activities of any person, or employee or agent of such person (regardless of whether such person is a tax exempt organization under section 501(c) of the Internal Revenue Code of 1986), who is engaged in the commercial development, manufacture, sale, importation, or distribution of a machine, manufacture, or composition of matter or the provision of pharmacy or clinical laboratory services (other than laboratory services provided in a physician's office), if such activities are —

(A) directly related to the commercial development, manufacture, sale, importation, or distribution of a machine, manufacture, or composition of matter or the provision of pharmacy or clinical laboratory services (other than clinical laboratory services provided in a physician's office); and

(B) regulated under the Federal Food, Drug, and Cosmetic Act, the Public Health Service Act, or the Clinical Laboratories Improvement Act.

(3) For purposes of this subsection:

(A) The term "body" means —

(i) a human body, organ, or cadaver; or

(ii) a nonhuman animal used in medical research or instruction directly relating to the treatment of humans.

(B) The term "medical activity" means the performance of a medical or surgical procedure on a body, but shall not include —

(i) the use of a patented machine, manufacture, or composition of matter in violation of such patent;

(ii) the practice of a patented use of a composition of matter in violation of such patent; or

(iii) the practice of a process in violation of a biotechnology patent.

(C) The term "medical practitioner" means any natural person who is —

(i) licensed by a State to provide the medical activity described under paragraph (1); or

(ii) acting under the direction of such natural person in the performance of the medical activity.

(D) The term "patented use of a composition of matter" does not include a claim for a method of performing a medical or surgical procedure on a body that recites the use of a composition of matter if the use of that composition of matter does not directly contribute to achievement of the objective of the claimed method.

(E) The term "professional affiliation" means staff privileges, medical staff membership, employment or contractual relationship, partnership or ownership interest, academic appointment, or other affiliation under which a medical practitioner provides a medical activity on behalf of, or in association with, a health care entity.

(F) The term "related health care entity" —

(i) means an entity with which a medical practitioner has a professional affiliation under which the medical practitioner performs a medical activity; and

(ii) includes without limitation such an affiliation with a nursing home, hospital, university, medical school, health maintenance organization, group medical practice, or a medical clinic.

(G) The term "State" means any State or territory of the United States, the District of Columbia, and the Commonwealth of Puerto Rico.

(4) This subsection shall not apply to any patent issued before the date of enactment of this subsection.

In statements made during the long session in which the Senate version of the amendment was passed, Senator Hatch, Chairman of the Senate Subcommittee on Patents, Copyrights and Trademarks, reiterated his opposition and voiced a commitment to reviewing the legislation at the first opportunity. *See* 142 CONG. REC. S. 11838, S. 11843 (Sept. 30, 1996) (statements of Sen. Hatch) ("This measure was added notwithstanding the fact that there were no Senate hearings, and over the objections of myself, the chairman of the Finance Committee and the U.S. Trade Representative. It is an unprecedented change to our patent code and it is my intention to closely scrutinize the implementation of this new law.... The provision would functionally eliminate the patenting of medical procedures."). Is Senator Hatch correct when he states that eliminating the remedies of 35 U.S.C. § 283 et seq. in suits against doctors and other medical practitioners "functionally eliminate[s]" medical procedure patents? What other classes of infringers are left? Note the amendment's *anti-researcher* exemption: commercial researchers are explicitly excluded from the no-remedies safe harbor the amendment creates. This may set a dangerous precedent in itself; many believe that a robust "research exemption" is needed to encourage R&D in fields where patents are present. *See* Chapter 8, *infra*.

NOTES

1.   The case of *Pallin v. Singer*, 36 U.S.P.Q.2d 1050 (D. Vt. 1995) demonstrates that medical procedure patents are becoming more widespread despite whatever doctrine *Morton* may have spawned. Although the opinion just cited in the *Pallin* case merely denied a summary judgment motion in a patent infringement suit, and even though the parties later stipulated to the patent's invalidity due to prior art uses of the claimed technique (see *Pallin v. Singer*, Consent Order, Mar. 28, 1996 (D. Vt. 1996), reported at 1996 WL 274407 (D. Vt.)), the case is noteworthy because no § 101 issue was raised, at least in the published opinions. It might be argued, therefore, that the case represents a tacit acceptance of the patentability of this subject matter. This is significant, because the patent at issue, granted to plaintiff Samuel Pallin (U.S. patent 5,080,111, "Method of Making Self-Sealing Episcleral Incision") covers a new way to make incisions in eye (primarily cataract) surgery — i.e., it is a clear example of a medical procedure patent. See Figure 2-7 below, which shows the shape of the incisions to be cut in the eye (labeled 18 in the Figure) according to the claimed technique.

The *Pallin* case was instrumental in the adoption of the amendments to 35 U.S.C. § 287 set forth at the beginning of this section.

2. The press has shown a steady interest in medical procedure patents. *See* Sabra Chartrand, *A Detection Method for Breast Tumors May Add Fire to a Debate Over Patents for Medical Procedures*, N.Y. TIMES, Jan. 30, 1995, at D2 (Professor Michael DeGregorio, inventor of U.S. Patent No. 5,384,260 (1995), a method of detecting breast cancer tumors that develop a resistance to Tamoxifen, expressed concern over the patenting of therapeutic methods, but was obligated to pursue the patent and assign the patent rights to Yale University.); Edward Felsenthal, *Medical Patents Trigger Debate Among Doctors*, WALL ST. J., Aug. 11, 1994, at B1; Lauran Neergaard, *Move to Patent Surgical Procedure Sparks Fight Royalties: Doctors Say Controlling the Way They Practice Medicine in Such a Way Is Unethical and Drives Up Health Care Costs*, L.A. TIMES, Apr. 2, 1995, at A14. For a good overview, see William D. Noonan, *Patenting Medical and Surgical Procedures*, 77 J. PAT. & TRADEMARK OFF. SOC'Y 651 (1995).

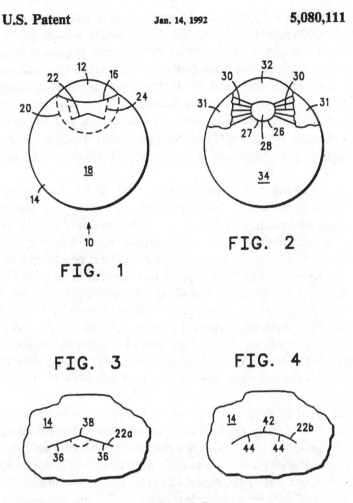

U.S. Patent   Jan. 14, 1992   5,080,111

Figure 2-7

3. For a very perceptive comment on an earlier version of this legislation, which concludes with a call for the centralized administration of medical procedure patents by clearinghouse organizations, to which physicians would be compelled to assign their medical procedure patents, see Joseph M. Reisman, *Physicians and Surgeons as Inventors: Reconciling Medical Process Patents and Medical Ethics*, 10 HIGH TECH. L.J. 355, 397-98 (1995):

> [T]he current debate over the patentability of medical processes and the ethical and conflict-of-interest objections raised by these patents are, by and large, merely objections to the ownership and enforcement of patents by practicing physicians. A mandatory assignment system limited to physician-inventors, therefore, could resolve much of the current debate. Such a mandatory assignment system, in which incentives to invent coexisted with safeguards against the violation of ethical norms, can be easily envisioned.

Organizations subject to the governance of a significant portion of the medical community (much like the AMA) could manage patent clearinghouses for the rights of otherwise independent physician-inventors. To ensure that all physicians participated in a clearinghouse, each organization would have to be approved by various state medical licensing boards. Furthermore, as a requirement to licensure, every physician would be required to assign any patent rights to one of the several state-approved clearinghouses. A university-affiliated physician would have the option of assigning her patent rights to the university, if it had been approved by the state.

Certain uniform rules would apply to all of the clearinghouses. Each would be required to offer all of its rights as a package to medical centers throughout the country. While each could employ different formulas to determine licensing rates, those rates would reflect only the size, location, or specialty of a potential licensee medical center, not the number of times a specific invention has been used by that hospital in the past. Meanwhile, member physician-inventors would be reimbursed on a per-use basis, and only medical records containing no identifiable information about individual patients (e.g., physicians' medical malpractice insurance records or hospitals' operating room logs) would be used to confirm the number of times a specific product or process was used. In this way, the invasions of patients' rights to privacy that most often result from enforcement of a patent could be avoided.

However, the details of each clearinghouse's licensing and enforcement scheme could be left to the individual organizations. For example, universities likely would simply retain their present technology transfer offices, but other organizations could look to their membership to strike an appropriate balance between profits and generosity. This variety would allow each physician to select an appropriate clearinghouse for his particular needs and desires. For example, if a physician wishes to license any future invention freely, he would select an appropriate clearinghouse. If, however, he wishes to recover research costs through patent rights, he could choose a clearinghouse with an appropriate licensing structure. Thus, by modeling their activities on existing technology transfer administrations, the proposed patent clearinghouses could become players in a dynamic market.

4. Compare Reisman's proposal with that in Note, *Ethical Considerations in the Patenting of Medical Processes*, 65 TEX. L. REV. 1139 (1987) ("The best way to balance the desires of medical researchers and investors on the one hand and the objections to medical process patents on the other is statutorily mandated universal licensing at a judicially determined fair price.").

5. Many foreign patent systems traditionally prohibit not only medical therapies and devices from being patented, but also pharmaceuticals. SCIENCE AND TECHNOLOGY: LESSONS FOR DEVELOPMENT POLICY (R. Evenson & G. Ranis eds.,

1990); J. Brodovsky, *The Mexican Pharmochemical and Pharmaceutical Industries*, in THE UNITED STATES AND MEXICO: FACE TO FACE WITH NEW TECHNOLOGY (C. Thorup ed., 1987). Even in Europe, under Article 54(2) of the European Patent Convention, no patents on medical processes are permitted. One policy behind this is that property rights should not prevent patients from having access to the very best medical treatment; humanitarian concerns, it is thought, "trump" the claims of a potential patentee.

In the United States, all inventions, including those related to medical devices and therapies, are treated equally under § 101; patents are not denied for "public health" reasons. However, courts do have broad discretion to consider the public interest when deciding whether to issue an injunction. In some cases courts have held that while an infringer must pay damages, the public interest in access to the invention outweighs the patentee's right to stop a competitor from producing the patented item. *See, e.g., Roche Prods., Inc. v. Bolar Pharmaceuticals, Inc.*, 733 F.2d 858 (Fed. Cir.), *cert. denied*, 469 U.S. 856, 865 (1984). *See also* Johnson, *Should Patents Preclude the Best Medical Treatment?*, TRIAL, March 1990, at 28, 31 (reviewing alternate view, that the nature of the invention is irrelevant to the issuance of an injunction); Evan Ackiron, Note, *Patents for Critical Pharmaceuticals: The AZT Case*, 17 AM. J.L. & MED. 145 (1991) (discussing various remedies in cases where critical drugs are subject to patent-related bottlenecks). See Chapter 9 for more on "public interest" issues in granting injunctions.

MORTON v. NEW YORK EYE INFIRMARY

17 F. Cas. 879 (C.C.S.D.N.Y. 1862)

[The court invalidated a patent on the method or process of anaesthetizing patients by administering ether in controlled dosages, primarily on the grounds that this was simply a new application of old knowledge about the effects of ether.]

Before dismissing this case, it may not be amiss to speak of the character of the discovery upon which the patent is founded. Its value in securing insensibility during the surgical operation, and thus saving the patient from sharp anguish while it is proceeding, and mitigating the shock to his system, which would otherwise be much greater, was proved on the trial by distinguished surgeons of the city of New York. They agreed in ranking it among the great discoveries of modern times; and one of them remarked that its value was too great to be estimated in dollars and cents. Its universal use, too, concurs to the same point. Its discoverer is entitled to be classed among the greatest benefactors of mankind. But the beneficent and imposing character of the discovery can not change the legal principles upon which the law of patents is founded .... [These principles] are inadequate to the protection of every discovery, by securing its exclusive control to the explorer to whose eye it may be first disclosed. A discovery may be brilliant and useful, and not patentable. No matter through what long, solitary vigils, or by what importunate efforts, the secret may have been wrung from the bosom of Nature, or to what useful purpose it may be applied. Something more is necessary. The new force or principle brought to light must be embodied and set to work, and can be patented only in connection or combination with the means by which, or the medium through which, it operates. Neither the natural functions of an animal upon which or through which it may be designed to operate, nor any of the useful purposes to which it may be applied, can form any essential parts of the combination, however they may illustrate and establish its usefulness. Motion for a new trial denied.

NOTES

1. The inventor/discoverer of controlled surgical uses of ether was not recognized with a patent, as the case shows. But he was enshrined on Boston's Public Garden, as Figure 2-8 (next page) shows. Morton was a Boston dentist who first discovered the usefulness of ether as an anesthetic when he used it on a patient while filling a tooth. See J.M. Fenster, *How Nobody Invented Anesthesia*, INVENTION & TECHNOLOGY, Summer 1996, at 24 (reviewing various claims to priority of invention).

2. When the court speaks of the "natural functions of an animal" as a factor which may *not* be considered in determining patentability, which "animal" is it referring to? Are there any special reasons to withhold patent protection for medical therapies that necessarily require human healing processes to operate effectively? Note that some doubt the existence of a general doctrine prohibiting medical procedure patents, and the widespread view that the *Morton* case originated such a doctrine. See William D. Noonan, *Patenting Medical and Surgical Procedures*, 77 J. PAT. & TRADEMARK OFF. SOC'Y 651, 658-61 (1995) (listing 48 selected medical process patents and maintaining that such patents are not a "recent phenomenon").

3. Oliver Wendell Holmes, Sr. coined the term "anaesthesia." See BLACK'S MEDICAL DICTIONARY 42 (W. Thompson ed., 34th ed. 1988).

Photograph by Beth Boyer

Dr. William T.G. Morton may have lost his patent suit, but the Boston dentist's work earned him a monument in the famous Boston Public Garden.

Figure 2-8

Chapter 3

UTILITY

A. INTRODUCTION

The Patent Act protects all inventions that are novel, *useful* and nonobvious. This chapter concentrates on the utility requirement.

At first glance it might seem as though this is a simple requirement to apply. After all, whether or not something is useful is normally easy to determine. In a sense patent law reflects this; utility is a relatively rare issue in the Patent Office, or defense by an accused infringer. But in another sense, there is more to it. Both conceptually and as borne out in the cases, some subtle issues lurk within the waters of utility.

Traditionally, utility has been thought to involve three major issues.

The first centers around whether an invention is operable or capable of any use. The inquiry here — called **general utility** — is whether the invention as claimed can really *do* anything. The second major issue is whether the invention works to solve the problem it is designed to solve. This **specific utility** requirement focuses on the operability of the invention to serve its intended purpose. The third issue, in some ways the most interesting, is called **beneficial utility**. It asks whether the intended purpose of the invention has some minimum social benefit, or whether it is completely harmful or deleterious. That is, if the invention does what it is supposed to, is it something that society wants done?

In modern practice, the first two issues usually arise in chemical cases and those involving biotechnology. Nevertheless, some understanding of general and specific utility outside these specialized contexts may be helpful.

In his landmark 1890 treatise, Professor William Robinson (then of Yale Law School, later Dean at the Catholic Law School) wrote that to be patentable, an invention must be more than "a mere curiosity, a scientific process exciting wonder yet not producing physical results, or [a] frivolous or trifling article or operation not aiding in the progress nor increasing the possession of the human race." 1 W. ROBINSON, TREATISE ON THE LAW OF PATENTS FOR USEFUL INVENTIONS 463 (1890).

In applying this approach, one might perhaps imagine a "machine" with working parts that did not really do anything; perhaps it just spins around, or oscillates back and forth for no particular purpose. Such a machine would fail the test of utility under § 101 of the Patent Act. Note that machines that serve only to amuse or entertain *are* deemed useful under the Patent Act. *See, e.g., Callison v. Dean*, 70 F.2d 55 (10th Cir. 1934) (upholding patent on "amusement devices of the type of aerial projectile targets with ball return ... particularly adapted for use with the amusement device ... in which a coin-controlled pistol may be caused to propel a ball to a target in which the balls, after striking the target, roll down an inclined plane into place to be loaded into the pistol ..."; "A device which may be used for innocent amusement possesses utility.").

Of course, a question that quickly springs to mind is why anyone would go through the bother and expense of applying for a patent when an invention has no apparent use. But one must keep in mind that inventors often suspect, but can't yet demonstrate, that a certain device has some real utility. While they are trying to verify their hunch, they sometimes file for a patent — to preserve priority, or beat out a competitor working on the same problem. Many utility cases arise this way.

Under the doctrine of specific utility, even if an invention is directed toward a certain function, it must actually perform that function. Otherwise it is not "useful" for achieving that function. A good example of this principle is the case of *Newman v. Quigg*, 877 F.2d 1575, 11 U.S.P.Q.2d (BNA) 1340 (Fed. Cir. 1989), where patent applicant Newman claimed an "Energy Generation System Having Higher Energy Output Than Input" — i.e., a "perpetual motion" machine. The Federal Circuit, in upholding the denial of Newman's patent, noted that the applicant had not rebutted data from tests performed by the National Bureau of Standards showing that, as feared, the device did not function perpetually. In short, it had no utility.

NOTES

1. *See also In re Perrigo*, 48 F.2d 965, 9 U.S.P.Q. (BNA) 152 (C.C.P.A. 1931) (affirming rejection of claims to "a method and apparatus for accumulating and transforming ether electric energy"); *Ex parte Heicklin*, 16 U.S.P.Q.2d (BNA) 1463 (Bd. Pat. App. & Interferences 1990) (incredible claims, here for method to retard the aging process, must be substantiated or a lack of utility rejection is appropriate).

2. In all cases except those involving drugs, the burden of proof is on the Patent Office to show that a claimed invention does not have utility. Only where there is a reasonable doubt as to the truth of the applicant's statements regarding utility does the burden shift to the applicant. *See In re Perrigo, supra.*

Where an applicant claims a drug or other therapeutic device, the Patent Office applies specific guidelines. *See* Examiner Guidelines for Biotech Applications, excerpted below following *In re Brana*.

3. In *Ex parte Cheeseborough*, 1869 Comm'n Dec. 18, 19 (1869), the patent applicant sought a patent for a method to prevent canals from freezing by running steam pipes through them. Applicant appealed a rejection by the examiner on the ground that the invention lacked utility and practicality. The Commissioner of Patents overturned the rejection and granted the patent, stating that

> the Patent Office should only see that the purpose proposed, if accomplished, would be useful, or that the plan does not show the absence of some part obviously essential to any end whatever. Beyond this it can only oppose

the opinion of man to man — an opinion by which, if all our great inventions had been tried when first presented to the office prior the public, the great majority of them would have been strangled at birth by the unfriendly hand of adverse criticism.

See also Ex parte McKay, 200 U.S.P.Q. (BNA) 324 (P.T.O. Bd. App. 1975) (claims for obtaining oxygen from extraterrestrial materials and producing materials on the moon upheld over lack of utility rejection; although "practical considerations would dictate against its commercial exploitation on earth," this "is not the standard by which the statutory requirement of utility is to be measured."). How do the *Cheeseborough* and *McKay* cases differ from the *Newman* case?

4. For an argument that the utility requirement diminishes incentives for "revolutionary" inventions, see Oddi, *Beyond Obviousness: Invention Protection in the Twenty-First Century*, 38 Am. U. L. Rev. 1097, 1127 (1989) (arguing that utility requirement and statutory classifications under § 101 [i.e., process, machine, manufacture, etc.] discriminate against revolutionary inventions, and calling for special protection on revolutionary inventions to offset these factors).

RELIANCE NOVELTY CORP. v. DWORZEK

80 F. 902 (N.D. Cal. 1897)

The bill charges the infringement of letters patent No. 26,684, issued to Benny J. Wertheimer, for a design upon the cases of coin-controlled machines, generally known as "nickel in the slot machines," which, in the case at bar, are of the kind commonly known as "card-playing slot machines."

Several objections are made by the defendants to the application for a preliminary injunction. It is claimed that [plaintiff's machine] has no element of utility, but is used on a gambling device.

The design covered by complainant's patent is placed on a case, with a glass front, containing the coin-controlled machine referred to. The losses or winnings of the player are determined by the combinations formed by the cards which ultimately rest face upright in the case. The machines are used principally in saloons, cigar stands, and other such places of resort by the frequenters and visitors thereto. The winnings of the successful player consist generally in cigars or drinks. The complainant claims, however, that these coin-controlled, card-playing machines, inclosed by its design case, may be put to other uses, among which is the exhibition of photographs, kinetoscope pictures, automatic toys, and views of celebrated places and persons. But its own affidavits show that the only use to which the card-playing machines containing its design case have been put is for gambling purposes.

It is a general principle, based upon public policy, that the patent laws of the United States do not authorize the issue of a patent for an invention which is injurious to the morals, health, or good order of society.

In Simonds' Summary of the Law of Patents (page 211) he says:

[I]t is not at all unreasonable to suppose that the legislator who drafted the [statute] meant that the word "useful" should have substantially the same meaning here [in the design patent statute] that it has in the part of the act creating utility patents — that is, that the things presented for patent shall be designed for some useful purpose, in distinction from a hurtful, frivolous, or immoral purpose.

I shall, therefore, deny the application for a preliminary injunction.

NOTES

A frequently quoted statement of the test of beneficial utility is drawn from Justice Story's opinion in *Bedford v. Hunt*, 3 F. Cas. 37, 1 Robb, Pat. Cas. 148 (C.C.D. Mass. 1817):

By useful invention, in the statute, is meant such a one as may be applied to some beneficial use in society, in contradistinction to an invention, which is injurious to the morals, the health, or the good order of society. It is not necessary to establish, that the invention is of such general utility, as to supersede all other inventions now in practice to accomplish the same purpose. It is sufficient, that it has no obnoxious or mischievous tendency, that it may be applied to practical uses, and that so far as it is applied, it is salutary. If its practical utility be very limited, it will follow, that it will be of little or no profit to the inventor; and if it be trifling, it will sink into utter neglect. The law, however, does not look to the degree of utility; it simply requires, that it shall be capable of use, and that the use is such as sound morals and policy do not discountenance or prohibit.

Story proposes that the market will sort out the truly useful inventions. Why not stretch this logic further, and eliminate the utility requirement altogether? Why might eliminating this requirement and leaving utility to the "market test" be detrimental? The first case in the next section confronts these questions head-on.

B. UTILITY IN CHEMICAL AND BIOTECHNOLOGICAL CASES

Because of the nature of chemical research, chemists often develop a chemical compound without a particular purpose in mind. Often a chemist works with a family of related compounds, trying to synthesize one which, because of the properties it shares with other compounds in the family, is thought likely to be useful for something. The chemist might have a particular goal when she sets out, such as the discovery of a compound that will treat a particular disease. Alternatively, she may be exploring a general class of compounds whose properties suggest they might eventually serve some as yet unspecified purpose. Either way, chemists often synthesize compounds which they believe might be useful someday for something, but for which no particular use is known.

Likewise, in biotechnology scientists often identify interesting research subjects whose use is not known or fully understood. For example, scientists might take interest because a gene seems to be present in many diseased cells, even though the protein product that the gene codes for is as yet unknown.

In both cases, when researchers apply for patents, the applicants run headlong into the utility requirement, as the following case demonstrates.

BRENNER v. MANSON

383 U.S. 519, 148 U.S.P.Q. (BNA) 689 (1966)

A Patent Office examiner denied Manson's application, and the denial was affirmed by the Board of Appeals within the Patent Office. The ground for rejection was the failure "to disclose any utility for" the chemical compound produced by the process. This omission was not cured, in the opinion of the Patent Office, by Manson's reference to an article in the November 1956 issue of the Journal of Organic Chemistry, 21 J. Org. Chem. 1333-1335, which revealed that steroids of a class which included the compound in question were undergoing screening for possible tumor-inhibiting effects in mice, and that a homologue [1] adjacent to Manson's steroid had proven effective in that role. Said the Board of Appeals, "It is our view that the statutory requirement of usefulness of a product cannot be presumed merely because it happens to be closely related to another compound which is known to be useful."

The Court of Customs and Patent Appeals (hereinafter CCPA) reversed [, stating] "where a claimed process produces a known product it is not necessary to show utility for the product," so long as the product "is not alleged to be detrimental to the public interest."

Our starting point is the proposition, neither disputed nor disputable, that one may patent only that which is "useful." [T]he concept of utility has maintained a central place in all of our patent legislation, beginning with the first patent law in 1790 and culminating in the present [§ 101].

As is so often the case, however, a simple, everyday word can be pregnant with ambiguity when applied to the facts of life. That this is so is demonstrated by the present conflict between the Patent Office and the CCPA over how the test is to be applied to a chemical process which yields an already known product whose utility — other than as a possible object of scientific inquiry — has not yet been evidenced. It was not long ago that agency and court seemed of one mind on the question. In [one case] the court affirmed rejection by the Patent Office

---

[1] "A homologous series is a family of chemically related compounds, the composition of which varies from member to member by [a given increment] .... Chemists knowing the properties of one member of a series would in general know what to expect in adjacent members."

of both process and product claims. It noted that "no use for the products claimed to be developed by the processes had been shown in the specification." It held that "It was never intended that a patent be granted upon a product, or a process producing a product, unless such product be useful."

The Patent Office has remained steadfast in this view. The CCPA, however, has moved sharply away from [it]. The trend began in *Application of Nelson*, 47 C.C.P.A. (Pat.) 1031, 280 F.2d 172. There, the court reversed the Patent Office's rejection of a claim on a process yielding chemical intermediates "useful to chemists doing research on steroids," despite the absence of evidence that any of the steroids thus ultimately produced were themselves "useful." The trend has accelerated, culminating in the present case where the court held it sufficient that a process produces the result intended and is not "detrimental to the public interest."

Respondent does not — at least in the first instance — rest upon the extreme proposition, advanced by the court below, that a novel chemical process is patentable so long as it yields the intended product and so long as the product is not itself "detrimental." Nor does he commit the outcome of his claim to the slightly more conventional proposition that any process is "useful" within the meaning of § 101 if it produces a compound whose potential usefulness is under investigation by serious scientific researchers, although he urges this position, too, as an alternative basis for affirming the decision. Rather, he begins with the much more orthodox argument that his process has a specific utility which would entitle him to [pursue a patent] even under the Patent Office's reading of § 101. The claim is that the supporting affidavits, by reference to Ringold's 1956 article, reveal that an adjacent homologue of the steroid yielded by his process has been demonstrated to have tumor-inhibiting effects in mice, and that this discloses the requisite utility. We do not accept any of these theories as an adequate basis for overriding the determination of the Patent Office that the "utility" requirement has not been met.

Even on the assumption that the process would be patentable were respondent to show that the steroid produced had a tumor-inhibiting effect in mice, we would not overrule the Patent Office finding that respondent has not made such a showing. The Patent Office held that, despite the reference to the adjacent homologue, respondent's papers did not disclose a sufficient likelihood that the steroid yielded by his process would have similar tumor-inhibiting characteristics. Indeed, respondent himself recognized that the presumption that adjacent homologues have the same utility has been challenged in the steroid field because of "a greater known unpredictability of compounds in that field." In these circumstances and in this technical area, we would not overturn the finding of the Primary Examiner, affirmed by the Board of Appeals and not challenged by the CCPA.

The second and third points of respondent's argument present issues of much importance. Is a chemical process "useful" within the meaning of § 101 either

(1) because it works — i.e., produces the intended product? or (2) because the compound yielded belongs to a class of compounds now the subject of serious scientific investigation? These contentions present the basic problem for our adjudication. Since we find no specific assistance in the legislative materials underlying § 101, we are remitted to an analysis of the problem in light of the general intent of Congress, the purposes of the patent system, and the implications of a decision one way or the other.

In support of his plea that we attenuate the requirement of "utility," respondent relies upon Justice Story's well-known statement that a "useful" invention is one "which may be applied to a beneficial use in society, in contradistinction to an invention injurious to the morals, health, or good order of society, or frivolous and insignificant" [2] — and upon the assertion that to do so would encourage inventors of new processes to publicize the event for the benefit of the entire scientific community, thus widening the search for uses and increasing the fund of scientific knowledge. Justice Story's language sheds little light on our subject. Narrowly read, it does no more than compel us to decide whether the invention in question is "frivolous and insignificant" — a query no easier of application than the one built into the statute. Read more broadly, so as to allow the patenting of any invention not positively harmful to society, it places such a special meaning on the word "useful" that we cannot accept it in the absence of evidence that Congress so intended. There are, after all, many things in this world which may not be considered "useful" but which, nevertheless, are totally without a capacity for harm.

Whatever weight is attached to the value of encouraging disclosure and of inhibiting secrecy, we believe a more compelling consideration is that a process patent in the chemical field, which has not been developed and pointed to the degree of specific utility, creates a monopoly of knowledge which should be granted only if clearly commanded by the statute. Until the process claim has been reduced to production of a product shown to be useful, the metes and bounds of that monopoly are not capable of precise delineation. It may engross a vast, unknown, and perhaps unknowable area. Such a patent may confer power to block off whole areas of scientific development, without compensating benefit to the public. The basic *quid pro quo* contemplated by the Constitution and the Congress for granting a patent monopoly is the benefit derived by the public from an invention with substantial utility. Unless and until a process is refined and developed to this point — where specific benefit exists in currently available form — there is insufficient justification for permitting an applicant to engross what may prove to be a broad field.

---

[2] Note on the Patent Laws, 3 Wheat. App. 13, 24. See also Justice Story's decisions on circuit in *Lowell v. Lewis*, 15 Fed. Cas. 1018 (No. 8568) (C.C.D. Mass. (1817)), and *Bedford v. Hunt*, 3 Fed. Cas. 37 (No. 1217) (C.C.D. Mass. (1817)).

These arguments for and against the patentability of a process which either has no known use or is useful only in the sense that it may be an object of scientific research would apply equally to the patenting of the product produced by the process. Respondent appears to concede that with respect to a product, as opposed to a process, Congress has struck the balance on the side of nonpatentability unless "utility" is shown. Indeed, the decisions of the CCPA are in accord with the view that a product may not be patented absent a showing of utility greater than any adduced in the present case. We find absolutely no warrant for the proposition that although Congress intended that no patent be granted on a chemical compound whose sole "utility" consists of its potential role as an object of use-testing, a different set rules was meant to apply to the process which yielded the unpatentable product. That proposition seems to us little more than an attempt to evade the impact of the rules which concededly govern patentability of the product itself.

This is not to say that we mean to disparage the importance of contributions to the fund of scientific information short of the invention of something "useful," or that we are blind to the prospect that what now seems without "use" may tomorrow command the grateful attention of the public. But a patent is not a hunting license. It is not a reward for the search, but compensation for its successful conclusion. "[A] patent system must be related to the world of commerce rather than to the realm of philosophy...."

The judgment of the CCPA is Reversed.

NOTES

1. Assume there was a market for Manson's research, i.e., that he could have licensed his results to other interested firms. Does this alone establish utility? Since Manson had found a steroid compound that was a homologue of a compound known to be useful, he had obviously increased the probability that this compound was useful. Another firm might well be willing to pay for this information. Is that enough? *See In re Kirk*, 376 F.2d 936, 942, 153 U.S.P.Q. 48, 54 (C.C.P.A. 1967) (stating that chemical compound was not presumed useful under § 101 merely because it was similar to other useful compounds). What is the difference between research results valuable only as information and results that are themselves precursors to an actual commercial product?

2. In an article by Eric Mirabel, *Practical Utility Is a Useless Concept*, 36 AM. U. L. REV. 811 (1987), the author argues that the doctrine of "practical utility" announced in *Manson* is inconsistent with the history and tradition of the utility requirement.

3. In Note, *Requirements for Patenting Chemical Intermediates: Do They Accomplish the Statutory Goals?*, 29 ST. LOUIS U. L.J. 191 (1984), the author discusses the development of the utility and nonobvious requirements as they relate to chemical intermediates. He concludes his analysis of current utility doctrine in the following passage:

> The underlying policy of the patent system indicates that the current approach to patenting chemical intermediates is not best suited for the advancement of science. Under the current system, novel, nonobvious chemical compounds must have a demonstrated particular use in order to receive patent protection. This implies that the discovery of a new chemical compound, and the related synthetic techniques employed to attain the new chemical intermediate, will not be disseminated when the end product does not meet the utility requirement. The advancement of science is impeded under such a scheme. In the discovery of a new chemical intermediate, there are several pieces of information that could advance the field of chemistry. The first is the existence of a new chemical compound. The second is the synthetic technique employed in arriving at this novel compound since the novel compound may have been developed through a novel technique that could be of valuable assistance to all chemists. The third is the technique employed in arriving at the end product. The end product or the technique so employed also may be novel and, therefore, worthy of scientific recognition. The inventor who has thus made these significant contributions presently will not be granted a patent until a practical use is discovered for the end product of the reaction scheme.
>
> The better approach would [allow] ... [an] inventor ... to patent a novel, nonobvious chemical intermediate when that intermediate does *in fact* produce an end product. Accordingly, the inventor would be fully compensated for his efforts even though he would not be required to establish a practical utility for the end product. He then would be more willing, as would an industrial supporter, to disseminate the information regarding the discovery.

4. The concept of a "use patent" is described in Merges & Nelson, *On the Complex Economics of Patent Scope*, 90 COLUM. L. REV. 800 (1990), where the authors discuss an anomaly alluded to in Justice Harlan's dissent in *Brenner* (excluded from the excerpt of the case above): an inventor who obtains a patent for a product, e.g., a particular molecule, has the right to exclude all others from making, using or selling that product for *any* and all purposes, including purposes that the inventor did not herself discover or invent. For example, a patented compound created for its use as a leather tanning agent might turn out to be an effective anti-AIDS drug. If so, the patentee would have the right to sell the drug as an AIDS treatment. Indeed, the patentee could exclude all others from this market — including the person who discovered that the leather tanning compound had anti-AIDS properties. Note that the utility requirement is met so long as the patentee shows *any* specific utility for the chemical when the patent is first filed

— in our example, when the leather tanning property of the compound is discovered. Others have responded to the anomaly by calling for a special type of patent in these situations, a "new use" patent.

New use patents already exist in a limited way. In our example, the one who discovers the anti-AIDS property of the leather tanning agent can obtain a *process* patent for "the process of using [the leather tanning compound] to treat AIDS." *See Rohm & Haas Co. v. Roberts Chem. Co.*, 245 F.2d 693, 113 U.S.P.Q. (BNA) 423 (4th Cir. 1957) (upholding defendant's patent on use of a well-known product as a fungicide); 1 D. CHISUM, PATENTS § 1.03[8] (1978 & Supp. 1989) (collecting other cases on this point). This is in essence only an improvement patent; the discoverer would still have to obtain a license from the patentee to use the compound for treatment of AIDS. But the reverse is also true; unlike the example outlined above, if the one who discovered the leather tanning agent's anti-AIDS properties obtained a process patent, the patentee would have to obtain a license from the improver to have the right to use the compound to treat AIDS.

5. Utility for pharmaceutical products can be established by animal testing. *See* Examiner Guidelines for Biotech Applications, excerpted below following *In re Brana*.

Until recently, there were doubts about whether the standards evolved in chemical cases also applied to cases involving biotechnology. The next case, and the PTO Guidelines that were issued soon thereafter, went a long way toward answering these questions.

In re BRANA

51 F.3d 1560, 34 U.S.P.Q.2d 1436 (Fed. Cir. 1995)

PLAGER, J.

Miguel F. Brana et al. (applicants), appeal the March 19, 1993 decision of the United States Patent and Trademark Office (PTO) Board of Patent Appeals and Interferences (Board), in Appeal No. 92-1196. The Board affirmed the examiner's rejection of claims 10-13 of patent application Serial No. 533,944 under 35 U.S.C. Section 112 Para. 1 (1988). The examiner's rejection, upon which the Board relied in rendering its decision, was based specifically on a challenge to the utility of the claimed compounds and the amount of experimentation necessary to use the compounds. We conclude the Board erred, and reverse.

I. BACKGROUND

On June 30, 1988, applicants filed patent application Serial No. 213,690 (the '690 application) directed to 5-nitrobenzo [de]isoquinoline-1,3-dione compounds, for use as antitumor substances, having the following formula:

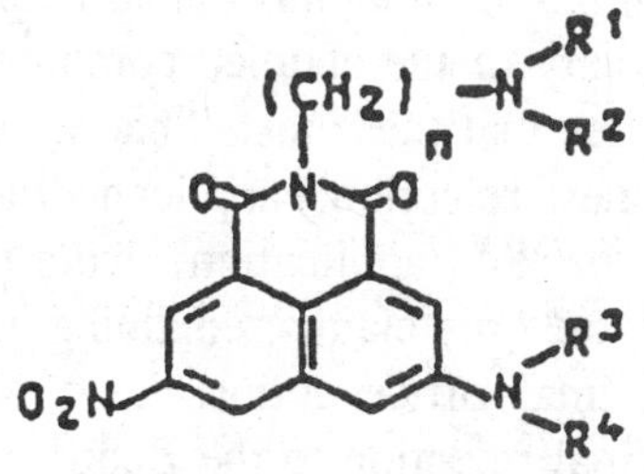

Figure 3-1

where N is 1 or 2, R^1 and R^2 are identical or different and are each hydrogen, C1-C6-alkyl, C1-C6-hydroxyalkyl, pyrrolidinyl, morpholino, piperidinyl or piperacinyl, and R^3 and R^4 are identical or different and are each hydrogen, C1-C6-alkyl, C1-C6-acyl, C2-C7-alkoxycarbonyl, ureyl, aminocarbonyl or C2-C7-alkylaminocarbonyl. These claimed compounds differ from several prior art benzo [de]isoquinoline-1,3-dione compounds due to the presence of a nitro group (O_2N) at the 5-position and an amino or other amino group ($NR^3 R^4$) at the 8-position of the isoquinoline ring.

The specification states that these non-symmetrical substitutions at the 5- and 8-positions produce compounds with "a better action and a better action spectrum as antitumor substances" than known benzo [de]isoquinolines, namely those in K.D. Paull et al., Computer Assisted Structure-Activity Correlations, Drug Research, 34(II), 1243-46 (1984) (Paull). Paull describes a computer-assisted evaluation of benzo [de]isoquinoline-1,3-diones and related compounds which have been screened for antitumor activity by testing their efficacy *in vivo*[3] against two specific implanted murine (i.e., utilizing mice as test subjects) lymphocytic leukemias, P388 and L1210.[4] These two *in vivo* tests are widely used by the National Cancer Institute (NCI) to measure the antitumor properties of a compound. Paull noted that one compound in particular, benzo [de]isoquino-line-1,3(2H)dione,5-amino-2(2-dimethyl-aminoethyl [sic]) (hereinafter "NSC 308847"), was found to show excellent activity against these two specific tumor models. Based on their analysis, compound NSC 308847 was selected for further studies by NCI. In addition to comparing the effectiveness of the claimed com-

---

[3] *In vivo* means "[i]n the living body, referring to a process occurring therein." Steadman's Medical Dictionary 798 (25th ed. 1990). *In vitro* means "[i]n an artificial environment, referring to a process or reaction occurring therein, as in a test tube or culture media." *Id.*

[4] The analysis in Paull consisted of grouping the previously-tested compounds into groups based on common structural features and cross-referencing the various groups, in light of the success rates of the group as a whole, to determine specific compounds that may be effective in treating tumors.

pounds with structurally similar compounds in Paull, applicants' patent specification illustrates the cytotoxicity of the claimed compounds against human tumor
cells, *in vitro*, and concludes that these tests "had a good action." ...

[After an initial obviousness rejection,] applicants filed a continuation application, Serial No. 533,944 (the '944 application), from the above-mentioned '690
application. Claims 10-13, the only claims remaining in the continuation application, were rejected in a final office action dated May 1, 1991. Applicants
appealed the examiner's final rejection to the Board.

In his answer to the applicants' appeal brief, the examiner stated that the final
rejection was based on 35 U.S.C. Section 112 Para. 1. The examiner first noted
that the specification failed to describe any specific disease against which the
claimed compounds were active. Furthermore, the examiner concluded that the
prior art tests performed in Paull and the tests disclosed in the specification were
not sufficient to establish a reasonable expectation that the claimed compounds
had a practical utility (i.e., antitumor activity in humans).

... [T]he Board affirmed the examiner's final rejection. The three-page opinion,
which lacked any additional analysis, relied entirely on the examiner's reasoning.
Although noting that it also would have been proper for the examiner to reject the
claims under 35 U.S.C. Section 101, the Board affirmed solely on the basis of
the Examiner's Section 112 Para. 1 rejection. This appeal followed.

II. DISCUSSION

At issue in this case is an important question of the legal constraints on patent
office examination practice and policy. The question is, with regard to pharmaceutical inventions, what must the applicant prove regarding the practical utility
or usefulness of the invention for which patent protection is sought. This is not
a new issue; it is one which we would have thought had been settled by case law
years ago. We note the Commissioner has recently addressed this question in his
Examiner Guidelines for Biotech Applications, see 60 Fed. Reg. 97 (1995); 49
Pat. Trademark & Copyright J. (BNA) No. 1210, at 234 (Jan. 5, 1995).

The requirement that an invention have utility is found in 35 U.S.C. Section
101: "Whoever invents ... any new and *useful* ... composition of matter ... may
obtain a patent therefor...." (emphasis added). It is also implicit in Section 112
Para. 1, which reads:

> The specification shall contain a written description of the invention, and
> of the manner and process of making and using it, in such full, clear,
> concise, and exact terms as to enable any person skilled in the art to which
> it pertains, or with which it is most nearly connected, to make and use the
> same, and shall set forth the best mode contemplated by the inventor of
> carrying out his invention.

Obviously, if a claimed invention does not have utility, the specification cannot
enable one to use it.

As noted, although the examiner and the Board both mentioned Section 101, and the rejection appears to be based on the issue of whether the compounds had a practical utility, a Section 101 issue, the rejection according to the Board stands on the requirements of Section 112 Para. 1. It is to that provision that we address ourselves.[5] The Board gives two reasons for the rejection; we will consider these in turn.

1

... [T]he Commissioner argues that the disclosed uses in the '944 application, namely the "treatment of diseases" and "antitumor substances," are similar to the nebulous disclosure found insufficient in *In re Kirk*, 376 F.2d 936, 153 U.S.P.Q. 48 (C.C.P.A. 1967). This argument is not without merit.

In *Kirk* applicants claimed a new class of steroid compounds. One of the alleged utilities disclosed in the specification was that these compounds possessed "high biological activity." *Id.* at 938, 153 U.S.P.Q. at 50. The specification, however, failed to disclose which biological properties made the compounds useful. Moreover, the court found that known specific uses of similar compounds did not cure this defect since there was no disclosure in the specification that the properties of the claimed compounds were the same as those of the known similar compounds. *Id.* at 942, 153 U.S.P.Q. at 53. Furthermore, it was not alleged that one of skill in the art would have known of any specific uses, and therefore, the court concluded this alleged use was too obscure to enable one of skill in the art to use the claimed invention. *See also Kawai v. Metlesics*, 480 F.2d 880, 178 U.S.P.Q. 158 (C.C.P.A. 1973).

Kirk would potentially be dispositive of this case were the above-mentioned language the only assertion of utility found in the '944 application. Applicants' specification, however, also states that the claimed compounds have "a better action and a better action spectrum as antitumor substances" than known compounds, specifically those analyzed in Paull. As previously noted ..., Paull grouped various benzo [de]isoquinoline-1,3-diones, which had previously been tested *in vivo* for antitumor activity against two lymphocytic leukemia tumor models (P388 and L1210), into various structural classifications and analyzed the test results of the groups (i.e., what percent of the compounds in the particular group showed success against the tumor models). Since one of the tested compounds, NSC 308847, was found to be highly effective against these two lymphocytic leukemia tumor models, applicants' favorable comparison implicitly asserts that their claimed compounds are highly effective (i.e., useful) against lymphocytic leukemia. An alleged use against this particular type of cancer is much more

---

[5] This court's predecessor has determined that absence of utility can be the basis of a rejection under both 35 U.S.C. Section 101 and Section 112 Para. 1 ... [citations omitted]. Since the Board affirmed the examiner's rejection based solely on Section 112 Para. 1, however, our review is limited only to whether the application complies with Section 112 Para. 1.

specific than the vaguely intimated uses rejected by the courts in *Kirk* and *Kawai*....

The Commissioner contends, however, that P388 and L1210 are not diseases since the only way an animal can get sick from P388 is by a direct injection of the cell line. The Commissioner therefore concludes that applicants' reference to Paull in their specification does not provide a specific disease against which the claimed compounds can be used. We disagree.

As applicants point out, the P388 and L1210 cell lines, though technically labeled tumor models, were originally derived from lymphocytic leukemias in mice. Therefore, the P388 and L1210 cell lines do represent actual specific lymphocytic tumors; these models will produce this particular disease once implanted in mice. If applicants were required to wait until an animal naturally developed this specific tumor before testing the effectiveness of a compound against the tumor *in vivo*, as would be implied from the Commissioner's argument, there would be no effective way to test compounds *in vivo* on a large scale.

We conclude that these tumor models represent a specific disease against which the claimed compounds are alleged to be effective. Accordingly, in light of the explicit reference to Paull, applicants' specification alleges a sufficiently specific use.

2

The second basis for the Board's rejection was that, even if the specification did allege a specific use, applicants failed to prove that the claimed compounds are useful. Citing various references,[6] the Board found, and the Commissioner now argues, that the tests offered by the applicants to prove utility were inadequate to convince one of ordinary skill in the art that the claimed compounds are useful as antitumor agents.

This court's predecessor has stated:

> [A] specification disclosure which contains a teaching of the manner and process of making and using the invention in terms which correspond in scope to those used in describing and defining the subject matter sought to be patented must be taken as in compliance with the enabling requirement of the first paragraph of Section 112 unless there is reason to doubt the objective truth of the statements contained therein which must be relied on for enabling support.

In re Marzocchi, 439 F.2d 220, 223, 169 U.S.P.Q. 367, 369 (C.C.P.A. 1971). From this it follows that the PTO has the initial burden of challenging a pre-

---

[6] See Pazdur et al., *Correlation of Murine Antitumor Models in Predicting Clinical Drug Activity in Non-Small Cell Lung Cancer: A Six Year Experience*, 3 Proceedings Am. Soc. Clin. Oncology 219 (1984); Martin et al., *Role of Murine Tumor Models in Cancer Research*, 46 Cancer Research 2189 (April 1986).

sumptively correct assertion of utility in the disclosure. *Id.* at 224, 169 U.S.P.Q. at 370. Only after the PTO provides evidence showing that one of ordinary skill in the art would reasonably doubt the asserted utility does the burden shift to the applicant to provide rebuttal evidence sufficient to convince such a person of the invention's asserted utility. *See In re Bundy*, 642 F.2d 430, 433, 209 U.S.P.Q. 48, 51 (C.C.P.A. 1981).

The PTO has not met this initial burden. The references cited by the Board, Pazdur and Martin, do not question the usefulness of any compound as an antitumor agent or provide any other evidence to cause one of skill in the art to question the asserted utility of applicants' compounds. Rather, these references merely discuss the therapeutic predictive value of *in vivo* murine tests — relevant only if applicants must prove the ultimate value in humans of their asserted utility. Likewise, we do not find that the nature of applicants' invention alone would cause one of skill in the art to reasonably doubt the asserted usefulness.

The purpose of treating cancer with chemical compounds does not suggest an inherently unbelievable undertaking or involve implausible scientific principles. Modern science has previously identified numerous successful chemotherapeutic agents. In addition, the prior art, specifically Zee Cheng et al. [U.S. Patent No. 4,614,820], discloses structurally similar compounds to those claimed by the applicants which have been proven *in vivo* to be effective as chemotherapeutic agents against various tumor models.

Taking these facts — the nature of the invention and the PTO's proffered evidence — into consideration we conclude that one skilled in the art would be without basis to reasonably doubt applicants' asserted utility on its face. The PTO thus has not satisfied its initial burden....

We do not rest our decision there, however. Even if one skilled in the art would have reasonably questioned the asserted utility, i.e., even if the PTO met its initial burden thereby shifting the burden to the applicants to offer rebuttal evidence, applicants proffered sufficient evidence to convince one of skill in the art of the asserted utility. In particular, applicants provided through Dr. Kluge's declaration[7] test results showing that several compounds within the scope of the claims exhibited significant antitumor activity against the L1210 standard tumor model *in vivo*. Such evidence alone should have been sufficient to satisfy applicants' burden.

---

[7] The declaration of Michael Kluge was signed and dated June 19, 1991. This declaration listed test results (i.e. antitumor activity) of the claimed compounds, *in vivo*, against L1210 tumor cells and concluded that these compounds would likely be clinically useful as anti-cancer agents. Enablement, or utility, is determined as of the application filing date. *In re Glass*, 492 F.2d 1228, 1232, 181 U.S.P.Q. 31, 34 (C.C.P.A. 1974). The Kluge declaration, though dated after applicants' filing date, can be used to substantiate any doubts as to the asserted utility since this pertains to the accuracy of a statement already in the specification. *In re Marzocchi*, 439 F.2d at 224 n.4, 169 U.S.P.Q. at 370 n.4. It does not render an insufficient disclosure enabling, but instead goes to prove that the disclosure was in fact enabling when filed (i.e., demonstrated utility).

The prior art further supports the conclusion that one skilled in the art would be convinced of the applicants' asserted utility. As previously mentioned, prior art — Zee Cheng et al. and Paull — disclosed structurally similar compounds which were proven *in vivo* against various tumor models to be effective as chemotherapeutic agents. Although it is true that minor changes in chemical compounds can radically alter their effects on the human body, *Kawai*, 480 F.2d at 891, 178 U.S.P.Q. at 167, evidence of success in structurally similar compounds is relevant in determining whether one skilled in the art would believe an asserted utility. *See Rey-Bellet v. Engelhardt*, 493 F.2d 1380, 181 U.S.P.Q. 453 (C.C.P.A. 1974); *Kawai*, 480 F.2d 880, 178 U.S.P.Q. 158.

The Commissioner counters that such *in vivo* tests in animals are only preclinical tests to determine whether a compound is suitable for processing in the second stage of testing, by which he apparently means *in vivo* testing in humans, and therefore are not reasonably predictive of the success of the claimed compounds for treating cancer in humans. The Commissioner, as did the Board, confuses the requirements under the law for obtaining a patent with the requirements for obtaining government approval to market a particular drug for human consumption. *See Scott v. Finney*, 34 F.3d 1058, 1063, 32 U.S.P.Q.2d 1115, 1120 (Fed. Cir. 1994) ("Testing for the full safety and effectiveness of a prosthetic device is more properly left to the Food and Drug Administration (FDA). Title 35 does not demand that such human testing occur within the confines of Patent and Trademark Office (PTO) proceedings.").

Our court's predecessor has determined that proof of an alleged pharmaceutical property for a compound by statistically significant tests with standard experimental animals is sufficient to establish utility. *In re Krimmel*, 292 F.2d 948, 953, 130 U.S.P.Q. 215, 219 (C.C.P.A. 1961); *see also In re Bergel*, 292 F.2d 958, 130 U.S.P.Q. 205 (C.C.P.A. 1961). In concluding that similar *in vivo* tests were adequate proof of utility the court in *In re Krimmel* stated:

> We hold as we do because it is our firm conviction that one who has taught the public that a compound exhibits some desirable pharmaceutical property in a standard experimental animal has made a significant and useful contribution to the art, even though it may eventually appear that the compound is without value in the treatment of humans.

Krimmel, 292 F.2d at 953, 130 U.S.P.Q. at 219. Moreover, NCI apparently believes these tests are statistically significant because it has explicitly recognized both the P388 and L1210 murine tumor models as standard screening tests for determining whether new compounds may be useful as antitumor agents.

....

On the basis of animal studies, and controlled testing in a limited number of humans (referred to as Phase I testing), the Food and Drug Administration may authorize Phase II clinical studies. See 21 U.S.C. Section 355(i)(1); 5 C.F.R. Section 312.23(a)(5), (a)(8) (1994). Authorization for a Phase II study means that the drug may be administered to a larger number of humans, but still under strictly supervised conditions. The purpose of the Phase II study is to determine primarily the safety of the drug when administered to a larger human population, as well as its potential efficacy under different dosage regimes. See 21 C.F.R. Section 312.21(b).

FDA approval, however, is not a prerequisite for finding a compound useful within the meaning of the patent laws. *Scott*, 34 F.3d 1058, 1063, 32 U.S.P.Q.2d 1115, 1120. Usefulness in patent law, and in particular in the context of pharmaceutical inventions, necessarily includes the expectation of further research and development. The stage at which an invention in this field becomes useful is well before it is ready to be administered to humans. Were we to require Phase II testing in order to prove utility, the associated costs would prevent many companies from obtaining patent protection on promising new inventions, thereby eliminating an incentive to pursue, through research and development, potential cures in many crucial areas such as the treatment of cancer.

In view of all the foregoing, we conclude that applicants' disclosure complies with the requirements of 35 U.S.C. Section 112 Para. 1....

NOTES

1. Why doesn't the court at least cite *Brenner*? How is this case different from *Brenner*? Is it important that the specific examiner's rejection at issue in this case cited to § 112 instead of § 101? What does the court's opinion say about this issue?

2. Recall the court's statements that further research and development will be necessary even after a biotechnology product is found useful. Granting a patent at this early stage will necessarily reduce the competition among firms to pursue this further R&D; in general, only the patentee will have an incentive to go forward. The economics of this situation are described below in "Note on Races, Rent Dissipation, and the Economics of the Utility Requirement."

The new "Examiner Guidelines for Biotech Applications," mentioned in the *Brana* opinion, liberalized treatment of biotechnology applications. They grew out of a series of public hearings at which members of the biotechnology industry stressed the importance of patents for early-round financing of startup companies. The chief criticism of the Patent Office was that application of an overly restrictive utility requirement chilled investment in the early stages of a company's life, by withholding the promise of exclusivity associated with a patent for too long. The argument was that the utility requirement placed biotechnology companies in a Catch-22: establishing utility required elaborate clinical testing, which was possible only if investors had the security of a patent. Thus the argument was that the investment required to secure a patent was not generally available to small companies until after a patent was in hand. *See, e.g.,* Biotechology Industry Organization, *Critical Synergy: The Biotechnology Industry and Intellectual*

Property Protection, Presentations of the Intellectual Property Committee of the Biotechnology Industry Organization at the October 17, 1994 Hearing of the U.S. Patent and Trademark Office. How are these complaints reflected in the following excerpts from the new Guidelines?

From U.S. Patent and Trademark Office, *Utility Examination Guidelines*, 60 Fed. Reg. 36263 (July 14, 1995):

Guidelines for Examination of Applications for Compliance With the Utility Requirement

A. *Introduction*

The following guidelines establish the policies and procedures to be followed by Office personnel in the evaluation of any application for compliance with the utility requirements of 35 U.S.C. 101 and 112. The guidelines also address issues that may arise during examination of applications claiming protection for inventions in the field of biotechnology and human therapy. The guidelines are accompanied by an overview of applicable legal precedent governing the utility requirement. The guidelines have been promulgated to assist Office personnel in their review of applications for compliance with the utility requirement. The guidelines and the legal analysis do not alter the substantive requirements of 35 U.S.C. 101 and 112, nor are they designed to obviate review of applications for compliance with this statutory requirement.

B. *Examination Guidelines for the Utility Requirement*

Office personnel shall adhere to the following procedures when reviewing applications for compliance with the "useful invention" ("utility") requirement of 35 U.S.C. 101 and 35 U.S.C. 112, first paragraph.

1. Read the specification, including the claims, to:

(a) Determine what the applicant has invented, noting any specific embodiments of the invention;

(b) Ensure that the claims define statutory subject matter (e.g., a process, machine, manufacture, or composition of matter);

(c) Note if applicant has disclosed any specific reasons why the invention is believed to be "useful."

2. Review the specification and claims to determine if the applicant has asserted any credible utility for the claimed invention:

(a) If the applicant has asserted that the claimed invention is useful for any particular purpose (i.e., a "specific utility") and that assertion would be considered credible by a person of ordinary skill in the art, do not impose a rejection based on lack of utility. Credibility is to be assessed from the perspective of one of ordinary skill in the art in view of any evidence of record (e.g., data, statements, opinions, references, etc.) that is relevant to the applicant's assertions. An applicant must provide only one credible assertion of specific utility for any claimed invention to satisfy the utility requirement.

(b) If the invention has a well-established utility, regardless of any assertion made by the applicant, do not impose a rejection based on lack of utility. An invention has a well-established utility if a person of ordinary skill in the art would immediately appreciate why the invention is useful based on the characteristics of the invention (e.g., properties of a product or obvious application of a process).

(c) If the applicant has not asserted any specific utility for the claimed invention and it does not have a well-established utility, impose a rejection under section 101, emphasizing that the applicant has not disclosed a specific utility for the invention. Also impose a separate rejection under section 112, first paragraph, on the basis that the applicant has not shown how to use the invention due to lack of disclosure of a specific utility. The sections 101 and 112 rejections should shift the burden to the applicant to:

— Explicitly identify a specific utility for the claimed invention, and
— Indicate where support for the asserted utility can be found in the specification.

Review the subsequently asserted utility by the applicant using the standard outlined in paragraph (2)(a) above, and ensure that it is fully supported by the original disclosure.

3. If no assertion of specific utility for the claimed invention made by the applicant is credible, and the claimed invention does not have a well-established utility, reject the claim(s) under section 101 on the grounds that the invention as claimed lacks utility. Also reject the claims under section 112, first paragraph, on the basis that the disclosure fails to teach how to use the invention as claimed. The section 112, first paragraph, rejection imposed in conjunction with a section 101 rejection should incorporate by reference the grounds of the corresponding section 101 rejection and should be set out as a rejection distinct from any other rejection under section 112, first paragraph, not based on lack of utility for the claimed invention.

To be considered appropriate by the Office, any rejection based on lack of utility must include the following elements:

(a) A prima facie showing that the claimed invention has no utility.

A prima facie showing of no utility must establish that it is more likely than not that a person skilled in the art would not consider credible any specific utility asserted by the applicant for the claimed invention. A prima facie showing must contain the following elements:

(i) A well-reasoned statement that clearly sets forth the reasoning used in concluding that the asserted utility is not credible;

(ii) Support for factual findings relied upon in reaching this conclusion; and

(iii) Support for any conclusions regarding evidence provided by the applicant in support of an asserted utility.

(b) Specific evidence that supports any fact-based assertions needed to establish the prima facie showing.

Whenever possible, Office personnel must provide documentary evidence (e.g., scientific or technical journals, excerpts from treatises or books, or U.S. or foreign patents) as the form of support used in establishing the factual basis of a prima facie showing of no utility according to items (a)(ii) and (a)(iii) above. If documentary evidence is not available, Office personnel shall note this fact and specifically explain the scientific basis for the factual conclusions relied on in sections (a)(ii) and (a)(iii).

4. A rejection based on lack of utility should not be maintained if an asserted utility for the claimed invention would be considered credible by a person of ordinary skill in the art in view of all evidence of record.

Once a prima facie showing of no utility has been properly established, the applicant bears the burden of rebutting it. The applicant can do this by amending the claims, by providing reasoning or arguments, or by providing evidence in the form of a declaration under 37 CFR 1.132 or a printed publication, that rebuts the basis or logic of the prima facie showing. If the applicant responds to the prima facie rejection, Office personnel shall review the original disclosure, any evidence relied upon in establishing the prima facie showing, any claim amendments and any new reasoning or evidence provided by the applicant in support of an asserted utility. It is essential for Office personnel to recognize, fully consider and respond to each substantive element of any response to a rejection based on lack of utility. Only where the totality of the record continues to show that the asserted utility is not credible should a rejection based on lack of utility be maintained.

If the applicant satisfactorily rebuts a prima facie rejection based on lack of utility under section 101, withdraw the section 101 rejection and the corresponding rejection imposed under section 112, first paragraph, per paragraph (3) above.

Office personnel are reminded that they must treat as true a statement of fact made by an applicant in relation to an asserted utility, unless countervailing evidence can be provided that shows that one of ordinary skill in the art would have a legitimate basis to doubt the credibility of such a statement. Similarly, Office personnel must accept an opinion from a qualified expert that is based upon relevant facts whose accuracy is not being questioned; it is improper to disregard the opinion solely because of a disagreement over the significance or meaning of the facts offered.

From U.S. Patent and Trademark Office, *Overview of Legal Precedent Governing the Utility Requirement*, reprinted in 49 PAT. TRADEMARK & COPYRIGHT J. 234 (1995):

III. *Special Considerations for Asserted Therapeutic Pharmacological Utilities*

The Federal courts have consistently reversed rejections by the Office asserting a lack of utility under Section 101 for inventions claiming a pharmacological or therapeutic utility where an applicant has provided evidence supporting such a utility. In view of this, Examiners should be particularly careful in their review of evidence provided in support of an asserted therapeutic or pharmacological utility.

A. *A Reasonable Correlation Between Evidence and Asserted Utility Is Sufficient*

As a general matter, evidence of pharmacological or other biological activity of a compound will be relevant to an asserted therapeutic use if there is a reasonable correlation between the activity in question and the asserted utility. The applicant does not have to prove that there is a statistically proven correlation between characteristics of a compound and the asserted use, nor does he or she have to provide actual evidence of success in treating humans where such a utility is asserted.

B. *Structural Similarity to Useful Products*

The courts have on several occasions found evidence of structural similarity to known compounds with particular therapeutic or pharmacological uses as supporting therapeutic utility of a newly claimed compound. Such evidence, when provided by an applicant in support of an assertion of utility, should be given appropriate weight in determining whether one skilled in the art would find the asserted utility credible.

C. *Data from In Vitro and Animal Testing Is Generally Sufficient to Support Therapeutic Utility*

Data generated using *in vitro* assays and testing in animals almost invariably will be sufficient to support an asserted therapeutic or pharmacological utility. In no case has a Federal court required an applicant to support an asserted utility with data from human clinical trials.

If an applicant provides data from *in vitro* and animal tests to support an asserted utility, the Examiner should determine if the tests, including the test parameters and choice of animal, would be viewed by one skilled in the art as being reasonably predictive of the asserted utility. If so, and the data supplied is consistent with the asserted utility, the Examiner should not maintain a rejection under Section 101. This approach is to be followed not only in cases where there are art-recognized animal models for assessing utility in human disease and treatment, but also where no such validation of a specific test has been performed. Thus, if one skilled in the art would accept the animal tests as being reasonably predictive of utility in humans, they should be considered sufficient to support the credibility of the asserted utility. Examiners should be careful not to find evidence unpersuasive simply because no animal model for the human disease condition had been established prior to the filing of the application.

D. *Human Clinical Data*

There is no decisional law that requires an applicant to provide data from human clinical trials to establish utility for an invention related to treatment of human disorders, even with respect to situations where no art-recognized animal models existed for the human disease encompassed by the claims. Examiners should not impose on applicants the unnecessary burden of providing evidence from human clinical trials. Examiners should note that before a drug can enter human clinical trials, the sponsor (e.g., often the applicant) must establish a sufficient basis to those especially skilled in the art (e.g., the Food and Drug Administration) that the drug will be effective to some degree in treating the stated disorder. Thus, as a general rule, if an applicant has initiated human clinical trials for a product or process used for treating an indication, the subject of that trial has met the burden of being reasonably predictive of utility.

NOTE

The PTO's legal analysis states that evidence that a particular compound is structurally similar to related compounds "should be given appropriate weight" in determining utility. What would this weight be, in light of *Brenner*?

MERGES, INTELLECTUAL PROPERTY IN HIGHER LIFE FORMS: THE PATENT SYSTEM AND CONTROVERSIAL TECHNOLOGIES, 47 Md. L. Rev. 1051, 1062-68 (1988)

What the opponents of biotechnology seek — to deny patents for subject matter they consider immoral — is not unknown in the history of patent law. From the early nineteenth century until midway through this century courts were often willing to withhold patents on inventions they considered immoral. These inventions fell chiefly into two classes: (1) inventions used to defraud buyers, and (2) machines used for gambling. Moral worth proved to be a difficult test of patentability — a fact which should give pause to those anxious to revive it.

The concept of immoral subject matter is thought to have originated in dictum from a Joseph Story opinion. [I.e., *Bedford v. Hunt*, described in a note *supra*.] As examples [of non-useful inventions], he cited patents to "poison people, or to promote debauchery, or to facilitate private assassination."

This doctrine was often invoked in the late nineteenth century to deny patents on gambling devices. Interestingly, it was a successful bar to patentability even where inventions appeared to be useful for things other than gambling. *See, e.g.,* *Schultz v. Holtz*, 82 F. 448 (N.D. Cal. 1897) (patent on coin return device for coin-operated machines denied because it had application to slot machines); *National Automatic Device Corp. v. Lloyd*, 40 F. 89, 90 (N.D. Ill. 1889) (patent on toy horse race course denied on evidence that toy course was used in bars for betting purposes). Patents were struck down on this basis well into the twentieth century, see, e.g., *Meyer v. Buckley Mfg. Co.*, 15 F. Supp. 640, 641 (N.D. Ill. 1936) (patent denied on "game of chance" vending machine, where user inserted coin and tried to manipulate miniature steam shovel to scoop up a toy), and even as late as 1941, in a pinball machine patent case, the Seventh Circuit was careful to note the distinction between playing pinball and gambling. *Chicago Patent v. Genco*, 124 F.2d 725, 728 (7th Cir. 1941) (upholding patent on pinball machine). By the 1970s, however, the courts were regularly upholding patents on gambling devices — both because gambling was no longer seen as a major moral issue, and because courts had become more wary of denying patents on the basis of an indeterminate moral standard. *See, e.g., Ex parte Murphy*, 200 U.S.P.Q. (BNA) 801, 803 (1977) (upholding claim for "one-armed bandit").

The fight against immoral inventions was not limited to patents for gambling devices. Another line of cases denied patents for inventions that could be used only to defraud. In one leading case, the Second Circuit invalidated a patent on a process for artificially producing spots on domestic tobacco, finding that the sole use for the process was to make domestic tobacco resemble fine grades of imported tobacco. *Richard v. Du Bon*, 103 F. 868, 873 (2d Cir. 1900). This was in keeping with other cases holding that patents could be granted only for devices having no fraudulent uses.

Cases on medicinal products make up a special class of "fraudulent use" cases. Beginning in the nineteenth century, courts were wary of placing the government's imprimatur on medicines and devices hawked to an unsuspecting public in the free-wheeling days before the establishment of an effective Food and Drug Administration (FDA). The result was a higher standard of utility for health-related inventions, vestiges of which can still be seen in patent cases and patent office practices. Brand, *Utility in a Pharmaceutical Patent*, 39 FOOD DRUG COSM. L.J. 480 (1984).

Now that a powerful FDA has far-reaching powers to regulate drugs and medical devices, however, courts are increasingly willing to focus on functional utility rather than clinical safety when medical patents are at issue. The rationale for this more limited role is to avoid duplication of effort. As one court stated, "[T]o require the Patent Office to make an affirmative finding as to the safety of a drug for human use would work a serious overlapping of the respective jurisdictions of the Patent Office and the FDA." *Carter-Wallace, Inc. v. Riverton Labs, Inc.*, 433 F.2d 1034, 1039 n.7 (2d Cir. 1970).

What conclusions can be drawn from the attempts of the courts to enforce moral norms by denying patents? First, as in the case of gambling devices, moral norms — or at least the courts' perceptions of them — change over time. Gambling is simply not perceived (by most) as a pernicious social ill in the current age — perhaps because other problems now seem so much worse. But other technologies once thought very wrong are now accepted as commonplace, e.g., birth control.

[E]ven conceding that biotechnology is analogous to gambling or selling fake medicines, another problem remains: what are the limits of the immorality test? How far into the future can the patent challenger look for the immoral effects of an invention, and what consensus version of morality can the courts rely on?

For example, historians and sociologists have long noted the profound social changes that accompanied the invention of the automobile. Some of these changes had unquestionable moral dimensions, such as the impact of automobiles on the incidence of premarital sex. Assuming these changes could have been foreseen, immoral use might have been raised as a reason not to enforce a patent on the automobile. A host of other technologies can be thought of in this vein: e.g., cattle prods (sometimes used in torture) and abortion-inducing drugs (safer than procedures, but considered immoral by some).

[P]atent protection for a new technology normally should not be denied on the basis of speculation about potential negative consequences, such as those suggested by opponents of animal patents. The patent system normally is not the proper place to conduct technology assessment. Its purpose is much simpler — "to promote the progress of science and the useful arts," according to the Constitution.

Second, patents on animals should not be excluded because of arguments about their potential social consequences. Those problems, if they eventually arise, should be dealt with outside the patent law. The FDA, for example, now handles questions about the safety and efficacy of drugs; likewise the considerable regulatory structure that has grown up around biotechnology is the proper place to address concerns about potential deleterious effects of animal patents.

NOTES

1. *See* W. ROBINSON, THE LAW OF PATENTS FOR USEFUL INVENTIONS 340 (1890) (urging courts to consider total effects of invention upon maker, operator, and consumer before granting patent).

2. From *Whistler Corp. v. Autotronics, Inc.*, 14 U.S.P.Q.2d (BNA) 1885 (N.D. Tex. 1988):

> This is a patent infringement action brought by Whistler Corporation ("Whistler"), contending defendants are liable for infringing U.S. Patent No. 4,315,261 ("the '261 patent"), entitled "Radar Signal Detector." The case was tried to the court, which now enters judgment in favor of Whistler for the reasons set forth in this memorandum opinion and order.
>
> ... In denying Whistler's prior preliminary injunction application, the court, in connection with the public interest factor, noted the seeming incongruity of asking a court of law to protect a device used to circumvent

the law. Notwithstanding Whistler's evidence that the instant detectors have other uses, the court remains of the view that the primary and almost exclusive purpose for the radar detectors in question is to circumvent law enforcement attempts to detect and apprehend those who violate the law. Although the court seriously questions its being required to referee a contest among entities that manufacture and sell such products, the court concludes that the matter is one for the legislatures of the states, or for the Congress, to decide. Stated another way, only two states have seen fit to prohibit such devices. Unless and until detectors are banned outright, or Congress acts to withdraw patent protection for them, radar detector patentees are entitled to the protection of the patent laws.

Perhaps seizing upon the observation made by the court at the preliminary injunction stage, defendants argue that the '261 patent thus lacks utility. The court disagrees, however, that defendants have proven lack of utility in the sense contemplated by 35 U.S.C. § 101. The Patent and Trademark Office determined that the '261 invention had utility. Absent clear and convincing evidence to the contrary, this court cannot and should not substitute its own views in place of those of the PTO, the several legislatures, or the Congress.

PROBLEM: cDNA SEQUENCES

Craig Venter, a scientist at the National Institutes of Health, began a project in 1991 to obtain the genetic sequences for many of the natural chemical compounds or proteins that work in the human brain. His plan was to take advantage of the fact that of the many DNA sequences in human genetic material, only those that "code" for operational proteins are found in a certain form — the "cDNA" form. The "c" in cDNA stands for complimentary. A complimentary DNA sequence is one that matches to the "genetic messenger" carrying the code for a particular gene, called messenger RNA or mRNA. The mRNA is constructed at the site of the gene and is transported to the protein-creating site in the cell — the ribosome. (The cDNA sequence is constructed by "matching up" chemicals called base pairs with the base pairs comprising the mRNA sequence; the "matching up" occurs because of the DNA's double helix structure.) Scientists believe that only 3% of the DNA in the body actually "codes" for some useful protein — the other 97% is a mystery.

Venter's project was to get a listing of the cDNA sequences that match to the mRNA for each gene in the active, protein-encoding DNA sequences in a human brain. Getting all the "raw" sequences together was fairly straight-forward; he used widely-available "libraries" of all the cDNA's found to date in brain tissue. (These are made by working backward from the mRNA sequences that can be found in the relevant cells.) His contribution was to partially "sequence" the cDNA — to obtain a base pair by base pair "listing" for as many cDNAs as he could. Before his work, there were libraries of cDNA fragments, but no one had obtained detailed base pair sequences for each fragment.

In practice, he only had to sequence a portion of the cDNA segments, and with that portion the gene sequence itself, the actual gene, could be identified or reconstructed. (He called the partial sequences "expressed sequence tags," or ESTs.) This effort began as one part of the larger project to sequence the entire human genome.

In a patent application, Venter claims each of the ESTs he has produced. He also claims fragments of the ESTs, complimentary versions of each, and other variants. In addition, he claims groups of ESTs — called "panels" — for use in screening tissue samples and the like.

Venter claims there is utility for his invention. Specifically, he asserts that the ESTs can be used to (1) map chromosomes, i.e., help give a general idea of the location of the genes on a chromosome; (2) identify tissue types (specifically, be used to tell whether a given sample of tissue comes from the brain or not); and (3) identify gene regions associated with a disease, by drawing cDNA from patients, matching it with its associated EST, and seeing if the EST identifies a particular gene region unique to those with the disease.

Has Venter in fact recited utility? Are the suggested applications "too remote" from known, practical applications? Under the reasoning in *Brenner*, what is sacrificed if patents are allowed on these ESTs before clearcut, practical utility has been conclusively demonstrated? *See* L. Roberts, *Genome Patent Fight Erupts*, 254 Sci. 181 (11 Oct. 1991).

Consider by comparison a case on chemical intermediates holding that no utility was present. The court said a chemical that is useful only because it leads to an ultimately useful chemical is not *itself* useful under the Patent Act. *In re Joly*, 376 F.2d 906, 153 U.S.P.Q. (BNA) (C.C.P.A. 1967).

NOTE

The Venter application was ultimately dropped by the NIH. *See* Rebecca S. Eisenberg & Robert P. Merges, *Opinion Letter as to the Patentability of Certain Inventions Associated with the Identification of Partial cDNA Sequences*, 23 AM. INTELL. PROP. L. ASS'N Q.J. 1 (1995) ("cDNA Opinion Letter"). Even so, because private firms are in hot pursuit of gene sequences and fragments such as those claimed in the Venter application, the issues may be with us for some time. In that spirit, consider the following comments on utility from the cDNA Opinion Letter:

> [T]he disclosed utilities that are most vulnerable to challenge are those that either (1) do not indicate a specific purpose for which the inventions may be used or (2) depend for their operability on the success of experiments that have not been performed and are not certain to work in the minds of other practitioners of ordinary skill in the field. The former category would seem to include the claimed utilities as diagnostic probes, in genetic linkage analysis, as probes to locate gene regions associated with genetic disease, for regulation of gene expression through antisense and triple helix methods, and

for differentiating tissue types. Even if these asserted utilities no longer trigger the heightened skepticism as to operability and enablement recently applied by the PTO to pharmaceutical and therapeutic inventions, they remain vulnerable to challenge on the ground that undue experimentation would be necessary in order to determine which if any diagnostic or therapeutic purposes any of the ESTs might serve. Yet each of these utilities is described in broad, general terms and in purely prophetic examples, unsupported by specific experimental data that would identify the significance of any particular sequence to any particular disease.

We lack the technical expertise to evaluate which of the remaining utilities would be met with skepticism by skilled persons in the field or would require undue experimentation to carry out. Uses of the disclosed sequences as probes for diagnosing disease gene regions or to control gene expression through triple helix formation or DNA or RNA antisense molecules seem particularly vulnerable to challenge on this basis. Each of these utilities seems to require a subsequent research effort that appears fraught with uncertainty on the basis of the limited information provided in the specification and the state of the art.

The asserted utility of panels of sequences for tissue typing or for forensic identification purposes may also be vulnerable on this ground. The utility of the sequences in tissue typing depends on the sequences being variably expressed in different types of tissue. The specification states that subtractive hybridization was used to selectively remove sequences shared by a cDNA library from a human lung fibroblast cell line, but it does not indicate which of the remaining sequences is unique to brain tissue. Similarly, the utility of the sequences for forensic identification purposes depends on their being polymorphic. The specification states that 85% of the sequences appear to come from noncoding regions and that polymorphisms are particularly common in noncoding regions, but it does not indicate which, if any, of the sequences is in fact polymorphic. Perhaps these difficulties can be overcome by using panels that are so large that the likelihood of variable expression by tissue type or polymorphisms across individuals becomes overwhelming. But in that case the asserted utilities would only seem to support the patentability of these large panels, and not of smaller panels or of individual sequences.

A related problem is that the disclosure gives only limited guidance as to which of the sequences (or which combinations of sequences) are suitable for which of these uses. The process of selection may itself involve undue experimentation. As Examiner Martinell stated in reference to the panel claims,

[t]he panel of oligonucleotides in claim 22 has no patentable utility because the instant application fails to disclose a single such panel out of

the astronomical number of such panels possible and disclose any use for such a putative panel in its currently available form.

Moreover, even if the disclosure is fully enabling as to how to select appropriate sequences or panels, the disclosed utilities will only support the patentability of those sequences or panels that are useful for those purposes and not the others. To the extent that the disclosed utilities work only for some of the sequences or only for some panels of sequences, the claims are overly broad.

Of all the asserted utilities for the ESTs, the most credibly operable and enabled are the use as probes to obtain full cDNA sequences and the use as chromosome markers. Although only a small handful of cDNAs corresponding to ESTs had actually been fully sequenced as of the filing date, the same procedure could be readily followed by other skilled persons in the field if they were motivated to do so. Similarly, although only a small fraction of the ESTs had actually been mapped to chromosomes as of the filing date, mapping the others according to the methods disclosed in the specification, although perhaps tedious, seems unlikely to involve more than routine experimentation. But these uses may be particularly vulnerable to challenge under *Brenner v. Manson* as representing utility only as an object of study in subsequent research rather than showing "specific benefit ... in currently available form."

Use of the ESTs as probes to obtain full cDNA sequences has no practical benefit unless and until the full sequences themselves may be used for some purpose beyond research. Subsequent research may well prove some of the genes useful for diagnostic or therapeutic purposes, but the information disclosed in the specification fails to identify which of the genes will be useful, or for which purposes. Practical utility of the sequences awaits determination of the function of the genes they are associated with, thus implicating the concern for premature filing underlying the decisions in *Brenner v. Manson* and *In re Ziegler*.

This concern with premature filing seems particularly on target in this context because it parallels the reactions of scientists to the NIH filings. Scientists quoted in the popular and scientific press repeatedly expressed an intuition that NIH was claiming too much in light of the very preliminary information that they had disclosed. It seems likely that the PTO and the courts might have a similar reaction, and that a utility rejection would present an appealing doctrinal basis for expressing that view.

cDNA Opinion Letter, *supra*, at 16-19. Note that even if patents are not available, trade secrecy provides an alternative form of protection. Indeed, proprietary genome databases are currently licensed on this basis. *See, e.g.*, Elyse Tanouye, *Code Crackers: SmithKline Beecham Leads in Race to Use Genetics to Find Drugs*, WALL ST. J., Nov. 24, 1995.

NOTE ON RACES, RENT DISSIPATION, AND THE ECONOMICS OF THE UTILITY REQUIREMENT

The utility requirement closely parallels other rules that encourage races to claim valuable resources. Indeed, races of this type have generated an interesting body of legal and economic commentary. To understand it, and to see how this kind of analysis applies to the cDNA case, a few definitions are in order.

A government-granted property right such as a patent creates supra-competitive returns: profits above those that would be available under perfect competition. Such a right — together with other government-created protections from open competition — is said by economists to create a **rent**.

Obviously, rents are valuable. Once firms are aware of them, they can be expected to spend money to pursue them. Under some circumstances, in fact, firms will spend up to the expected value of the rent in pursuit of it. *See generally* THRAINN EGGERTSON, ECONOMIC BEHAVIOR AND INSTITUTIONS 84-91 (1990). This in some sense dilutes the effectiveness of the rent, which explains why the whole process is called **rent dissipation**. Even worse, where multiple firms are aware of a rent, *each one* may spend this amount (or close to it) to pursue it. Thus the overall effect of the rent might be highly wasteful indeed: with each firm investing up to the expected value of the rent, the total collective expenditure may exceed the value of the rent! (This obviously assumes certain facts about the firms' knowledge of each others' actions and/or the impact of a firm's decision regarding whether to seek the rent upon the expected value(s) of the other firms.) *See id.* at 93. *See generally* TOWARD A THEORY OF THE RENT-SEEKING SOCIETY (James Buchanan, Robert Tollison & Gordon Tullock eds., 1980) (emphasizing pursuit of government-granted rents).

The literature on rent-seeking describes many cases where occupancy or use requirements are put in place as conditions for perfecting title to a claim. In general, these use requirements are condemned; they are said to encourage inefficient expenditures. *See, e.g.*, Terry L. Anderson & Peter J. Hill, *The Race for Property Rights*, 33 J.L. & ECON. 177 (1990) (pointing out the inefficiency of land claiming systems under which claimants farm land and make improvements not because these activities make economic sense in themselves but because they are required to secure claims). *See generally* David D. Haddock, *First Possession Versus Optimal Timing: Limiting the Dissipation of Economic Value*, 64 WASH. U. L.Q. 775 (1986).

But, as Richard Posner has pointed out, "it is not always inefficient to condition a property right on use." RICHARD A. POSNER, ECONOMIC ANALYSIS OF LAW (4th ed. 1992), at 49 (illustrating thesis with example of trademark law, which requires actual use of trademark to prevent expenditure of resources on dreaming up and stockpiling potential trademarks). This point is formalized and generalized in a helpful recent contribution by Dean Lueck, *The Rule of First Possession and the Design of the Law*, 38 J.L. & ECON. 393 (1995).

A recent contribution applies the literature on rent dissipation to the problem of cDNA patents. Matthew Erramouspe, Comment, *Staking Patent Claims on the Human Blueprint: Rewards and Rent-Dissipating Races*, 43 UCLA L. REV. 961 (1996). This Comment begins with the observation that wasteful "races" are proliferating in biotechnology. In the case of both individual genes, and the entire human genome, many teams are racing to obtain sequences and file patents on them. In addition, the author argues, the "homogeneity" of the researchers exacerbates the rent dissipation. To solve the problem, this Comment proposes rewarding not the discovery of sequences per se, but the use of different *techniques* to obtain them. The author assumes that there will be greater variety in the choice of techniques than in the discovered sequences themselves, and hence that this approach will lead to less rent dissipation. *Id.* at 996-97.

The Comment has certainly diagnosed the problem with the Venter patents. But, even though the solution does have some merit, it seems quite at odds with the caselaw, such as *Brenner*. (It may also be wrong in its assumption regarding heterogenous techniques; many believe that basic lab protocols in biotechnology are widely shared.) True, *Brenner* evinces a concern with filing too early; it implicitly seeks to prevent racing at the very early conceptual stage. *Brenner* does not, however, permit a drastic reconceptualization of the patent reward — such as focusing on research procedures instead of results — in pursuit of the goal of discouraging filing until later in the R&D process. (In advocating this approach, the Comment shares some characteristics with a prior article setting forth a general theory of patent law as aimed at minimizing rent dissipation. *See* Mark Grady & Jay Alexander, *Patent Law and Rent Dissipation*, 78 VA. L. REV. 305 (1992); *cf.* Robert P. Merges, *Rent Control in the Patent District: Observations on the Grady-Alexander Thesis*, 78 VA. L. REV. 359 (1992).)

After *Brenner*, and more recently *Brana*, all we have to work with is the claimed subject matter itself and the requirement of "practical utility." To that end, consider the cDNA Opinion Letter described earlier, which emphasizes detailed issues and problems regarding the workability of the various claimed embodiments of the invention at issue. The important point is to prevent too-rapid racing at the early, conceptual stage of the invention process. As the Opinion Letter illustrates, conventional utility doctrine gives courts the tools to do so.

All in all, the rent dissipation discussion illuminates a key feature of the utility doctrine: the temporal element. By showing the costs of encouraging filing "too early," this discussion highlights the importance of timing in the process from basic research through development, patent filing, and product scale-up. One important element is, however, obscured by this attention to timing. That is the issue of multiple utilities, which reduces to a question of the commensurateness between research and reward, or the proper scope of the property right.

Although the utilities mentioned in the Venter application — gene mapping and, possibly, diagnosis — are perhaps plausible utilities, no one doubts that the *real* usefulness of a cDNA sequence comes after one identifies what the gene which is represented by the cDNA actually codes for; that is, the protein product of the gene. Whether it is a hormone, structural protein, or even disease-causing agent, the gene product is "where the action is" in terms of developing therapies. From this perspective, the problem with the utility doctrine in the Venter case is clear: all the applicant need disclose is some "nominal" utility. Once he or she does so, assuming the other statutory tests of patentability are met, the utility requirement is met. Thus, having met the test for *legal* utility, the inventor can carry out the search for *real* utility. Where the ratio of nominal to real utility is very low, utility doctrine arguably goes awry.

Although some might defend even nominal utility on the grounds that it puts an early end to a wasteful race, there are two good reasons to doubt the wisdom of this approach. (1) Because nominal utilities are easy to concoct, and because many researchers are amply positioned to concoct them, requiring only nominal utility comes too close to permitting patents on pure concepts. Nominal utility, in other words, rewards research too early in the R&D process. (2) Arguably, patent law takes as a given that firms will naturally race to claim patents. Instead of trying to prevent this in every case, the law instead harnesses the self-interest of firms to the social good. By requiring researchers to obtain some useful result, the law insures that the costs of research are not entirely wasted. Firms may aim at different utilities, for one thing. For another, the annals of research are full of examples of serendipitous discoveries. And finally, as the market for so-called "negative know-how" attests, there is economic value in knowing which approaches do *not* work, i.e., in research that reveals a lack of utility. The upshot is that, unlike expenditures to stake a claim on land, multiple, duplicative expenditures to meet the utility test may result in social benefits. (Note that in effect this argument runs counter to the main thrust of the rent dissipation literature; instead of trying to forestall wasteful, duplicative investment, it *channels* investment into research that might yield valuable — albeit serendipitous — results.) *See generally* Robert P. Merges, *Rent Control, supra. See also* RICHARD A. POSNER, *supra* (using example of requirement that frontier land be occupied to show that "use" requirements may serve a valuable goal, in that case settlement of frontier).

If one were to adopt the notion that only real, and not nominal, utility ought to be rewarded, a threshold test would be required. When the asserted utility is only a small fraction of the real, anticipated utility, it would be deemed nominal. In such a case, how would you go about structuring the doctrine to achieve the proper result? Consider these options:

- Declare that nominal utility fails to meet the requirements of *Brenner* because it is tantamount only to a "hunting license," which the Court condemned in that case;
- Declare the sequence itself obvious and permit only "method of using" claims;
- Allow a patent on the sequence, but grant "new use" (improvement) patents liberally to follow-on inventors.

NOTES

1. Despite the uncertainty regarding patents on gene fragments, databases containing many such fragments — including companies associated with Craig Venter himself — are in great demand by researchers. *See, e.g.*, *Genome Technology Agreement*, WALL ST. J., July 17, 1996, at B1, col. 3 (describing licensing agreement granting access to gene database owned by Human Genome Sciences, Inc.). Do such agreements, reached in the absence of patents, suggest anything about the necessity or desirability of allowing patents on these gene fragments?

2. *Utility and Priority.* The recent case of *In re Ziegler*, 992 F.2d 1197 (Fed. Cir. 1993), illustrates an important context in which utility issues often arise. *Ziegler* involved an appeal from a rejection of a U.S. patent application claiming priority in the discovery of polypropylene on the basis of a German patent application filed in 1954. The examiner rejected the claims at issue in part on the ground that the German application failed to disclose a practical utility for polypropylene. That application disclosed that polypropylene is "plastic-like" and that it may be pressed into a flexible film with a characteristic infrared spectrum. A previous court in another proceeding had rejected Ziegler's argument that the disclosure that polypropylene is "plastic-like" established its utility, and Ziegler was therefore precluded from relitigating this issue. Thus, the only remaining question was whether the disclosure that polypropylene is solid and that it may be pressed into a flexible film with a characteristic infrared spectrum was sufficient to establish a practical utility for the material. In affirming the PTO's determination that it did not, the Federal Circuit echoed the concerns over premature filings expressed by the Supreme Court in *Brenner v. Manson*:

> We are convinced that, at best, Ziegler was on the way to discovering a practical utility for polypropylene at the time of the filing of the German application; but in that application Ziegler had not yet gotten there.

Id. at 1203. The court concluded:

> While we are cognizant of Ziegler's noteworthy contributions to polymer chemistry, we must nevertheless abide by the principle underlying 35 U.S.C. § 101 that a patent "is not a reward for the search, but compensation for its successful conclusion."

Id., quoting *Brenner v. Manson*, 383 U.S. at 586.

Chapter 4

NOVELTY AND STATUTORY BARS

[A]ntiquity envies new improvements, and novelty is not content to add without defacing.

> — Francis Bacon[1]

The thing that hath been, it is that which shall be; and that which is done is that which shall be done: and there is no new thing under the sun. Is there anything whereof it may be said, See this is new? It hath been already of old time, which was before us.

> — Ecclesiastes 1:9, 10

In delay there lies no plenty.

> — William Shakespeare
> Twelfth Night, Act II, Scene 3

A. INTRODUCTION

To obtain a patent, you must do something *new*. This is bedrock patent law, and has been for a long time, at least since the seventeenth century. But from this simple idea — or, more properly, the statute which embodies it, 35 U.S.C. § 102 — springs a host of detailed issues. Our job in this chapter is to make sense of these issues, and (we hope) see how they relate to the central concept of newness in patent law.

Before delving into these details, however, we might first pause to reflect on why novelty is required at all. Consider the following passage from a stellar nineteenth century treatise:

An inventor does not become entitled to a patent merely by exercising his creative faculties in the production of an art [i.e., process] or instrument. The consideration for the grant of his exclusive privilege is the benefit which he confers upon the public by placing in their hands a means through the use of which their wants may be supplied. If the same means has already been made available to them by the inventive genius of a prior inventor, or if though they receive it first from him it is incapable of useful application, no benefit results to them from his inventive act and there is no consideration for his patent. When this want of consideration becomes apparent before a

---

[1] Quoted in 2 THE GREAT IDEAS: A SYNTOPICON OF GREAT BOOKS OF THE WESTERN WORLD (M. Adler ed., 1955), at 444.

patent has been granted it will be refused; when afterward, the patent is defeated.

1 W. ROBINSON, THE LAW OF PATENTS FOR USEFUL INVENTIONS § 221 (1890), at 305. Robinson analogizes the novelty of an invention to the consideration necessary to make a contract binding. This analogy makes the policy rationale behind the novelty requirement clear: society's contract with the inventor is binding because the inventor has given something of value (due to its newness) in exchange for the patent. Note that in this relationship, society is represented by the patent examiner. Even though he or she is society's "agent," however, the examiner may have different incentives than society at large. This is only one reason why the patent "contract" is an unusual one; it also helps explain why judicial review of issued patents is necessary.

1. OVERVIEW: BASIC DISTINCTIONS UNDER § 102

We now turn to the details of the patent law's "newness" requirements. We begin with the statute itself, 35 U.S.C. § 102:

§ 102. CONDITIONS FOR PATENTABILITY; NOVELTY AND LOSS OF RIGHT TO PATENT

A person shall be entitled to a patent unless —

(a) the invention was known or used by others in this country, or patented or described in a printed publication in this or a foreign country, before the invention thereof by the applicant for patent, or

(b) the invention was patented or described in a printed publication in this or a foreign country or in public use or on sale in this country, more than one year prior to the date of the application for patent in the United States, or

(c) he has abandoned the invention, or

(d) the invention was first patented or caused to be patented, or was the subject of an inventor's certificate, by the applicant or his legal representative or assigns in a foreign country prior to the date of the application for patent or inventor's certificate filed more than twelve months before the filing of the application in the United States, or

(e) the invention was described in a patent granted on an application for patent by another filed in the United States before the invention thereof by the applicant for patent, or on an international application by another who has fulfilled the requirements of [the U.S. version of the Patent Cooperation Treaty] before the invention thereof by the applicant for patent, or

(f) he did not himself invent the subject matter sought to be patented, or

(g) before the applicant's invention thereof the invention was made in this country by another who had not abandoned, suppressed, or concealed it. In determining priority of invention there shall be considered not only the respective dates of conception and reduction to practice of the invention, but also the reasonable diligence of one who was first to conceive and last to reduce to practice, from a time prior to conception by the other.

The single most important feature of § 102 is its repeated use of the words "the invention." One receives a patent unless *the invention* is known or used or patented or described in a publication (§ 102(a)); or *the invention* was abandoned (§ 102(c)); or *the invention* was described in a patent filed by another prior to the date of invention (§ 102(e)). In each case one who seeks a patent can be thwarted if his or her invention was somehow publicly available prior to some important date — either the date of invention (e.g., § 102(a)), or a year before filing a patent application (e.g., § 102(b)).

The phrase "the invention" means "any device substantially identical to the one constructed by the applicant." How identical does it have to be? As a preliminary matter, at least as alike as would justify calling it the same "invention." To be more precise, we will have to look at some cases dealing with what is known as the "identity" requirement. This we will do in Part B of this chapter.

The next major point to note about § 102 is that it really deals with two distinct sets of issues, one related to the date of *invention* and the other related to the applicant's *filing date*. The first set of issues, those related to the date of invention, falls under the heading of **novelty**. This makes sense, since questions such as "did someone else publish the same idea earlier?" obviously bear on whether the inventor was the first to hit upon that idea.

The second set of issues, those related to the *filing* date, are known as **statutory bars**, or the "loss of right" provisions as they are called in the statutory title to § 102. A quick look at § 102(b) reveals why they are called statutory bars; no patent will issue if, more than a year before the applicant's *filing date*, certain events occur (e.g., description in a printed publication, public use or sale). These events, then, "bar" the applicant from obtaining a patent.

In a sense, of course, the events referred to in § 102(a) also bar an applicant from obtaining a patent. But the difference is that § 102(a) events bar the patent because the inventor was *not first*, and § 102(b) events bar a patent because the inventor *did not apply for a patent soon enough*. Section 102(a), the novelty provision, seems fair because it simply codifies the principle that an inventor must come up with something new to deserve a patent. But § 102(b) is different; it says that even if an inventor comes up with something new, if she *waits too long* in filing a patent application, she will lose her right to the patent. Under § 102(b), the period by which "too long" is judged is more than a year prior to the filing of a patent application. (That is, the inventor has one year from the occurrence of one of the events specified in § 102(b) to file a patent application.) It is the arbitrary quality of the one-year time measure that gives § 102(b) and the other loss of right provisions their more "technical" quality, and leads us to characterize them as "statutory bars."

Thus the essence of novelty is being first with an invention, and the essence of the statutory bars is being quick to apply for a patent on that invention. Because of this difference, what is referred to as **"the critical date"** differs for the two sets of requirements. For novelty, the critical date is the date of invention. For statutory bars, the critical date is exactly one year prior to the filing of a patent application.

Another essential distinction between the novelty and statutory bar provisions of § 102 is that the former apply only to others besides the inventor, while the latter apply to everyone *including* the inventor. In other words, an inventor cannot defeat her own novelty by taking some action, such as publishing an article describing her invention. In a sense, this simply follows from the concept of novelty; it would not make sense to say an inventor was not first with an invention because she herself arrived at the same invention earlier. But an inventor *can* cause a statutory bar by her own actions — putting an invention on sale, for instance, more than a year prior to filing a patent application (§ 102(b)). In fact, many statutory bar cases involve actions taken by the inventor. (As Shakespeare says: "[T]hat we but teach Bloody instructions, which, being taught, return, to plague the inventor; this even-handed justice Commends the ingredients of our poison'd chalice to our own lips." *Macbeth*, I.vii.1.)

This highlights the different policies behind the two sets of rules. Novelty, by awarding the first inventor, ensures that society receives something new when it grants a patent. The statutory bars, on the other hand, reward *early disclosure*, by penalizing an inventor who waits too long to file a patent application. Early filing has three primary benefits: (1) it cuts down on the possibility that others will rely on a publicly available invention and later find out it is patented; (2) it encourages the prompt disclosure of new technical information, since patents are published when issued; and (3) it helps to limit the effective period of the inventor's monopoly, by encouraging her to start the clock of patent protection running as soon after the making of the invention as possible. *See generally* Note, *New Guidelines for Applying the "On Sale" Bar to Patentability*, 24 STAN. L. REV. 730, 732-35 (1972).

It may help your understanding of the issues covered in this chapter to think of § 102 as containing variations along four dimensions: (1) *type* of prior art reference (publication, use, etc.); (2) *persons* covered (inventor, inventor and others, only others); (3) *place* where prior art takes place (U.S. or elsewhere); and (4) *date* of prior art reference. The "prior art chart" at the end of this chapter summarizes how §§ 102(a) and (b) vary along these dimensions.

2. INTERNATIONAL CONSIDERATIONS: NOVELTY AND PRIORITY

Under § 102(a) of the Act, novelty is defined according to the date of invention. And § 102(g), which deals with prior invention by another, also refers to this date. The single greatest difference between the U.S. patent system and those of the rest of the world is in these two sections. For in almost every other country, an applicant's novelty is measured as of the *filing* date. Likewise in most other countries the question of who invented first, the subject of our § 102(g) is, strictly speaking, irrelevant; the only relevant question is who *filed* first. As a consequence, priority disputes — involved disputes over who was the first inventor, resolved under U.S. law by a procedure known as an interference (discussed in Section C of this chapter) — are unknown in Europe, Japan, and virtually every other country. The first to file wins the patent, and that is the end of the question. One outgrowth of this difference is that in Europe, Japan and almost every other country, the critical date with respect to novelty is the date the patent application was filed.

Another difference between the U.S. and most other countries is that many countries use the same date for novelty and the statutory bars — the date of filing. In Europe and (for the most part) Japan, as well as most other countries, the date of filing is the critical date for novelty purposes. This means that if an invention was known or used by others, or described in a printed publication, or the like, anytime before the filing date, no patent will issue.[2] This differs from U.S. law in two ways, one of which we have already touched on. This is the fact that under § 102(a) of the U.S. Patent Act, the critical date is the date of invention. Since invention will always occur before (or, at the very least, on the same day as) filing, the U.S. system removes much prior art that other systems must consider in judging novelty. (To see why, recall that moving the critical date backward, as U.S. law does with respect to other countries, diminishes the amount of time there was before the critical date; and the less time there is before this date, the fewer publications, prior uses, etc., there will be.)

The second way these other systems differ from that of the U.S. is that they have no separate critical date for statutory bars. They use the filing date as the only critical date that matters. Recall that the purpose behind the statutory bars is to encourage inventors to file for patents soon after making an invention. Under the European and Japanese systems, the critical date for both novelty and the statutory bars is the filing date rather than either the date of invention or one year before filing. Hence, the European and Japanese systems combine the features of our novelty and statutory bar provisions in a single requirement, which combines what we call novelty and statutory bars, and which is based on the date of filing.

From a practical point of view, this difference affects the life of a patent practitioner in very profound ways. First and foremost, it means that even though the statutory bars give some "protection" under U.S. law for public disclosure or use after invention but before filing, there is no such protection in Europe and Japan. This stems from the fact that only the filing date matters under the patent laws of these countries. Thus there is (generally speaking) no **grace period** under

---

[2]There are some minor exceptions in Japan. *See* EXAMINATION GUIDELINES FOR PATENT AND UTILITY MODELS IN JAPAN (AIPPI Japan 1994), Sec. II, Ch. 1, at 1-10.

these systems. Even if one has solid proof of the date of invention, one must still make haste to the patent office, since any public activity — by the inventor or a third party — prior to the date of filing can disqualify the invention from patentability. Contrast this with the statutory bars, whose critical date of one year prior to filing gives the patentee one year from the date of public disclosure to file for a patent.

For example, if a scientist invents something in the U.S. and publishes an article describing it on January 1, 1993, she has a one-year *grace period* in which to file. Her invention is patentable if she files on or before January 1, 1994. This follows from the fact that the statutory bar provisions of the U.S. Patent Act make an invention unpatentable if it is described in a printed publication more than one year before filing a patent on it. In the U.S., in other words, publication starts a one-year clock running. As long as the inventor files for a U.S. patent before the clock runs out, her rights are preserved. By contrast, in Europe and Japan under current law there is *no clock*, no grace period. Publication before filing destroys patentability. Thus it is *critical* under these patent systems to file first and publish later. Unless the U.S. government is successful in current efforts to convince these countries to adopt a grace period, U.S. practitioners must adapt to this system if worldwide patent rights are to be preserved.

In the U.S., it is important to note, the statutory bar clock can be set running by the activities of a third party — e.g., the publication of an article describing the invention or the offering of the invention for sale by an independent third party. Thus, an inventor can never rely completely on the statutory bar grace period. That is, an applicant does not *always* have a year after the date of invention before the statutory bars take effect, since a third party may have performed some act that sets the clock running even before the applicant in question made her invention. Nevertheless, there is some breathing room, and as a practical matter, in most cases the breathing room will be the full year when no one else has thought of or disclosed the same invention. In other words, third-party statutory bars are relatively rare.

Whatever the benefits of the grace period in the U.S., it is critical to understand that there is only a very limited grace period in Europe and Japan. In Europe, a grace period of six months is granted when someone steals an invention, or when an invention is displayed at an Exhibition licensed by the European Patent Office. *See* Article 54 of the European Patent Convention.

In summary, the grace period provided by § 102(b) should *not* be relied on when international rights are desired. Because this is often the case, it can be said that the grace period implicit in the statutory bars of § 102(b) is not as important as it was when the U.S. economy was more isolated from the rest of the world.

We turn now to an outline of § 102.

3. A SCHEMATIC REPRESENTATION OF § 102(a) and (b)

Beginning in Section B of this chapter, we consider the nuts and bolts of novelty and statutory bars. Many pitfalls await us here; this is one of the knottiest sections in the entire patent statute. To make the exposition in this and following sections clear, we must somehow break § 102 into its smallest components. The version of § 102 reproduced below does this, by compacting each element in the statute. We will refer to this "102 Schematic" throughout this chapter:

Schematic Representation of § 102

§ 102(a): Novelty

[1] No patent if, before date of invention, invention$_a$ —
   [A] known or
   [B] used
      [C] by others
      [D] in this country, or
[2] invention$_a$ —
   [A] patented or
   [B] described in a printed publication
      [C] anywhere.

§ 102(b): Statutory Bars

[1] No patent if, more than one year prior to application, invention$_b$
   [A] patented or
   [B] described in printed publication
      [C] anywhere, or
[2] invention$_b$ —
   [A] in public use or
   [B] on sale
      [C] in this country.

The terminology "invention$_a$" and "invention$_b$" is meant to signify that the definition of "invention" is different for § 102(a) and § 102(b). This is explained below in the sections on "The Identity Requirement" in Sections B and C of this chapter.

The "Critical Date" and "References"

In § 102, dates are all-important. One's ability to obtain a patent very often depends critically on the effective date assigned to a piece of the prior art.

These "pieces" of the prior art, by the way, are called "references." A reference can be a prior article or patent, a previous public use or demonstration, or anything else encompassed by the terminology of § 102. Most frequently, however, "reference" is used to refer to a printed source, such as a prior publication or patent.

Section 102(a) makes the date of *invention* the key date; if a prior art reference is assigned a date earlier than the date of invention, then the invention is anticipated by the reference. So under § 102(a), we are comparing (1) the invention date against (2) the reference date. In the realm of § 102(a), then, the *invention date* is the **critical date**. If inventor A has a date of invention of June 1, 1990, for instance, this is the critical date for novelty purposes. A scholarly article in a scientific journal with an effective date of June 2 will *not* anticipate the invention — it is made public *after* the critical date.

Section 102(b), concerned as it is with encouraging prompt filing, focusses on another date: the date one year prior to the filing of the inventor's patent application. If a reference has an effective date more than a year before filing, the patent is barred. When § 102(b) statutory bar issues are at stake, then, we compare (1) the date exactly one year prior to filing against (2) the reference date. In the example just mentioned, assume the inventor files for a patent on September 1, 1990. The **critical date** for § 102(b) purposes in this case is thus September 1, *1989*. (Recall that § 102(b) actually says "*more than* one year" before filing.) Any reference appearing *before* the critical date will create a statutory bar which prevents the inventor from obtaining a patent. Thus a reference whose effective date is August 31 *will* create a statutory bar. But the same reference, if its effective date were September 1, or September 2, or later, will not. This, incidentally, is the source of the grace period. The inventor knows if she publishes on September 2 that she must file a patent application within a year. She has a one-year grace period, in other words, because there can be no statutory bar by a publication *less than* a year before filing. The "bar" begins when the grace period ends.

B. SECTION 102(a): THE NOVELTY REQUIREMENT

1. THE IDENTITY REQUIREMENT UNDER § 102(a)

As the Schematic Representation of § 102 shows, there are many phrases in § 102(a) that recur in § 102(b). As we shall see, these phrases do not always mean the same thing in both sections. An important example of this is the phrase "the invention" in the two sections. There are two different tests for determining when a prior art reference is sufficient (i.e., complete and detailed enough) to preclude patentability. (Thus the terminology "invention$_a$" and "invention$_b$" in the 102 Schematic above.)

We deal here with the identity requirement for § 102(a); the § 102(b) identity issue is discussed below in Section C of this chapter.

Note two points about the following case: first, two patents are involved, the "051" and "977" patents. Second, the accused infringer, Park, defends by saying these patents are invalid because they lack novelty under § 102(a). The issue in the case is whether the cited references are enough to show that the patents lack novelty — i.e., whether the references describe the same invention as that claimed in the patents. Put another way, the issue is whether these references "anticipate" the claimed inventions.

STRUCTURAL RUBBER PRODUCTS CO. v. PARK RUBBER CO.

749 F.2d 707, 223 U.S.P.Q. (BNA) 1264 (Fed. Cir. 1984)

Structural Rubber Products Co. appeals from the judgment of the District Court holding Park not liable for infringement of U.S. Patent Nos. 3,843,051 and 4,117,977, owned by appellant. The district court's judgment is based on invalidity of the patents for lack of novelty (35 U.S.C. § 102) in accordance with an answer given by a jury within a special verdict.

Structural argues that the district court erred in failing to grant its motion for judgment notwithstanding the verdict because there was no evidence to support the lack of novelty defense with respect to either patent.

The two patents in suit are directed to highway railroad crossings having a moisture-proof traffic surface designed primarily to prevent the degradation of track subgrade. The crossing is formed by a number of rectangular tubes aligned in the direction of the train track, which are covered by a resilient waterproof lamina. The inventor named in the two patents in suit is Jacob Whitlock, an officer and principal shareholder of Structural. The first of the two patents, U.S. Patent No. 3,843,051, issued October 23, 1974, discloses a crossing formed of a middle section, which fits between the two rails, and two side sections, which run from the outer side of each rail to the main roadway. To insure a water-tight seal between the rails and the crossing, the center section is oversized and must be bowed for insertion, thereby providing a compression fit as shown [in Figure 4-1].

The side portions (not illustrated [in Figure 4-1]) are firmly anchored to the railroad ties at their outermost edge to prevent lateral movement and form a tight seal against the rail. To extend the crossing portions end-to-end down the track, an overlapping splicer piece is disclosed and claimed in the patent. Claim 9, used during trial as representative of the invention, is [excerpted] below:

> In a highway railway crossing, ... a pair of elongated composite members arranged in abutting end-to-end relation and positionable between the rails and overlying a plurality of the rail supporting ties, each composite member comprising a one-piece upper lamina of resilient moisture-proof material having recessed, compressible elongated side edges for resilient sealing engagement with web portions of the rails, *a plurality of elongated reinforcing elements arranged in laterally spaced substantially parallel relation,* ... and *splicer means* [illustrated in Figure 4-2] *interconnecting the corresponding reinforcing elements, the splicer means for each pair of aligned reinforcing elements* extending longitudinally of the elements a substantial distance in opposite directions from the joint.

The [italicized] portions are significant to our decision.

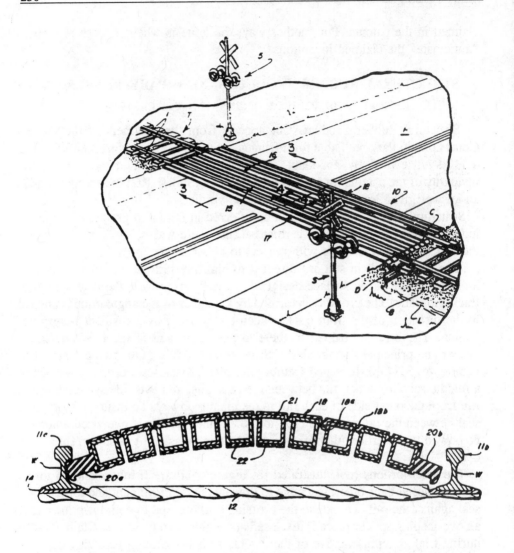

Figure 4-1

The second patent, U.S. Patent No. 4,117,977, issued October 3, 1978, discloses an improvement on the invention of the '051 patent. To facilitate the manufacture and installation of the crossing, the center section is divided into two halves. As shown [in Figure 4-3] an overlapping tongue-in-groove structure is present at the center joint to prevent any potential leakage.

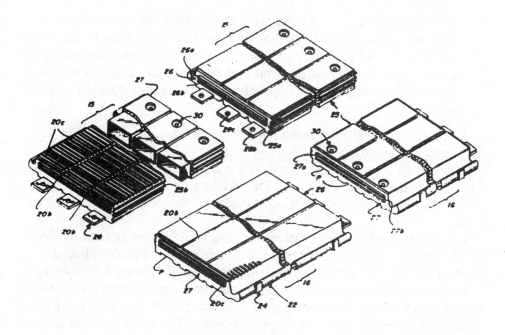

Figure 4-2

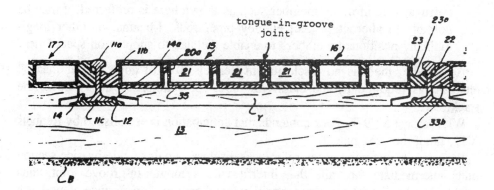

Figure 4-3

The halves of the center section are oversized so that a compression seal is created at the junction of the halves, and between the outer edges of the halves and the rails. Representative claim 14, used at trial, is [excerpted] below:

> In a highway crossing for a railroad wherein each of a pair of rails has a base section and a head section interconnected by a web section ..., the combination comprising: *at least one pair of elongated laterally-resilient gage section units adapted to be arranged in side-by-side relation intermediate the rails*, said units having corresponding elongated inner faces in

abutting relation, ... each unit having an elongated outer face adapted to be disposed adjacent the web section of a rail and in substantial engagement therewith and *an inner face provided with projecting segments constructed unitary with the gage section unit that interfit in an elongated tongue-in-groove relationship with corresponding segments of the adjacent unit of said pair* ....

Again, [italics have] been added to point out the elements of the claim which are principally in issue.

Based on the answers of the jury the court entered judgment in favor of Park. The district court denied the motion for JNOV on the novelty issue. On appeal, Park contends that the lack of novelty verdict is supported by substantial evidence.

The reference which Park contends supports the jury's verdict that the invention of the '051 patent lacks novelty is U.S. Patent No. 2,828,079, issued to C. H. Rennels, for a rubber railroad crossing as shown [in Figure 4-4, next page].

Rennels '079 discloses a crossing with a one-piece rubber center section which is reinforced by a corrugated metal plate, in contrast to the "plurality of elongated reinforcing elements" called for in the '051 claims. The specification of Rennels '079, however, states:

> Those skilled in the art will also recognize that while a longitudinally corrugated reinforcing member such as shown here is preferred, it may be possible to alternately [sic] employ pipe, rods, I-beams, or other longitudinally positioned members to enable the slab to support on spaced ties.

Admittedly, there is no disclosure in Rennels '079 of any "splicer means" element, as required by the claims in '051, for splicing sections "down the track."

With respect to '977, Park contends that anticipation is established by Rennels '079, [and] the '051 patent.

Park admits that none of the references discloses a pair of side-by-side section units intermediate the rails that interfit with a tongue-in-groove joint, thus confirming the district court's recognition that there was "an absence of evidence on the [novelty] issue."

A review of the evidence set out above leaves no room for doubt that Structural's attack on the judgment was well founded and that its motion for JNOV should have been granted. This court has repeatedly stated that the defense of lack of novelty (i.e., "anticipation") can only be established by a single prior art reference which discloses each and every element of the claimed invention. *RCA Corp. v. Applied Digital Data Systems, Inc.*, 730 F.2d 1440, 1444, 221 U.S.P.Q. 385, 388 (Fed. Cir. 1984).

The statutory language mandates such an approach. Section 102 speaks in terms of the invention having been known or used by others, or patented or described in a printed publication. Moreover, Section 103 provides that a patent may not

March 25, 1958   C. H. RENNELS   2,828,080

RAILROAD CROSSING STRUCTURE
Filed May 10, 1954

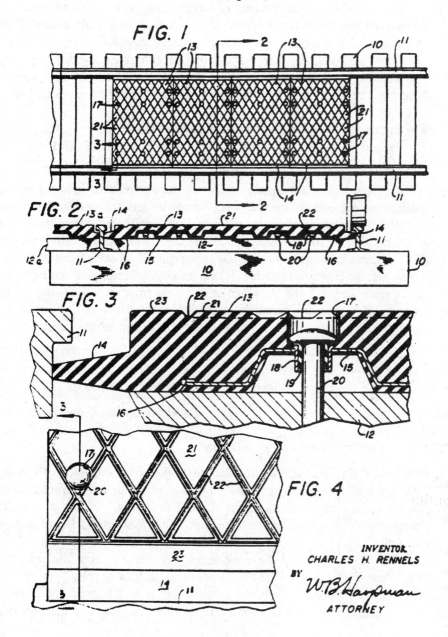

INVENTOR
CHARLES H. RENNELS
BY
W.B. Harpman
ATTORNEY

Figure 4-4

be obtained "though the invention is not *identically* disclosed or described as set forth in Section 102" (emphasis added). In view of Park's admissions that no single prior art reference discloses each element of any claim of either '051 or '977, the defense of invalidity for lack of novelty fails as a matter of law.

Park characterized the differences over the prior art here as "insubstantial" or "clearly obvious," and argues that the inventions, therefore, are not novel. However, Park misconstrues [the] import of [the earlier cases on this point]. While the teaching in the prior reference need not be *ipsissimis verbis*, nevertheless, there must be a teaching with respect to the entirety of the claimed invention.

Park's arguments are indistinguishable from statements made by the district court in *Connell v. Sears, Roebuck & Co.* [quoted in 722 F.2d 1542, 220 U.S.P.Q. (BNA) 193 (Fed. Cir. 1983)], which this court rejected as follows:

> The opinion says anticipation may be shown by less than "complete anticipation" if one of ordinary skill may in reliance on the prior art "complete the work required for the invention," and that "it is sufficient for an anticipation 'if the general aspects are the same and the differences in minor matters is only such as would suggest itself to one of ordinary skill in the art.'" Those statements relate to obviousness, not anticipation. Anticipation requires the presence in a single prior art disclosure of all elements of a claimed invention arranged as in the claim. A prior art disclosure that "almost" meets that standard may render the claim invalid under § 103; it does not "anticipate."

722 F.2d at 1548, 220 U.S.P.Q. at 198. Thus, Park's arguments can not substitute for the absence of evidence of an anticipatory reference.

Reversed, vacated, and remanded.

NOTES

1. *Every Element Test.* The court states that "the defense of lack of novelty (i.e., 'anticipation') can only be established by a single prior art reference which discloses each and every element of the claimed invention." It then goes on to hold that the trial court should have granted the plaintiff/patentee's JNOV motion to overturn the jury verdict finding anticipation. What were the elements of the claimed inventions? Which of these elements was missing from the prior art reference asserted by the defendant as establishing lack of novelty?

A good way to approach problems of this sort is to construct the kind of "comparison chart" described in Chapter 1. Here is a comparison chart for this case:

	Whitlock '051 Patent	Whitlock '977 Patent	Rennels Patent
Elements			
1. Grade crossing cover laid over ties and between rails	X	X	X
2. Interfitting "splicer means" to connect segments of the grade crossing cover to one another lengthwise	X	X	—
3. Two-piece construction, with tongue-in-groove joinder of two pieces	—	X	—
4. Corrugated metal "cap" on top of rubber or other material laid between the tracks	—	—	X

This makes clear what element was missing from the Rennels patent (the "splicer" means), and thus why the '051 patent was novel.

The diagram also demonstrates several other points. Recall that Whitlock's second patent, the '977 patent, is, as the court states, an improvement patent which teaches a two-piece construction for grade crossing protection units. Specifically, the '977 design uses a "tongue-in-groove" joint to connect each half of the grade crossing units. In the court's analysis of the novelty of the '977 patent it is clear that the '051 patent is available as prior art against the '977 patent *even though they were both issued to the same inventor.* As the diagram shows, the '977 patent claims subject matter distinct from, and therefore novel over, the '051 patent. The basic insight of the '051 patent is that track covers can be formed by modules spliced together down the length of the track. The '977 patent builds on this by adding two-piece construction to each module. The two halves make the track cover easier to install, while still providing a tight fit.

As we shall see in Chapter 7, there are some interesting twists when an inventor files two patent applications at or near the same time and one contains material that would be *obvious* in light of the other. To summarize that discussion, it is possible for the inventor in that situation to obtain both patents by "disclaiming" a portion of the second, obvious, one. No such compromise is possible when the second application includes material that is anticipated in (i.e., lacks novelty because of) the first, however. This is why the '051 patent must be analyzed to determine whether the invention claimed in the '977 patent is novel or not.

The second point to notice in the diagram is that the list of elements in the two patents to Whitlock are drawn from the *claims.* This is the essence of novelty: comparing the claims of the patent in issue to the information contained in the cited references. *See, e.g.*, *De La Vergne Bottle & Seal Co. v. Valentine Blatz Brewing Co.*, 66 F. 765 (7th Cir. 1895) (differences between inventor's actual practice and prior art reference irrelevant; relevant comparison is between claimed invention and prior art). In the *Structural Rubber* case we are dealing primarily with one cited reference, the patent to Rennels. Thus we are comparing the claims in the two Whitlock patents to the information in the Rennels patent. (We also analyze the claims of the Whitlock '977 patent against the totality of information in the Whitlock '051 patent.) But note the court's discussion of the paragraph from Rennels' specification which suggests the possibility of using "pipe, rods, I-beams, or other longitudinally [i.e., length-wise] positioned members to enable the slab to support itself on spaced ties." Although the court ultimately concludes this information is not enough to anticipate the '051 patent, the court also recognizes that this information is relevant to the determination of novelty. In other words, *all the information* in the Rennels patent — including all statements in the specification — must be analyzed to see if it anticipates the invention claimed in the '051 patent to Whitlock. Thus it is clear that, when confronted with a patent reference, call it *A*, said to defeat the novelty of an invention claimed in patent *B*, the *entire disclosure in A* must be compared with *the claims in B* to determine novelty.

The source for this, of course, is once again the statute; § 102(a) says that the novelty of "an invention" (measured by its claims) may be defeated by "a patent," which can only mean *all* the information contained in that patent. To see why, note that § 102(a) refers to "patent or printed publication," a reference which implies that all published information is to be considered when determining novelty. Would it make sense to consider everything in a printed publication, e.g., a scientific article, but only the claims in a patent, as relevant in deciding whether a particular invention was new or not? Would that put too much stress on what the author of the prior patent chose to claim, as opposed to disclose, in the prior patent?

2. *Merging of Distinct Issues.* One must be careful in reading the older cases, because they tended to collapse together two and sometimes three issues we now consider quite distinct: novelty (§ 102(a) of the 1952 Act), statutory bars (§ 102(b) of the 1952 Act) and nonobviousness (§ 103 of the 1952 Act). *Cf. RCA Corp. v. Applied Digital Data Sys.*, 730 F.2d 1440, 221 U.S.P.Q. (BNA) 385 (Fed. Cir. 1984) (Kashiwa, J., dissenting, arguing that Court of Claims precedent adopted "equivalency" test for anticipation); *American Seating Co. v. National Seating Co.*, 586 F. Supp. 611, 199 U.S.P.Q. (BNA) 257 (6th Cir. 1978) ("This Court has repeatedly defined the proper standard with respect to anticipation as requiring that all elements of a patented device *or their equivalent* be found in a single pre-existing structure or description").

3. *A Classic Statement. Knapp v. Morss,* 150 U.S. 221 (1893), is often quoted for the following passage:

There is another test as to the validity of the second claim. If the Balch, Everett, Wilson, or Ferris patents, ... were subsequent in date to that of the Hall patent, they would constitute an infringement thereof, for the rule is well established that "that which infringes, if later, would anticipate if earlier." *Peters v. Active Mfg. Co.*, 129 U.S. 530, 537 [1889].

The analogy between infringement (the subject of Chapter 8) and anticipation has been addressed by the Federal Circuit, which added the following refinement to the rule:

While "the classic test of anticipation" was indeed as stated, under the current statute "anticipation" does not carry the same meaning as before, and the "classic test" must be modified to: That which would *literally* infringe if later in time anticipates if earlier than the date of invention.

Lewmar Marine, Inc. v. Barient, Inc., 827 F.2d 744, 747, 3 U.S.P.Q.2d 1766; *See also* Wepner, *The Patent Invalidity/Infringement Parallel: Symmetry or Semantics?*, 93 DICK. L. REV. 67 (1988). Note that the "classic" test *would* be an accurate statement of the identity test for purposes of the statutory bars, § 102(b). See Section C of this chapter.

4. *Comparative Note.* In Japan, a "substantial identity" rule is applied in testing novelty; this is a more "relaxed" standard, according to one commentator. *See* Takenaka, *The Substantial Identity Rule Under the Japanese Novelty Standard*, 9 UCLA PAC. BASIN L.J. 220, 222 (1991).

2. THE "ENABLEMENT STANDARD" FOR ANTICIPATION

In *Dewey & Almy Chem. Co. v. Mimex Co.*, 124 F.2d 986, 52 U.S.P.Q. (BNA) 138 (2d Cir. 1942), Judge Learned Hand wrote:

No doctrine of the patent law is better established than that a prior patent or other publication to be an anticipation must bear within its four corners adequate directions for the practice of the patent invalidated. If the earlier disclosure offers no more than a starting point for further experiments, if its teaching will sometimes succeed and sometimes fail, if it does not inform the art without more how to practice the new invention, it has not correspondingly enriched the store of common knowledge, and it is not an anticipation.

Despite the seeming clarity of this "four corners" test, it is not always easy to apply. Consider the following excerpt. When reading the case, remember that a "series circuit" is an electrical circuit where the electrons follow only one path, e.g., one wire connected to a power source and an electrical appliance. A "parallel circuit" is a circuit with multiple paths having a common voltage source, e.g., the typical lighting circuits in a house. *See* BUREAU OF NAVAL PERSONNEL, BASIC ELECTRICITY (Dover ed. 1970), at 57, 85.

In re GRAVES

69 F.3d 1147, 36 U.S.P.Q.2d 1697 (Fed. Cir. 1995)

RICH, CIRCUIT JUDGE.

[T]he Board affirmed the examiner's final rejection of claims 4-6 of [Graves'] application, entitled "Power Interconnect Tester." The Board affirmed the rejection of claims 4 and 6 under 35 U.S.C. § 102(b) as being anticipated by Rockwell et al., U.S. Patent No. 4,399,400 (Rockwell), and affirmed the rejection of claim 5 under section 102(b) as being anticipated by Coben, U.S. Patent No. 4,814,693 (Coben). We affirm.

The claimed invention is a device and method for testing electrical systems by applying signals, checking for the continued presence of those applied signals, identifying points or wires that are shorted, recording such data, and comparing that data to previously recorded data to check for the presence of errors. Independent claims 4, 5, and 6 are the only claims remaining in the application.

Our first task on the merits is to decide whether the PTO's rejection of claims 4 and 6 under section 102(b), as being anticipated by Rockwell, was proper. Claim[ ] 4 read[s] as follows:

> 4. A test system and method for testing the integrity of the interconnections of electronic systems by testing for continuity from each point on the interconnect of an electronic system under test simultaneously to multiple selected power, ground and other connection points or wires, comprising the steps of:
>
> (a) controllably applying a test signal sequen[t]ially to each point on the interconnect of the electronic system under test;
> (b) simultaneously monitoring the selected multiple connection points or wires for presence of the test signal which is applied sequen[t]ially to each point on the interconnect of the system under test;
> (c) identifying each interconnect point and selected multiple connection point or wire which are connected or shorted together; and
> (d) comparing test data to records of the system under test for errors.

The Board found that Rockwell teaches continuity testing of wire harnesses and using scanners to apply test signals and to monitor their presence. According to the Board, Rockwell teaches obtaining test data and comparing it to known good data. The Board also found that Rockwell describes an interface adapter, a processor unit, a read-only memory, a recorder, a frequency shifted key modulator, and a power supply. In view of the above, the Board concluded that Rockwell meets all of the limitations of claims 4 and 6 and thereby anticipates these claims. We agree and accordingly affirm the rejection.

The dissent expresses the view that Rockwell fails to teach element (b) of claim 4. This raises two issues: proper construction of claim 4 and what Rockwell teaches.

As construed by the dissent, element (b) requires the simultaneous monitoring of each of multiple connection points or wires (i.e., each of multiple output points). The Board, on the other hand, construed element (b) to require the simultaneous monitoring of input and output points, but not necessarily the simultaneous monitoring of an input point and multiple output points. We conclude that the Board properly gave claim 4 as broad a reading as possible not inconsistent with the applicant's disclosure.

Even assuming, however, that the dissent's construction of claim 4 is correct, Rockwell nevertheless anticipates claim 4, even if it does not specifically disclose simultaneous monitoring of the output points, if simultaneous or parallel monitoring is within the knowledge of a skilled artisan. *See, e.g., In re LeGrice*, 301 F.2d 929, 133 U.S.P.Q. 365 (C.C.P.A. 1962) (A reference anticipates a claim if it discloses the claimed invention "such that a skilled artisan could take its teachings in combination with his own knowledge of the particular art and be in possession of the invention." *Id.* at 936, 133 U.S.P.Q. at 372; *In re Donohue*, 766 F.2d 531, 533, 226 U.S.P.Q. 619, 621 (Fed. Cir. 1985) (same).

Even the applicant, in item 12 of his request for reconsideration of the Board's 30 September 1994 decision, stated that one with knowledge of "basic electronics and simple logic" would understand the difference between the operation of the series circuit of Rockwell and the parallel circuit of the claimed invention. Thus, even under the dissent's construction of claim 4, the Board correctly held that a skilled artisan could take Rockwell's teachings in combination with his own knowledge and be in possession of the device of applicant's claim 4.

[Affirmed.]

NIES, SENIOR CIRCUIT JUDGE, dissenting in part.

I would reverse the Board's decision that claim 4 is anticipated by Rockwell. Claim 4 requires "simultaneously monitoring the selected multiple connection points or wires for presence of the test signal." I construe that claim language to mean that multiple points must be monitored for the test signal, a single test signal, at the same time — i.e., "simultaneously." The Board concluded that Rockwell taught this claim element "[s]ince continuity testing requires that the input and output points be simultaneously selected for application of an input potential and an output 'ground' potential." Under this construction, with which the majority apparently agrees, the word "simultaneously" is rendered superfluous. It is axiomatic that, in a continuity test of a wire, one must monitor the connection point at the same time the test signal is applied.

Regarding the construction of claim 4, the majority states:

The Board, on the other hand, construed element (b) to require the simultaneous monitoring of input and output points, but not necessarily the simultaneous monitoring of an input point and multiple output points. We conclude that the Board properly gave claim 4 as broad a reading as possible not inconsistent with the applicant's disclosure.

While I agree with the majority's restatement of the Board's construction, that construction is inconsistent with plain language of the specification. Graves' specification clearly states, in several different places, the "one-to-many" concept of applying a single test signal and simultaneously monitoring multiple points for the presence of the test signal. For example, the specification recites:

> No prior test systems or methods util[i]ze the present invention's technique for testing the integrity of an electronic system's interconnections versus selected multiple connection points or wires. The technique comprises applying a test signal sequen[t]ially while simultaneously monitoring all the selected multiple points for the presence of said test signal, thus indicating continuity to the single point under test.

The Rockwell reference does not anticipate claim 4 because it does not teach monitoring multiple points simultaneously. Rather, the Rockwell reference teaches checking continuity of a wire harness from a single input point to a single output point. Thus, while the Rockwell reference teaches monitoring multiple points, it teaches doing so one wire at a time, not testing multiple wires simultaneously.

Remarkably, the majority opts to overlook this fatal shortfall and concludes that "Rockwell meets all of the limitations" of claim 4.

While basic circuit knowledge encompasses the difference between a series circuit and a parallel circuit, the majority concludes that a skilled artisan (who undoubtedly would have that basic knowledge) would, after reading Rockwell, ipso facto be in possession of the claimed invention at the time the invention was made. Doing so is purely hindsight evaluation of the claims, and improperly minimizes Graves' invention.

––––––––

Besides the intrinsic difficulty of applying the enablement standard, there are two other considerations that cloud its application: (1) extrinsic evidence to interpret the reference; and (2) incorporation by reference of ancillary documents.

A recent case of note on the use of extrinsic evidence is *Ciba-Geigy Corp. v. Alza Corp.*, 864 F. Supp. 429, 33 U.S.P.Q.2d 1018 (D.N.J. 1994). This case dealt with the validity of a basic patent on the transdermal nicotine patch, a simple concept that has helped deliver many from the clutches of nicotine addiction. The patent was anticipated, defendant asserted, by virtue of a letter to the editor of *Nature* magazine by a Dr. Cecil Fox. In the letter, which was published more than a year prior to plaintiff's patent application (see the sections on the Statutory Bars, below), Dr. Fox discussed various ways nicotine could be introduced into the bloodstream:

> Alternative routes of drug administration more cosmetic than chewing tobacco or snuffs should be developed so that the nicotine addict has alternatives to cigarettes. Nicotine chewing gum has had limited success, but may soon

become available worldwide. Another alternative might be transdermal application much in the manner of nitroglycerine [sic] and scopolomine [sic] [motion sickness] patches. Nicotine "inhalers" might also be feasible if dosage could be adjusted. I would appreciate receiving correspondence from individuals or groups actively engaged in finding alternative methods of nicotine delivery in humans.

Cecil H. Fox, *Nicotine Delivery*, NATURE, Jan. 19, 1984, at 205.

To show the adequacy of this letter as an anticipating reference, defendants introduced extrinsic evidence, in the form of an affidavit from a noted expert on transdermal patches, Dr. Brian Barry. Dr. Barry asserted not only that in general one skilled in the art could have substituted nicotine as the active ingredient in a then-existing transdermal patch, but also that he in fact had done so, substituting nicotine in a transdermal nitroglycerine patch of a type known and available when the Fox letter was published in 1984. For guidance in conducting this substitution, according to the court,

> Dr. Barry looked to the following items of extrinsic evidence to interpret the Fox letter: 1. Articles that discuss how much nicotine must be present in the bloodstream to have an effect on the body. 2. The Transderm-Nitro leaflet to learn how much nitroglycerin was contained in this patch.

864 F. Supp. 429, 436.

The district court found that it was appropriate to consider both the testimony of Dr. Barry and his use of extrinsic references in deciding the issue of anticipation:

> Extrinsic evidence may be considered to explain, but not expand on, the meaning of an anticipatory reference. *In re Baxter Travenol Labs*, 952 F.2d 388, 390 (Fed. Cir. 1991); *Scripps Clinic & Research Fdn. v. Genentech Inc.*, 927 F.2d 1565, 1576 (Fed. Cir. 1991) .... Specifically, the Court may look to extrinsic evidence to learn how the person of ordinary skill would interpret an anticipatory reference:
>
>> It is sometimes appropriate to consider extrinsic evidence to explain the disclosure of a reference. Such factual elaboration is necessarily of limited scope and probative value, for a finding of anticipation requires that all aspects of the claimed invention were already described in a single reference: a finding that is not supportable if it is necessary to prove facts beyond those disclosed in the reference in order to meet the claim limitations. The role of extrinsic evidence is to educate the decision-maker to what the reference means to persons of ordinary skill in the field of the invention, not to fill gaps in the reference. *Scripps Clinic [supra]* at 1576.

The extrinsic evidence relied on by Dr. Barry does not expand the Fox letter but merely reveals the technical knowledge available to persons of ordinary skill in the field. A person of ordinary skill in this field would inherently know where to look to learn about nicotine levels in blood and would know to look at the leaflet to learn how big the drug reservoir was in an existing patch. This extrinsic evidence does no more than indicate knowledge readily available to persons of ordinary skill in the field. It is therefore, appropriate, to consider this extrinsic evidence when interpreting the Fox letter.

864 F. Supp. 429, 436-37.

NOTES

1. The Supreme Court in *Seymour v. Osborne*, 78 U.S. (11 Wall.) 516 (1870) stated:

Patented inventions cannot be superseded [i.e., anticipated] ... unless the description and drawings [of the reference] contain and exhibit a substantial representation of the patented improvement in such full, clear and exact terms as to enable any person skilled in the art or science to which it appertains to make, construct and practice the invention to the same practical extent as they would be enabled to do if the information was derived from a prior patent. Mere vague and general representations will not support such a defense.

See also Paperless Accounting, Inc. v. Bay Area Rapid Transit Sys., 804 F.2d 659, 665, 231 U.S.P.Q. 649, 653 (Fed. Cir. 1986) (stating that "even if the claimed invention is disclosed in a printed publication, that disclosure will not suffice as prior art if it was not enabling.").

2. In White, *The Novelty-Destroying Disclosure: Some Recent Decisions*, 9 EUR. INTELL. PROP. REV. 315, 318 (1990), the author describes the tension between the British cases, some of which have adopted the theory that a disclosure need not be enabling, and those of the European Patent Organization, a centralized Europe-wide patent examining bureau which has consistently adhered to the enablement standard.

TITANIUM METALS CORP. v. BANNER
778 F.2d 775, 227 U.S.P.Q. (BNA) 773 (Fed. Cir. 1985)

This appeal is from an Order of the United States District Court for the District of Columbia in a civil action brought pursuant to 35 U.S.C. 145 against Donald W. Banner as Commissioner of Patents and Trademarks authorizing the Commissioner to issue to appellee a patent containing claims for [a] "TITANIUM ALLOY." The Commissioner has appealed. We reverse.

The inventors, Loren C. Covington and Howard R. Palmer, employees of appellee to whom they have assigned their invention and the application thereon, filed an application [in] 1974 to patent an alloy they developed. The application involved on this appeal is a continuation-in-part thereof, filed [in] 1975, containing the claims on appeal. The alloy is made primarily of titanium (Ti) and contains small amounts of nickel (Ni) and molybdenum (Mo) as alloying ingredients to give the alloy certain desirable properties, particularly corrosion resistance in hot brine solutions, while retaining workability so that articles such as tubing can be fabricated from it by rolling, welding and other techniques. The inventors apparently also found that iron content should be limited, iron being an undesired impurity rather than an alloying ingredient. They determined the permissible ranges of the components, above and below which the desired properties were not obtained. A precise definition of the invention sought to be patented is found in the claims, [two of which are] set forth below.

1. A titanium base alloy consisting essentially by weight of about 0.6% to 0.9% nickel, 0.2% to 0.4% molybdenum, up to 0.2% maximum iron, balance titanium, said alloy being characterized by good corrosion resistance in hot brine environments.

2. A titanium base alloy as set forth in Claim 1 having up to 0.1% iron, balance titanium.

The examiner's final rejection was on the grounds that claims 1 and 2 are anticipated (fully met) by an article by Kalabukhova and Mikheyew, Investigation of the Mechanical Properties of Ti-Mo-Ni Alloys, Russian Metallurgy (Metally) No. 3, pages 130-133 (1970) (in the court below and hereinafter called "the Russian article") under 35 U.S.C. 102. The board affirmed the examiner's rejection.

The Russian article is short (3 pages), highly technical, and contains 10 graphs as part of the discussion. As its title indicates, it relates to ternary [i.e., three-part] Ti-Mo-Ni alloys, the subject of the application at bar. The examiner and the board both found that it would disclose to one skilled in the art an alloy on which claims 1 and 2 read, so that those claims would not be allowable under the statute because of lack of novelty of their subject matter. Since the article does not specifically disclose such an alloy in words, a little thinking is required about what it would disclose to one knowledgeable about Ti-Ni-Mo alloys. The PTO did that thinking as follows:

[Graph] 1c [left graph in middle row of six graphs in Figure 4-5] shows data for the ternary titanium alloy which contains Mo and Ni in the ratio of 1:3. Amongst the actual points on the graph is one at 1% Mo + Ni [third tiny circle from left; on graph line marked "16"]. At this point, the amounts of Mo and Ni would be 0.25% and 0.75% respectively. A similar point appears on the graph shown in [the graph on the left in the bottom row of Figure 4-5, point corresponding to first tiny square in upper left corner]. Appellants do not deny that the data points are disclosed in the reference.

On that basis, the board found that the claimed alloys were not new, because they were disclosed in the prior art. It having been argued that the Russian article contains no disclosure of corrosion-resistant properties of any of the alloys, the

Fig. 1. Effect of Alloy
Composition on the
Ultimate Strength,
Yield Point and
Elongation of Ti-Mo-Ni
Alloys for Mo:Ri Ratios
of 3:1, 1:1 and 1:3
(a, b and c respectively)
and for Binary Ti-Ni
Alloys (d).

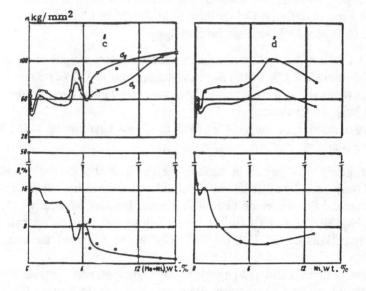

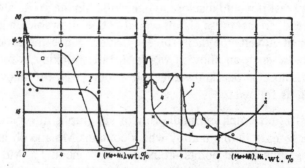

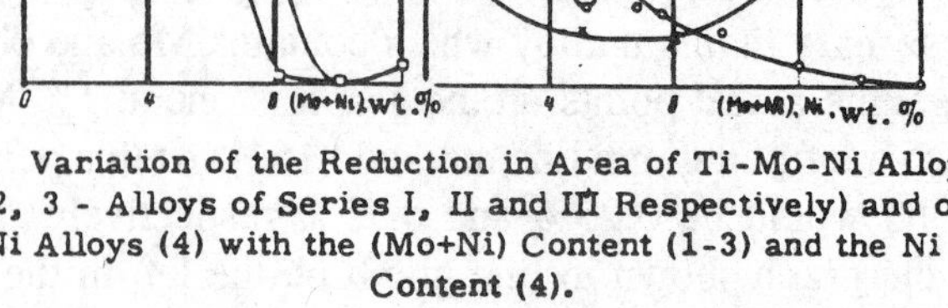

Fig. 2. Variation of the Reduction in Area of Ti-Mo-Ni Alloys
(1, 2, 3 - Alloys of Series I, II and III Respectively) and of
Ti-Ni Alloys (4) with the (Mo+Ni) Content (1-3) and the Ni
Content (4).

Figure 4-5

board held: "The fact that a particular property or the end use for this alloy as contemplated by appellants was not recognized in the article is of no consequence."

It therefore held the Russian article to be an anticipation, noting that although the article does not discuss corrosion resistance, it does disclose other properties such as strength and ductility. The PTO further points out that the authors of the reference must have made the alloys to obtain the data points.

We are left in no doubt that the court was impressed by the totality of the evidence that the applicants for patent had discovered or invented and disclosed knowledge which is not to be found in the reference, nor do we have any doubt about that ourselves. But those facts are beside the point. The patent law imposes certain fundamental conditions for patentability, paramount among them being the condition that what is sought to be patented, as determined by the claims, be new.

Section 102, the usual basis for rejection for lack of novelty or anticipation, lays down certain principles for determining novelty, among which are the provisions in § 102(a) and (b) that the claimed invention has *not* been "described in a printed publication in this or a foreign country," either (a) before the invention by the applicant or (b) more than one year before the application date to which he is entitled (strictly a "loss of right" provision similar to novelty). Either provision applies in this case, the Russian article having come 5 years prior to the filing date and its status as "prior art" not being questioned. The PTO was never specific as to what part of § 102 applies, merely rejecting on § 102. The question, therefore, is whether claims 1 and 2 encompass and, if allowed, would enable plaintiff-appellee to exclude others from making, using, or selling an alloy *described* in the Russian article.

To answer the question we need only turn to the affidavit of James A. Hall, a metallurgist employed by appellee, who undertook to analyze the Russian article disclosure by calculating the ingredient percentages shown in the graph data points, which he presented in tabular form. There are 15 items in his table. The second item shows a titanium base alloy containing 0.25% by weight Mo and 0.75% Ni and this is squarely within the ranges of 0.2-0.4% Mo and 0.6-0.9% Ni of claims 1 and 2. As to that disclosed alloy of the prior art, there can be no question that claims 1 and 2 read on it and would be infringed by anyone making, using, or selling it. Therefore, *the statute prohibits* a patent containing them.

By reason of the court's quotations from cases holding that a reference is not an anticipation which does not enable one skilled in the art to practice the claimed invention, it appears that the trial court thought there was some deficiency in the Russian article on that score. Enablement in this case involves only being able to make the alloy, given the ingredients and their proportions without more. The evidence here, however, clearly answers that question in two ways. Appellee's own patent application does not undertake to tell anyone how to make the alloy it describes and seeks to patent. It assumes that those skilled in the art would know how. Secondly, appellee's expert, Dr. Williams, testified on cross examination that given the alloy information in the Russian article, he would know how to prepare the alloys "by at least three techniques." Enablement is not a problem in this case.

As we read the situation, the court was misled by the arguments and evidence to the effect that the inventors here found out and disclosed in their application many things that one cannot learn from reading the Russian article and that this was sufficient in law to justify granting them a patent for their contributions — such things as what good corrosion resistance the claimed alloys have against hot brine, which possibly was not known, and the range limits of the Ni and Mo content, outside of which that resistance diminishes, which are teachings of very useful information. These things the applicants teach the art and the Russian article does not. But throughout the trial counsel never came to grips with the real issues: (1) what do the claims cover and (2) is what they cover new? Under the laws Congress wrote, they must be considered. Congress has not seen fit to permit the patenting of an old alloy, known to others through a printed publication, by one who has discovered its corrosion resistance or other useful properties, or has found out to what extent one can modify the composition of the alloy without losing such properties.

It is an elementary principle of patent law that when, as by a recitation of ranges or otherwise, a claim covers several compositions, the claim is "anticipated" if *one* of them is in the prior art. *In re Petering*, 301 F.2d 676, 682, 133 U.S.P.Q. 275, 280 (C.C.P.A. 1962).

For all of the foregoing reasons, the court below committed clear error and legal error in authorizing the issuance of a patent on claims 1 and 2 since, properly construed, they are anticipated under § 102 by the Russian article which admittedly discloses an alloy on which these claims read.

NOTES

1. Near the end of the preceding case, Judge Rich states that when "a claim covers several compositions, the claim is 'anticipated' if *one* of them is in the prior art." (Emphasis in original.) Patent lawyers often speak of "genus" and "species" to describe the relationship between references such as the Russian article and a claimed invention. The patent, that is, claimed a *class* of compounds of which the article's disclosed compound was a member. An example of a genus would be "clothing"; species would include "shirts," "shorts," and "socks." In these terms, one lesson of the *Titanium Metals* case is that a prior art reference disclosing "socks" could anticipate a claim in a subsequent patent application to "clothing." Stated technically, a prior art reference that discloses a species anticipates a later claim to a genus that includes that species. (The drafting solution to this problem involves changing the definition of the genus.)

Would the opposite be true — that a prior *genus* anticipates a later *species*? At first blush, it might seem this should indeed be the case. But where a species has significant and unpredictable advantages over the other members of the genus, it has been held to be novel. *See, e.g.*, 2 D. CHISUM, PATENTS § 3.02[2] (1978 & Supp. 1991):

It is well settled that a valid patent may issue for a nonobvious improvement on a prior patented invention, even though the improvement falls within the claims of that prior patent. This suggests that a prior genus which does not explicitly disclose a species does not anticipate a later claim to that species. The genus, if later, would not infringe the species claim, at least not in all cases. Hence, it does not anticipate. However, the prior genus will often render a later species claim obvious under Section 103. To avoid such a rejection, the applicant would have to demonstrate that the particular species had unique and unexpected advantages or properties that distinguish it from other species within the prior genus.

(Footnotes omitted.) For an application of this principle in the context of § 103 nonobviousness, see *In re Baird*, 16 F.3d 380, 29 U.S.P.Q.2d 1550 (Fed. Cir. 1994) (prior patent disclosing generic formula does not render obvious later claim to small group of high-performance compounds embraced by the formula).

2. European courts treat genus/species issues in much the same way as their U.S. counterparts. *See, e.g.,* Vivian, *Novelty and Selection Inventions*, 20 INT'L REV. IND. PROP. & COPYRIGHT L. 303 (1989):

[The House of Lords has made several pronouncements on inventions where a limited number of members of a class have been "selected" for their useful properties and made the subject of claims in a new patent.]

First, [the Lords] confirmed the view ... that the discovery that a previously disclosed or known substance has some advantage or useful quality not previously recognized does not give the right to a patent.

Second, for there to be a selection invention it does not matter whether the class disclosed in the earlier document is described by a general formula or ... if the compounds are specifically enumerated.

Third, the size of the initial group or class is not in itself decisive as to the question of [anticipation by] prior publication. The selection may be one from a class of ten million or one from a class of two. The House of Lords did however observe that the size of the class might be relevant to obviousness and that question may in turn depend in part upon whether the later invention relates to the same field as that occupied by the prior invention. In other words, would a skilled man look for the advantages he desires to produce in the area occupied by the prior invention?

3. A special form of genus claim, termed a "Markush expression," is often encountered in patent law. Such claims take the form of an expression such as "An X selected from the group consisting of A, B, and C," where X describes the functional class to which A, B, and C belong. These claims are often, but certainly not always, used in patents to chemical compositions. There is, for example, the famous patent claiming a cigarette filter made of cheese, whose claim 2 reads: "A cigarette filter according to claim 1, in which the cheese comprises grated particles of cheese selected from the group consisting of Parmesan, Romano, Swiss and cheddar cheeses." U.S. Patent 3,234,948, to Stebbings, cited in R. FABER, LANDIS ON MECHANICS OF PATENT CLAIM DRAFTING § 50 (3d ed. 1990).

"New Use" Patents

At one point in the preceding case, the court states:

> Congress has not seen fit to permit the patenting of an old alloy, known to others through a printed publication, by one who has discovered its corrosion resistance or other useful properties, or has found out to what extent one can modify the composition of the alloy without losing such properties.

In what sense is the discovery of a new property of an old material not novel? Does it make sense to place the emphasis on the material's *structure*, as opposed to its properties, qualities, uses, etc.? This doctrine has a long history. *See Ansonia Brass & Co. v. Electric Supply Co.*, 144 U.S. 11, 18 (1892) (prior art showing use of paint and fibrous material to insulate electrical wires anticipates claim to such materials as insulation for electric light wires).

Consider an example. Suppose Inventor *B* discovers that a well-known chemical composition used for tanning leather is effective as a treatment for AIDS. If Inventor *B* seeks to patent the composition itself, she will be met with a novelty rejection; the *structure* of the composition being well known, it is irrelevant whether a new use has been found for it. *See, e.g., Verdegaal Bros. v. Union Oil Co. of Cal.*, 814 F.2d 628, 2 U.S.P.Q.2d (BNA) 1051 (Fed. Cir. 1987) (prior art description of process anticipates patentee's claims to same process used for new and different effect). This is a simple application of the classic infringement test: that which infringes, if later, anticipates, if earlier. Since use of a chemical compound for unforeseen use *X* would infringe a patent on that compound, it follows that description of a compound for any purpose anticipates a claim to that compound for unforeseen use *X*. (Recall this rule from the discussion of utility in Chapter 3.) Logical consistency, however, comes at a price here, for it has been noted that neither of these rules seem adapted to optimizing the combination of (1) research into new compounds, and (2) research into new uses for old compounds. One commentator has noted:

> The most serious objection to compound protection, as it now exists in practice, is that routine patenting of new chemical compounds is permitted. This rewards the person who conceives the structure of the new compound, which is usually not a very creative step. In most cases the "new" compound is a member of a known class of compounds and is closely related in structure to known members.

Marquis, *An Economic Analysis of the Patentability of Chemical Compounds*, 63 J. PAT. OFF. SOC'Y 3, 42 (1981).

In our example, Inventor *B* can obtain a *process* patent for "the process of using [the leather tanning compound] to treat AIDS." Section 100(b) of the Patent Act permits this in its definition of "process": "The term 'process' ... includes a new use of a known ... composition of matter, or material." 35 U.S.C. § 100(b) (1986). *See Rohm & Haas Co. v. Roberts Chem. Co.*, 245 F.2d 693, 113 U.S.P.Q. (BNA) 423 (4th Cir. 1957) (upholding defendant's patent on use of a well-known product as a fungicide); 1 D. CHISUM, PATENTS § 1.03[8] (1978 & Supp. 1989) (collecting other cases on this point). Some members of the pharmaceutical and chemical industries have argued that new use/process patents do not give enough of an incentive to pursue research into new applications for old drugs and chemicals.

One reason for this is that new use/process patents often raise vexing questions about the patentee's right to prevent others from selling the old compound. A patentee's competitors may, for instance, purportedly sell the old compound for a non-infringing use, knowing full well that buyers will apply it to the patentee's newly-discovered use.[3] The patent statute includes a detailed provision to deal with this problem.[4]

Note that even if a process patent does issue for the new use in our example, it is in essence only an improvement patent; Inventor *B* would have to obtain a license if Inventor *A*, the inventor of the compound for leather-tanning purposes, had a *product* patent on the structure of *compound* X. But the reverse is also true; if Inventor *B* obtained a process patent, Inventor *A* would have to obtain a license from Inventor *B* to have the right to use the compound to treat AIDS. For comments on these and related matters, see Merges & Nelson, *On the Complex Economics of Patent Scope*, 90 COLUM. L. REV. 839, 860-62 (1990).

Some form of protection for the discovery of new uses is essential, since this is such a prominent branch of chemical research. Marshall, *Penn Charges Retin-A Inventor with Conflict*, 247 SCI. 1028 (2 Mar. 1990) (inventor of Retin-A compound, who co-owns patent with university on use of compound for treating acne, filed his own "new use" patent for application of compound for fighting wrinkles). The Patent Office and the courts have consequently found ways around the

---

[3] *See Rohm & Haas Co. v. Dawson Chem. Co.*, 448 U.S. 176 (1980). This problem is exacerbated in the pharmaceutical field because doctors have traditionally been free to prescribe whatever medication they see fit. Thus where a drug known for treatment of disease *A* is discovered to be an effective treatment for disease *B*, a doctor may write out a prescription for the drug "for disease *A*" while in actuality intending to treat the patient for disease *B*. This freedom of action on the part of doctors limits the effectiveness of a process patent for treatment of drug *B*, and may also limit the effectiveness of a combination patent where the extra ingredient combined with the drug is known by doctors to add little to its effectiveness in treating disease *B*. *See generally* Jacobs, *A Patent Attorney's View*, in *Seminar on Pharmaceutical Invention*, 48 J. PAT. OFF. SOC'Y 663, 666 (1965).

[4] *See* 35 U.S.C. § 271 (1985 & Supp. 1988); *Rohm & Haas Co.*, *supra*; Chapter 8 (contributory infringement), and Chapter 11 (patent misuse).

per se prohibition against product patents for new uses. This is especially true where an earlier inventor has a product patent on the compound; the patent system seems to recognize the inequity of granting a compound's inventor a monopoly over uses she did not discover.

For example, a patent on a new use for an old compound will often be allowed if the compound is combined with other compounds and claimed as a new "combination." Protection of a new use via combination claims has been allowed where the old compound is combined with a second active ingredient, or with an ingredient that enhances the effect of the old compound.[5]

In still other cases, a patent will be allowed where only very minor structural changes to the old compound are made.[6] The new variant of the old compound will receive an independent product patent, even if the inventor substitutes or changes the position of only one side-group or atom in a molecule.[7]

Eli Lilly & Co. v. Generix Drug Sales, Inc., 460 F.2d 1096 (5th Cir. 1972), for instance, dealt with Lilly's successful analgesic Darvon. Darvon grew out of a major push in the pharmaceutical industry to discover a non-addictive substitute for morphine in the late 1940s and early 1950s. During this period, scientists submitted hundreds of compounds for clinical testing. One scientist published a report listing a number of compounds he had synthesized. In the course of investigating this work, an Eli Lilly scientist synthesized analogues to some of the published compounds. One demonstrated superior analgesic effects, and later turned out to be non-addictive. Thus Darvon was born. In an infringement action, Lilly defended a charge that its Darvon patent was obvious, noting that even though its compound was made by changing only two functional groups in the prior art, the unpredictability of analgesic compound behavior rendered its discovery nonobvious. The court agreed: In the case of Darvon, "the process of

---

[5] *See* Gaumont, *Patentability and Patent Scope of Pharmaceutical Inventions*, 13 INT'L REV. INDUSTRIAL PROP. & COPYRIGHT L. 431, 450 (1982). *Cf. In re Tuominen*, 671 F.2d 1359 (C.C.P.A. 1982) (upholding rejection of claims for sunscreen compound since prior art taught other therapeutic uses for compound and patentee had not distinguished sunscreen "carrier" ingredients from carriers used in other therapeutic applications).

[6] *See In re Merck & Co.*, 800 F.2d 1091, 231 U.S.P.Q (BNA) 375 (Fed. Cir. 1986); *Pfizer, Inc. v. Int'l Rectifier Corp.*, 545 F. Supp. 486 (C.D. Cal. 1980) (minor variation in tetracycline compound patentable due to surprisingly good anti-microbial activity); 2 D. CHISUM 5.04[6] (1978, rev. 1992). The "doctrine of slight changes," as this practice is known, applies to mechanical inventions as well. *See H. K. Regar & Sons v. Scott & Williams*, 63 F.2d 229, 231 (2d Cir. 1933) (L. Hand, J.) ("When old devices are changed at all, the change may be dictated by a new conception, which it took originality to conceive. Strictly, the old device is not then put to a new use; the new use begets a new device. In such cases it requires but little physical change to make an invention.").

[7] *See* P. GRUBB, PATENTS FOR CHEMISTS 153 (1982) ("Perhaps the closest that a new compound can be to the prior art is ... when the new compound is an optically active [isomer of the old compound].... The only way in which an optical isomer can be patentable is if it has surprisingly superior properties ...").

chemical synthesis constituted only a preliminary portion of the invention process, [which also involved] extensive biological testing." 460 F.2d at 1101. Thus, given the "lack of predictability" in this field, the compound was patentable despite its structural similarity to the prior art.

The "doctrine of slight changes" has been criticized, however; patentability is made to turn on the fortuitous event of discovering a minor structural variation that will not alter the operability of the compound.[8] In some cases, owing to the delicate structure-function relationship of pharmacologically active compounds, the compound will not work with even the most minor change.

In such a case, the inventor is out of luck. A good example can be found in the case of *In re Thuau*, 135 F.2d 344 (C.C.P.A. 1943). Urbain Thuau had filed a patent application claiming a compound comprised of metacresolsufonic acid and an aldehyde, useful in the treatment of diseases of the cervix. Unfortunately for him, the very same compound had long been used in the leather tanning industry. The court affirmed the Patent Office's rejection of Thuau's claims.

> That appellant has made a valuable discovery in the new use of the composition here involved we have no doubt, and it is unfortunate for him if he cannot make claims adequate to protect such discovery, but to hold that every new use of an old composition may be the subject of a patent upon the composition would lead to endless confusion and go far to destroy the benefits of our patent laws.

135 F.2d at 347. The court was especially concerned with the confusion that might result if, for example, a compound traditionally sold by a chemical supplier for the old use were purchased by pharmacies for the newly discovered therapeutic use; in *Thuau*, the tannery supplier then might be liable for patent infringement even though it had been selling the same compound for years.

The anomalies of pharmaceutical patents have attracted a number of proposed reforms. In an opinion denying the patentability of a structurally obvious variant of an old compound, one court proposed that the solution might be to eliminate patents on compounds altogether, rewarding each inventor with a *process* patent only on the application she has discovered.

> It is basic to the grant of a patent that the scope of a patent should not exceed the scope of invention. If what makes a structurally obvious chemical substance patentable is the new and unobvious properties or uses discovered by the first person to compound the substance, the discoverer should have protection on what he discovered, *i.e.*, the new properties of the substance, but should not be entitled to a 17-year monopoly on the substance itself....

---

[8] *See* Hoxie, *A Patent Attorney's View*, in *Seminar on Chemical Invention*, 48 J. PAT. OFF. SOC'Y 630, 638 (1965) ("This ... has led to inequitable results in that of two discoveries of equal value and 'inventiveness,' one may be patentable and the other not depending on whether or not the 'gimmick' novelty [i.e., minor structural variation] can be supplied.").

We think that the purposes of the patent law will be adequately served if patents on compounds which are structurally obvious from the prior art are limited to method [i.e., process] patents directed to the new and useful characteristic or property which is the essence of the discovery or invention.

Monsanto Co. v. Rohm & Haas Co., 312 F. Supp. 778, 790-91 (E.D. Pa. 1970), *aff'd on other grounds,* 456 F.2d 592 (3d Cir.), *cert. denied,* 407 U.S. 934 (1972). *See also* Comment, *Uses, New Uses and Chemical Patents — A Proposal*, 1968 WIS. L. REV. 901, 915 (1968) (proposing abolition of product patents on compounds in favor of patents on methods of production and methods of using — two species of process patents).

Another commentator, Marquis, notes that the creative step in pharmaceutical research is often the discovery of the new use, rather than the synthesis of the old compound or a minor variation on it. *See* Marquis, *supra*, at 42. He therefore proposes a slightly different solution: permit patents specifically for new uses. *Id.*

These are helpful suggestions on ways to ascertain the proper scope of pharmaceutical inventions. What they have in common is an emphasis on limiting claim scope to what the inventor actually discovered. It might be useful to emphasize that this is the objective of any project to circumscribe pharmaceutical claims. A simple way to acknowledge this is to shift the emphasis to the inventor's *disclosure*. In *Thuau*, for instance, it was clear that what the inventor had discovered was a new use. Ultimately, this is what his claims should have reflected. The preferred way to do this would have been to grant Thuau a *process* patent. This would limit him to what he disclosed — a new application of, or way to use, the old compound.

For information on the European approach to these problems, see European Patent Office, Enlarged Board of Appeal, Decision No. G05/83, "Eisai," 1985 J. EURO. PAT. OFF. 64 (holding new use of therapeutic drug patentable in process form); Patterson, *The Patentability of Further Uses of Known Product Under the EPC*, 13 EURO. INTELL. PROP. REV. 16 (1991) (noting cases extending the "Eisai" case beyond therapeutic uses).

NOTES

1. *Canadian Patent Office record, Vol. 117, No. 19, 9 May 1989:*

Claims of the following type will now be permitted:

(a) When the invention is a novel compound X or novel composition Y:

(1) Compound X (composition Y) for the use of...
(2) The use of compound X (composition Y) for...
(3) The method of using compound X (composition Y) comprising...(set forth various steps of method).

(b) When the invention is a known compound Z or known composition W having a novel utility:

(1) Compound Z (composition W) for the (new) use of...

(2) Use of compound Z (composition W) for the (new) use

2. From the Defendant's argument in *Hotchkiss v. Greenwood*, 52 U.S. 248 (1850), argued by Daniel Webster:

> There are some cases of the application of old inventions to obvious new uses for which courts have refused to sustain a patent. Or the case of a double use, where no new manufacture or a cheapening of the old is the result. [But this] is a strange claim, to say the least of it. According to the principle of the claim, one man may claim a patent for making a stove of sheet-iron; another may claim a patent for making stoves of cast-iron; another may claim a patent for making stoves of copper; and each may claim, not the right to make a stove of a particular form and shape only, or by any peculiar process of making, but the exclusive right to make all sorts and shapes of stoves out of the particular material named. So another man claims the exclusive right of using ice to cool water; another claims the exclusive right to use ice for cooling wine; another, to use of the same article to cool brandy; and a physician claims the exclusive right to use the article of ice to cool a fevered patient's head.

From the opinion of the Court:

> If new effects are produced by an old machine in its unaltered state, no patent can be supported for it, as such a patent would be for an effect only. So in the new use of medicines or compositions. Suppose the world were better informed than it is how to prepare Dr. Jayne's feverpowder, and an ingenious physician should find out that it was a specific cure for a consumption, if given in particular quantities; could he have a patent for the sole use of Jayne's powders in consumption, or to be given in particular quantities? I think it must be conceded that such a patent would be void, and yet the use of the medicine would be new, and the effect of it as materially different from what is now known, as life is from death.

See also S. BEDINI, THOMAS JEFFERSON, MAN OF SCIENCE 208 (1990) (describing Jefferson's opposition to patents that claimed a new use of an old structure).

3. THE "INHERENCY" DOCTRINE

TILGHMAN v. PROCTOR

102 U.S. 707 (1880)

[This is a suit in equity brought by Richard A. Tilghman, against William Proctor, James Gamble, W. A. Proctor, James N. Gamble, and George H. Proctor, complaining of their infringement of letters-patent No. 11,766, granted to him for a process for obtaining free fat acids and glycerine from fatty bodies. The answer denies the validity of the letters and the alleged infringement of them. On a final hearing upon the pleadings and proofs, the bill was dismissed, and he appealed.]

The patent in question relates to the treatment of fats and oils, and is for a process of separating their component parts so as to render them better adapted to the uses of the arts. It was discovered by Chevreul, an eminent French chemist, as early as 1813, that ordinary fat, tallow, and oil are regular chemical compounds, consisting of a base which has been termed glycerine, and of different acids, termed generally fat acids, but specifically, stearic, margaric, and oleic acids. These acids, in combination severally with glycerine, form stearine, margarine, and oleine. They are found in different proportions in the various neutral fats and oils; stearine predominating in some, margarine in others, and oleine in others. When separated from their base (glycerine), they take up an equivalent of water, and are called free fat acids. In this state they are in a condition for being utilized in the arts. The stearic and margaric acids form a whitish, semi-transparent, hard substance, which is manufactured into candles. They are separated from the oleic acid, which is a thin oily fluid, by hydrostatic or other powerful pressure; the oleine being used for manufacturing soap, and other purposes. The base, glycerine, when purified, has come to be quite a desirable article for many uses.

The complainant's patent has but a single claim, the words of which are as follows: "Having now described the nature of my said invention, and the manner of performing the same, I hereby declare that I claim, as of my invention, the manufacturing of fat acids and glycerine from fatty bodies by the action of water at a high temperature and pressure." [See Figure 4-6.]

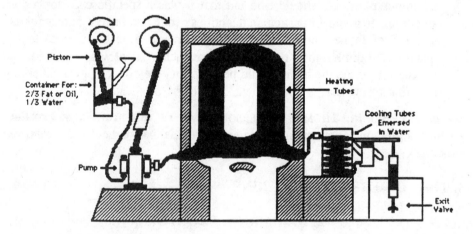

Figure 4-6

[Defendants argued Tilghman's patent was anticipated by the working of a steam engine invented by one Perkins.] We do not regard the accidental formation of fat acid in Perkins's steam cylinder from the tallow introduced to lubricate the piston (if the scum which rose on the water issuing from the ejection pipe was fat acid) as of any consequence in this inquiry. What the process was by which it was generated or formed was never fully understood. Those engaged in the art of making candles, or in any other art in which fat acids are desirable, certainly never derived the least hint from this accidental phenomenon in regard to any practicable process for manufacturing such acids.

The accidental effects produced in Daniell's water barometer and in Walther's process for purifying fats and oils preparatory to soap-making, are of the same character. They revealed no process for the manufacture of fat acids. If the acids were accidentally and unwittingly produced, whilst the operators were in pursuit of other and different results, without exciting attention and without its even being known what was done or how it had been done, it would be absurd to say that this was an anticipation of Tilghman's discovery.

Nor do we regard the patent of Manicler, which was taken out in 1826, as anticipating the process of Tilghman. It is true that he directs a mixture of fat with about one-quarter of its weight of water to be placed in a boiler, and subjected to a heat sufficient to create a pressure equal to one atmosphere above the natural atmospheric pressure (or about 250° Fah.); the boiler being provided with a safety-valve which would secure that degree of pressure. But, subject to this pressure, the patent directed that the mixture should be made to boil, and of course that the water should be converted into steam. It is probable, therefore, that any decomposition of the fat which may have been produced by this process was due to the steam formed and passing through the fat, as no means appears to have been adopted for keeping up the mixture of the fat and water. But we have no evidence that the process was ever successful in practice.

It is unnecessary to examine in detail other alleged anticipations of Tilghman's process. We believe that we have specified the most prominent and reliable instances.

The decree of the Circuit Court will be reversed.

NOTES

1. *Anticipation by Accident.* The holding of the Court with respect to the Perkins, Daniell and Walther devices has come to be known as the doctrine of accidental anticipation. *See In re Marshall,* 578 F.2d 301, 198 U.S.P.Q. (BNA) 334 (C.C.P.A. 1978) ("An accidental or unwitting duplication of an invention cannot constitute an anticipation."). *But see International Nickel Co. v. Ford Motor Co.,* 166 F. Supp. 551, 560-61, 119 U.S.P.Q. (BNA) 72 (S.D.N.Y. 1958) (dictum: "[A] prior use of a product deliberately created may constitute an anticipation, though the full benefits accruing therefrom may not be fully appreciated or even recognized.").

As to the merits of the "accidental anticipation" doctrine, consider the following passage:

[I]n practice, in other forms ... it sometimes happened that the glass, by mistake, ran down on to and over the point of union with the platinum, thus realizing ... the construction of the patent. But no such accidental and fugitive occurrence is of account.... Not only was it not understood or appreciated, but it was actually made the ground of rejection [on the assembly line], the lamp, when it happened, being regarded as imperfect and thrown out. It thus gave nothing to the world, standing in the way of discovery, indeed, instead of promoting it and is thus entitled to no consideration.

Edison Elec. Light Co. v. Novelty Incandescent Lamp Co., 167 F. 977, 980 (3d Cir. 1909). Note that in this case the defendant, Novelty, was trying to defeat the novelty of Thomas Edison's light bulb patent. But Novelty was defeated when this novelty was not defeated(!).

The case was one of many in which Edison's companies shut down competition in the early light bulb industry. *See* A. BRIGHT, THE ELECTRIC-LAMP INDUSTRY: TECHNOLOGICAL CHANGE AND ECONOMIC DEVELOPMENT FROM 1800 TO 1947, at 89 (1949). On General Electric's need to catch up technologically after the Edison patent expired in 1894, see T. HUGHES, AMERICAN GENESIS: A CENTURY OF INVENTION AND TECHNOLOGICAL ENTHUSIASM, 1870-1970, at 166-67 (1989).

2. *A Swiftian Comment.* Jonathan Swift, in a letter to Mr. Delany (1718), wrote (at p. 1, line 25): "'Tis never by invention got; Men have it when they know it not." He was speaking of humor, but § 102 was inherent in what he said.

In re SEABORG
328 F.2d 996, 140 U.S.P.Q. (BNA) 662 (C.C.P.A. 1964)

The application and the claims in issue relate to a new transuranic element having atomic number 95, now known as Americium (Am), to isotopes thereof, and to methods of producing and purifying said element and compositions thereof. Two isotopes of Americium are disclosed, Americium 241 and 242. Two general methods of synthesizing element 95 are set forth, namely (1) bombardment of plutonium with deuterons or neutrons; and (2) in a neutronic reactor operated at a relatively high power level (about 200 kw) for an extended period of time (approximately 100 days). A suitable reactor is said to be that described in Fermi et al. application Serial No. 568,904, filed December 19, 1944, which is now U.S. Patent No. 2,708,656.

The claims in issue read simply:

1. Element 95.
2. The isotope of element 95 having the mass number 241.

There is but a single ground of rejection involving the above claims, i.e., unpatentability over the Fermi et al. patent, for the reason that element 95 must be inherently produced in the operation of the reactor disclosed therein.

The Fermi et al. patent discloses several nuclear reactors. The patent does not mention elements 95 and 96. The claims in issue were first rejected on the Fermi patent. The specific basis for the examiner's rejection on Fermi was the exemplary statement of reactor operation contained in the [Fermi] patent, namely:

> After operation of the reactor for a sufficient length of time for an amount of 94^{239} to be created sufficient for chemical separation, such as, for example, 100 days at 500 kilowatts, the reactor is shut down by inserting the control rod fully into the reactor. After about one-half hour's wait, during which all delayed neutron emission will have ceased and the more highly radioactive materials decayed sufficiently, the reactor may be unloaded.
> ... After 100 days' operation the aging period may be about 30 days.

Appellant, however, asserts in his brief:

> ... The statements are exemplary only. [T]he maximum amount of americium 241 that could have been produced in the reactor operated for 100 days at 500 kilowatts power can be calculated to be 6.15×10^{-9} gram. Thus the reactor could have produced no more than one billionth [sic][1] of a gram of americium-241, and this one billionth of a gram would have been distributed throughout forty tons of intensely radioactive uranium reactor fuel. This amount of an unknown, unconcentrated isotope, if present, would have been undetectable....

The position of the Patent Office is stated in the solicitor's brief as follows:

> ... Since the products produced in a neutronic reactor depend upon the manner of operation, and appellant does not and cannot really challenge the findings of similarity between appellant's process and Fermi's process, the inference that the claimed product is inherently produced is reasonable and logical.

The record before us is replete with showings that the claimed product, if it was produced in the Fermi process, was produced in such minuscule amounts and under such conditions that its presence was undetectable.

We also agree with the summary statement in appellant's brief that:

> ... There is no positive evidence that americium was produced inherently in the natural uranium fuel by the operation of the reactor for the times and at the intensity mentioned in the exemplary statement relied upon by the Patent Office. The calculations, however, that the maximum amount of americium-241 which could have been produced by the operation of the reactor disclosed in the Fermi Patent for 100 days at 500 kilowatts would have been one billionth of one gram (1/1,000,000,000 gram), show that the

---

[1] It would appear that appellant meant "one one-hundred millionth" rather than "one billionth," since 6.15×10^{-9} gram amounts to more than *six* billionths of a gram.

element, if produced was produced in the most minute quantities. If the one billionth of a gram were produced, it would have been completely undetectable, since it would have been diluted with the 40 tons of intensely radioactive uranium fuel which made up the reactor. The possibility that although a minute amount of americium may have been produced in the Fermi reactor, it was not identified (nor could it have been identified) would preclude the application of the Fermi patent as a reference to anticipate the present invention.

For the foregoing reasons, the decision of the board is reversed.

NOTES

1. Recall the discussion in Chapter 2 of the issue of software patents, and whether mathematical algorithms are discovered or invented. Compare algorithms in this respect with chemical elements such as that claimed in the preceding case. In what sense are elements "invented" when they can be isolated only with monumental human intervention? Is there any difference, in economic terms, between a naturally occurring plant, hidden in a remote valley in the Antarctic, which would require a $12 million expedition to locate, and a transuranic element that requires a $12 million experiment to isolate? Should the answer to the preceding question determine the patentability of these items? If not, what should? See generally Chapter 2. *See also* Bloomberg, *Novelty of Claims Covering Recombinant Proteins*, in 6TH ANN. BIOTECH. LAW INST. 157 (B. Cunningham, M. Epstein & R. Seide eds., 1990).

2. From *In re Wiegand*, 182 F.2d 633 (C.C.P.A. 1950), a leading early inherency case, cited and discussed in an omitted part of the preceding case:

[Applicant filed a patent for "Carbon Black," used in the manufacture of rubber, paint and ink. He claimed "a furnace carbon black comprising not less than 97% fixed carbon and having a surface area within the range extending from 7.5 to 10 acres per pound." This claim form — drafted in terms of carbon composition and surface area — was necessitated by the extremely fine size of the carbon particles, which were made in a special furnace by flash-burning a stream of petroleum-derived hydrocarbon gas at high velocity and turbulence. The examiner rejected the application as anticipated by U.S. Patent 1,909,163 to Brownlee. Brownlee described a *process* for making hydrocarbons by positioning burners to produce "a swirling movement of the combustible mixture and flame ...."]

Both the Primary Examiner and the board [of Patent Appeals and Interferences in the Patent Office] were of the opinion that Brownlee's patented product ... would inherently possess the same properties as those embraced in the product defined in appellants' claims because of the similarity of the process of the appellants to that of Brownlee ....

We think it must be said that the inferences [drawn by the board] are logical and proper, and we can find no reasonable ground for disagreement with them.

3. The court in *Seaborg* states that although the Fermi reactor probably produced element 95, "its presence was undetectable." How does this differ from the separation of fat acids and glycerine produced accidentally by the prior art processes in the *Tilghman* case? Should the concept of accidental prior use be predicated on (1) lack of knowledge regarding what is produced; (2) undetectability of what is produced; or (3) something else? *See* Kilyk, *Accidental Prior Use*, 64 J. PAT. OFF. SOC'Y 392 (1982) ("The *Tilghman* rule ... can be stated as follows: Single, appreciated prior uses and prior uses that were a consistent result of that which was intended, regardless of appreciation so long as the involved product in issue is known ..., are anticipatory.").

4. *Close to the Nerve.* A recent case illustrates the close calls that abound in the area of inherency. In *Electro Medical Sys., S.A. v. Cooper Life Sciences, Inc.*, 34 F.3d 1048, 32 U.S.P.Q.2d 1017 (Fed. Cir. 1994), declaratory judgment plaintiff alleged the invalidity of one claim of defendant's patent on air abrasive equipment used to clean teeth. Defendant/patentee's invention discharged water along with a pressurized gas (usually air); it operated using unpressurized water. According to plaintiff, a prior patent to Ruemelin for a blasting and spraying gun utilizing pressurized liquid anticipated because, even though the normal use of the spray gun was with high liquid pressures, the gun as described "could be set to any water pressures." Since "any pressures" included "no pressure," the argument went, the prior patent anticipated the claims. The court disagreed.

> We do not agree that the subject matter of the claim was anticipated. "The mere fact that a certain thing may result from a given set of circumstances is insufficient to prove anticipation." *Continental Can Co. v. Monsanto Co.*, 948 F.2d 1264, 1268-69, 20 U.S.P.Q.2d 1746, 1749 (Fed. Cir. 1991) (quoting *In re Oelrich*, 666 F.2d 578, 581, 212 U.S.P.Q. 323, 326 (C.C.P.A. 1981)) .... EMS was required to prove that an unpressurized flow is necessarily present in the Ruemelin disclosure, and that it would be so recognized by persons of ordinary skill. *Id.* at 1268, 20 U.S.P.Q.2d at 1749. EMS did not discharge its burden; thus, the district court properly concluded that EMS failed to prove invalidity of [the claim].

34 F.3d 1048, 1052.

4. NOVELTY AND THE ECONOMICS OF "SEARCH"

A "lack of knowledge" standard, suggested in the note following *Seaborg*, might seem to make sense; after all, if someone was not trying to make something or produce some effect, it might seem illogical to say that something or that effect is "in the prior art." Yet the weakness of this line of thought is revealed if we keep in mind the *purpose* of the entire inquiry. We want to know if the later invention is a new structure, so it is that invention which should be the focus of our analysis. We should determine whether, if we asked those who "accidentally" reached the results we are interested in, they would be able to tell us they had or had not. It is *not* essential that they intended to achieve the results they achieved, that they knew precisely what they had, or even that the "accident" occurred on every attempt. The important thing is that, given a claim to structure X, we ask whether any identical structure existed before.

One way to justify this conclusion is by appeal to an economic model which views technological research and development (R&D) activities as a "search" process. In these models, firms search the research horizon for new products and improvements to old ones. Search can be instigated by an external shock, such as the introduction of a new product by a competitor. Or it can come about in an effort to stay ahead of the competition. In either case, search will be undertaken up to the point where it is no longer worth it — that is, when the cost of engaging in more search just equals the anticipated benefits of further search. H. Simon, *Theories of Bounded Rationality*, in 2 MODELS OF BOUNDED RATIONALITY: BEHAVIORAL ECONOMICS AND BUSINESS ORGANIZATION 408, 410 (1982) (describing class of models of decisions under uncertainty where decisionmaker's task "is to find the alternative [choice of action] that maximizes his expected profit net of search cost"); F. MACHLUP, THE ECONOMICS OF INFORMATION AND HUMAN CAPITAL 25-26 (1984) ("Economic decisionmakers as a rule seek more knowledge when they think that the cost of acquiring it will be less than the disadvantages due to their ignorance and uncertainty."); Stigler, *The Economics of Information*, 69 J. POL. ECON. 213 (1961); JACK HIRSHLEIFER & JOHN G. RILEY, THE ANALYTICS OF UNCERTAINTY AND INFORMATION 183 (1992). An example of these sorts of models from outside the R&D context comes from the literature on job searching, which models jobseekers' investments in information to reduce uncertainty about possible openings and wages; *see* F. MACHLUP, *supra*, 78-99; McCall, *Economics of Information and Job Search*, 84 Q.J. ECON. 113 (1970).

At the same time, since search is conducted on a step-by-step basis, there are opportunities to learn from the last "round" of searching, which can make the next round more efficient. For an important treatment of the "focusing" effect such iterative decisionmaking can have on research and development, see Nelson, *The Role of Knowledge in R&D Efficiency*, 47 Q.J. ECON. 459 (1982) (constructing a "search" model showing how firms refine their approach to R&D with experience). *See generally* R. NELSON & S. WINTER, AN EVOLUTIONARY THEORY OF ECONOMIC CHANGE (1982) (making extensive use of models and simulations where firms modify their search for new products and processes over time based on past experience).

A loose application of these search models to the problem of novelty in patent law provides a rationale for the doctrines we have been discussing. The role of novelty, in this view, is to discourage inventors from inventing when the results they seek already exist. (An alternative way to state this is that society wishes to reward only those technologies that are in fact new.) Make a reasonable assumption (here comes the economics!): that the cost of searching for a new technology by conducting R&D is higher than finding out about the same technology from someone who has already done their own R&D (or otherwise figured it out). Then the novelty doctrines begin to make sense, since they refuse to protect an invention that someone has already made. In other words, they encourage the (relatively) cheaper approach of finding out what is already available in the prior art. And in turn they discourage wasteful and duplicative R&D.

This may sound reasonable, but can it explain the accidental prior use doctrine? Perhaps. The key is to picture an inventor who is thinking of searching for an invention. She can either (i) perform original research towards the desired goal; or (ii) use some existing knowledge to figure out a solution. If novelty doctrines were such that only explicitly described and understood prior art could defeat a patent application, inventors would choose (i) more frequently. This is in fact the rule of *Tilghman*. But if novelty doctrines instead held that even where a researcher in the prior art did not understand what she had achieved, the fact that she had achieved a result places that result in the prior art, inventors would choose option (ii) more frequently — they would broaden their examination of the prior art considerably. That is, because in this hypothetical regime the rule is that a result need not be understood for it to bar a subsequent patent, inventors would be encouraged to inquire more deeply into the prior art. They would ask of it not only "has X been invented yet?," but also "have the conditions for X been in place in any art, such that X must have been produced?" You might picture the difference between these two questions as follows. Imagine our inventor addressing a crowd of artisans. She can ask "Has anyone here ever seen X (the invention she is searching for)?," *or* she can ask this question *and* the following: "Has anyone here ever done anything that might bring about X?" In terms of a search model, the *Tilghman* rule permits our inventor to limit her search of the prior art by asking only the first question. The *Seaborg* rule requires her to ask the second one as well.

Now of course one might well believe that this hypothetical rule, the one requiring broader inquiry of the prior art, is a bad rule, for the following reason. While it may be possible for an inventor to ask of the prior art "have you seen an X?," where X is described functionally as a solution to a particular problem she faces, it may be onerous to require her to ask the additional question, i.e., whether the prior art shows that the *conditions* for X have ever existed. This is because it may be impossible to predict what those conditions are *before* achieving invention X herself. Consequently, the alternative regime would in fact require an exhaustive search throughout the prior art, without any promise that our inventor would recognize the conditions for her solution if she came across them. This would be both wasteful and pointless.

In terms of the search model, then, the *Tilghman* rule seems to make sense. It says: where you know what you are looking for, explore the prior art to see if it has been done. But there is no need to exhaustively read the tea leaves of the prior art in search of information you could not even recognize if you found it.

The same reasoning applies to the result in *Seaborg* of course; there, it was simply unclear whether the claimed element was routinely produced in Fermi's prior art reactor. The issue then becomes almost metaphysical: if prior art appears in a physically unreachable locale, is it still prior art? The court's answer — no, of course not — makes sense in that no amount of exploration of the prior art would have revealed Seaborg's invention. Original search — R&D — was the only way to this result, so it makes no sense to discourage this search by withholding a patent.

To summarize: in *Tilghman*, original R&D was the only *feasible* way to the result desired, and in *Seaborg*, it was the only *possible* way. In both cases, a search for new technologies — original R&D — was therefore encouraged.

NOTES

1. The preceding analysis applies only when the invention whose novelty we are determining is a *structure* — i.e., something described in a product patent. As noted in preceding discussions of new uses for chemicals, the patent statute expressly permits *process* claims in the form "the use of [old product] *X* for new use *Y*." 35 U.S.C. § 100(b). Can you explain this legal rule in terms of the model just described? Keep in mind that the process claim to a new use is more valuable than no patent at all, but less valuable than a claim to the product *per se*. (In fact, if there is a preexisting patent on the product, the new use process patent will infringe it, and a blocking patents situation will arise.) How could one justify such an "intermediate" level of reward for this kind of search behavior? Note also that this set of legal rules is one example of the emerging literature on the economics of split or divided entitlements.

2. Notice that when claims to a structure are involved, novelty doctrine ignores the *properties* or characteristics associated with the structure. The logic behind this is simple: when claiming a structure, one is entitled to reap the benefits of any properties known to attach to the structure when the patent is applied for, as well as those properties discovered later. (This is subject to the restriction that discoverers of new properties may obtain process patents for their invention of the use of old product *X* for new application *Y*, but recall that this creates a blocking patents situation rather than giving the new discoverer absolute rights over the new use.) Thus the *scope* of a patent for a structure — i.e., a product patent — is quite broad, covering as it does even unforeseen uses. The doctrine that any identical structure disclosed in the prior art ought to bar such a product patent represents the *quid pro quo* for such broad protection. Broad protection, in other words, implies broad anticipation. See *Titanium Metals, supra*.

This symmetry is one of many examples of the way patent law attempts to balance the magnitude of the reward to the inventor, here measured in terms of patent scope, against the costs to society, here the large number of improvement products covered by the patentee's scope, and thus unavailable at competitive prices during the term of the patent.

3. For an interesting argument that a "low" standard of novelty will induce socially beneficial disclosure of new information, without high social costs, see Scotchmer & Green, *Novelty and Disclosure in Patent Law*, 21 RAND J. ECON. 131 (1990).

C. PATENTS AND PRINTED PUBLICATIONS UNDER §§ 102(a) AND 102(b)

Recall the following portions of the 102 Schematic:

§ 102(a): Novelty

....

[2] No patent if, before date of invention, invention$_a$ —

   [A] *patented* or
   [B] *described in a printed publication*
     [C] anywhere.

§ 102(b): Statutory Bars

[1] No patent if, more than one year prior to application, invention$_b$

   [A] *patented* or
   [B] *described in printed publication*
     [C] anywhere ...

The portions of the 102 Schematic reproduced above illustrate that although each element of prior art has quite distinct characteristics under §§ 102(a) and 102(b), two categories of § 102(a) prior art — patents and printed publications, 102(a)[2][A] and [B] in the Schematic — also appear in § 102(b) (to be precise, in § 102(b)[1][A] and [B]). The categories are modified by different requirements in the two sections; 102(a) bars a patent if any prior art in the categories is found which predates the invention, while § 102(b) prohibits a patent when prior art in the categories was available more than one year prior to the filing of a patent application. But the categories themselves are the same — viz, *patents and printed publications*. A common meaning has been ascribed to the phrase "patent or printed publication" in the two sections. Thus it is economical to consider in one combined section a key question that arises under both § 102(a) and § 102(b): what qualifies as a "patent or printed publication"?

1. "PATENTED"

The following cases interpret the meaning of "patented" in §§ 102(a) and 102(b), which element is present as § 102(a)[2][A] and § 102(b)[1][A] in the 102

Schematic. Note that under both §§ 102(a) and 102(b), a patent is effective as a reference "in this or a foreign country" ("anywhere" in elements § 102(a)[2][C] and § 102(b)[1][C] of the Schematic).

REEVES BROS. v. UNITED STATES LAMINATING CORP.

282 F. Supp. 118, 157 U.S.P.Q. (BNA) 235 (E.D.N.Y. 1966),
aff'd, 417 F.2d 869 (2d Cir. 1969)

This action involves two inventions made by John W. Dickey, upon which three patents were issued and duly assigned to Reeves Brothers, Inc. The First Patent (No. 2,957,793) relates to lamination of polyurethane foam to fabric by the use of flame heat. The Second Patent (No. 3,057,766) relates to an improvement in the method and apparatus for such lamination. The Third Patent (No. Re. 25,493) is a reissue of the Second Patent.

The Gebrauchsmuster as Anticipation

[I]t is proper to [begin by analyzing] the effect of the Gebrauchsmuster 1,691,026 (hereinafter referred to as "GM") issued by Germany in January, 1955, which defendants claim falls within the purview of Section 102(a) and (b) [and invalidates plaintiff's patents]. The questions which arise are whether (1) the GM is a patent within the purview of Section 102(a) and (b); (2) the GM as a patent constitutes anticipation only for what is claimed or also for what is disclosed; and (3) the GM actually anticipates the Dickey invention.

A patent has been repeatedly defined as a franchise granting the right to exclude everyone from making, using or selling the patented invention without the permission of the patentee. According to the testimony of the experts, a Gebrauchsmuster is registered under the German law after an application is filed in the German Patent Office. If the application meets the requirements of form and content, the GM is issued without any novelty search and is accompanied by the publication of an official notice in the German Official Gazette that it has been so issued. There is no requirement of nonobviousness in order to obtain a GM, and its purpose is to enable the applicant to obtain a speedy protection for a new article and if desirable, to concurrently seek a regular patent, a procedure which would consume much more time. After registration the specifications and claims become available to the public and anyone has free and open access to the same. The GM was not a printed publication at any time and is referred to as a utility model. It is limited to a maximum of six years instead of eighteen years, covers only articles and never can cover processes.

By a directive issued to its examiners in 1965, the United States Patent Office resolved certain prior inconsistent practices as to the treatment of GMs and stated that GMs may be considered as patents for anticipation purposes within the purview of Section 102. Plaintiff, however, contends that the words "patented ... in a foreign country" (as used in Section 102(a) and (b) of Article 35 of the Patent Act of 1952) have been taken without change from several of the prior enactments from as early as the Act of 1836, and that the legislative history of the various patent acts shows that Congress accorded no consideration to the enactment in various foreign countries of Utility Model Laws that came into existence in the latter part of the Nineteenth Century.

No place in the Patent Act or elsewhere did Congress indicate that only certain types or classes of patents may be considered under Section 102(a) and (b), and it did not distinguish between one particular type of foreign patent and another. If in effect the foreign document grants a patent right to exclude others from producing, using, or selling the invention, process, or article for a specified period of time, it clearly falls within the accepted definition of a patent which may be considered under Section 102(a) and (b). Accordingly, a GM must be deemed an effective patent under the above section as of its registration date.

Another problem results from the necessity of determining to what extent a GM may be used as an anticipatory reference under Section 102(a) and (b). There is respectable authority to the effect that under this section an American patent is a reference not only for its claims but also for its disclosures as revealed in its specifications. But this principle is apparently not applicable to foreign patents which, for anticipation purposes, are limited to their claims and cannot be used as references for the disclosures in their specifications. *American Tri-Ergon Corp. v. Paramount Publix Corp.*, 2 Cir. 1934, 71 F.2d 153, *reversed on other grounds*, 1935, 294 U.S. 464, 55 S. Ct. 449, 79 L. Ed. 997. So that what is publicly known or used but not printed in a foreign country is not a bar to an American patent.

The Court concludes that for anticipation purposes under Section 102 a GM, which is a foreign patent but not a printed publication, is a reference only for what is patented, i.e., for what it claims and not for what is disclosed in its specifications. This is consistent with the language of Section 102(a) and (b) which juxtaposes "patented ... in a foreign country" with the phrase "described in a printed publication in ... a foreign country." To permit the effect of such a foreign patent to extend beyond what is actually patented, would appear to indirectly effectuate a form of use and knowledge in a foreign country which is not statutorily allowable as an anticipatory reference to an American patent.

NOTES

1. *Still Good Law?* The portion of the preceding case holding that a foreign utility model is valid prior art only for what it claims has been ignored in some cases, and distinguished in others. *See Littlefuse, Inc. v. Bel Fuse, Inc.*, 21 U.S.P.Q.2d (BNA) 1293 (D.N.J. 1991) (finding Japanese utility model publication relevant prior art for what it discloses as well as what it claims; *Reeves* not cited). *But see Bendix Corp. v. Balax, Inc.*, 421 F.2d 809, 164 U.S.P.Q. (BNA) 485 (7th Cir. 1970) (foreign utility model specification can be resorted to for interpreting claims in the utility model); *Max Daetwyler Corp. v. Input Graphics, Inc.*, 583 F. Supp. 446, 455, 222 U.S.P.Q. 150 (E.D. Pa. 1984) ("If the claims of the GM do not disclose the invention of the American patent but the drawings or specifications of the GM do disclose the invention, the American patent is not anticipated by the GM. The specifications and drawings in the GM can only be considered under § 102(b) to the extent that they help to explain the claims of the GM.").

2. *Utility Models.* Utility models, or "petty patents," such as the German Gebrauchsmuster bear many similarities to full-fledged patents, the major difference usually being that they carry a shorter term of protection. But another form of patent-like protection, the design registration or German "Geschmacksmuster" is more problematical as a "patent" for § 102(a) and (b) purposes. This is a limited legal exclusion, available upon registration, which prevents others from copying the registered design but which does not protect against independent creation of a design. Despite these differences, cases have held that this form of protection amounts to a patent for purposes of § 102(a) and § 102(d) of the Act. *See In re Talbott*, 443 F.2d 1397, 170 U.S.P.Q. (BNA) 281 (C.C.P.A. 1971); *In re Carlson*, 983 F.2d 1032, 1038, 25 U.S.P.Q.2d 1207 (Fed. Cir. 1992). *See generally* Bleistein, *The German Law on "Gebrauchsmuster,"* 19 J. PAT. OFF. SOC'Y 126 (1937).

3. *Rationale for Reeves.* Note the court's literal reading of § 102(a), which permits the court to conclude that "patented" in §§ 102(a) and 102(b) means only that subject matter *claimed* in the prior art reference patent counts as novelty-defeating or statutory bar-raising subject matter. Thus a patent which describes fully invention A, but does not claim it, cannot destroy the novelty of a later patent application claiming invention A. Note that by its terms this argument would apply to U.S. patents as well, but this is clearly not the rule. *See, e.g.*, the *Structural Rubber Products* case earlier in this chapter.

Most researchers are accustomed to searching the relevant literature in their field to keep abreast with developments. To many, a thorough review of the literature includes both recent technical journals and recently-issued patents. And it can be assumed that they read more than the claims when they peruse these patents. (In fact it can be assumed they usually skip the claims — leave them to the lawyers!) If the researchers themselves do not distinguish between "publications" and patents, why should patent law make this distinction? Alternatively, is there any reason to think that the cost of searching patent disclosures is higher than the cost of reviewing technical journals and other publications? What about a patent that is published in a journal, or summarized in a commercial information service — does it suddenly become an effective reference for all it discloses when published in this alternative forum, whereas it would be effective only for what it claims otherwise?

In addition, the court in *Reeves* voices the fear that interpreting "patented" to mean "disclosed or claimed in a patent" would impermissibly impinge on the implicit policy of the "known or used" elements in §§ 102(a) and (b). This is because "known or used" is modified by "in this country" (element 102(a)[1][D] in the Schematic), whereas "patented" is not. In the court's analysis, the broader interpretation of "patented" — i.e., "disclosed in a patent" — is the equivalent of "known or used." The court is thus worried that broadening the meaning of "patented" in § 102(a) would make some *foreign* "known or used" material into viable prior art, in violation of § 102(a)'s requirement that only material "known or used" *in this country* should be within the prior art. The problem with this reasoning is that there is still plenty of material that will be "known or used" which *will not* be "disclosed in a patent." The two categories would remain distinct. Thus the broader interpretation does not undercut completely the policy implicit in the domestic-only "known or used" prior art category.

2. "PRINTED PUBLICATIONS"

Here we consider the meaning of "printed publication" under §§ 102(a) and 102(b), Schematic 102(a)[2][B] and 102(b)[1][B]. We begin our discussion of this topic with the following gem from Judge Learned Hand. (Walter Bagehot, who wrote that "Writers, like teeth, are divided into incisors and grinders," would no doubt classify Hand among the incisors.)

JOCKMUS v. LEVITON

28 F.2d 812 (2d Cir. 1928)

L. HAND, CIRCUIT JUDGE.

[Plaintiff, holder of a patent on an adjustable lightbulb holder in the shape of a candle, sued defendant for infringement. Defendant asserted lack of novelty, in that plaintiff's invention was anticipated by a product pictured in a commercial catalogue distributed to French customers of a German firm. From a judgment of validity and infringement, defendant appeals.]

We are content to follow the ruling that a catalogue distributed generally to a trade is a publication within Revised Statutes § 4886, 35 U.S.C.A. § 31. The aggregate of the[] [older] authorities is not so imposing as to cause us any hesitation. While it is true that the phrase, "printed publication," presupposes enough currency to make the work part of the possessions of the art, it demands no more. A single copy in a library, though more permanent, is far less fitted to inform the craft than a catalogue freely circulated, however ephemeral its existence; for the catalogue goes direct to those whose interests make them likely to observe and remember whatever it may contain that is new and useful.

Whether the cut, No. 712, in Gogarten & Schmidt's 1908 catalogue, was a sufficient disclosure is another matter. If the claims be strictly limited, it certainly was not, because it did not show how the end of the upper leg was fastened to the stud — whether as the plaintiff does it, or as the defendant, or in some other way. But, if the claims be read as they must be to cover the supposed infringement, we do not see what can be thought missing. That it was an adjustable candle socket the text itself declares; how its adjustment was to be made the cut makes plain beyond chance of mistake. The socket at the top is plainly for a bulb and the screw thread at the bottom to fit upon the pipe terminal. The jacket was represented [in illustrations], and the whole of this very simple invention was before the reader at a glance. We know of no rule that figures can never of themselves be an adequate anticipation of mechanical inventions, as of course they must be of designs, and we can see no reason for importing into the statute an arbitrary distinction, unrelated to its purposes. Words have their equivocations quite as much as figures; the question always must be what the art necessarily gathered from what appeared.

Whether the catalogue was in fact distributed generally, and when, are different questions. That it was printed in 1908 no one can reasonably doubt; it was a trade catalogue, meant to pass current for a season and to be superseded, as its successor of 1910 in this very case bears witness. To suppose that it bore an earlier date than that at which it first appeared contradicts all we know about merchandising; it might be post-dated like a motor car, but never the opposite. It is of course conceivable that, though printed, it was never distributed, or that the distribution was too limited to be a "publication." As to the last we can scarcely undertake to set a limit. Schmidt [from the firm that sent the catalogues] says that perhaps 1,000 went out. Far less would have served; the 50 which was his lower limit were quite enough. To be sure the fact of any distribution at all rests upon the uncorroborated testimony of him and Scharpe, because there was further documentary corroboration of neither, though each was explicit in his recollection, and each had had first hand knowledge. This would not be enough, if the catalogue itself were not produced, bearing its own evidence of existence since 1908, but no one can seriously suppose that such a document, printed in quantity, was intended to be kept secret; its whole purpose was to be spread broadcast as far as possible. It had been printed at some expense in French for French customers, and, unless some accident happened to prevent, it would in due course have gone upon its intended errand. To prove that no accident did happen, and that it did reach its destination we have, it is true, only oral, though entirely disinterested, testimony; but it is a mistake to assume that, even under the extraordinarily severe tests applied to the proof of anticipation, every step must be buttressed by documents. That some documents are necessary, perhaps, may be the rule; but, when the documents go so far as here, the ritual, if there is any, is satisfied, and the question is merely whether any doubt remains. We think that to entertain a scruple in a case so fortified is to catch at straws.

Decree reversed, and bill dismissed, for noninfringement.

NOTES

1. The *Jockmus* case is often cited for its definition of a publication. *See, e.g.*, 1 D. CHISUM, PATENTS § 3.04[2] (1978 & Supp. 1991).

2. Note that one who wishes to publish information to keep others from patenting it can take advantage of a statutory invention registration under the Patent Act. *See* Klivans, *Comment: Use of Statutory Invention Registration*, 73 J. PAT. & TRADEMARK OFF. SOC'Y 731 (1992).

In re HALL

781 F.2d 897, 228 U.S.P.Q. (BNA) 453 (Fed. Cir. 1986)

This is an appeal from the decision of the U.S. Patent and Trademark Office's (PTO) former Board of Appeals, adhered to on reconsideration by the Board of Patent Appeals and Interferences (board), sustaining the final rejection of claims 1-25 of [Hall's] reissue [a]pplication, based principally on a "printed publication" bar under 35 U.S.C. § 102(b). The reference is a doctoral thesis. Because appellant concedes that his claims are unpatentable if the thesis is available as a "printed publication" more than one year prior to the application's effective filing date of February 27, 1979, the only issue is whether the thesis is available as such a printed publication. On the record before us, we affirm the board's decision.

A protest was filed during prosecution of appellant's reissue application which included in an appendix a copy of the dissertation "1,4-*a*-Glucanglukohydrolase ein amylotylisches Enzym ..." by Peter Foldi (Foldi thesis or dissertation). The record indicates that in September 1977, Foldi submitted his dissertation to the Department of Chemistry and Pharmacy at Freiburg University in the Federal Republic of Germany, and that Foldi was awarded a doctorate degree on November 2, 1977.

Certain affidavits from Dr. Erich Will, who is the director and manager of the Loan Department of the Library of Freiburg University, have been relied upon by the examiner and the board in reaching their decisions. One document, styled a "Declaration" and signed by Dr. Will, states that:

> [I]n November 1977[,] copies of the dissertation FOLDI ... were received in the library of Freiburg University, and in ... December 1977 copies of the said dissertation were freely made available to the faculty and student body of Freiburg University as well as to the general public.

In an August 28, 1981 letter responding to an inquiry from a German corporation, Dr. Will said that the Freiburg University library was able to make the Foldi dissertation "available to our readers as early as 1977."

The examiner made a final rejection of the application claims. He said: "On the basis of the instant record it is reasonable to assume that the Foldi thesis was available (accessible) prior to February 27, 1979."

By letter, the PTO's Scientific Library asked Dr. Will whether the Foldi dissertation was made available to the public by being cataloged and placed in the main collection. Dr. Will replied in an October 20, 1983 letter, as translated:

> Our dissertations, thus also the Foldi dissertation, are indexed in a special dissertations catalogue, which is part of the general users' catalogue. In the stacks they are likewise set apart in a special dissertation section, which is part of the general stacks.

In response to a further inquiry by the PTO's Scientific Library requesting (1) the exact date of indexing and cataloging of the Foldi dissertation or (2) "the time such procedures normally take," Dr. Will replied in a June 18, 1984 letter:

The Library copies of the Foldi dissertation were sent to us by the faculty on November 4, 1977. Accordingly, the dissertation most probably was available for general use toward the beginning of the month of December, 1977.

The board held that the unrebutted evidence of record was sufficient to conclude that the Foldi dissertation had an effective date as prior art more than one year prior to the filing date of the appellant's initial application.

On appeal, appellant raises two arguments: (1) the § 102(b) "printed publication" bar requires that the publication be accessible to the interested public, but there is no evidence that the dissertation was properly indexed in the library catalog prior to the critical date; and (2) even if the Foldi thesis were cataloged prior to the critical date, the presence of a single cataloged thesis in one university library does not constitute sufficient accessibility of the publication's teachings to those interested in the art exercising reasonable diligence.

The [printed publication] bar is grounded on the principle that once an invention is in the public domain, it is no longer patentable by anyone.

The statutory phrase "printed publication" has been interpreted to give effect to ongoing advances in the technologies of data storage, retrieval, and dissemination. Because there are many ways in which a reference may be disseminated to the interested public, "public accessibility" has been called the touchstone in determining whether a reference constitutes a "printed publication" bar under 35 U.S.C. § 102(b). The § 102 publication bar is a legal determination based on underlying fact issues, and therefore must be approached on a case-by-case basis. The proponent of the publication bar must show that prior to the critical date the reference was sufficiently accessible, at least to the public interested in the art, so that such a one by examining the reference could make the claimed invention without further research or experimentation.

[A]ppellant argues that the Foldi thesis was not shown to be accessible because Dr. Will's affidavits do not say when the thesis was indexed in the library catalog and do not chronicle the procedures for receiving and processing a thesis in the library.

[A]ppellant would have it that accessibility can only be shown by evidence establishing a *specific* date of cataloging and shelving before the critical date. While such evidence would be desirable, in lending greater certainty to the accessibility determination, the realities of routine business practice counsel against requiring such evidence. The probative value of routine business practice to show the performance of a specific act has long been recognized. *See, e.g.*, 1 Wigmore, *Evidence* § 92 (1940); rule 406, Fed. R. Evid. Therefore, we conclude that competent evidence of the general library practice may be relied upon to establish an approximate time when a thesis became accessible.

We agree with the board that the evidence of record consisting of Dr. Will's affidavits establishes a prima facie case for unpatentability of the claims under the § 102(b) publication bar. It is a case which stands unrebutted.

Accordingly, the board's decision sustaining the rejection of appellant's claims is *affirmed*.

NOTES

1. Compare the preceding case with *Aluminum Co. of Am. v. Reynolds Metal Co.*, 14 U.S.P.Q.2d 1170 (N.D. Ill. 1990) (patentee's "progress letter," mailed to 33 recipients without secrecy notice, still not a printed publication for § 102(b) purposes, since it was *implicitly* confidential). Why is the number of copies of a document not the main factor in determining publication? *Cf.* Comment, *In re Cronyn: Can Student Theses Bar Patent Applications*, 18 J.C. & U.L. 105 (1991) (discussing *In re Cronyn*, 890 F.2d 1158 (Fed. Cir. 1989), which held that three theses filed in a shoebox in a chemistry-department library were not prior art under § 102(a)).

2. A publication becomes public when it becomes available to at least one member of "the general public." Thus a magazine or technical journal is effective as of its date of publication, i.e., when someone first receives it, rather than the date a manuscript was sent to the publisher or the date the journal or magazine was mailed. As was said in *In re Schlittler*, 234 F.2d 882, 110 U.S.P.Q. (BNA) 304 (C.C.P.A. 1956):

> [T]he mere placing of a manuscript in the hands of a publisher does not necessarily make it available to the public within the meaning of [the] authorities [reviewed].

After *Schlittler*, mere reception of a manuscript by a publisher does not constitute "publication" under § 102(a) or (b). Actual publication — i.e., receipt by subscribers — is required. *See, e.g., Protein Found., Inc. v. Brenner*, 147 U.S.P.Q. (BNA) 429 (1965); U.S. PATENT AND TRADEMARK OFFICE, MANUAL OF PATENT EXAMINING PROCEDURES § 706.02 (5th rev. ed. 1991); *Ex parte Hudson*, 18 U.S.P.Q.2d (BNA) 1322 (Bd. App. & Int. 1990). Is a grant proposal sent to a limited number of expert reviewers a publication under § 102(a)? *See E.I. duPont de Nemours & Co. v. Cetus Corp.*, 19 U.S.P.Q.2d (BNA) 1174 (N.D. Cal. 1990) (yes). Note that a portion of the *Schlittler* case has been overturned. *See In re Borst*, 345 F.2d 851, 145 U.S.P.Q. (BNA) 554 (C.C.P.A. 1965) (no reduction to practice necessary for publication to anticipate). Although at least one recent case suggests that scientific research grant applications are prior art, one recent article suggests this is not a general rule. Hodgins & Matula, *Government Grant Applications, Despite E.I. duPont de Nemours v. Cetus, Are Not Necessarily Prior Art*, 74 J. PAT. & TRADEMARK OFF. SOC'Y 241 (1992).

D. SECTION 102(a): "KNOWN OR USED ..."

Recall the following excerpt from our Schematic diagram of § 102:

§ 102(a): Novelty

[1] No patent if, before date of invention, invention$_a$ —
  [A] known or
  [B] used
    [C] by others
    [D] in this country ...

In this section, we examine the meaning of "known or used" in § 102(a).

NATIONAL TRACTOR PULLERS ASS'N v. WATKINS
205 U.S.P.Q. (BNA) 892 (N.D. Ill. 1980)

This is an action for declaration of invalidity and noninfringement of U.S. Patent 3,491,590 brought by the plaintiff, National Tractor Pullers Association, Inc., ("NTPA") against the patentee and owner of the patent, Mr. Billy K. Watkins. Defendant has filed a counterclaim for infringement.

The patent in suit is entitled "Power Stopper Weight Transfer Apparatus," and relates to devices commonly known as tractor pulling sleds. Such devices are used at pulling contests where competing tractor or truck owners test their machines against other machines by pulling a sled device down a track from a starting line towards a finish line. The sled device is designed to increase the resistance of the sled to being pulled in relation to the distance from the starting line. The resistance eventually exceeds the pulling power of the contestants' machines and thereby brings those machines to a halt.

[Plaintiff filed suit seeking to invalidate defendant's patent for a tractor sled. Defendant's design used a pulley system to progressively increase the weight on the tractor sled as it moved from the starting point, until the sled stopped. The tractor that went the greatest distance would then be the winner. See Figure 4-7, which shows a drawing from the Watkins patent and Mr. Watkins' sled in action. (The inventor himself is pictured alongside the sled.)

[One of plaintiff's arguments regarding invalidity was that defendant's device had been "known or used" prior to its invention by defendant. Among other evidence introduced on this point was a series of exhibits that plaintiff had submitted to the Patent Office in connection with its efforts to invalidate the patent during reissue proceedings initiated by the defendant. (Reissue and reexamination proceedings are discussed in Chapter 10.)]

A portion of the protestor's submission [in the reissue proceeding in the Patent Office] alleged that a sled substantially the same as Mr. Watkins' sled, but wheel-driven, had previously been invented by Messrs. Huls, Harms, and Sage some time in 1963 or 1964. The affidavits submitted by the protestors referred to drawings that had been made by Mr. Huls in 1963 or 1964 on a tablecloth in his

Jan. 27, 1970   **B. K. WATKINS**   **3,491,590**

POWER STOPPER WEIGHT TRANSFER APPARATUS
Filed April 24, 1968

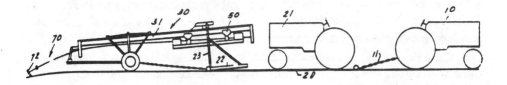

Figure 4-7

mother's kitchen. None of the alleged original drawings remain. However, in 1977, at the request of plaintiff's attorney, Mr. Huls attempted to recreate those drawings. Mr. Huls' drawing abilities being limited, Mr. Irwin was engaged to prepare formal drawings in 1977 which purported to be examples of what Mr. Huls had attempted to draw in 1963-64.

The Huls, Harms, and Sage affidavits state that the purported 1963-64 device was never built and that the group thereafter proceeded to build [another type of] machine, the Harms hydraulic device.

Watkins responded to the protestor's submission arguing that the 1963-64 Huls, Harms, Sage activities did not constitute prior art under 35 U.S.C. § 102; that there was no evidence of a prior device or public knowledge.

[T]he examiner found that [the] Huls 1963-64 activities did not constitute prior art.

The no longer existing alleged tablecloth drawings were never available to the public. They were drawn on the underside of the tablecloth and remained in the kitchen of Mr. Huls mother's home and were never printed nor otherwise published before being destroyed. The device was never constructed or reduced to practice and at least one participant in those activities, Mr. Merle K. Sage, testified at his deposition that the device allegedly shown in the 1977 Huls drawings could not be constructed as shown. The Irwin 1977 drawings did not exist prior to Mr. Watkins conception and reduction to practice, and do not purport to be identical with any drawings that ever existed prior to 1977.

That which is alleged to be prior art must have its prior art existence and relevancy established by clear and convincing evidence.

In order to qualify as prior art under 35 U.S.C. § 102, the art must be art which was known before the invention by the patentee. Prior knowledge as set forth in 35 U.S.C. § 102(a) must be prior public knowledge, that is knowledge which is reasonably accessible to the public.

The knowledge required by § 102(a) involves some type of public disclosure and is not satisfied by knowledge of a single person, or a few persons working together. *Filterite Corp. v. Tate Eng'g, Inc.*, 318 F. Supp. 584, 167 U.S.P.Q. 450 (D.C. Md. 1970), *aff'd*, 447 F.2d 62, 170 U.S.P.Q. 190 (4th Cir. 1971); *Union Carbide Corp. v. Filtrol Corp.*, 170 U.S.P.Q. 482 (C.D. Cal. 1971), *aff'd*, 179 U.S.P.Q. 209 (9th Cir. 1973). This court finds that the 1963-64 alleged Huls-Harms-Sage activities do not qualify as prior art as found by the Patent Office.

NOTES

1. The case most cited as the origin of the *"public"* knowledge or use requirement is *Pennock v. Dialogue*, 27 U.S. 1 (1829). But this case is actually not so much concerned with the novelty-defeating effects of public knowledge or use as with their effect as a statutory bar. The *Pennock* case is therefore reproduced below in Section E.3.

2. "Known ... by others" suggests that any prior conceptualization, if discovered, should be in the prior art. Why isn't the inquiry in the preceding case about whether Huls and friends *thought of* the Watkins device; why the emphasis on the drawings? Why is it not enough that the invention has been considered by "he who sits obscure in the exceeding lustre and the pure intense irradiation of mind." (Shelley, on Coleridge, Letter to Maria Gisborne (1820), 1.202). Likewise, of what significance is it that the tablecloth with the drawing of the design was destroyed? Would it make any difference if it were still in existence? If no one knew what had happened to it?

These questions were addressed in the Supreme Court case of *Gayler v. Wilder*, 51 U.S. (10 How.) 477 (1850). In *Gayler*, the Court considered whether a prior art device built by one Connor, which had been lost and whose details of construction had been forgotten by all concerned, anticipated the patented invention at issue in the case.

> [I]f the Connor safe had passed away from the memory of Connor himself, and of those who had seen it, and the safe itself had disappeared, the

knowledge of the improvement was as completely lost as if it had never been discovered. The public could derive no benefit from it until it was discovered by another inventor. And if [the patentee] made his discovery by his own efforts, without any knowledge of Connor's, he invented an improvement that was then new, and at that time unknown ....

51 U.S. at 495. Two dissenters from the majority opinion pointed out problems with this holding. Justice McLean made the pragmatic point that it was impossible to be sure that the patentee had not somehow learned of Connor's prior art safe. (Indeed, some have argued that § 102(a) in effect *presumes* that the second inventor learned of the prior invention, and disposes of the need to *prove* that this was so. *See, e.g.*, *Dayton Eng'g Labs. v. Kent*, 260 F. 187 (E.D. Pa. 1919) ("A fair presumption arises that the applicant has not invented what has been made the subject of public description, and he cannot have been the first inventor of what was in prior use ....")). The other dissenter, Justice Daniel, said that an invention once "given to the public" could not be withdrawn, even though the public had in effect "lost" what it had been given.

The views of the majority and the dissents might be characterized as "relative" vs. "unqualified" novelty. Which makes more sense? What quantum of proof ought to be required that a device or process has truly been "lost"? Does it make more sense from the point of view of administrative efficiency to *presume* that technology, once created, is never completely lost, thus saving the expense of proving the nonexistence of once-extant devices and processes? If so, why make this presumption conclusive; why not simply create a strong presumption that this is so, but allow the patentee to show that there was no conceivably feasible way to gain access to a particular piece of prior art?

The holding in *Gayler* was questioned in a later Supreme Court case, *Coffin v. Ogden*, 85 U.S. (18 Wall.) 120, 125 (1874) (emphasizing the necessity of a reduction to practice of the prior art device, but questioning the soundness of the "lost art" aspect of *Gayler*).

ROSAIRE v. BAROID SALES DIVISION, NATIONAL LEAD CO.

218 F.2d 72, 104 U.S.P.Q. 100 (5th Cir. 1955)

In this suit for patent infringement there is presented to us for determination the correctness of the judgment of the trial court, based on findings of fact and conclusions of law, holding that the two patents involved in the litigation were invalid and void and that furthermore there had been no infringement by defendant.

The Rosaire and Horvitz patents relate to methods of prospecting for oil or other hydrocarbons. The inventions are based upon the assumption that gases have emanated from deposits of hydrocarbons which have been trapped in the earth and that these emanations have modified the surrounding rock. The methods claimed involve the steps of taking a number of samples of soil from formations which are not themselves productive of hydrocarbons, either over a horizontal area or vertically down a well bore, treating each sample, as by grinding and heating in a closed vessel, to cause entrained or absorbed hydrocarbons therein to evolve as a gas, quantitatively measuring the amount of hydrocarbon gas so evolved from each sample, and correlating the measurements with the locations from which the samples were taken.

Plaintiff claims that in 1936 he and Horvitz invented this new method of prospecting for oil. In due course the two patents in suit, Nos. 2,192,525 and 2,324,085, were issued thereon. Horvitz assigned his interest to Rosaire.

In view of the fact that the trial court's judgment that the patents were invalid, would of course dispose of [this infringement suit] if correct, we turn our attention to this issue. [Appellee argues] that work carried on by one Teplitz for the Gulf Oil Corporation invalidated both patents by reason of the relevant provisions of the patent laws which state that an invention is not patentable if it "was known or used by others in this country" before the patentee's invention thereof. 35 U.S.C.A. § 102(a). Appellee contends that Teplitz and his coworkers knew and extensively used in the field the same alleged inventions before any date asserted by Rosaire and Horvitz.

On this point appellant himself in his brief admits that "Teplitz conceived of the idea of extracting and quantitatively measuring entrained or absorbed gas from the samples of rock, rather than relying upon the free gas in the samples. We do not deny that Teplitz conceived of the methods of the patents in suit." And further appellant makes the following admission: "We admit that the Teplitz-Gulf work was done before Rosaire and Horvitz conceived of the inventions. We will show, however, that Gulf did not apply for patent until 1939, did not publish Teplitz's ideas, and did not otherwise give the public the benefit of the experimental work."

The question as to whether the work of Teplitz was "an unsuccessful experiment," as claimed by appellant, or was a successful trial of the method in question and a reduction of that method to actual practice, as contended by appellee, is, of course, a question of fact. On this point the trial court made the following finding of fact:

> I find as a fact that Abraham J. Teplitz and his coworkers with Gulf Oil Corporation and its Research Department during 1935 and early 1936, before any date claimed by Rosaire, spent more than a year in the oil fields and adjacent territory around Palestine, Texas [see Figures 4-8(a) and (b)], taking and analyzing samples both over an area and down drill holes, exactly as called for in the claims of the patents which Rosaire and Horvitz subsequently applied for and which are here in suit. This Teplitz work was a successful and adequate field trial of the prospecting method involved and a reduction to practice of that method. The work was performed in the field under ordinary conditions without any deliberate attempt at concealment or effort to exclude the public and without any instructions of secrecy to the employees performing the work.

The Hub of East Texas

120 Miles
Southeast From
DALLAS

151 Miles
North From
HOUSTON

POPULATION 15,000

Combined Capital
of Four Banks
$375,000.00
Surplus, $350,000
Deposits, $3,000,000
1927 Assessed Property
Value $7,637,415

Shop and General Offices Missouri Pacific Lines.

Anderson County
Population 35,000
Land Area 695,905 Acres
4,399 Individual Farms.
Highway 43 open from Laredo to the East via Palestine.

New $300,000 Bridge over Trinity River Traversable All Year Round.

For Further Information Address
CHAMBER OF COMMERCE
PALESTINE, TEXAS.

Figure 4-8a

Dallas 120 miles

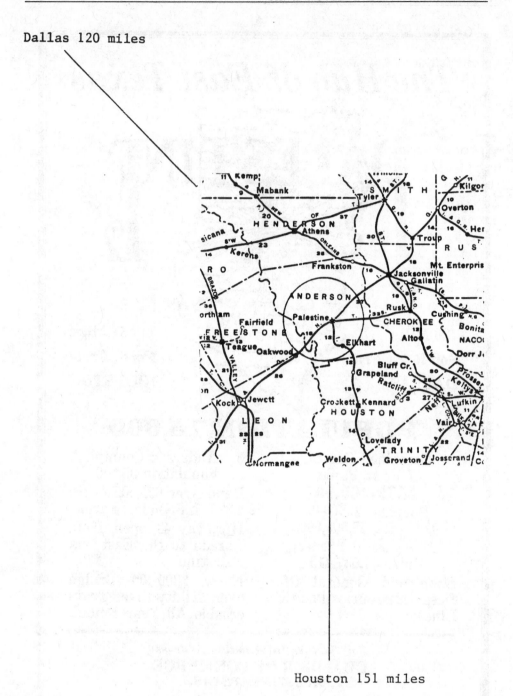

Houston 151 miles

Figure 4-8b

As we view it, if the court's findings of fact are correct then under the statute as construed by the courts, we must affirm the finding of the trial court that appellee's patents were invalid.

[T]here was sufficient evidence to sustain the finding of the trial court that there was more here than an unsuccessful or incomplete experiment. It is clear that the work was not carried forward, but that appears to be a result of two things: (1) that the geographical area did not lend itself properly to the test, and (2) that the "entire gas prospecting program was therefore suspended in September of 1936, in order that the accumulated information might be thoroughly reviewed." It will be noted that the program was not suspended to test the worth of the method but to examine the data that was produced by use of the method involved.

With respect to the argument advanced by appellant that the lack of publication of Teplitz's work deprived an alleged infringer of the defense of prior use, we find no case which constrains us to hold that where such work was done openly and in the ordinary course of the activities of the employer, a large producing company in the oil industry, the statute is to be so modified by construction as to require some affirmative act to bring the work to the attention of the public at large.

While there is authority for the proposition that one of the basic principles underlying the patent laws is the enrichment of the art, and that a patent is given to encourage disclosure of inventions, no case we have found requires a holding that, under the circumstances that attended the work of Teplitz, the fact of public knowledge must be shown before it can be urged to invalidate a subsequent patent.

NOTES

1. In *W.L. Gore & Assocs. v. Garlock, Inc.*, 721 F.2d 1540, 1548, 220 U.S.P.Q. (BNA) 303 (1983), the Federal Circuit had this to say about "secret" prior use, where patentee Gore argued that prior use by another of a machine conforming to the elements of Gore's claim was nonpublic and therefore non-anticipatory:

> The nonsecret use of a claimed process in the usual course of producing articles for commercial purposes is a public use. *Electric Storage Battery Co. v. Shimadzu*, 307 U.S. 5, 20, 41 U.S.P.Q. 155, 161 (1939) .... Thus it cannot be said that the district court erred in determining that the invention set forth in claim 1 of '566 patent was known or used by others under § 102(a), as evidenced by ... operation of the 401 machine before Dr. Gore's asserted date of that invention.

2. *Abandoned Experiments.* From *Picard v. United Aircraft Corp.*, 128 F.2d 632, 53 U.S.P.Q. (BNA) 563 (2d Cir. 1942) (L. Hand, J.):

> It is true that another's experiment, imperfect and never perfected, will not serve either as an anticipation or as part of the prior art, for it has not

served to enrich it. The patented invention does not become "known" by such a use or sale, or by anything of which the art cannot take hold and make use as it stands. But the mere fact that an earlier "machine" or "manufacture," sold or used, was an experiment does not prevent its becoming an anticipation or a part of the prior art, provided it was perfected and thereafter became publicly known. Whether it does become so depends upon how far it becomes a part of the stock of knowledge of the art in question. Judged by that standard, the Curtiss engine [prior art reference] was not an "abandoned experiment"; it had been perfected; it had withstood a severer test than was necessary in use; it had been sold; it remained permanently accessible to the art, a contribution to the sum of knowledge so far as it went.

See also *Corona Cord Tire Co. v. Dovan Chem. Corp.*, 276 U.S. 358, 384-85 (1928), where the Court held that commercial sales were not necessary for a completed experiment to constitute a "public use" under the Patent Act: "It is not an abandoned experiment because he confines his use of the [product] thus produced to his laboratory or his lecture room."

3. Public Equals Nonsecret. The very generous view of what it means for a disclosure to be "public" was criticized in a Comment:

The term "public" ... seems merely to mean "not secret." It is unnecessary to show that the previous discovery was ever used commercially, that it was in fact observable by the public if such a process or device would not normally be so viewed, or that it was known to more than a few persons. This construction of the term "public" seems questionable, since it may result in the denial of a patent even though the subsequent inventor has conferred a benefit by filing the invention with the public records.

Comment, *Prior Art in the Patent Law*, 73 HARV. L. REV. 369, 373 (1959). The author goes on to propose a "higher standard of knowledge or use," arguing that

an invention should be considered "known or used" only if it was so widely known or used that an ordinary skilled worker exercising reasonable diligence to learn the state of the art would have discovered, recognized, and been able to construct the invention.

Id., at 373.

Would someone exercising "reasonable diligence" have discovered the prior art in *Rosaire*? In *National Tractor Pullers*? What if person *A* were located geographically close to an obscure prior art reference, and person *B* was far away. Would the patentability of the same invention be different for the two? If the prior art in question was a device constructed by *C*, would she be barred from continued use of her device in the face of a patent to person *B*, whose invention was only patentable because she (*C*) was so far away it was not "reasonable" for *B* to know about it?

Even accepting the premise that only "reasonably discoverable" prior art ought to be held against an inventor, how does one measure "reasonableness" here? If inventor *A* is a huge multinational conglomerate, and inventor *B* is a home hobbyist with a workbench in the basement, should "reasonable diligence" be defined alike for both? If not, *A*, the large company, in effect faces a higher standard of patentable novelty than *B*. Is this a good idea? If we adopt it, should the scope of patents issued to the *A*'s and *B*'s of the world be the same, or should *B*'s patent, being easier to get, be limited in some fashion — e.g., by making it effective only in one state or region? Note the concept of "local novelty" is not unknown in the patent systems of the world. *See, e.g.*, Cohn, *Nature and Origins of Israeli Patent Law*, PAT. WORLD, Apr. 1991, at 2 (local novelty in effect in Israel in early part of country's history).

Section 102(a): "In This Country"

An invention is anticipated if "known or used by others *in this country*." This domestic knowledge or use requirement, element § 102(a)[1][D] in the 102 Schematic, is explored in the following case and notes.

WESTINGHOUSE MACHINE CO. v. GENERAL ELECTRIC CO.
207 F. 75 (2d. Cir. 1913)

This case grows out of an interference in the Patent Office entitled *De Kando v. Armstrong*, which was decided adversely to De Kando and his assignee, the Westinghouse Machine Company. [Armstrong, who assigned to General Electric, relied on his filing date, June 28, 1905, as his date of invention.]

Quoting from the opinion below the facts there found are:

> That De Kando actually made his invention in a foreign country and reduced it to actual practice and put it in actual use, prior to the spring of 1904 on the Valtellina Railway in Italy. That on March, 1904, Waterman went from the United States to Europe and met De Kando at Budapest, where the details of the invention were explained to him, and then, proceeding to Italy, Waterman saw the invention in actual use. In addition De Kando then furnished Waterman with an elaborate written description of the invention.

> It appears from the evidence that Waterman was learned and skilled and fully capable of fully understanding and that he did understand the invention. Waterman therefore "knew" that the invention had been actually made and reduced to successful practice. That Waterman not only brought the information he had gained in Europe with him to the United States, when he arrived May 5, 1904, but also the said written description of such invention and notes which he had made relating to such invention while in Europe. That Waterman made a written report as to this invention to Stillwell June 7, 1904, and during the year following he described same in the United States

to a number of electrical engineers of standing, all capable of understanding same, and June 19, 1905, Waterman explained the invention to the American Institute of Electrical Engineers in the United States. Prior to 1901 or 1902 Armstrong had conceived the same invention and in June, 1905, he filed his application for a patent.

[The court further finds that] [t]he knowledge of De Kando's invention and its use abroad was communicated by De Kando to Waterman for the specific purpose of introducing such knowledge into the United States and of having the invention put into use in the United States.

The proposition of law for which complainants contend is that De Kando's date of [first use] in this country is May, 1904, when Waterman, arriving here with knowledge of the completed invention, disclosed that knowledge to others here skilled in the art capable of understanding the same. That by reason of his knowledge and disclosures to others in this country prior to June 28, 1905, the invention was "known" in the legal sense in this country before Armstrong's application was filed.

[T]he Patent Law is contained in many sections, and they must be construed together to get at the precise code which they set forth. Section 4886 [of the 1870 Patent Act] states generally the conditions which must exist in order to entitle an inventor to the grant of a patent. Section 4923 deals specifically with the effect of knowledge and use in a foreign country, and it makes no distinction whether such use is made or such knowledge is acquired by persons who, after using the thing or acquiring the knowledge, remain abroad or come here. This section (4923) provides that the patent taken out by an applicant for the same thing here shall not be void on account of such knowledge or use unless the invention had been patented or described in a printed publication. As we construe this section, reduction to practice in a foreign country can never operate to destroy a patent applied for here, however widely known such reduction to practice may be, either among foreigners or among persons living here, unless the invention be patented or described in a printed publication.

The decree is affirmed.

NOTES

1. Why is § 102(a) "known or used," 102 Schematic 102(a)[1][A] and [B], the only prior art category that might apply here? Why wasn't Waterman's presentation to the American Institute of Electrical Engineers sufficient to anticipate Armstrong? (See the last paragraph of the opinion.) These considerations are moot in light of the Uruguay Round (see Section K below) and were arguably moot under pre-Uruguay Round law as well. *See* Badie, *Hints to Foreign Inventors: You Can Protect Your Invention Date*, 75 J. PAT. & TRADEMARK OFF. SOC'Y 651 (1993).

2. Does the holding above make sense in light of the policies discussed earlier, e.g., the concurrence by Justice Daniel in *Gayler v. Wilder*, or the opinion in the *Rosaire* case? It would appear to be quite illogical to hold that *any domestic* prior knowledge or use, no matter how obscure, is valid prior art, while *any foreign* knowledge or use, no matter how widely trumpeted — even in the U.S. — is not. This is not the only "anti-foreign" bias in the Patent Act, however; see below, the section on "Foreign Activities and Interferences."

3. The emphasis in the preceding case on a reduction to practice (defined and discussed in detail in Section J.4 of this chapter) precedes *In re Borst*, 345 F.2d 851, 145 U.S.P.Q. (BNA) 554 (C.C.P.A. 1965) (no reduction to practice necessary for reference to anticipate), and hence perhaps a court would look upon the same facts differently today.

4. The President's Commission on the Patent System in 1966 recommended abolition of the "foreign bias" in § 102(a):

> Foreign knowledge, use and sale would be included as prior art. Present arbitrary geographical distinctions would be eliminated.... The anomaly of excluding, from prior art, public knowledge, use or sale in a border town of Mexico or Canada, and including the same kind of disclosure in Alaska or Hawaii, would be eliminated .... [This change] would be another step toward conformity with European patent laws and would promote acceptance of a common definition of universal prior art.

PRESIDENT'S COMMISSION ON THE PATENT SYSTEM, "TO PROMOTE THE PROGRESS OF ... USEFUL ARTS" IN AN AGE OF EXPLODING TECHNOLOGY 6 (1966). *See generally* Chisum, *Foreign Activity: Its Effect on Patentability Under United States Law*, 11 INT'L REV. INDUS. PROP. & COPYRIGHT L. 26 (1980).

E. SECTION 102(b): THE STATUTORY BARS

> Ideas won't keep. Something must be done about them.
>
> — Alfred North Whitehead
> Dialogues

1. THE IDENTITY REQUIREMENT UNDER § 102(b)

Although both §§ 102(a) and 102(b) speak in terms of "the invention," it is generally recognized that what constitutes a sufficient invention is different for the two sections. In other words, the phrase "the invention" in § 102(a) has been interpreted to mean something different from the same phrase in § 102(b). (Thus the terminology "invention$_a$" and "invention$_b$" in the 102 Schematic above.)

DIX-SEAL CORP. v. NEW HAVEN TRAP ROCK CO.

236 F. Supp. 914, 144 U.S.P.Q. (BNA) 57 (D. Conn. 1964)

This is a suit for infringement of a patent for a "HOT BITUMINOUS SUR-
FACE TREATMENT AND PROCESS." Patent No. 2,884,841, was issued to
its inventor Dickinson [in] 1959, on an application filed by him on August 21,
1957. The patent was then assigned to the plaintiff. The original defendants are
two Connecticut corporations who have admittedly used the patented process for
many years. A third defendant, the State of Connecticut, was brought into the
action after its inception.

The defendants have set forth in their answer a series of defenses to the
infringement claim. They have challenged the validity of the patent on the ground
that plaintiff's invention was described in a printed publication and/or was in
public use for more than one year prior to the filing of the patent application
[under § 102(b)].

The plaintiff has argued that the section is not applicable here [because] for a
public use or a printed publication to defeat the validity of his patent it must be
identical with the patented process, and that such identity has not been established

The first patent act, the Patent Act of 1790, 1 Stat. 109, followed closely its
English counterpart and contained the requirement that the invention must not
have been "before known or used." Only three years later, however, the clause
was enlarged to "not known or used before the application." Patent Act of 1793,
1 Stat. 318. It was this part of the act which was the forerunner of the present
§ 102(b), and the introduction of that specific time period points up a distinction
in the patent act which has often been overlooked. Section 102(b) is concerned
with the actions of the inventor once he makes an invention that is novel and
patentable. It imposes a condition that the inventor act with deliberate speed in
filing his patent application or his rights to a legal monopoly will be barred.

The dual purposes of preventing exploitation and giving the public the fruits
of the discovery as soon as possible were reiterated by the Second Circuit in
Metallizing Engineering Co. v. Kenyon Bearing & Auto Parts Co., 153 F.2d 516
(2d Cir.), *cert. denied*, 328 U.S. 840, 66 S. Ct. 1016, 90 L. Ed. 1615 (1946).

> [I]t is a condition upon an inventor's right to a patent that he shall not ex-
> ploit his discovery competitively after it is ready for patenting; he must
> content himself with either secrecy, or legal monopoly. It is true that for the
> limited period of two years he was allowed to do so [under an old Patent
> Act] possibly in order to give him time to prepare an application; and even
> that has been recently cut down by half. But if he goes beyond that period
> of probation, he forfeits his right regardless of how little the public may
> have learned about the invention.

The plaintiff's first contention is that there was a lack of identity between [his
own] prior uses of the mix [on various jobs] and the patented process. The
plaintiff not only maintains that § 102(b) requires a greater degree of identity than

that required for infringement purposes, but claims that defendants must prove that the public uses were exactly identical. This raises an interesting question concerning the interpretation of the statutory section.

As authority for his contention of law, the plaintiff relies on *Draper v. Wattles*, 7 Fed. Cas. 1061 (No. 4,073) (C.C.D. Mass.1878). There the court stated at p. 1063:

> The sale or use, to defeat the patent, must have been of the thing patented; and we are of opinion that, in order to defeat the patent, it is not enough to prove that the inventor has sold an earlier and less perfect article — that is, less perfect in the sense of the patent law, even if the thing sold would be within the claim of the patent. In other words, the test is not, necessarily, whether the article sold would infringe the invention by embodying a part of it, but whether it is the invention — that is, embodies the whole of it. The law does not intend to say that a patentee dedicates to the public whatever he sells more than two years before he applies for a patent, but that he dedicates his invention if he sells it for that period.

But in *Draper*, the court itself noted that there was a substantial and "patentable" difference between the prior use and the patent. In comparing the two, the court said at p. 1062: "We think it very doubtful whether in that form the ring would have gone into general use, and that the last and patented article would not be a patentable improvement upon it." Thus the statement of the law, which was novel at that time, as far as I could determine, was not necessary for the decision.

Support for the plaintiff's argument is also sought to be drawn from *Chicopee Mfg. Co. v. Columbus Fiber Mills Co.*, 165 F. Supp. 307 (M.D. Ga.1958). There the court suggest[ed] that "the language of 35 U.S.C.A. § 103 refers to Section 102 as requiring that the invention be 'identically disclosed.'" That statutory construction suggested in *Chicopee* was subsequently specifically rejected by a reasoned decision in *Bros., Inc. v. Browning Mfg. Co.*, 317 F.2d 413 (8th Cir.), *cert. denied*, 375 U.S. 825 (1963). In the *Bros.* case, the plaintiff had distributed a pamphlet with a brief description of his invention more than one year prior to his patent application. This was cited as a printed publication under § 102(b). The plaintiff, as in the case before this court, argued that § 103 imposed an exact identity test on § 102(b). The court in holding the patent invalid because of the publication rejected the exact identity test and used the legislative history of § 103 to show that there was no intention by Congress in passing § 103 to change the § 102(b) standards.

In none of these cases did the court rely upon a rule of precise identity to uphold the patent in question. Thus, I do not feel compelled to decide that complete identity of prior public use is necessary to bar a later patent. Nor am I persuaded to do so. The better rule, supported by the weight of authority, is set forth in 1 Walker, Patents 355-56 (Dellers ed. 1937):

Precise identity between the thing covered by the patent, and the thing which the inventor allowed to be in public use or on sale more than two years before he applied for that patent, is not necessary to constitute constructive abandonment of the invention covered by the latter. It is enough if the two devices are substantially the same, or if the advance from one to the other did not amount to invention, but it is not enough that the two devices perform the same function, and are somewhat similar in construction and in mode of operation.

The Supreme Court opinion in *Hall v. Macneale*, 107 U.S. 90 (1882), probably marks the beginning of this approach. There the court, in discussing the form of the invention that had been in public use, said at p. 97:

The invention was complete in those safes. It was capable of producing the results sought to be accomplished, though not as thoroughly as with the use of welded steel and iron plates.

There was a distinct difference between the patented invention and that earlier form, but its prior use was still held to defeat patentability.

If exact identity were required, § 102(b) would become a paper defense, for then what is earlier put in use with minor changes later could be patented and that which the law intended the public to have would be considered an infringement.

The balance between encouragement of technological advancement by granting a legal monopoly to one who "invents ... any new and useful process," (35 U.S.C. § 101) and the interest of the public in having new inventions promptly available has been struck by Congress. Once the year in which to prepare and file his application has passed, the employment of a standard of patentability less stringent against the first inventor than against these others would seem to impair, if not defeat, congressional policy. There should be no distinction between prior art of the inventor's own making and that of others.

While the theory upon which an inventor may lose his right to obtain a patent may in some respects be different from that which would preclude a right from ever arising, the underlying policies supporting both theories are the same. What has passed into public use may not thereafter be withdrawn by anyone, including the inventor, into a legally sanctioned monopoly. There must be a further development which would merit such a privilege.

NOTES

1. The Federal Circuit has adopted the same test for identity, as is evident from this excerpt from *In re Hamilton*, 882 F.2d 1576, 1583, 11 U.S.P.Q.2d (BNA) 1890 (Fed. Cir. 1989):

[The applicant] has failed to rebut the prima facie showing that the offer to [the buyer] placed his invention "on sale" within the meaning of 35 U.S.C. § 102(b). He does not contest the board's determination that the claims to vertically perforated forms *would have been obvious* in view of the horizontally perforated forms offered for sale.

(Emphasis added.) One of the Federal Circuit's predecessor courts, the Court of Claims, had made a similar holding. *See Tri-Wall Containers, Inc. v. United States*, 408 F.2d 748, 161 U.S.P.Q. (BNA) 116 (Ct. Cl.), *cert. denied*, 396 U.S. 828 (1969).

2. One commentator warns that it is dangerous to file a patent application which claims both pre-critical date devices and patentable (nonobvious) improvements thereon, because then *all* the claims are at risk of being barred by § 102(b). The preferable course, he suggests, is to file "[a] disclosure that contains a description of the pre-critical date device and an explanation of the reasons for the improvement(s) made thereon," while claiming only the latter. Colman, *Identity Tolerance: Under the "On-Sale" and "Public Use" Provisions of Section 102(b)*, 54 J. PAT. OFF. SOC'Y 23, 50 (1972).

3. The court in *Dix-Seal* rejects the view of *Draper v. Wattles*, 7 Fed. Cas. 1061, 1063 (No. 4,073) (C.C.D. Mass. 1878), which was that "The sale or use, to defeat the patent, must have been of the thing patented ...." Some courts continue to adhere to this view, although usually in dictum or without much reflection. *See, e.g., Delong v. Raymond Int'l, Inc.*, 622 F.2d 1135, 206 U.S.P.Q. (BNA) 97 (3d Cir. 1980); 2 D. CHISUM, PATENTS § 6.02[3] (1978 & Supp. 1991). Cases such as *Dix-Seal*, however, express the better view.

4. It has been pointed out that the "looser" identity test for § 102(b) articulated in cases such as *Dix-Seal* tends to collapse the § 102(b) "identity" inquiry into the § 103 obviousness inquiry. While this is true, it is defensible for the reasons set forth in *Dix-Seal*; namely, that a "strict" identity test would essentially render § 102(b) ineffective as a statutory bar, since an inventor would only have to change one insignificant feature of the invention to escape from the bar of § 102(b). Nonetheless, it must be pointed out that the § 102(b) identity test does not completely mirror the § 103 inquiry (which is explored in Chapter 5). This is because the identity test under § 102(b) is applied as of the date of the event giving rise to the alleged bar — e.g., public use or sale — rather than the date of invention of the improvement claimed in the patent more than one year after this event. Thus, any post-critical date improvement in the device publicly used or sold before the critical date will be tested for § 102(b) identity as of the date of the pre-critical date event. If the improvement is patentably distinct — i.e., nonobvious — over the prior art pre-critical date event *as of the date of that event*, the improvement will be deemed to have failed the § 102(b) identity test. (Compare this with the nonobviousness inquiry regarding the improvement, which asks whether that improvement was obvious *as of its date of invention*.) The identity test under § 102(b) makes it easier to avoid a statutory bar than nonobviousness, since the former test is applied to an earlier time when there is less prior art and thus less knowledge in the field of invention in general.

2. SECTION 102(b): REVIEW OF PATENTS AND PRINTED PUBLICATIONS

In this section we begin our discussion of the categories of § 102(b) prior art.

The first of these categories are those identified in elements § 102(b)[1][A] and [1][B] — patents and printed publications. Fortunately, and atypically, these terms are given the same meaning in § 102(b) that they are given in § 102(a). In other words, elements § 102(b)[1][A] and [1][B] in the Schematic are the same as the corresponding elements under § 102(a), namely § 102(a)[2][A] and [2][B], discussed above in Section C. Both categories are applied without any geographic boundary; a publication or patent anywhere in the world counts as prior art under § 102(b), just as it does under § 102(a).

Of course, although the *categories* are the same, the critical dates under the two sections are different. Thus, although "printed publication" means the same thing under § 102(a) and § 102(b), only publications with an effective date more than one year prior to the filing of a patent application touch off a statutory bar under § 102(b),[9] while publications with dates before the date of invention can anticipate (i.e., deprive of novelty) an invention under § 102(a).

One more point to keep in mind is that § 102(a) refers only to patents and publications authored by *others* (Schematic § 102(a)[1][C]); the inventor herself cannot anticipate her own invention. But under § 102(b), prior art is not restricted to works produced by others. Prior patents and publications of the inventor count as prior art, too. Thus, an inventor can create a statutory bar *with her own work* if it is patented or published before the critical date.

In fact, this is the most common form of § 102(b) prior art. And it is easy to see why. Statutory bar prior art produced by those other than the inventor — call it third party § 102(b) prior art — will very often *also* qualify as § 102(a) prior art. For example, a publication by a third party more than a year before an inventor files a patent application will often in addition represent publication prior to the inventor's date of *invention*. Put another way, the third party act often has two effects: it defeats novelty under § 102(a), and it acts as a statutory bar under § 102(b). Note that when this is so, the Patent Office and the courts sometimes do not bother to point out that the prior art invalidates the patent under *both* § 102(a) and § 102(b), since *either* is a sufficient ground in itself. (But see *In re Hall* above, where the court does note that the dissertation, if a "publication," supports rejection of the patent application under either § 102(a) or (b).) *Cf.*

---

[9] With one minor exception:

> Where the last day of the year dated from the date of publication falls on a Saturday, Sunday or Federal holiday, the publication is not a statutory bar under 35 U.S.C. 102(b) if the application was filed on the next succeeding business day ....

U.S. PATENT AND TRADEMARK OFFICE, MANUAL OF PATENT EXAMINING PROCEDURES § 706.02 (5th Rev. 1983 & Supp. 1989). Isn't patent law great?

Vick, *Publish* and *Perish: The Printed Publication as a Bar to Patentability*, 18 AM. INTELL. PROP. L. ASS'N Q.J. 235 (1990).

3. SECTION 102(b): "IN PUBLIC USE OR ON SALE ..."

We now consider elements of prior art set forth in the following excerpt from the Schematic:

§ 102(b): Statutory Bars

[2] No patent if, more than year prior to application, invention$_b$ ...

    [A] in public use or
    [B] on sale
      [C] in this country.

The following case was the first to clearly distinguish between novelty and statutory bar issues. It also added a critical interpretive gloss on a clause in the 1793 Act regarding pre-application activity.

PENNOCK v. DIALOGUE
27 U.S. 1 (1829)

MR. JUSTICE STORY delivered the opinion of the Court.

This is a writ of error to the circuit court of Pennsylvania. The original action was brought by the plaintiffs in error for an asserted violation of a patent, granted to them on the 6th of July, 1818, for a new and useful improvement in the art of making leather tubes or hose, for conveying air, water, and other fluids. [A] verdict was found for the defendant, upon which judgment passed in his favour; and the correctness of that judgment is now in controversy before this court.

At the trial, a bill of exceptions was taken to an opinion delivered by the court, in the charge to the jury, as follows, viz.

> That the law arising upon the case was, that if an inventor makes his discovery public, looks on and permits others freely to use it, without objection or assertion of claim to the invention, of which the public might take notice; he abandons the inchoate right to the exclusive use of the invention, to which a patent would have entitled him had it been applied for before such use. And, that it makes no difference in the principle, that the article so publicly used, and afterwards patented, was made by a particular individual, who did so by the private permission of the inventor. And thereupon, did charge the jury, *that if the evidence brings the case within the principle which had been stated*, the court were of opinion that the plaintiffs were not entitled to a verdict.

The single question then is, whether the charge of the court was correct in point of law. It has not been, and indeed cannot be denied, that an inventor may abandon his invention, and surrender or dedicate it to the public. This inchoate right, thus once gone, cannot afterwards be resumed at his pleasure; for, where gifts are once made to the public in this way, they become absolute. Thus, if a man dedicates a way, or other easement to the public, it is supposed to carry with it a permanent right of user. The question which generally arises at trials, is a question of fact, rather than of law; whether the acts or acquiescence of the party furnish in the given case, satisfactory proof of an abandonment or dedication of the invention to the public. But when all the facts are given, there does not seem any reason why the court may not state the legal conclusion deducible from them. In this view of the matter, the only question would be, whether, upon general principles, the facts stated by the court would justify the conclusion.

The patent act, of the 21st of February, 1793, ch. 11, prescribes the terms and conditions and manner of obtaining patents for inventions; and proof of a strict compliance with them lies at the foundation of the title acquired by the patentee. The first section provides,

> that when any person or persons, being a citizen or citizens of the United States, shall allege that he or they have invented any new or useful art, machine, manufacture, or composition of matter, or any new or useful improvement on any art, machine, or composition of matter, *not known or used before the application*; and shall present a petition to the secretary of state, signifying a desire of obtaining an exclusive property in the same, and praying that a patent may be granted therefor [a patent shall issue].

The third section provides, "that every inventor, before he can receive a patent, shall swear, or affirm, that he does verily believe that he is the true inventor or discoverer of the art, machine, or improvement for which he solicits a patent." The sixth section provides that the defendant shall be permitted to give in defence, to any action brought against him for an infringement of the patent, among other things, "that the thing thus secured by patent was not originally discovered by the patentee, *but had been in use*, or had been described in some public work, *anterior to the supposed discovery of the patentee.*"

By the very terms of the first section of our statute, the secretary of state is authorised to grant a patent to any citizen applying for the same, who shall allege that he has invented a new and useful art, machine, &c. &c. "*not known or used before the application.*" The authority is a limited one, and the party must bring himself within the terms, before he can derive any title to demand, or to hold a patent. What then is the true meaning of the words "*not known or used before the application*"? They cannot mean that the thing invented was not known or used before the application by the inventor himself, for that would be to prohibit him from the only means of obtaining a patent. The use, as well as the knowledge of his invention, must be indispensable to enable him to ascertain its competency to the end proposed, as well as to perfect its component parts. The words then, to have any rational interpretation, must mean, not known or used by others, before the application. But how known or used? If it were necessary, as it well might be, to employ others to assist in the original structure or use by the inventor himself; or if before his application for a patent his invention should be pirated by another, or used without his consent; it can scarcely be supposed, that the legislature had within its contemplation such knowledge or use.

We think, then, the true meaning must be, not known or used by the public, before the application. And, thus construed, there is much reason for the limitation thus imposed by the act. While one great object was, by holding out a reasonable reward to inventors, and giving them an exclusive right to their inventions for a limited period, to stimulate the efforts of genius; the main object was "to promote the progress of science and useful arts;" and this could be done best, by giving the public at large a right to make, construct, use, and vend the thing invented, at as early a period as possible; having a due regard to the rights of the inventor. If an inventor should be permitted to hold back from the knowledge of the public the secrets of his invention; if he should for a long period of years retain the monopoly, and make, and sell his invention publicly, and thus gather the whole profits of it, relying upon his superior skill and knowledge of the structure; and then, and then only, when the danger of competition should force him to secure the exclusive right, he should be allowed to take out a patent, and thus exclude the public from any farther use than what should be derived under it during his fourteen years; it would materially retard the progress of science and the useful arts, and give a premium to those who should be least prompt to communicate their discoveries.

A provision, therefore, that should withhold from an inventor the privilege of an exclusive right, unless he should, as early as he should allow the public use, put the public in possession of his secret, and commence the running of the period, that should limit that right; would not be deemed unreasonable. It might be expected to find a place in a wise prospective legislation on such a subject. If it was already found in the jurisprudence of the mother country [i.e., Great Britain], and had not been considered inconvenient there; it would not be unnatural that it should find a place in our own.

Now, in point of fact, the statute of 21 Jac. ch. 3, commonly called the statute of monopolies, does contain exactly such a provision. That act, after prohibiting monopolies generally, contains, in the sixth section, an exception in favour of "letters patent and grants of privileges for *fourteen years or under*, of the sole working or making of any manner of new manufactures within this realm, to the true and first inventor and inventors of such manufactures, which *others, at the time of making such letters patent and grants, shall not use.*" Lord Coke, in his commentary upon this clause or proviso, (3 Inst. 184,) says that the letters patent "must be of such manufactures, which *any other at the time of making such letters patent did not use*; for albeit it were newly invented, yet if any other did use it at the making of the letters patent, or grant of the privilege, it is declared and enacted to be void by this act." The use here referred to has always been understood to be a public use, and not a private or surreptitious use in fraud of the inventor.

The words of our statute are not identical with those of the statute of James, but it can scarcely admit of doubt, that they must have been within the contemplation of those by whom it was framed, as well as the construction which had been put upon them by Lord Coke. But if there were no such illustrative comment, it is difficult to conceive how any other interpretation could fairly be put upon these words. We are not at liberty to reject words which are sensible in the place where they occur, merely because they may be thought, in some cases, to import a hardship, or tie up beneficial rights within very close limits. If an invention is used by the public, with the consent of the inventor, at the time of his application for a patent; how can the court say, that his case is, nevertheless, such as the act was intended to protect? If such a public use is not a use within the meaning of the statute, what other use is? If it be a use within the meaning of the statute, how can the court extract the case from its operation, and support a patent, where the suggestions of the patentee are not true, and the conditions on which alone the grant was authorised to be made, do not exist? In such a case, if the court could perceive no reason for the restrictions, the will of the legislature must still be obeyed. It cannot and ought not to be disregarded, where it plainly applies to the case. But if the restriction may be perceived to have a foundation in sound policy, and be an effectual means of accomplishing the legislative objects, by bringing inventions early into public and unrestricted use; and above all, if such policy has been avowed and acted upon in like cases in laws having similar objects; there is very urgent reason to suppose, that the act in those terms embodies the real legislative intent, and ought to receive that construction. It is not wholly insignificant in this point of view, that the first patent act passed by congress on this subject, (act of 1790, ch. 34, [ch. 7.) which the present act repeals, uses the words "*not known or used before,*" without adding the words "*the application;*" and in connection with the structure of the sentence in which they stand, might have been referred either to the time of the invention, or of the application. The addition of the latter words in the patent act of 1793, must, therefore, have been introduced, ex industria, and with the cautious intention to clear away a doubt, and fix the original and deliberate meaning of the legislature. The only real doubt which has arisen upon this exposition of the statute, has been created by the words of the sixth section already quoted. That section admits the party sued to give in his defence as a bar, that "the thing thus secured by patent was not originally discovered by the patentee, but had been in use *anterior to the supposed discovery* of the patentee.*" It has been asked, if the legislature intended to bar the party from a patent in consequence of a mere prior use, although he was the inventor; why were not the words "anterior *to the application*" substituted, instead of "anterior to the *supposed discovery*"? If a mere use of the thing invented before the application were sufficient to bar the right, then, although the party may have been the first and true inventor, if another person, either innocently as a second inventor, or piratically, were to use it without the knowledge of the first inventor; his right would be gone. In respect to a use by piracy, it is not clear that any such fraudulent use is within the intent of the statute; and upon general principles it might well be held excluded. In respect to the case of a second invention, it is questionable at least, whether, if by such second invention a public use was already acquired, it could be deemed a case within the protection of the act. If the public were already in possession and common use of an invention fairly and without fraud, there might be sound reason for presuming, that the legislature did not intend to grant an exclusive right to any one to monopolize that which was already common. There would be no quid pro quo — no price for the exclusive right or monopoly conferred upon the inventor for fourteen years.

Be this as it may, it is certain that the sixth section is not necessarily repugnant to the construction which the words of the first section require and justify. The sixth section certainly does not enumerate all the defences which a party may make in a suit brought against him for violating a patent. One obvious omission is, where he uses it under a license or grant from the inventor. The sixth section in the clause under consideration, may well be deemed merely affirmative of what would be the result from the general principles of law applicable to other parts of the statute. It gives the right to the *first* and true inventor and to him only; if known or used before his supposed discovery he is not the *first*, although he may be a *true* inventor; and that is the case to which the clause looks. But it is not inconsistent with this doctrine, that although he is the *first*, as well as the *true* inventor, yet if he shall put it into public use, or sell it for public use before he applies for a patent, that this should furnish another bar to his claim. In this view an interpretation is given to every clause of the statute without introducing any inconsistency, or interfering with the ordinary meaning of its language. No public policy is overlooked; and no injury can ordinarily occur to the first inventor, which is not in some sort the result of his own laches or voluntary inaction.

It is admitted that the subject is not wholly free from difficulties; but upon most deliberate consideration we are all of opinion, that the true construction of the act is, that the first inventor cannot acquire a good title to a patent; if he suffers the thing invented to go into public use, or to be publicly sold for use, before he makes application for a patent. His voluntary act or acquiescence in the public sale and use is an abandonment of his right; or rather creates a disability to comply with the terms and conditions on which alone the secretary of state is authorized to grant him a patent.

The opinion of the circuit court was therefore perfectly correct; and the judgment is affirmed with costs.

NOTES

1. The Court states, speaking of section one of the 1793 Act:

They cannot mean that the thing invented was not known or used before the application by the inventor himself, for that would be to prohibit him from the only means of obtaining a patent.... The words then, to have any rational interpretation, must mean, not known or used *by others*, before the application.

Story adds another major interpretive gloss to the patent act by holding that section one applied only to a *public* use.

To understand Story's interpretation, you must do two things: keep in mind his goal in the case and forget about the Patent Act we have today.

Story's goal is to find a statutory basis for what we would today call a statutory bar. He clearly does not want inventors, such as the one in the case, to exploit their inventions for long periods of time and only later apply for a patent. Encouraging early filing is the mainspring of the case.

The reason you must forget about today's Patent Act to understand the case is that many of the concepts Story introduced in his opinion have since been applied to *both* § 102(a) (novelty) and § 102(b) (statutory bars).

The difficulty in Story's approach to the statute, as he concedes, stems from section six, which sets forth defenses under the Act. This sounds like a fine source for a statutory bar — which is what Story is searching for. Unfortunately, the critical date under this provision was the date of "discovery," i.e., invention: "that the thing thus secured by patent ... had been in use, or had been described in some public work, anterior to the supposed discovery of the patentee." This eliminates the clause as the source of a possible statutory bar. (Do you see why?) Thus he must struggle to avoid the possible interpretation that section six *negates* any statutory bar, by being the exclusive source of any defenses under the Act, while basing his holding on the existence of a statutory bar in *section one*. He does this by construing section *one* as the statutory bar provision, and essentially saying that section six restates the principle of novelty stated in sections one and three (via the oath). Does he simply "fudge" this issue or are you convinced?

The anomaly of an inventor defeating her own novelty necessitates that the phrase "by others" be read into section one. Although this is the origin of the "by others" terminology in the current § 102(a) (element 102(a)[1][C] in the Schematic), keep in mind that the critical date under section one of the 1793 Act is the date of *application*; today § 102(a)'s critical date is the date of *invention*. So what is "by others" doing in a provision that must, if Story is to achieve his goal, amount to a statutory bar? (Remember, if the policy of early disclosure informs the statutory bars, it must be possible for the inventor's own acts of publication or public use to bar a patent — hence the anomaly of reading "by others" into the statutory bar provisions.) The answer is that this terminology must mean something different to Story than it does in today's § 102(a). It may, for instance, simply reiterate the *publicness* requirement Story finds in section one; to be "known or used by others" excludes the inventor's private use. Note that this interpretation, if true, differs from today's use of "by others" in § 102(a). Today, "known or used by others" means some *other* person must *independently* invent (and publicly know, use, publish, or patent) the same invention before the person who seeks a patent. Perhaps to Story, "known or used [by others]" in the 1793 Act meant that the inventor who seeks a patent somehow publicly used his or her invention so that it became known to others. On this view, the "known or used [by others]" interpretation reiterates the "public [due to the inventor's own activities]" interpretation of section one. This is supported by some language in the case.

Note in any event that the "public" requirement Story found in section one (essentially a statutory bar section) is now applied to both §§ 102(a) (novelty) and (b). Other concepts introduced in this opinion have been similarly adapted and transferred.

2. Story emphasizes throughout the opinion the policy underlying his interpretation of section one: to promote early disclosure. According to Story, how is this different from the policy underlying section six? Why are these policies furthered by emphasizing, respectively, the date of *application* (section one, 1793 Act) and the date of "*discovery*" (section six, 1793 Act)?

a. Public Use

EGBERT v. LIPPMANN

104 U.S. 333 (1881)

This suit was brought for an alleged infringement of the complainant's reissued letters-patent, No. 5216, dated Jan. 7, 1873, for an improvement in corset-springs. [A corset is shown in Figure 4-9 next page.]

The original letters were issued to Samuel H. Barnes. The reissue was made to the complainant, under her then name, Frances Lee Barnes, executrix of the original patentee.

> The specification for the reissue declares: —
>
> This invention consists in forming the springs of corsets of two or more metallic plates, placed one upon another, and so connected as to prevent them from sliding off each other laterally or edgewise, and at the same time admit of their playing or sliding upon each other, in the direction of their length or longitudinally, whereby their flexibility and elasticity are greatly increased, while at the same time much strength is obtained. [See Figure 4-10.]

The bill alleges that Barnes was the original and first inventor of the improvement covered by the reissued letters-patent, and that it had not, at the time of his application for the original letters, been for more than two years in public use or on sale, with his consent or allowance.

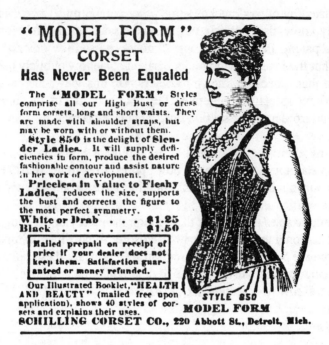

Figure 4-9

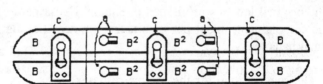

One set of corset springs, composed of two metallic plates, BB², and held together with rivets. The rivets, a, allow the metals to play against one another while the rivets, c, keep the corset springs from becoming detached.

Figure 4-10

The answer takes issue on this averment and also denies infringement. On a final hearing the court dismissed the bill, and the complainant appealed.

We have to consider whether the defence that the patented invention had, with the consent of the inventor, been publicly used for more than two years prior to his application for the original letters, is sustained by the testimony in the record.

[The patent statute] render[s] letters-patent invalid if the invention which they cover was in public use, with the consent and allowance of the inventor, for more than two years prior to his application. Since the passage of the act of 1839 it has been strenuously contended that the public use of an invention for more than two years before such application, even without his consent and allowance, renders the letters-patent therefor void.

It is unnecessary in this case to decide this question, for the alleged use of the invention covered by the letters-patent to Barnes is conceded to have been with his express consent.

The evidence on which the defendants rely to establish a prior public use of the invention consists mainly of the testimony of the complainant.

She testifies that Barnes invented the improvement covered by his patent between January and May, 1855; that between the dates named the witness and her friend Miss Cugier were complaining of the breaking of their corset-steels. Barnes, who was present, and was an intimate friend of the witness, said he thought he could make her a pair that would not break. At their next interview he presented her with a pair of corset-steels which he himself had made. The witness wore these steels a long time. In 1858 Barnes made and presented to her another pair, which she also wore a long time. When the corsets in which these steels were used wore out, the witness ripped them open and took out the steels and put them in new corsets. This was done several times.

It is admitted, and, in fact, is asserted, by complainant, that these steels embodied the invention afterwards patented by Barnes and covered by the reissued letters-patent on which this suit is brought.

Joseph H. Sturgis, another witness for complainant, testifies that in 1863 Barnes spoke to him about two inventions made by himself, one of which was a corset-steel, and that he went to the house of Barnes to see them. Before this time, and after the transactions testified to by the complainant, Barnes and [the complainant] had intermarried. Barnes said his wife had a pair of steels made according to his invention in the corsets which she was then wearing, and if she would take them off he would show them to [Sturgis]. Mrs. Barnes went out, and returned with a pair of corsets and a pair of scissors, and ripped the corsets open and took out the steels. Barnes then explained to witness how they were made and used.

The question for our decision is, whether this testimony shows a public use within the meaning of the statute.

We observe, in the first place, that to constitute the public use of an invention it is not necessary that more than one of the patented articles should be publicly used. The use of a great number may tend to strengthen the proof, but one well-defined case of such use is just as effectual to annul the patent as many. For instance, if the inventor of a mower, a printing press, or a railway-car makes and sells only one of the articles invented by him, and allows the vendee to use it for two years, without restriction or limitation, the use is just as public as if he had sold and allowed the use of a great number.

We remark, secondly, that, whether the use of an invention is public or private does not necessarily depend upon the number of persons to whom its use is known. If an inventor, having made his device, gives or sells it to another, to be used by the donee or vendee, without limitation or restriction, or injunction of secrecy, and it is so used, such use is public, even though the use and knowledge of the use may be confined to one person.

We say, thirdly, that some inventions are by their very character only capable of being used where they cannot be seen or observed by the public eye. An invention may consist of a lever or spring, hidden in the running gear of a watch, or of a rachet, shaft, or cog-wheel covered from view in the recesses of a machine for spinning or weaving. Nevertheless, if its inventor sells a machine of which his invention forms a part, and allows it to be used without restriction of any kind, the use is a public one. So, on the other hand, a use necessarily open to public view, if made in good faith solely to test the qualities of the invention, and for the purpose of experiment, is not a public use within the meaning of the statute.

Tested by these principles, we think the evidence of the complainant herself shows that for more than two years before the application for the original letters there was, by the consent and allowance of Barnes, a public use of the invention, covered by them. He made and gave to her two pairs of corset-steels, constructed according to his device, one in 1855 and one in 1858. They were presented to her for use. He imposed no obligation of secrecy, nor any condition or restriction whatever. They were not presented for the purpose of experiment, nor to test their qualities. No such claim is set up in her testimony. The invention was at the time complete, and there is no evidence that it was afterwards changed or improved. The donee of the steels used them for years for the purpose and in the manner designed by the inventor. They were not capable of any other use. She might have exhibited them to any person, or made other steels of the same kind, and used or sold them without violating any condition or restriction imposed on her by the inventor.

According to the testimony of the complainant, the invention was completed and put to use in 1855. The inventor slept on his rights for eleven years. Letters-patent were not applied for till March, 1866. In the mean time, the invention had found its way into general, and almost universal, use. A great part of the record is taken up with the testimony of the manufacturers and venders of corset-steels, showing that before he applied for letters the principle of his device was almost universally used in the manufacture of corset-steels. It is fair to presume that having learned from this general use that there was some value in his invention, he attempted to resume, by his application, what by his acts he had clearly dedicated to the public.

We are of opinion that the defence of two years' public use, by the consent and allowance of the inventor, before he made application for letters-patent, is satisfactorily established by the evidence.

Decree affirmed.

MR. JUSTICE MILLER dissenting.

A private use with consent, which could lead to no copy or reproduction of the machine, which taught the nature of the invention to no one but the party to whom such consent was given, which left the public at large as ignorant of this as it was before the author's discovery, was no abandonment to the public, and did not defeat his claim for a patent. If the little steel spring inserted in a single pair of corsets, and used by only one woman, covered by her outer-clothing, and in a position always withheld from public observation, is a *public* use of that piece of steel, I am at a loss to know the line between a private and a public use.

NOTES

1. In what sense was Frances Lee (later Barnes) using the corset steels (i.e., springs) "publicly"? Why does it not matter how many people use the invention for purposes of deciding if the use was public? Compare this holding to that of the court in *Rosaire* in Section D above.

2. The Court emphasizes that Ms. Barnes never entered into a confidentiality agreement with the inventor. But the Court also relates that the two later married. Does Barnes have a reasonable argument that although no *express* "injunction of secrecy" was made, nonetheless an *implied* requirement of secrecy, or at least an implied agreement that Mr. Barnes' permission was needed before she disclosed the invention, could be inferred from the surrounding circumstances: i.e., an invention, of an intimate nature, by a boyfriend (later husband), disclosed to few people, etc.? Justice Miller, in dissent, added: "It may well be imagined that a prohibition to the party so permitted [to use the springs] against her use of the steel spring to public observation, would have been supposed to be a piece of irony." 104 U.S. (14 Otto), at 339. Perhaps the embarrassment of asking was enough to keep Mr. Barnes from requesting that Frances Lee not show the invention to anyone. Of course, if given the choice between a statutory bar to his invention and a permanent bar to his marriage, Barnes no doubt made the right choice.

3. In *Hall v. MacNeale*, 107 U.S. (17 Otto) 90 (1883), Hall had in 1866 received a patent on improvements in the door and walls of burglar-proof safes. The question before the Court was whether the use of certain earlier-model safes before the critical date was *public* enough to create a statutory bar. The Court held:

> The construction and arrangement and purpose and mode of operation and use of the [hidden feature] in the safes were necessarily known to the workmen who put them in. They were, it is true, hidden from view, after the safes were completed, and it required a destruction of the safe to bring them into view. But this was no concealment of them or use of them in secret. They had no more concealment than was inseparable form any legitimate use of them.

For several Learned Hand opinions on public use, see *A. Schraeder Sons v. Wein Sales Corp.*, 9 F.2d 306, 308 (2d Cir. 1925) ("Considering that the whole work was experimental, and that only ... two [employees] had access to it, we think that it was unnecessary to exact from [one] a formal pledge of secrecy. It was implicit in the situation."); *Peerless Roll Leaf Co. v. H. Griffin & Sons*, 29 F.2d 646, 649 (2d Cir. 1928) ("When the number of [employees] is limited to as few as are necessary to practice [the invention] at all, when customers and the public generally are excluded, and adequate precautions are taken to prevent dispersion of the knowledge until at least two years before application is made [i.e., the statutory bar under the then-applicable statute], it seems to us enough, whether a formal pledge of secrecy be exacted or not.... [T]he knowledge of the necessary workmen not explicitly pledged to secrecy does not make the use public.").

W.L. Gore & Associates v. Garlock, Inc., 721 F.2d 1540, 220 U.S.P.Q. (BNA) 303 (Fed. Cir. 1983). [Plaintiff's patents, including U.S. Patent 3,953,566 ('566) to a process for stretching Teflon — polytetrafluoroethylene, or PTFE — to produce an industrial tape, were asserted against defendant, who argued that a third party from New Zealand, John Cropper, had licensed a similar process to another company, and that the Cropper process was used to make tape prior to the critical date of May 21, 1969, one year before plaintiff Gore's filing date of May 21, 1970.]

In 1966, Cropper developed and constructed a machine for producing stretched and unstretched PTFE thread seal tape. In 1967, Cropper sent a letter to a company in Massachusetts, offering to sell his machine, describing its operation, and enclosing a photo. Nothing came of that letter. There is no evidence and no finding that the present inventions thereby became known or used in this country.

In 1968, Cropper sold his machine to Budd, which at some point thereafter used it to produce and sell PTFE thread seal tape. The sales agreement between Cropper and Budd provided that Budd would not "divulge to any person or persons other than its own employees or employees of its affiliated corporations any of the said know-how or any details whatsoever relating to the apparatus." Budd told its employees the Cropper machine was confidential and required them to sign confidentiality agreements. Budd otherwise treated the Cropper machine like its other manufacturing equipment.

A former Budd employee said Budd made no effort to keep the secret. That Budd did not keep the machine hidden from employees legally bound to keep their knowledge confidential does not evidence a failure to maintain the secret. Similarly, that DuPont employees were shown the machine to see if they could help increase its speed does not itself establish a breach of the secrecy agreement. There is no evidence of when that viewing occurred. There is no evidence that a viewer of the machine could thereby learn anything of which process, among all possible processes, the machine is being used to practice. As Cropper testified, looking at the machine in operation does not reveal whether it is stretching, and if so, at what speed. Nor does looking disclose whether the crystallinity and temperature elements of the invention set forth in the claims are involved. There is no evidence that Budd's secret use of the Cropper machine made knowledge of the claimed process accessible to the public.

The district court held all claims of the '566 patent invalid under 102(b), because "the invention" was "in public use [and] on sale" by Budd more than one year before Gore's application for patent. [I]t was error to hold that Budd's activity with the Cropper machine, as above indicated, was a "public" use of the processes claimed in the '566 patent, that activity having been secret, not public.

Assuming, arguendo, that Budd sold tape produced on the Cropper machine before October 1969, and that that tape was made by a process set forth in a claim of the '566 patent, the issue under § 102(b) is whether that sale would defeat Dr. Gore's right to a patent on the process inventions set forth in the claims.

If Budd offered and sold anything, it was only tape, not whatever process was used in producing it. Neither party contends, and there was no evidence, that the public could learn the claimed process by examining the tape. If Budd and Cropper commercialized the tape, that could result in a forfeiture of a patent granted them for their process on an application filed by them more than a year later. There is no reason or statutory basis, however, on which Budd's and Cropper's secret commercialization of a process, if established, could be held a bar to the grant of a patent to Gore on that process.

Early public disclosure is a linchpin of the patent system. As between a prior inventor who benefits from a process by selling its product but suppresses, conceals, or otherwise keeps the process from the public, and a later inventor who promptly files a patent application from which the public will gain a disclosure of the process, the law favors the latter. The district court therefore erred as a matter of law in applying the statute and in its determination that Budd's secret use of the Cropper machine and sale of tape rendered all process claims of the '566 patent invalid under § 102(b).

NOTES

1. In the final paragraph of the preceding excerpt, the court states that as between a prior inventor who commercializes a process yet keeps it secret, and a later inventor who promptly files a patent application on the same invention, the law favors the latter. This policy is expressed in § 102(g), considered in this chapter, below. Is it clear that this policy — which is used to settle *priority* disputes between two inventors — is the right one to apply when trying to determine whether a single inventor ought to get a patent in light of the prior art? If the point is that the public could not gain access to the process invention simply by

using the product it produced, why is secrecy a necessary element at all; isn't inaccessibility of the process inherent in the fact that only the product is sold? *Compare Gillman v. Stern*, 114 F.2d 28 (2d Cir. 1940) (sale of products made with a secret machine renders the machine abandoned under § 102(g); see Section J below). *See generally* Robbins, *The Rights of a First Inventor-Trade Secret User As Against Those of the Second Inventor-Patentee (Part I)*, 61 J. PAT. OFF. SOC'Y 574, 591 (1979); De Jonghe, *When Is Commercial Use a 102(b) Bar?*, 51 J. PAT. OFF. SOC'Y 706 (1969) (arguing that public use should mean that public has enough access to an invention to practice it; short of this, any use should not be considered public). Note that, in the main case, Cropper and Budd's activities implicate the on-sale bar as well as the public use bar.

2. The reason that secret yet commercial third-party use presents a problematical statutory bar under § 102(b) is that such use does not implicate the monopoly-extension policy at issue when the applicant herself conducts the secret commercial use. In other words, pre-critical date secret use by a third party in no way extends the applicant's monopoly period. Since the applicant by definition cannot know of a secret third-party use (if she did it would not be secret), she cannot be spurred by that use into filing earlier than she would otherwise. Assume for example that inventor *A* has no knowledge of *B*'s secret employment, beginning January 1, 1990, of a process similar to one *A* has invented. There is no way for *A* to know that her critical date has in effect been *moved up* by *B*'s secret but commercial use of the process. Thus if *A*'s first public use or sale of the process she invented occurs on March 1, 1990, she would be expected to use this as her critical date. That is, she would be expected to measure her "grace period" from this date. She knows that if she files any later than March 1, 1991, she runs the risk of a statutory bar in the form of her March 1, 1990 public use.

But *B*'s public use of the process — i.e., her secret but commercial employment of it — will destroy *A*'s expectations. Assume, for example, that *A* finally filed for a patent on her process on February 1, 1991. Although her own use on March 1, 1990 is before the critical date, a use she did not know about — *B*'s — may come to haunt her. Should it? See below, Section E.3.d.

3. In one case a third party had in effect stolen the invention from the inventor whose later patent application was allegedly barred by the thief's prior use; the court held that the prior use nonetheless constituted a statutory bar to the true inventor's later application. *Lorenz v. Colgate-Palmolive-Peet Co.*, 167 F.2d 423, 77 U.S.P.Q. (BNA) 138 (3d Cir. 1948): "There is not a single word in the statute which would tend to put an inventor, whose disclosures have been pirated, in any different position from one who has permitted the use of his process."

MOLECULON RESEARCH CORP. v. CBS, INC.

793 F.2d 1261, 229 U.S.P.Q. (BNA) 805 (Fed. Cir. 1986)

This is an appeal from the judgment of the District Court holding claims 3-5 and 9 of Moleculon Research Corporation's U.S. Patent No. 3,655,201 ('201 patent) valid and infringed by certain of the well-known Rubik's Cube puzzles. We affirm in part, vacate in part, and remand.

Moleculon, as assignee of the '201 patent which issued to Larry D. Nichols, sued CBS Inc., as successor to the Ideal Toy Corporation, alleging infringement of claims 3, 4, 5, 6, and 9 of the '201 patent.

A puzzle enthusiast since childhood, Nichols, in the summer of 1957, conceived of a three-dimensional puzzle capable of rotational movement. He envisioned an assembly of eight cubes attached in a 2 x 2 x 2 arrangement, with each of the six faces of the composite cube distinguished by a different color and the individual cubes being capable of rotation in sets of four around one of three mutually perpendicular axes.

During the period 1957-1962, while doing graduate work in organic chemistry, Nichols constructed several paper models of his puzzle, making cubes of heavy file-card type paper and affixing small magnets to the inside of the cubes. Although these models confirmed the feasibility of Nichols' conception, they lacked durability. A few close friends, including two roommates and a colleague in the chemistry department, had occasion to see one of these paper models in Nichols' room and Nichols explained its operation to at least one of them.

In 1962, Nichols accepted employment as a research scientist at Moleculon. In 1968, Nichols constructed a working wood block prototype of his puzzle which he usually kept at home but on occasion brought into his office. In January 1969, Dr. Obermayer, the president of Moleculon, entered Nichols' office and happened to see the model sitting on his desk. Obermayer expressed immediate interest in the puzzle and Nichols explained its workings. Obermayer asked whether Nichols intended to commercialize the puzzle. When Nichols said no, Obermayer suggested that Moleculon try to do so. In March 1969, Nichols assigned all his rights in the puzzle invention to Moleculon in return for a share of any proceeds of commercialization. On March 7, 1969, Moleculon sent Parker Brothers an actual model and a description of the cube puzzle. In the next three years, Moleculon contacted between fifty and sixty toy and game manufacturers, including Ideal. Ideal responded to the effect that it did not currently have an interest in marketing the puzzle. Moleculon itself did not succeed in marketing the Nichols cube.

On March 3, 1970, Nichols filed on behalf of Moleculon a patent application covering his invention. The '201 patent issued on April 11, 1972.

The subject matter of the '201 patent, in its preferred embodiment, is a cube puzzle composed of eight smaller cubelets that may be rotated in groups of four adjacent cubes, and a method by which the sets of cubes may be rotated, first to randomize, and then to restore a predetermined pattern on the six faces of the composite cube.

The accused products are the well-known 3 x 3 x 3 Rubik's Cube puzzle, two 2 x 2 x 2 variations and a 4 x 4 x 4 Rubik's Revenge. These puzzles externally appear as composite cubes composed of smaller cubes or cubelets.

Internal inspection reveals that the composite cube is not composed of true six-sided cubelets but rather is composed of an internal mechanism holding together cubelet shells which have one or more external faces and permitting sets of cubelets to be rotated about an axis.

[At issue is whether] the district court erred in holding that the claimed invention was not in public use nor on sale within the meaning of 35 U.S.C. § 102(b).

CBS argues that the subject matter of the '201 patent was in "public use" and "on sale" by Nichols, prior to the March 3, 1969 critical date (i.e., one year prior to filing of the patent application), thus rendering the patent invalid under section 102(b).

CBS labels as public use Nichols' displaying of the models to other persons (such as his colleagues at school) without any mention of secrecy. CBS ascribes only commercial purpose and intent to Obermayer's use of the wood model and argues that a conclusion of barring public use under § 102(b) is compelled. We disagree.

CBS urges that the decision in *Egbert v. Lippmann*, 104 U.S. 333 (1881), compels a conclusion of public use in the present case.

The district court distinguished *Egbert* because here Nichols had not given over the invention for free and unrestricted use by another person. Based on the personal relationships and surrounding circumstances, the court found that Nichols at all times retained control over the puzzle's use and the distribution of information concerning it. The court characterized Nichols' use as private and for his own enjoyment. We see neither legal error in the analysis nor clear error in the findings.

As for Obermayer's brief use of the puzzle, the court found that Nichols retained control even though he and Obermayer had not entered into any express confidentiality agreement. The court held, and we agree, that the presence or absence of such an agreement is not determinative of the public use issue. *See TP Laboratories, Inc. v. Professional Positioners, Inc.*, 724 F.2d 965, 972, 220 U.S.P.Q. 577, 583 (Fed. Cir.), *cert. denied*, 105 S. Ct. 108 (1984). It is one factor to be considered in assessing all the evidence. There can be no question that the court looked at the totality of evidence, and evaluated that evidence in view of time, place, and circumstances.

With regard to the question of control, CBS complains that "[t]he record is devoid of any testimony from the friends, associates and fellow workers who saw Nichols' cube and to whom its operation was explained." The simple answer is that CBS had the burden at trial to prove public use with facts supported by clear and convincing evidence.

Accordingly, we sustain the district court's determination that the claims are not invalid under section 102(b). [Remanded on infringement issue.]

NOTES

1. *Scrambling Egbert?* The district court distinguished *Egbert* on the ground that there the invention had been given over for "free and unrestricted use by another person." It then cited the "personal relationship" between Obermayer (the user) and the inventor. Would the *Egbert* court accept that the open availability of the model on the inventor's desk, and the employer-employee relationship in this case compare favorably with the concealed use and admittedly close relationship in *Egbert*?

2. *How Many in Your Party?* The Federal Circuit recently distinguished *Moleculon* in a case where the invention was demonstrated not at work but at a party attended by twenty or thirty friends. In *Beachcombers, Int'l, Inc. v. WildeWood Creative Prods., Inc.*, 31 F.3d 1154, 31 U.S.P.Q.2d 1653 (Fed. Cir. 1994), the court upheld a jury verdict that the invention had been in public use, emphasizing some subtle differences in the facts of the two cases:

> [I]n *Moleculon* the court found that the inventor at all times retained control over the use of the device as well as over the distribution of information concerning it.... Here, there was evidence upon which the jury could have reasonably concluded that [the inventor, Carolyn] Bennett did not retain control over the use of the device and the future dissemination of information about it — Bennet's testimony that her purpose in demonstrating the device at her party was to ... garner feedback, that she never imposed any secrecy or confidentiality obligations, and [one of her guest's] testimony to the effect that she [the guest] did not believe she was subject to any secrecy or confidentiality restrictions — notwithstanding the closeness and ongoing nature of Bennett's relationship with her guests.

31 F.3d at 1160, 31 U.S.P.Q.2d at 1657-58. Would you assume that friends would keep a secret more readily than co-workers? Would it matter whether the secret involved matters related to work or a personal invention project? *See AMP, Inc. v. Fujitsu Microelectronics, Inc.*, 853 F. Supp. 808, 817, 31 U.S.P.Q.2d 1705 (M.D. Pa. 1994) (presentations to potential customers before critical date held not a public use; although plaintiff did not introduce evidence of written confidentiality agreements, court stated that plaintiff's testimony was sufficient proof of a "confidentiality requirement," and that in addition "the AMP presenters gave those in attendance no samples or written material detailing the concept"; "Here, [the court concluded,] the restrictions were clear and the attempt to disseminate information was considerably limited," and therefore there was no public use as a matter of law).

3. *Administrative Proceedings.* The Patent Office will consider evidence submitted by those who believe an application has been filed covering subject matter that was used publicly prior to the critical date. Under the procedure set forth in 37 C.F.R. § 1.292 (1996), an examiner who receives a petition for a "Public Use

Proceeding" must first determine whether the information submitted makes out a prima facie case that the invention is barred under § 102(b). If so, a hearing may be held. Notice must be given to the applicant.

4. Foreign Use as a Bar? A recent Note argues that the "in this country" limitation of § 102(b) is "outmoded" in light of contemporary international trade. *See* Note, *Bridge Over Troubled Water: Extending the Public Use Bar to Foreign Countries*, 1987 DET. C.L. REV. 65 (1987).

The Problem of Widely Known But Contractually Confidential Information

With growing sophistication about the legal status of prior art has come an increase in the use of confidentiality agreements. In addition to preserving trade secret status (on which, see ROBERT MERGES, PETER MENELL, MARK LEMLEY & THOMAS JORDE, INTELLECTUAL PROPERTY IN THE NEW TECHNOLOGICAL AGE ch. 2 (forthcoming 1997), confidentiality agreements insure that inventions demonstrated or information disclosed does not rise to the level of a "public use" under 35 U.S.C. § 102(b). For the most part, for the reasons articulated in the cases in this section, this makes sense.

At some point, however, the very widespread use of contractual confidentiality agreements could undermine the effectiveness of § 102(b). Imagine for example a scientific journal, in form and appearance interchangeable with others of its ilk, but which differs in one key respect: it is (purportedly, at least) licensed, and not sold. Furthermore, one of the restrictions laid out in the license is that the subscriber/licensee agrees to keep the information in the journal private and confidential. Putting aside the objections of scientists and others who undoubtedly believe in the efficacy of a wide-open "public domain" of information, there is no reason why such a scheme might not be attempted.

Indeed, in the brave new world of electronic networks, and especially the Internet and World Wide Web, such a distribution strategy is becoming easier. This is because, unlike with traditional "over the counter" sales of magazines and other vehicles embodying intellectual content, it is a trivial task for distributors of electronic material to create at least the semblance of a bargain or contract with each individual consumer of the material. Indeed, access to many internet addresses and "Web sites" is already conditioned on agreement to certain terms: that a viewer supply his or her e-mail address, for example, or fill out a brief form describing his or her demographic characteristics. It is no large leap to imagine confidentiality provisions in such cyber-agreements. In light of recent cases finding such agreements fully enforceable, the future of contracting in the interactive media seems bright indeed. *See ProCD, Inc. v. Zeidenberg*, 86 F.3d 1447, 39 U.S.P.Q.2d 1161 (7th Cir. 1996).

The consequences of such agreements for patent policy may not be so bright. If one can simultaneously disclose information and yet keep it out of the public domain/prior art, the "public use" category of § 102(b) prior art may shrink dramatically. If one views this provision as a way of limiting the amount of detrimental reliance third parties may place on disclosed information, the brave new world of electronic confidentiality may not pose a problem. This is because no one could reasonably rely on the public availability of information disclosed explicitly with notice of its confidential nature.

But of course another policy behind § 102(b) — one that extends to the on-sale bar as well as the public use bar — is to encourage early filing of patent applications. An intended corollary of this policy is to prevent a patentee from profiting from an invention for a period much longer than the statutory patent term, now twenty years from the filing date. Widespread but confidential disclosure threatens to undermine this policy foundation of § 102(b). An inventor can disclose information and yet keep it secret in the technical legal sense of the statute and caselaw. This may disseminate information about the concept, build early demand for it, and possibly even lead to feedback that will improve it. And this will all come about free of any statutory bar consequences.

Doctrine may catch up with these developments, however. It is conceivable that a court would negate the patent law effect of a purported confidential disclosure agreement if it were contained in a ubiquitous source relied on by an industry. It is also possible that a court would take into account the very difficult enforcement problems that accompany electronic confidentiality agreements, and thereby conclude that the disclosure was not, effectively speaking, confidential at all. *Cf.* Robert P. Merges, *Intellectual Property and Digital Content: Notes on a Scorecard*, 2 CYBERSPACE LAW. 18 (1996) (arguing that state-granted property rights can never be fully duplicated or supplanted by contract, at least without stretching the concept of contract so fully as to re-invent property rights).

In the meantime, we await the arrival of the first case touching on these issues. It will usher in a new era of interesting issues and practical strategies.

b. On Sale

FMC CORP. v. HENNESSY INDUSTRIES

650 F. Supp. 688, 2 U.S.P.Q.2d (BNA) 1479 (N.D. Ill. 1986)

Hennessy Industries, Inc. ("Hennessy/Coats") is the assignee of three patents on power tire changers which it claims are infringed by tire changers sold by FMC Corporation ("FMC/Vulcan"). FMC/Vulcan denies infringement. It further contends that each of the patents is invalid.

Predecessors of the present Hennessy Industries, Inc. were distributors for an Iowa company, Coats Company, which manufactured manual and semi-power tire changers. In January 1962 Hennessy Industries, Inc. acquired the assets of Coats Company and thereafter continued to manufacture and distribute tire changers under the Coats trade name. Manual and semi-power tire changers had become increasingly popular after the Second World War, after the introduction of safety rims increased the physical effort necessary to remove a tire from a wheel.

Tubeless tires were introduced in 1954 and their removal was even more difficult. Their increasing use created a potential and growing market for full-power tire changers.

The first, and by far most important, of [Coats' patents] was the Tabordon patent 3,255,801, filed March 14, 1962, issued June 14, 1966, and now expired ('801 patent). Hennessy/Coats claims that it first learned only after this litigation was filed of a semi-power version sold prior to March 14, 1961 (the critical date for purposes of 35 U.S.C. § 102), and that it then promptly disclaimed claim 1, the only claim which arguably but by no means certainly was anticipated by the earlier device. FMC/Vulcan does not argue, at least not seriously, that the Tabordon full-power tire changer was anticipated by prior art other than by the semi-power device. It contends, however, that the full-power tire changer was in public use or on sale in this country more than one year prior to the date of application, in contravention of 35 U.S.C. § 102(b). [Two later full power models are shown in Figure 4-11, next page; one sold by Hennessy/Coats is on the left, and FMC's is on the right.]

That takes us, then, both to a determination of what happened in northern Wisconsin during the late winter of 1961, as reconstructed a score or more years later, and what people knew or should have known about those happenings. A determination of the primary facts leads to the application of a legal standard about which there can be relatively little room for argument: whether the evidence supporting facts establishing a statutory bar is so clear and convincing that it overcomes the presumption of [patent] validity.

[The inventor] Tabordon lived in Casco, Wisconsin, where for a number of years he bought and sold cattle and, thereafter, in the '50s or earlier, made tire changing tools of his own devising in his barn. The devising was solo; he sometimes had a helper to construct the equipment he sold. Tabordon had some knowledge of patents, including the concept of a statutory bar and the desirability of establishing a record of when he conceived of an idea, and, through a Green Bay, Wisconsin, patent attorney, Stanley Binish, he had filed and prosecuted prior patent applications. The record does not establish, however, that he had any real understanding of what was patentable, as opposed to what he considered a good idea, or that he understood the legal meaning or implications of claims language, reduction to practice, and the like.

Well prior to the critical date, Tabordon developed and sold the "EZ tire changer:" a semi-power tire changer with diametrically opposed upper and lower bead breakers (shoes to break the tire bead from the rim) powered by a single power source to break the beads loose in a single-powered operation through the use of a pneumatic piston. That semi-power device anticipated (and not just arguably) claim 1, which Hennessy now disclaims. FMC contends that [a] full-power tire changer was also in public use or on sale before the critical date.

We turn, then, to the evidence concerning the first contention relating to public use or sale. Here the court relies more on documentary evidence than testimony, or at least testimony which is not otherwise corroborated by the paper record. We

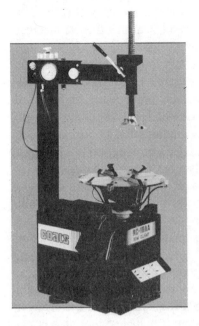

Figure 4-11

do know that Tabordon was producing the semi-power unit, the EZ tire changer, by at least late 1960. An August, 1960 photograph depicts the machine. Further, Tabordon entered into a distribution agreement for that unit and any improvements on October 31, 1960. An advertisement for that unit appeared as early as January, 1961. Tabordon tire changers were on display at a Milwaukee trade show at the beginning of March, 1961, and also by that time a promotional piece had been prepared.

The chronology of the full power machine is less certain. Some things are certain. An affidavit filed in [a] 1965 interference proceeding pushes possible reduction to practice back to December, 1960. Tabordon sent himself a January 28, 1961 sketch of the full-power by registered mail on January 31, 1961. Sometime in February, 1961 Gerald Simonar had such a unit for use at his service station in Luxemburg, Wisconsin. Tabordon himself, back at the time of the application, represented that the first sale was March 15, 1961, although he asked that the application be completed by March 1, 1962, for "business reasons." James Hennessy, prior to the application, represented to Hennessy/Coats patent counsel that the sale was on March 24, 1961. William Ballo obtained by purchase a full-power tire changer, probably on March 27, 1961.

Hennessy/Coats argues that the machine was not reduced to practice until some indefinite time because of design problems with the cable mechanism which rotated the spindle, as well as other problems which persisted into the first commercial Coats model. FMC/Vulcan contends that the use of the tire changer at the Simonar service station was a public use prior to the critical date. The court disagrees with both contentions. The evidence is clear that the tire changer at the service station did change tires as it was designed to do. It was not, however, very dependable, Simonar did not use it very long, and Tabordon came in to tinker with it. Tabordon left the machine at the service station to see how well it would operate in a commercial environment, a practice he has followed with various other tire tools in the past. Simonar got some use from it at no expense to him, but he did not purchase it or pay anything for its use, and there never was any intention that he do so. Tabordon, after a brief period, took it back for more tinkering. This court finds, accordingly, that the tire changer was by then reduced to practice but that the use was not a public use acting as a statutory bar.

The use at the Simonar service station was in a somewhat public place, but testing on the commercial premises of another, to his benefit, does not alone create a public use bar.

That February, 1961 use does, however, reflect the rather confined time frame upon which the parties necessarily focussed in contending that a critical event occurred (or did not occur) before March 14, 1961. If the full-power tire changer had been previously reduced to practice, as this court believes, then it was not only offered for sale but sold to William Ballo by no later than March 27, 1961, when he took delivery of a full-power machine. Does the evidence, clearly and convincingly, establish a statutory bar event two weeks or more before? This court is persuaded that it establishes two such events.

Tabordon had developed a full-power machine at the end of 1959 or shortly thereafter, which he abandoned as too slow and cannibalized for parts. He thereafter developed the semi-power. By October, 1960 that device, termed the EZ tire changer by the principals of Continental Distributor, was susceptible to commercial exploitation. What the status of the relevant full-power was at that time is unclear. Tabordon claimed that there was no full-power device prior to the January 28, 1961 sketch. Other evidence indicates that the principals of Continental Distributors had seen some kind of prototype prior to one of them contracting with Tabordon on October 31, 1960, and it was the expectation of a full-power which fueled their enthusiasm. The then distributor of the EZ tire changer began to solicit sales of that semi-power device, had a brochure printed and placed advertisements. They continued to press, however, for the full-power machine and Tabordon, strapped for funds, sought to accommodate them.

An offer for sale required two happenings: the availability of a unit and the offer of it for sale. The availability depended upon Tabordon. The offer for sale depended upon the distributors, and Tabordon had little knowledge about what they were doing and when. Promotional material, advertisements and displays were solely up to them. For both Tabordon and the distributors it was very much a shoestring operation. The two or so salespersons picked up units from Tabordon for cash and then peddled them to service stations and the like by demonstrations of tire changers mounted on a trailer hitched to the back of an automobile.

David D. Baldwin, self-styled national sales manager, attended the Wisconsin Petroleum Association trade show in Milwaukee on March 1 and 2, 1961, where Continental Distributors had a booth. There can be no real dispute about the date or the attendance. Both are documented. Nor is there any real dispute that such a demonstration of the full-power would be a statutory bar. *Faulkner v. Baldwin Piano & Organ Co.*, 561 F.2d 677, 684 (7th Cir. 1977), *cert. denied*, 435 U.S. 905 (1978). The dispute centers on what was demonstrated there. Tabordon had no recollection, but, in view of his isolation from any sales effort, that is not surprising. Baldwin, both at deposition and at trial, was certain that he demonstrated the full-power at the trade show and that he had a full-power brochure for that purpose. No such brochure has been located but it is highly probable that such a brochure was prepared some time, given the distributors' interest in the full-power. Continental Distributors' payments support the conclusion that the EZ brochure was prepared in the fall of 1960 and that a second brochure was prepared in early 1961. Finally, in view of the nature and location of the trade show and the immediacy of the Ballo sale, it is highly probable that the distributors should have wanted to demonstrate the full-power, which was at most a few days from initial sale.

This court is also persuaded that the full-power was demonstrated to Ballo on March 11, 1961. Tabordon had earlier received a check for $500 from Continental Distributors, which could have been in payment for demonstration tire changers, although at his deposition he claimed it was a loan. At his deposition Ballo believed a $25 check with a March 11 date to John P. Hillmer was a downpayment, with delivery on March 27, 1961. At trial he was far more uncertain. Both he and Hillmer agreed, however, that Ballo bought the tire changer as a result of a demonstration in south Milwaukee. It may well have been that the first check was for accessories (although the two checks appear to approach the expectable selling price of a full-power), but the evidence strongly supports the conclusion that Ballo was solicited but once, that being March 11, 1961; it is clear that he purchased a full-power; and the logical conclusion is that the full-power was demonstrated on March 11, at which time he agreed to purchase it for later delivery. That sequence may possibly explain Tabordon's reference on one occasion to March 15, 1961 as the critical date (a date when Continental Distributors apparently paid Tabordon for four machines) and on another occasion to March 24, 1961 (when he may have delivered the full-power to Hillmer).

NOTES

1. What is the critical date in this case?
2. Why did the court hold that the installation of the tire changer in the Simonar service station was not a public use under § 102(b)? Compare this with

cases from the previous section of this chapter, such as *Egbert* and *Moleculon*. And see *City of Elizabeth*, below (on experimental public use).

3. From this case, it appears difficult to separate "public use" considerations from "on sale" considerations. Indeed, they are often intertwined. But it is important to remember that *either* event — a use or a sale — will trigger the statutory bar.

4. It is important to note the distinction between the *sale* of a product or process made in conformity with a patent, and the *licensing or assignment* of a patent. In the former case, the subject matter of the sale is something produced *according to* an invention; in the latter, it is the *invention itself* that is the subject of the transaction. Only the former transaction is a statutory bar event. Licensing and assignment of patents or patent applications do not qualify as "placing the invention on sale" for purposes of § 102(b). *See Moleculon, supra:* "[T]he district court held that ... an assignment or sale of the rights in the invention and potential patent rights is not a sale of 'the invention' within the meaning of section 102(b). We agree." 229 U.S.P.Q (BNA) at 809. *See generally* D. CHISUM, PATENTS § 6.02 (1978 & Supp. 1996).

5. The court in *FMC* states at one point: "An offer for sale required two happenings: the availability of a unit and the offer of it for sale." The case that follows, and associated notes, explore the necessity of the first of these elements for an on-sale bar.

c. The Relevance of Reduction to Practice

UMC ELECTRONICS CO. v. UNITED STATES
816 F.2d 647, 2 U.S.P.Q.2d (BNA) 1465 (Fed. Cir. 1987)

UMC Electronics Company brought this action, pursuant to 28 U.S.C. § 1498(a), to recover compensation for use of its patented invention by the United States. UMC is the owner of Patent No. 3,643,513, issued February 22, 1972, by assignment from the inventor Preston Weaver. The United States Claims Court, 8 Cl. Ct. 604, 228 U.S.P.Q. 396 (1985), upheld the validity of all claims. We reverse the Claims Court's holding that the patented invention was not on sale within the meaning of 35 U.S.C. 102(b).

The claimed invention is an aviation counting accelerometer (ACA), a device for sensing and for recording the number of times an aircraft has been subjected to predetermined levels of acceleration. The sensor component is mounted on the aircraft in a direction to measure acceleration loading and is connected electrically to the recorder component. Records produced by an ACA can indicate an aircraft's remaining useful life and show the need for structural inspection, overhaul, or rotation to less demanding service. [A diagram of the ACA is shown in Figure 4-12, next page.]

The patent application which became the patent in this suit ('513) was filed on August 1, 1968. Under 35 U.S.C. § 102(b), the commercial exploitation and the

U.S. Patent   Feb. 22, 1972   3,643,513

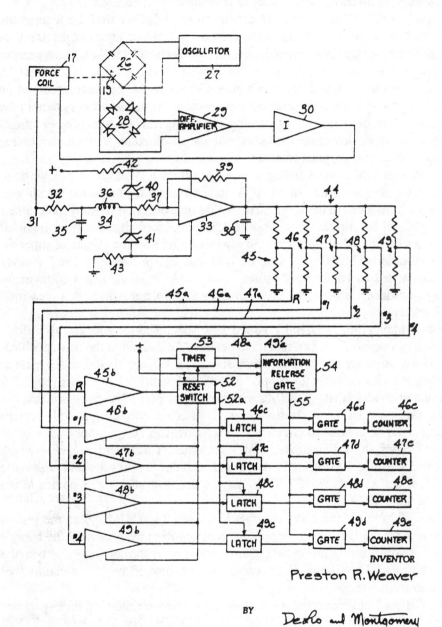

INVENTOR

Preston R. Weaver

BY

Deolo and Montgomery

ATTORNEYS

Figure 4-12

state of development of the invention one year before the filing of the application
for the subject invention are critical to resolution of the on-sale issue.

In early 1967, UMC concluded that its model UMC-A would not meet the
Navy's performance specification required by [a new] contract. [T]he UMC-A
accelerometer utilized, as part of its sensor, an electro-mechanical transducer to
mechanically generate signals that indicate levels of acceleration. [T]he UMC-A
device sometimes counted and sometimes did not count the same acceleration
load. The problem lay in the inherent frequency of the mass-spring system in the
transducer. The devices could not distinguish between acceleration due to inflight
maneuvers, which determines actual stress, and acceleration from other sources,
e.g., windgusts or weapons release.

To prevent UMC from losing the ACA contract, Weaver began work to
improve the sensor portion of an ACA and conceived his invention which uses
an analog transducer in the sensor. An analog transducer electrically generates a
varying signal (in contrast to the mechanically produced signal of prior devices)
which can be filtered electronically to selectively remove the effects of superimposed vibrations. The Claims Court found that in April-May of 1967 Weaver
built and tested an engineering prototype of his ACA containing a commercial
analog transducer, a filter, a timing circuit and a voltage sensor that measured
one load level.

In late May, 1967, the Navy issued new specifications and in July, 1967,
requested proposals from contractors to deliver ACA's built to the new specification. UMC responded to the request on July 27, 1967, the final date for making
a proposal, with an offer to supply $1,668,743 worth of its improved ACA
(hereinafter model UMC-B). UMC represented as part of its proposal that the
sensor portion "has been constructed and tested in conjunction with voltage
sensing and time controlled circuitry." In response to a Navy inquiry, on August
2, 1967, after the critical date, UMC submitted a technical proposal which
described the model UMC-B in detail and included test results and schematic
drawings. On August 9, 1967, UMC gave a demonstration of its device to the
Navy at the UMC facility.

[UMC did not get the Navy contract.] In June, 1980, UMC filed the instant
action against the United States seeking compensation by reason of the Navy's
alleged use of its invention [in the systems produced by the company that won the
1967 contract.] The Claims Court upheld the validity of the patent claims [but
found no infringement.]

The Claims Court analyzed the on-sale bar under the following three-part test
set out in *In re Corcoran*, 640 F.2d 1331, 1333-34, 208 U.S.P.Q. 867, 870
(C.C.P.A. 1981), taken from *Timely Prods. Corp. v. Arron*, 523 F.2d 288, 302,
187 U.S.P.Q. 257, 267-68 (2d Cir. 1975):

> (1) The complete invention claimed must have been embodied in or obvious
> in view of the thing offered for sale.

(2) The invention must have been tested sufficiently to verify that it is operable and commercially marketable. This is simply another way of expressing the principle that an invention cannot be offered for sale until it is completed, which requires not merely its conception but its reduction to practice.

(3) Finally, the sale must be primarily for profit rather than for experimental purposes.

[The trial court had found a reduction to practice (element (2)), but no physical embodiment of the invention in the thing offered for sale (element (1)). The Federal Circuit found this inconsistent, and concluded that there had not in fact been a reduction to practice. Having so concluded, the court turned to the question whether this by itself removed UMC from the effects of the § 102(b) on-sale bar.]

Whether a reduction to practice is a requirement of the on-sale bar of 35 U.S.C. § 102(b) requires a review of our precedent. However, the issue has been directly addressed by this court or its predecessors in only two cases, [*Barmag Barmer Maschinenfabrik AG v. Murata Mach., Ltd.*, 731 F.2d 831, 221 U.S.P.Q. 561 (Fed. Cir. 1984)] and *General Electric Co. v. United States*, 654 F.2d 55, 60-61, 211 U.S.P.Q. 867, 872-73 (Ct. Cl. 1981) (en banc), although the issue has surfaced in others. In *General Electric Co.*, the Court of Claims, one of this court's predecessors, analyzed an on-sale bar issue by focusing on the policies underlying the bar to determine whether application of the bar would further those policies. Those policies were stated to be:

> First, there is a policy against removing inventions from the public which the public has justifiably come to believe are freely available to all as a consequence of prolonged sales activity. Next, there is a policy favoring prompt and widespread disclosure of new inventions to the public. The inventor is forced to file promptly or risk possible forfeiture of his invention [patent] rights due to prior sales. A third policy is to prevent the inventor from commercially exploiting the exclusivity of his invention substantially beyond the statutorily authorized 17-year period. The on-sale bar forces the inventor to choose between seeking patent protection promptly following sales activity or taking his chances with his competitors without the benefit of patent protection. The fourth and final identifiable policy is to give the inventor a reasonable amount of time following sales activity (set by statute as 1 year) to determine whether a patent is a worthwhile investment. This benefits the public because it tends to minimize the filing of inventions [sic] of only marginal public interest.

654 F.2d at 61, 211 U.S.P.Q. at 873 (citations omitted). On the facts of that case, the court held that the policies were violated and that there was a reduction to practice before the critical date.

In *Barmag*, the court went out of its way to reserve the question whether a physical embodiment should be a requirement of the on-sale bar in all cases. Without a physical embodiment, as stated above, there can be no reduction to practice.

Contrary to the Claims Court's interpretation, *Barmag* did not suggest that an embodiment might not be required only in instances where there had been actual sales of goods. An *offer* to sell a later-claimed invention may be sufficient to invoke the bar whether the offer is accepted or rejected.

Adoption of a "sufficiently" reduced-to-practice requirement is in fact an abandonment of reduction to practice as that term is used in other contexts. This court observed in *Barmag*, 731 F.2d at 838 n.6, 221 U.S.P.Q. at 567 n.6, that our case law does not support a variegated definition of reduction to practice. At this point, we point out that "reduction to practice" is a term of art which developed in connection with interference practice to determine priority of invention between rival claimants. [See Section J.4, this chapter.]

Finally, a major flaw in reduction to practice as a per se requirement of the on-sale bar in all cases is disclosed by a close analysis of *Timely Products*, the leading case which purports to adopt that requirement. A significant development with respect to the scope of section 102(b) occurred in a series of decisions beginning with those of another of our predecessors, the Court of Customs and Patent Appeals, when it recognized the operation of the bar in conjunction with the obviousness determination under section 103. Implicit in the operation of a sections 102(b)/103 bar is the *absence* of reduction to practice of the *claimed invention* as a requirement for the bar to operate. The invention, i.e., as claimed with all elements, is not the subject of the sale. If it were, section 103 would not be involved. With respect to non-claimed subject matter of the sale in a sections 102(b)/103 situation, it is meaningless to speak of "reduction to practice" of what was sold. "Reduction to practice" relates only to the precise invention expressed *in a claim*. Thus, the second requirement of *Timely Products*, reduction to practice of the *claimed invention*, is inherently inconsistent with the first requirement under which the bar is applicable if the claimed invention is merely "obvious in view of the thing offered for sale."

In view of all of the above considerations, we conclude that reduction to practice of the claimed invention has not been and should not be made an absolute requirement of the on-sale bar.

We hasten to add, however, that we do not intend to sanction attacks on patents on the ground that the inventor or another offered for sale, before the critical date, the mere concept of the invention. Nor should inventors be forced to rush into the Patent and Trademark Office prematurely. On the other hand, we reject UMC's position that as a matter of law no on-sale bar is possible unless the claimed invention has been reduced to practice in the interference sense.

We do not reject "reduction to practice" as an important analytical tool in an on-sale analysis. A holding that there has or has not been a reduction to practice of the claimed invention before the critical date may well determine whether the claimed invention was in fact the subject of the sale or offer to sell or whether a sale was primarily for an experimental purpose. Thus, we simply say here that the on-sale bar does not necessarily turn on whether there was or was not a reduction to practice of the claimed invention. All of the circumstances surrounding the sale or offer to sell, including the stage of development of the invention and the nature of the invention, must be considered and weighed against the policies underlying section 102(b).

The above conclusion does not lend itself to formulation into a set of precise requirements such as that attempted by the *Timely Products* court. However, we point out certain critical considerations in the on-sale determination and the respective burdens of proof which have already been established in our precedent. Thus, without question, the challenger has the burden of proving that there was a definite sale or offer to sell more than one year before the application for the subject patent, and that the subject matter of the sale or offer to sell fully anticipated the claimed invention or would have rendered the claimed invention obvious by its addition to the prior art. If these facts are established, the patent owner is called upon to come forward with an explanation of the circumstances surrounding what would otherwise appear to be commercialization outside the grace period. The possibilities of such circumstances cannot possibly be enumerated. If the inventor had merely a conception or was working towards development of that conception, it can be said there is not yet any "invention" which could be placed on sale. A sale made because the purchaser was participating in experimental testing creates no on-sale bar.

The issue of whether an invention is on-sale is a question of law. *Barmag*, 731 F.2d at 836-37, 221 U.S.P.Q. at 565-66. Because the Claims Court's factual findings are not disputed, and the issue may be resolved by application of the proper rule of law to those findings, we need not remand.

UMC made a definite offer to sell its later patented UMC-B accelerometer to the Navy more than one year prior to the date of the application for the patent in suit. In its bid, UMC specified a price of $404.00 for each sensor component of the ACA and $271.00 for the compatible recorder component. The total contract price was in excess of $1.6 million. This written offer which revealed use of the analog transducer in the ACA was supplied on July 27, 1967. UMC admits that the offer it made was for profit, not to conduct experiments.

UMC's activities evidence, at least *prima facie*, an attempt to commercialize the invention of the '513 patent by bidding on a large government contract more than one year prior to the filing of the underlying application and thereby to expand the grace period in contravention of the policies underlying the statute.

Countering the *prima facie* case, UMC offers only the purely technical objection that no complete embodiment of the invention existed at the time of the sale. In this case, that circumstance is unavailing when we look at the realities of the development of this invention. [T]he contract was not a research and development contract, and UMC admits that the offer it made was for profit, not to conduct experimental work.

SMITH, CIRCUIT JUDGE, dissenting.

The panel majority correctly holds that the thing offered for sale by UMC was not reduced to practice by the critical date. That should be the end of the inquiry. The law is clear, and the parties agree, that the on-sale bar cannot be invoked without a reduction to practice. The panel majority, however, without being asked by the parties, asks whether reduction to practice "should" be required for the on-sale bar, and concludes that there should be no such requirement, notwithstanding the binding precedent to the contrary.

Section 102(b) is in the nature of a statute of limitations, enacted to implement the policy that those who seek the benefits of the patent grant must act promptly after the invention has been placed in possession of the public. Failure to act within 1 year forfeits the opportunity to obtain a patent.

As in statutes of limitation generally, the start of a statutory bar must be reasonably clear at the time it occurs. The long history of section 102(b), which effects the irretrievable loss of a valuable right, shows judicial and congressional recognition of this need for reasonable certainty.

It was never the purpose of section 102(b) to force premature entry into the patent system upon inventors who are still developing their inventions. The public interest is not served by a system that wastes the resources of inventors or by "the waste of Patent Office resources in processing half-baked inventions."

I agree with the panel majority that, for purposes of sections 102(b)/103, it is not required that the *claimed* invention must be reduced to practice and offered for sale. It is sufficient that the claimed invention "must have been embodied in *or obvious in view of the thing* offered for sale."

The difficulty postulated by the panel majority, that sections 102(b)/103 could not be applied if the thing offered must be reduced to practice, fails to materialize in real life. The first inquiry is whether the *thing offered* has been reduced to practice by the critical date and, thus, become prior art under section 102(b). Reduction to practice has occurred if one of the "things" offered has ever been completed or built and shown to work. Only then is it necessary to compare the *claims* to the prior art for determination of obviousness under section 103.

In the present case, the Claims Court applied a prototype as prior art against UMC's claimed invention, but held that the claimed invention would not have been obvious in view of the prototype. Similarly, if the thing offered on July 27 had been reduced to practice, the thing offered would have been available as prior art against UMC's claimed invention under sections 102(b)/103. However, the thing offered was not reduced to practice by the critical date, and it did not become part of the prior art under sections 102(b)/103.

It is the users of the patent system who will suffer the impact of the panel majority decision. The question is not theoretical; it is of great practical importance.

Those inventors who have sought financing, or who have contacted potential customers, or who have engaged in other normal business activities before they have made a workable device will not know how the time limit for filing a patent application will be measured or where the line will be drawn between raw idea and proved invention. Inventors do not normally try to patent something they have not yet found workable. Most inventors do not hire a patent lawyer until they know they have something that works, by which time, according to the panel majority, it may be too late.

NOTES

1. *Reduction to Practice and Interferences.* In Section J.4 of this chapter, the importance of reduction to practice and its place in interferences are described.

2. *Applying the Test.* Under the court's test, would it raise a statutory bar issue to offer to sell a "black box" invention of undescribed proportions to a gullible purchaser? Would it matter if seller of the "black box" had conceived the details of the invention? If the box itself contained nothing at all? In a related vein, under the test announced in the case, when would you advise a client to begin running her "statutory bar clock" — when she discussed the market for a potential invention with a potential buyer of one or more embodiments of it? When she put in a bid on a project to commence in several years' time, on the basis of a hoped-for but not yet conceived cost-saving invention that will permit a good rate of profit under the bid? For more, see the fine article by Rooklidge & Von Hoffman, *Reduction to Practice, Experimental Use and the "On Sale" and "Public Use" Bars to Patentability*, 63 St. JOHN'S L. REV. 1 (1988) (critiquing *UMC* test).

3. *Policies.* For a detailed discussion of the policies behind the on-sale bar, see Barrett, *New Guidelines for Applying the On Sale Bar to Patentability*, 24 STAN. L. REV. 730, 732-35 (1972). More recently, a sophisticated review of post-*UMC* Federal Circuit jurisprudence concluded that in applying these policies the court has "succumbed to the temptation of discretion in on-sale doctrine," making the law in this area hopelessly uncertain. Thomas K. Landry, *Certainty and Discretion in Patent Law: The On Sale Bar, the Doctrine of Equivalents, and Judicial Power in the Federal Circuit*, 67 S. CAL. L. REV. 1151, 1154 (1994). Landry argues persuasively that in pursuing its vision of a just result in individual cases — guided by the policies identified in *UMC* — the Federal Circuit has sacrificed far too much certainty and predictability. He proposes a return to the "on hand" standard discussed in *Timely Products*, or at least to the reduction to practice requirement jettisoned in *UMC*.

4. *Application.* The *UMC* standard has now been applied in a number of settings. *See, e.g., Ferag AG v. Quipp, Inc.,* 45 F.3d 1562, 33 U.S.P.Q.2d 1562, 1568 (Fed. Cir. 1995) (fact that customer who specified functional features required did not know precise parameters of newspaper conveyor system is irrelevant; only material issue is that patentee decided to meet customer's order with later-claimed invention, which created a § 102(b) bar); *Robotic Vision Sys., Inc. v. View Eng'g, Inc.,* 39 U.S.P.Q.2d 1167 (C.D. Cal. 1996) (invention for method of inspecting computer chips was on sale despite fact that software to

implement main inventive concept of scanning a full tray of chips was not yet installed on critical date). The *Ferag* case is also important for its holding that, even though the seller/patentee and product distributor had partially overlapping ownership, the offer for sale of the later-patented invention was not an "in house" transaction exempt from the on-sale bar. *Ferag, supra*, 45 F.3d at 1567. On this issue of mutual ownership, see 2 DONALD CHISUM, PATENTS 6.02[6][d] (1978 & Supp. 1996).

5. *Barred by a Thief?* The law seems unclear on the question whether public use by one who steals an invention creates a statutory bar for the innocent, non-consenting inventor. *See* 2 DONALD CHISUM, PATENTS § 6.02[5][c] (1978 & Supp. 1996) (collecting cases). What do you think? (Keep in mind the various policies behind § 102(b), especially the non-extension of patent term and third-party reliance concepts.)

KING INSTRUMENT CORP. v. OTARI CORP.

767 F.2d 853, 226 U.S.P.Q. (BNA) 402 (Fed. Cir. 1985)

King Instrument Corporation (King), the plaintiff below, charged Otari Corporation (Otari) with infringement of [two patents, including] its 3,737,358 ('358) [patent] issued June 5, 1973. King now appeals from final judgment by the United States District Court for the Northern District of California, following a bench trial, that held the '358 patent invalid because the invention claimed was found to be "on sale" under 35 U.S.C. § 102(b). We affirm.

The patents at issue relate to an automated apparatus for loading magnetic (blank or pre-recorded audio or video) tape into closed cassettes. Before loading, a closed cassette consists of an outer plastic case containing two winding hubs (spools) and a short length of leader tape wound around each hub. After loading, the finished product has a much longer length of magnetic supply ("use") tape which has been spliced to the leader tape. The patents claim an apparatus for automatically cutting, splicing, and winding magnetic use tape into closed cassettes.

The device disclosed in the '358 patent has been called a "shift block" machine. The assembly disclosed consists of two splicing blocks. The first block has two tape-receiving grooves, and the second block has one tape-receiving groove. Although using a different mechanism, the unclaimed operating sequence is generally the same as in the swing arm machine [claimed in U.S. Patent 3,637,153, the other patent at issue in the case, and shown in Figure 4-13].

The leader tape lies across both blocks whereupon it is cut into two sections by a knife unit. A means is provided for moving one block relative to the other (*i.e.*, horizontally pulling out one block — "shifting") so as to selectively align the second groove of the first block which supports the use tape with the single groove of the second block which supports one end of the leader tape. A splicing tape dispenser splices the leader tape and use tape. The tape is wound and then severed at a predetermined length. The block shifts back to its original position,

U.S. Patent   Jan 25, 1972   **3,637,153**

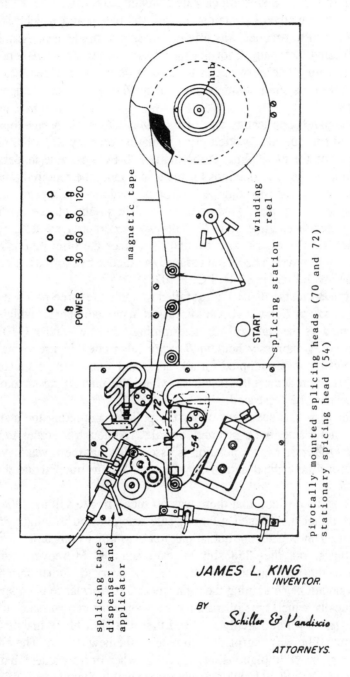

Figure 4-13

aligning and splicing the wound tape with the other "forgotten" leader end.

In holding the '358 shift block patent invalid, the district court found that a device which embodied the claims of the '358 patent and which had been previously reduced to practice was offered for sale to the Morningstar Division of Data Packaging Company (Morningstar) prior to May 27, 1970 (one year prior to the '358 filing date). Except as to its on sale defense, Otari was summarily denied relief on its other counterclaims for invalidity and noninfringement of the '358 patent.

The '358 patent application was filed on May 27, 1971. A tape loading device was offered for sale in a written price quotation on May 22, 1970 to Morningstar. The offer for two "King Turbo-matic 300-EC" cassette loaders contained a description of the specifications for the leader tape, the required power supply, a discount for two of Morningstar's old tape loaders, and a price quotation for a spare automatic splicer. This offer resulted in an acceptance confirmed by a purchase order dated June 8, 1970. The two loaders arrived at Morningstar on June 17, 1970. The district court found that, since the offer embodied the '358 claimed invention which had been reduced to practice by April 27, 1970, the '358 patent was invalid under 35 U.S.C. § 102(b).

King argues that the district court failed to apply the three-part test enunciated in *Timely Products Corp. v. Arron* [discussed in preceding case] which it says this court adopted as the standard for determining "on sale" under § 102(b). However, this court expressly held in *Barmag* [also cited in preceding case] that *Timely Products* is not adopted for all cases, and a less stringent standard might be appropriate in some circumstances where the underlying statutory policies might otherwise be frustrated.

An offer to sell is sufficient under the policies animating the statute, which proscribes not a sale, but a placing "on sale." Although it argues in the context of *Timely Products*, King's position is essentially that there was never an offer of sale before the critical date, nor was the '358 invention reduced to practice before that date.

To support its position that there was no such offer to sell the '358 invention, King asserts that the alleged offer for sale was phrased in language consistent with that used in concurrent quotations made to other companies for the swing arm machines, not the '358 shift block machines. Moreover, there was no reference in the offer as to how the machine worked. Other purchasers who received quotations containing the same general performance language could not say specifically which type of machine was being offered for sale. Robert Hunt of Morningstar, who allegedly received the '358 shift block machines in June, 1970, admitted he was "surprised" to receive the new device. The alleged offer becomes even more ambiguous, argues King, when one considers that the earlier swing arm and later shift block machines were both referred to as a "King Turbo-matic Cassette Loader 300 EC." It is said, therefore, that no intent existed to make such an offer, nothing in the offer identified the subject matter of the invention, and no notice was given to the purchaser that a new or different machine existed.

While a bare, unexplained offer, not explicitly shown to be of the new invention, may be insufficient, the totality of the circumstances must always be considered in order to ascertain whether an offer of the new invention was in fact made. *Accord Barmag, supra.* When an executory sales contract is entered into (or offered) before the critical date, the purchaser must know how the invention embodied in the offer will perform. The policies underlying the on sale bar, however, concentrate on the attempt by the inventor to exploit his invention, not whether the potential purchaser was cognizant of the invention. Accordingly, the purchaser need not have actual knowledge of the invention for it to be on sale. In this case, from the descriptions contained in the quotation (*e.g.*, "The loader measures tape in one foot increments from 2 feet to 999 feet"), the purchaser generally knew how the machine would perform. King's argument that nothing in the quotation distinguishes the offer from any other offer for a swing arm machine is inaccurate. Comparison of the Morningstar quotation to those made to other companies reveals that only the offer to Morningstar included a 40% allowance for old machines. Although this distinction does not establish the existence of an offer to replace old swing arm machine with a "new" type of machine, such a possibility is another factor for the trier to consider.

As evidence that no offer was made before the critical date, King also argues that Morningstar did not receive two shift block machines in June 1970, but in fact received two swing arm machines embodying the invention claimed in the [other] patent [at issue in the case]. However, Hunt of Morningstar was convinced that the two machines received on June 17, 1970 were horizontal shift block machines. Review of Hunt's testimony shows that he was continuously connected with the cassette winding operation during this period of time. His unbiased live testimony is a sufficient basis for the district court to have concluded that the machines received embodied the '358 shift block invention. The fact that Morningstar received two shift block machines is further support that the earlier ambiguous offer made on May 22, 1970 was in fact for shift block machines. [Reversed and remanded on this point.]

NOTES

1. How does the holding in this case square with the holding in *UMC Electronics*, above? Do they further the same policy goal? Of the policies enunciated in the *Timely Products* case (set out in *UMC*, above), how much weight do courts give number four, i.e., providing the inventor "a reasonable amount of time following sales activity (set by statute as one year) to determine whether a patent is a worthwhile investment"?

2. An offer, under basic contract law, must be specific as to its subject matter. But as the preceding case shows, this does not mean the offer must contain detailed specifications. This leaves a good deal of scope for application of the holding in the preceding case. Indeed, taking this case together with the preceding one (*UMC Electronics*), inventors would be wise to assume the statutory bar period begins running as soon as *almost any* effort is made to commercialize the products of an invention. *Cf.* Comment, Envirotech v. Westech Engineering: *The On-Sale Bar to Patentability and Executory Sales Offers*, 75 MINN. L. REV. 1505 (1991) (arguing for strong adherence to the policy-based analysis of on-sale bars).

Lest the student come to the view that the policy-based approach of *UMC Electronics* has now been collapsed into two simple elements — potential availability of the invention, plus a sale or offer for sale — consider the following excerpt.

––––––––––

From *Mahurkar v. Impra, Inc.*, 71 F.3d 1573, 37 U.S.P.Q.2d 1138 (Fed. Cir. 1995) (Plager, J.):

[Mahurkar owned a patent on medical catheters; for more facts, and a related case, *see Vas-Cath v. Mahurkar*, in Chapter 6.]

... On February 1, 1982, prior to filing any applications for the patents at issue in this appeal, Mahurkar granted an exclusive license to Quinton to make, use, and sell these double lumen catheters. Paragraph 2.8 of the License Agreement conditioned Quinton's exclusive status on it marketing Mahurkar's catheters by September 30, 1982.

As of August 1982, Quinton had not yet made any sales of the double lumen catheters, purportedly due to its inability to make the catheters in accordance with Mahurkar's specifications. In an effort to maintain its status as an exclusive licensee, Wayne Quinton, the chief executive officer of Quinton, contacted Christopher Blagg, a longstanding acquaintance and the executive director of Northwest Kidney Center (Northwest), and asked Blagg to buy 20 of these catheters from Quinton as a personal favor. Despite the fact that Northwest did not use this type of catheter, as it sent its patients to hospitals for catheter insertion, Blagg authorized the purchase. Northwest subsequently received a bill for the purchase of 20 catheters at $20 each. Northwest never paid this bill, but the record shows that Northwest received and paid for two prototype catheters on August 31, 1982 (Northwest transaction).

Upon receipt, Dr. Tom Sawyer, chief staff physician at Northwest, stored the catheters in a cabinet where they remained, unused, as of the commencement of this litigation. The catheters had a number of serious defects, which would have increased the risk of injury to patients using the catheters for dialysis. The instructions accompanying both of the catheters directed the user to sterilize them in an autoclave at 250 degrees for 30 minutes before insertion in a patient. The district court found that treating the catheters according to these instructions would have melted the catheters, or at least deformed them, rendering them unusable.

Mahurkar protested to Quinton that the Northwest transaction was a sham, and that he was therefore entitled per paragraph 2.8 of the License Agreement to terminate Quinton's status as an exclusive licensee. The parties ultimately settled their dispute, and throughout all relevant times Quinton has continued to retain exclusive rights under the License Agreement. Quinton eventually introduced Mahurkar's catheters into the market for widespread commercialization in April 1983.

On October 3, 1983, more than one year after the Northwest transaction but less than one year from the time Mahurkar's catheters were first commercially marketed, Mahurkar filed a design patent application .... On August 15, 1984, Mahurkar filed a utility application [that relied on the design patent application filing date; *see Vas-Cath*, Chapter 6].

As we have repeatedly said, whether a device has been placed on sale is not subject to a mechanical rule. On the contrary, the on-sale determination depends on the totality of the circumstances, considered in view of the policies underlying section 102(b). Our court has stressed that commercialization is the central focus for determining whether the patented invention has been placed on sale. Because we conclude that Quinton's sale to Northwest was a sham that did not result in "commercialization" of the invention or place it in the public domain, no section 102(b) sale occurred even though the prototype was a reduction to practice of the invention. We believe that the relevant facts indicate that no commercialization took place here. Quinton did not advertise the catheters, nor offer them to anyone but Blagg prior to the critical date. The Northwest transaction was a special deal made in an attempt to satisfy the requirements of a licensing agreement, not a sale made on ordinary commercial terms. Mahurkar did not believe that Quinton had a marketable product that could be offered to customers.

No members of the public outside of Northwest were likely aware of the transaction at all. If they had been aware, the circumstances of the transaction indicated that it was a sham transaction designed to satisfy a licensing agreement, rather than an ordinary commercial sale that would indicate that the invention was in the public domain.

That the Northwest transaction was not a section 102(b) sale is also consistent with encouraging the prompt and widespread disclosure of inventions and allowing an inventor a reasonable amount of time following sales activity to determine the potential value of a patent. The Northwest transaction was not "sales activity" that helped the inventor determine the value of a patent. Selling two unmarketable prototypes with instructions that made them unusable could not provide information as to the value of a patent. This suggests that the transaction did not impermissibly extend the one-year period allowed for inventors to evaluate the value of a patent before filing an application.

NOTE

Irreconcilable Differences? After *UMC*, reduction to practice is not required to prove a statutory bar; but after *Mahurkar*, sale of a reduced-to-practice but nonfunctional prototype cuts in favor of the applicant/patentee. After *King*, an offer for sale is sufficient; after *Mahurkar*, a bona fide sale under the Uniform Commercial Code (which the district court below had found and the Federal Circuit took as a given) may not be enough to trigger the on-sale bar.

d. The Experimental Use Exception

CITY OF ELIZABETH v. AMERICAN NICHOLSON PAVEMENT CO.

97 U.S. 126 (1877)

This suit was brought by the American Nicholson Pavement Company against the city of Elizabeth, N.J., upon a patent issued to Samuel Nicholson, dated Aug. 20, 1867, for a new and improved wooden pavement, being a second reissue of a patent issued to said Nicholson Aug. 8, 1854. The reissued patent was extended in 1868 for a further term of seven years. [I]n the specification, it is declared that the nature and object of the invention consists in providing a process or mode of constructing wooden block pavements upon a foundation along a street or roadway with facility, cheapness, and accuracy, and also in the creation and construction of such a wooden pavement as shall be comparatively permanent and durable, by so uniting and combining all its parts, both superstructure and foundation, as to provide against the slipping of the horses' feet, against noise, against unequal wear, and against rot and consequent sinking away from below. Two plans of making this pavement are specified. Both require a proper foundation on which to lay the blocks, consisting of tarred-paper or hydraulic cement covering the surface of the road-bed to the depth of about two inches, or of a flooring of boards or plank, also covered with tar, or other preventive of moisture. On this foundation, one plan is to set square blocks on end arranged like a checker-board, the alternate rows being shorter than the others, so as to leave narrow grooves or channel-ways to be filled with small broken stone or gravel, and then pouring over the whole melted tar or pitch, whereby the cavities are all filled and cemented together. The other plan is, to arrange the blocks in rows transversely across the street, separated a small space (of about an inch) by strips of board at the bottom, which serve to keep the blocks at a uniform distance apart, and then filling these spaces with the same material as before. The blocks forming the pavement are about eight inches high. The alternate rows of short blocks in the first plan and the strips of board in the second plan should not be higher than four inches.

The bill charges that the defendants infringed this patent by laying down wooden pavements in the city of Elizabeth, N.J., constructed in substantial conformity with the process patented, and prays an account of profits, and an injunction.

The defendants answered in due course, admitting that they had constructed, and were still constructing, wooden pavements in Elizabeth, but alleging that they were constructed in accordance with a patent granted to John W. Brocklebank and Charles Trainer, dated Jan. 12, 1869, and denied that it infringed upon the complainant.

They also denied that there was any novelty in the alleged invention of Nicholson, and specified a number of English and other patents which exhibited, as they claimed, every substantial and material part thereof which was claimed as new.

They also averred that the alleged invention of Nicholson was in public use, with his consent and allowance, for six years before he applied for a patent, on a certain avenue in Boston called the Mill-dam and contended that said public use worked an abandonment of the pretended invention.

These several issues, together with the question of profits, and liability on the part of the several defendants to respond thereto, are the subjects in controversy before us.

We do not think that the defence of want of novelty has been successfully made out. Nicholson's invention dates back as early as 1847 or 1848. He filed a *caveat* in the Patent Office, in August, 1847, in which the checker-board pavement is fully described; and he constructed a small patch of pavement of both kinds, by way of experiment, in June or July, 1848, in a street near Boston, which comprised all the peculiarities afterwards described in his patent; and the experiment was a successful one. Before that period, we do not discover in any of the forms of pavements adduced as anticipations of his, any one that sufficiently resembles it to deprive him of the claim to its invention. As claimed by him, it is a combination of different parts or elements, consisting, as the appellant's counsel, with sufficient accuracy for the purposes of this case, enumerates them, 1st, of the foundation prepared to exclude moisture from beneath; 2d, the parallel-sided blocks; 3d, the strips between these blocks, to keep them at a uniform distance and to create a space to be filled with gravel and tar; and, 4th, the filling. Though it may be true that every one of these elements had been employed before, in one kind of pavement or another, yet they had never been used in the same combination and put together in the same manner as Nicholson combined and arranged them, so as to make a pavement like his. The one which makes the nearest approach to it, and might, perhaps, be deemed sufficiently like to deprive Nicholson of the merit of invention, is that of John Hosking, which, in one form, consisted of alternate rows of short and long blocks, the latter partially resting on the former by their being mutually rabbeted so as to fit together. The spaces thus formed between the longer blocks, and on the top of the shorter ones, were filled with loose stone and cement or asphalt, substantially the same as in Nicholson's pavement. It would be very difficult to sustain Nicholson's patent if Hosking's stood in his way. But the only evidence of the invention of the latter is derived from an English patent, the specification of which was not enrolled until March, 1850, nearly two years after Nicholson had put his pavement down in its completed form, by way of experiment, in Boston. A foreign patent, or other foreign printed publication describing an invention, is no defence to a suit upon a patent of the United States, unless published anterior to the making of the invention or discovery secured by the latter, provided that the American patentee, at the time of making application for his patent, believed himself to be the first inventor or discoverer of the thing patented. He is obliged to make oath to such belief when he applies for his patent; and it will be presumed that such was his belief, until the contrary is proven. Since nothing appears to show that Nicholson had any knowledge of Hosking's invention or patent prior to his application for a patent in March, 1854, and since the evidence is very full to the effect that he had made his invention as early as 1848, the patent of Hosking cannot avail the defence in this suit.

The next question to be considered is, whether Nicholson's invention was in public use or on sale, with his consent and allowance, for more than two years prior to his application for a patent, within the meaning of the sixth, seventh, and fifteenth sections of the act of 1836, as qualified by the seventh section of the act of 1839, which were the acts in force in 1854, when he obtained his patent. It is contended by the appellants that the pavement which Nicholson put down by way of experiment, on Mill-dam Avenue in Boston, in 1848, was publicly used for the space of six years before his application for a patent, and that this was a public use within the meaning of the law.

To determine this question, it is necessary to examine the circumstances under which this pavement was put down, and the object and purpose that Nicholson had in view. It is perfectly clear from the evidence that he did not intend to abandon his right to a patent. He had filed a *caveat* in August, 1847, and he constructed the pavement in question by way of experiment, for the purpose of testing its qualities. The road in which it was put down, though a public road, belonged to the Boston and Roxbury Mill Corporation, which received toll for its use; and Nicholson was a stockholder and treasurer of the corporation. The pavement in question was about seventy-five feet in length, and was laid adjoining to the toll-gate and in front of the toll-house. It was constructed by Nicholson at his own expense, and was placed by him where it was, in order to see the effect upon it of heavily loaded wagons, and of varied and constant use; and also to ascertain its durability, and liability to decay. Joseph L. Lang, who was toll-collector for many years, commencing in 1849, familiar with the road before that time, and with this pavement from the time of its origin, testified as follows:

> Mr. Nicholson was there almost daily, and when he came he would examine the pavement, would often walk over it, cane in hand, striking it with his cane, and making particular examination of its condition. He asked me very often how people liked it, and asked me a great many questions about it. I have heard him say a number of times that this was his first experiment with

this pavement, and he thought that it was wearing very well. The circumstances that made this locality desirable for the purpose of obtaining a satisfactory test of the durability and value of the pavement were: that there would be a better chance to lay it there; he would have more room and a better chance than in the city; and, besides, it was a place where most everybody went over it, rich and poor. It was a great thoroughfare out of Boston. It was frequently travelled by teams having a load of five or six tons, and some larger. As these teams usually stopped at the toll-house, and started again, the stopping and starting would make as severe a trial to the pavement as it could be put to.

This evidence is corroborated by that of several other witnesses in the cause; the result of the whole being that Nicholson merely intended this piece of pavement as an experiment, to test its usefulness and durability. Was this a public use, within the meaning of the law?

An abandonment of an invention to the public may be evinced by the conduct of the inventor at any time, even within the two years named in the law. The effect of the law is, that no such consequence will necessarily follow from the invention being in public use or on sale, with the inventor's consent and allowance, at any time within two years before his application; but that, if the invention is in public use or on sale prior to that time, it will be conclusive evidence of abandonment, and the patent will be void.

But, in this case, it becomes important to inquire what is such a public use as will have the effect referred to. That the use of the pavement in question was public in one sense cannot be disputed. But can it be said that the invention was in public use? The use of an invention by the inventor himself, or of any other person under his direction, by way of experiment, and in order to bring the invention to perfection, has never been regarded as such a use. Curtis, Patents, sect. 381; *Shaw v. Cooper*, [32 U.S.] 7 Pet. 292 [1833].

Now, the nature of a street pavement is such that it cannot be experimented upon satisfactorily except on a highway, which is always public.

When the subject of invention is a machine, it may be tested and tried in a building, either with or without closed doors. In either case, such use is not a public use, within the meaning of the statute, so long as the inventor is engaged, in good faith, in testing its operation. He may see cause to alter it and improve it, or not. His experiments will reveal the fact whether any and what alterations may be necessary. If durability is one of the qualities to be attained, a long period, perhaps years, may be necessary to enable the inventor to discover whether his purpose is accomplished. And though, during all that period, he may not find that any changes are necessary, yet he may be justly said to be using his machine only by way of experiment; and no one would say that such a use, pursued with a *bona fide* intent of testing the qualities of the machine, would be a public use, within the meaning of the statute. So long as he does not voluntarily allow others to make it and use it, and so long as it is not on sale for general use, he keeps the invention under his own control, and does not lose his title to a patent.

It would not be necessary, in such a case, that the machine should be put up and used only in the inventor's own shop or premises. He may have it put up and used in the premises of another, and the use may inure to the benefit of the owner of the establishment. Still, if used under the surveillance of the inventor, and for the purpose of enabling him to test the machine, and ascertain whether it will answer the purpose intended, and make such alterations and improvements as experience demonstrates to be necessary, it will still be a mere experimental use, and not a public use, within the meaning of the statute.

Whilst the supposed machine is in such experimental use, the public may be incidentally deriving a benefit from it. If it be a grist-mill, or a carding-machine, customers from the surrounding country may enjoy the use of it by having their grain made into flour, or their wool into rolls, and still it will not be in public use, within the meaning of the law.

But if the inventor allows his machine to be used by other persons generally, either with or without compensation, or if it is, with his consent, put on sale for such use, then it will be in public use and on public sale, within the meaning of the law.

If, now, we apply the same principles to this case, the analogy will be seen at once. Nicholson wished to experiment on his pavement. He believed it to be a good thing, but he was not sure; and the only mode in which he could test it was to place a specimen of it in a public roadway. He did this at his own expense, and with the consent of the owners of the road. Durability was one of the qualities to be attained. He wanted to know whether his pavement would stand, and whether it would resist decay. Its character for durability could not be ascertained without its being subjected to use for a considerable time. He subjected it to such use, in good faith, for the simple purpose of ascertaining whether it was what he claimed it to be. Did he do any thing more than the inventor of the supposed machine might do, in testing his invention? The public had the incidental use of the pavement, it is true; but was the invention in public use, within the meaning of the statute? We think not. The proprietors of the road alone used the invention, and used it at Nicholson's request, by way of experiment. The only way in which they could use it was by allowing the public to pass over the pavement.

Had the city of Boston, or other parties, used the invention, by laying down the pavement in other streets and places, with Nicholson's consent and allowance, then, indeed, the invention itself would have been in public use, within the meaning of the law; but this was not the case. Nicholson did not sell it, nor allow others to use it or sell it. He did not let it go beyond his control. He did nothing that indicated any intent to do so. He kept it under his own eyes, and never for a moment abandoned the intent to obtain a patent for it.

In this connection, it is proper to make another remark. It is not a public knowledge of his invention that precludes the inventor from obtaining a patent for it, but a public use or sale of it. In England, formerly, as well as under our Patent Act of 1793, if an inventor did not keep his invention secret, if a knowledge of it became public before his application for a patent, he could not obtain one. To be patentable, an invention must not have been known or used before the application; but this has not been the law of this country since the passage of the act of 1836, and it has been very much qualified in England. *Lewis v. Marling*, 10 B. & C. 22. Therefore, if it were true that during the whole period in which the pavement was used, the public knew how it was constructed, it would make no difference in the result.

It is sometimes said that an inventor acquires an undue advantage over the public by delaying to take out a patent, inasmuch as he thereby preserves the monopoly to himself for a longer period than is allowed by the policy of the law; but this cannot be said with justice when the delay is occasioned by a *bona fide* effort to bring his invention to perfection, or to ascertain whether it will answer the purpose intended. His monopoly only continues for the allotted period, in any event; and it is the interest of the public, as well as himself, that the invention should be perfect and properly tested, before a patent is granted for it. Any attempt to use it for a profit, and not by way of experiment, for a longer period than two years before the application, would deprive the inventor of his right to a patent.

NOTES

1. *Experimental Evidence.* Compare the facts in the preceding case to those in *Egbert v. Lippmann, supra,* the "corset case." How did Nicholson's actions in this case differ from those of Barnes in the *Egbert* case? What evidence did Nicholson have regarding his six-year pre-filing period that Barnes did not have for his comparably long period? Also, compare the facts in this case to those in *FMC Corp. v. Hennessey Indus.,* the "power tire changer" case. What did the inventor in that case (Tabordon) do that differed from Nicholson's activities here, and how did that bring about a § 102(b) bar in that case? *See also Baxter v. Cobe Labs., Inc.,* 39 U.S.P.Q.2d 1437 (Fed. Cir. 1996).

2. *Historical Notes.* Notice that the patent in this case was (1) reissued (twice); and (2) "extended."

(1) Reissue: An interesting historical account describes the growth of the reissue as an abusive tool in the mid-nineteenth century, and the eventual elimination of most abuses with the passage of the precursor to today's reissue statute (described in Chapter 10, Reissue and Reexamination). *See* Dood, *Pursuing the Essence of Inventions: Reissuing Patents in the Nineteenth Century,* 32 TECH. & CULT. 999, 1007 (1991) (graph of reissues sought as percentage of outstanding patents peaks in late 1870s at approximately 1.2% before settling into modern level of less than .1%).

(2) Extension: The first patent act, Act of April 10, 1790, ch. 7, 1 Stat. 109, adopted the same patent term as the British Statute of Monopolies of 1624, 21

Jac. 1, ch. 3 — 14 years. This was based on the notion that a patent should protect an inventor for a period equal to two terms of a standard British trade apprenticeship of seven years. *See* White, *Why a Seventeen Year Patent?*, 38 J. PAT. OFF. SOC'Y 839 (1956). In the Patent Act of 1836 — which reinstituted the examination system in the original 1790 Act — a seven-year renewal term was added, making the total possible term 21 years. The old 17-year term in the U.S. was the result of a compromise between the House, which wanted to retain the 14 plus 7 term, and the Senate, which wanted to eliminate the renewal term. Economists have long noted that a uniform term sometimes rewards inventors too much, and sometimes gives too little incentive; some have proposed to "craft" individual terms to fit individual inventions. *See, e.g.*, W. NORDHAUS, INVENTION, GROWTH, AND WELFARE (1969) (economic model deriving optimal patent term under different circumstances). For an argument that a good deal of such "crafting" goes on via doctrines defining a patent's scope, see Merges & Nelson, *On the Complex Economics of Patent Scope*, 90 COLUM. L. REV. 839 (1990).

3. *Helping Hand.* In commenting on this case, Learned Hand made the following remarks:

> There are occasional expressions in the books which read as though the period of experiment is only that during which the inventor is trying to reduce the invention to a stable form, to adapt it completely to its purposes: but we should hesitate to hold that this privilege is so limited. For example, in *Elizabeth* ..., it did not appear that Nicholson, the inventor, delayed for any other reason than to learn how well his pavement would wear; apparently it was already as good as he hoped to make it. At any rate we shall assume that an inventor may wait longer, may wait until he learns whether his invention is enough value to justify an application for a patent. On this view he may test it, not only to put it in its definitive form, but to see whether his ideas are worth exploiting.

Aerovox Corp. v. Polymet Mfg. Corp., 67 F.2d 860, 862 (2d Cir. 1933). *But cf.* 2 D. CHISUM, PATENTS § 6.02[7] (1978 & Supp. 1991) ("[T]he Supreme Court cases seem to indicate that a period of public use to test the qualities and practical utility of an invention will be excused so long as such use is confined to what is reasonably necessary under the circumstances.").

MANVILLE SALES CORP. v. PARAMOUNT SYSTEMS

917 F.2d 544, 16 U.S.P.Q.2d (BNA) 1587 (Fed. Cir. 1990)

Paramount Systems, Inc. (Paramount), Robert S. Butterworth, and Anthony J. DiSimone appeal the District Court['s] judgment awarding Manville Sales Corporation (Manville) damages for infringement of U.S. Patent No. 3,847,333 (the '333 patent). Appellants contend that the district court erred in holding that the '333 patent was not invalid because the court erroneously concluded that the invention was not on sale nor in public use prior to the section 102(b) bar date, February 5, 1972.

In early 1971, a Manville division was awarded a subcontract to supply the luminaire assembly for a 150-foot tall, three-foot diameter lighting pole to be installed in the Fort Steele Rest Area along a highway near Rawlins, Wyoming. The assembly was installed, but failed in September, 1971.

Later that same month, Manville's research manager, Robert Zeller, conceived of a new self-centering luminaire assembly design capable of travelling readily up and down a pole, thereby providing reliable accessibility for maintenance to the luminaires. The invention had "iris" guide arms, whereas the prior art device installed in Wyoming had vertical guide arms. The guide arms are intended to apply forces between the light pole and the luminaire support such that the assembly maintains a centered position while travelling up and down the pole. By late October, Zeller had constructed a working model of the new design and had installed it on a test pole at Manville's R&D center in Ohio.

On October 29, 1971, after the new design proved operable on the test pole, Zeller sought permission from a Wyoming state official to try his new iris arm design as a substitute for the vertical guide arm device previously installed that had failed. With his request, Zeller sent a drawing that included a confidentiality notice. Wyoming law preserved the confidentiality of such drawings.

In response to Zeller's request, a Wyoming official conditionally approved payment for the new design subject to its performing satisfactorily, after installation.

The district court found that "contemporaneous 1971 documents and the testimony demonstrate that no one could have known at that time whether the new iris arm would work as intended at Fort Steele." Manville asserts that the new design's durability in weather conditions was unknown, and that Manville sought to install the new iris arm to test it under wind, cold and corrosive atmospheric conditions.

Zeller installed the iris arm device at the rest area in November, 1971 when it was not yet open to the public. In March, 1972, Zeller was notified by a Manville sales representative that supports that attach the luminaires to the ring had fallen off due to severe weather conditions. Zeller returned to Wyoming that month to fix the supports. After Zeller lowered the assembly, he concluded that the iris arms worked properly even after the Wyoming winter and despite the luminaire-to-ring support failure. On his way back to Ohio, Zeller stopped in Cheyenne and sought state approval for purchase of the iris arm device as fulfilling the original contract. In April, 1972, Wyoming officials inspected the device and authorized payment. The rest area was opened to the public in June, 1972.

Meanwhile, on February 7, 1972, Zeller had begun pursuing an iris arm design for two-foot diameter poles. Manville subsequently delayed shipments of lowering devices so that the new iris arms could be included. On March 10, 1972, Manville approved the iris arms for commercial use. Manville began notifying its sales staff of the decision to use the iris arms on March 15, 1972, and the iris arms first appeared in Manville's owners' manuals one week later. On April 20, 1972, Manville installed an iris arm in Nebraska. A patent application was filed on February 5, 1973, that later issued as the '333 patent.

[Paramount copied the Zeller/Manville design.] Manville filed suit against Paramount alleging infringement of the '333 patent. The district court concluded that the '333 patent was not invalid under 35 U.S.C. § 102(b) due to an on sale or public use bar because Manville's Wyoming activities constituted experimental use. Accordingly, the court entered judgment against Appellants and awarded damages to Manville.

In order to determine whether an invention was on sale or in public use, we must consider how the totality of the circumstances comports with the policies underlying the on sale and public use bars. This approach is necessary because "the policies or purposes underlying the on sale bar, in effect, define it." On the facts of the instant case, these underlying policies do not support the invalidation of the '333 patent because of an on sale or public use bar, nor can we conclude that the district court's underlying fact findings were clearly erroneous.

First, Manville did nothing to lead the public to believe that its iris arm invention was in "the public domain." On the contrary, Manville conveyed to a Wyoming official that its use of the invention on one pole at one site in Wyoming was experimental. Although Manville did not advise anyone else that its use was experimental and was not intended to release its invention into the public domain, the particular circumstances made such efforts unnecessary. Manville marked its design drawing with a confidentiality notice before disclosing it to a Wyoming official, and Wyoming law prohibited officials from disclosing confidential information to the public. *Compare Hycor Corp. v. Schlueter Co.*, 740 F.2d 1529, 1535, 222 U.S.P.Q. (BNA) 553, 558 (Fed. Cir. 1984) (affirming a section 102(b) bar and noting that users lacked any secrecy obligations). Additionally, the invention was mounted atop a 150-foot tall pole in a rest area still closed to the public, making it very unlikely that the public would even see the new design. We therefore conclude that there was no conduct by Manville that would lead the "public" to reasonably believe the invention was in the public domain. Nor is there any indication that the public had such a perception.

Second, Manville did not attempt to extend the patent term by commercially exploiting its invention more than one year before it filed a patent application. Manville retained ownership of the lowering device and did not notify its sales personnel about the invention, or initiate a sales campaign to market the iris arm design until March of 1972, after it first determined, based on inspecting the Fort Steele device, that the iris arms worked for their intended purpose. *Compare U.S. Environmental Products Inc. v. Westall*, 911 F.2d 713, 15 U.S.P.Q.2d (BNA) 1898 (Fed. Cir. 1990) (affirming a section 102(b) bar and noting the patent holder did not retain control over the invention and initiated promotional efforts during the asserted experimental use period). Moreover, although Manville eventually received compensation for the iris arm device in fulfillment of its original contract with Wyoming, a sale that is primarily for experimental purposes, as opposed to commercial exploitation, does not raise an on sale bar. *See Baker Oil Tools, Inc. v. Geo Vann, Inc.*, 828 F.2d 1558, 1563, 4 U.S.P.Q.2d (BNA) 1210, 1213 (Fed. Cir. 1987). Because Manville did not attempt to use the invention when it first bid on the Wyoming contract, and did not offer to sell the iris arm to anyone else until after it was tested in the cold, rain, snow, and wind — an environment in which it was designed to operate — we must agree with the district court that experimentation, and not profit, was the primary motive behind Manville's Wyoming use.

Finally, Manville's actions are entirely consistent with the policy "favoring prompt and widespread disclosure of inventions." The iris arm device was specifically designed to withstand year around weather. Prior to its testing in the winter environment, there really was no basis for confidence by the inventor that the invention would perform as intended, and hence no proven invention to disclose. The evidence indicates, moreover, that once the outdoor tests were complete, and the invention was found to work as intended, Manville acted within the statutorily prescribed period in disclosing the invention, once tested, to the public.

Contrary to Appellants' argument, merely because Manville also tested the invention briefly in Ohio does not mean Manville had ascertained whether the invention was operable for its intended purpose in its intended environment. When durability in an outdoor environment is inherent to the purpose of an invention, then further testing to determine the invention's ability to serve that purpose will not subject the invention to a section 102(b) bar. *See City of Elizabeth v. American Nicholson Pavement Co.*

Nor is this a case of a patentee attempting, after the fact, to portray his earlier actions as experimental use. As the district court correctly found, a Manville internal company memorandum, dated February 29, 1972, makes clear that at the time of the Wyoming activities, Manville considered them to be experimental. The memo, captioned "State of Wyo — Our experimental HMO installation," discussed problems with the installation, referring to "the 100 m.p.h. steady winds that area can experience," and noting that "forces occur on top of that pole that cannot be factory tested."

Accordingly, we conclude that Appellants have failed to establish a "public use or on sale" bar to the granting of a valid patent under section 102(b).

Affirmed in part and reversed in part.

NOTES

1. *TP Labs. v. Professional Positioners, Inc.*, 724 F.2d 965, 220 U.S.P.Q. (BNA) 577 (Fed. Cir. 1984), presented the Federal Circuit with another set of on-sale facts. The plaintiff/patentee admitted that the inventor — a Dr. H. Kesling — used the claimed dental appliance on three orthodontal patients before the critical date, but asserted that its use was experimental. In the course of its opinion, the Federal Circuit court stated:

[A] pledge of confidentiality is indicative of the inventor's continued control which here is established inherently by the dentist-patient relationship of the parties. Nothing in the inventor's use of the device on his patients (or the transfer to them) is inconsistent with experimentation. Similarly, the routine checking of patients by one of the other ... orthodontists does not indicate the inventor's lack of control or abandonment to the public.

The patient records discussed above indicate that treatment to correct such orthodontal irregularities can range from two to six years. Moreover, while results appeared to be good within six months' use by one patient, the variable of patient cooperation cannot be checked by one patient alone. Use on three patients is not an obviously excessive number. In other words, the test for success of the improvement was not whether it could be used at all, but whether it could be said to work better on patients than a positioner without [its main feature]. Again, as in *City of Elizabeth*, the test of necessity had to run for a considerable time and on several patients before the inventor could know whether "it was what he claimed it to be" and would "answer the purpose intended."

A factor in favor of the patentee is that during this critical time the inventor had readily available all of the facilities of TP to commercially exploit the device. Yet, no positioners [meeting the terms of the claims] were offered [to] competing orthodontists, despite the fact this was one facet of the inventor's total business activity. Further, the inventor made no extra charge for fitting the three patients with the improved positioners, although that in itself is not critical. The facts here indicate the inventor was testing the device, not the market. No commercial exploitation having been made to even a small degree prior to filing the patent application, the underlying policy of prohibiting an extension of the term is clearly not offended in this respect.

Indeed, none of the policies which underlie the public use bar and which, in effect, define it have been shown to be violated. At most, the record shows that the uses were not secret, but when the evidence as to the facts of use by the inventor is considered as a whole, we conclude that appellees failed to prove that the inventor made a public use of the subject invention within the meaning of 35 U.S.C. § 102(b). The patent may not be held invalid on this ground.

See also United States Envtl. Prods., Inc. v. Westall, 911 F.2d 713, 715-16, 15 U.S.P.Q.2d (BNA) 1898 (Fed. Cir. 1990) (contract between inventor and city which forbade experiments on installed unit without city engineer's permission led to finding of no experimental use and thus statutory bar).

2. The close relationship between reduction to practice under § 102(b) and experimental use should be apparent at this point. If a device has been reduced to practice, it logically follows that no more experimentation was necessary to see that the device worked as intended.

This issue came up in an interesting context in *Baker Oil Tools, Inc. v. Geo-Vann, Inc.*, 828 F.2d 1558, 4 U.S.P.Q.2d (BNA) 1210 (Fed. Cir. 1987). In this case the patentee had asserted, in connection with an interference proceeding, that prior to June 7, 1971, it had achieved a reduction to practice of certain versions of the claimed device, a gravel-packing machine used in oil drilling. Baker filed for a patent on February 17, 1972. The trial court held that the reduction to practice established a public use or on sale bar, in light of evidence that the patentee had tested the device before February of 1971 at well sites where it was doing work for Chevron and Signal Oil Corporation. The Federal Circuit reversed this aspect of the trial court's ruling:

> We agree with Baker Oil that the district court erred in law in its interpretation of these interference proceedings. Baker Oil's assertion before the PTO that the early device was reduced to practice should not have been given preclusive or estoppel effect. It may of course be considered as a factor in determining whether the pre-critical date uses were indeed primarily experimental, ... and Baker Oil concedes in its brief that appellees "are entitled to use the statements made in the interference as some evidence tending to refute assertions of experimentation," but it did not of itself establish that a completed invention existed at that time.

828 F.2d at 1562. On reduction to practice as an issue under the "on sale" bar, see *UMC Electronics*, and notes, above.

3. An important early Federal Circuit case is *In re Smith*, 714 F.2d 1127, 1135, 218 U.S.P.Q. (BNA) 976, 983 (Fed. Cir. 1983). In *Smith*, the Court of Appeals for the Federal Circuit invalidated a patent, finding a market test of a consumer good to be a barring "public use." The court cited as crucial to its decision the fact that the inventor was not constantly present to monitor the distribution, the lack of confidentiality agreements with the participants, the testing of features unclaimed in the patent application, and the fact that the prototype which was tested underwent little change in its evolution into the final product. Using the purpose test, the court refused to characterize the market testing as experimental, finding instead that it was commercially exploitative. It was pointed out in a dissent by Judge Nichols that it is almost impossible for a court to draw a line between "market" and "product" testing. *Id.* at 1138-39 (Nichols, J., dissenting). In this regard, see *Johnson & Johnson v. Kendall Co.*, 215 F. Supp. 124 (N.D. Ill. 1963) (distribution of free samples; experimental use upheld), *rev'd on other grounds*, 327 F.2d 391 (7th Cir.), *cert. denied*, 377 U.S. 934 (1964).

4. There is a fair-sized literature on the on-sale problem, reflecting both its popularity as a defense and the recent spate of cases dealing with it. *See* Welch, *Patent Law's Ephemeral Experimental Use Doctrine*, 11 U. TOLEDO L. REV. 865-92 (1980); Note, *The Public Use Bar to Patentability: Two New Approaches* *to the Experimental Use Exception*, 52 MINN. L. REV. 851 (1968); Pigott, *The Concepts of Public Use and Sale*, 49 J. PAT. OFF. SOC'Y 399, 411-26 (1967).

From *Lough v. Brunswick Corp.*, 86 F.3d 1113, 39 U.S.P.Q.2d 1100 (Fed. Cir. 1996):

[Plaintiff, the holder of U.S. Patent 4,848,775 for seal assemblies in the stern drive portion of inboard/outboard boat motors[10] sued the alleged infringer. After the trial court entered judgment on a jury verdict in favor of the patent holder, the Federal Circuit, per Judge Lourie, held that the patent was invalid under the public use bar, despite plaintiff's evidence that public use prior to the critical date was for experimental purposes.]

Neither party disputes that Lough's prototypes were in use before the critical date. Thus, both parties agree that the issue presented on appeal is whether the jury properly decided that the use of Lough's six prototypes in 1986, prior to the critical date, constituted experimental use so as to negate the conclusion of public use. Whether an invention was in public use prior to the critical date within the meaning of § 102(b) is a question of law.

To determine whether a use is "experimental," a question of law, the totality of the circumstances must be considered, including various objective indicia of experimentation surrounding the use, such as the number of prototypes and duration of testing, whether records or progress reports were made concerning the testing, the existence of a secrecy agreement between the patentee and the party performing the testing, whether the patentee received compensation for the use of the invention, and the extent of control the inventor maintained over the testing.... The last factor of control is critically important, because, if the inventor has no control over the alleged experiments, he is not experimenting. If he does not inquire about the testing or receive reports concerning the results, similarly, he is not experimenting.

In order to justify a determination that legally sufficient experimentation has occurred, there must be present certain minimal indicia. The framework might be quite formal, as may be expected when large corporations conduct experiments, governed by contracts and explicit written obligations. When individual inventors or small business units are involved, however, less formal and seemingly casual experiments can be expected. Such less formal experiments may be deemed legally sufficient to avoid the public use bar, but only if they demonstrate the presence of the same basic elements that are required to validate any experimental program. Our case law sets out these elements.

---

[10] Special thanks to F. Bruce Merges, Sr., of BayFlite Marine, Fort Lauderdale, Florida, whose family business technical training program — in particular, the special boat washing internship — allowed the author to understand the finer points of boats and motors.

Here, Lough either admits or does not dispute the following facts. In the spring of 1986, he noted that the upper seal assembly in Brunswick inboard/outboard boats was failing due to galvanic corrosion between the annular seal and the aperture provided for the upper seal assembly in the aluminum bell housing. He solved this problem by isolating the annular seal from the aluminum bell housing in order to prevent corrosion. After some trial and error, Lough made six prototypes. He installed the first prototype in his own boat. Lough testified at trial that after the first prototype had been in his boat for three months and he determined that it worked, he provided the other prototypes to friends and acquaintances in order to find out if the upper seal assemblies would work as well in their boats as it had worked in his boat. Lough installed one prototype in the boat of his friend, Tom Nikla. A prototype was also installed in the boat of Jim Yow, co-owner of the dealership where Lough worked. Lough installed a fourth prototype in [the boat of] one of the dealership's customers who had considerable problems with corrosion in his stern drive unit. The final two prototypes were given to friends who were employed at a different marina in Florida. These friends installed one prototype in the boat of Mark Liberman, a local charter guide. They installed the other prototype in a demonstration boat at their marina. Subsequently, this boat was sold. Neither Lough nor his friends knew what happened with either the prototype or the demonstration boat after the boat was sold. After providing the five prototypes to these third parties, Lough neither asked for nor received any comments concerning the operability of these prototypes.

Accepting that the jury found these facts, which either were undisputed or were as asserted by Lough, it cannot be reasonably disputed that Lough's use of the invention was not "experimental" so as to negate a conclusion of public use. It is true that Lough did not receive any compensation for the use of the prototypes. He did not place the seal assembly on sale before applying for a patent. Lough's lack of commercialization, however, is not dispositive of the public use question in view of his failure to present objective evidence of experimentation. Lough kept no records of the alleged testing.... He provided the seal assemblies to friends and acquaintances, but without any provision for follow-up involvement by him in assessment of the events occurring during the alleged experiments, and at least one seal was installed in a boat that was later sold to strangers. Thus, Lough did not maintain any supervision and control over the seals during the alleged testing.

Lough argues that other evidence supports a finding that his uses were experimental, including his own testimony that the prototypes were installed for experimental purposes and the fact that the prototypes were used in such a manner that they were unlikely to be seen by the public.... In addition, the fact that the prototypes were unlikely to be seen by the public does not support Lough's position. As the Supreme Court stated in *Egbert v. Lippmann*:

[S]ome inventions are by their very character only capable of being used where they cannot be seen or observed by the public eye. [...]

We therefore hold that the jury had no legal basis to conclude that the uses of Lough's prototypes were experimental and that the prototypes were not in public use prior to the critical date. Our holding is consistent with the policy underlying the experimental use negation, that of providing an inventor time to determine if the invention is suitable for its intended purpose, i.e., to reduce the invention to practice. Lough's activities clearly were not consistent with that policy.

PLAGER, CIRCUIT JUDGE, dissenting.

This is not a contest between Evinrude (Outboard Marine Corporation) and Mercury Marine (Brunswick), the two big competitors in this field, to see who can market a better engine. If it were, we could expect the combination of engineering and legal staffs on each side to be punctilious about observing the niceties of our prior opinions on how to conduct experiments so as to avoid any possible running afoul of the public use bar. No, this is a home-made improvement by a man with only a high school education who worked on boats and boat engines, including his own, where he kept encountering the problem with these shaft seals that Mercury Marine had failed to solve. He solved it by trial and error, with an ingenious bushing of his own design, and, on his grandfather's metal lathe, after several tries, fashioned a half-dozen prototype seals that looked like they might do the job.

Of course it would have been better for all concerned (except perhaps for Mercury Marine) if Mr. Lough had read our prior opinions before he became an inventor. Then he might have kept detailed lab notes setting out the problem and the possible solutions, and he wisely would have obtained written confidentiality agreements from those allowed to see or use his prototypes. Had he studied our cases first, he no doubt would have developed a detailed questionnaire for the persons to whom he provided the seals, and he would have insisted on periodic written reports. In other words, he would have put in the set of tight controls the majority would have wanted. Instead, he did what seemed appropriate in the setting in which he worked: he waited to hear from his test cases what problems might emerge, and, hearing none, at least none that convinced him he was on the wrong track, he accepted some friendly advice and proceeded to patent his invention.

Yes, he failed to conduct his testing, his experiments, with the careful attention we lawyers, with our clean and dry hands, have come to prefer. But, under all the facts and circumstances, it is more likely than not that he was testing and perfecting his device, rather than simply making it available gratis to members of the general public for what the law calls "public use.'" The jury chose to accept Lough's view of the events, and under that view there was more than enough evidence to support a jury finding that he was testing and perfecting his invention during much of the period leading up to the time he applied for his patent.

NOTE

Good Cases Make Hard Law. If you were the judge in this case, how would you have decided it? Should it matter that the inventor, Lough, was a "little guy" and not employed by a major boat company? Should patent law make extra concessions for small inventors, who are not "repeat players" in the patent game, and may not have the resources to research legal requirements and comply with them? (Note the special filing fees and other reduced administrative fees for small inventors in 35 U.S.C. § 41 (fees, etc.)). Would flexible doctrine for small inventors lead to inconsistent results and strategic behavior by large players?

NOTE, THE VALIDITY OF PATENTS AFTER MARKET TESTING: A NEW AND IMPROVED EXPERIMENTAL USE DOCTRINE?, 85 Colum. L. Rev. 371 (1985)

The cost of developing and introducing new products is enormous and the rate of new product failure is alarmingly high.[1] Academicians and marketing professionals point to inadequate or ineffective product and market testing as one of the causes of these problems.[2] Current law discourages market testing, however, by excluding it from the category of experimentation considered permissible prior to patent application. Certain products by their nature require experimentation outside the laboratory; the law as currently interpreted tends to discriminate against these products by creating a high risk that experimentation outside the lab will result in the later invalidation of a patent.

Due to a high product failure rate, the costs of national new product launches are enormous. It is also very expensive to determine a product's optimal market positioning and bundle of product features. Why not encourage market testing techniques that by discovering product flaws and suggesting product modifications before launch, prevent wasteful expenditure of resources on products that may prove to be unsuccessful? Many products benefit from both laboratory and market testing, and the cost of research arbitrarily confined solely to a laboratory setting "will be greater and the results less dependable" than that of a mixed experimen-

---

[1]See P. KOTLER, MARKETING MANAGEMENT 310-12 (1983); Crawford, *Marketing Research and the New Product Failure Rate*, 41 J. MARKETING 51-61 (1977); N.Y. TIMES, Oct. 12, 1983, at D12, col. 2.

[2]See G. URBAN & J. HAUSER, DESIGN AND MARKETING OF NEW PRODUCTS 31-59 (1980) (discussing how successfully to develop, test, and launch new products). A major form of product testing is market testing outside of the laboratory. This Note refers to in home use or industrial site tests and tests at simulated home or industrial use sites, collectively, as "market tests." In contrast, full-scale sales efforts for a new product restricted to one or more geographical markets — test markets — are referred to as "test marketing."

tal program that also includes a typical in-home, on-site, or simulated use test. Indeed, a highly respected empirical study of the new product development process has determined that market testing all new products prior to full-scale test marketing saves in excess of one million dollars and six months of development time for each new product.[3]

Allowing the inventor the time to perfect his invention benefits both the inventor and society. Society has an interest in receiving inventions that have been perfected. Under existing law, however, an inventor fearing that his activity could be deemed a barring public use might have to apply for a patent prematurely, and only then do his experimentation and market testing. If imperfect inventions are rushed to the patent office or into the marketplace without adequate experimentation, the inventor may eventually find that he has patented a worthless concept, or, if he later improves upon his invention, he may be forced to apply for a series of patents or to modify his original application through a continuation-in-part proceeding. Because of the uncertainty of a continuation-in-part proceeding, the inventor may have his patent invalidated as a result of an earlier, but unintentional, public use. Forcing the inventor to apply for a series of patents is also problematic because it may result in inadequate patent protection, and if the patent protection available is not effective and predictable, society will receive fewer inventions.

Market testing can have three different purposes: to gather feedback on the product, to gauge demand, and to stimulate demand. Only the first two activities are experimental and therefore ought to be entitled to the protection of the experimental use doctrine.

If the market testing is shown to have an experimental purpose and is deemed not commercially exploitative, the inventor may still be subject to a claim of detrimental public reliance. At this stage the publicness of use becomes crucial to the analysis, and the publicness issue should be explicitly analyzed by the courts. Inventors must show that the type of testing undertaken meets the reasonableness test, which balances the likelihood of detrimental public reliance against the possibility of effectively testing the product in a nonpublic setting. An inventor's testimony on the lack of satisfactory nonpublic testing alternatives should be given weight on this issue.

There are market tests in which the chance of detrimental public reliance is negligible and in which confidentiality pledges and inventor presence would ruin the spontaneity of the tests and thereby undermine their effectiveness. In the typical case, a manufacturer distributes samples of a possibly patentable product to a selected group of potential home users. Even without the secrecy restrictions and inventor presence there is little chance of detrimental public reliance because these users generally cannot manufacture the product and are not likely to communicate with persons who can. If reverse engineering is not possible then

---

[3]G. URBAN & J. HAUSER, *supra* note [2] at 57-58.

certainly the degree of publicness is of little concern. Different considerations exist in an industrial setting where the tester-users or plant visitors may be actual or potential competitors of the inventor or prospective customers with manufacturing capabilities. In these cases, security precautions such as secrecy agreements, inventor presence, and careful collection of all unused samples or prototypes may be necessary to avoid detrimental public reliance.

The number of claims based on alleged detrimental public reliance could be reduced by providing for a patent office-sanctioned system of notice to third parties similar to the current patent pending and patent issued markings.[4] A simple marking reading "patent to be applied for" would go a long way toward eliminating the possibility that detrimental public reliance would occur during the experimental process.

[I]f commercial exploitation during product development occurs for a period longer than the one year statutory grace period, it is illogical to invalidate his patent under the public use bar if the inventor can be prevented from extending the seventeen year life of his patent. Rather than invalidating the entire patent because of the possibility that the inventor may get more than seventeen years of protected commercial exploitation, it is more sensible to uphold the validity of the patent and focus instead on preventing the extension. This could be accomplished by forcing patent applicants to make an election on their patent applications: either choose to follow the traditional pattern — granting them seventeen years of protection from the date of patent award — or choose to have the seventeen years run from the date of application. If an inventor were to choose the latter alternative he would be allowed to protect himself from public use bar claims based on commercial exploitation by filing his application earlier, upon reduction to practice of any patentable subject matter. The inventor then could experiment while continuing commercial exploitation.

NOTES

1. The author of the preceding Note (written before the patent term was changed to 20 years from filing) states that continuation-in-part applications are no solution to the market testing dilemma, because of the "uncertainty of a continuation proceeding," i.e., the possible effect of the "new matter" rule of 35 U.S.C. § 120 ("[N]ew matter" is matter "involving a departure from or an addition to the original disclosure." 37 C.F.R. § 1.118(a) (1996)). New matter is only entitled to the filing date of the CIP application and not the filing date of the original or "parent" application. *See In re Scheiber*, 587 F.2d 59 (C.C.P.A. 1978). This suggests that in the cases the author is worried about, priority of invention may be sacrificed if an applicant cannot claim the benefit of an earlier filing date — which, in turn, suggests that others are working in the same field. If those making the

---

[4] There is little danger of improper use because, already, the markings of "patent applied for" and "patent pending" cannot be used under false pretenses. See 35 U.S.C. § 292 (1982).

prior art disclosures which create the applicant's need for early priority are competitors of the applicant, they will surely be introducing products of their own onto the market. Because of this, the public would seem to be on the verge of receiving the new and improved product that is the subject of the CIP application. Why should the public in effect protect the inventor against intervening prior art by granting a patent, when the applicant's competitors are about to introduce the same product on the market, perhaps without even seeking a patent? In other words, why preserve the priority of an applicant who is disposed to test her product extensively when another inventor is willing to publicize, and perhaps market, her invention at or near the same time as the applicant?

2. Regarding the author's proposals for legislative change, note that two key policies are addressed: preventing detrimental public reliance, and preventing an unwarranted extension of the patent term. Do they also address the other relevant policies in this area: permitting the patentee time to evaluate the invention, and favoring prompt and widespread disclosure of inventions? As to this latter policy, note the author's insistence that testing need not be done in a way that discloses the features of the product to the public. It would seem, then, that a long "grace period" for market testing would protect an inventor while keeping the details of the invention from the public. Do the benefits of such disclosure outweigh the costs identified by the author in an on-sale rule that reduces the incentive to conduct market testing on products? Recall the discussion of the key importance of the *disclosure* of technological information in patent law in Chapter 1. But keep in mind also that long pendency in the Patent Office, an accepted fact of life, probably does much more to dampen disclosure than any pre-market (secret) testing an applicant may do.

e. Third Party Statutory Bar Activity

GENERAL ELECTRIC CO. v. UNITED STATES

654 F.2d 55, 211 U.S.P.Q. (BNA) 867 (Ct. Cl. 1981)

This suit is brought by plaintiff, General Electric Company (GE), seeking reasonable and entire compensation for the alleged unauthorized use by or for the United States of the invention described in and covered by United States Patent No. 3,203,259 (' 259 patent).

United States Patent No. 3,203,259 (the "Lemmerman patent"), entitled "Viscous Damped Sensing Device," issued on August 31, 1965 in the name of Harold H. P. Lemmerman as the sole inventor, on an application filed December 31, 1956. GE is, and has been since the issuance thereof, the assignee and sole owner of the Lemmerman patent.

GE alleged in its petition that the invention covered by the Lemmerman patent has been manufactured or used by or for the Government in connection with gyroscopes furnished by [five contractors].

The Government filed its answer, denying infringement and validity. The Government [amended its answer and] amplified its pleading with respect to the alleged sale or offering for sale of devices covered by the patent, by GE and others, more than a year prior to the date on which the application for patent was filed by GE.

Defendant contends that the invention covered by each claim of the '259 patent was in public use or on sale by Control Engineering Corporation (CEC) prior to December 31, 1955 (more than 1 year prior to the December 31, 1956 filing date of the '259 patent application). Accordingly, defendant contends that all claims in the patent are invalid under § 102(b) of the Patent Act. We accept that argument (and therefore go no further).

The evidence establishes that in 1954, CEC began developing a rate gyro designated as the GR-J1.

The drawings and the unrebutted testimony of many witnesses clearly established that the GR-J1 had complementary rotor and stator vanes which cooperated with a low viscosity fluid to provide the required damping force. The correspondence between the GR-J1 and the invention recited in the '259 patent was so obvious that plaintiff conceded prior to trial that claims 1-7, 12, 13, and 15 read on the GR-J1 gyro. Accordingly, with respect to these claims, anticipation is conclusively established, provided the gyros were on sale or sold prior to December 31, 1955. [The court also finds that the devices produced by CEC met the limitations of other claims in the '259 patent.]

If it is found that the GR-J1 model was "on sale," within the meaning of 35 U.S.C. § 102(b), more than a year prior to the filing of the Lemmerman patent application, all claims of the patent which read on the GR-J1 are invalid.

The evidence established that, during the manufacture of the early production lot of GR-J1 gyros, CEC personnel visited a number of potential customers across the country in an effort to obtain orders for CEC's new GR-J1 gyro. As a result of this effort, CEC subsequently received orders from seven different companies for the purchase of one or more GR-J1 gyroscopes. With the exception of one order which was cancelled prior to delivery, all orders were filled by delivery of GR-J1 gyroscopes prior to December 31, 1955, which period is more than a year prior to the filing date of the Lemmerman application.

For each completed sale, CEC made about a 20-25 percent profit over the cost of components and assembly labor. Thus, it is evident that the items were not experimental or undeveloped devices. They were priced for sale and sold in a competitive market.

[P]laintiff contends that some of the deliveries were on a consignment basis and, therefore, were not sales. However, not all of the orders were filled on a consignment basis. Since some were actually sold, the bar is created, since it is well established that even a single sale is sufficient to invalidate a patent under § 102(b) of the Patent Act, see, e. g., *Tool Research & Engineering Corp. v. Honcor Corp.*, 367 F.2d 449, 453, 151 U.S.P.Q. 236, 241 (9th Cir. 1966), *cert. denied*, 387 U.S. 919, 87 S. Ct. 2032, 18 L. Ed. 2d 972 (1967). Moreover, the mere fact that a sale is made conditional upon the subjective satisfaction of the buyer or that the item is shipped on a consignment basis, does not automatically remove the transaction from either a sale or "on sale" within the meaning of section 102(b).

[The court discusses the policies behind the on-sale bar.] Where the sale is by one other than the inventor (one not under the inventor's control), it would seem that the policy against extended commercial exploitation and the policy favoring the filing of only worthwhile inventions could be said not to apply. Nevertheless, it is well established that a placing of the invention "on sale" by an unrelated third party more than 1 year prior to the filing of an application for patent by another has the effect under § 102(b) of invalidating a patent directed to that invention. See, e.g., *CTS Corp. v. Piher International Corp.*, 527 F.2d 95, 102, 188 U.S.P.Q. 419, 425 (7th Cir. 1975), *cert. denied*, 424 U.S. 978, 96 S. Ct. 1485, 47 L. Ed. 2d 748 (1976). Accordingly, Congress should be held to have concluded, at the least, that the policy against removing inventions from the public domain and the policy favoring early patent filing are of sufficient importance in and of themselves to invalidate a patent where the invention is sold by one other than the inventor or one under his control.

The record reveals that CEC's so-called "paddle-damping" gyro on which, as we have said, the Lemmerman claims read, was adequately reduced to practice prior to CEC's pre-December 31, 1955 sales and offers-to-sell. The device was plainly shown to be operable and useable commercially, at least in non-combat conditions, which is enough for our purposes because the Lemmerman claims do not recite a specific use and that invention, as claimed, may be used in non-military and non-combat systems.

For these reasons, the '259 patent is invalid, under Section 102(b), because the invention was on sale and in public use in this country more than one year prior to the application date of the patent (December 31, 1956).

NOTES

1. Rationale. One commentator argues that the two § 102(b) policies identified by the court in *General Electric* — avoidance of detrimental public reliance and encouragement of early patent filing/disclosure — are not in fact advanced when third-party on-sale activity is allowed to operate as a statutory bar. *See* Pitlick, *"On Sale" Activities of an Independent Third Party Inventor, Or — Whose Widget Is It?*, 64 J. PAT. OFF. SOC'Y 138 (1982). Pitlick argues that the early disclosure rationale "would frustrate the policy of giving an inventor a one year grace period in which to file a patent application after he has put the invention 'on sale.'" *Id.* at 151. As to the reliance argument, he states: "As this policy relates to *public* reliance, it is clear that third party 'on sale' activities, before they may bar the inventor-applicant or patentee, must be such that that part of the public which would have an interest in the subject matter, becomes informed of the invention." (Emphasis in original; footnote omitted.) The author goes on to call for a change in third-party on-sale cases: permit only *public* on-sale activities involving reduced-to-practice inventions to operate as a statutory bar. Although this treatment is admittedly different from that of first-party on-sale cases, it is argued that the change is supported by the reliance policy; without public sales, there is no opportunity for the public to begin relying on the free availability of the invention, and thus no chance that anyone's reliance will be frustrated when a patent issues on the invention based on a patent application filed more than a year after the third-party on-sale activity. *Cf. W.L. Gore & Assocs. v. Garlock, Inc.*, 721 F.2d 1540, 1548, 220 U.S.P.Q. (BNA) 303 (1983) ("There is no reason or statutory basis, however, on which Budd's and Cropper's [third party] secret commercialization of a process, if established, could be held a bar to the grant of a patent to Gore on that process.").

2. *Reduction to Practice*. Of course, the discussion of reduction to practice in the preceding case, and in the Pitlick article just cited, came before *UMC Electronics*, *supra*. Should a reduction to practice be required even after *UMC* in "third-party" on-sale cases?

3. *A Rare Bird?* Keep in mind that the facts in *General Electric* were rather unusual. Although the patentee sued the government for infringement, a substantial number of codefendants, drawn from the same industry as the patentee, were named in the suit as well. This made it possible for the defendant (the government) to thoroughly research a wide range of third-party activity involving the general area of technology at issue in the suit. This will seldom be the case; the average defendant will be hard-pressed to come up with evidence concerning the intimate details of product development at a number of firms that compete with the patentee. This is perhaps one reason why evidence of third-party sale and use is rarely introduced in patent cases.

To the extent that such evidence can be found, it will be expensive to find. There are of course no public records of such information, unless published accounts of development efforts can be located, and third-party firms can usually be expected to keep such information from the public to protect trade secrets, among other reasons. As a consequence, it will be costly to ferret out such information by third-party interrogatories, depositions, and the like.

If this is true, it can be surmised that only in the most critical cases — perhaps those with potentially huge damage awards looming — will an effort be made to locate such evidence. In terms of the economic "search" model described in Section B.4 above, a patent infringement defendant will be willing to invest in the search for such information only if the benefit — in the form of reduced losses due to not losing the infringement suit — makes it worthwhile. For this reason alone, although cases involving this issue can be expected to be rare, they can also be expected to be high-damage cases, where a large amount of money is at stake.

4. SUMMARY

§§ 102(a) and (b) Prior Art Chart & Problems

Table 4-1 is a chart designed to help you identify the categories of prior art under §§ 102(a) and (b), and keep track of their various reqirements.

102	Was Invention:	By:	In:	Before:	If yes:
					N
a	known	others	U.S.	date of invention	O
a	used	others	U.S.	date of invention	
a	patented	others	any country	date of invention	P
a	published	others	any country	date of invention	A
b	patented	anybody	any country	1 year prior to filing	T
b	published	anybody	any country	1 year prior to filing	E
b	in public use	anybody	U.S.	1 year prior to filing	N
b	on sale	anybody	U.S.	1 year prior to filing	T

Table 4-1

The following problems should help you review this material, to be sure you understand it.

PROBLEMS

Statement

Alice, an engineer, and her lab assistant Beverly, work for a large American auto manufacturer. Believing there is a long-felt need in the marketplace for American cars with the safety records of some European cars, Alice sets out to build less expensive and easier to install airbags. Alice begins her experiments in January of 1992. She knows other car manufacturers all over the world are working on similar experiments. Late on the evening of April 14, 1992, just after Beverly has left for the night, Alice hits on what she believes to be the right mix of material and design.

Due to delays in the legal department of the car manufacturer, a patent is not filed until June 15, 1993.

Will any of the following activities create problems under 102(a) and 102(b)?

1. Alice's employer began experimentation with the airbag in May of 1992.

2. Alice's employer installed the new airbag into its show cars displayed at the annual Detroit Auto Show. The show was attended by over 100,000 people and press from around the world in the period between June 1-14, 1992. The airbag was not described or deployed at the show.

3. "Merciless Bends," a German auto maker, developed a strikingly similar airbag in January of 1990. Management decided not to use the new airbag, at least for the time being.

4. Rhonda, a Japanese car manufacturer, also developed an airbag which closely resembled Alice's in May of 1992. Rhonda applied for a Japanese patent on June 1, 1992. The patent has not issued at this time.

5. Rhonda Car Co. applies for a U.S. patent in July of 1992. At that time, the company announces in commercials across the U.S. and Canada, "Rhonda is making it safer to drive." The commercial also depicts a 1993 Rhonda crashing into a wall and a dummy being saved from destruction by the deployment of a new airbag. A viewer could not tell the difference between the old and the new airbags, but the commercial goes on to say, "This is the new Rhonda TX4000 airbag, made with a new material and designed to be cheaper to install."

6. Not wanting to lose out to Rhonda once again, Alice's employer begins a widespread campaign to sell cars with its new airbag. The ad campaign begins July 16, 1992 and the first sale of a car with the new airbag is July 20, 1992. The car sold is a 1993 model.

7. In France, driving safety is becoming a large concern now that the British, who drive on the left side of the road, are coming through the Chunnel at alarming rates. The French daily *Le Monde* devotes half of the front page on June 1, 1992 to an article on new automotive safety devices. The article was submitted on April 1, and sent to engineers for review, before the June 1 publication date. Due to excellent investigative reporting, the article discloses that German auto makers came up with an inexpensive and easy to install airbag years ago, but never sought a patent on it, nor did they use it. Technical specifications for the airbag were printed on page 47 of the newspaper. Alice does not speak French.

8. Charlie, a plumber with a knack for inventing useful things, began working on an airbag for his own 1979 American car in 1989. He came up with a workable model and installed it himself in November 1989. When his daughter turned 16, he gave his old car to her, and bought a used 1984 American car for himself. He installed one of his airbags in that car as well.

9. Charlie's daughter was in an accident in February of 1992 and the airbag deployed, saving her life. The police at the scene were amazed a car so old could have an airbag. Charlie explained his invention to them and offered to install similar airbags at no charge in all police vehicles in their small community of Algonquit, Maine. The installations occurred on May 20, 1992.

Discussion

1. 102(a) — No problems here. Activity comes after date of invention, and, if Alice is involved, inventor cannot defeat her own novelty anyway.

    102(b) — No statutory bars. Assuming the experimentation is secret, it does not fall under element 102(b)[2][A], "in public use ... in this country." Even if not secret, there could be an experimental use exception.

2. 102(a) — The display of the cars with the airbags is after the date of invention, and is made by the inventor, so there is no novelty problem.

    102(b) — There are possible statutory bar problems. If the mere installation of an airbag is considered a public use, the car company will not be able to get the patent. *Compare Egbert, Manville Sales.* This is because of 102(b)[2][A] and [C]: the auto show was in the United States.

    If the installation is not considered a public use, though, there is no statutory bar problem here.

3. 102(a) — There is no *novelty* problem because although the airbag was invented by someone before Alice, the invention was not known or used publicly, elements 102(a)[1][A] and [B]. But § 102(g) *is* a problem.

    102(b) — There is no statutory bar, since Merciless Bends never applied for a patent nor did it use publicly or sell the device.

4. 102(a) — Rhonda's invention is in May 1992. This is after Alice's invention of January 1992, so there is no novelty problem.

    102(b) — There is no statutory bar, even though Rhonda applied for a patent in Japan. This is because under 102(b)[1][A][C], the patent would have to be issued somewhere in the world, not merely filed for, for there to be a statutory bar to Alice's application. *But cf.* § 102(e), described below in this chapter.

5. 102(a) — This activity comes after the date of invention; no problem.

    102(b) — Rhonda's ads do come under the 102(b)[B] category. The airbag is on sale within the meaning of the statute. The on-sale activity takes place in July, which is less than one year prior to Alice's application the following June. Therefore, there is no statutory bar.

6. 102(a) — An inventor cannot destroy her own novelty by her own work on the same invention, so novelty is not implicated.

    102(b) — Alice's employer puts the airbag "on sale" within the meaning of 102(b)[2][B] on July 16, 1992. This is less than one year prior to her filing date, so they do not create a statutory bar for themselves. But there is no *guarantee* of a full one-year grace period. To see how third parties can in effect shorten an inventor's grace period, imagine that the Rhonda Co. had begun its ad campaign in May of 1992, Alice's company would have one year from that date to file. Note that had Alice's company offered the car for sale 32 days earlier, its own activities would have prevented the issuance of a patent. It is of no consequence that the car was sold on July 20; the date the car was offered for sale is what is important in this case, because the offer came before the sale. It is also immaterial that the model year of the car was 1993.

7.   102(a) — The publication of the article comes after Alice's date of invention, so there appears to be no novelty problem. If the rule of *In re Schlittler* is applied, the sending of the article to reviewers before its formal publication will probably not matter; its effective date will be the publication date. Even if the author took no steps to keep secret his or her research for the article, and this research was therefore "public" in some minimal sense, this would at most be a public knowledge or use which is not prior art since not "in this country."

102(b) — There is a statutory bar here. The story in the French paper is a "description in a printed publication" "more than one year prior to application." This comes under 102(b)[1][B]. It is immaterial that the German company never applied for a patent and that Alice does not speak French. This activity is a statutory bar to Alice's patent application.

8.   102(a) — Charlie may have publicly used the same invention in the U.S. prior to Alice's invention. If so, her invention lacks novelty. The key question is whether installation of the airbag in his own car was a "public" use. It is likely that even if Charlie were the only person to ever ride in his car, his daughter probably transported friends in her car. Without any restrictions on the passengers, the use could be deemed public, even though the airbag was undetectable unless deployed. *See Egbert.*

102(b) — The use, if public, is also a statutory bar since it occurred more than one year prior to Alice's date of invention.

9.   102(a) — The deployment of the airbag is a public use of the invention prior to Alice's date of invention and so anticipates her invention, i.e., defeats its novelty.

102(b) — The public use, and the (arguable) offer to sell come more than a year before Alice files for her patent, and so will be a statutory bar. (The offers, if gratuitous, would trigger an interesting application of the policy-based analysis in cases such as *UMC Electronics*; query whether they were "offers for *sale*.")

Additional Questions

1. Given the above facts, and assuming Charlie has not applied for a patent by February of 1993, who gets a patent in the U.S. for the new airbags?

2. Who applies for and owns the patent for the airbag Alice invents?

3. Who is named the inventor on that application?

Answers

1. No one gets the patent. The French article prevents Alice from receiving a patent, Alice's prior invention prevents Rhonda from getting a patent in the U.S. and Charlie's activities were his own statutory bar.

2. Alice's employer applies for the patent, but she must be named an inventor. She very likely has signed a contract obligating her to assign the invention to the company; even without this, they may well own the rights under the theory that she has been "employed to invent" just such a device. If she has not signed an agreement, and she is deemed not one employed to invent, the company still retains the right to use the invention under the so-called "shop right." (These issues are discussed in more detail in Chapter 11, Section B, *Assignment and Ownership*.)

3. Alice and Beverly are probably both named as inventors. It is of no consequence that Beverly was not in the lab at the time Alice actually hit on the right design, if she contributed substantially to the design. Her contributions would probably be enough to include her as inventor. *See* 35 U.S.C. § 116.

F. SECTION 102(c): ABANDONMENT

MACBETH-EVANS GLASS CO. v. GENERAL ELECTRIC CO.

246 F. 695 (6th Cir. 1917)

This was a suit for infringement of letters patent reissue 13,766, bearing date July 7, 1914, to George A. Macbeth, assignor to Macbeth-Evans Glass Company. The invention relates to a "method and batch or mixture for making glass for illuminating purposes such as in electric and other shades and globes." According to the facts George A. Macbeth discovered and perfected the formula and process in issue prior to the fall of 1903. About the fall of that year, the appellant company (with which Macbeth was connected as president and stockholder) commenced to use the formula and process "as secret inventions for making illuminating glass," and thereafter continued such use until the application of Macbeth for the original letters patent (No. 1,097,600) was filed, May 9, 1913. Throughout this period the products of the formula and process were "put upon the market and sold in this country in large quantities as regular articles of trade and commerce."

In May, 1910, one of the plaintiff company's employees, who had been intrusted with the secrets of the invention set out in the reissued letters patent, left the company's employ and without its knowledge and in fraud of its rights disclosed these secrets to officials of the Jefferson Glass Company; and that company began a secret use of the invention and continued such use until after application was made for the patent as stated, May 9, 1913.

On the last-mentioned date, appellant commenced an action in the state of Pennsylvania, against its former employe and the Jefferson Glass Company, praying injunction against disclosures of the secrets to others and further manufacture and sale of glass under the secret formula and process.... [D]ecree was entered in that court enjoining defendants from making any glass "by substantially said secret process and formula and from disclosing the same to others." This decree was affirmed by the Supreme Court of Pennsylvania.

The instant case was heard below upon the facts thus in substance stated. The District Judge entered a decree adjudging the patent in suit to be void "because the discovery was used in the manner stated in the stipulation for almost ten years before the patent in suit was applied for, and was therefore abandoned, and also because the invention described in the patent was in public use more than two years prior to the application of (for) the patent"; accordingly, the bill was dismissed. The Macbeth-Evans Glass Company appeals.

The question is whether one who has discovered and perfected an invention can employ it secretly more than nine years for purposes only of profit, and then, upon encountering difficulty in preserving his secret, rightfully secure a patent, and thus in effect extend his previous monopoly for the further period fixed by the patent laws. Are both of these courses consistent with a reasonable interpretation of the constitutional provision and the statutes of the United States in relation to patents?

It is earnestly contended for appellant that its rights under the patent in issue are to be tested (1) by the use that was made of the invention, rather than of the product of the invention, prior to the application for a patent, and (2) by the acts if any of appellant and its assignor Macbeth, which would evince an intent to abandon the invention as distinguished from the right to patent the invention. The argument is that, when the acts of Macbeth and appellant are tested by the language of the patent laws, the secret use made of the invention could not have been a public use, and the constant effort made to preserve the secret was inconsistent with intent to abandon the invention; and consequently that the public use and the abandonment contemplated by the patent laws are inapplicable to the present case. The statutory provisions relied on are sections 4886 and 4920, Rev. Stat. (16 Stat. § 24). Section 4886 provides [a novelty requirement and a two year statutory bar.]

Section 4920 enumerates "special matters" which in an action for infringement may upon notice be proved under the general issue, and among them:

Fifth. That it [the invention or discovery] had been in public use or on sale in this country, for more than two years before his application for a patent, or had been abandoned to the public.

These provisions at once define a public purpose and the restrictions under which it is intended to be accomplished. The subject is a broad one; but the compass of the present case is restricted. No decision has come to our attention upon facts precisely like those here involved; in a word, the case is sui generis. It is not necessary, we may observe, to consider the portion of the decision below which deals with the question of public use. Our consideration will be limited to questions pertinent to abandonment.

In considering the subject of abandonment we assume that the patent is for a process which is not unitary with the product. If, indeed, this patent is for a process, and if the process and the product are distinct inventions separately patentable (as has been held in more or less analogous situations), there are some difficulties in the way of concluding that secret use of the process resulting in public use and sale of the product constitutes the statutory public use of the invention. It is these difficulties which we pass by when we make, for the purpose of the opinion, the assumption just stated [i.e., that public use of the product based on a process invention is not the issue in this case].

It is in substance urged for appellee that there is distinct inconsistency between the right to a trade secret and the right to a patent; and that Macbeth, having elected to use his invention as a trade secret for some ten years instead of applying for a patent, could not under settled principles of the doctrine of election turn around and assert the inconsistent right to a patent. Macbeth, like any inventor of a new and useful object, possessed the right to practice his invention in secret and for profit, though the secret was the sole source of protection for the invention. He had no right to exclude others from legitimate discovery and use of the invention, but he had an inchoate right to the exclusive use of the invention, which right, apart from the issues of the instant case, he might have perfected and made absolute by proceeding in the manner required by the patent laws; and while this was the only step open to him to secure the absolute right to exclude others, yet he failed to take the step. Hence the controversy as to inconsistency of rights must relate to the unpatented invention and so present the question, whether there is inconsistency between the right to practice an invention in secret without limit of time and for profit and the right to obtain a patent on the invention. Counsel for appellant say that these rights are different but not inconsistent. Such rights are important here only in their relation to a patentable invention. In this relation they seem to us to be inconsistent; inherently considered, their use can lead only to opposed ends — the one to reject and the other to seek a patent. The test of this will be aided by contrasting what was admittedly done in the exercise of the first of these rights with the claimed retention of the other.

When Macbeth perfected his invention in 1903 he and his company evidently concluded to control and use it for purposes of profit, and to work out these ends by practicing the invention in secret and placing the product on public sale. The plain object of such a course was to exclude others from using the invention and to secure its benefits for themselves. The adoption of this course signified by necessary implication a belief that the nature of the invention would enable them in this way to protect it for a substantial period of time, if not for a longer time than could be secured under the patent laws. The result shows that their belief was justified for a period of nearly ten years. True, it is admitted and rightly that the inventor and his company adopted and pursued this plan with knowledge that the invention, as already pointed out, furnished them no protection against use by others who might honestly discover it. This, however, inevitably concedes an intent either to abandon the right to secure protection under the patent laws, or to retain such right and if necessity should arise then to obtain through a patent a practical extension of any previous exclusive use (secured through secrecy) into a total period beyond the express limitation fixed by those laws. If the first of these hypotheses be the true one, it is not easy to see how the right to secure patent protection survived. The second hypothesis presents the two rights claimed and which it is said could not both be retained because of their inconsistency.

The conduct of the parties in carrying out the scheme of secret use and profit is appropriate evidence of its object and effect. It would be a contradiction to say that an inventor could both give up and hold the right to secure a patent. Here we have a continuous and uniform course of conduct for upwards of nine years; this would certainly be sufficient in any other sort of controversy to establish a definite intent; and, as if to accentuate their intent, the present inventor and his assignee engaged in serious litigation to maintain their scheme of secret use. It is impossible to see how such a course of conduct is reconcilable with a subsisting purpose to adhere to the right to secure a patent; it has every token of practical repudiation of such a purpose. Admittedly, we may repeat, these things were all done in the exercise of the right to adopt and pursue the scheme of secret use and profit; and it will not escape attention that the logic of this admission would lead to the same result as respects a purpose to retain the right to a patent if the plan had been pursued for a much longer time.

If then we assume that the course adopted by the present inventor and his assignee did not contemplate an intent to abandon the right to secure a patent, it certainly did contemplate an indefinite delay in disclosure of the invention and a practical and substantial enlargement of any period of monopoly recognized by statute. Can it be doubted that this was opposed to a declared and subsisting public policy?

Enough, however, has been shown of the practical construction and effect of the right to practice an invention in secret and for profit and the right to obtain a patent on the invention fairly to test the soundness of the claim that the rights are not inconsistent. They of course are now to be considered with reference to a scheme which includes an effort to secure a patent. And so regarded we may safely add to what we have already said of these rights that the first is in its nature and essence susceptible of exercise only in a way to evade, or at least unduly to delay, a disclosure of the invention in the interest of science and the useful arts, and with an intent to expand the statutory period of monopoly and thereby reap additional profits. The second is a means simply to acquire a monopoly subject to all the conditions and limitations of the patent laws. Such rights in our opinion are inconsistent in themselves — notably in the matter of profits available through use as distinguished from sale of the invention — and in their respective relations to the patent laws. It is not conceivable that an inventor can consistently hold both rights throughout the same period of time, where the design is to use them for purposes and with results like or similar to those here shown. We understand the rule of election to be broad enough to reach such rights as these. And we think that in this case Macbeth was put to a choice, an election.

True, as we have seen, it is contended that the efforts made here to preserve the secret were not reconcilable with an intent to abandon the invention. This is based on the theory that in the absence of intervening rights of other inventors a perfected invention may in point of time be indefinitely used in secret and for profit and also in entire consistency with the right to secure a patent on the invention; in a word, that persistence in such secret use, no matter for what length of time, will not justify an inference of abandonment of the invention. The abandonment contemplated by the patent laws naturally has reference to the advantages and protection alike which are obtainable under those laws. Abandonment in this sense must have been intended to signify a relinquishment of patent privileges. *Kendall v. Winsor*, 62 U.S. (21 How.) 322, 329 [(1858)].

Otherwise stated, abandonment of patent privileges is in every sense material to the patent laws tantamount to abandonment of the invention itself; and, of course, proof of such relinquishment or abandonment may be shown by conduct inconsistent with any other purpose.

Appellant also contends, it is true, that it is necessary to prove abandonment of the invention to the public. There could be no abandonment that would not inure to the benefit of the public, since the public could be the only possible beneficiary of such a relinquishment; this would be equally true if the invention were cast away or destroyed and the circumstances of the act or conduct of the inventor were consistent only with an intent to abandon the invention. This we think fairly accounts for the use of the words "had been abandoned to the public." Paragraph 5, § 4920. The views thus expressed are fortified by the rule that abandonment may take place at any time. *Elizabeth v. Pavement Co.* That rule differs and ought to differ from the statutory rule enacted with reference to the public use of an invention or the act of placing it on sale, since abandonment in itself signifies surrender of the right to a patent. This would seem to indicate a strong reason, if not the very reason, for the omission to prescribe a distinct period within which a patent must be applied for after an invention is perfected. Further, the fact that the public may in some such instances lose the advantages of inventions cannot impair the force and effect of the inventor's conduct, for in all instances abandonment in terms prevents the issue of a patent.

We are thus led to conclude that whatever view may be taken of the conditions existing at the time the patent in suit was applied for, the invention had been abandoned.

NOTES

1. *In Contrast*. The related case of *Kendall v. Windsor*, 62 U.S. (21 How.) 322 (1858), cited in the preceding case, was about a patent on a machine for making draft animal harnesses. The defendant, in an effort to invalidate plaintiff's patent, argued that plaintiff had commercialized harnesses made with the machine prior to filing for a patent, and had declared to several people that he preferred not to patent his invention. Plaintiff countered by arguing that he had indeed intended to obtain a patent, but that one of his employees had left with the design and given it to defendant, despite a pledge of secrecy to plaintiff. On appeal from a jury verdict for the plaintiff, the Supreme Court affirmed.

> [T]he inventor who designedly, and with the view of applying it indefinitely and exclusively for his own profit, withholds his invention from the public, comes not within the policy or objects of the Constitution or acts of Congress .... But [this policy] ... by no means forbid[s] a delay requisite for completing an invention, or for a test of its value or success by a series of sufficient and practical experiments....
>
> It is the unquestionable right of every inventor to confer gratuitously the benefits of his ingenuity upon the public, and this he may do either by express declaration or by conduct equally significant with language — such, for instance, as an acquiescence, with full knowledge in the use of his invention by others; or he may forfeit his rights as an inventor by a willful or negligent postponement of his claims, or by an attempt to withhold the benefit of his improvement from the public until a similar or the same improvement should have been made and introduced by others ....

2. *Interrelated Sections*. As the *Kendall* case, and the main case above, show, § 102(c) overlaps to a large extent with § 102(b). Events giving rise to a statutory bar under § 102(b), in other words, are implicitly taken to be an abandonment of the right to obtain a patent. Indeed, the most frequent acts of abandonment are precisely those covered in § 102(b) — publication, public use, and early commercialization. Because of this, § 102(c) is not very often invoked. For example, in the *MacBeth-Evans Glass* case, the court had to decide the case on grounds of abandonment because the secret yet commercial use of the invention in question did not qualify under then-existing law as a public use. Today, the result in the case would probably be the same, but the secret commercial use might be deemed a public use under § 102(b). *See W.L. Gore & Assocs. v. Garlock, Inc.*, 721 F.2d 1540, 1548, 220 U.S.P.Q. (BNA) 303 (1983) (dictum: "If Budd and

Cropper commercialized the tape, that could result in a forfeiture of a patent granted them for their [tape-making] process on an application filed by them more than a year later.").

3. What's Left? But what independent content can be given to § 102(c)? In what situations might an inventor be said to have "abandoned" her invention *without* meeting the criteria of § 102(b)? Three possibilities have been suggested: (A) Abandonment prior to the expiration of the one-year grace period under § 102(b); (B) Abandonment without any publication, public use, or sale; and (C) Abandonment by implication in a lapsed patent application or in unclaimed material disclosed in a related patent application.

(A) Abandonment Prior to Grace Period. It has been held that no abandonment should normally be inferred if an applicant files within the one-year § 102(b) grace period. *Mendenhall v. Astec Indus.*, 13 U.S.P.Q.2d (BNA) 1913 (E.D. Tenn. 1988), *aff'd in unpublished opinion*, 887 F.2d 1094, 13 U.S.P.Q.2d (BNA) 1956 (Fed. Cir. 1989) ("It would defeat the purpose of section 102(b) if the Court were to construe section 102(c) ... so as to find abandonment based solely on a delay in filing of less than one year."). Yet the court in *Mendenhall* went on to note that "to establish abandonment within this one year period, it must be proven that the inventor expressly and publicly renounced his intention to apply for a patent, under circumstances such that others would reasonably be led to rely upon that renunciation." Note that this latter point restates a key policy of the § 102(b) statutory bar provision: protecting the reliance interest of others when unclaimed technology is made public.

(B) Abandonment Without Publication, Public Use, or Sale. It should be clear by now that the secret but commercial use of an invention by the inventor — such as in *MacBeth-Evans Glass* — would today qualify as a public use under § 102(b). But what if the inventor makes no attempt to commercialize the invention or the things made by the invention? In other words, should prolonged, secret, but non-commercial use preclude an applicant from obtaining a patent? In *Bates v. Coe,* 98 U.S. (8 Otto) 31 (1878), the Supreme Court suggested that it should not. "Inventors may," the Court declared, "keep their inventions secret; ... they do not forfeit their right to apply for a patent, unless another in the meantime has made the invention, and secured by patent the exclusive right to ... the patented improvement." *Id.* at 46. The *MacBeth-Evans Glass* case, however, suggests otherwise. There, as we have seen, the court concluded that it could not characterize the inventor's activities (i.e., secret commercial use) as public; but it held that those activities constituted abandonment instead. Applying this logic to the modern situation, a court might well say that secret non-commercial use for a prolonged period constitutes abandonment under § 102(c) even though it is not a public use under § 102(b). Note that this issue is very closely related to the situation where two inventors are vying for priority, one of whom has used the invention in secret for some time. This is discussed below in Section J.3.

(C) Abandonment Via a Patent or Application. There are two other possible forms of abandonment. An applicant may discontinue the prosecution of her application at any time prior to issue. Such a discontinuance is termed an abandonment by the Patent Office. Is such an abandonment for Patent Office purposes an abandonment under § 102(c)? The answer is unclear. *Compare Peterson v. Fee Int'l Ltd.*, 381 F. Supp. 1071, 1079, 182 U.S.P.Q. 264 (W.D. Okla. 1974) (abandoned application does not bar later patent application for improved version of same invention) *with USM Corp. v. SPS Techs., Inc.*, 514 F. Supp. 213, 241, 211 U.S.P.Q. (BNA) 112 (N.D. Ill. 1981), *rev'd on other grounds*, 649 F.2d 505, 216 U.S.P.Q. (BNA) 959 (7th Cir. 1982), *cert. denied*, 462 U.S. 1107 (1983), *appeal after remand*, 770 F.2d 1035, 226 U.S.P.Q. (BNA) 1038 (Fed. Cir. 1985) (patentee's patent invalid due to inequitable conduct, which consisted of patentee's failure to disclose that claimed subject matter had been the subject of an earlier abandoned application: "subject matter once abandoned may not lawfully be resurrected and recaptured in a later filed patent application"). *See generally* 2 DONALD CHISUM, PATENTS § 6.03[2] (1978 & Supp. 1991). Because applications are kept secret by the Patent Office, the protection of the public's reliance interest is not implicated in these cases. Thus, so long as there is no secret commercial use (i.e., no patent term extension issue), it is difficult to see why an abandoned application ought to give rise to a § 102(c) abandonment bar.

A second abandonment issue is raised when a patentee discloses but does not claim subject matter in an earlier application, call it Application *A*, and then claims it in a subsequently-filed application, call it Application *B*. Until 1971, it was often held that Application *B* was barred under § 102(c) and its predecessors; then, in *In re Gibbs*, 473 F.2d 486, 168 U.S.P.Q. (BNA) 578 (C.C.P.A. 1971), this line of cases was reversed. It is the law now that disclosures made in Application *A* do not bar claims to the same subject matter in Application *B* *unless* Application *A* has become prior art under § 102(b) — i.e., unless Application *B* is filed more than one year after the *issuance* of Application *A*.

G. SECTION 102(d): PRIOR FOREIGN FILING

Section 102(d) reads as follows (note the insertion of schematic numbering and lettering):

§ 102. Conditions for patentability; novelty and loss of right to patent

A person shall be entitled to a patent unless —

(d) [1] the invention was [2] first patented or caused to be patented, or was the subject of an inventor's certificate, by the applicant or his legal representatives or assigns [a] in a foreign country [b] prior to the date of the application for patent in this country [3] on an application for patent or inventor's certifi-

cate [a] filed more than twelve months before the filing of the application in
the United States ....

Although perhaps confusing at first glance, this section actually sets forth a
fairly clear statutory bar condition: file an application in the U.S. within a year
of applying for a patent *anywhere else*. By doing this, one prevents the occurrence of the statutory bar event of this section — the *issuance* of a non-U.S.
patent which was applied for more than a year before a U.S. application was
filed.

In terms of the schematic elements identified above, § 102(d) requires three
main things: that [1] the same invention be [2] first patented [a] in a foreign
country [b] prior to the date of the U.S. application [3] on an application [a] filed
more than twelve months before the filing date of the U.S. application.

The final two elements can be confusing, because they are stated in the section
in the reverse order of their actual temporal sequence. It might be better to
understand § 102(d) as requiring three things, in this order: (1) same invention,
(2) applied for in a foreign country more than twelve months before being applied
for in the U.S., and (3) resulting in the issuance of a foreign patent before the
filing of a U.S. patent application. Note that *both* foreign events must occur
before the U.S. filing: the foreign application (at least a year before U.S. filing)
and the issuance of the foreign patent. The next case applies these elements, and
explores the degree of overlap required between the first-filed foreign application
and its U.S. counterpart.

In re KATHAWALA

9 F.3d 942, 28 U.S.P.Q.2d 1785 (Fed. Cir. 1993)

LOURIE, J.

Applicant Faizulla G. Kathawala [a Sandoz, Inc. researcher] appeals from the
July 17, 1992 decision of the U.S. Patent and Trademark Office (PTO) Board of
Patent Appeals and Interferences, [which] affirm[ed] the examiner's final rejec-
tion of claims 1, 2, and 19-21 of application Serial No. 772,288, entitled "Indole
Analogs of Mevalonolactone and Derivatives Thereof," as unpatentable under 35
U.S.C. Section 102(d) (1988) over Greek Patent 79,042 and Spanish Patent
443,668. We affirm.

BACKGROUND

Kathawala's invention relates to a group of new compounds having the ability
to inhibit a key enzyme in the biosynthesis of cholesterol. Claims 1 and 2 of the
application are directed to the compounds per se, claim 19 is directed to a
pharmaceutical composition containing the compounds, and claims 20 and 21 are
directed to methods of using the compounds for inhibition of cholesterol biosynthesis and treatment of atherosclerosis.

Kathawala filed the instant application on April 11, 1985, more than one year after he filed counterpart applications in Greece and Spain on November 21, 1983. Kathawala initially filed an application in the U.S. on November 22, 1982, claiming most of the same compounds as in the instant application. When he filed abroad, however, in 1983, he expanded his claims to include certain ester derivatives of the originally claimed compounds. It is claims to those esters, which Kathawala made the subject of a subsequent continuation-in-part application, the application now before us, that are at issue here.

Both foreign patents issued prior to the instant application in the U.S., the Greek patent on October 2, 1984, and the Spanish patent on January 21, 1985. The specifications of the Greek and Spanish patents are substantially the same as that of the U.S. application, both disclosing the same compounds, compositions, and methods of use. The Greek patent contains claims directed to the compounds, compositions, methods of use, and processes for making the compounds. The Spanish patent contains only "process of making" claims.

Because Kathawala filed his U.S. application claiming the esters more than one year after he filed his corresponding foreign applications, and those foreign applications issued as patents prior to the U.S. filing date, the examiner rejected the claims under 35 U.S.C. Section 102(d), which precludes issuance of a patent when

> the invention was first patented or caused to be patented ... by the applicant or his legal representatives or assigns in a foreign country prior to the date of the application for patent in this country on an application for patent ... filed more than twelve months before the filing of the application in the United States.

35 U.S.C. Section 102(d). The examiner rejected each of the claims over the Greek patent, and claims 1 and 2, the compound claims, over the Spanish patent.

Kathawala appealed to the Board, arguing with respect to the rejection over the Greek patent that his invention was not "patented" in Greece under section 102(d) because the compound, composition, and method of use claims in the Greek patent were invalid under Greek law as directed to non-statutory subject matter. Kathawala also argued that the examiner's rejection based on the Spanish patent was erroneous because, although that patent issued and was enforceable prior to the U.S. filing date, the specification was not publicly available until August 1, 1985, the date on which the notice of the Spanish patent grant was officially published, which was after the U.S. filing date. Thus, Kathawala argues, the compositions were not "patented" for purposes of section 102(d). Kathawala further argued that the "invention ... patented" in Spain was not the same "invention" claimed in the U.S. application because the Spanish patent claimed processes for making the compounds, and claims 1 and 2 were directed to the compounds themselves.

DISCUSSION

Turning first to the Greek patent, there is no dispute that it contains claims directed to the same invention as that of Kathawala's U.S. application. Kathawala argues, however, that his invention was not first "patented" in Greece under section 102(d) because the compound, composition, and method of use claims are invalid under Greek patent law as directed to non-statutory subject matter. According to Kathawala, only his process claims are valid under Greek law. Kathawala thus argues that the validity of his claims under Greek patent law determines whether his invention was "patented" in Greece within the meaning of section 102(d) prior to his U.S. filing date.

We disagree. Even assuming that Kathawala's compound, composition, and method of use claims are not enforceable in Greece, a matter on which we will not speculate, the controlling fact for purposes of section 102(d) is that the Greek patent issued containing claims directed to the same invention as that of the U.S. application. When a foreign patent issues with claims directed to the same invention as the U.S. application, the invention is "patented" within the meaning of section 102(d); validity of the foreign claims is irrelevant.

The PTO should be able to accept at face value the grant of the Greek patent claiming subject matter corresponding to that claimed in a U.S. application, without engaging in an extensive exploration of fine points of foreign law. The claims appear in the Greek patent because the applicant put them there. He cannot claim exemption from the consequences of his own actions.

Also before us is the rejection of claims 1 and 2, the compound claims, based on the Spanish patent. Kathawala argues that this rejection was erroneous for two reasons. First, Kathawala asserts that although the Spanish patent was granted and enforceable prior to the U.S. filing date, it was not published until after that date. Kathawala thus argues that his invention was not "patented" in Spain until the publication date of the Spanish patent. Second, Kathawala argues that the "invention" of claims 1 and 2, the compounds themselves, is not the same "invention … patented" in Spain under section 102(d), that compositions are a separate invention from processes.

We reject both arguments of Kathawala. With regard to the first argument, Kathawala concedes that the Spanish patent issued and was enforceable on January 21, 1985, a date prior to the U.S. filing date. Kathawala nevertheless asserts that the effective date of a foreign patent for purposes of Section 102(d), the date on which an invention is "patented," is not the date the foreign patent issues and becomes enforceable, but the date on which it becomes publicly available.

[C]ontrary to Kathawala's argument, it is irrelevant under section 102(d) whether the Spanish patent was publicly available prior to the U.S. filing date. Rather, the Board correctly concluded that an invention is "patented" in a foreign country under section 102(d) when the patentee's rights under the patent become fixed. *See* Marina V. Schneller, *Patenting and Filing Abroad as a Bar to U.S.*

Patent Grant — History, Purpose and Sanctions of 35 U.S.C. Section 102(d), 11 Int'l Rev. Indus. Prop. & Copyright L. 324, 345 (1980) ("[T]he date upon which the foreign patent is 'patented,' within the meaning of 35 U.S.C. Section 102(d), is the date upon which the rights to enforce the foreign patent first accrue to the U.S. applicant ... [and] the publication date of the foreign patent is irrelevant...").

Kathawala's second argument is that the "invention" patented in Spain is not the same "invention" claimed in claims 1 and 2. Kathawala argues that each claim defines a separate invention, and since the Spanish claims are directed to processes for making the subject compounds, and claims 1 and 2 of the instant application are directed to the compounds themselves, the "invention" patented in Spain is not the same "invention" as that of claims 1 and 2. Hence Kathawala urges that the rejection of claims 1 and 2 under section 102(d) based on the Spanish patent was erroneous.

We do not agree. It is a truism that a claim defines an invention, and a claim to a composition is indeed different from a claim to a process. However, we cannot let rigid definitions be used in situations to which they don't apply to produce absurd results. The word "invention" in the Patent Act has many meanings depending on the context. In the present context, it must have a meaning consistent with the policy and purpose behind section 102(d), which is to require applicants for patent in the United States to exercise reasonable promptness in filing their applications after they have filed and obtained foreign patents.

Kathawala made an "invention" relating to a group of new compounds. He filed applications in Greece and Spain disclosing his invention as consisting of four different aspects: compounds, compositions, methods of use, and processes of making the compounds. While Kathawala had the potential to claim each of those aspects, and did so in his Greek application, he chose to claim only the processes in Spain because, he asserts, pharmaceutical compositions and methods of use were not patentable under Spanish patent law during the relevant time period.

Kathawala's understandable decision not to claim the compounds in Spain, however, does not permit him to evade the statutory bar by arguing that the Spanish Patent Office would not have allowed such claims. Similarly, neither would it have mattered if Kathawala had applied for compound claims and the Spanish Patent Office had rejected them. What is controlling is that the application that Kathawala filed in Spain disclosed and provided the opportunity to claim all aspects of his invention, including the compounds.

It would be contrary to the policy of the statute to permit an applicant to file a foreign application on an invention that may be claimed by four related types of claims, obtain a grant of whatever patent rights were available in the foreign country, and then file an application in the United States, after the foreign patent has issued and more than one year after the foreign filing date on the same invention, with claims directed to those aspects of the invention which were unpatentable in the foreign country. That would permit grant of a U.S. patent on what is essentially the same "invention" as that patented in the foreign country and would frustrate the policy underlying section 102(d), which is to encourage the filing of applications in the United States within a year of the foreign filing of a counterpart patent application. An applicant cannot evade the statutory bar by citing alleged defects of foreign law concerning scope of patentable subject matter.

NOTES

1. The § 102(d) statutory bar has traditionally been quite rare, given the factual predicates. *See* KENNETH J. BURCHFIEL, BIOTECHNOLOGY AND THE FEDERAL CIRCUIT 73 (1995) (noting "remarkably short time" for issuance of Greek and Spanish patents in *Kathawala*). Yet Judge Lourie's approach in *Kathawala*, which lightens the emphasis on identity of claims between the foreign patent and U.S. application, could result in a modest expansion of this form of prior art. Some have doubted the wisdom of *Kathawala* for this very reason. *See id.* at 72-77 (criticizing statements in *Kathawala* minimizing distinction between disclosed and claimed subject matter in foreign patents).

2. If, as seems the case, the policy behind § 102(d) is to encourage early filing in the U.S., why distinguish, as Kathawala urges in its appeal to the Federal Circuit, between what is disclosed and what is claimed in a foreign patent application? How is disclosure within the U.S. encouraged when no U.S. application need be filed unless an equivalent foreign application *claims* the same subject matter?

3. In modern European patent law, and indeed the law of most major industrialized countries, patent applications are routinely published eighteen months after they are filed. In such a world, what role does § 102(d) play? Is it only to encourage U.S. dissemination earlier than the eighteenth month after foreign filing? If so, does this assume (counter to the facts) that applications in the U.S. normally result in issued patents within 6 months of filing? If dissemination in the U.S. is the goal, why not simply go to a system where the U.S. Patent Office publishes U.S. applications eighteen months after filing? *Cf.* Chisum, *Foreign Activity: Its Effect on Patentability Under United States Law*, 11 INT'L REV. IND. PROP. & COPYRIGHT L. 324 (1980) (concluding that § 102(d) is faulty because it focuses on foreign *issue* date instead of exclusively on foreign filing date; suggesting that 102(d) be changed to make foreign applications effective prior art one year after they are filed). *See also* Daus, *Comment: Certain Laid-Open Applications as 35 U.S.C. 102(d) Bars*, 69 J. PAT. & TRADEMARK OFF. SOC'Y 717 (1987) (proposing that key date for § 102(d) bar be the date of first publication of a foreign patent, usually eighteen months after filing).

4. Since pendency times in Europe can also be substantial, it must be noted that the events of § 102(d) may not be all that common. That is, it is not the rule that an earlier-filed foreign application routinely results in an earlier-issued foreign patent. This is especially true in those countries where the patent applicant can delay issuance by delaying the time when active examination of the application will occur; this is the case for applications filed under the European Patent Convention and in Japan, for instance. No statutory bar results when the foreign patent issues after the U.S. patent issues, regardless of when the foreign and U.S. applications are filed.

5. Section 102(d) is related to the provision assuring priority dates for foreign inventors under the Paris Convention, codified in the United States in 35 U.S.C. § 119. This is discussed below in Section K.1 of this chapter. In general, § 119 provides a "safe harbor" for foreign applicants if they file in the U.S. within one year of filing in another country that is a party to the Paris Convention.

6. The "identity of invention" for § 102(d) was at issue in *Ex parte Appeal No. 242-47*, 196 U.S.P.Q. (BNA) 828 (Pat. Off. Bd. App. 1976):

> Nor are we persuaded that a foreign patent which is a bar under 35 U.S.C. 102(d) cannot be combined with other patents or literature references to bar a patent on subject matter which would have been obvious from the barred subject matter in the light of other references.

Note that the more liberal identity test suggested in this passage comports with that which has been adopted for § 102(b). See Section E.1, above.

PROBLEMS: § 102(d)

Statement

Under the following hypotheticals, is Jan's United States patent application barred under 102(d)?

1. Jan, a French inventor, developed a new type of food processor which packages food, in addition to dicing, slicing and making puree. She files a French patent application June 17, 1990 which is issued October 15, 1992. On July 8, 1991 she files for a U.S. patent.

2. Jan files her Japanese patent application June 17, 1990 which is issued January 1, 1991. On June 18, 1991 Jan files her United States patent application.

3. Jan files her French patent application June 17, 1990. The French application is still pending when she files for a U.S. patent on June 21, 1991.

4. Jan files a patent application in Estonia on June 17, 1990. It issues on October 15, 1990. She files her U.S. patent application May 14, 1991.

Discussion

1. Jan escapes a § 102(d) problem because the French patent application did not issue before her U.S. filing date.

2.   Jan's United States patent is barred since her filing of the Japanese appli-
      cation predated her United States application by more than twelve months
      and since it issued as a Japanese patent before she filed in the United
      States.

3.   Jan escapes a § 102(d) bar since no foreign patent was issued before her
      United States filing date. This is despite the fact that her United States
      filing date is more than a year after her foreign filing date. But note that
      she would lose the benefit of her foreign filing date under the Paris
      Convention in this case; see Section K, below.

4.   Jan avoids a § 102(d) bar because the Estonian patent application was not
      filed more than a year before her United States patent application. This
      is despite the fact that the Estonian patent issued prior to her U.S. filing
      date. (Do you see why this result is necessary for compliance with the
      Paris Convention "priority year"?)

H. SECTION 102(e): DISCLOSURES IN EARLIER-FILED APPLICATIONS

ALEXANDER MILBURN CO. v. DAVIS-BOURNONVILLE CO.
270 U.S. 390 (1926)

MR. JUSTICE HOLMES delivered the opinion of the Court.

This is a suit for the infringement of the plaintiff's patent for an improvement
in welding and cutting apparatus alleged to have been the invention of one
Whitford. The suit embraced other matters but this is the only one material here.
The defense is that Whitford was not the first inventor of the thing patented, and
the answer gives notice that to prove the invalidity of the patent, evidence will
be offered that one Clifford invented the thing, his patent being referred to and
identified. The application for the plaintiff's patent was filed on March 4, 1911,
and the patent was issued June 4, 1912. There was no evidence carrying Whitford's invention further back. Clifford's application was filed on January 31,
1911, before Whitford's, and his patent was issued on February 6, 1912. It is not
disputed that this application gave a complete and adequate description of the
thing patented to Whitford, but it did not claim it. The District Court gave the
plaintiff a decree, holding that, while Clifford might have added this claim to his
application, yet as he did not, he was not a prior inventor. The decree was
affirmed by the [Second] Circuit Court of Appeals. There is a conflict between
this decision and those of other Circuit Courts of Appeals, especially the Sixth.
Lemley v. Dobson-Evans Co., 243 Fed. 391 [6th Cir. 1915]. *Naceskid Service
Chain Co. v. Perdue*, 1 Fed. (2d) 924 [6th Cir. 1924]. Therefore a writ of
certiorari was granted by this Court.

The patent law authorizes a person who has invented an improvement like the
present, "not known or used by others in this country, before his invention,"

&c., to obtain a patent for it. Rev. Sts. § 4886, amended, March 3, 1897. Among the defences to a suit for infringement, the fourth specified by the statute is that the patentee "was not the original and first inventor or discoverer of any material and substantial part of the thing patented." Rev. Sts. § 4920, amended, March 3, 1897. Taking these words in their natural sense as they would be read by the common man, obviously one is not the first inventor if, as was the case here, somebody else has made a complete and adequate description of the thing claimed before the earliest moment to which the alleged inventor can carry his invention back. But the words cannot be taken quite so simply. In view of the gain to the public that the patent laws mean to secure we assume for purposes of decision that it would have been no bar to Whitford's patent if Clifford had written out his prior description and kept it in his portfolio uncommunicated to anyone. More than that, since the decision in the case of *The Cornplanter Patent*, 23 Wall. [90 U.S.] 181 [1874], it is said, at all events for many years, the Patent Office has made no search among abandoned patent applications, and by the words of the statute a previous foreign invention does not invalidate a patent granted here if it has not been patented or described in a printed publication. Rev. Sts. § 4923. See *Westinghouse Machine Co. v. General Electric Co.*, 207 Fed. 75 [2d Cir. 1913]. These analogies prevailed in the minds of the Courts below.

On the other hand, publication in a periodical is a bar. This as it seems to us is more than an arbitrary enactment, and illustrates, as does the rule concerning previous public use, the principle that, subject to the exceptions mentioned, one really must be the first inventor in order to be entitled to a patent. *Coffin v. Ogden*, 18 Wall. [85 U.S.] 120 [1873]. We understand the Circuit Court of Appeals to admit that if Whitford had not applied for his patent until after the issue to Clifford, the disclosure by the latter would have had the same effect as the publication of the same words in a periodical, although not made the basis of a claim. The invention is made public property as much in the one case as in the other. But if this be true, as we think that it is, it seems to us that a sound distinction cannot be taken between that case and a patent applied for before but not granted until after a second patent is sought. The delays of the patent office ought not to cut down the effect of what has been done. The description shows that Whitford was not the first inventor. Clifford had done all that he could do to make his description public. He had taken steps that would make it public as soon at the Patent Office did its work, although, of course, amendments might be required of him before the end could be reached. We see no reason in the words or policy of the law for allowing Whitford to profit by the delay and make himself out to be the first inventor when he was not so in fact, when Clifford had shown knowledge inconsistent with the allowance of Whitford's claim, *[Webster] Loom Co. v. Higgins*, 105 U.S. 580 [1891], and when otherwise the publication of his patent would abandon the thing described to the public unless it already was old.

The question is not whether Clifford showed himself by the description to be the first inventor. By putting it in that form it is comparatively easy to take the next step and say that he is not an inventor in the sense of the statute unless he makes a claim. The question is whether Clifford's disclosure made it impossible for Whitford to claim the invention at a later date. The disclosure would have had the same effect as at present if Clifford had added to his description a statement that he did not claim the thing described because he abandoned it or because he believed it to be old. It is not necessary to show who did invent the thing in order to show that Whitford did not.

It is said that without a claim the thing described is not reduced to practice. But this seems to us to rest on a false theory helped out by the fiction that by a claim it is reduced to practice. A new application and a claim may be based on the original description within two years, and the original priority established notwithstanding intervening claims. A description that would bar a patent if printed in a periodical or in an issued patent is equally effective in an application so far as reduction to practice goes.

As to the analogies relied upon below, the disregard of abandoned patent applications, however explained, cannot be taken to establish a principle beyond the rule as actually applied. As an empirical rule it no doubt is convenient if not necessary to the Patent Office, and we are not disposed to disturb it, although we infer that originally the practice of the Office was different. The policy of the statute as to foreign inventions obviously stands on its own footing and cannot be applied to domestic affairs. The fundamental rule we repeat is that the patentee must be the first inventor. The qualifications in aid of a wish to encourage improvements or to avoid laborious investigations do not prevent the rule from applying here.

Decree reversed.

NOTES

1. *Clarifying the Case.* Why was there no priority contest — or "interference" — declared between the two parties? "The question," said the Court, "is whether Clifford's *disclosure* made it impossible for Whitford to *claim* the invention at a later date." (Emphasis added.) *See* 35 U.S.C. § 135 (1988) (interferences require overlap in *claims*). Interference proceedings are discussed in Section J.1 later in this chapter.

2. *Clarifying Its Logic.* Recall *In re Schlittler*, 234 F.2d 882, 110 U.S.P.Q. (BNA) 304 (C.C.P.A. 1956): "[T]he mere placing of a manuscript in the hands of a publisher does not necessarily make it available to the public." Are patents different? Does the *Alexander Milburn* rule further the same policy as the § 102(a) ruling in *Schlittler* (nonremoval from the public domain), or some other policy (e.g., "first to invent")?

3. *Critiques of the Milburn Rule.* Criticism of the *Milburn* rule is common. *See, e.g.*, Leuzzi, *A Re-evaluation of the Use of 35 U.S.C. 102(e), Secret Prior Art, in Obviousness Determinations*, 29 IDEA 167, 170 (1988-89):

The "rationale" of *Milburn* has been explained as residing in the theory of Patent Office delay, i.e., "but for" the delays in the Patent Office, the patent would have been prior art known to the public as of the filing date .... Thus arose the fiction that the § 102(e) patent could be treated as if it had issued on its filing date. Clearly, this is a fiction that finds no basis in fact for as any patent practitioner knows, the Patent Office rarely considers a patent application for several months. Even when allowed on a first action, the delays attendant in the mails and obtaining payment of the official fees can take weeks and the actual issuance and publication of the patent often will not occur until months after the applicant is notified that he has allowable the subject matter.

See also Wegner, *Patent Law Simplification and the Geneva Patent Convention*, 14 Am. Intell. Prop. J. 154, 176 (1986):

"Secret" prior art is a contradiction in terms. Prior "art" should refer to the *known* (or at least knowable) state of the art at the time the invention is made: at the time of the invention, was the sum total of knowledge from public use, printed publications, and patents *then available* such that the claimed invention would have been *at that time* [novel or] obvious to the worker with ordinary skill in the art?

(The full implications of foreign-filed applications and their U.S. prior art status under the Paris Convention on international priority are discussed in Section K below.) *See also* C. Douglass Thomas, *Secret Prior Art — Get Your Priorities Straight!*, 9 Harv. J. L. & Tech. 147 (1996) (arguing for novelty-only standard, and characterizing § 102(e) as a priority, not a novelty, provision).

As the excerpt by Wegner demonstrates, the harshest criticism of § 102(e) has been aimed at its use as a source of prior art under § 103, nonobviousness. (We discuss this topic in Chapter 5, Section C.4, below.) The use of secret prior art to defeat novelty is perhaps less unfair; without § 102(e), patents would issue to later-filing applicants covering material disclosed earlier. This might be quite harsh from the point of view of the earlier-filing applicant. By merely failing to *claim* certain subject matter, she would be forced to recognize the property rights of an admittedly later-filing applicant, who in many cases would in fact be a second-in-time inventor. She might even be forced to license from the later applicant technology which she herself developed at an earlier date! While in some sense this criticism applies to the case where the later-filing applicant's invention is only *obvious* from the disclosure of the earlier application, it seems less unfair to subject the earlier applicant to the property rights of the second applicant in the case where the earlier disclosure and later claim are identical. In the obviousness situation, the later applicant has contributed at least some independent inventive work beyond what the earlier applicant had herself invented. Thus, from a "labor theory" perspective, there is perhaps more justification for the grant of a patent to the second-filed applicant where her invention is merely obvious, rather than fully anticipated (i.e., not novel) in light of the earlier applicant's invention. Thus under the European Patent Convention, subject matter disclosed but not claimed in a prior patent application will defeat later claims to the same subject matter only if the prior disclosure and later claims are identical. That is, no "secret prior art" can render a later claim obvious. See EPC Articles 54 & 56.

4. Provisional Rejections. Section 706.02 of the Manual of Patent Examining Procedure authorizes the making of "provisional" rejections under 35 U.S.C. §§ 102(e), 103. Examiners may "provisionally reject claims not patentably distinct from the disclosure in a co-pending application having an earlier U.S. filing date." *Id. See In re Bartfeld*, 925 F.2d 1450, 17 U.S.P.Q.2d (BNA) 1885 (Fed. Cir. 1991).

The rejection is termed "provisional" because the prior filed application that discloses the invention or makes it obvious must of course eventually issue as a patent to be a true § 102(e) reference.

5. Provisional Applications. Are provisional patent applications (see Chapter 1) filed under the post-GATT § 111(b) effective prior art under § 102(e) as of their filing date? Most seem to think so. *See, e.g.*, Charles E. Van Horn, *Practicalities and Potential Pitfalls When Using Provisional Patent Applications*, 22 AM. INTELL. PROP. L. ASS'N Q.J. 259 (1994). For a contrary view, emphasizing that provisional patent applications cannot mature into issued patents (directly), see Andrew J. Patch, *Provisional Patent Applications and 35 U.S.C. 102(e) in View of* Milburn, Hilmer, *and* Wertheim, 77 J. PAT. & TRADEMARK OFF. SOC'Y 339 (1995).

6. Foreign Priority and § 102(e). The "secret" nature of § 102(e) prior art stems from the fact that a patent's disclosures are given prior art effect as of the date the patent application was filed. The filing date is not difficult to determine where a U.S. patent application matures into an issued patent. But what about a U.S. patent that is applied for based on the priority date of a patent application filed in a foreign country? The answer requires us to anticipate some material from the following section in this chapter.

Under the Paris Convention for the Protection of Intellectual Property (Paris Convention), signed in 1883, countries which are members of the Convention must respect the filing date of an application filed in another member country by nationals (basically, citizens) of that member country, so long as a related application is filed in the first country within one year. *See id.*, §§ 4(A)(1) & 4(C)(1). This Convention principle is embodied in § 119 of the U.S. Patent Statute. The first date is referred to as the "foreign priority date," or the "Convention priority date."

Several cases have now held that the application date mentioned in § 102(e) refers to the *U.S. application date*, rather than the filing date of the foreign application on which § 119 priority is premised. *See, e.g., In re Hilmer*, 359 F.2d 859, 149 U.S.P.Q. (BNA) 480 (C.C.P.A. 1966) (*Hilmer I*). In *Hilmer I*, Judge Rich, then of the CCPA, held that a U.S. patent was effective prior art only as of the U.S. filing date; the foreign priority date otherwise established by § 119 is to be disregarded for purposes of § 102(e). (The later opinion in this case, *In re Hilmer*, 424 F.2d 1108, 165 U.S.P.Q. (BNA) 155 (C.C.P.A. 1970) (*Hilmer II*), dealt with the effect of § 119 on § 102(g) prior art, which concerns prior inventions by another; this is discussed in the section on priority later in this chapter.)

The converse situation was addressed in *In re Gosteli*, 872 F.2d 1008, 10 U.S.P.Q.2d (BNA) 1614 (Fed. Cir. 1989), which held that a foreign priority date can be relied on by an applicant seeking to escape from the effect of a § 102(e) reference, so long as the foreign application that is the basis for the assertion of priority contains disclosures adequate to support the claims whose novelty or nonobviousness are in question due to the earlier-filed U.S. application disclosing similar subject matter. *See generally* Rollins, *35 U.S.C. 119 — Description and Enablement Requirements*, 67 J. PAT. OFF. SOC'Y 386, 386 (1985).

Section 102(e) creates some interesting problems when a patent application is filed under the Patent Cooperation Treaty (PCT) (see Section K below). In general, the application date for § 102(e) purposes is the date on which the PCT application enters the U.S. "national stage" of prosecution under 35 U.S.C. §§ 371(1), 371(2), and 371(4). *See* U.S. DEPARTMENT OF COMMERCE, MANUAL OF PATENT EXAMINING PROCEDURE § 1896 (6th rev. ed. 1995) (available via the World Wide Web at http://www.upto.com).

7. *More on Interferences and § 102(e).* Section 102(e) might appear to offer some solace to an inventor who feared losing an interference: if she files first and discloses the subject matter concerning which she fears she will fail in establishing priority, she could at least bar the other person from obtaining a patent (under § 102(e)) by *disclosing* the subject matter. This strategy would fail, however, because the other inventor could use Rule 131 to antedate ("swear behind") the § 102(e) reference. For more on Rule 131 practice, see Section L, below.

COMPARATIVE AND PHILOSOPHICAL NOTE ON § 102(e)

Under the European Patent Convention and Japanese patent law, an earlier patent applicant who discloses an invention obtains "senior rights" against a later applicant who discloses and claims the same thing. The later applicant will not get a patent, due to the disclosure of the same invention in the earlier application. *See* CONVENTION ON THE GRANT OF EUROPEAN PATENTS (EUROPEAN PATENT CONVENTION), Articles 54 & 56 (1973); T. TANABE & H. WEGNER, JAPANESE PATENT LAW § 130, at 58 (1979). As stated, this is no different from the principle embodied in § 102(e) of U.S. law. Also similar is the effective date of the earlier-filed application as a prior art reference: its filing date. But in Japan and Europe there is a critical difference: the disclosures of the earlier-filed application can *only* be used when the later-filed application claims the same exact invention. Not covered in these systems is a later-filed application claiming an invention that is obvious in light of the disclosures of the earlier-filed application. This is a major departure from U.S. law.

Another difference in Japan and Europe is that the earlier-filed application need never issue as a patent. Since in these systems all applications are published eighteen months after they are filed, the question of their issuance is irrelevant. Thus there is no European or Japanese analogue to the "provisional" rejection under § 102(e) of U.S. law.

The characterization of this rule as a "senior right" is telling. Under this conception, the key fact concerning the earlier-filed disclosure is that it was first arrived at by the earlier applicant. Thus this party ought to have a "senior right" as against a later applicant who claims the same subject matter. The quite primitive sense of justice behind the rule is clear: why should a later inventor who just happens to claim something I came up with first be able to assert a property right over me for that something? Indeed, this very point is made by the noted philosopher Robert Nozick, who claims that an independent inventor should *always* have a right to practice her invention — presumably, even if she made her invention later, not earlier. *See* R. NOZICK, ANARCHY, STATE AND UTOPIA (1974), at 181-82:

> The theme of someone worsening another's situation by depriving him of something he would otherwise possess may also illuminate the example of patents. An inventor's patent does not deprive others of an object which would not exist if not for the inventor. Yet patents would have this effect on others who independently invent the object. Therefore, these independent inventors, upon whom the burden of proving independent discovery may rest, should not be excluded from utilizing their own invention as they wish (including selling it to others).

This analysis helps us to see the differences between the American rule and that applied in Europe and Japan. In those systems, earlier-filed applications defeat later-filed applications claiming the *same invention*; they do not defeat later-filed applications claiming different, but obvious, inventions. In terms of Nozick's phraseology, the later-filing applicant would not be depriving the earlier filer of anything, since the one who filed later did come up with something new as compared to the earlier filer. Note that the key to this way of examining the problem is to compare the claims of the two applicants — the one who filed earlier, and the one who filed later.

The rule in the U.S., of course, is different; here, a later-filed application claiming different, but obvious, subject matter *is* defeated by the earlier-filed application. Clearly, the foregoing analysis, taken literally, cannot be used to support this rule, since the later-filer is not in fact claiming the same invention as disclosed by the earlier-filer. In Nozick's terminology, the later-filer who obtains exclusive patent rights over her invention would not be able to prevent the earlier filer from using "her own" invention, since the later-filed application does not claim this invention — it claims instead an obvious variant on the earlier-filer's "own" invention.

But one feature of the foregoing analysis is its emphasis on whether anyone is harmed by the later-filer's assertion of exclusive rights. It may be argued that there is some harm in the second situation that is not redressed by the European/Japanese rule. The harm in this case is not the assertion of rights (by the later-filer) over the earlier-filer's "own" invention, but rather the assertion of rights by the later-filer over an as-yet-unmade invention that was an obvious extension from what the earlier filer had done. In other words, the harm is the removal from public use of an easily-discoverable variant on the work done by the earlier filer. Admittedly, this is not the same degree of harm done by preventing the earlier filer from using "her own" invention. But it is arguably a harm nonetheless. (Indeed, the entire rationale for the nonobviousness standard turns on the fact that society seeks to reward only those inventive efforts having a certain "degree of difficulty.")

Note that in this alternative analysis based on Nozick, we are no longer balancing only the rights of the earlier and later filers. We are also taking into account the unformed or inchoate rights of the public in the nebulous yet important domain of inventions made obvious by the prior art. Under this analysis, if prior art is important enough to prevent an identical invention from being claimed over the objection of an earlier inventor, it is important enough to prevent the patenting of obvious variants on prior inventions, due to the equally powerful interests of the public in keeping a subsequent "inventor" from impinging on the public domain.

A final word may be said concerning all this, however. While the philosophical arguments pro and con the issue of "secret prior art" may be fun to make, one must never lose sight of the pragmatic implications of the current § 102(e) rule: greater uncertainty, for longer periods of time, for each patent applicant. Because of the "provisional" nature of § 102(e) rejections, a U.S. patent applicant claiming certain subject matter who files later than an earlier applicant who merely discloses that subject matter must wait until the Patent Office makes a final disposition of that earlier application. Not until then does the later-filer know for sure whether the § 102(e) rejection is going to "stick." And of course, the greater the number of potential § 102(e) references, the greater this uncertainty. Thus the U.S. rule embodied in § 102(e), which significantly expands the possible number of patent-defeating references by including those which make the applicant's invention obvious, may be said to so increase uncertainty that it is not worth the extra justice it provides. Thus we may agree with the principled defense of the current § 102(e) above, and yet concede that the fairness *in the individual case* implicit in extending Nozick's rationale to include nonobviousness considerations is not worth the cost *imposed on all applicants*.

Administrative efficiency, in other words, might dictate a slightly sub-optimal rule that costs less overall. The European/Japanese alternative might well be such a rule. It is perhaps for this reason that calls are currently being made to revamp § 102(e) along these lines.

PROBLEMS: § 102(e)

Statement

Stan, an electronics technician, developed an anti-squelch device for boat radios. His United States patent application, filed December 21, 1957, also disclosed but did not claim an ultra-sensitive radio tuner. Ohm Industrial, a Missouri electronics company, had been working on an identical radio tuner independently and filed its United States patent application December 22, 1957. Stan's patent issued December 21, 1958 and Ohm's issued December 22, 1958. In 1970 Ohm sues Yo-Yo Dyne, a radio manufacturer, for infringement.

1. Does Yo-Yo Dyne have a § 102(e) defense to infringement?

2. What if Ohm's radio tuner was not identical to that disclosed in Stan's patent but only obvious in light of it? What argument could Yo-Yo Dyne make?

3. What if Ohm's patent issued one day before Stan's patent?

Discussion

1. Under § 102(e), Stan's patent is effective prior art as of his filing dates; thus Yo-Yo Dyne can invalidate Ohm's patent under § 102(e).

2. In this case Stan's patent also invalidates Ohm's patent. However, Stan's patent must be used as prior art to defeat nonobviousness under § 103. See Chapter 5, Section C.

3. Stan's patent is still considered effective prior art as of his filing date. Since his filing date precedes Ohm's filing date, Ohm's patent may still be invalid. The issuance date is not critical to § 102(e). But Ohm could attempt to prove that it invented before Stan's filing date, by antedating or "swearing behind" this reference using Rule 131. See Section L, below.

I. SECTION 102(f): DERIVATION FROM ANOTHER

Patent Act § 102(f) states that a "person shall be entitled to a patent unless … he did not himself invent the subject matter sought to be patented …."

CAMPBELL v. SPECTRUM AUTOMATION CO.

513 F.2d 932, 185 U.S.P.Q. (BNA) 718 (6th Cir. 1975)

Milford A. Campbell, the patentee of United States patent No. 3,002,600, brought this action against Spectrum Automation (Spectrum) for infringement.

Spectrum counterclaimed, contending that the patent was invalid and that it therefore could not be infringed. District Judge Cornelia G. Kennedy held the patent to be invalid on a number of grounds. We affirm on one of these grounds that Campbell was not the inventor of the patent in suit.

The patent discloses an article that is used in material handling as a flexible feed track. Briefly described, wire is wound in closely adjacent loops around a square or rectangular mandrel and then coated with a flexible covering such as polyvinyl chloride. It is necessary to machine a groove through the length of this assembly to remove the article from the mandrel. Besides serving the purpose of releasing the assembly from the mandrel, the groove provides a useful access to the interior of the feed track. The resulting product, known as "Open-Flex," consists of individual metal segments bound together by the flexible coating. This invention is described in claim 3 as follows:

> 3. A flexible feed track for delivering articles by gravity along an irregular path comprising a plurality of hollow formed, segmental frame members disposed side by side along the length of said track and joined together by a bonded flexible coating, said frame members and said coating defining a way for articles to be delivered by said track, each of said frame members having spring-like characteristics so as to alter the cross-section defined thereby when a force is applied thereto and return to its original shape when the force is removed so as to cooperate with the inherent flexibility of said coating to permit said track to be formed torsionally and accurately as required to conduct said articles along a desired path of travel.

The two principals in this action, Richard Zimmerman and Campbell, both possess a high degree of technical expertise in this area. Zimmerman, who is now president of Spectrum, originally worked for Campbell and Campbell Machines Company during the period when Open-Flex was conceived. Later he formed his own company, Spectrum, and began to produce the product "Maxi-Flex," which Campbell contends infringes the patent in suit.

The only issue which we reach on this appeal concerns the identity of the true inventor of the flexible feed track. In the counterclaim for declaratory judgment of invalidity, Zimmerman alleged that he, not Campbell, was the true inventor of Open-Flex. If this is true, the patent would be invalid under the provisions of 35 U.S.C. § 102(f), which states that a "person shall be entitled to a patent unless ... he did not himself invent the subject matter sought to be patented ...."

The testimony in the District Court concerning inventorship is summarized in the following paragraphs. In early 1958, Campbell Machines Company received a purchase order for a number of storage feeders. Zimmerman was given the job of preparing the manufacturing information for the feeders and releasing the designs to the production shop. Although most of the feeder components were standard and had been produced previously, the lack of working space in the plant where the feeders were to be installed necessitated a new style of feed track.

Open-Flex was designed to fill this need. There is conflicting testimony as to the source of this idea and its reduction to practice. Campbell testified that confronted with this problem, he conceived the invention of Open-Flex just as it was later manufactured and patented, and that he gave full directions to Zimmerman as to how to manufacture it. These directions, he said, included the slot and were complete in all respects. Judge Kennedy found this testimony not to be credible and expressly stated that: "The Court does not believe Mr. Campbell's testimony."

Zimmerman's testimony included an express denial that he had ever been given such directions by Campbell. Zimmerman testified that he discussed with his father, who was an experienced and skilled tool and die maker, the problem of providing a flexible feed track to carry out the feeding function. Although the younger Zimmerman was also a tool and die maker, he did not know at that time that a spring could be wound in a rectangular shape. In the discussion with his father, Zimmerman reviewed hoses and tubes which use a spring wire spirally-wound body covered with a flexible coating, such as a vacuum hose. While with a previous employer Zimmerman had seen spirally-wound feed track or feed chutes. These were sometimes wrapped with electrical tape. Zimmerman's father was wearing a spring tension belt buckle at that time with a rectangular cross-section. From this belt buckle Zimmerman conceived the idea of a spirally-wound, rectangularly-shaped feed track, a flexible feed track with a rectangular cross-section. Zimmerman's father helped Zimmerman wind such a track which Zimmerman then showed to Campbell.

[The trial court] made a finding of fact that Zimmerman's testimony was a true statement of the events described, saying "The Court believes the testimony of Mr. Zimmerman."

The winding of the coil is only part of the invention. After the coil is wound it must be removed from the mandrel. Zimmerman's version, which also was corroborated by a coworker, was that "the slot was incorporated into the manufacturing process because of the inability to get the wound wire spring off the square mandrel." [The trial court judge] accepted this version and discredited Campbell's testimony that "the slot was a part of his original invention as he conceived it."

When the slot is created, the coherent spring is severed into as many segments as there are loops. To keep these from falling apart the flexible coating is applied prior to the slotting operation. Judge Kennedy credited the testimony that this process was conceived by Zimmerman, rather than by any action on the part of Campbell.

Neither party had strong supporting evidence to corroborate his oral testimony. Neither Campbell nor Zimmerman had notes, journals or other records of their work. The corroboration which did exist supported Zimmerman. He produced a photograph of his father, taken at about the time of the invention, which showed his father standing in front of a lathe, wearing the rectangular shaped, spiral wound belt buckle. This belt buckle was introduced into the record as an exhibit, was a part of the evidence considered by [the judge] and has been examined by this court.

Zimmerman's testimony concerning this belt buckle was as follows:

Q Now, what instructions if any did Mr. Campbell give you to make the first model?

A None.

Q How and when did you get the concept of making a spiral wound spring feed tube with coating?

A I conceived the basic idea at the home of my parents while discussing the problem of flexible feed track with my father.

Q Now, I show you Exhibit 45 and ask you what relation if any does that exhibit have with the making of the first open-flex model?

A This particular exhibit is a belt my father was wearing that Friday night that we discussed the flexible feed track problem. Actually, my sight of the spring wire-wound buckle was the starting concept of coming up with an answer for flexible feed track. I had never seen rectangularly wound springs before and this particular belt buckle caused me to ask my father why we couldn't wind such a rectangular spring, and his indication was, at that point was there was no reason as long as the lathe and the spring winding attachment could be adapted to it.

Q Now, is there any relation between the belt of Exhibit 45 and 44?

A Exhibit 44, the picture of my father, shows him wearing the belt.

Another witness, who was also employed by Campbell Machines Company at the time of the invention, corroborated the testimony that the covering did not bond to the first prototype, and that the slot was machined primarily for the purpose of removing the track from the mandrel, both in accordance with Zimmerman's testimony.

The District Court recognized that this corroboration was circumstantial, but found that in view of all the evidence Spectrum had met the "heavy burden" of proving that Zimmerman, not Campbell, was the true inventor.

Campbell contends that, in spite of the express factual findings of the District Court, the validity of the patent is established as a matter of law by the statutory presumption of validity, 35 U.S.C. § 282, and by the related requirement that oral testimony must be corroborated.

We conclude that the clear and convincing standard should be applied in the present case.

Campbell's assertion that the proof is insufficient as a matter of law because of the need for corroboration also must fail. While it is true that uncorroborated testimony is highly suspect, the fact finder takes this into account by application of a strict standard of proof.

Professor Wigmore approves of this rule, and further explains its rationale.

When a prior use is asserted (a situation analogous to the present case), the assertion of the rival claimant that his conception and use of the invention were prior in time will often describe conduct and events taking place in the privacy of his own workshop or home. Such assertions are easy to make and hard to meet. Accordingly, a rule of practice has grown up in the United States Patent Office declaring that the alleged inventor's uncorroborated testimony will not suffice. But this rule has not been definitely sanctioned by the Federal Supreme Court. Nor should it be. There can be no need for such a rule of law ..., especially where the evidence is weighed by a seasoned official acting without a jury. If the official does not believe the claimant's assertion, his own reasoning suffices to support his judgment of credibility. If he does believe the assertion, he should not be hampered by a fixed rule of thumb interfering with that judgment. That he should be cautious in relying on such assertions, is unquestioned.... (Footnotes omitted.) 7 Wigmore, Evidence § 2065a.

It is to be emphasized that in the present case there is not a complete lack of corroboration. The circumstantial evidence heretofore summarized in this opinion, including the father's belt buckle, substantiates Zimmerman's testimony. We hold that [the trial court's] findings of fact and determinations of credibility, coupled with the corroboration, sustain the heavy burden necessary to establish that Zimmerman, not Campbell, is the true inventor.

Since the patent is invalid because Campbell is not the true inventor, it is unnecessary to reach the other issues of validity or infringement decided adversely to Campbell in the District Court.

Affirmed.

NOTES

1. *Derivation.* Section 102(f) states that a "person shall be entitled to a patent unless ... he did not himself invent the subject matter sought to be patented." When it is determined that a patent applicant "did not himself invent" the claimed invention, the applicant is said to have "derived" the invention from someone else.

2. *Carrying the Burden.* As the *Campbell* case suggests, the party who raises a § 102(f) defense faces a stiff burden of proof. In *Pentech Int'l v. Hayduchok*, 18 U.S.P.Q.2d 1337 (S.D.N.Y. 1990), defendant, an accused infringer, asserted that plaintiff-patentee had derived his invention from work of another. In disposing of this issue, the court stated the burden of proof as follows:

Where a patent has issued to one claiming to be the inventor, there is a strong presumption that the patent holder was the original inventor, and the burden to establish the contrary rests upon the challenger. Once again, the challenger must prove prior invention by clear and convincing evidence.

Plaintiff sought to prove that defendants did not invent the patented product, but rather derived it from the G-Pen and Giodi products. To support a finding of derivation, a challenger to a patent must demonstrate both that the invention was previously conceived by another person and that the complete conception was communicated to the patentee. *Amax Fly Ash Corp. v. U.S.*, 514 F.2d 1041, 1047 (Ct. Cl. 1975); *Johnson & Johnson v. W.L. Gore & Assocs., Inc.*, 436 F. Supp. 704, 711 (D.C. Del. 1977). Because I find that plaintiff has not proven prior invention of the patented technology, the derivation challenge fails. There has not been an adequate showing that the [102(f) references] were identical to those disclosed in the patent.

How "complete" must be the conception communicated to the patentee for there to be derivation? *See, e.g., Amax Fly Ash Corp. v. United States*, cited in the passage above (in § 102(f) case, it would be insufficient merely to show prior knowledge of the broad idea of the patented invention; Government was required to show, in addition to the broad idea, that there was a realization, in finite terms, of the means or process steps by which the desired result of extinguishing a certain type of fire would be achieved); *Benchcraft, Inc. v. Broyhill Furniture Indus.*, 681 F. Supp. 1190, 7 U.S.P.Q.2d 1257 (N.D. Miss. 1988) (design patent case: Although alleged inventor of patented design for sofa and loveseat admitted that photographs of existing sofa comprised inspiration for design and that he used photographs of existing sofa to verify and clarify certain aspects of his design, alleged infringers of patent had not established that patented design was derived from photographs rather than invented, as they had failed to establish photographs disclosed each and every element of the patented design). *See generally Agawam Co. v. Jordan*, 74 U.S. (7 Wall.) 583, 19 L. Ed. 177 (1869) (conception communicated must be enough to enable one of ordinary skill in the art to construct and successfully operate the invention).

3. *Deriving Over the Ocean.* An important issue in derivation cases is whether acts done abroad may be introduced to establish the elements of derivation. The problem with such evidence is that it appears to run afoul of § 104 of the U.S. Patent Act, which prohibits evidence of foreign activities to establish priority under § 102(g) (see the following section of this chapter). The following excerpt clarifies this issue:

> It should be noted that proof of acts abroad is not barred when the object is not to establish a date of invention, that is when the object is not to antedate a printed publication or public use or the date of invention of another; in a case where an applicant for patent, in an interference, is trying to show that the adverse party was not an inventor at all but derived the invention from him, the fact that the events took place in a foreign country would be immaterial.

Federico, *Commentary on the New Patent Act*, 35 U.S.C.A. (1952), at 24. *See also Hedgewick v. Akers*, 497 F.2d 905, 908, 182 U.S.P.Q. (BNA) 167

(C.C.P.A. 1974) ("[T]he testimony presented on behalf of Hedgewick relating to acts, knowledge, or use of the invention in Canada was admissible for the purpose of the derivation issue").

4. *A Note on Shop Rights and Joint Inventors*. Under some circumstances, an employer who employs someone specifically to invent retains a "shop right" in the employee's inventions even if the employee is not under a contractual duty to assign inventions to the employer. Why did Campbell not argue that his company had a shop right in Zimmerman's invention? (Hint: look at Zimmerman's job description.)

It is also possible in some cases for those in Zimmerman's position to argue that they are joint inventors with the patentee. Each joint inventor has an undivided partial interest in the invention, and each can exploit it fully without permission of the other joint owner(s). For more on this, and the shop right mentioned above, see Chapter 11, Section B. Nevertheless, it is quite clear that ownership must never be confused with inventorship. For example, in *O.M.S., Inc. v. Dormont Mfg. Co.*, 39 U.S.P.Q.2d 1151, 1152 (W.D. Pa. 1996), a case in which an inventor named his business partners as co-inventors because "that's the way we did things [in our partnership]," the court awarded summary judgment of invalidity under § 102(f) for misjoinder of inventors.

How do written employment/assignment agreements interact with § 102(f) challenges? *Cf. Q.G. Prods., Inc. v. Shorty, Inc.*, 992, F.3d 1211, 26 U.S.P.Q.2d 1778, 1781 (Fed. Cir. 1993) (court applies doctrine of assignor estoppel (see Chapter 11) to prevent assignor from challenging validity of patent under § 102(f) by virtue of alleged exclusion of an inventor from patent application). Should assignees be permitted to eliminate a § 102(f) defense by contract? If they could not, how would that affect the market for assignable inventions?

A Case Study of Derivation: The Original Digital Computer

A famous instance of derivation involved the first multi-purpose, programmable digital computers. Two early researchers at the University of Pennsylvania, Echert and Mauchly, filed a patent covering this technology, which they claimed to have developed in the course of constructing their ENIAC computer. But in a later patent suit, a district court in Minnesota determined that in fact the two inventors had derived some of their ideas from Professor John Atanasoff, a researcher at Iowa State University. *See Iowa State Univ. Research Found. v. Sperry Rand Corp.*, 444 F.2d 406, 170 U.S.P.Q. (BNA) 374 (4th Cir. 1971), affirming in part the unpublished trial court opinion. For a thorough review of the matter, which supports the trial court's decision on derivation, see A. BURKS & A.W. BURKS, THE FIRST ELECTRONIC COMPUTER: THE ATANASOFF STORY (1988). *See also* C. MOLLENHOFF, ATANASOFF: FORGOTTEN FATHER OF THE COMPUTER (1988). According to a review of the first volume,

> Burks and Burks do not expect their readers to be persuaded merely by the
> court decision. They conduct a new trial in Atanasoff's defense for the

benefit of historians and members of the computer community, focusing on the technical details of inventions and prior work by both Atanasoff and Mauchly. With ample photographs and illustrations, as well as extensive quotations from the court testimony, they fulfill their promise to show that the courts can work through complex technical decisions (and that scientists can tutor judges in the essential details of research and development). Burks and Burks conclude that [Atanasoff's computer] was a special-purpose device that later gave rise to ENIAC; Mauchly's "crime" was a failure to acknowledge Atanasoff's earlier work.

L. Caporael, *Book Review*, 31 TECH. & CULT. 199 (1990).

Interestingly, the lack of a basic patent on digital computer design may actually have helped speed the development of the industry. *See* Merges & Nelson, *On the Complex Economics of Patent Scope*, 90 COLUM. L. REV. 839 (1990).

J. PRIORITY

Priority is a single concept that unifies a host of issues. The concept is simple: in a world where inventors race against each other as well as the advancing tide of prior art, precise rules must guarantee that the first inventor wins over the second, and that an inventor "wins" over some disclosure in the prior art that came after her invention.

In the first part of this section, we will concentrate on the rules for priority among competing inventors. Later, we take up questions concerning an inventor's date of invention as compared to the effective date of a potentially invalidating prior art reference. Throughout, you should keep in mind that the current American rule on priority — a strict "first to invent" rule — permeates our patent law, and that proposals to change to the international standard "first to file" rule, although likely to be accepted in the U.S. in the future, must come to grips with the importance of this concept in our law. While there are compelling reasons to advocate a change to "first to file," the transitional costs and problems will not be trivial.

1. SECTION 102(g): THE BASIC RULE OF PRIORITY

We begin with a map through the elements of § 102(g), in the form of the now-familiar schematic diagram:

§ 102. Novelty and loss of right

An inventor shall be entitled to a patent unless —

(g) [1] before the applicant's invention thereof the invention was [2] made in this country [3] by another who had not [a] abandoned, suppressed, or concealed it. [4] In determining priority of invention there shall be considered not only [a] the respective dates of [i] conception and [ii] reduction to practice of the invention, but also [b] the reasonable diligence of one who [i] was first to conceive and [ii] last to reduce to practice, [iii] from a time prior to conception by the other.

Although there are a number of fine points (some discussed below), this section states a basic set of rules. These are: (1) As between two claimants to priority, the first inventor wins, so long as (2) she does not abandon, suppress or conceal. In determining who is the first inventor, generally the first to embody the invention in an actual working version (i.e., the first to "reduce to practice") is the winner. The only exception is stated in the second sentence of § 102(g), schematic elements § 102(g)[4][a] and [b]: if the second to reduce to practice is the first to think up (conceive) the invention, she *may* be permitted to "backdate" her date of invention to the time she conceived of the idea for the invention. Whether or not she can take advantage of her earlier date of conception depends on her diligence and the date of the other inventor's conception. The details of this rule, and its rationale, are explained below.

We begin our exploration of § 102(g) by looking at the origins of the basic rules on priority. One note on terminology: an interference "count" is a claim shared in common by the parties to the interference, i.e., a claim that each party asserts should issue in a patent to them.

TOWNSEND v. SMITH

36 F.2d 292, 17 C.C.P.A. 647 (1929)

Interference proceeding between Harry P. Townsend and Henry L. Smith. Decision for the latter, and the former appeals. Reversed and rendered.

Harry P. Townsend, the appellant, presented his application to the Patent Office on January 13, 1922, praying that a patent might be issued to him on improvements in machines for cutting multiple threads on wood screws. On December 8, 1924, an interference proceeding was instituted and declared between his application and a patent issued to one Henry L. Smith, the appellee, No. 1,452,986, granted April 24, 1923, for a similar invention. The interference counts are seven in number.

The Examiner of Interferences rendered a decision awarding priority of invention to said Townsend on July 10, 1926. On appeal, the Board of Examiners in Chief rendered a decision on April 15, 1927, reversing the said decision of the Examiner of Interferences, and which decision of said board was afterward, on December 7, 1927, affirmed by the Commissioner of Patents. From the decision of said Commissioner this appeal was perfected.

The sole question at issue in this case is the question of priority as between the appellant and appellee. Townsend claims to have conceived the idea of his invention on or about June 1, 1921. The Examiner of Interferences found that he had done so, while the Board of Examiners in Chief and the Commissioner of

Patents, respectively, held that he had not proved such conception by such clear and convincing evidence as is required in such cases.

As both applications were co-pending at the time of the inadvertent issuance of the patent to appellee, and as but a short time intervened between the respective dates of application, the burden upon the appellant to prove prior conception is slight, and it is sufficient if he establish his case by a mere preponderance of the evidence. Having this rule, which we consider to be a reasonable one, in mind, we have examined the record carefully to ascertain what the facts are in this regard. The three tribunals in the Patent Office differing in their views as to what this evidence shows, the rule does not obtain here that obtains where all the tribunals agree, namely, that it must clearly and affirmatively appear that there has been some oversight, or mistake, or wrong construction of material facts, or some mistake or misapplication of some controlling principle of law, to justify this court in reversing the decision appealed from.

Townsend testifies that, while building wood screw threaders for the Ewing Bolt & Screw Company, on or about June 1, 1921, there was trouble with one of his screw threading machines. Townsend was an experienced builder of such machines, and understood them thoroughly at that time. He states that one of the gears had been cut with the wrong number of teeth, with the result that the threading tool, on the moment of initiating each cut on the screw blank, did not start in the same spot that it formerly did, and made a new mark each time the tool passed over the screw. He conceived the idea at the time, and mentioned it to the workmen around him, that this was the way to make a double threaded screw. At that time he was well acquainted with the Caldwell invention of double threaded wood screws. He says he explained it to two workmen, Pond and Clark, but that these men did not recollect it, except Clark recollected that some of the gears were cut wrong. He changed the machine at that time, putting on another gear, after which it cut single threaded screws, as it should have. He states that he thought nothing more about it until October 21, 1921, when he visited [Swift] and Caldwell at Providence, in answer to a letter informing him that they were interested in a machine for cutting a double threaded screw. He then promised them he would change one of his single threaded wood screw machines, which he was building for a Japanese order, and make it into a double threaded screw machine; he did this on or about the 10th or 11th of November, 1921, and wrote to Swift November 14th to come and see the machine. On the same day he wrote out the details of his invention for his attorney, for the purpose of making application for a patent. On November 21st the machine was demonstrated, and was afterwards changed back to a single thread machine and shipped to Japan on November 30, 1921. It is said by the Board of Examiners in Chief and the Commissioner that this testimony lacks corroboration of any kind. Townsend testifies that he did not know that a man by the name of Oscar J. Reeves had witnessed this occurrence of June 1st until about six weeks before the time of the hearing in May, 1925, but that Reeves, at that time, told him he had been present. The Board of Examiners in Chief and the Commissioner both reject the testimony of Reeves on the ground that it is not in harmony with Townsend's testimony, and is not to be relied upon as corroborative. Reeves is not related to either of the parties, and has no interest in the result of the proceeding. He testifies he was not well, and, in order to put in the time, on frequent occasions visited Townsend's shop where he was much interested in the operation of automatic machinery; that some time before June 17, 1921, which date he fixes by the fact that a short time thereafter he purchased a car and went to the country for his health, staying all summer, he was in Townsend's shop, and Townsend and his helpers were having trouble with a screw threading machine; that they had a wrong set of gearing in the machine which caused it to cut a double thread screw instead of a single thread; that Townsend made adjustments on the machine, and explained each adjustment to those about the machine; that he said at that time the trouble was caused by a wrong set of gears in the machine; that he explained to the men the changes he would have to make on the machine before it was ready for shipment, and so adjusted it that it worked before the witness left, making a single threaded screw after adjustment. Reeves testified, on being shown the drawings, that the adjustments were made on [certain] gears, which are the gears involved in the issue before us. On cross-examination he stated that double threaded screws were made with the machine, at that time, before the gears were changed, and that some of these were distributed among the bystanders. [A drawing of Smith's version of the invention is reproduced in Figure 4-14, next page.]

It is said that, because Reeves goes further in this matter than Townsend, and states that double threaded screws were actually made and distributed at that time, that he must be in error; that his testimony is in conflict with that of Townsend in this respect; and that therefore it should be rejected as corroboration.

The rule is well settled in this jurisdiction as to what is required to constitute a conception and disclosure of an invention. It is well stated in *Mergenthaler v. Scudder*, 11 App. D.C. 264 [(1897)]. A complete conception as defined in an issue of priority of invention is a matter of fact, and must be clearly established by proof. The conception of the invention consists in the complete performance of the mental part of the inventive art. All that remains to be accomplished in order to perfect the act or instrument belongs to the department of construction, not invention. It is therefore the formation in the mind of the inventor of a definite and permanent idea of the complete and operative invention as it is thereafter to be applied in practice that constitutes an available conception within the meaning of the patent law. A priority of conception is established when the invention is made sufficiently plain to enable those skilled in the art to understand it.

Does the alleged conception and disclosure of Townsend, in June, meet these requirements? We are inclined to the belief that it does. It will be remembered that Townsend, accidentally, it is true, had before him, at the time he claims to have conceived the invention, a machine which was actually cutting the threads upon the screw blank in the same manner as the final invention. The only thing required to change the single thread screw machine to a double thread screw

Apr. 24, 1923   H. L. SMITH   1,452,986

OPERATING MECHANISM FOR WOOD SCREW MACHINES
Filed Jan. 3, 1922

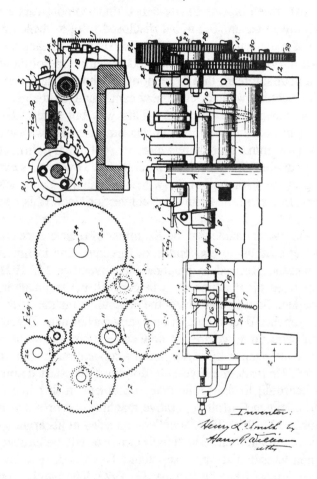

Figure 4-14

machine was the change in gears, which was already an accomplished fact by the error that had occurred. There can be no doubt that Townsend, and those about him, understood perfectly, at that time, just how such a machine could be constructed. This is not such a case as arises when an alleged inventor mentally conceives of some invention and makes an oral disclosure to another, which disclosure may or may not be complete. Here the parties had a complete working model, and there was nothing left to the imagination. The demonstration and disclosure were complete. We can see no reason for discarding the testimony of Reeves on the theory that he testifies screws were made and distributed, while Townsend does not. Townsend did not deny that this happened, nor did any one else. The fact that Reeves went further than Townsend in this regard is not a sufficient fact upon which we should conclude that he committed perjury or was totally mistaken in all that he said.

Another circumstance which leads us to believe Townsend's story has foundation is the fact that, when he was finally called upon to construct a machine on the Swift and Caldwell order, Townsend disclosed fully to those men just how he proposed to make the machine. He went to his shop, according to the testimony of Clark, and informed him that he wanted to set up one of the machines in the shop to cut a double thread; that thereupon the witness Clark and Townsend, "simply took the machine we had, cut a new cam, changed the gears, and cut a double thread on our regular machine." This was but a few days after his interview with Swift and Caldwell, and at this time the idea was so well developed in Townsend's mind that there were no preliminary difficulties in the preparation of the double threaded screw machine. In Townsend's explanation to Swift, according to the testimony of the witness, John W. Caldwell, Townsend was definite and clear as to the method of converting one of his own machines for this purpose.

For these reasons we conclude that the Examiner of Interference correctly held that Townsend had established conception of this invention in June, 1921. It is agreed that Townsend reduced to practice on November 14, 1921, when he prepared and operated his machine. It is held by all the tribunals in the Patent Office that appellee, Smith, conceived the invention on the 19th or 20th of October, 1921. Appellee does not insist upon any earlier date. Whether this was the exact date of conception we are not now called upon to say, in view of our conclusion in the matter generally. After Smith's conception, no question is raised as to his diligence. He made the necessary drawings and started construction of his machine. According to the preliminary statement in this interference, the appellee, Smith, completed a fully operative machine and operated the same on or about December 12, 1921. This, appellee concedes in his argument, he must rely upon as his date for formal reduction to practice. His preliminary statement is his pleading and he is bound by it. Appellant, Townsend, filed his application for a patent in the Patent Office on January 13, 1922. The Smith application was made on January 3, 1922. No question arises in the case as to the diligence of either Townsend or Smith after October, 1921, when they were each requested to prepare plans for double threaded screw machines by the Commercial Service Company. From that time forward each party moved with all the diligence required by the law.

From what has been said it appears that the appellant, Townsend, was the first to conceive and the first to reduce to practice. This being so, and there being no abandonment or negligence since reduction to practice, Townsend is entitled to priority. It has been argued that after Townsend's conception in June, 1921, he did nothing until October 21, 1921, and that this should be considered such failure to act promptly as to deprive him of the benefit of a claim of priority of conception. We do not understand this to be the law. Where an inventor has established priority of conception, disclosure and reduction to practice, in the absence of any clearly proved abandonment, his right to a patent has not become forfeited either to the public or to his rival. It has been held that a lapse of two years between a reduction to practice and the filing of an application, does not, in itself, constitute an abandonment. *Rolfe v. Hoffman*, 26 App. D.C. 336 [(1905)].

Townsend had a right, after having conceived and disclosed his invention, to wait until October and he did not forfeit his right to apply for a patent thereby unless someone else, in the meantime, had made the same invention and secured by patent the exclusive right to make, use and sell it. *Bates v. Coe*, 98 U.S. 31, 25 L. Ed. 68 [(1878)]; *Mason v. Hepburn*, 13 App. D.C. 86 [(1898)].

We are of the opinion that the Examiner of Interferences arrived at the correct conclusion in the matter, and the decision of the Commissioner of Patents is therefore reversed and priority is awarded to Townsend, the appellant.

NOTES

1. *Burdens of Proof.* As is so often the case with disputes centering on complex issues of fact, presumptions and burdens are very important to the outcome of many interferences. Note how they played a role in the *Townsend* case. There is an elaborate body of law allocating burdens in contemporary interferences. Much depends on whether the interference involves two applications or an application and an issued patent, and on when the respective applications or patents were filed. *See* 37 C.F.R. § 1.608 (1996) (applicant must make prima facie showing of priority to go forward against patentee); 37 C.F.R. § 1.617 (1996) ("If in the opinion of the administrative patent judge the evidence fails to show that the applicant is prima facie entitled to a judgment relative to the patentee, the administrative patent judge shall, concurrently with the notice declaring the interference, enter an order stating the reasons for the opinion and directing the applicant, within a time set in the order, to show cause why summary judgment should not be entered against the applicant."). *See generally* 3 D. CHISUM, PATENTS § 10.03[1][c] (1978 & Supp. 1996). Some courts had held that an applicant who *files* after another inventor's patent *issues* bears the burden of showing priority "beyond a reasonable doubt." However this practice ended in 1993 with the Federal Circuit decision of *Price v. Symsek*, 988 F.2d 1187, 26 U.S.P.Q.2d 1031 (Fed. Cir. 1993) (announcing "clear and convincing evidence" standard for such cases).

2. *What Cost Fairness?* Even garden variety priority disputes such as the one at issue in *Townsend* are costly to resolve. While economists have noted the subtle effects of priority rules, see, e.g., Suzanne Scotchmer & Jerry Green, *Novelty and Disclosure in Patent Law*, 21 RAND J. ECON. 131 (1990), the most obvious feature of the "first to invent" rule is that it is expensive to administer. Even assuming that it is more fair to reward the true first inventor, is the extra fairness worth the cost? In contemplating this issue, consider the following costs of the interference system:

- The average cost of an interference that goes to a final hearing was $100,000 in the early 1990s; for others, the average cost is estimated at $25,000, see Charles R.B. Macedo, *First-to-File: Is American Adoption of the International Standard in Patent Law Worth the Price?*, 18 AM. INTELL. PROP. L. ASS'N Q.J. 193 (1990).
- The total amount spent on interferences was estimated to be over $15 million per year, *id.*; and
- Uncertainty regarding priority, all during prosecution and up to one year after patent issues.

Some at least have argued that these costs do not buy much, since it is very rare for an interference to award priority to the junior party. This means that most interferences yield the same result as a first-to-file rule — at a much higher price. *See* The Patent Harmonization Act of 1992: Hearings on H.R. 4978 – S. 2605, Joint Hearings Before the Senate Judiciary Subcommittee on Patents, Copyrights and Trademarks and the House Judiciary Subcommittee on Courts, Intellectual Property and the Administration, 102d Cong., 2d Sess. 83 (1992) (statement of Robert P. Merges), summarized at 44 BNA PAT. TRADEMARK & COPYRIGHT J. 3 (May 7, 1992). For an interesting article arguing that the U.S. first-to-invent system encourages cross-licensing to settle potentially costly interferences, thereby unwittingly supporting cooperative inter-firm R&D, see William Kingston, *Is the United States Right about "First-to-Invent"?*, 14 EURO. INTELL. PROP. REV. 223 (1992). *But cf.* Robert P. Merges, *Intellectual Property and the Costs of Commercial Exchange: A Review Essay* (book review), 93 MICH. L. REV. 1570 (1995) (describing growth of inter-firm R&D internationally, without assistance from first-to-invent rules).

Although § 102(g) is most often invoked to resolve priority disputes between two rivals claimants to the same invention, it can also serve as a defense. An accused infringer can assert that the patentee did not invent first, pointing to prior invention by someone else — a third party. The following case is of this sort. It also serves as a good introduction to the concept of concealment (§ 102(g)[3][a] in the schematic).

INTERNATIONAL GLASS CO. v. UNITED STATES
408 F.2d 395, 161 U.S.P.Q. (BNA) 116 (Ct. Cl. 1969)

This is a patent suit under 28 U.S.C. § 1498 to recover "reasonable and entire compensation" for alleged unauthorized use for the Government of plaintiff's patented invention. Only the issue of liability is before the court; accounting, if any, is deferred to later proceedings. Plaintiff contends that claims 1-4 and 6 of its patent are infringed by Boeing Aircraft Company (hereafter "Boeing") and Rohr Corporation (hereafter "Rohr"), both of which made airplane parts for defendant within the statutory recovery period.

The issues before the court [include] patent validity under 35 U.S.C. §§ 102 and 103. In particular, defendant contends that claims 1-4 are invalid under sections 102(g) and 103.

Patent in Suit

The patent in suit, issued in 1953 to plaintiff and entitled "Mounting Method," relates to method and apparatus for holding workpieces, such as gem stones, to a work station for treatment, such as grinding, polishing or buffing. In essence, the workpiece is frozen to the station. The patent specification says:

> This invention is concerned with a method for temporarily mounting work pieces, *particularly of minute dimension, and hence, difficulty manageable* [sic!], for application of treatments requiring exposure of at least some of the surfaces of the work. The invention is particularly useful in connection with the grinding and polishing or buffing of materials such as glass, plastics and/or metal in the manufacture of ornamental and industrial jewels, imitation stones, lens, [sic] beads, bearings, buttons and the like.
>
> Work to be treated is bonded in accordance with this invention to a work support with a low temperature bond induced by interposing a film of a material which is liquid at normal room temperatures, preferably water, between the work piece and work support and freezing the liquid into an ice bond, if it be water, which is maintained during manufacturing operations performed on remaining exposed surfaces of the work. *The work is quickly released merely by melting the ice bond by application of heat.*
>
> While water or any aqueous vehicle is the most inexpensive and satisfactory bonding material for use in my invention, I do not exclude the use of other materials, liquid at normal room temperatures and having freezing points at or above about 32° F., for example, acetic acid, benzol, glycerine, and some of the relatively high freezing point oils. [Emphasis added].

One embodiment of an apparatus for practicing the invention (illustrated in [Figure 4-15, next page]) comprises a metal rod, called a dopstick, mounted in a housing. The rod has a conical-shaped depression, or dop, at its lower end for receiving a gem stone. A refrigerant chamber surrounds the lower part of the dopstick; the upper part is offset like a crank handle for rotation by an indexing device to turn the workpiece. In operation, before a gem stone is mounted at the end of the dopstick, water is sprayed onto the surface of the conical recess. With the stone inserted, refrigerant is circulated through the housing. Since the dopstick is metal, a good heat conductor, the water is frozen quickly and the stone secured in place. The stone is buffed or polished by an abrasive belt, then the dopstick is rotated, thereby to expose the stone's different facets for treatment. Thereafter, the ice bond is thawed either by passing warm fluid through the refrigerant chamber or by applying "localized" heat to the ice bond. The stone is then turned over and refrozen into place or another stone inserted.

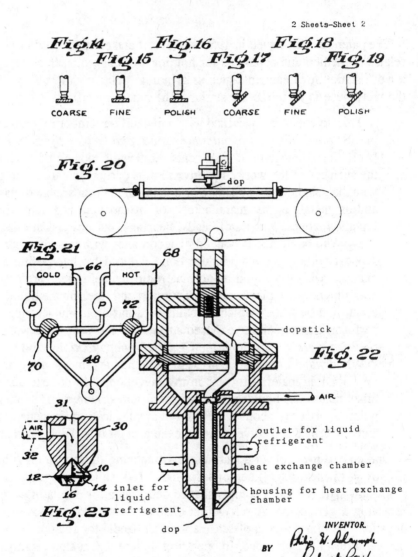

June 16, 1953   P. W. DALRYMPLE   2,641,879

MOUNTING METHOD
Filed JULY 11, 1951

2 Sheets-Sheet 2

Figure 4-15

The only apparatus disclosed in the patent specification for applying "localized" heat is a "high frequency coil" into which the lower end of the dopstick is mounted. When energized, the coil heats the dopstick. By applying "localized" heat, rather than discontinuing refrigerant flow and warming the refrigerant chamber, a workpiece can be released quickly, turned or replaced, and refrozen without interrupting the refrigeration process. According to the patentee, this technique, as opposed to warming the refrigerant chamber, is "more efficient," is preferred, and is the subject of claim 6, later discussed in detail.

The patent has 11 claims, both to apparatus and method. Only claims 1-4 and 6, all to method, are in issue, claim 1 [is] representative:

> 1. The method of temporarily rigidly mounting difficultly manageable work-pieces on supports for application of precision treatments to exposed surfaces of the mounted work-pieces, which comprises
>
> interposing a material which is liquid at normal room temperature between and in contact with a work-piece and a work-receiving surface of a work-support at a temperature not substantially exceeding normal room temperature, and withdrawing heat from said liquid at least in part by conduction through said support until said liquid is frozen at a temperature below room temperature, and forms a rigid work-piece-to-support frozen bond and thereafter treating an exposed surface of the work-piece while maintaining the temperature of said bond below the freezing point of said material.

Claim 3 is similar to claim 1 but specifies the "liquid" as "water" and states that the temperature of the bond is maintained "below 0° C." which is the freezing point of water. Claims 2 and 4 are similar to claims 1 and 3, respectively, but add as a final step "breaking the bond by applying heat" to thaw the ice.

Plaintiff introduced no evidence at trial that the patented apparatus and method were ever used by the jewelry industry, nor that a license was ever granted under the patent, though plaintiff, without success, solicited licenses from several companies in various industries, including the aircraft industry. The patent is thus a "paper patent."

The Alleged Infringing Process

The process used by Boeing and Rohr and alleged to infringe is the so-called "ice chuck" process for machining honeycomb material. Honeycomb, as the name implies, is an open-celled structure with thin aluminum or steel walls, about 0.001 to about 0.005 inches (1 to 5 mils) thick. Honeycomb is strong in compression in the direction parallel to the cell walls and is very light per unit volume. It is therefore a useful support filler to sandwich between upper and lower surfaces of airfoils, such as helicopter rotor blades. Honeycomb comes in pieces about 5 feet long and several inches thick. Before useful as filler, the pieces must be shaped by machining to the contour of the airfoil. Machining is difficult, however, since honeycomb is fragile and the cell walls are easily torn or deformed by usual grinding or cutting. Also, pieces cannot be anchored as in usual machining operations, e.g., by clamps, without damaging cell walls.

The ice-chuck method is a solution to difficulties of machining honeycomb. Boeing's method in essence is to fill up the honeycomb with water, freeze it solid to a work platform, then machine the frozen block to proper contour. The block is then thawed, the honeycomb piece turned over, and the process repeated. The final honeycomb piece thus has the proper shape for airfoil filler. In short, Boeing's method does two things: It secures the honeycomb to a work platform, thus solving the clamping problem; and the ice which fills all the cells of the honeycomb supports the cell walls during machining to prevent tearing or distorting.

Plaintiff concedes that its patent specification does not expressly disclose honeycomb among the other workpieces to which its process and apparatus are applicable. And indeed honeycomb as a workpiece is very unlike gem stones in size and structure. However, plaintiff says the patent claims, properly construed, read on the Boeing and Rohr processes because honeycomb pieces are "difficultly manageable workpieces"; the honeycomb surfaces are given "precision treatment"; and in all other respects, the accused processes respond to the method steps recited in the claims.

Validity of Claims 1 to 4

A principal defense is that the accused ice-chuck process was used by others who did not abandon, suppress or conceal it before the patentee's invention was made. 35 U.S.C. § 102(g). Thus, so defendant argues, claims 1-4 are invalid. The defense is based on testimony of Frank Sciaronni, a witness at trial, and on stipulated testimony of others, including one Kenneth Speck. Sciaronni, a diemaker, was in 1946 superintendent of the experimental helicopter division, McDonnell Aircraft Corporation (hereafter "McDonnell"), St. Louis, Missouri. While working on construction of a helicopter blade, Sciaronni used a process, similar to the Boeing ice-chuck process, to machine honeycomb. Speck, a machine shop foreman at McDonnell, also used a similar process in 1950. The circumstances under which the process was used by Sciaronni and Speck are summarized here.

In July 1946, Sciaronni was asked by a McDonnell engineer, working on a helicopter project, to shape a piece of plastic honeycomb material to proper contour to fill a helicopter blade. Recognizing the difficulties of machining honeycomb, Sciaronni first tried filling the honeycomb, before machining, with cerrobend, a solder-like material which melts in hot water. Cerrobend and its properties were well known at that time. He machined the cerrobend-honeycomb block to proper contour, then removed the cerrobend by melting, leaving a properly shaped honeycomb piece. However, because of residual impurities of cerrobend left on the edges of the honeycomb, the honeycomb did not bond well to the top and bottom surfaces of the helicopter rotor blade when sandwiched therebetween.

About a week later, Sciaronni was again asked to machine a piece of honeycomb, this time aluminum rather than plastic. Recalling the problems of using cerrobend, Sciaronni decided to use frozen water rather than cerrobend to fill up the honeycomb. Sciaronni testified that he got the idea to use water from seeing rivets frozen to the bottom of a pan in a refrigerator at McDonnell. The rivets were frozen prior to use with a rivet gun to minimize crushing or deforming when forced into place. The rivets froze to the pan much like ice cube trays freeze to the freezer compartment of an ordinary home refrigerator. Sciaronni built a crude plywood tub on which the honeycomb was placed, filled with water, frozen solid, and machined similarly to the Boeing process here in issue. He showed the finished honeycomb piece to several McDonnell personnel, including a patent engineer, and explained the machining process used. The piece so-machined ultimately was used with an experimental helicopter in flight tests in late 1946.

In 1950, during performance of another contract to build helicopters, [Speck, another McDonnell employee, used a similar approach]. Speck proceeded in much the same manner as had Sciaronni four years earlier. He first used cerrobend to fill honeycomb; and because of the problems it created in later bonding the honeycomb to the rotor blade, he turned to the ice-chuck method, substantially as performed by Sciaronni in 1946, after recalling an earlier experience of freezing rubber before cutting it. Sciaronni then told Speck that he (Sciaronni) had used the same ice-chuck process four years earlier; and, together, they machined several pieces of honeycomb for the new helicopter blade. Sciaronni and Speck in 1950 told Williams, the machine shop superintendent, and Walter Burke, president of McDonnell, about the process and showed them honeycomb pieces shaped thereby.

A patent application was never filed on the Sciaronni-Speck method, although notebook records were kept by Sciaronni in 1946. The records, however, were personal and were not submitted to patent counsel or supervisory personnel at McDonnell for further evaluation. Although Sciaronni testified that the method was used from time to time at McDonnell up to 1952 to make small samples of honeycomb, there is no evidence that the method was used by anyone at McDonnell after 1950 to make finished honeycomb filler; that the method was described in any document or report; or that knowledge of the method was ever disseminated outside McDonnell, though it was apparently not considered proprietary information.

Defendant does not contend that the activities of Sciaronni in 1946, and Speck and Sciaronni in 1950, constitute prior knowledge or use by others of the ice-chuck method within the meaning of 35 U.S.C. § 102(a); but rather it contends that such activities constitute prior invention in this country by others "who had not abandoned, suppressed, or concealed it." 35 U.S.C. § 102(g). The distinction is important since, unlike the defense under section 102(a) where prior knowledge and use must be "public" at the time the patented invention is made (*Gayler v. Wilder*, 51 U.S. (10 How.) 477 (1850)), prior invention under section 102(g) requires only that the invention be complete, *i.e.*, conceived and reduced to practice, and not abandoned, suppressed or concealed. Section 102(g) most commonly applies to priority disputes in U.S. Patent Office interference proceedings. However, it may also be an appropriate defense to patent validity in infringement litigation where a patent application was never filed by the prior inventor. *Engelhardt v. Judd*, 369 F.2d 408, 411, 151 U.S.P.Q. 732, 735 (C.C.P.A. 1966).

The evidence is clear that Sciaronni in 1946 and Speck in 1950 conceived and reduced to practice the ice-chuck process substantially like the Boeing process here in issue.[1] The question remains, however, whether they abandoned, suppressed or concealed their process within the meaning of section 102(g). The courts have consistently held that an invention, though completed, is deemed abandoned, suppressed, or concealed if, within a reasonable time after completion, no steps are taken to make the invention publicly known. *Kendall v. Winsor*, 62 U.S. (21 How.) 322 (1858); *Mason v. Hepburn*, 13 App. D.C. 86 (1898). Thus, failure to file a patent application (*Mason, supra*); to describe the invention in a publicly disseminated document; or to use the invention publicly (*Allinson Mfg. Co. v. Ideal Filter Co.*, 21 F.2d 22 (8th Cir. 1927), have been held to constitute abandonment, suppression or concealment. See also *Lyon v. Bausch & Lomb*, 224 F.2d 530, 106 U.S.P.Q. 1 (2d Cir. 1955), *cert. denied*, 350 U.S. 911 (1955). Neither Sciaronni, Speck, nor anyone else at McDonnell

---

[1]Plaintiff contends that the Sciaronni-Speck work "amounted to no more than an abandoned experiment and a dismissal [sic!] commercial failure." However, reduction to practice of a process requires only that it be "successfully performed." The Sciaronni-Speck work meets such criterion. Further, commercial use is not necessary to establish actual reduction to practice.

Plaintiff also contends that the Sciaronni-Speck process was materially different from the Boeing process. In particular, plaintiff says Sciaronni and Speck did not continuously cool the ice bond between the honeycomb block and the work platform to which it was frozen to maintain its temperature below 0° C. during machining. This is crucial, says plaintiff, since otherwise the bonds tend to melt and become "progressively weaker." Plaintiff even suggests that it is for this reason Speck and Sciaronni, and others at McDonnell, discarded their process after 1950.

The record does not support plaintiff. While it is true neither Speck nor Sciaronni continuously cooled their honeycomb-ice blocks during machining, they were aware of the problem of premature thawing of the bonds. Speck said, in his stipulated testimony, that he and Sciaronni "hurried across the shop with the frozen honeycomb to get the frozen block to the router before the ice melted." Yet, despite no cooling during machining, Speck said, "the ice block containing honeycomb remained adhered to the flat plate ..." and "the adhesive qualities of the ice kept the honeycomb rigidly bonded to the plate." Speck further noted, "after completing the shaping operation on the router, Mr. Sciaronni and myself decided to let the frozen block remain on the plate to see how long it would take the ice to melt. From this observation, we realized that it was not necessary to run as we did from the refrigerator to the routing machine. The ice took a comparatively long time to melt." Had premature thawing of ice bonds been a problem faced by Sciaronni or Speck in 1946 or 1950, it would seem the obvious solution was to use additional refrigeration.

took steps, after 1946 or 1950, to make public the results of their ice-chuck process. Their work lay dormant, did not enrich the art, and thus "remained secret, effectively concealed and suppressed until exhumed by ... [defendant] for the defense of this case." [*Carter Products v. Colgate-Palmolive Co.*, 130 F. Supp. 557, 104 U.S.P.Q. 314 (D. Md. 1955)], at 569. Defendant therefore has failed to make out a defense under 35 U.S.C. § 102(g).

NOTES

1. *The § 102(g) Two-Step.* Section 102(g) can be confusing because it seems to perform two different functions: it sorts out priority, and it serves as a source of novelty — defeating prior art. *Townsend, supra,* illustrates the former; *International Glass*, the latter. One way to square these disparate roles is to think of a priority contest as a case where each claimant is trying to defeat the other's novelty. Priority follows, in that, presumably, removing the other claimant's reference removes the last obstacle to patentability.

2. *Details.* It is important to keep in mind several points regarding third party § 102(g) lack-of-novelty defenses, i.e., cases like the preceding one where an accused infringer relies on a third party's prior invention to invalidate a patentee's patent. First, a § 102(g) lack-of-novelty defense, as the *International Glass* court points out,

> [is] unlike a defense under section 102(a) where prior knowledge and use must be "public" at the time the patented invention is made ..., [since] prior invention under section 102(g) requires only that the invention be complete, *i.e.*, conceived and reduced to practice, and not abandoned, suppressed or concealed.

408 F.2d at 402. In that there is no need to prove prior public knowledge or use, the 102(g) defense is easier to make out than a § 102(a) "prior knowledge or use" defense. Completely private uses of a prior invention may be enough to make out the § 102(g) defense. But if the prior invention has been "abandoned, suppressed or concealed," the invention will *not* be considered a prior art reference and the defense will not stand. Abandonment, suppression or concealment, according to the preceding case, can be shown several ways, including

> failure to file a patent application ...; to describe the invention in a publicly disseminated document; or to use the invention publicly.

408 F.2d at 403. Consequently, it should be clear that despite the lack of a "publicness" requirement under § 102(g), this defense will not always be available: prior inventions will often be deemed "abandoned, suppressed or concealed."

Finally, note the importance of corroborating evidence in this case. We will see that this is an important issue in many cases in this section.

3. *Comparing to* § *102(e).* The foregoing might be reassuring to those troubled by the thought that a completely *private* use of an invention could defeat the novelty of a subsequently invented product or process. But there is another — and much more important — source of such "secret prior art," the previously filed patent application. As the *International Glass* court notes, there is no abandonment under § 102(g) when the prior inventor has filed an application. Such a situation is dealt with in § 102(e) of the patent statute, which is covered in Section H of this chapter, above.

4. *Why Doesn't* § *102(g) "Swallow" All of* § *102?* One thought that occurs to many students when they first delve into § 102 is that subsection (g) seems to subsume all the other subsections. The idea is that, before there is a public use, publication or patent under subsections (a) and (b), or a prior-filed patent application under subsection (e), or *any* reference for that matter, there had to be prior invention. While in a sense this is true, the details of subsection (g) show that the other subsections are far from superfluous.

First, recall that (g) requires prior *invention*, defined as conception plus reduction to practice. As we have seen, e.g., in *UMC Electronics*, no reduction to practice is required for § 102(a) and (b) references. And it can be difficult to prove pre-filing reduction to practice. *See* 3 D. CHISUM, PATENTS §§ 10.03[1][c] & 10.06 (1978 & Supp. 1996).

Second, as we have also seen, § 102(e) applies when a prior-filed application discloses but does not claim an invention. By contrast, § 102(g) requires that when two patents or applications are involved, both applications (or an application and an issued patent) must *claim* the same invention. *See Sun Studs, Inc. v. ATA Equip. Leasing, Inc.*, 872 F.2d 978, 983-84; 10 U.S.P.Q.2d (BNA) 1338 (Fed. Cir. 1989).

Third, § 102(g) applies only to prior inventions "in this country" (schematic [2]); there is no such limitation on prior art patents and printed publications under §§ 102(a) and (b).

Last but not least, there is the important issue of cost, explored in the following section.

2. AN ECONOMIC PERSPECTIVE ON "THIRD PARTY" § 102(g) PRIOR ART

It is possible to analyze an accused infringer's use of a third party's prior invention under § 102(g) in terms of the "search" model presented earlier in Section B.4 of this chapter. (For a discussion of § 102(g) in the context of priority disputes between inventors, see Section J, later in this chapter.) Recall that for the most part, we ignored in that model the cost of searching — i.e., of acquiring the information in the prior art reference. That is what permitted us, for example, to justify those cases holding that one copy of a student thesis in an obscure library halfway around the world qualifies as prior art. It is tempting to carry over this assumption as we begin our analysis of third-party § 102(g) prior art. The problem with this is that in such a case *any* invention which might be invalidated under § 102(g) would never be made! The inventor, who as we have said has a major incentive to seek out even obscure information, would discover anything a later potential infringer would discover. With this information, accompanied by the knowledge of what standards a court will use in determining novelty and nonobviousness, the inventor will know that her invention is not patentable in light of someone else's prior invention. She will thus decide not to pursue the patent. And, assuming the reward of a patent is an important component of the overall set of incentives available to the inventor, she may wind up deciding *not to pursue the invention*.

This is not what really happens, of course; if it were, we would never see cases like *International Glass*. So let's get more realistic. What happens if, in looking at § 102(g), we introduce the cost factor into the model?

An in-depth analysis of the impact of costly information would consider the precise characteristics of the information in question. But this will be practically impossible in most situations. Instead, we will assume a simplified world where there are only two possible cost levels associated with investigating prior art references, a low cost and a high cost. You might think of the low cost as the typical real-world cost of looking up a patent or printed publication on some electronic database or in a library; call it $15.00. Note that this is the cost of examining the typical reference under §§ 102(a) and 102(b) of the Patent Act. In contrast, think of the high cost as the cost of investigating a possible prior invention. This might be either the cost of "looking behind" a patent or printed publication to discover actual invention dates, or the cost of finding out about an invention not otherwise reported in a patent or publication. Investigating actual invention dates might involve extensive inquiries, by phone or in person, of those working in the relevant field during the period of interest; the cost of follow-up calls to track down leads; and perhaps the cost of a personal visit to the prior inventor to obtain documentation and personal information concerning the invention date. All this might cost at least $200.00, and possibly as much as $2,000 or more.

To determine the impact of the availability of § 102(g) prior art, we must answer this question: When would it be worth it for an alleged infringer to spend the extra money to investigate prior invention?

The answer: when the investigation is worth the reward. *See In re Bass*, 474 F.2d 1276, 1286 n. 7, 177 U.S.P.Q. (BNA) 178 (C.C.P.A. 1973) (Rich, J.: reason why §§ 102(g)/103 defenses were not used much in preceding 20 years is because "it is a rare case where the effort of going back to the date of invention of a prior inventor is worth the cost."). And since the reward is the invalidation of the patentee's patent, this boils down to: when the patented invention is very valuable to the accused infringer.

As a consequence, the availability of § 102(g) prior art will *not* impact inventive efforts in a negative way, at least when the value of the invention is roughly the same to the patentee as to the infringer. This is because, with this key assumption, § *102(g) prior art will only be asserted when a highly valuable invention is at issue*. And when this is true, presumably the patentee will consider the risk of invalidation worth it, since the patent in question will be a valuable one. It is as if you said to the patentee: this patent might be invalidated by art you would find expensive to discover, but only if it turns out to be a valuable patent. The patentee might be expected to reply: fine, I'll take that chance; the only time it will be realized is if my invention turns out to be valuable, and then the risk will probably be worth it. Thus § 102(g) will not be expected to unduly dampen inventive effort. It is as if the inventor purchased an "option" to keep the possibility of a valid property right alive; by filing an application, which makes sense given what the inventor knows, protection is secured even though later investigation may yield information that undermines the value of the patent. On options theory generally, which may have wide application here, see LENOS TRIGEORGIS, REAL OPTIONS (1996).

The high cost also explains why the Patent Office will only rarely discover third party § 102(g) prior art. It makes no sense for the Patent Office, which is in a poor position to evaluate the potential value of patents, to spend huge amounts of money exhaustively researching the prior art for each patent application.

The only caveat involves the assumption that the patentee and accused infringer value the invention equally. If they do not, and specifically if the accused infringer values it more highly, she will be willing to spend more to have the patent invalidated than the patentee would find comfortable. In this case the extra risk of invalidation might, if the patentee had known about it ahead of time, dissuade her from patenting the invention or pursuing the research that led to it in the first place. But one might note two points by way of defense of § 102(g) in this connection.

First, this would seem a rare case. Although competitors might value a technology differently, we would not expect the difference to be too significant in too many cases. After all, there is some baseline value for a technology, even if it only stems from potential royalty income generated by licensing it to competitors.

Second, in those cases where the infringer actually values the technology more highly, society is better off if she spends the money to have the patent invalidated. In such a case, the expenditure will simply be the "price of admission" to a state of affairs where the party who values the asset more highly ends up owning it. To look at the problem another way, note that society benefits greatly when an inventor does an incomplete search of the prior art relative to the value of her invention. For when this happens, a later accused infringer can be expected to search the prior art more diligently and possibly find a "smoking gun." The ultimate beneficiary of such a sequence of events, of course, is society in general, which now gets the invention free of the inventor's patent claims. If both the infringer and the inventor continue to compete in the market for the now-unpatented invention, we will receive it at a competitive rather than a monopolistic price.

In general, from the perspective of economics, this is a preferable state. From the point of view of the patentee, however, it is anything but. Recall that the risk of invalidation is proportional to the value of the invention; so much so, that an inventor would presumably be willing to take the higher risk of invalidation when her patent is a valuable one. And, perhaps importantly, when the patentee knows even before filing that her invention will be valuable, she may do some preliminary § 102(g) investigating on her own to determine whether it is worthwhile patenting and commercializing the invention.

Because the risk of invalidation grows with the value of the invention, the patentee will not often be deterred by this risk. Only when she places a lower valuation on the invention compared to the infringer would we expect the patentee to so resent the availability of § 102(g) prior art that she would have given up the invention if she knew an accused infringer would investigate this source of prior art.

However, there is one more twist that might still save § 102(g) in those cases where the patentee values the invention less highly than the accused infringer. If the accused infringer could make a payment to the patentee in exchange for the right to use the invention, and thereby save the expense of investigating facts to invalidate the patent, everyone would be better off: the technological asset would wind up in the hands of the person who valued it most highly, and the patentee would receive some compensation for it. (Note that for this to work, the cost of acquiring the information must be less than or equal to the patentee's valuation of the invention, which suggests this may be a rare case since the patentee's valuation would hardly be worth the cost of patenting the invention in the first place.) Thus, in theory, even in these cases the patentee is not left with nothing, and § 102(g) can be at least partially defended.

Note that, still in theory, we would expect to see a certain number of infringement suits settled *before* the accused infringer spends the money to investigate prior inventive activity under § 102(g). And, in fact, we do observe such settlements, all the time. Note well the fact that when such settlements can be attributed to § 102(g), the parties are wise to transfer the money among themselves, where it might lead to more research and development, rather than to the legal profession, where it will only be spent foolishly on mahogany desks and AIPLA junkets. Would you feel so positive about a payment from the patentee to the prior inventor, the third party whose work created the § 102(g) reference? If not, why not?

To summarize, then, § 102(g) will not in retrospect seem too draconian to most inventors, since it will only be raised when a valuable invention is at issue, and hence the risk of invalidation appears worth taking. And in those cases where, in retrospect, § 102(g) makes the inventor sorry she ever pursued the invention because the risk of invalidation is not worth it to her, society stands to benefit because the accused infringer, who values the invention more highly, might use § 102(g) as a lever to pry it from the grips of the patentee. In such cases, the patentee would be wise to settle with the accused infringer, and at least have something to show for the ordeal.

3. SCHEMATIC § 102(g)[3][a]: "ABANDONED, SUPPRESSED, OR CONCEALED"

In the following case, note who is the "senior party" and who is the "junior party." A senior party is one who *files* first.

PEELER v. MILLER

535 F.2d 647, 190 U.S.P.Q. (BNA) 117 (C.C.P.A. 1976)

RICH, JUDGE.

The senior party, Peeler, Godfrey, and Furby (Peeler), [co-inventors on U.S. Patent No. 3,591,506, entitled "Functional Fluids Containing Halocarbons for Preventing Cavitation Damage," issued July 6, 1971, on an application filed January 4, 1968, assigned to Chevron Research Company] appeals from the decision of the Patent and Trademark Office (PTO) Board of Patent Interferences (board) awarding priority of invention in five counts to the junior party, Miller, [who on April 27, 1970 filed application serial No. 32,344, entitled "Functional Fluid Compositions Containing Fluro Alkanes," which is assigned to Monsanto Company.] We reverse.

The Subject Matter

Counts 6 and 8 adequately describe the subject matter:

> 6. A power transmission fluid consisting essentially of a major portion of a phosphate ester having a tendency to cause cavitation erosion damage, and as an additive effective in reducing such damage, from 0.01 to 10% by weight of a halocarbon containing only halogen atoms and at least one carbon atom having a boiling point below 75° C, wherein the halogen substituents on said halocarbon are chlorine, bromine or fluorine or combinations thereof.

> 8. A method of inhibiting cavitation damage to a hydraulic system utilizing a hydraulic fluid consisting essentially of a major portion of a phosphate ester, which method comprises maintaining in said hydraulic fluid by addition 0.01 to 10% by weight of a halocarbon containing only halogen atoms and at least one carbon atom having a boiling point below 75° C, wherein the halogen substituents on said halocarbon are chlorine, bromine or fluorine or combinations thereof.

The Evidence

Peeler took no testimony and relied on his filing date. Miller submitted testimony in the form of affidavits from himself, various Monsanto colleagues, and William Black, the Monsanto patent attorney who prepared and filed Miller's application. Miller's efforts, culminating in this invention, began in the fall of 1964 when he became aware of serious hydraulic valve leakage in British "Trident" aircraft using Monsanto's SKYDROL 500A brand hydraulic fluid. He concluded that cavitation [i.e., formation of gas-filled pockets] was responsible for the problem and began the search for a fluid additive to overcome the problem.

In 1965, in ultrasonic vibrating probe tests, in which a soft metal tip is vibrated at high frequency in a beaker containing SKYDROL 500A and the additive under test and the loss of metal from the tip measured, it was found that water as an additive would reduce cavitation damage substantially. This laboratory finding was confirmed in use in the Trident aircraft. In March 1966 Miller thought of using FREON 11 (the DuPont trademark for trichloromonofluoromethane) as the additive and also other halocarbons, which are fire-resistant and, like water, have high volatility in relation to the base fluid, as anti-cavitation additives. On March 8 Miller instructed a colleague (Stainbrook) to conduct ultrasonic vibrating probe tests using FREON 11 as the additive. Stainbrook performed one control run and one run with FREON 11 as the additive on that day. Stainbrook's affidavit and Miller's March 14 notebook page indicate that FREON 11 significantly reduced erosion of the probe tip in the experiment. In his notebook entry Miller indicated, "To better assess such additives, we are setting up hermetically sealed sample containers." The record does not show that hermetically sealed containers were subsequently used by Miller.

On April 5, 1966, Miller submitted a "preliminary disclosure of invention," which his superiors in the Research Department of Monsanto's Organic Chemicals Division rated "A (Ready (to file))" on April 18, 1966. Presumably, this disclosure was forwarded to Monsanto's patent department for action soon thereafter, but the record does not show when this occurred.

From the time when Miller's invention disclosure was rated "A (Ready)," more than four years elapsed until Miller's filing date. Miller continued working on cavitation inhibitors of undisclosed nature during this time, and in September 1966 he gave presentations at several U.S. aviation industry meetings on Monsanto's solution of the Trident valve damage problem. Stainbrook stated that he ran vibrating probe tests in October 1967 using FREON 112(a) (apparently tetrachlorodifluoroethane) as the additive and that he informed Miller of his results. What Miller did with this information is not indicated in the record. Meanwhile, there is no evidence of action in Monsanto's patent department until the arrival of Mr. Black in October 1968, some two and a half years after Miller's alleged actual reduction to practice. Mr. Black's affidavit states in material part: He was employed by Monsanto on October 14, 1968. He was assigned responsibility for the following areas: Petroleum Additives, Functional Fluids, Polyphenyl Ethers [&] Synthetic Lubricants. He was assigned four areas because the three attorneys who had previously handled them had resigned in the previous four months. He recalls that as of January 1969 he was responsible for: 1) about 60 to 70 pending U.S. Applications, 2) over 400 foreign pending applications, 3) over 100 active invention disclosures of which 27 were A ready to file [and] 21 were A not ready to file.

He recalls that as of that date, "(Miller's) invention disclosure ... was in order of filing priority, 31st on the list out of 48 cases." He generally filed invention disclosures according to their order of priority.

The Board Opinions

The board majority found that Miller had actually reduced the invention of the counts to practice in April 1966 and that he had not abandoned, suppressed, or concealed the invention within the meaning of 35 U.S.C. § 102(g). The majority found that Miller's March 1966 vibrating probe tests were sufficient to show that the invention was suitable for the use set forth in the counts, i.e., cavitation inhibition in hydraulic systems. The tests were held not to have been abandoned experiments. The majority rejected Peeler's claim that Miller had suppressed the invention, on the basis that there was no evidence that Miller intended to suppress the invention or in fact did so. [One dissenter on the Board concluded that Miller had abandoned or suppressed the invention.]

Opinion

While we agree with the board majority that Miller proved by a preponderance of the evidence that he had actually reduced the invention to practice in March 1966, we also agree with the dissenting member of the board that Miller must be deemed to have suppressed the invention under 35 U.S.C. § 102(g) through the behavior of his assignee. Perforce, the decision of the board must be reversed. We reach both issues, since without an actual reduction to practice there is no invention in existence which can be abandoned, suppressed, or concealed under § 102(g).

Peeler argues that the one successful vibrating probe test relied upon by Miller to establish an actual reduction to practice was preliminary in nature and failed to show that the invention would work "as intended to work in its practical contemplated use, i.e., as an aircraft hydraulic fluid ...." Peeler also urges us to find that a single successful test is insufficient to establish reproducibility of results and that the probe test was an abandoned experiment because Miller lacked conviction of success.

We note that the counts are not directed to aircraft hydraulic systems, which are special environments with high speed flow and extremes of temperature and pressure causing accelerated wear of valves and other hydraulic system components, but to hydraulic systems generally. Thus Miller need show only that his invention is suitable for reducing cavitation damage in any hydraulic system. [I]t may be true that the vibrating probe test is a rapid screening method for choosing candidates for more rigorous testing, but that does not vitiate the conclusion by Miller that the vibrating probe test was considered in 1966 by those in the art, based in part on the knowledge that the success of water as an additive was predicted by the probe test, to simulate conditions which would cause valve damage in aircraft. Miller's comment in the March 14 notebook entry indicating a need "to better assess such additives" does not, it seems to us, indicate that he considered FREON 11 unsuitable.

Finally, we hold that the March 1966 probe test was not an abandoned experiment. Except for Miller's September 1966 presentation, the record is devoid of any activity with respect to the invention by Miller personally after he filed the invention disclosure. This lack of activity is understandable in light of the realities of corporate research. Once he filed his invention disclosure with his superiors, Miller was finished with the invention. He had other work to do. If Monsanto desired protection for its employee's invention, any further action was in the hands of people other than Miller. That Stainbrook performed tests in 1967 on additives which the dissenting board member said were outside the scope of the counts is of no moment. There is no evidence that Miller changed his mind about the efficacy of the additives he found. In some cases the passage of a long period between reduction to practice and filing raises an inference that the purported reduction to practice was an abandoned experiment. This inference, however, only arises where there is doubt that the activities relied on constitute a reduction to practice. We have no reason to doubt that Miller considered his invention successful when he filed his invention disclosure; subsequent corporate inactivity does not raise the inference that Miller later thought his work incomplete or unsuccessful. As indicated infra, this passage of time redounds to the detriment of Monsanto, but not because of an inference that there was no reduction of the invention to practice.

Determining whether a de facto first inventor, Miller in this case, should also be considered the de jure first inventor under § 102 requires resolution of the policy question: which of the rival inventors has the greater right to a patent? *Brokaw v. Vogel*, 429 F.2d 476, 57 C.C.P.A. 1296 (1970). Under the facts of this case and the public policy inherent in § 102(g), we hold that the evidence has raised an inference of suppression of the invention by Miller's assignee, Monsanto, the real party in interest, which has not been rebutted. Monsanto's conduct is, of course, imputable to Miller under elementary legal principles. *In re Clark*, 522 F.2d 623 (C.C.P.A. 1975).

The evidence here is striking in its paucity. There is no evidence that Miller (or Monsanto) was spurred into filing his application by knowledge of Peeler's invention; spurring, however, is not an essential element of suppression. *Young v. Dworkin*, [489 F.2d 1277 (C.C.P.A. 1974)]. Neither Miller nor anyone else at Monsanto appears to have had any specific intent to suppress or conceal the invention. But proof of specific intent to suppress is not necessary where the time between actual reduction to practice and filing is unreasonable. This unreasonable delay may raise an inference of intent to suppress. *Young v. Dworkin*, *supra*, 489 F.2d at 1281 n. 3. The evidence shows, however, that over four years elapsed between the rating of Miller's invention disclosure "A (Ready)" and Miller's filing date and that much, if not all, of the delay occurred while the disclosure lay dormant in Monsanto's patent department.

In our opinion, a four-year delay from the time an inventor is satisfied with his invention and completes his work on it and the time his assignee-employer files a patent application is, prima facie, unreasonably long in an interference with a party who filed first. The circumstances surrounding the delay and Monsanto's attempted justification thereof serve only to persuade us of the correctness of our opinion. We make no criticism of Mr. Black; getting Miller's application filed in the time he did may have been an extraordinary effort. Monsanto, however, can take no comfort in that, since its neglect of Miller's application for the 2½ years preceding Mr. Black's arrival and its failure to replace two of the three attorneys who resigned were at least partial causes of the backlog which greeted Mr. Black.

Miller and the board majority rely heavily on the statement, often repeated in varying language by this court, that "Mere delay, without more, is not sufficient to establish suppression or concealment." *Young v. Dworkin, supra,* 489 F.2d at 1281, and cases cited therein. What we are deciding here is that Monsanto's delay is not "mere delay" and that Monsanto's justification for the delay is inadequate to overcome the inference of suppression created by its excessive delay. Surely, the word "mere" does not imply a total absence of a limit on the duration of the delay. "Mere" is a chameleonic word, whose meaning depends on the circumstances.

As Mr. Justice Holmes said in *Towne v. Eisner,* 245 U.S. 418, 425, 38 S. Ct. 158, 159, 62 L. Ed. 372 (1918), "A word is not a crystal, transparent and unchanged, it is the skin of a living thought and may vary greatly in color and content according to the circumstances and the time in which it is used." The living thought clothed by the phrase "mere delay" is not susceptible of discernment as an absolute matter. Whether any delay is "mere" in contemplation of law is a policy decision that can be made only on a case-by-case basis. A delay may be of no legal consequence because it is not long enough. Or the delay may be excused by activities of the inventor or his assignee during the delay period. See, e.g., *Frey v. Wagner,* 87 F.2d 212, 24 C.C.P.A. 823 (1937). There may be other factors. At least since *Mason v. Hepburn,* 13 App. D.C. 86 (1898), the courts have implemented a public policy favoring, in interference situations, the party who expeditiously starts his invention on the path to public disclosure through the issuance of patents by filing a patent application. This policy is now implemented through § 102(g) even as it was in *Mason v. Hepburn* prior to that statute, by denying de jure first inventor status to de facto first inventors who, or whose assignees, frustrate this policy.

Reversed.

NOTES

1. *Time Line.* It can be helpful to sketch out a time line of the major events in an interference. For example, here is one for the preceding case:

Peeler: -- X ----------------------------------
                                                   1/4/68
                                            Files application

Miller: ------ X ----------------- X ---------------------------- X ----------------------
         (Conceives?)   4/18/66   4/27/70
                           Reduction to practice   Files Application

2. *Declaring Interferences*. In this case, both Peeler (the senior party) and Miller (the junior party) had filed applications; thus the interference was declared between two pending applications. Compare this with the situation in *Townsend v. Smith*, above.

Sections 1.604 and 1.607 of the Patent Office Regulations (37 C.F.R. §§ 1.604, 1.607 (1996)) cover the declaration of interferences in these and other circumstances.

§ 1.604. Request for interference between applications by an applicant.

(a) An applicant may seek to have an interference declared with an application of another by,

(1) Suggesting a proposed count and presenting at least one claim corresponding to the proposed count or identifying at least one claim in its application that corresponds to the proposed count,

(2) Identifying the other application and, if known, a claim in the other application which corresponds to the proposed count, and

(3) Explaining why an interference should be declared.

(b) When an applicant presents a claim known to the applicant to define the same patentable invention claimed in a pending application of another, the applicant shall identify that pending application, unless the claim is presented in response to a suggestion by the examiner. The examiner shall notify the Commissioner of any instance where it appears an applicant may have failed to comply with the provisions of this paragraph.

§ 1.607. Request by applicant for interference with patent.

(a) An applicant may seek to have an interference declared between an application and an unexpired patent by,

(1) Identifying the patent,

(2) Presenting a proposed count,

(3) Identifying at least one claim in the patent corresponding to the proposed count,

(4) Presenting at least one claim corresponding to the proposed count or identifying at least one claim already pending in its application that corresponds to the proposed count, and, if any claim of the patent or application identified

as corresponding to the proposed count does not correspond exactly to the proposed count, explaining why each such claim corresponds to the proposed count, and

(5) Applying the terms of any application claim,

   (i) Identified as corresponding to the count, and

   (ii) Not previously in the application

to the disclosure of the application.

(6) Explaining how the requirements of 35 U.S.C. 135(b) are met, if the claim presented or identified under paragraph (a)(4) of this section was not present in the application until more than one year after the issue date of the patent.

(b) When an applicant seeks an interference with a patent, examination of the application, including any appeal to the Board, shall be conducted with special dispatch within the Patent and Trademark Office. The examiner shall determine whether there is interfering subject matter claimed in the application and the patent which is patentable to the applicant subject to a judgment in an interference. If the examiner determines that there is any interfering subject matter, an interference will be declared. If the examiner determines that there is no interfering subject matter, the examiner shall state the reasons why an interference is not being declared and otherwise act on the application.

(c) When an applicant presents a claim which corresponds exactly or substantially to a claim of a patent, the applicant shall identify the patent and the number of the patent claim, unless the claim is presented in response to a suggestion by the examiner. The examiner shall notify the Commissioner of any instance where an applicant fails to identify the patent.

(d) A notice that an applicant is seeking to provoke an interference with a patent will be placed in the file of the patent and a copy of the notice will be sent to the patentee. The identity of the applicant will not be disclosed unless an interference is declared. If a final decision is made not to declare an interference, a notice to that effect will be placed in the patent file and will be sent to the patentee.

See also 37 C.F.R § 1.601 (definitions); 1.605(a) (examiner may suggest interference to applicant); § 1.608 (prima facie showing by applicant in case of interference between application and issued patent); and § 1.606 (requirement of patentability of count). Note also that under § 135(b) of the Patent Act, an applicant may not claim subject matter that is the same as that contained in the claim(s) of an issued patent more than a year after the patent issues.

3. *New Rules.* For an introduction to the "new" interference rules, see Gholz, *Interference Practice Under the New Rules* (PRACTICING LAW INSTITUTE, PATENT SERIES NO. 213, 1985) at 365:

A recurrent theme in the "legislative history" of the new rules is that the average pendency time of interference under the new rules should be dramatically less than the average pendency time of interference under the old rules. One of the major innovations made to achieve this goal is the assignment of each interference to a single examiner-in-chief for "case management." (Some, but not all, of the "old rule" interference are also being assigned to a single examiner-in-chief for "case management.")

The singleton examiner-in-chief has the authority to enter "all interlocutory orders in the interference," including decisions on "preliminary motions." [He or she] has authority to set the times in each interference "on a case-by-case basis after consultation with counsel." (This should avoid the long dead periods often [encountered under the old rules.])

Reform continues apace. *See* Charles L. Gholz, *Practicing Under the New Patent Interference Rules and New Rule 131*, 77 J. PAT. & TRADEMARK OFF. SOC'Y 858 (1995).

4. *Collusive Settlements*. The Patent Act recognizes that the settlement of an interference dispute presents an excellent opportunity for two competitors to engage in anticompetitive behavior, e.g., market division, price fixing or the like. Thus, § 135(c) requires all agreements entered into as part of an interference settlement to be recorded in the Patent Office, where it is available for inspection by government agencies and others who show "good cause."

———

The following case deals with the same issue as that raised in *Peeler*. But you will find that this issue is intertwined with another, related issue, which is considered in depth in the following section of this chapter — the question of *diligence* by one who is first to conceive but last to reduce to practice. (This is especially apparent in the concurrence and dissent.) See note 1 following the case if you find this discussion confusing.

PAULIK v. RIZKALLA

760 F.2d 1270; 226 U.S.P.Q. (BNA) 224 (Fed. Cir. 1985)

NEWMAN, CIRCUIT JUDGE [writing for the court en banc].

This appeal is from the decision of the United States Patent and Trademark Office Board of Patent Interferences (Board), awarding priority of invention to the senior party Nabil Rizkalla and Charles N. Winnick (Rizkalla), on the ground that the junior party and de facto first inventors Frank E. Paulik and Robert G. Schultz (Paulik) has suppressed or concealed the invention within the meaning of 35 U.S.C. § 102(g). We vacate this decision and remand to the Board.

Rizkalla's patent application has the effective filing date of March 10, 1975, its parent application. Paulik's patent application was filed on June 30, 1975. The interference count is for a catalytic process for producing alkylidene diesters such as ethylidene diacetate, which is useful to prepare vinyl acetate and acetic acid.

Paulik presented deposition testimony and exhibits in support of his claim to priority; Rizkalla chose to rely solely on his filing date.

The Board held and Rizkalla does not dispute that Paulik reduced the invention of the count to practice in November 1970 and again in April 1971. On about November 20, 1970, Paulik submitted a "Preliminary Disclosure of Invention" to the Patent Department of his assignee, the Monsanto Company. The disclosure was assigned a priority designation of "B," which Paulik states meant that the case would "be taken up in the ordinary course for review and filing."

Despite occasional prodding from the inventors, and periodic review by the patent staff and by company management, this disclosure had a lower priority than other patent work. Evidence of the demands of other projects on related technology was offered to justify the patent staff's delay in acting on this invention, along with evidence that the inventors and assignee continued to be interested in the technology and that the invention disclosure was retained in active status.

In January or February of 1975, the assignee's patent solicitor started to work toward the filing of the patent application; drafts of the application were prepared, and additional laboratory experiments were requested by the patent solicitor and were duly carried out by an inventor. The evidentiary sufficiency of these activities was challenged by Rizkalla, but the Board made no findings thereon, on the basis that these activities were not pertinent to the determination of priority. The Board held that [Paulik was not only the first to conceive but he was also the first to reduce to practice.]

The Board then held that Paulik's four-year delay from reduction to practice to his filing date was prima facie suppression or concealment under the first clause of section 102(g), that since Paulik had reduced the invention to practice in 1971 and 1972 [i.e., first] he was barred by the second clause of section 102(g) from proving reasonable diligence leading to his 1975 filing [i.e., because he was first to conceive and first to reduce to practice], and that in any event the intervening activities were insufficient to excuse the delay. The Board refused to considered Paulik's evidence of renewed patent-related activity.

According to this decision, once suppression or concealment is established, this inference cannot be overcome by the junior party to an interference. There is no statutory or judicial precedent that requires this result, and there is sound reason to reject it.

United States patent law embraces the principle that the patent right is granted to the first inventor rather than the first to file a patent application.[1] The law does not inquire as to the fits and starts by which an invention is made. The historic jurisprudence from which 35 U.S.C. § 102(g) flowed reminds us that

---

[1] As observed by the Industrial Research Institute, a first-to-invent system "respects the value of the individual in American tradition and avoids inequities which can result from a 'race to the Patent Office.'" Final Report of the Advisory Committee on Industrial Innovation, U.S. of Chamber Commerce, Sept. 1979, p. 174.

"the mere lapse of time" will not prevent the inventor from receiving a patent." *Mason v. Hepburn*, 13 App. D.C. 86, 91, 1898 C.D. 510, 513 (1898). The sole exception to this principle resides in section 102(g) and the exigencies of the priority contest.

There is no impediment in the law to holding that a long period of inactivity need not be a fatal forfeiture, if the first inventor resumes work on the invention before the second inventor enters the field. We deem this result to be a fairer implementation of national patent policy, while in full accord with the letter and spirit of section 102(g).

The Board misapplied the rule that the first inventor does not have to show activity following reduction to practice to mean that the first inventor will not be allowed to show such activity. Such a showing may serve either of two purposes: to rebut an inference of abandonment, suppression, or concealment; or as evidence of renewed activity with respect to the invention. Otherwise, if an inventor were to set an invention aside for "too long" and later resume work and diligently develop and seek to patent it, according to the Board he would always be worse off than if he never did the early work, even as against a much later entrant.

Such a restrictive rule would merely add to the burden of those charged with the nation's technological growth. Invention is not a neat process. The value of early work may not be recognized or, for many reasons, it may not become practically useful, until months or years later. Following the Board's decision, any "too long" delay would constitute a forfeiture fatal in a priority contest, even if terminated by extensive and productive work done long before the newcomer entered the field.

We do not suggest that the first inventor should be entitled to rely for priority purposes on his early reduction to practice if the intervening inactivity lasts "too long," as that principle has evolved in a century of judicial analysis. Precedent did not deal with the facts at bar. There is no authority that would estop Paulik from relying on his resumed activities in order to pre-date Rizkalla's earliest date. We hold that such resumed activity must be considered as evidence of priority of invention. Should Paulik demonstrate that he had renewed activity on the invention and that he proceeded diligently to filing his patent application, starting before the earliest date to which Rizkalla is entitled — all in accordance with established principles of interference practice — we hold that Paulik is not prejudiced by the fact that he had reduced the invention to practice some years earlier.

This appeal presents a question not previously treated by this court or, indeed, in the historical jurisprudence on suppression or concealment. We take this opportunity to clarify an apparent misperception of certain opinions of our predecessor court which the Board has cited in support of its holding.

From the earliest decisions, a distinction has been drawn between deliberate suppression or concealment of an invention, and the legal inference of suppression or concealment based on "too long" a delay in filing the patent application.

Both types of situations were considered by the courts before the 1952 Patent Act, and both are encompassed in 35 U.S.C. § 102(g). The result is consistent over this entire period — loss of the first inventor's priority as against an intervening second inventor — and has consistently been based on equitable principles and public policy as applied to the facts of each case.

The earliest decisions dealt primarily with deliberate concealment. In 1858, the Supreme Court in *Kendal v. Winsor*, 62 U.S. (21 How.) 322, 328 (1858) held that an inventor who "designedly, and with the view of applying it indefinitely and exclusively for his own profit, withholds his invention from the public" impedes "the progress of science and the useful arts."

In *Mason v. Hepburn, supra*, the classical case on inferred as contrasted with deliberate suppression or concealment, Hepburn was granted a patent in September 1894. Spurred by this news, Mason filed his patent application in December 1894. In an interference, Mason demonstrated that he had built a working model in 1887 but showed no activity during the seven years thereafter. The court held that although Mason may have negligently rather than willfully concealed his invention, the "indifference, supineness, or wilful act" of a first inventor is the basis for "the equity" that favors the second inventor when that person made and disclosed the invention during the prolonged inactivity of the first inventor. 13 App. D.C. at 96, 1898 C.D. at 517.

The legislative history of section 102(g) makes clear that its purpose was not to change the law. The pre-1952 cases all dealt with situations whereby a later inventor made the same invention during a period of either prolonged inactivity or deliberate concealment by the first inventor, after knowledge of which (usually, but not always, by the issuance of a patent to the second inventor) the first inventor was "spurred" into asserting patient rights, unsuccessfully.

The decisions after the 1952 Act followed a similar pattern, as the courts considered whether to extinguish a first inventor's priority under section 102(g). The cases show either intentional concealment or an unduly long delay after the first inventor's reduction to practice. Some cases excused the delay, and some did not. [The court then reviews a series of cases, including *Peeler* and *Horwath v. Lee*, 564 F.2d 948, 195 U.S.P.Q. 701 (C.C.P.A. 1977).]

The decisions applying section 102(g) balanced the law and policy favoring the first person to make an invention, against equitable considerations when more than one person had made the same invention: in each case where the court deprived the de facto first inventor of the right to the patent, the second inventor had entered the field during a period of either inactivity or deliberate concealment by the first inventor. Often the first inventor had been spurred to file a patent application by news of the second inventor's activities. Although "spurring" is not necessary to a finding of suppression or concealment, see *Young v. Dworkin*, 489 F.2d at 1281, 180 U.S.P.Q. at 391-92 and citations therein, the courts' frequent references to spurring indicate their concern with this equitable factor.

In no case where the first inventor had waited "too long" did he end his period of inactivity before the second inventor appeared. We affirm the long-standing rule that too long a delay may bar the first inventor from reliance on an early reduction to practice in a priority contest. But we hold that the first inventor will not be barred from relying on later, resumed activity antedating an opponent's entry into the field, merely because the work done before the delay occurred was sufficient to amount to a reduction to practice.

This result furthers the basic purpose of the patent system. The exclusive right, constitutionally derived, was for the national purpose of advancing the useful arts — the process today called technological innovation. As implemented by the patent statute, the grant of the right to exclude carries the obligation to disclose the workings of the invention, thereby adding to the store of knowledge without diminishing the patent-supported incentive to innovate.

But the obligation to disclose is not the principal reason for a patent system; indeed, it is a rare invention that cannot be deciphered more readily from its commercial embodiment than from the printed patent. The reason for the patent system is to encourage innovation and its fruits: new jobs and new industries, new consumer goods and trade benefits. We must keep this purpose in plain view as we consider the consequences of interpretations of the patent law such as in the Board's decision.

A foreseeable consequence of the Board's ruling is to discourage inventors and their supporters from working on projects that had been "too long" set aside, because of the impossibility of relying, in a priority contest, on either their original work or their renewed work. This curious result is neither fair nor in the public interest. We do not see that the public interest is served by placing so severe a sanction on failure to file premature patent applications on immature inventions of unknown value. In reversing the Board's decision we do not hold that such inventions are necessarily entitled to the benefits of their earliest dates in a priority contest; we hold only that they are not barred from entitlement to their dates of renewed activity.

Having established the principle that Paulik, although not entitled to rely on his early work, is entitled to rely on his renewed activity, we vacate the decision of the Board and, in the interest of justice, remand to the PTO for new interference proceedings in accordance with this principle.

RICH, CIRCUIT JUDGE, concurring.

I am in full agreement with Judge Newman's opinion. I write in order to express some additional thoughts respecting 35 U.S.C. 102(g) as a member of the group which drafted that section, which was new in the Patent Act of 1952, our current statute.

The Words "suppressed, or concealed" in § 102(g) Have No Definite Meaning

These words were included in the section with no other intention than to codify pre-existing case law pertaining to priority determinations in interferences or infringement suits.

As Judge Newman has pointed out, the numerous CCPA/CAFC cases have applied equitable principles on a case-by-case basis to these priority problems. Doing the same here, the only sanction it is proper to apply against Paulik is to deprive him of the right, as against Rizkalla, to rely on the date of his earlier reduction to practice in establishing "priority" because of the long delay thereafter, while sustaining his right to rely on the time of his revived activity if it is connected by diligence to his filing date. If that revival date antedates the earliest date established by Rizkalla, given that diligence, Paulik is entitled to the priority award. This procedure would be far from novel. It is exactly what was stated to be the law over a century ago in *Farmer v. Brush*, 1881 C.D. 5 (digested in fn. 1, Robinson [on Patents] § 390 [1890]).

In short, "suppressed or concealed" means only what courts say it means in each case. It is like deciding obviousness or negligence. No prior case — as can be assumed from the fact that this is a case of first impression, nothing to the contrary having appeared — compels the meaning which has been given to these words by the Board herein. Deciding whether a party has "suppressed or concealed" is arriving at a conclusion of law, not finding a fact. In each case, the question is whether the facts as to what was or was not done lead to the legal conclusion of "suppressed, or concealed."

To put the finger on the crucial flaw in the Board's reasoning, I find it in these statements:

> We agree with Rizkalla that even if Paulik demonstrates continuous activity from prior to the Rizkalla effective filing date to his filing date that such would have no bearing on ... priority.

> It is of no significance in the case of a party who is not the last to reduce to practice.

It must be recognized that we are deciding a priority issue: which party is to be regarded as the "first" inventor in law, regardless of fact. The award, as the CCPA several times decided, should be to the one most deserving from a policy standpoint. In deciding who is prior in law, every fact has a "bearing" and is of "significance" and must be weighed on the scales of justice. It is of the utmost significance here whether Paulik was actively proceeding to patent his invention prior to any date established by Rizkalla, and thus the first to be on the way to giving the public the benefit of the invention. That is what a "priority" decision is all about.

With respect to the Board's playing with the words of paragraph (g), it was, of course, trying to make something out of the phrase "the reasonable diligence of one who was first to conceive and last to reduce to practice," in effect saying that Paulik's diligence from before Rizkalla's earliest date to Paulik's filing date is of "no significance" because Paulik was not the last but the first to reduce to practice! But the reason (g) was worded as it was, as I have explained above, is that it was an effort to restate concisely fundamental interference or priority law.

In that law, it was, and still is, an elementary principle that one who is both the first to conceive and first to reduce to practice does not have to show diligence at all. To take a statement that diligence shall be considered in the situation where it had long been required and turn it into a prohibition to consider it, or a ground for refusing to consider it, is about as perverse a construction as can be imagined. The old rule just stated does not, of course, apply here to Paulik's need to show diligence connecting his revived activity from just prior to Rizkalla's earliest proven date to his filing date or a reduction to practice, according to the establishing law. The statute does not deal with the situation here.

An inventor can delay as long as he likes, in the absence of commercialization (see *Metallizing Engineering Co. v. Kenyon Bearing and Auto Parts Co.*, 153 F.2d 516, 68 U.S.P.Q. 54, *cert. den.*, 328 U.S. 840 (1946)), if he is willing to risk having to show in an interference or in facing a defense of prior invention that he has the better right to the patent as between the contesting parties. On the facts shown by the present record, Paulik appears to have the better right when equities, rather than statements in opinions on unlike fact situations, are considered. And, finally, there is a question of fairness; why should Paulik be penalized for having done early work if, without reliance on it, he is still ahead of Rizkalla? There is more to § 102(g) than its bare words, namely, over a century of carefully thought out case law which must not be ignored in construing it.

FRIEDMAN, CIRCUIT JUDGE (with whom DAVIS, KASHIWA, BENNETT and MILLER, Circuit Judges, join), dissenting.

I think that in awarding priority to Rizkalla, the Board properly applied section 102(g) and the pertinent precedents of this court. I therefore would affirm.

Two decisions of the Court of Customs and Patent Appeals, *Peeler v. Miller*, 535 F.2d 647, 190 U.S.P.Q. 117 (C.C.P.A. 1976), and *Shindelar v. Holdeman*, 628 F.2d 1337, 207 U.S.P.Q. 112 (C.C.P.A. 1980), *cert. denied*, 451 U.S. 984 (1981), held that an unreasonable delay between the reduction to practice and the filing of the patent application constituted "suppression" of the invention under section 102(g) that barred the earlier but suppressing inventor from obtaining priority in an interference proceeding over the later inventor.

The facts in *Peeler* are virtually identical to those here.

In *Shindelar*, the Court of Customs and Patent Appeals upheld a decision of the Board of Patent Interferences that a delay of two years and five months between the patent attorney's receipt from the inventor of the information necessary to prepare the patent application and the filing of the application constituted suppression of the invention under 35 U.S.C. § 102(g). In holding that that delay was "unreasonably long," the court concluded that "there is no reasonable basis on which to differentiate this case from *Peeler v. Miller*, and the same result is therefore compelled, i.e., a holding of suppression as a matter of law." 628 F.2d at 1342, 207 U.S.P.Q. at 117.

The court does not deny that Paulik's four-year delay constituted prima facie suppression. Indeed, it could do so only by overruling *Peeler* and *Shindelar*.

I do not think that the language in section 102(g) leaves any room for considering the respective equities of (i) an earlier inventor who admittedly has suppressed or concealed his invention for an unreasonably long period and (ii) a later inventor who acted promptly in seeking the patent and was, in fact, first to file. Section 102(g) speaks in clear, simple, prohibitory terms. An inventor who has "abandoned, suppressed, or concealed" his invention is not entitled to priority as against a subsequent inventor who has not engaged in that conduct. Congress itself has made the judgment that in that situation the equities lie with the second inventor, not with the first. Under the statute, there is no room for the Board or the court to second-guess that congressional determination on the basis of the tribunal's own perception of where the equities lie in a particular case.

NOTES

1. *Working by Analogy.* Strictly speaking, the technical question of diligence in § 102(g) (i.e., schematic element 102(g)[4][b]) has nothing to do with the question of abandonment, suppression or concealment (schematic § 102(g)[3][a]). However, as we saw in *Peeler*, the acts and intentions of one accused of concealment — what might colloquially be termed her "diligence" — are important considerations in deciding the issue of abandonment, suppression or concealment. The difference between the two is this: The technical question of diligence (element [4][b]) comes into play *only* when, as between two inventors, one conceives first but reduces to practice second. (See Section J.4.b.iii, below.) The more colloquial "diligence" issue, considered in the preceding case, applies any time there is an assertion of abandonment, suppression or concealment (element [3][a]). In these cases — *Peeler* being a good example — we are concerned with whether the first inventor (i.e., the first to both conceive *and* reduce to practice) has concealed her invention, which necessarily leads us to inquire about her acts and motives — loosely speaking, into her "diligence," again, using that term in its non-technical (non-§ 102(g)[4][b]) sense. In other words, there is an analogy between the technical use of diligence, and diligence as a concept useful in determining abandonment. The analogy is so close, in fact, that the court, and especially the concurrence and dissent, in the preceding case apply a good deal of element [4][b] diligence analysis to the distinct question of whether the inventor abandoned (under [3][a]). If this is confusing, look at the schematic above. We will see how technical diligence ([4][b]) works in Section J.4.b.iii, below.

2. *Is Abandonment a "Relative" Term, or Once and For All?* In an omitted portion of the opinion, the court stated:

> The Board's decision converted the case law's estoppel against reliance on Paulik's early work for priority purposes [i.e., the "estoppel" provided by schematic element § 102(g)[4][b]], into a forfeiture encompassing Paulik's later work, even if the later work commenced before the earliest activity of Rizkalla.

Then the court states:

> [I]f an inventor were to set an invention aside for "too long" and later
> resume work and diligently develop and seek to patent it, according to the
> Board he would always be worse off than if he never did the early work,
> even as against a much later entrant.

In other words, after *Paulik*, § 102(g) concealment is not once and for all, in the
sense that deciding whether inventor *A* has concealed is crucially dependent on
what actions inventor *B* takes, and when she takes them. Note how the dissent
resists this notion, arguing instead that concealment is "binary": either you have
concealed or you have not; concealment does not come and go depending on your
actions relative to another inventor. In a word, the difference between the
majority and dissent is this: the majority sees concealment as a flexible doctrine
to be used in the overall task of assessing which inventor deserves priority; while
the dissent sees it as a distinct event that extinguishes an inventor's claim to
priority once and for all, more akin in a way to a statutory bar. Like a statutory
bar, the goal is to encourage early completion of the work, and early filing. Does
it put a dent in the dissent's view that the party who supposedly concealed here,
Paulik, was in fact the first to file? Does the "good act" of resuming work and
filing first extinguish the "bad act" of the earlier abandonment?

3. *Counts.* The preceding opinion refers to "interference counts." Each count
represents a quasi-claim defining the particular invention whose priority is under
review in the interference. A count is usually distilled from the claims made by
the rival inventors. It serves to define the boundaries of the interference. *See
generally* 37 C.F.R. § 1.601(f) (1995).

4. *Excusing Delay.* In *Lutzker v. Plet*, decided after *Paulik*, the Federal Circuit
stated:

> An inference of suppression or concealment may be overcome with evidence
> that the reason for the delay was to perfect the invention. See, for example,
> *Dewey v. Lawton*, 347 F.2d 629, 632, 146 U.S.P.Q. 187, 189-90 (C.C.P.A.
> 1965), which permitted "testing and refinement" of the invention for more
> than one year after reduction to practice; and *Schnick v. Fenn*, 277 F.2d
> 935, 941-42, 125 U.S.P.Q. 567, 573-74 (C.C.P.A. 1960), which permitted
> a delay of about eleven months after reduction to practice while "continuing
> 'the development of the best design'" in further perfecting the invention.
> When, however, the delay is caused by working on refinements and im-
> provements which are not reflected in the final patent application, the delay
> will not be excused. See *Horwath v. Lee*, 564 F.2d at 952, 195 U.S.P.Q. at
> 706. Further, when the activities which cause the delay go to commercializa-
> tion of the invention, the delay will not be excused. See *Fitzgerald v. Arbib*,
> 268 F.2d 763, 766, 122 U.S.P.Q. 530, 532 (C.C.P.A. 1959).

843 F.2d 1364, 6 U.S.P.Q.2d 1370 (Fed. Cir. 1988). *Cf. Connin v. Andrews*,
223 U.S.P.Q. 243 (Pat. & Trademark Off. Bd. Pat. Inf. 1984) (where a first

inventor who waited "too long" was nevertheless the first to file a patent application, the Board treated the filing of the application [which is called "constructive reduction to practice"; see below] as evidence negating suppression despite the long period of inactivity, and permitted the delaying senior party to rely on his early work).

Trade Secrets, § 102(g), and the Software Industry

The rule announced in the *Peeler* case above has for the most part been followed. In general, to amount to a loss of right to a patent in favor of a later inventor, suppression or concealment must be deliberate or intentional, *Piher, S.A. v. CTS Corp.*, 664 F.2d 122 (7th Cir. 1981), although, as in the *Peeler* case reproduced above, lengthy delay between the making of the invention and filing for a patent can give rise to an inference of concealment. *See, e.g., Horwath v. Lee*, 564 F.2d 948 (C.C.P.A. 1977) (the longer an inventor delays in filing application, the greater are the equities that may be raised on behalf of one who made the same invention and promptly filed); *Brokaw v. Vogel*, 429 F.2d 476, 57 C.C.P.A. 1296 (C.C.P.A. 1970) (five-year delay was too long). *But see Cochran v. Kresock*, 530 F.2d 385 (C.C.P.A. 1976) ("mere delay, without more," is not enough); *Peeler, supra* (balancing delay with earlier re-entry into the field and earlier filing).

It is important to grasp the impact of these cases. An inventor who keeps an invention secret by plan may lose her right to a patent in a priority contest. In addition, she may wind up infringing the patent of the party who won priority. In such a case, the second inventor/first filer will have in effect barred the first inventor from using her own invention.

On the other hand, in those cases where the first inventor's actions are not deemed intentional, or her delay in filing for a patent is not deemed excessive, under the rule in *Peeler*, her invention will defeat the novelty of the second inventor's patent application due to § 102(g). In such a case, the prior invention is a form of "secret" prior art. Many have criticized the use of non-public technology as prior art under §§ 102(a) and 102(g). *See, e.g.*, Note, *Patent Law in the Context of Corporate Research*, 8 J. CORP. L. 498 (1983):

> Establishing a standard for patentability in which an applicant's invention is evaluated … against secret prior art is disastrous for "the innovative spirit the patent laws are intended to kindle." Such a standard for patentability also runs counter to the objectives of the patent system as outlined in a 1956 congressional study: "[The patent system] aims to prevent the creation of an industry permeated by the intense secrecy with regard to its processes which characterized the Medieval guilds and which can only retard the realization by the public of the results of scientific progress." … It is ridiculous to force corporations to suppress such valuable information ….

Judge Learned Hand of the Second Circuit delivered an important opinion on the issue of prior invention in *Gillman v. Stern*, 114 F.2d 28 (2d Cir. 1940). He held that a completed invention will be deemed abandoned, suppressed, or concealed if no steps are taken to make the invention publicly known within a reasonable time. The inventor, Haas, kept his invention completely secret from the outside world, including his employees and his wife. The court held that such a secret invention could not be prior art. An important point regarding *Gillman* is that the invention at issue was a pneumatic "puffing" machine for quilting. Only the *output* of the machine — its products — was offered for sale; the machine itself "was always kept as strictly secret as possible, consistently with its exploitation." 114 F.2d at 30. *Gillman* has been called a good example of a "non-informing public use" case. Robbins, *The Rights of a First Inventor-Trade Secret User As Against Those of the Second Inventor-Patentee (Part I)*, 61 J. PAT. OFF. SOC'Y 574, 591 (1979); *see also* Burke, *The 'Non-informing Public Use' Concept and Its Application to Patent-Trade Secret Conflicts*, 45 ALB. L. REV. 1060 (1981). Such cases are to be distinguished from "hidden public use" cases, where the article in question is openly used, but it is impossible to determine its qualities from an inspection of it. Unlike the "non-informing" use, the "hidden use" has been said not to comprise abandonment, suppression or concealment. The rationale is that the "hidden use" is hidden only because of the nature of the invention, and not because of any intentional concealment by the inventor. Just because the inventor's black box cannot be pierced by observers, the argument runs, does not mean that it is being consciously concealed by the inventor.

Many have argued that in terms of the incentives that the patent system tries to create, cases such as *Gillman* make a good deal of sense. An inventor who files an application ought not to be stymied by prior work she had no way of discovering. This is especially true of cases such as *Peeler*, where the first inventor delayed filing for a patent for a long time, *see Lutzker v. Plet*, 843 F.2d 1364, 6 U.S.P.Q.2d 1370 (Fed. Cir. 1988) (delay of 51 months between reduction of invention to practice and first disclosure of the patent was unreasonably long and gave rise to inference of intent to abandon, suppress, or conceal the invention), and even more so of those cases where the second inventor's patent application "spurred" the first inventor into filing. *See, e.g.*, *Nelson v. Lenning*, 96 F.2d 508, 25 C.C.P.A. 1119 (C.C.P.A. 1938). The same general point is made in criticism of § 102(e) secret prior art, discussed above. *See, e.g.*, Wegner, *Patent Law Simplification and the Geneva Patent Convention*, 14 AM. INTELL. PROP. J. 154, 176-82 (1986). Indeed, the "search model" discussed earlier in this chapter might be said to support such cases, since no amount of research by a potential inventor could uncover this sort of prior art. Consequently, society would want it to be affirmatively disclosed as soon as possible.

But from another perspective, cases such as *Gillman* are troubling. To rule that secret use renders a prior invention "abandoned, suppressed or concealed" under § 102(g) is to *punish* those who elect to keep their inventions as trade secrets. Under *Gillman* and related cases, a later inventor who files a patent application can avoid the prior art effect of earlier secret uses by arguing that the earlier inventor "abandoned, suppressed or concealed" the invention. This removes it from the definition of prior art under § 102(g), and clears the way for the later inventor/patent applicant to obtain a patent. (Note that this *assumes* that the earlier use of the secret invention will not constitute § 102(a) "known or used by others" prior art; it should be clear to you that, in cases like those of the preceding section, there is a strong possibility that § 102(a) would not defeat novelty, given the prevailing interpretation of knowledge or use as implying some degree of "publicity.")

The rule proposed in *Gillman* is troubling because many industries rely heavily on trade secret protection to appropriate the value of their research and development. *See, e.g.*, Levin, Klevorick, Nelson & Winter, *Appropriating the Returns from Industrial Research and Development*, 1987 BROOKINGS PAP. ECON. ACTIVITY 783 (1987) (reporting results of extensive empirical survey of research and development personnel at U.S. corporations; many industries value trade secrets more highly than patents as appropriability mechanism, although non-legal techniques such as lead time advantages were valued most highly in most industries). Also, although several cases have held that state trade secret law may co-exist with federal patent law, *see, e.g.*, *Kewanee Oil Co. v. Bicron Corp.*, 416 U.S. 470 (1974), § 102(g)'s implicit "punishment" for those who elect trade secret protection raises the question how far the patent statute can go in disfavoring state-law forms of protection.

Trade secret protection has been important in the software industry, for example. As a consequence of § 102(g) and the growing importance of patents in this industry, some commentators have shown concern that software creators who keep their software as trade secrets could wind up having to license a later inventor of the same software, or even being forced to stop using their software altogether. *See* Gates, *Trade Secret Software: Is It Prior Art?*, 6 COMPUTER LAWYER 11 (1989). One commentator has noted, however, that patentees may be loath to risk having their patents invalidated by bringing infringement suits against such prior users, a risk that is presumably large in light of the equities favoring the earlier trade secret user. Consequently, according to this commentator, we would expect to see a settlement of any such dispute, perhaps by cross-licenses. Jorda, *The Rights of the First Inventor-Trade Secret User as Against Those of the Second Inventor-Patentee (Part II)*, 61 J. PAT. OFF. SOC'Y 593, 601 (1979).

Fortunately, the suggested rule in *Gillman* has not yet clearly prevailed. The Federal Circuit has held, for instance, that merely because research is secret does not mean it has necessarily been "abandoned, suppressed or concealed" under § 102(g). *See E.I. duPont de Nemours & Co. v. Phillips Petr. Co.*, 849 F.2d 1430 (Fed. Cir.), *cert. denied*, 109 S. Ct. 542 (1988).

Can you think of a way to protect the prior inventor's rights over her technology while still giving voice to the patent system's policy of promoting disclosure of inventions? Note that the software industry is currently undergoing a transition from being a non-patent industry to one where patents are important.

(See Chapter 2 for details.) Since many software firms have come to rely on trade secret protection, some may be hurt by the § 102(g) rule during the transitional period. Is there a way to afford them temporary relief, either through interpretation of the statute or by legislation?

Note, too, that the decision in *Paulik* could provide some relief. At least if the longstanding trade secret user begins to move toward filing a patent, her prior lack of patent-related activity will not necessarily be held against her under *Paulik*.

Finally, note that the system of "prior user" rights in Europe protects the rights of first inventors/later filers in those countries. Prior inventors are allowed to continue their use of the invention after a patent issues to the second inventor. *See* Neukom, *A Prior User Right for the Community Patent Convention*, 5 EUR. INTELL. PROP. REV. 165 (1990); Brownlee, *Trade Secret Use of Patentable Inventions, Prior User Rights and Patent Law Harmonization*, 72 J. PAT. & TRADEMARK OFF. SOC'Y 523 (1990). Would this rule make sense for the U.S. also? *See, e.g.*, Committee on the Judiciary, Subcomm. on Intellectual Property and Judicial Administration, U.S. House of Representatives, Hearings on Prior User Rights, Sept. 13, 1994 (Statement of Prof. Robert Merges) (defending concept of prior user rights, especially if accompanied by explicit "one-way" transferability provision); Kyla Harriel, *Prior User Rights in a First-to-Invent Patent System: Why Not?*, 36 IDEA 543 (1996).

NOTE

For more on trade secrets, see Chapter 12.

4. CONCEPTION, REDUCTION TO PRACTICE, AND DILIGENCE: SCHEMATIC § 102(g)[4]

The second sentence of § 102(g) is given below in the schematic form:

> [4] In determining priority of invention there shall be considered not only [a] the respective dates of [i] conception and [ii] reduction to practice of the invention, but also [b] the reasonable diligence of one who [i] was first to conceive and [ii] last to reduce to practice, [iii] from a time prior to conception by the other.

As we shall see, there are really three critical events listed in this provision. Again, in terms of the schematic, these are: the dates of ([a][i]) conception and ([a][ii]) reduction to practice, and ([b]) the reasonable diligence of one who is first to conceive and last to reduce to practice. We shall consider these three events in the sections that follow. For reasons that will soon be clear, we begin with reduction to practice.

a. Reduction to Practice

DSL DYNAMIC SCIENCES LTD. v. UNION SWITCH
& SIGNAL, INC.

928 F.2d 1122, 18 U.S.P.Q.2d 1152 (Fed. Cir. 1991)

DSL Dynamic Sciences Ltd. (DSL) appeals from the [district court decision] in a patent interference proceeding under 35 U.S.C. § 146, awarding priority of invention to Union Switch & Signal, Inc. (Union Switch). We affirm.

Background

The present case relates to "coupler mount assemblies," which are essentially clamps, used to attach various equipment to a railway car coupler. The assembly engages relief holes located in the side of a standard railway car coupler so as to grasp the side of the coupler without interfering with the ability to use the coupler to attach the railway car to another railway car. An example of the type of equipment mounted on the coupler mount assembly is a brake pressure monitor, which measures the brake pressure at the end of a train and transmits the brake pressure measurement to a receiver located in the locomotive.

DSL is the assignee of U.S. Patent No. 4,520,662 (Schmid patent), which issued on June 4, 1985 to Hartmut Schmid, and is based on an application filed on September 9, 1983. Union Switch is the assignee of U.S. Patent Application serial No. 593,778 (Blosnick application), which was filed on March 27, 1984 in the names of Robert Blosnick and James Toms. On April 4, 1986, the Patent and Trademark Office (PTO) declared [an] interference between the Schmid patent and the Blosnick application.[1]

Because the activity relating to conception and reduction to practice by Schmid was performed in Canada, DSL is prevented by 35 U.S.C. § 104 from establish-

---

[1] [From the text of the opinion:] The sole count remaining when the case was heard by the Board of Patent Appeals and Interferences (Board) was the following:

A coupler mount assembly for use with a railway vehicle coupler including a side wall having a convex exterior surface that is provided with a first pair of vertically aligned and spaced-apart relief holes adjacent the coupler tip, and a second pair of vertically aligned and spaced-apart relief holes adjacent the coupler base, said coupler mount assembly being adapted to mount an equipment housing on the coupler and comprising: first and second jaw means, each of which includes a hook; support means to which the equipment housing may be secured, said support means additionally supporting said first and second jaw means for movement relative to each other and so that the hooks thereof project from said support means and face each other; and clamping means supported by said support means for drawing said first and second jaw means toward each other, whereby said hooks of said first and second jaw means clamp an intermediate portion of the coupler sidewall between the first and second relief hole pairs when said hook of said first jaw means has been inserted into one hole of the first relief hole pair and said hook of said second jaw means has been inserted into a corresponding hole of the second relief hole pair.

ing an invention date earlier than its filing date of September 9, 1983, and that is the date it has relied on throughout the proceedings. Union Switch, on the other hand, maintained before the Board a conception date of January, 1983, and a reduction to practice date of no later than May, 1983.

As evidence to support its claim of reduction to practice, Union Switch presented evidence that around April 1, 1983, the inventors Blosnick and Toms tested a prototype of their invention by mounting the prototype on a railway car coupler and stepping on it. It also presented evidence of tests that were performed on actual moving trains during May of 1983. Three of these tests, which are referred to in the record as "Test Nos. 3, 4 and 5," involved the use of a prototype of the coupler mount assembly on cabooses of trains over distances of 144 miles (Test No. 3), 457 miles (Test No. 4), and 108 miles (Test No. 5). The performance of the prototype in each case was documented with pictures and written reports.

Before the Board, DSL argued that the prototypes used by Union Switch in early 1983 did not fall within the scope of the count and therefore were insufficient to reduce to practice the invention of the count. The Board disagreed, and in a decision dated March 29, 1989, found that Union Switch had established an invention date of no later than May of 1983, and therefore was entitled to priority of the invention of the count.

Before the district court, DSL continued to attack the sufficiency of Union Switch's evidence of its reduction to practice, but presented a new theory in doing so. Specifically, DSL argued that the tests were not performed in the intended environment of a coupler mount assembly, and therefore were not sufficient to establish reduction to practice.

In support of this argument, DSL offered testimony that the purpose of the equipment supported by a coupler mount assembly is to obviate the need for a caboose at the end of a train, and that, therefore, the coupler mount assemblies of the count would never in reality be attached to a caboose, but generally would be attached to the coupler of a freight car. [Union Switch argued that this evidence must be excluded under § 146, which provides for limited district court review of a Patent Office interference decision.]

Opinion

[I]t is our opinion that even if [DSL's] testimony had been presented, Union Switch would still have been entitled to the award of priority of invention. The issue of reduction to practice is a question of law which this court reviews de novo. *Hybritech Inc. v. Monoclonal Antibodies, Inc.*, 802 F.2d 1367, 1376, 231 U.S.P.Q. 81, 87 (Fed. Cir. 1986), *cert. denied*, 480 U.S. 947, 107 S. Ct. 1606, 94 L. Ed. 2d 792 (1987).

It is true, as DSL points out, that proof of actual reduction to practice requires a showing that "the embodiment relied upon as evidence of priority actually worked for its intended purpose." *Newkirk v. Lulejian*, 825 F.2d 1581, 1582, 3

U.S.P.Q.2d 1793, 1794 (Fed. Cir. 1987). This is so even if the "intended purpose" is not explicitly set forth in the counts of the interference. On the other hand, tests performed outside the intended environment can be sufficient to show reduction to practice if the testing conditions are sufficiently similar to those of the intended environment.

The burden of proof here was initially on Union Switch to prove an actual reduction to practice. Thus, for Union Switch to prevail, it must show one of two things: (1) that use of a coupler mount assembly with a caboose is an intended purpose of the coupler mount assembly, or (2) that if use with a caboose is not an intended use of a coupler mount assembly, the tests performed on a caboose coupler sufficiently simulated the conditions present on a freight car coupler to adequately show reduction of the invention to practice.

The tests performed by Union Switch were extensive. The reports prepared after each test show in detail the distance travelled between various checkpoints and the average speed between the checkpoints. The total distance travelled by the trains in Tests Nos. 3, 4 and 5 was over 700 miles. The average speed was often over 40 miles per hour, and for one 30-minute period was 56 miles per hour. Importantly, a unit was mounted on the coupler mount assembly to measure the forces applied to the assembly. The report for Test No. 4 indicates that the "vibration equipment showed shocks of over 15 G's," but that the coupler mount assembly still operated successfully.

Thus, even accepting DSL's argument that coupler mount assemblies are not intended for use on cabooses, we are convinced that the train tests were sufficient to reduce the invention to practice. We are of the opinion that Union Switch's train tests, which applied forces "in excess of 15 G's," sufficiently approximated the condition of "loads to 20 g" which Schmid indicates a coupler mount assembly must withstand on a non-cushioned rail car such as a freight car.

With respect to the proffered testimony of Mr. Starr, some cases have held that events occurring after an alleged actual reduction to practice can call into question whether reduction to practice has in fact occurred. However, there is certainly no requirement that an invention, when tested, be in a commercially satisfactory stage of development in order to reduce the invention to practice. A failure of several commercial devices allegedly made according to the Blosnick application long after the reduction to practice is insufficient to convince us that a device, meeting the limitations of the count, was not adequately tested to establish a reduction to practice.

For the above reasons, the decision of the district court is

Affirmed.

NOTES

1. *Elements of the Count.* The court states that "the device tested by Union Switch in May of 1983 fell within the scope of the count." What if it did not; specifically, what if an element of the count was missing in the device that was reduced to practice on the date shown? *See Akers v. Papst*, 113 F.2d 136, 27 C.C.P.A. 1400 (C.C.P.A. 1940) (to establish reduction to practice it must appear that the device tested included all elements of the count).

2. Priority Puzzle. Why did DSL have to rely on its filing date for priority? As discussed in Section K.4 below, under the version of § 104 of the Patent Act in effect when this case was decided, only acts performed in the United States could be introduced as evidence of conception and reduction to practice. As a result, foreign applicants had to rely on their U.S. filing date as their sole priority date. One effect of the post-Uruguay Round GATT amendments to U.S. patent law was to remedy this blatant U.S.-inventor advantage. Would DSL be assured of winning under the new (post-GATT) version of § 104?

3. Corroboration. Corroboration was an issue in the preceding case; it often is. The general rule, as stated, is that some testimony other than that of the inventor is necessary to establish each of the key inventive dates (i.e., conception, reduction to practice, and activities showing diligence). The idea is to ensure, by proof that could not have been fabricated or falsified, that the inventor actually prepared the invention and knew it would work. *Mikus v. Wachtel*, 504 F.2d 1150 (C.C.P.A. 1974). A wide range of evidence may be introduced for this purpose; it may be established by documentary evidence and the activities of others. *Gianladis v. Kass*, 324 F.2d 322, 51 C.C.P.A. 753 (1963). Nevertheless, when the invention involves intricate machinery or sophisticated processes, more is required for reduction to practice than in cases in which invention is comparatively simple. *Honeywell, Inc. v. Diamond*, 499 F. Supp. 924 (D.D.C. 1980).

Perhaps the best advice in this connection comes from the Bible: "Now go, write it before them in a table, and note it in a book." *Isaiah* 30:8. An inventor's notebook records, witnessed by someone else in the research department, are often determinative in these cases. *See, e.g., Peeler v. Miller*, above.

In *De Solms v. Schoenwald*, 15 U.S.P.Q.2d (BNA) 1507 (Pat. Off. Bd. App. & Int. 1990), the Board held that "De Solms has established conception of the invention of count 1 by September 17, 1981, when De Solms began the preparation of 6-amino-benzothiazole-2-sulfonamide, as corroborated by Christy and Smith." The other inventor in the interference, Schoenwald, had argued that De Solms' proof of reduction to practice and utility depended critically on some tests done by a colleague, one Sondey, and that no corroborating evidence was introduced to support these tests. The Board rejected the argument:

> Schoenwald's argument that there is no corroboration of Sondey's work in evaluating compound L-646,465-00F01 for carbonic anhydrase enzyme inhibition activity is not persuasive. Sondey is not an inventor, and it is well settled that the purpose of the corroboration requirement is to verify the testimony of the inventor. We reject Schoenwald's argument, that the Sondey's [sic] testimony must be corroborated even though he is not an inventor, as contrary to interference law. See III RIVISE AND CAESAR,

INTERFERENCE LAW AND PRACTICE, § 539 (Michie Co. 1947) and the cases cited therein.

The Board went on to state:

> Similarly, Schoenwald's argument that Sondey does not state that he showed or sent the information to anyone and De Solms does not indicate she ever received it is not persuasive. In our view it is unnecessary for the test results to be communicated to De Solms to establish a reduction to practice. Since De Solms had a conception of the invention by her preparation and identification of the compound coupled with her expectation of carbonic anhydrase enzyme inhibiting activity, the work of Sondey in evaluating the compound accrued to De Solms' benefit whether she knew about it or not. The evidence shows that Sondey was an employee of Merck, that he reduced the invention to practice in the course of his employment and that he has not contested the designation of De Solms as the inventor. The evidence satisfies us that the reduction to practice was on De Solms' behalf by persons authorized to do so.

3. *Post-Reduction Activities.* Where there is reasonable doubt whether there has been an actual reduction to practice, courts have found it appropriate to inquire into the inventor's subsequent conduct to determine if the acts relied on as a reduction to practice amount only to an abandoned experiment. *Hughes Aircraft Co. v. General Instrument Corp.*, 374 F. Supp. 1166 (D. Del. 1974).

4. *Commercial Viability.* There is no requirement that a prior invention be commercialized in order to be reduced to practice; the key is whether the invention has reached the point where practical business people would take the risk of commercializing the invention. *Friction Div. Prods., Inc. v. E.I. DuPont de Nemours & Co.*, 658 F. Supp. 998 (D. Del. 1987).

5. *Recognition of Invention's Features.* You must understand what you have invented to claim conception and/or reduction to practice. In *Knorr v. Pearson*, 671 F.2d 1368 (C.C.P.A. 1982), for instance, it was held that even assuming the claimant established inherent formation of claimed features, his failure to appreciate that phenomenon defeated his alleged prior conception and reduction to practice, and his subsequent recognition of the phenomenon and subsequent successful tests were irrelevant. Note the similarities between this and the concept of "accidental anticipation," discussed earlier in this chapter in connection with the case of *Tilghman v. Proctor.*

6. *No Concealment Without Reduction to Practice.* In general, the question of whether an invention has been abandoned, suppressed or concealed under § 102(g) is quite distinct from issues of technical priority under that section. But in one respect, there is a relationship between the two. Courts have held that without an actual reduction to practice there is no invention in existence that can be abandoned, suppressed or concealed under § 102(g). *See, e.g., Peeler v. Miller*, above. An interesting feature of these cases is that inventors, in seeking

priority, argue for a *later* reduction to practice than the one they might be entitled to, because concealment cannot begin until an invention has been reduced to practice.

i. Constructive Reduction to Practice

There are several references in the preceding cases to a "constructive reduction to practice." This is a term of art, which means the preparation of a patent application. *See* 1 RIVISE & CAESAR, INTERFERENCE LAW AND PRACTICE, §§ 130, 154 (Michie Co. 1940). As you might have inferred, the drafting of a well-prepared patent application is tantamount to an effective reduction to practice. The rationale for this is confidence in the technical sufficiency of the patent specification.

This confidence is well-placed, *if* the inventor meets the requirements of § 112 of the Patent Act. This is because, under this section, the disclosure in a patent specification must be so complete that it enables one skilled in the art to make and use the invention. (See Chapter 6.) Courts have consistently held that a patent application must be enabling for the application to constitute a constructive reduction to practice. *See, e.g., Feldman v. Aunstrup*, 517 F.2d 1351, 186 U.S.P.Q. (BNA) 108 (C.C.P.A. 1975), *cert. denied*, 424 U.S. 912 (1976); 3 D. CHISUM, PATENTS § 10.05[5] (1978 & Supp. 1991). Thus, if the inventor writes a truly enabling disclosure, the specification should be just as useful to the art as a completed invention. (More so, perhaps; it is much easier to FAX a specification than transport many inventions.)

Note well that this applies *only* to patent applications. *See, e.g., In re Schlittler*, 234 F.2d 882, 43 C.C.P.A. 986 (1956) (a printed publication or manuscript submitted for publication does not constitute a reduction to practice of claimed invention described therein but constitutes only evidence of conception); *Kear v. Roder*, 115 F.2d 810, 47 U.S.P.Q. (BNA) 458 (C.C.P.A. 1940) (publication of an invention by an inventor in a bulletin or a magazine is not in law a "constructive reduction to practice" of the invention thus disclosed). It might well be asked, however, why special preference should be shown for patent applications. Why, for instance, cannot a scientific or technical article, which meets the enablement requirement, be considered a constructive reduction to practice? Why is the *form* of technical disclosure — the patent specification — the dominant consideration?

Courts have given a curious answer. In *Kear, supra*, the court stated that in an interference it was not necessary to permit a publication to serve as a constructive reduction to practice, since the parties could easily present details concerning the completion of an invention. But this *assumes* that only those publications prepared after construction of the invention could meet the enablement requirement. It thus assumes away the difficult question: how could a patent specification be enabling without construction of the invention?

No matter how one approaches the problem, the existing cases seem problematic. Unless writing "Patent Specification" at the top of a technical article confers some greater descriptive content, there is no reason to treat an article not in specification form any differently. This is especially relevant in areas such as biotechnology. In these fields, scientist/inventors often race not only to patent their inventions but to publish their results. Thus these researchers often submit essentially the same manuscript to their patent attorneys and a scientific publication. It is published in similar form (except that the attorney adds patent claims). Why should a scientist who chose not to file an application, or who delayed filing (e.g., because she was willing to forego European and Japanese protection and therefore availed herself of the one-year U.S. grace period) be deemed not to have reduced to practice by virtue of her choice? One possible counterargument is that the "magical" effect of filing a patent application is justified as a way to encourage applicants to get into the patent system. This "disclosure theory"-based view of the matter, however, ignores the fact that technology is equally well disclosed in a scientific publication. After all, the idea behind the disclosure theory of patents is to encourage disclosure of inventions *that would not otherwise be disclosed*. This is not pertinent where a full-blown scientific publication is already in the hands of experts in the field.

ii. Effect of the Provisional Patent Application

Constructive reduction to practice will only become more important with the advent of the provisional patent application under § 111(b). There seems to be no reason why a provisional patent application cannot serve this function. The practical benefit of filing early is that it increases the chance of being designated the senior party in a subsequent interference. In the past, the stiff requirements of filing a full-blown application, together with the high cost, kept many inventors from filing too early. All this changed with the post-GATT creation of provisional applications. Now, one can expect much more use of early filing to constructively reduce an inventive concept to practice. *See* Peter G. Dilworth, *Some Suggestions for Maximizing the Benefits of the Provisional Application*, 78 J. PAT. & TRADEMARK OFF. SOC'Y 233, 234 (1996).

b. Conception and Diligence

CHRISTIE v. SEYBOLD
55 F. 69 (6th Cir. 1893)

Statement of facts by TAFT, CIRCUIT JUDGE:

This was an appeal from a decree of the circuit court of the United States for the district of Kentucky, directing the commissioner of patents to issue a patent to Charles Seybold, the appellee and complainant below, for a device in a power press used in bookbinding, whereby the platen is "detachably connected with power-driving mechanism and provided with a balancing weight." The bill was filed below under section 4915 of the Revised Statutes [1870 Act; predecessor to Patent Act § 146].

The appellant, Christie, who was respondent below, secured a patent, one claim of which covered the device which Seybold averred that he first invented. Seybold filed his application June 6, 1889, and Christie, his, June 7, 1889. An interference was declared between them in the patent office, on the following claim:

> In a power press a platen detachably connected with the power-driving mechanism and provided with a counterbalancing weight.

The commissioner decided the interference proceeding in favor of Christie, and issued a patent to him, rejecting Seybold's application. Christie lives in Kentucky, and Seybold therefore began proceedings against him in that district.

The invention in controversy was an improvement in presses used by bookbinders for compressing the signature bundle into a solid form, about which is applied the cover to make the complete book. The platen is the upper plate of the press. As the signature bundles vary much in size, it is of advantage to move the platen up and down in the press quickly in order to give space for the insertion of the bundle under it. The mechanism used for producing a strong pressure, whether it be a screw or other means, has a slow movement. If the platen is rigidly connected with this power-pressure mechanism, it cannot be moved upward or downward to release the bundle or readjust the space for a different bundle with much greater rapidity than when pressure is being applied. The improvement was in so detaching the platen from the power-pressure mechanism as to allow it to move up and down independent of that mechanism, and, by means of counterbalancing weights, to render its movement very easy.

Christie's patent [see Figure 4-16] consisted of a press frame [Element 11 in Figure 4-16] with a platen [5] moving up and down between the sides of the frame as guides, and having rigidly attached to its upper side a rack bar [6], which, extending up through the top of the press frame, engaged above with a pinion or small cogwheel [17] mounted upon a shaft journaled in two upright brackets fixed to the top of the press frame. To the same shaft were keyed ratchet wheels, which, by means of pawls and a lever [18], were rotated, driving the pinion, forcing downward the rack bar, and bringing the required pressure on the platen. On top of the rack bar was a cross bar, to the ends of which were attached cords passing up over pulleys journaled in upright posts supported on the top of the press frame, and carrying counterbalancing weights equal to the weight of the platen. The pawls which were engaged with a ratchet wheel to produce a rotary motion, forcing down the platen, might be thrown out of engagement with the ratchet wheel, and then the platen might be moved up or down easily by the aid of the counterbalancing weight. In doing so, of course, the pinion and ratchet wheels turned with the movement of the rack bar, but offered no obstruction to the upward or downward movement of the platen.

W. H. CHRISITE.
BOOK BINDER'S PRESS.

No. 450,882.   Patented Apr. 21, 1891.

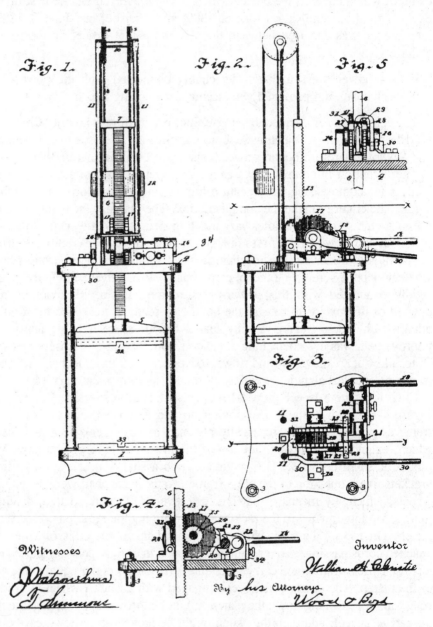

Figure 4-16

The facts with reference to the invention by the two parties were as follows:

Seybold conceived of his invention in October, 1885, and made a rough sketch of it, which he showed to several persons in January, 1886. He was a machinist and inventor, and engaged in manufacturing numbering machines, perforators, cutting machines, graining machines, polishing machines, sandpaper machines, and general repair work. At the time of his conception he says that he did not have the proper tools in his shop to make the machine. It would have required a planer, a long lathe, and a boring mill. He did not have the requisite tools until he moved into his new shop, in the month of March, 1889. From October, 1885, until October, 1888, he did nothing towards reducing his machine to practice. At the latter date he had full-sized drawings made, and his first machine was made in April, 1889. He applied for a patent June 6, 1889. The only reason which Seybold gave in the interference proceedings in the patent office for the delay in reducing his machine to practice was that he did not have the necessary tools or room in his shop. On the hearing below, another deposition was taken, in which he gave an additional reason. His evidence was as follows:

> A. Because my financial condition was such that I could not possibly buy those tools.... It would have been possible for me to order the press built by some other party; but as it has been my object to construct this press to be put on the market, and knowing the prices of presses built by my competitors, I found it impossible to build the press at the competition figure if ordered to be built in outside shops.
>
> Q. The reason, then, that you did not have a press built shortly after you had invented the same, was because there would have been no profit in it for you? Is this correct or not?
>
> A. Yes, sir.

Christie claimed to have conceived of his invention in the summer of 1886. He had working drawings made and patterns ordered for the production of his press in the spring and early summer of 1888, and his press was completed about July 12th of that year. The machine was set up and put in operation in the Methodist Book Concern of Cincinnati about that date, and continued in operation until the bill herein was filed. A second machine was built in October, and put in operation in that building. He filed an application for a patent June 7, 1889.

The court below held that Seybold was the first and true inventor of the machine, and entered a decree directing the commissioner of patents to issue a patent to him. The decree was based on the finding that while Seybold's device disclosed, "in a power press, a platen detachably connected with the power-driving mechanism," Christie's device did not.

TAFT, CIRCUIT JUDGE, (after stating the facts.)

The questions arising in this case, covered by the assignments in error, are two: First, does Christie's invention or device show, "in a power press, a platen detachably connected with the power-driving mechanism and provided with a counterbalancing weight?" and, second, if it does, which one of the two, Seybold or Christie, was the first or true inventor, within the meaning of the patent laws?

[The court decided two preliminary issues: first that the parties were permitted to raise the issue of whether the Christie device was within the "issue" or count of the interference; and second, that Christie's specification was sufficient to permit him to claim a power press with a platen "detachably connected" and balanced by counterweights.]

For these reasons we are unable to agree with the learned judge below in respect to the ground upon which he placed his decision. We are therefore brought to consider the question which, in the view he took of the case, he did not find it necessary to pass upon, — that is, who was the first and true inventor of that feature which we have found to be common to the two devices, and which is here the subject of controversy?

The patent statutes have always required such particularity of description in the applications for a patent as to leave no doubt that in the eye of the law he is the first and true inventor who first reduces the conception of a new invention or discovery to practical and operative form. In *Bedford v. Hunt*, 1 Mason, 302-304 [3 F. Cas. 37, 1 Robb, Pat. Cas. 148 (C.C.D. Mass. 1817)], Mr. Justice Story said: "The first inventor who has put the invention into practice, and he only is entitled to a patent."

And again, on page 305, he says:

> The intent of the statute was to guard against defeating patents by the setting up of a prior invention which had never been reduced to practice. If it were the mere speculation of a philosopher or a mechanician, which had never been tried by the test of experience, and never put into actual operation by him, the law would not deprive a subsequent inventor, who had employed his labors and his talents in putting it into practice, of the reward due to his ingenuity and enterprise.

So in *Agawam Co. v. Jordan*, 7 Wall. 583, Mr. Justice Clifford states the rule as follows:

> The settled rule of law is that whoever first perfects a machine is entitled to a patent, and is the real inventor, although others may have previously had the idea, and made some experiments towards putting it in practice. He is the inventor, and is entitled to the patent, who first brought the machine to perfection, and made it capable of useful operation.

This is the general rule, and had no exception under the statutes in force down to the act of July 4, 1836, (5 St. p. 117.) The fifteenth section of that act, in specifying the defenses which a defendant might set up in an action for infringement, permitted him to plead that the patentee "had surreptitiously and unjustly obtained the patent for that which was in fact invented or discovered by another who was using reasonable diligence in adapting and perfecting the same." The effect of the change made by the act of 1836 was considered by Mr. Justice Story in the case of *Reed v. Cutter*, 1 Story, 590 [20 F. Cas. 435, No. 11,645 (C.C.D. Mass. 1841)], where, referring to the words "was using reasonable diligence in adapting and perfecting his invention," he said:

> These latter words were copied from the fifteenth section of the act of 1836, c. 357, and constitute a qualification of the preceding language of that section; so that an inventor who has first actually perfected his invention will not be deemed to have surreptitiously or unjustly obtained a patent for that which was in fact first invented by another, unless the latter was at that time using reasonable diligence in adapting and perfecting the same. And this I take to be clearly the law; for he is the first inventor in the sense of the act, and entitled to a patent for his invention, who has first adapted and perfected the same to use; and until the invention is so perfected and adapted for use it is not patentable. An imperfect and incomplete invention, existing in mere theory or in intellectual notion, or in uncertain experiments, and not actually reduced to practice, and embodied in some distinct machinery, apparatus, manufacture, or composition of matter, is not, and indeed cannot be, patentable under our patent acts, since it is utterly impossible, under such circumstances, to comply with the fundamental requisites of those acts. In a race of diligence between two independent inventors, he who first reduces his invention to a fixed, positive, and practical form would seem to be entitled to a priority of right to a patent therefor. The clause now under consideration seems to qualify that right by providing that in such case he who invents first shall have the prior right, if he is using reasonable diligence in adapting and perfecting the same, although the second inventor has, in fact, first perfected the same, and reduced the same to practice in a positive form. It thus gives full effect to the well-known maxim that he has the better right who is prior in point of time, namely, in making the discovery or invention.

Reed v. Cutter is a leading case, and has been followed by Mr. Justice Clifford in *White v. Allen*, 2 Cliff. 224, 2 Fish. Pat. Cas. 440 [29 F. Cas. 969, No. 17,535 (C.C.D. Mass. 1863)], and in later cases.

It is obvious from the foregoing that the man who first reduces an invention to practice is prima facie the first and true inventor, but that the man who first conceives, and, in a mental sense, first invents, a machine, art, or composition of matter, may date his patentable invention back to the time of its conception, if he connects the conception with its reduction to practice by reasonable diligence on his part, so that they are substantially one continuous act. The burden is on the second reducer to practice to show the prior conception, and to establish the connection between that conception and his reduction to practice by proof of due diligence. It has sometimes been held, in the decisions in the patent office, that the necessity for diligence on the part of the first conceiver does not arise until the date of the second conception; but this, we think, cannot be supported on principle. The diligence of the first reducer to practice is necessarily immaterial. It is not a race of diligence between the two inventors in the sense that the right to the patent is to be determined by comparing the diligence of the two, because the first reducer to practice, no matter what his diligence or want of it, is prior in right unless the first conceiver was using reasonable diligence at the time of the second conception and the first reduction to practice. The reasonable diligence of the first conceiver must be pending at the time of the second conception, and must therefore be prior to it. Reasonable diligence by the first conceiver, beginning when his rival enters the field, could only carry his invention back to the date of the second conception, and in the race from that time the second conceiver must win because of his first reduction to practice. The elaborate opinion of the commissioner of patents, Mr. Mitchell, in the interference proceeding between Christie and Seybold, reported in 54 O.G. [Off. Gaz. of the Pat. Off.] 957, cites all the authorities, and is quite convincing on this point. We fully concur therein. As Christie reduced the invention to practice nearly a year before Seybold's press was made, the burden is on Seybold to show that from the time of his original conception, which antedated that of Christie, he was using reasonable diligence in adapting and perfecting his idea to practical use. Has he sustained that burden? It is quite clear to us that he has not. The question of reasonable diligence in any case depends, of course, upon all the circumstances. A complicated invention, requiring many experiments and much study to give it practical form, would reasonably delay a reduction to practice after the first conception for a greater length of time than where the idea and the machine embodying it were of a simple character. Then, too, the sickness of the inventor, his poverty, and his engagement in other inventions of a similar kind are all circumstances which may affect the question of reasonable diligence.

In this case, Seybold's first conception was in October, 1885, and he did not reduce his machine to practical form until April, 1889, three years and a half later. He made a rough sketch in January, 1886, which he subsequently lost. In October, 1888, three years after his first conception, he had working drawings made, and six months later a press was manufactured. His excuse for his delay is that until the spring of 1889 he could not afford to buy the necessary tools for the manufacture of the press, and, if he had been able to do so, his shop was not large enough to permit the use of them. He does not say, however, that he had not the means to have the press made at some other shop, where the proper tools were to be had, but, on the contrary, intimates that he might have done so, but for the fact that there would have been no profit for him to sell machines made by others according to his invention. Now, we do not think this a good excuse for failing to make at least one machine, in accordance with his conception. It is as much as to say that in his view his new conception, when reduced to practice, would not have sufficient value and utility to bring him any return commensurate with the outlay required to reduce it to practice, and in consequence he indefinitely postponed putting it into practical form until circumstances should change. This is a temporary abandonment of the idea, and is not the due diligence which entitles him to the favor of the public, for whose benefit, primarily, the patent laws were enacted, (*Wright v. Postel*, 44 Fed. Rep. 352 [(C.C.E.D. Pa. 1890)].)

It can hardly be claimed that the rough sketch made by Seybold of his proposed press in January, 1886, was a reduction to practice. It has been held in many cases that drawings, much more complete than the one here testified to, are not reductions to practice, as against a subsequent conceiver who first made an actual, operative machine.

On the whole case we find, therefore, that Seybold is not the true and first inventor. The decree of the court below is reversed, with instructions to dismiss the bill at the costs of the complainant.

NOTES

The Rule of Priority. Judge (later President, then Justice) Taft states the rule of priority in our law quite succinctly:

> [T]he man who first reduces an invention to practice is prima facie the first and true inventor, but ... the man who first conceives, and, in a mental sense, first invents, a machine, art, or composition of matter, may date his patentable invention back to the time of its conception, if he connects the conception with its reduction to practice by reasonable diligence on his part, so that they are substantially one continuous act.

Another way of stating this is as follows: The first reducer to practice has priority, *unless* the second reducer to practice can prove (1) that she conceived first *and* (2) that she used "reasonable diligence" in reducing her conception to practice. (The time frame for measuring this diligence, i.e., when it must begin, is discussed below.)

Another classic statement of the priority rule appears in *Laas v. Scott*, 161 F. 122, 126 (C.C.E.D. Wis. 1908):

> Under our patent system, he who first arrives at a complete conception of the inventive thought is entitled to recognition and reward, unless and until the interest of the public is compromised by his lack of diligence in demonstrating that his invention is capable of useful operation. The public may justly demand of the inventor who seeks a legal monopoly that within a reasonable time the invention be brought to such a state of perfection as to be adapted to actual use. To that extent the public interest is paramount. Actual reduction to practice is preferable to that which is constructive merely, as more to the interest of the public and reasonable indulgence ought to be extended to one pursuing that course in good faith. Therefore the inventor who first reduces the discovery to practical operation is held to be prima facie the true inventor, without regard to the date of his conception. But the earlier inventor may overcome this presumption and prevail, if he can show by satisfactory evidence continuous diligence to perfect and utilize

the invention. Thus with nicety and fairness has the law adjusted the respective rights of rival inventors consistently with the general welfare. When the inventor who is first to conceive is also the first to reduce to practice within the statutory period, he is clearly entitled to priority, although a junior inventor may anticipate him by earlier application at the Patent Office, and may have secured letters patent.

i. Conception in Detail

GOULD v. SCHAWLOW
363 F.2d 908, 150 U.S.P.Q. 634 (C.C.P.A. 1966)

Gould appeals from the decision of the Board of Patent Interferences which awarded priority of invention of the subject matter set forth in four counts to the senior party, Schawlow and Townes (Schawlow). [W]e affirm.

The invention relates to an apparatus for light amplification by stimulated emission of radiation, better known by the acronym "laser."

It appears that amplification of electromagnetic radiation by stimulated emission of radiation was first realized on a practical basis by devices operating in the microwave frequency range. The laser is described in the record as an extension of the maser principle to optical wavelengths, i.e. infrared, visible and ultraviolet light. No matter in what portion of the electromagnetic spectrum it is designed to operate, it appears that the heart of a maser-like device is a working medium, generally a gas or solid, containing atoms or molecules which have one or more sets of energy levels. Unlike the situation ordinarily prevailing in a volume of matter at equilibrium, where the lower energy states of the material will be more heavily populated with atoms or molecules than the higher energy levels, the laser working medium contains material in which a higher energy level is populated by a significantly greater number of atoms than is a lower energy level of the material. A working medium in such a non-equilibrium condition is said to have an "inverted population" [or] "negative temperature." The means used to excite or "pump" the working medium to create an inverted population of atoms or molecules may comprise a source of electromagnetic energy, for example, a strong light of suitable wavelength directed at the working medium.

The record also shows that a medium in which a population inversion exists may be stimulated to emit its stored energy by wave energy (microwave energy in a "maser" and light energy in a "laser") of the frequency corresponding to the energy separation of the inverted pair of energy levels, thus amplifying the stimulating signal. In marked contrast to white light from the sun or an electric light bulb, which consists of a whole spectrum of colors and which is emitted in a random, non-directional manner when excited atoms spontaneously return to a lower energy level, the light radiation emerging from the laser device here under conditions of stimulated emission is both "temporally coherent" (a term used to describe the monochromatic nature of the emitted light) and "spatially coherent" (a term used to describe the tendency of the emergent light to undergo little divergence or spreading).

The counts of the interference relate to a laser comprising an active medium with the requisite energy level characteristics, means for pumping that medium, and a cavity resonator to enhance the laser operation. The cavity employed in microwave masers which characteristically has dimensions of the order of one wavelength, e.g. 1-100 centimeters, cannot be conveniently employed in light amplifiers because of the shortness of light wavelengths. Rather, a cavity is utilized which has dimensions on the order of thousands or more of light wavelengths. Typically, the cavity defined by the counts is formed by a pair of spaced, plane, parallel optical reflectors, at least one of which is partially transparent, and side members through which pumping energy is admitted and some of the spontaneous and undesired stimulated emission, deviating in its travel from an axis perpendicular to the reflecting end plates, is allowed to escape. The desired output beam of the laser is built up or amplified by repeated passes back and forth along the axis perpendicular to the reflecting end plates, ultimately passing out of the cavity through the partially transparent end reflecting member in coherent form.

With the advent of devices capable of amplifying radiation other than microwaves, the term "maser" has assumed a more general meaning — molecular amplification by stimulated emission of radiation. The Schawlow patent uses the expression "optical maser" to denote an apparatus performing the function of the "laser." As a consequence, the counts employ the expression "maser." Count 1 is representative:

> 1. A maser generator comprising a chamber having end reflective parallel members and side members, a negative temperature medium disposed within said chamber, and means arranged about said chamber for pumping said medium, said side members being transparent to the pumping energy and transparent to or absorptive of other energy radiated thereat ....

Both Schawlow and Gould rely on their filing dates of July 30, 1958, and April 6, 1959, respectively, for constructive reduction to practice of the subject matter in interference, neither party alleging an actual reduction to practice prior to those dates. Under such circumstances it is, of course, well established interference law that the junior party, here Gould, must prove by a preponderance of the evidence (1) conception of the invention prior to July 30, 1958, and (2) reasonable diligence in reducing it to practice commencing from a time just prior to July 30, 1958, to his filing date of April 6, 1959. 35 U.S.C. 102(g). The board found that Gould had failed to prove either conception or diligence. We shall consider those issues separately.

Conception

In attempting to discharge his burden of proof, Gould relies primarily on his own testimony coupled with Exhibit 1, which is a bound notebook identified as notebook #1. Pages 1 to 9, the only pages relevant here, were witnessed November 13, 1957, by a notary public. The notary testified that, while he did not read the contents of that notebook and would not have understood them had he tried to do so, "those pages were full" at the time he signed on the margins. The board, but for two "insignificant exceptions" relating to additions Gould admitted making after the date of notarization, accepted Exhibit 1 as a "genuine and authentic document existing substantially as when notarized."

However, the board held that pages 1 to 9 of Exhibit 1 did not disclose "an operative embodiment of the subject matter of the counts," stating:

> In particular, the notebook No. 1 does not specifically indicate how the pump light is to be applied to the active medium nor that the sides of the cavity are transparent to the laser light. Gould himself testified that the disclosure of the Notebook No. 1 does not explicitly show a laser with "side members being transparent to the pumping energy and transparent to or absorptive of other energy radiated thereat" although he did indicate his belief that it was obvious that such was the construction of the side members of the apparatus of Figure 1 of the disclosure. Although it is urged that one skilled in the art would realize that the walls of the tube illustrated on page 1 of Notebook No. 1 were non-reflective and, specifically, were transparent to both pumping and laser light, we are not prepared to accept this unsubstantiated conclusion.

Set forth below [is the] text in Gould's notebook which he relies on to establish conception:

> Some rough calculations on the feasibility of a LASER: Light Amplification by Stimulated Emission of Radiation[.] [C]onceive a tube terminated by optically flat, partially reflecting parallel mirrors. The mirrors might be silvered or multilayer interference reflectors. The latter are almost lossless and may have high reflectance depending on the number of layers. A practical achievement is 98% in the visible for a 7-layer reflector....
>
> Consider a plane standing wave in the tube. There is the effect of a closed cavity; since the wavelength is small the diffraction and hence the lateral loss is negligible.
>
> If the tube contains an excess of atoms in a higher electronic state, a plane travelling wave may grow by inducing transitions in the atoms, which must add energy to the wave ....
>
> There are several possibilities for excitation:
>
> A. Optical excitation from an external discharge....

B. The (coherent) beam of light would emerge from the partially transmitting mirrors as a wave which was plane to within a fraction of wavelength, that is the beam would have an angular divergence 10^{-5} or better. At
a distance of one kilometer the beam would have broadened 1 centimeter.
Thus the beam could travel long distances essentially unweakened. Application to communication, radar etc. are obvious....

It is true, as the board noted, that Gould has conceded that his notebook
disclosure does not state "in so many words" that the side walls of the contemplated device are "transparent to the pumping energy and transparent to or
absorptive of other energy radiated thereat," as count 1 [of the interference]
requires. However, Gould submits that "even a relatively untrained layman"
should be able to understand that the disclosed apparatus meets the terms of the
counts in those respects, and that the board erred in failing to consider expert
testimony on that issue.

We think it is clear from the contentions of the parties and the expert testimony that the pages of Exhibit 1 are susceptible of numerous interpretations, each
ostensibly plausible, as to what was actually in Gould's mind when he wrote
those pages. In our opinion, Gould's notebook #1 is too ambiguous to justify the
conclusion that he possessed "a definite and permanent idea of the complete and
operative invention," or that he made his invention "sufficiently plain to enable
those skilled in the art to understand it." *See Townsend v. Smith*, 36 F.2d 292,
17 C.C.P.A. 647.

As was stated in *Mergenthaler v. Scudder*, 11 App. D.C. 264:

> ... But if drawings be exhibited and relied on, as evidence of the conception
> of the invention, they must show a complete conception, free from ambigu-
> ity or doubt, and such as would enable the inventor or others skilled in the
> art to reduce the conception to practice without any further exercise of
> inventive skill.

We agree with the board that Gould has not proved by a preponderance of the
evidence that his conception of the laser device described in Exhibit 1 included
side members which are non-reflective, viz. transparent to or absorptive of other
energy, particularly undesired stimulated laser light, radiated thereat.

But even assuming for purpose of discussion, as did the board, that Gould
properly discharged his burden of proving conception of the invention, which we
do not think is the case, he still must prove reasonable diligence in reducing that
conception to practice in order to prevail. [The court concluded that, despite
Gould's testimony that he worked more than one thousand hours on the invention
during the period from his conception to his reduction to practice, he had not
shown "specific activity" that proved diligence during that period.]

Affirmed.

NOTES

1. *More on Gould.* Although he lost the preceding interference, Gould received a number of important patents on basic laser technology based on the same early research and disclosure, including the "optical pumping" technique. *See Gould v. Quigg*, 822 F.2d 1074, 3 U.S.P.Q.2d (BNA) 1302 (Fed. Cir. 1987); *Gould v. Control Laser Corp.*, 705 F.2d 1340, 217 U.S.P.Q. (BNA) 985 (Fed. Cir.), *cert. denied*, 464 U.S. 935 (1983); *In re Gould*, 673 F.2d 1385, 213 U.S.P.Q. (BNA) 628 (C.C.P.A. 1982); *Gould v. Hellwarth*, 472 F.2d 1383, 176 U.S.P.Q. (BNA) 515 (C.C.P.A. 1973). *See generally* J. HECHT & D. TERESI, LASER: SUPERTOOL OF THE 1980s (1982) at 53-58 (recounting Gould's invention of laser as graduate student at Columbia in late 1950s, where Townes was a professor; describing the inept advice that Gould had to construct a working model before he could apply for a patent). The first page of Gould's notebook description of the laser, notarized by a Bronx candy store owner, is on display in the Smithsonian Institution.

2. *Definition of Conception.* Conception has been defined as "the formation in the mind of the inventor of a definite idea of a complete and operative invention as it is thereafter to be reduced to practice." The date of conception is therefore the date when the inventive idea is "crystallized in all of its essential attributes and becomes so clearly defined in the mind of the inventor as to be capable of being converted to reality and reduced to practice by the inventor or by one skilled in the art." *Technitrol, Inc. v. United States*, 440 F.2d 1363 (Ct. Cl. 1971). An alternative, and oft-cited, formulation defines it as

> the complete performance of the mental part of the inventive act. All that remains to be accomplished in order to perfect the act or instrument belongs to the department of construction, not invention. It is, therefore, the formation in the mind of the inventor of a definite and permanent idea of the complete and operative invention as it is thereafter to be applied in practice that constitutes an available conception within the meaning of the patent law.

Mergenthaler v. Scudder, 11 App. D.C. 264, 1897 C.D. 724 (D.C. Cir. 1897). *See also Standard Oil Co. v. Montedison, S.p.A.*, 494 F. Supp. 370 (D.C. Del. 1980), *aff'd*, 664 F.2d 356 (3d Cir. 1981), *cert. denied*, 456 U.S. 915 (1982) (conception is "definite and permanent idea" of complete and operative invention as it is thereafter to be applied in practice). *Cf. In re Tansel*, 253 F.2d 241, 117 U.S.P.Q. (BNA) 188 (C.C.P.A. 1958) (the final size and shape of every part, and location of every nut, screw and bolt, need not be exactly foreseen before conception of an apparatus can be said to be complete; and it is sufficient if the inventor discloses enough to enable person of ordinary skill in art to construct apparatus without extensive research or experimentation).

3. *Effect of Provisional Applications.* It has been suggested that now, with the advent of the provisional patent application under § 111(b), inventors should file a provisional application upon conception of an invention. In addition to establishing the earliest possible date for purposes both of priority and prior art effect (i.e., creating prior art for others), it is said that such an application might also be found to establish a constructive reduction to practice. Peter G. Dilworth, *Some Suggestions for Maximizing the Benefits of the Provisional Application*, 78 J. PAT. & TRADEMARK OFF. SOC'Y 233 (1996). And finally, of course, it is cheap: currently (1996) $150, or $75 for "small entity." *Id.*; *see* 35 U.S.C. § 41 (1996) (various PTO fees).

FIERS v. REVEL

984 F.2d 1164 (Fed. Cir. 1993)

LOURIE, CIRCUIT JUDGE.

Walter C. Fiers, Michel Revel, and Pierre Tiollais appeal from the June 5, 1991 decision of the Patent and Trademark Office Board of Patent Appeals and Interferences, awarding priority of invention in a three-way interference proceeding, No. 101,096, to Haruo Sugano, Masami Muramatsu, and Tadatsugu Taniguchi (Sugano). We affirm.

BACKGROUND

This interference among three foreign inventive entities relates to the DNA which codes for human fibroblast beta-interferon (β-IF), a protein that promotes viral resistance in human tissue. It involves a single count which reads:

> "A DNA which consists essentially of a DNA which codes for a human fibroblast interferon-beta polypeptide."

The parties filed U.S. patent applications as follows: Sugano on October 27, 1980, Fiers on April 3, 1981, and Revel and Tiollais (Revel) on September 28, 1982. Sugano claimed the benefit of his March 19, 1980 Japanese filing date, Revel claimed the benefit of his November 21, 1979 Israeli filing date, and Fiers sought to establish priority under 35 U.S.C. § 102(g) based on prior conception coupled with diligence up to his British filing date on April 3, 1980.

Sugano's Japanese application disclosed the complete nucleotide sequence of a DNA coding for β-IF and a method for isolating that DNA. Revel's Israeli application disclosed a method for isolating a fragment of the DNA coding for β-IF as well as a method for isolating messenger RNA (mRNA) coding for β-IF, but did not disclose a complete DNA sequence coding for β-IF.[1] Fiers, who was working abroad, based his case for priority on an alleged conception either in September 1979 or in January 1980, when his ideas were brought into the

---

[1]Revel's method involved preparing a cDNA library of clones from the mRNA of cells induced to produce β-IF, screening each clone for hybridization to mRNA from induced cells, eluting the hybridized mRNA, and assaying the eluted mRNAs for β-IF activity.

United States, coupled with diligence toward a constructive reduction to practice on April 3, 1980, when he filed a British application disclosing the complete nucleotide sequence of a DNA coding for β-IF. According to Fiers, his conception of the DNA of the count occurred when two American scientists, Walter Gilbert and Phillip Sharp, to whom he revealed outside of the United States a proposed method for isolating DNA coding for β-IF brought the protocol back to the United States. Fiers submitted affidavits from Gilbert and Sharp averring that, based on Fiers' proposed protocol, one of ordinary skill in the art would have been able to isolate β-IF DNA without undue experimentation. On February 26, 1980, Fiers' patent attorney brought into the United States a draft patent application disclosing Fiers' method, but not the nucleotide sequence for the DNA.

The Board awarded priority of invention to Sugano, concluding that (1) Sugano was entitled to the benefit of his March 19, 1980 Japanese filing date, (2) Fiers was entitled to the benefit of his April 3, 1980 British filing date, but did not prove conception of the DNA of the count prior to that date, and (3) Revel was not entitled to the benefit of his November 21, 1979 Israeli filing date. The Board based its conclusions on the disclosure or failure to disclose the complete nucleotide sequence of a DNA coding for β-IF.

DISCUSSION

Fiers' Case for Priority

The Board held that Fiers failed to establish conception in the United States prior to his April 3, 1980 British filing date. Specifically, the Board determined that Fiers' disclosure of a method for isolating the DNA of the count, along with expert testimony that his method would have enabled one of ordinary skill in the art to produce that DNA, did not establish conception, since "success was not assured or certain until the [β-IF] gene was in fact isolated and its sequence known." The Board relied on our opinion in *Amgen Inc. v. Chugai Pharmaceutical Co.*, 927 F.2d 1200, 18 U.S.P.Q.2d 1016 (Fed. Cir. 1991), in which we addressed the requirements necessary to establish conception of a purified DNA sequence coding for a specific protein. Accordingly, the Board held that Fiers was entitled only to the benefit of his April 3, 1980 British application date because only that application disclosed the complete nucleotide sequence of the DNA coding for β-IF. That date was subsequent to Sugano's March 1980 Japanese priority date.

Fiers argues that the Board erroneously determined that *Amgen* controls this case. According to Fiers, the Board incorrectly interpreted *Amgen* as establishing a rule that a DNA coding for a protein cannot be conceived until one knows the nucleotide sequence of that DNA. Fiers argues that this court decided *Amgen* on its particular facts and that this case is distinguishable. Fiers' position is that we intended to limit *Amgen* to cases in which isolation of a DNA was attended by serious difficulties such as those confronting the scientists searching for the DNA coding for erythropoietin (EPO), e.g., screening a genomic DNA library with fully degenerate probes. According to Fiers, his method could have been easily carried out by one of ordinary skill in the art.[2] Fiers also argues that *Amgen* held that a conception of a DNA can occur if one defines it by its method of preparation. Fiers suggests that the standard for proving conception of a DNA by its method of preparation is essentially the same as that for proving that the method is enabling. Fiers thus urges us to conclude that since his method was enabling for the DNA of the count, he conceived it in the United States when Gilbert and Sharp entered the country with the knowledge of, and detailed notes concerning, Fiers' process for obtaining it.

Conception is a question of law that we review de novo. *Hybritech Inc. v. Monoclonal Antibodies, Inc.*, 802 F.2d 1367, 231 U.S.P.Q. 81, 87 (Fed. Cir. 1986) (citing *Barmag Barmer Maschinenfabrik AG v. Murata Machinery, Ltd*[.], 731 F.2d 831, 837, 221 U.S.P.Q. 561, 565 (Fed. Cir. 1984)). Although *Amgen* was the first case in which we discussed conception of a DNA sequence coding for a specific protein, we were not writing on a clean slate. We stated:

> Conception does not occur unless one has a mental picture of the structure of the chemical, or is able to define it by its method of preparation, its physical or chemical properties, or whatever characteristics sufficiently distinguish it. It is not sufficient to define it solely by its principal biological property, e.g., encoding human erythropoietin, because an alleged conception having no more specificity than that is simply a wish to know the identity of any material with that biological property. We hold that when an inventor is unable to envision the detailed chemical structure of the gene so as to distinguish it from other materials, as well as a method for obtaining it, conception has not been achieved until reduction to practice has occurred, i.e., until after the gene has been isolated.

927 F.2d at 1206, 18 U.S.P.Q.2d at 1021. We thus determined that, irrespective of the complexity or simplicity of the method of isolation employed, conception of a DNA, like conception of any chemical substance, requires a definition of that substance other than by its functional utility.

Fiers' attempt to distinguish *Amgen* therefore is incorrect. We also reject Fiers' argument that the existence of a workable method for preparing a DNA establishes conception of that material. Our statement in *Amgen* that conception may occur, *inter alia*, when one is able to define a chemical by its method of preparation requires that the DNA be claimed by its method of preparation. We

---

[2] Fiers' method involved screening a cDNA library which he maintains is smaller and less complex than a genomic DNA library. Fiers also contends that his screening techniques were routine to those skilled in the art, while those skilled in the art lacked experience screening with fully degenerate probes. Fiers also notes that, in contrast to the situation with EPO in which erroneous amino acid sequence information had been published, the first thirteen amino acids of β-IF were known to the art.

recognized that, in addition to being claimable by structure or physical properties, a chemical material can be claimed by means of a process. A product-by-process claim normally is an after-the-fact definition, used after one has obtained a material by a particular process. Before reduction to practice, conception only of a process for making a substance, without a conception of a structural or equivalent definition of that substance, can at most constitute a conception of the substance claimed as a process. Conception of a substance claimed per se without reference to a process requires conception of its structure, name, formula, or definitive chemical or physical properties.

The present count is to a product, a DNA which codes for β-IF; it is a claim to a product having a particular biological activity or function, and in *Amgen*, we held that such a product is not conceived until one can define it other than by its biological activity or function. The difficulty that would arise if we were to hold that a conception occurs when one has only the idea of a compound, defining it by its hoped-for function, is that would-be inventors would file patent applications before they had made their inventions and before they could describe them. That is not consistent with the statute or the policy behind the statute, which is to promote disclosure of inventions, not of research plans. While one does not need to have carried out one's invention before filing a patent application, one does need to be able to describe that invention with particularity.

Fiers has devoted a considerable portion of his briefs to arguing that his method was enabling. The issue here, however, is conception of the DNA of the count, not enablement. Enablement concerns teaching one of ordinary skill in the art how to practice the claimed invention. See 35 U.S.C. § 112 (1988); *Amgen*, 927 F.2d at 1212, 18 U.S.P.Q.2d at 1026. Since Fiers seeks to establish priority under section 102(g), the controlling issue here is whether he conceived a DNA coding for β-IF, not whether his method was enabling.

We conclude that the Board correctly decided that conception of the DNA of the count did not occur upon conception of a method for obtaining it. Fiers is entitled only to the benefit of his April 3, 1980 British filing date, since he did not conceive the DNA of the count under section 102(g) prior to that date.

Revel's Case for Priority

[Revel's application was found wanting under the written description requirement, see Chapter 6, because it merely described a potential method for isolating the sequence, rather than a description of the DNA itself.]

Sugano's Case for Priority

[The court awarded priority to Sugano. It concluded that he was entitled to rely on his disclosure as enabling since it sets forth a detailed teaching of a method for obtaining a DNA coding for β-IF, as well as the sequence of the gene itself.]

CONCLUSION

The Board correctly awarded priority of invention to Sugano. Accordingly, the decision of the Board is

Affirmed.

NOTES

1. *"I Didn't Think of It Until I Had Done It."* *Fiers* illustrates a curious doctrine that has grown up in recent years surrounding the issue of conception in biotechnology cases. Several cases have held (or assumed) that in biotechnology the precise structure of a DNA sequence is not conceived when the gene's function is understood, but when something more is known about it — typically, its structure. Of course, knowing the structure means it is reduced to practice. Fiers sought to distinguish the decision in *Amgen, Inc. v. Chugai Pharmaceutical Co.*, 927 F.2d 122, *cert. denied sub nom. Genetics Institute, Inc. v. Amgen, Inc.*, 112 S. Ct. 169 (1991) (sequence not conceived when its functional utility is grasped, but only when something more is known, e.g., structure or method of preparation), arguing that in contrast to the uncertainties attending the method disclosed there (screening a genomic DNA library with fully degenerate probes to find the EPO gene), his own method for finding the β-IF gene could have been easily carried out by one of ordinary skill in the art. The Federal Circuit rejected this narrow reading of *Amgen*, holding that "irrespective of the complexity or simplicity of the method of isolation employed, conception of a DNA, like conception of any chemical substance, requires a definition of that substance other than by its functional utility." *Id.* at 1169. In other words, proof that the applicants were in possession of an operative method of obtaining the DNA was not sufficient to establish conception of the DNA itself. Conception only of a process for making the DNA would at most support a subsequent product-by-process claim to the DNA obtained by the disclosed process, and would not support a broader claim to the DNA itself without limitation as to the means by which it is obtained.

This holding was premised on the policy underlying the utility doctrine (see Chapter 3): discouraging filing "too early" in the research process. *Id.* at 1169. Yet such a notion seems at odds with other cases on conception which hold, for instance, that "[c]onception is complete when one of ordinary skill in the art could construct the apparatus without unduly extensive research or experimentation." *Sewall v. Walters*, 21 F.3d 411, 30 U.S.P.Q.2d 1356, 1358-59 (Fed. Cir. 1994). *See also Burroughs Wellcome Co. v. Barr Labs., Inc.*, 40 F.3d 1223, 1228, 32 U.S.P.Q.2d 1915, 1919 (Fed. Cir. 1994) ("[A]n inventor need not know that his invention will work for conception to be complete"; "He need only show that he had the idea; the discovery that an invention actually works is part of its reduction to practice."). The *Burroughs-Wellcome* case contains an especially valuable discussion attempting to reconcile the "simultaneous conception and reduction to practice cases" with more mainstream conception cases. The portion of this opinion dealing with inventorship issues is reproduced in Section C of Chapter 7.

2. Old § 104 at Work. Notice the details of Fiers' priority case. He sought to establish priority by proving that he was first to conceive of the invention and was diligent thereafter up to his British filing date. His British application included a disclosure of the complete DNA sequence for the gene. He claimed that his conception occurred when he disclosed a method for isolating the gene to American scientists who brought his protocol back to the U.S. (Why was this necessary under old § 104?) These scientists submitted affidavits stating that the protocol was enabling — i.e., that one of ordinary skill in the field would have been able to follow the protocol to isolate β-IF DNA without undue experimentation. The court accepted that communication to U.S. nationals could establish domestic conception under the old § 104.

ii. Note on Mental Versus Tangible Invention

A classic definition was provided by Professor William Robinson:

> [T]he mental part of the inventive act ... is an exercise of the creative faculties, generating an idea which is clearly recognized and comprehended by the inventor, and is both complete in itself and capable of application to a practical result.... Two ideas are present to the mind of the inventor: (1) The idea of an end to be accomplished; (2) The idea of a means by which that end can be attained. The same ideas are manifest in the invention when reduced to practice and engaged in the production of its appropriate result.

1 W. ROBINSON, ROBINSON ON PATENTS §§ 86-87 (1890). Robinson also reveals what might be termed his "mentalist" or psychological bias when he states: "To him alone whose mind conceives the perfect, practical, operative idea, — that idea which, when embodied in tangible materials, will accomplish the desired result, — belongs the right of the inventor and the credit of performing the inventive act." *Id.*, at § 80 (footnote omitted). In other sections, Professor Robinson develops his view that the mental component is the essence of invention. With Browning, he believes in the significance of one who is "stung by the splendour of a sudden thought." (Robert Browning, *A Death in the Desert* 1, 59). This view has some interesting implications.

For example, Robinson believes that the reduction of an idea to practice is mere *evidence* of the true invention: "[I]t is evident that no idea can be embodied in a practical art or instrument until it is sufficiently developed in the mind of the inventor to be thus applied." *Id.*, at § 80 n. 2. In Robinson's view, this explains cases such as *Tilghman v. Proctor*, Section B.3 above, where an "accidental" prior discovery is held not to preclude the patentability of an invention. The prior discovery, not being appreciated or understood, does not even qualify as an invention in Robinson's eyes. Thus it cannot properly be considered true prior art.

The Robinsonian or "mentalist" view of invention has a worthy adversary, a noted figure in the history of patent law: Judge (later Justice) Joseph Story. Confronted with the argument that, as he put it, "[a]n invention is the finding out by some effort of the understanding," Judge Story stated:

> It does not appear to me ... that this mode of reasoning upon the metaphysical nature, or the abstract definition of an invention, can justly be applied to cases under the Patent Act. That Act proceeds upon the language of common sense and common life, and has nothing mysterious or equivocal in it.... The thing to be patented is not a mere elementary principle, or intellectual discovery, but a principle put in practice, and applied to some art, machine, manufacture, or composition of matter.... The law looks to the fact, and not to the process by which it is accomplished. It gives the first inventor or discoverer of the thing, the exclusive right, and asks nothing as to the mode or extent of his genius to conceive or execute it.

Earle v. Sawyer, 1 Robb's Pat. Cas. 490, 494, 4 Mason Pat. Cas. 1, 8 F. Cas. 254, No. 4,247 (C.C.D. Mass. 1825). According to Story, this emphasis on the *fact* of invention — the actual artifact produced by the inventor — explains why the law rewards a lucky, serendipitous invention, equally as well as one whose conception was arduous and whose execution required painstaking care. It is the invention — the "fact" or "thing" — that matters in the eyes of the law. In these matters, a philosopher might tag Story as either a pragmatist or perhaps a materialist.

As interesting as this contrast is, it must be noted that both of these towering figures arrive more at less at the same destination: a focus on the invention itself, the actual artifact. For Robinson, of course, this is important only as an indirect indicator of true invention, i.e., conception in the mind of the inventor; while for Story, it is the physical device, the thing itself, that is of value to society and hence of interest to the law. But both recognize the legal primacy of the inventor's artifact. This accords well with the general tenor of patent jurisprudence in this country, which sees patents as a way to advance technology, rather than as a way to reward meritorious thoughts in engineering and applied science.

iii. Diligence in Detail

Recall the § 102(g) schematic, from above:

> [4] In determining priority of invention there shall be considered not only [a] the respective dates of [i] conception and [ii] reduction to practice of the invention, but also [b] the reasonable diligence of one who [i] was first to conceive and [ii] last to reduce to practice, [iii] from a time prior to conception by the other.

We now consider element [b], the concept of reasonable diligence.

In the case that follows, you will notice that elements [b][i] and [ii] are present, i.e., the junior party (second to file) alleges earlier conception but later reduction to practice. The discussion of element [b][iii] may be confusing, however. In the statute, diligence is measured "from a time prior to conception by the other," i.e., prior to conception by the first to reduce to practice, the senior party in the case. But in the following case, the period of diligence, you will see, is measured from the date of the first reducer's filing of a patent application. The discrepancy stems from two additional legal rules that you must be aware of.

The first is that, where a priority claimant cannot establish a date of conception, the date of reduction to practice is taken as the conception date. In other words, where for some reason no evidence can be introduced on the subject of conception, the conception date is "collapsed" into the reduction to practice date — actual or constructive. *Bates v. Coe*, 98 U.S. 31, 34 (1878). *See generally* Note, *Date of Invention: The Varying Standards of Proof*, 57 GEO. L.J. 162 (1968). This affects the measurement of the diligence period under element [b][iii]. Recall that this element requires diligence on the part of the first to conceive but last to reduce to practice, beginning just prior to the conception date of the second to conceive but first to reduce to practice. In cases such as the one that follows, the reduction to practice date is taken as the conception date for the person who is second to conceive but first to reduce to practice. Because of cases such as this one, patent lawyers often state that the diligence period begins just prior to the second-reducer's "entry into the field." *See, e.g., Brown v. Barton*, 102 F.2d 193, 197, 41 U.S.P.Q. (BNA) 99 (C.C.P.A. 1939); 3 D. CHISUM, PATENTS § 10.03[1][b] (1978 & Supp. 1991).

The second rule concerns foreign inventors. In the following case, the first reducer to practice is a Japanese national, claiming a patent based on work done in Japan. As we shall see, under the version of § 104 of the Patent Act in effect when this case was decided, only acts performed in the United States could be introduced as evidence of conception and reduction to practice. As a result, foreign applicants at the time had to rely on their U.S. filing date as their sole priority date. For inventors from NAFTA and WTO countries, this of course has now changed. See below, Section K.4. (Recall that the date of filing establishes a "constructive" reduction to practice in the absence of other evidence regarding reduction to practice.) Note also that the interference was disposed of under 37 C.F.R. § 1.617, "Summary Judgment Against Applicant." *See* 37 C.F.R. § 1.617 (1996).

To summarize: in the following case, the foreign applicant is precluded from introducing evidence of conception or actual reduction to practice, since these events took place overseas. As a result, his U.S. filing date, i.e., his date of constructive reduction to practice, is used as the beginning point of the diligence inquiry for the other inventor under the priority rules in § 102(g), specifically schematic element [b][iii].

GRIFFITH v. KANAMARU

816 F.2d 624, 2 U.S.P.Q.2d 1361 (Fed. Cir. 1987)

Owen W. Griffith (Griffith) appeals the decision of the Board of Patent Appeals and Interferences (board) that Griffith failed to establish a prima facie case that he is entitled to an award of priority against the filing date of Tsuneo Kanamaru, et al. (Kanamaru) for a patent on aminocarnitine compounds. We affirm.

Background

This patent interference case involves the application of Griffith, an Associate Professor in the Department of Biochemistry at Cornell University Medical College, for a patent on an aminocarnitine compound, useful in the treatment of diabetes, and a patent issued for the same invention to Kanamaru, an employee of Takeda Chemical Industries. The inventors assigned their rights to the inventions to the Cornell Research Foundation, Inc. (Cornell) and to Takeda Chemical Industries, respectively. The technology established by this invention is not at issue in this appeal and is therefore not described further.

Griffith had established conception by June 30, 1981, and reduction to practice on January 11, 1984. Kanamaru filed for a United States patent on November 17, 1982. The board found, however, that Griffith failed to establish reasonable diligence for a prima facie case of prior invention and issued an order to show cause under 37 C.F.R. § 1.617 as to why summary judgment should not be issued.

The board considered the additional evidence submitted by Griffith pursuant to the show cause order and decided that Griffith failed to establish a prima facie case for priority against Kanamaru's filing date. This result was based on the board's conclusion that Griffith's explanation for inactivity between June 15, 1983, and September 13, 1983, failed to provide a legally sufficient excuse to satisfy the "reasonable diligence" requirement of 35 U.S.C. § 102(g). Griffith appeals on the issue of reasonable diligence.

Analysis

This is a case of first impression and presents the novel circumstances of a university suggesting that it is reasonable for the public to wait for disclosure until the most satisfactory funding arrangements are made. The applicable law is the "reasonable diligence" standard contained in 35 U.S.C. § 102(g), and we must determine the appropriate role of the courts in construing this exception to the ordinary first-in-time rule. As a preliminary matter we note that, although the board focused on the June 1983 to September 1983 lapse in work, and Griffith's reasons for this lapse, Griffith is burdened with establishing a prima facie case of reasonable diligence from immediately before Kanamaru's filing date of November 17, 1982, until Griffith's reduction to practice on January 11, 1984. 35 U.S.C. § 102(g).

On appeal, Griffith presents two grounds intended to justify his inactivity on the aminocarnitine project between June 15, 1983, and September 13, 1983. The first is that, notwithstanding Cornell University's extraordinary endowment, it is reasonable, and as a policy matter desirable, for Cornell to require Griffith and other research scientists to obtain funding from outside the university. The second reason Griffith presents is that he reasonably waited for Ms. Debora Jenkins to matriculate in the Fall of 1983 to assist with the project. He had promised her she should have that task which she needed to qualify for her degree. We reject these arguments and conclude that Griffith has failed to establish grounds to excuse his inactivity prior to reduction to practice.

The reasonable diligence standard balances the interest in rewarding and encouraging invention with the public's interest in the earliest possible disclosure of innovation. Griffith must account for the entire period from just before Kanamaru's filing date until his [i.e., Griffith's] reduction to practice. 3 D. Chisum, Patents § 10.07 at 10-120 (1986). As one of our predecessor courts has noted:

> Public policy favors the early disclosure of inventions. This underlies the requirement for "reasonable diligence" in reducing an invention to practice, not unlike the requirement that, to avoid a holding of suppression or concealment, there be no unreasonable delay in filing an application once there has been a reduction to practice.

Naber v. Cricchi, 567 F.2d 382, 385 n. 5, 196 U.S.P.Q. 294, 297 n. 5 (C.C.P.A. 1977), *cert. denied*, 439 U.S. 826, 99 S. Ct. 98, 58 L. Ed. 2d 119 (1978) (citation omitted).

The board in this case was, but not properly, asked to pass judgment on the reasonableness of Cornell's policy regarding outside funding of research. The correct inquiry is rather whether it is reasonable for Cornell to require the public to wait for the innovation, given the well settled policy in favor of early disclosure. As the board notes, Chief Judge Markey has called early public disclosure the "linchpin of the patent system." *Horwath v. Lee*, 564 F.2d 948, 950, 195 U.S.P.Q. 701, 703 (C.C.P.A. 1977). A review of caselaw on excuses for inactivity in reduction to practice reveals a common thread that courts may consider the reasonable everyday problems and limitations encountered by an inventor. See, e.g., *Bey v. Kollonitsch*, 806 F.2d 1024, 231 U.S.P.Q. 967 (Fed. Cir. 1986) (delay in filing excused where attorney worked on a group of related applications and other applications contributed substantially to the preparation of Bey's application); *Reed v. Tornqvist*, 436 F.2d 501, 168 U.S.P.Q. 462 (C.C.P.A. 1971) (concluding it is not unreasonable for inventor to delay completing a patent application until after returning from a three week vacation in Sweden, extended by illness of inventor's father); *Keizer v. Bradley*, 270 F.2d 396, 47 C.C.P.A. 709, 123 U.S.P.Q. 215 (1959) (delay excused where inventor, after producing a component for a color television, delayed filing to produce an appropriate receiver for testing the component); *Courson v. O'Connor*, 227 F. 890, 894 (7th Cir. 1915) ("exercise of reasonable diligence ... does not require an inventor to devote his entire time thereto, or to abandon his ordinary means of livelihood"); *De Wallace v. Scott*, 15 App. D.C. 157 (1899) (where applicant made bona fide attempts to perfect his invention, applicant's poor health, responsibility to feed his family, and daily job demands excused his delay in reducing his invention to practice).

Griffith argues that the admitted inactivity of three months between June 15, 1983, and September 13, 1983, which he attributes to Cornell's "reasonable" policy requiring outside funding and to Griffith's "reasonable" decision to delay until a graduate student arrived, falls within legal precedent excusing inactivity in the diligence context. We disagree. We first note that, in regard to waiting for a graduate student, Griffith does not even suggest that he faced a genuine shortage of personnel. He does not suggest that Ms. Jenkins was the only person capable of carrying on with the aminocarnitine experiment. We can see no application of precedent to suggest that the convenience of the timing of the semester schedule justifies a three-month delay for the purpose of reasonable diligence. Neither do we believe that this excuse, absent even a suggestion by Griffith that Jenkins was uniquely qualified to do his research, is reasonable.

Griffith's second contention that it was reasonable for Cornell to require outside funding, therefore causing a delay in order to apply for such funds, is also insufficient to excuse his inactivity. The crux of Griffith's argument is that outside funding is desirable as a form of peer review, or monitoring of the worthiness of a given project. He also suggests that, as a policy matter, universities should not be treated as businesses, which ultimately would detract from scholarly inquiry. Griffith states that these considerations, if accepted as valid, would fit within the scope of the caselaw excusing inactivity for "reasonable" delays in reduction to practice and filing.

Griffith's excuses sound more in the nature of commercial development, not accepted as an excuse for delay, than the "hardship" cases most commonly found and discussed *supra*. Delays in reduction to practice caused by an inventor's efforts to refine an invention to the most marketable and profitable form have not been accepted as sufficient excuses for inactivity.

Cornell University has made a clear decision against funding Griffith's project in order to avoid the risks and distractions, albeit different in each case, that would result from directly financing these inventions. Griffith has placed in the record, and relies on, an able article by President Bok of Harvard, *Business and the Academy*, Harvard Magazine, May-June 1981, 31. Bok is explaining the policy issues respecting academic funding of scientific research, for the benefit of Harvard's alumni who must, of course, make up by their contributions the University's annual deficit. While much academic research could produce a profit, pursuit of such profit may be business inappropriate for a university, though it would be right and proper for a commercial organization. For example, it might produce conflicts between the roles of scientists as inventors and developers against their roles as members of the university faculty. However large the university's endowment may be, it may be better to enlist private funding and let this source of funds develop the commercial utilization of any invention as perhaps, the beneficial owner. If there is a patent, the source of funds may end up assignee of the patent. It seems also implicit in this policy choice that faculty members may not be allowed single-minded pursuit of reduction to practice whenever they conceive some idea of value, and at times the rights of other inventors may obtain a priority that a single-minded pursuit would have averted. Bok says diligent reduction to practice, to satisfy the patent laws, may interfere with a faculty member's other duties. Bok is asking the approval of his alumni, not of the courts. The management of great universities is one thing, at least, the courts have not taken over and do not deem themselves qualified to undertake. Bok does not ask that the patent laws or other intellectual property law be skewed or slanted to enable the university to have its cake and eat it too, i.e., to act in a noncommercial manner and yet preserve the pecuniary rewards of commercial exploitation for itself.

If, as we are asked to assume, Cornell also follows the policy Bok has so well articulated, it seems evident that Cornell has consciously chosen to assume the risk that priority in the invention might be lost to an outside inventor, yet, having chosen a noncommercial policy, it asks us to save it the property that would have inured to it if it had acted in single-minded pursuit of gain.

Although we agree with the board's conclusion, it is appropriate to go further and consider other circumstances as they apply to the reasonable diligence analysis of 35 U.S.C. § 102(g). The record reveals that from the relevant period of November 17, 1982 (Kanamaru's filing date), to September 13, 1983 (when Griffith renewed his efforts towards reduction to practice), Griffith interrupted and often put aside the aminocarnitine project to work on other experiments. Between June 1982 and June 1983 Griffith admits that, at the request of the chairman of his department, he was primarily engaged in an unrelated research project on mitochondrial glutathione metabolism. Griffith also put aside the aminocarnitine experiment to work on a grant proposal on an unrelated project. Griffith's statement in the record that his unrelated grant application, if granted, might "support" a future grant request directed to the aminocarnitine project does not overcome the conclusion that he preferred one project over another and was not "continuously" or "reasonably" diligent. Griffith made only minimal efforts to secure funding directly for the aminocarnitine project.

The conclusion we reach from the record is that the aminocarnitine project was second and often third priority in laboratory research as well as the solicitation of funds. We agree that Griffith failed to establish a prima facie case of reasonable diligence or a legally sufficient excuse for inactivity to establish priority over Kanamaru.

Griffith has failed to establish a prima facie case of "reasonable diligence" to establish grounds for the award of priority as against Kanamaru's filing date.

NOTES

1. *Common Conceptual Mistakes Regarding Reasonable Diligence.* Students, and even lawyers and courts, sometimes make mistakes when talking about diligence. Here are some of the common ones:

a. *Diligence Only Relevant in One Situation.* Diligence in the sense of element [b][iii] of § 102(g) is relevant *only* when one party to the interference claims an earlier conception date, but a later reduction to practice date. Where one party is both the first to conceive and the first to reduce to practice, that party has priority — period. (But recall that under the case of *Paulik v. Rizkalla*, Section J.3 above, there is still the possibility that this party will lose priority by waiting too long, after reduction to practice, to file a patent application.) In such a case, § 102(g) is uninterested in any inquiry into the reasonable diligence of this inventor. That is, there may be a very long and unexplained delay between the first inventor's conception and reduction to practice. But as long as the inventor was first on both, there is no viable priority issue under § 102(g). As the Bible says, "The race is not to the swift, nor the battle to the strong" (*Ecclesiastes* 9:11).

b. *No "Diligence Contest."* The wording of the statute makes clear that only *one party's* diligence is relevant: the first to conceive but second to reduce to practice. It is this person's activities (and inactivity) that is the subject of the reasonable diligence standard of element [b][iii]. Thus the behavior of the second to conceive but first to reduce to practice has no relevance under this section of the statute. An unexplained delay of many years between the conception and reduction to practice of this party does not affect the outcome of the case. Only the first to conceive must account for her behavior during the critical period. *See Steinberg v. Seitz*, 517 F.2d 1359, 1364, 186 U.S.P.Q. (BNA) 209 (C.C.P.A. 1975); 3 D. CHISUM, PATENTS § 10.03[1][a] (1978 & Supp. 1991). Again, though, compare *Paulik* above; the first inventor may face an abandonment problem if there is delay between reduction to practice and filing.

c. *Critical Period Not Flexible.* There is no flexibility regarding the period during which diligence must be shown. The Patent Act says this period *begins* "just prior" to the second-reducer's conception, and *ends* with the first-conceiver's reduction to practice. No amount of diligence commencing after the beginning point in this period matters in the eyes of the law. Thus an impeccably diligent inventor who was first to conceive will not prevail if her diligence begins even one day after the conception date of one who conceives second but reduces to practice first.

2. *Other Excuses for Inactivity.* Although the preceding case, as the court noted, presented an issue of first impression (the status of university grant-seeking activities vis-à-vis diligence), inventors have argued that many similar activities establish diligence. Aside from attempts to commercialize the invention — which do *not* establish diligence, as the court noted — inventors have asserted the following: (1) poverty and illness (generally a valid excuse for lapses in dili-

gence); (2) regular employment (valid excuse); and (3) overworked patent attorney (valid excuse). But courts have held that the following are not valid excuses for lapses in diligence: (1) doubts about value or feasibility; and (2) work on other inventions. *See* 3 D. CHISUM, PATENTS § 10.07[4] (1978 & Supp. 1991).

iv. Note on the Multiple Interference Paradox

For the most part, we have been concerned up to this point with interferences between only two parties. While these are quite frequent, there are also a good number of interferences involving more than two parties. A good example is the five party interference over the invention of polypropylene. *See Standard Oil Co. v. Montedison, S.p.A.*, 494 F. Supp. 370, 374, 206 U.S.P.Q. 676 (D. Del. 1980). Such an interference can be expected to crop up whenever several teams of researchers are racing toward a common goal. A more recent example involves the invention of "warm" superconducting materials in the late 1980s. *See* Robert Pool, *Superconductor Patents: Four Groups Duke It Out*, 245 SCI. 931 (1989).

These multi-party interferences can be exceedingly expensive. The polypropylene interference, for example, was declared in 1958 and resolved by the District Court only in 1980. Final resolution of the matter came in 1989, more than thirty years after the invention was made! *See United States Steel Corp. v. Phillips Petr. Co.*, 865 F.2d 1247, 9 U.S.P.Q. 2d (BNA) 1461 (Fed. Cir. 1989) (upholding Phillips' polypropylene product patent).

In general, interferences with three or more parties are no different than those with only two. In most cases, the question of priority is resolved by the application of the rules outlined above.

However, under a rare set of circumstances, these interferences can lead to a stalemate where no single party has clear priority. This results from the structure of the priority rules. While this is far from common, it has elicited interesting commentary — as much a function of the intellectually interesting nature of the "paradox" as of its practical importance.

To illustrate the kind of paradox the priority rules can produce, consider three inventors, *A*, *B* and *C*. *A* conceives of an invention at time *T1*. *B* conceives at time *T2*. At time *T3*, *A* begins a period of continuous diligence leading up to a reduction to practice. Meanwhile a third inventor, *C*, conceives at *T4*. At *T5*, inventor *B* begins a period of diligence that continues through her reduction to practice. *C* reduces to practice at *T6*, but was not continuously diligent from conception to reduction to practice. At *T7*, *B* reduces to practice. Finally, *A* reduces to practice at *T8*. The following diagram illustrates this sequence of events; CO is conception, D ——> means continuous diligence, and R is reduction to practice. (This notation may be helpful as you sketch out various priority situations.)

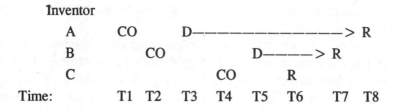

Inventor

A	CO		D———————————> R					
B		CO			D———> R			
C				CO	R			
Time:		T1	T2	T3	T4	T5	T6	T7	T8

In an interference between *A* and *B*, *B* wins because *A* was first to conceive and last to reduce to practice, but has not shown diligence since just prior to *B*'s conception. In an interference between *B* and *C*, *C* wins for the same reason: as between *B* and *C*, *B* was first to conceive and last to reduce to practice, but cannot show diligence since just prior to *C*'s conception. Finally, in an interference between *A* and *C*, *A* wins, since as between them *A* was first to conceive and last to reduce to practice *and* *A* can show diligence since before *C*'s entry into the field. This is the paradox: no single party beats the other two cleanly. *See* Ferrill, *An Anomalous Situation in the Law of Interference as Applied in Multi-party Cases*, 33 J. PAT. OFF. SOC'Y 457 (1951). It has been shown by means of a wonderfully clever use of axiomatic logic that there is a whole family of interferences — potentially infinite in number! — that can yield the paradox. *See* Stern, *Priority Paradoxes in Patent Law*, 16 VAND. L. REV. 131 (1962).

Several proposed solutions have been offered to resolve the paradox. The first is simply to award the patent to no one. *See* Stern, *supra*, at 140. The second is to eliminate the party with the worst claim to priority — on broadly equitable grounds — and resolve the remaining two-party interference. *Id.*, at 140 n. 39. Inventor *B* in our example is perhaps a good candidate for elimination, since she was neither first to conceive nor first to reduce to practice. Third, it has been suggested that the interference be turned into a pure race of conception or reduction to practice. *Id.*, at 141. Finally, it has been suggested that the impasse be resolved by making the interference a race of diligence. In the example above, then, *A* would win the three-party interference. *Id.*, at 143. As before *A* beats *C*. But under the modified rule, *A* beats *B* also. This is because *A*'s diligence commenced just prior to *B*'s *diligence*, and under the modified rule this is enough. (That is, unlike under the current rule, *A*'s diligence need not commence prior to *B*'s conception; only prior to her diligence.) One sad result of adopting the first to file rule: all this wonderful analysis would become irrelevant!

K. INTERNATIONAL PRIORITY

Patent lawyers often encounter inventions with worldwide commercial potential. Because patent law jurisdiction for the most part still follows national boundaries, such inventions must be protected by a series of national patents. (The exception is the European countries that have adopted the Community Patent Convention; these countries have agreed to recognize a single, Community-wide patent, a system scheduled to begin to take effect soon after the publication of this book.)

Patent lawyers face two problems in coordinating the prosecution of a series of national patents. First, a common priority date must be obtained, to insure that protection will be uniform and unaffected by prior art with an effective date before one or more of the national patent applications. Also, a common date will insure that prosecution of a patent in Country *A* does not somehow compromise the patentability of the invention in Country *B*. Second, the patent lawyer has to deal with the logistics of international protection; she must oversee multiple filings in diverse languages in numerous countries. The wide variations in national practices, and the high cost of conducting a large-scale application barrage, make this one of the more challenging professional tasks in patent law.

Fortunately, two international agreements make these tasks a bit more tolerable. First is the Paris Convention, a longstanding international organization created by treaty in 1886 whose primary function is to guarantee a uniform worldwide priority date across all member countries. An applicant may file in any member country of the Convention up to one year after an initial (typically home-country) filing without losing the priority date of the initial filing. The second international agreement is the Patent Cooperation Treaty, or PCT, which streamlines the filing of multiple national patent applications. Each agreement in its own way is an indispensable tool of the patent trade. Although detailed discussion of the agreements is beyond the scope of this volume, a few words about the essential features of each is in order, especially as they relate to priority issues.

1. THE PARIS CONVENTION

The Paris Convention was signed in 1883, a product of the first true "internationalization" wave in the field of patent law. Paris Convention for the Protection of Industrial Property, as last revised, July 14, 1967, 21 U.S.T. 1583, T.I.A.S. No. 6295, 828 U.N.T.S. 305, (last revision, sometimes referred to as the "Stockholm" revision, entered into force April 26, 1970). Its primary function is to define a common priority date so that one may file an application in one member state and have the benefit of that same filing date when filing later in another member state. One purpose of this is to prevent interlopers from copying patents applied for or issued in one state and claiming them as their own in another, before the legitimate owner has time to file in the other country.

The key provision in the Convention as regards priority is Article 4 of the Convention. The relevant excerpts from this section are set out below. Note that the "Union" refers to the so-called Paris Union, the organization formed by all who signed the Convention.

Article 4, Section A

A(1) Any person who has duly filed an application for a patent, or for the registration of a utility model, or of an industrial design, or of a trademark, in one of the countries of the Union, or his successor in title, shall enjoy, for the purpose of filing in the other countries, a right of priority in the periods hereinafter fixed.

A(2) Any filing that is equivalent to a regular national filing under the domestic legislation of any country of the Union or under bilateral or multilateral treaties concluded between countries of the Union shall be recognized as giving rise to the right of priority.

A(3) By a regular national filing is meant any filing that is adequate to establish the date on which the application was filed in the country concerned, whatever may be the subsequent fate of the application.

Article 4, Section B

B. Consequently, any subsequent filing in any of the other countries of the Union before the expiration of the periods referred to above shall not be invalidated by reason of any acts accomplished in the interval, in particular, another filing, the publication or exploitation of the invention, the putting on sale of copies of the design, or the use of the mark, and such acts cannot give rise to any third-party right or any right of personal possession. Rights acquired by third parties before the date of the first application that serves as the basis for the right of priority are reserved in accordance with the domestic legislation of each country of the Union.

Article 4, Section C

C(1) The periods of priority referred to above shall be twelve months for patents and utility models, and six months for industrial designs and trademarks.

C(2) These periods shall start from the date of filing of the first application; the day of filing shall not be included in the period.

C(3) If the last day of the period is an official holiday, or a day when the Office is not open for the filing of applications in the country where protection is claimed, the period shall be extended until the first following working day.

Several points are worth noting from the text of the Convention. First, the filing date that counts is any filing that is adequate to establish a filing date regardless of the outcome of the priority patent application. In other words, if a patent fails to issue from the first application, this is not fatal to applications filed in other countries within the one-year period. (The subsequent applications are not "dependent" on the ultimate fate of the initial or *priority* filing, in other words.) This section is also generally understood to mean that a utility model may claim priority from a patent application, and an industrial design may claim priority from a utility model.

Second, Article 4B spells out the *effects* of the right of priority. It states that filing patent applications, publishing, or exploiting an invention will not cause a loss of priority for subsequent applications so long as these acts are done *after* the initial filing and the subsequent filings are made before the end of the Convention priority period.

Third, note the language in Article 4B stating that "such acts cannot give rise to any third-party right." This is related to a set of rights that has little counterpart in current American law: the rights of independent inventors. In Europe, for example, an independent inventor may have the right to continue to use her invention despite the fact that a patentee has obtained a patent on the same invention. Compare this to the discussion earlier in this chapter regarding the issue of "abandonment, suppression or concealment" under § 102(g) of the U.S. Patent Act. The only "third-party" rights in U.S. law are those in § 252 of the U.S. patent statute, which gives courts discretion to recognize the rights of independent inventors who invent and commercialize after a patentee's original patent is issued but prior to a reissue of that patent with broader scope. *See, e.g.*, *Mine Safety Appliances Co. v. Becton Dickinson & Co.*, 17 U.S.P.Q.2d 1642 (S.D.N.Y. 1990). This topic is discussed in Chapter 10. (There is also a very limited set of "intervening rights" under the new patent term provision, 35 U.S.C. § 154. *See* Uruguay Round Agreements Act, § 532, 108 Stat. at 4985 (acts begun, or investments made, before June 8, 1995 yield only "equitable remuneration" for patentee whose term was extended retroactively under the Act (URAA)).

Unlike the U.S. then, the concept of third-party rights has much broader application in Europe and Japan. *See* European Patent Convention (EPC), Article 38 ("Right based on prior use and right of personal possession"); Patents Act 1977 (United Kingdom), § 64 ("Right to continue use begun before priority date"); T. TANABE & H. WEGNER, JAPANESE PATENT LAW § 841 (1984) ("Prior Use License of Right"). These countries grant third-party rights outside the context of reissue patents, for example protecting the right of an independent inventor to continue using her invention despite the issuance of a valid patent covering it. Typically these prior user rights protect only inventors who begin working an invention before the other inventor files a patent application, and then only to the extent that those independent inventors continue working the invention in the same manner. Such a right, in other words, "protects only the doing of the same act of infringement as was done (or prepared for) before the priority date; allowing the user no freedom to modify or develop his activities." 1 M. VITORIA ET AL., ENCYCLOPEDIA OF UNITED KINGDOM AND EUROPEAN PATENT LAW § 4-311 (1977 & Supp. 1991).

Article 4B of the Convention states that no third-party rights shall arise during the priority period protected by Article 4. That is, in a country where "intervening" third-party rights are granted prior to the filing of an application, no such rights shall accrue to independent inventors who begin use of their independent inventions after the priority filing date but before the filing in the home country, i.e., up to one year later. As the leading handbook on the Paris Convention states, commenting on the transition from the old version of this section to the current one,

> [t]he importance of the right of priority granted by the Convention was limited as long as rights of third parties originating in the priority period were expressly reserved. This reservation was generally interpreted as, for example, enabling third parties who had worked an invention during the priority period or who had obtained knowledge of the invention during that period to use or continue to use it even in the face of a patent granted on the basis of a priority right. The reservation was abolished by the Revision Conference of London in 1934, which replaced it by a sentence with the opposite effect ....

G. BODENHAUSEN, GUIDE TO THE APPLICATION OF THE PARIS CONVENTION FOR THE PROTECTION OF INDUSTRIAL PROPERTY 42 (1968).

In addition to setting up a uniform international priority scheme, the Paris Convention also establishes minimum standards of protection that must be recognized by all signatories in their national laws. For example, it sets limits on domestic legislation concerning compulsory licensing and forfeiture of rights (Article 5); requires that states protect industrial designs (Article 5^{quinques}); and the like. *See generally* G. BODENHAUSEN, *supra*; Gansser, *Violations of the Paris Convention for the Protection of Industrial Property*, 11 INT'L REV. INDUS. PROP. COPYRIGHT L. (IIC) 1 (1980).

Notice of Priority Filing

There is one important "catch" in the Paris Convention that has the potential to undermine all the benefits it provides. Under Article 4D(1), inventors wishing to take advantage of the Convention "shall be required to make a declaration indicating the date of such filing and the country in which it was made." Furthermore, this section permits each country to determine "the latest date on which such declaration must be made." As a consequence, one must be aware of the priority notification requirements of any country one wishes to file in. As an example, one Japanese case is reported where an applicant stated the wrong country of priority filing (France instead of Switzerland), and the Japanese Patent Office refused to recognize the priority date because of the applicant's failure to comply strictly with Japanese requirements. *See* T. TANABE & H. WEGNER, JAPANESE PATENT PRACTICE 133 (1986); *but cf. In re Tangsrud*, 184 U.S.P.Q. (BNA) 746 (Comm'r Pat. 1973) (stating, in opinion refusing to grant request to extend time for appeal from Board of Appeals decisions, that applicant need not file copy of foreign counterpart application within one year of the filing of that foreign application, but instead may file within one year of filing of U.S. application).

2. THE PATENT COOPERATION TREATY (PCT)

The PCT was signed in 1970. The Patent Cooperation Treaty, opened for signature June 19, 1970, 28 U.S.T. 7645, T.I.A.S. No. 8733 (entered into force Jan. 24, 1978). Its major purpose is to streamline the early prosecution stages of patent applications filed in numerous countries. It is often described as a clearing-house for international patent applications. As a practical matter, its major advantage is that it gives an inventor (and her patent lawyer) more of a precious commodity in the prosecution of an application destined for many countries: time. The signatories to the PCT have agreed to permit an applicant to wait for up to thirty months after the initial filing of a patent application in one country to begin the in-depth prosecution of the application in other countries. This allows the inventor more time, compared to non-PCT prosecution, in which to test the product, decide which countries' protection is worthwhile, and pay the patent office filing fees in the various countries. For these reasons, the PCT is growing in popularity and is expected to be an important member of the future patent lawyer's bag of tricks.

There are two main parts of the PCT. Chapter 1 provides that an applicant who files in a national patent office may elect within twelve months to add a PCT filing. The PCT filing is simply an additional filing in any national patent office designated in the PCT. In this case, the applicant has up to twenty months from the initial filing to request that the PCT preliminary prosecution procedure be initiated. At that time, the applicant must also select the PCT member nations that the applicant wishes to be covered under the PCT filing. Note that Chapter 1 preserves the applicant's priority date (in PCT member countries), without having to begin active prosecution, for eight months longer than the simple Paris Convention priority period.

Chapter 2 of the PCT extends the election period to thirty months. To qualify under Chapter 2, the applicant must make her PCT filing at most five months after the first national filing. Chapter 2 gives an inventor an extra eighteen months, compared to the Paris Convention, to select countries for coverage and to initiate multiple national prosecutions.

The extra time is a substantial advantage. Besides simply delaying the expenditure of filing and examination fees, the PCT allows an inventor a significant extra period to assess the technical merits and commercial potential of the invention. This extra time helps the inventor save wasted filing fees for inventions that fail to blossom; for those that show great promise, the various patent applications that grow out of the PCT filing can be tailored to reflect the commercially significant embodiments that have emerged from the extensive testing.

3. FOREIGN FILING LICENSES

The U.S. Patent Act reflects the fundamental fact that technology is important not only to inventors, but to the country as a whole. Specifically, the Act has provisions which permit the U.S. government to review all applications for their potential impact on national security. The Patent Act states that before filing a foreign counterpart application for inventions made in the United States, the application must be authorized by a license obtained from the Commissioner of Patents. 35 U.S.C. § 184; *see Coleman Instruments, Inc.*, 338 F.2d 573 (7th Cir. 1964) (purpose of § 184 is to protect national defense information). The Commissioner's license does not authorize the sale or use of technical data in a foreign country. Separate approvals are required from the appropriate export agency. The license simply provides permission to file a foreign application.

Rules promulgated by the Commissioner provide that if a foreign filing license is not issued within six months from the U.S. filing date, foreign counterparts may be filed without penalty unless a secrecy order has been issued by the Patent Office at the time of filing. 37 C.F.R. § 5.11 (1990). In practice, foreign filing licenses are routinely sent with the official filing receipt for the patent application. Note that an expedited foreign filing license may be received prior to filing a patent application with documentation of the material to be covered in the patent application. 37 C.F.R. § 5.13 (1990). Once the license is granted, it covers additional subject matter to the extent the new material does not pose a need for a national security review or change the nature of the subject matter on which the application was filed. *See generally Minnesota Mining & Mfg. Co. v. Norton Co.*, 426 F.2d 1117 (7th Cir.), *cert. denied*, 401 U.S. 925 (1970) (describing liberal rules for filing late license request where tardiness caused by inadvertence).

4. OVERSEAS ACTIVITIES AND U.S. INTERFERENCES: § 104 OF THE ACT

One of the most stubborn remnants of patent law's "mercantilist" roots, § 104 of the Act, persisted until 1994. Under the old version of this section, proof of two key dates in the inventive process — conception and reduction to practice — was possible only for those who had made their inventions in the United States. The effect of this section was to limit foreign inventors to their first filing date in any dispute over priority. This proved to be a major handicap, since in many cases a U.S. inventor prevailed on the basis of conception and/or reduction to practice evidence, while the foreign inventor (who might well have actually conceived and/or reduced to practice earlier) could only use his or her filing date as the earliest date of invention. Despite some heroic efforts in the caselaw to establish foreign inventors' contact with the U.S., § 104 gave very favorable treatment to inventions made in the U.S. *See, e.g., Holmwood v. Sugavanam*, 948 F.2d 1236, 20 U.S.P.Q.2d 1712, 1713 (Fed. Cir. 1991) (accepting for purposes of domestic reduction to practice evidence that interference party sent claimed fungicide into the U.S. to verify positive test results obtained previously in Germany). *But see Fiers v. Revel*, 984 F.2d 1164, 25 U.S.P.Q.2d 1601 (Fed. Cir. 1993) (communication of method for isolating DNA sequence to U.S. scientists did establish presence in U.S., but method alone did not constitute conception or reduction to practice of DNA sequence). *See generally* Badie, *Hints*

to Foreign Inventors: You Can Protect Your Invention Date, 75 J. PAT. & TRADE-
MARK OFF. SOC'Y 651 (1993), and correspondence at 76 J. PAT. & TRADEMARK
OFF. SOC'Y 174 (1994).

After years of intensive lobbying, North American, European and Japanese
forces were finally able to wrest a change in § 104 from the U.S. The U.S.
patent community, which had long resisted such a change, stated several objections to the use of foreign evidence of inventive acts. Perhaps the best summary
of the precise concerns expressed can be found in the detailed provisions of the
new § 104, which, following amendments under the North American Free Trade
Agreement (NAFTA) of 1993 (North American Free Trade Agreement, Dec. 17,
1992, Can.-Mex.-U.S., 32 I.L.M. 296 and 32 I.L.M. 605 (1993)) and the TRIPs
Uruguay Round agreement of 1994 (see Chapter 1), reads as follows:

§ 104. Invention made abroad

(a) *In general*.

(1) *Proceedings*. In proceedings in the Patent and Trademark Office, in
the courts, and before any other competent authority, an applicant for a
patent, or a patentee, may not establish a date of invention by reference to
knowledge or use thereof, or other activity with respect thereto, in a foreign
country other than a NAFTA country or a WTO member country, except as
provided in sections 119 and 365 of this title.

(2) *Rights*. If an invention was made by a person, civil or military —

(A) while domiciled in the United States, and serving in any other country in connection with operations by or on behalf of the United States,

(B) while domiciled in a NAFTA country and serving in another
country in connection with operations by or on behalf of that NAFTA
country, or

(C) while domiciled in a WTO member country and serving in another
country in connection with operations by or on behalf of that WTO
member country,

that person shall be entitled to the same rights of priority in the United
States with respect to such invention as if such invention had been made in
the United States, that NAFTA country, or that WTO member country, as
the case may be.

(3) *Use of information*. To the extent that any information in a NAFTA
country or a WTO member country concerning knowledge, use, or other
activity relevant to proving or disproving a date of invention has not been
made available for use in a proceeding in the Patent and Trademark Office,
a court, or any other competent authority to the same extent as such information could be made available in the United States, the Commissioner,
court, or such other authority shall draw appropriate inferences, or take

other action permitted by statute, rule, or regulation, in favor of the party that requested the information in the proceeding.

(b) *Definitions*. As used in this section —

(1) the term "NAFTA country" has the meaning given that term in section 2(4) of the North American Free Trade Agreement Implementation Act; and

(2) the term "WTO member country" has the meaning given that term in section 2(10) of the Uruguay Round Agreements Act.

35 U.S.C. § 104 (as amended by P.L. 103-182, Dec. 8, 1993, § 331, 107 Stat. 2113; P.L. 103-465, Dec. 8, 1994, § 531(a), 108 Stat. 4982).

Under this provision, inventors from all GATT signatory nations (i.e., WTO members), together with NAFTA members, may introduce evidence of foreign inventive activities to prove priority in the United States. Inventors from other countries, however, must still rely only on their filing date. *See* 37 C.F.R. § 1.624 (1996) ("Preliminary Statement; Invention Made in a Place Other than the United States, a NAFTA Country, or a WTO Member Country"). While it is difficult to say at this time precisely how many interferences will be affected, it is clear that the new § 104 works a major change in U.S. law. Even so, it is not quite true that foreign inventors are on exactly equal footing with their American counterparts. Most important, note the ability of a court to draw negative inferences in cases where less than complete information regarding inventive activities is made available in the U.S. proceeding. It will be interesting to watch the caselaw develop on this and related issues.

The § 102(g) Conundrum

The new § 104 allows a foreign inventor to gain priority over one asserting domestic U.S. activity. However, some have pointed out that a domestic U.S. inventor who loses an interference might still be entitled to a U.S. patent. While such an argument might seem bizarre, it is at least plausible due to an oversight on the part of the drafters of the Uruguay Round Amendments Act (URAA): the failure to amend § 102(g).

Recall that § 102(g) precludes issuance of a patent where an invention was made by another *in this country*. Since the "in this country" language in § 102(g) was left undisturbed by the URAA, it might be argued that interference evidence of the winning (foreign) party's foreign inventive acts may not be cited against the losing (domestic U.S.) party under § 102(g). The loser could then simply re-file his or her patent, and, it is argued, the examiner would have no statutory basis on which to reject the loser's new patent application. (How would the loser get around the winner's patent application and/or granted patent?)

One proposed solution to this conundrum is to rely on the doctrine of *interference estoppel*. Under this doctrine, the loser of an interference is estopped from arguing the patentability of the same or similar subject matter as that awarded to the winner. There are doubts, however, concerning the scope of this doctrine.

See, e.g., In re Deckler, 977 F.2d 1449 (Fed. Cir. 1992) (finding interference estoppel in a case where the losing party purportedly conceded that the subject matter of the newly submitted claims was not patentably distinct from the subject matter awarded to the winner); Harold C. Wegner, *Trips Boomerang — Obligations for Domestic Reform*, 29 VAND. J. TRANSNAT'L L. 535, 550 (1996) (expressing doubts about the prospects of interference estoppel as a way to prevent anomalous results in cases involving § 102(g) and new § 104).

NOTE

Background. For background information, consult Marshall A. Leaffer, *Protecting United States Intellectual Property Rights: Towards a New Bilateralism*, 76 IOWA L. REV. 273 (1991) (describing the GATT system and the basic principles to which GATT adheres in the international trade of goods).

L. RULE 131: QUASI-INTERFERENCES BETWEEN A PATENT AND PRIOR ART

The conceptual framework developed to cover interference issues, and reflected in current § 102(g), has proven useful in other contexts. Perhaps the most important of these is the issue of whether an invention came earlier than a prior art reference. We have seen the importance of the "critical date" for purposes of § 102. Aside from the statutory bars of § 102(b), whose critical dates are measured from the filing of an application, the other provisions of § 102 (e.g., subsections (a) and (e)) take as their critical date the date of *invention*. The question has often arisen, what is the date of invention for purposes of these provisions of § 102? The answer that has been settled on is to apply the § 102(g) concepts of conception, diligence, and reduction to practice, by analogy.

These principles are contained in a very important Patent Office rule, known as Rule 131, codified at 37 C.F.R. § 1.131. The purpose of the rule is to allow a patent applicant to show invention before the date of a prior art reference — to "swear behind" or "antedate" the reference. The rule reads as follows:

§ 1.131. Affidavit or declaration of prior invention to overcome cited patent or publication.

(a)(1) When any claim of an application or a patent under reexamination is rejected under 35 U.S.C. 102(a) or (e), or 35 U.S.C. 103 based on a U.S. patent to another which is prior art under 35 U.S.C. 102(a) or (e) and which substantially shows or describes but does not claim the same patentable invention, as defined in 37 C.F.R. 1.601(n), or on reference to a foreign patent or to a printed publication, the inventor of the subject matter of the rejected claim, the owner of the patent under reexamination, or the party qualified under 37 C.F.R. 1.42, 1.43 or 1.47, may submit an appropriate oath or declaration to overcome the patent or publication. The oath or declaration must include facts showing a completion of the invention in this country or in a NAFTA or WTO member country before the filing date of the application on which the U.S. patent issued, or before the date of the foreign patent, or before the date of the printed publication. When an appropriate oath or declaration is made, the patent or publication cited shall not bar the grant of a patent to the inventor or the confirmation of the patentability of the claims of the patent, unless the date of such patent or printed publication is more than one year prior to the date on which the inventor's or patent owner's application was filed in this country.

(2) A date of completion of the invention may not be established under this section before December 8, 1993, in a NAFTA country, or before January 1, 1996, in a WTO Member country other than a NAFTA country.

(b) The showing of facts shall be such, in character and weight, as to establish reduction to practice prior to the effective date of the reference, or conception of the invention prior to the effective date of the reference coupled with due diligence from prior to said date to a subsequent reduction to practice or to the filing of the application. Original exhibits of drawings or records, or photocopies thereof, must accompany and form part of the affidavit or declaration of their absence satisfactorily explained.

37 C.F.R. § 1.131 (1996).

Several issues commonly arise in connection with what is known as Rule 131 Practice:

• *Rule 131 Not an Interference.* Often the reference sought to be avoided by a Rule 131 affidavit is another U.S patent or application. In such a case, the courts have made clear that if the "reference" patent *claims* the same subject matter as the applicant submitting the affidavit, an interference must be declared. The test for determining whether the two patents claim the "same invention" is spelled out in 37 C.F.R. § 1.601(n) (1990), which was promulgated in response to *In re Eickmayer*, 602 F.2d 974, 202 U.S.P.Q. (BNA) 655 (C.C.P.A. 1979) (error for examiner to reject Rule 131 affidavit on grounds of same subject matter but not declare an interference). *See generally In re Zletz*, 893 F.2d 319, 322-23, 13 U.S.P.Q. 2d (BNA) 1320, 1322-23 (Fed. Cir. 1989) ("[W]hen the subject matter sought to be antedated is claimed in the reference patent, Rule 131 is not available and an interference must be had to determine priority.").

• *Sufficiency of Alleged Facts.* One must do more than simply make flat allegations such as "I reduced to practice prior to the effective date of the reference." As one court put it, "The Patent Office must have such facts as will enable it and its reviewing courts to judge whether there was construction and when it occurred, or whether there was diligence." *In re Harry*, 333 F.2d 920, 922, 142 U.S.P.Q. (BNA) 164 (C.C.P.A. 1964). Given these facts, a court will apply the same rules regarding conception, diligence, etc., as it does for an interference. *See, e.g., In re Mulder*, 716 F.2d 1542, 1545, 219 U.S.P.Q. 189 (Fed. Cir. 1983) (shortness of period during which applicant cannot show diligence — two days — does not excuse the break and thus applicant has not established priority; Rule 131 case, see below). Note that false statements in a Rule 131 affidavit can have severe consequences — for example, the patent may be declared invalid and an antitrust cause of action may lie with accused infringers for intentionally fraudulent procurement of the patent. See Chapter 7.

• *Partial Versus Whole Invention.* Where an applicant claims more subject matter than a reference discloses, must the applicant prove that she possessed her entire invention prior to the effective date of the reference, or only that portion of her invention disclosed in the reference? The courts have answered: only that portion disclosed in the reference. Thus in *In re Stempel*, 241 F.2d 755, 113 U.S.P.Q. (BNA) 77 (C.C.P.A. 1957), an applicant was permitted to file a Rule 131 affidavit showing reduction to practice of that portion of his application disclosed but not claimed in a reference patent. Specifically, the applicant was permitted to show reduction to practice of one chemical species prior to the date a reference patent was issued disclosing that same species. This was despite the fact that the applicant could not prove reduction to practice of the entire chemical genus claimed in his patent on the date the reference patent issued. The celebrated *Stempel* rule has been expanded to cover the situation where a reference discloses a compound but not a specific utility for it. The court in *In re Moore*, 444 F.2d 572, 170 U.S.P.Q. (BNA) 260 (C.C.P.A. 1971), held that an applicant who synthesized a compound prior to the effective date of a publication disclosing the compound could remove the reference publication with a Rule 131 affidavit. This despite the fact that the applicant had not determined a specific utility at the time he synthesized the compound.

• *Reference Removed if Obvious From Inventor's Work.* Where a reference reveals an embodiment that is not identical to, but would be obvious in light of, the applicant's invention, the reference can be removed by a Rule 131 affidavit. Another way of stating this is that the law applies an "obviousness" test of possession with respect to the invention described in the affidavit when comparing that invention to the matter described in the reference. *See, e.g., In re Dardick*, 496 F.2d 1234, 181 U.S.P.Q. (BNA) 834 (C.C.P.A. 1974). *See generally* 1 D. Chisum, Patents § 3.08[1][b] (1978 & Supp. 1991).

Discussion of this "possession" test, or enablement standard, is joined with another important issue in the following case: the use of a *foreign filing* to overcome a prior art reference. Note that § 120 of the Act allows an applicant to rely on an earlier-filed U.S. application for priority; the opinion discusses the relationship between § 119 and this section.

In re GOSTELI

872 F.2d 1008, 10 U.S.P.Q.2d 1614 (Fed. Cir. 1989)

The decision of the United States Patent and Trademark Office (PTO) Board of Patent Appeals and Interferences (Board), affirming the examiner's final rejection of claims 48-51 in the patent application of Jacques Gosteli [et al.] [hereinafter Gosteli or Applicants], under 35 U.S.C. § 102(e) (1982), is affirmed.

Gosteli's patent application discloses [certain] compounds having antibiotic properties. The claimed compounds are chemical intermediates used in the preparation of antibiotics known as 2-penems. Claims 48 and 49 are Markush-type genus claims, and dependent claims 50 and 51 are subgenus claims, each consisting of 21 specific chemical species. The examiner rejected claims 48-51 under section 102(e) as being anticipated by United States Patent No. 4,155,912 (Menard). Menard discloses, but does not claim, a first species, that is within the scope of claims 48 and 50, and a second species that is within the scope of claims 49 and 51.

Attempting to antedate Menard, Gosteli claimed the benefit, under 35 U.S.C. § 119 (1982), of their Luxembourg patent application's foreign priority date. The disclosure of the Luxembourg application is not as complete as that of Gosteli's United States application. The Luxembourg application discloses a subgenus of the genus claimed in the United States application and specifically describes the two chemical species disclosed by Menard. Menard's effective date is December 14, 1977, seven months after the May 9, 1977, filing date of Gosteli's Luxembourg application, but five months before Gosteli's May 4, 1978, United States filing date. Thus, Menard is not an effective reference under section 102(e) if Applicants are entitled to their Luxembourg priority date.

The Board denied Gosteli the benefit of their Luxembourg priority date reasoning that:

> [Gosteli's] problem in attempting to antedate the Menard reference is that their Luxembourg priority application does not disclose the "same invention" in a manner that complies with the first paragraph of 35 U.S.C. 112 as is claimed in the claims on appeal (48-51). In other words, claims 48-51 contain considerable subject matter which is not disclosed in the Luxembourg application.... Since [Gosteli's] Luxembourg application does not provide a written description of the entire subject matter set forth in the appealed claims 48-51, as required by the first paragraph of 35 U.S.C. 112, we have concluded that claims 48-51 have an effective filing date as of the May 4, 1978 filing date of [Gosteli's] grandparent [i.e., first U.S.] application and not as of the Luxembourg filing date. Accordingly, [Applicants have] not antedated the Menard reference.

Alternatively, Gosteli attempted to swear behind Menard by using declarations submitted under 37 C.F.R. § 1.131 (1988) (Rule 131). The Board rejected the use of Rule 131, because "the declaration does not ... contain 'facts showing a completion of the invention in this country before the filing date of' Menard."

Claims 48-51 of Gosteli's application stand rejected under section 102(e) as anticipated by Menard. The two chemical species disclosed by Gosteli's Luxembourg priority application are disclosed by Menard and also fall within the scope of the claims on appeal. Section 102(e) bars the issuance of a patent if its generic claims are anticipated by prior art disclosing individual chemical species. *See, e.g., In re Slayter*, 276 F.2d 408, 411, 125 U.S.P.Q. 345, 347 (C.C.P.A. 1960) (stating that species anticipate a generic claim). The parties agree that Menard is an effective anticipatory prior art reference unless Applicants are entitled to their Luxembourg priority date.

Generally, an applicant may antedate prior art by relying on the benefit of a previously filed foreign application to establish an effective date earlier than that of the reference. See 35 U.S.C. § 119; *In re Wertheim*, 541 F.2d 257, 261, 191 U.S.P.Q. 90, 95-96 (C.C.P.A. 1976); Rollins, *35 U.S.C. 119-Description and Enablement Requirements*, 67 J.Pat.Off.Soc'y 386, 386 (1985). Under section 119, the claims set forth in a United States application are entitled to the benefit of a foreign priority date if the corresponding foreign application supports the claims in the manner required by section 112, ¶ 1. *Wertheim*, 541 F.2d at 261-62, 191 U.S.P.Q. at 95-96; *Kawai v. Metlesics*, 480 F.2d 880, 887-89, 178 U.S.P.Q. 158, 164-65 (C.C.P.A. 1973) [see Chapter 6, Enablement].

Gosteli contends that their rights under section 119 are determined by focusing on (1) what is the subject matter disclosed in the Luxembourg priority application, and (2) whether that subject matter removes Menard. We disagree with Gosteli's reading of section 119. The statute provides, in pertinent part:

> An application for patent for an invention filed in this country by any person
> who has ... previously regularly filed an application for a patent for the
> same invention in a foreign country ... shall have the same effect as the
> same application would have if filed in this country on the date on which the
> application for patent for the same invention was first filed in such foreign
> country....

The reference to the "invention" in section 119 clearly refers to what the claims define, not what is disclosed in the foreign application. *Cf. In re Scheiber*, 587 F.2d 59, 61, 199 U.S.P.Q. 782, 784 (C.C.P.A. 1978) (stating that "invention" as used in 35 U.S.C. § 120 refers to what is claimed). Section 119 provides that a foreign application "shall have the same effect" as if it had been filed in the United States. 35 U.S.C. § 119. Accordingly, if the effective filing date of what is claimed in a United States application is at issue, to preserve symmetry of treatment between sections 120 and 119, the foreign priority application must be examined to ascertain if it supports, within the meaning of section 112, ¶ 1, what is claimed in the United States application. Compare *Kawai*, 480 F.2d at 886, 178 U.S.P.Q. at 162-63 (construing the section 112, ¶ 1 requirements of section 119) with *Scheiber*, 587 F.2d at 62, 199 U.S.P.Q. at 784-85 (construing the section 112, ¶ 1 requirements of section 120).

At oral argument, the government conceded that if Gosteli claims the species disclosed in the Luxembourg application, they would be entitled to the foreign priority date with regard to those claims. Thus, Menard would be ineffective as a reference against those claimed species, or any other claim properly supported by the Luxembourg disclosure as required by section 112, ¶ 1. We conclude, therefore, that claims 48-51 are entitled to the benefit of their foreign priority date under section 119 only if the foreign priority application properly supports them as required by section 112, ¶ 1. An application relying on the benefit of an earlier filing date in the United States would receive the same treatment under 35 U.S.C. § 120. See *Kawai*, 480 F.2d at 886, 178 U.S.P.Q. at 163.

As an alternative position, Gosteli contends that they can swear behind Menard, under Rule 131, by establishing a constructive reduction to practice in this country based on their foreign priority date of the two species disclosed by Menard. They reason that the use of a foreign priority date to establish the reduction to practice component for a Rule 131(b) showing is authorized by *In re Mulder*, 716 F.2d 1542, 1544-46, 219 U.S.P.Q. 189, 192-94 (Fed.Cir.1983), and therefore, showing priority with respect only to as much of the invention as Menard discloses is needed. Gosteli cites the rationale in *In re Stempel*, 241 F.2d 755, 760, 113 U.S.P.Q. 77, 81 (C.C.P.A. 1957), in support of their reasoning. We disagree.

Rule 131 requirements are quite specific. To antedate a prior art reference, the applicant submits an oath or declaration alleging acts that establish a completion of the invention in this country before the effective date of the prior art. 37 C.F.R. § 1.131(a).

The requirements and operation of section 119 differ from those of Rule 131. *Cf. Scheiber*, 587 F.2d at 61-62, 199 U.S.P.Q. at 784 (explaining a similar contrast between section 120 and Rule 131). Rule 131 provides a mechanism for removing specific prior art references, whereas section 119 is concerned only with an applicant's effective filing date. Because section 119, unlike Rule 131, operates independently of the prior art, it is appropriate that the showing required under section 119 differs from that required under Rule 131.

This case is distinguishable from *Mulder*. Gosteli's declarations make no mention of acts in this country. Gosteli relies on their Luxembourg application for a constructive reduction to practice date for the two chemical species at issue. That reliance is misplaced. *Mulder* is not purely a section 119 case. In *Mulder*, the conception date was based on activity in the United States, a date earlier than the prior art. Mulder was permitted to establish a constructive reduction to practice date based on his foreign filing. However, the constructive reduction to practice date was after the prior art. Rule 131 permitted Mulder to swear behind the reference, from the constructive reduction to practice date back to his conception date. The use of a foreign filing date in such circumstances is not inconsistent with our decisions. In *Mulder*, there was no dispute about compliance with the section 112 requirements subsumed in section 119. See *Mulder*, 716 F.2d at 1543, 219 U.S.P.Q. at 191 (stating that "[t]here is no question that applicants complied with all the formalities required by § 119 and related PTO rules").

Gosteli does not point to any activity inside the United States. Furthermore, Gosteli would not need activity in this country if section 119 gave them the benefit of an effective foreign filing date prior to Menard. Under these circumstances, Rule 131 is irrelevant. Thus, we affirm the Board; Gosteli cannot use the Rule 131 declarations filed to swear behind Menard.

[The court then reviewed the Patent Office's determination that the Luxembourg application did not fully enable the claims in the U.S. application under § 112 of the Act; it affirmed the Patent Office's finding.]

The Board's decision is

Affirmed.

NOTES

1. In *In re Mulder*, 716 F.2d 1542, 219 U.S.P.Q. 189 (Fed. Cir. 1983), cited in the preceding case, the Federal Circuit decided that despite the apparent roadblock presented by § 104, an applicant could rely on his foreign priority date to establish reduction to practice for purposes of a Rule 131 affidavit. Judge Rich, writing for the court, defended the holding as consistent with the basic purpose of § 119.

> We hold that [§ 119] entitles appellants to rely on their Netherlands filing date for a constructive reduction to practice. Section 119 is a "patent-saving" provision for the benefit of applicants, and an applicant is entitled to rely on it as a constructive reduction to practice to overcome the date of a reference under Rule 131. If entitlement to a foreign filing date can completely overcome a reference we see no reason why it cannot overcome a reference by providing the constructive reduction to practice element of proof required by Rule 131. It is a statutory priority right which cannot be interfered with by a construction placed on a PTO rule.

Id., 716 F.2d at 1545, citation omitted.

Note how the *Gosteli* court distinguishes *Mulder*; are you persuaded?

2. Check Gosteli's Luxembourg and U.S. filing dates. Assuming Luxembourg is a member of the Paris Convention (it is), how close was Gosteli's U.S. filing to losing the benefit of the Luxembourg filing date under the priority-preserving provision of the Paris Convention?

3. *See generally* Stringham, *Foreign Priority*, 15 J. PAT. OFF. SOC'Y 990 (1933) (arguing that Convention application should be effective on its filing date regardless of what claims it includes); Rollins, *35 U.S.C. 119-Description and Enablement Requirements*, 67 J. PAT. OFF. SOC'Y 386 (1985).

M. FOREIGN PRIORITY AND PRIOR ART EFFECTIVE DATES

In the previous section we discussed how an applicant can use Rule 131 to antedate prior art having an effective date earlier than the applicant's filing date. In this section we turn to a refinement on this issue: attempts to invalidate a patent application by referring back from a later-filed U.S. patent to its original foreign (i.e., Paris Convention) filing date. That is, we are concerned here with whether a prior art reference can have the benefit of a foreign "priority" date in proving invalidity, just as a U.S. application can have in proving priority. In this way, the issue is the reverse of a Rule 131 situation, where one seeks to establish priority (and hence patent validity) by antedating a prior art reference. We are concerned instead with attempts to establish the *invalidity* of an application by asserting that a prior art reference — another patent — has an effective date that is earlier than the patentee's date of invention. For this reason the arguments considered in this section are often called "defensive" or "patent-defeating" priority arguments. Thus, these arguments are *not* the normal ones seen so far, whereby an applicant or patentee seeks to establish priority by antedating a reference — i.e., "offensive," or patent-validating, priority arguments.

As the following cases show, the logic is simple: if a patentee can rely on a foreign filing date to establish *priority*, one seeking to *defeat* a patent can rely on the foreign filing date of a reference patent to establish *invalidity*.

One other issue must be mentioned by way of introduction. These cases are nominally concerned with issues covered in the next chapter, nonobviousness. As we shall see in that chapter, § 103, the statutory nonobviousness requirement, permits the Patent Office and courts to combine references drawn from all categories of § 102 prior art to establish that the claimed invention, though novel under § 102, is obvious in light of the prior art taken as a whole. Because the parties in the following cases stipulated that, if the contested prior art could be considered, the invention at issue would have been obvious under the Act, the real issue in the cases is whether the asserted prior art can be considered at all. Thus there are no difficult § 103 issues here.

In re HILMER (HILMER I)

259 F.2d 859, 149 U.S.P.Q. (BNA) 480 (C.C.P.A. 1966)

RICH, JUDGE.

The sole issue is whether a majority of the Patent Office Board of Appeals erred in overturning a consistent administrative practice and interpretation of the law of nearly forty years standing by giving a United States patent effect as prior art as of a foreign filing date to which the patentee of the reference was entitled under 35 U.S.C. 119.

Because it held that a U.S. patent, cited as a prior art reference under 35 U.S.C. 102(e) and 103, is effective as of its foreign "convention" filing date, relying on 35 U.S.C. 119, the board affirmed the rejection of claims 10, 16, and 17 of application serial No. 750,887, filed July 25, 1958, for certain sulfonyl ureas.

This opinion explains why, on the basis of legislative history, we hold that section 119 does not modify the express provision of section 102(e) that a reference patent is effective as of the date the application for it was "filed in the United States."

The two "references" relied on are:

Habicht 2,962,530 Nov. 29, 1960 (filed in the United States January 23, 1958, found to be entitled to priority as of the date of filing in Switzerland on January 24, 1957);

Wagner et al. 2,975,212 March 14, 1961 (filed in the United States May 1, 1957).

The rejection here is the aftermath of an interference between appellants and Habicht, a priority dispute in which Habicht was the winning party on a single count. He won because appellants conceded priority of the invention of the count to him. The earliest date asserted by appellants for their invention is their German filing date, July 31, 1957, which, we note, is a few months later than Habicht's priority date of January 24, 1957.

After termination of the interference and the return of this application to the examiner for further ex parte prosecution, the examiner rejected the appealed claims on Habicht, as a primary reference, in view of Wagner et al., as a secondary reference, holding the claimed compounds to be "unpatentable [i.e., obvious under § 103 of the Patent Act] over the primary reference in view of the secondary reference which renders them obvious to one of ordinary skill in the art."

Appellants appealed to the board contending, inter alia, that:

> the appellants' German application was filed subsequent to the Swiss filing date (of Habicht) but prior to the U.S. filing date of the Habicht application. The appellants now maintain that the Habicht disclosure cannot be utilized as anticipatory in view of 35 U.S.C. 119 which is entitled "Benefit of Earlier Filing Date in Foreign Countries: Right of Priority." This section defines the rights of foreign applicants and more specifically defines those rights with respect to dates to which they are entitled if this same privilege is awarded to citizens of the United States. There is no question (but) that Section 119 only deals with "right of priority." The section does not provide for the use of a U.S. patent as an anticipatory reference as of its foreign filing date.

We can now summarize the issue and simultaneously state the board's decision. Continuing the above quotation, the board said:

> The Examiner insists, however, that the effective date of the Habicht patent is January 24, 1957, the date of an application filed in Switzerland which is

claimed by Habicht under 35 U.S.C. 119. Appellants have not overcome this earlier date of Habicht. The issue is hence presented of whether the foreign priority date of a United States patent can be used as the effective filing date of the patent when it is used as a reference. Our conclusion is that the priority date governs.

This is the decision alleged to be in error.

We think it was error.

The board's construction is based on the idea that the language of the statute is plain, that it means what it says, and that what it says is that the application filed abroad is to have the same effect as though it were filed here — for all purposes. We can reverse the statement to say that the actual U.S. application is to have the same effect as though it were filed in the U.S. on the day when the foreign application was filed, the whole thing being a question of effective date. We take it either way because it makes no difference here.

Before getting into history, we note first that there is in the very words of the statute a refutation of this literalism. It says "shall have the same effect" and it then says "but" for several situations it shall not have the same effect, namely, it does not enjoy the foreign date with respect to any of the patent-defeating provisions based on publication or patenting anywhere in the world or public use or being on sale in this country more than one year before the date of actual filing in this country.

As to the other statute involved, we point out that the words of section 102(e), which the board "simply" reads together with section 119, also seem plain. Perhaps they mean precisely what they say in specifying, as an express patent-defeating provision, an application by another describing the invention but only as of the date it is "filed in the United States."

The great logical flaw we see in the board's reasoning is in its premise (or is it an a priori conclusion?) that "these two provisions must be read together." Doing so, it says 119 in effect destroys the plain meaning of 102(e) but the board will not indulge the reverse construction in which the plain words of 102(e) limit the apparent meaning of 119. We see no reason for reading these two provisions together and the board has stated none. We believe, with the dissenting board member, that 119 and 102(e) deal with unrelated concepts and further that the historical origins of the two sections show neither was intended to affect the other, wherefore they should not be read together in violation of the most basic rule of statutory construction, the "master rule," of carrying out the legislative intent.

[The court begins by noting the Board's emphasis on § 119's statement that a U.S. application claiming foreign priority "shall have the same effect as the same application would have if filed in this country on the date on which the application for patent for the same invention was first filed in such foreign country." After reviewing the history of the predecessors to § 119, the court turns to recent legislative history and then its criticism of the Board's reasoning.]

We need not guess what Congress has since believed to be the meaning of the disputed words in section 119, for it has spoken clearly. World wars interfere with normal commerce in industrial property. The one-year period of priority being too short for people in "enemy" countries, we had after World War I a Nolan Act (41 Stat. 1313, Mar. 3, 1921) and after World War II a Boykin Act. Foreign countries had reciprocal acts. One purpose was to extend the period of priority. House Report No. 1498, January 28, 1946, by Mr. Boykin, accompanied H.R. 5223 which became Public Law 690 of the 79th Cong., 2d Sess., Aug. 8, 1946, 60 Stat. 940. Section 1 of the bill, the report says, was to extend "the so-called period of priority," which then existed under R.S. 4887. On p. 3 the report says:

> In this connection, it may be observed that the portion of the statute which provides that the filing of a foreign application — shall have the same force and effect as the same application would have if filed in this country on the date on which the application for patent for the same invention, discovery, or design was first filed in such foreign country — is intended to mean "shall have the same force and effect," etc., insofar as applicant's right to a patent is concerned. This statutory provision has no bearing upon the right of another party to a patent except in the case of an interference where the two parties are claiming the same patentable invention.

U.S. Code Congressional Service 1946, p. 1493.

For the foregoing reasons, we are clearly of the opinion that section 119 is not to be read as anything more than it was originally intended to be by its drafters, the Commission appointed under the 1898 Act of Congress, namely, a revision of our statutes to provide for a right of priority in conformity with the International Convention, for the benefit of United States citizens, by creating the necessary reciprocity with foreign members of the then Paris Union.

[The court then turns to § 102(e).] We need not go into the reasoning of the *Milburn* case [*Alexander Milburn Co. v. Davis-Bournonville Co.*, 270 U.S. 390 (1926), discussed earlier in Section H of this chapter] which has its weaknesses, because all that matters is the rule of law it established: That a complete description of an invention in a U.S. patent application, filed before the date of invention of another, if it matures into a patent, may be used to show that that other was not the first inventor. This was a patent-defeating, judge-made rule and now is section 102(e). The rule has been expanded somewhat subsequent to 1926 so that the reference patent may be used as of its U.S. filing date as a general prior art reference [i.e., under § 103 as well as § 102; see Chapter 5].

What has always been pointed out in attacks on the *Milburn* rule, or in attempts to limit it, is that it uses, as prior knowledge, information which was secret at the time as of which it is used — the contents of U.S. patent applications which are preserved in secrecy, generally speaking, 35 U.S.C. 122. This is true, and we think there is some validity to the argument that that which is secret should be in a different category from knowledge which is public. Nevertheless we have the rule. However, we are not disposed to extend that rule, which applies to the date of filing applications in the United States, the actual filing date when the disclosure is on deposit in the U.S. Patent Office and on its way, in due course, to publication in an issued patent.

The board's new view, as expressed in this case, has the practical potential effect of pushing back the date of the unpublished, secret disclosures, which ultimately have effect as prior art references in the form of U.S. patents, by the full one-year priority period of section 119. We think the *Milburn* rule, as codified in section 102(e), goes far enough in that direction. We see no valid reason to go further, certainly no compelling reason.

Section 104

It seems clear to us that the prohibitions of 104, the limitations in sections 102(a) and 102(g) to "in this country," and the specifying in 102(e) of an application filed "in the United States" clearly demonstrates a policy in our patent statutes to the effect that knowledge and acts in a foreign country are not to defeat the rights of applicants for patents, except as applicants may become involved in priority disputes. We think it follows that section 119 must be interpreted as giving only a positive right or benefit to an applicant who has first filed abroad to protect him against possible intervening patent-defeating events in obtaining a patent. Heretofore it has always been so interpreted with the minor exceptions, of little value as precedents, hereinafter discussed. So construed, it has no effect on the effective date of a U.S. patent as a reference under section 102(e).

Section 120

At oral argument the Patent Office Solicitor argued by "analogy" from 35 U.S.C. 120 (a section which he said gives one U.S. application the benefit of an earlier U.S. application under specified circumstances for all purposes) that section 119 should similarly give to a patent, used as a reference under section 102(e), effect as of an earlier foreign filing date.

One aspect of [this issue] is that sections 119 and 120 contain the "same phrase," namely "shall have the same effect."

We find no substance in this argument because: (1) as above pointed out, out statute law makes a clear distinction between acts abroad and acts here except for patents and printed publications. Section 120, following policy in sections 102(a), (e) and (g) and 104, contains the limitation to applications "filed in the United States," excluding foreign applications from its scope. (2) Use of the same expression is mere happenstance and no reason to transfer the meaning and effect of section 120 as to U.S. filing dates to section 119 with respect to foreign filing dates. Section 120 was not drafted until 49 years after the predecessor of section 119 was in the statute. [Case remanded.]

In re HILMER (HILMER II)

424 F.2d 1108, 165 U.S.P.Q. (BNA) 255 (C.C.P.A. 1970)

RICH, ACTING CHIEF JUDGE.

This is a sequel to our opinion in *In re Hilmer*, 359 F.2d 859 53 C.C.P.A. 1288, (1966) (herein *"Hilmer I"*), familiarity with which is assumed.

In *Hilmer I*, under the heading "Reason for Remand," we pointed out that as to claims 10 and 16 there was a rejection with which the board had not dealt and remanded the case for clarification of the board's position "on the rejection of claims 10 and 16 as 'unpatentable over' the [patent to Habicht] in view of Wagner et al."

In *Hilmer I*, the question we decided was whether the Habicht patent was effective as a prior art reference under 35 U.S.C. 102(e) as of the Swiss filing date. We held that it was not and that it was "prior art" under 102(e) only as of the U.S. filing date, which date Hilmer could overcome by being entitled to rely on the filing date of his German application to show his date of invention. This disposed of a rejection predicated on the disclosure of the Habicht patent, as a primary reference, coupled with a secondary prior art patent to Wagner et al. (herein "Wagner").

The board's conclusion [below] was that the subject matter of claim 1, the compound claimed, is prior art against Hilmer. As to the basis on which it can be considered to be, or treated as, prior art, the board divided.

> Note must be taken of the fact that the rejection here is under 103 for obviousness wherefore it is clear that the subject matter of the appealed claims is different from the subject matter of Habicht's claim 1, allegedly, however, only in an obvious way by reason of the further disclosures of Wagner. Were the appealed claims to the same subject matter, it seems clear that Hilmer, because he conceded priority to Habicht, would not be entitled to them and Hilmer appears to have admitted as much throughout this appeal. But, it is contended, the situation is different when the claims on appeal are to different subject matter.

We turn now to the reasoning by which the board majority arrived at the conclusion that the compound of Habicht claim 1 is in the prior art — i.e., ahead of Hilmer's German filing date — and usable with the Wagner patent to support a section 103 obviousness rejection. We note at the outset that the board majority in no way relied on what occurred in the interference, on the concession of priority, or on any estoppel growing out of the interference.

Before examining the board majority's statutory theory, we will recall the fact that in *Hilmer I* we dealt with another statutory theory that by combining 102(e) and 119 a U.S. patent had an effective date as a prior art reference for all it discloses as of its foreign convention filing date. We reversed that holding and remanded. We now are presented with another theory that by combining 102(g) with 119 at least the claimed subject matter of a U.S. patent is prior art as of the convention filing date.

The board majority [stated its theory] as follows:

> While Section 102(g) refers to the prior invention as made "in this country," this limitation is removed as to application filing date by Section 119 of the statute which provides that an application for a patent for an invention shall have the same effect as though filed in this country on the date a prior application was filed in a foreign country, under the conditions prescribed. That this is the effect of Section 119 is also evident from Section 104. The Habicht invention is ... entitled to the filing date of the application in Switzerland as its date of invention in this country. Hence, we conclude on the basis of Section 102(g) and Section 119 that the claimed subject matter of the Habicht patent is available for use against the present application (as patent-defeating prior art) as of the date of the application filed in Switzerland.

We disagree with this line of reasoning.

In *Hilmer I* we explained at length why we could not accept similar reasoning about 119 which was there alleged to remove or qualify the limitation in 102(e) to the date when an application was filed "in the United States." For the same reasons we hold, contrary to the ipse dixit of the board, that 119 does not remove the limitation of 102(g) found in the phrase "in this country."

We disagree with the board that such an effect "is also evident from Section 104." Section 104 merely states that, except as provided by 119, an applicant or patentee may not establish a date of invention "by reference to knowledge or use thereof, or other activity" in a foreign country. Thus 119 and 104 relate, respectively, only to what an applicant or patentee may and may not do to protect himself against patent-defeating events occurring between his invention date and his U.S. filing date. Moreover, we discussed 104 and 102(a), (e), and (g) in *Hilmer I* and there showed that they indicate an intention on the part of Congress that knowledge and acts in a foreign country are not to defeat the rights of an applicant for a patent, except as the applicant may become involved in a priority dispute with another applicant entitled to 119 benefits. The present appeal does not involve a priority dispute.

As we understand the meaning of the term "priority," it refers either (a) to the issue which exists in the interference proceedings, namely, which of two or more rival inventors attempting to patent the same invention shall be deemed prior or first in law and entitled to the patent or (b) preservation of an effective filing date during a period such as the "convention" year as against acts which would otherwise bar the grant of a patent, for the protection of an applicant against loss of right to a patent. Nothing we have seen tends to indicate that this matter of "priority" has ever been intended to modify the long-standing provisions of our statutes as to what shall be deemed "prior art" under 103.

NOTES

1. *Hilmer, Right or Wrong?* In both *Hilmer I & II*, the Patent Office made novel arguments to expand the scope of the prior art, and hence reduce the amount of possibly patentable subject matter. In each case, the court rejected the proffered argument on a number of grounds. Do you agree with the court's reasoning? Or do you believe symmetry requires that if a patentee can antedate a reference, the Patent Office (or an accused infringer) should be permitted to antedate an application (or a patent)?

2. *Distinguishing the Issues in Hilmer I and II.* Both the *Hilmer* cases are about trying to use § 119 "defensively," to defeat patent rights. In *Hilmer I*, § 119 was invoked to "back date" a U.S. application. The theory was that § 119 gives a foreign priority application under the Paris Convention the "same effect" as if it had been filed in the U.S., and that therefore § 119 could be used to extend the U.S. filing date *backward* to the foreign priority filing date. No soap, said the CCPA. In *Hilmer II*, the Patent Office tried again, this time combining § 119 with § 102(g). The theory was that § 119 could be used to establish a foreign filing date as a constructive reduction to practice, thereby "back dating" a U.S. reference patent to its first foreign filing date. In effect, this argument would convert any foreign filing into a § 102(g) "prior invention" reference. Again the CCPA refused to go along, emphasizing that § 119 was a priority-preserving device and should not be converted into patent-defeating device.

The Federal Circuit recently squashed a similar attempt to tie together § 102(g) and § 102(e). In *Sun Studs, Inc. v. ATA Equip. Leasing, Inc.*, 872 F.2d 978, 983-84; 10 U.S.P.Q.2d (BNA) 1338 (Fed. Cir. 1989), ATA, the accused infringer, argued that Sun Stud's patent (to Mason) was invalid because of a patent to Mouat. Unfortunately for ATA, Mouat's effective date came after Sun Stud's date of conception. ATA argued nevertheless that Mouat *conceived* before Mason, and that therefore under § 102(g) Mouat invalidated Mason. The disclosure in Mouat's patent was introduced to show this. The Federal Circuit viewed this as a § 102(e) — not § 102(g) — reference.

> Both sides appear to have confused interference practice under § 102(g) with prior art status under § 102(e). The Mouat reference, as the district court held, does not describe or claim the identical invention to Mason. It is not prior art under § 102(g), but under § 102(e).

PROBLEMS: RULE 131

Suzanne files a patent in the U.S. claiming a method for producing a monoclonal antibody for antigens produced by the common cold virus. Her U.S. filing date is March 1, 1993. Her laboratory notebooks record that she reduced her invention to practice on November 22, 1989. The notebook also shows she conceived her invention on September 1, 1989. Scientists all over the world as well as in the United States are working on just such an antibody. Can Suzanne antedate their references? If so, what procedure should she use?

1. Kurt's patent was filed in Germany on October 21, 1991. It issued February 28, 1993. Kurt's patent discloses and claims Suzanne's discovery.

2. Sergei's thesis, indexed and shelved in an obscure library in Karaganga, Kazakhstan on January 1, 1992, discloses the antibody procedure.

3. Victor's patent was filed in the United States on January 1, 1991. The patent issued on May 1, 1993. Victor's patent claims and discloses the antibody procedure.

4. Jane's patent was filed in the United States on October 31, 1990. The patent issued on January 15, 1993. Jane's patent discloses but does not claim Suzanne's antibody discovery.

Discussion

1. Kurt's patent issued in Germany before Suzanne filed. However, Suzanne may still antedate this patent using Rule 131. Even though Kurt's patent claims the same monoclonal antibody procedure, there will be no U.S. interference procedure because Kurt's patent issued in Germany. Suzanne can easily antedate the effective date of Kurt's patent (February 28, 1993) by relying on her reduction to practice date, November 22, 1989.

2. At first glance, it appears Suzanne can easily antedate Sergei's thesis based on her reduction to practice date of November 22, 1989. But Sergei's thesis was available more than one year before Suzanne filed for her application. Under Rule 131, Suzanne may only antedate the prior art reference if she filed within a year of its publication. This encourages early filing. The key point is that one may not antedate a statutory bar reference. Suzanne's patent is barred. Note that if she had filed her patent application before January 2, 1993, Sergei's thesis would not be a statutory bar. Suzanne could then use Rule 131 to antedate Sergei's effective date of January 1, 1992.

3. Suzanne may not use Rule 131 to antedate Victor's prior art reference. The reason for this is that Rule 131 may only be used to antedate those references which disclose but do not claim the subject invention (as in the first example, with Jane's invention). Here, Victor both claimed and disclosed the same invention as Suzanne. Therefore, she may not antedate his reference. There will be an interference instead.

4. In order for Suzanne to "swear behind" or antedate Jane's prior art reference, she must use Rule 131. Under this rule, Suzanne must make an oath or declaration as to the facts showing a completion of the invention in the United States before the filing date of Jane's invention, since

the effective date of Jane's patent is its *filing* date under § 102(e). Suzanne can swear to an invention date before Jane's because of the records in her lab book. Specifically, Suzanne can antedate Jane's filing date by showing conception prior to that filing date, plus diligence from just prior to the effective date of the reference (i.e., Jane's filing date) until Suzanne's reduction to practice on November 22. If she can show diligence during this period, she will antedate Jane's patent application.

Therefore, assuming Suzanne can show she used due diligence to obtain her patent before October 31, 1990, she can use Rule 131 to antedate Jane's reference and will not be barred from the grant of a patent.

Chapter 5

NONOBVIOUSNESS

A. THE BASIC *GRAHAM* INQUIRY

Preceding chapters have shown that the Patent Office grants a patent when an inventor can show that her invention is at least minimally useful (i.e., meets the test of utility), and that nothing else quite like it can be found in the prior art (i.e., it is novel). In this chapter we consider the third basic requirement of patentability, that the invention be "nonobvious."

Nonobviousness can be thought of as a kind of "nontriviality" requirement. Many patent lawyers consider this the most important requirement; it has been called "the ultimate condition of patentability." NONOBVIOUSNESS — THE ULTIMATE CONDITION OF PATENTABILITY (J. Witherspoon ed. 1980). This is because nonobviousness attempts to measure an even more abstract quality than novelty or utility: the *technical accomplishment* reflected in an invention. This requirement asks in essence whether an invention is a big enough technical advance to merit the award of a patent. The theory is that even if an invention is new and useful, it does not deserve a patent if it represents merely a trivial step forward in the art. This is why nonobviousness is the final gatekeeper of the patent system.

The test of nonobviousness has a long history, and it is difficult to understand its current role in patent law without some knowledge of this historical background. (For much more detailed treatments, see Kitch, Graham v. John Deere: *New Standards for Patents*, 1966 SUP. CT. REV. 293 (1966).) Until 1850, courts tested only for novelty and utility. Kitch, *New Standards, supra,* at 304. *See also* Mintz, *The Standard of Patentability in the United States — Another Point of View,* 1977 DET. C.L. REV. 755, 765 (1977). But in *Hotchkiss v. Greenwood,* 52 U.S. 248 (1850), the Supreme Court denied a patent for applying an old method of making wood cabinet knobs to clay knobs, finding the process lacked "that degree of skill and ingenuity which constitute essential elements of every invention." 52 U.S. 248, 266. Later, the Court adopted the *Hotchkiss* language and the added hurdle to patentability it implied; henceforth, inventions had to embody some degree of "skill and ingenuity," or inventiveness. (Kitch concludes that the invention test was actually added to patent law only when the *Hotchkiss* holding was applied in the case of *Collar Co. v. Van Deusen,* 90 U.S. (23 Wall.) 530 (1875). Kitch, *New Standards, supra,* at 318.)

As time went on, it became clear that the judge-made test of invention was highly abstract; judges tended to phrase it differently and apply it unevenly in various cases. *See, e.g., Harries v. Air King Prods.,* 183 F.2d 158, 86 U.S.P.Q. (BNA) 57 (2d Cir. 1950) (L. Hand, J.) (invention is "as fugitive, impalpable, wayward and vague a phantom as exists in the whole paraphanelia of legal concepts"). It is thus not surprising that the patent community welcomed the opportunity for clarification provided by the general recodification of patent law in 1952. Section 103 of the 1952 Act was the first formal attempt to structure judicial thinking about obviousness. It reads:

> A patent may not be obtained [even though the invention is novel under § 102 of the Act], if the differences between the subject matter sought to be patented and the prior art are such that the subject matter as a whole would have been obvious at the time the invention was made to a person having ordinary skill in the art to which said subject matter pertains.

35 U.S.C. § 103 (1996).

On its face, § 103 appears to give the invention test a much more solid footing. It supplies both a yardstick to compare the invention with — the whole of the prior art — and a fictional artisan — the person "skilled in the art" — to apply that prior art to the problem addressed in the patent. By contrast, the old invention test asked whether the claimed subject matter showed "invention," that special quality which made a new thing patentable — what one court called "that impalpable something." *McClain v. Ortmayer*, 141 U.S. 419, 427 (1891). The essence of the statutory test is that it provides a frame of comparison: It tells the judge what to look at, and from what perspective, in order to determine if the invention is obvious.

But even after the enactment of the 1952 Act, it was still debatable whether the standard of nonobviousness had changed. *See* Rich, *Congressional Intent — Or, Who Wrote the Patent Act of 1952?*, in NONOBVIOUSNESS, *supra*, 1:1, 1:11-1:12. This was partly the result of ambiguities surrounding the passage of the new statute: It was unclear whether the new Act simply re-stated pre-1952 law or actually changed it. Although the commentary written by the authors of the 1952 Act shows that it was intended to end the confusion surrounding the invention requirement (*see* Federico, *Origins of Section 103*, 5 AM. PAT. L.Q.J. 87 (1977), *reprinted in* Rich, *Why and How § 103 Came to Be*, in NONOBVIOUSNESS, *supra*, at 1:201), some federal circuits thought there had been no change.

The Supreme Court finally addressed the issue in 1966, when it decided *Graham v. John Deere* — the starting point for all contemporary discussion of § 103.

GRAHAM v. JOHN DEERE CO.

383 U.S. 1, 148 U.S.P.Q. (BNA) 459 (1966)

[Together with *Calmar, Inc. v. Cook Chem. Co.*, and *Colgate-Palmolive Co. v. Cook Chem. Co.*, also on certiorari to the same Court.]

MR. JUSTICE CLARK delivered the opinion of the Court.

After a lapse of 15 years, the Court again focuses its attention on the patentability of inventions under the standard of Art. I, § 8, cl. 8, of the Constitution and under the conditions prescribed by the laws of the United States. Since our last expression on patent validity, *A. & P. Tea Co. v. Supermarket Corp.*, 340 U.S. 147 (1950), the Congress has for the first time expressly added a third statutory dimension to the two requirements of novelty and utility that had been the sole statutory test since the Patent Act of 1793. This is the test of obviousness, *i.e.*, whether "the subject matter sought to be patented and the prior art are such that the subject matter as a whole would have been obvious at the time the invention was made to a person having ordinary skill in the art to which said subject matter pertains. Patentability shall not be negatived by the manner in which the invention was made." § 103 of the Patent Act of 1952, 35 U.S.C. § 103 (1964 ed.).

The questions, involved in each of the companion cases before us, are what effect the 1952 Act had upon traditional statutory and judicial tests of patentability and what definitive tests are now required. We have concluded that the 1952 Act was intended to codify judicial precedents embracing the principle long ago announced by this Court in *Hotchkiss v. Greenwood*, 11 How. 248 [52 U.S.] (1851), and that, while the clear language of § 103 places emphasis on an inquiry into obviousness, the general level of innovation necessary to sustain patentability remains the same.

I
The Cases

(a). *Graham v. John Deere Co.*, an infringement suit by petitioners, presents a conflict between two Circuits over the validity of a single patent on a "Clamp for Vibrating Shank Plows." The invention, a combination of old mechanical elements, involves a device designed to absorb shock from plow shanks as they plow through rocky soil and thus to prevent damage to the plow. We granted certiorari [to resolve a conflict between two circuit court decisions regarding the same patent]. Although we have determined that neither Circuit applied the correct test, we conclude that the patent is invalid under § 103.

(b). *Calmar, Inc. v. Cook Chemical Co.*, and *Colgate-Palmolive Co. v. Cook Chemical Co.*, were separate declaratory judgment actions, but were filed contemporaneously. Petitioner in *Calmar* is the manufacturer of a finger operated sprayer with a "hold-down" cap of the type commonly seen on grocers' shelves inserted in bottles of insecticides and other liquids prior to shipment. Petitioner in *Colgate-Palmolive* is a purchaser of the sprayers and uses them in the distribution of its products. Each action sought a declaration of invalidity and noninfringement of a patent on similar sprayers issued to Cook Chemical as assignee of Baxter I. Scoggin, Jr., the inventor. By cross-action, Cook Chemical claimed infringement. The actions were consolidated for trial and the patent was sustained by the District Court. The Court of Appeals affirmed, and we reverse.

Manifestly, the validity of each of these patents turns on the facts. The basic problems, however, are the same in each case and require initially a discussion of the constitutional and statutory provisions covering the patentability of the inventions.

II

At the outset it must be remembered that the federal patent power stems from a specific constitutional provision which authorizes the Congress "To promote the Progress of ... useful Arts, by securing for limited Times to ... Inventors the exclusive Right to their ... Discoveries." Art. I, § 8, cl. 8. The clause is both a grant of power and a limitation. This qualified authority, unlike the power often exercised in the sixteenth and seventeenth centuries by the English Crown, is limited to the promotion of advances in the "useful arts." It was written against the backdrop of the practices — eventually curtailed by the Statute of Monopolies — of the Crown in granting monopolies to court favorites in goods or businesses which had long before been enjoyed by the public. See Meinhardt, Inventions, Patents and Monopoly, pp. 30-35 (London, 1946). The Congress in the exercise of the patent power may not overreach the restraints imposed by the stated constitutional purpose. Nor may it enlarge the patent monopoly without regard to the innovation, advancement or social benefit gained thereby. Moreover, Congress may not authorize the issuance of patents whose effects are to remove existent knowledge from the public domain, or to restrict free access to materials already available. Innovation, advancement, and things which add to the sum of useful knowledge are inherent requisites in a patent system which by constitutional command must "promote the Progress of ... useful Arts." This is the *standard* expressed in the Constitution and it may not be ignored. And it is in this light that patent validity "requires reference to a standard written into the Constitution." *A. & P. Tea Co. v. Supermarket Corp.*, *supra*, at 154 (concurring opinion).

Within the limits of the constitutional grant, the Congress may, of course, implement the stated purpose of the Framers by selecting the policy which in its judgment best effectuates the constitutional aim. This is but a corollary to the grant to Congress of any Article I power. *Gibbons v. Ogden*, 9 Wheat. [22 U.S.] 1 [1824]. Within the scope established by the Constitution, Congress may set out conditions and tests for patentability. *McClurg v. Kingsland*, 1 How. [42 U.S.] 202, 206 [1843]. It is the duty of the Commissioner of Patents and of the courts in the administration of the patent system to give effect to the constitutional standard by appropriate application, in each case, of the statutory scheme of the Congress.

Congress quickly responded to the bidding of the Constitution by enacting the Patent Act of 1790 during the second session of the First Congress. It created an agency in the Department of State headed by the Secretary of State, the Secretary of the Department of War and the Attorney General, any two of whom could issue a patent for a period not exceeding 14 years to any petitioner that "hath ... invented or discovered any useful art, manufacture, ... or device, or any improvement therein not before known or used" if the board found that "the invention or discovery [was] sufficiently useful and important...." 1 Stat. 110. This group, whose members administered the patent system along with their other public duties, was known by its own designation as "Commissioners for the Promotion of Useful Arts."

Thomas Jefferson, who as Secretary of State was a member of the group, was its moving spirit and might well be called the "first administrator of our patent system." See Federico, *Operation of the Patent Act of 1790*, 18 J. PAT. OFF. SOC. 237, 238 (1936). He was not only an administrator of the patent system under the 1790 Act, but was also the author of the 1793 Patent Act. In addition, Jefferson was himself an inventor of great note. His unpatented improvements on plows, to mention but one line of his inventions, won acclaim and recognition on both sides of the Atlantic. Because of his active interest and influence in the early development of the patent system, Jefferson's views on the general nature of the limited patent monopoly under the Constitution, as well as his conclusions as to conditions for patentability under the statutory scheme, are worthy of note.

Jefferson, like other Americans, had an instinctive aversion to monopolies. It was a monopoly on tea that sparked the Revolution and Jefferson certainly did not favor an equivalent form of monopoly under the new government. His abhorrence of monopoly extended initially to patents as well. From France, he wrote to Madison (July 1788) urging a Bill of Rights provision restricting monopoly, and as against the argument that limited monopoly might serve to incite "ingenuity," he argued forcefully that "the benefit even of limited monopolies is too doubtful to be opposed to that of their general suppression," V Writings of Thomas Jefferson, at 47 (Ford ed., 1895).

His views ripened, however, and in another letter to Madison (Aug. 1789) after the drafting of the Bill of Rights, Jefferson stated that he would have been pleased by an express provision in this form:

> "Art. 9. Monopolies may be allowed to persons for their own productions in literature & their own inventions in the arts, for a term not exceeding __ years but for no longer term & no other purpose." *Id.*, at 113.

And he later wrote:

> "Certainly an inventor ought to be allowed a right to the benefit of his invention for some certain time.... Nobody wishes more than I do that ingenuity should receive a liberal encouragement." Letter to Oliver Evans (May 1807), V Writings of Thomas Jefferson, at 75-76 (Washington ed.).

Jefferson's philosophy on the nature and purpose of the patent monopoly is expressed in a letter to Isaac McPherson (Aug. 1813), a portion of which we set out in the margin.[1] He rejected a natural-rights theory in intellectual property

---

[1] "Stable ownership is the gift of social law, and is given late in the progress of society. It

rights and clearly recognized the social and economic rationale of the patent system. The patent monopoly was not designed to secure to the inventor his natural right in his discoveries. Rather, it was a reward, an inducement, to bring forth new knowledge. The grant of an exclusive right to an invention was the creation of society — at odds with the inherent free nature of disclosed ideas — and was not to be freely given. Only inventions and discoveries which furthered human knowledge, and were new and useful, justified the special inducement of a limited private monopoly. Jefferson did not believe in granting patents for small details, obvious improvements, or frivolous devices. His writings evidence his insistence upon a high level of patentability.

As a member of the patent board for several years, Jefferson saw clearly the difficulty in "drawing a line between the things which are worth to the public the embarrassment of an exclusive patent, and those which are not." The board on which he served sought to draw such a line and formulated several rules which are preserved in Jefferson's correspondence.[2] Despite the board's efforts, Jefferson saw "with what slow progress a system of general rules could be matured." Because of the "abundance" of cases and the fact that the investigations occupied "more time of the members of the board than they could spare from higher duties, the whole was turned over to the judiciary, to be matured into

---

would be curious then, if an idea, the fugitive fermentation of an individual brain, could, of natural right, be claimed in exclusive and stable property. If nature has made any one thing less susceptible than all others of exclusive property, it is the action of the thinking power called an idea, which an individual may exclusively possess as long as he keeps it to himself; but the moment it is divulged, it forces itself into the possession of every one, and the receiver cannot dispossess himself of it. Its peculiar character, too, is that no one possesses the less, because every other possesses the whole of it. He who receives an idea from me, receives instruction himself without lessening mine; as he who lights his taper at mine, receives light without darkening me. That ideas should freely spread from one to another over the globe, for the moral and mutual instruction of man, and improvement of his condition, seems to have been peculiarly and benevolently designed by nature, when she made them, like fire, expansible over all space, without lessening their density in any point, and like the air in which we breathe, move, and have our physical being, incapable of confinement or exclusive appropriation. Inventions then cannot, in nature, be a subject of property. Society may give an exclusive right to the profits arising from them, as an encouragement to men to pursue ideas which may produce utility, but this may or may not be done, according to the will and convenience of the society, without claim or complaint from any body." VI Writings of Thomas Jefferson, at 180-181 (Washington ed.).

[2] "[A] machine of which we are possessed, might be applied by every man to any use of which it is susceptible." Letter to Isaac McPherson, *supra*, at 181.

"[A] change of material should not give title to a patent. As the making a ploughshare of cast rather than of wrought iron; a comb of iron instead of horn or of ivory ...." *Ibid*.

"[A] mere change of form should give no right to a patent, as a high-quartered shoe instead of a low one; a round hat instead of a three-square; or a square bucket instead of a round one." *Id.*, at 181-182.

"[A combined use of old implements.] A man has a right to use a saw, an axe, a plane separately; may he not combine their uses on the same piece of wood?" Letter to Oliver Evans (Jan. 1814), VI Writings of Thomas Jefferson, at 298 (Washington ed.).

a system, under which every one might know when his actions were safe and lawful." Letter to McPherson, *supra*, at 181, 182. Apparently Congress agreed with Jefferson and the board that the courts should develop additional conditions for patentability. Although the Patent Act was amended, revised or codified some 50 times between 1790 and 1950, Congress steered clear of a statutory set of requirements other than the bare novelty and utility tests reformulated in Jefferson's draft of the 1793 Patent Act.

III

The difficulty of formulating conditions for patentability was heightened by the generality of the constitutional grant and the statutes implementing it, together with the underlying policy of the patent system that "the things which are worth to the public the embarrassment of an exclusive patent," as Jefferson put it, must outweigh the restrictive effect of the limited patent monopoly. The inherent problem was to develop some means of weeding out those inventions which would not be disclosed or devised but for the inducement of a patent.

This Court formulated a general condition of patentability in 1851 in *Hotchkiss v. Greenwood*, 11 How. 248 [52 U.S. (1851)]. The patent involved a mere substitution of materials — porcelain or clay for wood or metal in doorknobs — and the Court condemned it, holding:

> "[U]nless more ingenuity and skill ... were required ... than were possessed by an ordinary mechanic acquainted with the business, there was an absence of that degree of skill and ingenuity which constitute essential elements of every invention. In other words, the improvement is the work of the skilful mechanic, not that of the inventor." At p. 267.

Hotchkiss, by positing the condition that a patentable invention evidence more ingenuity and skill than that possessed by an ordinary mechanic acquainted with the business, merely distinguished between new and useful innovations that were capable of sustaining a patent and those that were not. The *Hotchkiss* test laid the cornerstone of the judicial evolution suggested by Jefferson and left to the courts by Congress. The language in the case, and in those which followed, gave birth to "invention" as a word of legal art signifying patentable inventions. Yet, as this Court has observed, "[t]he truth is the word [invention] cannot be defined in such manner as to afford any substantial aid in determining whether a particular device involves an exercise of the inventive faculty or not." *McClain v. Ortmayer*, 141 U.S. 419, 427 (1891); *A. & P. Tea Co. v. Supermarket Corp.*, *supra*, at 151. Its use as a label brought about a large variety of opinions as to its meaning both in the Patent Office, in the courts, and at the bar. The *Hotchkiss* formulation, however, lies not in any label, but in its functional approach to questions of patentability. In practice, *Hotchkiss* has required a comparison between the subject matter of the patent, or patent application, and the background skill of the calling. It has been from this comparison that patentability was in each case determined.

IV
The 1952 Patent Act

The Act sets out the conditions of patentability in three sections. An analysis of the structure of these three sections indicates that patentability is dependent upon three explicit conditions: novelty and utility as articulated and defined in § 101 and § 102, and non-obviousness, the new statutory formulation, as set out in § 103. The first two sections, which trace closely the 1874 codification, express the "new and useful" tests which have always existed in the statutory scheme and, for our purposes here, need no clarification. The pivotal section around which the present controversy centers is § 103. It provides:

> § 103. Conditions for patentability; non-obvious subject matter
>
> A patent may not be obtained though the invention is not identically disclosed or described as set forth in section 102 of this title, if the differences between the subject matter sought to be patented and the prior art are such that the subject matter as a whole would have been obvious at the time the invention was made to a person having ordinary skill in the art to which said subject matter pertains. Patentability shall not be negatived by the manner in which the invention was made.

The section is cast in relatively unambiguous terms. Patentability is to depend, in addition to novelty and utility, upon the "non-obvious" nature of the "subject matter sought to be patented" to a person having ordinary skill in the pertinent art.

The first sentence of this section is strongly reminiscent of the language in *Hotchkiss*. Both formulations place emphasis on the pertinent art existing at the time the invention was made and both are implicitly tied to advances in that art. The major distinction is that Congress has emphasized "nonobviousness" as the operative test of the section, rather than the less definite "invention" language of *Hotchkiss* that Congress thought had led to "a large variety" of expressions in decisions and writings. Senate and House Reports, S. Rep. No. 1979, 82d Cong., 2d Sess. (1952); H.R. Rep. No. 1923, 82d Cong., 2d Sess. (1952), reflect this emphasis in these terms:

> Section 103, for the first time in our statute, provides a condition which exists in the law and has existed for more than 100 years, but only by reason of decisions of the courts. An invention which has been made, and which is new in the sense that the same thing has not been made before, may still not be patentable if the difference between the new thing and what was known before is not considered sufficiently great to warrant a patent. That has been expressed in a large variety of ways in decisions of the courts and in

writings. Section 103 states this requirement in the title. It refers to the difference between the subject matter sought to be patented and the prior art, meaning what was known before as described in section 102. If this difference is such that the subject matter as a whole would have been obvious at the time to a person skilled in the art, then the subject matter cannot be patented.

That provision paraphrases language which has often been used in decisions of the courts, and the section is added to the statute for uniformity and definiteness. This section should have a stabilizing effect and minimize great departures which have appeared in some cases." H.R. Rep., *supra*, at 7; S. Rep., *supra*, at 6.

It is undisputed that this section was, for the first time, a statutory expression of an additional requirement for patentability, originally expressed in *Hotchkiss*. It also seems apparent that Congress intended by the last sentence of § 103 to abolish the test it believed this Court announced in the controversial phrase "flash of creative genius," used in *Cuno Corp. v. Automatic Devices Corp.*, 314 U.S. 84 (1941).[3]

It is contended, however, by some of the parties and by several of the *amici* that the first sentence of § 103 was intended to sweep away judicial precedents and to lower the level of patentability. Others contend that the Congress intended to codify the essential purpose reflected in existing judicial precedents — the rejection of insignificant variations and innovations of a commonplace sort — and also to focus inquiries under § 103 upon nonobviousness, rather than upon "invention," as a means of achieving more stability and predictability in determining patentability and validity.

The Reviser's Note to this section, with apparent reference to *Hotchkiss*, recognizes that judicial requirements as to "lack of patentable novelty [have] been followed since at least as early as 1850." The note indicates that the section was

---

[3] The sentence in which the phrase occurs reads: "[T]he new device, however useful it may be, must reveal the flash of creative genius, not merely the skill of the calling." At p. 91. Although some writers and lower courts found in the language connotations as to the frame of mind of the inventors, none were so intended. The opinion approved *Hotchkiss* specifically, and the reference to "flash of creative genius" was but a rhetorical embellishment of language going back to 1833. Cf. "exercise of genius," *Shaw v. Cooper*, 7 Pet. [32 U.S.] 292 [(1833)]; "inventive genius," *Reckendorfer v. Faber*, 92 U.S. 347 (1876); *Concrete Appliances Co. v. Gomery*, 269 U.S. 177 [(1925)]; "flash of thought," *Densmore v. Scofield*, 102 U.S. 375 (1880); "intuitive genius," *Potts v. Creager*, 155 U.S. 597 (1895). Rather than establishing a more exacting standard, *Cuno* merely rhetorically restated the requirement that the subject matter sought to be patented must be beyond the skill of the calling. It was the device, not the invention, that had to reveal the "flash of creative genius." See Boyajian, *The Flash of Creative Genius, An Alternative Interpretation*, 25 J. PAT. OFF. SOC. 776, 780, 781 (1943); *Pacific Contact Laboratories, Inc. v. Solex Laboratories, Inc.*, 209 F.2d 529, 533 [(9th Cir. 1954)]; *Brown & Sharpe Mfg. Co. v. Kar Engineering Co.*, 154 F.2d 48, 51-52 [(11th Cir. 1946)]; *In re Shortell*, 31 C.C.P.A. (Pat.) 1062, 1069, 142 F.2d 292, 295-296 [(C.C.P.A. 1944)].

inserted because it "may have some stabilizing effect, and also to serve as a basis for the addition at a later time of some criteria which may be worked out."

We believe that this legislative history, as well as other sources,[4] shows that the revision was not intended by Congress to change the general level of patentable invention. We conclude that the section was intended merely as a codification of judicial precedents embracing the *Hotchkiss* condition, with congressional directions that inquiries into the obviousness of the subject matter sought to be patented are a prerequisite to patentability.

V

Approached in this light, the § 103 additional condition, when followed realistically, will permit a more practical test of patentability. The emphasis on nonobviousness is one of inquiry, not quality, and, as such, comports with the constitutional strictures.

While the ultimate question of patent validity is one of law, *A. & P. Tea Co. v. Supermarket Corp.*, *supra*, at 155, the § 103 condition, which is but one of three conditions, each of which must be satisfied, lends itself to several basic factual inquiries. Under § 103, the scope and content of the prior art are to be determined; differences between the prior art and the claims at issue are to be ascertained; and the level of ordinary skill in the pertinent art resolved. Against this background, the obviousness or nonobviousness of the subject matter is determined. Such secondary considerations as commercial success, long felt but unsolved needs, failure of others, etc., might be utilized to give light to the circumstances surrounding the origin of the subject matter sought to be patented. As indicia of obviousness or nonobviousness, these inquiries may have relevancy. See Note, *Subtests of "Nonobviousness": A Nontechnical Approach to Patent Validity*, 112 U. Pa. L. Rev. 1169 (1964).

This is not to say, however, that there will not be difficulties in applying the nonobviousness test. What is obvious is not a question upon which there is likely to be uniformity of thought in every given factual context. The difficulties, however, are comparable to those encountered daily by the courts in such frames of reference as negligence and scienter, and should be amenable to a case-by-case development. We believe that strict observance of the requirements laid down here will result in that uniformity and definiteness which Congress called for in the 1952 Act.

While we have focused attention on the appropriate standard to be applied by the courts, it must be remembered that the primary responsibility for sifting out unpatentable material lies in the Patent Office. To await litigation is — for all

---

[4] *See* Efforts to Establish a Statutory Standard of Invention, Study No. 7, Senate Subcommittee on Patents, Trademarks, and Copyrights, 85th Cong., 1st Sess. (Committee Print, 1958); Hearings, Subcommittee No. 3, House Committee on the Judiciary, on H.R. 3760, 82d Cong., 1st Sess. (1951).

practical purposes — to debilitate the patent system. We have observed a notorious difference between the standards applied by the Patent Office and by the courts. While many reasons can be adduced to explain the discrepancy, one may well be the free rein often exercised by Examiners in their use of the concept of "invention." In this connection we note that the Patent Office is confronted with a most difficult task. Almost 100,000 applications for patents are filed each year. Of these, about 50,000 are granted and the backlog now runs well over 200,000. 1965 Annual Report of the Commissioner of Patents 13-14. This is itself a compelling reason for the Commissioner to strictly adhere to the 1952 Act as interpreted here. This would, we believe, not only expedite disposition but bring about a closer concurrence between administrative and judicial precedent.

We have been urged to find in § 103 a relaxed standard, supposedly a congressional reaction to the "increased standard" applied by this Court in its decisions over the last 20 or 30 years. The standard has remained invariable in this Court. Technology, however, has advanced — and with remarkable rapidity in the last 50 years. Moreover, the ambit of applicable art in given fields of science has widened by disciplines unheard of a half century ago. It is but an evenhanded application to require that those persons granted the benefit of a patent monopoly be charged with an awareness of these changed conditions. The same is true of the less technical, but still useful arts. He who seeks to build a better mousetrap today has a long path to tread before reaching the Patent Office.

VI

We now turn to the application of the conditions found necessary for patentability to the cases involved here:

A. *The Patent in Issue in* Graham v. John Deere Co.

This patent, No. 2,627,798 (hereinafter called the '798 patent) relates to a spring clamp which permits plow shanks to be pushed upward when they hit obstructions in the soil, and then springs the shanks back into normal position when the obstruction is passed over. The device, which we show diagrammatically in the accompanying sketches [see Figure 5-1, next page], is fixed to the plow frame as a unit. The mechanism around which the controversy centers is basically a hinge. The top half of it, known as the upper plate is a heavy metal piece clamped to the plow frame and is stationary relative to the plow frame. The lower half of the hinge, known as the hinge plate, is connected to the rear of the upper plate by a hinge pin and rotates downward with respect to it. The shank, which is bolted to the forward end of the hinge plate, runs beneath the plate and parallel to it for about nine inches, passes through a stirrup, and then continues backward for several feet curving down toward the ground. The chisel, which does the actual plowing, is attached to the rear end of the shank. As the plow frame is pulled forward, the chisel rips through the soil, thereby plowing it. [See

Figure 1. – GRAHAM '798 PATENT

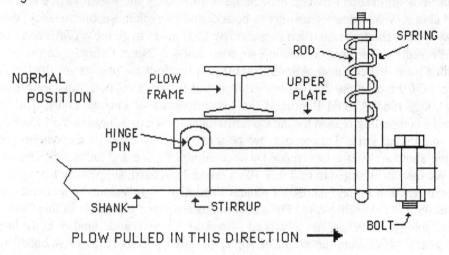

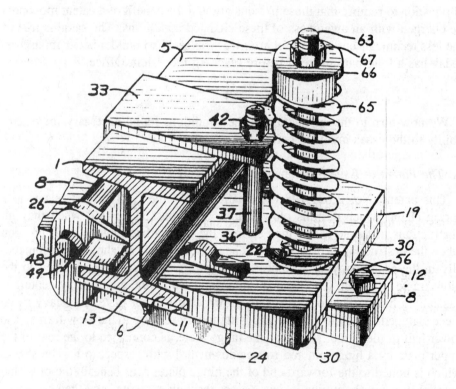

Figure 5-1

Figure 5-2, next page.] In the normal position, the hinge plate and the shank are kept tight against the upper plate by a spring, which is atop the upper plate. A rod runs through the center of the spring, extending down through holes in both plates and the shank. Its upper end is bolted to the top of the spring while its lower end is hooked against the underside of the shank.

When the chisel hits a rock or other obstruction in the soil, the obstruction forces the chisel and the rear portion of the shank to move upward. The shank is pivoted against the rear of the hinge plate and pries open the hinge against the closing tendency of the spring. This closing tendency is caused by the fact that, as the hinge is opened, the connecting rod is pulled downward and the spring is compressed. When the obstruction is passed over, the upward force on the chisel disappears and the spring pulls the shank and hinge plate back into their original position. The lower, rear portion of the hinge plate is constructed in the form of a stirrup which brackets the shank, passing around and beneath it. The shank fits loosely into the stirrup (permitting a slight up and down play). The stirrup is designed to prevent the shank from recoiling away from the hinge plate, and thus prevents excessive strain on the shank near its bolted connection. The stirrup also girds the shank, preventing it from fishtailing from side to side.

In practical use, a number of spring-hinge-shank combinations are clamped to a plow frame, forming a set of ground-working chisels capable of withstanding the shock of rocks and other obstructions in the soil without breaking the shanks. [See Figure 5-2, next page.]

Background of the Patent

Chisel plows, as they are called, were developed for plowing in areas where the ground is relatively free from rocks or stones. Originally, the shanks were rigidly attached to the plow frames. When such plows were used in the rocky, glacial soils of some of the Northern States, they were found to have serious defects. As the chisels hit buried rocks, a vibratory motion was set up and tremendous forces were transmitted to the shank near its connection to the frame. The shanks would break. Graham, one of the petitioners, sought to meet that problem, and in 1950 obtained a patent, U.S. No. 2,493,811 (hereinafter '811), on a spring clamp which solved some of the difficulties. Graham and his companies manufactured and sold the '811 clamps. In 1950, Graham modified the '811 structure and filed for a patent. That patent, the one in issue, was granted in 1953. This suit against competing plow manufacturers resulted from charges by petitioners that several of respondents' devices infringed the '798 patent.

The Prior Art

Five prior patents indicating the state of the art were cited by the Patent Office in the prosecution of the '798 application. Four of these patents, 10 other United States patents and two prior-use spring-clamp arrangements not of record in the

150F Series Flexible Chisel Plows have wheel-carried, offset-hinged outriggers. They are made in 14-, 16-, 18-, 20-, and 22-foot sizes. Shown here with flat cushion-spring standards which are recommended for rocky soil conditions.

Source: John Deere Co.

Figure 5-2

'798 file wrapper were relied upon by respondents as revealing the prior art. The District Court and the Court of Appeals found that the prior art "as a whole in one form or another contains all of the mechanical elements of the '798 Patent." One of the prior-use clamp devices not before the Patent Examiner — Glencoe — was found to have "all of the elements."

We confine our discussion to the prior patent of Graham, '811, and to the Glencoe clamp device, both among the references asserted by respondents. The Graham '811 and '798 patent devices are similar in all elements, save two: (1) the stirrup and the bolted connection of the shank to the hinge plate do not appear in '811; and (2) the position of the shank is reversed, being placed in patent '811 above the hinge plate, sandwiched between it and the upper plate. The shank is held in place by the spring rod which is hooked against the bottom of the hinge plate passing through a slot in the shank. [See Figure 5-3.] Other differences are of no consequence to our examination. In practice the '811 patent arrangement permitted the shank to wobble or fishtail because it was not rigidly fixed to the hinge plate; moreover, as the hinge plate was below the shank, the latter caused wear on the upper plate, a member difficult to repair or replace.

Graham's '798 patent application contained 12 claims. All were rejected as not distinguished from the Graham '811 patent. The inverted position of the shank was specifically rejected as was the bolting of the shank to the hinge plate. The Patent Office examiner found these to be "matters of design well within the expected skill of the art and devoid of invention." Graham withdrew the original claims and substituted the two new ones which are substantially those in issue here. His contention was that wear was reduced in patent '798 between the shank and the heel or rear of the upper plate.[5] He also emphasized several new features, the relevant one here being that the bolt used to connect the hinge plate and shank maintained the upper face of the shank in continuing and constant contact with the underface of the hinge plate.

Graham did not urge before the Patent Office the greater "flexing" qualities of the '798 patent arrangement which he so heavily relied on in the courts. The sole element in patent '798 which petitioners argue before us is the interchanging of the shank and hinge plate and the consequences flowing from this arrangement. The contention is that this arrangement — which petitioners claim is not disclosed in the prior art — permits the shank to flex under stress for its *entire* length. As we have sketched (see sketch, "Graham '798 Patent" in [Figure 5-3]), when the chisel hits an obstruction the resultant force (A) pushes the rear of the shank

---

[5] In '811, where the shank was above the hinge plate, an upward movement of the chisel forced the shank up against the underside of the rear of the upper plate. The upper plate thus provided the fulcrum about which the hinge was pried open. Because of this, as well as the location of the hinge pin, the shank rubbed against the heel of the upper plate causing wear both to the plate and to the shank. By relocating the hinge pin and by placing the hinge plate between the shank and the upper plate, as in '798, the rubbing was eliminated and the wear point was changed to the hinge plate, a member more easily removed or replaced for repair.

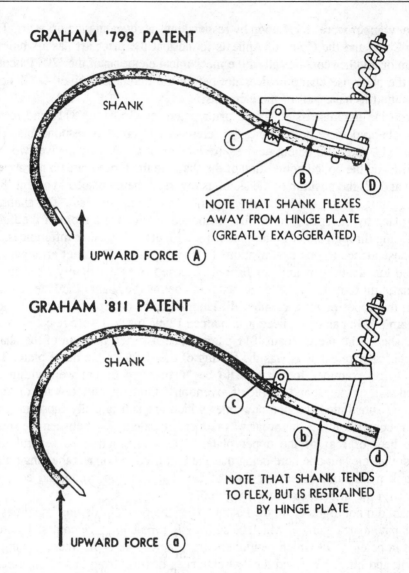

GRAHAM '798 PATENT

SHANK

C

B

D

NOTE THAT SHANK FLEXES
AWAY FROM HINGE PLATE
(GREATLY EXAGGERATED)

UPWARD FORCE Ⓐ

GRAHAM '811 PATENT

SHANK

c

b

d

NOTE THAT SHANK TENDS
TO FLEX, BUT IS RESTRAINED
BY HINGE PLATE

UPWARD FORCE ⓐ

Figure 5-3

upward and the shank pivots against the rear of the hinge plate at (C). The
natural tendency is for that portion of the shank between the pivot point and the
bolted connection (i.e., between C and D) to bow downward and away from the
hinge plate. The maximum distance (B) that the shank moves away from the plate
is slight — for emphasis, greatly exaggerated in the sketches. This is so because
of the strength of the shank and the short — nine inches or so — length of that
portion of the shank between (C) and (D). On the contrary, in patent '811 (see
sketch, "Graham '811 Patent" in [Figure 5-3]), the pivot point is the upper plate

at point (c); and while the tendency for the shank to bow between points (c) and (d) is the same as in '798, the shank is restricted because of the underlying hinge plate and cannot flex as freely. In practical effect, the shank flexes only between points (a) and (c), and not along the entire length of the shank, as in '798. Petitioners say that this difference in flex, though small, effectively absorbs the tremendous forces of the shock of obstructions whereas prior art arrangements failed.

The Obviousness of the Differences

We cannot agree with petitioners. We assume that the prior art does not disclose such an arrangement as petitioners claim in patent '798. Still we do not believe that the argument on which petitioners' contention is bottomed supports the validity of the patent. The tendency of the shank to flex is the same in all cases. If free-flexing, as petitioners now argue, is the crucial difference above the prior art, then it appears evident that the desired result would be obtainable by not boxing the shank within the confines of the hinge. The only other effective place available in the arrangement was to attach it below the hinge plate and run it through a stirrup or bracket that would not disturb its flexing qualities. Certainly a person having ordinary skill in the prior art, given the fact that the flex in the shank could be utilized more effectively if allowed to run the entire length of the shank, would immediately see that the thing to do was what Graham did, i.e., invert the shank and the hinge plate.

Petitioners' argument basing validity on the free-flex theory raised for the first time on appeal is reminiscent of *Lincoln Engineering Co. v. Stewart-Warner Corp.*, 303 U.S. 545 (1938), where the Court called such an effort "an afterthought. No such function ... is hinted at in the specifications of the patent. If this were so vital an element in the functioning of the apparatus it is strange that all mention of it was omitted." At p. 550. No "flexing" argument was raised in the Patent Office. Indeed, the trial judge specifically found that "flexing is not a claim of the patent in suit ..." and would not permit interrogation as to flexing in the accused devices. Moreover, the clear testimony of petitioners' experts shows that the flexing advantages flowing from the '798 arrangement are not, in fact, a significant feature in the patent.

We find no nonobvious facets in the '798 arrangement. The wear and repair claims were sufficient to overcome the patent examiner's original conclusions as to the validity of the patent. However, some of the prior art, notably Glencoe, was not before him. There the hinge plate is below the shank but, as the courts below found, all of the elements in the '798 patent are present in the Glencoe structure. Furthermore, even though the position of the shank and hinge plate appears reversed in Glencoe, the mechanical operation is identical. The shank there pivots about the underside of the stirrup, which in Glencoe is *above* the shank. In other words, the stirrup in Glencoe serves exactly the same function as the heel of the hinge plate in '798. The mere shifting of the wear point to the heel of the '798 hinge plate from the stirrup of Glencoe — itself a part of the hinge plate — presents no operative mechanical distinctions, much less nonobvious differences.

B. *The Patent in Issue in* Calmar, Inc. *v.* Cook Chemical Co., *and in* Colgate-Palmolive Co. *v.* Cook Chemical Co.

The single patent[6] involved in these cases relates to a plastic finger sprayer with a "hold-down" lid used as a built-in dispenser for containers or bottles packaging liquid products, principally household insecticides. Only the first two of the four claims in the patent are involved here and we, therefore, limit our discussion to them.

In essence the device here combines a finger-operated pump sprayer, mounted in a container or bottle by means of a container cap, with a plastic overcap which screws over the top of and depresses the sprayer (see [top of Figure 5-4, next page, "SCOGGIN PATENT" drawing]). The pump sprayer passes through the container cap and extends down into the liquid in the container; the overcap fits over the pump sprayer and screws down on the outside of a collar mounting or retainer which is molded around the body of the sprayer. When the overcap is screwed down on this collar mounting a seal is formed by the engagement of a circular ridge or rib located above the threads on the collar mounting with a mating shoulder located inside the overcap above its threads.[7] The overcap, as it is screwed down, depresses the pump plunger rendering the pump inoperable and when the seal is effected, any liquid which might seep into the overcap through or around the pump is prevented from leaking out of the overcap. The overcap serves also to protect the sprayer head and prevent damage to it during shipment or merchandising. When the overcap is in place it does not reach the cap of the container or bottle and in no way engages it since a slight space is left between those two pieces.

The device, called a shipper-sprayer in the industry, is sold as an integrated unit with the overcap in place enabling the insecticide manufacturer to install it on the container or bottle of liquid in a single operation in an automated bottling process. The ultimate consumer simply unscrews and discards the overcap, the pump plunger springs up and the sprayer is ready for use.

---

[6] The patent is U.S. No. 2,870,943 issued in 1959 to Cook Chemical Co. as assignee of Baxter I. Scoggin, Jr., the inventor. In [*Calmar v. Cook Chemical*] Calmar is the manufacturer of an alleged infringing device, and, in [*Colgate-Palmolive v. Cook Chemical*] Colgate is a customer of Calmar and user of its device.

[7] Our discussion here relates to the overcap seal. The container itself is sealed in the customary way through the use of a container gasket located between the container and the container cap.

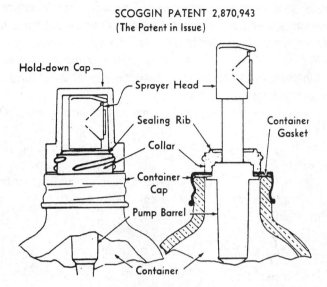

SCOGGIN PATENT 2,870,943
(The Patent in Issue)

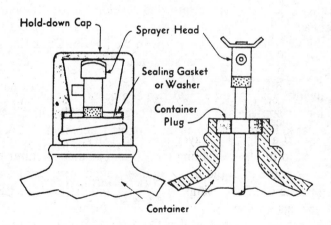

MELLON PATENT 2,586,687
(Prior art 1952)

Figure 5-4

The Background of the Patent

For many years manufacturers engaged in the insecticide business had faced a serious problem in developing sprayers that could be integrated with the containers or bottles in which the insecticides were marketed. Originally, insecticides were applied through the use of tin sprayers, not supplied by the manufacturer. In 1947, Cook Chemical, an insecticide manufacturer, began to furnish its customers with plastic pump dispensers purchased from Calmar. The dispenser was an unpatented finger-operated device mounted in a perforated cardboard holder and hung over the neck of the bottle or container. It was necessary for the ultimate consumer to remove the cap of the container and insert and attach the sprayer to the latter for use.

Hanging the sprayer on the side of the container or bottle was both expensive and troublesome. Packaging for shipment had to be a hand operation, and breakage and pilferage as well as the loss of the sprayer during shipment and retail display often occurred. Cook Chemical urged Calmar to develop an integrated sprayer that could be mounted directly in a container or bottle during the automated filling process and that would not leak during shipment or retail handling. Calmar did develop some such devices but for various reasons they were not completely successful. The situation was aggravated in 1954 by the entry of Colgate-Palmolive into the insecticide trade with its product marketed in aerosol spray cans. These containers, which used compressed gas as a propellent to dispense the liquid, did not require pump sprayers.

During the same year Calmar was acquired by the Drackett Company. Cook Chemical became apprehensive of its source of supply for pump sprayers and decided to manufacture its own through a subsidiary, Bakan Plastics, Inc. Initially, it copied its design from the unpatented Calmar sprayer, but an officer of Cook Chemical, Scoggin, was assigned to develop a more efficient device. By 1956 Scoggin had perfected the shipper-sprayer in suit and a patent was granted in 1959 to Cook Chemical as his assignee. In the interim Cook Chemical began to use Scoggin's device and also marketed it to the trade. The device was well received and soon became widely used.

In the meanwhile, Calmar employed two engineers, Corsette and Cooprider, to perfect a shipper-sprayer and by 1958 it began to market its SS-40, a device very much similar to Scoggin's. When the Scoggin patent issued, Cook Chemical charged Calmar's SS-40 with infringement and this suit followed.

The Opinions of the District Court and the
Court of Appeals

At the outset it is well to point up that the parties have always disagreed as to the scope and definition of the invention claimed in the patent in suit. Cook Chemical contends that the invention encompasses a unique combination of admittedly old elements and that patentability is found in the result produced. Its expert testified that the invention was "the first commercially successful, inexpensive integrated shipping closure pump unit which permitted automated assembly with a container of household insecticide or similar liquids to produce a practical, ready-to-use package which could be shipped without external leakage and which was so organized that the pump unit with its hold-down cap could be itself assembled and sealed and then later assembled and sealed on the container without breaking the first seal." Cook Chemical stresses the long-felt need in the industry for such a device; the inability of others to produce it; and its commercial success — all of which, contends Cook, evidences the nonobvious nature of the device at the time it was developed. On the other hand, Calmar says that the differences between Scoggin's shipper-sprayer and the prior art relate only to the design of the overcap and that the differences are so inconsequential that the device as a whole would have been obvious at the time of its invention to a person having ordinary skill in the art.

Both courts accepted Cook Chemical's contentions. While the exact basis of the District Court's holding is uncertain, the court did find the subject matter of the patent new, useful and nonobvious. It concluded that Scoggin "had produced a sealed and protected sprayer unit which the manufacturer need only screw onto the top of its container in much the same fashion as a simple metal cap." Its decision seems to be bottomed on the finding that the Scoggin sprayer solved the long-standing problem that had confronted the industry. The Court of Appeals also found validity in the "novel 'marriage' of the sprayer with the insecticide container" which took years in discovery and in "the immediate commercial success" which it enjoyed. While finding that the individual elements of the invention were "not novel per se" the court found "nothing in the prior art suggesting Scoggin's unique combination of these old features ... as would solve the ... problems which for years beset the insecticide industry." It concluded that "the ... [device] meets the exacting standard required for a combination of old elements to rise to the level of patentable invention by fulfilling the long-felt need with an economical, efficient, utilitarian apparatus which achieved novel results and immediate commercial success."

The Prior Art

Only two of the five prior art patents cited by the Patent Office Examiner in the prosecution of Scoggin's application are necessary to our discussion, i.e., Lohse U.S. Patent No. 2,119,884 (1938) and Mellon U.S. Patent No. 2,586,687 (1952). Others are cited by Calmar that were not before the Examiner, but of these our purposes require discussion of only the Livingstone U.S. Patent No. 2,715,480 (1953). Simplified drawings of each of these patents are reproduced in [Figures 5-4 and 5-5], for comparison and description.

The Lohse patent [top of Figure 5-5] is a shipper-sprayer designed to perform the same function as Scoggin's device. The differences, recognized by the District Court, are found in the overcap seal which in Lohse is formed by the skirt of the overcap engaging a washer or gasket which rests upon the upper surface of the container cap. The court emphasized that in Lohse "[there] are no seals above the threads and below the sprayer head."

The Mellon patent [bottom of Figure 5-4], however, discloses the idea of effecting a seal above the threads of the overcap. Mellon's device, likewise a shipper-sprayer, differs from Scoggin's in that its overcap screws directly on the

LOHSE PATENT 2,119,884
(Prior art 1938)

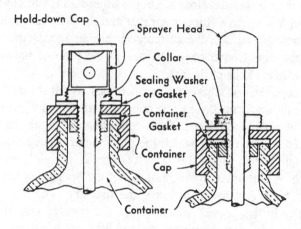

LIVINGSTONE PATENT 2,715,480
(Prior art 1953)

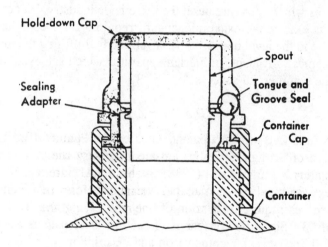

Figure 5-5

container, and a gasket, rather than a rib, is used to effect the seal.

Finally, Livingstone [Figure 5-5] shows a seal above the threads accomplished without the use of a gasket or washer.[8] Although Livingstone's arrangement was

---

[8] While the sealing feature was not specifically claimed in the Livingstone patent, it was

designed to cover and protect pouring spouts, his sealing feature is strikingly similar to Scoggin's. Livingstone uses a tongue and groove technique in which the tongue, located on the upper surface of the collar, fits into a groove on the inside of the overcap. Scoggin employed the rib and shoulder seal in the identical position and with less efficiency because the Livingstone technique is inherently a more stable structure, forming an interlock that withstands distortion of the overcap when subjected to rough handling. Indeed, Cook Chemical has now incorporated the Livingstone closure into its own shipper-sprayers as had Calmar in its SS-40.

The Invalidity of the Patent

Let us first return to the fundamental disagreement between the parties. Cook Chemical, as we noted at the outset, urges that the invention must be viewed as the overall combination, or — putting it in the language of the statute — that we must consider the subject matter sought to be patented taken as a whole. With this position, taken in the abstract, there is, of course, no quibble. But the history of the prosecution of the Scoggin application in the Patent Office reveals a substantial divergence in respondent's present position.

As originally submitted, the Scoggin application contained 15 claims which in very broad terms claimed the entire combination of spray pump and overcap. No mention of, or claim for, the sealing features was made. All 15 claims were rejected by the Examiner because (1) the applicant was vague and indefinite as to what the invention was, and (2) the claims were met by Lohse. Scoggin canceled these claims and submitted new ones. Upon a further series of rejections and new submissions, the Patent Office Examiner, after an office interview, at last relented. It is crystal clear that after the first rejection, Scoggin relied entirely upon the sealing arrangement as the exclusive patentable difference in his combination. It is likewise clear that it was on that feature that the Examiner allowed the claims. In fact, in a letter accompanying the final submission of claims, Scoggin, through his attorney, stated that "agreement was reached between the Honorable Examiner and applicant's attorney relative to *limitations* which must be in the claims in order to define novelty over the previously applied disclosure of Lohse when considered in view of the newly cited patents of Mellon and Darley, Jr." (Italics added.)

Moreover, those limitations were specifically spelled out as (1) the use of a rib seal and (2) an overcap whose lower edge did not contact the container cap. Mellon was distinguished, as [another patent to] the Darley, on the basis that although it disclosed a hold-down cap with a seal located above the threads, it did not disclose a rib seal disposed in such position as to cause the lower peripheral edge of the overcap "to be maintained out of contacting relationship with [the

---

disclosed in the drawings and specifications. Under long-settled law the feature became public property. *Miller v. Brass Co.*, 104 U.S. 350, 352 (1882).

container] cap … when … [the overcap] was screwed [on] tightly.…" Scoggin maintained that the "obvious modification" of Lohse in view of Mellon would be merely to place the Lohse gasket above the threads with the lower edge of the overcap remaining in tight contact with the container cap or neck of the container itself. In other words, the Scoggin invention was limited to the use of a rib — rather than a washer or gasket — and the existence of a slight space between the overcap and the container cap.

It is, of course, well settled that an invention is construed not only in the light of the claims, but also with reference to the file wrapper or prosecution history in the Patent Office. *Hogg v. Emerson*, 11 How. 587 [52 U.S.] (1850); *Crawford v. Heysinger*, 123 U.S. 589 (1887). Claims as allowed must be read and interpreted with reference to rejected ones and to the state of the prior art; and claims that have been narrowed in order to obtain the issuance of a patent by distinguishing the prior art cannot be sustained to cover that which was previously by limitation eliminated from the patent. *Powers-Kennedy Co. v. Concrete Co.*, 282 U.S. 175, 185-186 (1930); *Schriber Co. v. Cleveland Trust Co.*, 311 U.S. 211, 220-221 (1940).

Here, the patentee obtained his patent only by accepting the limitations imposed by the Examiner. The claims were carefully drafted to reflect these limitations and Cook Chemical is not now free to assert a broader view of Scoggin's invention. The subject matter as a whole reduces, then, to the distinguishing features clearly incorporated into the claims. We now turn to those features.

As to the space between the skirt of the overcap and the container cap, the District Court found:

> Certainly without a space so described, there could be no inner seal within the cap, but such a space is not new or novel, but it is necessary to the formation of the seal within the hold-down cap.
>
> *To me this language is descriptive of an element of the patent but not a part of the invention.* It is too simple, really, to require much discussion. In this device the hold-down cap was intended to perform two functions — to hold down the sprayer head and to form a solid tight seal between the shoulder and the collar below. In assembling the element it is necessary to provide this space in order to form the seal." (Italics added.)

The court correctly viewed the significance of that feature. We are at a loss to explain the Examiner's allowance on the basis of such a distinction. Scoggin was able to convince the Examiner that Mellon's cap contacted the bottle neck while his did not. Although the drawings included in the Mellon application show that the cap might touch the neck of the bottle when fully screwed down, there is nothing — absolutely nothing — which indicates that the cap was designed at any time to *engage* the bottle neck. It is palpably evident that Mellon embodies a seal formed by a gasket compressed between the cap and the bottle neck. It follows that the cap in Mellon will not seal if it does not bear down on the gasket and this would be impractical, if not impossible, under the construction urged by Scoggin before the Examiner. Moreover, the space so strongly asserted by Cook Chemical appears quite plainly on the Livingstone device, a reference not cited by the Examiner.

The substitution of a rib built into a collar likewise presents no patentable difference above the prior art. It was fully disclosed and dedicated to the public in the Livingstone patent. Cook Chemical argues, however, that Livingstone is not in the *pertinent* prior art because it relates to liquid containers having pouring spouts rather than pump sprayers. Apart from the fact that respondent made no such objection to similar references cited by the Examiner, so restricted a view of the applicable prior art is not justified. The problems confronting Scoggin and the insecticide industry were not insecticide problems; they were mechanical closure problems. Closure devices in such a closely related art as pouring spouts for liquid containers are at the very least pertinent references. See, II Walker on Patents § 260 (Deller ed. 1937).

Cook Chemical insists, however, that the development of a workable shipper-sprayer eluded Calmar, who had long and unsuccessfully sought to solve the problem. And, further, that the long-felt need in the industry for a device such as Scoggin's together with its wide commercial success supports its patentability. These legal inferences or subtests do focus attention on economic and motivational rather than technical issues and are, therefore, more susceptible of judicial treatment than are the highly technical facts often present in patent litigation. See Judge Learned Hand in *Reiner v. I. Leon Co.*, 285 F.2d 501, 504 (1960). See also Note, *Subtests of "Nonobviousness": A Nontechnical Approach to Patent Validity*, 112 U. PA. L. REV. 1169 (1964). Such inquiries may lend a helping hand to the judiciary which, as Mr. Justice Frankfurter observed, is most ill-fitted to discharge the technological duties cast upon it by patent legislation. *Marconi Wireless Co. v. United States*, 320 U.S. 1, 60 (1943). They may also serve to "guard against slipping into use of hindsight," *Monroe Auto Equipment Co. v. Heckethorn Mfg. & Sup. Co.*, 332 F.2d 406, 412 (1964), and to resist the temptation to read into the prior art the teachings of the invention in issue.

However, these factors do not, in the circumstances of this case, tip the scales of patentability. The Scoggin invention, as limited by the Patent Office and accepted by Scoggin, rests upon exceedingly small and quite nontechnical mechanical differences in a device which was old in the art. At the latest, those differences were rendered apparent in 1953 by the appearance of the Livingstone patent, and unsuccessful attempts to reach a solution to the problems confronting Scoggin made before that time became wholly irrelevant. It is also irrelevant that no one apparently chose to avail himself of knowledge stored in the Patent Office and readily available by the simple expedient of conducting a patent search — a prudent and nowadays common preliminary to well organized research. *Mast, Foos & Co. v. Stover Mfg. Co.*, 177 U.S. 485 (1900). To us, the limited claims of the Scoggin patent are clearly evident from the prior art as it stood at the time of the invention.

We conclude that the claims in issue in the Scoggin patent must fall as not meeting the test of § 103, since the differences between them and the pertinent prior art would have been obvious to a person reasonably skilled in that art.

The judgment of the Court of Appeals in [*Graham v. John Deere*] is affirmed. The judgment of the Court of Appeals in [*Calmar v. Cook Chemical*] and [*Colgate-Palmolive v. Cook Chemical*] is reversed and the cases remanded to the District Court for disposition not inconsistent with this opinion.

NOTES

1. At the outset, the Court states that Congress intended § 103 as a codification of existing precedent. Later, it notes that the second sentence of § 103 was inserted explicitly to overrule the *Cuno Engineering* case. Can these points be reconciled?

2. The Court states that it is proper in interpreting the Graham '798 claims to refer to the prosecution history (or "file wrapper") of the patent. We will see that this is an important tool in the law of infringement in Chapter 8.

3. The "subtests" of nonobviousness the Court refers to have had a major impact on the law concerning § 103 in the Federal Circuit, as the cases below in Section B of this chapter attest.

UNITED STATES v. ADAMS
383 U.S. 39, 148 U.S.P.Q. (BNA) 479 (1966)

This is a companion case to *Graham v. John Deere Co.*, decided this day along with *Calmar, Inc. v. Cook Chemical Co.* and *Colgate-Palmolive Co. v. Cook Chemical Co.* The United States seeks review of a judgment of the Court of Claims, holding valid and infringed a patent on a wet battery issued to Adams. This suit under 28 U.S.C. § 1498 was brought by Adams and others holding an interest in the patent against the Government charging both infringement and breach of an implied contract to pay compensation for the use of the invention. The Government challenged the validity of the patent, denied that it had been infringed or that any contract for its use had ever existed. The Trial Commissioner held that the patent was valid and infringed in part but that no contract, express or implied, had been established. The Court of Claims adopted these findings. The United States sought certiorari [which we granted] in order to settle the important issues of patentability presented by the four cases. We affirm.

I
The Patent in Issue and Its Background

The patent under consideration, U.S. No. 2,322,210, was issued in 1943 upon an application filed in December 1941 by Adams. It relates to a nonrechargeable, as opposed to a storage, electrical battery. Stated simply, the battery comprises two electrodes — one made of magnesium, the other of cuprous chloride —

which are placed in a container. The electrolyte, or battery fluid, used may be either plain or salt water. [See Figure 5-6, next page.]

The specifications of the patent state that the object of the invention is to provide constant voltage and current without the use of acids, conventionally employed in storage batteries, and without the generation of dangerous fumes. Another object is "to provide a battery which is relatively light in weight with respect to capacity" and which "may be manufactured and distributed to the trade in a dry condition and rendered serviceable by merely filling the container with water." Following the specifications, which also set out a specific embodiment of the invention, there appear 11 claims. Of these, principal reliance has been placed upon Claims 1 and 10, which read:

> 1. A battery comprising a liquid container, a magnesium electropositive electrode inside the container and having an exterior terminal, a fused cuprous chloride electronegative electrode, and a terminal connected with said electronegative electrode.
> 10. In a battery, the combination of a magnesium electropositive electrode, and an electronegative electrode comprising cuprous chloride fused with a carbon catalytic agent.

For several years prior to filing his application for the patent, Adams had worked in his home experimenting on the development of a wet battery. He found that when cuprous chloride and magnesium were used as electrodes in an electrolyte of either plain water or salt water an improved battery resulted.

The Adams invention was the first practical, water-activated, constant potential battery which could be fabricated and stored indefinitely without any fluid in its cells. It was activated within 30 minutes merely by adding water. Once activated, the battery continued to deliver electricity at a voltage which remained essentially constant regardless of the rate at which current was withdrawn. Furthermore, its capacity for generating current was exceptionally large in comparison to its size and weight. The battery was also quite efficient in that substantially its full capacity could be obtained over a wide range of currents. One disadvantage, however, was that once activated the battery could not be shut off; the chemical reactions in the battery continued even though current was not withdrawn. Nevertheless, these chemical reactions were highly exothermic, liberating large quantities of heat during operation. As a result, the battery performed with little effect on its voltage or current in very low temperatures. Relatively high temperatures would not damage the battery. Consequently, the battery was operable from 65° below zero Fahrenheit to 200° Fahrenheit.

Less than a month after filing for his patent, Adams brought his discovery to the attention of the Army and Navy. Arrangements were quickly made for demonstrations before the experts of the United States Army Signal Corps. The Signal Corps scientists who observed the demonstrations and who conducted further tests themselves did not believe the battery was workable. Almost a year later, in December 1942, Dr. George Vinal, an eminent government expert with

June 22, 1943
B. N. ADAMS
2,322,210
BATTERY
Filed Dec. 18, 1941
Fig. 1.
-
+
extention of electro-positive electrode
copper terminal
electro-positive electrode of Mg
electro-negative electrode
copper coil
Fig. 2.
Fig. 3.
10
12
26
28
44
20
42
34
14
Detail of Terminals
18
32
26
10
24
38
36
40
Bert N. Adams,
INVENTOR.
BY
Victor J. Evans & Co.
ATTORNEYS

Figure 5-6

the National Bureau of Standards, still expressed doubts. He felt that Adams was making “unusually large claims” for “high watt hour output per unit weight,” and

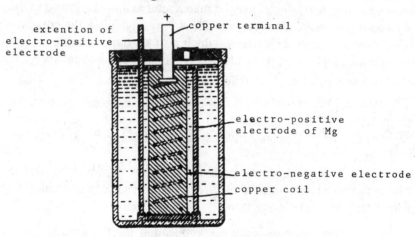

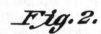

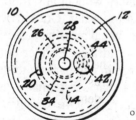

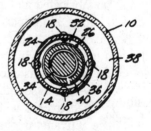

he found "far from convincing" the graphical data submitted by the inventor showing the battery's constant voltage and capacity characteristics. He recommended, "Until the inventor can present more convincing data about the performance of his [battery] cell, I see no reason to consider it further."

However, in November 1943, at the height of World War II, the Signal Corps concluded that the battery was feasible. The Government thereafter entered into contracts with various battery companies for its procurement. The battery was found adaptable to many uses. Indeed, by 1956 it was noted that "[t]here can be no doubt that the addition of water activated batteries to the family of power sources has brought about developments which would otherwise have been technically or economically impractical." See Tenth Annual Battery Research and Development Conference, Signal Corps Engineering Laboratories, Fort Monmouth, N.J., p. 25 (1956).

Surprisingly, the Government did not notify Adams of its changed views nor of the use to which it was putting his device, despite his repeated requests. In 1955, upon examination of a battery produced for the Government by the Burgess Company, he first learned of the Government's action. His request for compensation was denied in 1960, resulting in this suit.

II
The Prior Art

The basic idea of chemical generation of electricity is, of course, quite old. Batteries trace back to the epic discovery by the Italian scientist Volta in 1795, who found that when two dissimilar metals are placed in an electrically conductive fluid an electromotive force is set up and electricity generated. Essentially, the basic elements of a chemical battery are a pair of electrodes of different electrochemical properties and an electrolyte which is either a liquid (in "wet" batteries) or a moist paste of various substances (in the so-called "dry-cell" batteries). Various materials which may be employed as electrodes, various electrolyte possibilities and many combinations of these elements have been the object of considerable experiment for almost 175 years. See generally, Vinal, Primary Batteries (New York 1950).

At trial, the Government introduced in evidence 24 patents and treatises as representing the art as it stood in 1938, the time of the Adams invention. Here, however, the Government has relied primarily upon only six of these references which we may summarize as follows.

The Niaudet treatise describes the Marie Davy cell invented in 1860 and De La Rue's variations on it. The battery comprises a zinc anode and a silver chloride cathode. Although it seems to have been capable of working in an electrolyte of pure water, Niaudet says the battery was of "little interest" until De La Rue used a solution of ammonium chloride as an electrolyte. Niaudet also states that "[t]he capital advantage of this battery, as in all where zinc with sal ammoniac [ammonium chloride solution] is used, consists in the absence of any local or internal action as long as the electric circuit is open; in other words, this battery does not work upon itself." Hayes likewise discloses the De La Rue zinc-silver chloride cell, but with certain mechanical differences designed to restrict the battery from continuing to act upon itself.

The Wood patent is relied upon by the Government as teaching the substitution of magnesium, as in the Adams patent, for zinc. Wood's patent, issued in 1928, states: "It would seem that a relatively high voltage primary cell would be obtained by using ... magnesium as the ... [positive] electrode and I am aware that attempts have been made to develop such a cell. As far as I am aware, however, these have all been unsuccessful, and it has been generally accepted that magnesium could not be commercially utilized as a primary cell electrode." Wood recognized that the difficulty with magnesium electrodes is their suscepti-bility to chemical corrosion by the action of acid or ammonium chloride electro-lytes. Wood's solution to this problem was to use a "neutral electrolyte containing a strong soluble oxidizing agent adapted to reduce the rate of corrosion of the magnesium electrode on open circuit." There is no indication of its use with cuprous chloride, nor was there any indication that a magnesium battery could be water-activated.

The Codd treatise is also cited as authority for the substitution of magnesium. However, Codd simply lists magnesium in an electromotive series table, a tabulation of electrochemical substances in descending order of their relative electropositivity. He also refers to magnesium in an example designed to show that various substances are more electropositive than others, but the discussion involves a cell containing an acid which would destroy magnesium within minutes. In short, Codd indicates, by inference, only that magnesium is a theor-etically desirable electrode by virtue of its highly electropositive character. He does not teach that magnesium could be combined in a water-activated battery or that a battery using magnesium would have the properties of the Adams device. Nor does he suggest, as the Government indicates, that cuprous chloride could be substituted for silver chloride. He merely refers to the cuprous *ion* — a generic term which includes an infinite number of copper compounds — and in no way suggests that cuprous chloride could be employed in a battery.

The Government then cites the Wensky patent which was issued in Great Britain in 1891. The patent relates to the use of cuprous chloride as a depolariz-ing agent. The specifications of his patent disclose a battery comprising zinc and copper electrodes, the cuprous chloride being added as a salt in an electrolyte solution containing zinc chloride as well. While Wensky recognized that cuprous chloride could be used in a constant-current cell, there is no indication that he taught a water-activated system or that magnesium could be incorporated in his battery.

Finally, the Skrivanoff patent depended upon by the Government relates to a battery designed to give intermittent, as opposed to continuous, service. While the patent claims magnesium as an electrode, it specifies that the electrolyte to be used in conjunction with it must be a solution of "alcoline, chloro-chromate, or a permanganate strengthened with sulphuric acid." The cathode was a copper or carbon electrode faced with a paste of "phosphoric acid, amorphous phosphorous, metallic copper in spangles, and cuprous chloride." This paste is to be mixed with hot sulfuric acid before applying to the electrode. The Government's expert testified in trial that he had no information as to whether the cathode, as placed in the battery, would, after having been mixed with the other chemicals pre-scribed, actually contain cuprous chloride. Furthermore, respondents' expert testified, without contradiction, that he had attempted to assemble a battery made in accordance with Skrivanoff's teachings, but was met first with a fire when he sought to make the cathode, and then with an explosion when he attempted to assemble the complete battery.

III

The Validity of the Patent

The Government challenges the validity of the Adams patent on grounds of lack of novelty under 35 U.S.C. § 102(a) (1964 ed.) as well as obviousness under 35 U.S.C. § 103 (1964 ed.). As we have seen in *Graham v. John Deere Co.*, *ante*, p. 1, novelty and nonobviousness — as well as utility — are separate tests of patentability and all must be satisfied in a valid patent.

The Government concludes that wet batteries comprising a zinc anode and silver chloride cathode are old in the art; and that the prior art shows that magnesium may be substituted for zinc and cuprous chloride for silver chloride. Hence, it argues that the "combination of magnesium and cuprous chloride in the Adams battery was not patentable because it represented either no change or an insignificant change as compared to prior battery designs." And, despite "the fact that, wholly unexpectedly, the battery showed certain valuable operating advan-tages over other batteries [these advantages] would certainly not justify a patent on the essentially old formula."

There are several basic errors in the Government's position. First, the fact that the Adams battery is water-activated sets his device apart from the prior art. It is true that Claims 1 and 10, *supra*, do not mention a water electrolyte, but, as we have noted, a stated object of the invention was to provide a battery rendered serviceable by the mere addition of water. While the claims of a patent limit the invention, and specifications cannot be utilized to expand the patent monopoly, *Burns v. Meyer*, 100 U.S. 671, 672 (1880); *McCarty v. Lehigh Valley R. Co.*, 160 U.S. 110, 116 (1895), it is fundamental that claims are to be construed in the light of the specifications and both are to be read with a view to ascertaining the invention, *Seymour v. Osborne*, 11 Wall. 516, 547 (1871); *Schriber-Schroth Co. v. Cleveland Trust Co.*, 311 U.S. 211 (1940); *Schering Corp. v. Gilbert*, 153 F.2d 428 (1946). Taken together with the stated object of disclosing a water-activated cell, the lack of reference to any electrolyte in Claims 1 and 10 indicates that water alone could be used. Furthermore, of the 11 claims in issue, three of the narrower ones include references to specific electrolyte solutions comprising water and certain salts. The obvious implication from the absence of any mention of an electrolyte — a necessary element in any battery — in the other eight claims reinforces this conclusion. It is evident that respondents' present reliance upon this feature was not the afterthought of an astute patent trial lawyer. In his first contact with the Government less than a month after the patent application was filed, Adams pointed out that "no acids, alkalines or any other liquid other than plain water is used in this cell. Water does not have to be distilled...." Letter to Charles F. Kettering (January 7, 1942).

Nor is *Sinclair & Carroll Co. v. Interchemical Corp.*, 325 U.S. 327 (1945), apposite here. There the patentee had developed a rapidly drying printing ink. All that was needed to produce such an ink was a solvent which evaporated quickly upon heating. Knowing that the boiling point of a solvent is an indication of its rate of evaporation, the patentee merely made selections from a list of solvents and their boiling points. This was no more than "selecting the last piece to put into the last opening in a jig-saw puzzle." 325 U.S., at 335. Indeed, the Government's reliance upon *Sinclair & Carroll* points up the fallacy of the underlying premise of its case. The solvent in *Sinclair & Carroll* had no functional relation to the printing ink involved. It served only as an inert carrier. The choice of solvent was dictated by known, required properties. Here, however, the Adams battery is shown to embrace elements having an interdependent functional relationship. It begs the question, and overlooks the holding of the Commissioner and the Court of Claims, to state merely that magnesium and cuprous chloride were individually known battery components. If such a combination is novel, the issue is whether bringing them together as taught by Adams was obvious in the light of the prior art.

We believe that the Court of Claims was correct in concluding that the Adams battery is novel. Skrivanoff disclosed the use of magnesium in an electrolyte completely different from that used in Adams. As we have mentioned, it is even open to doubt whether cuprous chloride was a functional element in Skrivanoff. In view of the unchallenged testimony that the Skrivanoff formulation was both dangerous and inoperable, it seems anomalous to suggest that it is an anticipation of Adams. An inoperable invention or one which fails to achieve its intended result does not negative novelty. *Smith v. Snow*, 294 U.S. 1, 17 (1935).

Nor is the Government's contention that the electrodes of Adams were mere substitutions of pre-existing battery designs supported by the prior art. If the use of magnesium for zinc and cuprous chloride for silver chloride were merely equivalent substitutions, it would follow that the resulting device — Adams' — would have equivalent operating characteristics. But it does not. The court below found, and the Government apparently admits, that the Adams battery "wholly unexpectedly" has shown "certain valuable operating advantages over other batteries" while those from which it is claimed to have been copied were long ago discarded. Moreover, most of the batteries relied upon by the Government were of a completely different type designed to give intermittent power and characterized by an absence of internal action when not in use. Some provided current at voltages which declined fairly proportionately with time. Others were so-called standard cells which, though producing a constant voltage, were of use principally for calibration or measurement purposes. Such cells cannot be used as sources of power. For these reasons we find no equivalency.

We conclude the Adams battery was also nonobvious. As we have seen, the operating characteristics of the Adams battery have been shown to have been unexpected and to have far surpassed then-existing wet batteries. Despite the fact that each of the elements of the Adams battery was well known in the prior art, to combine them as did Adams required that a person reasonably skilled in the prior art must ignore that (1) batteries which continued to operate on an open circuit and which heated in normal use were not practical; and (2) water-activated batteries were successful only when combined with electrolytes detrimental to the use of magnesium. These long-accepted factors, when taken together, would, we believe, deter any investigation into such a combination as is used by Adams. This is not to say that one who merely finds new uses for old inventions by shutting his eyes to their prior disadvantages thereby discovers a patentable innovation. We do say, however, that known disadvantages in old devices which would naturally discourage the search for new inventions may be taken into account in determining obviousness.

Nor are these the only factors bearing on the question of obviousness. We have seen that at the time Adams perfected his invention noted experts expressed disbelief in it. Several of the same experts subsequently recognized the significance of the Adams invention, some even patenting improvements on the same system. Fischbach et al., U.S. Patent No. 2,636,060 (1953). Furthermore, in a crowded art replete with a century and a half of advancement, the Patent Office found not one reference to cite against the Adams application. Against the subsequently issued improvement patents to Fischbach, *supra*, and to Chubb, U.S. Reissue Patent No. 23,883 (1954), it found but three references prior to Adams — none of which are relied upon by the Government.

We conclude that the Adams patent is valid. The judgment of the Court of Claims is affirmed.

It is so ordered.

NOTES

1. *"The Trilogy."* The three preceding cases — *Graham*, *Cook Chemical* and *Adams* — are often referred to as "the trilogy." Coming as they did after a prolonged era in the Supreme Court that the patent bar perceived (with some reason) as anti-patent, these three cases were thought to mark a watershed in the treatment of patents in our highest court. *See generally* NONOBVIOUSNESS, *supra*.

2. *Bert's Travails.* The fascinating story of Bert Adams, inventor of the battery at issue in the preceding case, is told in R. GAUSEWITZ, PATENT PENDING: TODAY'S INVENTORS AND THEIR INVENTIONS 54-66 (1983). Bert's story includes the following items, among many others: (1) he invented the battery at issue one

night when ash from his cigarette accidentally fell into a batch of cuprous chloride he was cooking on the kitchen stove as part of one of his many experiments; (2) he originally disclosed his invention to the government during World War II as part of the patriotic inventors' war effort known as the National Inventors Council; (3) the Army declined an initial settlement offer for $25,000; and (4) the most effective part of the Supreme Court oral argument for Adams was demonstration of a model of the battery powering a small lightbulb, which continued to shine all during the argument for Adams and the government's rebuttal argument.

3. *No Single Reference.* The Court states, referring to the Codd reference:

> He does not teach that magnesium could be combined in a water-activated battery or that a battery using magnesium would have the properties of the Adams device.

This presages a general doctrine developed more fully by the Federal Circuit, to the effect that nonobviousness will be difficult to make out if a single reference suggests combining the features in the prior art actually combined in the invention at issue. *See In re Geiger*, 815 F.2d 686, 688, 2 U.S.P.Q.2d (BNA) 1276, 1278 (Fed. Cir. 1987) (obviousness cannot be established by combining pieces of prior art absent some "teaching, suggestion, or incentive supporting the combination"). The Court adds: "These long-accepted factors [in the art], when taken together, would, we believe, deter any investigation into such a combination as is used by Adams." This concept, of an inventor exploring ground even when the art "teaches away" from it, has proved a powerful argument to patentees. *See, e.g., In re Fine*, 837 F.2d 1071, 5 U.S.P.Q.2d 1596 (BNA) (Fed. Cir. 1988).

4. *Post*-Graham *Developments.* The Supreme Court arguably undercut some of the positive statements in *Graham* in two post-*Graham* cases. Both cases referred to the old invention test. But since both involved the distinct issue of "combination patents," the patent bar concluded that they did not signify any retrenchment from the principles of *Graham*. The Court in these cases reaffirmed the enigmatic "synergism" test for combination patents, which required an unexpected result or effect to flow from a combination of old components or techniques. If the combination failed to exhibit any properties beyond what might be expected, no patent would issue. *See Anderson's-Black Rock, Inc. v. Pavement Salvage Co.*, 396 U.S. 57 (1969); *Sakraida v. Ag-Pro, Inc.*, 425 U.S. 273 (1976). *See generally* 1 D. DUNNER ET AL., PATENT LAW PERSPECTIVES § 2.6 [2.-1-2] (2d ed. 1970 & Supp. 1990).

The Supreme Court held in *Anderson's-Black Rock* that, to be patentable, a new combination of old elements had to demonstrate "synergism," i.e., a new function or effect not predictable from the aggregation of the individual elements. The invention at issue was a paving machine containing a heating element to make smooth seams between adjoining strips of pavement. The Supreme Court invalidated the patent on the machine because the aggregation of old techniques lacked synergism; the new combination worked just as one would predict, given what was known about its individual components. *Id.*, at 282. *Sakraida v. Ag-Pro, Inc.*, *supra*, presented similar facts. The patent covered a customized barn for dairy cows, with sloped floors and water storage tanks to make waste clean-up simpler. *Id.*, at 274. The Supreme Court reiterated the synergism principle in these words:

> Though doubtless a matter of great convenience, producing a desired result in a cheaper and faster way, and enjoying commercial success, Dairy Establishments [patentee] "did not produce a 'new or different function' ... within the test of validity of combination patents." *Anderson's-Black Rock Pavement Co.* [396 U.S. 57] at 60 ... These desirable benefits "without invention will not make patentability." *A&P Tea Co. v. Supermarket Equip. Corp.*, 340 U.S. 147 at 153.

Id., at 282-83. The reference to the *A&P* case, *Great Atl. & Pac. Tea Co. v. Supermarket Equip. Corp.*, 340 U.S. 147 (1950), was especially disappointing to those who saw *Graham* as the end of anti-patent sentiment in the Supreme Court, since *A&P* was widely thought to represent the most unreasonable application of the synergism requirement. Some patent lawyers even feared that the Court was once again establishing a very high standard of patentability for all inventions. *See, e.g.*, 1 D. DUNNER ET AL., *supra*, at 2-414 through 2-415 (1986) ("*A&P* represented the culmination of subjective, hindsight-ridden and inconsistent judicial determinations of what is 'an invention'"). Even more frustrating for patent lawyers, the decisive impetus behind the drafting of § 103 had been a desire to overturn the *A&P* decision. *See* Rich, *Congressional Intent — Or, Who Wrote the Patent Act of 1952?*, in NONOBVIOUSNESS, *supra*, at 1:1, 1:7-1:8.

1. A NOTE ON THE ECONOMIC FUNCTION OF § 103

The cases we have seen so far in this chapter, and indeed the Patent Act itself, view the nonobviousness requirement as a gatekeeper: which inventions will be "let through" (receive patents), and which will not? The approach taken in this note is to approach the problem from a different point of view: to treat nonobviousness as a legal rule that influences behavior — specifically, the decisions of research and development (R&D) personnel to pursue or ignore specific research projects. Thus the nonobviousness standard is seen as an instrument for encouraging researchers to pursue projects whose success appears highly uncertain at the outset. Viewed this way, we ask whether the § 103 standard in fact serves the purpose of encouraging risky research.

The model and discussion in this brief note suggest that the answer — perhaps surprisingly — is to a large extent *no*. Under some realistic assumptions, we will see that § 103 actually has a bigger effect on decisions regarding which technologies to *develop* than regarding which research projects to pursue in the first place.

Thus, although § 103 does influence the amount and direction of research, it has more influence on the decision to scale up and commercialize a technology.

The cases hold that no patent will issue if, just prior to the invention, there was a "reasonable probability of success"[1] that the invention would work, as judged by someone "skilled in the art." If there was *no* reasonable probability of success, the resulting invention deserves a patent.[2] That is, an invention must be downright *im*probable for it to be patentable.[3]

The probability of the invention is viewed from the perspective of an ordinary skilled artisan,[4] *not* from the perspective of the actual inventor.

The standard discussed in this note is as follows: reward one who successfully invents when *the uncertainty facing him or her makes it more likely than not that the invention won't succeed.* Uncertainty under this standard is measured from the perspective of the average skilled inventor in the field. Again, the question we are interested in is this: does this standard actually encourage risky research, given what we know about actual R&D operations?

One can construct a simple formal model of the decision whether to pursue a research project, to explore the effects of the nonobviousness standard on the *incentives* facing a prospective researcher/inventor. Begin by imagining an inventor facing the choice of whether to attempt preliminary experimentation on the invention or not.[5] The next stage of the model presents another decision:

---

[1] *See, e.g., PPG Indus., Inc. v. Guardian Indus. Corp.*, 75 F.3d 1558, 1566 (Fed. Cir. 1996); *In re Merck & Co.*, 800 F.2d 1091, 1097, 231 U.S.P.Q. 375 (Fed. Cir. 1986) (the standard for obviousness is not "absolute predictability, [but] only a reasonable expectation that the beneficial result will be achieved..."); *Loctite Corp. v. Ultraseal*, 781 F.2d 861, 874, 228 U.S.P.Q. 90 (Fed. Cir. 1985) (obviousness is an objective standard, and it is only material what a person of ordinary skill would have thought).

[2] *See, e.g., W.L. Gore & Assocs. v. Garlock, Inc.*, 220 U.S.P.Q. (BNA) 303, 312 (Fed. Cir. 1983) (upholding nonobviousness of invention, since "there was no testimony and no finding that one skilled in the art would transfer conventional thermoplastic processes to those for unsintered PTFE [polytetrafluoroethylene, i.e., "Gore-tex"], *or would have been able to predict what would happen if they did.*") (emphasis added); *Ex parte Old*, 229 U.S.P.Q. 196, 200 (BNA) (Pat. Off. Bd. App. & Int. 1985) (reversing final rejection by patent examiner for obviousness, because "he himself does not urge that the character of [the invention] ... could be predicted ...").

[3] *See, e.g., Continental Oil Co. v. Witco Chem. Corp.*, 179 U.S.P.Q. (BNA) 200, 204 (7th Cir. 1973) (invalidating patent for invention that was "[a]t most ... somewhat doubtful until after an experiment had been made").

[4] Under the statute, a "person having ordinary skill in the art," 35 U.S.C. § 103 (1988) — thus the acronym "PHOSITA." *See* Tresansky, *PHOSITA — The Ubiquitous and Enigmatic Person in Patent Law*, 73 J. PAT. & TRADEMARK OFF. SOC'Y 37 (1991).

[5] This corresponds roughly to a common stage in research and development (R&D) projects: the preliminary screening of candidate technologies, or preliminary investigation of a technology for a suspected or hoped for quality. *See, e.g.,* S. Wiggins, *The Pharmaceutical Research and Development Decision Process*, in DRUGS AND HEALTH 55, 58 (J. Helms ed., 1981) (hereafter referred to as Wiggins, *R&D Process*) ("The screening procedure is a low-cost method of separating compounds that warrant more careful testing from toxic substances and from substances that have no observable

whether to develop the nascent invention. See Figure 5-7. By separating the invention process into two steps, the model tries to "unpack" some features of the conventional (implicit) model of invention, and thus capture a bit more of the complexity of the invention process.

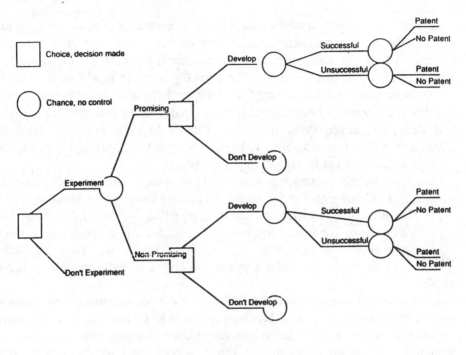

BASIC DECISION TREE

Figure 5-7

In this two-step decision model, the inventor makes an *initial* estimate of the potential returns from the inventive process, prior to beginning any experimenta-

pharmacological action."); F. Scherer, *Antitrust and Patent Policies*, in INNOVATION, ECONOMIC CHANGE AND TECHNOLOGY POLICIES 293, 304 (K. Stroetman ed., 1977) (responding to quote from the economist Joseph Schumpeter on the risk-seeking nature of most entrepreneurs, stating "My impression is that most research and development in large industrial corporations, including pharmaceutical firms, is conducted following a more careful calculation of costs, potential benefits, and success probabilities than Schumpeter assumed. But on this I could be wrong."). *Cf.* Mansfield, *How Economists See R&D*, HARV. BUS. REV., Nov.-Dec. 1981, at 98 (reporting results of empirical research indicating that although economic evaluations based on quantitative techniques increase a project's chances of commercial success, some managers are reluctant to adopt project selection methods).

tion.[6] This is equivalent to the common situation of the R&D manager deciding whether it is even worthwhile to begin to explore a research area.[7] If she decides the preliminary experimentation is worthwhile, she is faced with a second choice when that experimentation is successfully completed: to develop the invention, or to abandon it.[8]

An important feature of this model is that the researcher does not know at the time that the initial experiment is undertaken whether it will be a success or not. She may have some idea, or even a strong belief; but until the experiment is actually performed, there is no way of knowing whether it will work. This is important because of a key assumption in the model: that a patent is much more valuable if it covers a product which is successful in the marketplace. This is equivalent to assuming that a patent has little or no value in and of itself; its value stems solely from its ability to prevent competitors from appropriating the intrinsic benefits of the invention which the patent protects.

As a result of this assumption, and in light of some reasonable values for the probabilities of each event in the model, increasing the payoff associated with a patent strengthens the reward to successful innovation, but not as directly as one might think at first. The researcher knows that neither a promising experimental result nor a successful innovation are certain at the outset. Thus the added financial return that accompanies a patent has only a *contingent* value; it is not certain.

Again, this may seem obvious. But when some reasonable numbers are plugged into the basic model, it quickly becomes apparent just how limited the incentive effect of a patent is. To take a reasonable case, suppose the probability of obtaining a promising experimental result is 50%, and the probability of a commercially successful project is 40%. Suppose further that through experience we know that the probability of obtaining a promising experimental result is 70%

---

[6] *See* F. KNIGHT, RISK, UNCERTAINTY AND PROFIT 318 (1921):

Though we cannot describe a new invention in advance without making it ... yet it is possible in a large degree to offset ignorance with knowledge and behave intelligently with regard to the future. The changes [i.e., advances] are in large part the result of deliberate application of resources to bring them about, and in the large if not in a particular instance, the results of such activity can be so far foreseen that it is even possible to hire men and borrow capital at fixed remunerations for the purpose of carrying it on.

[7] *See, e.g.*, Wiggins, *R&D Process, supra*, at 63 ("at some point the [researcher] who has the [research] idea goes to the head of his or her research unit and suggests that the idea be pursued in a formal project. This is the *primary* source of all new research projects undertaken by pharmaceutical companies.").

[8] The use of project "hurdles" or decision points in the pharmaceutical industry is described in Wiggins, *R&D Process, supra*, at 70. One researcher finds that for a majority of inventors, patents act primarily as an incentive to commercialize, rather than invent. *See* Sirilli, *Patents and Inventors: An Empirical Study*, 16 RES. POL'Y 157, 164 (1987).

when the project turns out to be a commercial success. (That is, in looking back over data from past projects, we know that of all projects that were ultimately successful, the initial experiment produced promising results 70% of the time.) The chances of obtaining a patent for a product that is a commercial success is 50%. See Figure 5-8. Finally, assume that the award of a patent increases the financial payoff of a successful invention by 20%; we can say that without a patent, the payoff for a successful invention is $1,000, but with a patent it would be $1,200.[9] (There is a net return of zero if the initial experiment does not produce promising results, or if the experiment is promising but turns out to yield a commercially unsuccessful product.)

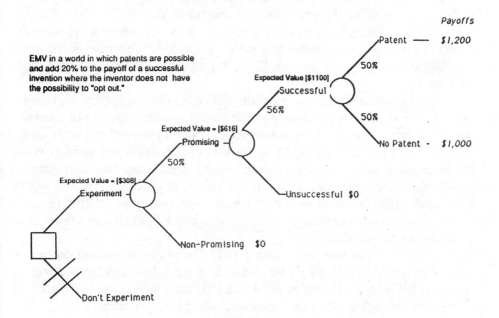

Figure 5-8

With these numbers, the extra incentive offered by a patent can be analyzed. If we allow the decisionmaker to decide whether to continue with the project after

---

[9] This is a conservative estimate of the average value of a patent to the average patentee, since it has been found that the average patent increases the imitation cost only modestly, see Mansfield, Schwartz & Wagner, *Imitation Costs and Patents: An Empirical Study*, 91 ECON. J. 907, 913 (1981) (survey of R&D personnel in random sample of companies produced result that patents caused a "median estimated increase in [the cost of imitation] of 11%").

the initial experiment,[10] the incentive effect of a patent becomes clear. The inventor can re-assess her original decision to pursue the project in light of the results of the initial experiment. Given the figures discussed above, the inventor will be facing one of two situations after the initial experiment. If the experiment produced promising results, the inventor will increase her estimate of the chances of commercial success because of the additional information that the experiment was successful. Her initial estimate was that the chance of a successful project was 40%; she will *raise* this estimate in light of the promising experimental results. Specifically, the probability of a successful project increases to 56% — up from the original estimate of 40% before the experimental results were known.[11] Likewise, if the experiment had produced *unpromising* results, the probability of a successful project would drop to 24%.

In such a two-step decision, the expected value of a patent that increases the payoff of a successful project by 20% (to $1,200) is $308, and the expected value without the possibility of a patent is $280. Thus there is a $28 "plus factor" from the patent.

Under plausible assumptions, then, the incentive effect of a patent is relatively modest. The availability of a patent would only change the behavior of a rational decisionmaker in cases where the expected value of the project without the possibility of a patent is slightly below the cost of undertaking the project. While this of course depends on the magnitude of the patent's contribution to expected payoff, under plausible assumptions of this magnitude the incentive effect will be quite small. This finding conforms to the views of some research and development managers, who consider patentability as a factor — albeit only one of many — in selecting research projects.

But what does this have to do with § 103? The answer is that adjustments in the probability of obtaining a patent — that is, in the § 103 standard — affect the final payoffs. So through this model we can get some idea of how changing the § 103 standard would affect the incentives facing R&D managers.

---

[10] This corresponds with how R&D decisions are actually made in many instances. *See* Mansfield & Wagner, *Organizational and Strategic Factors Associated with Probabilities of Success in Industrial R&D*, 48 J. BUS. 179 (1975) (reporting survey of R&D decisionmaking in 20 large corporations, where three identifiable stages are common: technical completion, commercialization, and evaluation or profitability). Indeed, we know from the literature on "options theory" that managers strive to arrange R&D — and in fact *all* capital-intensive projects — so as to preserve flexibility. There is value in being able to "opt out" of an R&D project in midstream. *See* LENOS TRIGEORGIS, REAL OPTIONS 58-68 (1996).

[11] Although it is intuitive that the chance of success would increase given a promising result, a precise figure for the increase can be arrived at using Bayes' Theorem. This allows us to calculate the probability of commercial success given a promising experiment, when we have available the data stated in the text. *See generally* H. RAIFFA, DECISION ANALYSIS: INTRODUCTORY LECTURES ON CHOICES UNDER UNCERTAINTY 14-20 (1968). The figures in the text were arrived at using this theorem.

It is not difficult to show with this model that it would take a very severe increase in the probability of obtaining a patent — i.e., a radical lowering of the standard of patentability — to significantly affect a potential researcher's incentives. The reason is the structure of the model, which dampens the incentive effect from the patent by making experimental success the key to commercial success. In other words, all the incentive in the world won't help if your technology won't work. And in fact, because it is relatively cheap (in the model anyway) to see if your technology holds any promise, the lure of a patent has little to do with inspiring you to do that preliminary research in the first place. Since this is true, it follows that even severe slackening of the patentability standard under § 103 will not have an overwhelming effect on incentives to invent.

Another perhaps surprising point that emerges from this brief model is that patents may have a greater impact on incentives to *develop* than incentives to invent. Once a promising result is in hand, the heightened payoff from a patent more directly affects the expected value of developing the product. This is because the incentive is much less "diluted." If the researcher knows from past experience that a promising experimental result is more likely to result in a commercially successful product, she can revise her estimate of the chance of success *given* a promising result. Because the researcher's estimate of the probability of receiving a high payoff rises after a successful experiment, her expected value rises as well. *This* is the point at which the patent has the most direct effect: providing an incentive to develop. It is because the experimental results are promising that the researcher revises her estimate of the probability of a successful innovation; hence the enhanced payoff from a patent enters into her expected value assessment with less "dilution" and a higher probability.[12]

This meshes with the experience and opinion of many R&D managers. They often state that patents have only a small role in decisions regarding initial experimentation or research, but that patents play a larger part in decisions about which technologies to develop and market.

a. Should the § 103 Standard Be Adjusted for Abnormally Expensive Inventions?

Under current doctrine, nonobviousness is based on *technical uncertainty* — the degree of uncertainty attending a certain experiment, prototype or inventive concept. And for the most part, that is the proper measure of patentability. But when initial experiments are extremely costly, normal levels of risk aversion give

---

[12] Interestingly, this premise was well stated in the celebrated concurrence of Judge Frank in *Picard v. United Aircraft Corp.*, 128 F.2d 632, 642-43 (2d Cir. 1942) ("But if we never needed, or do not now need, patents as bait for inventors, we may still need them, in some instances, as a lure to investors."). *See also* F. Machlup, *Patents*, in 2 ENCYCLOPAEDIA OF THE SOCIAL SCIENCES 461, 467 (1968) (stating that one theory of the patent system is that it gives incentives to develop technology).

such experiments a higher degree of perceived risk than they otherwise would have. Lowering the standard of patentability is therefore an appropriate response.

One easy way to think about high-cost research projects starts from the premise that they can lead to more unpredictable results. To put the matter in simple formal terms, high-cost projects have a very large *statistical variance* compared to low-cost projects. Inventors trying to decide whether to pursue a high-risk project will thus face more variance. In such a situation, economic theory, empirical research and common sense all suggest that when deciding on these projects, the benefits will be heavily "diluted" by the extra risk. It is a basic assumption, in other words, that a decisionmaker's aversion to risk increases as the variance in outcomes increases. Assuming that society values inventions in a risk-neutral way, the result will be fewer high-variance (i.e., high-risk) invention projects than the preferred number.

The policy solution is easy to envision: create some extra incentive to offset the inventor's lower perceived utility. This might take a number of forms. For example, the initial experimentation stage of the high-risk project could be subsidized by the government. Government funding of basic research is one instance of this; basic research projects often involve high costs and potentially high but quite uncertain rewards. *See* Nelson, *The Simple Economics of Basic Scientific Research*, 67 J. POL. ECON. 297 (1959); *cf.* Robert P. Merges, *Property Rights Theory and the Commons: The Case of Scientific Research*, 13 SOC. PHIL. & POL'Y 145 (1996) (informal appropriability mechanisms provide incentive to perform basic research).

In addition, a patent-related policy solution is possible. This would involve creating an extra-high payoff for those successful projects whose inventors faced a high-variance project. Because perceived payoff is a combination of dollar payoffs and probabilities, this could be achieved by either augmenting the potential profit from a patent or by increasing the probability of obtaining one. Naturally in this note we focus on the latter alternative. Although, as mentioned above, the effects of any patent-related incentive on initial decisions to invent are quite limited, some marginal inventors might be swayed by the extra reward. Thus it is at least worth attempting.

One practical way to assess whether a project involved a high degree of risk is to look at the cost. If the project was very costly relative to others in the industry, it is a good candidate for the extra "risk bonus" discussed here.[13] Although the cost of research has never been part of the formal analysis of nonobviousness, some decisions have noted that the expenditure of a large amount

---

[13] This bears a close relationship to a point made by the economist F.M. Scherer: patents are especially defensible where they award inventions whose costs are high relative to their benefits. *See* F. SCHERER, INDUSTRIAL MARKET STRUCTURE AND ECONOMIC PERFORMANCE 448 (2d ed. 1980) (innovations with low potential benefits relative to costs need promise of a patent to be worthwhile). The proposal outlined here merely stresses that what is important is *perceived* costs — which may be a function of risk aversion when variance is high — as compared to benefits.

of money tends to show that an invention is not obvious.[14] Thus there is some support for the idea that courts have already recognized the high-cost case as special when applying § 103. The discussion here confirms the wisdom of this practice. It would be better for inventors if the courts made this practice explicit in the patentability jurisprudence.[15]

To entertain such a notion, one need not suggest that Congress should change the statutory standard. An *interpretation* of the current standard that recognizes the central place of uncertainty would do the job. If one sees nonobviousness as a test of whether an invention entailed a high degree of technical uncertainty at its outset, the adjustment suggested here makes sense. In the case of an inexpensive or moderately expensive research project, the inquiry need go no further than technical uncertainty. But for a high-cost research project, one whose cost is much higher than the average project in the industry, we must also take account of the fact that a reduction in *perceived payoffs* makes the project look less attractive to the reasonably skilled inventor.

The notion of including cost as a component of technical uncertainty may be disquieting. After all, it might be thought that if the end result of a certain experiment is obvious, it is no less obvious simply because it may be very expensive to verify. The high cost, it will be argued, does not make the result any less likely. But a little reflection reveals that there is a relationship between

---

[14] *Panduit Corp. v. Dennison Mfg.*, 774 F.2d 1082, 1089, 227 U.S.P.Q. 337 (Fed. Cir. 1985) (fact that patent holder took seven years and spent millions of dollars is evidence that prior art did not render invention obvious); *Hardinge Bros. v. Marr Oil Heat Mach. Corp.*, 27 F.2d 779, 781 (7th Cir. 1928) (fact that patentee and infringer both made long and expensive experiments in an effort to make an oil burner with a cover on it, is evidence that invention was not obvious); *Bethlehem Steel Co. v. Nelies-Bement-Pond Co.*, 166 F. 880 (C.C.D.N.J. 1909) (patentee shows that he spent between $50,000 and $125,000 "perfecting" his invention; the court, in invalidating the patent, found that the actual experimentation was extremely limited, the large amounts of money were spent after the invention was made, and were merely to fine tune it; decision implies that had the money been expended for the original research, it would have been relevant); *Edoco Tech. Prods., Inc. v. Peter Kiewit Sons Co.*, 313 F. Supp. 1081, 1086 (C.D. Cal. 1970) (the fact that the invention achieved immediate commercial success, solved a long-felt need, others failed to solve the need, others copied the invention, and a long and expensive period of experimentation was required to solve the problem were all considered to be evidence of nonobviousness). *Cf. Eli Lilly & Co. v. Generix Drug Sales*, 460 F.2d 1096, 1103, 174 U.S.P.Q. 65 (5th Cir. 1972) (inventor who undertook costly and painstaking research in developing propoxyphene hydrochloride should be rewarded with a product patent; a use or process patent would be insufficient incentive and would discourage the inspiration process); *United States v. Ciba-Geigy Corp.*, 508 F. Supp. 1157, 1168, 211 U.S.P.Q. 529 (D.N.J. 1981) (for patent relating to hydrochlorothiazide, the costly research undertaken should be rewarded with a product patent).

[15] *Cf.* Oddi, *Beyond Obviousness: Invention Protection in the Twenty-First Century*, 38 AM. U. L. REV. 1097, 1127 (1989) (suggesting that courts ought to consider "qualitative and quantitative investment in research and development" as an additional objective factor in determining nonobviousness).

predictability and cost, especially when cost is very high. The reason, once again, involves risk aversion.

The greater the divergence between potential outcomes, the more would a risk averse person's preference for a choice diverge from a risk-neutral assessment of expected value. One could model this as a reduction in the perceived payoffs from the risky activity. It would be easy, however, to treat the payoff as constant and say instead that the risk aversion lowers the anticipated *probability* of the positive payoff. Viewed this way, the suggestion made here simply brings the law's treatment of the high-cost project into line with its treatment of the low-cost project. A slight "risk-adjustment" is added to make up for the effect of the project's high cost on *perceived* technical uncertainty.

b. The "Obvious to Try" Doctrine

Since the early 1960s,[16] the courts have been ruling consistently that obvious to try is not the standard of patentability.[17] The uncertainty-based view of nonobviousness espoused here explains these cases.

In one group of obvious to try cases, prior art suggests that a certain area should be investigated, but the resulting invention is either not suggested in the prior art, or has unexpected properties. For example, in *Novo Industri A/S v. Travenol Labs.*,[18] the court upheld the patentability of a species of fungus that produced an enzyme used for making cheese, holding that while it was obvious to examine this species along with others, the results obtained were unexpectedly good. Again, courts do not ask for certainty of success; an invention is obvious if the resulting invention does not differ significantly from what was suggested in the prior art or the inventor was reasonably certain that she would succeed.

The law is more complicated when the prior art suggests that the inventor either try a number of choices or vary a number of parameters.[19] In *In re*

---

[16] At one time, obvious to try was an accepted standard of obviousness, and even a showing by the applicant that unexpected results were reached or success was unlikely would not defeat a finding of lack of invention. *Mandel Bros. v. Wallace*, 335 U.S. 291, 295, 69 S. Ct. 73, 75 (1948) (patent for an improved anti-perspirant declared invalid due to lack of invention).

[17] *See, e.g., In re Fine*, 837 F.2d 1071, 1075, 5 U.S.P.Q.2d 1596 (Fed. Cir. 1988) (claims of application for patent for system for detecting and measuring small quantities of nitrogen compounds held not obvious because none of prior art, alone or in combination, suggests the claimed invention — at most they made it obvious to try); *Merck & Co. v. Biocraft Labs.*, 690 F. Supp. 1376, 1382 (D.N.J. 1988), *rev'd*, *Merck & Co. v. Biocraft Labs.*, 874 F.2d 804, 807, 10 U.S.P.Q.2d 1843 (Fed. Cir. 1989) (In an infringement action, the court held that patent for an orally administered diuretic was nonobvious, since prior art suggested that it would be obvious to try combining certain compounds, but it did not teach the unique combinations of drugs as outlined in the patent in question).

[18] *Novo Industri A/S v. Travenol Labs.*, 677 F.2d 1202, 1208, 215 U.S.P.Q. 412 (7th Cir. 1982) (patent involving the identification of a fungus species which produces a milk-coagulating enzyme needed for the production of cheese held not obvious because, although it was obvious to try the particular fungus species, the results were totally unexpected).

[19] *See, e.g., Uniroyal v. Rudkin-Wiley Corp.*, 837 F.2d 1044, 1053, 5 U.S.P.Q.2d 1434 (Fed.

O'Farrell, the court ruled that an invention is merely obvious to try when the prior art "gave either no indication of which parameters are critical or no direction as to which of many possible choices is likely to be successful."[20] As this case shows, the courts are not clear as to how many parameters need to vary, or how many permutations are necessary to render an invention nonobvious. It has been held, however, that "routine optimization" is not tantamount to nonobviousness.[21] Instead, the court has focused on the amount of guidance the prior art gives, which steers the inquiry back to the reasonable certainty of success standard. If the worker is forced to run through so many permutations that she does not expect to succeed, then the invention should be nonobvious.[22]

In *Merck & Co. v. Biocraft Labs.*,[23] the prior art suggested 1200 combinations, but the invention was found to be obvious because each of the combinations was expected to be effective, thus rendering any of the 1200 obvious.

Based on the recent obvious to try cases, it seems that the standard is a subset of the reasonable expectation of success standard. If an inventor is faced with a large number of variables, and the prior art does not provide enough guidance to narrow those down to a manageable level, then an inventive step is needed to proceed. Consequently, the skilled worker could not be reasonably certain of success, and any useful products that turn up are patentable. On the other hand, if the number of possible permutations has been limited by the prior art, then a mechanic could plod through them one at a time and be reasonably certain of success.

Cir. 1988) (patent infringement suit concerning an air-deflecting device for reducing wind resistance encountered by tractor-trailer trucks is remanded because district court incorrectly applied obvious standard by using "obvious to try" reasoning; the lower court rejected the patent as obvious even after finding that beyond the prior art, "experimentation [would be needed] to extract the exact parameters that would make the device work," and after holding that "even an expert would be unable to predict the result an aerodynamic device would have on a tractor-trailer vehicle."); *In re Antonie*, 559 F.2d 618, 620, 195 U.S.P.Q. 6 (C.C.P.A. 1977) (patent application for rotating biological contactor apparatus held not obvious, merely obvious to try, because inventor varied every parameter of a system in order to optimize the effectiveness of the system without guidance from the prior art as to which parameters to vary or how to vary them); *Polaroid Corp. v. Eastman Kodak*, 641 F. Supp. 828, 853, 228 U.S.P.Q. 305 (D. Mass. 1986) (Polaroid's patents for film and camera were held valid because: "[t]he fact that one skilled in the art would consider as possible candidates in an extensive search the mordants disclosed in these references does not meet the standard of obviousness").

[20] 853 F.2d 894, 7 U.S.P.Q.2d 1673 (Fed. Cir. 1988).

[21] *In re Kulling*, 897 F.2d 1147, 14 U.S.P.Q.2d (BNA) 1056, 1058 (Fed. Cir. 1990). *See also Ex parte Sugimoto*, 14 U.S.P.Q.2d 1312 (Bd. Pat. App. & Int. 1990) (invention involving routine substitution would have been obvious).

[22] *Ex parte Erlish*, 3 U.S.P.Q.2d 1011 (PTO Bd. Pat. App. & Int'f 1987); *Ex parte Allen*, 2 U.S.P.Q.2d 1425 (PTO Bd. Pat. App. & Int. 1987), *aff'd in unpublished opinion*, 846 F.2d 77 (Fed. Cir. 1988).

[23] 874 F.2d 804, 10 U.S.P.Q.2d 1843 (Fed. Cir. 1989).

Clearly, these cases are pushing towards a recognition that systematic research *in and of itself* does not make the resulting inventions obvious. And this in turn can be seen as a validation of the point made above, that high-cost research deserves an extra "boost" via adjustments in the patentability standard. Although, as the model shows, this basic experimentation receives little extra encouragement from adjustments in the patent standard, there is a small effect in a desirable direction.

In addition, the obvious to try cases support the notion that patents encourage development more than early research. The systematic exploration of a field, with the knowledge that if one "slogs through" the candidates a successful result is likely, is very much the essence of the "development" phase of "research and development." Thus the obvious to try cases are in a sense direct examples of the point made earlier: that patents give the biggest "push" to technological ideas which have already been "blocked out," and which then need to be scaled up and implemented. The research behind the obvious to try cases, in other words, follows the pattern of development work rather than early research. As such, it is clear from the discussion above that this is precisely the kind of endeavor that patents can encourage most effectively.

2. SUGGESTIONS IN THE PRIOR ART

Quite frequently, an invention is asserted to be obvious in light of a combination of prior art references. Device A, for instance, may disclose elements 1, 2 and 3; publication B may reveal elements 4, 5 and 6; and patent C may disclose elements 7 and 8. In light of these references, it may be asserted that invention D, whose claims include elements 1, 4, and 7, is obvious. Is it?

The Federal Circuit has provided a good deal of illumination on this problem, which was a source of great consternation before 1982. (*Cf.*, *e.g.*, *Anderson's-Black Rock, Inc. v. Pavement Salvage Co.*, 396 U.S. 57 (1969); *Sakraida v. Ag-Pro, Inc.*, 425 U.S. 273 (1976), both expounding the now-discredited "synergism" theory of combination inventions). The court has emphasized that inventions which purportedly combine isolated features from various aspects of the prior art must be judged by the same standards as other inventions. The court has stated, for instance, that there must be "something in the prior art as a whole to suggest the desirability, and thus the obviousness, of making the combination." *Lindemann Maschinenfabrik GmbH v. American Hoist & Derrick Co.*, 730 F.2d 1452, 1462, 221 U.S.P.Q. (BNA) 481, 488 (Fed. Cir. 1984).

In cases such as *Interconnect Planning Corp. v. Feil*, 774 F.2d 1132, 227 U.S.P.Q. (BNA) 543 (Fed. Cir. 1985), the Federal Circuit has clarified the issue further, by providing a useful procedure for assessing nonobviousness in such situations. In *Interconnect*, the court stated the appropriate standard as follows:

> The claims here at issue are directed to a combination of known components of telephone systems in an admittedly new way to achieve a new total system. Neither the district court in its opinion, nor the defendants, identi-

fied any suggestion in the prior art that the components be combined as they were by Feil or that such combination could achieve the advantages of the Feil system.

774 F.2d at 1143. The court has expanded on this, noting that "[w]hen it is necessary to select elements of various teachings in order to form the claimed invention, we ascertain whether there is any suggestion or motivation in the prior art to make the selection made by the applicant." *In re Gorman*, 933 F.2d 982, 986, 18 U.S.P.Q.2d 1885 (Fed. Cir. 1991). *Cf. In re Geiger*, 815 F.2d 686, 688, 2 U.S.P.Q.2d (BNA) 1276, 1278 (Fed. Cir. 1987) (obviousness cannot be established by combining pieces of prior art absent some "teaching, suggestion, or incentive supporting the combination").

The cases make clear that a reference must not only suggest additions or modifications, but also must suggest that such changes would be successful. A good example is the case of *In re O'Farrell*, 853 F.2d 894, 7 U.S.P.Q.2d (BNA) 1673 (Fed. Cir. 1988), an important biotechnology case. O'Farrell, Polisky and Gelfand were co-inventors of a method to control the expression of cloned genes in a bacterium. Unfortunately, the prior art included a published article which made their invention obvious. (The article was co-authored by two of the three inventors, Polisky and Gelfand, and a third scientist, Bishop.) The court stated in this connection:

> We agree with the board [of Patent Appeals and Interferences] that appellants' claimed invention would have been obvious in light of the Polisky reference [i.e., Polisky, Gelfand and Bishop] alone or in combination with [a second reference] within the meaning of § 103. Polisky contained detailed enabling methodology for practicing the claimed invention, a suggestion to modify the prior art to practice the claimed invention, and evidence suggesting that it would be successful.

This test was applied in an important commercial context in the following case.

In re VAECK

947 F.2d 488, 20 U.S.P.Q.2d 1438 (Fed. Cir. 1991)

RICH, J.

This appeal is from the September 12, 1990 decision of the Patent and Trademark Office (PTO) Board of Patent Appeals and Interferences (Board), affirming the examiner's rejection of [almost all] claims ... of [appellant's] application ..., filed March 4, 1987, ... as unpatentable under 35 U.S.C. 103 .... We reverse the § 103 rejection.

BACKGROUND

A. *The Invention*

The claimed invention is directed to the use of genetic engineering techniques for production of proteins that are toxic to insects such as larvae of mosquitos and black flies. These swamp-dwelling pests are the source of numerous human health problems, including malaria. It is known that certain species of the naturally-occurring Bacillus genus of bacteria produce proteins ("endotoxins") that are toxic to these insects. Prior art methods of combatting the insects involved spreading or spraying crystalline spores of the insecticidal Bacillus proteins over swamps. The spores were environmentally unstable, however, and would often sink to the bottom of a swamp before being consumed, thus rendering this method prohibitively expensive. Hence the need for a lower-cost method of producing the insecticidal Bacillus proteins in high volume, with application in a more stable vehicle.

As described by appellants, the claimed subject matter meets this need by providing for the production of the insecticidal Bacillus proteins within host cyanobacteria. Although both cyanobacteria and bacteria are members of the procaryote kingdom [i.e., organisms without a cell nucleus, as opposed to eucaryotes], the cyanobacteria (which in the past have been referred to as "blue-green algae") are unique among procaryotes in that the cyanobacteria are capable of oxygenic photosynthesis. The cyanobacteria grow on top of swamps where they are consumed by mosquitos and black flies. Thus, when Bacillus proteins are produced within transformed cyanobacterial hosts [i.e., when the Bacillus genes for those proteins have been successfully taken up by the foreign cyanobacteria and the genetic material has been made a permanent part of that host organism, to be replicated when it reproduces] according to the claimed invention, the presence of the insecticide in the food of the targeted insects advantageously guarantees direct uptake by the insects.

More particularly, the subject matter of the application on appeal includes a chimeric (i.e., hybrid) gene comprising (1) a gene derived from a bacterium of the Bacillus genus whose product is an insecticidal protein, united with (2) a DNA promoter effective for expressing the Bacillus gene in a host cyanobacterium, so as to produce the desired insecticidal protein.

....

D. *The Grounds of Rejection*

1. *The § 103 Rejections*

Claims 1-6, 16-21, 33-38, 47-48 and 52 (which include all independent claims in the application) were rejected as unpatentable under 35 U.S.C. 103 based upon Dzelzkalns [reference] in view of Sekar I or Sekar II and Ganesan [references]. The examiner stated that Dzelzkalns discloses a chimeric gene capable of being highly expressed in a cyanobacterium, said gene comprising a promoter region effective for expression in a cyanobacterium operably linked to a structural gene encoding [a protein called chloramphenicol acetyl transferase, abbreviated "CAT"]. The examiner acknowledged [the differences between the proteins, but] pointed out [that] Sekar I, Sekar II, and Ganesan teach genes encoding insecticidally active proteins produced by Bacillus, and the advantages of expressing such genes in ... hosts [from another species] to obtain larger quantities of the protein. The examiner contended that it would have been obvious to one of ordinary skill in the art to substitute the Bacillus genes taught by Sekar I, Sekar II, and Ganesan for the CAT gene in ... Dzelzkalns [reference] in order to obtain high level expression of the Bacillus genes in the transformed cyanobacteria. The examiner further contended that it would have been obvious to use cyanobacteria as [a host] for expression of the claimed genes ....

OPINION

A. *Obviousness*

We first address whether the PTO erred in rejecting the claims on appeal as prima facie obvious within the meaning of 35 U.S.C. 103. Obviousness is a legal question which this court independently reviews, though based upon underlying factual findings which we review under the clearly erroneous standard.

Where claimed subject matter has been rejected as obvious in view of a combination of prior art references, a proper analysis under § 103 requires, *inter alia*, consideration of two factors: (1) whether the prior art would have suggested to those of ordinary skill in the art that they should make the claimed composition or device, or carry out the claimed process; and (2) whether the prior art would also have revealed that in so making or carrying out, those of ordinary skill would have a reasonable expectation of success. See *In re Dow Chemical Co.*, 837 F.2d 469, 473, 5 U.S.P.Q.2d 1529, 1531 (Fed. Cir. 1988). Both the suggestion and the reasonable expectation of success must be founded in the prior art, not in the applicant's disclosure. *Id.*

We agree with appellants that the PTO has not established the prima facie obviousness of the claimed subject matter. The prior art simply does not disclose or suggest the expression in cyanobacteria of a chimeric gene encoding an insecticidally active protein, or convey to those of ordinary skill a reasonable expectation of success in doing so. More particularly, there is no suggestion in Dzelzkalns, the primary reference cited against all claims, of substituting in the disclosed plasmid a structural gene encoding Bacillus insecticidal proteins for the CAT gene utilized for selection purposes. The expression of antibiotic resistance-conferring genes in cyanobacteria, without more, does not render obvious the expression of unrelated genes in cyanobacteria for unrelated purposes.

The PTO argues that the substitution of insecticidal Bacillus genes for CAT marker genes in cyanobacteria is suggested by the secondary references Sekar I, Sekar II, and Ganesan, which collectively disclose expression of genes encoding Bacillus insecticidal proteins in two species of host Bacillus bacteria (B. megaterium and B. subtilis) as well as in the bacterium E. coli. While these references disclose expression of Bacillus genes encoding insecticidal proteins in certain transformed bacterial hosts, nowhere do these references disclose or suggest expression of such genes in transformed cyanobacterial hosts.

To remedy this deficiency, the PTO emphasizes similarity between bacteria and cyanobacteria, namely, that these are both procaryotic organisms, and argues that this fact would suggest to those of ordinary skill the use of cyanobacteria as hosts for expression of the claimed chimeric genes. While it is true that bacteria and cyanobacteria are now both classified as procaryotes, that fact alone is not sufficient to motivate the art worker as the PTO contends. As the PTO concedes, cyanobacteria and bacteria are not identical; they are classified as two separate divisions of the kingdom Procaryotae. Moreover, it is only in recent years that the biology of cyanobacteria has been clarified, as evidenced by references in the prior art to "blue-green algae." Such evidence of recent uncertainty regarding the biology of cyanobacteria tends to rebut, rather than support, the PTO's position that one would consider the cyanobacteria effectively interchangeable with bacteria as hosts for expression of the claimed gene.

....

The PTO asks us to agree that the prior art would lead those of ordinary skill to conclude that cyanobacteria are attractive hosts for expression of any and all heterologous genes. Again, we can not. The relevant prior art does indicate that cyanobacteria are attractive hosts for expression of both native and heterologous [i.e. foreign] genes involved in photosynthesis (not surprisingly, for the capability of undergoing oxygenic photosynthesis is what makes the cyanobacteria unique among procaryotes). However, these references do not suggest that cyanobacteria would be equally attractive hosts for expression of unrelated heterologous genes, such as the claimed genes encoding Bacillus insecticidal proteins.

In [In re] O'Farrell [853 F.2d 894, 7 U.S.P.Q.2d (BNA) 1673 (Fed. Cir. 1988)], this court affirmed an obviousness rejection of a claim to a method for producing a "predetermined protein in a stable form" in a transformed bacterial host. 853 F.2d at 895, 7 U.S.P.Q.2d at 1674.... The main difference between the prior art and the claim at issue was that in Polisky [reference], the heterologous gene was a gene for ribosomal RNA, while the claimed invention substituted a gene coding for a predetermined protein. Id. at 901, 7 U.S.P.Q.2d at 1679. Although, as the appellants therein pointed out, the ribosomal RNA gene is not normally translated into protein, Polisky mentioned preliminary evidence that the transcript of the ribosomal RNA gene was translated into protein, and further predicted that if a gene coding for a protein were to be substituted, extensive translation might result. Id. We thus affirmed, explaining that

> the prior art explicitly suggested the substitution that is the difference between the claimed invention and the prior art, and presented preliminary evidence suggesting that the [claimed] method could be used to make proteins....
>
> ... Polisky contained detailed enabling methodology for practicing the claimed invention, a suggestion to modify the prior art to practice the claimed invention, and evidence suggesting that it would be successful.

Id. at 901-02, 7 U.S.P.Q.2d at 1679-80.

In contrast with the situation in *O'Farrell*, the prior art in this case offers no suggestion, explicit or implicit, of the substitution that is the difference between the claimed invention and the prior art. Moreover, the "reasonable expectation of success" that was present in *O'Farrell* is not present here. Accordingly, we reverse the § 103 rejections.

Even though the "suggestion test," as this approach has been called, has been applied consistently by the courts, it leaves some interesting questions open. For instance, several cases hold that even an "implicit" suggestion to combine references, or to modify the teachings of a single reference, is enough to make the resulting invention obvious. *See In re Hauserman*, 15 U.S.P.Q.2d (BNA) 1157, disposition reported at 892 F.2d 1049 (Fed. Cir. 1989) (unpublished) ("Nor is there any suggestion in [the reference], *either explicit or implicit*, which would have motivated one skilled in the art to provide" the claimed feature.) (emphasis added). These cases raise the difficult issue of what is enough to constitute an "implicit suggestion," motivation, or incentive — and how such a standard can be kept from undermining the entire "suggestion or motivation" concept. A suggestion which is merely implicit, in other words, seems to carry one away from the idea that references must refer to possible combination or extension *on their face* to make out a case of obviousness. On the other hand, doing away with the implicit suggestion idea would seem to doom accused infringers to lengthy searches for prior art that says what anyone in the field knows — e.g., that a new type of automobile engine would be enhanced by greater gas mileage. In such cases, it seems quite reasonable for courts to maintain that a reference implicitly calls for further optimization along lines that are well-recognized in the art — i.e., that certain new combinations are obvious even *without* an explicit suggestion that they be pursued. *Cf.* KENNETH J. BURCHFIEL, BIOTECHNOLOGY AND THE FEDERAL CIRCUIT § 6.2 (1995) (criticizing the Federal Circuit's reliance on motivation, and arguing that the seminal *Hotchkiss* case might go the other way under this test).

In one view, the two-part suggestion test simply reiterates the doctrine that "obvious to try" is *not* the proper standard under § 103. The second requirement, a "reasonable expectation of success," mandates that results, and not just approaches, must be predictable to defeat a patent claim. In light of the earlier discussion in Section A.1, "A Note on the Economic Function of § 103," ask yourself whether this makes sense. One issue to think about is the *number* of avenues that might reasonably be tried, and the *cost* of each. If the cost of trying the available research avenues is not too high — either because there are very few of them or because the aggregate cost of exploring them all is low — should we award a patent? Under this approach, what is missing from the opinion in *Vaeck* is a description of how expensive it was for Vaeck *et al.* to find out whether the Bacillus genes would be expressed in cyanobacteria. Should we just assume high cost in an "infant industry" such as biotechnology? For how long?

From *Lamb-Weston, Inc. v. McCain Foods, Ltd.*, 78 F.3d 540, 37 U.S.P.Q.2d
1856 (Fed. Cir. 1996):

[Patentee of lattice-shape, waffle-cut partially fried potato product sued competitor for infringement; infringer counterclaimed for invalidity under § 103.
In January 1980, an independent inventor named Matsler demonstrated his
proprietary potato slicing apparatus to the plaintiff/patentee, Lamb-Weston.
Although 98% of the waffle fry slices were unusable, Lamb-Weston began
negotiations with Mr. Matsler's patent attorney to license the technology.
Instead of contracting with Lamb-Weston, however, Mr. Matsler licensed
his invention to a Lamb-Weston competitor. To demonstrate his invention
to this competitor, Matsler fried some of his potato slices and distributed
them to customers at a local restaurant. In February 1980, Lamb-Weston
received a letter from Mr. Jayne, another inventor, offering to confidentially
disclose *his* waffle fry cutting apparatus. In March 1980, Lamb-Weston
evaluated Mr. Jayne's machine, but found it unacceptable. Lamb-Weston
terminated communications with Mr. Jayne, and began developing its own
machine, starting with a commercial machine for making waffle-style potato
chips and adapting it to make waffle fries. Lamb-Weston started testing its
waffle fries in 1980 and began selling them in late 1983 under the trademark
"CrissCut." In August 1983, Lamb-Weston filed a patent application in the
United States Patent and Trademark Office (PTO) on the waffle-cut potato
product, the slicing apparatus, and the process for making the fries. Lamb-
Weston separated the process claims out of the application; this divisional
application resulted in the '084 patent, the patent in dispute in this case. Although waffle-cut french fried were known in the art, and par-boiling
machines were as well, the '084 patent claims them in combination. The
district court invalidated the patent, however, holding that the Matsler and
Jayne slicing devices provided the motivation for a person of ordinary skill
in the art to combine the known waffle-cut potato chips with the particular
patented process for producing frozen, parfried, and reconstituted waffle
fries. *Lamb-Weston, Inc. v. McCain Foods, Inc.*, 818 F. Supp. 1376, 1390
(E.D. Wash. 1993).]

This court finds it unnecessary to examine the appropriateness of the
Matsler and Jayne slicing devices as prior art, although protected under
nondisclosure agreements, to provide this motivation to combine [see below,
section on 102(f)/103 prior art]. We find it is the potato products resulting
from these slicing devices, and not merely the devices themselves, that
create the motivation to combine. Unlike the slicing apparatus, the potato
products were not subject to confidentiality agreements. In addition to the
prior art cited to the examiner during prosecution, the district court found
that waffle fries were available at restaurants as early as 1935.

The Matsler and Jayne waffle-shaped potato slices themselves were not
subject to nondisclosure agreements. In fact, Matsler and a representative

from J.R. Simplot distributed waffle-shaped potato fries at a Dairy Queen for a test. Jayne sent pictures of waffle-sliced potatoes from his machine to manufacturers, including Lamb-Weston. These disclosures were not secret. Therefore, these disclosures fall within the terms of prior art defined by section 102(a) or section 102(g).

Although the district court should have found the motivation to combine without examining the Matsler and Jayne devices, the district court reached the correct conclusion of obviousness.

Ample prior art suggests a motivation to cook potato products of various shapes using a parfry process. For example, the Strong patent describes a parfry process used on shoe-string french fries. The Matsler and Jayne potato products, however, supplied waffle-shaped potato products of the appropriate thickness for the known parfry process. The motivation to combine arose, therefore, because the size and shape of Matsler and Jayne potato products suggested application of the parfry process to thicker products.

The motivation to parfry the Matsler and Jayne potato products in making the claimed invention derives from (1) the extensive prior art disclosing the desirability of parfrying potato products, and (2) the suitability of the Matsler and Jayne potato products for the parfry process. The evidence of prior use and sale of waffle fries and parfried potato products, in addition to the Matsler and Jayne potato slices, provides sufficient motivation to combine the known waffle-cut shape and the parfry cooking method of the Strong patent. This combination renders the '084 patent obvious.

Affirmed and vacated.

PAULINE NEWMAN, CIRCUIT JUDGE, dissenting.

The panel majority finds "motivation" simply in its observation that raw and fully cooked waffle-cut potatoes existed in the prior art, apparently holding that the mere thickness of these known products as compared with potato chips is the "motivation" that made obvious the invention of a previously unknown product, as described in claims 1 and 4 of the patent in suit. The panel majority holds that this new product would have been obvious, despite the failure of the industry to have produced it, the several years of experimentation and development incurred by Lamb-Weston, and the absence of teaching or suggestion in the prior art as to what to make and how to make it. Lamb-Weston's recognition of the potential of its proposed new product is not the teaching, suggestion, or motivation that precedent requires.... Indeed, the long existence of raw and fully cooked waffle-cut potatoes if anything weighs against the obviousness of producing such a product in partially fried and frozen form. Commercial success, failure of others, and copying, are all evidence of unobviousness, not obviousness. *See Graham* ....

From *In re Beattie*, 974 F.2d 1309, 24 U.S.P.Q.2d 1040 (Fed. Cir. 1992) (Archer, J.):

Beattie's application, entitled "Apparatus and Method for Reading and Playing Music on Keyboard or Stringed Instruments," claims a marker intended to rest on the keys of a piano or other keyboard or fretboard instrument and to facilitate the reading and playing of music. The marker consists of a horizontal and a vertical portion. Displayed on the horizontal portion is the traditional musical notation C D E F G A B corresponding to the seven tones of the diatonic scale played by the white keys that make up an octave on a piano. The vertical portion displays numbers, preferably 0 1 2 3 4 5 6 7 8 9 10 11, and corresponds to the twelve half-tones of the chromatic scale played by the white and black keys that together make up an octave.

United States Patent No. 1,725,844 to Barnes discloses a marker corresponding to a keyboard with a horizontal portion displaying traditional alphabetical notation and a vertical portion displaying that alphabetical notation plus attendant sharps and flats: C; C-Sharp or D-Flat; D; D-Sharp or E-Flat; E; F; F-Sharp or G-Flat; G; G-Sharp or A-Flat; A; A-Sharp or B-Flat; B.

United States Patent No. 566,388 to Eschemann teaches a musical marking system with a lower register displaying the traditional seven letters on the white keys and those letters with attendant sharps and flats on the black keys of the octave and an upper register with a numerical rather than alphabetical notation. Specifically, the traditional letters are represented as numbers one through seven with attendant sharps and flats indicated as those numbers outlined to correspond to the twelve tones of the octave: 1 1 2 2 3 4 4 5 5 6 6 7.

United States Patent No. 608,771 to Guilford discloses a system of musical notation that identifies the series of twelve half-tones of the chromatic scale with numbers 1 2 3 4 5 6 7 8 9 10 11 12. Guilford characterizes alphabetical notation with sharps and flats as "perplexing and irrational."

The board affirmed the examiner's rejection of claims 1 through 7 under 35 U.S.C. § 103 as obvious in view of the combined teachings of Barnes, Eschemann and Guilford. The board concluded that Eschemann taught a marking system displaying a combination of two different notations, viz., alphabetical and numerical, and then determined that it would have been obvious to substitute the 1 2 3 4 5 6 7 8 9 10 11 12 numerical notation of Guilford for the 1 1 2 2 3 4 4 5 5 6 6 7 numerical notation of Eschemann.

The question here is whether the board correctly held that it would have been obvious to one having ordinary skill in the art to combine the references in order to meet the claimed invention. Beattie contends that the board, in arriving at its conclusion of obviousness, did not accord due weight to the notion that Guilford teaches away from the claimed combination and that the declarations of seven music teachers provide convincing evidence of non-obviousness of the invention.

Eschemann displays on the lower register of his marking system the traditional letters alone and those letters with attendant sharps and flats for "those familiar with the ordinary musical notation." On the upper register, Eschemann displays 1 1 2 2 3 4 4 5 5 6 6 7 "for those unfamiliar with the theory of music." Eschemann, then, provides the suggestion to retain traditional alphabetical notation when introducing a new numerical notation.

Guilford teaches the advantages of a dodecatonic twelve tone music theory over the traditional heptatonic seven and twelve tone music theories. Specifically, Guilford discloses the deficiencies of traditional music theory of twelve tones based on a notation system having only seven intervals thus requiring five sharps and flats. He arrives at a "simple and rational" solution by utilizing the uniform series of numbers 1 2 3 4 5 6 7 8 9 10 11 12 instead of the "perplexing and irrational" system of C, C#/Db, D, D#/Eb, E, F, F#/Gb, G, G #/Ab, A, A#/Bb, B. This reference suggests the desirability of implementing a simple numerical alternative to the complex alphabetical music notation.

Armed with a reference teaching the old alphabetical notation on a marking system with a new numerical notation in one hand and a reference teaching a different numerical notation in the other hand, the obviousness of substituting Guilford's numerical twelve tone system for Eschemann's numerical twelve tone system to arrive at Beattie's claimed invention is clearly established.

[T]he absence of a single express teaching of a marker with the two theories combined does not make impossible a sound prima facie case of obviousness. As long as some motivation or suggestion to combine the references is provided by the prior art taken as a whole, the law does not require that the references be combined for the reasons contemplated by the inventor.

CLEVENGER, CIRCUIT JUDGE, dissenting respectfully.

The majority correctly points to nothing in the Eschemann or Barnes references that would provide a suggestion to combine them with Guilford. The majority cannot find such a suggestion in the Eschemann or Barnes markers because both registers of these markers are written in heptatonic notation, i.e., with seven primary tones and five secondary tones. There is no indication in either reference that these markers should or could incorporate the dodecatonic notation disclosed in Guilford. Consequently, if Guilford is to be combined with either Eschemann or Barnes, it is because Guilford provides the requisite suggestion.

Guilford describes traditional pitch notation as "a perplexing and irrational system of sharps, flats, and naturals" such that "the same tone has many different symbols." He finds the traditional five line staff bothersome because it notates, at most, only one and one-third octaves of the more than seven octave musical range.... Guilford more than fails to suggest using the traditional system of notation in combination with his own system of notation as Beattie has done. Rather, Guilford actively rejects the traditional alphabetical notational system and proposes his system as a replacement. In so doing, Guilford removes any basis of finding a suggestion to combine his system of notation with any other system, including the traditional alphabetic system of notation used in the lower portions of both the Eschemann and Barnes markers.

The Board did not examine these unmistakable teachings of Guilford. Instead, it merely asserted that an artisan would have seen the need to merge Guilford with the other prior art. The Board thus committed clear error by misreading the factual content of the prior art.

NOTES

1. *Sharp Test, or Flat?* Notice that the suggestion/motivation test produces deep splits in many cases (*Lamb-Weston, Beattie*). Does that indicate anything about the sufficiency or coherence of the test? Or does it show that, no matter what the doctrinal flavor of the day, obviousness has a subtle bouquet that defies straightforward classifications? How would the issue of "costliness to try" described in the note after *In re Vaeck* change the analysis in *Beattie*?

2. To some extent, the suggestion test seems to track the practice of actual inventors. Consider the following description of the research methodology of Lee de Forest, a towering figure in the early days of radio technology:

> [H]e concentrated on improving wireless detectors, or receivers. "I began," he recalled, "a serious, systemized search through *Science Abstracts, Wiedemann's Annalen, Comptus Rendus*, and other physics journals, seeking to find *some hint or suggestion* that might possibly be a clue to the development of a new device which could be used as a detector for the reception of wireless signals." He probably also scanned the technical journals, such as *Electrical World & Engineer* ....

T. HUGHES, AMERICAN GENESIS: A CENTURY OF INVENTION AND TECHNOLOGICAL ENTHUSIASM 61-62 (1989).

If an inventor, like De Forest, found nothing to suggest a certain combination, it would seem anomalous to call this invention obvious. The Federal Circuit cases say precisely this, for the most part, except where the literature as a whole or the general skill level makes such a suggestion unnecessary. (De Forest, for example, probably only tackled cutting-edge problems.) Given the complexity of the problem, can we assume that if De Forest had found a suggestion to *try* a particular approach, he could have done so for little cost and with a high chance of success?

B. THE OBJECTIVE OR SECONDARY FACTORS

Recall from *Graham, supra*, the Court's statement that "Such secondary considerations as commercial success, long felt but unsolved needs, failure of others, etc., might be utilized to give light to the circumstances surrounding the origin of the subject matter sought to be patented. As indicia of obviousness or nonobviousness, these inquiries may have relevancy." 383 U.S. 1, 17-18. From this brief mention, the "secondary factors," or "objective indicia," as they are often called by the Federal Circuit, have grown in stature to the point where they now occupy a central place in § 103 determinations.

HYBRITECH, INC. v. MONOCLONAL ANTIBODIES, INC.

802 F.2d 1367, 231 U.S.P.Q. 81 (Fed. Cir. 1986),
cert. denied, 480 U.S. 947 (1987)

RICH, CIRCUIT JUDGE.

This appeal is from the decision of the United States District Court for the Northern District of California, in favor of defendant Monoclonal Antibodies, Inc. (Monoclonal) holding that all 29 claims of plaintiff's patent No. 4,376,110 entitled "Immunometric Assays Using Monoclonal Antibodies" ('110 patent), issued to Dr. Gary S. David and Howard E. Greene and assigned to Hybritech Incorporated (Hybritech), are invalid for obviousness under § 103. We reverse and remand.

Background

Vertebrates defend themselves against invasion by microorganisms by producing antibodies, proteins which can complex with the invading microorganisms and target them for destruction or removal. In fact, any foreign molecule of sufficient size can act as a stimulus for antibody production. Such foreign molecules, or antigens, bear particular sites or epitopes that represent antibody recognition sites. B cell lymphocytes, the cells that actually produce antibodies, recognize and respond to an epitope on an antigen by reproducing or cloning themselves and then producing antibodies specific to that epitope. Even if the antigen is highly purified, the lymphocytes will produce antibodies specific to different epitopes on the antigen and so produce antibodies with different specificities. Furthermore, because the body is exposed to many different antigens, the blood of a vertebrate will contain antibodies to many different antigenic substances.

Scientists and clinicians have long employed the ability of antibodies to recognize and complex with antigens as a tool to identify or label particular cells or molecules and to separate them from a mixture. Their source of antibodies has been primarily the serum separated from the blood of a vertebrate immunized or exposed to the antigen. Serum, however, contains a mixture of antibodies directed to numerous antigens and to any number of epitopes on a particular antigen.

Because such a mixture of antibodies arises from many different clones of lymph-ocytes, it is called "polyclonal."

Recent technological advances have made it possible to isolate and cultivate a single clone of lymphocytes to obtain a virtually unlimited supply of antibodies specific to one particular epitope. These antibodies, known as "monoclonal antibodies" because they arise from a single clone of lymphocytes, are produced by a relatively new technology known as the hybridoma. Hybridomas are produced by fusing a particular cancer cell, the myeloma cell, with spleen cells from a mouse that has been injected or immunized with the antigen. These fusions are isolated by transferring them to a growth fluid that kills off the unfused cancer cells, the unfused spleen cells dying off by themselves. The fused hybrid spleen and myeloma cells, called hybridomas, produce antibodies to the antigen initially injected into the mouse. The growth fluid containing the hybrid-omas is then diluted and put into individual test tubes or wells so that there is only one hybridoma per tube or well. Each hybridoma then reproduces itself and these identical hybridomas each produce identical monoclonal antibodies having the same affinity and specificity. In this way, a virtually unlimited supply of identical antibodies is created, directed to only one epitope on an antigen rather than, as with polyclonal antibodies, to many different epitopes on many different antigens.

In addition to the specificity of antibodies to particular epitopes discussed above, antibodies also have a characteristic "sensitivity," the ability to detect and react to antigens. Sensitivity is expressed in terms of "affinity": the greater an antibody's ability to bind with a particular antigen, the greater the antibody's affinity. The strength of that antibody-antigen bond is in part dependent upon the antibody's "affinity constant," expressed in liters per mole, for the antigen.

Immunoassays, the subject matter of the '110 patent, are diagnostic methods for determining the presence or amount of antigen in body fluids such as blood or urine by employing the ability of an antibody to recognize and bind to an antigen. Generally, the extent to which the antibody binds to the antigen to be quantitated is an indication of the amount of antigen present in the fluid. Label-ling the antibody or, in some cases, the antigen, with either a radioactive sub-stance, I^{125}, or an enzyme makes possible the detection of the antibody-antigen complex. In an extreme case, where the fluid sample contains a very low level of the antigen, binding might not occur unless the antibodies selected or "screen-ed" for the procedure are highly sensitive.

In the case of a "competitive" immunoassay, a labelled antigen reagent is bound to a limited and known quantity of antibody reagent. After that reaction reaches equilibrium, the antigen to be detected is added to the mixture and competes with the labelled antigen for the limited number of antibody binding sites. The amount of labelled antigen reagent displaced, if any, in this second reaction indicates the quantity of the antigen to be detected present in the fluid sample. All of the antigen attached to the antibody will be labelled antigen if there is no antigen in the test fluid sample. The advantage of this method is that only a small amount of antibody is needed, its drawback, generally, that the system must reach equilibrium, and thus produces results slowly.

In the case of a "sandwich" assay, otherwise known as an immunometric assay, a quantity of unlabelled antibody reagent is bound to a solid support surface such as the inside wall of a test tube containing a complex of the fluid sample containing the antigen to be detected and a labelled antibody reagent. The result is an insoluble three part complex referred to as a sandwich having antibody bread and antigen filling.

The advantage of the sandwich assay is that it is fast and simple, its drawback that enormous quantities of antibodies are needed.

Hybritech

Hybritech, started in 1978 and joined thereafter by coinventors Green and Dr. David, has, since 1979, been in the business of developing diagnostic kits employing monoclonal antibodies that detect numerous antigens and thus a broad range of conditions such as pregnancy, cancer, growth hormone deficiency, or hepatitis. Examples of antigens include influenza viruses, immunoglobulin E (IgE) which indicates allergic reaction, human chorionic gonadotropin (HCG) which indicates pregnancy, and prostatic acid phosphatase (PAP) which indicates prostate cancer, to name a few. Dr. Adams, a business-experienced scientist, joined the company in May 1980 as head of research and development. The '110 patent, application for which was filed August 4, 1980, issued March 8, 1983, with claims defining a variety of sandwich assays using monoclonal antibodies. Claim 19, apparently the broadest of the twenty-nine in the patent, is directed generally to a sandwich assay.[1]

Hybritech sued Monoclonal for damages and an injunction alleging that the manufacture and sale of Monoclonal's diagnostic kits infringed the '110 patent.

The district court held that the claimed subject matter of the '110 patent was neither conceived nor actually reduced to practice before May 1980, and was anticipated under § 102(g) by the actual reduction to practice of the invention by Drs. Uotila and Ruoslahti at the La Jolla Cancer Research Foundation (LJCRF) as early as November of 1979 and by the actual reduction to practice of the invention by Drs. Oi and Herzenberg (Oi/Herzenberg work) at the Stanford

---

[1] Claim 19 Reads:

19. In an immunometric assay to determine the presence or concentration of an antigenic substance in a sample of a fluid comprising forming a ternary complex of a first labelled antibody, said antigenic substance, and a second antibody said second antibody being bound to a solid carrier insoluble in said fluid wherein the presence of the antigenic substance in the samples is determined by measuring either the amount of labelled antibody bound to the solid carrier or the amount of unreacted labelled antibody, the improvement comprising employing monoclonal antibodies having an affinity for the antigenic substance of at least about 10^8 liters/mole for each of said labelled antibody and said antibody bound to a solid carrier.

University Laboratory as early as July 1978, later published in December of 1979.

The district court also held the claims of the '110 patent invalid for obviousness from the Oi/Herzenberg work in view of (1) a February 1979 article by M.E. Frankel and W. Gerhard (Frankel article) which discloses high-affinity monoclonal antibodies, and apparently in view of numerous other references including: (2) the work of Nobel Prize winners G. Kohler and C. Milstein disclosing a Nobel Prize-worthy method for producing monoclonal antibodies in vitro (outside the body) published in an August 7, 1975, article; (3) U.S. Patent No. 4,244,940 issued to Jeong et al. disclosing a simultaneous polyclonal assay (Jeong), U.S. Patent No. 4,098,876 to Piasio et al. disclosing a reverse polyclonal sandwich assay (Piasio), U.S. Patent No. 4,016,143 to Schurrs et al. disclosing a forward polyclonal sandwich assay (Schurrs); (4) a July 1979 publication by A.C. Cuello et al. disclosing the use of monoclonal antibodies in competitive assays; and (5) eight articles dated between January 1979 and March 6, 1980, "predicting" that monoclonal antibodies would be used in future immunoassays.

A. *The References*

1. *Kohler and Milstein's Nobel Prize-Winning Work: Producing Monoclonal Antibodies In Vitro for the First Time*

In early immunoassay work, polyclonal antibodies produced in vivo (in the body) in mice were used to bind with the antigen to be detected in the body fluid sample. Mice were immunized by injection with antigen so that the lymphocytes in their bodies produced antibodies that attacked the injected antigen. Those polyclonal antibodies were withdrawn from the animal's blood and used in immunoassays. The major problem was that when the mice's immune systems changed or the mice died, the antibodies changed or died too; supply was limited and uncertain.

As the examiner was aware, Kohler and Milstein developed a technique not only for producing antibodies in vitro, independent of a living body, thus eliminating dependence on a particular animal, but for in vitro production of monoclonal antibodies by hybridomas, discussed in the Background section, *supra*.

Given that sandwich assays require enormous amounts of antibodies, companies like appellant and appellee, which utilize monoclonal antibodies for sandwich assays, would not be in business were it not for the work of Kohler and Milstein.

3. *The Work of Drs. Oi and Herzenberg at the Stanford University Laboratory in 1978 Published in December 1979*

Drs. Oi and Herzenberg used monoclonal antibodies to "map" epitopes or determine the number and location of different antibody binding sites on a known quantity of IgE antigen by attaching to it an antibody bound to a carrier and exposing that antigen to other monoclonal antibodies. The antibodies either attached to epitopes on the antigen or were blocked from doing so by the other monoclonal antibodies, depending on the location and number of epitopes; if the epitopes on the antigen were too close together and the number of antibodies too great, few antibodies would bind to the antigen. Hybritech points out that both Dr. Herzenberg and Dr. Oi testified that their work did not involve determining the presence or quantity of antigen, that they had no idea what the affinities of the monoclonal antibodies used were, and that those values were never calculated.

One unsigned, unwitnessed page from three large laboratory notebooks, which Hybritech argues is insufficient because it does not identify the chemical reagents or protocol used, was relied on by Monoclonal to establish actual reduction to practice of the Oi/Herzenberg work in 1978 to establish a case of § 102(g) prior invention by another. The district court agreed with Monoclonal that the Oi/Herzenberg work anticipated the claimed invention and, in addition, combined this work with the Frankel publication to hold that the claimed subject matter was obvious under § 103.

5. *The Cuello Article and the Jeong, Piasio, and Schurr Patents Considered by the Examiner*

Cuello, dated July 1979, states that it describes the usefulness of monoclonal antibodies in the characterization and localization of neurotransmitters such as Substance P, a peptide clearly associated with the transmission of primary sensory information in the spinal cord. The article discloses producing monoclonal antibodies from hybrid myelomas (hybridomas), their use in conventional radioimmunoassay techniques, and the benefits from doing so which flow from the ability to derive permanent cell lines capable of continuous production of highly specific antibodies.

The district court found that the examiner twice rejected all of the claims of the '110 patent based on Cuello alone or in combination with the Jeong, Piasio, and Schurr references which disclose various sandwich assays using polyclonal antibodies. The court also found that the examiner allowed the claims after they were amended to include the 10^8 affinity limitation and after Richard Bartholomew, a Hybritech employee, submitted an affidavit alleging the advantages of using monoclonal rather than polyclonal antibodies in sandwich assays.

Apparently based on the testimony of Monoclonal's expert witness Judith Blakemore, a named inventor of the Jeong patent, the district court stated that the "reasons for allowance were not well-founded because (1) the alleged advantages were expected as naturally flowing from the well-known natural characteristics of monoclonal antibodies ...; (2) ... were not significant ...; or (3) were at best minor," although they were "argued to the examiner as if they were" important. These were Monoclonal's words from its pretrial submission adopted by the court.

OPINION

Notwithstanding that the introduction of prior art not before the examiner may facilitate the challenger's meeting the burden of proof on invalidity, the presumption [of validity under § 282] remains intact and on the challenger throughout the litigation, and the clear and convincing standard does not change.

[After concluding that the district court's finding of anticipation was not supported by the evidence, the court moved on to the question of obviousness.]

IV. *Obviousness, 35 U.S.C. § 103*

A section 103 obviousness determination — whether the claimed invention would have been (not "would be" as the court repeatedly stated because Monoclonal's pretrial papers used that improper language) obvious at the time the invention was made is reviewed free of the clearly erroneous standard although the underlying factual inquiries — scope and content of the prior art, level of ordinary skill in the art, and differences between the prior art and the claimed invention — integral parts of the subjective determination involved in § 103, are reviewed under that standard. Objective evidence such as commercial success, failure of others, long-felt need, and unexpected results must be considered before a conclusion on obviousness is reached and is not merely "icing on the cake," as the district court stated at trial.

1. *The Eight Articles "Predicting" Widespread Use of Monoclonal Antibodies*

Before discussing the more pertinent references in this case — the Oi/Herzenberg and Frankel works — we cull the other prior art references relied on by the trial court.

First, the latest four of the eight articles that the court stated were of the "utmost importance" because they "predicted" that the breakthrough in production of monoclonal antibodies by Kohler and Milstein would lead to widespread use of monoclonal antibodies in immunoassays are neither 102(a)/103 nor 102(b)/103 prior art because they are dated between late 1979 and March 6, 1980, well after the date of conception and within one year of the filing date of the '110 patent.

The earliest four of the eight articles, on the other hand, although clearly prior art, discuss production of monoclonal antibodies — admittedly old after Kohler and Milstein showed how to produce them — but none discloses sandwich assays. At most, these articles are invitations to try monoclonal antibodies in immunoassays but do not suggest how that end might be accomplished. To the extent the district court relied upon these references to establish that it would have been obvious to try monoclonal antibodies of 10^8 liters/mole affinity in a sandwich immunoassay that detects the presence of or quantitates antigen, the court was in error. See *Jones v. Hardy*, 727 F.2d 1524, 1530, 220 U.S.P.Q. 1021, 1026 (Fed.

Cir. 1984) ("Obvious to try" is improper consideration in adjudicating obviousness issue).[2]

2. *The Kohler and Milstein Work, the Cuello Article and the Jeong, Piasio, and Schurr Patents Considered by the Examiner*

The district court's finding that Kohler and Milstein developed a method for producing monoclonal antibodies in vitro is correct, but that finding proves no more; although it made possible all later work in that it paved the way for a supply of monoclonal antibodies, it indisputably does not suggest using monoclonal antibodies in a sandwich assay in accordance with the invention claimed in the '110 patent.

The Cuello reference discloses monoclonal antibodies but not in a sandwich assay. The competitive assay in Cuello, moreover, uses only one monoclonal antibody and thus in no way suggests the claimed invention wherein a ternary complex of two monoclonal antibodies and an antigen form a sandwich. Furthermore, the court did not explain how this art, by itself or in combination with any of the other art, suggests the claimed subject matter and thus why that combination would have been obvious. We are of the opinion that it does not.

The district court correctly found that the use of polyclonal antibodies in sandwich assays was well known. The Jeong patent discloses the use of polyclonal antibodies in a simultaneous sandwich assay, with no suggestion that monoclonal antibodies be so used. It is prior art by virtue of § 102(e), application for the patent having been filed September 5, 1978, its effective date as a reference. The Piasio patent, disclosing a reverse sandwich assay using polyclonal antibodies, and Schurrs, disclosing a forward sandwich assay using the same, both § 102(a) prior art, are likewise devoid of any suggestion that monoclonal antibodies can be used in a similar fashion.

3. *The Oi/Herzenberg Work and the Frankel Article*

Clearly, the most pertinent items of prior art not cited by the examiner are the Oi/Herzenberg work, as described *supra*, and the Frankel article. [T]he Oi/Herzenberg work involved mapping epitopes on a known quantity of antigen [, i.e., determining the surface structure of an antigen]. It was not concerned with and does not disclose using monoclonal antibodies of at least 10^8 liters/mole affinity. Oi and Herzenberg testified that they did not know the affinity of the antibodies

---

[2] Finding 10 [in the trial court's opinion], which states that the invention was contemporaneously developed and disclosed in at least five publications and patent applications not listed above and dated well after the filing date of the '110 patent but before its issuance is irrelevant for purposes of the hypothesis based on the three factual inquiries required by § 103. [S]imultaneous development may or may not be indicative of obviousness, the latter being the case here for the above reasons and because the other evidence of nonobviousness is adequate, such occurrences having been provided for in 35 U.S.C. § 135 [on interferences].

used, and [an expert] testified that nowhere in that work is there mention of monoclonal antibody affinity of at least 10^8 liters/mole. On this basis, we conclude that the Oi/Herzenberg work is qualitatively different than the claimed invention; the former is directed to mapping epitopes on a known quantity of antigen and the latter to determining the "presence or concentration of an antigenic substance in a sample of fluid...." We disagree with Monoclonal that these are "essentially the same thing." Furthermore, it is perfectly clear that this work in no way suggests using monoclonal antibodies of the affinity claimed in the '110 patent. It is because of these differences between the Oi/Herzenberg work and the claimed invention that the fact that an antigen was sandwiched between two monoclonal antibodies in the course of Oi's and Herzenberg's work is not sufficient basis to conclude that the claimed invention would have been obvious at the time it was made to a person of ordinary skill in the art.

Likewise, a conclusion that the invention would have been obvious cannot properly be reached when the Oi/Herzenberg work is considered in view of the Frankel article. Frankel teaches a method for rapid determination of affinity constants for monoclonal antibodies, some of which clearly have affinities of the order defined by the claims, but does not in any way suggest using two of those antibodies in a sandwich to assay an antigen by forming a ternary complex of labelled antibody, the antigenic substance, and a bound antibody wherein the presence of the antigenic substance is determined by measuring either the amount of labelled antibody bound to a solid carrier or the amount of unreacted labelled antibody. The mere existence of prior art disclosing how to measure the affinity of high affinity monoclonal antibodies is insufficient to support a holding of obviousness. Hybritech's claims define a process that employs monoclonal antibodies, and does not merely claim antibodies of high affinity. In view of the fact that the Oi/Herzenberg work is not directed to an assay as claimed and does not disclose antibodies of at least 10^8 liters/mole affinity, and further that Frankel fails to suggest using such antibodies in a sandwich assay, the Frankel article does not compensate for the substantial difference between the Oi/Herzenberg work and the claimed subject matter, and therefore those references in combination cannot support a holding of obviousness.

4. Objective Evidence of Nonobviousness

In one part of its opinion the court found that "the commercial success of the kits may well be attributed to the business expertise and acumen of the plaintiff's personnel, together with its capital base and marketing abilities" and later that "[w]here commercial success is based on the sudden availability of starting materials, in this instance the availability of monoclonal antibodies as a result of the Kohler and Milstein discovery, business acumen, marketing ability, and capital sources, no causal relationship is proven." (Citation omitted.)

i. *Commercial Success: Hybritech's Diagnostic Kits Grabbed a Substantial Market Share*

The undisputed evidence is that Hybritech's diagnostic kits had a substantial market impact. The first diagnostic kit sales occurring in mid-1981, sales increased seven million dollars in just over one year, from $6.9 million in 1983 to an estimated $14.5 million in 1984; sales in 1980 were nonexistent. Competing with products from industry giants such as Abbott Labs, Hoffman LaRoche, Becton-Dickinson, and Baxter-Travenol, Hybritech's HCG kit became the market leader with roughly twenty-five percent of the market at the expense of market shares of the other companies. Its PAP kit ranks second only to a product sold by Dupont's New England Nuclear, surpassing products from Baxter-Travenol, Abbott, and others. Hybritech's other kits, indisputably embodying the invention claimed in the '110 patent, obtained similar substantial market positions.

Although the district court did not provide its insights into why commercial success was due to business acumen and not to the merits of the claimed invention, Monoclonal urges in support that it was due to Hybritech's spending disproportionate sums on marketing, 25-30% of income. The undisputed evidence was that expenditures of mature companies in this field are between 17 and 32%. Furthermore, the record shows that advertising makes those in the industry — hospitals, doctors, and clinical laboratories — aware of the diagnostic kits but does not make these potential users buy them; the products have to work, and there is no evidence that that is not the case here or that the success was not due to the merits of the claimed sandwich assays — clearly contrary to the district court's finding.

The trial court's finding that the "sudden availability of monoclonals" was the reason for the commercial success of Hybritech's diagnostic kits is unsupported by the record and clearly erroneous. Monoclonal admits that monoclonal antibodies were available in the United States in 1978, and the evidence clearly reflects that. Thus, at least three years passed between the time monoclonal antibodies were available in adequate supply and the time Hybritech began selling its kits. Especially in the fast-moving biotechnology field, as the evidence shows, that is anything but sudden availability.

ii. *Unexpected Advantages*

Hybritech points to the testimony of three witnesses skilled in the diagnostic field who state that, based on tests done in their laboratories as a result of real-world comparisons in the normal course of research, the diagnostic kits that embody the '110 invention unexpectedly solved longstanding problems. Dr. Hussa, the head of a large referral laboratory and a world-wide consultant, testified that until Hybritech introduced its kits, he and others were very skeptical and had almost exclusively used competitive assays with a radioactive tracer (RIAs). In relation to an HCG Hybritech kit, he testified that he had first thought that the Hybritech HCG kit would not give accurate results for low antigen concentrations because that condition is indicated in the Hybritech kit by a low radioactivity reading, a reading difficult to differentiate from control samples containing no antigen. He also stated that in the past, RIA kits falsely detected HCG in nonpregnant women, a condition which would indicate cancer and surgery. He stated that when he employed the Hybritech HCG kit in such instances it demonstrated, correctly and absent any difficulty interpreting the data, that no HCG was present.

Having considered the evidence of nonobviousness required by § 103 and *Graham* [*v. John Deere*], we hold, as a matter of law, that the claimed subject matter of the '110 patent would not have been obvious to one of ordinary skill in the art at the time the invention was made and therefore reverse the court's judgment to the contrary. The large number of references, as a whole, relied upon by the district court to show obviousness, about twenty in number, skirt all around but do not as a whole suggest the claimed invention, which they must, to overcome the presumed validity. Focusing on the obviousness of substitutions and differences instead of on the invention as a whole, as the district court did in frequently describing the claimed invention as the mere substitution of monoclonal for polyclonal antibodies in a sandwich assay, was a legally improper way to simplify the difficult determination of obviousness.

With respect to the objective indicia of nonobviousness, while there is evidence that marketing and financing played a role in the success of Hybritech's kits, as they do with any product, it is clear to us on the entire record that the commercial success here was due to the merits of the claimed invention. It cannot be argued on this record that Hybritech's success would have been as great and as prolonged as admittedly it has been if that success were not due to the merits of the invention. The evidence is that these kits compete successfully with numerous others for the trust of persons who have to make fast, accurate, and safe diagnoses. This is not the kind of merchandise that can be sold by advertising hyperbole.

[In the final part of its opinion, the court rejects appellee's assertion that the patentee had not provided an enabling disclosure for its claims.]

CONCLUSION

The judgment of the district court holding the patent in suit invalid is reversed in all respects, and the case is remanded for a determination of the issue of infringement which the court held was moot.

NOTES

1. *Skilled in the Art.* In comparing the inventions at issue in *Graham* and the preceding case, it is apparent that they spring from quite different fields. *See* Note, *Hybritech, Inc. v. Monoclonal Antibodies, Inc.: Are Courts Promoting Progress in Rapidly Expanding Scientific Fields?*, 5 GA. ST. U. L. REV. 639 (1989) (noting complex nature of technology, and suggesting alternative system for protection of such inventions). How then does the law purport to apply a single standard of patent validity under § 103? One way the courts and Patent Office can take account of these differences is via the statutory element providing that nonobviousness is to be judged from the perspective of "one skilled in the art." In *Environmental Designs, Ltd. v. Union Oil Co.*, 713 F.2d 693, 696, 218 U.S.P.Q. (BNA) 865, 868 (Fed. Cir. 1983), *cert. denied*, 464 U.S. 1043 (1984), the court provided a list of factors relevant to a determination of the level of skill in the art:

(1) educational level of the inventor;
(2) type of problems encountered in the art;
(3) prior art solutions to the problems;
(4) rapidity with which innovations are made;
(5) sophistication of the technology; and
(6) educational level of active workers in the field.

These factors can be used to implicitly adjust the standard of nonobviousness. But flexibility regarding what contitutes skill contrasts with the treatment of another essential element from § 103 and *Graham*: the "scope and content of the prior art." No adjustments are made in this regard; the skilled artisan of § 103 is expected to know *everything* that is within the prior art. *See In re GPAC, Inc.*, 57 F.3d 1573, 35 U.S.P.Q.2d 1116 (Fed. Cir. 1995); Section C.1, below.

2. *Nonobviousness: Analysis or Conclusion?* Sometimes it seems as though the very idea of a uniform "standard" under § 103 is misleading. In reading cases on nonobviousness, one can get the impression that the legal decisionmaker simply arrived at a conclusion and added the rationale later. It is certainly true, as Learned Hand put it, that

> [T]here will remain cases where we can only fall back upon such good sense as we may have.... There comes a point when the question must be resolved by a subjective opinion as to what seems an easy step and what does not. We must try to correct our standard by such objective references as we can, but in the end the judgment will appear, and no doubt be, to a large extent personal, and in that sense arbitrary.

Kirsch Mfg. Co. v. Gould Mersereau Co., 6 F.2d 793, 794 (2d Cir. 1925).

For further illustration of how slippery this issue can be, consider the following comments from a dissenting opinion by Judge Rich, author of the *Hybritech* opinion.

> I am constrained to dissent from the majority's holding that the six claims in suit are not invalid for obviousness in view of the prior art under 35 U.S.C. § 103.
>
> The majority opinion, after obviously careful consideration of the facts, preliminarily arrives at the conclusion that the claims in suit define only obvious subject matter and then reverses that conclusion because of the

"secondary considerations," which I shall discuss further, concluding that "this is one of those cases where the evidence of secondary considerations 'may ... establish that an invention appearing to have been obvious in light of the prior art is not.' *Stratoflex* [*Inc. v. Aeroquip Corp.*], 713 F.2d at 1538 [218 U.S.P.Q. 871, 879 (Fed. Cir. 1983)]." This is my point of disagreement. This is not one of these cases because, also per *Stratoflex*, a nexus is required between the invention disclosed in plaintiff's patent and the secondary considerations. No such nexus exists here.

The majority, like the trial judge, has been led astray and has assumed that the patent in suit is on some imaginary "system" for detecting flaws, which has enjoyed commercial success in the hands of Alco and was copied by Westinghouse, thus changing the prima facie obvious invention into a patentable invention.

As the prosecution history shows, by a series of amendments the claims acquired a kind of life of their own, divorced from the disclosure of the patent's specification.... Unsupported claim limitations should be ignored in appraising commercial success....

Long prior to [the] supposed invention [at issue here], the ultrasonic detection of flaws in metal parts was a highly developed and sophisticated art. [The] filing date was Dec. 3, 1973. Over ten years before that, Gunkel taught the use of multiple transducers operating simultaneously, longitudinally of and around tubular articles such as pipe, but on the outside, to detect flaws with use of electrical analysis means to combine and correlate the data produced by the transducers and their related pickups, to detect and appraise the nature of flaws. Gunkel proposed using as many as four transducers generating as many different modes of signals to get as many different kinds of data. The Nimrod disclosure shows the use of ultrasonic testing conducted from the inside of a bore of a shaft, as in the '006 patent, through which the transducers are moved longitudinally and angularly rotated.

I reiterate that the only commercial success of the system relied on below is that company's testing of a total of, perhaps, 100 rotors. That testing was necessarily done by using the system, not merely the device shown in the patent, which in itself cannot test anything. There is no showing that the tests were accurate and there is considerable evidence that they may not have been. All we know is that [the patentee] was hired to do them because their customers considered them competent. To my mind, that is no proof that [its] success in getting that much testing business was due to the invention disclosed in Smith's patent. All it can do is position transducers in a bore and tell you where they are. That had been done in the prior art. One always has to know where the transducers are or it is impossible to determine where the flaws, if any, are. The accuracy with which it does so depends entirely on the refinement of the machining by which the locator is manufactured. The Nimrod boresonic device was said to be just as accurate, if not more so. All the rest — the interpretation of the signals to acquire some intelligence and the apparatus and instrumentation essential thereto — was the common knowledge of the ultrasonic nondestructive testing art....

Alco Standard Corp. v. Tennessee Valley Auth., 808 F.2d 1490, 1504-11, 1 U.S.P.Q.2d 1337 (Fed. Cir. 1986).

After comparing the majority opinion in *Hybritech* and the dissent just excerpted — both written by the eminent Judge Rich — you will perhaps understand why nonobviousness can be so unpredictable. But if you find yourself "at sea" while reading cases in this area, do not lose sight of the fact that there is an underlying rationale for the entire § 103 inquiry — the notion that not all novel inventions (under § 102) deserve patent protection. For attempts to construct theories about why this goal is worthwhile, see the excerpt at the beginning of this chapter. *See also* F. SCHERER, INDUSTRIAL MARKET STRUCTURE AND ECONOMIC PERFORMANCE 440 (2d ed. 1980) (describing the ideal patent system as one which rewards *only* "patent-induced" inventions, i.e., those that would have gone undiscovered but for the reward of a patent). *Cf.* J. MOKYR, THE LEVER OF RICHES: TECHNOLOGICAL CREATIVITY AND ECONOMIC PROGRESS 252 (1990) (patent system justified by high-value, low probability innovations — when "a crackpot hits the jackpot").

3. *Fact or Law?* A long-simmering debate centers on whether nonobviousness is a question of law or fact. *See, e.g.*, Note, *Nonobviousness in Patent Law: A Question of Law or Fact*, 18 WM. & MARY L. REV. 612 (1977) (arguing that nonobviousness should be a pure fact question). The Federal Circuit's law and fact analysis has been justified on the grounds that it allows quick resolution of patent validity without necessitating that cases be remanded to the trial court, Note, *Panduit Corp. v. Denison Mfg. Co.: De Novo Review and the Federal Circuit's Application of the Clearly Erroneous Standard*, 36 AM. U. L. REV. 963 (1987), and that the court is more expert in patent law than trial courts, and thus should be permitted to resolve "mixed" questions of law and fact, to fulfill its statutory mandate of stabilizing patent law. *Cf.* Dreyfuss, *The Federal Circuit: A Case Study in Specialized Courts*, 64 N.Y.U. L. REV. 1 (1989).

The Federal Circuit has resolved the question by deciding that although nonobviousness is predicated on certain factual findings (i.e., the "four factors" introduced in the previous note), the ultimate legal conclusion of obviousness is scrutinized as a matter of law, *Panduit Corp. v. Dennison Mfg. Co.*, 810 F.2d 1561, 1568, 1 U.S.P.Q.2d 1593, 1597 (Fed. Cir.), *cert. denied*, 107 S. Ct. 2187 (1987). The Supreme Court has made clear, however, that although the fact/law distinction may appear somewhat arbitrary in this context, Rule 52 of the Federal Rules of Civil Procedure requires the Federal Circuit to clarify whether it is overturning a factual finding that is "clearly erroneous," or simply reversing a legal conclusion. *See Dennison Mfg. Co. v. Panduit Corp.*, 475 U.S. 809, 106 S. Ct. 1578 (1986), *vacating and remanding*, 774 F.2d 1082, 227 U.S.P.Q. (BNA) 337 (Fed. Cir. 1985). This was the first time the Supreme Court passed on a (quasi-) substantive issue in patent law since the Federal Circuit's formation in 1982 — in fact, since 1980, when it decided *Diamond v. Chakrabarty*, 447 U.S. 303 (1980). As mentioned, the Federal Circuit has now clarified that nonobviousness issues are matters of law, subject only to the lower standard used to review the legal conclusions of the district courts.

A Subtle — But Significant? — Shift Since Graham. In *Graham*, you may recall, the Supreme Court stated that the "secondary factors" of commercial success, long felt need, etc., "may have relevancy." 383 U.S. at 18. The Federal Circuit, by contrast, routinely speaks of these factors — under the rubric "object-ive evidence" — as a *required* fourth element in the § 103 analysis. *See, e.g., Greenwood v. Haitori Seiko Co.*, 900 F.2d 238, 241, 14 U.S.P.Q.2d 1474 (Fed. Cir. 1990):

> [C]ertain factual predicates are required before the legal conclusion of obviousness or nonobviousness can be reached.... The underlying factual determinations to be made are (1) the scope and content of the prior art, (2) the differences between the claimed invention and the prior art, (3) the level of ordinary skill in the art, and (4) objective evidence of non-obviousness, such as commercial success, long-felt but unsolved need, failure of others, copying, and unexpected results. *Graham v. John Deere Co.*, ... *Perkin-Elmer Corp.* [*v. Computervision Corp.*], 732 F.2d 888, 894, 221 U.S.P.Q. [(BNA) 669 (Fed. Cir.)] at 674[, *cert. denied*, 105 S. Ct. 187 (1984)].

The district courts are following this analysis, as would be expected. *See, e.g., Micro Motion, Inc. v. Exac Corp.*, 16 U.S.P.Q.2d (BNA) 1001, 1007-08 (N.D. Cal. 1990) (relying on "objective criteria" to find nonobviousness); *Joy Techs., Inc. v. Quigg*, 732 F. Supp. 227, 14 U.S.P.Q.2d (BNA) 1432 (D.D.C. 1990) (denying Patent Office's motion for summary judgment on obviousness grounds, due to applicant/plaintiff's evidence of secondary considerations).

The following excerpts from articles by Dreyfuss and Merges explore the significance of this shift.

1. SECONDARY FACTORS AND PREDICTABLE CASELAW

ROCHELLE DREYFUSS, THE FEDERAL CIRCUIT: A CASE STUDY IN SPECIALIZED COURTS, 64 N.Y.U. L. Rev. 1 (1989)*

Th[e] use of secondary considerations is not new to the CAFC. Rather, these considerations were previously accorded little weight because their appearance can sometimes be attributed to factors other than nonobviousness. For instance, commercial success may be due to the dominant market position of the patentee before the introduction of the new invention; the sudden ability to meet long felt

---

need could derive from other technological advances, unrelated to the inventor's contribution; acquiescence may be attributed to the relative cost of obtaining a license, as opposed to challenging the patent. Rather than reject these considerations entirely, the CAFC has recognized their importance in making the law precise and instead has sought to minimize the extent to which they can be misused. Thus, the court has elaborated a "nexus" requirement, which requires that before secondary considerations can be used to demonstrate nonobviousness, a showing must be made that their appearance is attributable to the inventive characteristics of the discovery as claimed in the patent. Secondary considerations do not constitute a complete answer to the problem posed by obviousness. It is, for instance, possible for a nonobvious invention to fail to present secondary considerations. Nonetheless, it is now less probable that a lower court will declare invalid the patent on an invention that, because of the insight of its inventor, met long felt need, enjoyed commercial success, or displayed other objective indicia of having made an important social contribution. Since it is likely that the inconsistent treatment of such inventions was the most destablizing element of the system, the CAFC has, in this area, made strides in achieving the appearance of precision.

....

The previous section discussed the Federal Circuit's accomplishments in developing a uniform, predictable law, without regard to the actual correctness of the results. Although precision is itself a goal worth attaining, especially for intercircuit actors such as technology consumers and producers, the court will not have fully achieved congressional goals unless it also develops accurate law. To measure the accuracy of the CAFC's opinions, I have tried to evaluate the extent to which the court has formulated rules that reflect sensitivity to the needs of the technology industry. I have also looked at the degree to which the court has attempted to advance what it regards as national policy.

1. Sensitivity to the Imperatives of Invention

An important factor in developing a patent law that accurately responds to the national goal of encouraging technological advances and inventiveness is an understanding of the dynamics of innovation. In many respects, the CAFC has displayed an exceptional appreciation of the fundamentals of technological development and has skillfully used its insights in structuring decisions.

The CAFC's tests for obviousness furnish excellent illustrations. As described previously, the regional courts had developed a subjective test for obviousness that led to imprecise results. Matters were, however, further complicated by decisions that required courts to apply special rules when the invention was considered a "combination" of known elements.

The CAFC has correctly diagnosed the problem. It has recognized that the regional courts had been given an impossible task, for virtually all inventions involve the combination of known elements. Some inventions are straightforward applications of previous technology while others are more complex. For example, the "Dairy Establishment" patent at issue in *Sakraida v. Ag Pro, Inc.* can clearly be analyzed as combining an inclined slope, water, and height to create an effective manure flusher. In other combinations, however, the ordinary observer will have difficulty discerning the elements involved. For example, the motion picture projector and the lightbulb do not appear to be combinations, yet Thomas Edison's papers reveal that he invented motion pictures by redesigning the phonograph and derived the lightbulb from the telegraph.

Armed with this intuition, the CAFC has realized that the law on combinations was misdirected. It is impossible to articulate a test to decide which patents call for special rules when every invention is, essentially, a combination.

The court's insight into inventiveness has enabled it to refine the test for obviousness in other important ways. First, realizing that creative inventors reason from previous developments, the CAFC now understands that prior art may actually lead inventors away from the invention; previous misunderstandings may make what would otherwise be a rather obvious invention, nonobvious. The court has directed lower courts, when reviewing prior art, to consider whether the inventor made his contribution by defying conventional wisdom.

Second, despite its general enthusiasm for secondary considerations, the court has rejected one objective criterion, that of simultaneous invention. Without an understanding of how invention takes place, a court might conclude that simultaneous development of an invention by several inventors proves its obviousness. Once the dynamics of invention are properly understood, however, it is easier to see that simultaneous, but nonobvious, inventions are perfectly possible. Inspiration in one field may depend heavily on knowledge uncovered elsewhere. Once an important advance has been made, the incorporation of that development into another field could occur to several minds without the incorporation itself being, in any sense, obvious.

Conclusion

I have used the experience of the CAFC to investigate the costs and benefits of specialization. On the whole, the CAFC experiment has worked well for patent law, which is now more uniform, easier to apply, and more responsive to national interests.

2. AN ECONOMIC CRITIQUE OF COMMERCIAL SUCCESS

MERGES, ECONOMIC PERSPECTIVES ON INNOVATION: PATENT STANDARDS AND COMMERCIAL SUCCESS, 76 Cal. L. Rev. 803 (1988)

Commercial success is a poor indicator of patentability because it depends for its effectiveness on a long chain of inferences, and because the links in the chain are often subject to doubt. This was one of the central insights of a seminal article on patentability, *Graham v. John Deere Co.: New Standards for Patents*, written by Edmund Kitch in 1966.[1] In it Kitch argued that commercial success was an unreliable indicator of nonobviousness. To make his point, Kitch identified four inferences a judge must make to work backward from evidence of market success to a conclusion of patentable invention:

First, that the commercial success is due to the innovation. Second, that ... potential commercial success was perceived before its development. Third, the potential commercial success having been perceived, it is likely that efforts were made [by a number of firms] to develop the improvement. Fourth, the efforts having been made by men of skill in the art, they failed because the patentee was the first to reduce his development to practice.

With only this last event as a starting point, a court is asked to reconstruct a long series of events, and, more importantly, to decide how much of the final success is attributable to each factor introduced along the way. Each inference is weak, because there are almost always several explanations why a product was successful or why other firms missed a market opportunity. Only the *last* piece of the puzzle is indisputably established; the goal of the exercise is reached through a series of inferences that only begins with this last piece. It is an altogether extraordinary job of factual reconstruction, one that reveals the falsity of the term "objective evidence," which is often used by proponents of the secondary considerations.

The second objection to the commercial success doctrine is that it assumes an overly simplistic model of innovation. In reconstructing the events from invention to commercial success, a judge relies on an *implicit model* of innovation, in which market needs are perceived equally by several firms, the firms race to innovate, and the patentee whose invention succeeds in the market is declared the winner. Of course, the model provides for alternative scenarios. A court could find, for example, that an invention was successful because of unpatented features, or because of the patentee's dominant position in an industry. But even in these cases, the starting point for analysis is to test the facts against the implicit model. Consequently, although the burden of proving facts is on the patentee, she is granted what amounts to a quasi-presumption of patentability because of the framework dictated by the commercial success doctrine. And as we have seen, this quasi-presumption appears to exercise considerable influence on the outcome of cases in the Federal Circuit.

At this point, several questions suggest themselves: how realistic is the model implicit in the commercial success doctrine? How much do we know about the innovation process, and does it support or undercut the model? While patent cases

---

[1] 1966 SUP. CT. REV. 293. This is still the most thoughtful and comprehensive statement of the role of the secondary considerations. *See also* Note, *A Critique of the Use of Secondary Considerations in Applying the Section 103 Nonobviousness Test for Patentability*, 28 B.C. L. REV. 359 (1987); Note, *The Standard of Patentability — Judicial Interpretation of Section 103 of the Patent Act*, 63 COLUM. L. REV. 306 (1963).

provide a good deal of *ad hoc* discussion of these issues, we must go beyond the cases for systematic answers to our questions.

The patent system, as we saw above, rewards invention directly, and innovation only indirectly. Economists since Schumpeter have distinguished between the two,[2] normally describing an *invention* as a technical idea that can lead to a new product or that can be used to solve an industrial problem. They reserve the term *innovation* for the introduction of a new technology — in the usual case, the arrival of an invention in commercialized form on the market.

In our critique of the secondary factors, we will look at two lines of economic analysis, one theoretical and the other empirical. The theoretical work presents a strong challenge to the "implicit model" of innovation reflected in the commercial success doctrine. It demonstrates that there are many situations where competing firms have sound economic reasons to eschew innovation opportunities, and many more where they will simply overlook them. Likewise, the implicit model underlying commercial success reflects the erroneous assumption that firms often have a great deal of information about what the market wants. As a consequence, a successful innovation may represent something other than a technical coup and hence is a poor proxy for the presence of a patentable technical advance.

The Empirical Evidence

Empirical research supports several general conclusions from the theoretical work on innovation. Specifically, a number of studies of successful innovations highlight the critical importance of an innovating firm's sensitivity and responsiveness to the market. User education, service, and field support are all critical to the success of an innovation, yet they are largely unrelated to the underlying technical advance embodied in the innovation itself. A simple conclusion follows from the literature on innovation: the relative importance of market-related factors, as opposed to sheer technical superiority, illustrates the dangers of relying on evidence of commercial success to prove nonobviousness.

These [empirical] studies have found that successful innovations usually spring from a combination of product development and market knowledge;[3] rarely does a successful innovation result from one of these two factors alone. Differences in the way firms explore these combinations lead to different innovational approaches and, ultimately, different degrees of success.

---

[2] *See* R. NELSON & S. WINTER, EVOLUTIONARY THEORY OF ECONOMIC CHANGE 263 (1982) (describing invention/innovation distinction dating from the work of the noted Austrian economist and student of technical change, Joseph Schumpeter).

[3] *See* K. PAVITT, THE CONDITIONS FOR SUCCESS IN TECHNOLOGICAL INNOVATION (1971); C. FREEMAN, THE ECONOMICS OF INDUSTRIAL INNOVATION (2d ed. 1982), at 124.

For example, a number of studies led by British economist Christopher Freeman reveal these patterns.[4] Freeman's group studied a large number of successful innovations in Great Britain. By pairing successful and unsuccessful innovations, they found that successful innovators incorporated a detailed understanding of consumer needs into their product development and marketing plans. Of the differences between success and failure, Freeman states that

> [t]hose which came through most strongly were directly related to marketing. In some cases they might be regarded as obvious, but the case studies showed that even the most obvious requirements were sometimes ignored. Successful attempts were distinguished frequently from failure by greater attention to the education of users, to publicity, to market forecasting and selling ... and to the understanding of user requirements.

A detailed study of 203 new products by R.B. Cooper and E.J. Kleinschmidt of the McMaster University Business School in Canada revealed a similar pattern.[5] Although Cooper and Kleinschmidt found that "product advantage" was the most important determinant of success, they also discovered that this variable had a number of dimensions. For the most part, product advantage was present when an innovation had unique features for the customer, was of higher quality than competitive products, and was *perceived* as superior to competitive products in some respect. But most importantly, they found that "technological characteristics of the product, such as the use of new or advanced technology, product innovativeness, and the role of industrial design do not appear to influence [the] Financial Performance [variables in their study]." In other words, there was not necessarily any strong relationship between technical achievement (i.e., invention) and a commercially successful innovation. The lesson for us is clear: the inferential link between success and patentability — the presence of a significant technical advance — is weak in many cases. As a result, it appears that this research undercuts one of the chief assumptions behind the use of commercial success to establish patentability.

In summary, the various empirical studies agree that successful new products are launched with detailed knowledge of market conditions. While technological enhancements are by no means insignificant — some of the studies actually *assume* appreciable advances in technology — the researchers consistently emphasize the market-orientation of successful new products.

---

[4] *See* C. FREEMAN, *supra*, at 124.

[5] Cooper & Kleinschmidt, *New Products: What Separates Winners from Losers?*, 4 J. PROD. INNOV. MANAG. 169 (1987) (describing Product "New Prod," study of 203 successful and unsuccessful innovations); Cooper & Kleinschmidt, *What Makes a New Product A Winner: Success Factors at the Project Level*, 17 R&D MANAGEMENT 175 (1987) (same study) [hereinafter Cooper & Kleinschmidt, *Success Factors*]; Cooper, *The Dimensions of Industrial New Product Success and Failure*, 43 J. MKTG. 93 (Summer 1979).

a. *The Superior Secondary Factor: Failure of Others*

[Merges goes on to argue that the failings of commercial success do not render all the secondary considerations useless.]

Unlike commercial success, the failure of others to make an invention proves *directly* that parallel research efforts were under way at a number of firms, and that one firm (the patentee) won the race to a common goal. So long as the race was long enough, and so long as there was a clear winner, it is difficult to find fault with such evidence as proof of patentability.[6] In fact, since the failure of others is often one of the inferential steps underlying the commercial success doctrine, it makes sense for courts to adopt a rule of thumb requiring the patentee in most cases to prove failure of others before commercial success will be given substantial weight.

For failure of others to be persuasive, however, a patentee must establish two preliminary facts. First, there must really be parallel research, research aimed at the same goal. If two runners are on tracks of differing length or terrain, they will not be in a true race. Second, the patented invention must be the result of more than minimal research efforts; the race must be over a fairly long distance. Quick results by one firm, followed in rapid succession by the same discovery at other firms, would tend to show that the problem being solved was trivial. The winner should not be judged on the basis of a sprint.[7] Although it is dangerous to make rigid rules, failure over a period of several years indicates that the problem's solution was nonobvious. No specific term should be set, however, because intensively researched problems might justify a shorter period. So long as the patentee shows that the invention resulted from a significant research effort, and other firms pursued similar research, failure of others will be a reliable secondary consideration in the determination of nonobviousness.

Perhaps no judge was more convinced of the reliability of this form of evidence than Learned Hand, as shown by the many opinions he wrote that mention it. Of course, Judge Hand's considerable influence extends throughout patent law, but he was especially ardent — and characteristically eloquent — in

---

[6] Many judges have sung the praises of long felt need. Justice William R. Day of the Supreme Court said: "It may be safely said that if those skilled in the mechanical arts are working in a given field and have failed after repeated efforts to discover a certain new and useful improvement, that he who first makes the discovery ... is entitled to protection as an inventor." *Expanded Metal Co. v. Bradford*, 214 U.S. 366, 381 (1908). *See also Krementz v. S. Cottle Co.*, 148 U.S. 556, 560 (1892). Recently, the Federal Circuit has shown a willingness to consider such evidence, but has at times appeared to relax one of the two elements conventionally required to establish it — actual parallel research.

[7] *See Ruben Condenser Co. v. Copeland Refrigeration Corp.*, 85 F.2d 537, 541 (2d Cir. 1936) (L. Hand, J.); *Clark v. Wright Aeronautical Corp.*, 162 F.2d 960, 966 (2d Cir. 1934) (L. Hand, J.). *See generally* P. BLAUSTEIN, LEARNED HAND ON PATENT LAW 107, 113-116 (1983) ("density" of efforts by others was crucial to Learned Hand's treatment of failure of others evidence).

championing the secondary factors, which he usually referred to under the rubric of "the history of the art." Although references to commercial success and licensing appear in some of Hand's opinions, for the most part he reserved his most sweeping support for evidence of long felt need and failure of others.[8]

Judge Hand's regard for the failure of others — and his skepticism about commercial success — shows through clearly in his opinions. Even "[a]mazing success," he wrote, is not enough. "[T]hat is not the test of the validity of a claim."[9] The more reliable test, as he described it in *Ruben Condensor Co. v. Aerovox Corp.*,[10] requires consideration of a series of preliminary factors before relying on commercial success:

> While it is always the safest course to test a putative invention by what went before and what came after, it is easy to be misled. Nothing is less reliable than uncritically to accept its welcome by the art, even though it displace what went before. If the machine or composition appears shortly after some obstacle to its creation, technical or economic, has been removed, we should scrutinize its success jealously.... We should ask how old was the need; for how long could known materials and processes have filled it; how long others had unsuccessfully tried for an answer. *If these conditions are fulfilled, success is a reliable touchstone*....[11]

Besides the analytical rigor it lends to the nonobviousness inquiry, evidence of the failure of others has another virtue: it is relatively easy to obtain. Almost all

---

[8] *See, e.g., Victor Talking Mach. Co. v. Carl Lindstrom Co.*, 279 Fed. 570, 571 (S.D.N.Y. 1913) (L. Hand, J.) (long felt need); *Hookless Fastener Co. v. G.E. Prentice Mfg. Co.*, 68 F.2d 940, 941 (2d Cir. 1934) (L. Hand, J.) (long felt need); *Auto Pneumatic Action Co. v. Kindler & Collins*, 247 Fed. 323, 327-328 (S.D.N.Y. 1917) (L. Hand, J.) (failure of others); *Todd Protecto-graph Co. v. Safe-Guard Check Writer Co.*, 291 Fed. 613, 614 (S.D.N.Y. 1923) (L. Hand, J.) (failure of others); *Lyon v. Bausch & Lomb Optical Co.*, 285 F.2d 501, 108 U.S.P.Q. (BNA) (2d Cir. 1960), *cert. denied*, 366 U.S. 929 (1961). And the judge meant *long* felt need; in cases where the need was shown to have been recognized for one to five years, he found it unpersuasive, except in the case of a patent relating to automobiles, in which he thought the intense concentration of inventive activity made a five year need significant. *See Hartford v. Moore*, 181 Fed. 132, 137 (S.D.N.Y. 1910) ("thousands and tens of thousands of skilled mechanics have become familiar with the whole mechanism" of the auto); P. BLAUSTEIN, *supra*, §§ 4.11-4.20 (1983) (summarizing cases decided by Judge Hand concerning long felt need). Even so, in another case Judge Hand held that a five-year need was impressive, given the fact that there was no evidence that others had tried and failed. *Safety Car Heating & Lighting Co. v. General Electric Co.*, 155 F.2d 937, 939 (2d Cir. 1946). *Cf. Nagy v. L. Mundet & Son, Inc.*, 101 F.2d 82 (2d Cir. 1939) (L. Hand, J.) ("It is not safe to assume, because a single manufacturer for a few years has not discovered an improvement, that it was beyond the powers of rather commonplace talent"; "The case is much stronger for an invention when it appears at the end of a period of active competition among several manufacturers ....").

[9] *Merit Mfg. Co. v. Hero Mfg. Co.*, 185 F.2d 350 (2d Cir. 1954).

[10] 77 F.2d 266 (2d Cir. 1935) (L. Hand, J.).

[11] *Id.*, 77 F.2d 266, 268 (emphasis added).

firms keep detailed records of their research to establish critical dates for patent priority. Patentees quite often investigate the research records of a defendant charged with patent infringement, since these records are highly relevant to questions of infringement, ordinary skill in the art, and parallel research activities. Moreover, a patentee trying to prove failure of others will often describe the research efforts of other firms besides the infringer. Finally, during its review of the patents and competitive products in the prior art a court will often take note of the inferior solutions to the problem in the prior art, as compared to the patentee's solution. Summarizing the availability of failure of others evidence, one ex-patent practitioner, Judge Connor of the Southern District of New York, observed:

> So in every case I tried, I looked desperately for evidence of trial and failure; if I found it, which I usually did, I hammered away at that one theme, almost to the disregard of everything else. And it succeeded to an amazing degree.[12]

Of course, an invention will not always follow upon the failure of others. In cases where a patentee is the first into a new field, this factor will not be available. But one must keep in mind that failure of others is not a *requirement* for patentability — only a superior indicator. Where a patentee is truly the first into a field, the technical merits of her invention can be expected to speak for themselves. While the courts must be careful to examine the competitive environment of even a pioneering invention, a breakthrough development in a new field should demonstrate nonobviousness even without any secondary consideration evidence. Thus the failure of others, while providing a good benchmark of nonobviousness for the normal invention, will not be an obstacle to patentability in the case of a significant advance into an uncharted technological field.

NOTE

Burchfiel states that the argument advanced in the passage above assumes (unrealistically) that competitors have available all relevant prior art. He believes that only if firms have access to each other's research results can we assume that the failure of others justifies the inference of nonobviousness. KENNETH J. BURCH-FIEL, BIOTECHNOLOGY AND THE FEDERAL CIRCUIT § 6.2 (1995). He is no doubt correct that inventors are often ignorant of their rivals' research, but it is not clear that proof of actual knowledge of competitive efforts would enhance the "failure of others" argument. The point is not that an inventor knows of competitive efforts; it is that, despite them, he or she reached the goal first, having set off from a common starting point provided by public domain information. The

---

[12]Connor, *Winning Patent Infringement Suits — The Art of Swimming Against the Tide*, in NONOBVIOUSNESS — THE ULTIMATE CONDITION OF PATENTABILITY (Witherspoon ed. 1980), at 4:401-4:406.

failure of others demonstrates that the work of one researcher, alone and perhaps ignorant of others, was a significant step forward.

C. THE "SCOPE AND CONTENT OF THE PRIOR ART"

1. THE "WINSLOW TABLEAU"

Fred Winslow solved a recurring problem in the packaging industry: how to take a stack of plastic bags, ready for packing, and open the topmost bag in the stack to fill it. To do this, he used a jet of air to fill the top bag. His device held the top bag in place by means of a flap on one side of the bag's opening. The flap had one or more holes, and rods passed through the holes. The flap was perforated so that it could be torn away after the bag was filled.

The patent examiner rejected his claims to an apparatus for opening and filling bags, citing three primary references, patents to Gerbe, Hellman and Rhoades.

Gerbe discloses a bag-filling machine in which a clamp holds the topmost bag by the bottom of the bag's opening, much like one would hold a bag with one hand to fill it. Gerbe uses special bags, however; the top of the bag's opening is crescent shaped, to keep it out of the clamp. Air is then blown into it to open it for filling.

Hellman describes a bagging system where the bags are hung vertically from a rod, like a beach bag hung from a nail. The rod is tipped at a slight angle from the horizontal, to allow a weight to slide down the rod and clamp one side of the bag to hold it open. One side of the opening on the bags is longer than the other, making a flap. It is these flaps that are pierced by the rod. As the bags slide down the rod, an air blast opens the next one in line, an item is dropped into the bag, and the weight of the item tears the flap and the bag falls into a hopper. The specific thing to be bagged in the Hellman system is piston rings, so there is plenty of weight to tear the flaps.

Rhoades discloses a way to suspend paper bags. The bags are hung vertically and pushed by a spring against a piercing point. The piercing point passes through the crescent-shaped opening of one side of the bag and pierces the other side, holding it against the other bags in the stack. The other side of the bag, the one with the crescent opening, is not pierced, so it hangs open.

In re WINSLOW

365 F.2d 1017, 151 U.S.P.Q. (BNA) 48 (C.C.P.A. 1966)

RICH, JUDGE, delivered the opinion of the court:

Appellant presents the usual argument that hindsight reconstruction has been employed by the examiner and the board. We disagree with that position. We think the proper way to apply the 103 obviousness test to a case like this is to first picture the inventor as working in his shop with the prior art references — which he is presumed to know — hanging on the walls around him. One then notes that what applicant Winslow built here he admits is basically a Gerbe bag holder having [an] air-blast bag opening to which he has added two bag retaining pins. If there were any bag holding problem in the Gerbe machine when plastic bags were used, their flaps being gripped only by spring pressure between the top and bottom plates, Winslow would have said to himself, "Now what can I do to hold them more securely?" Looking around the walls, he would see Hellman's envelopes with holes in their flaps hung on a rod. He would then say to himself, "Ha! I can punch holes in my bags and put a little rod (pin) through the holes. That will hold them! After filling the bags, I'll pull them off the pins as does Hellman. Scoring the flap should make tearing easier."

Thus does appellant make his claimed invention merely by applying knowledge clearly present in the prior art. Section 103 requires us to presume full knowledge by the inventor of the prior art in the field of his endeavor. We see no "hindsight reconstruction" here, but only selection and application by the examiner of very pertinent art. That is his duty.

The decision of the board is affirmed.

SMITH, JUDGE, dissenting.

What appellant discovered had not occurred to Gerbe, the most recent inventor of subject matter closest to that here claimed. I assume that the Gerbe device is operable. Appellant, however, points out several practical difficulties inherent in the Gerbe construction which appellant proposes to eliminate. The end stop in Gerbe requires a degree of longitudinal rigidity in the bags, lest they tend to crumple against it as the successive uppermost bags are removed. Gerbe thus found it necessary to bow the stack of bags by providing special edge supports to assure such rigidity. Also, the stop is not seen to be of any help in retaining an inflated bag. Since the frictional hold exerted by the tongue of the bag may not be great, it may well yield to a sliding force such as might be exerted by an operator's thumb on a repetitive basis. Thus, concern is justified that the air blast could blow the bag away before it could be filled. Also, in Gerbe the stack of bags is held by friction only. The success of the clamping action requires that each bag assert a frictional force against the next bag yet the top bag must be easily removed without upsetting the clamping action. The removal of the top bag may well cause several bags to follow thus upsetting the clamping action.

To say that a pin cooperating with aligning holes in a bag flap extension is the obvious answer to eliminating the drawbacks in Gerbe, is, I think, an unwarranted simplification which results only from hindsight reasoning. A comparison of the respective devices clearly indicates the differences between appellant's device and those of Hellman and Gerbe.

The problem as I see it is that the simplicity of appellant's device has obscured the unobvious merits of appellant's improvement over prior art devices. I would reverse the decision of the board.

NOTES

1. *Judge Smith.* The author of the dissent in this case, Judge Arthur Smith, wrote many influential opinions in patent cases during his long and illustrious career as a judge in the CCPA. He also wrote a fine casebook in the field.

2. *The "Winslow Tableau" and "Superperson" in the Art.* The image of the inventor at work in her workshop, prior art spread out around the walls, has proved to be a compelling one. But for criticism of this aspect of nonobviousness doctrine, see Ebert, *Superperson and the Prior Art*, 67 J. PAT. OFF. SOC'Y 657 (1985). This article proposes that courts' presumption that a skilled artisan knows everything in a field should be restricted by taking account of cognitive limitations of real people.

Just how broad *is* the tableau with which the inventor is assumed to be familiar? That is the question we turn to next.

2. ANALOGOUS ARTS

GEORGE J. MEYER MANUFACTURING CO. v. SAN MARINO ELECTRONIC CORP.

422 F.2d 1285, 165 U.S.P.Q. (BNA) 23 (9th Cir. 1970)

Plaintiff[-appellee], San Marino Electronic Corporation (San Marino) manufactures empty bottle inspection machines. Defendant [-appellant], Geo. J. Meyer Manufacturing Co. (Meyer) manufactures a bottle inspection machine designated the Mark IV which is designed in part according to the teachings of U.S. Patent No. 3,133,640 (No. '640).

At the time of the issuance of Patent No. '640 there was an unfilled need for a device which would rapidly and efficiently inspect empty bottles and detect foreign particles in them. Meyer's Mark IV based in part on Patent No. '640 filled this need and was a commercial success.

The patent in suit envisages a device which may be described: At the bottom is a light source, over which is a glass light diffuser. Over that is the bottle to be inspected and over the bottle is a lens which focuses the diffused light passing through the bottle to a revolving reticle [defined below]. The light as it is affected by the reticle strikes a photo-electric cell. The centers of the light source, the opal glass diffuser, the reticle and the photo-electric cell all have a common vertical axis.

The reticle is a disc divided into alternating opaque and translucent pie-shaped segments of equal area. The patent illustrates a reticle which has seven opaque and seven translucent segments and which revolves 167 times per second.

As the bottle passes over the light source, an examination occurs. This examination continues during the time that the center of the bottle is being conveyed from a position approximately one-sixteenth of an inch in front of the center of the light source to one-sixteenth of an inch beyond the center of the light source. The reticle makes at least one complete revolution during this period of time.

If the bottle is clean and clear then, since the quantity of light does not change as the reticle turns[,] a maximum and relatively constant amount of light passes through the reticle to the photocell and produces a relatively high direct current. Under these conditions the direct current circuit operates to prevent the reject mechanism from acting. If, however, the bottle itself is sufficiently opaque, or if a relatively large foreign object restricts the passage of light, then the direct current produced by the photocell is reduced and at a predetermined level of reduction the direct current circuit causes the bottle to be rejected.

If there is a foreign object in the bottle of a size too small to reduce the direct current output of the photocell to the predetermined level of reduction the bottle will be rejected by the alternating current circuit. As the reticle rotates any foreign particle in the bottle will be alternately covered and uncovered. When the foreign object is covered by an opaque section of the reticle, then a maximum amount of light passes through the unobstructed translucent segments. This amount of light is diminished when the foreign object restricts the passage of light through one of the translucent segments. As a result of the operation of the reticle, light in varying intensities strikes the photocell which in turn emits energy in the form of an alternating current signal. The frequency of the alternating current signal generated by a small particle in the bottle is different from the frequency generated by the edge of the bottle and variations in the general background of the bottle such as those caused by the edge, lettering or differences in the thickness or coloring of the glass. The circuits are designed to discriminate among alternating currents of different frequencies and the circuit is tuned to select, for rejection purposes, the frequency generated by the foreign object in the bottle. As a result of this frequency discrimination the reject mechanism operates in the presence of a foreign object of relatively small size, but does not operate to reject bottles because of the effects produced by the general background. The use of the alternating current signal to discriminate among these several effects was a substantial improvement in the prior art.

It is not claimed that there was anything new in the electrical circuits employed, but it is claimed that the [combination described above] did constitute an invention. The evidence shows, and the district court found, that no such technique had been employed in the bottle inspection field. In the star tracking and missile tracking field however multislit scanners similar to that used by Meyer had been used to convert radiations from a star or missile into an alternating current and to distinguish by electrical circuity between the signal given by the star or the missile and signals produced by the general background. The heart of the district court's decision is contained in the following findings and conclusions.

> If the missile and star tracking field cannot be properly considered with the bottle inspection field as a single art of detecting objects in a field of view by electro-optical techniques, the system disclosed and claimed in the '640 patent constitutes an invention over the prior art relating to bottle inspection, and the patent is valid.

The nature of the art we are here concerned with is the detection of foreign objects in a field of view by electro-optical techniques, rather than being limited to the bottle inspection field.

Under the circumstances of this case what is the "art to which said subject matter pertains?" Meyer takes the position which we think untenable that the relevant art is the art of bottle inspection. The very narrow approach suggested by Meyer has been rejected in this Circuit. In *Aerotec Industries of California v. Pacific Scientific Company*, 381 F.2d 795 (9 Cir. 1967) the court held that the concept of a spring wound reel which can be caused to lock up when it is suddenly accelerated, the locking mechanism being operated by the inertia of a member built into the reel for that purpose, as it had been applied to trolley catchers was relevant to a similar device used in a harness for airplane pilots. Under this decision we cannot confine our consideration here to the field of bottle inspection but must venture somewhere beyond that field to determine the area of the relevant art.

It may be that at an earlier time in our history most inventions relating to locks were made by locksmiths and most inventions relative to plows were arrived at by those who made or used plows. At that time and in those days perhaps the "subject matter" of the invention was the lock or plow and the "art" the art of lock and plow making. In today's world, a world of extensive and rapid communication of scientific and industrial knowledge[,] a world of institutions of higher learning and private laboratories which gather men of all disciplines and direct their talents not only to the discovery of basic truths but to the solutions of specific problems, the questions arising in a particular industry are answered not only by those who have learned the lessons of that industry but also by those trained in scientific fields having no necessary relationship to the particular industry. These considerations lead us to believe that today the word "art" includes not only the knowledge accumulated with respect to a problem in a particular industry but that accumulated in those scientific fields the techniques of which have been commonly employed to solve problems of a similar kind in the particular and closely related fields. In the bottle inspection field the sciences of optics and electronics had been widely used and as new electronic and optical techniques were developed to solve, in related fields, problems of the kind presented by bottle inspection, then those techniques became part of the relevant art. We agree with the trial court's finding [that]

Electro-optical systems for the detection of objects in the sky, detection of material moving on a conveyor, detection of the presence of objects moving on the ground, and detection of objects in a container, all are systems which reside in an analogous art, and such systems employ similar elements in a similar relationship for a similar purpose. Further, such systems are related by the end object of seeking to detect an object having distinct light or dark characteristics in a background of different light or dark characteristics.

This approach to the problem, if not required, is at least foreshadowed by the language of Mr. Justice Clark, speaking for the Supreme Court in *Graham v. John Deere Co.*, 383 U.S. 1 at page 19:

> Moreover, the ambit of applicable art in given fields of science has widened by disciplines unheard of a half century ago. It is but an evenhanded application to require that those persons granted the benefit of a patent monopoly be charged with an awareness of these changed conditions. The same is true of the less technical, but still useful arts. He who seeks to build a better mousetrap today has a long path to tread before reaching the Patent Office.

Meyer relies upon *Sperry Products, Inc. v. Aluminum Company of America*, 171 F. Supp. 901 at p. 911 (N.D. Ohio 1959). In that case the patent in suit used a pulse echo method employing sound waves to detect flaws in metal. The analogous art was claimed to be a device using the pulse method employing electro-magnetic waves to detect ionized layers in the atmosphere. In both cases the pulse echo method was used but in one case the problem involved solid matter and variations in its composition while in the other the problem did not relate to the composition of the matter (the atmospheric particles) or the uniformity of it, but rather to the electrical charge possessed by the particles. In the one case sound pulses were used, in the other electro-magnetic pulses. The problem of the bottle inspector and the missile tracker is the same — to detect any light giving or light interrupting foreign objects against a background.

Assuming that the relevant art includes star and missile tracking, is patent No. '640 valid as a combination patent? We think not.

NOTES

1. *Related Cases.* In *A.J. Deer Co. v. United States Slicing Mach. Co.*, 21 F.2d 812, 813 (7th Cir. 1927), the court stated:

> If the elements and purposes in one art are related and similar to those in another art, and because and by reason of that relation and similarity make an appeal to the mind of a person having mechanical skill and knowledge of the purposes of the other art, then we are of opinion that such arts must be said to be analogous, and, if the converse is true, they are nonanalogous arts.

In *Automatic Arc Welding Corp. v. A.O. Smith Corp.*, 60 F.2d 740 (7th Cir. 1932), patents in the electric arc lighting field were included in the prior art for an arc welding invention. In the course of its opinion, the court distinguished the holding in the *Slicing Machine* case just quoted from:

> In the *Slicing Machine Case*, the court was considering the analogies in the meat slicing and the saw log cutting arts. While in one sense it might be said there was a common art — the cutting or slicing art — it was developed in different industries — the meat slicing industry and the lumber industry. There is a vast difference in the size of a saw log and a slab of bacon. There

is likewise great difference in the structure and solidity of meat and saw logs. There was similarity, it is true, between the machinery which the inventor in the saw log industry had designed for cutting saw logs into lumber and that used by the inventor of the meat cutting machine for cutting slabs of bacon.

But would one who was confronted by the problem of slicing bacon be chargeable with the state of the art as it had developed in the saw log business? The court answered, "No." Why not a similar answer here? Our reply is — Because of greater similarity in the two problems and the greater similarity of means adopted by the electrical engineer to solve the similar problems.

Analogous Arts in the Federal Circuit

Although the *Slicing-Arc Welding* line of cases is still the starting point, they have been succeeded by more recent cases which introduce a slight twist to the basic standard. The twist originated in *In re Wood*, 599 F.2d 1032, 1036, 202 U.S.P.Q. (BNA) 171, 174 (C.C.P.A. 1979):

> The determination that a reference is from a nonanalogous art is therefore two-fold. First, we decide if the reference is within the field of the inventor's endeavor. If it is not, we proceed to determine whether the reference is reasonably pertinent to the particular problem with which the inventor was involved.

The *Wood* test was adopted by the Federal Circuit in *In re Deminski*, 796 F.2d 436, 442, 230 U.S.P.Q. 313 (Fed. Cir. 1986) (reciting *Wood* "two-step" test, but finding that prior art at issue satisfied first step), and has been used since then. *See, e.g., In re Gorman*, 933 F.2d 982, 18 U.S.P.Q.2d 1885 (Fed. Cir. 1991).

Although the *Wood* test adds a two-step analysis, notice that it actually works no change on the older line of cases, since the ultimate question in close cases remains whether an inventor, in solving the problem before her, would reasonably have consulted a particular source of prior art. The *problem-solving* focus, in other words, stays the same. *See Jergens v. McKasy*, 927 F.2d 1552, 18 U.S.P.Q.2d (BNA) 1031 (Fed. Cir. 1991) (dragon windsock not prior art for hunting decoy invention). The following case and excerpt show application of the test to recent fact patterns.

In re CLAY

966 F.2d 656, 23 U.S.P.Q.2d 1058 (Fed. Cir. 1992)

[This case involved claims for a process for storing refined liquid hydrocarbon products, e.g., refined gasoline, in a storage tank having dead volume between tank bottom and outlet port. The examiner and Board found the claims unpatentable because of the prior art. The prior art references were (1) U.S. Patent 4,683,949 (Sydansk), also assigned to Clay's assignee, Marathon Oil Company, which discloses a process for reducing the permeability of hydrocarbon-bearing formations and thus improving oil production, using a gel similar to that in Clay's invention; and (2) a patent to Hetherington.]

Clay argues that the claims at issue were improperly rejected over Hetherington and Sydansk, because Sydansk is nonanalogous art. Whether a reference in the prior art is "analogous" is a fact question. *Panduit Corp. v. Dennison Mfg.*, 810 F.2d 1561, 1568 n. 9, 1 U.S.P.Q.2d 1593, 1597 n. 9 (Fed. Cir.), *cert. denied*, 481 U.S. 1052, 107 S. Ct. 2187, 95 L. Ed. 2d 843 (1987). Thus, we review the Board's decision on this point under the clearly erroneous standard.

Two criteria have evolved for determining whether prior art is analogous: (1) whether the art is from the same field of endeavor, regardless of the problem addressed, and (2) if the reference is not within the field of the inventor's endeavor, whether the reference still is reasonably pertinent to the particular problem with which the inventor is involved. *In re Deminski*, 796 F.2d 436, 442, 230 U.S.P.Q. 313, 315 (Fed. Cir. 1986).

The Board found Sydansk to be within the field of Clay's endeavor because, as the Examiner stated,

> one of ordinary skill in the art would certainly glean from [Sydansk] that the rigid gel as taught therein would have a number of applications within the manipulation of the storage and processing of hydrocarbon liquids ... [and that] the gel as taught in Sydansk would be expected to function in a similar manner as the bladders in the Hetherington patent.

These findings are clearly erroneous.

The PTO argues that Sydansk and Clay's inventions are part of a common endeavor — "maximizing withdrawal of petroleum stored in petroleum reservoirs." However, Sydansk cannot be considered to be within Clay's field of endeavor merely because both relate to the petroleum industry. Sydansk teaches the use of a gel in unconfined and irregular volumes within generally underground natural oil-bearing formations to channel flow in a desired direction; Clay teaches the introduction of gel to the confined dead volume of a man-made storage tank. The Sydansk process operates in extreme conditions, with petroleum formation temperatures as high as 115 degrees C and at significant well bore pressures; Clay's process apparently operates at ambient temperature and atmospheric pressure. Clay's field of endeavor is the storage of refined liquid hydrocarbons. The field of endeavor of Sydansk's invention, on the other hand, is the extraction of crude petroleum. The Board clearly erred in considering Sydansk to be within the same field of endeavor as Clay's.

Even though the art disclosed in Sydansk is not within Clay's field of endeavor, the reference may still properly be combined with Hetherington if it is reasonably pertinent to the problem Clay attempts to solve. *In re Wood*, [*supra*]. A reference is reasonably pertinent if, even though it may be in a different field from that of the inventor's endeavor, it is one which, because of the matter with which it deals, logically would have commended itself to an inventor's attention in considering his problem. Thus, the purposes of both the invention and the prior art are important in determining whether the reference is reasonably pertinent to the problem the invention attempts to solve. If a reference disclosure has the same purpose as the claimed invention, the reference relates to the same problem, and that fact supports use of that reference in an obviousness rejection. An inventor may well have been motivated to consider the reference when making his invention. If it is directed to a different purpose, the inventor would accordingly have had less motivation or occasion to consider it.

Sydansk's gel treatment of underground formations functions to fill anomalies so as to improve flow profiles and sweep efficiencies of injection and production fluids through a formation, while Clay's gel functions to displace liquid product from the dead volume of a storage tank. Sydansk is concerned with plugging formation anomalies so that fluid is subsequently diverted by the gel into the formation matrix, thereby forcing bypassed oil contained in the matrix toward a production well. Sydansk is faced with the problem of recovering oil from rock, i.e., from a matrix which is porous, permeable sedimentary rock of a subterranean formation where water has channeled through formation anomalies and bypassed oil present in the matrix. Such a problem is not reasonably pertinent to the particular problem with which Clay was involved — preventing loss of stored product to tank dead volume while preventing contamination of such product. Moreover, the subterranean formation of Sydansk is not structurally similar to, does not operate under the same temperature and pressure as, and does not function like Clay's storage tanks.

A person having ordinary skill in the art would not reasonably have expected to solve the problem of dead volume in tanks for storing refined petroleum by considering a reference dealing with plugging underground formation anomalies. The Board's finding to the contrary is clearly erroneous. Since Sydansk is non-analogous art, the rejection over Hetherington in view of Sydansk cannot be sustained.

———

From *Wang Laboratories, Inc. v. Toshiba, Inc.*, 993 F.2d 858, 864-65, 26 U.S.P.Q.2d 1767 (Fed. Cir. 1993):

[The patentee held two patents on single in-line memory modules (SIMMs) having eight data memory chips capable of storing 8-bit binary words or bytes, plus a ninth chip, which functions as a check or parity bit for error detection.]

[Defendants, accused infringers] Toshiba and NEC argue that the claims in suit are invalid for obviousness under 35 U.S.C. § 103 (1988). Specifically, they state that the claimed subject matter would have been obvious in view of U.S. Patent 4,281,392 assigned to Allen-Bradley Company, sales of Allen-Bradley's X9 SIMMs, and Texas Instruments 1982 MOS Memory Data Book....

Appellants assert that Allen-Bradley's '392 patent and its commercial counterpart, the X9 SIMM, are analogous to the claimed subject matter, and accordingly that they are effective to render the claims in suit invalid. However, because of the adequate jury instruction concerning analogous art, we will presume that the Allen-Bradley art was found to be non-analogous to the claimed subject matter. The question then is whether that finding is supported by substantial evidence. We conclude that there was substantial evidence.

Analogous art is that which is relevant to a consideration of obviousness under section 103. "Whether something legally within the prior art is 'analogous' is a fact question...." *Panduit Corp. v. Dennison Mfg. Co.*, 810 F.2d 1561, 1568 n. 9, 1 U.S.P.Q.2d 1593, 1597 n. 9 (Fed. Cir.), *cert. denied*, 481 U.S. 1052, 107 S. Ct. 2187, 95 L. Ed. 2d 843 (1987). Two criteria are relevant in determining whether prior art is analogous: (1) whether the art is from the same field of endeavor, regardless of the problem addressed, and (2) if the art is not within the same field of endeavor, whether it is still reasonably pertinent to the particular problem to be solved. *In re Clay*, 966 F.2d 656, 658-59, 23 U.S.P.Q.2d 1058, 1060 (Fed. Cir. 1992) (citations omitted).

The '392 patent is entitled "Memory Circuit for Programmable Machines"; it discloses a SIMM containing nine memory chips, eight for storing data and one for error detection, mounted in a single row. In the late 1970's, Allen-Bradley manufactured and sold the X9 SIMM for use in its 9-bit programmable controller. This product consisted of nine memory chips encapsulated in ceramic dual in-line packages (ceramic DIPs) mounted on an epoxy-glass printed circuit board substrate.

The Allen-Bradley art is not in the same field of endeavor as the claimed subject matter merely because it relates to memories. It involves memory circuits in which modules of varying sizes may be added or replaced; in contrast, the subject patents teach compact modular memories. Thus, based on the evidence of record, the jury could reasonably have found that the first criterion of the analogous art test has not been met and that the prior art and the claimed subject matter are not in the same field of endeavor.

Even though the Allen-Bradley art is not within the relevant field of endeavor, it may still be analogous if it is reasonably pertinent to the problem the inventor attempted to solve. *Id.* at 659, 23 U.S.P.Q.2d at 1060-61 (citation omitted). "A reference is reasonably pertinent if, even though it may be in a different field from that of the inventor's endeavor, it is one which, because of the matter with which it deals, logically would have commended itself to an inventor's attention in considering his problem." *Id.* at 659, 23 U.S.P.Q.2d at 1061. However, given the jury's ultimate conclusion, we presume that the jury decided that the Allen-Bradley art was not reasonably pertinent. The question then is whether that conclusion is supported by substantial evidence.

Dr. Jeffrey Frey, Wang's technical expert, testified that the Allen-Bradley technology, including the SIMM described in the patent and the X9, was not pertinent to the field of personal computers for which Wang's SIMMs were designed. Although Wang's patents do not mention the term "personal computer," Dr. Frey stated that "[t]he entire context of the patent[s] — in the application of the memories, units of nine, dynamic memories — indicates they're meant for use in personal computers." Dr. Frey further testified that the Allen-Bradley module was developed for use in a controller of large industrial machinery and could not be used in a personal computer. He also stated that the Allen-Bradley patent teaches the use of Static Random-Access-Memories (SRAMs) or Read-Only-Memories (ROMs) and does not suggest the use of Dynamic Random-Access-Memories (DRAMs) as taught by Wang. As Dr. Frey stated, DRAMs are primarily used in personal computers (PCs), while SRAMs, which are larger and more expensive, are not used in PCs.

Wang's SIMMs were designed to provide compact computer memory with minimum size, low cost, easy repairability, and easy expandability. See '605 patent, col. 2, lines 61-64 ("By using the small D-RAMs and small capacitors, module 30 may have physical dimensions [on] the order of three-quarter inch by three inches while providing large memory capacity."). In contrast, the Allen-Bradley patent relates to a memory circuit for a larger, more costly industrial controller. SRAMs were used by Allen-Bradley because of their intended industrial environment. According to Dr. Frey, size was not a consideration in the Allen-Bradley work. Thus, there is substantial evidence in the record to support a finding that the Allen-Bradley prior art is not reasonably pertinent and is not analogous.

[From footnote 9:] Even if the Allen-Bradley art were analogous, there was substantial evidence before the jury of significant differences (e.g., substrate size, type of memory chip (SRAM v. DRAM), number of terminals, chip packaging, etc.) between what the Allen-Bradley art teaches and the claimed invention. As to the chip packaging, the testimony would support a jury finding that there was no suggestion or incentive to make the necessary combination of Allen-Bradley's ceramic DIP module with the disclosed Texas Instruments plastic leaded chip carrier at the time of the claimed invention. In addition, there was ample evidence presented to the jury as to the commercial success of the claimed invention. With these assumed jury-found factual underpinnings, its determination of nonobviousness must be affirmed as a matter of law.

NOTES

1. *Feat of Clay.* The *Clay* court characterized the two fields at issue (patented invention and prior art) as solving the problem of "dead volume in tanks for storing refined petroleum" versus "plugging underground formation anomalies."

Is it relevant that storage tanks for refined petroleum and maximizing underground output are both aspects of the oil business? Notice that the prior art reference at issue in *Clay* was assigned to the same firm that the inventor in the case worked for, Marathon Oil. Why was there no discussion of whether the engineers and technicians had any contact with each other, or were likely to? Is it possible to focus too much on the problem solved, and not enough on overall similarities in the arts or the fields of which they form a part?

2. *Analogous Arts in the On-Line Era.* Today, very powerful search engines such as "Web crawlers" can systematically riffle through astounding amounts of raw data. If researchers have these facilities available, and use them regularly, the number of arts that are analogous is in some sense irrelevant; as long as some part of a common vocabulary is shared across fields, the search engines will find all references to a particular term or concept if instructed to do so. Does this imply that the doctrine of analogous arts should be limited in the post-electronic network world? How would this be done; by inquiring into the general availability of information in a particular field on electronic networks? What would be required for the doctrine to be eliminated entirely?

The experience of engineers and inventors supports the problem-oriented view of relevant prior art "Invention can be seen as the process of solving new problems. Accounts of successful inventors often focus on their problem-solving techniques." T. HUGHES, AMERICAN GENESIS: A CENTURY OF INVENTION AND TECHNOLOGICAL ENTHUSIASM 53 (1989). In this stimulating book, Hughes recounts the example of the Wright brothers:

> [W]hen they became young bicycle manufacturers, they began looking for books on the subject [of flight]. In the spring of 1899 a book on ornithology suggested to them that birds could be the model for human flight.... After the analogy of birds and gliding men spurred their enthusiasm for gliding, they wrote to the Smithsonian Institution for references to books and articles on the problems.

Id. at 56-57. Clearly the relevant prior art in this case includes the literature on bird flight, not just the early literature on mechanized flight. Again, the proper focus should be the problem facing the inventor, not the industry classification of the field which primarily uses the invention. For a description of the flow of technical information across industries, see F.M. Scherer, *Interindustry Technology Flows in the United States*, 11 RES. POL'Y 227 (1982).

3. EXPLAINING THE DOCTRINE OF ANALOGOUS ARTS: WHY DIFFERENT STANDARDS FOR §§ 102 AND 103?

Recall from Chapter 4 that *everything* is relevant prior art for purposes of § 102 — there is no doctrine of "nonanalogous arts" to exclude novelty-defeating subject matter drawn from far distant and unrelated fields. Why should the standard be different for nonobviousness?

One rationale might center on the fact that § 103 requires some fairly fine linedrawing already in the form of the ultimate judgment regarding patentability. So an additional linedrawing exercise is consistent with the thrust of this section. By contrast, an assessment of which arts are analogous and which are not would add a very different dimension to the thrust of § 102, which (in theory anyway) is largely free of difficult linedrawing issues. Recall that analysis under § 102 is meant to have a rather "mechanical" quality: if a reference, properly within the prior art (e.g., effective before the critical date) discloses each element of the claimed invention, novelty is defeated. Plain and simple; no judgment calls.

In Chapter 4, the strict and mechanical rules governing § 102 issues were presented in detail. These rules can be defended on the ground that they made novelty and statutory bar determinations more predictable. Anyone who knows the rules, for instance, should be able to tell whether a prior art reference contains all the elements of a claimed invention, and whether that reference is properly within the prior art. Since this degree of certainty is impossible to obtain for the necessarily more open-textured nonobviousness inquiry, there is no harm in adopting a more realistic test of what falls within the prior art. In addition, it has been argued that in some cases a loose "standard" such as § 103 is easier to administer and otherwise makes more sense than a strict "rule" such as § 102. *See* Louis Kaplow, *Rules Versus Standards: An Economic Analysis*, 42 DUKE L.J. 557 (1992). One astute commentator has pointed out that standards can facilitate bargaining in some cases as well. *See* Jason Johnston, *Bargaining Under Rules Versus Standards*, 11 J. L. ECON. & ORG. 256 (1995).

Note, however, that the "realism" of the analogous arts test is tempered in several ways. Most importantly, as we shall see, once a reference is deemed to be within an analogous art, no attempt is made to determine whether it was "reasonably accessible" to one working in that art. So cases such as *In re Hall* — the lone copy of a thesis in an obscure library — are decided the same way under § 103 as under § 102. Second, as we shall also see, a series of cases have made clear that each category of prior art listed under § 102 is "fair game" for § 103 purposes. As you will recall, these categories include previously-filed patents (§ 102(e)) and prior invention by another (§ 102(g)), neither of which (in some cases) is even remotely accessible. So although the analogous arts doctrine somewhat reduces the universe of relevant prior art, § 103 is still a long way from any sort of reasonable accessibility test. The *categories* of prior art may still include difficult-to-access items (the clearest case being § 102(e)), even if a court finds that prior art in certain non-analogous *fields* should be excluded from the § 103 analysis. In other words, there is still a good deal of obscure prior art to worry about, just as there is under § 102.

4. SECTIONS 102 & 103 OVERLAP ISSUES

This section takes a close look at how the categories of prior art created in § 102 are used to specify "the scope and content of the prior art" under § 103.

HAZELTINE RESEARCH, INC. v. BRENNER
382 U.S. 252 (1965)

The sole question presented here is whether an application for patent pending in the Patent Office at the time a second application is filed constitutes part of the "prior art" as that term is used in 35 U.S.C. § 103.

The question arose in this way. On December 23, 1957, petitioner Robert Regis filed an application for a patent on a new and useful improvement on a microwave switch. On June 24, 1959, the Patent Examiner denied Regis' application on the ground that the invention was not one which was new or unobvious in light of the prior art and thus did not meet the standards set forth in § 103. The Examiner said that the invention was unpatentable because of the joint effect of the disclosures made by patents previously issued, one to Carlson (No. 2,491,644) and one to Wallace (No. 2,822,526). The Carlson patent had been issued on December 20, 1949, over eight years prior to Regis' application, and that patent is admittedly a part of the prior art insofar as Regis' invention is concerned. The Wallace patent, however, was pending in the Patent Office when the Regis application was filed. The Wallace application had been pending since March 24, 1954, nearly three years and nine months before Regis filed his application and the Wallace patent was issued on February 4, 1958, 43 days after Regis filed his application.

Petitioners' primary contention is that the term "prior art," as used in § 103, really means only art previously publicly known. In support of this position they refer to a statement in the legislative history which indicates that prior art means "what was known before as described in section 102." [H.R. Rep. No. 1923, 82d Cong., 2d Sess., p. 7 (1952).] They contend that the use of the word "known" indicates that Congress intended prior art to include only inventions or discoveries which were already publicly known at the time an invention was made.

If petitioners are correct in their interpretation of "prior art," then the Wallace invention, which was not publicly known at the time the Regis application was filed, would not be prior art with regard to Regis' invention. This is true because at the time Regis filed his application the Wallace invention, although pending in the Patent Office, had never been made public and the Patent Office was forbidden by statute from disclosing to the public, except in special circumstances, anything contained in the application.

The Commissioner, relying chiefly on *Alexander Milburn Co. v. Davis-Bournonville Co.*, 270 U.S. 390 [1926], contends that when a patent is issued, the disclosures contained in the patent become a part of the prior art as of the time the application was filed, not, as petitioners contend, at the time the patent is issued. In that case a patent was held invalid because, at the time it was applied for, there was already pending an application which completely and adequately described the invention. In holding that the issuance of a patent based on the first application barred the valid issuance of a patent based on the second application. Mr. Justice Holmes, speaking for the Court, said,

> The delays of the patent office ought not to cut down the effect of what has been done.... (The first applicant) had taken steps that would make it public as soon as the Patent Office did its work, although, of course, amendments might be required of him before the end could be reached. We see no reason in the words or policy of the law for allowing (the second applicant) to profit by the delay.... [270 U.S. at 401].

In its revision of the patent laws in 1952, Congress showed its approval of the holding in *Milburn* by adopting 35 U.S.C. § 102(e) which provides that a person shall be entitled to a patent unless "(e) the invention was described in a patent granted on an application for patent by another filed in the United States before the invention thereof by the application for patent." Petitioners suggest, however, that the question in this case is not answered by mere reference to § 102(e), because in *Milburn*, which gave rise to that section, the co-pending applications described the same identical invention. But here the Regis invention is not precisely the same as that contained in the Wallace patent, but is only made obvious by the Wallace patent in light of the Carlson patent. We agree with the Commissioner that this distinction is without significance here. While we think petitioners' argument with regard to § 102(e) is interesting, it provides no reason to depart from the plain holding and reasoning in the *Milburn* case. The basic reasoning upon which the Court decided the Milburn case applies equally well here. When Wallace filed his application, he had done what he could to add his disclosures to the prior art. The rest was up to the Patent Office. Had the Patent Office acted faster, had it issued Wallace's patent two months earlier, there would have been no question here.

To adopt the result contended for by petitioners would create an area where patents are awarded for unpatentable advances in the art. We see no reason to read into § 103 a restricted definition of "prior art" which would lower standards of patentability to such an extent that there might exist two patents where the Congress has plainly directed that there should be only one.

Affirmed.

———

The case that follows, decided by the CCPA shortly after *Hazeltine*, might be better understood if several terms are defined. The invention concerns a textile processing machine, more specifically for the "carding" of fibers, e.g., wool. The inventors found that if they suctioned off air at the intersection of two rollers — one of which is called a "lickerin" — they could reduce the amount of textile dust that escaped from the dust screen, and thereby improve the performance of the carding machine. Note too that a "plenum" is simply a filled airspace; it is the opposite of a vacuum. Thus the "lickerin plenum" referred to in the case is the non-vacuum airspace near the lickerin.

In re BASS

474 F.2d 1276, 177 U.S.P.Q. (BNA) 178 (C.C.P.A. 1973)

RICH, ACTING CHIEF JUDGE.

This appeal is from the decision of the Patent Office Board of Appeals affirming the examiner's rejection of claims 1-9 of application serial No. 623,721, filed March 16, 1967 [a continuation-in-part of an application filed October 11, 1965], for [an] "Air Control System for Carding Machines." All claims are rejected on the ground of obviousness in view of the following references:

Reiterer — 3,115,683; Dec. 31, 1963

Bass, Jr. et al. (Bass) — 3,315,320; Apr. 25, 1967 (filed Aug. 23, 1965)

Jenkins, Sr. (Jenkins) — 3,348,268; Oct. 24, 1967 (parent filed Oct. 13, 1964)

Fuji, Japanese Patent Application No. 1025/63, published Feb. 14, 1963.

The statutory basis of this rejection is primarily 35 U.S.C. 103. Additionally, however, 35 U.S.C. 102(g) is relied on to establish that the prior inventions of Bass and Jenkins, as shown in their patents, are "prior art."

The issues raised by this appeal are, first, whether § 102(g) makes available as "prior art," within the meaning of § 103, the prior invention of another who has not abandoned, suppressed or concealed it. The remaining issues are the obviousness of the subject matter of the several claims in view of the available prior art.

The Invention

The joint invention of applicants Bass, Jr., Jenkins, Sr., and Horvat is a vacuum system for controlling and collecting waste on carding machines. Carding is the process of cleaning, straightening, aligning, and forming textile fibers into slivers preparatory to spinning. [The claimed invention is designed to solve a longstanding problem in the carding art: the buildup of waste particles on the cloth being processed. These particles are made up of dirt, seeds, etc., which collect around the cloth because the rapidly spinning cylinders on the carding machine — through which the cloth or "web" is fed — cause a suction effect that pulls the waste particles into the space where the cloth is being processed.]

Directed to the solution of these problems, appellants describe their invention in general terms as follows:

> To this end, there is provided a unique combination of elements which cooperate with each other to minimize the air pressure beneath the main cylinder without reducing its speed and to control the disposition of waste

in the area beneath the main cylinder. More specifically, the invention comprises [1] an enclosure for the area beneath the main cylinder whereby it is rendered as airtight as practical, [2] means closely adjacent the transfer points of the web from the lickerin to the main cylinder and [3] from the main cylinder to the doffer for relieving or drawing off air pressure created through rotation of the main cylinder and lickerin to reduce the air pressure beneath the main cylinder and while also drawing off fly and lint released at said transfer points and preferably, [4] means carried by the screen beneath the main cylinder for controlling the flow of air currents toward the center of the carding machine and away from its edges whereby to further minimize the danger of "blowouts" carrying waste into the atmosphere. [Bracketed numbers ours.]

Claim[] 1 [is] representative[; it reads]:

1. A vacuum system for controlling and collecting waste on carding machines of the type having a lickerin, a main cylinder, a screen beneath the main cylinder, and a doffer roll; said device comprising:

(a) a source of suction;

(b) a first suction nozzle disposed above the lickerin and arranged adjacent the point where the surfaces of the lickerin and cylinder diverge to draw off surface air currents created through rotation of the lickerin and main cylinder;

(c) a second suction nozzle disposed between the main cylinder and the doffer adjacent the point where the surfaces of the doffer and main cylinder converge to draw off surface air currents generated through rotation of the main cylinder as well as lint and fly released at the transfer point of the web between the main cylinder and the doffer;

(d) said screen comprising:

(i) a frame having a longitudinal axis and including a pair of longitudinally extending parallel side members spaced from each other and on opposite sides of said longitudinal axis; and

(ii) channeling means extending between said side members channeling more of said air currents through said screen intermediate said side members than at said side members, said channeling means comprising a plurality of air obstructing elements, each element having a face, the faces of said air obstructing elements being narrower adjacent said longitudinal axis than adjacent said side members; and

(e) whereby air pressure in the area beneath the main cylinder is minimized and waste passing through the screen is collected in the central portion of the area beneath the main cylinder.

The References

Reiterer discloses the use of a suction nozzle adjacent the point where the lickerin and main cylinders diverge.

Bass essentially describes the lickerin suction nozzle used by appellants. The patentees are the present appellants Bass and Horvat.

Jenkins essentially shows the main cylinder screen used by appellants and the patentee is appellant Jenkins.

Fuji discloses the use of a suction nozzle at the point where the main cylinder and the doffer converge.

[The applicants filed a Rule 131 affadavit to antedate several references; see Chapter 4 for discussion of Rule 131.] As to the Bass and Jenkins references, the examiner said in his final rejection that while the affidavits may overcome them so far as 35 U.S.C. 102(e) is concerned, because the affidavits antedate the filing dates of those two patents, they are not overcome as disclosing prior inventions of "another" under 35 U.S.C. 102(g). He relied on the Board of Appeals decision in *Ex parte Robbins and Porter*, 156 U.S.P.Q. 707 (1967) [(where earlier-filed application of different inventive entity is antedated by Rule 131 affadavit, this eliminates the reference for § 102(e) purposes, but not necessarily under § 102(g); where affadavit and specification of earlier-filed application show that subject matter disclosed in earlier application was invented before subject matter claimed in later application, that earlier subject matter is available as a reference under § 102(g))]. The board then proceeded to a discussion and affirmance of the rejection of all claims for obviousness on the bases first above recited.

Appellants' argument in this court is along three lines. They argue unobviousness of the inventions of the appealed claims over all the references, unobviousness over the references exclusive of Bass and Jenkins, and the impropriety of using Bass and Jenkins as prior art under § 102(g). The last point certainly is the point principally argued.

Appellants' brief refers to the rejection in this case as "a section 102(g) rejection," which it is not, and we therefore clarify that matter at the outset. The rejection is for obviousness under § 103 based in part on alleged prior inventions of others which are deemed to be "prior art" within the meaning of that term in § 103 by virtue of § 102(g). The essence of appellants' argument against this use of § 102(g) is that it is concerned only with "identity of invention." They say, "The applicants' invention must be the same as the invention of another." Since that is obviously not the case here, so their argument runs, § 102(g) "is out and Rule 131 is in." Appellants argue that the *Robbins* case is distinguishable because it was a case of identical inventions. This, however, is not so. The examiner had rejected the claims, inter alia, for obviousness.

In addition to contending that § 102(g) "is out" because the application is claiming separate and distinct inventions from what is claimed in the Bass and Jenkins patents, appellants argue that they are not proper references "since applicants [Bass, Jenkins, and Horvat] were working together on a common project, as evidenced by the facts in the Rule 131 affidavit...." They then add that "the appellants freely admit that they did not invent the claimed subject matter of the Bass, Jr. patent or the Jenkins, Sr. patent...."

Opinion

§ 102(g) Prior Invention as "Prior Art" under § 103

Narrowly considered, the issue presented by the facts of this case is one of first impression in this court. This is by no means the first time we have passed on whether § 102(g) prior invention of another is prior art, as will be shown, or even the first time we have considered whether such prior invention can be combined with other prior art to sustain a § 103 obviousness rejection. However, it is the first time we have considered combining § 102(g) and § 103 in the context of an ex parte rejection entirely divorced from the award of priority in an interference which established the prior inventorship relied on in rejecting.

This court has several times approved of rejections based on a combination of § 102(g) with § 103. The first case so holding is believed to be *In re Gregg*, 244 F.2d 316, 113 U.S.P.Q. 526 (1957). [The court then reviews other prior cases, most involving "post-interference ex parte rejection," i.e., cases where a losing interference party filed a subsequent application on a related invention which was held to be obvious in light of the winning party's application.]

From the above decisions it is clear beyond question that in using § 102(g) prior art to support a rejection it has not been limited to situations involving "identity of invention," as appellants contend, but has repeatedly been used to support the rejection of claims to different but obvious inventions under § 103.

As a general proposition of law, and particularly considering the way in which full anticipation situations under § 102 shade into obviousness rejections under § 103 because of discernable differences, we cannot sanction an interpretation of the statute under which a prior invention is "prior art" under the former situation but not under the latter.

The situation presents a close parallel to the situation under § 102(e) which was dealt with by this court in *In re Harry*, 51 C.C.P.A. 1541, 333 F.2d 920, 142 U.S.P.Q. 164 (1964), and by the Supreme Court a year later in *Hazeltine Research, Inc. v. Brenner*, 382 U.S. 252, 147 U.S.P.Q. 429 (1965).

In *Harry*, in discussing the § 102(e) + § 103 rejection, our summation reads:

> In our opinion, the "prior art" referred to in § 103 includes, along with the patents, printed publications, public uses and sales of paragraphs (a) and (b) of section 102, prior invention as established by a copending application, if it becomes a patent, as contemplated by paragraph (e) and as held in the *Milburn* case. Such prior invention, as prior art, may be combined with other references to sustain a rejection for obviousness under section 103.

Such being the law as to prior invention established under § 102(e), as it surely is with the Supreme Court's approval, we see no reason a different rule should prevail when the prior invention is otherwise established, as by the circumstances of the case, an adverse ruling in an interference, admissions by the applicant, or otherwise the statutory basis for using the prior invention being § 102(g). [From note 7:] It may be wondered why, in the twenty years since § 102(g) came into effect, there have not been more adjudicated cases reported on it to show "prior art" in support of a § 103 rejection. The answer probably is that there are many other defenses much easier to establish and it is a rare case where the effort of going back to the date of invention of a prior inventor is worth the cost.

Having settled the question of law, it remains to determine what the evidence shows as to the priority of the Bass and Jenkins inventions, upon which their availability as prior art depends.

The earliest date of invention alleged by appellants for their combination is the date of conception, February 10, 1964. Reduction to practice is alleged in April 1964. Their effective filing date is October 11, 1965.

First, we consider Jenkins, asserted to be the prior inventor of the tapered bar screen element of the claimed combination. The affidavit evidence asserts that the screen was conceived "before December 6, 1963" and built according to a drawing dated December 5, 1963. It was installed in the first prototype of appellants' combination about April 17, 1964. Assuming that to be the first reduction to practice of the screen, as well as of the combination, the record contains an admission of its conception by Jenkins about two months before appellants claim to have conceived the combination. The Jenkins invention would appear, prima facie, to be prior on the basis of prior conception and simultaneous reduction to practice, which makes diligence irrelevant.

We turn now to the Bass and Horvat reference (Bass). The invention of these patentees is the "first suction nozzle," element "(b)" in claim 1, located at the lickerin end of the machine. The only argument the solicitor makes on the priority issue is that "the affidavits made no attempt to show that the invention of Bass and Horvat was not prior to the invention of appellants." We do not think it was incumbent on the applicants to prove it was not prior, merely because the Patent Office thinks it might have been.

Appellants' position with respect to Bass is "that the Bass, Jr. et al. [invention] and the instant combination were part of the same research and development program and were invented simultaneously, as opposed to the Patent Office's position that the Bass, Jr. et al. lickerin plenum was invented previous to the combination merely because it was filed first." Finding no substantial evidence of record tending to indicate priority in Bass, we believe the appellants' position to be sound. We therefore exclude Bass from consideration as prior art in passing on the obviousness rejection.

The Rejections of Claims

Claims 2, 3, 4, and 5 were rejected as obvious in view of Reiterer and Fuji. We have carefully considered appellants' argument but agree with the decision on obviousness and this rejection is affirmed.

The rejection of all remaining claims 1, 6, 7, 8, and 9, was predicated on Bass combined with Fuji, Jenkins being added in rejecting claims 1, 6, 7, and 9. With the elimination of the Bass reference, there is no suggestion in the remaining references applied of the suction means at the lickerin side of the carding machine and no basis for a holding of obviousness of the combination of which it is a principal element. It is, therefore, necessary to reverse the rejection of these claims.

Comments on Judge Baldwin's Concurring Opinion

The concurrence admits that lost counts in interference — which is but one way of establishing prior invention — are properly used as the basis for rejections, not only of the same invention but also of those obvious in view of the prior invention thus established. [I]t makes no sense to distinguish one prior invention from another according to the manner in which its priority has been established.

The concurrence worries about our decision making a lot of issued patents invalid, which presumably would not otherwise be. The concern is misdirected. Since we are making no change in the law — certainly no change as it is applied by other courts in infringement suits — no more patents will be invalid than is already the case.

BALDWIN, JUDGE, concurring, with whom ALMOND, J., joins.

On the basis of the *Milburn* case, which changed the effective date of a U.S. patent from its issue date to its filing date, the principal opinion would change the effective date of all U.S. references to the unknown point in time when their subject matter was invented. On the basis of cases dealing with the rejection of a losing interference party's claims over the lost counts, the principal opinion condones the rejection of one applicant's claims over the contents of a patent where the parties' cases had never been in interference and in fact could not be put into interference under well established law.

What has always been pointed out in attacks on the *Milburn* rule, or in attempts to limit it, is that it uses, as prior knowledge, information which was secret at the time as of which it is used. This is true, and we think there is some validity to the argument that that which is secret should be in a different category from knowledge which is public. Nevertheless we have the rule. However, we are not disposed to extend that rule, which applies to the date of filing [an] application in the United States, the actual filing date when the disclosure is on deposit in the U.S. Patent Office and on its way, in due course, to publication in an issued patent.

The board's new view, as expressed in this case, has the practical potential effect of pushing back the date of the unpublished, secret disclosures, which ultimately have effect as prior art references in the form of U.S. patents, by the full one-year priority period of section 119. We think the *Milburn* rule, as codified in section 102(e), goes far enough in that direction. We see no valid reason to go further, certainly no compelling reason.

To push the effective date of a non-anticipatory reference backwards beyond the point where the knowledge it contains was made public to the time when its author obtained that knowledge, as we are asked to do here, would be to extend the exception to the point where it essentially swallows the rule. Section 102(e) would be turned into mere surplusage, for the application date of the patent would no longer be important, except as showing a constructive reduction to practice and except insofar as it evidences an intent not to suppress, conceal or abandon.

NOTES

1. *Lost Counts.* Several of the cases referred to by the court concern the use of a lost interference count as prior art. This situation arises when two inventors, call them Abe and Betty, are in an interference, and Betty wins. Abe's application will then be rejected under § 102(g); by winning the interference, Betty has established that she is the first inventor of the subject matter, so Abe's application will be rejected for lack of novelty. This is the doctrine of lost counts: the interference counts Abe lost become effective prior art against his application.

What if Abe then files a new application, or an amended application, claiming something obvious in light of, but slightly different from, the subject matter of the interference counts? It will be rejected again, also on the basis of the lost counts doctrine. The majority opinion points out that the application of the lost counts doctrine in this context is a prototype, pointing the way to the full recognition of the § 102(g)/103 basis for invalidity.

2. *Similar Reasoning Extending § 102(b) to § 103 Cases.* In the same year as the *Hazeltine* case, the CCPA made clear that § 102(b) prior art was part of the "relevant prior art" under § 103. *In re Foster*, 343 F.2d 980, 988, 145 U.S.P.Q. (BNA) 166 (C.C.P.A. 1965):

> There appears to be no dispute about the operation of this statute in "complete anticipation" situations but the contention seems to be that 102(b) has no applicability where the invention is not completely disclosed in a single patent or publication, that is to say where the rejection involves the addition to the disclosure of the reference of the ordinary skill of the art or the disclosure of another reference which indicates what those of ordinary skill in the art are presumed to know, and to have known for more than a year before the application was filed. Upon a complete reexamination of this matter, we are convinced that the contention is contrary to the policy consideration which motivated the enactment by Congress of a statutory bar. On logic and principle we think this contention is unsound, and we also believe it is contrary to the patent law as it has actually existed since at least 1898.
>
> First, as to principle, since the purpose of the statute has always been to require filing of the application within the prescribed period after the time the public came into possession of the invention, we cannot see that it makes any difference how it came into such possession, whether by a public use,

a sale, a single patent or publication, or by combinations of one or more of the foregoing. In considering this principle we assume, of course, that by these means the invention has become obvious to that segment of the "public" having ordinary skill in the art. Once this has happened, the purpose of the law is to give the inventor only a year within which to file and this would seem to be liberal treatment. Whenever an applicant undertakes, under Rule 131, to swear back of a reference having an effective date more than a year before his filing date, he is automatically conceding that he made his invention more than a year before he filed. If the reference contains enough disclosure to make his invention obvious, the principle of the statute would seem to require denial of a patent to him. The same is true where a combination of two publications or patents makes the invention obvious and they both have dates more than a year before the filing date.

As to dealing with the express language of 102(b), for example, "described in a printed publication," technically, we see no reason to so read the words of the statute as to preclude the use of more than one reference; nor do we find in the context anything to show that "a printed publication" cannot include two or more printed publications. We do not have two publications here, but it is a common situation.

a. The "Personal Knowledge" Requirement

In the important case of *In re Clemens*, 622 F.2d 1029, 206 U.S.P.Q. (BNA) 289 (C.C.P.A. 1980), the court was confronted with a difficult § 102(g)/103 issue. The Patent Office Board of Appeals upheld the rejection of Clemens' patent application on the basis of a patent to Barrett, who filed earlier than Clemens. A complicating factor was that both Barrett and Clemens were doing research for the same company — so they were obligated to turn over the rights to their research to a common assignee. The CCPA nonetheless stated that the Barrett reference was prior art against Clemens — *if* it satisfied 102(g)'s prior invention standard. In that case, the court decided it did not:

> Because the record does not support a finding that Barrett made his invention before appellants [Clemens] made the invention ..., the present 35 U.S.C. 102(g)/103 rejection ... must fall.

622 F.2d 1029, 206 U.S.P.Q. at 299. But the principle was established that such prior invention, even if performed for the same company or in the same lab as the applicant's research, was prior art against the applicant.

In a further statement, which was dictum in light of the holding just referred to, the court distinguished the *Bass* case, *supra*, by noting that Clemens had actual knowledge of Barrett's research. The court continued:

> [W]here this other invention is unknown to both the applicant and the art at the time the applicant makes his invention, treating it as 35 U.S.C. 103 prior

art would establish a standard for patentability in which an applicant's contribution would be measured against secret prior art.

622 F.2d at 1040, 206 U.S.P.Q. (BNA) at 299. The court added that the creation of such categories of secret prior art was disfavored. *Id.*

An early Federal Circuit case, *Kimberly-Clark Corp. v. Johnson & Johnson Co.*, 745 F.2d 1437, 223 U.S.P.Q. 603 (Fed. Cir. 1984), presented a similar problem. In-house work by Champaigne and Mobley, researchers at Kimberly-Clark ("K-C"), was asserted as prior art against a claimed invention by Roeder, also a K-C employee, in the field of sanitary napkins. The court addressed two key issues: whether the asserted references qualified as prior art under § 102(g) (discussed below); and the correctness of the suggestion in *Clemens* that personal knowledge of another's invention was required to make that other invention effective prior art for purposes of § 102(g)/103 invalidity. On the question of the personal knowledge dictum in *Clemens*, the court stated:

> Both parties are citing *Clemens* for the legal proposition that personal knowledge of non-public work is sufficient to qualify that work as § 103 "prior art." ... As § 102(g) contains no personal knowledge requirement, the court's sole discussion of personal knowledge was dictum in the course of a discussion which distinguished the facts before it from those in a previous opinion of the court also dealing with §§ 102(g)/103, namely, *In re Bass*.

745 F.2d at 1445. This was emphasized in *E.I. Du Pont de Nemours & Co. v. Phillips Petr. Co.*, 849 F.2d 1430, 7 U.S.P.Q.2d (BNA) 1129 (Fed. Cir. 1988):

> *Kimberly-Clark* distinguished as dictum the *Clemens* requirement of applicant's personal knowledge because "§ 102(g) contains no personal knowledge requirement." 745 F.2d at 1445, 223 U.S.P.Q. at 607. Nor does § 102(g) contain a "known to the art" requirement apart from the requirement of no abandonment, suppression or concealment. Hence, the alternative *Clemens* requirement that the prior work be "known to the art" is also implicitly dismissed as dictum.

849 F.2d at 1437.

b. Details of § 102(g) Inquiry in the § 102(g)/103 Context

In *Kimberly-Clark, supra*, the court addressed the question of whether the cited § 102(g) reference had been abandoned, suppressed or concealed. (If it had been, of course, it would have been removed as a § 102(g) reference and hence would not have been within the prior art.) Discussing the specific references in the case, which dealt with a sanitary napkin invention with a new adhesive strip design, the court said in part:

> K-C relies on Roeder's [i.e., the patentee's] experimental conclusions on the location of the adhesive strips as proof of Roeder's prior reduction to

practice. Those Roeder conclusions, however, make no reference to the adhesive's multiple functions which the examiner, the board and the trial court correctly determined to be critical limitations of the '371 patent claims. We are therefore not persuaded that the record supports a reduction to practice of Roeder's claimed invention prior to Champaigne's filing date. Accordingly, the district court's finding that Champaigne's invention was a prior reduction to practice was not legally wrong. Since Champaigne's invention meets the other requirements of § 102(g) his work can be considered as prior art to Roeder under § 103.

[From footnote 1:] [T]he timely filing of a patent application, and subsequent issuance of a patent thereon, covering the Champaigne pad, constitutes sufficient proof that his invention was not abandoned, suppressed, or concealed.

The second item of K-C in-house work, that of Carolyn Mobley, consisted of laboratory experiments, documented in lab notebooks, designed to test various adhesive mixtures to find an adhesive composition that would alleviate the prior art problems ranging from insufficient tack to the undergarment to transfer of the adhesive to the undergarment.... While evidence of in-house testing may be prima facie evidence of conception, reduction to practice requires that an invention be sufficiently tested to demonstrate that it will work for its intended purpose. [T]he usefulness of the adhesive mixtures for their intended purpose was not inherently apparent, so that utility must have been demonstrated by actual testing of various adhesive mixtures. Mobley's experiments failed to set forth a single adhesive mixture that performed with sufficient success.... We hold the Mobley experiments were not prima facie evidence of a reduction to practice. Under § 102(g), proof of a conception alone does not suffice to establish Mobley's work as prior to Roeder's invention. We therefore agree with K-C that Mobley's work was unavailable as § 103 "prior art" under § 102(g).

745 F.2d at 1444-45.

The court in *E.I. Du Pont de Nemours & Co. v. Phillips Petr. Co.*, 849 F.2d 1430, 7 U.S.P.Q.2d (BNA) 1129 (Fed. Cir. 1988), also addressed the issue of whether there had been an abandonment, suppression or concealment:

[From footnote 7:] Because work is "secret" does not necessarily mean that it has been "abandoned, suppressed or concealed." The latter determination depends on the overall facts of each case. For example, the filing of a United States patent application, as Phillips did here, maintains the secrecy of work, but is a factor cutting against abandonment, suppression or concealment. In any event, Du Pont conceded that the prior Phillips work has not been abandoned, suppressed or concealed, e.g., it admits in its reply brief that the [reference] work is "available as a defense of prior invention under Section 102(g)." In that regard, the Phillips work was the subject of foreign patent applications, speeches at various conferences, and papers presented at American Chemical Society meetings.

[A]lthough *Kimberly-Clark* concluded there was no abandonment, suppression, or concealment because of a filed patent application that issued, *Kimberly-Clark* does not require that a patent application be filed or a patent be issued before § 102(g) prior work can qualify as § 103 prior art. Certainly the court in *Kimberly-Clark* was concerned about "secret prior art." Nevertheless the requirement of proving no abandonment, suppression, or concealment does mollify somewhat the "secret" nature of § 102(g) prior art. Despite its concern over "secret prior art," the court in *Kimberly-Clark* allowed prior work to be used as prior art in a § 103 context so long as it satisfied the requirements of § 102(g).

849 F.2d at 1437. For a case finding that several § 102(g) references had been abandoned, suppressed, or concealed, see *CSS Int'l Corp. v. Maul Tech. Co.*, 16 U.S.P.Q.2d 1657 (S.D. Ind. 1989), *aff'd on other grounds*, 17 U.S.P.Q.2d 1873 (Fed. Cir. 1990).

c. Fixing the "In-House" Prior Art Problem: Inventive Entities and the 1984 Amendment to § 103

As cases such as *Clemens* and *Kimberly-Clark* illustrate, a common source of § 102(g) prior art is research performed at the same company that employs the applicant or patentee. Because prior invention "of another" has been interpreted to mean invention of another inventor or "inventive entity," the work of a fellow employee is fair game under this section. On inventive entities, see the following section.

Cases such as *Clemens* show the problems this rule creates. There you may recall that the invention at issue ran into § 102(g) prior art that was created, *in part*, by the same inventor. This problem provides an opportunity to introduce a concept with general application throughout patent law: the "inventive entity."

The Inventive Entity

In patent law, different combinations of inventors comprise different "inventive entities." Thus researcher *A* working alone is a different inventive entity than researchers *A* and *B* working together. Likewise, the team of *A* and *B* is different from the team of *A*, *B* and *C*. The thought is that a particular combination of inventors working on a specific problem has a group identity with respect to that invention: they (or he or she) are its "inventor." Because "inventor" usually refers to a single person, however, we use the term "inventive entity" with respect to an invention created by a group.

The impact of the inventive entity concept is felt throughout patent law. For purposes of novelty, for instance, there is a longstanding rule that an inventor's own prior research may not anticipate her invention. When an inventive entity is involved, however, the rule is understood to mean only that an inventive entity cannot anticipate a later invention *by that same inventive entity*. Thus if there is any non-overlap between the members of the research team that produced the allegedly anticipatory work and the inventive entity of the claimed invention, anticipation *will* be a problem. So prior work by *A* and *B* may anticipate a later invention by *A* alone, or by *A*, *B* and *C*. *See, e.g.*, *In re Bass*, *supra*, where the court states: "[I]n situations involving cases filed by different inventive entities, regardless of ownership, sections 102 and 103 of 35 U.S.C. preclude the granting of two or more patents when directed to identical inventive concepts or when one of the concepts would be obvious in view of the other." 474 F.2d at 1292.

As this statement from *Bass* shows, the inventive entity idea is also applied for purposes of nonobviousness. *See, e.g.*, *In re O'Farrell*, 853 F.2d 894, 7 U.S.P.Q.2d (BNA) 1673 (Fed. Cir. 1988) (article by two of three co-inventors was § 102(a) prior art against their patent application). Note, however, that the inventive entity concept was never applied so harshly as to create a 102(g) or § 102(e)/103 rejection when a sole inventor files first, then files a related application with another inventor. According to the leading case of *In re Land & Rogers*, 368 F.2d 866, 879, 151 U.S.P.Q. (BNA) 621, 633 (C.C.P.A. 1966):

> When the joint and sole inventions are related, as they are here, inventor *A* commonly discloses the invention of *A* & *B* in the course of describing his sole invention and when he so describes the invention of *A* & *B* he is not disclosing "prior art" to the *A* & *B* invention, even if he has legal status as "another." [The reference to "another" is to that word as used in 35 U.S.C. 102(e) and (g).]

Despite this exception, the inventive entity concept has caused a good deal of trouble. Although the theory behind the the concept makes sense, it leads to some rather preposterous outcomes. For instance, in situations like that in *Clemens*, researcher *A*, working for the same company as researcher *B*, might find her research cited against *B*'s invention. (And after *Kimberly-Clark*, it is irrelevant whether *B* actually knew of *A*'s research.) Thus research done for the same corporation might in a sense wind up "cancelling itself out" when the company applied for patents. In the words of the Book of Common Prayer: "Thus were they stained with their own works ...."

Congress to the Rescue: The 1984 Amendments to § 103

In 1984, Congress put a halt to the anomaly by adding the following provision to the end of § 103 of the Patent Act:

> Subject matter developed by another person, which qualifies as prior art only under subsection (f) or (g) of this title, shall not preclude patentability under this section where the subject matter and the claimed invention were, at the time the invention was made, owned by the same person or subject to an obligation of assignment to the same person.

Patent Law Amendments Act of 1984, Pub. L. No. 98-622, § 104, 98 Stat. 3385, *reprinted in* 1984 U.S.C.C.A.N. 5827, 5833, codified at 35 U.S.C. § 103, ¶ 2 (1986 & Supp. VI 1990). This effectively reverses cases such as *Clemens* and *Bass* since they turned on references which were produced by researchers who had agreed to assign research results to the same company, and which qualified as prior art under § 102(g) of the Patent Act; the legislative history of the enactment makes this clear.

On the other hand, since the amendment was passed almost simultaneously with *Kimberly-Clark*, it is not clear whether the amendment was intended to change the result in that case as well. *Cf.* 2 D. CHISUM, PATENTS § 5.03[3][c][vi] (1978 & Supp. 1991). That is, it may still be argued that only the *Clemens* situation is affected by the new legislation. If so, prior work not commonly owned or subject to common assignment is *not* a proper basis for a § 103 rejection. By the same token, perhaps prior work about which the applicant has no actual knowledge is not effective prior art. Note, however, that the Patent Office does not subscribe to either of these views; it believes — with ample reason — that the 1984 amendments do not change the fact that § 102(g) prior art is fair game for § 103 purposes, so long as it does not fall within the commonly owned or assigned proviso of the 1984 Act. *See* 37 C.F.R. § 1.106(d) (1991). The language of the amendment would appear to support this view: it speaks of subject matter "which qualifies as prior art ... under subsection ... (g) of this title," and says that such a reference "shall not preclude patentability ... where the subject matter and the claimed invention were" commonly owned or assigned. There appears to be no reason why this should affect the basic premise of *Kimberly-Clark*, which simply determines what shall be subject matter "which qualifies as prior art" under § 102(g); only because this case fell into the exception stated in the amendment — "shall not preclude patentability where" it is commonly owned or assigned — is it changed by the amendment. Where the subject matter is not commonly owned or assigned, there is no reason it may not "qualif[y] as prior art ... under section 102(g)."

The wisdom of condoning another category of "secret" prior art has, of course, been criticized; it is a potential candidate for elimination in the context of international harmonization talks. *See* Section E below, *Taking an "Inventive Step" Overseas*.

d. An Economic Rationale for the 1984 Amendment to § 103

From an economic standpoint, the 1984 amendment to § 103 insures that information generated inside a firm cannot be used when judging the nonobviousness of that firm's own inventions. Since technical uncertainty — the thing nonobviousness seeks to measure, just prior to the inventor's successful research — is determined almost exclusively with reference to publicly-available information, nonobviousness does not penalize a firm for investments in private information. For the reasons discussed throughout the literature on such information, especially the work of Anthony Kronman, this rule makes a good deal of sense. Kronman theorized that the goal of contract rules governing what must be disclosed during negotiations is to protect investments in costly information, by not requiring disclosure, while insuring fairness by mandating that other information must be disclosed. *See* A. Kronman, *Mistake, Disclosure, Information and the Law of Contracts*, in THE ECONOMICS OF CONTRACT LAW 114 (1979). The idea is to protect costly investments made to generate private information.

In general, nonobviousness measures the chances of success, not against the inventor's subjective evaluation of the likelihood of success, but against the objective standard of the reasonably skilled worker in the field just prior to the commencement of the inventor's research. Because this hypothetical reasonably skilled artisan is endowed with only *publicly* available technical knowledge — the prior art — the proprietary knowledge of the actual inventor is immaterial to the obviousness inquiry. This encourages firms to invest in proprietary knowledge prior to the commencement of a particular invention project. In fact, since private knowledge is not held against the inventor when patentability is determined, the inventor can be expected to invest in such knowledge up to the point where its money value is just equal to the cost of obtaining more of it. *See* Stigler, *The Economics of Information*, 69 J. POL. ECON. 213 (1961). *Cf.* H. Simon, *Theories of Bounded Rationality*, in 2 MODELS OF BOUNDED RATIONALITY: BEHAVIORAL ECONOMICS AND BUSINESS ORGANIZATION 408, 410 (1982) (describing a class of models of decisions under uncertainty where decisionmaker's task "is to find the alternative [choice of action] that maximizes his expected profit net of search cost"). If this private knowledge were part of the prior art, the implicit cost of obtaining such knowledge would rise (due to its negative impact on patent possibilities, and hence overall earnings) and less would be produced. This would naturally affect the firm's decision to invest in such preliminary research. But it would also affect society at large, since much of this preliminary knowledge takes the form of basic research, which is often publicly disclosed, even when undertaken by private firms.

Of course, investment in such information might well affect the inventor's cost calculus. She will need to justify the expense by a reduction in costs or an increase in expected payoff. For example, if the preliminary research indicates that the project will not be a success, the inventor can avoid the expense of a failed project. On the other hand, preliminary research might lead to a larger expected payoff, e.g., by focussing the project on a more promising or profitable technology. For an important treatment of the "focusing" effect such iterative decisionmaking can have on research and development, see Nelson, *The Role of Knowledge in R&D Efficiency*, 47 Q. J. ECON. 459 (1982) (constructing a "search" model showing how firms refine their approach to R&D with experience). *See generally* R. NELSON & S. WINTER, AN EVOLUTIONARY THEORY OF ECONOMIC CHANGE (1982) (making extensive use of models and simulations where firms modify their search for new products and processes over time based on past experience).

In either case, the inventor who performs preliminary research has in effect
bought information. This is recognized in the economic literature on invention.
See, e.g., Mansfield, *How Economists See R&D*, HARV. BUS. REV., Nov.-Dec.
1981, at 98:

> Many ... [formal project selection] models fail to recognize that R&D is
> essentially a process of buying information, that unsuccessful projects can
> provide valuable information, and as a result that the real task is to facilitate
> sequential decision making under conditions of uncertainty.

The patent system should not — and does not, thanks to the 1984 amendment
— discourage this by including private information in the prior art against which
the ultimate invention is judged.

e. Extending *Hazeltine* and *Bass* to Other Categories of § 102 Prior Art

The basic premise of *Bass* is that "considering the way in which full anticipation situations under § 102 shade into obviousness rejections under § 103 because
of discernable differences, we cannot sanction an interpretation of the statute
under which a prior invention is 'prior art' under the former situation but not
under the latter." The following cases show the working out of this suggestion
for categories of prior art beyond § 102(g).

The Case of § 102(f)/103 Prior Art

One § 102 event whose status as a source of § 103 prior art has engendered
dispute is the requirement of subsection (f) that the patentee be the actual inventor
of the subject matter at issue. In a typical § 102(f) rejection, the applicant or
patentee is shown to have "derived" from another the invention sought to be
patented. *See, e.g., Campbell v. Spectrum Automation*, 513 F.2d 932, 185
U.S.P.Q. (BNA) 718 (6th Cir. 1975) (excerpted in Chapter 4); *Hedgewick v.
Akers*, 497 F.2d 905, 908, 182 U.S.P.Q. 167, 169 (C.C.P.A. 1974) ("Derivation
is shown by a prior, complete conception of the claimed subject matter and
communication of the complete conception to the party charged with derivation.")
If § 102(f) is included as § 103 prior art, then even though the entire invention
was not derived from another, if so much of the inventive concept was derived
as to make the remainder obvious to one skilled in the art, the invention would
be unpatentable under § 103. While the Federal Circuit has not ruled definitively
on this issue, it has suggested that § 102(f)/103 may well be a valid basis for
patent invalidity. *See Lamb-Weston, Inc. v. McCain Foods, Ltd.*, 78 F.3d 540,
544 fn. *.

So far, the Patent Office has shown a willingness to reject applications on the
basis of § 102(f)/103 obviousness. *See Ex parte Yoshino*, 227 U.S.P.Q. (BNA)
52, 54 (Pat. Off. Bd. App. & Int. 1985) (§ 102(f) is valid prior art category
under § 103). *See also Ex parte Stalego*, 154 U.S.P.Q. (BNA) 52, 53 (Pat. Off.

Bd. App. 1966); *Ex parte Thelin*, 152 U.S.P.Q. (BNA) 624, 625 (Pat. Off. Bd. App. 1966); 37 C.F.R. § 1.106(d) (1991).

The following scenario illustrates the impact of including "derived" information under § 102(f) in the relevant prior art for purposes of § 103:

> Inventor *A*, while visiting his friend *B* in Peoria, is told by *B* that he has discovered that by applying an aqueous solution of calcium bromide to warts, the warts are removed and do not reappear. *B*'s discovery is never published or disclosed to the public. Inventor *A* then tests out *B*'s discovery and confirms that aqueous calcium bromide is highly effective for removing warts. Inventor *A* then tests an aqueous solution of calcium chloride and finds that it is equally effective in wart removal.

Stiefel, *Section 102(f) as a Basis for Section 103 Prior Art — Myth or Reality*, 61 J. PAT. OFF. SOC'Y 734 (1979). *A*'s invention will be found obvious, since his substitution of calcium chloride would be obvious to one skilled in the art. For criticisms of § 102(f) subject matter as the basis of § 103 findings, see Janicke, *What Is "Prior Art" Under Section 103?: The Need for Policy Thought*, in NONOBVIOUSNESS — THE ULTIMATE CONDITION OF PATENTABILITY 5:105 (J. Witherspoon ed., 1980); Roth, *Obviousness Under Section 103*, 47 J. PAT. OFF. SOC'Y 811, 825 (1965).

Much of the criticism of § 102(f) prior art in the § 103 context emphasizes that it will cut down on the number of inventions patented, and hence disclosed to the public. But a very perceptive student note effectively rebuts this argument (and makes some other points worth noting as well):

> [S]ince the inventor always has the option of entirely suppressing his conception, a rule of law that allows the deriver to obtain a patent on the basis of derived information will inhibit disclosure of the information in any event. To put it otherwise, an inventor would be unlikely to disclose his work to anyone if the law permitted the deriving party to obtain a patent on obvious variants of the disclosed information; adoption of such a rule does not make disclosure any more likely. Collaborative pursuits — which could result in an earlier reduction to practice — thus will be inhibited. In economic terms, wasteful allocation of societal resources would result from efforts to prevent plagiarism of inventions.

Comment, *The Use of Derived Information as Prior Art Under Section 103 of the Patent Act*, 79 NW. U. L. REV. 423, 454 (1984). A further point in this connection is that, if anything, § 102(f) seems a more fair source of § 103 prior art than § 102(g), since the latter section really can result in "secret" prior art being used against the patentee or applicant.

Whatever the policy implications, the status of § 102(f) prior art under § 103 was seemingly resolved by the Patent Law Amendments Act of 1984: "Subject matter developed by another person, which qualifies as prior art only under subsection (f) or (g) of section 102 of this title, shall not preclude patentability under this section where" it is commonly owned or assigned. *See* the preceding section of this chapter. By fairly clear negative implication, the language of this bill suggests that § 102(f) is perfectly acceptable as a source of § 103 prior art, *except* where the derived information and the claimed invention are commonly owned at the time the invention is made.

Note, however, that even if § 102(f) is considered a valid source of prior art for purposes of § 103, the Patent Office recognizes that § 102(f) requires derivation of the invention *from another*. *See Ex parte Billottet*, 192 U.S.P.Q. (BNA) 413, 415-16 (Pat. Off. Bd. of App. 1976). In the case of partial overlap between an inventive entity claiming an invention and an inventive entity responsible for earlier research from whom the later entity allegedly derived enough to make their invention obvious, no § 102(f)/103 invalidity should result. *See* 2 D. CHISUM, PATENTS § 5.03[3][d] (1978 & Supp. 1991) (noting that "this would be an exception to the normal concept of separate 'inventive entities.'").

Special Rules for § 102(e)

Perhaps for obvious reasons, the rules on prior art and different inventive entities are softened somewhat in the case of § 102(e) prior art. As the Federal Circuit has stated:

> When the joint and sole inventions are related, as they are here, inventor *A* commonly discloses the invention of *A & B* in the course of describing his sole invention and when he so describes the invention of *A & B* he is not disclosing "prior art" to the *A & B* invention, even if he has legal status as "another"....

In re Kaplan, 789 F.2d 1574, 1576, 229 U.S.P.Q. (BNA) 678, 680 (Fed. Cir. 1986) (quoting *In re Land & Rogers*, 368 F.2d 866, 879, 151 U.S.P.Q. (BNA) 621, 633 (C.C.P.A. 1966)). The reason for this is simple: it would be almost impossible to ascertain in many cases which actually came first — *A*'s invention or *A & B*'s joint invention — and it would be quite unfair to in effect perform a mini-interference pitting *A* against her alter ego, *A & B*. Nonetheless, it must be admitted that this rule, however sensible, is an exception to the general theory of the inventive entity. But, as you should know by now, this is not the only area where patent law falls short of absolute symmetry — a good thing, as it turns out!

In *Applied Materials, Inc. v. Gemini Res. Corp.*, 835 F.2d 279, 281, 15 U.S.P.Q.2d 1816 (Fed. Cir. 1988), the court reiterated this theme:

> In this case the applications which matured into the '712 and '313 patents all grew from the same original application. Accordingly, if the invention claimed in the '313 patent is fully disclosed in the '712 patent, this invention had to be invented before the filing date of the '712 patent and the latter cannot be 102(e) prior art to the '313 patent.

See also Jackson Jordan, Inc. v. American Plasser Corp., 824 F.2d 977 n. 1 (Fed. Cir. 1987) (patent is not effective prior art reference if issued to same inventive entity less than one year prior to filing of application for patent at issue in the case). Note that, as the court in *Jackson Jordan* implied in dictum, a prior art reference which acts as a statutory bar can be effective against an inventor even if the reference was authored or invented by the same or a related inventive entity.

In a related case, the Federal Circuit has held that a § 102(e)/103 rejection is fundamentally different from a rejection for "double patenting" (a topic discussed in Chapter 7). *In re Bartfeld*, 925 F.2d 1450, 1453, 17 U.S.P.Q.2d 1885 (Fed. Cir. 1991) ("Given this fundamental difference between obviousness-type double patenting and § 102(e)/103 rejections, terminal disclaimers are neither appropriate nor available means for overcoming § 102(e)/103 rejections.").

The Federal Circuit has also recently elucidated the relationship between § 102(e) and § 102(g) in *Sun Studs, Inc. v. ATA Equip. Leasing, Inc.*, 872 F.2d 978, 983-84; 10 U.S.P.Q.2d (BNA) 1338 (Fed. Cir. 1989), *modified*, 872 F.2d 978, 11 U.S.P.Q.2d 1479 (Fed. Cir. 1989). Here an infringement defendant attempted to rely on the contents of a Mouat patent's specification to invalidate another patent, to Mason; Mouat, the reference patent, had a filing date *after* the filing date of the patent at issue, however, so the defendant asserted conception of the subject matter prior to Mouat's filing date. The court denied this attempt to, in effect, backdate the contents of a specification stating that it was an improper aggregation of § 102(e) and § 102(g) concepts:

> Both sides appear to have confused interference practice under § 102(g) with prior art status under § 102(e). The Mouat reference, as the district court held, does not describe or claim the identical invention to Mason. It is not prior art under § 102(g), but under § 102(e).... Under 35 U.S.C. § 102(e) the entire disclosure of Mouat's specification is effective as a reference, but only as of Mouat's filing date.

D. NONOBVIOUSNESS IN CASES INVOLVING CHEMISTRY AND BIOTECHNOLOGY

Inventions involving chemistry and biotechnology have a special status under § 103. The former have been the subject of an elaborate body of patent law — especially with regard to nonobviousness — since early in the twentieth century. It has been said, for instance, that

> [c]laims for chemical compounds present unique problems in applying the standard of nonobviousness or invention. Because of the unpredictable nature of chemical reactions, a newly-synthesized compound may be very similar in structure to known and existing compounds and yet exhibit very different properties. Further, many such new compounds are obvious in the sense that any competent chemist could have synthesized them if requested or motivated to do so. A key problem is whether a compound that is "chemically

obvious" in the above sense should be viewed as nonobvious for the purposes of the patent laws when the inventor shows that it possesses unexpected properties not in fact possessed by the prior art.

2 D. CHISUM, PATENTS § 5.04[6] (1978 & Supp. 1996).

This does not mean that the nonobviousness standard is any different for chemical inventions. *See In re Johnson*, 747 F.2d 1456, 1460, 223 U.S.P.Q. (BNA) 1260, 1263 (Fed. Cir. 1984) ("the requirement of unobviousness in the case of chemical inventions is the same as for other types of inventions."). The "unique problems" the field presents have not resulted in doctrinal developments fundamentally at odds with the basic structure of § 103. Instead, they have produced a rich body of caselaw which elaborates a series of detailed sub-rules meant to *apply* the principles of § 103 in the unique context of chemical inventions.

As for biotechnology, it was well recognized that a similarly elaborate body of law was developing in the 1980s and early 1990s, despite occasional admonitions from the courts that biotechnology was subject to the same standards as other branches of science and technology. Recently, however, Congress passed the Biotechnological Process Patents Act ("BPPA") of 1995, P.L. 104-41, § 1, 109 Stat. 351 ("BPPA"), codified at 35 U.S.C. § 103(b). The BPPA amended § 103 to provide a special standard of patentability for certain biotechnology-related inventions. Henceforth, under § 103 at least, patent law treats biotechnology very differently indeed. The next section will serve as an introduction to some of the intricacies of this emerging body of law.

1. BIOTECHNOLOGY

The following case is an important statement of § 103 principles as applied to inventions in the biotechnology industry. In the body of the opinion, and in the notes that follow, frequent reference is made to other important cases that are helping to shape this emergent legal specialty.

In re DEUEL

51 F.3d 1552, 34 U.S.P.Q.2d 1210 (Fed. Cir. 1995)

LOURIE, J.

Thomas F. Deuel, Yue-Sheng Li, Ned R. Siegel, and Peter G. Milner (collectively "Deuel") appeal from the November 30, 1993 decision of the U.S. Patent and Trademark Office Board of Patent Appeals and Interferences affirming the examiner's final rejection of claims 4-7 of application Serial No. 07/542,232, entitled "Heparin-Binding Growth Factor," as unpatentable on the ground of obviousness under 35 U.S.C. Section 103 (1988). *Ex parte Deuel*, 33 U.S.P.Q.2d 1445 (Bd. Pat. App. Int. 1993). Because the Board erred in concluding that Deuel's claims 5 and 7 directed to specific cDNA molecules would have been obvious in light of the applied references, and no other basis exists in the record to support the rejection with respect to claims 4 and 6 generically covering all possible DNA molecules coding for the disclosed proteins, we reverse.

BACKGROUND

The claimed invention relates to isolated and purified DNA and cDNA molecules encoding heparin-binding growth factors ("HBGFs"). [cDNA means "complementary DNA"; it can be thought of as the "genetic mirror image" of the functional part of a gene. Briefly, a gene is "transcribed" to form messenger RNA (mRNA), which carries the genetic information from its repository (in the nucleus of the cell, for eukaryotes such as humans) to the site where it is "translated" into one of the many proteins needed for an organism to function. The genetic complement to a piece of mRNA is called a cDNA. These are very useful in scientific research and now in commercial biotechnology as well.] HBGFs are proteins that stimulate mitogenic activity (cell division) and thus facilitate the repair or replacement of damaged or diseased tissue. DNA (deoxyribonucleic acid) is a generic term which encompasses an enormous number of complex macromolecules made up of nucleotide units. DNAs consist of four different nucleotides containing the nitrogenous bases adenine, guanine, cytosine, and thymine. A sequential grouping of three such nucleotides (a "codon") codes for one amino acid. A DNA's sequence of codons thus determines the sequence of amino acids assembled during protein synthesis. Since there are 64 possible codons, but only 20 natural amino acids, most amino acids are coded for by more than one codon. This is referred to as the "redundancy" or "degeneracy" of the genetic code.

DNA functions as a blueprint of an organism's genetic information. It is the major component of genes, which are located on chromosomes in the cell nucleus. Only a small part of chromosomal DNA encodes functional proteins.

Messenger ribonucleic acid ("mRNA") is a similar molecule that is made or transcribed from DNA as part of the process of protein synthesis. Complementary DNA ("cDNA") is a complementary copy ("clone") of mRNA, made in the laboratory by reverse transcription of mRNA. Like mRNA, cDNA contains only the protein-encoding regions of DNA. Thus, once a cDNA's nucleotide sequence is known, the amino acid sequence of the protein for which it codes may be predicted using the genetic code relationship between codons and amino acids. The reverse is not true, however, due to the degeneracy of the code. Many other DNAs may code for a particular protein. The functional relationships between DNA, mRNA, cDNA, and a protein may conveniently be expressed as follows:

Collections ("libraries") of DNA and cDNA molecules derived from various species may be constructed in the laboratory or obtained from commercial sources. Complementary DNA libraries contain a mixture of cDNA clones reverse-transcribed from the mRNAs found in a specific tissue source. Complementary DNA libraries are tissue-specific because proteins and their corresponding mRNAs are only made ("expressed") in specific tissues, depending upon the protein. Genomic DNA ("gDNA") libraries, by contrast, theoretically contain all of a species' chromosomal DNA. The molecules present in cDNA and DNA libraries may be of unknown function and chemical structure, and the proteins which they encode may be unknown. However, one may attempt to retrieve molecules of interest from cDNA or gDNA libraries by screening such libraries with a gene probe, which is a synthetic radiolabelled nucleic acid sequence designed to bond ("hybridize") with a target complementary base sequence. Such "gene cloning" techniques thus exploit the fact that the bases in DNA always hybridize in complementary pairs: adenine bonds with thymine and guanine bonds with cytosine. A gene probe for potentially isolating DNA or cDNA encoding a protein may be designed once the protein's amino acid sequence, or a portion thereof, is known.

As disclosed in Deuel's patent application, Deuel isolated and purified HBGF from bovine uterine tissue, found that it exhibited mitogenic activity, and determined the first 25 amino acids of the protein's N-terminal sequence.[1] Deuel then isolated a cDNA molecule encoding bovine uterine HBGF by screening a bovine uterine cDNA library with an oligonucleotide probe designed using the experimentally determined N-terminal sequence of the HBGF. Deuel purified and sequenced the cDNA molecule, which was found to consist of a sequence of 1196 nucleotide base pairs. From the cDNA's nucleotide sequence, Deuel then predicted the complete amino acid sequence of bovine uterine HBGF disclosed in Deuel's application.

Deuel also isolated a cDNA molecule encoding human placental HBGF by screening a human placental cDNA library using the isolated bovine uterine cDNA clone as a probe. Deuel purified and sequenced the human placental cDNA clone, which was found to consist of a sequence of 961 nucleotide base pairs. From the nucleotide sequence of the cDNA molecule encoding human placental HBGF, Deuel predicted the complete amino acid sequence of human placental HBGF disclosed in Deuel's application. The predicted human placental and bovine uterine HBGFs each have 168 amino acids and calculated molecular weights of 18.9 kD. Of the 168 amino acids present in the two HBGFs discovered by Deuel, 163 are identical. Deuel's application does not describe the chemical structure of, or state how to isolate and purify, any DNA or cDNA molecule except the disclosed human placental and bovine uterine cDNAs, which are the subject of claims 5 and 7.

Claims 4-7 on appeal are all independent claims and read, in relevant part, as follows:

> 4. A purified and isolated DNA sequence consisting of a sequence encoding human heparin binding growth factor of 168 amino acids having the following amino acid sequence:

---

[1] Deuel determined that the N-terminal sequence of bovine uterus HBGF is Gly - Lys - Lys - Glu - Lys - Pro - Glu - Lys - Lys - Val - Lys - Lys - Ser - Asp - Cys - Gly - Glu - Trp - Gln - Trp - Ser - Val - Cys - Val - Pro.

Met Gln Ala ... [remainder of 168 amino acid sequence].

5. The purified and isolated cDNA of human heparin-binding growth factor having the following nucleotide sequence:

GTCAAAGGCA ... [remainder of 961 nucleotide sequence].

6. A purified and isolated DNA sequence consisting of a sequence encoding bovine heparin binding growth factor of 168 amino acids having the following amino acid sequence:

Met Gln Thr ... [remainder of 168 amino acid sequence].

7. The purified and isolated cDNA of bovine heparin-binding growth factor having the following nucleotide sequence:

GAGTGGAGAG ... [remainder of 1196 nucleotide sequence].

Claims 4 and 6 generically encompass all isolated/purified DNA sequences (natural and synthetic) encoding human and bovine HBGFs, despite the fact that Deuel's application does not describe the chemical structure of, or tell how to obtain, any DNA or cDNA except the two disclosed cDNA molecules. Because of the redundancy of the genetic code, claims 4 and 6 each encompass an enormous number of DNA molecules, including the isolated/purified chromosomal DNAs encoding the human and bovine proteins. Claims 5 and 7, on the other hand, are directed to the specifically disclosed cDNA molecules encoding human and bovine HBGFs, respectively.

During prosecution, the examiner rejected claims 4-7 under 35 U.S.C. Section 103 as unpatentable over the combined teachings of Bohlen [European Patent Application No. 0326075, naming Peter Bohlen as inventor, published August 2, 1989] and Maniatis [Maniatis et al., Molecular Cloning: A Laboratory Manual, "Screening Bacteriophage [lambda] Libraries for Specific DNA Sequences by Recombination in Escherichia coli," Cold Spring Harbor Laboratory, New York, 1982, pp. 353-361.] The Bohlen reference discloses a group of protein growth factors designated as heparin-binding brain mitogens ("HBBMs") useful in treating burns and promoting the formation, maintenance, and repair of tissue, particularly neural tissue. Bohlen isolated three such HBBMs from human and bovine brain tissue. These proteins have respective molecular weights of 15 kD, 16 kD, and 18 kD. Bohlen determined the first 19 amino acids of the proteins' N-terminal sequences, which were found to be identical for human and bovine HBBMs. Bohlen teaches that HBBMs are brain-specific, and suggests that the proteins may be homologous between species. The reference provides no teachings concerning DNA or cDNA coding for HBBMs.

Maniatis describes a method of isolating DNAs or cDNAs by screening a DNA or CDNA library with a gene probe. The reference outlines a general technique for cloning a gene; it does not describe how to isolate a particular DNA or cDNA molecule. Maniatis does not discuss certain steps necessary to isolate a target cDNA, e.g., selecting a tissue-specific cDNA library containing a target cDNA and designing an oligonucleotide probe that will hybridize with the target cDNA.

The examiner asserted that, given Bohlen's disclosure of a heparin-binding protein and its N-terminal sequence and Maniatis's gene cloning method, it would have been prima facie obvious to one of ordinary skill in the art at the time of the invention to clone a gene for HBGF. According to the examiner, Bohlen's published N-terminal sequence would have motivated a person of ordinary skill in the art to clone such a gene because cloning the gene would allow recombinant production of HBGF, a useful protein. The examiner reasoned that a person of ordinary skill in the art could have designed a gene probe based on Bohlen's disclosed N-terminal sequence, then screened a DNA library in accordance with Maniatis's gene cloning method to isolate a gene encoding an HBGF. The examiner did not distinguish between claims 4 and 6 generically directed to all DNA sequences encoding human and bovine HBGFs and claims 5 and 7 reciting particular cDNAs.

In reply, Deuel argued, *inter alia*, that Bohlen teaches away from the claimed cDNA molecules because Bohlen suggests that HBBMs are brain-specific and, thus, a person of ordinary skill in the art would not have tried to isolate corresponding cDNA clones from human placental and bovine uterine cDNA libraries. The examiner made the rejection final, however, asserting that

> [t]he starting materials are not relevant in this case, because it was well known in the art at the time the invention was made that proteins, especially the general class of heparin binding proteins, are highly homologous between species and tissue type. It would have been entirely obvious to attempt to isolate a known protein from different tissue types and even different species.

No prior art was cited to support the proposition that it would have been obvious to screen human placental and bovine uterine cDNA libraries for the claimed cDNA clones. Presumably, the examiner was relying on Bohlen's suggestion that HBBMs may be homologous between species, although the examiner did not explain how homology between species suggests homology between tissue types.

The Board affirmed the examiner's final rejection. In its opening remarks, the Board noted that it is "constantly advised by the patent examiners, who are highly skilled in this art, that cloning procedures are routine in the art." According to the Board, "the examiners urge that when the sequence of a protein is placed into the public domain, the gene is also placed into the public domain because of the routine nature of cloning techniques." Addressing the rejection at issue, the Board determined that Bohlen's disclosure of the existence and isolation of HBBM, a functional protein, would also advise a person of ordinary skill in the art that a gene exists encoding HBBM. The Board found that a person of ordinary skill in the art would have been motivated to isolate such a gene because the protein has useful mitogenic properties, and isolating the gene for HBBM would permit large quantities of the protein to be produced for study and possible commercial use.

Like the examiner, the Board asserted, without explanation, that HBBMs are the same as HBGFs and that the genes encoding these proteins are identical. The Board concluded that "the Bohlen reference would have suggested to those of ordinary skill in this art that they should make the gene, and the Maniatis reference would have taught a technique for 'making' the gene with a reasonable expectation of success." Responding to Deuel's argument that the claimed cDNA clones were isolated from human placental and bovine uterine cDNA libraries, whereas the combined teachings of Bohlen and Maniatis would only have suggested screening a brain tissue cDNA library, the Board stated that "the claims before us are directed to the product and not the method of isolation. Appellants have not shown that the claimed DNA was not present in and could not have been readily isolated from the brain tissue utilized by Bohlen." Deuel now appeals.

DISCUSSION

On appeal, Deuel challenges the Board's determination that the applied references establish a prima facie case of obviousness. In response, the PTO maintains that the claimed invention would have been prima facie obvious over the combined teachings of Bohlen and Maniatis. Thus, the appeal raises the important question whether the combination of a prior art reference teaching a method of gene cloning, together with a reference disclosing a partial amino acid sequence of a protein, may render DNA and cDNA molecules encoding the protein prima facie obvious under Section 103.

Deuel argues that the PTO failed to follow the proper legal standard in determining that the claimed cDNA molecules would have been prima facie obvious despite the lack of structurally similar compounds in the prior art. Deuel argues that the PTO has not cited a reference teaching cDNA molecules, but instead has improperly rejected the claims based on the alleged obviousness of a method of making the molecules. We agree.

Because Deuel claims new chemical entities in structural terms, a prima facie case of unpatentability requires that the teachings of the prior art suggest the claimed compounds to a person of ordinary skill in the art. Normally a prima facie case of obviousness is based upon structural similarity, i.e., an established structural relationship between a prior art compound and the claimed compound. Structural relationships may provide the requisite motivation or suggestion to modify known compounds to obtain new compounds. For example, a prior art compound may suggest its homologs because homologs often have similar properties and therefore chemists of ordinary skill would ordinarily contemplate making them to try to obtain compounds with improved properties. Similarly, a known compound may suggest its analogs or isomers, either geometric isomers (cis v. trans) or position isomers (e.g., ortho v. para).

In all of these cases, however, the prior art teaches a specific, structurally-definable compound and the question becomes whether the prior art would have suggested making the specific molecular modifications necessary to achieve the claimed invention.

Here, the prior art does not disclose any relevant cDNA molecules, let alone close relatives of the specific, structurally-defined cDNA molecules of claims 5 and 7 that might render them obvious. Maniatis suggests an allegedly obvious process for trying to isolate cDNA molecules, but that, as we will indicate below, does not fill the gap regarding the subject matter of claims 5 and 7. Further, while the general idea of the claimed molecules, their function, and their general chemical nature may have been obvious from Bohlen's teachings, and the knowledge that some gene existed may have been clear, the precise cDNA molecules of claims 5 and 7 would not have been obvious over the Bohlen reference because Bohlen teaches proteins, not the claimed or closely related cDNA molecules. The redundancy of the genetic code precluded contemplation of or focus on the specific cDNA molecules of claims 5 and 7. Thus, one could not have conceived the subject matter of claims 5 and 7 based on the teachings in the cited prior art because, until the claimed molecules were actually isolated and purified, it would have been highly unlikely for one of ordinary skill in the art to contemplate what was ultimately obtained. What cannot be contemplated or conceived cannot be obvious.

The PTO's theory that one might have been motivated to try to do what Deuel in fact accomplished amounts to speculation and an impermissible hindsight reconstruction of the claimed invention. It also ignores the fact that claims 5 and 7 are limited to specific compounds, and any motivation that existed was a general one, to try to obtain a gene that was yet undefined and may have constituted many forms. A general motivation to search for some gene that exists does not necessarily make obvious a specifically-defined gene that is subsequently obtained as a result of that search. More is needed and it is not found here.

The genetic code relationship between proteins and nucleic acids does not overcome the deficiencies of the cited references. A prior art disclosure of the amino acid sequence of a protein does not necessarily render particular DNA molecules encoding the protein obvious because the redundancy of the genetic code permits one to hypothesize an enormous number of DNA sequences coding for the protein. No particular one of these DNAs can be obvious unless there is something in the prior art to lead to the particular DNA and indicate that it should be prepared. We recently held in *In re Baird*, 16 F.3d 380, 29 U.S.P.Q.2d 1550 (Fed. Cir. 1994), that a broad genus does not necessarily render obvious each compound within its scope. Similarly, knowledge of a protein does not give one a conception of a particular DNA encoding it. Thus, *a fortiori*, Bohlen's disclosure of the N-terminal portion of a protein, which the PTO urges is the same as HBGF, would not have suggested the particular cDNA molecules defined by claims 5 and 7. This is so even though one skilled in the art knew that some DNA, albeit not in purified and isolated form, did exist. The compounds of claims 5 and 7 are specific compounds not suggested by the prior art. A different result might pertain, however, if there were prior art, e.g., a protein of sufficiently small size and simplicity, so that lacking redundancy, each possible DNA would be obvious over the protein. *See In re Petering*, 301 F.2d 676 (C.C.P.A. 1962) (prior art reference disclosing limited genus of 20 compounds rendered every species within the genus unpatentable). That is not the case here.

The PTO's focus on known methods for potentially isolating the claimed DNA molecules is also misplaced because the claims at issue define compounds, not methods. See *In re Bell*, 991 F.2d 781, 785, 26 U.S.P.Q.2d 1529, 1532 (Fed. Cir. 1993). In *Bell*, the PTO asserted a rejection based upon the combination of a primary reference disclosing a protein (and its complete amino acid sequence) with a secondary reference describing a general method of gene cloning. We reversed the rejection, holding in part that "[t]he PTO's focus on Bell's method is misplaced. Bell does not claim a method. Bell claims compositions, and the issue is the obviousness of the claimed compositions, not of the method by which they are made." *Id.*

We today reaffirm the principle, stated in *Bell*, that the existence of a general method of isolating cDNA or DNA molecules is essentially irrelevant to the question whether the specific molecules themselves would have been obvious, in the absence of other prior art that suggests the claimed DNAs. A prior art disclosure of a process reciting a particular compound or obvious variant thereof as a product of the process is, of course, another matter, raising issues of anticipation under 35 U.S.C. Section 102 as well as obviousness under Section 103. Moreover, where there is prior art that suggests a claimed compound, the existence, or lack thereof, of an enabling process for making that compound is surely a factor in any patentability determination. There must, however, still be prior art that suggests the claimed compound in order for a prima facie case of obviousness to be made out; as we have already indicated, that prior art was lacking here with respect to claims 5 and 7. Thus, even if, as the examiner stated, the existence of general cloning techniques, coupled with knowledge of a protein's structure, might have provided motivation to prepare a cDNA or made it obvious to prepare a cDNA, that does not necessarily make obvious a particular claimed cDNA. "Obvious to try" has long been held not to constitute obviousness. *In re O'Farrell*, 853 F.2d 894, 903, 7 U.S.P.Q.2d 1673, 1680-81 (Fed. Cir. 1988). A general incentive does not make obvious a particular result, nor does the existence of techniques by which those efforts can be carried out. Thus, Maniatis's teachings, even in combination with Bohlen, fail to suggest the claimed invention.

The PTO argues that a compound may be defined by its process of preparation and therefore that a conceived process for making or isolating it provides a definition for it and can render it obvious. It cites *Amgen Inc. v. Chugai Pharmaceutical Co.*, 927 F.2d 1200, 18 U.S.P.Q.2d 1016 (Fed. Cir.), *cert. denied*, 502 U.S. 856 (1991), for that proposition. We disagree. The fact that one can conceive a general process in advance for preparing an undefined compound does not mean that a claimed specific compound was precisely envisioned and therefore obvious. A substance may indeed be defined by its process of preparation. That occurs, however, when it has already been prepared by that process and one therefore knows that the result of that process is the stated compound. The process is part of the definition of the compound. But that is not possible in advance, especially when the hypothetical process is only a general one. Thus, a conceived method of preparing some undefined DNA does not define it with the precision necessary to render it obvious over the protein it encodes. We did not state otherwise in *Amgen*. *See Amgen*, 927 F.2d at 1206-9, 18 U.S.P.Q.2d at 1021-23 (isolated/purified human gene held nonobvious; no conception of gene without envisioning its precise identity despite conception of general process of preparation).

We conclude that, because the applied references do not teach or suggest the claimed cDNA molecules, the final rejection of claims 5 and 7 must be reversed. *See also Bell*, 991 F.2d at 784-85, 26 U.S.P.Q.2d at 1531-32 (human DNA sequences encoding IGF proteins nonobvious over asserted combination of references showing gene cloning method and complete amino acid sequences of IGFs).

Claims 4 and 6 are of a different scope than claims 5 and 7. As is conceded by Deuel, they generically encompass all DNA sequences encoding human and bovine HBGFs. Written in such a result-oriented form, claims 4 and 6 are thus tantamount to the general idea of all genes encoding the protein, all solutions to the problem. Such an idea might have been obvious from the complete amino acid sequence of the protein, coupled with knowledge of the genetic code, because this information may have enabled a person of ordinary skill in the art to envision the idea of, and, perhaps with the aid of a computer, even identify all members of the claimed genus. The Bohlen reference, however, only discloses a partial amino acid sequence, and thus it appears that, based on the above analysis, the claimed genus would not have been obvious over this prior art disclosure. We will therefore also reverse the final rejection of claims 4 and 6 because neither the Board nor the patent examiner articulated any separate reasons for holding these claims unpatentable apart from the grounds discussed above.

The Board's decision affirming the final rejection of claims 4-7 is

Reversed.

NOTES

1. *A Fish Story.* *Deuel* can be understood in terms of a fishing scenario. Researchers "fish" for genes based on the amino acids in the protein whose genes they are searching for. They know that at least *one* sequence of base pairs exists, comprising the sought-after gene; the existence of the protein tells them this. It is as if a fisherman knows that he will catch *a* fish. What the *Deuel* court requires is for the researcher to predict the *actual* base pair sequence of the gene. This is akin to asking the fisherman exactly what kind of fish he will catch: bass or pike, large or small, markings, etc. Is this a sensible requirement? What justification is there for denying the researcher (or the fisherman) a property right simply because he can't describe the precise features of the molecule (or fish) he is searching for and is sure to find? For one suggestion, see Section 1.a, *supra*, on § 103 and abnormally expensive inventions.

2. *Ring a Bell?* The modern biotechnology industry is built around two different sets of technologies, monoclonal antibodies and recombinant DNA. Both of these are based on prior, more general advances in molecular biology and both were initially discovered and employed by scientists concerned with pure research. The Federal Circuit has been confronted by several challenges to patents based on these important technologies. So far, consistent with the "infant industry" stage thesis, the court has found the patents at issue valid despite the fact that the level of skill in this art continues to increase. *See, e.g., Hybritech, Inc. v. Monoclonal Antibodies, Inc.*, 802 F.2d 1367, 231 U.S.P.Q. (BNA) 81 (Fed. Cir. 1986), analyzed in Robert P. Merges, *Commercial Success and Patent Standards: Economic Perspectives on Innovation*, 76 CAL. L. REV. 803 (1988) (criticizing Federal Circuit opinion finding basic monoclonal antibody assay patent valid). Fortunately for the industry, an even broader patent on its other major technology — gene expression techniques — was rejected on obviousness grounds in 1988 because several of the inventors published results prior to the invention. *In re O'Farrell*, 853 F.2d 894, 7 U.S.P.Q.2d (BNA) 1673 (Fed. Cir. 1988). The investigators had discovered that a gene for a non-operational protein taken from a frog could be inserted into a bacterium and expressed there. 853 F.2d at 894, 7 U.S.P.Q.2d at 1674. On the basis of that research they filed a patent claiming a process for producing proteins that comprised "linking [a] natural or synthetic heterologous gene [i.e., one from a foreign source] ... to an indigenous [bacterium] gene portion ...." *Id*. The prior publication rendered the claimed invention obvious, the court said. In so doing, it was careful to note that it was *not* saying that the techniques of gene expression in general were unpatentable but only that the claims before it were too close to the description in the published article.

Any doubts about the court's budding biotechnology jurisprudence were settled when it decided *In re Bell*, 991 F.2d 781, 26 U.S.P.Q.2d (BNA) 1529 (Fed. Cir. 1993). Although other cases — some important — intervened between *O'Farrell* and *Bell*, the latter was the most significant opinion on biotechnology in some time. As such it was widely regarded as a bellwether of the court's current thinking on this important industry. As it turned out, those worried about *O'Farrell* had nothing to fear: *Bell* is in many ways a companion to *Hybritech*, and shows the same concern for the importance of patents in the biotechnology industry.

Bell involved a patent application claiming human gene sequences which code for insulin-like growth factors I and II (IGF-I and II). The examiner rejected the claims on grounds of obviousness, citing two publications by Rinderknecht disclosing amino acid sequences for IGF-I and IGF-II, and a patent to Weissman on a "Method for Cloning Genes." After the Board upheld the examiner, the applicants appealed. In a decision whose importance can hardly be overstated, the Federal Circuit reversed.

The court held that although Rinderknecht provided the structure of the protein, there were over 1000 possible nucleotide sequences that might code for it. 991 F.2d at 784. Given the nearly infinite number of possibilities suggested by the prior art, and the failure of the cited prior art to suggest which of those possibilities is the human sequence, the claimed sequences would not have been obvious. Further, the court stated, combining Rinderknecht with Weissman does not make the claimed sequences obvious, since Weissman does not expressly teach or fairly suggest that its general method for isolating genes should be combined with the disclosed protein of the Rinderknecht references. The Board clearly erred, the court continued, when it held that Weissman teaches toward, rather than away from, the claimed sequences. Therefore, the requisite teaching or suggestion to combine the teachings of the cited prior art references is absent. In the words of the court:

> It may be true that, knowing the structure of the protein, one can use the genetic code to hypothesize possible structures for the corresponding gene and that one thus has the potential for obtaining that gene. However, because of the degeneracy of the genetic code, there are a vast number of nucleotide sequences that might code for a specific protein. In the case of IGF, Bell has argued without contradiction that the Rinderknecht amino acid sequences could be coded for by more than 1036 different nucleotide sequences, only a few of which are the human sequences that Bell now claims. Therefore, given the nearly infinite number of possibilities suggested by the prior art, and the failure of the cited prior art to suggest which of those possibilities is the human sequence, the claimed sequences would not have been obvious.
>
> Bell does not claim all of the 1036 nucleic acids that might potentially code for IGF. Neither does Bell claim all nucleic acids coding for a protein having the biological activity of IGF. Rather, Bell claims only the human nucleic acid sequences coding for IGF. Absent anything in the cited prior art suggesting which of the 1036 possible sequences suggested by Rinderknecht corresponds to the IGF gene, the PTO has not met its burden of establishing that the prior art would have suggested the claimed sequences.

991 F.2d at 784.

This holding preserved in one stroke an important source of biotechnology patents — the systematic cloning of known proteins and protein fragments. Although several cases between *O'Farrell* and *Bell* held particular inventions obvious, such a holding from the Federal Circuit in this case would have raised the standard considerably in an area of research considered vital to biotechnology companies. The result, then, as in *Hybritech*, was to give the benefit of the doubt to the fledgling industry. Although at some point the level of skill will probably rise high enough to make inventions such as the one at issue in *Bell* legally obvious, for the time being the court has preserved the possibility of property rights in this important branch of the industry. Perhaps if this branch continues to be valuable, a decision that raises the standard of patentability here will cause problems for the industry. One suggestion is to give a slight "plus factor" to obvious but very expensive research. Robert P. Merges, *Uncertainty and the Standard of Patentability*, 7 HIGH TECH. L.J. 1 (1993). While inconsistent in some respects with a case here or there, this proposal has the virtue of both describing what the courts are actually doing in biotechnology cases (no small feat judging the vast pile of commentary growing up around these decisions) and providing a rationale for it. There is, furthermore, an historical argument to be made in favor of this approach: it appears to have been the (unarticulated) basis of the early era of chemical patent law. *Cf.* Robert P. Merges, Patent Law and Infant Industries: Chemical Industries and Biotechnology Compared (Working Paper 1996).

2. For a critique of *Deuel, Bell* and their ilk, see Anita Varma & David Abraham, *DNA Is Different: Legal Obviousness and the Balance Between Biotech Inventors and the Market*, 9 HARV. J.L. & TECH. 53, 55 (1996) ("In a series of recent decisions, the Federal Circuit has effectively tilted the balance far in favor of biotech patent applicants through its definition of the legal test of what constitutes a proper prima facie case of legal obviousness."). The authors advocate a solution that appears to be along the lines of a less stringent suggestion test. *See also* Brian C. Cannon, Note, *Toward a Clear Standard of Obviousness for Biotechnology Patents*, 79 CORNELL L. REV. 735 (1994). *But see* Stephen B. Maebius, *Patenting DNA Claims After In re Bell: How Much Better Off Are We?*, 76 J. PAT. & TRADEMARK OFF. SOC'Y 508 (1994) (pointing out fact-specific nature of the *Bell* holding). *Cf.* Robert Desmond, Comment, *Nothing Seems "Obvious" to the Court of Appeals for the Federal Circuit: The Federal Circuit, Unchecked by the Supreme Court, Transforms the Standard of Obviousness Under the Patent Law*, 26 LOY. L.A. L. REV. (1993).

Biotech Process Patents

New § 103(b) creates a relaxed standard of patentability for biotechnology-related inventions claimed as processes for making or using novel biotechnological compositions. It reads:

§ 103. Conditions for patentability; non-obvious subject matter

....

(b)(1) Notwithstanding subsection (a), and upon timely election by the applicant for patent to proceed under this subsection, a biotechnological process using or resulting in a composition of matter that is novel under section 102 and nonobvious under subsection (a) of this section shall be considered nonobvious if —

(A) claims to the process and the composition of matter are contained in either the same application for patent or in separate applications having the same effective filing date; and

(B) the composition of matter, and the process at the time it was invented, were owned by the same person or subject to an obligation of assignment to the same person.

(2) A patent issued on a process under paragraph (1) —

(A) shall also contain the claims to the composition of matter used in or made by that process, or

(B) shall, if such composition of matter is claimed in another patent, be set to expire on the same date as such other patent, notwithstanding section 154.

(3) For purposes of paragraph (1), the term "biotechnological process" means —

(A) a process of genetically altering or otherwise inducing a single- or multi-celled organism to —

(i) express an exogenous nucleotide sequence,

(ii) inhibit, eliminate, augment, or alter expression of an endogenous nucleotide sequence, or

(iii) express a specific physiological characteristic not naturally associated with said organism;

(B) cell fusion procedures yielding a cell line that expresses a specific protein, such as a monoclonal antibody; and

(C) a method of using a product produced by a process defined by subparagraph (A) or (B), or a combination of subparagraphs (A) and (B).

....

This Act has two primary effects: (1) it makes per se nonobvious certain process claims in biotechnology-related patents and patent applications; and (2) it adds an enormous amount of verbiage onto the previously concise structure of § 103 to do so.

Brief Analysis

The overall impact of new section 103(b) is quite modest. This is especially so compared to earlier bills, which would have applied to all patents. *See* KENNETH BURCHFIEL, BIOTECHNOLOGY AND THE FEDERAL CIRCUIT § 6.11(d) (1995) (criticizing earlier versions as too broad).

The key features of § 103 are that it: (1) applies only to "biotechnological process[es]," as defined with particularity in § 103(b)(3); (2) requires that the process "use[] or result[] in" a novel and nonobvious composition of matter, i.e., product; (3) ties the term of the process patent to the term of the underlying composition of matter patent; and (4) applies only when the product and process are developed by the same firm or research group.

The limitation to biotechnological processes ties § 103(b) tightly to conventional biotech research. This keeps a tight rein on the sweep of the section. While guardians of traditional standards will be grateful, the very specificity of the BPPA puts it at risk of becoming outdated in the future. Like the Semiconductor Chip Protection Act, which was tied to production techniques now largely outmoded, the BPPA may someday be made irrelevant by the march of technology. Indeed, the BPPA exercise helps us appreciate a major virtue of the Patent Act of 1952: its highly generalized statements of standards and principles. (*See, e.g.*, original §§ 101, 102, 103, 112, 154, and 271.) The generality of the basic provisions of the 1952 Act allowed it to grow organically — almost in a classically common law-like way — to encompass the coming of all manner of new technologies developed since its enactment.

The second and third requirements restrict the coverage of § 103(b) even more. They in effect subject inventions claimed as product/process pairs under the BPPA to "double patenting"-type treatment. (Specifically, it treats the process claims as subject to an "obviousness-type double patenting" analysis; See Chapter 7.) This means that, while the obvious process claim is allowed, its term of protection is linked to the term of the underlying product claim(s). If there are two separate patents, a "terminal disclaimer" is required so that they both expire on the same date. The upshot is that just as in the case of double patenting, the law trades a bit of extra scope for a bit shorter patent term. This statutory bargain limits the economic power bestowed on the inventor of a biotechnological product/process pair.

A Note on Political Economy

The BPPA also highlights the influence of specific industries on the development of intellectual property legislation. This is not a new development by any means. *See, e.g.*, Robert P. Merges, *Contracting Into Liability Rules: Collective Rights Organizations and Intellectual Property Rights*, CAL. L. REV. (1996) (summarizing literature on the political economy of intellectual property rights); Peter Menell, *The Challenges of Reforming Intellectual Property*, 94 COLUM. L. REV. 2644 (1994); Jessica Litman, *Copyright Legislation and Technological Change*, 68 OR. L. REV. 275 (1989) (arguing that copyright legislation is so complicated that Congress delegates it to industry representatives anyway). But together with certain other trends, such as the passage of firm-specific patent extensions ("private patent bills"), legislation such as this raises the possibility of a threat to traditional standards of generality and even-handedness. *See* Subcommittee on Patents, Copyrights and Trademarks, Committee on the Judiciary, U.S. Senate, Hearings on Patent Extensions, Aug. 1, 1991 (Statement of Prof. Robert P. Merges), at 1 ("Special requests [for extensions] recapitulate the history of our patent system, and remind us of the wisdom of resolving these issues inside the special institutions designed for them."). *See generally* Robert P. Merges, *The Economics of Intellectual Property Rights: An Overview and*

Guide to the Literature, J. ECON. CULTURE (1996) (emphasizing the attractiveness of intellectual property legislation, as a private redistribution of wealth in favor of strong interests, in an era when direct government expenditures are limited).

We turn now to a brief review of the Federal Circuit/PTO rift that preceded the BPPA.

Doctrinal/Administrative Background of the BPPA

To understand why Congress would tinker with the well-entrenched general principle stated in the former version of § 103 requires two things: a little history, and an appreciation for the "political economy" of intellectual property rights legislation.

The history leading up to the enactment of the BPPA is fraught with poorly reasoned cases, hardheaded administrative responses, and a general lack of interest in the economic effects of patent doctrine. Prior to *In re Ochiai*, below, and another recent case, *In re Brouwer*, 37 U.S.P.Q.2d 1663 (Fed. Cir. 1996), the Federal Circuit had upheld the Patent Office in several controversial cases involving process inventions. The most controversial was *In re Durden*, 763 F.2d 1406, 226 U.S.P.Q. 359 (Fed. Cir. 1985), where the Federal Circuit affirmed the rejection of claims to a method of making a compound using (1) a novel (and patented) chemical composition "starting material," and (2) a well-known (non-novel) process. The Federal Circuit approved of the Board's logic that, given the facts of this case, the novel starting material was of a member of class well known to work in the established process. It was as if, the opinion implies, someone had tried to claim a method for making cookies using a a new (and patented) type of dough (e.g., cucumber and peanut butter) in an otherwise old recipe (mix dough, separate into cookie-sized pieces, bake for 30 minutes at 350 degrees, etc.). The cookie dough might be new, but the "method of making cookies" using that new dough was obvious. In the court's words:

> [The applicant in *Durden*] filed a parent application ... "claiming novel oxime compounds, novel insecticidal carbamate compounds and a novel process for producing the carbamate compounds, employing the novel oxime compounds as the starting materials." A patent issued in 1980 on the parent application claiming carbamate compound products. A divisional application was filed claiming ... the process of making the novel carbamate products from the novel oxime starting materials and the one remaining claim now before us stands rejected as ... obvious....

> [T]here has been a failure to distinguish between novelty and unobviousness. Of course, an otherwise old process becomes a new process when a previously unknown starting material, for example, is used in it which is then subjected to a conventional manipulation or reaction to produce a product which may also be new, albeit the expected result of what is done. But it does not necessarily mean that the whole process had become unobvious in

the sense of § 103. In short, a new process may still be obvious ... notwithstanding the specific starting material or resulting product, or both, is not to be found in the prior art.

See generally Litman, *Obvious Process Rejections Under 35 U.S.C. 103*, 71 J. PAT. OFF. SOC'Y 775 (1989).

Two subsequent cases touch on this issue. In *In re Dillon, infra*, the court stated:

> We make no judgment as to the patentability of claims that Dillon might have made and properly argued to a method directed to the novel aspects of her invention, except to question the lack of logic in a claim to a method of reducing particulate emissions by combusting. Suffice it to say that we do not regard *Durden* [*In re Durden*, 763 F.2d 1406, 226 U.S.P.Q. 359 (Fed. Cir. 1985),] as authority to reject as obvious every method claim reading on an old type of process, such as mixing, reacting, reducing, etc. The materials used in a process as well as the result obtained therefrom, must be considered along with the specific nature of the process, and the fact that new or old, obvious or nonobvious, materials are used or result from the process are only factors to be considered, rather than conclusive indicators of the obviousness or nonobviousness of a claimed process. When any applicant presents and argues suitable method claims, they should be examined in light of all these relevant factors, free from any presumed controlling effect of *Durden*. *Durden* did not hold that all methods involving old process steps are obvious[;] the court in that case concluded that the particularly claimed process was obvious; it refused to adopt an unvarying rule that the fact that nonobvious starting materials and nonobvious products are involved ipso facto makes the process nonobvious. Such an invariant rule always leading to the opposite conclusion is also not the law. Thus, we reject the Commissioner's argument that we affirm the rejection of the method claims under the precedent of *Durden*.

919 F.2d at 695.

And in *In re Pleuddemann*, 910 F.2d 823, 15 U.S.P.Q.2d (BNA) 1738 (Fed. Cir. 1990) (Rich, J.), the court limited *Durden*'s application to claims covering a method of making, as opposed to those covering a method of using a certain substance. In *Pleuddemann* the applicant discovered certain organosilanes that were deemed patentable through the Examiner's allowance of claims to the organosilanes, per se. Claims to methods of use of these patentable organosilanes were denied. In discussing prior cases such as *In re Kuehl*, 475 F.2d 658, 177 U.S.P.Q. 250 (C.C.P.A. 1973), the court observed that there is a distinction that may be of significance between claims to a method of making a novel compound, that can be obvious though the compound itself is not, and claims to a method of using the compound.

> We have concluded, for reasons stated above, that the process-of-use claims are patentable and that it is not necessary to show unexpected utility in order

to show unobviousness. We would add, moreover, that in our view it is in the public interest to permit appellant to claim the process [of use] as well as the product. The result is to encourage a more detailed disclosure of the specific methods of using the novel composition he had invented in order to have support for the process claims.

The *Pleuddemann* and *Dillon* cases suggest the correct approach to the problem posed by *Durden*. It is an empty metaphysical game to question whether an old process, when used with novel starting materials or to produce a novel product, is itself new. In one sense, of course it is new; that precise process has never been employed before, by definition. The starting material or end product did not exist; so that precise process could not have either. But does that make the process new?

To take the opposite metaphysical tack, the answer is no. The essence of a process is its steps — its procedure for acting on starting materials or producing an end product. Only a new set of steps can constitute a new process. Merely applying the old steps to new things cannot be said to yield a new process. For example, consider an age-old recipe for baking fruit pies. If a clever botanist has crossed a banana with an orange, to produce a "banorange," does the use of the age-old recipe to make a banorange pie really contribute anything new? To put the problem in terms introduced at the beginning of this chapter: was there a significant degree of technical uncertainty just prior to first trying to make a banorange pie using the age-old recipe?

Simply posing the question this way reveals the wisdom of avoiding a *per se* rule either way. Rather than saying the process of applying the old recipe to the new fruit is *per se* old (because the underlying process is old), or *per se* new (because, of course, it has never been applied to the banorange before), we might more fruitfully (!) ask whether one skilled in the pie-baking art would have had a reasonable expectation that the recipe would be a success using the new fruit just prior to trying the recipe on the fruit. Perhaps something about this fruit would make the skilled chef worry that the old recipe would not work so well. (The banorange's consistency, for instance, might be different enough from that of all other fruit to raise a doubt that it would bake well.) Perhaps it would be expected to work just fine, as always. Only case-by-case inquiry, keeping the key question regarding technical certainty squarely in mind, can really carry out the purpose of § 103 in this context.

In any event, from the modest beginning in *Durden*, the Patent Office evolved a rather rigid per se rule: no patents for otherwise old processes used with novel starting materials. The patent bar was not pleased. *See, e.g.*, Kate Murashige, *Section 102/103 Issues in Biotechnology Patent Practice*, 16 AM. INTELL. L. ASS'N Q.J. 294, 310 (1989). Indeed, a two-pronged assault was launched. The campaign was so successful that two trophies ultimately resulted: new § 103(b) (above), and the *Ochiai* decision, excerpted below. (An interim victory was the decision in *In re Pleuddemann*, 910 F.2d 823, 15 U.S.P.Q.2d 1738 (Fed. Cir. 1990) (reversing process application rejection; distinguishing claims to "method of *using*" claims, such as those at issue, from "method of *making*" claims such as those in *Durden*). Can you see how clever drafting could take advantage of this distinction? Consider claims to a "method of using [x] to produce [y]."

In re OCHIAI

71 F.3d 1565, 37 U.S.P.Q.2d 1127 (Fed. Cir. 1995)

PER CURIAM.

This appeal is from the July 8, 1992, decision of the United States Patent and Trademark Office (PTO) Board of Patent Appeals and Interferences (Board) affirming the examiner's rejection of claims 6 through 10 of Michihiko Ochiai et al.'s (collectively "Ochiai") application serial no. 07/462,492, claiming priority from parent application serial no. 642,356, filed December 19, 1975, now U.S. Patent No. 4,098,888 (methods for the manufacture of cephems). *Ex parte Ochiai*, 24 U.S.P.Q.2d 1265 (Bd. Pat. App. & Int. 1992). The real party in interest is Takeda Chemical Industries, Ltd., the assignee of any patent issuing from the application.

The rejection of the above claims was predicated on an asserted view of the law of obviousness, per 35 U.S.C. § 103, in view of the combined teaching of six references. [U.S. Patent No. 3,167,549 to Hoover; U.S. Patent No. 3,338,897 to Takano et al.; U.S. Patent No. 3,360,515 to Takano et al.; U.S. Patent No. 4,024,133 to Cook et al.; U.S. Patent No. 4,024,134 to Gregson et al.; and Flynn, Cephalosporin and Penicillins 83-91 (1972).] Because, under the legally correct method for determining obviousness, the claimed process is not obvious in view of the cited prior art references, we reverse.

The Invention

Ochiai's application is directed to a process for using an acyl side chain from a particular type of organic acid having a 2-aminothiazolyl group, and a particular type of amine to make a particular cephem compound having antibiotic properties. Claim 6, the principal claim on appeal, [appears on the following page].

Ochiai's U.S. Patent No. 4,298,606 covers the cephem compound resulting from the process of claim 6, and Ochiai's U.S. Patent No. 4,203,899 covers the organic acid used in the process of claim 6. *Id.* at 1267. In other words, viewed as of the time the claimed process was invented, claim 6 recites a process of using a new, nonobvious acid to make a new, nonobvious cephem. The '606 and '899 patents, like the application at bar, claim priority from the December 1975 parent application.

The Rejection

The examiner rejected claims 6 through 10 as obvious in light of the combined teaching of the six references noted above. All six references, as Ochiai acknowl-

6. A process for preparing a cephem compound of the formula:

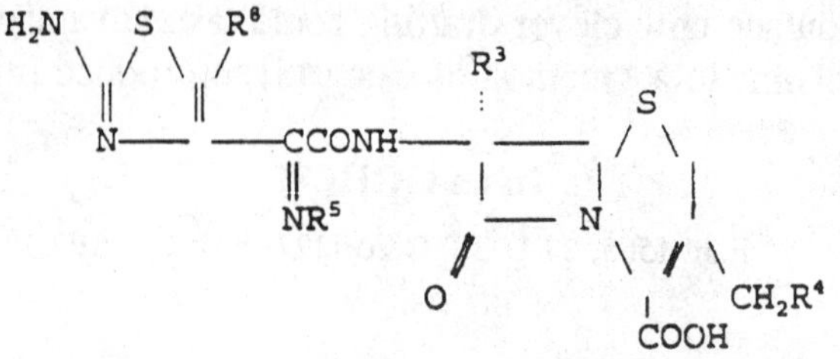

wherein R^3 is hydrogen or methoxy, R^4 is hydrogen or a residue of a nucleophilic compound, R^5 is hydroxyl or a protected hydroxyl, and R^8 is hydrogen or a halogen, or a pharmaceutically acceptable salt or ester thereof, which comprises introducing an acyl group of the formula:

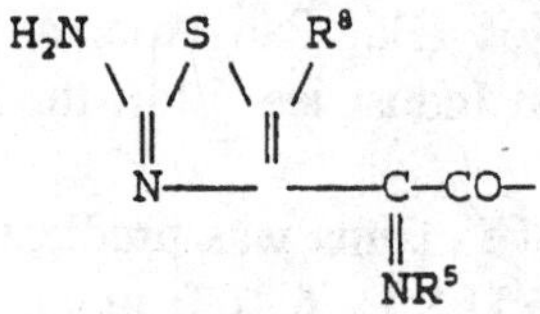

wherein R^5 and R^8 are as defined above into the amino group of the molecule of the formula:

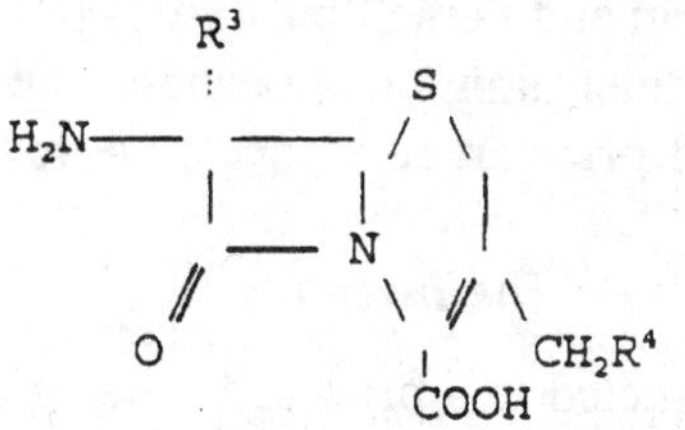

wherein R^3 and R^4 are as defined above or a salt or ester thereof.

Figure 5-9

edges, teach the use of a type of acid to make a type of cephem by a standard acylation reaction with the very same amine recited in claim 6. The examiner explained the rejections thusly in his answer to Ochiai's appeal to the Board:

> It must again be stressed that the citation of six references is to demonstrate convincingly that a standard, conventional process of preparing cephalosporin compounds is being claimed. The only difference between what is being claimed and the prior art is the selection of a slightly different acylation agent [i.e., acid] to result in a slightly different final product. The closest

prior art of the six references is represented by the Cook et al. 4,024,133 and Gregson et al. patent 4,024,134. These two references use [sic, are] quite similar in their disclosure, Cook being the most [sic, more] relevant. Both of these references generically disclose the "2-amino-thiazolyl" group which appellants seek to introduce....

....

The examiner recognizes that the specific "2 amino thiazolyl" moiety has not been specifically named in [the] Cook et al[.] patent. However, Cook et al. when viewed from the standpoint of one skilled in the art would recognize the use of "2-aminothiazolyl" if the final products sought were to contain this moiety. This merely states the obvious....

....

The facts presented here are identical to those that occurred in the *Durden* decision (*In re Durden* [763 F.2d 1406] 226 U.S.P.Q. 359). The acylating agent herein being used has been patented by appellants, see Ochia et al. 4,203,899. The final products have also been patented by appellants which appellants acknowledge, brief page 5 footnote 4. The only difference between the facts in *Durden* [...] and the instant situation is that appellants have not admitted on the record that the process is obvious. Appellants seek to distinguish the *Durden* decision based on this difference.[...]

On appeal, the Board affirmed the examiner's rejection. After reviewing the examiner's reliance on *In re Durden*, 763 F.2d 1406, 226 U.S.P.Q. 359 (Fed. Cir. 1985), and the "standard" nature of the acylation reaction disclosed in the rejected claims, the Board acknowledged Ochiai's contention that the fact that "neither the final product nor the method of introducing the particular [acid] component were known, obvious or even remotely suggested in the prior art ... should be dispositive of the obviousness of the invention" recited in claim 6. *Ochiai*, 24 U.S.P.Q.2d at 1267. The Board did not, however, find Ochiai's contention persuasive. According to the Board,

[w]e are not here concerned with the patentability of the starting materials, the final compounds or other processes of making the [cephem] compounds. We are concerned only with the claimed process and the patentability thereof. Cases such as *In re Larsen*, 292 F.2d 531, 49 C.C.P.A. 711, 130 U.S.P.Q. 209 (C.C.P.A. 1961); *In re Albertson*, 332 F.2d 379, 51 C.C.P.A. 1377, 141 U.S.P.Q. 730 (C.C.P.A. 1964) and, particularly, *In re Durden, supra*, all of which were directed to processes of making chemical compounds, are controlling herein.... In each case, a material A, either known or novel, was subjected to a standard process of reacting with a standard reactant, B, in order to produce the result expected from the reaction of A with B. Indeed in *Albertson* as in the instant case, the only manipulative step of the process is that which is embodied in the word "reacting."

Id. The Board also rejected Ochiai's assertion that cases such as *In re Pleuddemann*, 910 F.2d 823, 15 U.S.P.Q.2d 1738 (Fed. Cir. 1990), *In re Mancy*, 499 F.2d 1289, 182 U.S.P.Q. 303 (C.C.P.A. 1974), and *In re Kuehl*, 475 F.2d 658, 177 U.S.P.Q. 250 (C.C.P.A. 1973), are in tension with *Durden* and *Albertson* and counsel allowance of the rejected claims. Distinguishing *Pleuddemann*, *Mancy*, and *Kuehl* as "method of using" rather than "method of making" cases, the Board summarized its decision as follows:

> In the case before us, appellants have admitted the claims are directed to a process of making a desired AB product. The process steps, "introducing" A into AB or "reacting" A with B are standard processes used by practitioners in the prior art for reacting similar A moieties with the same B moiety. We are in agreement with the examiner that there is nothing unobvious in the particular process chosen and claimed by the appellants.

Ochiai appeals, contending that both the examiner and the Board failed to apply the proper test for obviousness established by *Graham v. John Deere Co.*, 383 U.S. 1, 86 S. Ct. 684, 15 L. Ed. 2d 545, 148 U.S.P.Q. 459 (1966), and its progeny. Specifically, according to Ochiai, both the examiner and the Board, on the assumption that our decision in *Durden* controlled the outcome of the instant case, failed to weigh the specific differences between the claimed invention — with all its limitations — and the prior art references, the so-called "second *Graham* factor."

The Solicitor, while defending the correctness of the Board's conclusion and, unlike the Board itself, doing so in the familiar terms of *Graham*, also asserts that a supposed irreconcilable conflict in our cases — between *Albertson* and *Durden*, on the one hand, and *Pleuddemann*, on the other — "makes it very difficult for patent attorneys to give cogent advice to clients or for patent examiners to render consistent decisions on the patentability (under § 103) of processes involving the use of new and unobvious starting materials." Unlike Ochiai, however, the Solicitor asks us to take the opportunity to reaffirm the vitality of *Albertson* and *Durden* in the course of deciding this appeal.

The Issue

The issue before this court is whether the Board erred in upholding the examiner's rejection of claim 6 as obvious under 35 U.S.C. § 103 in view of … *Durden* as interpreted by the PTO when neither the particular acid used nor the particular cephem produced is either taught or suggested by the art that predates the parent application.

The Analysis

The test of obviousness vel non is statutory. It requires that one compare the claim's "subject matter as a whole" with the prior art "to which said subject matter pertains." 35 U.S.C. § 103. The inquiry is thus highly fact-specific by design. This is so "whether the invention be a process for making or a process of using, or some other process." *Kuehl*, 475 F.2d at 665, 177 U.S.P.Q. at 255. When the references cited by the examiner fail to establish a prima facie case of obviousness, the rejection is improper and will be overturned.

Applying this statutory test to the art of record, we conclude that Ochiai's process invention as claimed is not prima facie obvious. The process invention Ochiai recites in claim 6 specifically requires use of none other than its new, nonobvious acid as one of the starting materials. One having no knowledge of this acid could hardly find it obvious to make any cephem using this acid as an acylating agent, much less the particular cephem recited in claim 6. In other words, it would not have been obvious to those of ordinary skill in the art to choose the particular acid of claim 6 as an acylating agent for the known amine for the simple reason that the particular acid was unknown but for Ochiai's disclosure in the '429 application. As one of our predecessor courts had occasion to observe, in a case involving a highly analogous set of facts, "one cannot choose from the unknown." *Mancy*, 499 F.2d at 1293, 182 U.S.P.Q. at 306. [In *Mancy*, the applicant claimed a process for using a newly discovered strain of the microorganism *Streptomyces* to produce a known antibiotic by means of conventional aerobic cultivation. 499 F.2d at 1290, 182 U.S.P.Q. at 304. The examiner rejected the claim, and the Board affirmed the rejection. The court reversed, concluding that [w]ithout *Streptomyces bifurcus*, strain DS 23,219, knowledge of which is supplied [only] by appellants' application and availability of which is supplied by appellants' deposit of the microorganism with the Department of Agriculture, one skilled in the art would not find it obvious to produce daunorubicin by aerobically cultivating *Streptomyces bifurcus*. *Id*. at 1292, 182 U.S.P.Q. at 305.]

In addition, although the prior art references the examiner discussed do indeed teach the use of various acids to make various cephems, they do not define a class of acids the knowledge of which would render obvious the use of Ochiai's specifically claimed acid. The Board noted that Ochiai's specifically claimed acid is "similar" to the acids used in the prior art. Likewise, the examiner asserted that the claimed acid was "slightly different" from those taught in the cited references. Neither characterization, however, can establish the obviousness of the use of a starting material that is new and nonobvious, both in general and in the claimed process. The mere chemical possibility that one of those prior art acids could be modified such that its use would lead to the particular cephem recited in claim 6 does not make the process recited in claim 6 obvious "unless the prior art suggested the desirability of [such a] modification." *In re Gordon*, 733 F.2d 900, 902, 221 U.S.P.Q. 1125, 1127 (Fed. Cir. 1984). As we noted above, the examiner discussed no references containing any suggestion or motivation either (a) to modify known acids to obtain the particular one recited in claim 6, or (b) to obtain the particular new and nonobvious cephem produced by the process of claim 6. In short, the prior art contains nothing at all to support the conclusion that the particular process recited in claim 6 is obvious.

The Alleged Conflict in Our Case Law

Both the Solicitor and Ochiai devote substantial portions of their briefs to purported demonstrations that our precedents on the obviousness vel non of chemical processes are, if not in conflict, at least in severe tension with one another and thus create unnecessary confusion.

Because the regime of section 103, much like the Fourth Amendment proscriptions against "unreasonable" searches and warrants issued upon less than "probable cause," mandates that legal outcomes turn on the close analysis of facts, reasonable persons may well disagree about the outcome of a given obviousness determination. These disagreements over the application of a legal rule can, however, be transformed into perceived "irreconcilable conflicts" between legal rules only when, as occurred here, examiners, members of the Board, and patent lawyers purport to find competing per se rules in our precedents and argue for rejection or allowance of a particular claim accordingly. We acknowledge that some generalized commentary found in these cases reviewing rejections of claims directed to chemical processes may, if viewed in isolation, have inadvertently provided encouragement to those who desire per se rules in this area. As the cases noted above make clear, however, this is not and has never been the law of section 103. Indeed, *Durden*, the very case relied on by the examiner and the Board for a purported per se rule, clearly states that there are no such per se rules.

The use of per se rules, while undoubtedly less laborious than a searching comparison of the claimed invention — including all its limitations — with the teachings of the prior art, flouts section 103 and the fundamental case law applying it. Per se rules that eliminate the need for fact-specific analysis of claims and prior art may be administratively convenient for PTO examiners and the Board. Indeed, they have been sanctioned by the Board as well. But reliance on per se rules of obviousness is legally incorrect and must cease. Any such administrative convenience is simply inconsistent with section 103, which, according to *Graham* and its progeny, entitles an applicant to issuance of an otherwise proper patent unless the PTO establishes that the invention as claimed in the application is obvious over cited prior art, based on the specific comparison of that prior art with claim limitations. We once again hold today that our precedents do not establish any per se rules of obviousness, just as those precedents themselves expressly declined to create such rules. Any conflicts as may be perceived to exist derive from an impermissible effort to extract per se rules from decisions that disavow precisely such extraction.

NOTES

1. *Too Late to Help?* Despite its clarity, *Ochiai* would have been more helpful if issued prior to passage of the BPPA, *supra*; it certainly seems a more even-handed solution to the problem of biotechnology process patents. Indeed, it is ironic that Congress passed the BPPA stating a per se rule, in light of the Federal Circuit's warning in *Ochiai* about the folly of such rules in § 103 analysis.

2. Rules Versus Standards. The Biotechnology Process Patent Amendments Act (*infra*) was passed largely at the insistence of the biotechnology industry, which felt that the Patent Office was suppressing meritorious inventions by applying a per se rule of unpatentability. The solution was to adopt the reverse per se rule; now all inventions in the legislatively defined class are automatically patentable.

The biotechnology industry argued strenuously that the Act was needed to restore certainty. This echoes a theme of the economic literature on the benefits (and costs) of clear ex ante rules. *See* Louis Kaplow, *Rules Versus Standards: An Economic Analysis*, 42 DUKE L.J. 557 (1992). The downside of such a rigid rule, of course, is that its application will at times yield unsatisfying results. In this respect the application of a standard — a general decisional framework, typical for example of common law doctrines — is superior. Cases such as *Ochiai* should put to rest the notion that the courts, in applying the very "standard-ish" § 103, will never allow patents on biotechnology processes whose only novel element is the starting materials. Equally important, the general § 103 standard would have allowed courts to deny patents for very modest adaptations of existing processes. The new legislation, however, eliminates that possibility.

2. CHEMISTRY

a. The Technological Landscape of the Chemical Industry

Chemical industries produce an incredibly diverse range of products, from bulk chemicals, like sulfuric acid, to synthetic materials, like plastics, to pharmaceuticals. (David Landes, the noted historian of technology, has called the business of chemical manufacture "the most miscellaneous of industries." D. LANDES, THE UNBOUND PROMETHEUS: TECHNOLOGICAL CHANGE AND INDUSTRIAL DEVELOPMENT IN WESTERN EUROPE FROM 1750 TO THE PRESENT 269 (1969)). And research is a cornerstone of these industries, which have been called the first science-based sector of the economy. *See* F. AFTALION, A HISTORY OF THE INTERNATIONAL CHEMICAL INDUSTRY (O. Benfey trans., 1991). Despite the diversity of products, however, invention in the chemical industries shares several key attributes. Research and development on new chemical products is subject to an unusual degree of uncertainty and costly experimentation, both because it is difficult to predict the precise chemical structure needed to achieve a given end and because the effects of using a new chemical substance in a particular way can be startling. C. TAYLOR & Z. SILBERSTON, THE ECONOMIC IMPACT OF THE PATENT SYSTEM: A STUDY OF THE BRITISH EXPERIENCE) 252 (1973) ("unpredictability [of the behavior of chemicals in the human body] is of a much higher order than that found in non-biological areas of chemical research — and very much higher than that in engineering fields"); 2 D. CHISUM, *supra* § 5.04[6]

("[A] newly-synthesized compound may be very similar in structure to known and existing compounds and yet exhibit very different properties."). *Cf.* H. Grabowski & J. Vernon, *The Pharmaceutical Industry*, in GOVERNMENT AND TECHNICAL PROGRESS 281, 294 (R. Nelson ed., 1980) ("the strategy of developing 'me too' products through molecular modification is neither costless nor always guaranteed to produce an effective substitute for an established product.").

Obviousness and enablement rules for chemical inventions reflect the accepted unpredictability of chemical inventions. *See, e.g., Studiengesellschaft Kohle mbH v. Eastman Kodak Co.*, 616 F.2d 1315, 1341, 206 U.S.P.Q. (BNA) 577, 600 (5th Cir.) ("[I]n catalytic chemistry, minor changes in components, their ratio, or the external condition of the reaction may produce major changes in the reaction itself."), *cert. denied*, 449 U.S. 1014, 208 U.S.P.Q. (BNA) 88 (1980); *In re Fisher*, 427 F.2d 833, 839, 166 U.S.P.Q. (BNA) 18, 24 (C.C.P.A. 1970) ("In cases involving unpredictable factors, such as most chemical reactions and physiological activity, the scope of enablement obviously varies inversely with the degree of unpredictability of the factors involved.").

Further, once a new product or use is discovered, it is easy for a competitor to replicate. Thus patent protection on products or novel ways of applying them is vital if the inventor is to reap returns. *See* C. TAYLOR & Z. SILBERSTON, *supra*, at 244-45; *see also* E. VON HIPPEL, THE SOURCES OF INNOVATION 66-67 (1988) (describing unusual strength of patents in pharmaceutical and chemical industries relative to other industries). In fact, the chemical industries are among the few that simply could not survive (at least as we know them) without patent protection. *See* Levin, Klevorick, Nelson & Winter, *Appropriating the Returns from Industrial Research and Development*, 1987 BROOKINGS PAPERS ECON. ACTIVITY 783 (1987) (reporting results of extensive empirical survey of research and development personnel at U.S. corporations, which shows that chemical-related industries rely most heavily on patents to protect inventions).

The growth of the chemical industries led to an ever-increasing demand for new product and process innovation — and hence to higher and higher levels of research and development (R&D) spending. Since patents are the most important protection for these investments, most new chemical products are patented. This, coupled with the highly competitive nature of the industry, results in a great deal of patent litigation. At bottom, it is this volume of litigation that has produced the elaborate doctrinal rules surrounding chemical products. Thus we can see the economic imperatives of these industries driving the development and elaboration of patent doctrine.

A Quick Word on Chemical Structure

A great deal of significance is attached to chemical structure in chemical nonobviousness cases. Thus it is useful to know a few facts about basic structural relationships. According to one source,

[a]mong the closest structural relationships are (in decreasing order): salts of acids and bases, geometrical isomers, positional isomers, homologues (for example, within the alkyl series), and adjacent halogen compounds....").
Chemical homologs, or members of a homologous group, are members of a related family of chemical compounds.

P. GRUBB, PATENTS FOR CHEMISTS 151 (1982). A salt is defined generally as a compound formed when one or more of the hydrogen atoms of an acid are replaced by one or more cations of the base. The common example is sodium chloride (NaCl) in which the hydrogen ions of hydrochloric acid (HCl) are replaced by the sodium ions (cations) of sodium hydroxide (NaOH). Thus sodium chloride is said to be a "salt of the hydrochloric acid." There is a great variety of salts because of the large number of acids and bases which have been characterized by chemists. *See, e.g., In re Jones*, 21 U.S.P.Q.2d 1941 (Fed. Cir. 1992) (salt of well known acid not obvious because not so closely related to other salts disclosed in other patents).

Salts are only one example of structurally related compounds. Another example is a homologous family, for instance, the alkanes, a group of hydrocarbon (i.e., hydrogen and oxygen-containing) compounds. Methane, whose chemical formula is CH_4, is the simplest alkane. Adding one carbon atom and two hydrogen atoms to methane's structure yields ethane, C_2H_6. Next in the homologous series is propane, C_3H_8. Then come butane (C_4H_{10}), pentane (C_5H_{12}), hexane (C_6H_{14}), and so on. The "formula" for this homologous series — known as the higher alkanes — is C_nH_{n+2}. *See* R. MORISON & R. BOYD, ORGANIC CHEMISTRY 79-80 (3d ed. 1973).

In the cases that follow, structural relationships such as those between the members of this series of compounds play an important role. In general, as you will see, the "closer" the relationship, the more likely that the newly-synthesized compound will be found obvious, or at least "prima facie" obvious. Although some of the cases involve compounds related in a well-established way, such as the alkanes just described, others have a less "formal" relationship. In fact, the very notion of which compounds are related can be quite complex; it often turns on expert testimony of chemists.

b. Chemical Nonobviousness: *Dillon* and Before

It is rare that the history and texture of an entire doctrinal area are summarized neatly in one case. But chemical nonobviousness is just such a situation; the single case is *In re Dillon*, the first case we will examine. Of course, the development of this doctrinal area long predates 1990, the date of the *en banc* Federal Circuit opinion in *Dillon*. But in many ways, this entire development is recapitulated in this single case. It thus serves as an excellent summary. As a consequence, if you will read only one case in this area, make it *Dillon* (but be sure to read the dissent too). If you plan to go further, *Dillon* will give you *entre* to the complexities of the discussion that follow.

In re DILLON

919 F.2d 688, 16 U.S.P.Q.2d 1897 (Fed. Cir. 1990),
cert. denied, 111 S. Ct. 1682 (1991)

[LOURIE, J., for the court en banc, joined by CHIEF JUDGE NIES and CIRCUIT JUDGES RICH, ARCHER, MAYER, MICHEL, PLAGER, CLEVENGER and RADER.]

[Appellant Diane M. Dillon originally claimed certain fuel compositions with a major component of a gasoline (or other hydrocarbon fuel) and a minor component of a tri- or tetra-orthoester that reduces soot emissions when the fuel is burned. The tri- or tetra-orthoester could be depicted, for example, as

$$
\begin{array}{ccc}
 & \text{C-``R''} & \\
 & | & \\
\text{``R''}_5 \text{---} & \text{C} & \text{--- ``R''} \\
 & | & \\
 & \text{C-``R''} &
\end{array}
$$

which are tri-orthoesters when three of the four "R" groups are bonded to the central carbon atom ("C") by an oxygen, e.g., $-O-R_5$, and which are tetra-orthoesters when all four of the "R" groups are bridged by oxygen. Footnote 2 of the opinion explains that "[t]ri-orthoesters have three -OR groups bonded to a central carbon atom, and the fourth carbon bond is to hydrogen or a hydrocarbon group (-R); they are represented as $C(R)(OR)_3$. Tetra-orthoesters have four -OR groups bonded to a central carbon atom, and are represented as $C(OR)_4$ ...." (Incidentally, this is a good example of the structural similarity in chemical compounds discussed above.)]

Prior art was discovered that anticipated the tri-orthoesters as fuel additives for dewatering the fuel, so appellant reformulated her claims so that only tetra-orthoesters were covered in the claims as appealed to the court.

The prior art tri-orthoester compositions contain the same amounts of tri-orthoester for dewatering fuel as one would use for the property not disclosed in the prior art, namely, appellant's soot reduction property. Secondary prior art was cited to show that a tri-orthoester suggests the use of a tetra-orthoester in related compositions, but not for the applicant's purpose of soot reduction.

The composition claims were rejected as obvious under 35 U.S.C. § 103 over two primary references — Sweeney U.S. patents 4,390,417 ('417) and 4,395,267 ('267) — in view of secondary references including Elliott U.S. Patent 3,903,006 and Howk U.S. Patent 2,840,613. Sweeney '417 discloses tri-orthoesters for dewatering fuel. Elliott equates tri-orthoesters and tetra-orthoesters as water scavengers in hydraulic (non-hydrocarbon) fluids. Howk equates tri- and tetra-orthoesters in a similar type of chemical reaction. The Board stated that the Elliott reference shows equivalence between tetra-orthoesters and tri-orthoesters, and that "it is clear from the combined teachings of these references ... that

[Dillon's tetra-orthoesters] would operate to remove water from non-aqueous liquids by the same mechanism as the orthoesters of Sweeney."

The Board stated that there was a "reasonable expectation" that the tri- and tetra-orthoester fuel compositions would have similar properties, based on "close structural and chemical similarity" between the tri- and tetra-orthoesters and the fact that both the prior art and Dillon use these compounds as "fuel additives." The Commissioner argues on appeal that the claimed compositions and method "would have been prima facie obvious from combined teachings of the references." On this reasoning, the Board held that unless Dillon showed some unexpected advantage or superiority of her claimed tetra-orthoester fuel compositions as compared with tri-orthoester fuel compositions, Dillon's new compositions as well as her claimed method of reducing particulate emissions are unpatentable for obviousness. It found that no such showing was made.

The Issue

The issue before this court is whether the Board erred in rejecting as obvious under 35 U.S.C. § 103 claims to Dillon's new compositions and to the new method of reducing particulate emissions, when the additives in the new compositions are structurally similar to additives in known compositions, having a different use, but the new method of reducing particulate emissions is neither taught nor suggested by the prior art.

The Broad Composition Claims

The Board found that the claims to compositions of a hydrocarbon fuel and a tetra-orthoester were prima facie obvious over Sweeney '417 and '267 in view of Elliott and Howk. We agree. Appellant argues that none of these references discloses or suggests the new use which she has discovered. That is, of course, true, but the composition claims are not limited to this new use; i.e., they are not physically or structurally distinguishable over the prior art compositions except with respect to the orthoester component. We believe that the PTO has established, through its combination of references, that there is a sufficiently close relationship between the tri-orthoesters and tetra-orthoesters (see the cited Elliott and Howk references) in the fuel oil art to create an expectation that hydrocarbon fuel compositions containing the tetra-[ortho]esters would have similar properties, including water scavenging, to like compositions containing the tri-orthoesters, and to provide the motivation to make such new compositions. Howk teaches use of both tri- and tetra-orthoesters in a similar type of chemical reaction. Elliott teaches their equivalence for a particular practical use.

Our case law well establishes that such a fact situation gives rise to a prima facie case of obviousness. See In re Shetty, 566 F.2d 81, 85, 195 U.S.P.Q. 753, 755-56 (C.C.P.A. 1977); In re Albrecht, 514 F.2d 1385, 1388, 185 U.S.P.Q. 590, 593 (C.C.P.A. 1975); In re Murch, 464 F.2d 1051, 1054, 175 U.S.P.Q. 89,

91 (C.C.P.A. 1972); *In re Hoch*, 428 F.2d 1341, 1343, 166 U.S.P.Q. 406, 409 (C.C.P.A. 1970).

Appellant cites *In re Wright*, 848 F.2d 1216, 1219, 6 U.S.P.Q.2d 1959, 1961 (Fed. Cir. 1988), for the proposition that a prima facie case of obviousness requires that the prior art suggest the claimed compositions' properties and the problem the applicant attempts to solve. The earlier panel opinion in this case, *In re Dillon*, 892 F.2d 1554, 13 U.S.P.Q.2d 1337 [Newman, J.] (now withdrawn), in fact stated "a prima facie case of obviousness is not deemed made unless both (1) the new compound or composition is structurally similar to the reference compound or composition and (2) there is some suggestion or expectation in the prior art that the new compound or composition will have the same or a similar utility as that discovered by the applicant." *Id.* at 1560, 13 U.S.P.Q.2d at 1341.

This court, in reconsidering this case in banc, reaffirms that structural similarity between claimed and prior art subject matter, proved by combining references or otherwise, where the prior art gives reason or motivation to make the claimed compositions, creates a prima facie case of obviousness, and that the burden (and opportunity) then falls on an applicant to rebut that prima facie case. Such rebuttal or argument can consist of a comparison of test data showing that the claimed compositions possess unexpectedly improved properties or properties that the prior art does not have (*In re Albrecht*, 514 F.2d 1389, 1396, 185 U.S.P.Q. 585, 590 (C.C.P.A. 1975); *Murch*, 464 F.2d at 1056, 175 U.S.P.Q. at 92), that the prior art is so deficient that there is no motivation to make what might otherwise appear to be obvious changes (*Albrecht*, 514 F.2d at 1396, 185 U.S.P.Q. at 590; *In re Stemniski*, 444 F.2d 581, 170 U.S.P.Q. 343 (C.C.P.A. 1971), *In re Ruschig*, 343 F.2d 965, 145 U.S.P.Q. 274 (C.C.P.A. 1965)), or any other argument or presentation of evidence that is pertinent. There is no question that all evidence of the properties of the claimed compositions and the prior art must be considered in determining the ultimate question of patentability, but it is also clear that the discovery that a claimed composition possesses a property not disclosed for the prior art subject matter, does not by itself defeat a prima facie case. *Shetty*, 566 F.2d at 86, 195 U.S.P.Q. at 756. Each situation must be considered on its own facts, but it is not necessary in order to establish a prima facie case of obviousness that both a structural similarity between a claimed and prior art compound (or a key component of a composition) be shown and that there be a suggestion in or expectation from the prior art that the claimed compound or composition will have the same or a similar utility as one newly discovered by applicant. To the extent that Wright suggests or holds to the contrary, it is hereby overruled. In particular, the statement that a prima facie obviousness rejection is not supported if no reference shows or suggests the newly-discovered properties and results of a claimed structure is not the law.

Under the facts we have concluded that a prima facie case has been established. The art provided the motivation to make the claimed compositions in the expectation that they would have similar properties. Appellant had the opportunity to rebut the prima facie case. She did not present any showing of data to the effect that her compositions had properties not possessed by the prior art compositions or that they possessed them to an unexpectedly greater degree. She attempted to refute the significance of the teachings of the prior art references. She did not succeed and we do not believe the PTO was in error in its decision.

Appellant points out that none of the references relates to the problem she confronted, citing *In re Wright*, and that the combination of references is based on hindsight. It is clear, however, that appellant's claims have to be considered as she has drafted them, i.e., as compositions consisting of a fuel and a tetra-orthoester, and that Sweeney '417 and '267 describe the combination of a liquid fuel with a related compound, a tri-orthoester. While Sweeney does not suggest appellant's use, her composition claims are not limited to that use; the claims merely recite compositions analogous to those in the Sweeney patents, and appellant has made no showing overcoming the prima facie presumption of similar properties for those analogous compositions. The mention in the appealed claims that the amount of orthoester must be sufficient to reduce particulate emissions is not a distinguishing limitation of the claims, unless that amount is different from the prior art and critical to the use of the claimed composition. See *In re Reni*, 419 F.2d 922, 925, 164 U.S.P.Q. 245, 247 (C.C.P.A. 1970). That is not the case here. The amount of ester recited in the dependent claims can be from 0.05-49%, a very broad range; a preferred range is .05-9%, compared with a percentage in Sweeney '417 approximately equimolar to the amounts of water in the fuel which the ester is intended to remove (.01-5%).

Appellant attacks the Elliott patent as non-analogous art, being in the field of hydraulic fluids rather than fuel combustion. We agree with the PTO that the field of relevant prior art need not be drawn so narrowly. [See] *In re Deminski*, [discussed in Section C.2, *supra* this chapter]. Following that test, one concerned with the field of fuel oils clearly is chargeable with knowledge of Sweeney '417, which discloses fuel compositions with tri-orthoesters for dewatering purposes, and chargeable with knowledge of other references to tri-orthoesters, including for use as dewatering agents for fluids, albeit other fluids. These references are "within the field of the inventor's endeavor." Moreover, the statement of equivalency between tri- and tetra-orthoesters in Elliott is not challenged. We therefore conclude that Elliott is not excludable from consideration as non-analogous art. It is evidence that supports the Board's holding that the prior art makes the claimed compositions obvious, a conclusion that appellant did not overcome.

Appellant urges that the Board erred in not considering the unexpected results produced by her invention and in not considering the claimed invention as a whole. The Board found, on the other hand, that no showing was made of unexpected results for the claimed compositions compared with the compositions of Sweeney. We agree. Clearly, in determining patentability the Board was obligated to consider all the evidence of the properties of the claimed invention as a whole, compared with those of the prior art. However, after the PTO made a showing that the prior art compositions suggested the claimed compositions, the burden was on the applicant to overcome the presumption of obviousness that was created, and that was not done. For example, she produced no evidence that her compositions possessed properties not possessed by the prior art compositions. Nor did she show that the prior art compositions and use were so lacking in significance that there was no motivation for others to make obvious variants. There was no attempt to argue the relative importance of the claimed compositions compared with the prior art. See *In re May*, 574 F.2d 1082, 1092-95, 197 U.S.P.Q. 601, 609-11 (C.C.P.A. 1978).

Appellant's patent application in fact included data showing that the prior art compositions containing tri-orthoesters had equivalent activity in reducing particulate emissions (she apparently was once claiming such compositions with either tri-orthoesters or tetra-orthoesters). She asserts that the examiner used her own showing of equivalence against her in violation of the rule of *In re Ruff*, 256 F.2d 590, 596, 118 U.S.P.Q. 340, 346 (C.C.P.A. 1958). While we caution against such a practice, it is clear to us that references by the PTO to the comparative data in the patent application were not employed as evidence of equivalence between the tri- and tetra-orthoesters; the PTO was simply pointing out that the applicant did not or apparently could not make a showing of superiority for the claimed tetra-ester compositions over the prior art tri-ester compositions.

The strong assertions by the dissent and its treatment of some of the case law impel us to make the following comments:

[T]he cases [cited in the dissent] establish that if an examiner considers that he has found prior art close enough to the claimed invention to give one skilled in the relevant chemical art the motivation to make close relatives (homologs, analogs, isomers, etc.) of the prior art compound(s), then there arises what has been called a presumption of obviousness or a prima facie case of obviousness. *In re Henze*, 181 F.2d 196, 85 U.S.P.Q. 261 (C.C.P.A. 1950); *In re Hass*, 141 F.2d 122, 127, 130, 60 U.S.P.Q. 544, 548, 552 (C.C.P.A. 1944). The burden then shifts to the applicant, who then can present arguments and/or data to show that what appears to be obvious, is not in fact that, when the invention is looked at as a whole. *In re Papesch*, 315 F.2d 381, 137 U.S.P.Q. 43 (C.C.P.A. 1963). The cases of *Hass* and *Henze* established the rule that, unless an applicant showed that the prior art compound lacked the property or advantage asserted for the claimed compound, the presumption of unpatentability was not overcome.

Exactly what facts constituted a prima facie case varied from case to case, but it was not the law that, where an applicant asserted that an invention possessed properties not known to be possessed by the prior art, no prima facie case was established unless the reference also showed the novel activity. There are cases, cited in the dissent, in which a prima facie case was not established based on lack of structural similarity. See *In re Grabiak*, 769 F.2d 729, 732, 226 U.S.P.Q. 870, 872 (Fed. Cir. 1985); *In re Taborsky*[,] 502 F.2d 775, 780-81, 183 U.S.P.Q. 50, 55 (C.C.P.A. 1974). Some of the cited cases also contained language suggesting that the fact that the claimed and the prior art compounds possessed the same activity were added factors in the establishment of the prima facie case. E.g., *In re Zeidler*, 682 F.2d 961, 966, 215 U.S.P.Q. 490, 494 (C.C.P.A. 1982); [many additional citations omitted]. Those cases did not say, however, as the dissent asserts, that, in the absence of the similarity of activities, there would have been no prima facie case.

For example, the dissent quotes a statement in *Grabiak* that "[w]hen chemical compounds have 'very close' structural similarities and similar utilities, without more a prima facie case may be made." 769 F.2d at 731, 226 U.S.P.Q. at 871. That case does not state, as implied by the dissent, that without the similarity of utilities, there would not have been a prima facie case. A conclusion based on one set of facts does not necessarily rule out a similar conclusion with slightly different facts.

We will not review all the cases cited in the dissent, but *Stemniski* is an important case, for it overruled *Henze* and *In re Riden*, 318 F.2d 761, 138 U.S.P.Q. 112 (C.C.P.A. 1963) (a case similar to *Henze*), "to the extent that [they] are inconsistent with the views expressed herein." 444 F.2d at 587, 170 U.S.P.Q. at 348. The views that were expressed therein were that:

> [w]here the prior art reference neither discloses nor suggests a utility for certain described compounds, why should it be said that a reference makes obvious to one of ordinary skill in the art an isomer, homolog or analog or related structure, when that mythical, but intensely practical, person knows of no "practical" reason to make the reference compounds, much less any structurally related compounds?

Id. at 586, 170 U.S.P.Q. at 347. Thus, *Stemniski*, rather than destroying the established practice of rejecting closely-related compounds as prima facie obvious, qualified it by holding that a presumption is not created when the reference compound is so lacking in any utility that there is no motivation to make close relatives.

Properties, therefore, are relevant to the creation of a prima facie case in the sense of affecting the motivation of a researcher to make compounds closely related to or suggested by a prior art compound, but it is not required, as stated in the dissent, that the prior art disclose or suggest the properties newly-discovered by an applicant in order for there to be a prima facie case of obviousness.

The dissent cites the seminal case of *Papesch*, suggesting that it rejected the principle that we now "adopt," thereby implying that we are weakening *Papesch*. We are doing nothing of the sort. *Papesch* indeed stated that a compound and all of its properties are inseparable and must be considered in the determination of obviousness. We heartily agree and intend not to retreat from *Papesch* one inch. *Papesch*, however, did not deal with the requirements for establishing a prima facie case, but whether the examiner had to consider the properties of an invention at all, when there was a presumption of obviousness. 315 F.2d at 391, 137 U.S.P.Q. at 51. The reference disclosed a lower homolog of the claimed compounds, so it was clear that impliedly a prima facie case existed; the question was whether, under those circumstances, the biological data were admissible at all. The court ruled that they were, *id.* at 391, 137 U.S.P.Q. at 51, and we agree with that result. The dissent quotes the brief passage at the end of the *Papesch* opinion to the effect that the prior art must "at least to a degree" disclose the applicant's desired property, *id.* at 392, 137 U.S.P.Q. at 52, but this brief mention was not central to the decision in that case and did not refer to the requirements of a prima facie case. *Papesch* is irrelevant to the question of the requirements for a prima facie case, which is the question we have here.

The dissent mentions positions advanced by the Commissioner, including citing the *In re Mod*, 408 F.2d 1055, 161 U.S.P.Q. 281 (C.C.P.A. 1969) and *In re de Montmollin*, 344 F.2d 976, 145 U.S.P.Q. 416 (C.C.P.A. 1965) decisions. We do not, however, in today's decision necessarily adopt any positions of the Commissioner other than those stated in our opinion and note that neither *Mod* nor *de Montmollin* dealt with the requirements of a prima facie case. They concerned the question whether the existence of a new property for claimed compounds in addition to a property common to both the claimed and related prior art compounds rendered the claimed compounds unobvious. We are not faced with that question today.

Another example of the lack of direct pertinence of a case quoted in the dissent is *May*, which the dissent cites as an example of the consistent line of decisions to the effect that "both structure and properties must be suggested in the prior art before a prima facie case of obviousness was deemed made." This case does not state that both structure and properties "must" be suggested. The claimed and prior art compositions were both disclosed as having analgesic activity; it was conceded that a prima facie case was made out, but the court concluded that applicants had rebutted the presumed expectation that structurally similar compounds have similar properties with a showing of an actual unexpected difference of properties between the claimed compound and the prior art. 574 F.2d at 1095, 197 U.S.P.Q. at 611. The applicant in that case thus made a showing that Dillon did not make in this case.

Properties must be considered in the overall evaluation of obviousness, and the lack of any disclosure of useful properties for a prior art compound may indicate a lack of motivation to make related compounds, thereby precluding a prima facie case, but it is not correct that similarity of structure and a suggestion of the activity of an applicant's compounds in the prior art are necessary before a prima facie case is established.

[From the dissent by NEWMAN, J., joined by COWEN, SENIOR CIRCUIT JUDGE, and MAYER, CIRCUIT JUDGE.]

The majority's holding that prima facie obviousness of new chemical compounds and compositions is determined based only on structural similarity to prior art compounds and compositions having a known use is reminiscent of the *"Hass-Henze* Doctrine" of earlier days. This doctrine was discarded thirty years ago, and although it resurfaced on occasion, its original sweep was superseded by many years of judicial analysis. Review of this analysis shows the courts' evolving understanding of the characteristics of chemical inventions, particularly the inseparability of chemical properties and chemical structure, and the legal consequences of this scientific fact.

Judicial decisions over the past three decades established the general rule that the determination of prima facie obviousness of new chemical compounds and compositions and their uses can not be based on chemical structure alone, but must also include consideration of all their properties, including those discovered by the applicant. This rule had important procedural and substantive consequences during patent examination, for it determined the kind of evidence and proof that was required of a patent applicant. The ruling of this in banc court changes what must be proved in order to patent a new chemical compound or composition, and thus changes what is patentable.

In accordance with the court's in banc holding, a new chemical compound or composition is not patentable even when the prior art does not suggest that the new chemical compound or composition would have the applicant's newly discovered property and use, unless the applicant makes the same showing that is required when the prior art does suggest the applicant's new property and use.

[From footnote 2:] The majority holds that a prima facie case of obviousness is made whenever the structure of the applicant's new compound or composition (or mechanical device) is "obvious" from that shown in the prior art, independent of whether the prior art suggests or makes obvious the applicant's newly discovered property and use. The majority allows an exception for situations where the prior art gives no "reason or motivation to make the claimed invention," and duly makes clear that this means motivation to make the new compound or composition for the prior art use, not for the applicant's newly discovered use. This exception comes into play only when the prior art structure has no known utility; and a few such situations are reported, e.g. *In re Stemniski*, 444 F.2d 581, 58 C.C.P.A. 1410, 170 U.S.P.Q. 343 (C.C.P.A. 1971) (prior art compounds used only as intermediates), and *In re Albrecht*, 514 F.2d 1389, 185 U.S.P.Q. 585 (C.C.P.A. 1975) (no practical utility). Thus, according to the majority, when the prior art chemical compound or composition has no known use, the prior art provides no "reason or motivation" to make a structurally similar new compound or composition; and in such case the prior art would not make a prima facie case of obviousness based on structural similarity alone.

While I welcome any reduction in the sweep of the court's holding, this exception is of trivial impact. In most cases the prior art compound or composition has some known use; and thus for most cases the majority's "motivation" test would be met based solely on similarity of structure. This is an important change of law. While the holdings of the prior law were not entirely consistent — see the various CCPA opinions discussed *post* — this en banc court now establishes the rule that will control all cases in the future.

The applicant is thus required to show "unexpected" properties and results, whether or not the prior art provides an expectation or suggestion of the properties and results disclosed in the patent application. And unless the applicant proves that the prior art structure does not actually possess the same unobvious property that the applicant discovered for the new structure, the court holds today that the new chemical compound or composition is not patentable. This is an incorrect application of the patent statute, and a rejection of the wisdom of precedent. Therefore, respectfully, I dissent.

[T]he question of whether there is a prima facie case of obviousness controls whether Dillon is required to prove that her newly discovered property of particulate (soot) reduction during combustion is not actually possessed by the prior art composition, when the prior art composition was not known or suggested to have this property. Dillon did not so prove, and the Commissioner urges that since Dillon's specification itself discloses that the prior art composition does possess this newly discovered property, the prima facie case based on structural similarity was not rebutted.

Heretofore, the courts generally recognized a controlling distinction between the two principal types of factual situations that arise when a patent applicant's new chemical compound or composition has a structure that is "similar" to chemical structures shown in the prior art: (1) those where the prior art suggests, at least in general terms, that the new chemical compound or composition will have the applicant's newly discovered property and use; and (2) those where it does not. These factual situations have had different consequences with respect to whether a prima facie case of obviousness was made. The difference turned on whether or not the structure and properties and use of a new chemical compound or composition were suggested in the prior art. The distinction determined whether the applicant was required to come forward with rebuttal evidence, which often was in the form of new technological information not known to the prior art, in order to establish an "unexpected" difference between the properties discovered by the applicant and those actually possessed by the prior art structure.

This distinction brought a consistent application of the law of 35 U.S.C. § 103 to the examination of chemical inventions, for it established the framework wherein the law was applied to the facts of each case. The court today rejects this distinction, holding in banc that it suffices to show prima facie obviousness whenever the prior art describes a similar chemical structure, provided only that the prior art gives some "reason or motivation" to make the claimed chemical structure, "regardless of the properties disclosed in the inventor's application," in the Commissioner's words.

[Judge Newman then describes the precedent at length, breaking up the rulings into two groups: (1) The "earlier period of modern chemistry," when " 'structural obviousness' alone was deemed to create a presumption of unpatentability"; and (2) the post-*Papesch* era, when "properties as well as structure were material to the patentability of new chemicals." In the elaboration of post-*Papesch* doctrine,

Judge Newman finds: "the utility discovered by the applicant must be at least suggested in the prior art, in order to establish prima facie unpatentability of new compounds and compositions that are structurally similar to known chemicals, is the common thread that ties most of the decisions of the CCPA and the Federal Circuit." She then reviews the individual cases in detail.]

The Commissioner raised the policy argument that Dillon is simply removing from the public an obvious variant of Sweeney's and Elliott's compositions, one that might be useful to scavenge water in fuels. In *Ruschig* the court had considered the argument, and remarked that the provision of adequate patent protection for the applicant's new compounds, not previously in existence and having a new and unobvious use, was favored over the "mere possibility that someone might wish to use some of them for some such [other] purpose." 343 F.2d at 979, 145 U.S.P.Q. at 286. This practical wisdom has been tested by long experience. It accords with judicial recognition that:

> Although there is a vast amount of knowledge about general relationships in the chemical arts, chemistry is still largely empirical, and there is often great difficulty in predicting precisely how a given compound will behave.

In re Carleton, 599 F.2d 1021, 1026, 202 U.S.P.Q. 165, 170 (C.C.P.A. 1979).

Granting Dillon a patent on her invention takes away nothing that the public already has; and the public receives not only the knowledge of Dillon's discovery, for abandoned patent applications are maintained in secrecy, but Dillon is not deprived of an incentive to discover and to commercialize this new product for this new use.

I would hold that a prima facie case of obviousness of a new chemical compound or composition requires consideration of not only the chemical structure but also the newly discovered properties, in light of the teachings and suggestions of the prior art.

NOTES

1. *Products Versus Uses.* A good deal of the tension in cases such as *Dillon* stems from the fact that while the commercial significance of chemical research resides in finding a composition with a valuable *use*, research sponsors (i.e., usually companies) want patent claims for *products*. Note the following passage from *Dillon*:

> While Sweeney does not suggest appellant's use, her composition claims are not limited to that use; the claims merely recite compositions analogous to those in the Sweeney patents, and appellant has made no showing overcoming the prima facie presumption of similar properties for those analogous compositions. The mention in the appealed claims that the amount of orthoester must be sufficient to reduce particulate emissions is not a distinguishing limitation of the claims, unless that amount is different from the prior art and critical to the use of the claimed composition.

919 F.2d at 693. In other words, Diane Dillon found a valuable new use for a family of compounds, but claimed not the right to use them for that purpose, but the right to exclude others from making, using or selling those compositions *for any purpose*. The fundamental problem in cases like these is this inconsistency between what is invented and what is claimed.

How did things get this way? The answer stems largely from the historical reality — and continuing perception — that product patents are better than any alternative. One such alternative, a "new use" patent on the use of old compound *X* for new use *Y*, is explicitly envisioned by the Patent Act; see § 100(b) ("The term 'process' means process, art or method, and includes a new use of a known process, machine, manufacture, composition of matter, or material."). But it has long been thought that such a claim provides a distinctively inferior brand of protection to a commercial product when compared to a straight product patent.

> In the field of drug patents today therapeutic value, not chemical composition, is the substance of all incentive to invent.... When ... a fresh, efficacious, undisclosed use is identified, its inventor deserves the full ambit of statutory protection. A limitation to "use" or process patentability, based solely on the existence of prior chemical formulations, would not accord with the basic constitutional power being exercised by the Congress to promote science and the useful arts.

Eli Lilly & Co. v. Generix Drug Sales, Inc., 460 F.2d 1096, 1103-04, 174 U.S.P.Q. (BNA) 65, 70-71 (5th Cir. 1972). *See also In re Ruschig*, 343 F.2d 965, 979, 145 U.S.P.Q. (BNA) 274, 286 (C.C.P.A. 1965) (similar holding; "[v]aluable inventions should be given protection of value in the real world of business and the courts"); *In re Papesch*, 315 F.2d 381, 391, 137 U.S.P.Q. (BNA) 43 (C.C.P.A. 1963) ("[Product] claims have well-recognized advantages to those in the business of making and selling compounds, in contrast to process-of-use claims, because competitors in the sale of compounds are not generally users."); D. SCHWARTZMAN, INNOVATION IN THE PHARMACEUTICAL INDUSTRY 167 (1979) ("It is generally true that process patents are not very effective.... The patent covering the chemical composition of the active ingredient thus is the significant one."); *see generally* Armitage & Ellis, *Chemical Patents in Europe*, 12 EUR. INTELL. PROP. REV. 119 (1990) (product patents should continue to be granted to inventor who pioneers a new structure, even though these patents cover unthought-of uses, because it is structural innovation that is most difficult and economically significant). According to the dissent in *Dillon*:

> *Ruschig* and other cases consistently rejected the proposition that claims to new compounds and compositions must contain a limitation to a specific use. Any change in this long-established practice requires careful thought.

Id. at 919 F.2d at 704, n.10. For more on this question, see the Comment following this section, *Do We Need New Use Protection?*

2. *Common Properties Cases*. The majority in the en banc *Dillon* opinion writes:

> [*In re Mod* and *In re de Montmollin*] concerned the question whether the existence of a new property for claimed compounds in addition to a property common to both the claimed and related prior art compounds rendered the claimed compounds unobvious. We are not faced with that question today.

Id. at 698. Meanwhile, we read in Judge Newman's dissent:

> The facts in *Mod* are indeed on all fours with the facts now before us. In *Mod* the court held that the apparently shared property of insecticidal activity sufficed to make Mod's new (but structurally similar) compounds unpatentable for obviousness, despite Mod's discovery that his new compounds had the new property of antimicrobial activity. In Dillon's case the court holds that the presumptively shared property of water sequestration suffices to make Dillon's new (but structurally similar) compositions unpatentable for obviousness, despite Dillon's discovery that her new compositions have the new property of soot reduction. In neither case did the prior art suggest or make obvious the applicant's newly discovered property.

Id. at 707 n.12.

On what grounds can Judge Lourie, writing for the majority, distinguish *Mod*? Was the soot-reduction property of Dillon's tetra-orthoesters not "new" given the prior art disclosure of the related property of water-scavenging? The dissent says soot reduction is a "new property" of the precise compositions, tetra-orthoesters and gasoline, claimed by Dillon: "It is undisputed," writes Judge Newman in dissent that "[the] combination [of Dillon's tetra-orthoester compounds] with hydrocarbon fuels, for any purpose, is not described in the prior art; nor is their use to reduce particulate emissions from combustion of hydrocarbon fuels." F.2d at 716. Who is right?

3. *New Properties*. What is a "new property," and what is not? Consider *In re de Montmollin*, 344 F.2d 976, 145 U.S.P.Q. (BNA) 416 (C.C.P.A. 1965). There an applicant presented a claim for a textile dye said to make both cotton and wool highly fade-resistant. It was rejected in light of structurally similar prior art known to be useful in dyeing wool. The CCPA upheld the rejection on the ground that the prior art references "provide more than adequate reason ... for making the present compounds." 344 F.2d at 978. *See also In re Hoch*, 428 F.2d 1341, 1343, 166 U.S.P.Q. (BNA) 406, 408-09 (C.C.P.A. 1970) (reference described a known compound and its use for "treatment of plant diseases"; court held that a prima facie case of obviousness was made as to the applicant's structurally similar compound disclosed to be useful as a herbicide, stating: "On the face of it, 'treatment of plant diseases' could mean usefulness in controlling plant-infesting organisms.... We are thus not persuaded that herbicidal properties are 'contraindicated' by the [prior art] patent.").

Despite the verbal sparring between the two opinion writers in *Dillon*, their disagreement seems to center on a legitimate issue: was it a nonobvious discovery that a compound closely similar to prior art compounds had a property (soot reduction), given that this property was seemingly related to a known property of the prior art (dewatering)? Was this a nontrivial advance over the prior art? Looked at this way, *Dillon* was a case that reveals the deeply subjective determinations that ultimately govern the fate of inventors in close cases on nonobviousness.

In a sense, when one boils down the majority opinion in *Dillon*, it seems to propose a common-sense test: has the applicant overcome the prima facie case, by disproving that the *property* is obvious in light of the prior art properties? (This is, of course, asked only when the structure *is* obvious in light of prior art structures.) Looked at this way, Judge Newman's opinion might be interpreted as proposing a novelty-only test for properties: if it is a new compound, no matter how closely related to old ones, and it demonstrates a new property, no matter how closely related to old properties, it is patentable. In other words, novel structure plus novel property equals nonobviousness.[24] The majority takes a different tack, focussing on the prima facie case, based on similar structure.

An extension of the majority opinion might even lead one to state that it in effect applies the basic logic of nonobviousness to the inquiry regarding properties. Under this interpretation, the *Dillon* opinion could be read as saying that a new property is not enough for a closely related compound; it must be a new and nonobvious property, one that is not too closely related to the properties revealed by the prior art. Of course, this is simply a restatement of the requirement spelled out in *Papesch*, that the applicant overcome the prima facie case against her by showing an unexpected property, or an unexpectedly high measure of a previously known property.

4. *Properties and the Harvard Note*. The interpretation of *Dillon* suggested in the preceding note is akin to the approach suggested in Note, *Standards of Obviousness and the Patentability of Chemical Compounds*, 87 HARV. L. REV. 607, 626-27 n.77 (1974), which calls for a comparison of the claimed compound's properties with those of the prior art structurally similar compounds. The Note would require two elements to be established: (1) that the claimed compound's property be "unexpected" in light of the prior art; and (2) that the unexpected property be "different in kind" from those of the prior art com-

---

[24] This is perhaps reflected in the following statement in the dissent:

In [*In re Shetty*, 566 F.2d 81, 195 U.S.P.Q. (BNA) 753 (C.C.P.A. 1977)] [the court held that] [t]he Patent Office has failed to show a reasonable expectation, or some predictability, that [a reference] compound would be an effective appetite suppressant if administered in the dosage disclosed by [another reference]. *Id.* at 86, 195 U.S.P.Q. at 756. In contrast, the majority today affirms the rejection of Dillon's claims, process and composition, although such "expectation" or "predictability" was, without dispute, absent.

919 F.2d at 712 (Newman, J., dissenting).

pounds. *Compare In re Mod*, 408 F.2d 1055, 161 U.S.P.Q. (BNA) 281 (C.C.P.A. 1969) (addition of one new property, antimicrobial activity, not enough where claimed compound is equally possessed of old property, insecticidal use, as prior art compound); *In re Albrecht*, 514 F.2d 1389, 185 U.S.P.Q. (BNA) 585 (C.C.P.A. 1975) (suggestion in prior art that structurally related compound would be poor choice for performing old use does not defeat patentability of novel but obvious compound found to have new use). See note below on *In re Merck*.

5. *The Inherency Puzzle.* The dissent in *Dillon* summarizes a long line of cases in the following passage:

> [R]ebuttal [of the prima facie case of obviousness] was generally presented in the form of comparative experimental data, whereby the inventor demonstrated that the properties of his or her new chemical compound or composition achieved some unobvious or unexpected result or advantage, as compared with the actual properties of the prior art structure. This rebuttal often required the inventor to go beyond the general teachings in the prior art, and prove that the prior art compound did not, in fact, possess the specific property and advantage of the new compound or composition. Such proofs were invariably required when the prior art suggested the general property and use discovered by the applicant.

919 F.2d at 699. The theory that led to the requirement of such rebuttal evidence was that even though the claimed compound may have been synthesized to take advantage of a new property, the old compounds in the art might also have possessed that property — and this fact may have been known in the art. Thus the applicant is required to show that the prior art compounds do not in fact possess the property in order to prevent the applicant from removing an obvious chemical variant with an obvious property from the public domain. *See, e.g., In re Jones*, 412 F.2d 241, 56 C.C.P.A. 1293, 162 U.S.P.Q. 224 (C.C.P.A. 1969). When the prior art compounds are not known to possess the property, however, the courts have generally held that no comparative testing is required. *See, e.g., In re Gordon*, 428 F.2d 854, 855, 166 U.S.P.Q. (BNA) 327, 329 (C.C.P.A. 1970) (since a prima facie case of obviousness was not made as to a new glass composition having new and unobvious properties, it was unnecessary for the applicant to prove whether the prior art composition had the same property (the ability to wet graphite) as the applicant's composition: "We agree that it is improper to require comparative evidence where a reference is devoid of any suggestion of the claimed invention.").

6. *A Comment on Inherency.* The problem with this line of cases is that they either go too far or not far enough. If the true discovery that leads an applicant to seek a patent is a new property, it should be irrelevant that the prior art compounds possess the same property. After all, no one knew that they did, presumably, before the applicant began her research. For the Patent Office and courts to now require her to go back to the prior art and disprove that it reflects her property is absurd since it is "hoisting her by her own petard," i.e., using her own discovery to test whether she has really made a discovery. Again, the problem stems from the fact that her commercially useful discovery involves a property or *use*, but her claims describe a compound or product. See Section D.3 below, *Do We Need "New Use" Protection?*

In addition, one should keep in mind that even if a new compound patent is granted, if the prior art compounds are also possessed of the same property as the now-patented compound, nothing is to stop a researcher from using the old compounds to take advantage of the new property. The "property right," in other words, does not cover the use (property), but the new structure. So why should we be concerned about a patent on one compound capable of performing a certain function when other prior art (and hence public domain) compounds can serve the same function? (Does the analysis change when the new compound is also the *optimal* one for taking advantage of the new property?)

On the other hand, if we are to take the "inherent property" theory seriously, the comparative testing requirement should not be restricted to the case where the prior art suggests the existence of the applicant's claimed property in the prior art compounds. For, suggested or not, if old compounds have an asserted property, it is just as much a removal from the public domain to allow an applicant to claim an obvious variant of those old compounds on the basis of an inherent (though unsuggested, i.e., unknown) property. In other words, even though the prior art would not lead one to believe that old compounds had property X, someone, someday, might have played with the old compounds and discovered this fact. The allowance of a patent on an obvious structural variant of these prior art compounds *theoretically* removes something from the public domain, for if someone does discover the new use inherent in the old compounds, the obvious but new compound would, by definition, be a logical candidate for exploration. The patent makes this impossible. And if the "theoretical" nature of this "removal" seems tenuous, remember cases such as *Rosaire* and *In re Hall* in Chapter 4, where very obscure prior art references were shown to defeat novelty just as surely as full page ads in *Science* or billboards in Fenway Park. If a "theoretical" (i.e., practically unimaginable) reference can defeat patentability, why not a theoretical (difficult to imagine) exploration of the prior art for undiscovered properties and obvious structural variants? *Cf. In re Chupp*, 816 F.2d 643, 647, 2 U.S.P.Q.2d (BNA) 1437, 1440 (Fed. Cir. 1987) (court disposed of the Commissioner's policy argument that grant of the composition claims would prevent the public from using Chupp's structurally obvious compound for the herbicidal uses shown in the prior art, with the remark that "the expectation that persons would want to use the compound to produce inferior results (or would want to fight lawsuits over such uses) is false."). What if the prior art compounds had been just as effective for the use discovered by the applicant, rather than inferior for that use, as the court found? What if the applicant's compounds were in fact better for the use disclosed in the prior art?

7. *Should the Inventor's Problem Affect Nonobviousness?* A minor theme in *Dillon* is the relevance of the problem solved by the inventor. Counsel for Dillon argued that the tetra-orthoesters she invented were not an obvious solution to the problem she was actually working on — soot reduction — although they might have been (more) obvious as solutions to the problem of dewatering fuel. The court in its en banc opinion replied to this argument:

> Appellant points out that none of the references relates to the problem she confronted, citing *In re Wright*, [848 F.2d 1216, 6 U.S.P.Q.2d (BNA) 1959 (Fed. Cir. 1988),] and that the combination of references is based on hindsight. It is clear, however, that appellant's claims have to be considered as she has drafted them, i.e., as compositions....

919 F.2d at 693-94.

The *Wright* case cited by the court occasioned a good deal of controversy when it was decided; it was specifically overruled in *Dillon*. *See* 919 F.2d at 694. *Wright* involved a claim to a carpenter's level including a cylindrical vessel containing the liquid "bubble" that indicates whether the thing being examined is level. The patent claimed a specific type of bubble cylinder — one that was barrel-shaped, with a pin in the middle. The prior art showed bubble cylinders having this shape and containing a pin, but noted that the pin was chosen as a solution to the problem of visibility. Wright, on the other hand, asserted that he had used a pin because it made possible a wider range of pitch measurements (because the bubble did not slide all the way to one side of the cylinder so easily). The court, in granting the claims, stated:

> The determination of whether a novel structure is or is not "obvious" requires cognizance of the properties of that structure and the problem which it solves, viewed in light of the teachings of the prior art.... The problem solved by the invention is always relevant.

848 F.2d at 1219, 6 U.S.P.Q.2d (BNA) at 1361.

The well-recognized criticism of this reasoning is that it has the potential to convert any obvious invention into a nonobvious one simply by allowing an inventor to assert that she chose the obvious modification of the prior art for a different purpose than was suggested in that art. Thus an obvious modification of an automobile engine which the prior art suggests as a way of reducing fuel emissions might be asserted to have been pursued because it made the engine quieter. *See generally* Rollins, *Was* Wright *Wrong?*, 71 J. PAT. & TRADEMARK OFF. SOC'Y 39 (1989); Silverberg, *Comment: The* Wright *Controversy*, 71 J. PAT. & TRADEMARK OFF. SOC'Y 575 (1989).

On the other hand, defenders of the approach taken in *Wright* point out that not *all* arguments regarding differences in the problem solved should be effective in overcoming § 103 rejections. *See* Welsh, *PTO Practice: Was* Wright *Right After All?*, 71 J. PAT. & TRADEMARK OFF. SOC'Y 568 (1989); Lastova, *Was* Wright *Right?*, 70 J. PAT. & TRADEMARK OFF. SOC'Y 386 (1988). Certainly if one follows the logic of *Papesch*, properties of a device (chemical or otherwise) are always relevant in determining obviousness. Hence why not consider the "property" of what problem the inventor was tackling? In addition, the approach in *Wright* stresses that if one is looking for a solution to problem *X*, one might not appreciate the significance of a novel structure that solves problem *Y*. If one is not motivated to make the structure in search of a solution to problem *Y*, that is, one may not appreciate that the structure solves this problem. Hence one may overlook the significance of the structure. The *Wright* opinion turns on the assumption that there is no real motivation to build the novel structure if all one has in mind is solving the old problem, i.e., problem *X*.

The disagreement over the importance of the problem faced by the inventor really boils down to two difficult empirical issues: (1) is the fact that a novel structure will likely solve problem *X* enough reason to build it, so that when one does one will have the chance to see that it solves problem *Y*?; and (2) assuming one did have reason to build the novel structure, would it be apparent at that time that it solved problem *Y*, *even to one who was not initially looking to solve that problem*?

8. *Stretching the Limits of the "Problem" Approach.* There is one appealing aspect to the approach taken in *Wright*, which is perhaps to be bemoaned in light of *Dillon*'s clear overruling of *Wright*.

A recent case involving Genentech illustrates the issue. Genentech had invented a recombinant DNA method for producing the human blood clotting protein factor VIII:C. *See Scripps Clinic & Research Found. v. Genentech, Inc.*, 666 F. Supp. 1379, 1390, 3 U.S.P.Q.2d (BNA) 1481, 1488 (N.D. Cal. 1987), *patent invalidated in Scripps Clinic & Research Found. v. Genentech, Inc.*, 707 F. Supp. 1547, 11 U.S.P.Q.2d (BNA) 1187 (N.D. Cal. 1989); *rev'd and remanded*, 18 U.S.P.Q.2d (BNA) 1001 (Fed. Cir. 1991).

Genentech's process had major advantages over an earlier, patented technique of purifying the substance drawn from natural blood. Genentech's process was not only better; it was completely different. Yet in the first part of the case, the court upheld the earlier patent, held by the Scripps Institute, on the ground that it was a legitimate product patent and thus Genentech's new method of producing it was an infringement. (The Federal Circuit remanded for consideration of whether Genentech should escape infringement under the "reverse doctrine of equivalents"; *see Scripps Clinic & Research Found. v. Genentech, Inc.*, 927 F.2d 1565, 18 U.S.P.Q.2d (BNA) 1001 (Fed. Cir 1991)); Merges, *A Brief Note on Blocking Patents and Reverse Equivalents: Biotechnology as an Example*, 73 J. PAT. & TRADEMARK OFF. SOC'Y 878 (1991).

The trial court had invalidated the Scripps patent, saying that it did not adequately disclose the purification method that Scripps itself judged best. The Federal Circuit reversed on this point, and remanded on the grounds just mentioned. But — except for the remand issue — the court did not disturb the trial court's holding that Genentech's recombinant technique infringed the product patent.

This is perhaps unfortunate social policy. It might well inhibit technical advance in biotechnology, where much invention involves improving ways to produce purified natural products. If the initial patent is granted on the product, rather than the process for making it, subsequent process research by others will be discouraged. This is a good example of a prospect that will likely reduce competition for improvements. While licensing by firms can mitigate this problem, there is no guarantee that this will take place at such an early stage in the industry. *See generally* Merges & Nelson, *On the Complex Economics of Patent Scope*, 90 COLUM. L. REV. 801 (1990).

An alternative solution to the problem is suggested by the approach taken in *Wright*. Since the essence of the recombinant version's advantage is that it is much cheaper to produce, it might make sense to grant Genentech a completely independent, non-subservient patent on its very structurally similar Factor VIII protein. The reasoning would be that, as in *Papesch*, *all* properties of the claimed protein must be taken into account — *including the cost of producing it!* It could be argued that this is no less a relevant property than its uses or the problem it was created to solve. And from a social policy perspective, this would make a great deal of sense since it would effectively overcome the true problem in the case: that property rights over an economically inferior product (the natural version) can be used to prevent the introduction of an economically superior product (the recombinant version). Thus while a biochemist might say that the two products are identical, an economist certainly would not. Why not pay attention to these differences too?

9. Functional Limitations. In an omitted portion of the opinion, the majority in *Dillon* states:

> The mention in the appealed claims that the amount of orthoester must be sufficient to reduce particulate emissions is not a distinguishing limitation of the claims, unless that amount is different from the prior art and critical to the use of the claimed composition. See *In re Reni*, 419 F.2d 922, 925, 57 C.C.P.A. 857, 164 U.S.P.Q. 245, 247 (C.C.P.A. 1970). That is not the case here.

919 F.2d at 693-94. This suggests that "functional" claim language cannot save a claim to an otherwise old composition. *Compare In re Duva*, 156 U.S.P.Q. (BNA) 90 (C.C.P.A. 1967) (holding that functional preamble to claim for old composition, i.e., "a composition *for* [a certain function]" could not be ignored in determining the obviousness of the claimed invention) *with Kropa v. Robie & Mahlman*, 187 F.2d 150, 88 U.S.P.Q. (BNA) 478 (C.C.P.A. 1951) (stating that whether or not preamble's functional limitation was to be used in interpreting claim depended on reason for its inclusion, i.e., to distinguish prior art, capture infringers, etc.).

Genus/Species Revisited

In re BAIRD

16 F.3d 380, 29 U.S.P.Q.2d 1550 (Fed. Cir. 1994)

LOURIE, J.

Applicants Brian W. Baird [et al.] appeal from the October 15, 1992 decision of the U.S. Patent and Trademark Office (PTO) Board of Patent Appeals and Interferences, affirming the examiner's final rejection of claims 1-5 of [Baird's] application, entitled "Flash Fusible Toner Resins," as unpatentable on the ground of obviousness under 35 U.S.C. Section 103 (1988). We reverse.

BACKGROUND

Baird's application is directed to a flash fusible toner comprising a polyester of bisphenol A and an aliphatic dicarboxylic acid. The application discloses that toners containing bisphenol A have optimal characteristics for flash fusing including, inter alia, high thermal stability and low critical surface energy.

Claim 1, the only claim at issue, reads as follows:

> 1. A flash fusible toner comprising a binder resin which is a bisphenol A polyester containing an aliphatic di [carboxylic] acid selected from the group consisting of succinic acid, glutaric acid and adipic acid.

Claim 1 stands rejected as obvious over U.S. Patent 4,634,649 to Knapp et al., which relates to developer compositions comprised of, inter alia, the polymeric esterification product of a dicarboxylic acid and a diphenol .... The Knapp formula contains a broad range of variables and thus encompasses a large number of different diphenols, one of which is bisphenol A, which is shown in Baird's application ....

Knapp also discloses [a generic formula for] dicarboxylic acids. Twenty typical dicarboxylic acids are recited, including succinic acid, glutaric acid, and adipic acid, the dicarboxylic acids recited in claim 1.

The examiner rejected claim 1 as obvious on the ground that Knapp specifically discloses as components of his esters the three dicarboxylic acids recited in claim 1 and a generic formula which encompasses bisphenol A. Recognizing that bisphenol A is defined when certain specific variables are chosen, the examiner reasoned that bisphenol A "may be easily derived from the generic formula of the diphenol in [Knapp] and all the motivation the worker of ordinary skill in the art needs to arrive at the particular polyester of the instant claim[] is to follow [that formula]."

The Board upheld the examiner's rejection. It rejected Baird's argument that there was no motivation for one to select bisphenol A from Knapp and summarily concluded that "the fact that [the claimed] binder resin is clearly encompassed by the generic disclosure of Knapp ... provides ample motivation for the selection of [the claimed composition]." Slip op. at 3.

DISCUSSION

We review an obviousness determination by the Board de novo, while we review underlying factual findings for clear error.

What a reference teaches is a question of fact. The fact that a claimed compound may be encompassed by a disclosed generic formula does not by itself render that compound obvious. *In re Jones*, 958 F.2d 347, 350, 21 U.S.P.Q.2d 1941, 1943 (Fed. Cir. 1992) (rejecting Commissioner's argument that "regardless [] how broad, a disclosure of a chemical genus renders obvious any species that happens to fall within it").

In the instant case, the generic diphenol formula disclosed in Knapp contains a large number of variables, and we estimate that it encompasses more than 100 million different diphenols, only one of which is bisphenol A. While the Knapp formula unquestionably encompasses bisphenol A when specific variables are chosen, there is nothing in the disclosure of Knapp suggesting that one should select such variables. Indeed, Knapp appears to teach away from the selection of bisphenol A by focusing on more complex diphenols .... Fifteen typical diphenols are recited. None of them, or any of the other preferred phenols recited above, is or suggests bisphenol A.

The Commissioner repeatedly emphasizes that many of the diphenols specifically enumerated in Knapp are derivatives of bisphenol A. He argues that Knapp thus suggests the selection of bisphenol A itself. We disagree, because, according to the specification, the diphenol in the esters of claim 1 can only be bisphenol A, not a bisphenol A derivative. While Knapp may suggest certain complex bisphenol A derivatives, it does not describe or suggest bisphenol A and therefore does not motivate the selection of bisphenol A.

Given the vast number of diphenols encompassed by the generic diphenol formula in Knapp, and the fact that the diphenols that Knapp specifically discloses to be "typical," "preferred," and "optimum" are different from and more complex than bisphenol A, we conclude that Knapp does not teach or fairly suggest the selection of bisphenol A. A disclosure of millions of compounds does not render obvious a claim to three compounds, particularly when that disclosure indicates a preference leading away from the claimed compounds.

NOTE

1. On one level, *Baird* makes sense; it seems unrealistic to hold a chemical researcher to the knowledge of a handful of compounds buried in the guts of an elaborate generic formula in a single reference. And yet, how does that differ from assuming access to other obscure references (e.g., *In re Hall*, Chapter 4, the "single copy of a German thesis" case)? Do we ask, in cases such as *Hall*, whether someone would have been "motivated" to seek out the reference? Or do we assume, canonically under § 102, that an available reference is accessible? Perhaps *Baird* and its predecessors in the chemical arts can be distinguished on the ground that the generic chemical formula cases involve an additional step. Not only must the researcher find the reference, but he or she must also "plug in" the correct variables to arrive at the compound later sought to be claimed. Still, if this is the point of distinction, how may one account for cases such as *Titanium Metal*, also in Chapter 4, which held that a single point on a graph that represented one of the claimed embodiments defeated the novelty of the claims at issue? If one in the art can be expected to look into the individual points on graphs, why not expect that same person to crank through the details of a generic chemical formula? Again, note that the formula in the reference in *Baird* had several *million* solutions, while the points on the graph in *Titanium Metal* were far less numerous.

2. The prior art patent cited in the case, U.S. Patent 4,634,649, was issued to Knapp *et al.* in 1987 and assigned to Xerox. It will expire in 2005 (under a post-GATT extension of its term, 20 years from its filing date). Does the *Baird* decision indicate that the inventors (or assignee) in the case must take out a license from Xerox to practice their invention? *See* Chapter 8, *Infringement*. Given that the Baird invention is a striking "species" in a very large genus, do Baird *et al.* have an argument that even if they appear to infringe, they should be let off the hook because their invention is so distinctive? *See id.*, discussion of the "Reverse Doctrine of Equivalents."

3. DO WE NEED "NEW USE" PROTECTION?

(The following is adapted from Merges & Nelson, *On the Complex Economics of Patent Scope*, 90 COLUM. L. REV. 839 (1990).)

In the case of new use inventions, the fundamental problem is the rule that a product patent covers all uses. [One problem with this is that it] may be difficult to monitor whether the compound is being used for the new (patented) application or for its old, well-established use. Consider the case of Urbaine Thuau, who filed a patent application containing product claims over a compound he had found useful in the treatment of cervical diseases. However, the compound itself was not new. It had long been used in the leather tanning industry. The Patent Office rejected the patent application, and the Court of Customs and Patent Appeals later affirmed.

> That appellant has made a valuable discovery in the new use of the composi-
> tion here involved we have no doubt, and it is unfortunate for him if he can
> not make claims adequate to protect such discovery, but to hold that every
> new use of an old composition may be the subject of a patent upon the
> composition would lead to endless confusion and go far to destroy the
> benefits of our patent laws.

In re Thuau, 135 F.2d 344, 347, 57 U.S.P.Q. (BNA) 324, 326 (1943). *Compare In re Duva*, 156 U.S.P.Q. (BNA) 90 (C.C.P.A. 1967) (holding that functional preamble to claim for old composition, i.e., "a composition *for* [a certain function]" could not be ignored in determining the obviousness of the claimed invention).

The court expressed particular concern with the "confusion" that might result if purchasers of the product for its newly discovered use bought it from the traditional suppliers. Although these suppliers might have no way of knowing what use the purchaser had in mind, if the new patent were granted, they would be liable nonetheless for patent infringement. While the patent statute includes a detailed provision to deal with this problem (35 U.S.C. § 271(c)), enforcing the rule may be quite difficult. *See, e.g., Thuau, supra*, 135 F.2d at 347, 57 U.S.P.Q. at 326. *See generally*, Merges, *Reflections on Current Legislation Affecting Patent Misuse*, 70 J. PAT. & TRADEMARK OFF. SOC'Y 793, 799-801 (1988).

In some cases, the courts have left patentees with no option but to pursue process claims. In *In re Shetty*, 566 F.2d 81, 195 U.S.P.Q. (BNA) 753 (C.C.P.A. 1977), for example, Shetty's new compounds were homologs of known compounds that were described in the prior art as antiviral agents, whereas Shetty's compounds were discovered to have appetite-suppressant activity. The court held that a prima facie case was made based on the close similarities of chemical structure. Since Shetty did not prove that there were actual differences in properties, the product or composition claims were not allowed. However, the *Shetty* court allowed the process claims (to the new use), without requiring proof that the old compounds did not have the same property as Shetty's. The court said:

> The Patent Office has failed to show a reasonable expectation, or some predictability, that [a reference] compound would be an effective appetite suppressant if administered in the dosage disclosed by [another reference].

566 F.2d at 86, 195 U.S.P.Q. (BNA) at 756.

Nonetheless, the *Shetty* solution has not been widely adopted, again because of the traditional fear that process patents were not as valuable as product patents.

Solutions have been proposed. In a ruling denying a product patent on an obvious variant of an old compound, the court proposed that the solution might be to eliminate patents on obvious variants of old compounds altogether, instead rewarding each inventor with a process patent on the application she has discovered.

> It is basic to the grant of a patent that the scope of a patent should not exceed the scope of invention. If what makes a structurally obvious chemical substance patentable is the new and unobvious properties or uses discovered by the first person to compound the substance, the discoverer should have protection on what he discovered, i.e. the new properties of the substance, but should not be entitled to a 17-year monopoly on the substance itself.... We think that the purposes of the patent law will be adequately served if

patents on compounds which are structurally obvious from the prior art are limited to method (i.e. process) patents directed to the new and useful characteristic or property which is the essence of the discovery or invention.

Monsanto Co. v. Rohm & Haas Co., 312 F. Supp. 778, 790-91, 164 U.S.P.Q. (BNA) 556, 566, 165 U.S.P.Q. (BNA) 683 (E.D. Pa. 1970) (Supp. op.), *aff'd on other grounds*, 456 F.2d 592, 172 U.S.P.Q. (BNA) 323 (3d Cir.), *cert. denied*, 407 U.S. 934, 174 U.S.P.Q. (BNA) 129 (1972); *see also* Comment, *Uses, New Uses and Chemical Patents — A Proposal*, 1968 WIS. L. REV. 901, 915 (proposing abolition of product patents on compounds in favor of patents on methods of production and methods of using — two species of process patents).

This suggestion has so far been ignored. In general, courts have yet to solve the problem of how to reward and thus give incentives to the discovery of new uses. While the problem is not confined to the realm of chemical substances, it crops up mostly here. For reasons which should be clear, granting process patents on new uses makes a good deal of sense, since it would bring the scope of the property right into line with the object of actual research. One must recognize, however, that in some cases enforcement problems may be formidable.

Overcoming Enforcement Issues

The enforcement problems attendant upon process patents are at the heart of arguments against relying on this form of protection. The disadvantages of process patents include the following: (1) Difficulty detecting infringement; (2) defects in infringement doctrines, leading to (3) necessity of inefficient multiple infringement suits; and (4) (until recently) better treatment for product patents when accused infringer imports product from a foreign country. Any proposal to strengthen the role of process patents in the protection of newly discovered uses for old products must address these issues.

The difficulty of detecting infringement was raised in the *Thuau* case, discussed above. The problem is that under a use patent only one use of a product is prohibited; thus the mere sale of the product by a competitor is not *per se* infringement since it might be in connection with an unrelated (and hence infringement-free) use. Because it is difficult for the patentee to obtain firm evidence regarding the ultimate use of the product, it is difficult to establish that the protected right — use of the product for a particular end — has been infringed by end-users.

To some extent, infringement doctrines assist the use-patentee here, but the problems with these doctrines pose the second obstacle to the widespread embrace of a process patent solution to the problem of new uses. For example, courts have held that any aid or encouragement given to end users to assist them or guide them toward using the purchased product for an infringing use is actionable by the patentee. *See generally* 5 D. CHISUM, PATENTS § 17.04[4] (1978 & Supp. 1991). But unfortunately the competitors of use-patentees are often aware of the detailed contours of contributory infringement doctrine. Hence they can insulate themselves from infringement liability by scrupulously refraining from any of the activities that have been found to constitute contributory infringement — even if they know full well that the product largely if not exclusively is being employed by end-users for the patented use.

This then leads to the third problem with use patents: enforcement costs. In the normal case, it will be too expensive for a use-patentee to detect infringement by end-users and then bring individual cases against them. The only economically feasible enforcement option — suits against manufacturers and distributors of the product employed for the infringing end use — is foreclosed by the problems with contributory infringement doctrine just outlined. The net result in many cases is that process patents for new uses are left unenforced — a situation not much different in practice from never granting such patents at all.

This problem is especially acute in the important field of pharmaceuticals. Because of the traditional deference given to doctors, FDA approval for a particular use (or "medical indication," as it is known) does not restrict a doctor from prescribing a drug for any purpose she sees fit. Pharmacists therefore do not police doctors' prescriptions. The result is that a doctor can easily prescribe a drug for a patented use, so long as the drug has also been approved by the FDA for some other, non-patented use. *See, e.g.*, Wheaton, *Generic Competition and Pharmaceutical Innovation: The Drug Price Competition and Patent Term Restoration Act of 1984*, 35 CATH. U. L. REV. 433 (1986). Despite these problems, however, some firms have made progress recently implementing plans to successfully enforce use patents. The most striking example is the Upjohn Corporation's use patent on the compound minoxidil, sold under the tradename "Rogaine" as a partial treatment for baldness. *See* F. Gebhart, *Upjohn Surprises Industry by Enforcing Minoxidil Patent*, DRUG TOPICS, April 3, 1989, at 50 (Upjohn suing "physicians, pharmacists, and clinics"; quoting company official: "Our position ... is that anyone who prescribes, uses, prepares or is involved with the topical application of minoxidil for hair growth violates our patents."). Rogaine is a classic "new use" story — it was a blood pressure drug which produced surprising hair growth in some patients during clinical trials. On the importance of research into new uses in this field, see DiMasi & Lasagna, *Development of Supplementary Indications for Already-Approved Drugs by the United States Pharmaceutical Industry*, 5 J. CLIN. RES. & PHARMACOEPIDEMIOLOGY 19 (1991).

Traditionally, there was a fourth problem with use patents, one they in fact shared with all process patents: they were not as effective when asserted against foreign infringers. This was because under the law protecting domestic patentees from infringing imports, products could be excluded no matter where they were manufactured, but products made from patented processes could not be; the theory was that the infringing act took place outside the reach of U.S. patent laws. *See* U.S. INTERNATIONAL TRADE COMMISSION, FOREIGN PROTECTION OF INTELLECTUAL PROPERTY RIGHTS AND THE EFFECT ON U.S. TRADE (1988). This problem was largely abrogated in 1988 with the passage of the process patent-related provisions (i.e., § 1342) of the Omnibus Trade and Competitiveness Act of 1988, P.L. 100-418, 102 Stat. 1107, 1212, codified at 19 U.S.C. § 1337, 35 U.S.C. § 271(g) (1986 & Supp. V) (new § 271(g): "[w]hoever ... imports into the United States or sells or uses within the United States a product which is made by a process patented in the United States shall be liable as an infringer...."). *Cf. Amgen, Inc. v. U.S. Int'l Trade Comm'n*, 902 F.2d 1532, 14 U.S.P.Q.2d 1734 (Fed. Cir. 1990) (holding that product made from host cell protected by U.S. product patent could not be excluded from U.S. since § 1337 only applies to *process* patents).

The Doctrine of "Slight Changes" and Composition Claims

The Patent Office has been more comfortable about giving a product patent for a new use of an old substance when the patent applicant has modified the substance. To some extent, this serves as a solution to the "new use" problem, since the modified substance is actually only a pretext for awarding a patent for the new use. There has been recognition, however, that this practice provides incentive for trivial or obvious modifications of an old compound, and results in the granting of a new product patent rather than a new use (or process) patent. *See* Hoxie, *A Patent Attorney's View*, in *Seminar on Chemical Invention*, 47 J. PAT. OFF. SOC'Y 630, 638 (1965) ("This ... has led to inequitable results in that of two discoveries of equal value and 'inventiveness,' one may be patented and the other not depending on whether or not the 'gimmick' novelty [i.e., minor structural variation] can be supplied."). Because of the unpredictability of structure-function relationships, then, the doctrine of slight changes is not a good general solution to the new use problem.

A related line of cases suggests another solution, but has many of the same problems. In these cases, old compounds are combined with other ingredients and claimed as a new composition. Since the important active ingredient is the old compound, these patents in effect award the discovery of a new use. *See, e.g.*, *In re Wiggins*, 397 F.2d 356, 158 U.S.P.Q. (BNA) 199 (C.C.P.A. 1968); P. GRUBB, PATENTS FOR CHEMISTS 158-159 (1982) ("A new composition may sometimes be claimed when the invention is really a new compound or a new use of an old compound.").

Some Slight Changes to Make Use Patents Useful

It should be clear that neither of the solutions just described are robust enough to truly address the fundamental cause of the new use dilemma: the conceptual divergence between what is invented (applications, or uses) and what is claimed (structures, or perhaps compositions). Something else needs to be done.

It is suggested that the necessary changes are not monumental. They are in fact minimal, entailing essentially only the following major points: (1) changes in the text or interpretation of § 271 on contributory infringement; (2) increased reliance on class actions against *defendant* classes of infringers; and (3) a bit of courage and imagination on the part of counsel in enforcing new use/process patents.

As to the first, the problems with contributory infringement doctrine are referred to above. These boil down to one issue: manufacturers — the only efficient class of defendants from the point of view of plaintiff/patentees — can insulate themselves from liability despite having knowledge, or having information that ought to charge them with knowledge, that many of their sales are being made into the market for the patented use. The simple way to address this problem is to change the presumption regarding infringement in such a situation. Where a seller/accused infringer is selling enough of the product to know or have reason to know that it is being applied to the patented use, there ought to be a presumption that the defendant has infringed. Thus no amount of insulation from contributory infringement ought to be effective if the *volume of sales* of the product is suspiciously high in light of the known demand for the product as applied to non-infringing uses. The sales volume, in other words, should act as a prima facie indication that the seller has infringed where it would be clear to the reasonable seller in this industry that at least a substantial proportion of its sales must be being applied to the patented end use.

The second change would involve only a slight extension of existing law. In at least one case, a court has certified a defendant class in a patent infringement suit. *See Technograph Printed Circuits, Ltd. v. Methode Electronics, Inc.*, 285 F. Supp. 714 (N.D. Ill. 1968) (certifying defendant class action in case involving patent infringement allegations against 80 defendants). *See generally* Note, *Defendant Class Actions*, 91 HARV. L. REV. 630 (1978) (commenting on notice problems: "In patent litigation, notice — perhaps combined with a form requesting specific information — may reveal whether many of the other class members [aside from the named, representative defendant] will face significantly greater liability than will the personal representative if the patent is held valid."). This precedent must be applied and extended if plaintiff/patentees are to be able to effectively enforce use patents. The reason is simple: the class action reduces the transaction costs of filing individual suits. And where individual end-users are involved, as described above, suits against end-users may ultimately be necessary to enforce a new use patent. Thus effective procedural devices must be used to reduce the transaction costs. Hence the defendant class action. This is a device which might have come in handy when Upjohn was enforcing its minoxidil process-of-use patent, as described earlier.

The third proposal outlined above involves no change in the law, yet it may be the hardest to achieve. The tools for enforcing use patents are in most cases ready at hand; what is needed most critically is the courage to apply them in a forceful and novel way. Until they are tried and tested by someone with the creativity to employ them, the conventional wisdom — that use patents are ineffective — will continue to be true by dint of inertia. Until this thinking is challenged, new use patents will continue to fulfill the bar's prophecy that they are useless. There is no enforcement, and hence no effective property right, without first the will to enforce. And until new use patents are enforced, we will continue to dance around the fundamental rift between uses invented in the lab and structures protected in the courts.

4. THE ROAD TO *DILLON*

a. The Early Days: Structure Is King

The *Hass-Henze* Doctrine

One of the earliest cases involving a denial of a claim to a chemical compound based upon close structural proximity is *Bender v. Hoffmann*, 1898 C.D. 262, discussed in Wegner, *Prima Facie Obviousness of Chemical Compounds*, 6 AM. PAT. L. ASS'N Q.J. 271, 272 (1978).

From at least the 1930's and for the next three decades, a preoccupation with "paper chemistry" dominated obviousness considerations. Looking only at the two-dimensional structural formula of the claimed compound versus the prior art, the question was one of relative closeness of two-dimensional structures, with a prior art adjacent homolog or position isomer almost always being fatal to patentability, as the claimed compound was "structurally obvious."

> [At this time] the main job of the Examiner was to identify the single closest structural formula in a prior art reference. Then, merely eyeballing that structure against the claim was virtually all that the Examiner needed to do under pre-*Papesch* case law. A seasoned Examiner could make a clear decision on obviousness of the claimed compound in virtually an instant, like a home plate umpire calling balls and strikes. If an adjacent homolog, it was a "strike" (unpatentable) right down the middle of the plate. If an added functional group was present, perhaps a "ball" (patentable).

H. WEGNER, CHEMICAL PATENT PRACTICE (1991).

The presumption of obviousness from close structural similarity stemmed from a pair of early cases, *In re Henze*, 181 F.2d 196, 85 U.S.P.Q. (BNA) 261 (C.C.P.A. 1950), and *In re Hass*, 141 F.2d 122, 127, 130, 60 U.S.P.Q. (BNA) 544, 548, 552 (C.C.P.A. 1944). These cases established the rule that, unless an applicant showed that the prior art compound lacked the property or advantage asserted for the claimed compound, the presumption of unpatentability for closely related compounds was not overcome. Without such a showing, structure was king, and no patent would issue. *See generally* Collins, *The Forgotten Chemistry of the Hass-Henze Doctrine*, 44 J. PAT. OFF. SOC'Y 284 (1962). In both cases, close homologs (described below) of prior art compounds were found obvious by the Patent Office, and the court affirmed the rejections.

b. The *Papesch* Revolution

Although the *Hass* and *Henze* cases suggested in dictum that the presumption of obviousness — the prima facie case — could be overcome by a showing regarding chemical properties, it was unclear whether this concept was binding or how it would be applied. The *Papesch* case clarified these issues, and ushered in the modern era of chemical nonobviousness.

In re PAPESCH

315 F.2d 381, 137 U.S.P.Q. 43 (C.C.P.A. 1963)

RICH, JUDGE.

This appeal is from the decision of the Patent Office Board of Appeals affirming the rejection of claims 1-3, the only claims presented in appellant's application for "2,4,6-TRIALKYLPYRAZOLO (4,3-d)-4,5,6,7-TETRAHYDRO-PYRIMIDINE-5,7-DIONES."

The specification, which is brief and occupies less than three pages of the printed record, states:

> The trialkyl compounds of this invention have been found to possess unexpectedly potent anti-inflammatory activity in contrast to the related trimethyl compound. The instant compounds are also diuretic agents.

[The claims were rejected as "obvious homologs" of compounds disclosed in a scientific publication by Robins.]

The case is argued on the assumption that a lower homolog of the claimed compounds is in the prior art and we shall proceed on that assumption. In other words, comparing the specific compound of claim 2 with the prior art, the compounds differ only in that where appellant has three ethyl groups the prior art has three methyl groups, a total difference of three -CH(2) groups. Whether this meets the usual definitions of "homology" (according to two additional references to chemical texts made of record by the Patent Office) we do not stop to consider inasmuch as appellant has not argued the point.

[Appellant's] affidavit reports comparative tests of the Robins et al. trimethyl compound and appellant's triethyl compound which show that the latter is an active anti-inflammatory agent while the prior art compound is completely inactive in that respect.

We have before us, therefore, a single clean-cut issue of law. The claims are rejected only on the ground that they are unpatentable over a single reference which discloses what is conceded to be a lower homolog of the claimed compounds and proof has been given showing that the compound of claim 2 possesses an advantageous pharmacological property shown not to be possessed by the prior art compound.

[The court discusses the *Hass-Henze* doctrine, and concludes:] What this comes down to, in final analysis, is a rather simple proposition: If that which appears, at first blush, to be obvious though new is shown by evidence not to be obvious, then the evidence prevails over surmise or unsupported contention and a rejection based on obviousness must fall. Many cases, both before and after the enactment of section 103, have been decided according to such reasoning.

[After completing its review of the prior cases, the court continues.] From the foregoing cases it will be seen that this and other courts, both before and after the enactment of section 103, have determined the unobviousness and patentability of new chemical compounds by taking into consideration their biological or pharmacological properties. Nine of the ten cases above considered, directly and indirectly, involved such properties. Patentability has not been determined on the basis of the obviousness of structure alone. In fact, where patentability was found in the above cases it was found in spite of close similarity of chemical structure, often much closer similarity than we have here.

Returning now to the decision of the board in this case, we think that it rests on one fundamental error of law, namely, the failure to take into consideration the biological or pharmaceutical property of the compounds as anti-inflammatory agents on the ground that to chemists the structure of the compounds would be so obvious as to be beyond doubt, and that a showing of such properties is to be used only to resolve doubt.

From the standpoint of patent law, a compound and all of its properties are inseparable; they are one and the same thing. The graphic formulae, the chemical nomenclature, the systems of classification and study such as the concepts of homology, isomerism, etc., are mere symbols by which compounds can be identified, classified, and compared. But a formula is not a compound and while it may serve in a claim to identify what is being patented, as the metes and bounds of a deed identify a plot of land, the thing that is patented is not the formula but the compound identified by it. And the patentability of the thing does not depend on the similarity of its formula to that of another compound but of the similarity of the former compound to the latter. There is no basis in law for ignoring any property in making such a comparison. An assumed similarity based on a comparison of formulae must give way to evidence that the assumption is erroneous.

The argument has been made that patentability is here being asserted only on the basis of one property, the anti-inflammatory activity, and that the compounds claimed and the compound of the prior art presumably have many properties in common. Presumably they do, but presumption is all we have here. The same is true of all of the compounds of the above cases which were held patentable over compounds of the prior art, many of which must have had more in common by way of properties than the compounds here because the relationships, structurally, were even closer than here.

As to the examiner's view that in a case such as this the applicant should claim his invention as a process utilizing the newly discovered property, the board appears to have ignored it, properly we think. It is contrary to practically all of the above decisions wherein no fault was found with granting product claims. Such claims have well-recognized advantages to those in the business of making and selling compounds, in contrast to process-of-use claims, because competitors in the sale of compounds are not generally users.

Reversed.

NOTES

1. *Structures, Properties, and New Uses.* Despite the dicta in *Hass* and *Henze*, the latter case implied that structure, and not properties, was the key to chemical nonobviousness. The reason: the logic of the prohibition on product patents for new uses.

> If by discovering useful properties of a new but adjacent member an applicant may escape the responsibility of showing that the same property is not inherent in an old homologue not heretofore *known* as useful for that purpose, the doctrine that a new use for an old product is not patentable would effectively be wiped out of the law of chemical patents. The principle is too firmly imbedded in our substantive patent law to permit such a result.

In re Henze, 181 F.2d at 202. Note how Judge Rich deals with this objection: he states that product patents have a distinct business advantage, in effect dismissing the new use problem on pragmatic grounds. See the preceding section, *Do We Need "New Use" Protection?*, for discussion and proposals regarding the pragmatic problems of new use patents.

2. *Applying Papesch.* One recent case, *In re Merck*, 800 F.2d 1091, 231 U.S.P.Q. (BNA) 375 (Fed. Cir. 1986), shows a routine application of the teachings of *Papesch*. It is also important for its statements regarding the "obvious to try" standard.

> The invention is directed to a method of treating human mental disorders; the method involves treating depression in humans by the oral administration of 5- (3-dimethylamino propylidene)dibenzo[a, d][1, 4]cycloheptadiene (commonly known as and hereafter referred to as "amitriptyline"), or the hydrochloride or hydrobromide salts thereof, in a particular dosage range.

A [prior art] patent to Rey-Bellet disclosed amitriptyline and its hydrochloride salt, and recited as properties a "manifold activity upon the central nervous system," as well as pharmacological and medicinal properties, such as "narcosis-potentiating, adrenolytic, sedative, antihistaminic, antiemetic, antipyretic and hypothermic." Rey-Bellet did not disclose or otherwise teach that amitriptyline possessed antidepressive properties. A prior art publication by Kuhn disclosed a compound called imipramine, and taught that the compound was a very effective antidepressant in humans. Imipramine, said the court, differs from the structure of amitriptyline only in the replacement of the unsaturated carbon atom in the center ring with a nitrogen atom. Next the court cited a prior art publication by Friedman, whose aim was "to survey the history of isosterism, to classify the varieties of isosteric replacements which are recorded in the literature, and to note the influence of these replacements on the biological activity of compounds." Friedman, however, did not disclose or otherwise teach as bioisosteric the interchange of the nitrogen and unsaturated carbon atoms. A prior art publication by Petersen, however, applied this theory to the substitution of an unsaturated carbon atom for a nitrogen atom in a biologically active compound, and showed the equivalence of the compounds. The court concluded:

> We see no clear error in the Board's determination as to the teachings of the prior art references, in combination. In view of these teachings, which show a close structural similarity and a similar use (psychotropic drugs) between amitriptyline and imipramine, one of ordinary skill in the medicinal chemical arts, possessed of the knowledge of the investigative techniques used in the field of drug design and pharmacological predictability, would have expected amitriptyline to resemble imipramine in the alleviation of depression in humans.
>
> [The court turns to appellants argument that the Board applied an impermissible "obvious to try" standard.] Clearly, amitriptyline and imipramine, both known psychotropic drugs, are closely structurally related. The expectation that the similar structures would behave similarly was suggested in [a prior art reference]. In combination with those teachings, the prior art teaching that the precise structural difference between amitriptyline and imipramine involves a known bioisosteric replacement provides sufficient basis for the required expectation of success, without resort to hindsight. Obviousness does not require absolute predictability. Only a reasonable expectation that the beneficial result will be achieved is necessary to show obviousness.

Note that one anomaly in the law that continues, however, If a structure exists in the prior art, even though no use was known for it, it anticipates a later product (structure) claim — a throwback, it seems, to the days when structure was king. *See In re Schoenwald*, 22 U.S.P.Q.2d (BNA) 1671 (Fed. Cir. 1992).

4. *Markush Groups.* Many chemical patent claims use a device known as a Markush group. In general, as discussed in Chapter 1, a Markush group has the form: "I claim [1] a solid, [2] together with a liquid, [3] acting together [for some purpose,] wherein the solid is selected from the group rock, wood and steel, and the liquid is selected from the group water, oil, and orange juice." In chemical cases, the Markush group claim will look like the following:

I claim —

$$-COR_a$$

wherein R_a is a member selected from the group consisting of -OH, $-OR_b$ or $-NR_c Rd$, R_b is a lower alkyl, lower alkoxy-lower alkyl, or trifluoromethyl-lower alkyl, R_c is hydrogen or a lower alkyl, and R_d is hydrogen, lower alkyl.

Some Markush groups can encompass thousands — even hundreds of thousands — of compounds. Is it surprising that such a claim could be allowed by a patent examiner? How could the applicant meet the burden of proving enablement under § 112 of the Patent Act? *See* Chapter 6. If the claims cover an infinite genus, does this imply that no one could patent any species within that genus, no matter how marvelous the properties of the newly discovered species?

The answer is generally no. Although a claimed invention — e.g., a particular compound — "reads on" and therefore infringes a claim in a prior patent, solid authority holds that the particular compound may still be patented as nonobvious. A "subservient patent" may be issued in such a case, so long as it discloses an improved feature. *See, e.g., Atlas Powder Co. v. E.I. Du Pont de Nemours & Co.*, 750 F.2d 1569, 1576-77, 224 U.S.P.Q. (BNA) 409, 413-14 (Fed. Cir. 1984). Nor does the fact that the subservient patentee has invented a nonobvious variant of a device covered by a broad patent mean that the broad patent is invalid for lack of enabling disclosure under 35 U.S.C. § 112. *See, e.g., B.G. Corp. v. Walter Kidde & Co.*, 79 F.2d 20, 22 (2d Cir. 1935) (L. Hand, J.) ("It is true that [the inventor of the spark plug] did not foresee the particular adaptability of his plug to the airplane.... Nevertheless, he did not shoot in the dark; he laid down with perfect certainty what he wished to accomplish and how.... [H]e is not charged with a prophetic understanding of the entire field of its usefulness."); *Amerace Corp. v. Ferro Corp.*, 532 F. Supp. 1188, 1201-02, 213 U.S.P.Q. (BNA) 1099, 1109-10 (N.D. Tex. 1982). And a subservient patent can prevent a dominant patent holder from practicing the particular improved feature claimed in the subservient patent because a patent grant is a right to *exclude*, not an affirmative right to practice an invention. See 35 U.S.C. § 154 (1988). Thus the dominant patentee can exclude the subservient patentee from practicing her invention at all, and the subservient patentee can exclude the dominant patentee from practicing her specific improved feature. See *Atlas Powder*, 750 F.2d at 1580, 224 U.S.P.Q. at 416; *Ziegler v. Phillips Petr. Co.*, 483 F.2d 858, 871-72, 177 U.S.P.Q. (BNA) 481, 489-90 (5th Cir.), *cert. denied*, 414 U.S. 1079, 180 U.S.P.Q. (BNA) 1 (1973); *cf. Cantrell v. Wallick*, 117 U.S. 689, 694 (1886) (Where one patent is an improvement on another patent, "neither of the two patentees can lawfully use the invention of the other without the other's consent."); *Cochrane v. Deener*, 94 U.S. 780, 787 (1877) ("One invention may include within it many others, and each and all may be valid at the same time."). For more on this, see Chapter 6, Section B.3.a, *Enablement and the Temporal Paradox*.

3. Chemical Intermediates. An important set of cases involves chemical intermediates. *See In re Lalu*, 747 F.2d 703, 223 U.S.P.Q. (BNA) 1257 (Fed. Cir. 1984). There the applicant claimed perfluoroalkyl sulfonyl chlorides and bromides having the formula:

$$C_nF_{2n+1}(CH_2) \begin{matrix} S & Z \\ O & \\ b & 2 \end{matrix}$$

wherein the perfluoroalkyl group $CnF2_{n+1}$ is defined by n being a number between 1 and 20, Z is a chlorine or bromine atom, and the bridging group $(CH_2)_b$ is defined by b being a number between 2 and 20. The application was rejected because of a prior patent to Oesterling, who disclosed homologous compounds, namely 1,1- dihydroperfluoroalkyl sulfonic acids having the formula:

$$C_nF_{2n+1}CH_2SO_3H$$

wherein C_nF_{2n+1} is a lower perfluoroalkyl group and the bridging group is a methylene (CH_2) group. The board, in affirming the examiner's rejection, said the close structural similarity between the reference sulfonyl chloride compounds and the claimed compounds was sufficient to raise the presumption of obviousness. According to the court,

> [a]ppellants argue that since several utilities were disclosed for the compounds claimed, and Oesterling teaches no significant properties or utility for the disclosed sulfonyl chlorides except as intermediates in the formation of the product sulfonic acids, the rejection of the instant claims is not proper.
>
> There is no disclosure that the Oesterling compounds would have any properties in common with those of appellants' compounds, as those properties of the former relate to the use of the compounds for base neutralization, catalysis, metal cleaning, and fuel. The mere fact that Oesterling's sulfonyl chlorides can be used as intermediates in the production of the corresponding sulfonic acids does not provide adequate motivation for one of ordinary skill in the art to stop the Oesterling synthesis and investigate the intermediate sulfonyl chlorides with an expectation of arriving at appellants' claimed sulfonyl halides for use as corrosion inhibiting agents, surface active agents, or leveling agents.

For more on the status of chemical intermediates, see *In re Surrey*, 319 F.2d 233 (C.C.P.A. 1963); *In re Druey*, 319 F.2d 237 (C.C.P.A. 1963); *In re Widmer*, 353 F.2d 752 (C.C.P.A. 1965). *See generally* Woessner, *Recent Decisions Affecting the Patentability of Chemical Intermediates*, 63 J. PAT. OFF. SOC'Y 258 (1981). For descriptions of these cases, and a proposed change in the rules affecting chemical intermediates, see Note, *Requirements for Patenting Chemical Intermediates: Do They Accomplish the Statutory Goals?*, 29 ST. LOUIS U. L.J. 191 (1984).

E. COMPARATIVE NOTE: TAKING AN "INVENTIVE STEP" OVERSEAS

For the most part, every major patent system in the world has evolved a standard that serves the function of the nonobviousness requirement in the United States. A final gatekeeper seems to be necessary to an effective modern patent system. Despite the broad similarity in purpose, however, we shall see that there are some interesting differences between the requirements in the various countries.

1. THE EUROPEAN COUNTRIES

In Europe the ultimate condition of patentability is the requirement that an applicant show an "inventive step." According to the European Patent Convention (EPC), which forms the basis for all major European countries' current domestic patent statutes,

> [a]n invention shall be considered as involving an inventive step if, having regard to the state of the art, it is not obvious to a person skilled in the art. If the state of the art also includes [previously filed European patent applications not yet issued as patents], these documents are not to be considered in deciding whether there has been an inventive step.

EPC, Article 56.

According to European practitioners, "[t]he objection to validity [in Article 56] is essentially that of obviousness." 1 ENCYCLOPEDIA OF U.K. AND EUROPEAN PATENT LAW § 5-201 (M. Vitoria et al. eds., 1977 & Supp. 1991). But there are a few differences between this provision and its counterpart in the U.S. Code, § 103.

The first difference appears in the second sentence of Article 56. Here previously-filed but not yet issued patent applications are removed from the prior art from which inventive step is determined. Contrast this with the U.S. rule, embodied in cases such as *In re Bass*, 474 F.2d 1276, 177 U.S.P.Q. (BNA) 178 (C.C.P.A. 1973), which states that these applications *are* effective prior art for § 103 purposes. Note that the European system does not remove these applications from the prior art for *novelty* purposes; Article 54 says that they are effective references for defeating novelty. In other words, the Europeans do follow the rule of *Alexander Milburn Co. v. Davis-Bournonville Co.*, 270 U.S. 390 (1926); they simply refused to extend it in the context of nonobviousness as did the U.S. courts in cases such as *Bass*. *See generally* Harrison, *Interference Issues in a First-to-File World: Interference Issues in Europe*, 18 AM. INTELL. PROP. L. ASS'N Q.J. 65 (1991).

Although Article 56 is largely silent about two important matters in § 103 — the level of skill in the art, and the time from which "inventiveness" is to be determined — it and the cases interpreting it do provide some guidance. As to the level of skill, the European view seems to parallel that in the U.S. *See Intermediate Layer for Reflector*, 1981, No. 10 OFFIC. J. EUR. PAT. OFF. 434, Case No. T 6/80 (Eur. Pat. Off. Tech. Bd. App., 13 May 1981) (using "person skilled in the art" standard); *Production of Hollow Thermoplastic Objects*, 1982, No. 7 OFFIC. J. EUR. PAT. OFF. 249, Case No. T 5/81 (Eur. Pat. Off. Tech. Bd. App., 4 March 1982) (same standard used, with admonition not to view prior art from perspective of inventor who has already envisioned invention). As the cases make clear, the level of skill varies depending on the field. *See, e.g., Genentech (Human*

Growth Hormone), [1989] Rep. Pat. Cas. 147 (Ct. App., U.K.) (very high level of skill in biotechnology field).

As to the time from which inventiveness is to be measured, again the European view is very similar to that in the U.S. As the text of Article 56 makes clear, all categories of Article 54 prior art (i.e., art or novelty purposes) *except* previously-filed patent applications are to be taken into account in determining whether an invention shows an inventive step. It follows logically that the priority date of the inventor's application would be the appropriate time from which to determine the presence of an inventive step; the cases bear this out. *See, e.g.*, *Metal Refining*, 1983, No. 4 OFFIC. J. EUR. PAT. OFF. 133, Case No. T 24/81 (Eur. Pat. Off. Tech. Bd. App., 13 Oct. 1982) (prior art must be viewed as it would be by the "skilled man" as of the priority date of inventor's application).

On the issue of what is to be deemed analogous prior art under the European system, it appears as though a "problem-oriented" rather than strictly professional field-oriented view has been adopted, as in the U.S. *See Cleaning Apparatus for Conveyor Belt*, 1982, No. 6 OFFIC. J. EUR. PAT. OFF. 225, Case No. T 32/81 (Tech. Bd. App. Eur. Pat. Off., 5 March 1982).

a. Relevancy of the Problem Solved

As discussed above in the notes to *In re Dillon*, the Federal Circuit has rejected the notion that the problem solved by the inventor is a relevant consideration in determining nonobviousness. The situation is different in Europe, at least on the face of it; and it is more complex.

A number of leading European decisions emphasize the importance of the "problem and solution" approach to determining the presence of an inventive step. The starting place for the analysis is the technical problem that the invention addresses and solves. The prior art is examined with an eye toward one question: was the solution of this problem obvious in light of what was known? *See Carbonless Copying Paper*, 1981, No. 7 OFFIC. J. EUR. PAT. OFF. 206 (Eur. Pat. Off. Tech. Bd. App., 6 Apr. 1981), *corrected at* 1981, No. 9 OFFIC. J. EUR. PAT. OFF. 349; *Metal Refining/BASF*, 1983, No. 4 OFFIC. J. EUR. PAT. OFF. 133, Case No. T 24/81 (Eur. Pat. Off. Tech. Bd. App., 13 Oct. 1982).

The main goal of the problem-and-solution approach seems to be to make the entire inventive step inquiry more objective. Just as § 103 ended the style of inquiry centered around the presence or absence of the almost magic quality of "invention," so Article 56 seeks to define more precisely what is being compared to what in determining whether an inventive step has been made. (In the case of Article 56, the problem addressed and solved in the claimed invention is compared to the prior art's teachings.)

There are, however, conflicting signals in the cases decided so far on one important issue. This is whether the skilled artisan is presumed to have the inventor's problem in mind when the court reconstructs that artisan's review of the prior art to see whether the inventor's solution was obvious. In the *Metal Refining* case, *supra*, for instance, the Board seemed to imply that the problem should be taken for granted; it stated that all previously published references and embodiments which suggest a solution to the skilled artisan must be considered, even when those references do not particularly emphasize the solution. On the other hand, in the *Thermoplastic Objects* case, *supra*, the Board pointed out that the teachings of a prior art document may have narrower implications for a skilled artisan who does not have the inventor's problem and solution in mind. The Board notes that in the case before it, however, the inventor was the first to perceive the problem that the invention solved. Thus perhaps in other cases, where the problem solved is well known, the prior art would have to be examined as if the skilled artisan had this problem in mind. This is supported by a case which held that the problem posed and solved by an invention must be significantly different than problems whose solutions are addressed in the prior art. *Light Reflecting Slats*, 1982, No. 11 OFFIC. J. EUR. PAT. OFF. 419, Case No. T 39/82 (Eur. Pat. Off. Tech. Bd. App., 30 July 1982). *Cf. Radio Receiver and Recorder*, Case No. T 54/85 (Eur. Pat. Off. Tech. Bd. App., 20 Jan. 1989) (abstract reprinted in 1 CHARTERED INSTITUTE OF PATENT AGENTS, EUROPEAN PATENTS SOURCEFINDER § T1368 (1988 & Supp. 1990)) (where prior art shows that invention is obvious solution for one problem addressed, but not for another problem solved by invention, invention has achieved an inventive step).

b. Combining References

In general, the European rules on combining references are similar to those applied by the U.S. Patent Office. *See, e.g.*, *Methylenebis (phenyl isocyanate)*, 1982, No. 10 OFFIC. J. EUR. PAT. OFF. 394, Case No. T 2/81 (Eur. Pat. Off. Tech. Bd. App., 1 July 1982) (it is inadmissible to combine unrelated references; but references may be considered jointly to verify a general trend or preference in the art). *See generally* Pagenberg, *Interference Issues in a First-to-File World: Introduction*, 19 AM. INTELL. PROP. L. ASS'N Q.J. 1 (1991) (discussing European Patent Office's cases prohibiting the creation of a "mosaic" of prior art references purporting to show obviousness of claimed invention).

According to one source, in Europe "[w]here those in the trade have known for years of the separate integers [i.e., elements] of an invention but have not seen fit to combine them it must support an argument that it is not obvious to do so and that the documents should not be read together." 1 ENCYCLOPEDIA OF U.K. AND EUROPEAN PATENT LAW § 5-204 (M. Vitoria et al. eds., 1977 & Supp. 1991), citing *Gas Purification*, 1987, No. 9 OFFIC. J. EUR. PAT. OFF. 405, Case No. T 271/84 (Eur. Pat. Off. Tech. Bd. App., 18 March 1986) (invention combined elements from three different procedures, at least two of which the prior art taught were incompatible).

c. "Obvious to Try"

Although the European case law, like its U.S. counterpart, makes predictability tantamount to obviousness (*see Plasmid pSG2*, 1988, No. 12 OFFIC. J. EUR. PAT. OFF. 452, Case No. T 162/86 (Eur. Pat. Off. Tech. Bd. App., 7 July 1987), the U.S. doctrine that an invention obvious to try is not, therefore, obvious has not always been followed in Europe. In *Electromagnetically Operated Switch/Allen-Bradley*, 1983, No. 1 OFFIC. J. EUR. PAT. OFF. 15, Case No. T 21/81 (Eur. Pat. Off. Tech. Bd. App., 10 Sept. 1982), the Board held that it is part of the normal activities of the person skilled in the art to select the most appropriate of a group of materials known as suitable for a particular purpose. And in several other early cases, the Board seemed to equate obvious to try with obvious, i.e., lacking in inventive step. *See Process/Fischer*, (unpublished), Case No. T 67/83 (Eur. Pat. Off. Tech. Bd. App., 1 Aug. 1984) (abstract reprinted in 1 CHARTERED INSTITUTE OF PATENT AGENTS, EUROPEAN PATENTS SOURCEBOOK § T 261 (1988 & Supp. 1990)); *Fibre Manufacture/Akzo*, 1987, No. 4 EUR. PAT. OFF. REP. 198, Case No. T 235/85 (Eur. Pat. Off. Tech. Bd. App., 10 Feb. 1987).

On the other hand, more recent cases seem to follow the U.S. approach; they emphasize that a reasonable prediction of success must accompany both the research path taken *and* the outcome. *See, e.g., Milk Production/Monsanto*, (unpublished), Case No. T 249/88 (Eur. Pat. Off. Tech. Bd. App., 14 Feb. 1989) (abstract reprinted in 1 CHARTERED INSTITUTE OF PATENT AGENTS, EUROPEAN PATENTS SOURCEBOOK § T 1411 (1988 & Supp. 1990)) (reasonable expectation of success must accompany not only approach but outcome); *Cracking Composition/Phillips Petroleum*, 1989, No. 4 EUR. PAT. OFF. REP. 207, Case No. T 247/87 (Eur. Pat. Off. Tech. Bd. App., 28 Apr. 1988) (obvious to try is not the proper inquiry; obvious that approach would succeed is proper).

d. Second Indications — The New Use Problem

Under the European Patent Convention, forms of medical treatment or therapy, as well as diagnostic methods, are not patentable subject matter. Article 52(4). But Article 54(5) modifies this rule by stating that it shall not apply to exclude the patentability of a substance or composition "for use in a method." Of course, as in the U.S., the general rule in Europe is that new chemical structures useful as pharmaceuticals are entitled to product patent protection. *See, e.g., Alpha-interferons/Biogen*, 1989, No. 11 OFFIC. J. EUR. PAT. OFF. 1, Case No. T 301/87 (Eur. Pat. Off. Tech. Bd. App., 16 Feb. 1989). But note that several members of the European Patent Convention have exercised their right under Article 167 of the Convention not to recognize the patentability of pharmaceutical products under their national patent laws. *See, e.g., Extension of Reservation Under Art. 167(2)(a) EPC by Spain*, 1987, No. 3 OFFIC. J. EUR. PAT. OFF. 93 (Eur. Pat. Off. Adm. Council, 5 Dec. 1986).

An early challenge to the patentability of pharmaceutical uses clarified the meaning of this section. In *Pyrrolidine Derivatives/Hoffman-La Roche*, 1984, No.

4 OFFIC. J. EUR. PAT. OFF. 164 (Eur. Pat. Off. Tech. Bd. App., 12 Jan. 1984), the Board held that a known compound claimed for a medical application — a so-called "first medical indication" — could be included in a method-of-use claim. The Board also confronted the question of the proper scope of such a claim. It held that the discoverer of the first medical use or indication was entitled to exclude others from using the same compound for *any* medical indication — even one the original discoverer did not know of at the time of her claim.

Next, the European Patent Office considered a closely related question: whether the discovery of a *second* medical use or indication warranted a method-of-use patent. The Enlarged Board of Appeal said yes in a series of cases. *See, e.g.*, *Second Medical Indication/Eisai*, 1985, No. 3 OFFIC. J. EUR. PAT. OFF. 64, Case No. Gr. 5/83 (Eur. Pat. Off. En. Bd. App., 5 Dec. 1984). This followed earlier decisions to the same effect by national courts in Germany and Switzerland, and rejected a decision of the courts in Great Britain to the opposite effect. *See Hydropyridine/Bayer*, 1984, No. 1 OFFIC. J. EUR. PAT. OFF. 26 (Bundesgerichtof, F.R.G., 20 Sept. 1983); *Hydropyridine/Bayer*, 1984, No. 5 OFFIC. J. EUR. PAT. OFF. 233 (Brit. Pat. Off., 2 Nov. 1982). The same reasoning has now been applied to animal therapies, also prohibited under Article 52; second "veterinary" indications are now upheld if claimed in method form. *See* the whimsically named *Pigs II/Duphar Int'l Res.*, 1989, No. 1 OFFIC. J. EUR. PAT. OFF. 24, Case No. T 19/86 (Eur. Pat. Off. Tech. Bd. App., 15 Oct. 1987) (therapeutic application of vaccine to new class of pigs — those testing positive for disease, instead of negative as in earlier uses — constitutes second medical indication).

Finally, the logic of this line of cases has been applied outside the context of medical uses. In *Novelty of Purpose in Patent Claim/Mobil*, 1990, No. 3 OFFIC. J. EUR. PAT. OFF. (headnote) (Eur. Pat. Off. En. Bd. App., 11 Dec. 1989), the Enlarged Board of Appeal upheld Mobil's claim on a new use of a known compound. The Board permitted Mobil to change the form of its claim from a strict compound to a method of using the compound, over the opposition of opponent Chevron Research. The Board specifically approved of the use form, treating it rather like a functional limitation. *See generally* Patterson, *The Patentability of Further Uses of Known Product Under the EPC*, 13 Eur. Intell. Prop. Rev. 16, 17 (1991). *Cf. Composition claims — Patent Office Notice*, EUR. INTELL. PROP. REV., July 1989, reprinting *Notice*, 117 CANADIAN PAT. OFF. REC. (9 May 1989) (stating intention to accept new use claims for compounds, including pharmaceuticals, despite prohibition from earlier case on medical therapy patents in EPC).

It should be clear from the preceding sections that the Europeans are closer to an understanding of the importance of "new use" claims as an appropriate form of protection. See Section D.3, *Do We Need "New Use" Protection?*, *supra*. But one troubling matter remains. If the discoverer of a first use is given broad product-like protection, as in *Pyrrolidine Derivatives*, *supra*, little research on new uses can be expected during the term of this original patent. *But see*

Marsico, *The Chemical-Pharmaceutical Product Patent: Absolute Protection, General Formulas and Sufficiency of Description*, 11 EUR. INTELL. PROP. REV. 397, 400 (1990) (advocating broad protection for discoverer of structure and new use, since this research makes possible research on subsequent uses). Why should the progressive treatment of new use inventions be limited to the case where the compound with a known use is unpatented? If a new use patent can be distinguished over prior art for novelty and inventive step purposes, why can't it be distinguished over an existing patent for infringement purposes? *Cf.* White, *The Novelty-Destroying Disclosure: Some Recent Decisions*, 9 EUR. INTELL. PROP. REV. 315, 320 (1990) (noting incongruity that one who uses patented invention for unrelated use can be deemed infringing even though under other circumstances new use claims would be allowed to that inventor). As long as broad protection is given to the discoverer of a first medical use, this inconsistency will remain.

e. Secondary Considerations

The European treatment of secondary considerations — commercial success, long-felt want, etc. — parallels that of the U.S. courts, but is in general slightly less receptive of them in important respects. In *Air Drying Apparatus/Grass-Hair Holding*, (unpublished decision), Case No. T 92/86 (Eur. Pat. Off. Tech. Bd. App., 5 Nov. 1987) (abstract reprinted in 1 CHARTERED INSTITUTE OF PATENT AGENTS, EUROPEAN PATENTS SOURCEBOOK § T 905 (1988 & Supp. 1990)), the Board acknowledged that commercial success evidence could be useful, so long as it related to the technical features of a claimed element and was the result of those features rather than other business factors. But the court refused to credit testimony regarding the accused infringer's copying of the product, since this one instance of copying was not enough to establish a general acknowledgement of the advantages of the claimed invention in the art. And the Board takes seriously the requirement that the proponent of the commercial success evidence — i.e., the applicant or patentee — rule out business factors as the cause of the patented product's success. *See Production of Explosive Fusecord/ICI*, 1987, No. 6 EUR. PAT. OFF. REP. 357, Case No. T 270/84 (Eur. Pat. Off. Tech. Bd. App., 1 Sept. 1987) (excluding evidence of commercial success because applicant had not carried burden of connecting it to technical merits of invention).

The cases reveal a greater solicitude for evidence that the invention met a long-felt need. *See, e.g., Packing Machine*, 1985, No. 5 OFFIC. J. EUR. PAT. OFF. 132, Case No. T 106/84 (Eur. Pat. Off. Tech. Bd. App., 25 Feb. 1985) (simple solution that met long-felt need indicates inventive step); *PABX/K. Paulsson et al.* (unpublished), Case No. T 13/88 (Eur. Pat. Off. Tech. Bd. App., 13 Mar. 1989), (abstract reprinted in 1 CHARTERED INSTITUTE OF PATENT AGENTS, EUROPEAN PATENTS SOURCEBOOK § T 1444 (1988 & Supp. 1990)) (patentability denied due to inadequacy of showing of long-felt want). And it is clear that a *long*-felt want is what the Board has in mind; a solution to a problem only recently recognized in the art does not qualify. *See Metal Refining/BASF*, 1983, No. 4

OFFIC. J. EUR. PAT. OFF. 133, Case No. T 24/81 (Eur. Pat. Off. Tech. Bd. App., 13 Oct. 1982). *See generally* H. ULLRICH, STANDARDS OF PATENTABILITY FOR EUROPEAN INVENTIONS 85-86, 89-91 (IIC STUDIES IN INDUSTRIAL PROPERTY AND COPYRIGHT LAW No. 1, 1977).

In some of the national courts, such as those of Great Britain, commercial success plays second chair to the lead role of other secondary factors. *See* 1 ENCYCLOPEDIA OF U.K. AND EUROPEAN PATENT LAW § 5-222 (M. Vitoria et al. eds., 1977 & Supp. 1991) (in Great Britain, cases state that "commercial success alone is 'of very little importance.' It must also be shown that there was a 'long-felt want' ..."); Cornish, *The Essential Criteria for Patentability of European Inventions: Novelty and Inventive Step*, 14 INT'L REV. INDUS. PROP. & COPYRIGHT L. 765 (1983); J. BOCHNOVIC, THE INVENTIVE STEP: ITS EVOLUTION IN CANADA, THE UNITED KINGDOM, AND THE UNITED STATES 72-75 (IIC Studies in Industrial Property and Copyright Law No. 5, 1982) (commercial success carries weight in British courts only when accompanied by evidence of failure of others to solve the problem).

For criticisms of the use of commercial success, and a plea for more reliance on the failure of others, see Merges, *Economic Perspectives on Innovation: Patent Standards and Commercial Success*, 76 CAL. L. REV. 803 (1988).

2. JAPAN

a. "Easily Made" Inventions Unpatentable

For the most part Japanese patent law follows the pattern of the U.S. and European systems. Obvious modifications — inventions which could be "easily made" by a worker of ordinary skill in the art — are unpatentable. *See* T. TANABE & H. WEGNER, JAPANESE PATENT LAW § 120 (1979). It is said by Tanabe and Wegner that Japanese obviousness doctrine shifts the attention away from the prior art, and inquires more starkly into the merits of the claimed invention standing alone. *Id.*

In one respect, Japanese law follows the European practice closely: patent applications filed before an inventor's application date are effective prior art as of the date of filing for novelty purposes only. *See* Japanese Patent Act § 29[bis], reprinted in TANABE & WEGNER, *supra*, § 130. Note that as in Europe and under § 102(e) of the U.S. Code, a prior-filed application must eventually be published to be effective prior art. TANABE & WEGNER, *supra*, at § 132. And, as under the 1984 amendments to § 103 of the U.S. Code, applications assigned to a single entity cannot be used as prior art under Article 29[bis]. TANABE & WEGNER, *supra*, at § 131.

b. *Koka*, or Meritorious Effect

One very distinctive feature of Japanese patent law bears a close resemblance to certain nonobviousness concepts in U.S. law: the *koka*, or meritorious effect.

A Japanese patent applicant must show that her invention has some meritorious effect not heretofore demonstrated in the prior art.

The *koka* requirement is closely tied to the Japanese rule that an inventor must identify the essence, or gist — in Japanese, the *yoshi* — of her invention. The gist is the structural difference or differences over the prior art; it is the "core idea" of the invention. The gist is important for purposes of the *koka* requirement because the *koka* must be defined in terms of the gist. That is, the gist of the invention must have some *koka*, or meritorious effect, compared to the prior art. If an invention demonstrates some meritorious effect but this effect does not grow out of the gist described by the inventor, the *koka* requirement has not been met and no patent will issue. TANABE & WEGNER, *supra*, at § 500.

The *koka* requirement as applied calls forth the same types of arguments made for nonobviousness in the U.S. Thus, old combinations and aggregations — *chikan* and *yoseatsume* — have no meritorious effect unless some new overall effect is shown for the combination. TANABE & WEGNER, *supra*, § 511.2, § 512. New uses for old products are apparently patentable. *See* TANABE & WEGNER, *supra*, § 513 (*"yoto-henko"*). In addition, "selection inventions" — the selection of a part of a prior art range — are patentable so long as the range selected shows remarkable and concrete advantages. TANABE & WEGNER, *supra*, at § 515; T. TANABE & H. WEGNER, JAPANESE PATENT PROCEDURE 137-38 (1986). *See generally* David J. Abraham, *Shinpo-sei: Japanese Inventive Step Meets U.S. Non-obviousness*, 77 J. PAT. & TRADEMARK OFF. SOC'Y 528, 538 (1995) ("There are also some differences between the Japanese and U.S. systems, particularly in the area of objective evidence of non-obviousness, i.e., *koka*, due to the great importance of them under the Japanese system.").

Practitioners note that is essential to tie the *koka* to the broadest claim in the patent or application. T. TANABE & H. WEGNER, JAPANESE PATENT PROCEDURE, at 103. In *The Wheel Rim Case*, showa 50 (Gyo-ke) 73, Tokyo High Court (Dec. 1980), the final rejection of an application was upheld on the basis of lack of *koka*. The applicant submitted a claim setting a range of values for one parameter for a formula for determining optimal wheel design in light of the problem of keeping a tire on the rim while the wheel is moving. But the applicant tested only one value of the formula, near the bottom of the claimed range, so the court held that the applicant had failed to tie his *koka* to the claims. While this case is more properly viewed as an enablement case (see Chapter 6), it demonstrates the importance of the *koka* requirement. The *koka*, then, must not only be present (and the invention thus nonobvious, when structure and *koka* are combined), but it must also be adequately described (and the claimed invention thus enabled by the specification).

DISCLOSURE AND ENABLEMENT

A. INTRODUCTION

The late eighteenth century saw a fundamental change in the conception of the inventor's contribution in exchange for a patent. Under the original patent systems, society's benefit was the introduction of a new art or technology into the country. By the late eighteenth century, the primary benefit was seen as the technological know-how behind the inventor's patent. The beneficiaries on this view were not just the public at large, but also (and more importantly) others skilled in the technical arts who could learn something from the patentee's invention. This was a major change in the economic role of patents, for it shifted the emphasis from the introduction of finished products into commerce to the introduction of new and useful *information* to the technical arts. This new emphasis on technical disclosure was manifested primarily in the increasingly stringent requirement that the applicant for a patent describe his invention clearly and completely, a development most often associated with the 1778 opinion of the well-respected Judge Mansfield in *Liardet v. Johnson. See* Adams & Averly, *The Patent Specification: The Role of Liardet v. Johnson,* 7 J. LEG. HIST. 156 (1986) (arguing in opposition to earlier writers that *Liardet* represented the culmination of eighteenth century trends rather than a sharp break with past practice).

This shift in emphasis addressed a complaint voiced by Lord Burghley over the original patent system — its dismal success rate in introducing new industries to the country. Perhaps paradoxically, the technical specification requirement, while recognizing that not every invention will lead to a new industry, may have more efficiently fostered the growth of industry as a whole, by ensuring that up-to-date technical information was disseminated rapidly after its creation. Certainly it can be argued that this "disclosure function" is one of the most important roles played by the patent system. *See, e.g.*, Trajtenberg, *A Penny for Your Quotes: Patent Citations and the Value of Innovations,* 21 RAND J. ECON. 172 (1990) (using patent citations as measure of invention's value); Scotchmer & Green, *Novelty and Disclosure in Patent Law,* 21 RAND J. ECON. 131 (1990) (modelling value of patent system partly on assumption that disclosure is useful to others working in the field).

The U.S. patent system recognized the importance of enabling disclosures from the beginning. As Donald Chisum writes:

> The statutory requirement of an enabling disclosure is truly ancient: it was stated in the first United States Patent Act in 1790. The 1790 Act even

stated a purpose of the requirement: "that the public may have the full benefit thereof, after the expiration of the patent term." The statement of purpose has since been dropped, but putting the invention in full possession of the public so the invention may be freely made and used after expiration of the patent is still a primary purpose of the requirement.

Chisum, *Comment: Anticipation, Obviousness, Enablement: An Eternal Golden Braid*, 15 AM. INTELL. PROP. L. ASS'N Q.J. 57 (1987). *See also* Woodward, *Definiteness and Particularity in Patent Claims*, 46 MICH. L. REV. 755 (1948).

The courts have applied this policy consistently. For example, in *O'Reilly v. Morse*, 56 U.S. (15 How.) 62 (1854), the Supreme Court considered a challenge to the scope of a claim in Samuel Morse's famous telegraphy patent. Morse claimed "the use of the motive power of the electric or galvanic current, which I call electro-magnetism, however developed for marking or printing intelligible characters ... at any distance[]." 56 U.S. at 112. In essence, Morse declared ownership of all methods of communicating at a distance using electromagnetic waves. But since he had not actually disclosed "all methods" in his specification, much less even imagined them, the Court ruled the claim invalid.

> [I]f the eighth claim of the patentee can be maintained, there was no necessity for any specification, further than to say that he had discovered that, by using the motive power of electro-magnetism, he could print intelligible characters at any distance.... [T]his claim can derive no aid from the specification filed. It is outside of [the specification], and the patentee claims beyond it.

56 U.S. at 119-20. In modern parlance, the patentee's disclosure was found to be nonenabling given the scope of his claims. (As we shall see, this claim might also be considered indefinite today, a wholly distinct defect; see Section C, below.) *See also McClain v. Ortmayer*, 141 U.S. 419, 424 (1891) ("The object of the patent law in requiring the patentee to 'particularly point out and distinctly claim the part, improvement or combination which he claims as his invention or discovery,' is not only to secure to him all to which he is entitled, but to apprise the public of what is still open to them.")

In light of the disclosure function, and of cases such as *Morse*, it might seem to make sense to limit the rights of a patentee to only those embodiments of the invention she has disclosed in her specification, i.e., those that she has actually created at the time the patent application is filed. But imitators would soon find some minor variation over the disclosed embodiments; with such an ultra-strict enablement principle, they would then have a nonenablement defense if the patentee tried to enforce the patent against their minor variation. Such a rule would soon render patents useless.

This was also recognized long ago in the United States. Consider for example a suit over a 1904 patent to King Gillette on the first disposable blade safety razor. *See* U.S. Patent 775,134, issued Nov. 15, 1904. One of the problems

Gillette faced was how to keep a very thin, detachable blade rigid during shaving. His solution, as described in his specification, was to " 'secure [the] blade to a holder ... [so that] it receives a degree of rigidity sufficient to make it practically operative.' " *See Gillette Safety Razor Co. v. Clark Blade & Razor Co.*, 187 F. 149, 156 (C.C.D.N.J. 1911), *aff'd*, 194 F. 421 (3d Cir. 1912). Claim two of the Gillette patent reads " '[I claim as] a new article of manufacture, a detachable razor-blade of such thinness and flexibility as to require external support to give rigidity to its cutting edge.' " *Id.* at 149.

Gillette's success drew imitators, including the Clark Blade and Razor Company. When Gillette sued for patent infringement, Clark claimed that Gillette's patent did not sufficiently describe all the possible embodiments of the blade and that, in particular, Clark's design fell outside the range of what Gillette's patent had described. The Third Circuit rejected this argument, quoting broad language from the Supreme Court:

> [C]laim 2 is not invalid ... for, if such were the law, patentability must have been denied to Elias Howe for "the grooved and eye-pointed needle" which constituted his seventh claim, and of which it was said [by the Supreme Court] in *Deering v. Winona*:
>
>> The invention of a needle with the eye near the point is the basis of all the sewing machines used, but the methods of operating such a needle are many; and, if Howe had been obliged to make his own method a part of every claim in which the needle was an element, his patent would have been practically worthless.

194 F. at 423 (citations omitted) (quoting *Deering v. Winona Harvester Works*, 155 U.S. 286, 302 (1894)).

The *Gillette* case illustrates that a patent's specification need not point out precisely how to make every device that would fall within its claims. Disclosure of an inventive concept or principle, whose precise contours are defined by the claims, is enough.

Contrasting *Morse* with *Gillette* frames the ever-present tension in the law of enablement: the desire to restrict the patentee's property right to that which she has actually invented, while at the same time guarding against too skimpy a right, which in fact would be no right at all given the ease of inventing around it.

ANATOMY OF § 112

Adequate disclosure is the heart of Patent Act § 112. This core concept finds its expression in four slightly different but closely related requirements in this section: (1) Enablement; (2) written description; (3) definiteness of claims; and (4) best mode. These elements of the disclosure requirement can be identified in the six paragraphs of § 112.

§ 112. Specification.

[¶ 1] The specification shall contain a written description of the invention, and of the manner and process of making and using it, in such full, clear, concise, and exact terms as to enable any person skilled in the art to which it pertains, or with which it is most nearly connected, to make and use the same, and shall set forth the best mode contemplated by the inventor of carrying out his invention.

[¶ 2] The specification shall conclude with one or more claims particularly pointing out and distinctly claiming the subject matter which the applicant regards as his invention.

[¶ 3] A claim may be written in independent or, if the nature of the case admits, in dependent or multiple dependent form.

[¶ 4] Subject to the following paragraph, a claim in dependent form shall contain a reference to a claim previously set forth and then specify a further limitation of the subject matter claimed. A claim in dependent form shall be construed to incorporate by reference all the limitations of the claim to which it refers.

[¶ 5] A claim in multiple dependent form shall contain a reference, in the alternative only, to more than one claim previously set forth and then specify a further limitation of the subject matter claimed. A multiple dependent claim shall not serve as a basis for any other multiple dependent claim. A multiple dependent claim shall be construed to incorporate by reference all the limitations of the particular claim in relation to which it is being considered.

[¶ 6] An element in a claim for a combination may be expressed as a means or step for performing a specified function without the recital of structure, material, or acts in support thereof, and such claim shall be construed to cover the corresponding structure, material, or acts described in the specification and equivalents thereof.

In the sections that follow, we consider each element of § 112 in some detail. But a brief orientation to the major requirements, found in ¶¶ 1 and 2, is in order.

Enablement. This requirement — set out in ¶ 1 — is the most important element of adequate disclosure under § 112. It requires the inventor to describe her invention clearly enough so that one skilled in her art can understand it well enough to make and use it. The description must be good enough to prevent the skilled artisan from having to undertake a great deal of experimentation to reproduce the claimed invention.

Written description. Although there is some confusion regarding the difference between this requirement and enablement, it is generally understood that in addition to enabling one skilled in the art to recreate the invention, the inventor must actually describe what she claims. This requirement comes into play when an inventor amends her application after the initial filing date; the focus is on whether the broadened claims find support in the disclosure of the original application. Like enablement, this element finds its expression in ¶ 1.

Claim definiteness. In addition to disclosing her invention, an inventor must, under ¶ 2, claim it in such a way that those who follow her can easily discern the boundaries of her legal right. She must demarcate clearly what she claims and what is left free to the public to use. Although the disclosure in the patent specification is often relied on to help interpret claim language, the definiteness requirement is essentially a matter of the clarity of claim language.

Best mode. Finally, an inventor must tell the public the best mode she knows for practicing the claimed invention. Of all the embodiments encompassed within the claims, she must state which one, if any, she believes is most effective. This subjective test, dependent on the inventor's knowledge and state of mind, is an important battleground in contemporary litigation.

B. ENABLEMENT

1. "UNDUE EXPERIMENTATION"

THE INCANDESCENT LAMP PATENT
159 U.S. 465 (1895)

This was a bill in equity, filed by the Consolidated Electric Light Company against the McKeesport Light Company, to recover damages for the infringement of letters patent No. 317,076, issued May 12, 1885, to the Electro-Dynamic Light Company, assignee of Sawyer and Man, for an electric light. The defendants justified [their actions] under certain patents to Thomas A. Edison, particularly No. 223,898, issued January 27, 1880; denied the novelty and utility of the complainants' patent, and averred that the same had been fraudulently and illegally procured. The real defendant was the Edison Electric Light Company, and the case involved a contest between what are known as the Sawyer and Man and the Edison systems of electric lighting.

In their application, Sawyer and Man stated that their invention related to "that class of electric lamps employing an incandescent conductor enclosed in a transparent, hermetically-sealed vessel or chamber, from which oxygen is excluded, and ... more especially to the incandescing conductor, its substance, its form, and its combination with the other elements composing the lamp. Its object is to secure a cheap and effective apparatus; and our improvement consists, first, of the combination, in a lamp chamber, composed wholly of glass, as described in patent No. 205,144, "upon which this patent was declared to be an improvement, "of an incandescing conductor of carbon made from a vegetable fibrous material, in contradistinction to a similar conductor made from mineral or gas carbon, and also in the form of such conductor so made from such vegetable carbon, and combined in the lighting circuit with the exhausted chamber of the lamp." [See Figure 6-1, next page.]

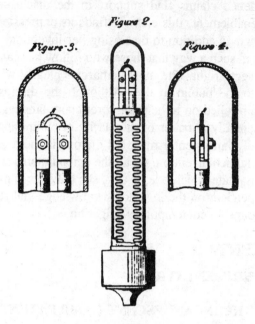

Sawyer and Man

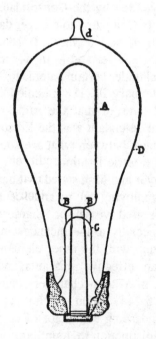

Edison

Figure 6-1

The specification further stated that:

> In the practice of our invention we have made use of carbonized paper, and
> also wood carbon. We have also used such conductors or burners of various
> shapes, such as pieces with their lower ends secured to their respective
> supports, and having their upper ends united so as to form an inverted V-
> shaped burner. We have also used conductors of varying contours — that is,
> with rectangular bends instead of curvilinear ones; but we prefer the arch
> shape.
>
> ... No especial description of making the illuminating carbon conductors,
> described in this specification and making the subject-matter of this im-
> provement, is thought necessary, as any of the ordinary methods of forming
> the material to be carbonized to the desired shape and size, and carbonizing
> it according to the methods in practice before the date of this improvement,
> may be adopted in the practice thereof by any one skilled in the arts apper-
> taining to the making of carbons for electric lighting or for other use in the
> arts.
>
> The advantages resulting from the manufacture of the carbon from
> vegetable fibrous or textile material instead of mineral or gas carbon are
> many. Among them may be mentioned the convenience afforded for cutting
> and making the conductor in the desired form and size, the purity and
> equality of the carbon obtained, its susceptibility to tempering, both as to
> hardness and resistance, and its toughness and durability.

The claims were as follows:

> 1. An incandescing conductor for an electric lamp, of carbonized fibrous
> or textile material and of an arch or horseshoe shape, substantially as
> hereinbefore set forth.
>
> 2. The combination, substantially as hereinbefore set forth, of an electric
> circuit and an incandescing conductor of carbonized fibrous material,
> included in and forming part of said circuit, and a transparent hermetically
> sealed chamber in which the conductor is enclosed.
>
> 3. The incandescing conductor for an electric lamp, formed of carbonized
> paper, substantially as described.

The commercial Edison lamp used by the appellee is composed of a burner, A
[see diagram], made of carbonized bamboo of a peculiar quality discovered by
Mr. Edison to be highly useful for the purpose, and having a length of about six
inches, a diameter of about five one thousandths of an inch, and an electrical
resistance of upwards of 100 ohms. This filament of carbon is bent into the form
of a loop, and its ends are secured by good electrical and mechanical connections
to two fine platinum wires B. These wires pass through a glass stem, C, the glass
being melted and fused upon the platinum wires. A glass globe, D, is fused to the
glass stem C. This glass globe has originally attached to it at the point d, [a] glass
tube, by means of which a connection is made with highly organized and refined

exhausting apparatus, which produces in the globe a high vacuum, whereupon the glass tube is melted off by a flame, and the globe is closed by the fusion of the glass at the point *d*.

Upon a hearing in the Circuit Court before Mr. Justice Bradley upon pleadings and proofs, the court held the patent to be invalid, and dismissed the bill. 40 Fed. Rep. 21. [C.C.W.D. Pa. (1889)]. Thereupon complainant appealed to this court.

MR. JUSTICE BROWN, after stating the case as above reported, delivered the opinion of the court.

In order to obtain a complete understanding of the scope of the Sawyer and Man patent, it is desirable to consider briefly the state of the art at the time the application was originally made, which was in January, 1880.

Two general forms of electric illumination had for many years been the subject of experiments more or less successful, one of which was known as the arc light, produced by the passage of a current of electricity between the points of two carbon pencils, placed end to end, and slightly separated from each other. In its passage from one point to the other through the air, the electric current took the form of an arc, and gave the name to the light. This form of light had been produced by Sir Humphry Davy as early as 1810, and by successive improvements in the carbon pencils and in their relative adjustment to each other, had come into general use as a means of lighting streets, halls, and other large spaces; but by reason of its intensity, the uncertain and flickering character of the light, and the rapid consumption of the carbon pencils, it was wholly unfitted for domestic use. The *second* form of illumination is what is known as the incandescent system, and consists generally in the passage of a current of electricity through a continuous strip or piece of refractory material, which is a conductor of electricity, but a poor conductor — in other words, a conductor offering a considerable resistance to the flow of the current through it. It was discovered early in this century that various substances might be heated to a white heat by passing a sufficiently strong current of electricity through them. The production of a light in this way does not in any manner depend upon the consumption or wearing away of the conductor, as it does in the arc light.

For many years prior to 1880, experiments had been made by a large number of persons, in various countries, with a view to the production of an incandescent light which could be made available for domestic purposes, and could compete with gas in the matter of expense. Owing partly to a failure to find a proper material, which should burn but not consume, partly to the difficulty of obtaining a perfect vacuum in the globe in which the light was suspended, and partly to a misapprehension of the true principle of incandescent lighting, these experiments had not been attended with success; although it had been demonstrated as early as 1845 that, whatever material was used, the conductor must be enclosed in an air-tight bulb [i.e., vacuum], to prevent it from being consumed by the oxygen in the atmosphere. The chief difficulty was that the carbon burners were subject to a rapid disintegration or evaporation, which electricians assumed was due to the disrupting action of the electric current, and, hence, the conclusion was reached that carbon contained in itself the elements of its own destruction, and was not a suitable material for the burner of an incandescent lamp.

It is admitted that the lamp described in the Sawyer and Man patent is no longer in use, and was never a commercial success; that it does not embody the principle of high resistance with a small illuminating surface; that it does not have the filament burner of the modern incandescent lamp; that the lamp chamber is defective, and that the lamp manufactured by the complainant and put upon the market is substantially the Edison lamp; but it is said that, in the conductor used by Edison, (a particular part of the stem of the bamboo lying directly beneath the silicious cuticle, the peculiar fitness for which purpose was undoubtedly discovered by him,) he made use of a fibrous or textile material, covered by the patent to Sawyer and Man, and is, therefore, an infringer. It was admitted, however, that the third claim — for a conductor of carbonized paper — was not infringed.

The two main defences to this patent are (1) that it is defective upon its face, in attempting to monopolize the use of all fibrous and textile materials for the purpose of electric illumination; and (2) that Sawyer and Man were not in fact the first to discover that these were better adapted than mineral carbons to such purposes.

Is the complainant entitled to a monopoly of all fibrous and textile materials for incandescent conductors? If the patentees had discovered in fibrous and textile substances a quality common to them all, or to them generally, as distinguishing them from other materials, such as minerals, etc., and such quality or characteristic adapted them peculiarly to incandescent conductors, such claim might not be too broad. If, for instance, minerals or porcelains had always been used for a particular purpose, and a person should take out a patent for a similar article of wood, and woods generally were adapted to that purpose, the claim might not be too broad, though defendant used wood of a different kind from that of the patentee. But if woods generally were not adapted to the purpose, and yet the patentee had discovered a wood possessing certain qualities, which gave it a peculiar fitness for such purpose, it would not constitute an infringement for another to discover and use a different kind of wood, which was found to contain similar or superior qualities. The present case is an apt illustration of this principle. Sawyer and Man supposed they had discovered in carbonized paper the best material for an incandescent conductor. Instead of confining themselves to carbonized paper, as they might properly have done, and in fact did in their third claim, they made a broad claim for every fibrous or textile material, when in fact an examination of over six thousand vegetable growths showed that none of them possessed the peculiar qualities that fitted them for that purpose. Was everybody then precluded by this broad claim from making further investigation? We think not.

The injustice of so holding is manifest in view of the experiments made, and continued for several months, by Mr. Edison and his assistants, among the different species of vegetable growth, for the purpose of ascertaining the one best adapted to an incandescent conductor. Of these he found suitable for his purpose [there were] only about three species of bamboo, one species of cane from the Valley of the Amazon, impossible to be procured in quantities on account of the climate, and one or two species of fibres from the agave family. Of the special bamboo, the walls of which have a thickness of about three-eighths of an inch, he used only about twenty-thousandths of an inch in thickness. In this portion of the bamboo the fibres are more nearly parallel, the cell walls are apparently smallest, and the pithy matter between the fibres is at its minimum. It seems that carbon filaments cannot be made of wood — that is, exogenous vegetable growth — because the fibres are not parallel and the longitudinal fibres are intercepted by radial fibres. The cells composing the fibres are all so large that the resulting carbon is very porous and friable. Lamps made of this material proved of no commercial value. After trying as many as thirty or forty different woods of exogenous growth, he gave them up as hopeless. But finally, while experimenting with a bamboo strip which formed the edge of a palmleaf fan, cut into filaments, he obtained surprising results. After microscopic examination of the material, he despatched a man to Japan to make arrangements for securing the bamboo in quantities. It seems that the characteristic of the bamboo which makes it particularly suitable is that the fibres run more nearly parallel than in other species of wood. Owing to this, it can be cut up into filaments having parallel fibres, running throughout their length, and producing a homogeneous carbon. There is no generic quality, however, in vegetable fibres, because they are fibrous, which adapts them to the purpose. Indeed, the fibres are rather a disadvantage. If the bamboo grew solid without fibres, but had its peculiar cellular formation, it would be a perfect material, and incandescent lamps would last at least six times as long as at present. All vegetable fibrous growths do not have a suitable cellular structure. In some the cells are so large that they are valueless for that purpose. No exogenous, and very few endogenous, growths are suitable. The messenger whom he despatched to different parts of Japan and China sent him about forty different kinds of bamboo, in such quantities as to enable him to make a number of lamps, and from a test of these different species he ascertained which was best for the purpose. From this it appears very clearly that there is no such quality common to fibrous and textile substances generally as makes them suitable for an incandescent conductor, and that the bamboo which was finally pitched upon, and is now generally used, was not selected because it was of vegetable growth, but because it contained certain peculiarities in its fibrous structure which distinguished it from every other fibrous substance. The question really is whether the imperfectly successful experiments of Sawyer and Man, with carbonized paper and wood carbon, conceding all that is claimed for them, authorize them to put under tribute the results of the brilliant discoveries made by others.

It is required by Rev. Stat. § 4888 that the application shall contain a written description of the device "and of the manner and process of making, constructing, compounding, and using it in such full, clear, concise, and exact terms as to enable any person, skilled in the art or science to which it appertains or with which it is most nearly connected, to make, construct, compound, and use the same." The object of this is to apprise the public of what the patentee claims as his own, the courts of what they are called upon to construe, and competing manufacturers and dealers of exactly what they are bound to avoid. *Grant v. Raymond*, 6 Pet. [31 U.S.] 218, 247 [1832]. If the description be so vague and uncertain that no one can tell, except by independent experiments, how to construct the patented device, the patent is void.

It was said by Mr. Chief Justice Taney in *Wood v. Underhill*, 5 How. [46 U.S.] 1, 5 [1857], with respect to a patented compound for the purpose of making brick or tile, which did not give the relative proportions of the different ingredients:

> But when the specification of a new composition of matter gives only the names of the substances which are to be mixed together, without stating any relative proportion, undoubtedly it would be the duty of the court to declare the patent void. And the same rule would prevail where it was apparent that the proportions were stated ambiguously and vaguely. For in such cases it would be evident, on the face of the specification, that no one could use the invention without first ascertaining, by experiment, the exact proportion of the different ingredients required to produce the result intended to be obtained .... And if, from the nature and character of the ingredients to be used, they are not susceptible of such exact description, the inventor is not entitled to a patent.

So in *Tyler v. Boston*, 7 Wall. [74 U.S.] 327, 330 [1868], wherein the plaintiff professed to have discovered a combination of fuel oil with the mineral and earthy oils, constituting a burning fluid, the patentee stated that the exact quantity of fuel oil, which is necessary to produce the most desirable compound, must be determined by experiment. And the court observed: "Where a patent is claimed for such a discovery it should state the component parts of the new manufacture claimed with clearness and precision, and not leave a person attempting to use the discovery to find it out 'by experiment.'" See also *Bene v. Jeantet*, 129 U.S. 683 [(1889)]; *Howard v. Detroit Stove Works*, 150 U.S. 164, 167 [(1893)]; *Schneider v. Lovell*, 10 Fed. Rep. 666 [C.C.S.D.N.Y. 1882]; *Welling v. Crane*, 14 Fed. Rep. 571 [C.C.D.N.J. 1882].

If Sawyer and Man had discovered that a certain carbonized paper would answer the purpose, their claim to all carbonized paper would, perhaps, not be extravagant; but the fact that paper happens to belong to the fibrous kingdom did not invest them with sovereignty over this entire kingdom, and thereby practically limit other experimenters to the domain of minerals.

In fact, such a construction of this patent as would exclude competitors from making use of any fibrous or textile material would probably defeat itself, since, if the patent were infringed by the use of any such material, it would be anticipated by proof of the prior use of any such material. In this connection it would appear, not only that wood charcoal had been constantly used since the days of Sir Humphry Davy for arc lighting, but that in the English patent to Greener and Staite of 1846, for an incandescent light, "charcoal, reduced to a state of powder," was one of the materials employed. So also, in the English patent of 1841 to De Moleyns, "a finely pulverized boxwood charcoal or plumbago" was used for an incandescent electric lamp. Indeed, in the experiments of Sir Humphry Davy, early in the century, pieces of well-burned charcoal were heated to a vivid whiteness by the electric current, and other experiments were made which evidently contemplated the use of charcoal heated to the point of incandescence. Mr. Broadnax, the attorney who prepared the application, it seems, was also of opinion that a broad claim for vegetable carbons could not be sustained because charcoal had been used before in incandescent lighting.

We are all agreed that the claims of this patent, with the exception of the third, are too indefinite to be the subject of a valid monopoly. For the reasons above stated the decree of the Circuit Court is

Affirmed.

NOTES

1. *Modern Equivalent.* The modern equivalent to old Rev. Stat. § 4888 is 35 U.S.C. § 112 (1986). The first paragraph of § 112 has been interpreted in such a way that three distinct requirements are now said to spring from it: (1) the written description requirement; (2) the clear claim requirement; and (3) the enablement requirement. *See* Section A, *Introduction*. Which of these requirements was at issue in *Incandescent Lamp*? More than one?

2. *The Key Concept: A Common Principle.* The Court states the fundamental premise of enablement doctrine in one passage, which is worth repeating because of its clarity:

> If, as before observed, there were some general quality, running through the whole fibrous and textile kingdom, which distinguished it from every other, and gave it a peculiar fitness for the particular purpose, the man who discovered such quality might justly be entitled to a patent; but that is not the case here. An examination of materials of this class carried on for months revealed nothing that seemed to be adapted to the purpose; .... Under these circumstances, to hold that one, who had discovered that a certain fibrous or textile material answered the required purpose, should obtain the right to exclude everybody from the whole domain of fibrous and textile materials, and thereby shut out any further efforts to discover a better specimen of that class than the patentee had employed, would be an unwarranted extension of his monopoly, and operate rather to discourage than to promote invention.

The key is the Court's focus on the discovery of a "general quality" that unites all the embodiments encompassed in the claim. This is perhaps best thought of as the "principle" of the invention. The Court suggests that *if such a quality or principle had been identified, and if* the inventors had spelled this out in their specification, then the claim to "all fibrous and textile material" would have been enabled. This is bedrock enablement doctrine. Note the close relationship between the claims and the specification in this doctrine. If the specification teaches enough to prove that there is a common quality running through the embodiments claimed, then those claims will be deemed enabled. But if, as here, the specification does not reveal a common quality present in the embodiments claimed, and does not even teach how to sift through those embodiments intelligently — i.e., without "undue experimentation" — the claims will be said to lack support in the specification, and will fall. The case of *Welling v. Crane*, 14 F. 571 (C.C.D.N.J. 1882), cited in the Court's opinion above, relies on this rationale; the court states: "If [the claim] fairly includes in the material to be used all animal or vegetable fibers, the patent must be declared void for claiming too much." 14 F. at 573.

3. *Rationale for Enablement*. The Court puts forth several rationales for the enablement requirement. For example, the Court asks: "Was everybody then precluded by this broad claim from making further investigation? We think not." What assumptions lie behind the statement? Why should the patent system be concerned with "further investigation"?

4. *Thomas Edison*. Edison's discovery that only a certain type of bamboo plant would work as a filament is an example of his exhaustive research efforts. Of course, the bamboo itself is not patentable, since it is a product of nature. (See Chapter 2 for a discussion of the anomalous nature of this doctrine as applied in cases such as this.) After isolating the precise type of bamboo that would work, Edison acted with characteristic speed on a characteristically grand scale: he tried to lock up as many acres of production of the bamboo as he could. *See* A. MILLARD, EDISON AND THE BUSINESS OF INNOVATION (1990). This is an example not only of backward (vertical) integration, but also of an attempt to protect the discovery of the bamboo indirectly; the large scale of the operation, together with the secrecy that surrounded it, was intended to dissuade others from trying to recreate the discovery of this one type of bamboo. *See generally* Teece, *Profiting from Technological Innovation: Implications for Integration, Collaboration, and Public Policy*, 15 RES. POL'Y 285 (1986) (describing the use of "co-specific assets" to appropriate the value of intellectual property). Thus Edison crafted a strategy to work around the fact that the bamboo itself could not be protected directly by an intellectual property right. *See also* Hirshleifer, *The Private and Social Value of Information and the Reward to Inventive Activity*, 61 AM. ECON. REV. 561 (1971) (positing reduced need for intellectual property protection, since inventors have "inside information" about their inventions, so they can reap gains by investing in assets that their inventions will make more valuable and selling short assets that their inventions will make less valuable).

5. *Invalidity Versus Non-Infringement*. The claims at issue would have been upheld, the Court suggested, if they had claimed only what Sawyer and Man had actually invented (carbonized paper incandescence); they were invalid, however, since it would take a good deal of additional experimentation to determine whether incandescing conductors could be made out of the many materials claimed. Did the Court invalidate the entire patent? Why did the Court not choose to "judicially narrow" the scope of the claims? After all, Sawyer and Man had apparently invented *something*. See below, Section B.3.a.

6. Background. For more on the early history of the lighting industry, see W. BRIGHT, THE ELECTRIC-LAMP INDUSTRY (1949), and W. MACLAREN, THE RISE OF THE ELECTRICAL INDUSTRY DURING THE NINETEENTH CENTURY (1943); A. MILLARD, *supra*.

7. Anticipation/Infringement. In the portion of the opinion dealing with the prior art work of Sir Humphry Davy and Greener and Staite, the Court implicitly invokes a maxim we saw in Chapter 4, and will see again in Chapter 8: That which anticipates, if earlier, infringes, if later. The point is made in this case in connection with the lack of enablement defense, but as we shall see it is often discussed when infringement is the central issue in a case.

In re FISHER

427 F.2d 833, 166 U.S.P.Q. (BNA) 18 (C.C.P.A. 1970)

This appeal is from the decision of the Patent Office Board of Appeals, which affirmed the rejection of claims 4 and 5, the only claims remaining in appellant's application serial No. 72,481, filed November 29, 1960, for Adrenal Gland Stimulating Concentrate and Method for the Preparation Thereof. [The application in issue was a C-I-P of a parent.]

The Disclosure

The instant specification relates to the preparation of substances containing adrenocorticotrophic hormones (ACTH) in a composition suitable for injection into human beings in the treatment of certain forms of arthritis and other human pathological conditions. It is stated that previous ACTH products were unsatisfactory for administration to humans because of their low potency, generally around 50% of "International Standard," [a potency measure determined by seeing how much hormone is produced when a given amount of the compound being investigated is administered] and because of their relatively high content of undesirable factors, notably posterior pituitary hormones which consist mainly of oxytocic and vasopressor [compounds]. A method is disclosed for producing ACTH preparations having potencies ranging from 111% to 230% of standard and containing no more than 0.08 units of vasopressin and no more than 0.05 units of oxytocin per International Unit of ACTH, which limits are said to be tolerable to humans. The method generally starts with frozen pituitary glands of hogs, sheep, beef [sic] or other animals, including whales. These glands are quick-thawed in an organic solvent to extract contaminated ACTH from the gland meat. A precipitate containing the active material is recovered, free of contaminants, by treatment with fractionating salts. The material is then subjected to hydrolysis, and an inactive fraction of hydrolized fragmented material is separated from a fraction containing the active substance. The active fraction is then adjusted to a pH above 2.8, the excess salts being separated from the concentrate of the active principle. Several variations of this procedure are set forth and six specific examples are given. The specification then states that the ACTH concentrate produced as described is found to contain peptides having free amino and carboxyl groups, and is further characterized

> by its solubility in glacial acetic acid and phenol; by its relative insolubility in other organic solvents; by its greater stability under acid conditions than under alkali conditions; by its susceptibility to attack by proteolytic enzymes and peptidases; and by its positive reaction to the Millon and xanthoproteic tests for tyrosine, the biuret test for peptide linkage, the ninhydrin test for free amino groups in the alpha position, the Sakaguchi test for guanidine groups, and the Hopkins-Gole and benzaldehyde tests for indole nuclei and tryptophane.

The specification then states that the product can be characterized structurally as a peptide containing a chain of identifiable amino acids.

The Claims

Appellant defines the subject matter sought to be patented as follows:

4. An adrenocorticotrophic [ACTH] hormone preparation containing at least 1 International Unit of ACTH per milligram and containing no more than 0.08 units of vasopressin and no more than 0.05 units of oxytocin per International Unit of ACTH, and being further characterized as containing as the active component of [a] polypeptide of at least 24 amino acids having the following sequence from the N terminus of the molecule; Serine, Tyrosine, Serine, Methionine, Glutamic Acid, Histadine, Phenylalanine, Arginine, Tryptophan, Glycine, Lysine, Proline, Valine, Glycine, Lysine, Lysine, Arginine, Arginine, Proline, Valine, Lysine, Valine, Tyrosine, Proline.

5. An adrenocorticotrophic hormone preparation containing at least 1 International Unit of ACTH per milligram and containing no more than 0.08 units of vasopressin and no more than 0.05 units of oxytocin per International Unit of ACTH, and being further characterized by its solubility in glacial acetic acid and phenol; by its relative insolubility in other organic solvents; by its greater stability under acid conditions than under alkali conditions; by its susceptibility to attack by proteolitic enzymes and peptidases; and by its positive reaction to the Millon and xanthoproteic tests for tyrosine, the biuret test for peptide linkages, and the ninhydrin test for free amino groups in the alpha position, the Sakaguchi test for guanidine groups,

and the Hopkins-Gole and benzaldehype tests for indole nuclei and trypto-phane.

Opinion

The rejection for insufficient disclosure

The examiner did not reject the claims for insufficient disclosure. This was first applied by the board.

The board stated: "[We] consider appellant's claims to be so broad that ... the specification lacks sufficient supporting description to comply with the requirements of 35 U.S.C. § 112, first paragraph." The board noted that the claims cover:

> substantially all "preparations" produced synthetically or by breakdown of the 39 amino acid polypeptides in any manner to form a polypeptide product of lesser molecular weight containing any number (claim 5) or at least 24 (claim 4) of the amino acids as long as the product exhibits, without the stated side effects, activity equal to at least 1 International Unit of ACTH per milligram.

We have already discussed [in an earlier part of the opinion not excerpted here], with respect to the parent application, the lack of teaching of how to obtain other-than-39 amino acid ACTHs. That discussion is fully applicable to the instant application, and we think the board was correct in finding insufficient disclosure due to this broad aspect of the claims.

The second aspect of breadth mentioned by the board in the quoted portion of its opinion has not yet been discussed. This is the problem arising from the potency recitation "at least 1 International Unit of ACTH per milligram." This is a so-called "open-ended" recitation. It has a lower limit but no upper limit. As previously mentioned, the specification discloses products having potencies from 111% to 230% of standard, which we understand to mean from 1.11 to 2.30 International Units of ACTH activity per milligram. The issue thus presented is whether an inventor who is the first to achieve a potency of greater than 1.0 for certain types of compositions, which potency was long desired because of its beneficial effect on humans, should be allowed to dominate *all* such compositions having potencies greater than 1.0, including future compositions having potencies far in excess of those obtainable from his teachings plus ordinary skill.

It is apparent that such an inventor should be allowed to dominate the future patentable inventions of others where those inventions were based in some way on his teachings. Such improvements, while unobvious from his teachings, are still within his contribution, since the improvement was made possible by his work. It is equally apparent, however, that he must not be permitted to achieve this dominance by claims which are insufficiently supported and hence not in compliance with the first paragraph of 35 U.S.C. § 112. That paragraph requires that the scope of the claims must bear a reasonable correlation to the scope of enablement provided by the specification to persons of ordinary skill in the art. In cases involving predictable factors, such as mechanical or electrical elements, a single embodiment provides broad enablement in the sense that, once imagined, other embodiments can be made without difficulty and their performance characteristics predicted by resort to known scientific laws. In cases involving unpredictable factors, such as most chemical reactions and physiological activity, the scope of enablement obviously varies inversely with the degree of unpredictability of the factors involved. In the present case we must conclude, on the record before us, that appellant has not enabled the preparation of ACTHs having potencies much greater than 2.3, and the claim recitations of potency of "at least 1" render the claims insufficiently supported under the first paragraph of 35 U.S.C. § 112.

Our conclusion is in no way opposed to the principles of the cases cited by appellant in support of his contention that he is entitled to coverage of the breadth now sought. *Farbenfabriken of Elberfeld Co. v. Kuehmsted* ("the aspirin case"), 171 Fed. 887 (N.D. Ill. 1909), *aff'd*, 179 Fed. 701 (7th Cir. 1910), *In re Williams*, 36 C.C.P.A. 756, 171 F.2d 319, 80 U.S.P.Q. 150 (1948), and *Parke, Davis & Co. v. Mulford & Co.*, 196 Fed. 496 (2d Cir. 1912), each involved claims to substantially pure compositions. Such claims do not present the same breadth problem as here, because in those cases the possible range of further purification was either small or nonexistent. Such claims have an inherent upper limit of 100% purity, whereas in the present case it would appear theoretically possible to achieve potencies far greater than those obtained by appellant. *Merck & Co. v. Olin Mathieson Chemical Corp.*, 253 F.2d 156, 116 U.S.P.Q. 484 (4th Cir. 1958), involved a claim reciting an activity of "at least 440 L.L.D. units per milligram," but no issue appears to have been raised regarding that recitation and the court's opinion does not consider it.

For the reasons given above, the decision of the board is affirmed.

NOTES

1. *Current Status of Fisher*. It is sometimes said that the doctrine enunciated in *Fisher*, often termed "undue breadth," is not a proper ground for invalidating a patent; only lack of enablement will do. *See, e.g., In re Hyatt*, 708 F.2d 712, 714, 218 U.S.P.Q. (BNA) 195 (Fed. Cir. 1983) (criticizing "undue breadth" rejections, and stating that such rejections are "more accurately, based on the first paragraph of § 112 [i.e., enablement]."). In any event, *Fisher* continues to be cited in enablement cases for the general proposition that the scope of enablement must be at least roughly commensurate with the scope of claims. *See, e.g., Scripps Clinic & Research Found. v. Genentech, Inc.*, 927 F.2d 1565, 1572, 18 U.S.P.Q.2d 1001, 18 U.S.P.Q.2d 1896 (Fed. Cir. 1991) (distinguishing facts in *Fisher* from facts at issue).

2. *More on the Rationale for Enablement.* The Court in the *Incandescent Lamp* case stated: "Was everybody then precluded by this broad claim from making further investigation? We think not." How do you square this statement with the following, from the preceding case:

> It is apparent that ... an inventor should be allowed to dominate the future patentable inventions of others where those inventions were based in some way on his teachings. Such improvements, *while unobvious from his teachings*, are still within his contribution, since the improvement was made possible by his work.

Can one reconcile the desire to encourage further research, enunciated in *Incandescent Lamp* case, with the policy of permitting broad claims even over nonobvious extensions of a basic inventive principle as stated in this passage? Is the issuance of "blocking patents" an attempt to accommodate these competing interests? See Section B.3.a below, comments on "blocking patents."

Amgen, Inc. v. Chugai Pharmaceutical Co., 927 F.2d 1200, 18 U.S.P.Q.2d 1016 (Fed. Cir. 1991) (Lourie, J.). [Plaintiff and defendant each held patents on technology related to the production of erythropoetin (EPO), a critical biological protein that stimulates production of red blood cells and is therefore effective in combatting anemia and related conditions. Plaintiff Amgen held a patent on a recombinant DNA version of EPO, while defendant Chugai held a license from codefendant Genetics Institute under a product patent for purified EPO made by concentrating the protein from natural sources. The trial court had held valid certain claims in defendant's patent, and ruled that plaintiff infringed; it also held certain claims in both patents were invalid for failure to enable. Plaintiff's recombinant EPO patent included the key claim 7, which reads: "7. A purified and isolated DNA sequence consisting essentially of a DNA sequence encoding a polypeptide having an amino acid sequence sufficiently duplicative of that of erythropoietin to allow possession of the biological property of causing bone marrow cells to increase production of reticulocytes and red blood cells, and to increase hemoglobin synthesis or iron uptake." The "biological property" language, together with the descriptions of the two key functions — blood cell production and iron uptake — was intended to broaden the claim so as to cover any functional substitute or "analog" for the natural EPO protein. The following excerpt comes from the discussion of the validity of claim 7 and related claims.]

> ... The essential question here is whether the scope of enablement of claim 7 is as broad as the scope of the claim. *See generally In re Fisher* ....
> The specification of [Amgen's] patent provides that:

>> [O]ne may readily design and manufacture genes coding for microbial expression of polypeptides having primary conformations which differ from that herein specified for mature EPO in terms of the identity or

location of one or more residues (e.g., substitutions, terminal and intermediate additions and deletions).
    ....

   DNA sequences provided by the present invention are thus seen to
comprehend all DNA sequences suitable for use in securing expression in
a procaryotic or eucaryotic host cell of a polypeptide product having at
least a part of the primary structural conformation and one or more of the
biological properties of erythropoietin ....

The district court found that over 3,600 different EPO analogs can be
made by substituting at only a single amino acid position, and over a million
different analogs can be made by substituting three amino acids. The patent
indicates that it embraces means for preparation of "numerous" polypeptide
analogs of EPO. Thus, the number of claimed DNA encoding sequences that
can produce an EPO-like product is potentially enormous.

In a deposition, Dr. Elliott, who was head of Amgen's EPO analog program, testified that he did not know whether the fifty to eighty EPO analogs
Amgen had made "had the biological property of causing bone marrow cells
to increase production of reticulocytes and red blood cells, and to increase
hemoglobin synthesis or iron uptake." Based on this evidence, the trial court
[found a lack of enablement]. In making this determination, the court relied
in particular on the lack of predictability in the art .... After five years of
experimentation, the court noted, "Amgen is still unable to specify which
analogs have the biological properties set forth in claim 7."

   ... [Although] it is not necessary that a patent applicant test all the
embodiments of his invention, *In re Angstadt*, 537 F.2d 498, 502, 190
U.S.P.Q. 214, 218 (C.C.P.A. 1976)[,] what is necessary is that he provide
a disclosure sufficient to enable one skilled in the art to carry out the
invention commensurate with the scope of his claims. For DNA sequences,
that means disclosing how to make and use enough sequences to justify grant
of the claims sought. Amgen has not done that here. It is well established
that a patent applicant is entitled to claim his invention generically, when he
describes it sufficiently to meet the requirements of Section 112. See *Utter
v. Hiraga*, 845 F.2d 993, 998, 6 U.S.P.Q.2d 1709, 1714 (Fed. Cir. 1988)
("A specification may, within the meaning of 35 U.S.C. § 112 ¶ 1, contain
a written description of a broadly claimed invention without describing all
species that claim encompasses.") Here, however, despite extensive statements in the specification concerning all the analogs of the EPO gene that
can be made, there is little enabling disclosure of particular analogs and how
to make them. Details for preparing only a few EPO analog genes are
disclosed. Amgen argues that this is sufficient to support its claims; we
disagree. This "disclosure" might well justify a generic claim encompassing
these and similar analogs, but it represents inadequate support for Amgen's
desire to claim all EPO gene analogs. There may be many other genetic

sequences that code for EPO-type products. Amgen has told how to make and use only a few of them and is therefore not entitled to claim all of them.

In affirming the district court's [invalidation of these] claims, we do not intend to imply that generic claims to genetic sequences cannot be valid where they are of a scope appropriate to the invention disclosed by an applicant. That is not the case here, where Amgen has claimed every possible analog of a gene containing about 4,000 nucleotides, with a disclosure only of how to make EPO and a very few analogs.

Considering the structural complexity of the EPO gene, the manifold possibilities for change in its structure, with attendant uncertainty as to what utility will be possessed by these analogs, we consider that more is needed concerning identifying the various analogs that are within the scope of the claim, methods for making them, and structural requirements for producing compounds with EPO-like activity. It is not sufficient, having made the gene and a handful of analogs whose activity has not been clearly ascertained, to claim all possible genetic sequences that have EPO-like activity. Under the circumstances, we find no error in the court's conclusion that the generic DNA sequence claims are invalid under Section 112.

From *In re Goodman*, 11 F.3d 1046, 29 U.S.P.Q.2d 2010 (Fed. Cir. 1993) (Rader, J.):

[Robert M. Goodman and coinventors appealed the rejection of claims 1-13 of application No. 07/507,380 (the '380 application) on grounds of lack of enablement. The claims were directed to a method of manufacturing mammalian peptides in plant cells by integrating a DNA construct encoding a peptide into plant cells. The DNA construct includes regulatory regions functional in the plant. The regulatory regions instruct the plant cell to transcribe the region of the DNA coding for the mammalian peptide. The method calls for harvesting the valuable peptide after translation of the transcribed messenger RNA.]

The specifications of the '282 patent [which issued from a parent of which the '380 application was a divisional] and the '380 application describe the claimed method in general terms, but provide only a single working example. The example describes the formation of an expression cassette with regulatory regions functional in tobacco plants and a structural gene coding for gamma-interferon. In the example the expression cassette is joined to a selectable marker to simplify isolation of plant cells that successfully integrate the construct. The selectable marker consists of regulatory regions functional in tobacco plants and a DNA sequence coding for a tetracycline resistance gene.

Claims 1-6 on appeal, however, purport to cover any desired mammalian peptide produced in any plant cell. Dependent claims 2-6 add [certain] limitations but in no way limit the type of mammalian peptide produced or the type of plant cell used.

Independent claim 1 provides:

1. A method for producing a mammalian peptide which comprises:

growing plant cells containing an integrated sequence comprising,

a first expression cassette having in the direction of transcription (1) a transcriptional and translational initiation region functional in said plant cells, (2) a structural gene coding for said mammalian peptide, and (3) a termination region,

whereby said structural gene is expressed to produce said mammalian peptide; and isolating said mammalian peptide substantially free of plant cell components.

The Board affirmed the Examiner's rejection of [the] claims under 35 U.S.C. Section 112, first paragraph. According to the Board, the specification did not enable one of ordinary skill in the art to produce any mammalian peptide with the claimed method on July 29, 1985, the effective filing date of the application. Regarding enablement, the Board stated:

[E]ven if one were to read into the claim recitation a limitation that the regulatory region was native either to the plant cell in question or the mammalian cell in question, the present specification would still lack adequate guidance to enable one of ordinary skill to extend [Goodman's] invention beyond the single working example.

According to the Board, Goodman's specification did not disclose the "plant functional" regulatory regions for plants beyond the single example. Thus, one of skill in the art could not replicate the invention in "all plants." Furthermore, the Board found that the specification taught only the Agrobacterium-mediated transformation method of plant transformation. This method works only with dicotyledonous plant cells, not all "plant cells."

Goodman's specification contains a single example of producing gamma-interferon in the dicotyledonous species, tobacco. This single example, however, does not enable a biotechnician of ordinary skill to produce any type of mammalian protein in any type of plant cell. The specification does not contain sufficient information to enable the broad scope of the claims. For instance, production of peptides in monocotyledonous plants involves extensive problems unaddressed by Goodman's specification.

In an effort to show that his recombinant methods achieved comparable results in monocots as well as the higher-ordered dicot plants, Goodman cites an article .... However, the article found limited success transforming asparagus cells using A. tumefaciens as a gene delivery system. The article expressly invited further "investigation" to determine whether the method works with monocots in general. [The court then reviews related articles.] Goodman's own 1987 article, *Gene Transfer in Crop Improvement*, 236 Science 48 (1987), underscores the "major block" to using the claimed method with monocot plant cells. Goodman reports:

> Although data have been cited that Agrobacterium can transfer T-DNA to monocotyledonous hosts, clear evidence of T-DNA integration exists only for asparagus, and, even in that case, no transformed plants have been described.

Id. at 52 (citation omitted).

Thus, even the references cited by Goodman to show enablement support the Board's position that great uncertainties encumbered Agrobacterium-mediated transformation in monocot plants at the time of filing. Goodman's 1987 article shows that the claimed invention did not overcome those uncertainties. Claims 6, 8, and 9 recite the Agrobacterium method of transformation. The record clearly supports the Board's determination that these claims are not enabled for the breadth of all varieties of plants.

In sum, this court discerns no error in the Board's conclusion of non-enablement. Goodman's specification does not enable one skilled in biotechnology in 1985 to practice the method for all "plant cells" as application claims 1-9 require. The record, especially Goodman's own article, shows the need for extensive experimentation to practice the claimed method for just a few plants, let alone all plant cells as broadly claimed in the application.

In re WANDS

858 F.2d 731, 8 U.S.P.Q.2d 1400 (Fed. Cir. 1988)

This appeal is from the decision of the Patent and Trademark Office (PTO) Board of Patent Appeals and Interferences (board) affirming the rejection of all remaining claims in appellant's application for a patent, entitled "Immunoassay Utilizing Monoclonal High Affinity IgM Antibodies." The rejection under 35 U.S.C. § 112, first paragraph, is based on the grounds that appellant's written specification would not enable a person skilled in the art to make the monoclonal antibodies that are needed to practice the claimed invention without undue experimentation. We reverse.

Background

The claimed invention involves immunoassay methods for the detection of hepatitis B surface antigen by using high-affinity monoclonal antibodies of the IgM isotype. Antibodies are a class of proteins (immunoglobulins) that help defend the body against invaders such as viruses and bacteria. An antibody has the potential to bind tightly to another molecule, which molecule is called an antigen. The body has the ability to make millions of different antibodies that bind to different antigens. However, it is only after exposure to an antigen that a complicated immune response leads to the production of antibodies against that antigen. For example, on the surface of hepatitis B virus particles there is a large protein called hepatitis B surface antigen (HBsAg). As its name implies, it is capable of serving as an antigen. During a hepatitis B infection (or when purified HBsAg is injected experimentally), the body begins to make antibodies that bind tightly and specifically to HBsAg. Such antibodies can be used as regents for sensitive diagnostic tests (e.g., to detect hepatitis B virus in blood and other tissues, a purpose of the claimed invention). A method for detecting or measuring antigens by using antibodies as reagents is called an immunoassay.

Normally, many different antibodies are produced against each antigen. One reason for this diversity is that different antibodies are produced that bind to different regions (determinants) of a large antigen molecule such as HBsAg. In addition, different antibodies may be produced that bind to the same determinant. These usually differ in the tightness with which they bind to the determinant. Affinity is a quantitative measure of the strength of antibody-antigen binding. Usually an antibody with a higher affinity for an antigen will be more useful for immunological diagnostic tests than one with a lower affinity. Another source of heterogeneity is that there are several immunoglobulin classes or isotypes. Immunoglobulin G (IgG) is the most common isotype in serum. Another isotype, immunoglobulin M (IgM), is prominent early in the immune response. IgM molecules are larger than IgG molecules, and have 10 antigen-binding sites instead of the 2 that are present in IgG. Most immunoassay methods use IgG, but the claimed invention uses only IgM antibodies.

For commercial applications there are many disadvantages to using antibodies from serum. Serum contains a complex mixture of antibodies against the antigen of interest within a much larger pool of antibodies directed at other antigens. These are available only in a limited supply that ends when the donor dies. The goal of monoclonal antibody technology is to produce an unlimited supply of a single purified antibody. [For a description of monoclonal antibody technology, see *Hybritech v. Monoclonal Antibodies, Inc.* in Chapter 5.]

The Claimed Invention

The claimed invention involves methods for the immunoassay of HBsAg by using high-affinity monoclonal IgM antibodies. Jack R. Wands and Vincent R. Zurawski, Jr., two of the three coinventors of the present application, disclosed methods for producing monoclonal antibodies against HBsAg in United States patent No. 4,271,145 (the '145 patent), entitled "Process for Producing Antibodies to Hepatitis Virus and Cell Lines Therefor," which patent issued on June 2, 1981. The '145 patent is incorporated by reference into the application on appeal. The specification of the '145 patent teaches a procedure for immunizing mice against HBsAg, and the use of lymphocytes from these mice to produce hybridomas that secrete monoclonal antibodies specific for HBsAg. The '145 patent discloses that this procedure yields both IgG and IgM antibodies with high-affinity binding to HBsAg. For the stated purpose of complying with the best mode requirement of 35 U.S.C. § 112, first paragraph, a hybridoma cell line that secretes IgM antibodies against HBsAg (the 1F8 cell line) was deposited at the American Type Culture Collection, a recognized cell depository, and became available to the public when the '145 patent issued.

The application on appeal claims methods for immunoassay of HBsAg using monoclonal antibodies such as those described in the '145 patent. Most immunoassay methods have used monoclonal antibodies of the IgG isotype. IgM antibodies were disfavored in the prior art because of their sensitivity to reducing agents and their tendency to self-aggregate and precipitate. Appellants found that their monoclonal IgM antibodies could be used for immunoassay of HbsAg with unexpectedly high sensitivity and specificity. Claims 1, 3, 7, 8, 14, and 15 are drawn to methods for the immunoassay of HBsAg using high-affinity IgM monoclonal antibodies. Claims 19 and 25-27 are for chemically modified (e.g., radioactively labeled) monoclonal IgM antibodies used in the assays. The broadest method claim reads:

> 1. An immunoassay method utilizing an antibody to assay for a substance comprising hepatitis B-surface antigen (HBsAg) determinants which comprises the steps of:
>
>> contacting a test sample containing said substance comprising HBsAg determinants with said antibody; and determining the presence of said substance in said sample; wherein said antibody is a monoclonal high affinity IgM antibody having a binding affinity constant for said HBsAg determinants of at least 109 M-1.

Claims 1, 3, 7, 8, 14, 15, 19, and 25-27 were rejected under 35 U.S.C. § 112, first paragraph, on the grounds that the disclosure would not enable a person skilled in the art to make and use the invention without undue experimentation. The rejection is directed solely to whether the specification enables one skilled in the art to make the monoclonal antibodies that are needed to practice the invention. The position of the PTO is that data presented by Wands show that the production of high-affinity IgM anti-HBsAg antibodies is unpredictable and unreliable, so that it would require undue experimentation for one skilled in the art to make the antibodies.

Enablement by Deposit of Microorganisms and Cell Lines

The first paragraph of 35 U.S.C. § 112 requires that the specification of a patent must enable a person skilled in the art to make and use the claimed invention. A patent need not disclose what is well known in the art. Although we review underlying facts found by the board under a "clearly erroneous" standard, we review enablement as a question of law.

Where an invention depends on the use of living materials such as microorganisms or cultured cells, it may be impossible to enable the public to make the invention (i.e., to obtain these living materials) solely by means of a written disclosure. One means that has been developed for complying with the enablement requirement is to deposit the living materials in cell depositories which will distribute samples to the public who wish to practice the invention after the patent issues. [*In re Argoudelis*, 434 F.2d 1390, 1392-93, 168 U.S.P.Q. 99, 101-02 (C.C.P.A. 1970).] Administrative guidelines and judicial decisions have clarified the conditions under which a deposit of organisms can satisfy the requirements of section 112. [*In re Lundak*, 773 F.2d 1216, 227 U.S.P.Q. 90 (Fed. Cir. 1985); *Feldman v. Aunstrup*, 517 F.2d 1351, 186 U.S.P.Q. 108 (C.C.P.A. 1975), *cert. denied*, 424 U.S. 912, 96 S. Ct. 1109, 47 L. Ed. 2d 316 (1976); MANUAL OF PATENT EXAMINING PROCEDURE (MPEP) 608.01(p)(C) (5th ed. rev. 1987). *See generally* Hampar, *Patenting of Recombinant DNA Technology: The Deposit Requirement*, 67 J. PAT. & TRADEMARK OFF. SOC'Y 569 (1985).] A deposit has been held necessary for enablement where the starting materials (i.e., the living cells used to practice the invention, or cells from which the required cells can be produced) are not readily available to the public. [*In re Jackson*, 217 U.S.P.Q. 804, 807-08 (Bd. App. 1982) (strains of a newly discovered species of bacteria isolated from nature); *Feldman*, 517 F.2d 1351, 186 U.S.P.Q. 108 (uncommon fungus isolated from nature).] Even when starting materials are available, a deposit has been necessary where it would require undue experimentation to make the cells of the invention from the starting materials. [*In re Forman*, 230 U.S.P.Q. 546, 547 (Bd. Pat. App. & Int. 1986) (genetically engineered bacteria where the specification provided insufficient information about the amount of time and effort required); *In re Lundak*, 773 F.2d 1216, 227 U.S.P.Q. 90 (unique cell line produced from another cell line by mutagenesis).]

Wands does not challenge the statements by the examiner to the effect that, although the deposited 1F8 line enables the public to perform immunoassays with antibodies produced by that single hybridoma, the deposit does not enable the generic claims that are on appeal. The examiner rejected the claims on the grounds that the written disclosure was not enabling and that the deposit was inadequate. Since we hold that the written disclosure fully enables the claimed invention, we need not reach the question of the adequacy of deposits.

Undue Experimentation

Although inventions involving microorganisms or other living cells often can be enabled by a deposit, a deposit is not always necessary to satisfy the enablement requirement. No deposit is necessary if the biological organisms can be obtained from readily available sources or derived from readily available starting materials through routine screening that does not require undue experimentation. Whether the specification in an application involving living cells (here, hybridomas) is enabled without a deposit must be decided on the facts of the particular case.

Appellants contend that their written specification fully enables the practice of their claimed invention because the monoclonal antibodies needed to perform the immunoassays can be made from readily available starting materials using methods that are well known in the monoclonal antibody art. There is no challenge to their contention that the starting materials (i.e., mice, HBsAg antigen, and myeloma cells) are available to the public. The PTO concedes that the methods used to prepare hybridomas and to screen them for high-affinity IgM antibodies against HBsAg were either well known in the monoclonal antibody art or adequately disclosed in the '145 patent and in the current application. The sole issue is whether, in this particular case, it would require undue experimentation to produce high-affinity IgM monoclonal antibodies.

Enablement is not precluded by the necessity for some experimentation such as routine screening. However, experimentation needed to practice the invention must not be undue experimentation. "The key word is 'undue,' not 'experimentation.'" [*In re Angstadt*, 537 F.2d 498, 504, 190 U.S.P.Q. (BNA) 214, 219 (C.C.P.A. 1976).]

The determination of what constitutes undue experimentation in a given case requires the application of a standard of reasonableness, having due regard for the nature of the invention and the state of the art.

> The test is not merely quantitative, since a considerable amount of experimentation is permissible, if it is merely routine, or if the specification in question provides a reasonable amount of guidance with respect to the direction in which the experimentation should proceed ....

[*In re Jackson*, 217 U.S.P.Q. (BNA) at 807.]

The term "undue experimentation" does not appear in the statute, but it is well established that enablement requires that the specification teach those in the art to make and use the invention without undue experimentation. Whether undue experimentation is needed is not a single, simple factual determination, but rather is a conclusion reached by weighing many factual considerations. The board concluded that undue experimentation would be needed to practice the invention on the basis of experimental data presented by Wands. These data are not in dispute. However, Wands and the board disagree strongly on the conclusion that should be drawn from that data.

Factors to be considered in determining whether a disclosure would require undue experimentation have been summarized by the board in *In re Forman*. They include (1) the quantity of experimentation necessary, (2) the amount of direction or guidance presented, (3) the presence or absence of working examples, (4) the nature of the invention, (5) the state of the prior art, (6) the relative skill of those in the art, (7) the predictability or unpredictability of the art, and (8) the breadth of the claims. [*In re Forman*, 230 U.S.P.Q. (BNA) at 547.]

[The court describes the steps leading up to the invention. The inventors first created hybridomas to produce antibodies to the HBsAg antigen. The hybridoma cells that secreted the desired antibodies were then isolated from the enormous number of other cells in the mixture. This was done through a series of screening procedures. Then the inventors isolated and cloned the desired hybridomas. The antibody from each hybridoma was assayed to determine whether it would bind to the antigen. As is expected in this art, most did not; these clones were discarded. The few highly effective hybridomas that were left were screened further to determine which had the high affinity desired by the inventors and stated as a limitation in their claims.]

During prosecution Wands submitted a declaration under 37 C.F.R. § 1.132 providing information about all of the hybridomas that appellants had produced before filing the patent application. The first four fusions were unsuccessful and produced no hybridomas. The next six fusion experiments all produced hybridomas that made antibodies specific for HBsAg. Antibodies that bound at least 10,000 cpm in the commercial radioimmunoassay [used in the second screening step] were classified as "high binders." Using this criterion, 143 high-binding hybridomas were obtained. In the declaration, Wands stated that

> It is generally accepted in the art that, among those antibodies which are binders with 50,000 cpm or higher, there is a very high likelihood that high affinity (Ka [greater than] 109 M-1-1) antibodies will be found. However, high affinity antibodies can also be found among high binders of between 10,000 and 50,000, as is clearly demonstrated in the Table. The PTO has not challenged this statement.

The declaration stated that a few of the high-binding monoclonal antibodies from two fusions were chosen for further screening. The remainder of the antibodies and the hybridomas that produced them were saved by freezing. Only nine antibodies were subjected to further analysis. Four (three from one fusion and one from another fusion) fell within the claims, that is, were IgM antibodies and had a binding affinity constant of at least 109 M-1-1. Of the remaining five antibodies, three were found to be IgG, while the other two were IgM for which the affinity constants were not measured (although both showed binding well above 50,000 cpm).

Apparently none of the frozen cell lines received any further analysis. The declaration explains that after useful high-affinity IgM monoclonal antibodies to HBsAg had been found, it was considered unnecessary to return to the stored antibodies to screen for more IgMs. Wands says that the existence of the stored hybridomas was disclosed to the PTO to comply with the requirement under 37 C.F.R. § 1.56 that applicants fully disclose all of their relevant data, and not just favorable results. How these stored hybridomas are viewed is central to the positions of the parties.

The position of the board emphasizes the fact that since the stored cell lines were not completely tested, there is no proof that any of them are IgM antibodies with a binding affinity constant of at least 109 M-1-1. Thus, only 4 out of 143 hybridomas, or 2.8 percent, were proved to fall within the claims. Furthermore, antibodies that were proved to be high-affinity IgM came from only 2 of 10 fusion experiments. These statistics are viewed by the board as evidence that appellants' methods were not predictable or reproducible. The board concludes that Wands' low rate of demonstrated success shows that a person skilled in the art would have to engage in undue experimentation in order to make antibodies that fall within the claims.

Wands views the data quite differently. Only nine hybridomas were actually analyzed beyond the initial screening for HBsAg binding. Of these, four produced antibodies that fell within the claims, a respectable 44 percent rate of success. (Furthermore, since the two additional IgM antibodies for which the affinity constants were never measured showed binding in excess of 50,000 cpm, it is likely that these also fall within the claims.) Wands argues that the remaining 134 unanalyzed, stored cell lines should not be written off as failures. Instead, if anything, they represent partial success. Each of the stored hybridomas had been shown to produce a high-binding antibody specific for HBsAg. Many of these antibodies showed binding above 50,000 cpm and are thus highly likely to have a binding affinity constant of at least 109 M-1-1. Extrapolating from the nine hybridomas that were screened for isotype (and from what is well known in the monoclonal antibody art about isotype frequency), it is reasonable to assume that the stored cells include some that produce IgM. Thus, if the 134 incompletely analyzed cell lines are considered at all, they provide some support (albeit without rigorous proof) to the view that hybridomas falling within the claims are not so rare that undue experimentation would be needed to make them.

The first four fusion attempts were failures, while high-binding antibodies were produced in the next six fusions. Appellants contend that the initial failures occurred because they had not yet learned to fuse cells successfully. Once they became skilled in the art, they invariably obtained numerous hybridomas that made high-binding antibodies against HBsAg and, in each fusion where they determined isotype and binding affinity they obtained hybridomas that fell within the claims.

We conclude that the board's interpretation of the data is erroneous. It is strained and unduly harsh to classify the stored cell lines (each of which was proved to make high-binding antibodies against HBsAg) as failures demonstrating that Wands' methods are unpredictable or unreliable. [From court's fn. 29: "Even if we were to accept the PTO's 2.8% success rate, we would not be required to reach a conclusion of undue experimentation. Such a determination must be made in view of the circumstances of each case and cannot be made solely by reference to a particular numerical cutoff."] At worst, they prove nothing at all about the probability of success, and merely show that appellants were prudent in not discarding cells that might someday prove useful. At best, they show that high-binding antibodies, the starting materials for IgM screening and Scatchard analysis, can be produced in large numbers. The PTO's position leads to the absurd conclusion that the more hybridomas an applicant makes and saves without testing, the less predictable the applicant's results become. Furthermore, Wands' explanation that the first four attempts at cell fusion failed only because they had not yet learned to perform fusions properly is reasonable in view of the fact that the next six fusions were all successful. The record indicates that cell fusion is a technique that is well known to those of ordinary skill in the monoclonal antibody art, and there has been no claim that the fusion step should be more difficult or unreliable where the antigen is HBsAg than it would be for other antigens.

The nature of monoclonal antibody technology is that it involves screening hybridomas to determine which ones secrete antibody with desired characteristics. Practitioners of this art are prepared to screen negative hybridomas in order to find one that makes the desired antibody. No evidence was presented by either party on how many hybridomas would be viewed by those in the art as requiring undue experimentation to screen. However, it seems unlikely that undue experimentation would be defined in terms of the number of hybridomas that were never screened. Furthermore, in the monoclonal antibody art it appears that an "experiment" is not simply the screening of a single hybridoma, but is rather the entire attempt to make a monoclonal antibody against a particular antigen. This process entails immunizing animals, fusing lymphocytes from the immunized animals with myeloma cells to make hybridomas, cloning the hybridomas, and screening the antibodies produced by the hybridomas for the desired characteristics. Wands carried out this entire procedure three times, and was successful each time in making at least one antibody that satisfied all of the claim limitations. Reasonably interpreted, Wands' record indicates that, in the production of high-affinity IgM antibodies against HBsAG, the amount of effort needed to obtain such antibodies is not excessive. Wands' evidence thus effectively rebuts the examiner's challenge to the enablement of their disclosure.

Reversed.

NOTES

1. *Newman, J., Dissenting.* Judge Newman concurred in the part of the opinion holding that no deposit of the cell lines was necessary. But she dissented on the ground that "Wands has not provided data sufficient to support the breadth of his generic claims." 858 F.2d at 741.

> The Commissioner deems the success rate to be four out of 143, or 2.8%; to which Wands responds with statistical analysis as to how unlikely it is that Wands selected the only four out of 143 that worked. Wands did not, however, prove the right point. The question is whether Wands, by testing nine out of 143 (the Commissioner points out that the randomness of the sample was not established), and finding that four out of the nine had the

desired properties, has provided sufficient experimental support for the breadth of the requested claims, in the context that "experiments in genetic engineering produce, at best, unpredictable results," quoting from *Ex parte Forman*, 230 U.S.P.Q. 546, 547 (Bd. Pat. App. & Int. 1986).

The premise of the patent system is that an inventor, having taught the world something it didn't know, is encouraged to make the product available for public and commercial benefit, by governmental grant of the right to exclude others from practice of that which the inventor has disclosed. The boundary defining the excludable subject matter must be carefully set: it must protect the inventor, so that commercial development is encouraged; but the claims must be commensurate with the inventor's contribution. Thus the specification and claims must meet the requirements of § 112. *In re Fisher* ....

It is incumbent upon Wands to provide reasonable support for the proposed breadth of his claims. I agree with the Commissioner that four exemplars shown to have the desired properties, out of the 143, do not provide adequate support.... Wands must provide sufficient data or authority to show that his results are reasonably predictable within the scope of the claimed generic invention, based on experiment and/or scientific theory. In my view he has not met this burden.

858 F.2d at 741-42. The *Forman* case cited by Judge Newman, *In re Forman*, 230 U.S.P.Q. 546, 547 (Bd. Pat. App. & Int. 1986), involved genetically engineered bacteria where the specification provided insufficient information about the amount of time and effort required.

2. Related Cases: "Inoperable Species." In *Atlas Powder Co. v. E.I. Du Pont de Nemours & Co.*, 750 F.2d 1569, 224 U.S.P.Q. 409 (Fed. Cir. 1984), the court affirmed a finding that Du Pont, the accused infringer, had not proved lack of enablement on the part of the patentee Atlas Powder. The patent, for explosive compounds, listed in its specification numerous salts, fuels and emulsifiers that could form thousands of emulsions, but gave no commensurate teaching as to which combinations would work. Du Pont had argued that its tests showed a 40% failure rate in constructing various embodiments of the claimed invention. The court rejected this "inoperable species" argument:

Of course, if the number of inoperative combinations becomes significant, and in effect forces one of ordinary skill in the art to experiment unduly in order to practice the claimed invention, the claims might indeed be invalid. See, e.g., *In re Cook*, 439 F.2d 730, 735, 169 U.S.P.Q. 298, 302 (1971). That, however, has not been shown to be the case here.... The district court also found that one skilled in the art would know how to modify slightly many of [the experimental] "failures" to form a better emulsion.

750 F.2d at 1576-77. *See also In re Cavallito*, 282 F.2d 357, 361, 127 U.S.P.Q. (BNA) 202, 205 (C.C.P.A. 1960) (claims covering generic class of several

hundred thousand possible compounds invalid because the applicant had identified only thirty specific operative compounds); 2 D. CHISUM, PATENTS § 7.03[7][c] (1978 & Supp. 1991) ("claim will be rejected if it is so broad as to read upon inoperative as well as operative subject matter"). *But cf. In re Dinh-Nguyen*, 492 F.2d 856, 858-59, 181 U.S.P.Q. 46, 48 (C.C.P.A. 1974) ("It is not a function of the claims to specifically exclude ... possible inoperative substances....").

In *Ex parte Jackson*, 217 U.S.P.Q. (BNA) 804, 806 (Pat. Off. Bd. App. 1982), the Board reversed the rejection of a claim to three specified strains of antibiotic-producing bacterium "and mutations thereof" since "mutations can be intentionally produced [and presumably tested for efficacy] by a variety of known procedures." A commentator recently suggested that the Board in *Jackson* would only require enabling screening procedures to indicate that "at least *some* such mutants would have the desired characteristic of producing the antibiotic." Lentz, *Adequacy of Disclosures of Biotechnology Inventions*, 16 AM. INTELL. PROP. L. ASS'N Q.J. 314, 324 (1989) (emphasis added).

3. *Enable Whom?* The following summarizes an important point in the law of enablement, which is especially relevant to highly sophisticated fields such as biotechnology:

> A patent specification is not addressed to judges or lawyers, but to those skilled in the art; it must be comprehensible to them, even though the unskilled may not be able to gather from it how to use the invention, and even if it is "all Greek" to the unskilled. *Mowry v. Whitney*, 81 U.S. 620, 644 (1872); *Webster Loom Co. v. Higgins*, 105 U.S. 580, 585-86 (1882); *[In re] Nelson*, 280 F.2d 172, 181 (C.C.P.A. 1960).

Gould v. Mossinghoff, 229 U.S.P.Q. 1 (D.D.C. 1985), *aff'd in part, vacated in part sub nom. Gould v. Quigg*, 822 F.2d 1074, 3 U.S.P.Q.2d (BNA) 1302 (Fed. Cir. 1987).

4. *The Microorganism Deposit.* The Court of Customs and Patent Appeals first addressed the adequacy of microorganism deposits under § 112 in *In re Argoudelis*, 434 F.2d 1390, 1392-93, 168 U.S.P.Q. 99, 101-02 (C.C.P.A. 1970). There a patent application claimed new antibiotic compounds and a process for preparing the compounds from microorganisms. The applicants deposited samples of their microorganisms in the permanent culture collection of the United States Department of Agriculture before the filing date of their patent application and referred to this deposit in the specification. At the request of the applicants, the depository agreed not to release the organism without their written permission until a patent issued. Reversing the PTO, the Court of Customs and Patent Appeals approved the use of a deposit to "disclose" a microorganism obtained from nature. The court held that § 112 did not require that the general public have access to the culture before the patent issued, reasoning that as long as the materials are available to the PTO during the pendency of the patent application, the disclosure is sufficient to demonstrate completion of the invention as of the filing date. Since patent applicants in other fields need not make their patent disclosures public unless and until a patent issues, the court felt that no earlier public disclosure should be required for microorganism-related inventions.

For the most recent Patent Office rules on deposit, see 37 C.F.R §§ 1.801-1.809 (1991).

Note that these rules reflect U.S. adherence to the international treaty on biological deposits — the "Budapest Treaty." *See* International Recognition of the Deposit of Microoogranisms for the Purposes of Patent Procedure, Apr. 28, 1977, 32 U.S.T. 1241, T.I.A.S. No. 9768. *See* 961 OFFIC. GAZETTE PAT. OFF. 21-36 (Aug. 23, 1977). The Budapest Treaty establishes minimum requirements for maintaining an international depository for microorganisms and authorizes such depositories to receive and store deposits and dispense samples in accordance with the Treaty and the patent laws of the signatory nations. 999 OFFIC. GAZETTE PAT. OFF. 2 (Oct. 7, 1980). *See generally* Meyer, *Problems and Issues in Depositing Microorganisms for Patent Purposes*, 65 J. PAT. OFF. SOC'Y 455 (1983) (discussing depository requirements under international treaties and section 112); Hampar, *Patenting of Recombinant DNA Technology: The Deposit Requirement*, 67 J. PAT. OFF. SOC'Y 569, 605-07 (1985).

5. *Predictable Versus Unpredictable Arts.* Element (7) in the laundry list of factors from *Forman*, cited and discussed in the preceding case, is the predictability of the art. Various fields of technology are often distinguished in this regard. The more predictable a field, the less disclosure is necessary to enable a broad claim or claim. *See, e.g., Spectra-Physics, Inc. v. Coherent, Inc.*, 827 F.2d 1524, 1533 (Fed. Cir. 1987) ("If an invention pertains to an art where the results are predictable, ... a broad claim can be enabled by disclosure of a single embodiment."). *Cf. In re Cook*, 439 F.2d 730, 734 (C.C.P.A. 1971) (pointing out that, in the case, "a dichotomy between predictable and unpredictable factors [*within*] any art ... [was] at the heart of much of the argument" that a single operative example was entitled to a broad claim).

This differentiation is illustrated in the PTO examination manual. See PATENT & TRADEMARK OFFICE, U.S. DEPARTMENT OF COMMERCE, MANUAL OF PATENT EXAMINING PROCEDURE § 706.03(z) (5th ed. rev. 9, 1988). The manual directs patent examiners as follows:

> In applications directed to inventions in arts where results are predictable, broad claims may properly be supported by the disclosure of a single species. However, in applications directed to inventions in arts where the results are unpredictable, the disclosure of a single species usually does not provide an adequate basis to support generic claims. This is because in arts such as chemistry it is not obvious from the disclosure of one species, what other species will work.

2. THE USES OF EXAMPLES IN THE SPECIFICATION

In re STRAHILEVITZ

668 F.2d 1229, 212 U.S.P.Q. 561 (C.C.P.A. 1982)

Invention

Appellant's invention relates to methods and devices for removing a hapten, antigen, or antibody from the blood of a living mammal.

A hapten is a small molecule which does not by itself produce antibodies but which, when conjugated to a carrier protein or other macro-molecular carrier, induces in a recipient animal or human the production of antibodies that are specific to the small molecule. For example, certain psychoactive drugs, such as LSD, heroin, and tetrahydrocannabinol, can function as haptens. When an antibody (a relatively large immunoprotein) contacts the hapten or antigen to which it is specific, it tightly binds the hapten or antigen. It is this specific binding property of antibodies which is used by appellant to remove haptens, antibodies, or antigens from blood. Claim 44, the broadest appealed claim, reads:

[44.] An immunological method for removing from a living mammal a hapten in the blood of said mammal, comprising connecting in the blood circulatory system of said mammal a hapten-removing device, said device comprising passage means for said blood; an antibody to said hapten in said device; and exposure means in said device for exposing said hapten to said antibody and for preventing said antibody from entering said circulatory system.

The examiner rejected the claims as based upon an insufficient disclosure under 35 U.S.C. § 112, first paragraph, stating:

The disclosure is essentially an invitation to experiment. No specific examples are given. No human treatment (in fact no animal treatment) is described. The specification is replete with statements as to what may be done. No dialysis or adsorption data (have) been presented.... (A)ppellant urges "nearly universal applicability" for selectively removing chemical species.

... If there is in fact universal applicability, with selectivity, appellant should have inserted numerous (50 to 100 for instance) examples into the specification.... Appellant urges that no working example is required and that instructions to a technician are not required. But it has already been pointed out that appellant believes his device has universal applications (and the claims are just about that broad). Admittedly, one skilled in the art is a Ph.D., but even with such a high level of skill, such a person would need detailed guidance to practice the claimed alleged universal invention.

The board took a somewhat different approach:

(A)ppellant admits ... the disclosure contains no "operative example." While we recognize that specific examples are not necessary to meet the requirements of Section 112, *In re Gay*, 50 C.C.P.A. 725, 309 F.2d 769, 135 U.S.P.Q. 311 (1962), when present, they do provide good evidence that the disclosure is enabling and that the invention may be performed without undue experimentation. In our view, the material most descriptive of the claimed methods and apparatus, is that presented in examples 12 and 13, wherein systems are defined for the removal of haptens, antigens and antibodies from the circulatory system. Here, appellant has presented no descriptive material that in our view is sufficient to provide a proper instruction in the manner of either developing the apparatus as claimed or the method of using same. The wide variety of variables that are inherent in the process, and for which the disclosure provides no basis for evaluation, leads us to the conclusion that operation of the method as claimed would involve an undue amount of experimentation and we will therefore sustain the rejection.

A threshold issue is whether the PTO met its burden of proof in calling into question the enablement of appellant's disclosure. This burden required that the PTO advance acceptable reasoning inconsistent with enablement. Thereupon, the burden would shift to appellant to show that one of ordinary skill in the art could have practiced the claimed invention without undue experimentation. *In re Sichert*, 566 F.2d 1154, 1161, 196 U.S.P.Q. 209, 215 (C.C.P.A. 1977).

We recognize that working examples are desirable in complex technologies and that detailed examples can satisfy the statutory enablement requirement. Indeed, the inclusion of such examples here might well have avoided a lengthy and, no doubt, expensive appeal. Nevertheless, as acknowledged by the board, examples are not required to satisfy section 112, first paragraph. See, e.g., *In re Stephens*, 529 F.2d 1343, 188 U.S.P.Q. 659 (C.C.P.A. 1976); *In re Borkowski*, 57 C.C.P.A. 946, 422 F.2d 904, 164 U.S.P.Q. 642 (1970).

Although the invention is applicable to a large variety of haptens and antigens, the examiner offered no reason why these different compounds would require different techniques or process parameters.

However, the examiner (and the board) also reasoned that enablement was not present because no dialysis or adsorption (of the antibody or antigen) data were presented, and we are persuaded that this was sufficient to shift the burden to appellant to establish that a person of ordinary skill in the art could have practiced the invention without undue experimentation.

Enablement

Appellant explains that his invention resides in combining the known prior art techniques of hemodialysis or hemoperfusion with immunochemical dialysis and immunochemical adsorption. He properly relies on literature citations to establish both the level of ordinary skill in the art and the fact that the techniques necessary to practice his invention were known in the art.

Appellant argues that methods for forming antibodies which are specific to particular haptens and antigens were well known prior to his filing date. In his specification, he states:

> Immunization of rabbits with conjugates in complete Freund's Adjuvant are carried out by a similar procedure to the one described by Strahilevitz et al., *supra*. The preparation of antisera and globulin fractions are also described in this reference.

He then gives a specific example of preparing an antibody to tetrahydrocannabinol, referring to a method described in Immunologic Methods in Steroid Determination (Peron & Caldwell ed. 1970) for conjugating the compound to a protein, and detailing the injection of "(r)abbits, sheep or other suitable animals" with the conjugate, giving concentration, dosage, and frequency of injection data.

[Another reference], cited in appellant's specification and made a part of the record in the parent application, details the preparation of protein-hapten conjugates, injection of the conjugates into animals, and recovery of antibodies to the haptens from the animals. It is clear from this disclosure that selection and preparation of related haptens, antigens, and antibodies involve routine and well-known techniques.

In example 13 of appellant's specification, appears the following statement:

> As shown in Figure 7, the apparatus for this method consists of a column 26 which includes a matrix 37 to which a binding species is linked. The binding species is a hapten, antigen (including a hapten conjugated to a carrier) or antibody which reacts specifically with the species which is to be removed from the blood. The linkage of the binding species to the matrix 37 may preferably be directly to the matrix, as when the matrix is made of a synthetic polymer such as polystyrene latex. The linkage may also be through a suitable solid phase coating on the matrix. The antibody is then linked to the coating by one of the known methods for the preparation of immunoadsorbents, for example by a modification of one of the methods of Campbell (Campbell et al., Proc. Nat. Acad. Sci., U.S.A., 37, p. 575 (1951); Malley and Campbell, J. Am. Chem. Soc. 85, p. 487 (1963)).

Additionally, appellant points out that appropriate matrices and techniques for binding antigens or antibodies thereto were well known in the art, as evidenced by Weetall, U.S. Patent No. 3,652,761, cited by the examiner in support of a rejection under 35 U.S.C. § 103 which was reversed by the board. Weetall discloses that it was known in the art to couple antigens to cellulose and its derivatives to remove antibodies from serum.

The position of the board and the Solicitor is that appellant has provided no disclosure regarding selection of the dialysis membranes required to practice the subject matter of claims 42, 43, 47, and 48. However, appellant's specification states:

> Such membranes, having various pore sizes, and thus which are permeable to molecules of various sizes are commercially available .... The semipermeable membrane is chosen to be of such a porosity and permeability as to be permeable to small molecules like the intoxicating hapten of interest, but is not permeable to large molecules present in the blood of the patient such as serum proteins. Selection of the membranes, therefore, is based upon their porosity and the relative molecular sizes of the antibody and the hapten or antigen. Weetall, *supra*.

[T]hese references clearly indicate that selection of semipermeable membranes on the basis of pore size, as suggested by appellant's specification, was a technique known in the art prior to appellant's filing date.

Appellant states that a person of ordinary skill in the art would know appropriate flow rates and other parameters for performing dialysis, citing [other references]. [One reference] teach[es] a method in which blood is passed through a column at 300 ml./min. for three hours to remove barbiturates from the blood. These references disclose typical dialysis and related data in methods similar to those of appellant. There is no reason to believe that these parameters would not also be applicable to appellant's methods, as he contends.

In view of all the foregoing, we hold that appellant's disclosure would have enabled a person of ordinary skill in the art to make and use appellant's invention without undue experimentation.

NOTES

1. *"Prophetic Examples."* Usually, the "examples" listed in a specification report actual laboratory or prototype testing results. Contrast this with the "examples" in the case just described. Example 13, for instance, was not what the courts would call a "working example," i.e., a report of actual results. It was really an *application* of the principle set forth in the specification, that certain "binding species" could be used to bind haptens and antigens and thereby remove the latter from the bloodstream. Example 13 sets forth one way of doing this — using a matrix of binding agents on the sides of a column. But no actual data are reported; no real experiments were run to test whether this application of the principle enunciated in the application actually worked.

This type of example has come to be called a "prophetic example." It is based on the notion that some applications of known techniques are so predictable that they can be "prophesied" by one skilled in the art. Prophetic examples can pose significant problems for enablement doctrine, since this doctrine is based on the notion that actual inventive work must lie behind the language in an applicant's claims. In essence, then, cases like *Strahilevitz* hold that an adequate description of purely *conceptual* inventive work can meet the requirements of Patent Act § 112.

On the Strahilevitz patent and the opportunity it offers biotechnology inventors to file patents before obtaining working examples, see P. Kelly, *Prophetic Patents in Biotechnology*, 8 BIO/TECH. 24, 25 (1990).

Note that the possibility of prophetic examples is implicit in the idea of a constructive reduction to practice. See Chapter 4, Section J.4.a; *Gould v. Quigg*, 822 F.2d 1074, 3 U.S.P.Q.2d 1302, 1304 (Fed. Cir. 1987).

The PTO Manual of Patent Examining Procedure (MPEP) § 608.01(p)(D) (5th ed. 1983), recognizes the acceptability of prophetic examples:

> Simulated or predicted test results and prophetical examples (paper examples) are permitted in patent applications. Working examples correspond to work actually performed and may describe tests which have actually been conducted and results that were achieved. Paper examples describe the manner and process of making an embodiment of the invention which has not actually been conducted. Paper examples should not be represented as work actually done. Paper examples should not be described using the past tense.

2. Related Cases. In re *Borkowski*, 422 F.2d 904, 908, 164 U.S.P.Q. 642 (C.C.P.A. 1970), also involved a specification with no working examples.

> [A] specification need not contain a working example if the invention is otherwise disclosed in such a manner that one skilled in the art will be able to practice it without an undue amount of experimentation. Here, while it may be that an "exemplary correlation" of parameters such as times of reaction and rates of reactant feed and product removal would give the worker in the art some useful information and provide a "jumping off place," we see no basis for concluding that without such information the worker in the art would not be enabled by the specification to practice the invention, i.e., to "balance" the several reactions involved in appellants' process. The "few hours" experimentation mentioned by the examiner certainly would not seem to be an undue amount of time considering the nature of the claimed invention.

In a sense, cases such as *Strahilevitz* are merely an extension of a basic tenet: that an applicant be entitled to claim the full scope of what she invented. A common application of this tenet is in the area of "pioneer" claims. *See, e.g., Morley Sewing Mach. Co. v. Lancaster*, 129 U.S. 263 (1889) (pioneer invention is entitled to a generic claim, under which will be included every species included within the genus); *Brush Elec. Co. v. Electric Imp. Co.*, 52 F. 965 (C.C.D. Cal. 1892); *American Bell Tel. Co. v. Spencer*, 8 F. 509 (C.C.D. Mass. 1881). It is often said in these cases that the inventor must not be coerced into reciting each and every embodiment (or "species") of the device framed by the generic claim. Cases dispensing with the requirement of a working example extend this reasoning to its limit, by holding that the inventor need not recite *any* actually constructed embodiment.

3. *Burden of Proof.* This case illustrates the burden of proof on the enablement issue during ex parte prosecution. If the patent examiner can point to a reasonable indication in the prior art that some embodiments of the claimed invention will be impossible to make without much more information than the inventor (or anyone else) knows, the claims will be narrowed. But if the examiner cannot point to such an indication in the prior art, Patent Office policy dictates that even very broad claims may be allowed. This means that claims to pioneer inventions often are allowed to cover ground that examiners *believe*, but cannot prove, is well beyond the area actually explored and disclosed by the inventor. *See In re Armbruster*, 512 F.2d 676, 680, 185 U.S.P.Q. (BNA) 152, 155 (C.C.P.A. 1975); *In re Geerdes*, 491 F.2d 1260, 1265, 180 U.S.P.Q. (BNA) 789, 793 (C.C.P.A. 1974). The rule puts the burden of *disproving* enablement on the examiner. The rationale is that any other rule would leave claim scope too much in the hands of individual examiners and their technological forecasting abilities. *See* Winner, *Enablement in Rapidly Developing Arts — Biotechnology*, 70 J. PAT. & TRADEMARK OFF. SOC'Y, 608, 619-23 (1988). The author of this article summarizes the somewhat conflicting cases on the topic, and concludes that "[t]o reject claims for lack of enablement of embodiments that were only imagined by the examiner does not seem fair." *Id.* at 622. Narrowing is left to the courts in particular infringement suits. *See* PATENT AND TRADEMARK OFFICE, U.S. DEP'T OF COMMERCE, MANUAL OF PATENT EXAMINING PROCEDURE § 706.03(d) (5th ed. rev. 1989) ("The fact that a claim is broad does not necessarily justify a rejection on the ground that the claim is vague and indefinite or incomplete. In non-chemical cases, a claim may, in general, be drawn as broadly as permitted by the prior art."); Levin, *Broader than the Disclosure in Chemical Cases*, 31 J. PAT. & TRADEMARK OFF. SOC'Y, 5, 7 (1949). Note that in appropriate cases, this narrowing can even take the form of excusing a clear infringement, under the "reverse doctrine of equivalents." *See In re Hogan*, 559 F.2d 595, 606, 194 U.S.P.Q. (BNA) 527, 537 (C.C.P.A. 1977) (suggesting this possibility in defense of placing burden on examiner to narrow scope in an application). On the reverse doctrine of equivalents, see Chapter 8.

In an infringement action where enablement (more properly, "non-enablement") is raised as a defense, "[t]he burden is on one challenging validity to show by clear and convincing evidence that the prophetic examples together with other parts of the specification are not enabling." *Atlas Powder Co. v. E.I. Du Pont de Nemours & Co.*, 750 F.2d 1569, 1577, 224 U.S.P.Q. 409 (Fed. Cir. 1984).

3. COMMENT: PROBLEMS IN ENABLEMENT, U.S. AND ABROAD

An example of the function and problems of enablement doctrine is the recent patent granted to Doctors Phillip Leder and Timothy Stewart of the Harvard Medical School for their successful work involving transgenic mice. They isolated a gene which is associated with cancer in mammals (including humans) and then injected the gene into a fertilized mouse egg, which yielded transgenic mice that are extremely sensitive to carcinogens. U.S. Patent No. 4,736,866. This makes the mice excellent animal "models" for studying cancer drugs. Leder and Stewart claimed not only the technique they had used, or the particular transgenic mouse variety they had created, but rather all "non-human transgenic mammals" produced by their technique. It may well turn out that their admittedly important discovery was indeed this broad. On the other hand, significant work may be required to obtain similar results in higher-order mammals. One wonders whether arguments by an accused infringer that she had to do considerable experimenting and problem-solving prior to producing a transgenic dog, or that she created a transgenic cat using a substantially different technique, would be sufficient to take her invention outside the Leder and Stuart claims.

In fact, the European Patent Office cited just these concerns when it rejected those claims in the Leder and Stuart patent that went beyond mice and rodents. Even though this decision was later overturned by the EPO Technical Board of Appeal, its reasoning is instructive. *See In re President & Fellows of Harvard College* (European Patent Office July 14, 1989), reported in 20 INT'L REV. INDUS. PROP. & COPYRIGHT L. 889, 895-96 (1989) ("Onco-Mouse" case), *rev'd*, OFFIC. J. EUR. PAT. OFF. (1990), in opinion reported in *Genetically Engineered Mouse May Be Patentable in Europe*, 40 PAT. TRADEMARK & COPYRIGHT J. (BNA) 535 (1990). From the 1989 decision:

> The invention as disclosed in its broadest concept ... relates to *any* oncogene and *any* conceivable mammalian animal. [The European Patent Code] relates to sufficiency [of disclosure] and it is important to note that this article is satisfied only if substantially any embodiment of the invention as defined in its broadest claim is capable of being realised on the basis of the disclosure.
>
> ....
>
> It is thus not believable that the skilled man would be able to transfer successfully the specific teachings of the present application to all kinds of mammalian animals ... without applying inventive skill or undue experimentation. Animals which have been used in the prior art are mainly mice and no instructions are to be found in the specification as to how success could be achieved with other mammalian animals.

It is difficult to resolve issues like these when a patent is filed; at that point, no one knows what future developments will follow or how difficult it will be to achieve them. Thus, there is an argument for granting a broad set of claims for pioneering inventions. Since the inventor may have enabled a broad new range of applications, courts reason, it is unfair to limit her to the precise embodiment through which she discovered the broader principle claimed. *See, e.g., In re Hogan*, 559 F.2d 595, 606, 194 U.S.P.Q. (BNA) 527, 537 (C.C.P.A. 1977); *In re Goffe*, 542 F.2d 564, 567, 191 U.S.P.Q. (BNA) 429, 431 (C.C.P.A. 1976). As one opinion put it,

> To restrict [a patentee] to the ... form disclosed ... would be a poor way to

stimulate invention, and particularly to encourage its early disclosure. To demand such restriction is merely to state a policy against broad protection for pioneer inventions, a policy both shortsighted and unsound from the standpoint of promoting progress in the useful arts, the constitutional purpose of the patent laws.

In re Hogan, 559 F.2d at 606, 194 U.S.P.Q. at 537.

As the European decision in the *Harvard Mouse* case points out, however, this liberal treatment of enablement has some pitfalls. As one illustration, consider the infamous Selden patent episode. The Selden patent on an automobile design had as its key claim the use of a light, gasoline-powered internal combustion engine. George Selden received a very broad patent in 1895 on the basic elements of the early automobile — "carriage," drive mechanism (transmission) and engine — that gave him a commanding position in the burgeoning automotive field. *See* U.S. Patent No. 549,160, issued Nov. 5, 1895; *Columbia Motor Car Co. v. C.A. Duerr & Co.*, 184 F. 893, 894 (2d Cir. 1911). The claim was quite general, failing to specify many important details about the engine. The Patent Office allowed that claim, and district courts upheld it twice, despite arguments that the broad idea was obvious, and that the engine referred to in the claim was of a particular kind not encompassing all the engines that were claimed to infringe. *See Electric Vehicle Co. v. Winton Motor-Carriage Co.*, 104 F. 814, 814-16 (C.C.S.D.N.Y. 1900); *Electric Vehicle Co. v. C.A. Duerr & Co.*, 172 F. 923 (C.C.S.D.N.Y. 1909), *rev'd sub nom. Columbia Motor Car Co. v. C.A. Duerr & Co.*, 184 F. 893 (2d Cir. 1911). Eventually, the Second Circuit drastically narrowed the claim, stating that it covered only the particular kind of gasoline engine used by Selden. *Columbia Motor Car Co.*, 184 F. at 908-09. In the meantime, the patent was used to elicit stiff licensing fees from the automobile industry, and may have slowed the rate of innovation in the early days of the industry. *See* Merges & Nelson, *On the Complex Economics of Patent Scope*, 90 COLUM. L. REV. 839 (1990).

Note that U.S. courts no longer narrow claims in infringement cases, as the court did in the Selden patent case. In fact, that case itself appears to fly in the face of Supreme Court precedent on the books when it was decided:

> [W]e know of no principle of law which would authorize us to read into a claim an element which is not present, for the purpose of making out a case of novelty or infringement. The difficulty is that if we once begin to include elements not mentioned in the claim in order to limit such claim and avoid a defense or anticipation, we should never know where to stop.

McCarty v. Lehigh Valley R. Co., 160 U.S. 110, 116 (1895). In any event, today the patent would either be submitted for reissue by the patentee or a request for reexamination would be made by the accused infringer. *See* Chapter 10, *Reissue and Reexamination*.

The practice of "judicial narrowing" of claims is still followed in some countries, however. *See* Fujino, *Broadly Written Claims Run Risk of Losing Everything*, PATENT WORLD (May 1992), at 38 (Japanese courts use examples in specification to narrow broad claims). T. TANABE & H. WEGNER, JAPANESE PATENT LAW § 035 (1979) (describing judicial narrowing in Japan, which stems at least partly from fact that Japanese courts cannot invalidate patents). *Cf. Texas Instruments v. United States Int'l Trade Comm'n*, 846 F.2d 1369, 1372, 6 U.S.P.Q.2d (BNA) 1886, 1889 (Fed. Cir. 1988) (suggesting that reverse doctrine of equivalents — which excuses infringer despite literal infringement — is appropriate where patent as granted included claim scope broader than disclosure really supported).

This tactic does save some patents from invalidity, and permits some accused devices to escape infringement. But cabining claim scope too closely has costs as well. A frequent criticism of the Japanese patent system, for example, is that it permits only very narrow claims. *See, e.g., Japanese Patent Policy, Hearing before the Subcomm. on Foreign Commerce and Tourism, United States Senate Comm. on Commerce, Science, and Transportation, Feb. 28, 1989,* 101st Cong., 1st Sess. (Hearing 101-19). And although this feature of Japanese patent law, if true, has several facets, an important one is that in Japan the equivalent of U.S. enablement doctrine is applied quite strictly — making it more difficult to obtain broad claims. *See* T. TANABE & H. WEGNER, JAPANESE PATENT LAW §§ 423, 725.2 (1979) (pointing out lack of doctrine of equivalents in Japanese law, and need for substantial working examples in application). This is said to permit the Japanese practice of surrounding a foreign-filed patent application with a large number of related applications, effectively reducing the foreign application to a worthless, narrow set of claims. *See Hearing, supra;* D. Spero, *Patent Protection or Piracy — A CEO Views Japan*, HARV. BUS. REV., Sept./Oct. 1990, at 58, 60 (article by president of Fusion Systems, Inc., a company which claims that Japanese competitors surrounded its Japanese patent application to neutralize it; states that Mitsubishi alone filed over 300 applications on technology related to Fusions' invention. Note that not all commentators agree on this characterization of Japanese patent law. *See, e.g., Fusion Systems,* Case Study, Harvard Business School (1990) (concluding that Fusion lost its right through ignorance of Japanese system rather than the biased nature of that system). If true, however, this criticism points out the dangers of restricting claim scope too much by very tight application of the doctrine of equivalents.

a. Enablement and the Temporal Paradox

Enablement must be established only as of the date the inventor filed for her patent. *In re Hogan*, 559 F.2d at 607, 194 U.S.P.Q. at 538. An inventor can properly claim subject matter that later turns out to be beyond her actual research, so long as her research enables one skilled in the art to make and use her claimed invention *as that invention was understood as of the filing date*. For example, consider an inventor who claims "crystalline polypropylene," and provides an enabling disclosure to make the substance which, on that date, everyone in the art would agree was "crystalline polypropylene." After the filing date, another researcher invents a radically new family of catalysts which for the first time make possible the production of polypropylene of high molecular weight and intrinsic viscosity — two properties that make the fiber commercially useful. It has been held that the inventor's original disclosure is sufficient to sustain a patent since it was enabling *as of the filing date*. The result is that the inventor's claims cover the later-developed, commercially useful form of the fiber. *Phillips Petr. Co. v. United States Steel Corp.*, 673 F. Supp. 1278, 1286, 1292, 6 U.S.P.Q.2d (BNA) 1065, 1068, 1074 (D. Del. 1987), *aff'd*, 865 F.2d 1247, 9 U.S.P.Q.2d (BNA) 1461 (Fed. Cir. 1989). According to the court in *Phillips*:

> Defendants' misdirected approach here is the same as that improperly relied upon by the PTO in *Hogan*. Defendants do not, as they cannot, argue that the 1953 specification fails to enable one skilled in the art to practice the claimed invention. That the '851 claim may cover a later version of the claimed composition (crystalline polypropylene with higher intrinsic viscosity and average molecular weight) relates to infringement, not to patentability. See *In re Hogan*, 559 F.2d at 607, 194 U.S.P.Q. at 538. To hold differently would, in the words of *Hogan*, "impose an impossible burden on inventors and thus on the patent system." 559 F.2d at 606, 194 U.S.P.Q. at 537.

865 F.2d at 1251-52. Note that the radically new catalysts here were the famous Ziegler catalysts, a breakthrough development in chemical process technology useful in a number of applications, especially the manufacture of synthetic fibers.

Several interesting points follow from *Phillips*. First, it helps explain an interesting conundrum: that an invention may both be nonobvious over a preceding invention, yet infringe that invention. The conundrum arises because the nonobvious (improvement) invention must come within the claims of the preceding (basic) invention, and therefore that preceding invention must enable the improvement, as it must enable any embodiment falling within the claims. But how can an improvement simultaneously be enabled by a basic invention yet be nonobvious in light of that invention?

The answer is in the temporal disparity between enablement and nonobviousness. Enablement is measured as of a patent's filing date. Thus the basic invention will be judged enabling if its teachings are sufficient to enable its claims as of the filing date. Nonobviousness, on the other hand, is measured as of the date of invention. Thus the improvement will be nonobvious if it was an unpredictable advance as of *its* date of invention.

To understand why this temporal disparity matters, consider the example of a basic invention — call it the invention of fuzzballs. The first creator of fuzzballs will be allowed to claim as a product all fuzzballs, limited only by the prior art on fuzzballs. Let us imagine the patent application on the basic fuzzball invention is filed in Year 1. This application will be tested for enablement as of the Year 1 filing date. If the applicant enables the art to make "fuzzballs" — *as that term is understood as of the filing date* — the claim will be allowed. Thus, if the creator of fuzzballs recites in her specification only examples of fuzzballs made from wool and cotton, this in no way limits her claim. It is simply the case that, as of the filing date, these are the only known fuzzballs. So we say, not that she has enabled only fuzzballs made from these materials, but that she has enabled fuzzballs generally — it's just that the term "fuzzballs" only includes these two types, as far as anyone knows as of the filing date.

Now imagine a later improvement: the invention of fuzzballs made from synthetic fibers, by another inventor, in Year 2. If the synthetic fuzzballs are accused of infringement, how will a court rule? A natural defense for the inventor of synthetic fuzzballs will be that the first inventor's "all fuzzballs" claim is not enabled by her specification. And if the second inventor has received a patent on her improved fuzzballs, this will, in her opinion, bolster her argument. For how could her synthetic fuzzballs be both nonobvious over the basic fuzzball patent, and an infringement of that patent, at the same time?

The key is that the content of the term "fuzzball" is measured as of different dates. The claim of the first patent to "all fuzzballs" is measured as of the filing date for that patent. Since the improvement fits that phrase, as it was understood at that (earlier) date, the improvement is enabled. *See Phillips, supra.* The strange thing is that the inventive content of the improvement is measured as of its invention date (for purposes of nonobviousness; see § 103), but it is compared to the term in the claim to see if it corresponds as of the earlier date. That is, it's as if someone asked on the filing date in Year 1, "Could you make a fuzzball with this patent?" where fuzzballs are made only of wool and cotton. The answer on the filing date would be yes. But the key is: *We do not change the question when we ask it later.* So when the later inventor discovers that fuzzballs can be made with synthetic fibers, we do not ask whether the basic patent filed in Year 1 enables the making of *synthetic* fuzzballs. We continue to ask whether it enabled the making of all fuzzballs, where the content of the term fuzzballs is measured as of the date of the original invention.

Thus the definition of fuzzballs used in the question, "Did you enable the making of all fuzzballs?" does not change over time, while the real working content of the phrase does, of course, continue to change, reflecting the inevitable growth of fuzzball technology. In this way, contributions which expand our understanding of the term "fuzzballs" are patentable, yet the test of whether the original claim enables the making of "all fuzzballs" is frozen in time. Thus can a basic patent both enable a later invention, yet not make that invention obvious. This is, of course, the common situation of blocking patents. *See B.G. Corp. v. Walter Kidde & Co.*, 79 F.2d 20, 22 (2d Cir. 1935) (L. Hand, J.) ("It is true that [the inventor of the spark plug] did not foresee the particular adaptability of his plug to the airplane .... Nevertheless, he did not shoot in the dark; he laid down with perfect certainty what he wished to accomplish and how .... [H]e is not charged with a prophetic understanding of the entire field of its usefulness."); *Amerace Corp. v. Ferro Corp.*, 532 F. Supp. 1188, 1201-02, 213 U.S.P.Q. (BNA) 1099, 1109-10 (N.D. Tex. 1982). An improvement patent can prevent a basic patent holder from practicing the particular improved feature claimed in the improvement (or subservient) patent because a patent grant is a right to *exclude*, not an affirmative right to practice an invention. *See* 35 U.S.C. § 154 (1988). Thus the dominant patentee can exclude the subservient patentee from practicing her invention at all, and the subservient patentee can exclude the dominant patentee from practicing her specific improved feature. *See Atlas Powder*, 750 F.2d at 1580, 224 U.S.P.Q. at 416; *Ziegler v. Phillips Petr. Co.*, 483 F.2d 858, 871-72, 177 U.S.P.Q. (BNA) 481, 489-90 (5th Cir.), *cert. denied*, 414 U.S. 1079, 180 U.S.P.Q. (BNA) 1 (1973); *cf. Cantrell v. Wallick*, 117 U.S. 689, 694 (1886) (Where one patent is an improvement on another patent, "neither of the two patentees can lawfully use the invention of the other without the other's consent."); *Cochrane v. Deener*, 94 U.S. 780, 787 (1877) ("One invention may include within it many others, and each and all may be valid at the same time.").

It is interesting to note how the enablement doctrine has served the development of a regime of property rights that in a rough way calibrates the reward to the inventive contribution. When a basic invention fully enables a later one, i.e., makes the later one predictable as of the filing date of the patent on the earlier one, the later one receives no patent (because it is obvious) and directly infringes the earlier one. This is the strongest form of property right, and might be termed "complete domination." The concept of "reasonable predictability" from cases such as *Wands* explains the result. It follows from this that an invention claimed in an improvement patent filed the same day as a basic patent cannot be both enabled by the basic patent and nonobvious over it, since in this case there is no "temporal disparity." If the basic patent enables as of that date — i.e., makes the improvement reasonably predictable — then the improvement cannot be nonobvious — i.e., not unpredictable in light of the basic patent.

The intermediate case is illustrated by *Phillips* or perhaps *Atlas Powder*. Here the later invention is said to be nonobvious in light of the first, so it merits an independent (though subservient) improvement patent. The temporal disparity between nonobviousness and enablement explains how the later invention can be enabled yet nonobvious in light of the earlier patented invention. This is an interim case; note how enablement doctrine adjusts to the need for a distinct, yet distinctly subservient, property right for the improvement invention. (Note too how this doctrine helps set up a situation where the two inventors are encouraged to bargain towards a license, a topic discussed in Chapter 11.)

The final case is where the "improvement" is really quite beyond the scope of the original invention altogether. In such a case, the improvement will not even be describable in the terms used in the original patent's claims. *See Texas Instruments v. United States Int'l Trade Comm'n*, 846 F.2d 1369, 1372, 6 U.S.P.Q.2d (BNA) 1886, 1889 (Fed. Cir. 1988), for a close call on this issue. This case illustrates that only the doctrine of equivalents will be capable of bringing the improvement within the scope of the original patent. And it has been suggested that the magnitude of the improvement's technological achievement be considered in determining infringement. *See Texas Instruments, supra*; Merges & Nelson, *On the Complex Economics of Patent Scope*, 90 COLUM. L. REV. 839 (1990). An interesting variant on this last case is where the improvement literally falls within the terms of the claim, but is in fact a very significant step forward from the invention claimed. This is an occasion for the "reverse doctrine of equivalents" discussed in Chapter 8.

b. Some Comparative Notes on Enablement

After noting that the "disclosure theory" is recognized as the leading justification for patents in Japan, a leading treatise on Japanese patent law summarizes the Japanese approach to enablement:

> In Japan, the domestic applicant tends towards the drafting of a relatively brief disclosure of the invention. This is not due to any motive to "hide" aspects of how to make and use the invention, but is more from the standpoint that making a detailed, technically beautiful description takes *time*. In a first-to-file system, an applicant who painstakingly drafts his application only to find that his competitor has raced to the Patent Office ... is hardly rewarded for such noble efforts of disclosure ....

T. TANABE & H. WEGNER, JAPANESE PATENT LAW § 420 (1979).

Although the Japanese enablement requirement is quite liberal, the authors suggest caution in cutting down the disclosure when an application is translated into Japanese and filed in Japan. One very good reason is that the addition of working examples after the initial filing may lead to the Japanese equivalent of prosecution history estoppel (see Chapter 8); the added examples may be taken as admissions that the originally filed application does not cover those embodiments, thus leading to a finding of noninfringement. *Id.*, at § 421.

In Europe, the rules on disclosure are quite similar to those in the U.S. For instance, in keeping with cases such as *Wands*, disclosure is measured by the standard of one skilled in the relevant art. *See* European Patent Convention, Article 83; *Alpha-interferons/Biogen*, 1989, No. 11 OFFIC. J. EUR. PAT. OFF. 1, Case No. T 301/87 (Eur. Pat. Off. Tech. Bd. App., 16 Feb. 1989) (invention sufficiently disclosed if at least one way of carrying out invention is indicated in specification; reproducibility of working examples not absolutely required); Szabo, *Patent Protection of Biotechnological Inventions — European Perspectives*, 21 INT'L REV. INDUS. PROP. & COPYRIGHT L. 468, 470 (1990) (EPO Board of Appeals decisions on "sufficiency of disclosure" generally hold that unavailability of starting materials or genetic precursors is not a reason to deny patents, as long as the selection procedure is described adequately).

The only truly distinctive feature of European enablement doctrine is its insistence that an inventor explicitly identify the problem she has solved in her specification. But even this requirement is in practice folded into the other, conventional, requirements such as patentable subject matter and inventive step. It has been held, for instance, that an application for an otherwise patentable invention may not be rejected for failure to state the problem solved, since an examiner must be able to infer a technical problem and solution from the existence of a patentable invention. *Containers/ICI*, 1982, No. 6 OFFIC. J. EUR. PAT. OFF. 211 (Eur. Pat. Off. Tech. Bd. App., 28 Oct. 1981).

C. THE WRITTEN DESCRIPTION REQUIREMENT

Cases involving the written description requirement of Patent Act § 112 are deeply intertwined with issues of priority, covered in § 120, and the question of "new matter," the subject of § 132. These sections read as follows:

§ 120. Benefit of Earlier Filing Date in the United States

An application for patent for an invention disclosed in the manner provided by the first paragraph of section 112 of this title in an application previously filed in the United States ..., which is filed by an inventor or inventors named in the previously filed application shall have the same effect as to such invention, as though filed on the date of the prior application, if filed before the patenting or abandonment of or termination of proceedings on the first application or on an application similarly entitled to the benefit of the filing date of the first application and if it contains a specific reference to the earlier filed application.

§ 132. Notice of rejection; reexamination

Whenever, on examination, any claim for a patent is rejected, or any objection or requirement made, the Commissioner shall notify the applicant thereof, stating the reasons for such rejection, or objection or requirement, together with such information and references as may be useful in judging of the propriety of continuing the prosecution of his application; and if after receiving such notice, the applicant persists in his claim for a patent, with or without amendment, the application shall be reexamined. No amendment shall introduce new matter into the disclosure of the invention.

In the case that follows, which is typical of written description cases, the issue is whether the first-filed application — the "priority application" — contains a disclosure adequate to support the claims contained in the patent that eventually issued.

VAS-CATH INC. v. MAHURKAR

935 F.2d 1555, 19 U.S.P.Q.2d 1111 (Fed. Cir. 1991)

[Plaintiff sued for a declaration that defendant Mahurkar's two utility patents were invalid.] In reaching its decision, the district court concluded that none of the twenty one claims of the two utility patents was entitled, under 35 U.S.C. § 120, to the benefit of the filing date of Mahurkar's earlier-filed United States design patent application ('081 design application), which comprised the same drawings as the utility patents, because the design application did not provide a "written description of the invention" as required by 35 U.S.C. § 112, first paragraph. We reverse the grant of summary judgment [of invalidity] with respect to all claims.

Mahurkar's catheter comprises a pair of tubes (lumens) designed to allow blood to be removed from an artery, processed in an apparatus that removes impurities, and returned close to the place of removal. Prior art catheters utilized concentric circular lumens, while Mahurkar's employs joined semi-circular tubes that come to a single tapered tip. Advantageously, the puncture area of Mahurkar's semicircular catheter is 42% less than that of a coaxial catheter carrying the same quantity of blood, and its conical tip yields low rates of injury to the blood. The prior art coaxial catheters are now obsolete; Mahurkar's catheters appear to represent more than half of the world's sales.

[The examiner recognized Mahurkar's design patent filing date as the priority date for his two utility patent applications. Plaintiff Vas-Cath's suit for invalidity was based on defendant's Canadian industrial patent application, which issued more than one year prior to Mahurkar's two U.S. utility patent applications and was therefore in the prior art as to the patents at issue in this case.] Vas-Cath's complaint alleged, inter alia, that the '329 and '141 patents [defendant's two U.S. utility patents] were both invalid as anticipated under 35 U.S.C. § 102(b) by [the] Canadian [design patent]. Vas-Cath's anticipation theory was premised on the argument that the '329 and '141 patents were not entitled under 35 U.S.C. § 120 to the filing date of the '081 design application because its drawings did not provide an adequate "written description" of the claimed invention as required by 35 U.S.C. § 112, first paragraph.

For purposes of the summary judgment motion, Mahurkar conceded that, if he could not antedate it, [the] Canadian [design patent] would represent an enabling and thus anticipating § 102(b) reference against the claims of his '329 and '141 utility patents. Thus, the question before the district court was whether the disclosure of the '081 design application, namely, the drawings without more, adequately meets the "written description" requirement also contained in § 112, first paragraph, so as to entitle Mahurkar to the benefit of the 1982 filing date of the '081 design application for his two utility patents and thereby antedate [the] Canadian [design patent].

The "Written Description" Requirement of § 112

The cases indicate that the "written description" requirement most often comes into play where claims not presented in the application when filed are presented thereafter. Alternatively, patent applicants often seek the benefit of the filing date of an earlier-filed foreign or United States application under 35 U.S.C. § 119 or

35 U.S.C. § 120, respectively, for claims of a later-filed application. The question raised by these situations is most often phrased as whether the application provides "adequate support" for the claim(s) at issue; it has also been analyzed in terms of "new matter" under 35 U.S.C. § 132. The "written description" question similarly arises in the interference context, where the issue is whether the specification of one party to the interference can support the claim(s) corresponding to the count(s) at issue, i.e., whether that party "can make the claim" corresponding to the interference count.

One may wonder what purpose a separate "written description" requirement serves, when the second paragraph of § 112 expressly requires that the applicant conclude his specification "with one or more claims particularly pointing out and distinctly claiming the subject matter which the applicant regards as his invention."

One explanation is historical: the "written description" requirement was a part of the patent statutes at a time before claims were required. A case in point is *Evans v. Eaton*, 20 U.S. (7 Wheat.) 356, 5 L. Ed. 472 (1822), in which the Supreme Court affirmed the circuit court's decision that the plaintiff's patent was "deficient," and that the plaintiff could not recover for infringement thereunder. The patent laws then in effect, namely the Patent Act of 1793, did not require claims, but did require, in [the] 3d section, that the patent applicant "deliver a written description of his invention, and of the manner of using, or process of compounding, the same, in such full, clear and exact terms, as to distinguish the same from all things before known, and to enable any person skilled in the art or science of which it is a branch, or with which it is most nearly connected, to make, compound and use the same...." *Id.* at 430. In view of this language, the Court concluded that the specification of a patent had two objects, the first of which was "to enable artisans to make and use [the invention]...." *Id.* at 433. The second object of the specification was to

> put the public in possession of what the party claims as his own invention, so as to ascertain if he claims anything that is in common use, or is already known, and to guard against prejudice or injury from the use of an invention which the party may otherwise innocently suppose not to be patented. It is, therefore, for the purpose of warning an innocent purchaser, or other person using a machine, of his infringement of the patent; and at the same time, of taking from the inventor the means of practising upon the credulity or the fears of other persons, by pretending that his invention is more than what it really is, or different from its ostensible objects, that the patentee is required to distinguish his invention in his specification.

Id. at 434.

A second, policy-based rationale for the inclusion in § 112 of both the first paragraph "written description" and the second paragraph "definiteness" requirements was set forth in *Rengo Co. v. Molins Mach. Co.*, 657 F.2d 535, 551, 211 U.S.P.Q. 303, 321 (3d Cir.), *cert. denied*, 454 U.S. 1055 (1981):

[The written description and definiteness standards,] while complementary, approach a similar problem from different directions. Adequate description of the invention guards against the inventor's overreaching by insisting that he recount his invention in such detail that his future claims can be determined to be encompassed within his original creation. The definiteness requirement shapes the future conduct of persons other than the inventor, by insisting that they receive notice of the scope of the patented device.

With respect to the first paragraph of § 112 the severability of its "written description" provision from its enablement ("make and use") provision was recognized by this court's predecessor, the Court of Customs and Patent Appeals, as early as *In re Ruschig*, 379 F.2d 990, 154 U.S.P.Q. 118 (C.C.P.A. 1967). The issue [in that case], as the court saw it, was one of fact: "Does the specification convey clearly to those skilled in the art, to whom it is addressed, in any way, the information that appellants invented that specific [claimed] compound?" *Id.* at 996, 154 U.S.P.Q. at 123.

In a 1971 case again involving chemical subject matter, the court expressly stated that "it is possible for a specification to enable the practice of an invention as broadly as it is claimed, and still not describe that invention." *In re DiLeone*, 436 F.2d 1404, 1405, 168 U.S.P.Q. 592, 593 (C.C.P.A. 1971). As an example, the court posited the situation "where the specification discusses only compound *A* and contains no broadening language of any kind. This might very well enable one skilled in the art to make and use compounds *B* and *C*; yet the class consisting of *A*, *B* and *C* has not been described." *Id.* at 1405 n.1, 168 U.S.P.Q. 593 n.1.

Since its inception, the Court of Appeals for the Federal Circuit has frequently addressed the "written description" requirement of § 112. A fairly uniform standard for determining compliance with the "written description" requirement has been maintained throughout: "Although [the applicant] does not have to describe exactly the subject matter claimed, ... the description must clearly allow persons of ordinary skill in the art to recognize that [he or she] invented what is claimed." *In re Gosteli*, 872 F.2d 1008, 1012, 10 U.S.P.Q.2d 1614, 1618 (Fed. Cir. 1989) (citations omitted).

The purpose of the "written description" requirement is broader than to merely explain how to "make and use"; the applicant must also convey with reasonable clarity to those skilled in the art that, as of the filing date sought, he or she was in possession of the invention. The invention is, for purposes of the "written description" inquiry, whatever is now claimed.

The District Court's Analysis

We agree with the district court's conclusion that drawings alone may be sufficient to provide the "written description of the invention" required by § 112, first paragraph.

Whether the drawings are those of a design application or a utility application is not determinative, although in most cases the latter are much more detailed. In the instant case, however, the design drawings are substantially identical to the utility application drawings.

We find the district court's concern with "what the invention is" misplaced, and its requirement that the '081 drawings "describe what is novel or important" legal error. There is "no legally recognizable or protected 'essential' element, 'gist' or 'heart' of the invention in a combination patent." *Aro Mfg. Co. v. Convertible Top Replacement Co.*, 365 U.S. 336, 345, 81 S. Ct. 599, 604, 5 L. Ed. 2d 592 (1961). "The invention" is defined by the claims on appeal. The instant claims do not recite only a pair of semi-circular lumens, or a conical tip, or a ratio at which the tip tapers, or the shape, size, and placement of the inlets and outlets; they claim a double lumen catheter having a combination of those features. That combination invention is what the '081 drawings show. As the district court itself recognized, "what Mahurkar eventually patented is exactly what the pictures in serial '081 show."

We find the "range of variation" question, much emphasized by the parties, more troublesome. The district court stated that "although Mahurkar's patents use the same diagrams, [the claims] contain limitations that did not follow ineluctably [i.e., inevitably] from the diagrams." As an example, the court stated (presumably with respect to independent claims 1 and 7 of the '329 patent) that the utility patents claim a return lumen that is "substantially greater than one-half but substantially less than a full diameter" after it makes the transition from semi-circular to circular cross-section, and the drawings of serial '081 fall in this range. But until the utility application was filed, nothing established that [the lumen] had to — for that matter that the utility patent would claim anything other than the precise ratio in the diagrams. Mahurkar argues that one of ordinary skill in this art, looking at the '081 drawings, would be able to derive the claimed range.

[The district court noted that several later patents issued to Mahurkar on improvements in the catheter, namely refinements of the dimensions of his device.] The district court erred in taking Mahurkar's other patents into account. Mahurkar's later patenting of inventions involving different range limitations is irrelevant to the issue at hand. Application sufficiency under § 112, first paragraph, must be judged as of the filing date.

United States Steel Corp. v. Phillips Petroleum Co.

The court further erred in applying a legal standard that essentially required the drawings of the '081 design application to necessarily exclude all diameters other than those within the claimed range. We question whether any drawing could ever do so. At least with respect to independent claims 1 and 7 of the '329 patent and claims depending therefrom, the proper test is whether the drawings conveyed with reasonable clarity to those of ordinary skill that Mahurkar had in fact invented the catheter recited in those claims, having (among several other limitations) a return lumen diameter substantially less than 1.0 but substantially greater than 0.5 times the diameter of the combined lumens. Consideration of what the drawings conveyed to persons of ordinary skill is essential. [Reversed and remanded.]

NOTES

1. From *Permutit v. Graver Corp.*, 284 U.S. 52 (1931), at 58:

> As the patentee has thus failed to give in the specification "a written description" and has likewise failed particularly to point out and distinctly claim the free zeolite bed, as "the part, improvement, or combination which he claims as his invention or discovery," the patent is void.

On drawings:

> Moreover, while drawings may be referred to for illustration and may be used as an aid in interpreting the specification or claim, they are of no avail where there is an entire absence of description of the alleged invention, or a failure to claim it.

284 U.S. at 60. Other older authority states the same basic theme, that adequate disclosure is necessary to support patentability. *See, e.g., Tyler v. Boston*, 7 Wall (74 U.S.) 327 (1869); *Gill v. Wells*, 22 Wall. (89 U.S.) 1 (1874). *See generally* 2 W. ROBINSON, THE LAW OF PATENTS § 484, at 73 (1890), where the author states:

> According to the statutes, the Description must contain full explanations of three different subjects: the invention itself; the manner of making it; and the mode of putting it to practical use, a complete knowledge upon all these points being necessary to render the invention available to the public without further experiment or exercise of inventive skill.

2. *Update.* On remand, Judge Frank Easterbrook of the Seventh Circuit, sitting by designation, had this to say about the trial evidence on the written description defense:

> Because a "specification is directed to one skilled in the art," *Hayes Microcomputer Products*, 982 F.2d [1527,] at 1533 [(Fed. Cir. 1992)], I must decide whether such a person would understand the drawings of the design application as showing that Mahurkar was in possession, when he filed the design application, of the features claimed in the utility application. The answer to that question must be "yes." The drawings accompanying the design and utility applications are identical (except for the addition of arrows and numbers to the utility drawings). The utility application simply lays out the details of what the design drawings show — to be precise, the utility claims narrate what features of the drawings are important, without adding

anything. I find that Mahurkar was in possession of the whole invention when he filed the design applications, and the drawings in the design application would have enabled a person of ordinary skill in the art to draft the written claims that appeared in the design application.

What the drawings show to a person skilled in the art is a question of fact, on which there was extensive testimony at trial. Mahurkar testified that any fool could see the import of the drawings — they are so clear that even a judge can tell what is going on. Tr. 127-28. In my first published opinion I wrote that Mahurkar plainly had possession of the invention and showed that invention in the drawings — "what Mahurkar eventually patented is exactly what the pictures in [the design applications] show," 745 F. Supp. at 523 — but I did not think them legally sufficient.

But of course judges and other amateurs in this technical field are not the right audience. During the trial each of Mahurkar's three experts in catheter design stepped through each of the elements in each claim of the '968 and '141 patents. Each expert was asked whether the claim could be seen in the design drawings. Each answered yes. Mahurkar's lawyers produced charts relating each element of each independent claim to a specific part of the drawings. The experts stated that this correspondence was accurate. I credit those answers, which when combined with the Federal Circuit's legal standard means that the design applications satisfy the written description requirement of § 112. Examiner Truluck, a person of ordinary skill in the art of catheter design, must have seen it too, for he allowed the utility application as a continuation of the design application.

In sum, I answer the questions posed by the Federal Circuit with the finding of fact that the design drawings clearly show that Mahurkar possessed the invention claimed in the '968 patent as of the date of the design filing and that the drawings conveyed with reasonable clarity to those of ordinary skill in the art that Mahurkar in fact invented the catheter recited in the utility claims ....

In re Mahurkar Double Lumen Hemodialysis Catheter Patent Litig., 831 F. Supp. 1354, 1361-62, 28 U.S.P.Q.2d 1801 (N.D. Ill. 1993) (Easterbrook, J., by designation).

3. *No Visible Means of Support?* In *Wang Labs., Inc. v. Toshiba, Inc.*, 993 F.2d 858, 865-66, 26 U.S.P.Q.2d 1767 (Fed. Cir. 1993), Judge Lourie, writing for a three-judge panel, addressed a written description defense:

[The patentee held two patents on single in-line memory modules (SIMMs) having eight data memory chips. One limitation in several of the issued claims recited "support means." Defendants Toshiba and NEC seized on this claim limitation as the basis of a written description defense.]

According to [defendant] NEC, the recitation of "support means for supporting the memory module at an angle with respect to the printed circuit motherboard" was not supported by the original Clayton application, and therefore the claims in both patents are invalid. NEC notes that "support means" was not recited in the original claims, but was added by amendment. It alleges that the specification describes the leads of the memory modules as having only an electrical function, not a mechanical, support function.

A patent specification is directed to one of ordinary skill in the art. It is also clear that "drawings alone may provide a 'written description' of an invention as required by § 112." *Vas-Cath*, 935 F.2d at 1565, 19 U.S.P.Q.2d at 1118. Dr. Frey testified that Figure 2 "show[s] terminals as leads, which are means of supporting the module." Additionally, Dr. Frey stated, when discussing whether leadless SIMMs are disclosed in the patents, that a person of ordinary skill in the art would know that a leadless SIMM includes a row of terminals "to mount and support that module." He went on to state that "it's the edge of the card and the terminals that support the module." The inventor, Mr. Clayton, also testified that on leaded SIMMs, the leads themselves are the support means, and that on leadless SIMMs, the bottom row of terminals constitutes the support means. Thus, there is substantial evidence in the record to support the conclusion that the support means element is adequately described in the specification by the disclosure of both leads and the terminal edge of the modules. NEC has not shown that the district court's denial of JNOV on the issue of failure to meet the written description requirement was incorrect.

4. For detailed discussions of written description issues, see Rollins, *35 U.S.C. 120 — The Description Requirement*, 64 J. PAT. OFF. SOC'Y 656 (1982); Walterscheid, *Insufficient Disclosure Rejections (Part III)*, 62 J. PAT. OFF. SOC'Y 261 (1980).

***Kennecott Corp. v. Kyocera International, Inc.*, 835 F.2d 1419, 5 U.S.P.Q.2d** (BNA) 1194 (Fed. Cir. 1987). [In its infringement suit against defendant Kyocera, plaintiff Kennecott stipulated that its '299 patent was invalid unless it had the benefit of the 1975 filing date of its '954 application, since sales activities in 1977 occurred more than one year prior to the filing of a continuation-in-part application in 1978. The patent claimed ceramic objects made from silicon carbide grains having a special microstructure — "equiaxed microstructure," meaning short, stubby "nonelongated" submicron size grains. The claims define the grains as having a ratio of maximum to minimum dimensions of not greater than 3:1.]

Pertinent undisputed or conceded facts include the following:

the high (over 95%) alpha silicon carbide ceramic body that is described in the '954 application has an equiaxed microstructure;

the '954 application does not mention the equiaxed microstructure of the high-alpha silicon carbide ceramic body, nor state the requirements for forming such microstructure;

the inventors knew that the high-alpha silicon carbide ceramic body had an equiaxed microstructure, and it was known that ceramics from high-alpha silicon carbide could have this structure;

examples 1-30 in the '954 application, all the examples using high-alpha silicon carbide, all produce a ceramic body having an equiaxed microstructure;

the method set forth in the '954 application using the high-alpha silicon carbide invariably produces a ceramic product having an equiaxed microstructure.

Kennecott asserts that the equiaxed microstructure is inherent in the structure produced in the '954 application, and that the '299 claims, which specifically name the equiaxed structure, therefore enjoy the benefit of the earlier filing date.

It was undisputed that the only written description in the '299 application that was not present in the original '954 disclosure was the description and pictures of the product's microstructure. Kennecott points to authority that the added description of a property of a previously disclosed product does not deprive claims to that product of the benefit of a prior disclosure of the product. Kyocera responds that because the '954 specification is silent as to the microstructure of the product, and because one would not know whether the product had an equiaxed microstructure merely by reading the specification, the specification is inadequate in law to support claims that require an equiaxed microstructure.

On the issue of sufficiency of the earlier disclosure, the body of precedent teaches that the legal conclusion depends on the particular facts. In *In re Edwards* [, 568 F.2d 1349, 1351, 196 U.S.P.Q. (BNA) 465, 467 (C.C.P.A. 1978)] the court considered a chemical compound that was not described in the earlier application, and stated that the earlier and later applications need not use the identical words, if the earlier application shows the subject matter that is claimed in the later application, with adequate direction as to how to obtain it. The court observed that the chemical reactions described in the earlier filing "will inherently produce, as the predominant component, the [later claimed] compound." 568 F.2d at 1352, 196 U.S.P.Q. at 467. The facts in *Edwards* are strongly analogous to those herein, for Kennecott's '954 examples 1-30 all produce a ceramic that has an equiaxed structure.

The facts before us ... are analogous to those discussed in *In re Reynolds*, 443 F.2d 384, 170 U.S.P.Q. 94 (C.C.P.A. 1971). In *Reynolds* the question was whether words describing a function that was inherent in the claimed product could be added to the specification by amendment, or whether such description was "new matter." ... It was concluded that the express description of the inherent property, since not "new matter," could be added to the specification with effect as of the original filing date.

... It was conceded that anyone with a microscope would see the microstructure of the product of the '954 application. The disclosure in a subsequent patent application of an inherent property of a product does not deprive that product of the benefit of an earlier filing date. [Reversed.]

NOTES

1. *Related Case.* In *In re Kaslow*, 707 F.2d 1366, 217 U.S.P.Q. (BNA) 1089 (Fed. Cir. 1983), the applicant attempted to overcome an obviousness rejection of his application claiming a computerized system for processing supermarket discount coupons. In his original specification, the applicant taught the use of computers to scan the digital product code on coupons, compare the code to the codes stored in the cash register for that customer's purchases, and make appropriate deductions from the purchase price. Since these steps were obvious in light of prior art systems, according to the court

> the appellant amended his claims to emphasize that the memory at each supermarket shall identify discount coupons according to individual manu-facturer and transmit this data from each supermarket to a central computer in order to provide an audit. This procedure would therefore eliminate the need for clearinghouses and prevent retailer fraud.

707 F.2d at 1371 (referring to the fraud committed by some supermarkets by, e.g., submitting coupons for reimbursement that had never actually been used to buy products). The court noted that although the original specification stated that "the summarized data may include data relating to the coupons honored in the various stores linked to [a] central computer, so that a check may be made on the overall volume of coupon traffic and the relative trading in of coupons issued by various manufacturers,"

> there is a considerable difference between simplifying auditing procedures [as the specification describes] and providing an audit. As pointed out by the examiner, an audit requires examination and verification of records for accuracy. The present invention, as disclosed, may aid in the auditing process, but it does not provide an audit.

707 F.2d at 1372. The court therefore held that the addition of the phrase "to provide an audit" to the claims was not supported by the original specification.

The court did not address whether the auditing step was an inherent property of the centralized computer system claimed. What do you think? Should it matter whether the perhaps inherent feature is the "point of novelty" which distinguishes the (amended) claimed invention from the prior art?

2. *Obviousness Standard for Written Description?* In *In re DiLeone (DiLeone I)*, 436 F.2d 1404, 1406-07 (C.C.P.A. 1971), Judge Baldwin, in dissent, stated

> [the Patent Office and examiner] have disputed the fact that *the scope of appellants' invention would be obvious from the language of the descrip-*

tion.... Keeping in mind the well known unpredictability of the chemical sciences, I find that the examiner's objections were reasonable. Beyond asserting that they are entitled to the broad claims they are seeking, appellants have not contradicted this position. Feeling, as I do, that the description requirement should serve to assure that one of ordinary skill in the pertinent art will in fact, be taught by a specification disclosure, I conclude that the disclosure before us does not adequately describe the subject matter being claimed.

(Emphasis added.)

This suggestion is echoed in *In re Smythe*, 480 F.2d 1376, 1383, 178 U.S.P.Q. (BNA) 279 (C.C.P.A. 1973), where the court rejected an argument that the applicant's claims to a sample analyzer using an "inert fluid" medium to separate ("segmentize") components of a sample were invalid because the original specification contained references only to "air or other gas" media. (In technical terms, "fluid" includes liquids while "gas" of course does not; thus the claims were indeed broader than the original specification.) The court provided an instructive statement on why the written description requirement was met:

> We are not saying that the disclosure of "air or other gas which is inert to the liquid" sample by itself is a description of the use of all "inert fluid" media. Rather, it is the description of the properties and functions of the "air or other gas" segmentizing medium described in appellants' specification which would suggest to a person skilled in the art that appellants' invention includes the use of "inert fluid" broadly. The Kessler patent is only some additional evidence of the knowledge of one skilled in the automatic sample analysis art, and as such it supports appellants' position that to such persons appellants' description conveys the idea of using inert fluids broadly.
>
> A hypothetical situation may make our point clear. If the original specification of a patent application on the scales of justice disclosed only a 1-pound "lead weight" as a counterbalance to determine the weight of a pound of flesh, we do not believe the applicant should be prevented, by the so-called "description requirement" of the first paragraph of § 112, or the prohibition against new matter of § 132, from later claiming the counterbalance as a "metal weight" or simply as a 1-pound "weight," although both "metal weight" and "weight" would indeed be progressively broader than "lead weight," including even such an undisclosed, but obviously art-recognized equivalent, "weight" as a pound of feathers. The broader claim language would be permitted because the description of the use and function of the lead weight as a scale [implied such substitutes].

But see In re Winkhaus, 527 F.2d 637, 640, 188 U.S.P.Q. (BNA) 129, 131 (C.C.P.A. 1975), ("That a person skilled in the art might realize from reading the disclosure that such a step is possible is not a sufficient indication to that person that that step is part of appellants' invention. Such an indication is the least that is required for a description of the invention under the first paragraph of § 112."); *In re Barker*, 559 F.2d 588, 593, 194 U.S.P.Q. (BNA) 470 (C.C.P.A. 1977) ("motivation and enablement are not the issues; description of the invention is").

3. *Inherency in Anticipation Context.* For discussion of inherency in the anticipation context, see Chapter 4, Section B.3, *Tilghman v. Proctor*, *In re Fermi*, and other cases. If one were to apply the standard for anticipation cases such as *Tilghman v. Proctor* to the preceding case, how would it be decided? Recall these factors: (1) knowledge of nature and properties of the device inherently containing the disputed subject matter; (2) reproducibility of the inherent structure or property.

COMMENT ON THE WRITTEN DESCRIPTION REQUIREMENT

There has been dispute concerning the written description requirement since its refinement and reemergence in the CCPA. *See* 2 DONALD CHISUM, PATENTS § 7.04[1][a] (1978 & Supp. 1996). The difficulty has always been to avoid two pitfalls: (1) to keep the requirement distinct from enablement, which has largely been achieved by shifting the focus from the broad sweep of the applicant's disclosure to the more narrow issue of his or her invention; and (2) to distinguish the description of the invention from the claims to the invention. The upshot of the doctrine's application is that the applicant must not only enable all subject matter later claimed but must also *describe* some subset of the disclosed information with more particularity in order to preserve the right to later claim some or all of the information in that subset.

The written description requirement creates an additional and more stringent disclosure requirement which is applied *on top of* the normal enablement requirement. Claim amendments must now not only be supported by the general enablement requirement in § 112 ¶ 6 but must also find a somewhat specific antecedent in the original specification indicating that the applicant has "possession" of the later-claimed subject matter. How specific? Consider two cases.

In *In re Wertheim*, 541 F.2d 257, 191 U.S.P.Q. 90 (C.C.P.A. 1976), the CCPA held that an original specification describing a process for freeze-drying coffee, yielding a solid concentration in the range of "25% – 60%" and giving specific examples of 36% and 50% failed to meet the written description test for later claims including a range of "at least 35%." In *Ralston Purina Co. v. Far-Mar-Co., Inc.*, 586 F. Supp. 1176 (D. Kan. 1984), *aff'd in part & rev'd in part*, 772 F.2d 1570, 227 U.S.P.Q. 177 (Fed. Cir. 1985), however, the Federal Circuit upheld several trial court findings that appear to push the limits of the doctrine. For example, the parent specification discloses that soybean meal "having a protein content of approximately 50% is the preferred meal component," and the claims as issued included "protein meal of at least about that of solvent extracted soybean meal" [i.e., 50%]. Likewise, the parent specification discloses that the subject mixture must be exposed to heat, which in Example 1 is said to be in the range of 212-380 degrees Fahrenheit; the claims included limitations such as "in excess of 212 degrees F." and "at least about 212 degrees F." Finally, the specification listed examples whose total moisture content was about 36%, and the court allowed claims to soy meal with total moisture of "at least about 25%."

The point of the case comparison is not to illustrate that individual cases pose difficult problems under § 112. This is to be expected. It is rather to demonstrate the difficulty of applying a standard that requires disclosure beyond that of the ordinary enablement requirement of § 112, and yet short of a requirement of actual claiming.

Coupled with the inherent difficulties of applying the test is the underlying question: what purpose is served by the written description requirement? The usual argument — that it gives notice to competitors concerning the scope of the applicant's intended claim scope — seems to miss the fact that parent patent applications are not disclosed. Currently, only issued patents are. Why require the disclosure of something that only later will become relevant? There is no chance of detrimental competitor reliance: all a competitor can realistically rely on are the claims, as present in the issued patents. Indeed, the rule against broadening reissues more than two years after a patent's issue date adequately addresses the reliance question. And, of course, the regular enablement requirement seeks to relate patent scope to the underlying value of the patentee's disclosure.

D. DEFINITE CLAIMS

The second paragraph of 35 U.S.C. § 112 reads:

> [¶ 2] The specification shall conclude with one or more claims particularly pointing out and distinctly claiming the subject matter which the applicant regards as his invention.

A good explanation of the rationale behind the second paragraph can be found in Justice Brandeis' opinion in *Permutit v. Graver Corp.*:

> The statute requires the patentee not only to explain the principle of his apparatus and to describe it in such terms that any person skilled in the art to which it appertains may construct and use it after the expiration of the patent, but also to inform the public during the life of the patent of the limits of the monopoly asserted, so that it may be known which features may be safely used or manufactured without a license and which may not.

284 U.S. 52 (1931), at 60.

Claims that are indefinite, in other words, do not give clear warning about the patentee's property rights. They fail to inform passersby whether they are trespassing or keeping a safe distance. Further, if patentees are allowed to be vague, they will have an incentive to do so, since vague claims will increase the de facto scope of a patent by forcing competitors to expand the "safe distance" they keep from the patentee's turf (claims). *See General Elec. Co. v. Wabash Appliance Corp.*, 304 U.S. 364 (1938) (rule requiring definite claims seeks to guard against unreasonable advantages to patentee and disadvantages to others arising from uncertainty concerning their rights).

This principle has deep roots. The Supreme Court, in *Evans v. Eaton*, 20 U.S. (7 Wheat.) 161, 5 L. Ed. 472 (1822), interpreted the disclosure section of the 1793 statute as having two purposes: (1) to make known the manner of constructing the invention in order to enable artisans to make and use it, and (2) to put the public in possession of what the party claims as his own invention in order to ascertain whether he claims anything in common use, or already known, and to protect the public from an inventor "pretending that his invention is more than what it really is, or different from its ostensible objects ...." *Id.* at 196.

These two policies have been carried forward into the present Patent Act. *In re Borkowski*, 422 F.2d 904, 909, 164 U.S.P.Q. (BNA) 642 (C.C.P.A. 1970), touched on the differences between non-enablement and lack of claim clarity:

> Thus, just as a claim which is of such breadth that it reads on subject matter disclosed in the prior art is rejected under 102 rather than under the second paragraph of 112, a claim which is of such breadth that it reads on subject matter as to which the specification is not "enabling" should be rejected under the first paragraph of 112 rather than the second. We do not intend hereby to suggest that rejections under 112 must be labeled "first paragraph" or "second paragraph." What we do suggest is that it should be made clear exactly which of the several requirements of 112 are thought not to have been met. Is the claim unclear or is the specification's disclosure inadequate to support it?

ORTHOKINETICS, INC. v. SAFETY TRAVEL CHAIRS, INC.

806 F.2d 1565, 1 U.S.P.Q.2d 1081 (Fed. Cir. 1986)

Orthokinetics appeals from [an] order granting a judgment notwithstanding the verdict (JNOV) holding that claims 1-5 of its U.S. Patent Re[issue] 30,867 ('867 patent) are invalid under 35 U.S.C. § 112. We reverse and remand with instructions to reinstate the jury verdicts.

Orthokinetics manufactures products for invalids and handicapped individuals, including pediatric wheelchairs. It is the assignee of the '867 patent reissued to Edward J. Gaffney (Gaffney) on February 16, 1982, entitled "Travel Chair."

The '867 reissue patent discloses a collapsible pediatric wheelchair which facilitates the placing of wheelchair-bound persons, particularly children, in and out of an automobile. Orthokinetics asserted infringement of claims 1 through 5 by Safety. Claim 1 reads:

> 1. In a wheel chair having a seat portion, a front leg portion, and a rear wheel assembly, the improvement wherein said front leg portion *is so dimen-*

sioned as to be insertable through the space between the doorframe of an automobile and one of the seats thereof whereby said front leg is placed in support relation to the automobile and will support the seat portion from the automobile in the course of subsequent movement of the wheel chair into the automobile, and the retractor means for assisting the attendant in retracting said rear wheel assembly upwardly independently of any change in the position of the front leg portion with respect to the seat portion while the front leg portion is supported on the automobile and to a position which clears the space beneath the rear end of the chair and permits the chair seat portion and retracted rear wheel assembly to be swung over and set upon said automobile seat.

[Emphasis added.]

Orthokinetics introduced the Travel Chair to the market in November of 1973. In 1978, Safety Travel Chairs, Inc. (STC) began to sell similar chairs.

The jury found that Safety failed to prove by clear and convincing evidence that the '867 patent was invalid because of claim language that does not particularly point out and distinctly claim the invention. 35 U.S.C. § 112, 2d ¶. The district court determined otherwise and granted Safety's motion for JNOV.

Claim 1, from which the rest of the claims depend, contains the limitation: "wherein said front leg portion is so dimensioned as to be insertable through the space between the doorframe of an automobile and one of the seats thereof." Noting the testimony of Orthokinetics' expert, Mr. Hobbs, who said the dimensions of the front legs depend upon the automobile the chair is designed to suit, the district court stated:

> [T]his testimony clearly and convincingly establishes that claim 1 of the ['867] patent does not describe the invention [fully]. The undisputed, specific testimony of Gaffney and Hobbs demonstrates that an individual desiring to build a non-infringing travel chair cannot tell whether that chair violates the ['867] patent until he constructs a model and tests the model on vehicles ranging from a Honda Civic to a Lincoln Continental to a Checker cab. Without those cars, "so dimensioned" is without meaning.

The foregoing statement [is] impermissible in law [because] it requires that claim 1 "describe" the invention, which is the role of the disclosure portion of the specification, not the role of the claims.

A decision on whether a claim is invalid under § 112, 2d ¶, requires a determination of whether those skilled in the art would understand what is claimed when the claim is read in light of the specification.

It is undisputed that the claims require that one desiring to build and use a travel chair must measure the space between the selected automobile's doorframe and its seat and then dimension the front legs of the travel chair so they will fit in that particular space in that particular automobile. Orthokinetics' witnesses, who were skilled in the art, testified that such a task is evident from the specification and that one of ordinary skill in the art would easily have been able to determine the appropriate dimensions. The jury had the right to credit that testimony and no reason exists for the district court to have simply discounted that testimony as "conclusory." The claims were intended to cover the use of the invention with various types of automobiles. That a particular chair on which the claims read may fit within some automobiles and not others is of no moment. The phrase "so dimensioned" is as accurate as the subject matter permits, automobiles being of various sizes. As long as those of ordinary skill in the art realized that the dimensions could be easily obtained, § 112, 2d ¶ requires nothing more. The patent law does not require that all possible lengths corresponding to the spaces in hundreds of different automobiles be listed in the patent, let alone that they be listed in the claims. Compliance with the second paragraph of § 112 is generally a question of law. On the record before us, we observe no failure of compliance with the statute, and thus no basis on § 112 grounds for disturbing the jury's verdict. The district court's grant of Safety's motion for JNOV for claim indefiniteness was in error and must be reversed.

NOTE

Definite Defined by Field. "[I]f the language is as precise as the subject matter permits, the courts can demand no more." *Georgia-Pacific Corp. v. United States Plywood Corp.*, 258 F.2d 124, 136, 118 U.S.P.Q. 122, 132 (2d Cir.), *cert. denied*, 358 U.S. 884 (1958). *See also Shatterproof Glass Corp. v. Libby-Owens-Ford, Inc.*, 758 F.2d 613 (Fed. Cir.), *cert. dismissed*, 106 S. Ct. 340 (1985). The standard to use in drafting is to ask whether an expert witness could convincingly testify that the allegedly vague language in the claim means something definite to people in the field. If a vague-sounding phrase — such as "substantially equal to," or "closely proximate to," or the like — translates into a workable distinction for artisans in this field, chances are it is not indefinite. *See, e.g., Rosemount, Inc. v. Beckman Indus.*, 727 F.2d 1540, 1546-47, 221 U.S.P.Q. 1, 7 (Fed. Cir. 1984) (phrase "close proximity" is "as precise as the subject matter permits").

Standard Oil Co. v. American Cyanamid Co., 585 F. Supp. 1481, 224 U.S.P.Q. 210 (E.D. La. 1984), *aff'd*, 774 F.2d 448, 227 U.S.P.Q. (BNA) 293 (Fed. Cir. 1985). This patent infringement action involved a catalytic process used primarily to manufacture acrylamide ($CH_2 = CH\text{-}CONH_2$), which is a valuable organic chemical with important commercial applications as a precursor for compounds used in pollution control, energy development, and the production of polymers used in municipal and industrial water treatment, pulp and paper processing, textile treatment, food processing, and other applications. The production of acrylamide is now a major competitive business in the United States.

Acrylamide is a monomer, made by combining a molecule of water with a molecule of acrylonitrile. Prior to the 1960s, acrylamide was produced by a two-step process, using sulfuric acid and ammonia. The two-step process had several drawbacks, consuming large quantities of sulfuric acid and ammonia while producing a relatively low yield of acrylamide and also resulting in a by-product (ammonium sulfate) not always easily or profitably disposed of.

Claim 2 of the Greene reissue patent at issue in the case was as follows:

> The process for hydrolyzing a nitrile ... comprising contacting said nitrile with water ... in the presence of copper ion, said copper ion being at least partially soluble in water, the nitrile or in both water and nitrile and said copper ion being composed of copper in a combined valence state of $Cu^\circ + Cu^+$, $Cu^\circ + Cu^{++}$, or $Cu^\circ + Cu^+ + Cu^{++}$ ....

The district court invalidated claim 2 of the patent, finding that the specification did not define the term "partially soluble" in claim 2:

> The term "partially soluble" is not defined in the patent, nor was a standard definition of that term offered by Sohio. However, the term "slightly soluble" did appear to have an established meaning at the relevant time, that is, in the mid-1960s. W.H. NEBERGALL & F.C. SCHMIDT, COLLEGE CHEMISTRY 662-76, 764-65 (1957).
>
> The Court has found no textbook definition of the term "partially soluble," however, and Dr. Greene has admitted that the term "partially soluble" is not defined in the patent specifications. She should, of course, have done so in the patent, and if this had been done, that definition would have been binding on this court.
>
> [Standard] argues that "at least partially soluble" would have the same meaning as "at least slightly soluble." This Court disagrees. Taken alone, the expert testimony on this point is far from conclusive. However, when read against the language of the reissue patent [and other testimony], to the effect that "partially soluble" suggests "considerable amounts" and "substantial amounts," respectively, [this argument] become more persuasive. To illustrate, the reissue patent specifications note that "... any cupric or cuprous salt may be used so long as it is at least slightly soluble ...", and that "... although CuCl, CuI, and CuCN are practically insoluble in water ... they can still catalyze the hydrolysis of nitriles to amides." It is subsequently noted that: "The amount of catalyst appears to have little or no effect on the conversion of nitrile to hydrolysis products. At the lower catalyst levels, however, the reaction times required for significant hydrolysis may be quite long."
>
> Obviously, Dr. Greene, aware of the meaning of "slightly soluble," having used it in the specifications, and conceding that she was "skilled in the art" of chemistry at the time, nevertheless elected to use another term, i.e. "partially soluble" when she stated Claim 2. Considering that she sought

to devise a process useful in her employer's business, and having noted that "lower catalyst levels" required "quite long" reaction times it can only be fairly concluded that she contemplated a process which required more than simply a "slightly soluble" ion; she required that the ion be "at least partially soluble." Thus, in effect Dr. Greene defined in Claim 2 a significant and substantial degree of solubility.

Because of this, the district court concluded, "there is obvious 'waffling' as to the meaning of ["partially soluble"]." Since there is "no generally accepted or textbook use of the term 'partially soluble'," the claim presents "an inherent ambiguity." Consequently, "There is no realistic way that 'those skilled in the art' could utilize the process as claimed in the patent." Although Dr. Greene "had the right, and the skill and background, to have defined the term," she chose not to; thus the term "is too vague to particularly point out and distinctly claim the subject matter which [Standard] claims as its invention," and the patent is invalid. 585 F. Supp. at 1490-91.

NOTES

1. *Squaring the Specification and Claims.* Although the minor difference between "slightly soluble" and "partially soluble" might seem a thin basis on which to invalidate a patent, the court in *Standard Oil* was no doubt correct in its reasoning. During prosecution of the patent, the examiner had rejected Standard Oil's proposed claim language which covered *insoluble* copper catalysts, on the ground that this claim was inconsistent with the specification which taught that the catalysts had to be at least "slightly soluble." So the patent attorney amended the claim by adding the "partially soluble" language discussed by the court. *See* 585 F. Supp. at 1483. But the amended language had no meaning in this field; without further elucidation, it was too unclear to adequately define the bounds of the patentee's claims.

This is one example of a situation that often arises during prosecution. The Patent Office strictly enforces its rule that all phrases used in the claims "must find clear support or antecedent basis in the description so that the meaning of the claims may be ascertainable by reference to the description." 37 C.F.R. § 1.75(d)(1) (1991). And, as the *Standard Oil* case makes clear, if the examiner misses a non-defined phrase in the claims, a court may not. On avoiding "no antecedent basis" rejections, see R. FABER, LANDIS ON THE MECHANICS OF PATENT CLAIM DRAFTING § 18, 23 (1990).

2. *"Interpreting Claims" Versus Reading-In Limitations.* It is often said when construing a patent's claims that limitations must not be read into the claims from the specification. This is true both when claims are being compared to a prior art reference (where perhaps the patentee would like to see such a limitation read in, to distinguish the claim from the subject matter in the reference), and when claims are being compared to a device accused of infringement (where reading in such limitations would, if permitted, be fatal to the patentee's infringement claim, because they bring the accused device outside the reach of the claims). *See*

Section B.3, *Comment: Problems in Enablement, U.S. and Abroad,* this chapter.

Yet it is also bedrock patent law that a claim is to be interpreted with the aid of the specification. *Standard Oil Co. v. American Cyanamid Co.*, 774 F.2d 448, 452, 227 U.S.P.Q. (BNA) 293 (Fed. Cir. 1985) ("The descriptive part of the specification aids in ascertaining the scope and meaning of the claims inasmuch as the words of the claims must be based upon the description. The specification is, thus, the primary basis for construing the claims."). *See also In re Marosi*, 710 F.2d 799, 218 U.S.P.Q. 289 (Fed. Cir. 1983) (sufficient guidance in specification to delineate meaning of claim phrase "substantially free of alkali metals" in process for synthesizing zeolitic compounds).

Can the two principles, "don't read in limitations" and "interpret claims in light of the specification," be reconciled? The cases suggest so, via the notion that it is only improper to import *extraneous* limitations from the specification into the claims. As the Federal Circuit expressed it in one case:

> It is entirely proper to use the specification to interpret what the patentee meant by a word or phrase in the claim. *See, e.g., Loctite Corp. v. Ultraseal Ltd.*, 781 F.2d 861, 867, 228 U.S.P.Q. 90, 93 (Fed. Cir. 1985). But this is not to be confused with adding an extraneous limitation appearing in the specification, which is improper. By "extraneous," we mean a limitation read into a claim from the specification wholly apart from any need to interpret what the patentee meant by particular words or phrases in the claim. "Where a specification does not require a limitation, that limitation should not be read from the specification into the claims." *Specialty Composites v. Cabot Corp.*, 845 F.2d 981, 987 (Fed. Cir. 1988).

E.I. Du Pont de Nemours & Co. v. Phillips Petr. Co., 849 F.2d 1430, 1433, 7 U.S.P.Q.2d 1129 (Fed. Cir. 1988). *See also Corning Glass Works v. Sumitomo Elec. U.S.A., Inc.*, 868 F.2d 1251, 1257, 9 U.S.P.Q.2d 1962 (Fed. Cir. 1989) ("This is not a case where 'extraneous' limitations from the specification are being read into the claim wholly apart from any need to interpret what the patentee meant by particular words or phrases in the claim.").

The problem with this, of course, is that it is not always clear how to distinguish between an extraneous limitation and a proper reference to the specification to construe a term in the claims. This is because, of necessity, "construing" a term often involves "limiting" it; definition is inherently a process of inclusion and exclusion. For more on this, see Chapter 8.

3. *The Acrylamide Story.* The acrylamide technology discussed in the excerpt from *Standard Oil* has an interesting technical and legal history. Until the 1960s, as the court points out, it was made in a two-step process using sulfuric acid and ammonia. Beginning in the mid-1960s, researchers at Standard Oil Company, American Cyanamid, and Dow Chemical began investigating ways to improve the traditional process, which consumed large amounts of inputs and left a byproduct that was difficult to dispose of. Building on the work of a Japanese chemist who discovered that water in combination with certain metals catalyzed the conversion,

inventors at the three companies came up with variants on a one-step process for converting acrylonitrile to acrylamide. *See Dow Chem. Co. v. American Cyanamid Co.*, 816 F.2d 617, 2 U.S.P.Q.2d (BNA) 1350 (Fed. Cir. 1987). At least two patented their inventions, claiming the use of copper in one form or another as the key catalytic agent. Standard Oil's patent claimed a process using a "copper ion," a charged form of the metal, as a catalyst. *Standard Oil Co. v. American Cyanamid Co.*, 774 F.2d at 450. American Cyanamid's process used an uncharged form of the metal. 774 F.2d at 451. Thus in an infringement action by Standard Oil against American Cyanamid, the court held that Cyanamid's process did not infringe Standard Oil's patent. Cyanamid fared less well as a defendant in a subsequent infringement suit involving related patents. *See Dow, supra*. In that case, Cyanamid conceded that its process would infringe patents held by Dow if Dow's patents were valid; but it argued that Dow's inventions were obvious in light of the prior art. *Dow Chem. Co. v. American Cyanamid Co.*, 816 F.2d at 617. The court found otherwise, holding that a prior patent teaching the use of copper for a related two-step process did not render Dow's 1969 invention obvious.

4. *"Saving" Claims from Invalidity.* Older cases were split on a practice now widely condemned: construing a patent narrowly, in some cases despite explicit claim language, to save it from invalidity or to permit an accused device to escape infringement. But now it is not permitted by U.S. courts, although it sometimes appears to be applied overseas. *See* Section B.3, *Comment: Problems in Enablement, U.S. and Abroad,* this chapter.

Functional Language in Claims

Functional language speaks of what a device *does*, rather than what it *is*. Terms such as "a clamp," "a screw," or "a latch" describe a structural feature of an invention, i.e., what that feature is. But a phrase such as "holding device," or "means for attaching" describe this same feature in terms of what it does. And these latter phrases are, of course, broader than the others; they include a nail, a Velcro closure, and indeed *any* way of attaching something to something else.

Earlier in the history of the patent system, functional language in claims was prohibited. As late as the 1940s, the Supreme Court was condemning such language, describing it as a technique designed solely to draft overly broad claims. *Halliburton Oil Well Cementing Co. v. Walker*, 329 U.S. 1 (1946) (invalidating as overly broad claim that read "means ... for tuning ..."). *See generally* R. FABER, LANDIS ON THE MECHANICS OF PATENT CLAIM DRAFTING § 34 (1990). Partly in response to the *Halliburton* case, the 1952 Patent Act explicitly codified the use of "means plus function" claims in then ¶ 3 of § 112, which is now ¶ 6. This section reads:

> An element in a claim for a combination may be expressed as a means or step for performing a specified function without the recital of structure, material, or acts in support thereof, and such claim shall be construed to

cover the corresponding structure, material, or acts described in the specification and equivalents thereof.

35 U.S.C. § 112 (1986 & Supp. VI 1991).

But even outside § 112, ¶6, functional language is now much more readily accepted by the Patent Office and the courts. Indeed, as the following passage from the pen of Learned Hand attests, it must be, at least to some extent, if patents are to serve their basic purpose:

A vast deal has been written about "functional" claims and it must be owned that much of it cannot be reconciled with the rest; yet, in spite of the fact that the latest decisions of the Supreme Court have declared with great strictness against them, we do not think that form is inevitably determinative of validity. The question always is whether such claims extend the monopoly beyond the "invention," and that is not to be determined so simply. An applicant for a patent must make "a written description" of "his invention or discovery" "in such full, clear, concise, and exact terms as to enable any person skilled in the art ... to make, construct, compound, and use the same;" and he must "particularly point out and distinctly claim the part, improvement, or combination which he claims as his invention or discovery." If the claims were limited to the "concise and exact terms" in which the specifications ordinarily describe a single example of the invention, few, if any, patents, would have value, for there are generally many variants well-known to the art, which will at once suggest themselves as practicable substitutes for the specific details of the machine or process so disclosed. It is the office of the claims to cover these, and it is usually exceedingly difficult, and sometimes impossible, to do so except in language that is to some degree "functional"; for obviously it is impossible to enumerate all possible variants. Indeed, some degree of permissible latitude would seem to follow from the doctrine of equivalents, which was devised to eke out verbal insufficiencies of claims. Since by virtue of that doctrine a claim will cover whatever will accomplish substantially the same result by substantially the same means, it cannot be that a claim becomes invalid when it states expressly what the courts would in any event imply.

"Functional" claims certainly fulfill one of the offices of claims in general, which is to advise the art of the scope of the monopoly; at least they do so unless ... they are too vague to be understood at all. Their vice is not that, but that they extend the monopoly beyond the proper limits of the "invention"; and to ascertain what those limits are, we always have to look to the contribution of the disclosure to the art. Almost all inventions are combinations of old elements, whose selection as a new unit gives them their only importance. Their combination is the end or purpose of the "invention": its "nature and design" which the applicant must state. The elements of the combination are the means by which that "nature and design" is realized; and nobody invades the patent who does not appropriate both end and means. To the extent to which variants, which will be serviceable as substitute means, are known to the art, and at once suggest themselves without need of further substantial experimentation, they are equivalents, and to extend the monopoly to them is not only justifiable but necessary to the protection of the inventor. However, although for these reasons it is possible for claims, "functional" in form, to be valid, verbally they do leave at large the means by which the "invention" is to be practised; they do not "distinctly claim the part, improvement, or combination which" the inventor "claims as his invention or discovery." On that account the patentee must be prepared to prove, if he would support them, that all practicable means, comprehended within the general language he has chosen, were in fact known and accessible to the art, and that their substitution for the specific details of the specifications, would at once suggest itself without further substantial experimentation.

Philip A. Hunt Co. v. Mallinckrodt Chem. Works, 177 F.2d 583, 585-86 (2d Cir. 1949) (L. Hand, J.). *See also In re Swinehart*, 439 F.2d 210, 169 U.S.P.Q. (BNA) 226 (C.C.P.A. 1971) (rejecting notion that functional language — in this case, the term "transparent" with respect to a new composition — is improper when "at the point of novelty," i.e., to describe the novel feature of the claimed invention; stating that functional language is a problem only when it causes claim to be indefinite or extends scope of claim beyond that which was disclosed in specification).

Despite the broad language of the 1952 statute, there are still some limits to means-plus-function claims. According to prevailing interpretations of § 112, ¶ 6, "single means" claims are invalid. These are claims to all ways of doing a specified function. Since the statutory language in ¶ 6 speaks of means-plus-function claims *in a combination*, a single-element claim drafted in means-plus-function format is thought to violate the statute. Thus a claim to "An apparatus for holding one thing to another, comprising means for attaching a first thing to a second thing" would be invalid as a single means claim. *See, e.g., In re Hyatt*, 708 F.2d 712-13 (Fed. Cir. 1985).

NOTES

1. *Anticipation and Claim Definiteness:* "Means plus function" claims raise two additional issues that have perplexed bench and bar: First, if a certain structure is disclosed in a specification, can that particular structure be "read in" to a claim to keep it from being anticipated by a prior art reference? Second, must the Patent Office search the prior art for any structure that is the equivalent of the structures encompassed by the means plus function claim?

As to the first question, the Court of Customs and Patent Appeals decided that supporting details in a specification could not be used to narrow the scope of a means plus function claim to avoid a prior art reference. Such a case would not be definite, because the crucial structural limitation imported from the specification to save them from a prior art reference, would not be apparent on the face of the claims. *In re Lundberg*, 244 F.2d 543, 548-49, 113 U.S.P.Q. (BNA) 530 (C.C.P.A. 1957).

As to the second question, the Federal Circuit recently held that the Patent Office must scrutinize the prior art for devices that meet the terms of a means plus function claim — i.e., for devices that are structurally equivalent under Patent Act § 112, ¶6. *In re Bond*, 910 F.2d 831, 15 U.S.P.Q.2d (BNA) 1566 (Fed. Cir. 1990).

The Patent Office has responded to *Bond* by issuing, in effect, a notice of nonacquiescence. *See* Patent Office Statement, reported at 43 PAT. TRADEMARK & COPYRIGHT J. (BNA) 161 (1992). The Office argued that *Bond* is (1) inconsistent with *Lundberg*, and (2) too difficult for examiners to apply properly. The inconsistency with *Lundberg* seems to be premised on the notion that because the court refused to inquire into the details of the device as described in Lundberg's specification, courts should likewise refuse to inquire into the details of devices disclosed in the prior art, for the purpose of determining patentability (i.e., novelty and nonobviousness). A recent commentary reveals some flaws in this thinking, and also criticizes the Office's workload argument against *Bond. See* Fisher, *Comments on Application of 35 U.S.C. 112, ¶6*, 44 PAT. TRADEMARK & COPYRIGHT J. (BNA) 46 (1992).

2. Means Claims and Infringement. An important question with respect to the means-plus-function claims authorized by § 112, ¶ 6 is their scope for infringement purposes. This is discussed below in Chapter 8, Section B.4.

E. THE BEST MODE REQUIREMENT

Recall the language of § 112:

> [¶ 1] The specification ... shall set forth the best mode contemplated by the inventor of carrying out his invention.

This frames the best mode requirement, an important source of duties for patent applicants, as the following cases show. When reading them, pay special attention to the ways in which the best mode requirement differs from the other statutory norms laid out in § 112.

RANDOMEX, INC. v. SCOPUS CORP.

849 F.2d 585, 7 U.S.P.Q.2d 1050 (Fed. Cir. 1988)

Randomex, Inc. appeals the final judgment of the district court dismissing Randomex's complaint because of the invalidity of United States Letters Patent No. 3,803,660 ('660) for failure to disclose the "best mode."

In mainframe computers information is stored on magnetic disks, several of which are housed in a disk pack. A small particle of dust or dirt on a disk may cause physical damage to the disk or loss of data. Before Randomex's invention, only large, nonportable machines were available to clean disk packs. The disk packs had to be transported to the machine which was undesirable because the delicate disks could be damaged in transit. All types of these various cleaning systems used some type of cloth or brush in conjunction with a cleaning fluid. One of the nonportable cleaning machines used a 91% alcohol solution to clean the disks; another used diluted surgical detergent.

The '660 patent is directed to a portable apparatus for cleaning disk packs. A disk pack is removed from the computer and placed in the apparatus where brushes wipe the disks clean, whereupon a cleaning solution is sprayed on the brushes to remove the accumulated dirt. Although the cleaning solution is not claimed specifically in the '660 patent, it is needed to practice the invention. Thus, the patent disclosed:

> [t]he cleaning solution employed should be of a type adequate to clean grease and oil from the disc surfaces, such as a 91 percent alcohol solution or a non-residue detergent solution such as Randomex Cleaner No. 50281.

Column 5, lines 49-53.

[At trial, the jury found in answer to interrogatory question 2 that one skilled in the art would not need to conduct an undue amount of experimentation to arrive at the applicant's best mode for practicing the invention. But in question 3, the jury found that the patentee deliberately failed to disclose the preferred diskcleaner formula in the specification to enhance their own sales. The judge construed the answer to question 3 as a finding that the patentee had not disclosed the best mode, invalidated the patent, and refused JNOV motions in this regard; Randomex appealed.]

The [district] court opined that Randomex "kept secret [its solution formula] in order to sell the product to users of its device." It concluded that "the fact that experimentation by obtaining a chemical analysis of plaintiff's Cleaner solution ... could reveal plaintiff's formula could not, as matter of law, satisfy the statutory requirement." It based its conclusion on the following factors: (1) Randomex was under no obligation to make its fluid available for such reverse engineering; (2) there was nothing to keep Randomex from changing its formula; and (3) a patent is supposed to fully educate the public for use following the expiration date and who, after seventeen years, could determine what had been plaintiff's proprietary Cleaner. The district court held, accordingly, that "[s]o far as best mode is concerned, the reference to 'Randomex cleaner No. 50281' was legally insufficient."

[After criticizing the district court's use of question 3 as a proxy for best mode findings, the court turns to its own analysis.] It is concealment of the best mode of practicing the claimed invention that section 112 ¶ 1 is designed to prohibit. Here the claimed invention is a portable machine for cleaning computer disk packs. Those of ordinary skill in this art are not users of the end device. The world is full of cleaning fluids produced by persons skilled in the cleaning fluid art, who know what are proper or improper uses for each cleaning fluid. It is absurd to postulate that persons skilled only in other arts would reverse engineer a particular cleaning fluid as a step to discover what other cleaning fluids would do the same work. Those skilled in other arts would simply ask those who knew. Thus, the answer to Q3 [i.e., question 3 in the interrogatories to the jury] is useless in determining whether the inventors failed to meet the best mode requirement, and the district court erred in relying on Q3 to invalidate the patent.

Although Q2 [question 2] is poorly framed and is directed more to enablement than best mode, we must determine if Q2 is so legally deficient that in answering that question the jury would have failed to make the underlying inquiries necessary to support its finding that the inventors fulfilled the best mode requirement. It is undisputed in this case that (1) a 91% alcohol solution was used in a prior art non-portable machine; (2) diluted surgical detergent — a non-residue detergent solution — was used in the prior art non-portable machines; (3) Randomex Cleaner No. 50281 is a non-residue detergent solution; (4) the applicant knew of no better non-residue detergent solution than Randomex Cleaner No. 50281; (6) the evidence tended to show that a 91% alcohol solution was the "worst mode," not the "best"; (7) Scopus easily "reverse engineered" Randomex's solution; (8) the inventor intentionally omitted the formula for Randomex Cleaner No. 50281 from the disclosure.

First, as an initial matter, "[is] the best mode requirement complied with when an inventor discloses his preferred embodiment indiscriminately with other possible embodiments?" 2 D. Chisum, Patents § 7.05[1] at 7-68 (1987). The Board of Patent Appeals and Interferences has stated:

> [t]here is no requirement in 35 U.S.C. 112 that an applicant point out which of his embodiments he considers his best mode; that the disclosure includes the best mode contemplated by the applicant is enough to satisfy the statute. There is no concealment of best mode here since one of ordinary skill in the art could readily determine the best operating mode....

Ernsthausen v. Nakayama, 1 U.S.P.Q.2d 1539, 1549 (Bd. Pat. App. Int. 1985), *aff'd*, 809 F.2d 787, 788 (Fed. Cir. 1986) (tables). As applicable to the facts of this case, we agree with this statement of the Board.

The disclosure of the 91% alcohol solution is suspect in light of evidence that one who used it might have had to contend with an explosion. Although the motive for including the 91% alcohol solution in the disclosure is not apparent, the solution was part of the prior art and suggested an easily procurable inferior substitute for the Randomex Cleaner No. 50281. The indiscriminate disclosure in this instance of the preferred cleaning fluid along with one other possible cleaning fluid satisfies the best mode requirement.

Second, the district court held that the reference to "Randomex Cleaner No. 50281" was legally insufficient. By this we assume the district court found that the quality of the disclosure was so poor as to effectively result in concealment. We disagree. The complete description is "a non-residue detergent solution such as Randomex Cleaner No. 50281." Although a trade name alone may be inappropriate in a best mode disclosure when suitable substitutes are unavailable, see *White Consolidated Indus., Inc. v. Vega Servo-Control, Inc.*, 713 F.2d 788, 791, 218 U.S.P.Q. 961, 963 (Fed. Cir. 1983), here, commercial substitutes were readily available in the prior art and the trade name is mere surplusage — an addition to the generic description. Contrary to the district court's conclusion, Randomex's disclosure was not an attempt to conceal its cleaning fluid formula; it disclosed the contents of the fluid as "a non-residue detergent solution," the same solution as the surgical detergent solution used in the prior art. The failure to disclose its cleaning fluid formula was, as the inventor and president of Randomex admitted, merely a public relations attempt to generate sales for its cleaning fluid; it disclosed the best mode of practicing its claimed invention using in conjunction with it a non-residue detergent solution.

[From footnote:] For example, if one should invent a new and improved internal combustion engine, the best mode requirement would require a patentee to divulge the fuel on which it would run best. This patentee, however, would not be required to disclose the formula for refining gasoline or any other petroleum product. Every requirement is met if the patentee truthfully stated that the engine ran smoothly and powerfully on Brand X super-premium lead free "or equal." Making engines and refining petroleum are different arts, and the person skilled in the art of making engines would probably buy the suggested gasoline. But if the hypothetical maker or user of the engine did not want to use the Brand X super-premium, he would then explore the "or equal" alternative of the patent disclosure. Practically speaking, he would not buy a test tube of Brand X gasoline and reverse engineer it to determine how Brand X refined it. He would ask dealers what other brands of gasoline are available that, in their view, would do for the patented engine what Brand X did. The user is not driven by lawyer's ideology. He is a person who elects practical means to accomplish practical ends.

As the jury found by answering Q2 in Randomex's favor, the patent disclosed the "best mode contemplated by the inventor of carrying out his invention," 35 U.S.C. § 112 ¶ 1, as directed to one of ordinary skill in the art. This invention neither added nor claimed to add anything to the prior art respecting cleaning fluid. If the disclosure in the '660 patent had truthfully said "the cleaning solution employed should be of a commercial type adequate to clean grease and oil from disk surfaces, i.e., a non-residue detergent solution such as Randomex Cleaner No. 50281, or equal," the best mode requirement would have been met without full disclosure of the formula. Because there is no dispute as to the underlying facts, it follows that nondisclosure of the formula per se did not rise to the level of violating the statutory requirement to disclose the best mode.

[From the dissent by JUDGE MAYER:]

I dissent because I see a sharper distinction between the best mode and enablement requirements of 35 U.S.C. § 112. Enablement and best mode are two separate and distinct elements of patentability. The enablement aspect requires a disclosure that will permit those skilled in the art, without undue experimentation, to make and practice the invention. The best mode clause insists on more: it requires "an inventor to disclose the best mode contemplated by him, as of the time he executes the application, of carrying out his invention." *In re Gay*, 309 F.2d at 772, 135 U.S.P.Q. at 315. It precludes "inventors from applying for patents while at the same time concealing from the public preferred embodiments of their inventions which they have in fact conceived." *Id*.

Here, prior to the patent application, one of the patentees and the president of Randomex, Ludka, had tried several different cleaning solutions in his quest for the one that worked best. Through experimentation, he learned that "there was a difference in effectiveness in detergent formulae percentages," and ultimately arrived at an optimum cleaning formula. As he admits, however, he intentionally refrained from disclosing the optimum formula so that the users of his cleaner would also purchase his cleaning solution. Ludka believed this intentional non-disclosure was "a good advertising gimmick" that would bring him additional profits from his invention.

The specification of the '660 patent sets out an undifferentiated list of apparently equally effective solutions, no one of which is highlighted as preferred over the others. There would be no problem with this if all of the suggested solutions worked equally well. But using the alcohol solution, an example of an unstated number of other cleaning solutions, did not work well and could produce dangerous fumes[. According to the trial court:]

> Ludka ... testified that in experimenting to find the best fluid, he abandoned alcohol after one try. While he maintained at the trial that alcohol was usable, neither he, nor plaintiff's expert, contradicted defendants' expert's testimony that, because plaintiff's device was enclosed, alcohol could produce dangerous fumes.

[The district court also quoted from a memo by Ludka stating that certain cleaning fluids could cause disk crashes and loss of data.] Thus, not only did Ludka fail to point out that the Randomex solution was the best mode, he also disclosed solutions that he knew could be harmful and even dangerous. This is the antithesis of the good-faith full disclosure that is mandated by section 112's best mode requirement.

It is irrelevant that there was a variety of non-residue detergent solutions on the market that might work because Ludka knew that among those available his was the most effective. Yet he only named it as one among many possible solutions, and then only by its trade name, not generically. He did not disclose which of the suggested modes was the "best mode contemplated by him" for practicing the invention. His disclosure does not satisfy section 112 because he buried his best mode in a list of less satisfactory ones.

NOTES

1. *Best Mode: A Higher Standard than Enablement?* Judge Mayer's dissent in *Scopus* expresses nicely the view that the best mode requirement imposes more exacting duties on the applicant than the general demands of enablement. A good summary of this view can be found in Comment, *Patent Law — Patent Law Policy and the Best Mode Requirement: Randomex, Inc. v. Scopus Corp.*, 14 J. CORP. L. 1015 (1989), which contains the following comment on the *Scopus* case:

> A showing that the formula was concealed intentionally to gain collateral profits should be a factor even if, as the *Randomex* court indicates, Scopus could reverse-engineer the cleaning fluid. Direct evidence of deliberate concealment should be considered independent of whether a disclosure enables those skilled in the art. Although this may increase the level of disclosure above the amount needed for enablement, the existing distinction between the best mode and enablement requirements should remain. If intentional concealment leads to a slightly higher required level of specificity, the inventor would think twice about less than full public disclosure. The public must receive the utmost benefit in exchange for granting the inventor a monopoly on an invention. Requiring a slightly higher level of specificity may make the inventor choose between patent or trade secret protection for his invention.

From one point of view this should be relatively uncontroversial: best mode must mean something more than mere enablement, or the statute would not include the best mode language. Yet, at the same time, the cases are less than cogent regarding the exact content of this requirement. The *Chemcast* case, next in this section, is an attempt to clear up these issues.

2. Related Cases. In *Scripps Clinic & Research Found. v. Genentech, Inc.*, 927 F.2d 1565, 1579-80, 18 U.S.P.Q.2d 1896 (Fed. Cir. 1991) the court reversed a district court finding that Scripps' patent on purified TPA protein was invalid for failure to disclose the best mode. Although Scripps' specification disclosed the use of monoclonal antibodies to isolate pure TPA from blood products, Genentech charged that the specification failed to disclose that Scripps researchers had found that one particular strain of antibodies — the "2.2.9" strain — was the most effective for this purpose. The Federal Circuit reversed, citing statements in *In re Wands*, 858 F.2d 731, 737-38, 8 U.S.P.Q.2d 1400, 1406-07 (Fed. Cir. 1988), that the laborious task of selecting appropriate monoclonal antibodies could be carried by those skilled in the art. Implicit in the court's holding was the notion that the 2.2.9 line of antibodies was no better than any others that could be isolated and selected by a skilled artisan. *Compare Northern Telecom, Inc. v. Datapoint Corp.*, 908 F.2d 931, 15 U.S.P.Q.2d (BNA) 1321 (Fed. Cir.), *cert. denied*, 111 S. Ct. 296 (1990) (invalidating patent on best mode grounds, where applicant failed to disclose, in patent claiming method for batch data processing, preferred magnetic tape consisting either of commercially available 3M brand tape or inventors' own re-engineered tape).

In *Spectra-Physics, Inc. v. Coherent, Inc.*, 827 F.2d 1524, 1532, 3 U.S.P.Q.2d (BNA) 1737 (Fed. Cir. 1987), the court invalidated certain claims in patents to

Hobart and Mefferd, assigned to defendant Coherent. The claims related to the solution of a sticky problem in laser technology: the "bunching" of gases toward one end of the gas-containing discharge tube which, when excited by a high-energy electrical discharge, emits the concentrated coherent light characteristic of a laser. The light is "focused" by a series of discs with holes in them, inside the discharge tube; the holes line up and point to the end of the tube, a bit like a telescope. Coherent's solution to the "gas bunching" problem was to place copper cups between the discs and the side of the discharge tubes; this helped conduct heat from the inside of the tube, which solved the "bunching" problem. In its specification, Coherent described soldering or brazing as the way to carry out the element in its claims reciting "means for" for attaching the cups to the tube wall. Plaintiff Spectra-Physics claimed, however, that Coherent had failed to disclose its preferred means for attaching the copper cups to the inside of the discharge tube — brazing with TiCuSil, a copper-silver composition, in a tightly-controlled "braze cycle." The court agreed:

> Coherent admits that its braze cycle is not disclosed in either patent nor is it contained in the prior art. Instead, it maintains that its braze cycle is unique to its ovens, and because the performance of industrial ovens varies considerably, the actual parameters would be meaningless to someone who used a different oven. In support of its position, Coherent cites *In re Gay*, 309 F.2d at 769, 135 U.S.P.Q. at 316, which states that "[n]ot every last detail is to be described, else patent specifications would turn into production specifications, which they were never meant to be." In doing so, however, Coherent was not discussing whether it had complied with the best mode requirement because the court had held in its favor on that issue; it was discussing whether it had complied with the enablement requirement on which the court had held against it.
>
> [F]ar from being a "production specification," Coherent did not disclose any details about its brazing process. It is this complete lack of detail which effectively resulted in its concealment.

827 F.2d at 1531, 3 U.S.P.Q.2d at 1741.

In re Nelson, 280 F.2d 172, 184, 126 U.S.P.Q. 242, 253 (C.C.P.A. 1960) (Rich, J.), cited in an excluded part of the dissent by Judge Mayer in *Scopus*, includes this instructive passage:

> One cannot read the wording of section 112 without appreciating that strong language has been used for the purpose of compelling complete disclosure. There always exists, on the part of some people, a selfish desire to obtain patent protection without making a full disclosure, which the law, in the public interest, must guard against.

3. *Where Did Best Mode Come From?* For a brief account of the statutory predecessors to the best mode requirement, see 2 D. CHISUM, PATENTS § 7.05 (1978 & Supp. 1991).

4. *"Updating" the Best Mode?* It is well settled that an applicant need not update the best mode recited in an application after filing but before issuance of a patent. *See, e.g., Carter-Wallace, Inc. v. Riverton Labs., Inc.*, 433 F.2d 1034, 1038, 167 U.S.P.Q. (BNA) 656 (2d Cir. 1970); *Spectra-Physics, supra*, 827 F.2d at 1535. But does this rule carry over to the situation where the inventor files a continuation-in-part (CIP) of an earlier application? *See* the *Transco Products* opinion below.

The best mode requirement also represents a problem for foreign applicants who base their U.S. priority on a previous foreign filing under § 119 of the Act. *See* Chapter 4, Section K. These applicants normally submit a direct translation of their foreign application, which typically fails to disclose a best mode since *only* the U.S. requires this to be disclosed. *See* Litman, *Problems with the Best Mode Requirement of 35 U.S.C. 112 in Applications Claiming Priority Under 35 U.S.C. 119 and 35 U.S.C. 120*, 61 J. PAT. OFF. SOC'Y 431 (1979) (Patent Act § 119 grants benefit of foreign filing date for priority only). *But see* Wegner & Pagenberg, *Paris Convention Priority: A Unique American Viewpoint Denying "The Same Effect" to the Foreign Filing*, 5 INT'L REV. OF INDUS. PROP. & COPY-RIGHT L. 361 (1974) (arguing that Paris Convention, to which U.S. belongs, should be interpreted to obviate this problem).

CHEMCAST CORP. v. ARCO INDUSTRIES

913 F.2d 923, 16 U.S.P.Q.2d 1033 (Fed. Cir. 1990)

Chemcast Corporation appeals the judgment of the United States District Court for the Eastern District of Michigan that Claim 6 of United States Patent No. 4,081,879 ('879 patent), the only claim in suit, is invalid because of the inventor's failure to disclose the best mode as required by 35 U.S.C. § 112. We affirm.

The '879 patent [to Chemcast founder Phillip L. Rubright] claims a sealing member in the form of a grommet or plug button that is designed to seal an opening in, for example, a sheet metal panel. Claim 6, the only claim in suit, depends from Claim 1.

> 1. A grommet for sealing an opening in a panel, said grommet comprising an annular base portion having a continuous circumferential and axial extending sealing band surface, an annular locking portion having a continuous circumferential and axial extending ridge portion approximately the same diameter as said sealing band surface, said sealing band surface constituting an axial extending continuation of said ridge portion, said locking portion and said base portion being in contact with each other and integrally bonded together, said base portion comprising an elastomeric material and said locking portion being more rigid than said base portion, whereby when the grommet is installed in a panel opening, the locking portion is inserted through the opening to a position on the opposite side of the panel from the base portion locking the grommet in place, and said sealing band surface

forms a complete seal continuously around the entire inner periphery of the panel opening.

6. The grommet as defined in claim 1 wherein the material forming said base portion has a durometer hardness reading of less than 60 Shore A and the material forming said locking portion has a durometer hardness reading of more than 70 Shore A.

[From footnote:] A device known as a durometer measures the hardness and softness of the materials used in the grommet. The Shore Instrument & Manufacturing Company is a leading manufacturer of durometers used for measuring rubber-like materials. A durometer referred to as a Shore A durometer measures soft, vulcanized rubber and all elastomeric materials, while a Shore D durometer measures rigid materials such as hard rubber and harder grades of plastic. The Shore B and Shore C durometers can be used to measure intermediate hardnesses. There is some overlap in the range of use of the durometers. A conversion chart is published by the Shore Instruments & Manufacturing Co. which shows that the range of 30 to 100 on the scale of a Shore A durometer corresponds to the range of 6 to 58 on a Shore D durometer.

The grommet of Claim 6 is referred to as a dual durometer grommet because it may be composed either of two materials that differ in hardness or of a single material that varies in hardness. In either case, the different hardnesses can be, and for a sufficiently large hardness differential must be, measured with different durometers: Shore A for the softer base portion and Shore D for the harder locking portion. The harder locking portion of the grommet is the focus of this case.

Chemcast sued Arco for infringement of Claim 6 of the '879 patent. Arco counterclaimed that the patent was invalid on several grounds, including Rubright's failure to comply with 35 U.S.C. § 112. The district court agreed. It held that, because the '879 patent did not either disclose the best mode contemplated by the inventor of carrying out the invention or particularly point out and distinctly claim the subject matter of the invention, Chemcast could not recover on its claim of infringement.

[The Federal Circuit remanded the case with instructions to the district court to revise its best mode analysis.] On remand, the court again invalidated the patent for failure to satisfy the best mode requirement. It made 47 factual findings detailing both what, at the time of filing the patent application, Rubright considered to be the best mode of practicing his claimed invention and what the specification as filed disclosed to one of ordinary skill in the art. According to the court, the principal shortcomings of the disclosure were its failure to specify (1) the particular type, (2) the hardness, and (3) the supplier and trade name, of the material used to make the locking portion of the grommet. Therefore, it held that the application as filed failed adequately to disclose the best mode of practicing the invention contemplated by Rubright. Chemcast appeals.

The best mode inquiry focuses on the inventor's state of mind as of the time he filed his application — a subjective, factual question. But this focus is not exclusive. Our statements that "there is no objective standard by which to judge the adequacy of a best mode disclosure," and that "only evidence of concealment (accidental or intentional) is to be considered," *In re Sherwood* [etc.], assumed that both the level of skill in the art and the scope of the claimed invention were additional, objective metes and bounds of a best mode disclosure.

Of necessity, the disclosure required by section 112 is directed to those skilled in the art. Therefore, one must consider the level of skill in the relevant art in determining whether a specification discloses the best mode. We have consistently recognized [this].

The other objective limitation on the extent of the disclosure required to comply with the best mode requirement is, of course, the scope of the claimed invention. Thus, in *Randomex*, the inventor's deliberate concealment of his cleaning fluid formula did not violate the best mode requirement because his "invention neither added nor claimed to add anything to the prior art respecting cleaning fluid." [And] in [*DeGeorge v. Bernier*, 768 F.2d 1318, 1324, 226 U.S.P.Q. 758, 763 (Fed. Cir. 1985),] we reversed a finding that an inventor's nondisclosure of unclaimed circuitry with which his claimed circuitry interfaced violated the best mode requirement: "Because the properly construed count does not include a word processor, failure to meet the best mode requirement here should not arise from an absence of information on the word processor."

In short, a proper best mode analysis has two components. The first is whether, at the time the inventor filed his patent application, he knew of a mode of practicing his claimed invention that he considered to be better than any other. This part of the inquiry is wholly subjective, and resolves whether the inventor must disclose any facts in addition to those sufficient for enablement. If the inventor in fact contemplated such a preferred mode, the second part of the analysis compares what he knew with what he disclosed — is the disclosure adequate to enable one skilled in the art to practice the best mode or, in other words, has the inventor "concealed" his preferred mode from the "public"? Assessing the adequacy of the disclosure, as opposed to its necessity, is largely an objective inquiry that depends upon the scope of the claimed invention and the level of skill in the art.

Notwithstanding the mixed nature of the best mode inquiry, and perhaps because of our routine focus on its subjective portion, we have consistently treated the question as a whole as factual. We adhere to that standard here, and review the district court's best mode determination accordingly.

Chemcast alleges that the trial court erred in its best mode analysis by failing to focus, as required, on the claimed invention and on whether the inventor, Rubright, concealed a better mode than he disclosed. Neither allegation has any merit. Chemcast first argues that, because the '879 patent does not claim any specific material for making the locking portion of the grommet, Rubright's failure to disclose the particular material that he thought worked the best does not violate the best mode requirement. This argument confuses best mode and enablement. A patent applicant must disclose the best mode of carrying out his claimed invention, not merely a mode of making and using what is claimed. A specification can be enabling yet fail to disclose an applicant's contemplated best mode. Indeed, most of the cases in which we have said that the best mode requirement was violated addressed situations where an inventor failed to disclose non-claimed elements that were nevertheless necessary to practice the best mode of carrying out the claimed invention.

Moreover, Chemcast is mistaken in its claim interpretation. While the critical limitation of Claim 6 is a hardness differential of 10 points on the Shore A scale between the grommet base and locking portions, and not a particular material type, some material meeting both this limitation and that of Claim 1, that "said base portion compris[e] an elastomeric material and said locking portion be[ ] more rigid than said base portion," is claimed. That the claim is broad is no reason to excuse noncompliance with the best mode requirement. Here, the information the applicant is accused of concealing is not merely necessary to practice the claimed invention; it also describes the preferred embodiment of a claimed element.

Chemcast's second argument is equally misplaced. The court devoted no fewer than 13 factual findings to what the inventor Rubright knew as of the filing date of the '879 application. Those findings focus, as did the parties, on the type, hardness, and supplier of the material used to make the locking portion of the grommet. The court found that Rubright selected the material for the locking portion, a rigid polyvinyl chloride (PVC) plastisol composition; knew that the preferred hardness of this material was 75 ± 5 Shore D; and purchased all of the grommet material under the trade name R-4467 from Reynosol Corporation (Reynosol), which had spent 750 man-hours developing the compound specifically for Chemcast. Furthermore, the court found that at the time the '879 application was filed, the only embodiment of the claimed invention known to Rubright was a grommet composed of R-4467, a rigid PVC plastisol composition with a locking portion hardness of 75 ± 5 Shore D.

In light of what Rubright knew, the specification, as issued, was manifestly deficient. It disclosed the following:

> The annular locking portion [ ] of the sealing member [ ] is preferably comprised of a rigid castable material, such as a castable resinous material, either a thermoplastic or thermosetting resin, or any mixtures thereof, for example, polyurethane or polyvinyl chloride. The [locking] portion [ ] also should be made of a material that is sufficiently hard and rigid so that it cannot be radially compressed, such as when it is inserted in the opening [ ] in the panel [ ]. Materials having a durometer hardness reading of 70 Shore A or harder are suitable in this regard.

Col. 4, 11.53-63. The material hardness (75 Shore D) and supplier/trade name (Reynosol compound R-4467) are not explicitly disclosed here or anywhere else in the specification. Nor, in light of the level of skill in the art, are they implicitly disclosed. Given the specification, one skilled in the art simply could not divine Rubright's preferred material hardness. The court found that "the specification of the open-ended range of materials of '70 Shore A or harder' conceals the best mode 75 Shore D material in part because materials of Shore A and Shore D hardnesses are recognized as different types of materials with different classes of physical properties." As for the specific supplier and trade name designation of the preferred material, the court found that disclosing a list of generic potential materials was "not an adequate disclosure of the best mode PVC Re[y]nosol Compound R-4467."

We agree. That "at least eight other PVC composition suppliers [] could have formulated satisfactory materials for the dual durometer grommet," does not, as Chemcast urges, excuse Rubright's concealment of his preferred material, and the only one of which he was aware. Again Chemcast confuses enablement and best mode. The question is not whether those skilled in the art could make or use the '879 grommet without knowledge of Reynosol compound R-4467; it is whether they could practice Rubright's contemplated best mode which, the court found, included specifically the Reynosol compound. Rubright knew that Reynosol had developed R-4467 specifically for Chemcast and had expended several months and many hundred man-hours in doing so. Because Chemcast used only R-4467, because certain characteristics of the grommet material were claimed elements of the '879 invention, and because Rubright himself did not know the formula, composition, or method of manufacture of R-4467, section 112 obligated Rubright to disclose the specific supplier and trade name of his preferred material.

Other facts Chemcast points to as obviating the need for Rubright's disclosure of "Reynosol R-4467" are simply irrelevant. That Reynosol considered the formulation of R-4467 a trade secret and that it offered the compound only to Chemcast do not bear on the state of Rubright's knowledge or the quality of his disclosure. First, it is undisputed that Rubright did not know either the precise formulation or method of manufacture of R-4467; he knew only that it was a rigid PVC plastisol composition denominated "R-4467" by Reynosol. Whatever the scope of Reynosol's asserted trade secret, to the extent it includes information known by Rubright that he considered part of his preferred mode, section 112 requires that he divulge it. See *White Consol. Indus. v. Vega Servo-Control*, 713 F.2d 788, 791 (Fed. Cir. 1983). Second, whether and to whom Reynosol chooses to sell its products cannot control the extent to which Rubright must disclose his best mode. Were this the law, inventors like Rubright could readily circumvent the best mode requirement by concluding sole-user agreements with the suppliers of their preferred materials.

Nor does the fact that Rubright developed his preferred mode with the requirements of a particular customer in mind excuse its concealment; compliance with section 112 does not turn on why or for whom an inventor develops his invention. An inventor need not disclose manufacturing data or the requirements of a particular customer if that information is not part of the best mode of practicing the claimed invention, but the converse also is true. Whether characterizable as "manufacturing data," "customer requirements," or even "trade secrets," information necessary to practice the best mode simply must be disclosed.

Given the specification and the level of skill or understanding in the art, skilled practitioners could neither have known what Rubright's contemplated best mode was nor have carried it out. Indeed, on these facts, they would not even have known where to look. This is not a case, like *Randomex*, where the inventor indiscriminately disclosed his preferred mode along with other possible modes. Rubright did not disclose his preferred mode at all. His preferred material hardness, 75 Shore D, is three hardness scales removed from the 70 Shore A hardness mentioned in the specification. Neither his preferred source, Reynosol Compound R-4467, nor any other is disclosed.

In this situation and on these facts, where the inventor has failed to disclose the only mode he ever contemplated of carrying out his invention, the best mode requirement is violated. Accordingly, the judgment of the district court is affirmed.

NOTES

1. *Chemcast Applied.* In *Amgen, Inc. v. Chugai Pharmaceutical Co.*, 18 U.S.P.Q.2d (BNA) 1016, 1025 (Fed. Cir. 1991), Judge Lourie of the Federal Circuit applied the two-step *Chemcast* test and found no best mode violation.

2. *Best Mode and Inequitable Conduct.* In *Consolidated Alum. Corp. v. Foseco Int'l Ltd.*, 910 F.2d 804 (Fed. Cir. 1990), the Federal Circuit held that plaintiff/patentee's intentional fraud in disclosing a fictitious process component during prosecution of their patent rendered that patent, as well as a series of related patents, invalid for inequitable conduct. See Chapter 7, Section A, *Inequitable Conduct*. This establishes a precedent that the intentional withholding or misrepresentation of the best mode may have grave consequences indeed. A recent Note criticized the extension of the "unclean hands" holding in this case to the related patents, arguing that although "the court should treat those with unclean hands firmly, refusing to enforce other related patents may have been a harsher decision than necessary." Note, *The Best Mode Requirement Refined: The Federal Circuit's Best Mode Standard, Mandate for Detail, and the Penalty for Nondisclosure*, 37 WAYNE L. REV. 1721, 1737 (1991).

1. COMMENT ON THE *CHEMCAST* CASE

The chief contribution of the *Chemcast* opinion is to clarify the relationship between two § 112 issues, enablement and best mode. In this regard, the two-step test for determining best mode is perhaps worth recalling:

> [A] proper best mode analysis has two components. The first is whether, at the time the inventor filed his patent application, he knew of a mode of practicing his claimed invention that he considered to be better than any other. This part of the inquiry is wholly subjective, and resolves whether the

inventor must disclose any facts in addition to those sufficient for enablement. If the inventor in fact contemplated such a preferred mode, the second part of the analysis compares what he knew with what he disclosed — is the disclosure adequate to enable one skilled in the art to practice the best mode or, in other words, has the inventor "concealed" his preferred mode from the "public"? Assessing the adequacy of the disclosure, as opposed to its necessity, is largely an objective inquiry that depends upon the scope of the claimed invention and the level of skill in the art.

Chemcast, supra, 913 F.2d 923, 927-28.

There are several points worth noting here. First, this test places a significant gloss on the text of the statute in that a best mode — and hence the disclosure of such — is not mandated for each patent application. Where an inventor has in mind a laundry list of interchangeable ways of carrying out the invention, or parameters for making or using a part of the invention, there is no need to highlight a best mode in the application. This is consistent with the *Randomex* case, set out above.

Second, the test relaxes the standard proposed in cases such as *In re Nelson* for adequate disclosure of the best mode. According to *Chemcast,* when there is a best mode one need only disclose it in a way that meets the enablement test under § 112. This is part of the objective half of the test: measuring the adequacy of the best mode disclosure according to whether it enables one skilled in the art to practice it. The other aspect of the objective component of the test — determining the best mode of carrying out the invention by looking to the claims, the technical definition of "the invention" — is straightforward.

There is a clear tension here between the two halves of the test. The subjective part seeks to punish a deliberate concealment. But the second part of the test poses a much more lenient standard for the *quality* of disclosure necessary to avoid a charge of concealment. By calling for disclosure that enables, the "objective" part of the test implicitly permits disclosure that requires significant (though not "undue") experimentation. That is, when there is a best mode, the applicant need only say "here is my best mode" — and then proceed to disclose it in rather general terms.

To see how this might be applied, consider the *Randomex* case again. In dissent, Judge Mayer (author of the two-part *Chemcast* test under discussion here) pointed out that the applicant had failed to disclose the best mode even though one was known to him. Recall that this was in contrast to the majority opinion, which held that disclosure of the best cleaning fluid in a list of possible fluids satisfied the best mode requirement. Under *Chemcast,* all that would be required of the inventor in this situation presumably would have been a brief reference in the list that the preferred fluid was the "best mode" or "best one" for carrying out the invention. Importantly, because the enablement standard is called for in the objective part of the *Chemcast* test, this would suffice if those skilled in the art were capable of deriving the formula of the preferred cleaner, and perhaps of figuring out *why* this was the best. In other words, the disclosure of the best mode would be considered adequate even if it left a good deal of follow-up work to those skilled in the art.

This is at odds with the subjective part of the test. It permits an applicant to conceal details of the best mode that can be derived by those skilled in the art — even if the inventor has a very good idea about those details. Thus once the best mode is identified, it can be described quite generally, which permits the retention of a good deal of "know how" surrounding the best mode. One might argue that this is inconsistent with the intent of the best mode; as pointed out in *Nelson*, the language of this requirement in § 112 seems to say clearly that a fairly high level of disclosure is necessary. It might even be argued that the *Chemcast* test converts the best mode requirement into a minimal addition to ordinary disclosure: simply identify the best mode (e.g., in a list of components, say "this one is best"), and then, if the disclosure in general conforms to the enablement requirement in § 112, best mode is automatically satisfied. As mentioned, this permits the concealment of a good deal of information. Although it is of some value for the applicant to identify which component works best, it might well be asked why the applicant should be permitted to then omit the full details of what she knows about that best mode. If, for instance, in a claim with a "means for attaching" element the inventor finds that a bolt and nut made of copper work best, why not require the applicant to state the full details on this score? The *Chemcast* test could well be interpreted to permit instead statements such as: "means may include screws, bolts (best mode), latches or the like, made of weather-resistant materials such as galvanized aluminum, copper, or the like." Is it really consistent with the spirit of the best mode requirement to allow the applicant to conceal these details, and only require her to state in general what the best mode is?

TRANSCO PRODUCTS INC. v. PERFORMANCE CONTRACTING, INC.

38 F.3d 551, 32 U.S.P.Q.2d 1077 (Fed. Cir. 1994),
cert. denied, 115 S. Ct. 1102 (1995)

RICH, CIRCUIT JUDGE.

Performance Contracting, Inc. and Performance Contracting Group, Inc. (collectively Performance) appeal the May 18, 1993, decision of the United States District Court for the Northern District of Illinois, holding by summary judgment claims 1-4 of U.S. Patent No. 4,009,735 (Pinsky patent) invalid on the basis of three violations of the best mode requirement of 35 U.S.C. § 112. The district court based two of these violations on Pinsky's failure to update his best mode disclosure upon filing a continuation application pursuant to 37 CFR § 1.60 (Rule 60). The district court based the third violation on Pinsky's failure to provide supplier/trade name information for a material recited in the claims and described in the specification.

Because the district court erred as a matter of law in holding that an applicant must update the best mode disclosure upon the filing of a continuing application containing no new matter, the district court's holding regarding the first two violations is reversed. In addition, because the district court improperly resolved a genuine issue of material fact on summary judgment to find the third violation, that part of the district court's holding is vacated and remanded for further proceedings in accordance with our discussion herein.

BACKGROUND

I. *The Pinsky Patent*

The Pinsky patent issued from a Rule 60 continuation application filed on October 2, 1974, which application claimed priority pursuant to 35 U.S.C. § 120 based on a parent application filed October 24, 1973. The Pinsky patent is directed generally to thermal insulation for vessels and piping within nuclear power plants. Fig. 1 of the Pinsky patent, which illustrates a pipe wrapped with thermal insulation according to the claimed invention, is set forth below [in Figure 6-2, next page] together with both Fig. 2, which illustrates the thermal insulation with a portion of the glass fiber cloth facing removed, and Fig. 3, which illustrates the quick release fastener used for the thermal insulation.

Claim 1, the only independent claim in the Pinsky patent, reads as follows, with the numerals in brackets referring to elements illustrated in the figures:

Readily removable and replaceable rewettable thermal insulation [2] for use on vessels and piping within reactor containment areas of nuclear power plants comprising high temperature resistant mineral fiber or glass fiber [12] encapsulated within rewettable, high temperature resistant, asbestos free glass cloth [14] held in place with a plurality of spaced quick release and engage fasteners [6], wherein the glass cloth can withstand repeated wettings from spray systems within the reactor containment areas of nuclear power plants and wherein the fasteners are two woven nylon, hook and loop mating strips [22, 24], wherein the glass cloth has a finish of a leachable, organic silicate carried in a fatty and mineral oil vehicle.

II. *District Court Proceedings*

Transco Products Inc. (Transco) began marketing thermal insulation for nuclear power plant containment areas as early as 1982. Performance notified Transco in three letters, dated February 13, March 8, and September 11, 1989, that Performance believed Transco was infringing the Pinsky patent. In response, Transco filed suit on October 25, 1989, seeking a declaratory judgment of invalidity, noninfringement, and unenforceability of the Pinsky patent. By counterclaim, Performance asserted the Pinsky patent against Transco, alleging that Transco's sale of insulation for nuclear power plant containment areas infringed claims 1-4.

U.S. Patent   Mar. 1, 1977   **4,009,735**

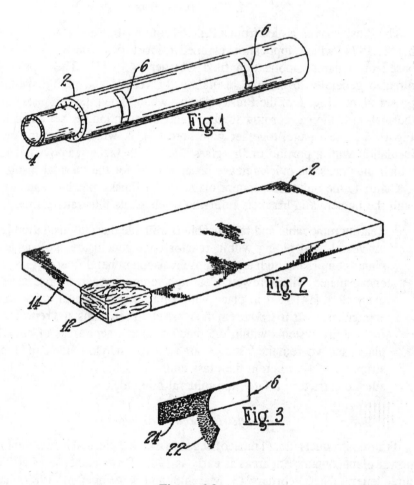

Figure 6-2

In the litigation that followed, Transco filed a motion for summary judgment of non-infringement of the Pinsky patent, and Performance filed a cross-motion for summary judgment of infringement. The district court denied both of these motions. *Transco Prods. Inc. v. Performance Contracting, Inc.*, 813 F. Supp. 613 (N.D. Ill. 1993). The district court, *sua sponte*, instructed the parties, however, to brief the issue of whether claims 1-4 of the Pinsky patent should be held invalid by summary judgment on the basis that the Pinsky patent fails to disclose the best mode of practicing the claimed invention. Following briefing, the district court issued the appealed decision holding the Pinsky patent invalid in view of three violations of the best mode requirement.

The district court based the first two best mode violations on knowledge Pinsky allegedly had at the time of filing his continuation application, but did not have at the time of filing the corresponding parent application. The district court found that Pinsky knew at the time of filing his continuation application that the use of stainless steel hooks for the fasteners (6), as opposed to the disclosed nylon-type hooks, constituted the best mode for carrying out the claimed invention. The district court also found that Pinsky knew at the time of filing his continuation application that the claimed fasteners should be placed longitudinally on the insulation with respect to the pipe, as opposed to circumferentially.

Of particular relevance to our disposition of this case, the district court found, and Transco does not dispute, that Pinsky did not consider either of the foregoing to be the best mode of practicing the claimed invention as of the filing date of the parent application. The district court stated, however, that the filing date of Pinsky's continuation application controlled, because, according to the district court, an applicant must update the best mode disclosure upon each filing of a continuing application. *Transco*, 821 F. Supp. at 550, 28 U.S.P.Q.2d at 1749. Accordingly, the district court held that Pinsky's failure to disclose this information in his continuation application was a violation of the best mode requirement.

Regarding the third violation, the district court found that Pinsky violated the best mode requirement by failing to disclose the commercial designation for a material that he described in the specification for use as the finished glass cloth (14). The district court found that Pinsky's description of the cloth was deficient and that Pinsky should have disclosed that the use of Burlington Industries' commercial 603A finished glass cloth constituted the best mode, since he knew this supplier/trade name information at the time of filing the parent application.

ANALYSIS

I. *Summary Judgment*

A motion for summary judgment is properly granted only when the pleadings, depositions, answers to interrogatories, and admissions on file, together with the affidavits, if any, show that there is no genuine issue as to any material fact and that the moving party is entitled to judgment as a matter of law. Fed. R. Civ. P. 56(c).

In reviewing the district court's grant of summary judgment, we must make an independent determination as to whether the standards of Rule 56(c) have been met. Reversal is required if the district court improperly determined any genuine issue of material fact or erred in holding that Transco was entitled to judgment as a matter of law.

II. *Continuing Applications and the Best Mode Requirement*

A. *Continuing Applications*

Prior to analyzing the particulars of this issue, we believe it necessary to recognize that there are various types of "continuing" applications that one may file at the PTO. See The Manual of Patent Examining Procedure (MPEP), §§ 201.03-201.13 (1988). An applicant may file a continuation, divisional, or continuation-in-part (CIP) application of a prior application, all of which the PTO characterizes as "continuing" applications. See MPEP § 201.11. In general, a continuing application is one filed during the pendency of another application which contains at least part of the disclosure of the other application and names at least one inventor in common with that application.

"Continuation" and "divisional" applications are alike in that they are both continuing applications based on the same disclosure as an earlier application. They differ, however, in what they claim. A "continuation" application claims the same invention claimed in an earlier application, although there may be some variation in the scope of the subject matter claimed. See MPEP § 201.07. A "divisional" application, on the other hand, is one carved out of an earlier application which disclosed and claimed more than one independent invention, the result being that the divisional application claims only one or more, but not all, of the independent inventions of the earlier application. See MPEP § 201.06. A "CIP" application is a continuing application containing a portion or all of the disclosure of an earlier application together with added matter not present in that earlier application. See MPEP § 201.08. The term "parent" is often used to refer to the immediately preceding application upon which a continuing application claims priority; the term "original" is used to refer to the first application in a chain of continuing applications. See MPEP §§ 201.04, 201.04(a).

The PTO has noted that the expressions "continuation," "divisional," and "continuation-in-part" are merely terms used for administrative convenience. See MPEP § 201.11. As explained more fully in Section II.B below, the bottom line is that, no matter what term is used to describe a continuing application, that application is entitled to the benefit of the filing date of an earlier application only as to common subject matter.

B. *Interplay of Section 120 and Section 112*

The district court held that an applicant must update the best mode disclosure upon filing any continuing application. The requirement that an applicant disclose the best mode for practicing the claimed invention is found in the first paragraph of section 112, which reads:

> *The specification* shall contain a written description of the invention, and of the manner and process of making and using it, in such full, clear, concise, and exact terms as to enable any person skilled in the art to which it pertains, or with which it is most nearly connected, to make and use the

same, and *shall set forth the best mode contemplated by the inventor of carrying out his invention.*

35 U.S.C. § 112, ¶ 1 (emphasis added).

On its face, section 112 does not distinguish between a parent application and continuing applications thereof. However, section 112 must be read in light of the other parts of Title 35, namely section 120, which governs the manner in which continuing applications are to be treated. Section 120 reads:

> An application for patent for an invention disclosed in the *manner provided by the first paragraph of section 112* of this title in an application previously filed in the United States, or as provided by section 363 of this title, which is filed by an inventor or inventors named in the previously filed application shall have the same effect, as to such invention, as though filed on the date of the prior application, if filed before the patenting or abandonment of or termination of proceedings on the first application or on an application similarly entitled to the benefit of the filing date of the first application and if it contains or is amended to contain a specific reference to the earlier filed application.

35 U.S.C. § 120 (emphasis added). In essence, "having the same effect" means having the benefit of the filing date of the earlier filed application.

The plain and unambiguous meaning of section 120 is that any application fulfilling the requirements therein "shall have the same effect" as if filed on the date of the application upon which it claims priority. The courts have repeatedly recognized this principle.

Section 120 appeared in the statutes for the first time in the Patent Act of 1952. Prior to 1952, continuing application practice was a creature of patent office practice and case law, and section 120 merely codified the procedural rights of an applicant with respect to this practice. Before section 120 was enacted, the Supreme Court noted that a continuing application and the application on which it is based are considered part of the same transaction constituting one continuous application. The legislative history of section 120 does not indicate any congressional intent to alter the Supreme Court's interpretation of continuing application practice. The Court of Customs and Patent Appeals (C.C.P.A.), a predecessor of this court, acknowledged that the state of the law regarding continuing application practice had not been changed by the enactment of section 120:

> The Supreme Court's explanation illuminates the meaning of "shall have the same effect" and clearly requires that we view appellants' applications as "parts of the same transaction" and "as constituting one continuous application" *for the continuing subject matter recited therein.*

Hogan, 559 F.2d at 604, 194 U.S.P.Q. at 535 (emphasis added). Thus, an application is entitled to the benefit of the filing date of an earlier application as to common subject matter. *See Weil v. Fritz*, 572 F.2d 856, 865 n. 16, 196 U.S.P.Q. 600, 608 n. 16 (C.C.P.A. 1978).

C. *Best Mode Requirement*

By use of the language "in the manner provided by the first paragraph of section 112," section 120 speaks of the first paragraph of section 112 as a whole.

Section 120 thus does not exempt the best mode requirement from its reach, and therefore this court must accept the plain and precise language of section 120 as encompassing the same. Accordingly, the date for evaluating a best mode disclosure in a continuing application is the date of the earlier application with respect to common subject matter.[1]

We note by analogy the manner in which the best mode requirement has been examined in other contexts. It has been held that the appropriate date for determining compliance with the best mode requirement for a reissue application is the filing date of the original application and not that of the reissue application. *Dow Chemical Co. v. American Cyanamid Co.*, 615 F. Supp. 471, 482, 229 U.S.P.Q. 171, 179 (E.D. La. 1985), *aff'd*, 816 F.2d 617, 2 U.S.P.Q.2d 1350 (Fed. Cir. 1987), *cert. denied*, 484 U.S. 849, 108 S. Ct. 149, 98 L. Ed. 2d 105 (1987). In a similar vein, it has been held that, in the context of a priority claim under 35 U.S.C. § 119, one looks to the foreign application and its filing date to determine the adequacy of the best mode disclosure and not to the filing date of the corresponding U.S. application.

Contrary to Transco's assertions, public policy does not demand that the public receive a new best mode disclosure in all continuing applications. Such a rule would subvert the patent system's goal of promoting the useful arts through encouraging early disclosure. An inventor's motivation to file early and then continue to test and improve upon his invention would be stifled by the knowledge that any progress that he made could preclude him from enjoying the procedural benefits available through continuing application practice. If he later developed better modes for practicing an invention adequately disclosed in an

---

[1] However, as mentioned earlier, a continuing application is entitled to rely on the filing date of an earlier application only with respect to subject matter common to both applications. The PTO acknowledges this principle in its discussion of CIP applications in the MPEP:

Any claim in a continuation-in-part application which is directed solely to subject matter adequately disclosed under 35 U.S.C. 112 in the parent application is entitled to the benefit of the filing date of the parent application. However, if a claim in a continuation-in-part application recites a feature which was not disclosed or adequately supported by a proper disclosure under 35 U.S.C. 112 in the parent application, but which was first introduced or adequately supported in the continuation-in-part application such a claim is entitled only to the filing date of the continuation-in-part application.

MPEP § 201.11. See P.J. Federico, "Commentary on the New Patent Act," 35 U.S.C.A. § 1 (1954), pp. 31-33.

earlier filed application, he would nonetheless have to redraft his disclosure to add these later-developments upon filing a continuing application.

The district court's comments regarding continuing application practice and new matter illustrate a misunderstanding of patent law and patent office practice. The subject matter that the district court believes Pinsky should have disclosed in his continuation application would clearly have constituted "new matter" pursuant to 35 U.S.C. § 132, 37 C.F.R. § 1.118, and MPEP §§ 608.04(a)-(c) and 706.03(o). It must be understood that the introduction of a new best mode disclosure would constitute the injection of "new matter" into the application and automatically deprive the applicant of the benefit of the earlier filing date of the parent or original application for any claim whose validity rests on the new best mode disclosure.

Moreover, imagine the practical implications if an applicant were forced to update the best mode disclosure upon each filing of a continuing application. Under current practice, the filing of many, if not most, continuing applications is merely a matter of form not requiring any input from the inventor. The best mode requirement, however, focuses on what the inventor knows. Thus, under the district court's holding, an attorney would necessarily be forced to discuss with an inventor any progress that has been made regarding the invention each time that a continuing application is filed, even when it is being filed merely for administrative convenience. This result would be completely contrary to current continuing application practice.

Furthermore, given that much of continuing application practice stems from actions taken by the PTO, it would be unfair to impose upon applicants an additional best mode burden. For example, when confronted with an application claiming more than one independent and distinct invention, an examiner often will impose a restriction requirement pursuant to 35 U.S.C. § 121 to ease the burden of examining that subject matter, thus forcing an applicant to file one or more divisional applications. In addition, an examiner also will often issue a final rejection and indicate that, if certain amendments are made to the claims in a continuation application filed pursuant to the streamlined procedures set forth in Rule 62, the examiner will allow those claims and pass them to issuance. Actions such as these, taken by the PTO primarily for administrative convenience, should not increase the burdens on an applicant regarding his ability to obtain patent protection.

Indeed, in this case, Pinsky filed his continuation application merely for the purpose of having the examiner consider an amendment to the claims proposed after final rejection in the parent application, but which was not entered in the parent application on the basis that it did not meet the procedural requirements of 37 CFR § 1.116. This is not an atypical chain of events. To impose upon an applicant the burden of updating the best mode disclosure under this type of circumstance would be unreasonable.

In conclusion, because the relevant date for evaluating a best mode disclosure is the date of the parent application, and because there is no dispute that Pinsky did not believe that the use of steel hooks and longitudinal fasteners constituted the best mode for practicing the claimed invention at the time Pinsky filed his parent application, reversal of these two best mode holdings is necessitated.

III. *Cloth Finish*

A. *Background*

The district court also found that Pinsky violated the best mode requirement by failing to provide supplier/trade name information for the finished glass cloth used in the preferred embodiment of his invention at the time he filed his parent application. The Pinsky patent provides the following description of the cloth at column 2, lines 32-45:

> The finish employed in this invention can vary widely. Generally, the finish is a leachable, organic silicate carried in a fatty and mineral oil vehicle. The finished fabric meets the requirements of U.S. Navy specification Mil-I-24244 with regard to chemical analysis and chemical resistance of materials used in the insulation of stainless steel, as well as the requirements of Coast Guard specification CFL-164.009 relating to incombustible materials. The glass cloth of this invention can withstand repeated wettings from spray systems within reactor containment areas of nuclear power plants and can withstand temperatures of 700 degrees F for at least 40 years.

The district court found the foregoing description of the finished glass cloth deficient in that Pinsky did not additionally disclose that the preferred cloth was Burlington Industries' 603A cloth, which was supplier/trade name information that Pinsky knew at the time of filing his parent application. For the reasons set forth below, we hold that the district court committed legal error when it resolved in this case, on summary judgment, a dispute as to a genuine issue of material fact, namely the adequacy of Pinsky's disclosure. We therefore vacate this part of the district court's decision and remand this issue to the district court for trial.

B. *Best Mode Requirement*

The determination as to whether the best mode requirement has been satisfied is a question of fact. The purpose of the best mode requirement is to "restrain inventors from applying for patents while at the same time concealing from the public preferred embodiments of their invention which they have in fact conceived." *In re Gay*, 309 F.2d 769, 772, 135 U.S.P.Q. 311, 315 (C.C.P.A. 1962). A holding of invalidity for failure to disclose the best mode requires clear and convincing evidence that the inventor both knew of and concealed a better mode of carrying out the claimed invention than was set forth in the specification. The burden of establishing invalidity by this standard lies with the party seeking such a holding, which in this case is Transco.

Performance does not dispute that Pinsky believed at the time that he filed the parent application that the use of a finished glass cloth like Burlington's 603A cloth constituted the best mode of practicing the claimed invention. The first part of *Chemcast's* two-step analysis therefore has been satisfied. Thus, the pertinent part of the *Chemcast* analysis at issue in this case is the second part dealing with the adequacy of Pinsky's disclosure. As will be illustrated below, there clearly existed before the district court a dispute as to the adequacy of Pinsky's disclosure, and the district court improperly resolved this issue on summary judgment.

[T]the district court erred in finding on summary judgment that such commercial information should have been provided in this particular case for Pinsky's disclosure to satisfy the adequacy prong of *Chemcast's* two-part test, as this was a fact issue highly disputed. The record evidence before the district court included a July 24, 1992, affidavit by a Mr. Vaughn, the director of research and development of Clark-Schwebel Fiber Glass Corp., one of the three major suppliers of finished glass cloth in the country. Vaughn's affidavit states, in particular, that "the description 'glass cloth having a finish of a leachable, organic silicate carried in a fatty and mineral oil vehicle' that is known to meet Mil-I-24244 and CFL-164.009 is an accurate description of glass cloth with a 603A finish" and is one "that one of ordinary skill in the art of finishes for glass cloth now, and in 1973, would understand to be a generic description of a 603A finish."

Rebuttal evidence included an affidavit of a Mr. Avery, the President of Transco, stating that "[i]n 1971-1974, I was someone skilled in the art of insulation" and that "[i]n the 1971-1974 time period and continuing to this day, I, and everyone I know in this industry, save Mr. Pinsky, have no idea (1) what a glass fabric is that has a finish of a leachable organic silicate carried in a fatty and mineral oil vehicle and that meets U.S. Navy Specification Mil-I-24244 and CFL-164.009 and (2) who makes and sells such a glass fabric." Avery's affidavit also takes specific issue with Vaughn's testimony. Performance counters that Avery is not technically qualified in the art and knows nothing about finishes.

Performance contends that, at the very least, the evidence it presented before the district court was sufficient to preclude summary judgment. We agree. The evidence outlined above illustrates that the district court was faced with a dispute as to a genuine issue of a material fact, namely, the adequacy of Pinsky's disclosure. As discussed previously, there must be no such disputes for summary judgment to be appropriate. Therefore, the district court committed legal error by resolving this issue on summary judgment.

NOTES

1. The result in *Transco* is arguably now mandated by the GATT TRIPs Agreement, at Article 29. *See* Roy E. Hofer & Ann Fitzgerald, *New Rules for Old Problems: Defining the Contours of the Best Mode Requirement in Patent Law*, 44 AM. U. L. REV. 2309, 2348 n.294 (1995).

2. Whose Knowledge Counts? Several cases have been decided recently on the issue of whose subjective knowledge regarding best mode counts for purposes of the defense. In *CPC Int'l, Inc. v. Archer Daniels Midland Co.*, 831 F. Supp. 1091, 1107-09, 30 U.S.P.Q.2d 1427 (D. Del. 1993), *aff'd per curiam in unpublished disposition*, 31 F.3d 1176 (Fed. Cir. 1994), the district court stated:

> ADM contends that because CPC failed to set forth the Swenson development work involving the scale-up of the Edwards invention, CPC knowingly failed to disclose the best mode of practicing the invention.
>
> Edwards completed his work on the continuous crystallization of dextrose by June, 1977, when he was transferred to another job at CPC and his work was placed in an inactive ideas file. CPC reactivated the work in 1979 and 1980, when it undertook the scale-up work with Swenson. CPC prepared and filed the patent application in December, 1980. There is no evidence to suggest that Edwards played a significant role in the preparation of the application or the drafting of the specifications, or that he was even aware of the Swenson work. Because CPC was primarily involved in the preparation and filing of the patent application, the purpose of the statute would not be served merely by looking to Edwards' intent at the time the application was filed. The Court must instead consider the information available to both Edwards and his agent, CPC, at the time they applied for the patent.
>
> In the patent specification, CPC described Edwards' invention without regard to shape or size of the vessel, the shape or size of the agitator, or the method of agitation. It reported it had found through experimental tests using turbine blades to produce agitation that "an impeller tip speed of about 60 cm/sec. separates the regions of surface reaction and diffusion-controlled crystal growth." CPC further noted that through further testing "it has been found that tip speeds in the range of 300-600 cm/sec. offer a reasonable compromise with regard to growth rate, nucleation rate, and cost-efficient mechanical agitation design."
>
> The patent does not refer to Swenson's scale-up work, which showed that Edwards' tip speeds — to which Edwards had ascribed an upper limit of 60 cm/sec. — were inoperative at the pilot-plant scale and that pilot plant tests were actually conducted at tip speeds ranging from 516 to 558 cm/sec. The identification and description of Edwards' work is thus the only mode for practicing the invention disclosed in the patent. ADM argues that Swenson's work is the best mode, as Edwards had recognized the need to scale up, as Swenson rejected Edwards' suggestion that tip speeds be limited to 60 cm/sec., and as CPC incorporated Swenson's tip speeds into claims 1 and 5 of the patent. More precisely, ADM contends that the process conditions developed during the Swenson pilot-plant studies were the best mode known to CPC at the time it filed the '172 patent application, and that CPC withheld this process information.

The Court concludes that the Swenson work was the best mode known to CPC for practicing the claimed invention and that the Swenson work was concealed from the public. CPC had taken Edwards' work to Swenson and invested time and money in a scale up in order to determine the efficacy of the process. That scale-up apparently demonstrated that the process would work on a commercial scale and it provided information to CPC on a method for implementing the process. CPC used that information to stretch its claims to cover that work, including expanding Edwards' claim for a tip speed from 60 cm/sec. to 600 cm/sec.

As noted above, it would have been apparent to CPC and others at the time that scaling up Edwards' work would have required an adjustment in Edwards' proposed optimum tip speed. By including a description of Edwards' work and failing to describe the Swenson scale up, CPC intentionally failed to disclose what it knew at the time was the best mode for implementing what it intended the invention to be, a commercial process.

But in *Glaxo Inc. v. Novopharm Ltd.*, 830 F. Supp. 871, 29 U.S.P.Q.2d 1126, 1134-35 (E.D.N.C. 1993), the court took another tack:

[Defendant] Novopharm argued at trial that the knowledge of Glaxo officials directly connected to the application for the patent should be imputed to [the inventor] Crookes for purposes of finding a best mode violation. This argument has some intuitive appeal, since it is Glaxo, and not Crookes individually, that both directed the patent prosecution and has enjoyed the monopoly the issued patent provides. If the court were to impute to Crookes the knowledge of [Glaxo employee] Brereton and those with whom he met prior to the patent application process, then clearly the court would be required to find a best mode violation. The statute refers only to the knowledge of the inventor, however, 35 U.S.C. Section 112, and the holding of the Federal Circuit in the *Texas Instruments* [*v. International Trade Comm'n*, 871 F.2d 1054 (Fed. Cir. 1989)] case does not permit using imputed knowledge to meet the requirement. The court concludes as a matter of law Novopharm failed to show the '431 patent should be invalidated based on a best mode violation.

What goal is served by imputing corporate knowledge to the defendant, as the court did in *CPC*? Does it make sense to shield large research groups from the effects of the inventive entity concept, as in § 103(c) (see Chapter 5), on the theory that research is actually done by teams rather than individuals, but ignore the shared information of a research team for purposes of the best mode defense? On the other hand, if the idea is to encourage the sharing of information, as in § 103, then it might make sense to limit the application of the best mode defense.

3. For useful recent commentary, see Jerry R. Selinger, *In Defense of "Best Mode": Preserving the Benefit of the Bargain for the Public*, 43 CATH. U. L. REV. 1071 (1994) (recounting history and defending best mode); David J. Weitz, *The*

Biological Deposit Requirement: A Means of Assuring Adequate Disclosure, 8 HIGH TECH. L.J. 275, 279 (1993) (proposing statutory best mode deposit requirement).

2. COMPARATIVE NOTES: BEST MODE

Strictly speaking, the U.S. patent system is the only one that has a best mode requirement. Under the GATT TRIPs Agreement, the signatories thereto are *permitted* to have a best mode requirement, but not required to do so. *See* Article 29. In the past, European and Japanese negotiators have proposed the elimination of the requirement from U.S. law in connection with discussions on international patent harmonization. *See* Note, *The Best Mode Requirement Refined: The Federal Circuit's Best Mode Standard, Mandate for Detail, and the Penalty for Nondisclosure*, 37 WAYNE L. REV. 1721, 1738 n.89 (1991).

Nevertheless, patent law in both Japan and Europe reflects some of the same underlying concerns as the U.S. best mode requirement, albeit in different doctrinal forms. In cases such as *Inadequate Description/Hakoune*, 1986, No. 11 OFFIC. J. EUR. PAT. OFF. 376 (Eur. Pat. Off. Tech. Bd. App., 14 July 1986), the EPO rejects patent applications for inadequate description where they fail to disclose sufficient details of how to perform the invention, in order to prevent competitors from copying.

Likewise the Japanese Patent Office *advises* applicants to include the best mode in their specification. T. TANABE & H. WEGNER, JAPANESE PATENT LAW § 422 (1979). Although not a formal requirement of patentability, commentators suggest that failure to include the best mode in the Japanese counterpart to an American invention may result in the judicial narrowing of the Japanese patent when it is issued and later infringed. *Id.* Note that the authors also point out a problem with the reverse scenario: whether a priority application filed in Japan which meets all U.S. requirements other than best mode is entitled to the Japanese priority date. They point to case law which suggests this might be a problem and criticize this result.

Chapter 7

MISCELLANEOUS INVALIDITY ISSUES

Once a patent applicant or patentee survives the major challenges to validity — lack of novelty, obviousness, and the like — it would seem she is in the clear. Not so. The gamut of invalidating doctrines runs wider, encompassing at least two other sets of issues: (1) inequitable conduct or "fraud on the Patent Office"; and (2) double patenting.

A. INEQUITABLE CONDUCT

The U.S. patent system relies exclusively on the applicant and the examiner to determine whether an invention is patentable, and if so, what its proper scope should be. Although the examiner is charged with the duty of making a search of the prior art, he or she cannot be expected in one search to duplicate the knowledge of the applicant regarding the particular field relating to an invention. For these reasons, and because applicants have an obvious incentive not to disclose prior art that would be damaging to their chances for a patent, applicants come before the Patent Office with a stiff duty of disclosure.

Because the patent system relies so much on conscientious disclosure, it necessarily metes out harsh punishment when this duty is breached. Thus a patent whose prosecution was marked by a significant nondisclosure receives the system's ultimate sanction — total unenforceability. Any lesser penalty, it is thought, would invite nondisclosure.

As often happens where high-stakes litigation is concerned, weighty public policy is harnessed to the interest of litigants; in this case, a doctrine designed to insure the integrity of the patent system becomes a powerful weapon in the hands of one accused of infringement. The reason why is the penalty. If an accused infringer can show some inequitable conduct during prosecution on the part of the patentee, the patent will be unenforceable: a complete defense to the charge of infringement. If some reference can be sniffed out that the patentee should have presented during prosecution, some information gleaned from the patentee's own research that the examiner perhaps should have been notified of, or some response to a patent examiner's action characterized as overly aggressive, the accused infringer may be off the hook. Thus have a patentee's competitors become the greatest watchdogs on the integrity of disclosure before the Patent Office. Indeed, the barking of these watchdogs has often kept patentees (and especially their lawyers) up at night, contemplating the ugly possibility that one more reference, one more lab result, should have been added to a patent application at the last minute, to keep the howling pack from the door once the hounds of litigation are let loose.

We begin our survey of the doctrinal landscape with an important early Federal Circuit case, *J.P. Stevens*. Then we move on to some detailed issues, and some more recent cases. One warning is in order, however, before we begin our excursion: this is a fast-changing area of law, and each case is unique, as befits a primarily *equitable* doctrine. So ultimately no more than rough patterns and general principles can be sketched. But be aware that the tone of more recent cases (especially the important *Kingsdown* decision, below) has changed somewhat since *J.P. Stevens*.

J.P. STEVENS & CO. v. LEX TEX LTD.

747 F.2d 1553, 223 U.S.P.Q. (BNA) 1089 (Fed. Cir. 1984)

Appeal from a final judgment of the District Court for the Southern District of Florida holding infringed, not invalid, and not unenforceable product claims 24, 26-27, and 31 of U.S. Patent No. 3,091,912 ('912 patent), issued on June 4, 1963 to Messrs. Stoddard and Seem, ultimately assigned to Lex Tex Ltd., Inc. (Lex Tex). Stevens [and other defendants] appeal those parts of the judgment holding that [inter alia] the claims were not unenforceable due to fraud on the Patent and Trademark Office (PTO). We reverse the portion of the final judgment holding that the claims in suit were not unenforceable.

[T]he district court determined that Stoddard and Seem (the '912 applicants) knew of and did not disclose during prosecution (1957 through 1963) British Patent No. 710,082 to Weiss (Weiss) and Italian Patent No. 531,481 to DaGasso (DaGasso). The court further determined, however, that there was no clear and convincing evidence of materiality or intent and, hence, no fraud on the PTO.

The '912 Patent

The '912 patent relates to reprocessing "torque stretch yarns," produced by twisting a multifilament yarn, heat setting the twist, and reverse twisting. Production of torque stretch yarns was the subject of three basic "single heater" patents involved in earlier phases of the litigation.

Torque stretch yarns possess certain properties that the processes claimed in the '912 patent were designed to improve by simultaneously applying heat and tension to the yarn in whatever correlation is required to produce desired effects. Different correlations produce different effects. Process claim 1 reads:

> 1. The method of processing multifilament "torque stretch yarn" whose stretch characteristics have been set at a given temperature comprising the steps of continuously advancing the yarn, controlling the degree of tension in said travelling yarn in at least one portion of its continuous travel, said tension being below the breaking tension of the structural elements of the yarn, heating said yarn during said portion of its continuous travel to a temperature not substantially greater than said given temperature and correlating the controlled tension and the heat imparted to said yarn with the

tensile force necessary to extend the yarn to the limit of its stretch characteristics and the tensile force necessary to extend the yarn to the yield point of
the structural elements of the yarn to thereby control the physical characteristics in the reprocessed yarn.

Other process claims specify the correlating criteria, add the step of controlling
tension in a second portion of the yarn's travel, or add a process of making
torque stretch yarn from multifilament yarn before performing the process set
forth in claim 1. The process claims were originally in suit but were withdrawn
after the Board opinion in a PTO reissue proceeding, discussed *infra*, determined
that most of them do not avoid the prior art.

The yarns produced by the processes of the '912 patent are asserted to have
uniform characteristics throughout their length. Moreover, the tendency of torque
stretch yarn randomly to "pigtail," i.e., the tendency of groups of opposed
spiralled formations to twist about themselves, is described as lessened. Product
claims 24, 26, 27, and 31, the only claims in suit, cover the yarn produced by
the foregoing processes, though not couched in product by process terminology.

Weiss and DaGasso Patents

The Weiss patent teaches that undesirable characteristics of stretch yarn made
by a prior twist-heat set-untwist batch method can be lessened by stretching the
yarn from 10% to 70% and steaming it in the stretched state for up to 30
minutes. The Weiss patent discloses a batch process, as opposed to the continuous
process of the '912 patent. The Weiss patent had counterparts in a number of
foreign countries, including the United States (U.S. Patent No. 2,765,505, issued
on October 16, 1956).

DaGasso teaches subjecting yarn made by a continuous twist-heat set-untwist
method to a second continuous process involving heat treatment followed by a
drawing action. The parties agree and the district court found that during heat
treatment the yarn is under positive tension.

Prosecution History of the '912 Patent

The application that resulted in the '912 patent ('912 application) was filed on
April 19, 1957, with process claims 1-23, product claims 24-29, and apparatus
claims 30-32, to which a fourth apparatus claim 33 was added by amendment
before the examiner's first Office Action. Pursuant to a restriction requirement
[i.e., requirement that splits an original application into several related ones] in
the first Office Action, apparatus claims 30-33 became claims 1-4 of Continuation-In-Part (CIP) application 682,724, filed September 9, 1957 and issued on
February 19, 1963, as U.S. Patent No. 3,077,724 ('724 patent). The specification
of application 682,724 ('724 application) is essentially identical to that of the '912
application.

[All the claims of the '912 application were eventually granted. Several, including most of the process claims, were invalidated in a subsequent reissue proceeding and appeal.]

"Inequitable Conduct"

"Common law fraud" requires (1) misrepresentation of a material fact, (2) intent to deceive or a state of mind so reckless respecting consequences as to be the equivalent of intent (scienter), (3) justifiable reliance on the misrepresentation by the party deceived, inducing him to act thereon, and (4) injury to the party deceived, resulting from reliance on the misrepresentation. *Norton v. Curtiss*, 433 F.2d 779, 793, 167 U.S.P.Q. 532, 543 (C.C.P.A. 1970).

Conduct before the PTO that may render a patent unenforceable is broader than "common law fraud." *Norton*, 433 F.2d at 793, 167 U.S.P.Q. at 543-44. It includes failure to disclose material information, or submission of false material information, with an intent to mislead. Because the "fraud" label can be confused with other forms of conduct, this opinion avoids that label and uses "inequitable conduct" as a more accurate description of the proscribed activity, it being understood that the term encompasses affirmative acts of commission, e.g., submission of false information, as well as omission, e.g., failure to disclose material information.

"Inequitable conduct" requires proof by clear and convincing evidence of a threshold degree of materiality of the nondisclosed or false information. It has been indicated that the threshold can be established by any of four tests: (1) objective "but for"; (2) subjective "but for"; (3) "but it may have been"; and (4) PTO Rule 1.56(a), i.e., whether there is a substantial likelihood that a reasonable examiner would have considered the omitted reference or false information important in deciding whether to allow the application to issue as a patent. [*American Hoist & Derrick Co. v. Sowa & Sons*, 725 F.2d 1350, 1362, 220 U.S.P.Q. (BNA) 763, 772-73 (Fed. Cir.), *cert. denied*, 105 S. Ct. 95 (1984)]. The PTO standard is the appropriate starting point because it is the broadest and because it most closely aligns with how one ought to conduct business with the PTO. *American Hoist*, 725 F.2d at 1363, 220 U.S.P.Q. at 773. Under the standard, a reference that would have been merely cumulative [i.e., one added to a list of other similarly relevant references] is not material.

"Inequitable conduct" also requires proof of a threshold intent. That intent need not be proven with direct evidence. It may be proven by showing acts the natural consequences of which are presumably intended by the actor. Proof of deliberate scheming is not needed; gross negligence is sufficient. Gross negligence is present when the actor, judged as a reasonable person in his position, should have known of the materiality of a withheld reference. On the other hand, simple negligence, oversight, or an erroneous judgment made in good faith, is insufficient.

Once the thresholds of materiality and intent are established, the court must balance them and determine as a matter of law whether the scales tilt to a conclusion that inequitable conduct occurred. If the court reaches that conclusion, it must hold that the patent claims at issue are unenforceable.

Whether the holding should be one of invalidity or unenforceability has had no practical significance in cases thus far presented to this court and has not therefore been addressed.

The Supreme Court has discussed inequitable conduct, as a defense to a claim of patent infringement, in terms of enforceability, see, e.g., *Precision Instrument Manufacturing Co. v. Automotive Maintenance Machinery Co.*, 324 U.S. 806, 814-16 (1945). In *Walker Process Equip., Inc. v. Food Mach. & Chem. Corp.*, 382 U.S. 172, 176 (1965), in addressing a claim for damages under § 4 of the Clayton Act based, inter alia, on alleged willfully fraudulent procurement of a patent, the Court spoke of "invalidity." Some courts have extrapolated from *Walker Process* two categories of defenses: (1) "fraud," rendering the patent invalid and (2) "other inequitable conduct," rendering the patent unenforceable.

Focusing on the effect of inequitable conduct as a defense, we conclude that it results in unenforceability.

Once a court concludes that inequitable conduct occurred, all the claims — not just the particular claims to which the inequitable conduct is directly connected — are unenforceable. As stated in *Gemveto Jewelry Co. v. Lambert Bros., Inc.*, 542 F. Supp. 933, 943, 216 U.S.P.Q. 976, 984 (S.D.N.Y. 1982):

> The gravamen of the fraud defense is that the patentee has failed to discharge his duty of dealing with the examiner in a manner free from the taint of "fraud or other inequitable conduct." If such conduct is established in connection with the prosecution of a patent, the fact that the lack of candor did not directly affect all the claims in the patent has never been the governing principle. It is the inequitable conduct that generates the unenforceability of the patent and we cannot think of any cases where a patentee partially escaped the consequences of his wrongful acts by arguing that he only committed acts of omission or commission with respect to a limited number of claims. It is an all or nothing proposition.

In this case, our analysis focuses on the process claims. We conclude that inequitable conduct occurred with respect to those claims and that the product claims in suit are therefore unenforceable.

Standard of Review

Materiality and intent are factual issues subject to the clearly erroneous standard of review. Thus, this court must affirm findings on materiality and intent unless it is left with a definite and firm conviction that error has occurred.

If the threshold of materiality and intent is crossed, we must determine, as a matter of law, whether inequitable conduct occurred.

Materiality of Weiss and DaGasso

The district court, essentially ignoring the PTO reissue proceeding, found that "[t]he Weiss and DaGasso patents are either not as material as other art cited by the PTO or there is [sic] competent conflicting opinions by reasonable experts such that the failure to cite Weiss and DaGasso cannot constitute intentional deception or gross negligence."

It found that the '912 invention differed from those of Weiss and DaGasso, and stated that "[t]his difference indicates that the inventions involved are significantly different, and the claim language that the patentees have been consistently relying on to distinguish their invention over Weiss and DaGasso has some genuine technological base."

Error resulted from a failure to give primary consideration to events involved in the PTO reissue proceeding. As stated above, the starting point for determining materiality is the PTO standard, i.e., a substantial likelihood that a reasonable examiner would have considered the nondisclosed information important in deciding whether to allow the application to issue as a patent. Consequently, the result of a PTO proceeding that assesses patentability in light of information not originally disclosed is of strong probative value in determining whether the nondisclosed information would have been material.

The rejections of the process claims in reliance on Weiss and DaGasso in the reissue proceeding indicate that those references were clearly important to the PTO in deciding that most of the process claims were unpatentable. Those references would have been equally important in the original prosecution of the '912 application. That importance, alone, establishes the materiality of those references — as long as the rejections were themselves reasonable. The latter condition, which is necessary to a finding under the PTO standard of materiality that a "reasonable examiner" would have considered the references important, is satisfied here. The process claims include the key step of subjecting a torque stretch yarn to a selected tension during heat treatment. That step is taught by Weiss and DaGasso, rendering them more material, or "important" under the PTO standard, than any of the references cited in the original prosecution or by the district court. It was clearly reasonable, therefore, for the examiner to make, and the Board for the most part to sustain, rejections of the process claims on Weiss and DaGasso.

The district court appears to have been persuaded by Lex Tex' argument that the process claimed in the '912 patent differed significantly from the processes of Weiss and DaGasso. Its process, says Lex Tex, involves "controlling" the tension by positively driven feed rolls whereby the tension can be increased or decreased. Though Weiss and DaGasso involve means to increase tension, says Lex Tex, they do not include feed rolls that can increase or decrease it, and the invention described in the '912 specification therefore differs from that described in the references. Lex Tex argues that claims are interpreted in light of the specification and that the "control" language of the claims must be therefore limited to means that can increase or decrease tension, i.e., positively driven feed rolls.

We disagree. Claims should be construed in light of the specification, but that does not mean that claims incorporate all disclosures in the specification. Moreover, nothing in the '912 specification requires that the process claims be limited to control means that can either increase or decrease tension (such as positively driven feed rolls). The specification discloses six general embodiments of the process invention, two that involve reducing tension and four that involve increasing tension after the torque stretch yarn is produced. The "controlling" limitation of the process claims reads on selecting a tension and applying heat — whether the tension be high or low. It does not require that the controlling means be capable of selectively accomplishing either an increase or decrease in tension. Indeed, the specification describes an option without feed rolls for simultaneous application of heat and tension.

The district court, in finding Weiss less relevant than [another reference], noted the continuous nature of the '912 process in comparison with Weiss' batch process. That Weiss involved a batch process does not require, however, a finding that Weiss was not material, or that it was less material than [this reference]. The difference between continuous and batch processes is merely one difference to consider in determining whether the claimed invention would have been nonobvious. That difference does not undermine the importance of Weiss' teaching of a simultaneous heat-tension treatment, an important aspect of the claims.

The district court also noted the possibilities that the primary examiner of the '912 patent: (1) knew of Weiss because he was also the primary examiner of the United States counterpart to Weiss and conducted prior art searches in classes that included Weiss; and (2) knew of DaGasso because he was also the primary examiner of the '724 application, in which DaGasso was cited. If the primary examiner actually knew about the Weiss and DaGasso references when examining the '912 application, that knowledge might preclude a finding of materiality. *Cf.*, *Orthopedic Equipment Co. v. All Orthopedic Appliances*, 707 F.2d 1376, 1383, 217 U.S.P.Q. 1281, 1286 (Fed. Cir. 1983) (nondisclosure not material because the examiner independently ascertained the existence of the undisclosed prior art). However, the district court did not find actual knowledge by the primary examiner — it merely noted possibilities and, where inequitable conduct is at issue, mere possibilities are insufficient. There is no evidence, and Lex Tex does not argue on appeal, that the primary examiner actually recalled the critical aspects of the U.S. Weiss or DaGasso patents. Nor is there evidence that the examiner principally responsible for examining the application, as opposed to the primary examiner, had knowledge of the references.

Intent

The district court found "no clear and convincing evidence that the applicants or their attorney, believing Weiss to be relevant, intentionally withheld it from the PTO or that they acted with recklessness or gross negligence," and it found "no evidence of deceptive intent with respect to the failure to cite DaGasso in the original application." In the latter regard, said the district court, "[t]he evidence does show ... that [applicants] believed that the claim limitations in the '912 were clearly and patentably distinguished from DaGasso."

Those findings must be determined to have been clearly erroneous. As stated above, threshold intent is established where an actor in an applicant's position would have reasonably known that the reference was material, e.g., that the reference would have been important to a reasonable examiner in deciding whether to allow the claims. Here, where none of the prior art cited during prosecution taught a key element of the claimed process invention, and where both Weiss and DaGasso taught that key element, the applicants for the '912 patent should have known that those references would be important to the PTO, especially in light of certain undisputed facts: (1) claim 4 of the '724 application was rejected on DaGasso; (2) licenses were taken under Weiss and foreign counterparts to Weiss; and (3) corresponding foreign applications were rejected on Weiss.

Original claim 4 of the '724 application and claim 30 of the '912 patent are similar. Each require treatment of torque stretch yarn with simultaneous heat and tension. Claim 4 of the '724 application (in partially amended form) was rejected on October 13, 1959, on DaGasso in view [of another reference]. Concerning the rejection, applicant Seem stated in internal correspondence that DaGasso "does disclose our can-can [double heater] type of apparatus to continuously produce and post treat torque stretch yarn." Though applicants further amended the claim in an effort to avoid the prior art, the claim was again rejected, on November 7, 1960, on the same references. The claim was then cancelled in favor of a new claim 5, which was subsequently amended and issued.

Fully aware of DaGasso and its materiality in relation to the application that resulted in the '724 patent, applicants should have known of its materiality in relation to the '912 application. Applicants nonetheless elected not to disclose DaGasso to the examiner of the latter application.

In March, 1957, Universal Winding Company, later Leesona Corporation (Universal), the then owner of the '912 application, introduced a machine for reprocessing torque stretch yarn. Heberlein, the owner of the Weiss patent, informed Universal that sale of the machine would be a contributory infringement of the Weiss process claims. Universal took a license under foreign counterparts to the Weiss patent. Fluflon, Ltd., a British company owned in part by Stoddard and Seem, also took a license under Weiss.

The district court discounted the effect of the Universal license, viewing it as merely an "economic decision based upon a desire to avoid costly litigation over the Weiss patent since it might be considered a dominating patent under the patent laws in Europe." There is no evidence, stated the district court, that such "business judgment" amounted to gross negligence or recklessness.

We agree that taking a license may have been an exercise in good business judgment. We find the consideration irrelevant, however, to a determination of whether the failure to disclose the licensed patent, Weiss, to the PTO during prosecution of the '912 application, was grossly negligent or otherwise "intentional."

The license agreements are virtually conclusive evidence that the applicants should have known of the materiality of Weiss. Applicants may have believed that the '912 process was patentable over Weiss, but that they took a license under it in connection with the sale of their machine that performed the '912 process evinces knowledge of Weiss' importance. A failure to disclose Weiss in view of that knowledge constitutes reckless disregard of the duty to disclose.

Japanese, German and British applications corresponding to the '912 application were filed during pendency of the latter. The Japanese and German applications were rejected in view of Weiss, and the Japanese application was eventually abandoned. The British counterpart was allowed despite the citation of Weiss.

The district court stated that "while the applicants were aware of the Weiss patent, there was no recognition on their part of its materiality or relevance [in the United States] because of the differences in the patent laws of these foreign countries as to disclosure, claims practice, forms of applications and standards of patentability."

Differences in foreign patent laws may in other contexts be important. They are not relevant in determining intent underlying a failure to disclose to the PTO. The controlling factor in that determination is found in the nondisclosed information itself. Whether the '912 applicants can be viewed as meeting the threshold of intent to mislead the PTO has nothing to do with rules governing disclosure, claims, applications and patentability in foreign lands. Whether Weiss should have been disclosed under those rules in those lands has no controlling effect on whether it should have been disclosed to the PTO here. That Weiss was cited and claims were rejected on Weiss in applications corresponding to the '912 application should have caused a reasonable applicant to have so recognized its materiality in the PTO as to have led to its disclosure. No requirement exists to disclose to the PTO all references cited against foreign corresponding applications; yet in the present circumstances the failure to cite Weiss in light of its citation in foreign lands is strong evidence of intent to mislead.

[The court then addressed defendant's argument that their good faith belief in the narrow construction of their claims exonerates them from inequitable conduct.] [A] good faith belief that claims should be narrowly construed to avoid uncited prior art will not necessarily or always preclude a finding of recklessness or gross negligence in failing to cite that art. The references may be important in assessing patentability, whatever may be the applicant's view. In *Driscoll v. Cebalo*, 731 F.2d 878, 221 U.S.P.Q. 745 (Fed. Cir. 1984), applicant cancelled a claim he believed was anticipated by a Canadian reference, replacing it with a claim that he believed avoided that reference. This court refused to give controlling effect to applicant's subjective determination that the new claim avoided the art. A finding of intent was reached in *Driscoll*, notwithstanding contemporaneous evidence that the applicant there did believe the new claim avoided the art. Here, where there is no evidence of good faith belief in the narrow claim interpretation, and there is contrary evidence, a finding is compelled that the intent element of inequitable conduct is clearly present.

Balancing Materiality and Intent

A high degree of materiality was present here. The PTO standard was easily met by the close relationship of the Weiss and DaGasso disclosures to the claims of the '912 patent, as reflected in the citation of Weiss and DaGasso by the reissue examiner.

There was also a relatively high degree of intent. If there were no deliberate scheming, there was clearly reckless or grossly negligent activity. Applicants clearly should have known of the materiality of Weiss and DaGasso, especially after they took licenses under Weiss and its counterparts, had their foreign applications rejected on Weiss, and had similar claims in their virtually identical CIP application rejected on DaGasso.

Balancing materiality and intent, we are compelled to conclude that "inequitable conduct" occurred. Accordingly, all claims of the patent must be held unenforceable.

NOTES

1. *Harsh Penalty.* As the court notes, the penalty for inequitable conduct regarding *any* claim of a patent is the unenforceability of the *entire patent* — a bitter pill indeed for the disappointed inventor, but a necessary tonic in a system where applicants carry so much of the burden of disclosure.

2. *Analogy to Common Law Fraud.* The court begins by setting out the elements required to prove fraud in a common law contracts case. The second element, "intent to deceive or a state of mind so reckless respecting consequences as to be the equivalent of intent (scienter)," is not in fact required in all contracts cases. Likewise, in most cases courts state that there must be an affirmative misrepresentation of material fact for a fraud defense to be made out. *See* A. FARNSWORTH, CONTRACTS § 4-12 (1982). If an innocent but material misrepresentation is actionable under contract law, and if an affirmative statement (rather than concealment) is a prerequisite for such an action, it is perhaps not entirely accurate to state, as the *Norton* case does, that patent-related inequitable conduct is a more rigorous standard of behavior; they are simply different.

Why should there be different rules for common law contract fraud and "fraud on the Patent Office"? The grant of a patent has been analogized to a contract between an inventor and society. If this analogy is extended, what place does it leave for differing standards of fraud? Note that in a private contract action, *either* intent or materiality is required; why a different standard in the patent system? How does the contract remedy — rescission of the contract, perhaps with restitution to the aggrieved victim of the misrepresentation — compare to the penalty in patent inequitable conduct cases?

1. NOTE ON SUPREME COURT PRECEDENT

In *Precision Instrument Mfg. Co. v. Automotive Maintenance Mach. Co.*, 324 U.S. 806 (1945), the Court invalidated a patent on the ground that the applicant had failed to disclose an alleged act of perjury committed during an interference proceeding. In the course of its opinion, the Court laid down some general principles that have often been cited:

> A patent by its very nature is affected with a public interest. As recognized by the Constitution, it is a special privilege.... At the same time, a patent is an exception to the general rule against monopolies and to the right to access to a free and open market. The far-reaching social and economic consequences of a patent, therefore, give the public a paramount interest in seeing that patent monopolies spring from backgrounds free from fraud or other inequitable conduct and that such monopolies are kept within their legitimate scope. The facts ... must accordingly be measured both by public and private standards of equity.

324 U.S. at 816.

> Those who have applications pending with the Patent Office or who are parties to Patent Office proceedings have an uncompromising duty to report to it all facts concerning possible fraud or inequitableness underlying the applications in issue. This duty is not excused by reasonable doubts as to the sufficiency of the proof of the inequitable conduct nor by resort to independent legal advice. Public interest demands that all facts relevant to such matters be submitted formally or informally to the Patent Office, which can then pass upon the sufficiency of the evidence. Only in this way can that agency act to safeguard the public in the first instance against fraudulent patent monopolies. Only in that way can the Patent Office and the public escape from being classed among the "mute and helpless victims of deception and fraud."

324 U.S. at 818. An interesting feature of the case is that Automotive, the patentee, had settled an interference dispute with the appellant Precision; because of this, the possible perjury came to light. The potential harm to the public interest from the settlement of interferences gave rise to Patent Act § 135(c), which requires a copy of any interference settlement agreement to be filed with the Patent Office.

In *Kingsland v. Dorsey*, 338 U.S. 318 (1949), the Supreme Court reinstated a decision by the Patent Office disbarring a patent attorney for fraud on the Patent Office growing out of some unusual circumstances. The attorney had apparently participated in a scheme to trumpet the merits of an invention by ghost-writing an article lauding the claimed invention and attributing the article to a putative "adversary" of the firm, a labor leader named Clarke active in the company's union. The entire scheme was revealed and harshly criticized in the Court's patent misuse/antitrust ruling in *Hazel-Atlas Glass Co. v. Hartford-Empire Co.*, 322 U.S. 238, 240-41 (1944); *see also* Note, *Compulsory Licensing by Antitrust Decree*, 56 YALE L.J. 77 (1946) (detailed description of administrative procedure set up to license bottle industry patents in the wake of *Hartford-Empire Co.* case; reprints portion of final district court consent decree in appendix). In reinstating the attorney's disbarment from the Patent Office bar, the Court commented on the perils of fraud before the Office:

> We agree with the following statement made by the Patent Office Committee on Enrollment and Disbarment that considered this case:
>
>> By reason of the nature of an application for patent, the relationship of attorneys to the Patent Office requires the highest degree of candor and good faith. In its relation to applicants, the Office ... must rely upon their integrity and deal with them in a spirit of trust and confidence ....
>
> It was the Commissioner, not the courts, that Congress made primarily responsible for protecting the public from the evil consequences that might result if practitioners should betray their high trust.
>
> After an examination of the record we are satisfied that the findings were amply supported .... The charge of unfairness in the hearings is, we think, wholly without support.

338 U.S. at 319-20. In an interesting dissent, Justice Douglas (usually no friend to patent lawyers) argued that "an accused lawyer may expect that he will not be condemned out of a capricious self-righteousness or denied the essentials of a fair hearing." 338 U.S. at 320.

Although *Precision Instrument, supra,* is often referred to as the first Supreme Court case dealing with fraud, the 1944 *Hartford Empire* case contains some strong language regarding the patent attorney's duty of disclosure. *See Hartford Empire,* 322 U.S. 238, at 245-46 ("Here, even if we consider nothing but Hartford's sworn admissions, we find a deliberately planned and carefully executed scheme to defraud not only the Patent Office but the Circuit Court of Appeals. Proof of the scheme, and of its complete success up to date, is conclusive."). And references to fraud on the Patent Office are not unknown before that time. *See Railroad Co. v. Dubois,* 79 U.S. (12 Wall.) 47 (1870) (infringement case where accused apparently argued fraudulent prosecution of derived invention; Court stated: "[D]efendants, when sued for an infringement, were not at liberty to set up as a defence that the patent had been fraudulently obtained, no fraud appearing upon its face.").

The infamous "planted article" in the *Hartford-Empire* case provided an occasion for a Supreme Court discourse on materiality:

> Whether or not it was the primary basis for that ruling, the article did impress the Court, as shown by the Court's opinion. Doubtless it is wholly impossible accurately to appraise the influence that the article exerted on the judges. But we do not think the circumstances call for such an attempted appraisal. Hartford's officials and lawyers thought the article material. They conceived it in an effort to persuade a hostile Patent Office to grant their patent application, and went to considerable trouble and expense to get it published. Having lost their infringement suit based on the patent in the District Court wherein they did not specifically emphasize the article, they urged the article upon the Circuit Court and prevailed. They are in no position now to dispute its effectiveness.

322 U.S. 238, 246-47.

NOTE

Fraudulent Procurement as Antitrust Violation. In *Walker Process Equip., Inc. v. Food Mach. & Chem. Corp.*, 382 U.S. 172, 147 U.S.P.Q. (BNA) 404 (1965), the Supreme Court held that the maintenance and enforcement of a patent obtained by fraud on the Patent Office may be the basis of an action under § 2 of the Sherman Act and therefore subject to a treble damage claim by an injured party under § 4 of the Clayton Act. As found by the trial court, and affirmed by the Seventh Circuit, defendant committed fraud by not disclosing a public use which would have been a statutory bar. *See* 335 F.2d 315 (7th Cir. 1964).

2. MATERIALITY

Cases such as *Stevens* — where an applicant suppresses or conveniently forgets a relevant prior art reference — are perhaps the classic instances of inequitable conduct. But a host of other acts and omissions can qualify as well, most typically (1) failure to note acts that may constitute public use and on-sale bars under Patent Act § 102(b); (2) false affidavits and declarations relating to dates of invention; and (3) presentation of "doctored" data in affidavits and declarations relating to comparative testing and embodiment examples. *Cf. Kangaroos U.S.A., Inc. v. Caldor, Inc.*, 778 F.2d 1571, 228 U.S.P.Q. (BNA) 32 (Fed. Cir. 1985) ("There is no reprieve from the duty of square dealing and full disclosure that rests on the patent practitioner in dealings with the PTO"; stating that inequitable conduct might consist of knowingly taking advantage of an examiner error in some phase of prosecution). Moreover, inequitable conduct can occur at almost any stage of a patent prosecution, and as a result of many activities carried on by patent lawyers. *See, e.g., Hewlett-Packard Co. v. Bausch & Lomb Inc.*, 882 F.2d

1556, 11 U.S.P.Q.2d (BNA) 1750 (Fed. Cir. 1989) (inequitable conduct during patent reissue proceeding renders *all* claims of patent invalid); *Northern Telecom, Inc. v. Datapoint Corp.*, 908 F.2d 931, 15 U.S.P.Q.2d (BNA) 1321 (Fed. Cir. 1990) (amendment to patent after notice of allowance but before issue fee is paid (Rule 312 amendment)).

MERCK & CO. v. DANBURY PHARMACAL, INC.
873 F.2d 1418, 10 U.S.P.Q.2d (BNA) 1682 (Fed. Cir. 1989)

[Merck's U.S. Patent 3,882,246 claimed a method of using cyclobenzaprine to treat certain types of skeletal muscle disorders. Defendant Danbury argued at trial that Merck engaged in inequitable conduct during the prosecution of the patent; the trial court agreed, declaring the patent unenforceable. The trial court found that when prosecuting its patent application Merck (1) withheld prior art references regarding amitriptyline, a pharmacologically similar compound; and (2) failed to disclose a shared side effect between amitriptyline and the claimed compound, cyclobenzaprine, namely that they both induce drowsiness. The trial court found that even in light of these two omissions, the claimed compound was not obvious under § 103 of the Patent Act. Nonetheless, it refused to tie this finding of nonobviousness to a finding that the nondisclosed information was immaterial for purposes of determining the inequitable conduct issue. Specifically, it refused to accept Merck's argument that the nondisclosed prior art was not material to the examiner's decision on the grounds that it did not deal with a major feature of the claimed invention, the compound's ability to relax muscle spasms without relaxing normal muscle activity, a quality known as muscle tone "selectivity." In its discussion on the materiality factor, the Federal Circuit made the following points.]

"Inequitable conduct resides in failure to disclose material information, or submission of false information, with an intent to deceive...." Merck mounts its major attack on the findings that the withheld prior art and its misrepresentations were material, saying that neither related to the selectivity of cyclobenzaprine.

Merck says the determinations of nonobviousness and materiality of the withheld prior art are inconsistent, because prior art that did not render the invention claimed in the '246 patent obvious (because selectivity was not "foreshadowed" in that art) could not be material. Second, in view of the claim limitation to selectivity, Merck argues that the withheld prior art is merely cumulative because neither of the two references considered by the examiner were selective.

First, Merck wrongly presupposes a "but for" standard of materiality. Materiality may be established, as it was here, by a showing that a reasonable examiner would consider the withheld prior art important in deciding whether to issue the patent. Here, as the district court correctly found, "amitriptyline's activity was comparable to cyclobenzaprine's," both having similar properties and effects.

Thus the withheld prior art would clearly have been important to a reasonable examiner.

Second, the withheld prior art is not merely cumulative because amitriptyline was, as indicated in Merck's own tests, by far the most relevant to skeletal muscle relaxation. To FDA, Merck disclosed amitriptyline, not the cited prior art to which it now says amitriptyline would have been merely cumulative. That the claimed invention may have been superior in one property to both the cited and withheld prior art may be a basis for patentability; it cannot serve automatically to render the withheld prior art either cumulative or immaterial.

Merck says its misrepresentation that cyclobenzaprine did not cause drowsiness is immaterial because drowsiness is unrelated to selectivity [and that] absence of a drowsiness effect was not relied on by the examiner in deciding to allow the '246 patent.

First, the [trial] court found that cyclobenzaprine's selectivity was related to the side effect of drowsiness. It stated that "[t]o the extent drowsiness falls within the spectrum of sedation, it appears ... that cyclobenzaprine produces sedative effects, although not muscle weakness," and thus "cyclobenzaprine's selectivity is limited to its operation without loss of normal muscle tone." Merck has not shown that finding to have been clearly erroneous or that the district court abused its discretion in so viewing the evidence. Merck was aware of the side effect of drowsiness and that it clearly resembles side effects ordinarily associated with nervous system depressants. Thus the court correctly cited a pattern of misrepresentations regarding cyclobenzaprine's freedom from the attendant side effects ordinarily associated with nervous system depressants.

[Second,] Merck again improperly argues for a "but for" standard of materiality in its assumption that the examiner did not rely on its drowsiness misrepresentation. To be material, a misrepresentation need not be relied on by the examiner in deciding to allow the patent. The matter misrepresented need only be within a reasonable examiner's realm of consideration.

NOTE

A Taint You Cannot Purge. In *A.B. Dick Co. v. Burroughs Corp.*, 798 F.2d 1392, 230 U.S.P.Q. (BNA) 849 (1986), the court held that the applicant's failure to disclose a material reference rendered the patent unenforceable even though (1) the examiner found the reference himself, and (2) amended versions of the affected claims were allowed after being rejected because of the reference. 798 F.2d at 1397-98. The case also supports the point made in *Danbury* that a reference need not render the claims unpatentable to be material. 798 F.2d at 1397.

From *Refac International, Ltd. v. Lotus Development Corp.*, 81 F.3d 1576, 38 U.S.P.Q.2d 1665 (Fed. Cir. 1996) (Lourie, J.):

The patent in suit, U.S. Patent 4,398,249, concerns a method of converting a software source code program to object code. During prosecution of the '249 patent, the examiner initially rejected the application, which was filed on August 12, 1970, under 35 U.S.C. § 112, ¶ 1, on the ground of inadequate disclosure. In response, a Rule 132 affidavit by·Pardo was submitted, averring that the application contained sufficient disclosure to enable any person skilled in the programming art to make and use the claimed invention.

[After another rejection,] the inventors' attorney proposed a strategy of filing affidavits from three people other than the inventors, with different experience and skill levels, attesting to the sufficiency of the disclosure. He requested that the inventors find three such people, and they recommended Peter H. Jones, a computer scientist or compiler writer; David H. Cikra, a computer programmer; and Robert F. Bullen, a supervisor of programmers. Affidavits from these three individuals were then filed ....

In response to these affidavits, the examiner issued a notice of allowance. Neither the inventors nor the affiants had disclosed to the U.S. Patent and Trademark Office ("PTO"), however, that each of the affiants had a prior association with the inventors' company, Lanpar, Ltd., or that they had pre-existing knowledge of a commercial embodiment of the invention ....

The rationale of *Paragon* [*Podiatry Lab., Inc. v. KLM Laboratories, Inc.*, 984 F.2d 1182, 25 U.S.P.Q.2d 1561 (Fed. Cir. 1993)] supports affirmance of the trial court's decision [that information regarding past association was material to the examiner's evaluation of the affidavit and that the inventors submitted the affidavit with an intent to mislead the PTO.] The fact that the conduct here consists of an omission rather than a misrepresentation does not compel a different result, as either may mislead an examiner. An examiner must be able to evaluate information in an affidavit in context, giving it the proper weight; both the materiality and the inference of intent arising from the omission in Jones's affidavit are enhanced by the otherwise detailed recitation of his employment history. The district court therefore did not abuse its discretion in concluding that the omission of information in Jones's affidavit relating to his status as a disinterested party was intended to mislead the PTO.

Refac also argues that Jones's affidavit was cumulative to Cikra's and Bullen's affidavits and that it was therefore not material as a matter of law. Refac relies on the following passage in *Molins* to support its argument: "If the information allegedly withheld is not as pertinent as that considered by the examiner, or is merely cumulative to that considered by the examiner, such information is not material." *Molins*, 48 F.3d at 1179, 33 U.S.P.Q.2d at 1827.

Lotus responds that the inventors should not be allowed to shield their inequitable conduct by arguing that the Jones affidavit was not the sole cause for allowance. Lotus states that such a policy would force an inquiry into the decision-making process of the examiner in every case in which inequitable conduct is alleged to have occurred.

The cited passage from *Molins* relates to cumulative prior art references, not to cumulative affidavits. Molins cited a discussion in Scripps that also related to cumulative references. We decline to place submitted cumulative affidavits in the same status as unsubmitted cumulative prior art. While it is not necessary to cite cumulative prior art because it adds nothing to what is already of record (although it may be prudent to do so), one cannot excuse the submission of a misleading affidavit on the ground that it was only cumulative. Affidavits are inherently material, even if only cumulative. The affirmative act of submitting an affidavit must be construed as being intended to be relied upon. It is not comparable to omitting an unnecessary act.

Whether or not Jones's affidavit was cumulative to that of Cikra's and Bullen's affidavits is also of no consequence. Since any one of the affidavits from Cikra, Bullen, and Jones may have resulted in an allowance of the claims, each affidavit ipso facto had a certain level of materiality.

Refac also argues that Jones's affidavit had no probative value and therefore cannot be used to infer an intent to mislead.

The inequitable conduct found by the district court in this case did not involve what is more commonly (but often unjustifiably) asserted as inequitable conduct, viz., failure to cite relevant prior art or making a material misrepresentation. Holding the omission of an aspect of one's employment history to be inequitable conduct might thus seem to be unduly severe, a heavy penalty for an arguably minor omission. However, the district court here made findings of materiality and intent to deceive, based partly on credibility findings, and, given our standard of review, we do not consider the findings to be clearly erroneous or the conclusion to be an abuse of discretion. We cannot hold as a matter of law that omission of a relevant part of one's employment history on an affidavit intended to show the adequacy of the patent specification to one of ordinary skill in the art, when such an affidavit by the inventor was earlier rejected, does not constitute inequitable conduct.

[*Affirmed.*]

NOTES

1. *No Paragon of Virtue.* In *Paragon Podiatry Lab., Inc. v. KLM Labs., Inc.*, 984 F.2d 1182, 25 U.S.P.Q.2d 1561 (Fed. Cir. 1993), the court affirmed a rare summary judgment disposition of invalidity on grounds of inequitable conduct. As in *Refac*, the applicant had submitted a false declaration that an affiant was a disinterested party. The court stated:

Paragon argues that any intent to mislead may not be "presumed" from the mere failure to disclose known highly material information. While a correct view of the law, that truism does not apply here. The inference arises not simply from the materiality of the affidavits, but from the affirmative acts of submitting them, their misleading character, and the inability of the examiner to investigate the facts. The natural consequence of these acts was to lead the examiner to believe that the affiants were "disinterested" parties, and the patentees were successful in that effort.

Id. at 1191.

a. The Standard of Materiality in the Patent Office

The test referred to in the excerpt from *Danbury* — whether a reasonable examiner would have considered a reference important in deciding to allow the application to issue as a patent — is the most frequently used test in recent years. *See, e.g., American Hoist & Derrick Co. v. Sowa & Sons, Inc.*, 725 F.2d 1350, 220 U.S.P.Q. (BNA) 763 (Fed. Cir.), *cert. denied*, 105 S. Ct. 95 (1984). It stems from a longstanding Patent Office Rule, Rule 56. Although now withdrawn (as explained below), the Rule animates many recent cases, and continues to some extent to rule from the grave. Here are pertinent excerpts from Rule 56:

37 C.F.R. 1.56. Duty of disclosure; fraud; striking or rejection of applications.

(a) A duty of candor and good faith toward the Patent and Trademark Office rests on the inventor, on each attorney or agent who prepares or prosecutes the application and on every other individual who is substantively involved in the preparation or prosecution of the application .... All such individuals have a duty to disclose to the Office information they are aware of which is material to the examination of the application. *Such information is material where there is a substantial likelihood that a reasonable examiner would consider it important in deciding whether to allow the application to issue as a patent.*

(Emphasis added.) In 1988, the PTO announced that it would no longer investigate and reject original or reissue applications under Rule 56. The primary reason given for this decision was that the Office was not well positioned to decide the "intent to mislead" issue that recent Federal Circuit decisions require for a finding of a inequitable conduct. PTO Notice Regarding Implementation of 37 C.F.R. § 1.56, 1095 O.G. 16 (Sept. 8, 1988) (citing *In re Harita*, 847 F.2d 801, 6 U.S.P.Q.2d 1930 (Fed. Cir. 1988), and *FMC Corp. v. Manitowoc Co.*, 835 F.2d 1411, 5 U.S.P.Q.2d 1112 (Fed. Cir. 1987)).

In 1989 the PTO announced a proposed new Rule 57 as a substitute for existing Rule 56. PTO, "Notice of Proposed Rule: Duty of Disclosure and

Practitioner Misconduct," 54 Fed. Reg. 11334 (March 17, 1989); this proposal has since been withdrawn. *See Proposed Rule 57 Withdrawn by Patent Office*, 40 PAT. TRADEMARK & COPYRIGHT J. (BNA) 323 (1990). The most important change in the short-lived proposal was in the standard of materiality of information that must be disclosed. Instead of the old Rule 56 standard of whether "there is a substantial likelihood that a reasonable examiner would consider it important in deciding whether to allow the application to issue as a patent," Rule 57 would have imposed a "but for" standard, requiring disclosure of information "which [an individual] knows or should have known would render unpatentable any pending claim."

Even after this proposal was announced, the Federal Circuit continued to apply the reasonable examiner standard. *See, e.g., Danbury, supra.* This is in keeping with precedent, which discouraged the applicant from acting as her own examiner by deciding whether information renders a claim unpatentable. In light of this precedent, even if the Patent Office someday adopts something like proposed Rule 57, practitioners will undoubtedly continue to err on the side of more disclosure; and the more cautious among them will probably still hew to the old Rule 56 standard and the cases that embody it. *See* Wegner, *Inequitable Conduct and the Proper Roles of Patent Attorney and Examiner in an Era of International Patent Harmonization*, 16 AM. INTELL. PROP. L. ASS'N Q.J. 38, 52-54 (1988) (describing expansion of duty of disclosure, suggesting changes in this area of law must be anticipated). *See also Patent and Trademark Office: Proposed Prima Facie Standard for Duty of Disclosure Draws Mixed Reaction*, 42 PAT. TRADEMARK & COPYRIGHT J. (BNA) 573 (Oct. 17, 1991) (summarizing public hearing on Patent Office proposal to amend Rule 56 to reflect a standard defining as "material" any reference that "is not cumulative to information already of record in the application, and (1) [which] creates, by itself or in combination with other information, a prima facie case of unpatentability of a claim; or (2) [which] supports a position of unpatentability taken by the Office which the applicant disputes, or it is inconsistent with a position in support of patentability on which the applicant relies."). The Patent Office has adopted this new "prima facie" test in its revised Rule 56. But some doubts apparently remain over the Office's procedure in adopting the new rule. *See Patent Office Adopts Inequitable Conduct Rules*, 43 PAT. TRADEMARK & COPYRIGHT J. 246 (1992); Moy, *The Effect of New Rule 56 on the Law of Inequitable Conduct*, 74 J. PAT. TRADEMARK OFF. SOC'Y 257 (1992) (arguing that new rule is outside PTO's rulemaking authority and predicting that courts will ignore it).

b. The Securities Law Analogy

One commentator commented on the origins of inequitable conduct as an extension of the theory behind "Rule 10b-5" liability in securities cases:

> Courts [in securities cases] have now adopted [a] test which is paraphrased in the test embodied in Rule 56. Under 10b-5 a fact is material "if there is

substantial likelihood that a reasonable [investor] would consider it important." But despite this similar criteria for materiality, the intent requirement under 10b-5 is distinctly different from that which the Federal Circuit has found sufficient in patent inequitable conduct cases. Under 10b-5 law, the defendant must have acted with scienter, defined as an intent to deceive or manipulate or defraud. [T]he Supreme Court [has] affirmed that an action for damages under 10b-5 would not lie in the absence of "an allegation of 'scienter.'" In doing so, the Court expressly rejected a test [championed] by the Securities Exchange Commission which proposed that civil liability could be imposed for negligent violation of Rule 10b-5 where "the defendant knew or could reasonably foresee that the plaintiff would rely on his conduct." One court offered the following explanation for the need of a duty of care on the part of the investor:

> Considered alone, the sweeping language of Rule 10b-5 creates an almost completely undefined liability. All that the rule requires for its vioation is that someone "do something bad" in connection with a purchase or sale or securities. Without further delineation, civil liability is formless.

The liability for "doing something bad" before the Patent Office seems equally formless today. Rule 10b-5 was instituted to protect ordinary investors from misrepresentation. One would not think that expert patent examiners require even greater protection.

Lynch, *An Argument for Eliminating the Defense of Patent Unenforceability Based on Inequitable Conduct*, 16 AM. INTELL. PROP. L. ASS'N Q.J. 7 (1988). *See* 17 C.F.R. 240.10b-5 (1989), promulgated by the Securities and Exchange Commission (the "SEC") under § 10(b) of the Securities Exchange Act of 1934. 15 U.S.C. 78j(b) (1988). Rule 10b-5 provides:

> It shall be unlawful for any person, directly or indirectly, by the use of any means or instrumentality of interstate commerce, or of the mails or of any facility of any national securities exchange,
>
> (a) To employ any device, scheme, or artifice to defraud,
> (b) To make any untrue statement of material fact or to omit to state a material fact necessary in order to make the statements made, in the light of the circumstances under which they were made, not misleading, or
> (c) To engage in any act, practice, or course of business which operates or would operate as a fraud or deceit upon any person in connection with the purchase or sale of any security.

17 C.F.R. 240.10b-5 (1989).

By way of preempting the objection that inequitable conduct really protects the *public* from invalid patents, Lynch asserts that to deprive an otherwise patentable invention of protection as the result of a "hypertechnical" inquiry is to undermine the real goals of the patent system. *Id.*

3. INTENT

KINGSDOWN MEDICAL CONSULTANTS, LTD.
v. HOLLISTER, INC.

863 F.2d 867, 9 U.S.P.Q.2d 1384 (Fed. Cir. 1988),
cert. denied, 490 U.S. 1067 (1989)

Kingsdown Medical Consultants, Ltd. and E.R. Squibb & Sons, Inc., (Kingsdown) appeal from a judgment of the United States District Court for the Northern District of Illinois, holding U.S. Patent No. 4,460,363 ('363) unenforceable because of inequitable conduct before the United States Patent and Trademark Office (PTO). We reverse and remand.

BACKGROUND

Kingsdown sued Hollister Incorporated (Hollister) for infringement of claims 2, 4, 5, 9, 10, 12, 13, 14, 16, 17, 18, 27, 28, and 29 of Kingsdown's '363 patent. The district court held the patent unenforceable because of Kingsdown's conduct in respect of claim 9 and reached no other issue.

The invention claimed in the '363 patent is a two-piece ostomy appliance for use by patients with openings in their abdominal walls for release of waste.

The two pieces of the appliance are a pad and a detachable pouch. The pad is secured to the patient's body encircling the abdominal wall opening. Matching coupling rings are attached to the pad and to the pouch. When engaged, the rings provide a water tight seal. Disengaging the rings allows for removal of the pouch.

The Prosecution History

Kingsdown filed its original patent application in February 1978. The '363 patent issued July 17, 1984. The intervening period of more than six-and-a-half years saw a complex prosecution, involving the submission, rejection, amendment, re-numbering, etc., of 118 claims, a continuation application, an appeal, a petition to make special, and citation and discussion of 44 references.

After a series of office actions and amendments, Kingsdown submitted claim 50. [C]laim 50 read:

> A coupling for an ostomy appliance comprising a pad or dressing having a generally circular aperture for passage of the stoma, said pad or dressing aperture encircled by a coupling member and an ostomy bag also having a generally circular aperture for passage of the stoma, said bag aperture encircled by a second coupling member, one of said coupling members being two opposed walls of closed looped annular [i.e., ring-like] channel form and the other coupling member of closed loop form having a rib or projec-

tion dimensioned to be gripped between the mutually (sic) opposed channel walls when said coupling members are connected, said rib or projection having a thin resilient deflectible seal strip extending therefrom, which, when said rib or projection is disposed between said walls, springs away therefrom to sealingly engage one of said walls, and in which each coupling member is formed of resilient synthetic plastics material.

The examiner found that claim 50 contained allowable subject matter, but rejected the claim for indefiniteness under 35 U.S.C. § 112, second paragraph, objecting to "encircled," because the coupling ring could not, in the examiner's view, "encircle" the aperture in the pad, the ring and aperture not being "coplanar." The examiner had not in earlier actions objected to "encircled" to describe similar relationships in other claims. Nor had the examiner found the identical "encircled" language indefinite in original claims 1 and 6 which were combined to form claim 50.

To render claim 50 definite, and thereby overcome the § 112 rejection, Kingsdown amended the claim. [A]mended claim 50 read:

A coupling for an ostomy appliance comprising a pad or dressing having a body contacting surface and an outer surface with a generally circular aperture for passage of the stoma extending through said pad or dressing, a coupling member extending outwardly from said outer pad or dressing surface and encircling the intersection of said aperture and said outer pad or dressing surface, and an ostomy bag also having a generally circular aperture in one bag wall for passage of the stoma with a second coupling member affixed to said bag wall around the periphery of said bag wall aperture and extending outwardly from said bag wall, one of said coupling members being two opposed walls of closed looped annular channel form and the other coupling member of closed loop form having a rib or projection dimensioned to be gripped between the mutually opposed channel walls when said coupling members are connected, said rib or projection having a thin resilient deflectible seal strip extending therefrom, which, when said rib or projection is disposed between said walls, springs away therefrom to sealingly engage one of said walls, and in which each coupling member is formed of resilient synthetic plastic material.

To avoid the § 112 rejection, Kingsdown had thus added the pad's two surfaces, replaced "aperture encircled," first occurrence, with "encircling the intersection of said aperture and said outer pad or dressing surface," and deleted "encircled," second occurrence. In an advisory action, the examiner said the changes in claim language overcame the § 112 rejection and that amended claim 50 would be allowable.

While Kingsdown's appeal of other rejected claims was pending, Kingsdown's patent attorney saw a two-piece ostomy appliance manufactured by Hollister.

Kingsdown engaged an outside counsel to file a continuation application and withdrew the appeal.

Thirty-four claims were filed with the continuation application, including new and never-before-examined claims and 22 claims indicated as corresponding to claims allowed in the parent application. In prosecuting the continuation, a total of 44 references, including 14 new references, were cited and 29 claims were substituted for the 34 earlier filed, making a total of 63 claims presented. Kingsdown submitted a two-column list, one column containing the claim numbers of 22 previously allowed claims, the other column containing the claim numbers of the 21 claims in the continuation application that corresponded to those previously allowed claims. That list indicated, incorrectly, that claim 43 in the continuation application corresponded to allowed claim 50 in the parent application. Claim 43 actually corresponded to the unamended claim 50 that had been rejected for indefiniteness under § 112. Claim 43 was renumbered as the present claim 9 in the '363 patent.

There was another claim 43. It was in the parent application and was combined with claim 55 of the parent application to form claim 61 in the continuation. Claim 55 contained the language of amended claim 50 relating to "encircled." It was allowed as submitted and was not involved in any discussion of indefiniteness. Claim 61 became claim 27 of the patent. Claim 27 reads as follows:

> An ostomy appliance comprising a pad or dressing having a body contacting surface and an outer surface with an aperture for passage of the stoma extending through said pad or dressing, a coupling member extending outwardly from said pad or dressing and encircling the intersection of said aperture and the outer surface of said pad or dressing and an ostomy bag also having an aperture in one bag wall for passage of the stoma with a second coupling member affixed to said bag wall around the periphery of said bag wall aperture and extending outwardly from said bag wall, said bag coupling member being two opposed walls of closed loop channel form and said pad or dressing coupling member being a closed loop form having a rib or projection dimensioned to be gripped between the opposed channel walls when said coupling members are connected, and a thin resilient seal strip extending at an angle radially inward from an inner surface of said rib or projection which engages the outer surface of said inner channel wall and wherein said rib or projection has a peripheral bead extending therefrom in a direction opposite said deflectible seal strip and said outer channel wall has a complementary bead on its inner surface, each of said two beads having an annular surface inclined to the common axis of said coupling members when connected, the arrangement being such that said two annular surfaces are in face-to-face contact when said two members are in their mutually coupled positions.

The district court rendered its opinion and announced its decision orally from the bench.

Having examined the prosecution history, the district court found that the examiner could have relied on the representation that claim 43 corresponded to allowable claim 50 and rejected Kingsdown's suggestion that the examiner must have made an independent examination of claim 43, because: (1) in the Notice of Allowance, the examiner said the claims were allowed "in view of applicant's communication of 2 July 8[2]"; (2) there was no evidence that the examiner had compared the language of amended claim 50 with that of claim 43; and (3) the examiner could justifiably rely on the representation because of an applicant's duty of candor.

The district court stated that the narrower language of amended claim 50 gave Hollister a possible defense, i.e., that Hollister's coupling member does not encircle the intersection of the aperture and the pad surface because it has an intervening "floating flange" member. The court inferred motive to deceive the PTO because Kingsdown's patent attorney viewed the Hollister appliance after he had amended claim 50 and before the continuation application was filed. The court expressly declined to make any finding on whether the accused device would or would not infringe any claims, but stated that Kingsdown's patent attorney must have perceived that Hollister would have a defense against infringement of the amended version of claim 50 that it would not have against the unamended version.

ISSUE

Whether the district court's finding of intent to deceive was clearly erroneous, rendering its determination that inequitable conduct occurred an abuse of discretion. [From footnote 5:] Because of our decision on intent, it is unnecessary to discuss materiality. *Allen Archery, Inc. v. Browning Mfg. Co.*, 819 F.2d 1087, 1094, 2 U.S.P.Q.2d 1490, 1495 (Fed. Cir. 1987).

OPINION

We confront a case of first impression, in which inequitable conduct has been held to reside in an incorrect inclusion in a continuation application of a claim that contained allowable subject matter, but had been rejected as indefinite in the parent application.

Inequitable conduct resides in failure to disclose material information, or submission of false material information, with an intent to deceive, and those two elements, materiality and intent, must be proven by clear and convincing evidence. *J.P. Stevens & Co., Inc. v. Lex Tex Ltd., Inc.*, 747 F.2d 1553, 1559, 223 U.S.P.Q. 1089, 1092 (Fed. Cir. 1984), *cert. denied*, 474 U.S. 822 (1985). The findings on materiality and intent are subject to the clearly erroneous standard of Rule 52(a) Fed. R. Civ. P. and are not to be disturbed unless this court has a definite and firm conviction that a mistake has been committed. *J.P. Stevens*, 747 F.2d at 1562, 223 U.S.P.Q. at 1094.

"To be guilty of inequitable conduct, one must have intended to act inequitably." *FMC Corp. v. Manitowoc Co., Inc.*, 835 F.2d 1411, 1415, 5 U.S.P.Q.2d 1112, 1115 (Fed. Cir. 1987). Kingsdown's attorney testified that he was not aware of the error until Hollister mentioned it in March 1987, and the experts for both parties testified that they saw no evidence of deceptive intent. As above indicated, the district court's finding of Kingsdown's intent to mislead is based on the alternative grounds of: (a) gross negligence; and (b) acts indicating an intent to deceive. Neither ground, however, supports a finding of intent in this case.

a. *Negligence*

The district court inferred intent based on what it perceived to be Kingsdown's gross negligence. Whether the intent element of inequitable conduct is present cannot always be inferred from a pattern of conduct that may be described as gross negligence. That conduct must be sufficient to require a finding of deceitful intent in the light of all the circumstances. We are not convinced that deceitful intent was present in Kingsdown's negligent filing of its continuation application or, in fact, that its conduct even rises to a level that would warrant the description "gross negligence."

It is well to be reminded of what actually occurred in this case — a ministerial act involving two claims, which, because both claims contained allowable subject matter, did not result in the patenting of anything anticipated or rendered obvious by anything in the prior art and thus took nothing from the public domain. In preparing and filing the continuation application, a newly-hired counsel for Kingsdown had two versions of "claim 50" in the parent application, an unamended rejected version and an amended allowed version. As is common, counsel renumbered and transferred into the continuation all (here, 22) claims "previously allowed." In filing its claim 43, it copied the "wrong," i.e., the rejected, version of claim 50. That error led to the incorrect listing of claim 43 as corresponding to allowed claim 50 and to incorporation of claim 43 as claim 9 in the patent. In approving the continuation for filing, Kingsdown's regular attorney did not, as the district court said, "catch" the mistake.

In view of the relative ease with which others also overlooked the differences in the claims, Kingsdown's failure to notice that claim 43 did not correspond to the amended and allowed version of claim 50 is insufficient to warrant a finding of an intent to deceive the PTO. Undisputed facts indicating that relative ease are: (1) the similarity in language of the two claims; (2) the use of the same claim number, 50, for the amended and unamended claims; (3) the multiplicity of claims involved in the prosecution of both applications; (4) the examiner's failure to reject claims using "encircled" in the parent application's first and second office actions, making its presence in claim 43 something less than a glaring error; (5) the two-year interval between the rejection/amendment of claim 50 and the filing of the continuation; (6) failure of the examiner to reject claim 43 under

§ 112 or to notice the differences between claim 43 and amended claim 50 during what must be presumed, absent contrary evidence, to have been an examination of the continuation; and (7) the failure of Hollister to notice the lack of correspondence between claim 43 and the amended version of claim 50 during three years of discovery and until after it had carefully and critically reviewed the file history 10 to 15 times with an eye toward litigation. That Kingsdown did not notice its mistake during more than one opportunity of doing so, does not in this case, and in view of Hollister's frequent and focused opportunities, establish that Kingsdown intended to deceive the PTO.

[W]e [do not] suggest that the presumed compliance of the examiner with his duty to examine the claims in a continuation would relieve an applicant of its duty to avoid mistakes in describing a submitted claim as corresponding to an allowed version of an earlier claim in the parent application. The district court correctly noted that an examiner has a right to expect candor from counsel. Its indication that examiners "must" rely on counsel's candor would be applicable, however, only when the examiner does not have the involved documents or information before him, as the examiner did here. Blind reliance on presumed candor would render examination unnecessary, and nothing in the statute or Manual of Patent Examining Procedure would justify reliance on counsel's candor as a substitute for an examiner's duty to examine the claims.

Thus the first basis for the district court's finding of deceitful intent (what it viewed as "gross negligence") cannot stand.

b. *Acts*

The district court also based its finding of deceitful intent on the separate and alternative inferences it drew from Kingsdown's acts in viewing the Hollister device, in desiring to obtain a patent that would "cover" that device, and in failing to disclaim or reissue after Hollister charged it with inequitable conduct. The district court limited its analysis here to claim 9 and amended claim 50.

It should be made clear at the outset of the present discussion that there is nothing improper, illegal or inequitable in filing a patent application for the purpose of obtaining a right to exclude a known competitor's product from the market; nor is it in any manner improper to amend or insert claims intended to cover a competitor's product the applicant's attorney has learned about during the prosecution of a patent application. Any such amendment or insertion must comply with all statutes and regulations, of course, but, if it does, its genesis in the marketplace is simply irrelevant and cannot of itself evidence deceitful intent.

The district court appears to have dealt with claim 9 in isolation because of Hollister's correct statement that when inequitable conduct occurs in relation to one claim the entire patent is unenforceable. *J.P. Stevens*, 747 F.2d at 1561, 223 U.S.P.Q. at 1093. But Hollister leapfrogs from that correct proposition to one that is incorrect, i.e., that courts may not look outside the involved claim in determining, in the first place, whether inequitable conduct did in fact occur at all. Claims are not born, and do not live, in isolation. Each is related to other claims, to the specification and drawings, to the prior art, to an attorney's remarks, to co-pending and continuing applications, and often, as here, to earlier or later versions of itself in light of amendments made to it. The district court accepted Hollister's argument that Kingsdown included claim 43 (unamended claim 50) in its continuing application because its chances of proving infringement of claim 43 were greater than would have been its chances of proving infringement of amended claim 50, in view of Hollister's "floating flange" argument against infringement of the latter. Neither the court nor Hollister tells us how Kingsdown could have known in July 1982 what Hollister's defense would be years later, when suit was filed.

Faced with Hollister's assertion that an experienced patent attorney would knowingly and intentionally transfer into a continuing application a claim earlier rejected for indefiniteness, without rearguing that the claim was not indefinite, the district court stated that "how an experienced patent attorney could allow such conduct to take place" gave it "the greatest difficulty." A knowing failure to disclose and knowingly false statements are always difficult to understand. However, a transfer of numerous claims en masse from a parent to a continuing application, as the district court stated, is a ministerial act. As such, it is more vulnerable to errors which by definition result from inattention, and is less likely to result from the scienter involved in the more egregious acts of omission and commission that have been seen as reflecting the deceitful intent element of inequitable conduct in our cases.

Because there has been no decision on whether any of claims 2, 4, 5, and 27 are infringed by Hollister's product, or on whether Kingsdown could have reasonably believed they are, it cannot at this stage be said that Kingsdown needed claim 9 to properly bring suit for infringement. If it did not, the district court's implication of sinister motivation and the court's inference of deceptive intent from Kingsdown's acts would collapse.

The district court, in finding intent, made a passing reference to Kingsdown's continuation of its suit after Hollister charged inequitable conduct. [A] suggestion that patentees should abandon their suits, or disclaim or reissue, in response to every charge of inequitable conduct raised by an alleged infringer would be nothing short of ridiculous. The right of patentees to resist such charges must not be chilled to extinction by fear that a failure to disclaim or reissue will be used against them as evidence that their original intent was deceitful. Nor is there in the record any basis for expecting that any such disclaimer or reissue would cause Hollister to drop its inequitable conduct defense or refrain from reliance on such remedial action as support for that defense. Kingsdown's belief in its innocence meant that a court test of the inequitable conduct charge was inevitable and appropriate. A requirement for disclaimer or reissue to avoid adverse inferences would merely encourage the present proliferation of inequitable conduct charges.

RESOLUTION OF CONFLICTING PRECEDENT

[From footnote:] Because precedent may not be changed by a panel [i.e., it requires action *in banc*], this section has been considered and decided by an *in banc* court.

"Gross Negligence" and the Intent Element of Inequitable Conduct

Some of our opinions have suggested that a finding of gross negligence compels a finding of an intent to deceive. Others have indicated that gross negligence alone does not mandate a finding of intent to deceive.

"Gross negligence" has been used as a label for various patterns of conduct. It is definable, however, only in terms of a particular act or acts viewed in light of all the circumstances. We adopt the view that a finding that particular conduct amounts to "gross negligence" does not of itself justify an inference of intent to deceive; the involved conduct, viewed in light of all the evidence, including evidence indicative of good faith, must indicate sufficient culpability to require a finding of intent to deceive.

Nature of Question

Some of our opinions have indicated that whether inequitable conduct occurred is a question of law. In *Gardco Mfg. Inc. v. Herst Lighting Co.*, 820 F.2d 1209, 1212, 2 U.S.P.Q.2d 2015, 2018 (Fed. Cir. 1987) (citing *Precision Instrument Mfg. Co. v. Automotive Maintenance Mach. Co.*, 324 U.S. 806 (1945)), the court indicated that the inequitable conduct question is equitable in nature. We adopt the latter view, i.e., that the ultimate question of whether inequitable conduct occurred is equitable in nature.

Standard of Review

As an equitable issue, inequitable conduct is committed to the discretion of the trial court and is reviewed by this court under an abuse of discretion standard. We, accordingly, will not simply substitute our judgment for that of the trial court in relation to inequitable conduct.

Effect of Inequitable Conduct

When a court has finally determined that inequitable conduct occurred in relation to one or more claims during prosecution of the patent application, the entire patent is rendered unenforceable. We, in banc, reaffirm that rule as set forth in *J.P. Stevens & Co. v. Lex Tex Ltd.*

CONCLUSION

Having determined that the district court's finding of intent is clearly errone-ous, the panel reverses the judgment based on a conclusion of inequitable conduct before the PTO and remands the case for such further proceedings as the district court may deem appropriate.

NOTES

1. *"An Absolute Plague."* "[T]he habit of charging inequitable conduct in almost every major patent case has become an absolute plague." *Burlington Indus. v. Dayco Corp.*, 849 F.2d 1418, 1422, 7 U.S.P.Q.2d 1158, 1161 (Fed. Cir. 1988).

2. *More on "Gross Negligence" and Intent.* In re Harita, 847 F.2d 801, 6 U.S.P.Q.2d (BNA) 1930 (Fed. Cir. 1988), the court states that "[w]e think that we should not infer merely from some vague thing called 'gross negligence' an intent ...." The court's decision in *FMC Corp. v. Manitowoc Co.*, 835 F.2d 1411, 5 U.S.P.Q.2d (BNA) 1112 (Fed. Cir. 1987) also supports this view:

> [A]n applicant who knew or should have known of the art or information, and of its materiality, is not automatically precluded thereby from an effort to convince the fact finder that the failure to disclose was nonetheless not due to an intent to mislead the PTO; i.e., that, in light of all the circumstances of the case, an inference of intent to mislead is not warranted. No single factor or combination [of] factors can be said always to require an inference of intent to mislead .... A mere denial of intent to mislead (which would defeat every effort to establish inequitable conduct) will not suffice ....

Similarly, in *Demaco Corp. v. F. Von Langsdorff Licensing Ltd.*, 851 F.2d 1387, 7 U.S.P.Q.2d (BNA) 1222, 1229 (Fed. Cir. 1988), the court suggested that a finding of gross negligence would not necessarily result in a finding of intent since "gross negligence [must be] of such gravity as to warrant the drawing therefrom of an inference of intent to deceive or mislead the PTO."

3. *Inequitable Conduct and The Best Mode Requirement.* In *Consolidated Alum. Corp. v. Foseco Int'l Ltd.*, 910 F.2d 804 (Fed. Cir. 1990), the Federal Circuit held that plaintiff/patentee's intentional fraud in disclosing a fictitious process component during prosecution of their patent rendered that patent, as well as a series of related patents, invalid for inequitable conduct. See Chapter 6, Section E, on the Best Mode requirement under § 112. This establishes a precedent that the intentional withholding or misrepresentation of the best mode may have grave consequences indeed. A recent Note criticized the extension of the inequitable conduct or "unclean hands" holding in this case to the related patents, arguing that although "the court should treat those with unclean hands firmly, refusing to enforce other related patents may have been a harsher decision that necessary." Note, *The Best Mode Requirement Refined: The Federal Circuit's Best Mode Standard, Mandate for Detail, and the Penalty for Nondisclosure*, 37 WAYNE L. REV. 1721, 1737 (1991).

4. For a good review of the background and development of the best mode defense, see Robert J. Goldman, *Evolution of the Inequitable Conduct Defense in Patent Litigation*, 7 HARV. J.L. & TECH. 37 (1993). Goodman argues that inequitable conduct doctrine has progressed through four stages, the penultimate one characterized by a very aggressive expansion of the concept. Now, he argues, the Federal Circuit has retrenched somewhat. He also advocates a more lenient standard of review, which he believes may cut down somewhat on the number of appeals involving inequitable conduct, if not the number of times it is used as a defense at trial.

B. DOUBLE PATENTING

Several doctrines conspire to raise the possibility that an inventor might extend her patent monopoly by filing a successive series of related patent applications after filing a patent for the basic inventive principle. An inventor's own prior work cannot be cited against her for purposes of novelty. Prior-filed patent applications of the same inventor are not prior art under § 102(e), which speaks in terms of pending applications "of another." And of course these same categories of prior art are excluded from any obviousness analysis. In fact, the only way an inventor's prior work (more properly, the prior work of the identical "inventive entity") can become prior art as to her (or them) is if it qualifies as a statutory bar — that is, if it is described in a patent, published, or placed on sale or in use more than a year before she (or they) files a patent application claiming the same invention or an obvious variant on it.

This leaves open the possibility that inventors will in effect extend the monopoly period on a basic invention by filing a series of related or improvement patent applications sometime before the critical date for statutory bar purposes (i.e., before the first patent reaches its one year issue date anniversary).

The doctrine of double patenting has been improvised, largely by courts, to prevent this scenario. This doctrine prohibits an inventor from extending the monopoly period by claiming the same invention more than once, i.e., in a later patent application. In addition, it has been extended to cover the situation where the later application claims not the same invention, but an obvious variation on it. In this situation, courts have devised the "terminal disclaimer," which requires the applicant to disclaim any portion of the statutory twenty-year-from-filing exclusivity period for the second patent that would run over the term of the first patent. In this way, applicants may file applications claiming obvious variants on a basic invention. While entitled to these claims on obvious variations (if otherwise patentable), the applicant will be limited to the term of the basic patent. Thus if a second patent, claiming subject matter obvious in light of that claimed in the first application, issues one year after that first application, the second patent will have a term shorter by one year than it otherwise would have had. It must expire, in other words, at the same time as the first patent. The patentee's terminal disclaimer, which would be required by the Patent Office in such a case, serves this function.

Special Patent Office rules apply when the Patent Office, and not the applicant, splits an original application into several related ones (a practice called "restriction"). Specifically, when the Office issues a restriction requirement, the later applications filed as a result of the restriction are not subject to the double patenting doctrine as long as their claims remain consonant with the restriction requirement.

1. THE BASICS OF DOUBLE PATENTING

MILLER v. EAGLE MANUFACTURING CO.

151 U.S. 186 (1894)

The appellee, as assignee of letters patent No. 222,767, dated December 16, 1879, and No. 242,497, dated June 7, 1881, issued to Edgar A. Wright, for certain new and useful improvements in wheeled cultivators, brought this suit against the appellants, who were the defendants in the court below, for the alleged infringement thereof.

[One defense] made in that court [was] that the invention shown in each of the patents in suit is identical.

The class of cultivators to which the Wright patents in question relate are of the ordinary character of wheeled, straddle-row cultivators, having vertical swinging beams, or drag bars, to carry the shovels or plows, suspended from an arch or frame, mounted on two wheels.

The patented device consists of a wire spring, attached to the swinging beam or plow bars, [which has] the double effect of either raising or depressing the beams carrying the [plows]. [The spring was designed to push the plows into the earth when the plow bar was in the down position, but to assist in raising the plow bar by exerting upward pressure when the bar was lifted slightly.]

In his original application, filed May 23, 1879, Wright fully described his improved device for use in connection with cultivators, and claimed for it, not only its lifting and depressing action, but also its lifting power, which increased as the [plow bars] were raised.

An interference with other pending applications being anticipated as to the broad claims of the invention, the application was divided, on November 12, 1879, for the purpose of obtaining one patent for the lifting and depressing effect of the spring on the [plow bars], and another for the lifting power of the spring, increasing as the [plow bars] rise; the latter being sought upon the original application, while the former was based upon the divisional application of November 12, 1879. Patent No. 222,767, for the double effect or duplex action of the improved spring, was granted on December 16, 1879. [The key claim in this patent reads: "In combination with a vertically swinging beam or drag bar, a spring, substantially as described and shown, arranged to urge the beam downward when in action, and urge it upward when it is lifted above the operative position."] [T]hereafter, on June 7, 1881, patent No. 242,497, for the single effect of increased lifting force in raising the plow [bars], was granted, after interference had been disposed of. [The key claim of the '497 patent reads: "In a cultivator, the combination of a vertically swinging drag bar or beam and a lifting spring, which acts with increasing force or effect on the beam as the latter rises, and vice versa."]

[At trial, the validity of both patents was sustained, and infringement found.]

The novelty of Wright's invention consists, as held by the court below, in the application of a double-acting spring to assist the operator in either lifting the plow beams, or the plows attached thereto, or in sinking them deeper in the earth, as occasion might require, while the cultivator is in service. The first patent, issued in 1879, covered both the lifting and depressing actions or operations, while the second patent covered only the lifting effect. The spring device which was designed to accomplish these effects or operations, is the same in both patents. The drawings in each of the patents are identical, and the specification in each is substantially the same. Under these circumstances can it be held that the second patent has any validity, or must it be treated as having been anticipated by the grant of the 1879 patent? If, upon a proper construction of the two patents they should be considered as covering the same invention, then the later must be declared void, under the well-settled rule that two valid patents for the same invention cannot be granted either to the same or to a different party.

In *James v. Campbell*, 104 U.S. [356,] 382 [1881], the court say[s]:

> It is hardly necessary to remark that a patentee could not include in a subsequent patent any invention embraced or described in a prior one, granted to himself, any more than he could an invention embraced or described in a prior patent granted to a third person; indeed, not so well, because he might get a patent for an invention before patented to a third person in this country, if he could show that he was the first and original inventor, and if he should have an interference declared.... If he was the author of any other invention than that which the specification describes and claims, though he might have asked to have it patented at the same time, and in the same patent, yet if he has not done so, and afterwards desires to secure it, he is bound to make a new and distinct specification for that purpose, and make it the subject of a new and different patent.

When a patentee anticipates himself, he cannot, in the nature of things, give validity to the second patent.

The result of the foregoing and other authorities is that no patent can issue for an invention actually covered by a former patent, especially to the same patentee, although the terms of the claims may differ; that the second patent, although containing a broader, more generic claim than the specific claims, contained in the prior patent, is also void; but that where the second patent covers matter described in the prior patent, essentially distinct and separable from the invention covered thereby, and claims made thereunder, its validity may be sustained.

In the last class of cases it must distinctly appear that the invention covered by the later patent was a separate invention, distinctly different and independent from that covered by the first patent; in other words, it must be something substantially different from that comprehended in the first patent. It must consist in something more than a mere distinction of the breadth or scope of the claims of each patent. If the case comes within the first or second of the above classes, the second patent is absolutely void.

The principal contention of the appellee is that the patent of 1881 covers a distinct and separate invention from the first.

A single invention may include both the machine and the manufacture it creates; and in such cases, if the inventions are really separable, the inventor may be entitled to a monopoly of each. It is settled, also, that an inventor may make a new improvement on his own invention of a patentable character, for which he may obtain a separate patent; and the cases cited by the appellee come to this point, and to this point only: That a letter patent may be granted where the invention is clearly distinct from, and independent of, one previously patented.

It clearly appears from a comparison of the two patents, and their respective specifications and drawings, that the first function or object of the patent of 1879, relating to the lifting power of the spring, is identical with the sole object or function covered by the patent of 1881, and that the improved device and combination for the accomplishment of the lifting operation are identical in both patents.

The invention covered by the first patent, as stated in the specification, consists in a spring which serves the double purpose of lifting or holding down the plows at will; and it is further stated that one spring may be adapted to serve all, or either one or more, of the offices above enumerated.

The patent of 1879 thus embraces both the lifting and the depressing effects or operations of the spring device, while that of 1881 seeks to cover only the increased lifting effect of the same device. The first patent clearly includes the second. No substantial distinction can be drawn between the two, which have the same element in combination, and the same spring arrangement and adjustment to accomplish precisely the same lifting effect, increasing as the beams are raised from their operative positions. The matter sought to be covered by the second patent is inseparably involved in the matter embraced in the former patent; and this, under the authorities, renders the second patent void.

If the two patents in question had been granted to different parties, it admits of no question that the last would have been held an infringement of the first, for the reason that the patent of 1879 just as clearly includes as a part of the invention the increased lifting effect of the spring device, increasing as the beams are raised, as that disclosed in the patent of 1881. It certainly did not involve patentable novelty to drop or omit from the patent a claim for the depressing action of the spring arrangement which might be effected by any mere mechanical contrivance.

[I]t is difficult to understand upon what principle the patentee can be allowed to withdraw from the operation of such prior patent, one of its distinct elements, and make it the subject of a second distinct patent. It is not the result, effect, or purpose to be accomplished which constitutes invention, or entitles a party to a patent, but the mechanical means or instrumentalities by which the object sought is to be attained; but a patentee cannot so split up his invention for the purpose of securing additional results, or of extending or of prolonging the life of any or all of its elemental parts. Patents cover the means employed to effect results.

The prior invention covered the means, and the only means, by which the results sought by the patent of 1881 were to be accomplished; and it is settled that the patentee of such prior device would be entitled to all of its uses, whether described or not. [A] single element or function of a patented invention cannot be made the subject of a separate and subsequent patent; and it therefore follows that this increased lifting effect of the spring device, sought to be covered by the 1881 patent, being clearly shown and described in the specification, drawings, and claims of the 1879 patent, was not the subject matter of a valid patent. [Reversed.]

NOTES

1. The Court states: "[N]o patent can issue for an invention actually covered by a former patent, especially to the same patentee ...." Here, both patents at issue were to the "same patentee," Wright. What if they had not been? What reasons for rejection/invalidity would exist, and under what circumstances? Consider (1) § 102(a)/§ 102(b); (2) § 102(e); (3) § 102(g); and (4) each combined with § 103. With all these grounds for invalidity, why is there a need for a special doctrine of "double patenting"?

2. *Same Invention Double Patenting.* Judge Learned Hand reiterated the *Miller* court's view of double patenting in *Traitel Marble Co. v. U.T. Hungerford Brass & Copper Co.*, 22 F.2d 259, 262 (2d Cir. 1927):

The defense is good only when the claims are the same, and the discussion in *Miller v. Eagle Mfg. Co.*, *supra*, was really of this point. As we have held that the original claims and the claims in suit are not the same, the defense fails. It is, indeed, quite true that Calkins gets a protection for more than 17 years for the continuous edged strip. He got it during the existence of the original generic claims, and he gets it from the claims in suit. Yet it is never an objection to an improvement patent that an earlier generic patent has covered the same structure, and each is valid, though taken out by a single inventor. *O'Reilly v. Morse*, [56 U.S.] 15 How. 62, 122, 133, 134 [1854]. This is precisely the same situation, except that, because the applications were copending, it is not necessary that the improvement should be an invention over the matters disclosed in the other application. In view of the fact that the date of issue of an application is beyond the control of the applicant, the chance of so extending the monopoly is disregarded, and it makes no difference which of the applications issues first. *Thomson-Houston Co. v. Ohio Brass Co.* (C.C.A.) 80 F. 712, 726, 727.

Note that several principles discussed by Judge Hand have changed; see the more recent cases that follow.

In re VOGEL

422 F.2d 438, 164 U.S.P.Q. 619 (C.C.P.A. 1970)

This appeal is from the decision of the Patent Office Board of Appeals affirming the rejection of all claims (7, 10 and 11) in appellants' patent application serial No. 338,158, filed January 16, 1964 ["the application"], for "Process of Preparing Packaged Meat Products for Prolonged Storage."

The ground of rejection for each claim is double patenting, based upon the claims of appellants' U.S. patent 3,124,462, issued March 10, 1964 ["the patent"], in view of a reference patent of Ellies, Re. 24,992, reissued May 30, 1961. No terminal disclaimer has been filed.

The Appealed Claims

Claims 7 and 10 are directed to a process of packaging meat generally. Claim 10 is illustrative:

10. A method for prolonging the storage life of packaged meat products comprising the steps of: removing meat from a freshly slaughtered carcass at substantially the body bleeding temperature thereof under ambient temperature conditions; comminuting the meat during an exposure period following slaughter while the meat is at a temperature between said bleeding and ambient temperatures; sealing the comminuted meat within a flexible packaging material having an oxygen permeability ranging from 0.01×10^{-10} to 0.1×10^{-10} cc.mm/sec/cm^2/cm Hg at 30 degrees C. during said exposure period and before the meat has declined in temperature to the ambient temperature; and rapidly reducing the temperature of the packaged meat to a storage temperature below the ambient temperature immediately following said packaging of the meat.

The invention is based on appellants' discovery that spoilage and discoloration of meat are markedly accelerated if the meat is allowed to reach ambient temperature before packaging.

Claim 11 is directed to a similar process specifically limited to beef.

Prior Art

The only reference of record is Ellies. Ellies teaches the use of meat-packaging material having the oxygen permeability range recited in the claims.

The Patent

Appellants' patent, which is not prior art, claims a method of processing pork. Claim 1 of the patent is illustrative.

> 1. A method of preparing pork products, comprising the steps of: bonding a freshly slaughtered carcass while still hot into trimmings; grinding desired carcass trimmings while still warm and fluent; mixing the ground trimmings while fluent and above approximately 80 degrees F., mixing [to] be completed not more than approximately 3½ hours after the carcass has been bled and stuffing the warm and fluent mixed trimmings into air impermeable casings.

The Board

The board characterized the rejection as follows:

> The sole ground of rejection is that claims 7, 10 and 11 are unpatentable over appellants' copending patented claims in Vogel et al., in view of Ellies. This is a double-patenting type rejection, whose statutory basis is 35 U.S.C. 101, as indicated in In re Ockert, 245 F.2d 467; 114 U.S.P.Q. 330 [C.C.P.A. 1957].

Thus the board viewed this case as involving "same invention" type double patenting. The board then discussed the differences between the appealed claims and the patent claims and found that the former did not define a "patentable advance" over the latter. It is thus clear that the board was not at all dealing with "same invention" type double patenting but with the "obvious variation" type. The board found that the appealed claims merely extended the pork process to beef, and that this was not a "patentable advance." [In support of its conclusion, the Board cited a dictionary definition of "sausage" which treats pork and beef as interchangeable.]

Opinion

The proceedings below in this case indicate the advisability of a restatement of the law of double patenting as enunciated by this court.

The first question in the analysis is: Is the same invention being claimed twice? 35 U.S.C. 101 prevents two patents from issuing on the same invention. By "same invention" we mean identical subject matter. Thus the invention defined by a claim reciting "halogen" is not the same as that defined by a claim reciting "chlorine," because the former is broader than the latter. On the other hand, claims may be differently worded and still define the same invention. Thus a claim reciting a length of "thirty-six inches" defines the same invention as a claim reciting a length of "three feet," if all other limitations are identical. In determining the meaning of a word in a claim, the specification may be examined. It must be borne in mind, however, especially in non-chemical cases, that the words in a claim are generally not limited in their meaning by what is shown in the disclosure. Occasionally the disclosure will serve as a dictionary for terms appearing in the claims, and in such instances the disclosure may be used in interpreting the coverage of the claim. A good test, and probably the only objective test, for "same invention," is whether one of the [two] claims [i.e., either the one in the application or the one in the patent] could be literally infringed without literally infringing the other. If it could be, the claims do not define identically the same invention. This is essentially the test applied in *In re Eckel*, 393 F.2d 848 (C.C.P.A. 1968). There the court rejected the idea of "colorable variation" as a comparison category and stated that inventions were either the same, or obvious variations, or unobvious variations. The court's holding in *Eckel* was that same invention means identically same invention.

If it is determined that the same invention is being claimed twice, 35 U.S.C. 101 forbids the grant of the second patent, regardless of the presence or absence of a terminal disclaimer. If the same invention is not being claimed twice, a second question must be asked.

The second analysis question is: Does any claim in the application define merely an obvious variation of an invention disclosed and claimed in the patent? In considering the question, the patent disclosure may not be used as prior art. This does not mean that the disclosure may not be used at all. As pointed out above, in certain instances it may be used as a dictionary to learn the meaning of terms in a claim. It may also be used as required to answer the second analysis question above. We recognize that it is most difficult, if not meaningless, to try to say what is or is not an obvious variation of a claim. A claim is a group of words defining only the boundary of the patent monopoly. It may not describe any physical thing and indeed may encompass physical things not yet dreamed of. How can it be obvious or not obvious to modify a legal boundary? The disclosure, however, sets forth at least one tangible embodiment within the claim, and it is less difficult and more meaningful to judge whether that thing has been modified in an obvious manner. It must be noted that this use of the disclosure is not in contravention of the cases forbidding its use as prior art, nor is it applying the patent as a reference under 35 U.S.C. 103, since only the disclosure of the invention claimed in the patent may be examined.

If the answer to the second question is no, there is no double patenting involved and no terminal disclaimer need be filed. If the answer is yes, a terminal disclaimer is required to prevent undue timewise extension of monopoly.

We now apply this analysis to the case before us.

The first question is: Is the same invention being claimed twice? The answer is no. The patent claims are limited to pork. Appealed claims 7 and 10 are limited to meat, which is not the same thing. Claims 7 and 10 could be infringed by many processes which would not infringe any of the patent claims. Claim 11 is limited to beef. Beef is not the same thing as pork.

We move to the second question: Does any appealed claim define merely an obvious variation of an invention disclosed and claimed in the patent? We must analyze the claims separately.

As to claim 11 the answer is no. This claim defines a process to be performed with beef. We must now determine how much of the patent disclosure pertains to the invention claimed in the patent, which is a process to be performed with pork, to which all the patent claims are limited. The specification begins with certain broad assertions about meat sausages. These assertions do not support [i.e., relate to] the patent claims. The patent claims recite "pork" and "pork" does not read on "meat." To consider these broad assertions would be using the patent as prior art, which it is not. The specification then states how the process is to be carried out with pork. This portion of the specification supports the patent claims and may be considered. It describes in tabular form the time and temperature limits associated with the pork process. Appealed claim 11, reciting beef, does not read on the pork process disclosed and claimed in the patent. Further, we conclude that claim 11 does not define merely an obvious variation of the pork process. The specific time and temperature considerations with respect to pork might not be applicable to beef. There is nothing in the record to indicate that the spoliation characteristics of the two meats are similar. Accordingly, claim 11 does not present any kind of double patenting situation.

Appealed claim 10, *supra*, will now be considered. It recites a process to be performed with "meat." "Meat" reads literally on pork. The only limitation appearing in claim 10 which is not disclosed in the available portion of the patent disclosure is the permeability range of the packaging material; but this is merely an obvious variation as shown by Ellies. The answer to the second analysis question, therefore, is yes, and the claim is not allowable in the absence of a terminal disclaimer. The correctness of this conclusion is demonstrated by observing that claim 10, by reciting "meat," includes pork. Its allowance for a full term would therefore extend the time of monopoly as to the pork process. It is further noted that viewing the inventions in reverse order, i.e. as though the broader claims issued first, does not reveal that the narrower (pork) process is in any way unobvious over the broader (meat) invention disclosed and claimed in the instant application. The same considerations and result apply to claim 7.

The decision of the board is affirmed as to claims 7 and 10 and reversed as to claim 11.

NOTES

1. *Statutory Basis, "Same Invention" Double Patenting.* The court states that "35 U.S.C. 101 prevents two patents from issuing on the same invention." This is because § 101 states that "*a* patent may be granted," suggesting that a multiplicity of patents may not issue on the same invention. *See, e.g., In re Boylan*, 392 F.2d 1017, 157 U.S.P.Q. (BNA) 370 (C.C.P.A. 1968).

2. *Comparing Claims.* Note the statement in the preceding case: "We recognize that it is most difficult, if not meaningless, to try to say what is or is not an obvious variation of a claim." Some useful guidance on the proper approach is then given. This has been supplemented by the following approach, described in *In re Braat*, 937 F.2d 589, 594 n.5, 19 U.S.P.Q.2d 1289 (Fed. Cir. 1991):

> In determining whether one claim is patentable in view of the subject matter of another claim, it is useful to compare the one claim with a tangible embodiment which is disclosed and which falls within the scope of the other claim. The patent disclosure must not be used as prior art.

3. *Terminal Disclaimer.* The court states that when an obvious variant of the patented invention is claimed in an application, "a terminal disclaimer is required to prevent undue timewise extension of monopoly." The statutory basis for such disclaimers is found in § 253 of the Patent Act, which reads as follows:

§ 253. Disclaimer

> Whenever, without any deceptive intention, a claim of a patent is invalid the remaining claims shall not thereby be rendered invalid. A patentee ... may, on payment of the fee required by law, make disclaimer of any complete claim, ... Such disclaimer shall be in writing, and recorded in the Patent and Trademark Office; and it shall thereafter be considered as part of the original patent ....
>
> In like manner any patentee or applicant may disclaim or dedicate to the public the entire term, or any terminal part of the term, of the patent granted or to be granted.

In his influential Commentary on the 1952 Patent Act, P.J. Federico, a senior patent examiner and one of the consultants to Congress who helped draft the 1952 Act, made the following observations:

> The second paragraph of section 253 is new .... Under this provision a patentee, either before or after the issue of the patent, may, for example, disclaim the last two or three years of the term of a patent, or may disclaim all the term of the patent after a specified date. No specific reason for this provision appears in the printed record, but its proponents contemplated that it might be effective in some instances, in combatting a defense of double patenting, to permit the patentee to cut back the term of a later issued patent so as to expire at the same time as the earlier issued patent and thus eliminate any charge of extension of monopoly.

Federico, *Commentary on the New Patent Act*, 35 U.S.C.A. at 49 (1952). Terminal disclaimers in the double-patenting context were expressly approved of in *In re Robeson*, 331 F.2d 610, 615, 141 U.S.P.Q. (BNA) 485 (C.C.P.A. 1964). *See* De Jonghe, *Double Patenting and Terminal Disclaimers*, 54 J. PAT. & TRADEMARK OFF. SOC'Y 627 (1972).

4. *Terminal Disclaimer Not an Admission of Obviousness.* The Federal Circuit has recently held that the filing of a terminal disclaimer is not an admission that the patent causing the disclaimer renders the second application obvious; it is merely a device to overcome a rejection. *Quad Envtl. Techs. Corp. v. Union San. Dist.*, 946 F.2d 870, 874, 20 U.S.P.Q.2d (BNA) 1392 (Fed. Cir. 1991):

> In legal principle, the filing of a terminal disclaimer simply serves the statutory function of removing the rejection of double patenting, and raises neither presumption nor estoppel on the merits of the rejection. It is improper to convert this simple expedient of "obviation" into an admission or acquiescence or estoppel on the merits.

5. *Other Policies.* The principal policy rationale for obviousness-type double patenting was well stated by Judge Rich in his concurring opinion in *In re Zickendraht*, 319 F.2d 225, 232, 138 U.S.P.Q. (BNA) 23, 27 (C.C.P.A. 1963):

> The public should ... be able to act on the assumption that upon the expiration of the patent it will be free to use not only the invention claimed in the patent but also modifications or variants which would have been obvious to those of ordinary skill in the art at the time the invention was made, taking into account the skill of the art and prior art other than the invention claimed in the issued patent.

Other policies were identified in *In re Robeson*, 331 F.2d 610, 615, 141 U.S.P.Q. (BNA) 485 (C.C.P.A. 1964):

> [E]xtension of monopoly is not the only objection to double patenting. Others include possible harassment by multiple assignees, inconvenience to the Patent Office, and the possibility that one might avoid the effect of file wrapper estoppel by filing a second application.

As to the first possibility, note that separate patents may of course be assigned separately, as the inventor chooses; an infringer caught in the web of the multiple patents would then have to deal with the threat of lawsuits from multiple sources. The second point refers to the doctrine whereby patentees in infringement actions are prohibited from asserting that an accused product infringes if the features of the accused product were specifically stated to be outside the scope of the patentee's claims during prosecution. See Chapter 8, Section B, *The Doctrine of Equivalents.*

6. *Different Statutory Category, Different Invention.* *Studiengesellschaft Kohle mbH v. Northern Petrochem. Co.*, 784 F.2d 351, 228 U.S.P.Q. 837 (Fed. Cir.), *cert. dismissed*, 478 U.S. 1028 (1986), presented an interesting double patenting issue. The plaintiff/patentee ("SGK") had obtained patents on both novel catalysts (the famous Zeigler catalysts, important in the synthetic fiber branch of the chemical industry), and on a process for making certain fibers using those catalysts. Defendant Northern claimed that this was double patenting. The Federal

Circuit disagreed, holding that the process claims were based on a different statutory category, and thus defined an invention different from that embraced by the catalyst (composition) claims. The court refused to consider the obviousness-type double patenting issue because the parties had not raised it. *See* Note, *Studiengesellschaft Kohle mbH v. Northern Petrochem. Corp.*, 36 AM. U. L. REV. 1041 (1987).

7. More Reading. Some fine points are discussed in Davs, *Double Patenting: More Is Not Always Better*, 73 J. PAT. TRADEMARK OFF. SOC'Y 740 (1992); WALTERSCHEID, *Historical Development of the Law of Double Patenting up through the 1952 Patent Act*, 4 AM. PAT. L. ASS'N Q.J. 243 (1976) (discussing early rulings in double patenting area); Gholz, *The Law of Double Patenting in the CCPA*, 4 AM. PAT. L. ASS'N Q.J. 261, 263 (1976) (discussing historical development of double patenting); Kuffner, *Double Patenting in the Courts of General Jurisdiction*, 4 AM. PAT. L. ASS'N Q.J. 283, 284-85 (1976).

In re KAPLAN

789 F.2d 1574, 229 U.S.P.Q. 678 (Fed. Cir. 1986)

RICH, CIRCUIT JUDGE.

This appeal is from the decision of the United States Patent and Trademark Office (PTO) Board of Patent Appeals and Interferences (board) rejecting the single claim of appellants' [Kaplan and Walker's] application serial No. 364,221, filed April 1, 1982, entitled "Homogeneous Liquid Phase Process for Making Alkane Polyols," on the sole ground of "double patenting, because it constitutes an improper extension of monopoly for an invention claimed by Kaplan." We reverse.

Background

The Kaplan and Walker application at bar and the cited Kaplan patent, No. 3,944,588, issued Mar. 16, 1976, to one of the appellants on an application filed Jan. 2, 1975, are both assigned to Union Carbide Corporation, the real party in interest. As is apparent, the Kaplan patent application [resulting in the Kaplan '588 patent] was pending only about fourteen and a half months. It was copending with the great-great-grandparent of the application at bar, filed Sept. 30, 1975. [The Kaplan '588 patent's] title is "Catalytic Process for Polyhydric Alcohols and Derivatives." The Kaplan patent contains one independent claim and thirteen dependent claims. The claims most relevant here are those incorporated in dependent claim 4, which is the only claim specifically relied on by the board to support its double patenting rejection. They read as follows:

> 1. The process of making alkane diols and triols having from 2 to 3 carbon atoms in the molecule which comprises reacting in a homogeneous liquid phase mixture of hydrogen and oxides of carbon in the presence of a rhodium carbonyl complex and a trialkanolamine borate at a pressure of

from about 1000 psia to about 50,000 psia correlated with a temperature of about 100 degrees C to about 375 degrees C sufficient to produce said diols and triols.

2. The process of claim 1 wherein the temperature is from about 100 degrees C to about 300 degrees C.

4. The process of claim 2 wherein the reaction is effected in the presence of an organic solvent.

Among organic solvents disclosed and specifically claimed in the Kaplan patent are two known as "tetraglyme" (in more explicit nomenclature, dimethyl ether of tetraethylene glycol) and sulfolane. Two of the Kaplan dependent claims (10 and 11) individually name these specific solvents, respectively. No claim in Kaplan calls for a solvent mixture, which is significant with respect to the double patenting rejection for reasons which will appear. There are, however, a number of examples of mixed solvents in Table VI of the Kaplan patent specification, particularly Example 45, upon which the board relied. Example 45 is specific to a mixture of "Tetraglyme/sulfolane (65/10)." The heading of Table VI is "Tri-isopropanolamine Borate in Mixed Solvents."

Against this much of the background, we now reproduce the single claim on appeal of this joint application of Kaplan and Walker which stands rejected for double patenting in view of claim 4 of the Kaplan patent:

> In the homogeneous liquid phase process of producing alkane polyols by the reaction of oxides of carbon and hydrogen in the presence of a rhodium catalyst in which rhodium is complexed with carbon monoxide to provide a rhodium carbonyl complex at a temperature between about 100 degrees C. to about 375 degrees C. and a pressure between about 1000 psia to about 50,000 psia, the improvement which comprises effecting said reaction in a solvent mixture of tetraglyme and sulfolane under conditions whereby such solvent mixture is essentially inert and the rate of formation of such alkane polyol is greater than would be obtained by effecting said reaction under equal conditions using tetraglyme or sulfolane as the solvent.

It will be observed from a comparison of this claim with the Kaplan claims reproduced above that the Kaplan and Walker (joint) claim at bar is, generally speaking, defined as an improvement on the Kaplan (sole) catalytic process of producing alkane polyols (diols and triols) by reacting hydrogen and carbon oxides (e.g., carbon monoxide) in an organic solvent. The reason why the process using the solvent mixture of the appealed claim was not claimed in the Kaplan patent, although it is disclosed in the patent specification, is that Kaplan alone was not the inventor of that process; it was the joint invention of Kaplan and Walker and therefore the application on appeal was filed. The reason it was disclosed in Kaplan's patent was that it was part of the "best mode" of practicing Kaplan's catalytic process. It is a given, of course, that a sole inventor and joint inventors including the sole inventor are separate "legal entities," a legal proposition from which certain legal consequences flow, *In re Land and Rogers*, 368 F.2d 866, 879, 151 U.S.P.Q. 621, 633 (C.C.P.A. 1966) "such as who must apply for patent." It is worth remembering an axiomatic statement on the same page of the *Land and Rogers* case, which is also applicable here:

> When the joint and sole inventions are related, as they are here, inventor A commonly discloses the invention of A & B in the course of describing his sole invention and when he so describes the invention of A & B he is not disclosing "prior art" to the A & B invention, even if he has legal status as "another." [The reference to "another" is to that word as used in 35 U.S.C. 102(e) and (g).]

The board [of appeals] entered its own rejection on the ground of double patenting. Applicants sought reconsideration by the board [and] then took this appeal.

To indicate the reasoning of the board, we quote most of the paragraph of its initial opinion in which it made its new rejection:

> [W]e reject claim 1 [there is no other] on the ground of double patenting, because it constitutes an improper extension of monopoly [of] an invention claimed by Kaplan.... [A]t least claim 4 of the Kaplan patent and appellant's claim 1 embrace common subject matter. Both claims are generic and both claims would be infringed by a process which utilized rhodium and trialkanolamine borate as the catalyst and a mixed solvent as the organic solvent. Example 45 of the Kaplan patent clearly shows that the term solvent, as used in Kaplan's claims is intended to embrace the mixed solvent of Example 45 [of the Kaplan '588 patent specification]. Further, appellants' claim 1 is sufficiently broad to encompass the use of a trialkanolamine borate in conjunction with the rhodium catalyst. Because both claims embrace the same subject matter, allowance of the instant application would amount to "double patenting of the improper extension of monopoly type" ....

[From footnote 2:] Just what the board meant by saying "both claims are generic" is not clear to us. The claims speak for themselves. Kaplan's claim 4 defines the solvent used in the process, which is the limitation under discussion by the board, as "an organic solvent." Appellants' claim on appeal defines the solvent as "a solvent mixture of tetraglyme and sulfolane." Far from being "generic," the latter looks very much like a quite specific species of the genus "organic solvent."

OPINION

We reverse the board's double patenting rejection essentially for two reasons: (1) It has confused double patenting with "domination" which, by itself, does not give rise to "double patenting" and (2) it has used the disclosure of appellants' joint invention in the Kaplan patent specification as though it were prior art, which it is not, to support the obviousness aspect of the rejection.

By domination we refer, in accordance with established patent law terminology, to that phenomenon, which grows out of the fact that patents have claims, whereunder one patent has a broad or "generic" claim which "reads on" an invention defined by a narrower or more specific claim in another patent, the former "dominating" the latter because the more narrowly claimed invention cannot be practiced without infringing the broader claim. To use the words of which the board seemed to be enamored, the broader claim "embraces" or "encompasses" the subject matter defined by the narrower claim. In possibly simpler terms, one patent dominates another if a claim of the first patent reads on a device built or process practiced according to the second patent disclosure. This commonplace situation is not, per se, double patenting as the board seemed to think.

Any patent granted on the application at bar will have the single claim on appeal which is expressly limited to carrying out the Kaplan process using the specific solvent mixture of tetraglyme and sulfolane invented by appellants. Is this an extension of a patent on Kaplan's invention — Kaplan who never conceived of using that mixture? When Kaplan's (sole) patent expires, and assuming appellants get their joint patent, the world will still be free to use (so far as these two patents go) the Kaplan process so long as appellants' solvent mixture is not used in it. Of course, it may be that everyone will want to use the improvement, but that is commonly the case when dominating patents expire with improvement patents still outstanding.

Obvious Variation of What Kaplan Claims

We turn now to consideration of the obviousness aspect of this obviousness-type double patenting rejection, which had to be based, of course, on what is claimed in the Kaplan patent. The board relied on Kaplan claim 4, which depends from claim 2, which depends from claim 1. These claims are set forth above. The board relied on the fact that claim 4 calls for "an organic solvent." The board did not say that the use of appellants' "solvent mixture of tetraglyme and sulfolane" would be obvious from claim 4. Indeed, in that portion of the board's opinion in which it reversed all of the examiner's rejections, the board held, on the record which contains appellants' declarations, that they, not Kaplan, invented the use of those mixed solvents, that appellants had antedated Kaplan as a reference under 35 U.S.C. § 102(e), that the Kaplan patent cannot be used to show obviousness under § 103, and that appellants' claim was not obvious from a cited patent to Pruett et al. It also reversed a rejection under §§ 102(g)/103 for obviousness which used Kaplan as the sole basis. Then it turned about and made an obviousness-type double patenting rejection based on Kaplan's claim 4. This rejection was predicated on the novel argument, particularly set out in the board's second opinion on rehearing, that Example 45 in Kaplan "provides some of the support for the term 'organic solvent' as used in claim 4 of the Kaplan patent."

Thus, after concluding that the Kaplan patent is not available to show obviousness of appellants' claimed process, the board has nevertheless used Kaplan to show obviousness in a double patenting context, for it relied on no other reference. Moreover, that part of the Kaplan disclosure used to do this is a description of appellants' joint invention. The board's claim-support theory does not suffice to justify this anomalous result. There is adequate support for the "organic solvent" limitation in claim 4 apart from appellants' specific mixed solvent invention, including the disclosure of the separate solvents in the mixture which are separately claimed by Kaplan. There is no way the board could have found appellants' claimed invention to be an obvious variation of what Kaplan claims except by treating the Kaplan patent disclosure as though it were prior art. This has repeatedly been held in our precedents to be impermissible. In effect, what the board did was to use a disclosure of appellants' own joint invention which had been incorporated in the Kaplan sole disclosure to show that their invention was but an obvious variation of Kaplan's claimed invention. That amounts to using an applicant's invention disclosure, which is not a 1-year time bar, as prior art against him. That is impermissible. [Reversed.]

NOTES

1. *Heart of the Disagreement.* The essence of the disagreement between the Federal Circuit and the Board of Appeals in this case is whether the earlier patent to Kaplan claims or merely discloses some of what is claimed by Kaplan and Walker. The Board argues that there is claim overlap, not merely that Kaplan discloses some of what Kaplan and Walker claim. In support of this argument, they turn to the definition of "organic solvent" in the Kaplan specification. They justify this as an attempt to clarify the meaning of that phrase. But the Federal Circuit sees it instead as reliance on the specification, rather than the claims, of Kaplan. This dispute — between "reading things into the claims from the specification" and merely "construing the claims in light of the specification" — is very often present in infringement cases where claim construction is an issue. See Chapter 8, Section A.

2. *Joint Inventors and Double Patenting.* In an omitted footnote in the preceding case, the court states:

> All applications involved in this case were filed and the Kaplan patent had issued before amendment of 35 U.S.C. § 116 by P.L. 98-622 of Nov. 8, 1984, sec. 104(a), 98 Stat. 3384, now paragraph one of 35 U.S.C. § 116, which reads:
>
> > When an invention is made by two or more persons jointly, they shall apply for patent jointly and each make the required oath, except as

otherwise provided in this title. Inventors may apply for a patent jointly even though (1) they did not physically work together or at the same time, (2) each did not make the same type or amount of contribution, or (3) each did not make a contribution to the subject matter of every claim of the patent.

The first sentence is the substance of the law at the times involved in this case. The second sentence is the liberalization added by the 1984 amendment, which, had it been available, might have obviated the problem in this case.

789 F.2d at 1575 n.1.

3. *Inventive Entities and Double Patenting.* Recall the following statement from the preceding case:

It is a given, of course, that a sole inventor and joint inventors including the sole inventor are separate "legal entities," a legal proposition from which certain legal consequences flow, *In re Land and Rogers*, 368 F.2d 866, 879, 151 U.S.P.Q. 621, 633 (C.C.P.A. 1966) "such as who must apply for patent."

Recall also the refinement on this principle discussed by the court, which originated in the *Land & Rogers* case: inventor *A*'s prior work (including filed patents) is not the work of "another" under Patent Act §§ 102(e) and 102(g) which can be cited against inventive entity *A & B*'s subsequent work.

However, as was discussed in Chapter 4, this is a limited refinement to the concept of inventive entities. In general, where different inventive entities are concerned, the caselaw prior to 1984 held that the work of one entity may be cited against that of another under §§ 102(e) and 102(g). See Chapter 4, Section B.4.

This has obvious ramifications in the double patenting context. For example, in *In re Fong*, 378 F.2d 977, 154 U.S.P.Q. (BNA) 25 (C.C.P.A. 1967), Fong, Brown, Wasley, Whitfield, & Miller filed a patent application on February 19, 1962, entitled "Continuous Shrinkproofing of Wool Textiles." This application described an adaptation of the basic process of U.S. Patent No. 3,078,138, which issued February 19, 1963, to Miller, Whitfield, and Wasley, on a method for shrink-proofing woolen textile material by forming a resin on its surface. The court held that the previously-filed application which resulted in the '138 patent was § 102(e) prior art against the later-filed, but copending, application for the continuous version of the process. It never reached the double patenting issue.

Note that even after the legislative changes to § 103 in 1984, the *Fong* case would come out the same. Recall from Chapter 4 that this legislation excludes patents and applications produced by different inventive entities but owned by or assigned to a common source (e.g., an employer) from being considered work by "another" under §§ 102(f) and 102(g) when deciding the issue of nonobviousness. Thus the application resulting in the '138 patent in *Fong* would still be prior art under § 102(e) against the later-filed application of the different inventive entity, even though all the named inventors on both applications worked for the same employer. *See Ex parte Bartfeld*, 16 U.S.P.Q.2d (BNA) 1714 (Pat. Off. Bd. App. Int. 1990) (a commonly-assigned application from a different inventive entity may be used as a § 102(e) reference; distinguishing § 102(e) from double patenting cases).

The 1984 legislation does provide some hope, however, for those who find themselves in the *Fong* situation. The key is to get out from under § 102(e); the way to do this is to file both patent applications on the same date. This eliminates the effect of § 102(e), which applies only to previously filed applications of another inventive entity. An alternative approach would be to file a single application for both the basic and improvement inventions. The 1984 amendments to § 116 now permit this.

Having escaped from the *Fong* holding, however, a group of applicants would nonetheless face another hurdle: double patenting. In *Fong*, as mentioned, this issue was never reached because of the availability of the previously-filed application as prior art. Were it not available, however, the question would be whether it must be treated as a previously-filed or at least as a copending application by the "same inventor." That is, having escaped the §§ 102(f) and 102(g) prior art effect by virtue of the legislation and the § 102(e) prior art effect by filing both applications at the same time, will the two sets of overlapping inventors now be treated as a single inventor who has filed two applications for related inventions — the classic obviousness-type double patenting scenario?

The answer is yes. The legislative history of the 1984 amendments to § 103 calls for the Patent Office to "reinstate" its practice of considering double patenting as a viable ground for rejection in such a case. *See* 130 CONG. REC. H10525 (daily ed., Oct. 1, 1984) (remarks of Representative Kastenmeier); SENATE COMMITTEE ON THE JUDICIARY, PATENT LAW AMENDMENTS ACT OF 1984, S. REP. 98-663, 98th Cong., 2d Sess. 8 (1984), *reprinted in* 1984 U.S.C.-C.A.N. 5834 (section-by-section analysis of the Patent Law Amendments of 1984).

The reference to "reinstating" double patenting stems from the fact that the Patent Office took this approach prior to the doctrinal expansion of § 103 prior art to include §§ 102(f) and 102(g). *See, e.g., In re Bowers*, 359 F.2d 886, 149 U.S.P.Q. (BNA) 570 (C.C.P.A. 1966); *In re Borcherdt*, 197 F.2d 550, 94 U.S.P.Q. (BNA) 175 (C.C.P.A. 1952); *and In re Borg*, 392 F.2d 642, 157 U.S.P.Q. (BNA) 359 (1968).

The Federal Circuit has acknowledged the effect of the 1984 legislation. In *In re Longi*, 759 F.2d 887, 893-94, 225 U.S.P.Q. (BNA) 645 (Fed. Cir. 1985), the court held that double patenting rejections were proper for copending applications of different inventive entities assigned to a common owner. In its opinion, the court discussed the rationale for such a holding:

Appellants ... maintain that the entire doctrine of double patenting of the obviousness type should not apply to commonly-owned applications with different inventive entities. A rejection based upon such a doctrine, appellants say, is unduly restrictive and discourages group research. Moreover, each inventor in a research department should be entitled to separate patents for his or her own independent contribution to the basic objective of the overall research project. Such a broad position has been previously rejected, and it is inconsistent with both our precedents and recent legislation.

Many times our predecessor court, the Court of Customs and Patent Appeals, has treated commonly-owned applications by different inventors as though they were filed by the same inventor, and then relied upon the doctrine of double patenting of the obviousness type to deny a second patent on subject matter not patentably distinct from the claims of the first patent.... *In re Rogers*, 394 F.2d 566, 55 C.C.P.A. 1092, 157 U.S.P.Q. 569 (1968); .... In fact, the appellant in *In re Rogers* made an argument similar to the one the present appellant makes here. In that case, Rogers asserted that the obviousness type double patenting rejection was "distressing" to corporate practitioners and did not take into account the considerable exchange of information between inventors. The result, as the argument goes, would be that a corporation would find itself in a "box" because patent protection for both inventions would not be possible.

As we declared in that case, appellants, and those in like situations, are not in an inescapable "box." *In re Rogers, supra*, 394 F.2d at 571, 157 U.S.P.Q. at 573. A patent may still issue if an applicant faced with such a rejection were to file a terminal disclaimer under 35 U.S.C. § 253, disclaiming "any terminal part of the term ... of the patent," thereby guaranteeing that the second patent would expire at the same time as the first patent. It is well-established that a common assignee is entitled to proceed with a terminal disclaimer to overcome a rejection based on double patenting of the obviousness type. Since the second patent would expire simultaneously with the first, this use of a terminal disclaimer is consistent with the policy that the public should be free to use the invention as well as any obvious modifications at the end of the patent's term.

2. ORDER OF FILING AND ISSUANCE

Most of the cases we have discussed so far follow this sequence: Application for Invention *A* filed on Date 1; Application for Invention *B* filed on Date 2; and (in many cases) patent for invention *A* issues on Date 3. The typical double patenting rejection involves the patentability of Invention *B* in light of the conflict between one or more of its claims and the claims of the patent or application on Invention *A*. (Note that although technically there is no double patenting issue until at least one of the applications issues as a patent, the Patent Office can provisionally reject an application because of a perceived double patenting prob-

lem with another application. *See* U.S. PATENT AND TRADEMARK OFFICE, MAN-
UAL OF PATENT EXAMINING PROCEDURE § 804 (5th ed. 1983 & rev. 5 1985)).
We discuss here two variants on this sequence:

- Variant 1: Applications for both inventions filed the same day.
- Variant 2: Patent for Invention *B* issues while application for Invention *A*
  still pending.

Variant 1

This is essentially the situation presented in *In re Newton*, 414 F.2d 1400, 163
U.S.P.Q. (BNA) 35 (C.C.P.A. 1969). There the court upheld the applicant's use
of a terminal disclaimer to overcome a double patenting rejection based on the
issuance of a patent resulting from the filing of a commonly-assigned application.
See also In re Frilette, 412 F.2d 269, 276, 162 U.S.P.Q. (BNA) 163 (C.C.P.A.
1969) (stating, in dictum, that neither common inventive entity nor even one or
more common members across inventive entities is necessary to overcome a
double patenting rejection with a terminal disclaimer; common assignment of the
application and the patent is all that is required).

Variant 2

This came up in *In re Borg*, 392 F.2d 642, 157 U.S.P.Q. (BNA) 359 (C.C.P.A.
1968). There the court upheld the applicant's use of a terminal disclaimer on the
first-filed application in light of the second-filed but already issued patent.
Implicit in this holding was the view that the order of filing is irrelevant; the
basic extension-of-monopoly logic applies whenever two patents have overlapping
subject matter. The following case presents an important recent elaboration on
this theme.

In re BRAAT

937 F.2d 589, 19 U.S.P.Q.2d 1289 (Fed. Cir. 1991)

[This case involved two inventors employed by U.S. Philips Corporation,
holder of the basic patents on compact disc (CD) technology.

[Braat applied for a patent on an enhanced version of a recording medium,
such as a CD, which could store more information than prior versions. The added
storage is obtained by packing the tracks on the disc more closely than in prior
art devices. Braat's real invention was in the way he overcame a major problem
in the prior art: the fact that, as tracks are placed more closely together, the
device used for reading them (typically a laser beam) begins to pick up information from more than one track — a situation known as "crosstalk." Braat solved
the crosstalk problem by using two different types of "read elements," the light-
sensing elements that pick up the information encoded on the tracks in the form
of reflected light. Braat realized that if every other track was encoded so as to
give off light recognized by only one of the "read elements," in technical terms,

light of differing "phase depths," the information on alternate tracks would never get confused. (His invention is analogous to writing text in two very closely packed columns, one column in French and the other English. If two readers are used, one of whom knows only French and the other only English, the columns are not likely to be confused, and more text can be placed on each page.)

[While Braat's application was pending, a patent issued to Dil, another inventor employed by Philips. Dil's patent (U.S. Patent No. 4,209,804) claimed a recording medium characterized by V-shaped tracks with sidewalls whose pitch was between 65 and 85 degrees, and which reflected light in a particular range of phase depths. Dependent claims 5 and 6 of the Dil patent claim embodiments of his device employing the alternate-track phase depth differences of the Braat application.]

RICH, J.

The crux of this appeal comes down to whether the Board erred in applying a "one-way" patentability determination instead of a "two-way" determination. The Board correctly found that the rejected claims of Braat are merely obvious variations of the invention described by dependent claims [5 and 6] of Dil. The only difference between the claims of Braat and claims [5 and 6] of Dil is [Braat's] omission of the requirement in the claims of Dil of information areas having side walls which are angled at a particular angle, and we do not think that omission of such a limitation in the present case would constitute an unobvious modification. The issue is whether the Board erred in concluding that such a one-way determination was all that was necessary or whether it was necessary to also determine whether the claims of Dil are patentably distinct from the invention described by the rejected claims of Braat; i.e., whether the addition in the claims of Dil of side walls which are angled at a particular angle was merely an obvious modification over the [alternate track encoding] invention claimed in Braat.

On appeal, Philips (the assignee) attempts to characterize the invention of Dil as an improvement over the invention of the Braat application, citing 3 D. Chisum Patents, § 9.03[2][c] (1990), entitled "Generic Claim Issuing After Later Filed Specific or Improvement Claim," as well as *In re Borah*, 354 F.2d 1009, 148 U.S.P.Q. 213 (C.C.P.A. 1966), for the proposition that when a later filed improvement patent issues before an earlier filed basic invention, a double patenting rejection is only proper against the claims to the basic invention if the improvement is not patentably distinct from the basic invention. The rationale behind this proposition is that an applicant (or applicants), who files applications for basic and improvement patents should not be penalized by the rate of progress of the applications through the PTO, a matter over which the applicant does not have complete control. See Chisum, *supra*. In this situation, the order of issuance is, in effect, ignored, and the relevant determination becomes whether the improvement is patentably distinct from the generic invention.

We hesitate to characterize the Dil invention as an "improvement" over the Braat invention. The word "improvement" implies that it was developed specifically for use with the "basic" invention, and thus must have come later in time. The Dil patent invention, however, is totally separate from that of Braat, and could conceivably have been developed earlier rather than later. The inventions of Dil and Braat are independent but when jointly used may complement each other, and it is for that reason that Dil disclosed the Braat invention in his own patent application and, in claims [5 and 6], claimed the use of the two inventions in combination. A better characterization of the relationship between the inventions is as combination/subcombination. Braat and Dil each developed separate subcombination inventions, which are described by their respective independent claims. Dil then combined these two subcombinations to form a third invention. This combination is described by dependent claims [5 and 6] of Dil.

However, we agree that the reasoning of *Borah* and Chisum, § 9.03[2][c] is applicable in the present case. Philips could not have included the claims of Dil in the Braat application, for Braat did not invent the subject matter of the Dil claims, i.e., information areas having V-shaped side walls at particular angles of inclination. Nor could Philips have included the claims of Braat in the Dil application, for Dil did not invent the subject matter of the Braat application, i.e., adjacent track segments of different phase depth. Philips filed the Braat and Dil applications so as to maintain proper inventorship, with claims directed to Braat's "subcombination" invention in the first application and claims directed to both Dil's "subcombination" invention and to the "combination" invention in the second application. Philips even acknowledged in Dil's application that part of the combination invention was invented by Braat, not Dil. It is not Philips' fault that the combination claims in the Dil patent issued first. Thus, a double patenting rejection is sustainable here only if claims [5 and 6] of Dil are not patentably distinct from the subject matter defined by the rejected claims of Braat, and the Board erred in sustaining the double patenting rejection without making such a "two-way" determination.

We are further convinced that claims [5 and 6] of Dil are patentably distinct from the subject matter defined by the claims of Braat. [These claims], of course, include the limitations of Dil's independent claim 1, which requires, among other things, V-shaped information areas with side walls having an angle of inclination, relative to the normal to the record carrier, of between 65 degrees and 85 degrees. There is nothing in the rejected claims of Braat which refers to any angling of the side walls of the information areas, much less the specific angles recited in claim 1 of Dil. Moreover, we note that in the preferred embodiment of the Braat application, the information areas are all rectangular, and have side walls which are not inclined relative to the normal to the carrier. Since the subject matter embraced by the rejected claims of Braat does not suggest the record carrier recited by claims [5 and 6] of Dil, we conclude that the claims of the Braat application and the Dil patent are patentably distinct, and that the double patenting rejection was in error.

It is true that allowance of the Braat application will result in some timewise extension of Philips' patent protection of the Dil structure. This is because Braat's claims dominate the invention of Dil claims [5 and 6]. As our predecessor court pointed out in *Borah*, "We see ... that as a matter of law the extension of protection objection is not necessarily controlling." 354 F.2d at 1017, 148 U.S.P.Q. at 220. [O]nly if the extension of patent right is unjustified is a double patenting rejection appropriate. There are situations where the extension is justified. See *Borah*; *In re Kaplan*. This case presents such a situation. [Reversed.]

NOTES

1. *Two-Way Street.* Dil issued first. And Braat was obvious in light of Dil. But, the court said, under the facts presented here, that is not all there is to it: Dil must also be obvious in light of *Braat* to sustain a double-patenting rejection. In other words, the Board erred in not conducting a "two-way" analysis.

Why? The policy rationale suggested by Chisum is to protect the applicant against the arbitrary vicissitudes of patent prosecution. The thought is that a species claim in a first-issued application may make obvious a genus (and hence much more valuable) claim in a later-issued application. The luck of the draw, in other words, would determine whether the inventor obtained the valuable broad coverage or only the less valuable specific coverage.

Note well the following elements in this case: (1) the "improvement" (or combination) application of Dil was filed *second* but issued *first*; (2) Dil and Braat had a common assignee, Philips, who was attempting to keep to accepted inventorship rules in filing the two applications as distinct inventions. What if the "improvement" had been filed first? And issued first? Or second? What if the same inventor or inventive entity had filed both; would this make any difference? What if Dil and Braat had worked for different companies and had not been under an obligation to assign to the same assignee; what rejection(s) would have been available for the Dil application and how would the analysis differ from that in the preceding case?

2. *Spoiled Braat?* Donald R. McPhail, in an article entitled *A Two-Way Test for Obviousness-Type Double Patenting*, 14 GEO. MASON L. REV. 691, 692 (1992), concludes that "[t]he proper standard for all questions of obviousness-type double patenting should remain the earlier one-way test." He reasons:

> Whether the earlier claims are patentable over the later claims is a moot question — those are not the claims that are going to serve to extend the period of the patent grant. It is the later claims that will enable an inventor to exclude others from practicing his invention. In the present case, patent protection for the invention defined by claims 5 and 6 of Dil, the optical disc identical to that of Braat but including the tracks having angled side walls, began in 1980. Even upon expiration of that patent in 1997, the public will be unable to make, use, or sell these discs absent a license from Braat. This is because any optical disc having all the features claimed in Dil will also necessarily possess all the features claimed in Braat. The Philips Corpora-

tion, assignee of both Braat and Dil, may therefore continue to exclude others from the Dil optical discs by means of the Braat patent; the net result of this being patent protection until 2009, when the Braat patent will expire. Philips Corporation has thus obtained nearly thirty years of patent rights to a single invention. For the doctrine of obviousness-type double patenting to serve its fundamental purpose, the only pertinent inquiry is the patentability of the later claims over the earlier claims.

Id. at 706-07. Should the fault of the inventor factor into the analysis, or only the effect on the public of the termwise extension of patents? *See* the excerpt from the *Goodman* case, just below.

3. *Genus/Species Revisited.* In *Ex parte Michno*, 38 U.S.P.Q.2d 1211, 1211-12 (Bd. Pat. App. & Int. 1993) (designated as nonprecedential), the Board revisited the issue of genus/species relationships in double patenting cases:

> [Applicant Michno claimed a photographic film with a silver halide emulsion layer, including a development inhibitor releasing coupler (DIR) compound.]
>
> ... [F]or purposes of resolving the double patenting issue presented on appeal, the relationship of the appealed claims to the patented claims is one of genus-species, i.e., the appealed claims dominate the patented claims.
>
> We are unaware of any judicial precedent which stands for the proposition that an obviousness-type double patenting situation automatically arises when a patent on a narrow invention issues during pendency of an application for a claimed invention which encompasses or dominates the narrow invention. The notion that a pending claim to a generic invention is necessarily patentably indistinct, in the sense of double patenting of the obviousness type, from a narrower patented claim encompassed by the pending generic claim was scotched by *In re Braat* ....
>
> We observe that the examiner does not actually confront appellants' representation that the appealed and patented claims involve different inventions, in that the selection of the particular inhibitor group for the DIRs of Michno's patented invention renders it unnecessary to employ the specific timing group required in the here claimed invention to yield the unexpected improvements obtained by the claimed invention. In short, the examiner did not provide a sufficient basis to support the conclusion that the claimed invention is an obvious variation of the patented invention.

4. *For Review.* Assuming Dil filed first, why was there no § 102(e) or 102(e)/103 rejection for Braat's application?

From *In re Goodman*, 11 F.3d 1046, 29 U.S.P.Q.2d 2010, 2012, 2015-16 (Fed. Cir. 1993):

The claims on appeal define a method of manufacturing mammalian peptides in plant cells. The method calls for integration into plant cells of a DNA construct encoding a mammalian peptide. This transferred DNA construct includes regulatory regions functional in the plant. The regulatory regions instruct the plant cell to transcribe the region of the DNA coding for the mammalian peptide. The method calls for harvesting the valuable peptide after translation of the transcribed messenger RNA.

The application claims an invention of broad scope — a method for producing mammalian peptides in plant cells. When the bacterium Agrobacterium tumefaciens infects a wound on a dicotyledonous plant, the bacterium attaches to the plant cell wall and introduces a particular piece of its Ti plasmid DNA into the plant cell. This piece of plasmid is the T-DNA (Transferred DNA). The T-DNA integrates into the nuclear genome of the plant cell. The plant cell then manufactures certain enzymes, encoded according to the T-DNA segment, for synthesis of tumor-specific compounds called opines.

Accordingly, upon insertion of a foreign DNA segment into the T-region of the Ti plasmid, the natural genetic transfer functions of these bacteria introduce the foreign segment into the plant cell genome. Using its own cell machinery, the plant cell then dutifully strives to transcribe the T-DNA segment and translate the peptide it encodes. Numerous factors affect successful transcription and translation, including the regulatory gene regions (i.e., initiation and termination sequences) preceding and following the T-DNA segment as well as intracellular compounds present during protein formation. If a stable translation product results, the peptide can be harvested from the plant cells.

The '380 application is a continuation of 06/760,236, which issued as U.S. Patent No. 4,956,282 (the '282 patent). The '282 patent claims a method for producing an interferon in dicotyledonous plant cells. Claim 1 of the '282 patent is identical to claim 8 of the '380 application except that application claim 8 specifies only "plant cells," rather than dicotyledonous plant cells. The '380 application thus has claims broader than those of the issued patent. Stated otherwise, the claims of the '282 patent are species of the genus claimed in the '380 application.

Application claim 9 is similarly identical to claim 2 of the '282 patent with the exception of the dicotyledonous limitation. Application claim 13 is identical to claim 3 of the '282 patent except that the '282 patent is limited to gamma-interferon rather than "an interferon." Accordingly, these claims also present genus-species relationships between the '380 application and the '282 patent.

The specifications of the '282 patent and the '380 application describe the claimed method in general terms, but provide only a single working example. The example describes the formation of an expression cassette with regulatory regions functional in tobacco plants and a structural gene coding for gamma-interferon. In the example the expression cassette is joined to a selectable marker to simplify isolation of plant cells that successfully integrate the construct. The selectable marker consists of regulatory regions functional in tobacco plants and a DNA sequence coding for a tetracycline resistance gene.

Claims 1-6 on appeal, however, purport to cover any desired mammalian peptide produced in any plant cell. Dependent claims 2-6 add limitations — such as specifying the use of a marker, Ti-plasmids, and T-DNA boundary regions — but in no way limit the type of mammalian peptide produced or the type of plant cell used.

Independent claim 7, claim 8 dependent therefrom, and claim 9 dependent from claim 8, specify an interferon as the mammalian protein produced by the method. None of the claims, however, limit the type of plant cell in the method.

The Board also affirmed the rejection of claims 1-13 under the doctrine of obviousness-type double patenting in light of claims 1-3 of the '282 patent. The Board held that the issuance of the present claims in the absence of a terminal disclaimer would grant an "unjustified timewise extension of right to exclude granted by a patent." *In re Schneller*, 397 F.2d 350, 354, 158 U.S.P.Q. 210, 214 (C.C.P.A. 1968) (emphasis added). The Board found that the conflicting claims are not patentably distinct from each other because both claim methods and expression cassettes for producing mammalian peptides in plant cells.

To prevent extension of the patent right beyond statutory limits, the doctrine of obviousness-type double patenting rejects application claims to subject matter different but not patentably distinct from the subject matter claimed in a prior patent. *In re Braat*, 937 F.2d 589, 592, 19 U.S.P.Q.2d 1289, 1291-92 (Fed. Cir. 1991). Obviousness-type double patenting is a question of law. *Texas Instruments Inc. v. International Trade Commission*, 988 F.2d 1165, 1179, 26 U.S.P.Q.2d 1018, 1029 (Fed. Cir. 1993).

The double patenting determination involves two inquiries. First, is the same invention claimed twice? *General Foods Corp. v. Studiengesellschaft Kohle mbH*, 972 F.2d 1272, 1278, 23 U.S.P.Q.2d 1839, 1843 (Fed. Cir. 1992). This inquiry hinges upon the scope of the claims in question. *Id.* at 1280. [T]he claimed inventions are not identical in scope.

If one claimed invention has a broader scope than the other, the court must proceed to a second inquiry: whether one claim defines merely an obvious variation of the other patent claim. *Vogel*, 422 F.2d at 441. Without a patentable distinction — because the pending claim defines merely an obvious variation of the patented claim — the patentee may overcome the double patenting rejection by filing a terminal disclaimer.

In *In re Braat*, 937 F.2d 589, 593 [19 U.S.P.Q.2d 1289] (Fed. Cir. 1991) ..., the later-filed application contained claims to a patentable combination that included a subcombination which was the subject of an independent prior application. Although the later-filed application became a patent first, this court did not reduce the term of the earlier-filed, but later issued, patent. This court did not require a terminal disclaimer because Braat's application was held up not by the applicant, but by "the rate of progress of the application through the PTO, over which the applicant does not have complete control." *Braat*, 937 F.2d at 593.

This case requires no "two-way" analysis. Although application claims 12 and 13 form the genus containing the species of patent claim 3, PTO actions did not dictate the rate of prosecution. Rather, appellant chose to file a continuation and seek early issuance of the narrow species claims. The appellant also chose to forego an immediate appeal to this court on its broader claims when it filed a continuation application. Moreover, appellant argues that a terminal disclaimer is unwarranted.

Appellant's position could extend the term of the patent grant for many cases in a similar posture. By adopting the easy course of filing a continuation or divisional application to gain a narrow claim, a patentee could gain an extension of the term on a species when the broad genus later issued. This practice would extend the exclusionary right past the 17-year limit mandated by Congress. Under Supreme Court precedent, only one patent can issue for each patentable invention. *Miller*, 151 U.S. at 197. A second application — "containing a broader claim, more generical in its character than the specific claim in the prior patent" — typically cannot support an independent valid patent. *Miller*, 151 U.S. at 198; *See Stanley*, 214 F.2d at 153.

Claim 12 and Claim 13 are generic to the species of invention covered by claim 3 of the patent. Thus, the generic invention is "anticipated" by the species of the patented invention. *Cf., Titanium Metals Corp. v. Banner*, 778 F.2d 775, 227 U.S.P.Q. 773 (Fed. Cir. 1985) (holding that an earlier species disclosure in the prior art defeats any generic claim). This court's predecessor has held that, without a terminal disclaimer, the species claims preclude issuance of the generic application.

Appellant chose to group claims 10-12 together, and indeed application claim 12 is dependent on application claim 11, which claim is dependent on application claim 10; therefore, these claims stand or fall together. It follows then that application claims 10 and 11 are — like claim 12 — not patentably distinct over patent claim 3. Because claim 12 must, in the absence of a terminal disclaimer, fall because of double patenting over the '282 patent, application claims 10-11 must likewise fall.

NOTE

GATT-TRIPs and Double Patenting. U.S. compliance with the TRIPs agreement brought patent terms measured from the date of filing, rather than issuance. This means that terminal disclaimers filed under double patenting practice will now be pegged to the filing date of the patent which creates the obviousness-type double patenting issue for the application. And now so-called "provisional" double patenting rejections will result in patent terms of a determinate length (assuming the first-issued patent was filed after the effective date of the URAA), since they are tied to the application dates and not the date of issuance, as in the past. *See* Kenneth J. Burchfiel, *U.S. GATT Legislation Changes Patent Term*, 77 J. PAT. & TRADEMARK OFF. SOC'Y 222, 225 (1995).

3. EFFECT OF PATENT OFFICE RESTRICTION REQUIREMENT

When a patent applicant includes subject matter which embraces more than one "independent and distinct" invention, the examiner may require the patentee to split the application into several applications. This is called a restriction requirement, and is authorized by § 121 of the Patent Act:

§ 121. Divisional applications

If two or more independent and distinct inventions are claimed in one application, the Commissioner may require the application to be restricted to one of the inventions. If the other invention is made the subject of a divisional application which complies with the requirements of section 120 of this title it shall be entitled to the benefit of the filing date of the original application. A patent issuing on an application with respect to which a requirement for restriction under this section has been made, or on an application filed as result of such requirement, shall not be used as a reference either in the Patent and Trademark Office or in the courts against a divisional application or against the original application or any patent issued on either of them, if the divisional application is filed before the issuance of the patent on the other application.... The validity of a patent shall not be questioned for failure of the Commissioner to require the application to be restricted to one invention.

35 U.S.C. § 121 (1986 & Supp. 1990). *See also* 37 C.F.R. 1.141 (1991) (definition of "independent and distinct" inventions). When a restriction requirement is imposed, the patent applicant must choose which of the several inventions she wishes to pursue as the subject of the original application, and which she will incorporate in a new "divisional" application or applications. This is referred to as an "election," and the applicant is then said to have both "elected" claims (which remain in her original application) and "unelected" claims (which appear in the divisional application(s)). *See* U.S. PATENT AND TRADEMARK OFFICE, MANUAL OF PATENT EXAMINING PROCEDURE § 802.01 (5th ed. 1983 & rev. 5 1985).

As we will see in the following case, a question has arisen concerning the third sentence of this section stating that the parent application "shall not be used as a reference." Specifically, the issue is whether and to what extent this applies to a divisional application rejected for obviousness-type double patenting. In general, the courts have held that such a rejection is as improper as a lack of novelty or obviousness rejection based on the § 121 reference, the parent application — *except* under certain circumstances. These circumstances generally revolve around the degree to which the contested application is a true divisional application from the parent. The following case represents recent thinking in this regard.

GERBER GARMENT TECHNOLOGY, INC.
v. LECTRA SYSTEMS

916 F.2d 683, 16 U.S.P.Q.2d 1436 (Fed. Cir. 1990)

The District Court granted Lectra's motion for summary judgment that claims 15 and 16 of the '154 patent are invalid for obviousness-type double patenting in view of claim 23 of United States Patent No. 3,495,492 ('492). Gerber appeals from the denial of its motion for preliminary injunction. We affirm.

On May 5, 1969 Gerber filed an original patent application. The Patent and Trademark Office (PTO) examiner imposed a restriction requirement between "Claims 1-11 and 16-28 drawn to a cutting apparatus" and "Claims 12-15 drawn to a work holding means." Gerber elected to prosecute the former claims and the application issued as the (now expired) '492 patent on February 17, 1970.

On February 2, 1970 Gerber had filed a continuation-in-part application directed to the "work holding means" of claims 12-15. [A continuation of this] latter application issued as the '154 patent on February 5, 1974.

Compliance with a restriction requirement means the claims in a divisional application must be consonant with those [originally filed and] not elected under that requirement. Noncompliance with the consonance requirement is normally detected by the PTO examiner. See Manual of Patent Examining Procedure (MPEP) § 804.01 (double patenting protection of Section 121 applies where the claims are not consonant with, i.e. "have been changed in material respects from," the claims subject to the restriction requirement). Examiners' compliance with MPEP § 804.01 may account for the absence of court decisions on the precise fact pattern before us and the consequent "first impression" status of the case in this court.

[On appeal,] Gerber mounts a dual attack. First, Gerber proffers an argument based on absolutism, i.e., that the third sentence of 35 U.S.C. § 121 absolutely precludes invalidity based on anything in the '492 patent because that patent cannot under any circumstances whatever be used as a "reference." Second, Gerber says claims 15 and 16 of the '154 patent are consonant with the claims not elected in its response to the restriction requirement. With admirable candor, Gerber does not challenge the view that obviousness-type double patenting is present if § 121 is rendered inapplicable by nonconsonance of Claims 15 and 16.

Section 121 provides for restriction when "independent and distinct inventions" are claimed in one application. The prohibition against use of a parent application "as a reference" against a divisional application applies only to the divisional applications that are "filed as a result of" a restriction requirement. Plain common sense dictates that a divisional application filed as a result of a restriction requirement may not contain claims drawn to the invention set forth in the claims elected and prosecuted to patent in the parent application. The divisional application must have claims drawn only to the "other invention." It is true that the disclosure in the patent containing the elected claims cannot be used as a "reference" on which to reject a claim in a divisional application under 35 U.S.C. § 103, for that disclosure is the applicant's and is not in the "prior art." That is not to say, however, that the elected claims may not be looked to in assessing compliance with the prohibition against claiming the same invention in two patents. In this regard, the phrase "obviousness type" may have been an unfortunate choice, for, as here, the claims in the divisional application may be actually drawn (though in variant language) to the same invention as that set forth in the elected claims. As discussed below, that phenomenon may be viewed as a failure to keep the claims in the divisional application "consonant."

Consonance requires that the line of demarcation between the "independent and distinct inventions" that prompted the restriction requirement be maintained. Though the claims may be amended, they must not be so amended as to bring them back over the line imposed in the restriction requirement. Where that line is crossed the prohibition of the third sentence of Section 121 does not apply.

The presence or absence of consonance will necessarily depend upon analysis of the involved claims. As a fall back position from its position that the '492 patent cannot be used for any purpose, Gerber says the district court erred in holding claims 15 and 16 of the '154 patent so like "cutting apparatus" claim 23 of the '492 patent as to be not consonant with the claims not elected in responding to the restriction requirement. Gerber says that claim 15 is directed to the subcombination of a work holding means in the "environment" of a machine having a cutting blade.

That "a tool in the form of a cutting blade" appears in the preamble of claim 15 is not determinative of whether it is a claim limitation. Where words in the preamble "are necessary to give meaning to the claim and properly define the invention," they are deemed limitations of the claim. The cutting blade is "necessary to give meaning" to claims 15 and 16 and "properly define the invention." The cutting blade appears not only in the preamble, but is referenced repeatedly in the body of the claim. It is integral to the claim itself. Moreover, Gerber's Remarks accompanying a May 7, 1973 amendment referred to the cutting blade as a limitation of claim 15 and relied on the cutting blade penetration of the support means to distinguish the prior art. Hence the cutting blade is not merely an aspect of the claim environment, but an affirmative limitation of claim 15. Claim 16 depends from claim 15 and thus incorporates all the limitations of that claim.

In its brief Gerber agrees that the cutting blade may be a claim limitation without which there can be no infringement. It then asserts that the cutting blade is not an element of the subcombination to which the claim is drawn, which is another way of stating its position that the cutting blade is part of the "environment."

When it made the cutting blade a limitation of claims 15 and 16 Gerber crossed back over the line of demarcation between the "cutting apparatus" claims and "work holding means" claims drawn by the examiner in the restriction requirement. Gerber originally included in the divisional/continuing applications (that resulted in the '154 patent) the claims to the work holding means. After numerous amendments, Gerber incorporated as a limitation the cutting blade of elected claim 23 of the '492 patent and thereby rendered claims 15 and 16 non-consonant with those not elected in its response to the restriction requirement.

[*Affirmed.*]

4. THE ECONOMIC RATIONALE FOR A VIGOROUS DOUBLE PATENTING DOCTRINE

The current rules on double patenting (and related § 102/103 doctrine) go a good ways toward overcoming the problems that the concept of multiple inventive entities poses in an era of largely group research. To summarize: group research resulting in multiple patents generally presents no § 102/103 problem so long as the research results are covered by a single patent *or* multiple patents are filed on the same day. (That is, § 102(e) is not a problem in these cases, and the 1984 amendments to § 103 eliminate the effect of §§ 102(f) and (g) where the applications are commonly assigned.) And as long as one is willing to use the device of a terminal disclaimer, commonly-assigned and copending applications will not run into obviousness-type double patenting problems. (Same invention-type double patenting remains a problem, however; *see In re Vogel.*) Moreover, simply because one application dominates the other does not necessarily imply that either or both will be properly subject to obviousness-type double patent rejections. *In re Kaplan; In re Braat.*

In the past ten or fifteen years, the economically oriented literature on patents has begun to reflect an increased understanding that the single patent, the single invention is very seldom the appropriate unit of analysis. The literature now recognizes a basic facet of technological change that has long been reflected in the details of patent statutes and doctrine: oftentimes a patent is part of a steady stream of inventions. Today's patent may well represent the development of yesterday's minor tributary. Or it may serve as the basis for tomorrow's coursing river. The variants are many. Whatever form it takes, however, technology progresses in highly intertwined, overlapping units.

This is a salutary situation. A review of the sequence of technical developments in many industries reveals a recurring pattern of basic inventions followed by myriad applications, improvements, and elaborations. Extremely broad scope for patents on basic inventions is problematical as it tends to slow the pace of the all-important secondary improvements. *See* Merges & Nelson, *On the Complex Economics of Patent Scope*, 90 COLUM. L. REV. 839 (1990). On the other hand, there are good economic reasons to make sure there are adequate rewards for true pioneers — those who create basic inventions. One rationale for limiting at least somewhat the scope of broad initial patents is that those who create pioneer inventions often have a head start in developing the applications and improvements to follow. *See* Merges & Nelson, *supra*; J. RABINOW, INVENTING FOR FUN AND PROFIT (1990) (statement by famous and prolific inventor that developing improvements is critical if an inventor is to reap rewards from any invention). The inventor of the basic technology, in other words, is well positioned in the race for improvements. *Cf.* Howard Chang, Patent Scope, Antitrust Policy and Cumulative Innovation, Harvard Program on Law and Economics, Working Paper (Jan. 15, 1991 draft) (describing model where pioneer inventor requires patent of broad scope to undertake research); Gilbert & Shapiro, *Optimal Patent Length and Breadth*, 21 RAND J. ECON. 106 (1990) (concluding that, under terms of their model, scope was more important than duration for patents, and thus optimal patent would often be infinitely long but narrow in scope).

Properly understood, the law of double patenting fits into this pattern. Double patenting allows a patentee to claim variants on an invention in separate but related applications. The doctrine involves something of a tradeoff: in exchange for more favorable treatment than a third-party improver, the inventor gives up the extra patent term that might have come with prosecution of a separate, later-filed application.

Double patenting doctrine contributes to this effect. It allows the inventor(s) of a basic technique to file patents on improvements while it is still pending. This even extends to the first year after the patent has issued (because the issued patent does not become a statutory bar until the end of that year, and the patent cannot be used as novelty-defeating prior art if issued to the same inventive entity.) In this way, patent doctrine helps a pioneer secure protection for improvements, while at the same time limiting the timewise duration of the basic patent. It also insures rapid disclosure of the basic patent, because the inventor need not keep it pending so as to add amendments to broaden it.

Double patenting allows a pioneer inventor to patent additional, follow-on inventions. By privileging the obvious follow-on inventions of the pioneer, double patenting doctrine gives a modest extra encouragement to the pioneer to follow through on the original research. In this way follow-on invention *by the original inventor* receives a special incentive. *See Quad Envt'l Techs. Corp. v. Union Sanitary Dist.*, 946 F.2d 870, 873, 20 U.S.P.Q.2d 1392, 1394 (Fed. Cir. 1991) ("Voluntary limitation of the term of the later-issued patent is a convenient response to an obvious-type double patenting rejection, when the requirement of common ownership is met. Any possible enlargement of the term of exclusivity is eliminated, while enabling some limited protection to a patentee's later developments.").

Of course, the incentive is limited because the term of protection for any follow-on work is linked to the term of the original, pioneering patent through the device of the terminal disclaimer. Terminal disclaimers, then, mitigate the incentive to create follow-on inventions, but not completely: it is still surely worth something for a pioneer inventor to bring further subject matter within the ambit of the pioneering patent, even though that subject matter describes modest advances that would have been obvious from the original research. In this way, double patenting is not unlike the institution of blocking patents. It represents a rather clever parsing of property rights over a family of inventions in an effort to calibrate incentives to encourage both original, breakthrough research and follow-on developments, improvements, and applications.

Double patenting thus allows a slight incentive bonus to the original patentee. This bonus is unavailable to competitors; any improvements they develop which are rendered obvious by the original patented invention will themselves be unpatentable. As a consequence, double patenting adds another reason to favor relatively narrow claim scope at the margin. Some recent literature on patent scope contends that there are cases where broad initial scope makes sense, due to the pioneer's need for enhanced incentives. Double patenting allows just such an incentive to the pioneer; in effect, the doctrine allows a pioneer to expand the scope of claims filed in an original application on a pioneering invention by filing separate applications related to the first (and limited to its term), which cover obvious applications or variants of the original.

These salutary effects are muted, however, in the presence of certain facts. Where different inventive entities are involved, identical filing dates are required to preserve the option of obtaining patent protection on obvious improvements by filing terminal disclaimers (*see In re Longi*, 759 F.2d 887, 893-94, 225 U.S.P.Q. (BNA) 645 (Fed. Cir. 1985) (double patenting rejection proper for copending applications of different inventive entities assigned to a common owner)); alternatively, proof (under Rule 131) that the second-filed application was actually invented first will do. In this case, the law thwarts the common assignee's attempts to add patents for improvements during the pendency of the basic patent application or immediately after issuance of a basic patent. To the extent this diminishes the ability of a pioneer company to take advantage of its research head start, it undermines the (socially beneficial) practice of limiting to some extent extremely broad scope for basic patents. The solution lies in extending the legislative approach of the 1984 amendments to § 103 — that is, ending the strict enforcement of prior art against related inventive entities for §§ 102(f) & (g)/103 purposes — to the § 102(e)/103 context. Pending applications assigned to the same inventive entity would no longer be viable prior art, and hence the only obstacle facing the inventor of an improvement to a commonly-assigned (and copending) application would be double patenting — which once again could be overcome with an appropriate terminal disclaimer.

Alternatively, rules on joining together two or more related applications into a single application could be used to obviate the double patenting problem.

Either approach makes sense. A firm that has been assigned the basic patent has a head start in researching improvements, and the law ought to accommodate this head start by permitting the filing of related improvement patents. At the same time, because of the economic importance of limiting the scope and term of the basic patent, the pioneer ought not receive automatic protection for a wide range of improvements simply by filing a very broad basic patent. The creator of the basic invention, in other words, ought to have to actually produce the improvements — just as anyone else would. (For an argument that the enablement doctrine should be framed so as to require more additional inventive work before many of these improvements can be claimed by the pioneer, see Merges & Nelson, *supra*). The double patenting doctrine cooperates nicely with this desire to at least modestly limit broad pioneer patent scope; it recognizes that pioneers will often begin research on improvements soon after making a basic invention, and permits them to file related patents on these improvements. It also prohibits the holder of the basic patent from stacking improvements on top of that basic patent to achieve several decades of dominance in a particular field — a result effectively blocked by requiring terminal disclaimers. The rules on double patenting, together with existing rules on related inventive entities and the changes thereto discussed here, provide a nice balance in this regard between the interests of the pioneer and society's desire to foster active competition in the development of improvements.

5. COMPARATIVE AND INTERNATIONAL RESTRICTION: "UNITY OF INVENTION"

Restriction and divisional applications are the U.S. version of an issue contested and discussed throughout the world, and generally referred to as "unity of invention." In general, European standards on which inventions may be claimed together are quite liberal, and the same is true in Japan. *See Benzyl Esters/Bayer*, 1983, No. 7 OFFIC. J. EUR. PAT. OFF. 274 (Eur. Pat. Off. Tech. Bd. App., 8 March 1983) (claims to chemical products, intermediates and process show common essential feature and hence meet unity requirements of European Patent Convention Article 82); T. TANABE & H. WEGNER, JAPANESE PATENT LAW § 220 (1979) (claims to product and process properly included in one patent, as are claims to "linked" genuses and related genus and species inventions).

An important practical point to note is that since the European and Japanese systems allow *assignees* to file applications in addition to inventors, related inventions of different inventive entities may be easily joined — a result similar to that following the 1984 amendments to 35 U.S.C. § 116, but perhaps even more liberal.

As concerns restriction, U.S. Patent Office regulations were slightly modified in 1978 when the U.S. adhered to the Patent Cooperation Treaty (PCT). *See* Comments on Adopted Rules, 43 Fed. Reg. 20458 (May 11, 1978) (commenting on new version of 37 C.F.R. § 1.141). Even so, the "unity" standard of the PCT is more liberal than the traditional "independent and distinct" standard of § 121 of the Patent Act. If there is a linking, common general inventive concept between the inventions of two different claims, then even if the inventions are "independent and distinct" under § 121, the two inventions are properly grouped together for purposes of PCT Rule 13. At least one case suggests that U.S. regulations were not modified enough to come into compliance with the PCT. *Caterpillar Tractor Co. v. Commissioner*, 650 F. Supp. 218, 231 U.S.P.Q. (BNA) 590 (E.D. Va. 1986), *rev'g In re Caterpillar Tractor Co.*, 228 U.S.P.Q. (BNA) 77 (Com'r Dec. on reconsideration 1985), *previous decision*, 226 U.S.P.Q. (BNA) 625 (Com'r Dec. 1985). If followed, this decision will mean that § 372(b)(2) of the Patent Act will allow applicants to circumvent the domestic rules for "unity" (i.e., restriction).

If international harmonization efforts are successful, the need for terminal disclaimers will be largely eliminated. This stems from the fact that under Japanese and European practice, a patent's duration is twenty years from the *filing* date. There is thus no "timewise extension" problem when obvious variants of a single invention are claimed in applications which are filed at approximately the same time.

Unity of invention, however, continues to be a hot topic in international harmonization debates. *See, e.g.*, L. Schroeder, *The Harmonization of Patent Laws*, in SECURING AND ENFORCING PATENT RIGHTS 473 (Am. Law Inst.-Am. Bar Ass'n 1990) (Course of Study No. C567) ("The approach taken [on unity] will be somewhat more liberal than our present system and will be more in keeping with the approach now taken by the European Patent Office.").

C. INVENTORSHIP AND MISJOINDER

1. INVENTORSHIP

§ 116. Inventors

When an invention is made by two or more persons jointly, they shall apply for patent jointly and each make the required oath, except as otherwise provided in this title. Inventors may apply for a patent jointly even though (1) they did not physically work together or at the same time, (2) each did not make the same type or amount of contribution, or (3) each did not make a contribution to the subject matter of every claim of the patent.

If a joint inventor refuses to join in an application for patent or cannot be found or reached after diligent effort, the application may be made by the other inventor on behalf of himself and the omitted inventor. The Commissioner, on proof of the pertinent facts and after such notice to the omitted inventor as he prescribes, may grant a patent to the inventor making the application, subject to the same rights which the omitted inventor would have had if he had been joined. The omitted inventor may subsequently join in the application.

Whenever through error a person is named in an application for patent as the inventor, or through error an inventor is not named in an application, and such error arose without any deceptive intention on his part, the Commissioner may permit the application to be amended accordingly, under such terms as he prescribes.

35 U.S.C. § 116 (1996).

BURROUGHS WELLCOME CO. v. BARR LABORATORIES, INC.

40 F.3d 1223, 32 U.S.P.Q.2d 1915 (Fed. Cir. 1994)

MAYER, CIRCUIT JUDGE.

Barr Laboratories, Inc., Novopharm, Inc., and Novopharm, Ltd., appeal the order of the United States District Court for the Eastern District of North Carolina granting the motion of Burroughs Wellcome Co. for judgment as a matter of law that six United States patents were not invalid and were infringed. We affirm in part, vacate in part, and remand.

Burroughs Wellcome Co. is the owner of six United States patents that cover various preparations of 3'-azidothymidine (AZT) and methods for using that drug in the treatment of persons infected with the human immunodeficiency virus (HIV). Each of these patents names the same five inventors — Janet Rideout, David Barry, Sandra Lehrman, Martha St. Clair, and Phillip Furman (Burroughs Wellcome inventors) — all of whom were employed by Burroughs Wellcome at the time the inventions were alleged to have been conceived. The defendants-appellants concede that all five are properly named as inventors on the patents.

Burroughs Wellcome's patents arise from the same parent application filed on September 17, 1985. Five of the patents relate to the use of AZT to treat patients infected with HIV or who have acquired immunodeficiency syndrome (AIDS). The other patent, the '750 patent, covers a method of using AZT to increase the T-lymphocyte count of persons infected with HIV.

In the early 1980s, scientists began to see patients with symptoms of an unknown disease of the immune system, now known as AIDS. The disease attacks and destroys certain white blood cells known as CD4 T-lymphocytes or T-cells, which form an important component of the body's immune system. The level of destruction eventually becomes so great that the immune system is no longer able to mount an effective response to infections that pose little threat to a healthy person.

In mid-1984, scientists discovered that AIDS was caused by a retrovirus, known as HTLV III or, more commonly today, HIV.

At about this time, scientists at the National Institutes of Health (NIH), led by Samuel Broder, were looking for effective AIDS therapies as well. Unlike Burroughs Wellcome, Broder and his colleagues used live HIV, and were able to develop a test that could demonstrate a compound's effectiveness against HIV in humans using a unique line of T-cell clones (the ATH8 cell line). The NIH scientists began to seek compounds from private pharmaceutical companies for screening in their cell line. After Burroughs Wellcome contacted Broder in the fall of 1984, he agreed to accept compounds from Burroughs Wellcome under code for testing against live HIV.

Burroughs Wellcome's Rideout selected AZT and a number of other compounds for testing in the murine [i.e., lab mouse] screens on October 29, 1984. The tests, performed at Burroughs Wellcome facilities by St. Clair, showed that AZT had significant activity against both murine retroviruses at low concentrations. In light of these positive results, the Burroughs Wellcome inventors met on December 5, 1984, to discuss patenting the use of AZT in the treatment of AIDS. Burroughs Wellcome's patent committee thereafter recommended that the company prepare a patent application for future filing. By February 6, 1985, the company had prepared a draft application for filing in the United Kingdom. The draft disclosed using AZT to treat patients infected with HIV, and set out various pharmaceutical formulations of the compound in an effective dosage range to treat HIV infection.

Two days earlier, on February 4, 1985, Burroughs Wellcome had sent a sample of AZT, identified only as Compound S, to Broder at NIH. In an accompanying letter, Lehrman told Broder of the results of the murine retrovirus tests and asked that he screen the compound for activity against HIV in the ATH8 cell line. Another NIH scientist, Hiroaka Mitsuya, performed the test in mid-February 1985, and found that Compound S was active against HIV. Broder informed Lehrman of the results by telephone on February 20, 1985. Burroughs Wellcome filed its patent application in the United Kingdom on March 16, 1985.

After Burroughs Wellcome learned that AZT was active against HIV, it began the process of obtaining Food and Drug Administration (FDA) approval for AZT as an AIDS therapy. As a part of the clinical trials leading to FDA approval, Broder and another NIH scientist, Robert Yarchoan, conducted a Phase I human patient study which showed that treatment with AZT could result in an increase in the patient's T-cell count. Broder reported this result to Lehrman on July 23, 1985. In 1987, the FDA approved AZT for marketing by Burroughs Wellcome; Burroughs Wellcome markets the drug for treatment of HIV infection under the trademark Retrovir.

On March 19, 1991, Barr Laboratories, Inc. (Barr) sought FDA approval to manufacture and market a generic version of AZT by filing an Abbreviated New Drug Application (ANDA) pursuant to 21 U.S.C. § 355(j) (1988). As part of the process, Barr certified to the FDA that Burroughs Wellcome's patents were invalid or were not infringed by the product described in its ANDA. After Barr informed Burroughs Wellcome of its action, Burroughs Wellcome commenced this case for patent infringement against Barr.

Barr filed a counterclaim under 35 U.S.C. § 256 (1988) seeking correction of the patents to list Broder and Mitsuya as coinventors. Barr admitted that its AZT product would infringe the patents, but contended that it did not because Barr had obtained a license to manufacture and sell AZT from the government, which should be deemed the owner of the interest of coinventors Broder and Mitsuya in the AZT patents. Burroughs Wellcome denied that Broder and Mitsuya were coinventors and also responded that the assertion of any rights of Broder, Mitsuya, or the government in the patents was barred by laches, estoppel, and waiver.

After more than three weeks of trial, while Burroughs Wellcome was still in the process of presenting its case, the district court granted Burroughs Wellcome's motion for judgment as a matter of law against all of the defendants, concluding that the Burroughs Wellcome inventors had conceived of the subject matter of the inventions at some time before February 6, 1985, without the assistance of Broder, Mitsuya, or Yarchoan. The court rejected the arguments of Barr and Novopharm that they should be allowed to present evidence that the Burroughs Wellcome inventors had no reasonable belief that the inventions would actually work — that AZT was in fact active against HIV — until they were told the results of the NIH testing.

The court also rejected Novopharm's argument that the Burroughs Wellcome inventors had not conceived the invention of the '750 patent — the use of AZT to increase a patient's T-cell count — before July 23, 1985, when Broder reported the results of the NIH patient study to Lehrman. The court concluded that the increase in T-cell count was an obvious phenomenon known to the inventors that would result from administration of AZT. And the district court denied Barr's renewed motion for partial summary judgment on Burroughs Wellcome's equitable defenses to its counterclaim for correction of the patents under section 256.

Discussion

The arguments of both Barr and Novopharm are directed to when the inventors conceived the invention. Burroughs Wellcome says it was before they learned the results of the NIH tests; Barr and Novopharm say that confirmation of the inventions' operability, which came from the NIH tests, was an essential part of the inventive process. If Burroughs Wellcome is right, then the patents name the proper inventors, they are not invalid, and the appellants are liable for infringement. If Barr and Novopharm are correct, then Broder, Mitsuya, and Yarchoan should have been named as joint inventors and the resolution of Burroughs Wellcome's infringement suits is premature.

A joint invention is the product of a collaboration between two or more persons working together to solve the problem addressed. 35 U.S.C. § 116 (1988); *Kimberly-Clark Corp. v. Procter & Gamble Distrib. Co.*, 973 F.2d 911, 917, 23 U.S.P.Q.2d 1921, 1926 (Fed. Cir. 1992). People may be joint inventors even though they do not physically work on the invention together or at the same time, and even though each does not make the same type or amount of contribution. 35 U.S.C. § 116. The statute does not set forth the minimum quality or quantity of contribution required for joint inventorship.

Conception is the touchstone of inventorship, the completion of the mental part of invention. *Sewall v. Walters*, 21 F.3d 411, 415, 30 U.S.P.Q.2d 1356, 1359 (Fed. Cir. 1994). It is "the formation in the mind of the inventor, of a definite and permanent idea of the complete and operative invention, as it is hereafter to be applied in practice." *Hybritech Inc. v. Monoclonal Antibodies, Inc.*, 802 F.2d 1367, 1376, 231 U.S.P.Q. 81, 87 (Fed. Cir. 1986) (citation omitted). Conception is complete only when the idea is so clearly defined in the inventor's mind that only ordinary skill would be necessary to reduce the invention to practice, without extensive research or experimentation. *Sewall*, 21 F.3d at 415, 30 U.S.P.Q.2d at 1359. Because it is a mental act, courts require corroborating evidence of a contemporaneous disclosure that would enable one skilled in the art to make the invention. *Coleman v. Dines*, 754 F.2d at 359, 224 U.S.P.Q. at 862.

Thus, the test for conception is whether the inventor had an idea that was definite and permanent enough that one skilled in the art could understand the invention; the inventor must prove his conception by corroborating evidence, preferably by showing a contemporaneous disclosure. An idea is definite and permanent when the inventor has a specific, settled idea, a particular solution to the problem at hand, not just a general goal or research plan he hopes to pursue. *See Fiers v. Revel*, 984 F.2d 1164, 1169, 25 U.S.P.Q.2d 1601, 1605 (Fed. Cir. 1993); *Amgen, Inc. v. Chugai Pharmaceutical Co.*, 927 F.2d 1200, 1206, 18 U.S.P.Q.2d 1016, 1021 (Fed. Cir. 1991) (no conception of chemical compound based solely on its biological activity). The conception analysis necessarily turns on the inventor's ability to describe his invention with particularity. Until he can do so, he cannot prove possession of the complete mental picture of the invention. These rules ensure that patent rights attach only when an idea is so far developed that the inventor can point to a definite, particular invention.

But an inventor need not know that his invention will work for conception to be complete. *Applegate v. Scherer*, 332 F.2d 571, 573, 141 U.S.P.Q. 796, 799 (C.C.P.A. 1964). He need only show that he had the idea; the discovery that an invention actually works is part of its reduction to practice. *Id.; see also Oka v. Youssefyeh*, 849 F.2d 581, 584 n. 1, 7 U.S.P.Q.2d 1169, 1171 n. 1 (Fed. Cir. 1988).

Barr and Novopharm suggest that the inventor's definite and permanent idea must include a reasonable expectation that the invention will work for its intended purpose. They argue that this expectation is of paramount importance when the invention deals with uncertain or experimental disciplines, where the inventor cannot reasonably believe an idea will be operable until some result supports that conclusion. Without some experimental confirmation, they suggest, the inventor has only a hope or an expectation, and has not yet conceived the invention in sufficiently definite and permanent form. But this is not the law. An inventor's belief that his invention will work or his reasons for choosing a particular approach are irrelevant to conception. *MacMillan v. Moffett*, 432 F.2d 1237, 1239, 167 U.S.P.Q. 550, 552 (C.C.P.A. 1970).

The Burroughs Wellcome inventors set out with the general goal of finding a method to treat AIDS, but by the time Broder confirmed that AZT was active against HIV, they had more than a general hope or expectation. They had thought of the particular antiviral agent with which they intended to address the problem, and had formulated the idea of the inventions to the point that they could express it clearly in the form of a draft patent application, which Barr and Novopharm concede would teach one skilled in the art to practice the inventions. The draft expressly discloses the intended use of AZT to treat AIDS. It sets out the compound's structure, which, along with at least one method of preparation, was already well known. The draft also discloses in detail both how to prepare a pharmaceutical formulation of AZT and how to use it to treat a patient infected with HIV. The listed dosages, dose forms, and routes of administration conform to those eventually approved by the FDA. The draft shows that the idea was clearly defined in the inventors' minds; all that remained was to reduce it to practice — to confirm its operability and bring it to market. *See Haskell v. Colebourne*, 671 F.2d 1362, 1365-66, 213 U.S.P.Q. 192, 194 (C.C.P.A. 1982) (enabling draft patent application sufficient to corroborate conception).

An examination of the events that followed the preparation of Burroughs Wellcome's draft confirms the soundness of the conception. Broder and Mitsuya received from Burroughs Wellcome a group of compounds, known to Broder and Mitsuya only by code names, selected for testing by the Burroughs Wellcome inventors. They then tested those compounds for activity against HIV in their patented cell line. The test results revealed for the first time that one of the compounds, later revealed to be AZT, was exceptionally active against the virus.

Here, though, the testing was brief, simply confirming the operability of what the draft application disclosed. True, the science surrounding HIV and AIDS was unpredictable and highly experimental at the time the Burroughs Wellcome scientists made the inventions. But what matters for conception is whether the inventors had a definite and permanent idea of the operative inventions. In this case, no prolonged period of extensive research, experiment, and modification followed the alleged conception. By all accounts, what followed was simply the normal course of clinical trials that mark the path of any drug to the marketplace.

That is not to say, however, that the NIH scientists merely acted as a "pair of hands" for the Burroughs Wellcome inventors. Broder and Mitsuya exercised considerable skill in conducting the tests, using their patented cell line to model the responses of human cells infected with HIV. Lehrman did suggest initial concentrations to Broder, but she hardly controlled the conduct of the testing, which necessarily involved interpretation of results for which Broder and Mitsuya, and very few others, were uniquely qualified. But because the testing confirmed the operability of the inventions, it showed that the Burroughs Wellcome inventors had a definite and permanent idea of the inventions. It was part of the reduction to practice and inured to the benefit of Burroughs Wellcome.

The question is not whether Burroughs Wellcome reasonably believed that the inventions would work for their intended purpose, the focus of the evidence offered by Barr and Novopharm, but whether the inventors had formed the idea of their use for that purpose in sufficiently final form that only the exercise of ordinary skill remained to reduce it to practice. *See MacMillan v. Moffett*, 432 F.2d at 1239, 167 U.S.P.Q. at 552 (Inventor's "reasons or lack of reasons for including U-5008 are not relevant to the question of conception. The important thing is that he did think in definite terms of the method claimed."). Whether or not Burroughs Wellcome believed the inventions would in fact work based on the mouse screens is irrelevant.

We do not know precisely when the inventors conceived their inventions, but the record shows that they had done so by the time they prepared the draft patent application that thoroughly and particularly set out the inventions as they would later be used. The district court correctly ruled that on this record, the NIH scientists were not joint inventors of these inventions.

The trial court's decision should be affirmed across the board because it correctly found that the Burroughs Wellcome inventors solely conceived and are entitled to the inventive benefit of all the claimed inventions.

NOTES

1. *A Cat Tail.* The principles of the preceding case were applied in an interesting setting in *Brown v. Regents of Univ. of Cal.*, 866 F. Supp. 439, 440-42, 31 U.S.P.Q.2d (BNA) 1463 (N.D. Cal.), *appeal dismissed*, 47 F.3d 1179 (Fed. Cir. 1994). In *Brown*, as in *Burroughs Wellcome*, the issue of inventorship arose indirectly as a defense: the accused infringer claimed immunity from suit by the patentee due to a license from the putative co-inventor, Brown. The following excerpt is drawn from the case.

> [O]n July 2, 1986, plaintiff took her sick cats to Dr. Neils C. Pedersen, a well-known animal virologist at the U.C. Davis School of Veterinary Medicine. Ms. Brown brought with her detailed observations and records that she had kept of her cats' illnesses. She told Dr. Pedersen that she believed that her cats were infected with a virus similar to the human AIDS virus. She further claims that she told Dr. Pedersen that she believed that the virus was a new, "slow-acting" lentivirus. Dr. Pedersen examined the cats, questioned Ms. Brown about the cats' histories, and drew blood samples from the cats.
>
> During 1986 and 1987, Dr. Pedersen and a colleague, Dr. Janet K. Yamamoto, performed extensive laboratory work which culminated in the development of methods for isolating a new virus, feline T-lymphotropic virus ("FTLV," "FIV"), in a substantially pure, nonnaturally occurring, form. Drs. Pedersen and Yamamoto also developed methods for detecting the presence of FIV in cats, as well as methods for vaccinating them against the virus. On August 26, 1987, they filed a patent application on these inventions. The '753 patent issued on August 6, 1991, and the '602 patent issued on June 2, 1992. The doctors assigned both patents to the University of California.
>
> The '753 patent claims FIV, a biologically active composition of matter ("biochemical compound") that has been isolated from cells grown in an in vitro culture. (See Amended Complaint, Ex. 1.) The '602 patent claims

methods for diagnosing an FIV infection by detecting in a clinical sample the presence of the virus itself or antibodies to the virus. (See Amended Complaint, Ex. 2.) The claimed novelty of the '602 patent is based on the isolation and purification of the new biochemical product covered by the '753 patent. Neither patent claims mere discovery of FIV.

While Dr. Pedersen widely and publicly credited Ms. Brown for her role in the discovery of FIV, it is undisputed that Ms. Brown played no role in the laboratory work required to isolate and purify the virus, and to develop methods for diagnosing it. (See, e.g., Reply 2-4.) Ms. Brown's central contention is essentially that she supplied the critical inventive contribution to the patents through her role in discovering the virus, and that the work of Drs. Pedersen and Yamamoto in isolating and purifying the virus was unoriginal.

In a passage that has been widely cited, one district court held that an individual must have played an "inventive" role in making an "original contribution" to the "final solution" of a problem to qualify as a joint inventor. *Monsanto Co. v. Kamp*, 269 F. Supp. 818, 824 (D.D.C. 1967).

Applying the principles set forth above, it is evident that Ms. Brown did not contribute to the conception of the inventions covered by the patents at issue in this case. [S]he at most played a substantial role in the discovery of FIV. The patents in this case do not claim discovery of the virus, however; they claim isolation and substantial purification of the virus, as well as methods for diagnosing the virus by detecting the presence of the virus itself, or antibodies to it, in a clinical sample. (See Defendants' Memo 15-16; Amended Complaint, Exs. 1, 2.)

As the patents cover biochemical substances, under *Amgen* and *Fiers*, they cannot have been conceived prior to their reduction to practice in the laboratory of Drs. Pedersen and Yamamoto. Ms. Brown is a nonscientist who played no role in the laboratory work involved in isolating the virus; therefore, regardless of the value of her research leads, she cannot be deemed to have contributed to the conception of the inventions covered by the patents. Her arguments as to the uninventiveness of Drs. Pedersen's and Yamamoto's contributions go to the validity of the patents in the first instance, not to her right to be named as a joint inventor thereon.

2. THE MISJOINDER DEFENSE

Section 256 of the 1952 Patent Act provides in pertinent part:

Whenever through error a person is named in an issued patent as the inventor, or through error an inventor is not named in an issued patent and such error arose without any deceptive intention on his part, the Commissioner may, on application of all the parties and assignees, with proof of the facts and such other requirements as may be imposed, issue a certificate correcting such error.

35 U.S.C. § 256 (1996). Out of this mild corrective, plaintiffs have tried to fashion an affirmative cause of action for misjoinder of inventions. The case and notes that follow describe the result.

GENERAL ELECTRIC CO. v. BRANDON

25 U.S.P.Q.2d 1885 (N.D.N.Y. 1992)

MCAVOY, DISTRICT JUDGE.

General Electric Company seeks a declaratory judgment that it is the rightful owner of United States Patent No. 4,436,311 ("the '311 Patent") which was issued to one of its former employees, Ronald E. Brandon (hereinafter Brandon). The complaint alleges that Brandon left GE in 1980, filed his patent application in 1982 and was issued the '311 Patent in 1984. It is alleged that the invention covered by the '311 Patent was made by GE employees or suggested by or derived from the work of GE employees.

The plaintiff contends that "the gist" of its complaint is that the patent was wrongfully issued in the name of defendant because it was based upon the work of other GE employees. The plaintiff states at p. 8 of its memo of law that "GE's complaint does not allege misappropriation of trade secrets.... Rather, GE's complaint alleges that because defendant Brandon had an obligation to disclose that information and assign the '311 Patent to GE, the '311 Patent rightfully belongs in equity to GE."

At one point in its memo of law the plaintiff argues that under 35 U.S.C. § 256 the court is empowered to correct the inventorship on an issued patent. Section 256 is nowhere mentioned in the complaint. The defendants have argued that the plaintiff has not pled the element of an action for correction of inventorship under § 256. They also argue that § 256 cannot be used as a vehicle for substituting inventors in the absence of innocent error in the joinder or non-joinder of inventors. However, as the plaintiff points out this second argument is based upon a reading of the statute prior to the 1982 amendment.

In *MCV, Inc. v. King-Seeley Thermos Co.*, 870 F.2d 1568, 1570-71 (Fed. Cir. 1989), the court held that a suit for a determination of inventorship and correction of a patent under § 256 is permissible .... The *MCV* court then reasoned that a resolution of the inventorship dispute would involve the definition of the invention and a determination of who in fact was the inventor — both substantive questions of patent law.

Prior to 1982, § 256 was interpreted as authorizing suits to correct joint inventorship disputes, but not suits to substitute one sole inventor for another. However, in 1982 the statute was amended to delete the "misjoinder" language. The legislative history indicates that "changes from a mistakenly identified sole inventor to different, but actual, joint inventors, [and] conversions from erroneously identified joint inventors to different but actual, sole inventor would also be permitted." 1982 U.S. Code Cong. and Adm. News, 765, 773. It is this amended statute upon which the plaintiff relies.

The other aspect of the defendants' argument — that is, that § 256 may only be used in the absence of "deceptive intention," and the plaintiff has alleged that defendants' error was not innocent — carries some strength. While it is true that § 256 requires that the error in designation be without "deceptive intention ... on his part," the statute does not provide any guidance as to whose intentions are at issue. This "deceptive intention" language was not changed in the 1982 amendment and there is only one case which directly deals with the issue.

In *Dee v. Aukerman*, 625 F. Supp. 1427 (S.D. Ohio 1986), the court discussed the origins of § 256 and found that its purpose was to correct innocent mistakes and prevent invalidation of patents.

A reading of the *MCV* decision suggests that a § 256 correction may only be obtained if the omission was completely "without deceptive intent." As to the question of whether the error was without deceptive intention, the court stated that "[o]ne answer would permit correction of the patent; the opposite answer could invalidate it." *MCV* at 1571. This statement is presumably based upon the premise that if the person who initially applied for the patent failed to include all true inventors the patent is invalidated, *see, e.g., Iowa State University Research Foundation, Inc. v. Sperry Rand Corp.*, 444 F.2d 406, 408 (4th Cir. 1971) (inclusion of more or less than the true inventors in a patent renders it void), and if invalidated a patent cannot be corrected.

Based upon the case law, at a minimum there must be a lack of deceptive intention on the part of the person originally named as the inventor. The statute allows for administrative correction of mistakes and specifically provides that if the error is correctible under § 256 the patent will not be invalidated. Here, not only has plaintiff not mentioned § 256 in the complaint, but the tenor of the complaint is that defendant did not mistakenly name himself as the sole inventor of the subject of the '311 Patent. Therefore, the plaintiff's argument under § 256 fails.

NOTE

General Electric was recently applied in *University of Colo. Found. v. American Cyanamid Co.*, 880 F. Supp. 1387, 35 U.S.P.Q.2d 1737, 1745-46 (D. Colo. 1995):

> Plaintiffs claim the naming of Dr. Ellenbogen as the inventor on the Patent is in violation of 35 U.S.C. Section 115. That section requires that "[t]he applicant shall make oath that he believes himself to be the original and first inventor of the ... composition of matter, or improvement thereof, for which he solicits a patent." 35 U.S.C. Section 115. Based on this alleged violation, Plaintiffs seek relief pursuant to 35 U.S.C. Section 256 in the form of "[a]n order revising the name of the inventor on the patent to name only the true inventors, namely Drs. Allen and Seligman," (Second Am. Compl. at 20).

Cyanamid claims Section 256 is intended to permit correction of inventorship where error is inadvertent and "without deceptive intent" and Plaintiffs' allegations of fraud on the part of Cyanamid render the section inapplicable. The rationale here is if the patentee applied for the patent with the deceptive intent of omitting an inventor, the patent is invalidated and cannot be corrected. See *General Elec. Co. v. Brandon* [*supra*].

Cyanamid acknowledges neither the Supreme Court nor the Federal Circuit has squarely addressed whether the words "without deceptive intent" in Section 256 refer to the patentee, the omitted inventor, or both. Nevertheless, Cyanamid argues case law from the district courts supports the position that Section 256 is inapplicable where a plaintiff alleges the defendant/patentee acted with deceptive intention when it failed to identify a true inventor.

The court in *General Electric*, however, determined the claim as if it had been framed under Section 256 and noted the "'deceptive intention' language was not changed in the 1982 amendment." [Because of a lack of support in the precedent,] I therefore conclude Section 256 is not applicable here where Plaintiffs seek correction based on Cyanamid's alleged fraud and deception.

See also McMurray v. Harwood, 870 F. Supp. 917, 919-20 (E.D. Wis. 1994) (§ 256 limited to correction of innocent errors and does not permit replacement of fraudulently named inventor with innocent inventor).

Chapter 8

INFRINGEMENT

Section 271(a) of the Patent Act covers infringement:

> Except as otherwise provided in this title, whoever without authority makes, uses, offers to sell, or sells any patented invention, within the United States or imports into the United States any patented invention during the term of the patent therefor, infringes the patent.

Note at the outset what the statute does *not* require: proof of "access" to the patented invention; and any *intent* to infringe. Both are irrelevant; the first because even independent invention is an infringement (unlike copyright law, where access is required and independent creation is a defense), and the second because the right to exclude does not depend upon the infringer's state of mind.

No better introduction to the basic issues of infringement can be found than the classic discussion in the following case.

AUTOGIRO CO. OF AMERICA v. UNITED STATES

384 F.2d 391, 155 U.S.P.Q. 697 (Ct. Cl. 1967)

[Plaintiff brought suit against the U.S. seeking compensation for infringement of sixteen of its patents on helicopter technology. The trial commissioner of the Court of Claims found fifteen of the patents valid and infringed. The court affirmed the findings as to eleven of the patents.]

The Patent Act of 1952 is the controlling law in this case. No previous patent act contained a section on infringement. Congress had always allowed the courts to settle the issue without any legislative guidelines. Section 271(a) which covers the type of infringement alleged here was not inserted in the Act to clarify any legal problems, but only as a codification of existing judicial determinations.

The claims of the patent provide the concise formal definition of the invention. They are the numbered paragraphs which "particularly point [ ] out and distinctly claim [ ] the subject matter which the applicant regards as his invention." 35 U.S.C. § 112. It is to these wordings that one must look to determine whether there has been infringement. Courts can neither broaden nor narrow the claims to give the patentee something different than what he has set forth. No matter how great the temptations of fairness or policy making, courts do not rework claims. They only interpret them. Although courts are confined by the language of the claims, they are not, however, confined to the language of the claims in interpreting their meaning.

Claims cannot be clear and unambiguous on their face. A comparison must exist. The lucidity of a claim is determined in light of what ideas it is trying to convey. Only by knowing the idea, can one decide how much shadow encumbers the reality.

The inability of words to achieve precision is none the less extant with patent claims than it is with statutes. The problem is likely more acute with claims. Statutes by definition are the reduction of ideas to print. Since the ability to verbalize is crucial in statutory enactment, legislators develop a facility with words not equally developed in inventors. An invention exists most importantly as a tangible structure or a series of drawings. A verbal portrayal is usually an afterthought written to satisfy the requirements of patent law. This conversion of machine to words allows for unintended idea gaps which cannot be satisfactorily filled. Often the invention is novel and words do not exist to describe it. The dictionary does not always keep abreast of the inventor. It cannot. Things are not made for the sake of words, but words for things. To overcome this lag, patent law allows the inventor to be his own lexicographer.

The necessity for a sensible and systematic approach to claim interpretation is axiomatic. The Alice-in-Wonderland view that something means whatever one chooses it to mean makes for enjoyable reading, but bad law. Claims are best construed in connection with the other parts of the patent instrument and with the circumstances surrounding the inception of the patent application.

II

In deriving the meaning of a claim, we inspect all useful documents and reach the "felt meaning" of the claim. In seeking this goal, we make use of three parts of the patent: the specification, the drawings, and the file wrapper.

Specification. — Section 112 of the 1952 Patent Act requires the specification to describe the manner and process of making and using the patent so that any person skilled in the patent's art may utilize it. In serving its statutory purpose, the specification aids in ascertaining the scope and meaning of the language employed in the claims inasmuch as words must be used in the same way in both the claims and the specification. The use of the specification as a concordance for the claim is accepted by almost every court, and is a basic concept of patent law. Most courts have simply stated that the specification is to be used to explain the claims; others have stated the proposition in different terms, but with the same effect.

Drawings. — The patent may contain drawings. 35 U.S.C. § 113. In those instances where a visual representation can flesh out words, drawings may be used in the same manner and with the same limitations as the specification. *Permutit Co. v. Graver Corp.*, 284 U.S. 52, 52 S. Ct. 53, 76 L. Ed. 163 (1931).

File wrapper. — The file wrapper contains the entire record of the proceedings in the Patent Office from the first application papers to the issued patent. Since all express representations of the patent applicant made to induce a patent grant are in the file wrapper, this material provides an accurate charting of the patent's pre-issuance history. [It can be used], like the specification and drawings, to determine the scope of claims. For example, the prior art cited in the file wrapper is used in this manner. [It] gives clues as to what the claims do not cover. *Westinghouse Electric & Mfg. Co. v. Formica Insulation Co.*, 266 U.S. 342 (1924).

III

The use of the various parts of the patent to determine the meaning of the claims is only half the process of determining patent infringement. The other half is "reading the claims on the accused structures." If the claims read literally on the accused structures, an initial hurdle in the test for infringement has been cleared. The race is not over; it has only started. To allow literality to satisfy the test for infringement would force the patent law to reward literary skill and not mechanical creativity. And since the law is to benefit the inventor's genius and not the scrivener's talents, claims must not only read literally on the accused structures, but also the structures must "do the same work, in substantially the same way, and accomplish substantially the same result." This approach of making literal overlap only a step and not the entire test of infringement has been consistently applied by the courts since *Westinghouse v. Boyden Power Brake Co.*, 170 U.S. 537, at 568 (1898).

If the claims do not read literally on the accused structures, infringement is not necessarily ruled out. The doctrine of equivalence casts around a claim a penumbra which also must be avoided if there is to be no infringement. It provides that a structure infringes, without there being literal overlap, if it performs substantially the same function in substantially the same way and for substantially the same purpose as the claims set forth.

Checking the subordination of substance to form and not depriving the inventor of the benefit of his invention cannot be standardized. The range of equivalence varies with each patent; however, some general guidelines can be drawn. One important guide is whether persons reasonably skilled in the art would have known of the interchangeability of an ingredient not contained in the patent with one that was. Another guide is the notion that pioneer patents are to be given wider ranges of equivalence than minor improvement patents. This statement is less a canon of construction and more a shorthand expression for the dictates of the law and the patents themselves. The doctrine of equivalence is subservient to file wrapper estoppel. [A claim] may not include within its range anything that would vitiate limitations expressed before the Patent Office. Thus a patent that has been severely limited to avoid the prior art will only have a small range between it and the point beyond which it violates file wrapper estoppel. Similarly a patent which is a major departure from the prior art will have a larger range in which equivalence can function. The scope of the patents also influences the range of equivalence. A pioneer patent which occupies symbolically a six-inch circle will have three inches of equivalence if its range is fifty percent. An improvement patent occupying a two-inch circle has only one inch of equivalence with the same range. Thus with relatively identical ranges, the scope of the patent provides the pioneer patent with absolutely a larger range of equivalence.

IV

In summary, the determination of patent infringement is a two-step process. First, the meaning of the claims in issue must be determined by a study of all relevant patent documents. Secondly, the claims must be read on the accused structures. In doing this, it is of little value that they read literally on the structures. What is crucial is that the structures must do the same work, in substantially the same way, and accomplish substantially the same result to constitute infringement. This is the general approach which this court uses to determine the infringement of all the patent claims properly before it in this case.

NOTES

1. *Some Refinements*. *Autogiro*'s framework can be fleshed out with the addition of several points.

a. *Claims*. Courts have sent conflicting signals on an important issue: whether the preamble to a claim is to be read as a limitation, or simply as descriptive prose introducing the real elements (and limitations) of the claimed invention. In *Loctite Corp. v. Ultraseal Ltd.*, 781 F.2d 861, 868, 228 U.S.P.Q. (BNA) 90 (Fed. Cir. 1985), one preamble phrase ("An anaerobic curing sealant ...") was found to be a limitation, while another ("adapted to remain in a [certain] state for prolonged periods of time while in contact with air and to polymerize ... in the absence of air and upon contact with metal surfaces ...") was not. *See also In re Stencel*, 828 F.2d 751, 4 U.S.P.Q.2d (BNA) 1071 (Fed. Cir. 1987) (obviousness issue: preamble recited limitation, rendering claimed invention nonobvious). *See generally Perkin-Elmer Corp. v. Computervision Corp.*, 732 F.2d 888, 896, 221 U.S.P.Q. (BNA) 669, 675-76 (Fed. Cir.), *cert. denied*, 105 S. Ct. 187 (1984) (preamble recites limitation only if necessary to give meaning to claimed structure).

Second, the "doctrine of claim differentiation" can be a helpful aid. This doctrine stems from the simple proposition that applicants do not use two claims where one will do. Hence it provides that if one claim includes a limitation and another omits it, the claims cover different subject matter. Limitations in one claim, in other words, will not be read into another claim. *See, e.g., Intellicall, Inc. v. Phonometrics, Inc.*, 952 F.2d 1384, 21 U.S.P.Q.2d (BNA) 1383 (Fed. Cir. 1992) (panel including retired Justice Thurgood Marshall discussed doctrine of claim differentiation and held it did not apply).

b. *Specification*. As *Autogiro* makes clear, courts often refer to the specification to define words and phrases used in the claims. But it is equally well established that limitations may not be "read into" the claims from the specification. As we will see (especially in *Unique Concepts*, below), the line between permissible interpretation and impermissible addition of limitations may seem illusory at times.

c. *Prosecution History.* One must be careful to distinguish two uses of a patent's prosecution history in construing claims. In all cases it is appropriate to see what the applicant said during prosecution as an aid in interpreting what the claims mean. If a certain term is referred to in a response to an office action (such as a rejection), for example, that may be helpful later in deciding whether an accused product really fits the definition of a term used in the claim. (See the *Unique Concepts* case below, for example). But after a court decides there is no literal infringement, and moves on to infringement under the doctrine of equivalents, the prosecution history can enter the analysis again. Under the doctrine of "prosecution history estoppel" (formerly "file wrapper estoppel," for the common name used at the Patent Office to a refer to the bundle of papers connected with a particular application), the patentee is estopped from "reclaiming" a meaning for a term or phrase that was specifically disclaimed during prosecution in order to avoid the prior art. We will see this in operation in several cases below, especially the *Prodyne* case.

2. *Matters of Law and Fact.* The first step, construing the scope of a claim, can be determined as a matter of law if the language of the claim is not disputed. However, "when the meaning of a term in the claim is disputed and extrinsic evidence is necessary to explain that term, then an underlying factual question arises, and construction of the claim should be left to the trier...." *Palumbo v. Don-Joy Co.*, 762 F.2d 969, 974, 226 U.S.P.Q. (BNA) 5 (Fed. Cir. 1985). This two-step analysis of patent infringement "applies whether claims are asserted to be infringed literally or by application of the doctrine of equivalents." *Texas Instruments v. United States Int'l Trade Comm'n*, 805 F.2d 1558, 1562 (Fed. Cir. 1986).

A. INTERPRETING THE CLAIM

UNIQUE CONCEPTS, INC. v. BROWN

939 F.2d 1558, 19 U.S.P.Q.2d 1500 (Fed. Cir. 1991)

LOURIE, CIRCUIT JUDGE.

Unique Concepts, Inc. and Floyd M. Baslow (collectively "Unique") appeal from the final judgment of the United States District Court for the Southern District of New York, holding that certain products produced by defendants (collectively "Brown") do not infringe Unique's patent. We affirm.

The Patent in Suit

Unique is the exclusive licensee under U.S. Patent 4,108,260 ('260 patent), issued April 19, 1977, and owned by Floyd M. Baslow. [T]he patent is directed to an "assembly of border pieces" used to attach a fabric wall covering to a wall.

The assembly is made up of a number of "right angle corner border pieces" and "linear border pieces" which are arranged so as to form a frame around the area of a wall to be covered.

Below is [Figure 8-1, next page] showing an exploded view of the border pieces [that form] the framework.

[As filed, the application] originally contained 14 claims. Claim 1, the only independent claim, recited an assembly comprising "linear border pieces and right angle corner border pieces," each of the border pieces having a raised face, a storage channel, and a keyway. The original claims of the Baslow application were rejected by the Patent and Trademark Office (PTO) as being unpatentable in view of various references. The Examiner found that the references "show frames including corners in arrangements similar to that of applicant...."

In response, the applicant amended his claims and argued against the references, stating that "[t]he main advantage of the present invention is that it greatly simplifies the mounting of a fabric covering.... Thus an amateur can practice the present invention...."

The next item in the file history is a notice of allowability together with an examiner's amendment canceling [certain] claims, and amending [others]. Claim 1, the sole independent claim [of the issued patent], reads:

> 1. An assembly of border pieces for creating a framework attachable to a wall or other flat surface for mounting a fabric sheet which is cut to dimensions at least sufficient to cover the surface, *said assembly comprising linear border pieces and right angle corner border pieces* which are arranged in end-to-end relation to define a framework that follows the perimeter of the area to be covered, *each piece* including a raised face, a storage channel running adjacent the outer edge of the piece and having a narrow inlet communicating with said face, the portion of the selvage [i.e., edge] of said sheet which includes fabric material in excess of that necessary to cover said surface being stuffed in said storage channel so that the exposed selvage of the sheet lies against said face to present a smooth appearance which extends to said inlet and is directly adjacent said perimeter, said linear pieces being formed of an integral one piece plastic material of sufficient elasticity to permit dilation of said inlet whereby said inlet may be temporarily expanded to admit said excess material and then contracted to retain said excess material in said storage channel.

(Emphasis added.)

The Proceedings in the District Court

Unique brought the present suit in 1986, alleging that certain products made by Brown infringed claims 1-3 of the '260 patent. Brown denied infringement. [T]he parties [stipulated that] the sole issue which remained was whether two of Brown's products (the "regular flat track with heel" and the "cove track")

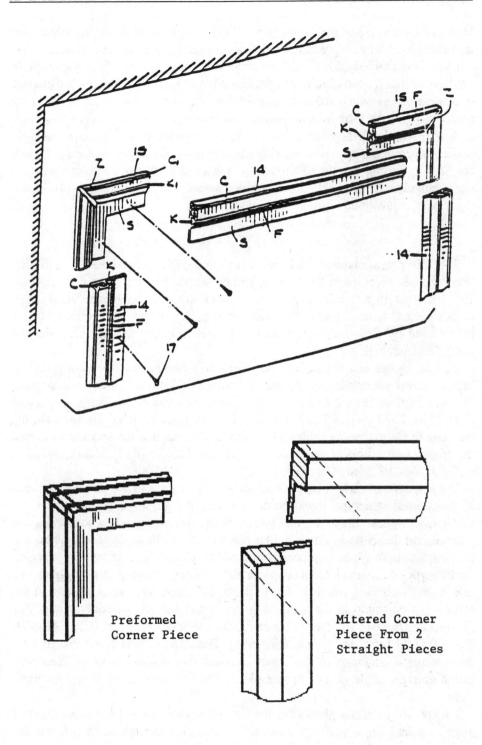

Preformed
Corner Piece

Mitered Corner
Piece From 2
Straight Pieces

Figure 8-1

infringed claims 1-3 of the '260 patent. Validity was not at issue; the stipulation prevented a claim interpretation which would render the claims invalid.

Brown maintained that its accused products do not infringe [because they] do not have corner pieces which were preformed at a right angle, but instead employ two linear pieces which are each mitered, i.e., cut at a 45 degree angle, and then placed together to form a right angle.

A trial was held, at which each party, by agreement, presented as its only witness a patent expert. After hearing the testimony, the judge entered judgment for Brown, finding that the mitered linear pieces used by Brown do not meet the claim language "right angle corner border pieces," either literally or under the doctrine of equivalents. Unique appealed.

DISCUSSION

The '260 patent claims a framework for mounting a fabric sheet "comprising linear border pieces and right angle corner border pieces." The district court found the patent not infringed because, inter alia, the language "right angle corner pieces" is limited to preformed corner pieces, whereas the mitered linear pieces used by Brown do not meet this limitation either literally or under the doctrine of equivalents.

Unique argues that the district court erred in finding that the claims do not literally cover assemblies having mitered corners. Claim construction is an issue of law, which we review de novo. *ZMI Corp. v. Cardiac Resuscitator Corp.*, 844 F.2d 1576, 1578, 6 U.S.P.Q.2d 1557, 1559 (Fed. Cir. 1988). To ascertain the meaning of claims, we consider three sources: the claims, the specification, and the prosecution history. *Loctite Corp. v. Ultraseal, Ltd.*, 781 F.2d 861, 867, 228 U.S.P.Q. 90, 93 (Fed. Cir. 1985).

The language of claim 1 makes unambiguous reference to two distinct elements of the claimed structure: linear border pieces and right angle corner pieces. If, as Unique argues, linear border pieces of framing material, whose ends are mitered, are the same as linear border pieces and a right angle corner piece, the recitation of both types of pieces is redundant. Unique's argument for merging the two types of claim elements into one also violates the oft-quoted "all elements rule," the essence of which is that to prove infringement, every element in the claim must be found in the accused device either literally or equivalently. *See SmithKline Diagnostics, Inc. v. Helena Laboratories Corp.*, 859 F.2d 878, 889, 8 U.S.P.Q.2d 1468, 1477 (Fed. Cir. 1988). The district court thus correctly held that the plain language of the claim includes two distinct types of elements, including right angle corner border pieces, thereby precluding literal infringement.

The specification also shows that the claim language "right angle corner border piece" means a single preformed piece. The specification repeatedly refers to the preformed pieces 15 and 16, using only the words "right angle" border pieces or "corner pieces." In addition, the drawings show only preformed corner pieces and no mitered pieces.

The specification does refer once to "improvise[d] corner pieces" as an alternative to the preformed pieces:

> Instead of using preformed right-angle corner pieces of the type previously disclosed, one may improvise corner pieces by miter-cutting the ends of a pair of short linear border pieces at right angles to each other and providing a space between the cut ends to define the necessary storage slot. For this purpose, a temporary spacer may be used to provide exactly the right amount of storage space. The advantage of such corner pieces resides in the fact that linear pieces may be mass-produced at low cost by continuous extrusion, whereas preformed corner pieces must be molded or otherwise fabricated by more expensive techniques. *On the other hand, a preformed corner piece is somewhat easier for a do-it-yourselfer to work with.*

Col. 8, lines 28-41 (emphasis added). However, this reference does not negate the claim language clearly reciting right angle corner pieces. This paragraph, rather than providing an illustration of a right angle corner border piece, as the dissent indicates, provides an alternative to it. The language right angle corner border piece is too clear to encompass linear pieces that are not right angle corner pieces. The fact that mitered linear border pieces meet to form a right angle corner does not make them right angle corner pieces, when the claim separately recites both linear border pieces and right angle corner border pieces. Such an interpretation would run counter to the clear meaning of the language. Linear border pieces are not right angle corner border pieces. Both types of pieces are required by the claim.

The statute requires that an inventor particularly point out and distinctly claim the subject matter of his invention. 35 U.S.C. § 112 (1988). It would run counter to this statutory provision for an applicant for patent to expressly state throughout his specification and in his claims that his invention includes right angle corner border pieces and then be allowed to avoid that claim limitation in a later infringement suit by pointing to one paragraph in his specification stating an alternative that lacks that limitation, and thus interpret the claim contrary to its plain meaning. Such a result would encourage an applicant to escape examination of a more broadly-claimed invention by filing narrow claims and then, after grant, asserting a broader scope of the claims based on a statement in the specification of an alternative never presented in the claims for examination.

The claims as granted contain the right angle corner border piece limitation. All the limitations of a claim must be considered meaningful, and Brown's avoidance of that limitation avoids literal infringement.

It is also well-established that subject matter disclosed but not claimed in a patent application is dedicated to the public. *Edward Miller & Co. v. Bridgeport Brass Co.*, 104 U.S. 350, 352, 26 L. Ed. 783 (1881). That is what occurred here. If Unique intended to claim mitered linear border pieces as an alternative to its right angle corner border pieces, it had to persuade the examiner to issue such a claim. As will be shown below, Unique failed to do so.

The prosecution history also supports the district court's decision. During the prosecution of the '260 patent, the examiner understood the right angle corner pieces of Claim 1 to be distinct from mitered linear pieces, because he initially rejected the claims, citing and referring to other references as showing preformed, right angle corner pieces or braces. The applicant overcame the rejection by arguing the advantage of simplification for the do-it-yourselfer. As noted in the specification, a preformed corner piece is one of the advantages of the invention making it attractive to the do-it-yourselfer.

There then occurred a telephone interview between the attorney and the examiner, following which the examiner canceled certain claims. Among the canceled claims was original Claim 9, which depended from original Claim 1 (also canceled) and recited short linear mitered pieces as forming a right angle corner piece.

The dissent relies upon Claim 9 to construe what is now Claim 1 as including linear pieces which are mitered to form a corner piece. It interprets "linear pieces whose ends are mitered" to be a species of generic Claim 1's "right angle corner border pieces," and therefore within its scope. Such a construction is unjustified because the language of Claim 1 is clear and is inconsistent with Claim 9 being dependent thereon.

The record contains no indication of what transpired in the interview and why Claim 9 was canceled. A plausible reason is that Claim 9 was canceled because it was not properly dependent upon original Claim 1. The court referred to Brown's expert, who stated that the claim was canceled because it did not encompass an invention suitable for a do-it-yourselfer. The dissent finds this expert testimony to be "wholly incredible." We do not know why Claim 9 was canceled and cannot speculate on the reasons for the cancellation; we can only interpret the clear language of the claims as granted.

When the language of a claim is clear, as here, and a different interpretation would render meaningless express claim limitations, we do not resort to speculative interpretation based on claims not granted. See *White v. Dunbar*, 119 U.S. 47, 52 (1886) ("The claim is a statutory requirement, prescribed for the very purpose of making the patentee define precisely what his invention is; and it is unjust to the public, as well as an evasion of the law, to construe it in a manner different from the plain import of its terms."). Our interpretation gives full effect to the recitation of two distinct elements in the claimed structure: linear border pieces and right angle corner border pieces. It also gives full effect to the specification and the expert testimony, and a reasonable interpretation of the prosecution history. [The court went on to find there was no infringement under the doctrine of equivalents; see below.]

Affirmed.

[From the dissent by JUDGE RICH:]

I would hold [that] claim 1 [was] literally infringed. (This assumes that defendants' assemblies have both corner border pieces (as distinct from "linear" border pieces) and linear border pieces, which I do not know to be the fact.)

In the present posture of this appeal, the sole question is whether the majority has correctly construed the meaning of a single limitation in claim 1, which claim is set forth in full in its opinion. That limitation is: "right-angle corner border pieces." I simply disagree with the majority's conclusions and with its attempted supporting reasoning. We arrive at different "plain meanings."

I fully agree with the majority's statement of the law respecting claim construction, a question of law we review de novo. We construe claims in the light of the language of the claim itself, the specification on which it is based, and the whole prosecution history. The majority has not properly done this and, in my judgment, has demonstrably come to a wrong conclusion. Significant statements in the specification and prosecution history are misapplied. I shall begin with the specification.

As the majority states, the specification first describes and illustrates the one-piece corner pieces 15 and 16, outside and inside corners respectively. True, these are the only corner pieces shown in drawings. Then the specification contains the significant statement quoted in the majority opinion from the patent at col. 8, lines 28-41. (My emphasis.):

> Instead of using *preformed* right-angle corner pieces of the type previously disclosed, one may improvise *corner pieces* by miter-cutting the ends of a pair of *short* linear border pieces placed *at right angles* to each other and providing a space between the cut ends to define the necessary storage slot. For this purpose, a temporary spacer may be used to provide exactly the right amount of storage space. The advantage of *such corner pieces* resides in the fact that linear pieces may be mass-produced at low cost by continuous extrusion, whereas *preformed* corner pieces must be molded or otherwise fabricated by more expensive techniques. On the other hand, a preformed corner piece is *somewhat* easier for a do-it-yourselfer to work with.

Perhaps this is a matter, on both sides, of seeing what you choose to see. Beyond question, however, the specification discloses two species of right-angle corner border pieces: (1) preformed one-piece and (2) mitered, short, linear pieces, arranged at right angles and properly spaced at their junction. The latter are to be joined to longer linear pieces. No drawing is needed to make (2) clear. In any case, there are always, in a single assembly, both corner pieces and linear pieces, even when the second species of corner is used.

Now I turn to the contents of the file-wrapper. From day one when the application was filed these two kinds of corners were not only described but claimed and we look to this, equally with the specification, to determine the correct construction of the claim 1 language. Original claim 1, as filed, used exactly the same terminology as patent claim 1, "right-angle corner border pieces." There were 14 original claims on day one. Among them was claim 9, depending from claim 1, reading:

> 9. An assembly as set forth in claim 1, wherein *said right-angle corner pieces are formed by a pair of short linear pieces whose ends are mitered and spaced from each other to define a slot therebetween* to receive the pucker of the selvage when the selvage is locked into the keyway. [My emphasis.]

Note that claim 9 is referring back to "right angle" corners *as described in claim 1* and is thus defining a species of that genus. Now, what does that tell one skilled in the art about the meaning of "right-angle corner border pieces"? It tells one that the claim 1 phrase is, and was clearly intended by the applicant to be, broad enough to cover the species recited in claim 9, which the majority says it does not cover. There is a genus-species relationship between the phrase in claim 1, which never changed throughout the prosecution, and the particular form of corner piece recited in claim 9.

I have to disagree with the majority's criticism or downplaying of my use of claim 9 as a construction aid in several particulars. The majority seems to start with an a priori assumption of what the "clear" language of claim 1 means. On the other hand, I am looking at the genealogical record of that claim to *find out* what it means.

The majority says, "we ... cannot speculate on the reasons for the cancellation" of claim 9 because we have no idea of the content of the 'phone conversation between the examiner and the attorney which led to cancellation, along with many other claims. I agree. The majority then *speculates* that it may have been an improper dependent claim, though it is not apparent why and the majority gives no reason. I don't care why (or whether) claim 9 was canceled — it was simply part of the original application and sheds a bright *light* on what claim 1 was intended to mean.

I see no significance to the fact that claim 9 was canceled because it *is* part of the prosecution history, *all* of which is clearly before us. The majority correctly states that we must consider the prosecution history, of which claim 9 is a significant part.

The majority opines that the alternative corner piece described in claim 9 has not been claimed and is therefore dedicated to the public. This strange position begs the question. Of course it has not been claimed *specifically*. The question, however, is whether it is covered by or included in claim 1, which I say it is. Therefore, its subject matter is not "dedicated to the public."

35 U.S.C. § 112, which requires claims, is irrelevant to a consideration of what claims mean. Since Brown's so-called "expert" — expert only in the sense he was a patent lawyer — knew no more than the members of this panel, his speculations are of no value to us. The citation of cases is also of no help in finding out what claims mean.

To me, claim 9 is the only evidence of record, except for the specification itself, which is of any value in construing claim 1, and I think it is of great value.

The majority seems to say that my construction of claim 1 "would render meaningless express claim limitations." I await enlightenment on what those "express limitations" are. I have already said that I read both *corner* pieces and *linear* pieces in claim 1. The debate here is over the kinds of corner pieces claim 1 covers. It is clear that it is not limited to unitary or preformed or one-piece corner pieces as shown in the drawings. That much is truly "clear."

Much has been made of the contention that using short mitered corner pieces is something that a "do-it-yourselfer" — an "amateur" — is unable to do. Defendants' expert speculated, with no support whatsoever, that, in his opinion, the examiner required claim 9 to be canceled because "it was simply not something that a do-it-yourselfer could do." Both defendants and the district court relied heavily on this testimony. I find this opinion testimony to be wholly incredible. The sole basis given by the expert for his opinion was the fact that claim 9 was canceled while claim 4 [which adds an element for storing excess fabric at the corners] was not. However, there is absolutely nothing in the record showing *why* the examiner allowed certain claims and canceled certain other claims.

The fact is that this whole "do-it-yourselfer" argument has been blown way out of proportion. The specification does not state that do-it-yourselfers are *incapable* of using mitered corner pieces; it merely states, as quoted above, that preformed corner pieces are "somewhat easier for a do-it-yourselfer to work with." Furthermore, the *only reference* to do-it-yourselfers during prosecution is a statement that certain known *prior art* arrangements are difficult for a do-it-yourselfer to use because the *fabric must be cut precisely to size* whereas according to the invention of the '260 patent, the fabric need merely be cut *roughly* to size, with the excess fabric being stuffed in the storage channel. This is equally true as to either kind of corner. To infer from this one statement that the claims must be limited to features not recited in the claims (i.e., *"preformed"* corner pieces) is contrary to established patent law practice.

Let us consider next another lesson about meaning to be learned from the specification. In the quotation above from column 8, in the opening sentence the drafter of the specification exhibits a clear consciousness of the distinction between "preformed right-angle corner pieces" and those made by mitering and placing at right angles two short pieces of linear border pieces. Claim 1 does not contain the limiting word "preformed" yet the majority, without justification, is reading it into the claim in holding that the claim does not cover corner pieces which are made up as clearly described in the specification.

I also point out that the term "right-angle" is not a limitation to *preformed* unitary pieces since the specification makes clear that the made-up variety of corners are also right-angle corner pieces when assembled.

The majority's argument based on alleged violation of the "all elements" rule is untenable. It overlooks the fact that the teaching in the specification is clear about making "corner pieces" by using two "*short* linear border pieces" (my emphasis) and then using such "improvised" *corner pieces in conjunction with linear pieces* to make the complete wall frame. Of course, it is the all-elements rule on which the defendants rely for non-infringement, arguing that they have no "corner pieces" when in fact they have a type of corner piece which is disclosed and claimed as an element of the combination of claim 1. I am not "merging the two types of claim elements into one" — whatever that may mean. I am simply saying that the element defined in claim 1 as "right-angle corner border pieces" is, as clearly shown by the patent and its prosecution history, a limitation generic to two types of corner pieces disclosed in the patent which is broad enough to read on defendants' structure because it is clearly *not* limited to "preformed" or "unitary" corner pieces, as held below and by the majority. That is the sum and substance of my position and it calls for reversal.

NOTE

From the Specification. The Baslow patent elaborates on the way the invention works:

> In securing the selvage [i.e., edge] of the fabric sheet to a border piece, the selvage is placed over the face and a zone thereon is trapped within the keyway by means of a compressible spline which overlies the selvage zone and is forced into the keyway through its inlet, the remaining tail of the selvage being stuffed into the storage channel whereby the exposed selvage presents a smooth appearance.

Baslow also states that the object of the invention is to "mak[e] it a simple matter to cover the wall surface with a fabric sheet"; that under his approach he intends the fabric to be installed "by means of simple tools whose use requires no special skills, whereby the sheet may be mounted on the framework quickly and without difficulty"; and that, "because of the complexities and skills entailed in known forms of fabric wallcovering systems, the homeowner has not heretofore been qualified to make his own installation. As a consequence, high quality fabric wall covering installations have been confined to those few who have the means to afford expensive professional assistance." Are these statements of any help in determining what Baslow meant when he claimed an "assembly comprising linear border pieces and right angle corner border pieces"?

Recall that the trial in the *Unique Concepts* case was quite streamlined: it was tried to a judge; each side presented only one expert witness; and there were a number of stipulations. The case that follows grew out of a more complex trial background, and contains directions for infringement cases of all varieties, large and small.

MARKMAN v. WESTVIEW INSTRUMENTS, INC.

116 S. Ct. 1384, 38 U.S.P.Q.2d 1461 (1996)

JUSTICE SOUTER delivered the opinion of the Court.

The question here is whether the interpretation of a so-called patent claim, the portion of the patent document that defines the scope of the patentee's rights, is a matter of law reserved entirely for the court, or subject to a Seventh Amendment guarantee that a jury will determine the meaning of any disputed term of art about which expert testimony is offered. We hold that the construction of a patent, including terms of art within its claim, is exclusively within the province of the court.

I

The Constitution empowers Congress "[t]o promote the Progress of Science and useful Arts, by securing for limited Times to Authors and Inventors the exclusive Right to their respective Writings and Discoveries." U.S. Const., Art. I, § 8, cl. 8. Congress first exercised this authority in 1790, when it provided for the issuance of "letters patent," Act of Apr. 10, 1790, ch. 7, § 1, 1 Stat. 109, which, like their modern counterparts, granted inventors "the right to exclude others from making, using, offering for sale, selling, or importing the patented invention," in exchange for full disclosure of an invention, H. Schwartz, Patent Law and Practice 1, 33 (2d ed. 1995). It has long been understood that a patent must describe the exact scope of an invention and its manufacture to "secure to [the patentee] all to which he is entitled, [and] to apprise the public of what is still open to them." *McClain v. Ortmayer*, 141 U.S. 419, 424, 12 S. Ct. 76, 77, 35 L. Ed. 800 (1891). Under the modern American system, these objectives are served by two distinct elements of a patent document. First, it contains a specification describing the invention "in such full, clear, concise, and exact terms as to enable any person skilled in the art ... to make and use the same." 35 U.S.C. § 112; see also 3 E. Lipscomb, Walker on Patents § 10:1, pp. 183-184 (3d ed. 1985) (Lipscomb) (listing the requirements for a specification). Second, a patent includes one or more "claims," which "particularly poin[t] out and distinctly clai[m] the subject matter which the applicant regards as his invention." 35 U.S.C. § 112. "A claim covers and secures a process, a machine, a manufacture, a composition of matter, or a design, but never the function or result of either, nor the scientific explanation of their operation." 6 Lipscomb § 21:17, at 315-316. The claim "define[s] the scope of a patent grant," 3 *id.*, § 11:1, at 280, and functions to forbid not only exact copies of an invention, but products that go to "the heart of the invention but avoid the literal language of the claim by making a noncritical change," Schwartz, *supra*, at 82.[1] In this

---

[1] Thus, for example, a claim for a ceiling fan with three blades attached to a solid rod connected to a motor would not only cover fans that take precisely this form, but would also cover a similar

opinion, the word "claim" is used only in this sense peculiar to patent law.

Characteristically, patent lawsuits charge what is known as infringement, Schwartz, *supra*, at 75, and rest on allegations that the defendant "without authority ma[de], use[d] or [sold the] patented invention, within the United States during the term of the patent therefor...." 35 U.S.C. § 271(a). Victory in an infringement suit requires a finding that the patent claim "covers the alleged infringer's product or process," which in turn necessitates a determination of "what the words in the claim mean." Schwartz, *supra*, at 80; see also 3 Lipscomb, § 11:2, at 288-290.

Petitioner in this infringement suit, Markman, owns United States Reissue Patent No. 33,054 for his "Inventory Control and Reporting System for Dry-cleaning Stores." The patent describes a system that can monitor and report the status, location, and movement of clothing in a dry-cleaning establishment. The Markman system consists of a keyboard and data processor to generate written records for each transaction, including a bar code readable by optical detectors operated by employees, who log the progress of clothing through the dry-cleaning process. Respondent Westview's product also includes a keyboard and processor, and it lists charges for the dry-cleaning services on bar-coded tickets that can be read by portable optical detectors.

Markman brought an infringement suit against Westview and Althon Enterprises, an operator of dry-cleaning establishments using Westview's products (collectively, Westview). Westview responded that Markman's patent is not infringed by its system because the latter functions merely to record an inventory of receivables by tracking invoices and transaction totals, rather than to record and track an inventory of articles of clothing. Part of the dispute hinged upon the meaning of the word "inventory," a term found in Markman's independent claim 1, which states that Markman's product can "maintain an inventory total" and "detect and localize spurious additions to inventory." The case was tried before a jury, which heard, among others, a witness produced by Markman who testified about the meaning of the claim language.

After the jury compared the patent to Westview's device, it found an infringement of Markman's independent claim 1 and dependent claim 10.[2] The District Court nevertheless granted Westview's deferred motion for judgment as a matter of law, one of its reasons being that the term "inventory" in Markman's patent encompasses "both cash inventory and the actual physical inventory of articles of clothing." 772 F. Supp. 1535, 1537-1538 (E.D. Pa. 1991). Under the trial court's construction of the patent, the production, sale, or use of a tracking

---

fan that includes some additional feature, e.g., such a fan with a cord or switch for turning it on and off, and may cover a product deviating from the core design in some noncritical way, e.g., a three-bladed ceiling fan with blades attached to a hollow rod connected to a motor. H. Schwartz, Patent Law and Practice 81-82 (2d ed. 1995).

[2] Dependent claim 10 specifies that, in the invention of claim 1, the input device is an alphanumeric keyboard in which single keys may be used to enter the attributes of the items in question.

system for dry cleaners would not infringe Markman's patent unless the product was capable of tracking articles of clothing throughout the cleaning process and generating reports about their status and location. Since Westview's system cannot do these things, the District Court directed a verdict on the ground that Westview's device does not have the "means to maintain an inventory total" and thus cannot "detect and localize spurious additions to inventory as well as spurious deletions therefrom," as required by claim 1. *Id.*, at 1537.

Markman appealed, arguing it was error for the District Court to substitute its construction of the disputed claim term "inventory" for the construction the jury had presumably given it. The United States Court of Appeals for the Federal Circuit affirmed, holding the interpretation of claim terms to be the exclusive province of the court and the Seventh Amendment to be consistent with that conclusion. 52 F.3d 967 (1995). Markman sought our review on each point, and we granted certiorari. 515 U.S. __, 116 S. Ct. 40, 132 L. Ed. 2d 921 (1995). We now affirm.

II

The Seventh Amendment provides that "[i]n Suits at common law, where the value in controversy shall exceed twenty dollars, the right of trial by jury shall be preserved...." U.S. Const., Amdt. 7. Since Justice Story's day, *United States v. Wonson*, 28 F. Cas. 745, 750 (No. 16,750) (CC Mass. 1812), we have understood that "[t]he right of trial by jury thus preserved is the right which existed under the English common law when the Amendment was adopted." *Baltimore & Carolina Line, Inc. v. Redman*, 295 U.S. 654, 657, 55 S. Ct. 890, 891, 79 L. Ed. 1636 (1935). In keeping with our long-standing adherence to this "historical test," Wolfram, *The Constitutional History of the Seventh Amendment*, 57 Minn. L. Rev. 639, 640-643 (1973), we ask, first, whether we are dealing with a cause of action that either was tried at law at the time of the Founding or is at least analogous to one that was, *see, e.g., Tull v. United States*, 481 U.S. 412, 417, 107 S. Ct. 1831, 1835, 95 L. Ed. 2d 365 (1987). If the action in question belongs in the law category, we then ask whether the particular trial decision must fall to the jury in order to preserve the substance of the common-law right as it existed in 1791. *See infra*, at 1389-1391.[3]

A

As to the first issue, going to the character of the cause of action, "[t]he form of our analysis is familiar. 'First we compare the statutory action to 18th-century actions brought in the courts of England prior to the merger of the courts of law

---

[3] Our formulations of the historical test do not deal with the possibility of conflict between actual English common law practice and American assumptions about what that practice was, or between English and American practices at the relevant time. No such complications arise in this case.

and equity.'" *Granfinanciera, S.A. v. Nordberg,* 492 U.S. 33, 42, 109 S. Ct. 2782, 2790, 106 L. Ed. 2d 26 (1989) (citation omitted). Equally familiar is the descent of today's patent infringement action from the infringement actions tried at law in the 18th century, and there is no dispute that infringement cases today must be tried to a jury, as their predecessors were more than two centuries ago. *See, e.g., Bramah v. Hardcastle,* 1 Carp. P.C. 168 (K.B. 1789).

B

This conclusion raises the second question, whether a particular issue occurring within a jury trial (here the construction of a patent claim) is itself necessarily a jury issue, the guarantee being essential to preserve the right to a jury's resolution of the ultimate dispute. In some instances the answer to this second question may be easy because of clear historical evidence that the very subsidiary question was so regarded under the English practice of leaving the issue for a jury. But when, as here, the old practice provides no clear answer, see *infra,* at 1391-1392, we are forced to make a judgment about the scope of the Seventh Amendment guarantee without the benefit of any foolproof test.

The Court has repeatedly said that the answer to the second question "must depend on whether the jury must shoulder this responsibility *as necessary to preserve the 'substance of the common-law right of trial by jury.'"* *Tull v. United States, supra,* at 426, 107 S. Ct., at 1840 (emphasis added) (quoting *Colgrove v. Battin,* 413 U.S. 149, 156, 93 S. Ct. 2448, 2452, 37 L. Ed. 2d 522 (1973)); see also *Baltimore & Carolina Line, supra,* at 657, 55 S. Ct., at 891. "'Only those incidents which are regarded as fundamental, as inherent in and of the essence of the system of trial by jury, are placed beyond the reach of the legislature.'" *Tull v. United States, supra,* at 426, 107 S. Ct., at 1840 (citations omitted); *see also Galloway v. United States,* 319 U.S. 372, 392, 63 S. Ct. 1077, 1088, 87 L. Ed. 1458 (1943).

The "substance of the common-law right" is, however, a pretty blunt instrument for drawing distinctions. We have tried to sharpen it, to be sure, by reference to the distinction between substance and procedure. See *Baltimore & Carolina Line, supra,* at 657, 55 S. Ct., at 891; *see also Galloway v. United States, supra,* at 390-391, 63 S. Ct., at 1087-1088; *Ex parte Peterson,* 253 U.S. 300, 309, 40 S. Ct. 543, 546, 64 L. Ed. 919 (1920); *Walker v. New Mexico & Southern Pacific R. Co.,* 165 U.S. 593, 596, 17 S. Ct. 421, 422, 41 L. Ed. 837 (1897); *but see Sun Oil Co. v. Wortman,* 486 U.S. 717, 727, 108 S. Ct. 2117, 2124, 100 L. Ed. 2d 743 (1988). We have also spoken of the line as one between issues of fact and law. *See Baltimore & Carolina Line, supra,* at 657, 55 S. Ct., at 891; see also *Ex parte Peterson, supra,* at 310, 40 S. Ct., at 546; *Walker v. New Mexico & Southern Pacific R. Co., supra,* at 597, 17 S. Ct., at 422; *but see Pullman-Standard v. Swint,* 456 U.S. 273, 288, 102 S. Ct. 1781, 1789, 72 L. Ed. 2d 66 (1982).

But the sounder course, when available, is to classify a mongrel practice (like construing a term of art following receipt of evidence) by using the historical method, much as we do in characterizing the suits and actions within which they arise. Where there is no exact antecedent, the best hope lies in comparing the modern practice to earlier ones whose allocation to court or jury we do know, *cf. Baltimore & Carolina Line, supra*, at 659, 660, 55 S. Ct., at 892, 893; *Dimick v. Schiedt*, 293 U.S. 474, 477, 482, 55 S. Ct. 296, 297, 79 L. Ed. 603 (1935), seeking the best analogy we can draw between an old and the new, see *Tull v. United States, supra*, at 420-421, 107 S. Ct., at 1836-1837 (we must search the English common law for "appropriate analogies" rather than a "precisely analogous common-law cause of action").

C

"Prior to 1790 nothing in the nature of a claim had appeared either in British patent practice or in that of the American states," Lutz, *Evolution of the Claims of U.S. Patents*, 20 J. Pat. Off. Soc. 134 (1938), and we have accordingly found no direct antecedent of modern claim construction in the historical sources. Claim practice did not achieve statutory recognition until the passage of the Act of 1836, Act of July 4, 1836, ch. 357, § 6, 5 Stat. 119, and inclusion of a claim did not become a statutory requirement until 1870, Act of July 8, 1870, ch. 230, § 26, 16 Stat. 201; see 1 A. Deller, Patent Claims § 4, p. 9 (2d ed. 1971). Although, as one historian has observed, as early as 1850 "judges were ... beginning to express more frequently the idea that in seeking to ascertain the invention 'claimed' in a patent the inquiry should be limited to interpreting the summary, or 'claim,'" Lutz, *supra*, at 145, "[t]he idea that the claim is just as important if not more important than the description and drawings did not develop until the Act of 1870 or thereabouts." Deller, *supra*, § 4, at 9.

At the time relevant for Seventh Amendment analogies, in contrast, it was the specification, itself a relatively new development, H. Dutton, The Patent System and Inventive Activity During the Industrial Revolution, 1750-1852, pp. 75-76 (1984), that represented the key to the patent. Thus, patent litigation in that early period was typified by so-called novelty actions, testing whether "any essential part of [the patent had been] disclosed to the public before," *Huddart v. Grimshaw*, Dav. Pat. Cas. 265, 298 (K.B. 1803), and "enablement" cases, in which juries were asked to determine whether the specification described the invention well enough to allow members of the appropriate trade to reproduce it, *see, e.g., Arkwright v. Nightingale*, Dav. Pat. Cas. 37, 60 (C.P. 1785).

The closest 18th-century analogue of modern claim construction seems, then, to have been the construction of specifications, and as to that function the mere smattering of patent cases that we have from this period[4] shows no established

---

[4] Before the turn of the century, "no more than twenty-two cases came before the superior courts of London." H. Dutton, The Patent System and Inventive Activity During the Industrial Revolution, 1750-1852, p. 71 (1984).

jury practice sufficient to support an argument by analogy that today's construction of a claim should be a guaranteed jury issue. Few of the case reports even touch upon the proper interpretation of disputed terms in the specifications at issue, *see, e.g., Bramah v. Hardcastle*, 1 Carp. P.C. 168 (K.B. 1789); *King v. Else*, 1 Carp. P.C. 103, Dav. Pat. Cas., 144 (K.B. 1785); *Dollond's Case*, 1 Carp. P.C. 28 (C.P. 1758); *Administrators of Calthorp v. Waymans*, 3 Keb. 710, 84 Eng. Rep. 966 (K.B. 1676), and none demonstrates that the definition of such a term was determined by the jury.[5] This absence of an established practice should not surprise us, given the primitive state of jury patent practice at the end of the 18th century, when juries were still new to the field. Although by 1791 more than a century had passed since the enactment of the Statute of Monopolies, which provided that the validity of any monopoly should be determined in accordance with the common law, patent litigation had remained within the jurisdiction of the Privy Council until 1752 and hence without the option of a jury trial. E. Walterscheid, *Early Evolution of the United States Patent Law: Antecedents (Part 3)*, 77 J. Pat. & Tm. Off. Soc. 771, 771-776 (1995). Indeed, the state of patent law in the common-law courts before 1800 led one historian to observe that "the reported cases are destitute of any decision of importance.... At the end of the eighteenth century, therefore, the Common Law Judges were left to pick up the threads of the principles of law without the aid of recent and reliable precedents." Hulme, *On the Consideration of the Patent Grant, Past and Present*, 13 L.Q. Rev. 313, 318 (1897). Earlier writers expressed similar discouragement at patent law's amorphous character,[6] and, as late as the 1830's, English commentators were irked by enduring confusion in the field. *See* Dutton, *supra*, at 69-70.

---

[5] Markman relies heavily upon Justice Buller's notes of Lord Mansfield's instructions in *Liardet v. Johnson* (K.B. 1778), in 1 J. Oldham, The Mansfield Manuscripts and the Growth of English Law in the Eighteenth Century 748 (1992). *Liardet* was an enablement case about the invention of stucco, in which a defendant asserted that the patent was invalid because it did not fully describe the appropriate method for producing the substance. Even setting aside concerns about the accuracy of the summary of the jury instructions provided for this case from outside the established reports, see 1 Oldham, *supra*, at 752, n. 11, it does not show that juries construed disputed terms in a patent. From its ambiguous references, e.g., *id.*, at 756 ("[Lord Mansfield] left to the jury 1st, on all objections made to exactness, certainty and propriety of the Specification, & whether any workman could make it by [the Specification]"), we cannot infer the existence of an established practice, *cf. Galloway v. United States*, 319 U.S. 372, 392, 63 S. Ct. 1077, 1088, 87 L. Ed. 1458 (1943) (expressing concern regarding the "uncertainty and the variety of conclusions which follows from an effort at purely historical accuracy"), especially when, as here, the inference is undermined by evidence that judges, rather than jurors, ordinarily construed written documents at the time. See *infra*, at 1393-1394.

[6] *See, e.g., Boulton and Watt v. Bull*, 2 H. Bl. 463, 491, 126 Eng. Rep. 651, 665 (C.P. 1795) (Eyre, C.J.) ("Patent rights are no where that I can find accurately discussed in our books"); Dutton, *supra*, n. 3, at 70-71 (quoting Abraham Weston as saying "it may with truth be said that the [Law] Books are silent on the subject [of patents] and furnish no clue to go by, in agitating the Question What is the Law of Patents?").

Markman seeks to supply what the early case reports lack in so many words by relying on decisions like *Turner v. Winter*, 1 T.R. 602, 99 Eng. Rep. 1274 (K.B. 1787), and *Arkwright v. Nightingale*, Dav. Pat. Cas. 37 (C.P. 1785), to argue that the 18th-century juries must have acted as definers of patent terms just to reach the verdicts we know they rendered in patent cases turning on enablement or novelty. But the conclusion simply does not follow. There is no more reason to infer that juries supplied plenary interpretation of written instruments in patent litigation than in other cases implicating the meaning of documentary terms, and we do know that in other kinds of cases during this period judges, not juries, ordinarily construed written documents.[7] The probability that the judges were doing the same thing in the patent litigation of the time is confirmed by the fact that as soon as the English reports did begin to describe the construction of patent documents, they show the judges construing the terms of the specifications. *See Bovill v. Moore*, Dav. Pat. Cas. 361, 399, 404 (C.P. 1816) (judge submits question of novelty to the jury only after explaining some of the language and "stat[ing] in what terms the specification runs"); *cf. Russell v. Cowley & Dixon*, Webs. Pat. Cas. 457, 467-470 (Exch. 1834) (construing the terms of the specification in reviewing a verdict); *Haworth v. Hardcastle*, Webs. Pat. Cas. 480, 484-485 (1834) (same). This evidence is in fact buttressed by cases from this Court; when they first reveal actual practice, the practice revealed is of the judge construing the patent. *See, e.g. Winans v. New York & Erie R. Co.*, 21 How. 88, 100, 16 L. Ed. 68 (1859); *Winans v. Denmead*, 15 How. 330, 338, 14 L. Ed. 717 (1854); *Hogg v. Emerson*, 6 How. 437, 484, 12 L. Ed. 505 (1848); *cf. Parker v. Hulme*, 18 F. Cas. 1138 (No. 10,740) (CC ED Pa. 1849). These indications of our patent practice are the more impressive for being all of a piece with what we know about the analogous contemporary practice of interpreting terms within a land patent, where it fell to the judge, not the jury, to construe the words.[8]

---

[7] *See, e.g.*, Devlin, *Jury Trial of Complex Cases: English Practice at the Time of the Seventh Amendment*, 80 Colum L. Rev. 43, 75 (1980); Weiner, *The Civil Jury Trial and the Law-Fact Distinction*, 54 Calif. L. Rev. 1867, 1932 (1966). For example, one historian observed that it was generally the practice of judges in the late 18th century "to keep the construction of writings out of the jury's hands and reserve it for themselves," a "safeguard" designed to prevent a jury from "constru[ing] or refin[ing] it at pleasure." 9 J. Wigmore, Evidence § 2461, p. 194 (J. Chadbourn rev. ed. 1981) (internal quotation marks omitted). The absence of any established practice supporting Markman's view is also shown by the disagreement between Justices Willis and Buller, reported in *Macbeath v. Haldimand*, 1 T.R. 173, 180-182, 99 Eng. Rep. 1036, 1040-1041 (K.B. 1786), as to whether juries could ever construe written documents when their meaning was disputed.

[8] As we noted in *Brown v. Huger*, 21 How. 305, 318, 16 L. Ed. 125 (1859): "With regard to the second part of this objection, that which claims for the jury the construction of the patent, we remark that the patent itself must be taken as evidence of its meaning; that, like other written instruments, it must be interpreted as a whole ... and the legal deductions drawn therefrom must be conformable with the scope and purpose of the entire document. This construction and these

D

Losing, then, on the contention that juries generally had interpretive responsibilities during the 18th century, Markman seeks a different anchor for analogy in the more modest contention that even if judges were charged with construing most terms in the patent, the art of defining terms of art employed in a specification fell within the province of the jury. Again, however, Markman has no authority from the period in question, but relies instead on the later case of *Neilson v. Harford*, Webs. Pat. Cas. 328 (Exch. 1841). There, an exchange between the judge and the lawyers indicated that although the construction of a patent was ordinarily for the court, *id.*, at 349 (Alderson, B.), judges should "leav[e] the question of words of art to the jury," *id.*, at 350 (Alderson, B.); *see also id.*, at 370 (judgment of the court); *Hill v. Evans*, 4 De. G.F. & J. 288, 293-294, 45 Eng. Rep. 1195, 1197 (Ch. 1862). Without, however, in any way disparaging the weight to which Baron Alderson's view is entitled, the most we can say is that an English report more than 70 years after the time that concerns us indicates an exception to what probably had been occurring earlier.[9] In place of Markman's inference that this exceptional practice existed in 1791 there is at best only a possibility that it did, and for anything more than a possibility we have found no scholarly authority.

III

Since evidence of common law practice at the time of the Framing does not entail application of the Seventh Amendment's jury guarantee to the construction of the claim document, we must look elsewhere to characterize this determination of meaning in order to allocate it as between court or jury. We accordingly consult existing precedent[10] and consider both the relative interpretive skills of judges and juries and the statutory policies that ought to be furthered by the allocation.

---

deductions we hold to be within the exclusive province of the court."

[9] In explaining that judges generally construed all terms in a written document at the end of the 18th century, one historian observed that "[i]nterpretation by local usage for example (today the plainest case of legitimate deviation from the normal standard) was still but making its way." 9 Wigmore, Evidence § 2461, at 195; *see also id.*, at 195, and n. 6 (providing examples of this practice). We need not in any event consider here whether our conclusion that the Seventh Amendment does not require terms of art in patent claims to be submitted to the jury supports a similar result in other types of cases.

[10] Because we conclude that our precedent supports classifying the question as one for the court, we need not decide either the extent to which the Seventh Amendment can be said to have crystallized a law/fact distinction, *cf. Ex parte Peterson*, 253 U.S. 300, 310, 40 S. Ct. 543, 546, 64 L. Ed. 919 (1920); *Walker v. New Mexico & Southern Pacific R. Co.*, 165 U.S. 593, 597, 17 S. Ct. 421, 422, 41 L. Ed. 837 (1897), or whether post-1791 precedent classifying an issue as one of fact would trigger the protections of the Seventh Amendment if (unlike this case) there were no more specific reason for decision.

A

The two elements of a simple patent case, construing the patent and determining whether infringement occurred, were characterized by the former patent practitioner, Justice Curtis.[11] "The first is a question of law, to be determined by the court, construing the letters-patent, and the description of the invention and specification of claim annexed to them. The second is a question of fact, to be submitted to a jury." *Winans v. Denmead*, 15 How., at 338; *see Winans v. New York & Erie R. Co.*, 21 How., at 100; *Hogg v. Emerson, supra*, at 484; *cf. Parker v. Hulme, supra*, at 1140.

In arguing for a different allocation of responsibility for the first question, Markman relies primarily on two cases, *Bischoff v. Wethered*, 9 Wall. 812, 19 L. Ed. 829 (1870), and *Tucker v. Spalding*, 13 Wall. 453, 20 L. Ed. 515 (1872). These are said to show that evidence of the meaning of patent terms was offered to 19th-century juries, and thus to imply that the meaning of a documentary term was a jury issue whenever it was subject to evidentiary proof. That is not what Markman's cases show, however.

In order to resolve the *Bischoff* suit implicating the construction of rival patents, we considered "whether the court below was bound to compare the two specifications, and to instruct the jury, as a matter of law, whether the inventions therein described were, or were not, identical." 9 Wall., at 813 (statement of the case). We said it was not bound to do that, on the ground that investing the court with so dispositive a role would improperly eliminate the jury's function in answering the ultimate question of infringement. On that ultimate issue, expert testimony had been admitted on "the nature of the various mechanisms or manufactures described in the different patents produced, and as to the identity or diversity between them." *Id.*, at 814. Although the jury's consideration of that expert testimony in resolving the question of infringement was said to impinge upon the well-established principle "that it is the province of the court, and not the jury, to construe the meaning of documentary evidence," *id.*, at 815, we decided that it was not so. We said that "the specifications ... profess to describe mechanisms and complicated machinery, chemical compositions and other manufactured products, which have their existence in pais, outside of the documents themselves; and which are commonly described by terms of the art or mystery to which they respectively belong; and these descriptions and terms of art often require peculiar knowledge and education to understand them aright.... Indeed, the whole subject-matter of a patent is an embodied conception outside of the patent itself.... This outward embodiment of the terms contained in the patent is the thing invented, and is to be properly sought, like the explanation of all latent ambiguities arising from the description of external things, by evidence in pais." *Ibid.*

---

[11] *See* 1 A Memoir of Benjamin Robbins Curtis, LL.D., 84 (B. Curtis ed. 1879); *cf. O'Reilly v. Morse*, 15 How. 62, 63, 14 L. Ed. 601 (1854) (noting his involvement in a patent case).

Bischoff does not then, as Markman contends, hold that the use of expert testimony about the meaning of terms of art requires the judge to submit the question of their construction to the jury. It is instead a case in which the Court drew a line between issues of document interpretation and product identification, and held that expert testimony was properly presented to the jury on the latter, ultimate issue, whether the physical objects produced by the patent were identical. The Court did not see the decision as bearing upon the appropriate treatment of disputed terms. As the opinion emphasized, the Court's "view of the case is not intended to, and does not, trench upon the doctrine that the construction of written instruments is the province of the court alone. *It is not the construction of the instrument*, but the character of the thing invented, which is sought in questions of identity and diversity of inventions." *Id.*, at 816 (emphasis added). *Tucker*, the second case proffered by Markman, is to the same effect. Its reasoning rested expressly on *Bischoff*, and it just as clearly noted that in addressing the ultimate issue of mixed fact and law, it was for the court to "lay down to the jury the law which should govern them." *Tucker, supra*, at 455.[12]

If the line drawn in these two opinions is a fine one, it is one that the Court has drawn repeatedly in explaining the respective roles of the jury and judge in patent cases, and one understood by commentators writing in the aftermath of the cases[13] Markman cites. Walker, for example, read *Bischoff* as holding that the question of novelty is not decided by a construction of the prior patent, "but depends rather upon the outward embodiment of the terms contained in the [prior patent]; and that such outward embodiment is to be properly sought, like the explanation of latent ambiguities arising from the description of external things, by evidence in pais." A. Walker, Patent Laws § 75, p. 68 (3d ed. 1895). He also emphasized in the same treatise that matters of claim construction, even those aided by expert testimony, are questions for the court:

> Questions of construction are questions of law for the judge, not questions of fact for the jury. As it cannot be expected, however, that judges will always possess the requisite knowledge of the meaning of the terms of art or science used in letters patent, it often becomes necessary that they should

---

[12] We are also unpersuaded by petitioner's heavy reliance upon the decision of Justice Story on circuit in *Washburn v. Gould*, 29 F. Cas. 312 (No. 17,214) (CC Mass. 1844). Although he wrote that "[t]he jury are to judge of the meaning of words of art, and technical phrases," *id.*, at 325, he did so in describing the decision in *Neilson v. Harford*, Webs. Pat. Cas. 328 (Exch. 1841), which we discuss, *supra*, at 1392, and, whether or not he agreed with *Neilson*, he stated, "[b]ut I do not proceed upon this ground." 29 F. Cas., at 325.

[13] *See, e.g., Coupe v. Royer*, 155 U.S. 565, 579-580, 15 S. Ct. 199, 205, 39 L. Ed. 263 (1895); *Silsby v. Foote*, 14 How. 218, 226, 14 L. Ed. 391 (1853); *Hogg v. Emerson*, 6 How. 437, 484, 12 L. Ed. 505 (1848); *cf. Brown v. Piper*, 91 U.S. 37, 41, 23 L. Ed. 200 (1875); *Winans v. New York & Erie R. Co.*, 21 How. 88, 100, 16 L. Ed. 68 (1859); *cf. also U.S. Industrial Chemicals, Inc. v. Carbide & Carbon Chemicals Corp.*, 315 U.S. 668, 678, 62 S. Ct. 839, 844, 86 L. Ed. 1105 (1942).

avail themselves of the light furnished by experts relevant to the significance of such words and phrases. The judges are not, however, obliged to blindly follow such testimony.

Id., § 189, at 173 (footnotes omitted).

Virtually the same description of the court's use of evidence in its interpretive role was set out in another contemporary treatise:

"*The duty of interpreting letters-patent has been committed to the courts.* A patent is a legal instrument, to be construed, like other legal instruments, according to its tenor.... Where technical terms are used, or where the qualities of substances or operations mentioned or any similar data necessary to the comprehension of the language of the patent are unknown to the judge, the testimony of witnesses may be received upon these subjects, and any other means of information be employed. But in the actual interpretation of the patent the court proceeds upon its own responsibility, as an arbiter of the law, giving to the patent its true and final character and force."

2 W. Robinson, Law of Patents § 732, pp. 481-483 (1890) (emphasis added). In sum, neither *Bischoff* nor *Tucker* indicates that juries resolved the meaning of terms of art in construing a patent, and neither case undercuts Justice Curtis's authority.

B

Where history and precedent provide no clear answers, functional considerations also play their part in the choice between judge and jury to define terms of art. We said in *Miller v. Fenton*, 474 U.S. 104, 114, 106 S. Ct. 445, 451, 88 L. Ed. 2d 405 (1985), that when an issue "falls somewhere between a pristine legal standard and a simple historical fact, the fact/law distinction at times has turned on a determination that, as a matter of the sound administration of justice, one judicial actor is better positioned than another to decide the issue in question." So it turns out here, for judges, not juries, are the better suited to find the acquired meaning of patent terms.

The construction of written instruments is one of those things that judges often do and are likely to do better than jurors unburdened by training in exegesis. Patent construction in particular "is a special occupation, requiring, like all others, special training and practice. The judge, from his training and discipline, is more likely to give a proper interpretation to such instruments than a jury; and he is, therefore, more likely to be right, in performing such a duty, than a jury can be expected to be." *Parker v. Hulme*, 18 F. Cas., at 1140. Such was the understanding nearly a century and a half ago, and there is no reason to weigh the respective strengths of judge and jury differently in relation to the modern claim; quite the contrary, for "the claims of patents have become highly technical in many respects as the result of special doctrines relating to the proper form and scope of claims that have been developed by the courts and the Patent Office." Woodward, *Definiteness and Particularity in Patent Claims*, 46 Mich. L. Rev. 755, 765 (1948).

Markman would trump these considerations with his argument that a jury should decide a question of meaning peculiar to a trade or profession simply because the question is a subject of testimony requiring credibility determinations, which are the jury's forte. It is, of course, true that credibility judgments have to be made about the experts who testify in patent cases, and in theory there could be a case in which a simple credibility judgment would suffice to choose between experts whose testimony was equally consistent with a patent's internal logic. But our own experience with document construction leaves us doubtful that trial courts will run into many cases like that. In the main, we expect, any credibility determinations will be subsumed within the necessarily sophisticated analysis of the whole document, required by the standard construction rule that a term can be defined only in a way that comports with the instrument as a whole. *See Bates v. Coe*, 98 U.S. 31, 38, 25 L. Ed. 68 (1878); 6 Lipscomb § 21:40, at 393; 2 Robinson, *supra*, § 734, at 484; *Woodward, supra*, at 765; *cf. U.S. Industrial Chemicals, Inc. v. Carbide & Carbon Chemicals Corp.*, 315 U.S. 668, 678, 62 S. Ct. 839, 844, 86 L. Ed. 1105 (1942); 6 Lipscomb at § 21:40, at 393. Thus, in these cases a jury's capabilities to evaluate demeanor, *cf. Miller, supra*, at 114, 117, 106 S. Ct., at 451, 453, to sense the "mainsprings of human conduct," *Commissioner v. Duberstein*, 363 U.S. 278, 289, 80 S. Ct. 1190, 1198, 4 L. Ed. 2d 1218 (1960), or to reflect community standards, *United States v. McConney*, 728 F.2d 1195, 1204 (C.A.9 1984) (en banc), are much less significant than a trained ability to evaluate the testimony in relation to the overall structure of the patent. The decisionmaker vested with the task of construing the patent is in the better position to ascertain whether an expert's proposed definition fully comports with the specification and claims and so will preserve the patent's internal coherence. We accordingly think there is suficient reason to treat construction of terms of art like many other responsibilities that we cede to a judge in the normal course of trial, notwithstanding its evidentiary underpinnings.

C

Finally, we see the importance of uniformity in the treatment of a given patent as an independent reason to allocate all issues of construction to the court. As we noted in *General Elec. Co. v. Wabash Appliance Corp.*, 304 U.S. 364, 369, 58 S. Ct. 899, 902, 82 L. Ed. 1402 (1938), "[t]he limits of a patent must be known for the protection of the patentee, the encouragement of the inventive genius of others and the assurance that the subject of the patent will be dedicated ultimately to the public." Otherwise, a "zone of uncertainty which enterprise and experimentation may enter only at the risk of infringement claims would discourage invention only a little less than unequivocal foreclosure of the field," *United Carbon Co. v. Binney & Smith Co.*, 317 U.S. 228, 236, 63 S. Ct. 165, 170, 87 L. Ed. 232 (1942), and "[t]he public [would] be deprived of rights supposed to belong to it, without being clearly told what it is that limits these rights." *Merrill v. Yeomans*, 94 U.S. 568, 573, 24 L. Ed. 235 (1877). It was just for the sake of such desirable uniformity that Congress created the Court of Appeals for the Federal Circuit as an exclusive appellate court for patent cases, H.R. Rep. No. 97-312, pp. 20-23 (1981), observing that increased uniformity would "strengthen the United States patent system in such a way as to foster technological growth and industrial innovation." *Id.*, at 20.

Uniformity would, however, be ill served by submitting issues of document construction to juries. Making them jury issues would not, to be sure, necessarily leave evidentiary questions of meaning wide open in every new court in which a patent might be litigated, for principles of issue preclusion would ordinarily foster uniformity. *Cf. Blonder-Tongue Laboratories, Inc. v. University of Ill. Foundation*, 402 U.S. 313, 91 S. Ct. 1434, 28 L. Ed. 2d 788 (1971). But whereas issue preclusion could not be asserted against new and independent infringement defendants even within a given jurisdiction, treating interpretive issues as purely legal will promote (though it will not guarantee) intrajurisdictional certainty through the application of *stare decisis* on those questions not yet subject to interjurisdictional uniformity under the authority of the single appeals court.

....

Accordingly, we hold that the interpretation of the word "inventory" in this case is an issue for the judge, not the jury, and affirm the decision of the Court of Appeals for the Federal Circuit.

It is so ordered.

NOTE

Quick Response. So-called *"Markman"* hearings are now an established part of patent law. *See, e.g., Ethicon Endo-Surgery, Inc. v. United States Surgical Corp.*, 93 F.3d 1572 (Fed. Cir. 1996); John B. Pegram, Markman *and Its Implications*, 78 J. PAT. & TRADEMARK OFF. SOC'Y 560 (1996). Indeed, it is essential to obtain the trial court's view on the meaning of the claims to determine what evidence to introduce at trial and how best to show infringement. *Id*. And, of course, it is imperative to find out whether the Federal Circuit differs on the meaning of claim terms. (Note the *de novo* standard of review in this connection.) Interlocutory appeals will surely become much more common as a consequence.

Approaches to Claim Interpretation: Corbin to Gadamer

The majority in *Unique Concepts* states:

> The fact that mitered linear border pieces meet to form a right angle corner does not make them right angle corner pieces, when the claim separately recites both linear border pieces and right angle corner border pieces. Such an interpretation would run counter to the clear meaning of the language. Linear border pieces are not right angle corner border pieces. Both types of pieces are required by the claim.

Then the dissent:

> There is a genus-species relationship between the phrase in claim 1 [i.e., "corner border pieces"], which never changed throughout the prosecution, and the particular form of corner piece recited in claim 9 [i.e., one made from joining the mitered edges of two short linear pieces].... Claim 1 does not contain the limiting word "preformed" yet the majority, without justification, is reading it into the claim in holding that the claim does not cover corner pieces which are made up as clearly described in the specification.

What is this dispute really about? It begins with the "clear meaning" of the claim language "corner border pieces." Once the majority has construed this phrase as a distinct element wholly separate from another element, linear pieces, the result of its resort to the specification and prosecution history is foreordained. This is because neither source can be used to change an otherwise "clear" interpretation of claim language. Note also that the majority does not view its approach as "reading in" a limitation from the specification. Yet at the same time its *construction* of the claim language does have the *effect* of *limiting* the meaning of the phrase "right angle corner piece." (Specifically, it limits it by excluding "mitered short linear pieces" from the class of items encompassed by the phrase.) Thus we have an excellent example of a recurring theme in claim interpretation: the thin and wavering line between improper "reading in" of limitations and perfectly proper "claim interpretation." Note finally the predictable way the dissent criticizes the majority's interpretation: "the majority, without justification, is reading [the limitation "preformed"] into the claim ...."

For his part, Judge Rich in dissent claims not to have made any initial determination of the meaning of the claim. He seeks its meaning in all the sources available: claim, specification, and prosecution history. This approach conflicts to some extent, however, with prior caselaw, which holds that resort to these sources is justified *only* when a claim is ambiguous "on its face." Thus the conflict between the dissent and the majority can be recast as one over whether the claim is ambiguous on its face.

The entire debate is reminiscent of positions taken in the law of contracts over the question of the parol evidence rule. Older cases held that written contracts whose terms were clear on their face could not be supplemented by evidence of prior oral or written negotiations between the parties — i.e., could not be augmented by evidence outside the "four corners" of the contract itself. The great contracts scholar Arthur Corbin, however, eventually convinced judges and lawyers that it was always necessary to refer to these "parol" sources to *initially determine* whether the contract language was ambiguous. Thus he forced the abandonment of the old "four corners" test, in favor of a much more liberal "all evidence of ambiguity" test. Not surprisingly, when courts have greater license to look for ambiguity, they find it more often; the rule excluding parol evidence has thus been weakened considerably. *See* Corbin, *The Interpretation of Words and the Parol Evidence Rule*, 50 CORNELL L.Q. 161 (1965). ("[E]xtrinsic evidence is always necessary in the interpretation of a written instrument: in determining the meaning and intention of the parties who executed or relied upon it, in applying it to the objects and persons involved in the litigation or otherwise disputed issues, in determining the specific legal operation that justice requires to be given to the written instrument."). *See also* Farnsworth, *"Meaning" in the Law of Contracts*, 76 YALE L.J. 939 (1967) ("Once it is recognized that all language is infected with ambiguity and vagueness, it is senseless to ask a court to determine whether particular language is 'ambiguous' or 'vague' as opposed to 'plain.'").

In terms of this debate, where does Judge Rich's dissent in *Unique Concepts* fall? (Recall his statement: "The majority seems to start with an a priori assumption of what the 'clear' language of claim 1 means.") Is it appropriate to search for ambiguity first, then resolve it, or should the law seek to minimize the occasions when ambiguity becomes a legal issue? Does the intention of the party — in this case, the patent applicant — provide a helpful touchstone for resolving the problem? Do you think the Baslow patent in the preceding case should cover linear border pieces with mitered edges? Should the burden be on the applicant to clarify her meaning, such that ambiguous claims will not be construed to cover an accused device falling within the "zone of ambiguity"?

The Farnsworth article cited earlier takes pains to state that even the liberal version of the parol evidence rule has limitations. To be precise, he says that parol evidence is properly excluded when it directly contradicts the language of the contract. Applying that thinking to the problem of claim interpretation, one might say that even Judge Rich's approach in *Unique Concepts* is limited in that no evidence from the specification or prosecution history could be used to directly contradict an element or limitation in a claim. A claim to a process including heat limitations (e.g., "not less than 112 degrees Centigrade") could not be *interpreted* (with the aid of one of these extrinsic sources) to mean there is no heat limitation.

Judge Lourie's approach in *Unique Concepts* would no doubt be consonant with this view. In fact, it can be argued that this is precisely how the majority in *Unique Concepts* viewed that case — as an attempt to obviate a claim limitation (to "straight and corner pieces") by citing language in the specification ("straight pieces can be used as corner pieces") that directly contradicts the "plain" or "clear" language of the claim. What do you think: is there a difference between the heat limitation case and the situation in *Unique Concepts*? If so, does it stem from the differing degrees of precision of the claim language in the two cases: "at least 112 degrees Centigrade" versus "straight and corner pieces"? Can a clear line be drawn between evidence that contradicts an apparently plain meaning and evidence that merely helps determine meaning in the first place?

Corbin introduces a distinction between interpretation and construction that might be useful for our purposes. According to Corbin, interpretation is "the process by which one person gives a meaning to the symbols of expression used by [another] person." In contrast, construction is the determination of a document's "legal operation — its effect upon the action of courts and administrative officials." This distinction mirrors the two-step approach to determining infringement that we have seen described and used in *Autogiro* and *Unique Concepts*. Under this approach, claims are first interpreted (with the aid of specification and prosecution history) and then construed (by applying them to the accused device). As an aside, recall the function of the § 112 "definiteness" requirement in this connection: to insure that claims are definite enough to give a potential infringer notice regarding the patentee's exclusive subject matter. In the terms introduced here, this can be viewed as a requirement that claims be *susceptible* of reasonable interpretation. If they are too vague to be interpreted, a court cannot be expected to apply them to an accused structure.

Reading patent cases on claim interpretation, one is struck by the fact that the judicial approaches often mirror the elaborate theories of those who devote full time to a study of language and its interpretation. One such theory which is worth introducing is that of the German philosopher of language, Hans-Georg Gadamer. In his *Truth and Method*, he has a great deal to say about how legal interpretation sheds light on the act of interpretation generally. Consider the following excerpt:

> [D]iscovering the meaning of a legal text and discovering how to apply it in a particular legal instance are not two separate actions, but one unitary process.
>
> ....
>
> The work of interpretation is to *concretize* the law in each specific case — i.e., it is a work of *application*.... Application does not mean first understanding a given universal in itself and then afterward applying it to a concrete case. It is the very understanding of the universal — the text — itself.

TRUTH AND METHOD 310, 329, 340 (J. Weinsheimer & D. Marshall trans., 2d rev. ed. 1989).

Without drawing any conclusions, consider the following points with these excerpts in mind.

When a judge says that an interpretation of a claim would "read in" illegitimate limitations, she may often have an eye toward the *effect* of this interpretation in the particular case — i.e., she may be collapsing step 1 (claim interpretation) into step 2 (applying it to the accused device, termed "construction" here). If there is disagreement whether a certain view of a claim is legitimate "interpretation" or illegitimate "reading in of limitations," it must often be rooted in different views of the *ultimate* question presented to the court: whether the accused device infringes or not. In the terms introduced earlier in discussing Corbin's views on parol evidence, we might say that these debates show the collapsing together of the supposedly distinct stages of interpretation and construction. If that were so, it would accord with Gadamer's view of legal interpretation: that it is *always* directed ultimately to application, that in fact only through application is there true interpretation or understanding.

Surely our experience confirms this: in interpreting a phrase we in effect create two classes, those items which fall within the phrase and those that are outside it. It is almost impossible in creating these classes to forget entirely the *reason* for the exercise — to determine whether one *particular* item of interest falls inside or outside. And so it is in claim interpretation. In creating the generalized "picture" of what the claim means, one may often be influenced by whether the picture shows the accused device inside the protected class or outside. Interpretation, in other words, will often co-exist with application. If Gadamer is right, this is not an occasion to lament the result-oriented approach of judges, but an occasion to reflect on the fact that correct legal interpretation is essentially *about* application, and cannot hope to be otherwise.

B. THE DOCTRINE OF EQUIVALENTS

Judge Learned Hand wrote:

> [A]fter all aids to interpretation have been exhausted, and the scope of the claims has been enlarged as far as the words can be stretched, on proper occasions courts make them cover more than their meaning will bear.

Royal Typewriter Co. v. Remington Rand, Inc., 168 F.2d 691, 692, 77 U.S.P.Q. (BNA) 517, 518 (2d Cir.), *cert. denied*, 335 U.S. 825, 79 U.S.P.Q. (BNA) 454 (1948).

In this section we explore this most contentious issue, the enlargement of patent claims beyond what "their [literal] meaning will bear" — the doctrine of equivalents. We begin with the remainder of the opinion in *Unique Concepts*, introduced above in Section A; then we consider the benchmark Supreme Court case in the area (*Graver Tank*), and recent Federal Circuit elaborations.

UNIQUE CONCEPTS, INC. v. BROWN
939 F.2d 1558, 19 U.S.P.Q.2d 1500 (Fed. Cir. 1991)

[See part I of this opinion in Section A above, and especially Figure 8-1 before reading this.]

With respect to infringement by equivalents, since Brown conceded that the "result" of the right angle corner piece of the accused device is substantially the same as that of Claims 1, 2, and 3, the district court held that "the result is substantially the same; however, the means and function of the patented and accused devices are not the same, negating a finding of equivalents."

The issue of law on this point is whether the trial court understood and properly applied the requisite elements for finding infringement by equivalence, i.e., determining whether the '260 patent and Brown's structure are substantially the same in function, way and result. *See Pennwalt Corp. v. Durand-Wayland, Inc.*, 833 F.2d 931, 934, 4 U.S.P.Q.2d 1737, 1739 (Fed. Cir. 1987) (en banc), *cert. denied*, 485 U.S. 961, 108 S. Ct. 1226, 99 L. Ed. 2d 426 (1988). On review of the record, we conclude that the court understood and correctly applied the appropriate test. The court-appointed expert told the judge that a finding of infringement by equivalents requires a determination whether the accused devices achieve substantially the same result and substantially the same function of the claimed invention, in substantially the same way. At trial, Unique's expert similarly testified.

The determination whether an accused device infringes the claims of a patent is one of fact, reviewed under the clearly erroneous standard. Therefore, we may reverse the district court's finding of no infringement only if we are left with a "definite and firm conviction that a mistake has been committed" by the trial court. The court explained that because Brown's device performs the function and achieves the result in a substantially different way, there was no infringement by Brown's frame of the '260 patent:

> One of the main objects of the invention was stated to be to make something useful for a do-it-yourselfer. In fact, claim 9, as originally presented, expressly called for mitered pieces and was canceled because it was not something that a do-it-yourselfer could do, according to [Brown's] expert witness. The accused device has a *different and complicated way* of doing what the right-angle piece does in the patented device. It is a lot simpler for the do-it-yourselfer to use the preformed right-angle pieces of the patented device and far more difficult to create corners by the mitered means used and the function of the accused device.

([E]mphasis added). This finding is supported by the testimony of Brown's expert as to the difference between mitered corners and preformed corners:

> In this particular case it is more than simply cutting two pieces because you have to cut four pieces to make two mates. You have the channel and the inlet that has to be made also. Additionally, you have to have a spacer and make the proper space so you can shove the little piece of selvage that's left over at the end and make a nice fine product. Additionally, you have to put that corner piece up in the right place in the right section. It is simply *quite a different procedure* to do all of this and to end up with the same result as a right-angle corner piece. I think you are doing something in a *completely different way*.

(Emphasis added). On review of the record, we see no clear error in the district court's findings.

GRAVER TANK & MFG. CO. v. LINDE AIR PRODUCTS CO.

339 U.S. 605 (1950)

MR. JUSTICE JACKSON delivered the opinion of the Court.

Linde Air Products Co., owner of the Jones patent for an electric welding process and for fluxes to be used therewith, brought an action for infringement against [Graver]. [Figure 8-2, next page, shows the Jones welding device in operation.] The trial court held four flux claims valid and infringed and certain other flux claims and all process claims invalid. The Court of Appeals affirmed

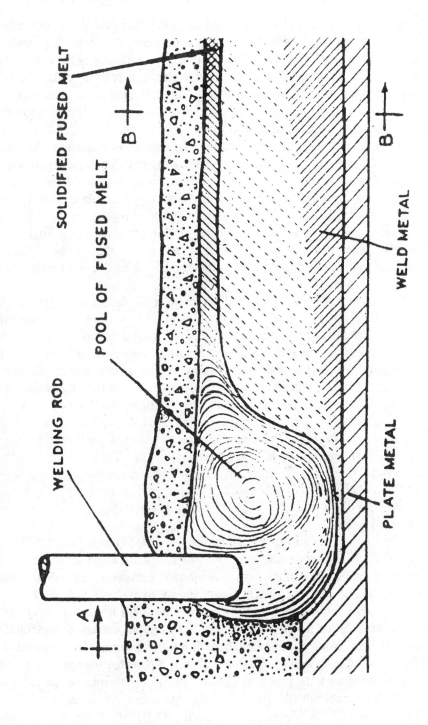

JONES ET AL PATENT NO 2043960

SOLIDIFIED FUSED MELT

POOL OF FUSED MELT

WELDING ROD

WELD METAL

PLATE METAL

Figure 8-2

findings of validity and infringement as to the four flux claims but reversed the trial court and held valid the process claims and the remaining contested flux claims. We granted certiorari, and reversed the judgment of the Court of Appeals insofar as it reversed that of the trial court, and reinstated the District Court decree. 336 U.S. 271. Rehearing was granted, limited to the question of infringement of the four valid flux claims and to the applicability of the doctrine of equivalents to findings of fact in this case.

At the outset it should be noted that the single issue before us is whether the trial court's holding that the four flux claims have been infringed will be sustained. Any issue as to the validity of these claims was unanimously determined by the previous decision in this Court and attack on their validity cannot be renewed now by reason of limitation on grant of rehearing.

In determining whether an accused device or composition infringes a valid patent, resort must be had in the first instance to the words of the claim. If accused matter falls clearly within the claim, infringement is made out and that is the end of it.

But courts have also recognized that to permit imitation of a patented invention which does not copy every literal detail would be to convert the protection of the patent grant into a hollow and useless thing. Such a limitation would leave room for — indeed encourage — the unscrupulous copyist to make unimportant and insubstantial changes and substitutions in the patent which, though adding nothing, would be enough to take the copied matter outside the claim, and hence outside the reach of law. One who seeks to pirate an invention, like one who seeks to pirate a copyrighted book or play, may be expected to introduce minor variations to conceal and shelter the piracy. Outright and forthright duplication is a dull and very rare type of infringement. To prohibit no other would place the inventor at the mercy of verbalism and would be subordinating substance to form. It would deprive him of the benefit of his invention and would foster concealment rather than disclosure of inventions, which is one of the primary purposes of the patent system.

The doctrine of equivalents evolved in response to this experience. The essence of the doctrine is that one may not practice a fraud on a patent. Originating almost a century ago in the case of *Winans v. Denmead*, [56 U.S.] 15 How. 330 [1853], it has been consistently applied by this Court and the lower federal courts, and continues today ready and available for utilization when the proper circumstances for its application arise. "To temper unsparing logic and prevent an infringer from stealing the benefit of the invention" [L. Hand in *Royal Typewriter Co. v. Remington Rand, supra*] a patentee may invoke this doctrine to proceed against the producer of a device "if it performs substantially the same function in substantially the same way to obtain the same result." *Sanitary Refrigerator Co. v. Winters*, 280 U.S. 30, 42 (1929). The theory on which it is founded is that "if two devices do the same work in substantially the same way, and accomplish substantially the same result, they are the same, even though they differ in name, form or shape." *Union Paper-Bag Machine Co. v. Murphy*, 97

U.S. 120, 125 [1877]. The doctrine operates not only in favor of the patentee of a pioneer or primary invention, but also for the patentee of a secondary invention consisting of a combination of old ingredients which produce new and useful results, *Imhaeuser v. Buerk*, 101 U.S. 647, 655 [1879], although the area of equivalence may vary under the circumstances. See *Continental Paper Bag Co. v. Eastern Paper Bag Co.*, 210 U.S. 405, 414-415 [1908] and cases cited; *Seymour v. Osborne*, [78 U.S.] 11 Wall. 516, 556 [1870]; *Gould v. Rees*, 15 Wall. [82 U.S.] 187, 192 [1872]. The wholesome realism of this doctrine is not always applied in favor of a patentee but is sometimes used against him. Thus, where a device is so far changed in principle from a patented article that it performs the same or a similar function in a substantially different way, but nevertheless falls within the literal words of the claim, the doctrine of equivalents may be used to restrict the claim and defeat the patentee's action for infringement. *Westinghouse v. Boyden Power Brake Co.*, 170 U.S. 537, 568 [1897]. In its early development, the doctrine was usually applied in cases involving devices where there was equivalence in mechanical components. Subsequently, however, the same principles were also applied to compositions, where there was equivalence between chemical ingredients. Today the doctrine is applied to mechanical or chemical equivalents in compositions or devices. Ellis, Patent Claims (1949) §§ 59-60.

What constitutes equivalency must be determined against the context of the patent, the prior art, and the particular circumstances of the case. Equivalence, in the patent law, is not the prisoner of a formula and is not an absolute to be considered in a vacuum. It does not require complete identity for every purpose and in every respect. In determining equivalents, things equal to the same thing may not be equal to each other and, by the same token, things for most purposes different may sometimes be equivalents. Consideration must be given to the purpose for which an ingredient is used in a patent, the qualities it has when combined with the other ingredients, and the function which it is intended to perform. An important factor is whether persons reasonably skilled in the art would have known of the interchangeability of an ingredient not contained in the patent with one that was.

A finding of equivalence is a determination of fact. Proof can be made in any form: through testimony of experts or others versed in the technology; by documents, including texts and treatises; and, of course, by the disclosures of the prior art. Like any other issue of fact, final determination requires a balancing of credibility, persuasiveness and weight of evidence. It is to be decided by the trial court and that court's decision, under general principles of appellate review, should not be disturbed unless clearly erroneous. Particularly is this so in a field where so much depends upon familiarity with specific scientific problems and principles not usually contained in the general storehouse of knowledge and experience.

In the case before us, we have two electric welding compositions or fluxes: the patented composition, Unionmelt Grade 20, and the accused composition, Lincolnweld 660. The patent under which Unionmelt is made claims essentially a combination of alkaline earth metal silicate and calcium fluoride; Unionmelt actually contains, however, silicates of calcium and magnesium, two alkaline earth metal silicates. Lincolnweld's composition is similar to Unionmelt's, except that it substitutes silicates of calcium and manganese — the latter not an alkaline earth metal — for silicates of calcium and magnesium. In all other respects, the two compositions are alike. The mechanical methods in which these compositions are employed are similar. They are identical in operation and produce the same kind and quality of weld.

The question which thus emerges is whether the substitution of the manganese which is not an alkaline earth metal for the magnesium which is, under the circumstances of this case, and in view of the technology and the prior art, is a change of such substance as to make the doctrine of equivalents inapplicable; or conversely, whether under the circumstances the change was so insubstantial that the trial court's invocation of the doctrine of equivalents was justified.

Without attempting to be all-inclusive, we note the following evidence in the record: Chemists familiar with the two fluxes testified that manganese and magnesium were similar in many of their reactions. There is testimony by a metallurgist that alkaline earth metals are often found in manganese ores in their natural state and that they serve the same purpose in the fluxes; and a chemist testified that "in the sense of the patent" manganese could be included as an alkaline earth metal. Much of this testimony was corroborated by reference to recognized texts on inorganic chemistry. Particularly important, in addition, were the disclosures of the prior art, also contained in the record. The Miller patent, No. 1,754,566, which preceded the patent in suit, taught the use of manganese silicate in welding fluxes. Manganese was similarly disclosed in the Armor patent, No. 1,467,825, which also described a welding composition. And the record contains no evidence of any kind to show that Lincolnweld was developed as the result of independent research or experiments.

It is not for this Court to even essay an independent evaluation of this evidence. This is the function of the trial court. And, as we have heretofore observed, "To no type of case is this ... more appropriately applicable than to the one before us, where the evidence is largely the testimony of experts as to which a trial court may be enlightened by scientific demonstrations. This trial occupied some three weeks, during which, as the record shows, the trial judge visited laboratories with counsel and experts to observe actual demonstrations of welding as taught by the patent and of the welding accused of infringing it, and of various stages of the prior art. He viewed motion pictures of various welding operations and tests and heard many experts and other witnesses." 336 U.S. 271, 274-275.

The trial judge found on the evidence before him that the Lincolnweld flux and the composition of the patent in suit are substantially identical in operation and in result. He found also that Lincolnweld is in all respects equivalent to Unionmelt for welding purposes. And he concluded that "for all practical purposes, manganese silicate can be efficiently and effectively substituted for calcium and magnesium silicates as the major constituent of the welding composition." These conclusions are adequately supported by the record; certainly they are not clearly erroneous.

It is difficult to conceive of a case more appropriate for application of the doctrine of equivalents. The disclosures of the prior art made clear that manganese silicate was a useful ingredient in welding compositions. Specialists familiar with the problems of welding compositions understood that manganese was equivalent to and could be substituted for magnesium in the composition of the patented flux and their observations were confirmed by the literature of chemistry. Without some explanation or indication that Lincolnweld was developed by independent research, the trial court could properly infer that the accused flux is the result of imitation rather than experimentation or invention. Though infringement was not literal, the changes which avoid literal infringement are colorable only. We conclude that the trial court's judgment of infringement respecting the four flux claims was proper, and we adhere to our prior decision on this aspect of the case.

Affirmed.

MR. JUSTICE BLACK, with whom MR. JUSTICE DOUGLAS concurs, dissenting.

I heartily agree with the Court that "fraud" is bad, "piracy" is evil, and "stealing" is reprehensible. But in this case, where petitioners are not charged with any such malevolence, these lofty principles do not justify the Court's sterilization of Acts of Congress and prior decisions, none of which are even mentioned in today's opinion.

The only patent claims involved here describe respondent's product as a flux "containing a major proportion of alkaline earth metal silicate." The trial court found that petitioners used a flux "composed principally of manganese silicate." Finding also that "manganese is not an alkaline earth metal," the trial court admitted that petitioners' flux did not "literally infringe" respondent's patent. Nevertheless it invoked the judicial "doctrine of equivalents" to broaden the claim for "alkaline earth metals" so as to embrace "manganese." On the ground that "the fact that manganese is a proper substitute ... is fully disclosed in the specification" of respondent's patent, it concluded that "no determination need be made whether it is a known chemical fact outside the teachings of the patent that manganese is an equivalent ...." Since today's affirmance unquestioningly follows the findings of the trial court, this Court necessarily relies on what the specifications revealed. In so doing, it violates a direct mandate of Congress without even discussing that mandate.

R.S. § 4888, as amended, 35 U.S.C. § 33 [now Patent Act § 112], provides that an applicant "shall particularly point out and distinctly claim the part, improvement, or combination which he claims as his invention or discovery." We have held in this very case that this statute precludes invoking the specifications to alter a claim free from ambiguous language, since "it is the claim which measures the grant to the patentee." 336 U.S. 271, 277. What is not specifically claimed is dedicated to the public. For the function of claims under R.S. § 4888, as we have frequently reiterated, is to exclude from the patent monopoly field all that is not specifically claimed, whatever may appear in the specifications. Today the Court tacitly rejects those cases. It departs from the underlying principle which, as the Court pointed out in *White v. Dunbar*, 119 U.S. 47, 51 [1886] forbids treating a patent claim

> like a nose of wax, which may be turned and twisted in any direction, by merely referring to the specification, so as to make it include something more than, or something different from, what its words express.... The claim is a statutory requirement, prescribed for the very purpose of making the patentee define precisely what his invention is; and it is unjust to the public, as well as an evasion of the law, to construe it in a manner different from the plain import of its terms.

Giving this patentee the benefit of a grant that it did not precisely claim is no less "unjust to the public" and no less an evasion of R.S. § 4888 merely because done in the name of the "doctrine of equivalents."

In seeking to justify its emasculation of R.S. § 4888 by parading potential hardships which literal enforcement might conceivably impose on patentees who had for some reason failed to claim complete protection for their discoveries, the Court fails even to mention the program for alleviation of such hardships which Congress itself has provided. 35 U.S.C. § 64 authorizes reissue of patents where a patent is "wholly or partly inoperative" due to certain errors arising from "inadvertence, accident, or mistake" of the patentee. And while the section does not expressly permit a patentee to expand his claim, this Court has reluctantly interpreted it to justify doing so. Like the Court's opinion, this congressional plan adequately protects patentees from "fraud," "piracy," and "stealing." Unlike the Court's opinion, it also protects business men from retroactive infringement suits and judicial expansion of a monopoly sphere beyond that which a patent expressly authorizes. The plan is just, fair, and reasonable. In effect it is nullified by this decision undercutting what the Court has heretofore recognized as wise safeguards. One need not be a prophet to suggest that today's rhapsody on the virtue of the "doctrine of equivalents" will make enlargement of patent claims the "rule" rather than the "exception."

Whatever the merits of the "doctrine of equivalents" where differences between the claims of a patent and the allegedly infringing product are de minimis, colorable only, and without substance, that doctrine should have no application to the facts of this case. For the differences between respondent's welding substance and petitioner's claimed flux were not nearly so slight. The claims relied upon here did not involve any mechanical structure or process where invention lay in the construction or method rather than in the materials used. Rather they were based wholly on using particular materials for a particular purpose. Respondent's assignors experimented with several metallic silicates, including that of manganese. According to the specifications (if these are to be considered) they concluded that while several were "more or less efficacious in our process, we prefer to use silicates of the alkaline earth metals." Several of their claims which this Court found too broad to be valid encompassed manganese silicate; the only claims found valid did not. Yet today the Court disregards that crucial deficiency, holding those claims infringed by a composition of which 88.49% by weight is manganese silicate.

In view of the intense study and experimentation of respondent's assignors with manganese silicate, it would be frivolous to contend that failure specifically to include that substance in a precise claim was unintentional. Nor does respondent attempt to give that or any other explanation for its omission. But the similar use of manganese in prior expired patents, referred to in the Court's opinion, raises far more than a suspicion that its elimination from the valid claims stemmed from fear that its inclusion by name might result in denial or subsequent invalidation of respondent's patent.

Under these circumstances I think petitioner had a right to act on the belief that this Court would follow the plain mandates of Congress that a patent's precise claims mark its monopoly boundaries, and that expansion of those claims to include manganese could be obtained only in a statutory reissue proceeding. The Court's ruling today sets the stage for more patent "fraud" and "piracy" against business than could be expected from faithful observance of the congressionally enacted plan to protect business against judicial expansion of precise patent claims. Hereafter a manufacturer cannot rely on what the language of a patent claims. He must be able, at the peril of heavy infringement damages, to forecast how far a court relatively unversed in a particular technological field will expand the claim's language after considering the testimony of technical experts in that field. To burden business enterprise on the assumption that men possess such a prescience bodes ill for the kind of competitive economy that is our professed goal.

The way specific problems are approached naturally has much to do with the decisions reached. A host of prior cases, to some of which I have referred, have treated the 17-year monopoly authorized by valid patents as a narrow exception to our competitive enterprise system. For that reason, they have emphasized the importance of leaving business men free to utilize all knowledge not preempted by the precise language of a patent claim.

The Court's approach today causes it to retreat from this sound principle. The damages retroactively assessed against petitioner for what was authorized until today are but the initial installment on the cost of that retreat.

Moreover, a doctrine which is said to protect against practicing "a fraud on a patent" is used to extend a patent to a composition which could not be patented. For manganese silicate had been covered by prior patents, now expired. Thus we end with a strange anomaly: a monopoly is obtained on an unpatented and unpatentable article.

NOTES

1. *Dissent Arguments.* The dissent makes several arguments. One is that "the similar use of manganese in prior expired patents" should prevent the patentee from claiming it. As a general matter this is a correct statement of law; the doctrine of equivalents may not be used to expand a claim to include structures described in the prior art. *See, e.g., Loctite Corp. v. Ultraseal Ltd.*, 781 F.2d 861, 870, 228 U.S.P.Q. (BNA) 90, 96 (Fed. Cir. 1985). In this case, however, the majority apparently concluded that although the accused product's welding flux was known in the prior art, no prior art reference taught the *combination* of this flux with the other elements of the claimed invention.

The dissent's second argument is that

> Whatever the merits of the "doctrine of equivalents" where differences between the claims of a patent and the allegedly infringing product are de minimis, colorable only, and without substance, that doctrine should have no application to the facts of this case. For the differences between respondent's welding substance and petitioner's claimed flux were not nearly so slight.

This kind of disagreement — over precisely how much the asserted equivalent varies from the claimed embodiments of the invention — is extremely common in doctrine of equivalents cases, as we shall see in this section. In this connection, recall the description of the doctrine of equivalents in the *Autogiro* case at the beginning of this chapter, with its reference to "adjusting" the range of equivalents to reflect the degree of inventive contribution reflected in the patented invention. Whether an invention qualifies for "pioneer" treatment (and hence a broad range of equivalents) is often disputed by litigants in infringement cases.

2. *Reissue and Equivalents.* For a contemporary statement of the view taken in the dissent, that reissue proceedings should be used in place of the doctrine of equivalents, see Adelman & Francione, *The Doctrine of Equivalents in Patent Law: Questions that Pennwalt Did Not Answer*, 137 U. PA. L. REV. 673 (1989). As we will see in Chapter 10, a reissue that seeks broadened claims must be filed within two years of the issuance of the patent. Is this one reason to maintain the doctrine, even with its flaws?

3. *Limitations on the Doctrine.* Equivalents do not extend (1) to cover an accused device in the prior art, and (2) to allow the patentee to recapture through equivalence certain coverage given up during prosecution. *Loctite Corp. v. Ultraseal Ltd.*, 781 F.2d 861, 870, 228 U.S.P.Q. 90, 96 (Fed. Cir. 1985).

———

Pennwalt v. Durand-Wayland, Inc., 833 F.2d 931, 4 U.S.P.Q.2d 1737 (Fed. Cir. 1987) (en banc), *cert. denied*, 108 S. Ct. 1226 (1988). Pennwalt had sued Durand-Wayland for infringing claims 1, 2, 10 and 18 of U.S. Patent No. 4,106,628 (the '628 patent) on an invention entitled "Sorter for Fruit and the

Like." Following a nonjury trial on the issues of patent infringement and validity, the district court issued an opinion concluding that the accused devices did not infringe any of the claims-at-issue, either literally or under the doctrine of equivalents. The Federal Circuit affirmed and, in the process, made the following influential comments on the relationship between claim elements and the doctrine of equivalents:

> The '628 patent claims a sorter. The principal object of the invention is to provide a rapid means for sorting items, such as fruit, by color, weight, or a combination of these two characteristics. The sorter recited in claims 1 and 2 conveys items along a track having an electronic-weighing device that produces an electrical signal proportional to the weight of the item, along with signal comparison means, clock means, position indicating means, and discharge means, each of which performs specified functions. The specification describes the details of a "hard-wired" network consisting of discrete electrical components which perform each step of the claims, e.g., by comparing the signals from the weighing device to reference signals and sending an appropriate signal at the proper time to discharge the item into the container corresponding to its weight. The combined sorter of claims 10 and 18 is a multifunctional apparatus whereby the item is conveyed across the weighing device and also carried past an optical scanner that produces an electrical signal proportional to the color of the item. The signals from the weighing device and color sensor are combined and an appropriate signal is sent at the proper time to discharge the item into the container corresponding to its color and weight.
>
> Durand-Wayland manufactures and sells two different types of sorting machines. The first accused device, the "Microsizer," sorts by weight only and employs software labeled either Version 2 or Version 5. The second accused device employs software labeled Version 6 and sorts by both color and weight through the use of the "Microsizer" in conjunction with a color detection apparatus called a "Microsorter."
>
> Under the doctrine of equivalents, infringement may be found (but not necessarily) if an accused device performs substantially the same overall function or work, in substantially the same way, to obtain substantially the same overall result as the claimed invention. That formulation, however, does not mean one can ignore claim limitations. As this court recently stated in *Perkin-Elmer Corp. v. Westinghouse Elec. Corp.*, 822 F.2d 1528, 3 U.S.P.Q.2d 1321 (Fed. Cir. 1987):
>
>> One must start with the claim, and though a "non-pioneer" invention may be entitled to some range of equivalents, a court may not, under the guise of applying the doctrine of equivalents, erase a plethora of meaningful structural and functional limitations of the claim on which the public is entitled to rely in avoiding infringement.... Though the doctrine of equivalents is designed to do equity, and to relieve an inventor from a

semantic strait jacket when equity requires, it is not designed to permit wholesale redrafting of a claim to cover non-equivalent devices, i.e., to permit a claim expansion that would encompass more than an insubstantial change.... [I]n applying the doctrine of equivalents, each limitation must be viewed in the context of the entire claim.... "It is ... well settled that each element of a claim is material and essential, and that in order for a court to find infringement, the plaintiff must show the presence of every element or its substantial equivalent in the accused device."

Pennwalt argues that the "accused machines simply do in a computer what the patent illustrates doing with hard-wired circuitry," and asserts that "this alone is insufficient to escape infringement." If Pennwalt was correct that the accused devices differ only in substituting a computer for hard-wired circuitry, it might have a stronger position for arguing that the accused devices infringe the claims. The claim limitations, however, require the performance of certain specified functions. Theoretically, a microprocessor could be programmed to perform those functions. However, the district court found that the microprocessor in the accused devices was not so programmed.

Since each of the claims-at-issue requires a position indicating means and the same analysis applies to each, we set forth only the relevant language of claim 10:

first position indicating means responsive to a signal from said clock means and said signal from said second comparison means for continuously indicating the position of an item to be sorted while the item is in transit between said optical detection means and said electronic weighing means, second position indicating means responsive to the signal from said clock means, the signal from said first comparison means and said first position indicating means for generating a signal continuously indicative of the position of an item to be sorted after said item has been weighed.

The testimony of Dr. Alford, Durand-Wayland's expert, was that the accused machine had no component which satisfied either of the above limitations defining position indicating means, and Pennwalt has admitted that the accused machines do not sort by keeping track of the physical location of an item in transit, continuously or otherwise, as required by each of these limitations.

[T]he facts here do not involve later-developed computer technology which should be deemed within the scope of the claims to avoid the pirating of an invention. On the contrary, the inventors could not obtain a patent with claims in which the functions were described more broadly. Having secured claims only by including very specific functional limitations, Pennwalt now seeks to avoid those very limitations under the doctrine of equivalents. This it cannot do. Simply put, the memory components of the Durand-Wayland sorter were not programmed to perform the same or an equivalent function of physically tracking the items to be sorted from the scanner to the scale or from the scale to its appropriate discharge point as required by the claims.

[From the Commentary by JUDGE NEWMAN:]

The majority can not be oblivious to the in banc weight of its opinion, or to the muddle of uncertainty that it will cause.

[One] subsidiary question raised by the majority opinion is: when is a "function" omitted? Is it omitted when it is consolidated with another "function," or when less than all the provisions of a complex claim clause are performed? What if the function is peripheral to the invention, or becomes superfluous due to unrelated technological advance? Is every descriptive word in a claim clause a "function"? Is every "function" a "limitation"?

In the accused device a modified electronic memory keeps track of the movement of the fruit, and indicates when it reaches the weighing means and the discharge bin; that is, it indicates when the fruit has reached the next stop in its passage through the device. But the "continuous" indication of the fruit's position while in transit is superfluous and is not done. (Both sides testified that "continuous" indication is not done, in either the Pennwalt commercial device or the accused device.)

According to the majority, because the position indication is not "continuous," a claimed "function" is not performed. All "functions" mentioned in claims are defined by the majority as essential, simply because they're there, whatever their role in the patented invention and whatever their part in the clause in which they appear. The majority states the sweeping rule that if "even a single function required by a claim or an equivalent function is not performed," that ends the inquiry under the doctrine of equivalents.

NOTES

1. *What Is an Element?* Judge (later Chief Judge) Nies wrote some additional views in *Pennwalt*, in which she stated the following point:

Every Supreme Court decision which has addressed the issue of infringement of a patent claim, beginning with *Prouty v. Draper*, 41 U.S. (16 Pet.) 335, 10 L. Ed. 985 (1842) — and the precedent is voluminous — has held that where a part of the claimed invention, that is, a limitation of the claim, is lacking in the accused device exactly or equivalently, there is no infringement.

833 F.2d at 950. Practitioners and judges have disputed what *Pennwalt* means when it speaks of a claim "element." As Judge Nies suggests, element means limitation. But, as we shall see in the *Corning Glass* case that follows, not every

case reflects this view. *See generally Perkin-Elmer Corp. v. Westinghouse Elec. Corp.*, 822 F.2d at 1533 n.9, 3 U.S.P.Q.2d at 1325 n.9. ("References to 'elements' can be misleading.... [C]larity is advanced when sufficient wording is employed to indicate when 'elements' is intended to mean a component ... of an embodiment of an invention and when it is intended to mean a feature set forth in or as a limitation in a claim.").

Perhaps an example will help to clarify the difference between an element and a limitation. Suppose a claim to a food processing method includes a step where the raw foodstuff is baked at high temperature. Suppose further that the claim includes the following parameters: baking between 150 and 250 degrees Centigrade, at a pressure of 3 atmospheres. One might say the baking step is an *element* of the claim, and the temperature and pressure ranges are *limitations*.

Now apply the analysis in the majority and dissenting opinions in *Pennwalt* to the following scenario. A competitor of the patentee holding this process patent bakes the raw foodstuff at 300 degrees Centigrade, under normal atmospheric pressure. Does this infringe the patent?

There are three views of the matter. One is that there is no infringement because the accused device has omitted an element of the claim — the pressure limitation. Here, of course, the "element" is interpreted synonymously with "limitation." Thus the "all element" rule of *Pennwalt* becomes the "all limitation" rule and the dissent's view seems warranted: there is not much difference (if any) between the doctrine of equivalents and literal infringement.

A second view is that although a limitation is missing in the accused device, all *elements* are present. The accused process includes a baking step, after all. Under this view, elements are not synonymous with limitations; limitations may partially comprise elements, or may "modify" them. In our example, infringement under the doctrine of equivalents might well be made out under this second view.

A third view might be as follows. The baking step is an element, as is the generic feature "baking at high temperature and higher than normal pressure." Under this view, there would be no infringement in the scenario put forth because the second specified feature of the element is missing in the accused device, which we said worked at normal atmospheric temperature.

If this is confusing, you are beginning to understand the doctrine of equivalents.

2. *Claims as Notice.* In her dissent, Judge Nies writes:

> As a matter of due process under the fifth amendment, reasonable notice must be given to the public of what conduct must be avoided. Whether in civil or criminal proceedings, it is unequivocally established that that basic right to notice applies.... An infringement standard as vague as application of the "invention as a whole," which permits claim limitations to be read out of the claim, would nullify the statutory requirement and violate due process.

833 F.2d at 954. If this argument is accepted, what does it say about "secret" prior art under § 102(e), about which, by definition, an inventor can have no notice? Obscure references under other subsections of § 102 would also raise this question. Is there a difference between a lack of notice regarding a piece of prior art and lack of notice to competitors regarding the coverage of claims in an issued patent?

HILTON DAVIS CHEMICAL CO. v. WARNER-JENKINSON CO.

62 F.3d 1512, 35 U.S.P.Q.2d 1641 (Fed. Cir. 1995),
cert. granted, 116 S. Ct. 1014 (1996)

PER CURIAM.

Hilton Davis Chemical Co. sued Warner-Jenkinson Co., Inc. for infringement of U.S. Patent No. 4,560,746 (the '746 patent). The jury found that the '746 patent was not invalid and that Warner-Jenkinson infringed under the doctrine of equivalents. The trial court entered judgment on the jury verdict. *Hilton Davis Chem. Co. v. Warner-Jenkinson Co.*, No. C-1-91-218 (S.D. Ohio June 22, 1992). Because substantial evidence supports the jury verdict of infringement, the court en banc affirms.

BACKGROUND

Hilton Davis and Warner-Jenkinson manufacture dyes, including FD & C (food, drug, and cosmetic) Red Dye # 40 and Yellow Dye # 6. The process of making these dyes yields impurities as byproducts. Manufacturers must remove these impurities from the dyes to meet stringent governmental requirements for food and drug purity. Historically, Hilton Davis and Warner-Jenkinson used an expensive and wasteful process known as "salting out" to purify the dyes. The '746 patent, assigned to Hilton Davis, discloses an improved purification process that replaces salting out with "ultrafiltration." Ultrafiltration uses osmosis to separate components of a solution by drawing some of the components, but not others, through a membrane. Thus, the '746 process filters impure dye solution through a membrane at certain pressures, pHs, and pore diameters. Impurities, but not dye molecules, pass through the membrane, leaving a high purity dye product.

Hilton Davis began its search for an alternative to the salting out process in 1982. The co-inventors of the '746 process, Drs. Cook and Rebhahn, led this project for Hilton Davis. The inventors decided to investigate a membrane separation process. Dr. Cook then hired Osmonics, Inc., a filtration equipment manufacturer, to test the process on a Hilton Davis Red Dye # 40 solution which had been disclosed to Osmonics under a secrecy agreement. The first test, in August 1982, did not succeed. Dr. Cook then instructed Osmonics to perform a second Red Dye # 40 test with specified changes in the test membrane and filtration procedures. This second test, in October 1982, succeeded. Osmonics successfully purified Hilton Davis Yellow Dye # 6 under Dr. Cook's instructions in January 1983.

The inventors filed their initial patent application based on the October 1982 and January 1983 test results. After further in-house testing by Dr. Cook, the inventors filed a continuation-in-part application claiming a broader range of membrane pore sizes. The '746 patent issued in 1985.

The '746 patent claims a process for purifying commercial dyes including Red Dye # 40 and Yellow Dye # 6. Claim 1, the only independent claim at issue, appears in Jepson form. *See In re Jepson*, 1917 C.D. 62, 243 O.G. 525 (Ass't Comm'r Patents 1917). Claim 1 recites:

> In a process for the purification of a dye selected from [a group including Red Dye # 40 and Yellow Dye # 6] ... the improvement which comprises:
>
> subjecting an aqueous solution ... to ultrafiltration through a membrane having a *nominal pore diameter of 5-15 Angstroms* under a hydrostatic pressure of *approximately 200 to 400 p.s.i.g.*, at a *pH from approximately 6.0 to 9.0*, to thereby cause separation of said impurities from said dye, said impurities of a molecular size smaller than the nominal pore diameter passing [through] said membrane and said dye remaining in the concentrate, and when substantially all said impurities have been removed from said concentrate ... recovering said dye, in approximately 90% purity from said concentrate by evaporation of said concentrate to dryness.

(Emphasis added.) The inventors added the phrase "at a pH from approximately 6.0 to 9.0" during prosecution to distinguish U.S. Patent 4,189,380 to Booth et al. (the Booth patent). The Booth patent discloses an ultrafiltration process that, among other differences from the '746 process, operates at a pH above 9 and preferably between 11 and 13.

Warner-Jenkinson developed its accused ultrafiltration process for Red Dye # 40 and Yellow Dye # 6 in 1986. Like the '746 process, Warner-Jenkinson's accused process included ultrafiltration through a membrane. At trial, Hilton Davis showed that Warner-Jenkinson's process operated at pressures somewhere in a range of 200 to nearly 500 p.s.i.g. and a pH of 5. While Hilton Davis did not present actual pore size measurements for Warner-Jenkinson's membrane, several experts testified that a membrane collecting Red Dye # 40 and Yellow Dye # 6 would have a nominal pore diameter of 5 to 15 Angstroms.

In 1982, Warner-Jenkinson had tested a membrane separation process on a dye solution that had already been salted out. Warner-Jenkinson, like Hilton Davis, hired Osmonics under a secrecy agreement to perform its test. Osmonics performed the Warner-Jenkinson test in August 1982, one week before it performed the first Hilton Davis test. The Warner-Jenkinson test was not successful, however, because it did not produce a sufficiently pure dye. After the unsuccessful test, Warner-Jenkinson ceased work on filtration of Red Dye # 40 and Yellow Dye # 6 until 1986.

Warner-Jenkinson did not learn of the '746 patent until October 1986, after it had begun commercial use of its ultrafiltration process to purify Red Dye # 40. Hilton Davis learned of Warner-Jenkinson's process in 1989 and sued Warner-Jenkinson for patent infringement in 1991.

After considering extensive evidence offered over nine days, the jury found that the '746 patent was not invalid and that Warner-Jenkinson infringed under the doctrine of equivalents. The jury found that Warner-Jenkinson did not willfully infringe, however, and awarded only 20% of Hilton Davis' request in damages. The district court then denied Warner-Jenkinson's post-trial motions, and entered a permanent injunction prohibiting Warner-Jenkinson from practicing ultrafiltration except at pressures above 500 p.s.i.g. and pHs above 9.01.

Warner-Jenkinson appealed the infringement and validity findings. After a panel of this court heard oral argument on July 9, 1993, the court en banc decided to rehear the appeal to consider the important issues raised concerning the doctrine of equivalents. This court asked the parties to brief three questions: 1. Does a finding of infringement under the doctrine of equivalents require anything in addition to proof of the facts that there are the same or substantially the same (a) function, (b) way, and (c) result, the so-called triple identity test of *Graver Tank [& Manufacturing Co.] v. Linde Air Products Co.*, 339 U.S. 605 [70 S. Ct. 854, 94 L. Ed. 1097] (1950), and cases relied on therein? If yes, what? 2. Is the issue of infringement under the doctrine of equivalents an equitable remedy to be decided by the court, or is it, like literal infringement, an issue of fact to be submitted to the jury in a jury case? 3. Is application of the doctrine of equivalents by the trial court to find infringement of the patentee's right to exclude, when there is no literal infringement of the claim, discretionary in accordance with the circumstances of the case? Oral argument directed to the en banc questions occurred on March 7, 1994.

DISCUSSION

I

This case presents an opportunity to restate — not to revise — the test for infringement under the doctrine of equivalents. Courts have applied the doctrine of equivalents to protect the substance of the patentee's right to exclude since the first few decades after enactment of the Patent Act of 1790, ch. 7, 1 Stat. 109. Sitting as Circuit Justice, Justice Story, the leading intellectual property scholar of that era, stated: "Mere colorable differences, or slight improvements, cannot shake the right of the original inventor." *Odiorne v. Winkley*, 18 F. Cas. 581, 582 (C.C.D. Mass. 1814) (No. 10,432) (Story, C.J.). Indeed, the Supreme Court has consistently recognized the doctrine of equivalents as a protection for patent owners. *See, e.g., Winans v. Denmead*, 56 U.S. (15 How.) 330, 343, 14 L. Ed. 717 (1854); *Sewall v. Jones*, 91 U.S. 171, 184, 23 L. Ed. 275 (1875); *Sanitary Refrigerator Co. v. Winters*, 280 U.S. 30, 41-42, 50 S. Ct. 9, 12-13, 74 L. Ed. 147 (1929). Often the Supreme Court noted that an accused product or process, to avoid infringement under the doctrine, must include "substantial and not merely colorable" differences from the patent claims. *Singer Mfg. Co. v. Cramer*, 192 U.S. 265, 286, 24 S. Ct. 291, 299, 48 L. Ed. 437 (1904); *see also McCormick v. Talcott*, 61 U.S. (20 How.) 402, 405, 15 L. Ed. 930 (1858); *Duff v. Sterling Pump Co.*, 107 U.S. 636, 639, 2 S. Ct. 487, 490, 27 L. Ed. 517 (1883).

The Supreme Court mapped the modern contours of the doctrine of equivalents in its landmark *Graver Tank* decision. *Graver Tank & Mfg. Co. v. Linde Air Prods. Co.*, 339 U.S. 605, 70 S. Ct. 854, 94 L. Ed. 1097 (1950). In *Graver Tank*, the Court addressed whether Graver Tank's use of a particular electric welding flux infringed Linde Company's patent. The patent claimed "essentially a combination of alkaline earth metal silicate and calcium fluoride." *Id.* at 610, 70 S. Ct. at 857. Graver Tank's accused flux substituted "silicates of calcium and manganese — the latter not an alkaline earth metal — for silicates of calcium and magnesium." *Id.* Because only exact duplicates literally infringe, *id.* at 607, 70 S. Ct. at 855-56, the Court recognized that infringement depended on the longstanding doctrine of equivalents. *Id.* at 608, 70 S. Ct. at 856.

In explaining the bases for the doctrine, the Supreme Court observed that limiting enforcement of exclusive patent rights to literal infringement "would place the inventor at the mercy of verbalism and would be subordinating substance to form." *Graver Tank*, 339 U.S. at 607, 70 S. Ct. at 856. Such a limitation, the Court reasoned, might even encourage infringers "to make unimportant and insubstantial changes and substitutions in the patent which, though adding nothing, would be enough ... [to evade] the reach of law." *Id.*

Based on these predicates, the Supreme Court concluded, the doctrine applies if, and only if, the differences between the claimed and accused products or processes are insubstantial. *Graver Tank*, 339 U.S. at 610, 70 S. Ct. at 857. The Court expressed the doctrine in the following terms for the *Graver Tank* case:

> The question which thus emerges is whether the substitution of the manganese which is not an alkaline earth metal for the magnesium which is, under the circumstances of this case, and in view of the technology and prior art, is a change of such substance as to make the doctrine of equivalents inapplicable; or conversely, whether under the circumstances the change was so insubstantial that the trial court's invocation of the doctrine of equivalents was justified.

Id. The Court defined the doctrine of equivalents in terms of the substantiality of the differences between the claimed and accused products or processes. The Supreme Court in *Graver Tank* thus made insubstantial differences the necessary predicate for infringement under the doctrine of equivalents.

In recent decisions, this court has also stressed the significance of this "insubstantial differences" standard. *Valmont Indus., Inc. v. Reinke Mfg. Co.*, 983 F.2d 1039, 1043, 25 U.S.P.Q.2d 1451, 1454 (Fed. Cir. 1993); *Charles Greiner & Co.*

v. Mari-Med Mfg., Inc., 962 F.2d 1031, 1036, 22 U.S.P.Q.2d 1526, 1529 (Fed. Cir. 1992); [etc.] In many of these cases, this court also relied on the so-called triple identity, or function-way-result, test to measure the substantiality of the differences. *Valmont*, 983 F.2d at 1043.... With this case, this court explicitly holds that the application of the doctrine of equivalents rests on the substantiality of the differences between the claimed and accused products or processes, assessed according to an objective standard.

II

In applying the doctrine of equivalents, it is often enough to assess whether the claimed and accused products or processes include substantially the same function, way, and result. Courts recognized this principle as early as 1817, when Justice Bushrod Washington, riding circuit, instructed a jury that "[w]here the [claimed and accused] machines are substantially the same, and operate in the same manner, to produce the same result, they must be in principle the same." *Gray v. James*, 10 F. Cas. 1015, 1016 (C.C.D. Pa. 1817) (No. 5,718); *see also Sanitary Refrigerator*, 280 U.S. at 42, 50 S. Ct. at 13 (*"[G]enerally speaking*, one device is an infringement of another 'if it performs substantially the same function in substantially the same way to obtain the same result.' ... [The patent claim] is nevertheless infringed by a device in which there is no substantial departure from the description in the patent, but a mere colorable departure therefrom.") (quoting *Machine Co. v. Murphy*, 97 U.S. 120, 125, 24 L. Ed. 935 (1877)) (emphasis added). Because examination of function, way, and result often discloses the substantiality of the differences between the accused and claimed products or processes, many courts, including the Supreme Court itself, have used this formulation to describe the doctrine of equivalents. *See, e.g., Graver Tank*, 339 U.S. at 608, 70 S. Ct. at 856 (quoting *Sanitary Refrigerator*, 280 U.S. at 42, 50 S. Ct. at 13); *Machine Co. v. Murphy*, 97 U.S. at 125, 24 L. Ed. 935.

It goes too far, however, to describe the function-way-result test as "the" test for equivalency announced by *Graver Tank*. The function-way-result test often suffices to assess equivalency because similarity of function, way, and result leaves little room for doubt that only insubstantial differences distinguish the accused product or process from the claims. But evaluation of function, way, and result does not necessarily end the inquiry. Indeed, the Supreme Court explained that the function-way-result test arose in an era characterized by relatively simple mechanical technology. *Graver Tank*, 339 U.S. at 609, 70 S. Ct. at 856-57 (reciting history of doctrine). As technology becomes more sophisticated, and the innovative process more complex, the function-way-result test may not invariably suffice to show the substantiality of the differences.

Thus evidence beyond function, way, and result is also relevant to the doctrine of equivalents. In *Graver Tank*, the Supreme Court identified and relied on factors in addition to similarity of function, way, and result. The Court considered that persons reasonably skilled in the art knew that the manganese in the accused flux was interchangeable for the magnesium in the claimed flux. 339 U.S. at 609, 612, 70 S. Ct. at 856-57, 858. The Court also permitted the fact-finder to infer infringing "imitation" from the lack of evidence that the accused infringer independently developed its flux. *Id.* at 612, 70 S. Ct. at 858.

The Supreme Court's reliance in *Graver Tank* on factors other than function, way, and result endorses consideration of all evidence relevant to the substantiality of the differences. Because "[e]quivalence, in the patent law, is not the prisoner of a formula," *id.* at 609, 70 S. Ct. at 856, the available relevant evidence may vary from case to case. When a trial record presents only evidence of function, way, and result, then application of the doctrine will necessarily rest on function, way, and result alone. When a record presents other evidence relevant to the substantiality of the differences, however, the fact-finder must consider it.

In either event, the vantage point of one of ordinary skill in the relevant art provides the perspective for assessing the substantiality of the differences. *Valmont*, 983 F.2d at 1043. The test is objective, with proof of the substantiality of the differences resting on objective evidence rather than unexplained subjective conclusions, whether offered by an expert witness or otherwise.

According to the Supreme Court, "[a]n important factor" to be considered, quite apart from function, way, and result, "is whether persons reasonably skilled in the art would have known of the interchangeability of an ingredient not contained in the patent with one that was." *Graver Tank*, 339 U.S. at 609, 70 S. Ct. at 857. The precedent of this court has also stressed the importance of evidence of known interchangeability to show infringement under the doctrine. *See Corning Glass Works v. Sumitomo Elec. U.S.A., Inc.*, 868 F.2d 1251, 1261, 9 U.S.P.Q.2d 1962, 1969 (Fed. Cir. 1989); *Thomas & Betts Corp. v. Litton Sys., Inc.*, 720 F.2d 1572, 1579, 220 U.S.P.Q. 1, 6 (Fed. Cir. 1983). The known interchangeability of the accused and claimed elements is potent evidence that one of ordinary skill in the relevant art would have considered the change insubstantial. Without such evidence, the patentee will need other objective technological evidence demonstrating that the substitute nevertheless represents a change that the ordinary artisan would have considered insubstantial at the time of infringement.

Evidence of copying is also relevant to infringement under the doctrine of equivalents, see *Graver Tank*, 339 U.S. at 612, 70 S. Ct. at 858, not because the doctrine of equivalents rests on the subjective awareness or motivation of the accused infringer, but rather because copying suggests that the differences between the claimed and accused products or processes — measured objectively — are insubstantial. When an attempt to copy occurs, the fact-finder may infer that the copyist, presumably one of some skill in the art, has made a fair copy, with only insubstantial changes. Such an inference, of course, would not dominate the doctrine of equivalents analysis. Instead, where the inference arises, it must be weighed together with the other evidence relevant to the substantiality of the differences.

By considering evidence of copying, however, the Supreme Court did not imply that infringement under the doctrine requires bad faith or some other subjective component. Intent is not an element of infringement. *See, e.g., Kewanee Oil Co. v. Bicron Corp.*, 416 U.S. 470, 478, 94 S. Ct. 1879, 1884, 40 L. Ed. 2d 315 (1974). A patent owner may exclude others from practicing the claimed invention, regardless of whether infringers even know of the patent: This question [of infringement] is one irrespective of motive. The defendant may have infringed without intending, or even knowing it; but he is not, on that account, the less an infringer. His motives and knowledge may affect the question of damages, to swell or reduce them; but the immediate question is the simple one, has he infringed? *Parker v. Hulme*, 18 F. Cas. 1138, 1143 (C.C. E.D. Pa. 1849) (No. 10,740); *see also Kewanee*, 416 U.S. at 478, 94 S. Ct. at 1884; *Intel Corp. v. United States Int'l Trade Comm'n*, 946 F.2d 821, 832, 20 U.S.P.Q.2d 1161, 1171 (Fed. Cir. 1991). The Supreme Court, in the exegesis of the doctrine in *Graver Tank*, notably does not mention a threshold showing of bad faith or evil intent. Proof of bad faith by an infringer may entitle the patent owner to enhanced damages and attorney fees for willful infringement under 35 U.S.C. §§ 284-285 (1988). Evidence of culpable conduct, however, is not a prerequisite nor necessary for application of the doctrine.

The Supreme Court applied the doctrine of equivalents in *Graver Tank* to prevent "fraud on a patent," 339 U.S. at 608, 70 S. Ct. at 856, not fraud by the accused infringer. As *Graver Tank* demonstrates, preventing "fraud on a patent" involves an objective assessment of the substantiality of the differences between the claimed and accused products or processes. The doctrine of equivalents does not rely on the subjective awareness or intent of the accused infringer. While the doctrine discourages the "unscrupulous copyist," 339 U.S. at 607, 70 S. Ct. at 856, its reach is not so limited. Thus, lack of substantial differences, not the accused infringer's motives or intent, triggers application of the doctrine of equivalents.

Evidence of "designing around" the patent claims is also relevant to the question of infringement under the doctrine. The ability of the public successfully to design around — to use the patent disclosure to design a product or process that does not infringe, but like the claimed invention, is an improvement over the prior art — is one of the important public benefits that justify awarding the patent owner exclusive rights to his invention. Designing around "is the stuff of which competition is made and is supposed to benefit the consumer." *State Indus., Inc. v. A.O. Smith Corp.*, 751 F.2d 1226, 1236, 224 U.S.P.Q. 418, 424 (Fed. Cir. 1985). When a competitor becomes aware of a patent, and attempts to design around its claims, the fact-finder may infer that the competitor, presumably one of skill in the art, has designed substantial changes into the new product to avoid infringement. Again, the strength of this inference may vary from case to case. Evidence of designing around therefore weighs against finding infringement under the doctrine of equivalents.

Evidence that the accused infringer developed its product or process through independent research is not directly relevant to the question of infringement under the doctrine of equivalents.[1] Independent development is not designing around. Independent development means that the accused infringer had no knowledge of the patented invention when it developed its product or process. Without knowledge, the independent developer could not have set out to make its product or process either similar to or different from the claimed invention. Unlike copying or designing around, therefore, independent development itself provides no information about the substantiality of the differences. Furthermore, because intent is not an element of infringement, independent development does not excuse infringement of the patent owner's right to exclude. *See Parker v. Hulme*, 18 F. Cas. at 1143. An independently developed product or process that falls within the patent claims or includes only insubstantial differences nevertheless infringes. *See Kewanee*, 416 U.S. at 478, 94 S. Ct. at 1884. In sum, those who make only insubstantial changes to a patented product or process are liable for infringement, regardless of their awareness of the patent and its disclosure.

III

Infringement, whether literal or under the doctrine of equivalents, is a question of fact. *Winans v. Denmead*, 56 U.S. (15 How.) at 338, 14 L. Ed. 717 .... The Supreme Court made this abundantly clear in *Graver Tank*:

> A finding of equivalence is a determination of fact. Proof can be made in any form: through testimony of experts or others versed in the technology; by documents, including texts and treatises; and, of course, by the disclosures of the prior art. Like any other issue of fact, final determination requires a balancing of credibility, persuasiveness and weight of evidence. [When tried to the trial court, it] is to be decided by the trial court and that court's decision, under general principles of appellate review, should not be disturbed unless clearly erroneous. Particularly is this so in a field where so much depends upon familiarity with specific scientific problems and principles not usually contained in the general storehouse of knowledge and experience.

---

[1]Evidence of independent development is highly relevant, however, to refute a patent owner's contention that the doctrine of equivalents applies because the accused infringer copied, that is, intentionally appropriated the substance of the claimed invention. In *Graver Tank*, the Supreme Court linked the fact-finder's inference of copying to independent research. 339 U.S. at 612, 70 S. Ct. at 858. Because the record lacked evidence of independent development, the fact-finder could infer copying or "imitation." *Id*. When the patent owner asserts copying, evidence that the accused infringer developed its product or process without knowing of the patent becomes relevant in rebuttal. For this reason, the fact-finder must consider any evidence of independent development in a case where the patent owner alleges copying as probative of infringement under the doctrine of equivalents.

339 U.S. at 609-10, 70 S. Ct. at 857. The Supreme Court thus reemphasized that infringement under the doctrine of equivalents is an issue of fact. When infringement is tried to the court, as in *Graver Tank*, an appellate court reviews the trial court's infringement finding for clear error. When tried to a jury, an appellate court reviews the jury verdict for lack of substantial evidence. *See, e.g., Genentech, Inc. v. Wellcome Found. Ltd.*, 29 F.3d 1555, 1565, 31 U.S.P.Q.2d 1161, 1168-69 (Fed. Cir. 1994).

In several recent opinions, this court has referred to the doctrine of equivalents as "equitable."[2] The term "equitable" can have many meanings. The Supreme Court explained in *Graver Tank* that the doctrine prevents the unfairness of depriving the patent owner of effective protection of its invention, 339 U.S. at 607, 70 S. Ct. at 855-56, thereby achieving a fair or "equitable" result. Thus, in doctrine of equivalents cases, this court's allusions to equity invoke equity in its broadest sense — equity as general fairness. While recognizing the equity, or fairness, promoted by the doctrine of equivalents, furthermore, the Supreme Court stated unequivocally that application of the doctrine is a question of fact. *Id.* at 609, 70 S. Ct. at 856-57. This court has followed. *SRI*, 775 F.2d at 1118 ("It is settled that the question of infringement (literal or by equivalents) is factual. *Graver Tank*.").

By referring to the doctrine as a doctrine of fairness, neither the Supreme Court nor this court has invoked the myriad implications of an alternative to legal remedies. In addition, neither the Supreme Court nor this court has invoked equity in the technical sense of a set of principles originating in England to compensate for the historically harsh rules of common law. *Graver Tank* does not discuss any of the principles commonly attending the chancellor's invocation of equitable power, such as the "clean hands" doctrine, the elevated burden of proof, the abuse of discretion standard of review, or the mandatory balancing of the equities. Indeed, the Supreme Court has more than once stated that every patent owner is entitled to invoke the doctrine of equivalents — a proposition inimical to the hypothesis that the doctrine is equitable. *See Sanitary Refrigerator*, 280 U.S. at 42, 50 S. Ct. at 13; *Seymour v. Osborne*, 78 U.S. (11 Wall.) 516, 556, 20 L. Ed. 33 (1871) ("Patentees ... are entitled in all cases to invoke to

---

[2] *See Valmont Indus., Inc. v. Reinke Mfg. Co.*, 983 F.2d 1039, 1043 n. 1, 25 U.S.P.Q.2d 1451, 1454 n. 1 (Fed. Cir. 1993) ("the doctrine 'is designed to do equity [but] it is not designed ... to permit a claim expansion that would encompass more than an insubstantial change'") (quoting *Perkin-Elmer Corp. v. Westinghouse Elec. Corp.*, 822 F.2d 1528, 1532, 3 U.S.P.Q.2d 1321, 1324 (Fed. Cir. 1987)); *Texas Instruments Inc. v. United States Int'l Trade Comm'n*, 988 F.2d 1165, 1173, 26 U.S.P.Q.2d 1018, 1024 (Fed. Cir. 1993) ("the doctrine of equivalents has been 'judicially devised to do equity'") (quoting *Loctite Corp. v. Ultraseal, Ltd.*, 781 F.2d 861, 870, 228 U.S.P.Q. 90, 96 (Fed. Cir. 1985)); *Charles Greiner & Co. v. Mari-Med Mfg., Inc.*, 962 F.2d 1031, 1036, 22 U.S.P.Q.2d 1526, 1529 (Fed. Cir. 1992) ("careful confinement of the doctrine of equivalents to its proper equitable role ... promotes certainty and clarity in determining the scope of patent rights"); *London v. Carson Pirie Scott & Co.*, 946 F.2d 1534, 1538, 20 U.S.P.Q.2d 1456, 1458 (Fed. Cir. 1991) ("this equitable doctrine evolved from a balancing of competing policies").

some extent the doctrine of equivalents...."). Moreover, the Supreme Court in *Graver Tank* credited the origin of the doctrine of equivalents to its own decision in *Winans v. Denmead* — a case at law, not equity. *See Graver Tank*, 339 U.S. at 608, 70 S. Ct. at 856; *Winans v. Denmead*, 56 U.S. (15 How.) at 338, 14 L. Ed. 717. Therefore, by its terms, *Graver Tank* did not impliedly transform a legal basis for recovery into an equitable one. In short, the Supreme Court's cases on the doctrine of equivalents foreclose a holding that the doctrine is a matter of equity to be applied at the court's discretion.

IV

In answer to the first question posed by this court en banc, a finding of infringement under the doctrine of equivalents requires proof of insubstantial differences between the claimed and accused products or processes. Often the function-way-result test will suffice to show the extent of the differences. In such cases, the parties will understandably focus on the evidence of function, way, and result, and the fact-finder will apply the doctrine based on that evidence. Other factors, however, such as evidence of copying or designing around, may also inform the test for infringement under the doctrine of equivalents. No judge can anticipate whether such other factors will arise in a given case. Instead, the presence of such factors will depend on the way the parties frame their arguments. Neither the Supreme Court nor this court limits the types of evidence that either party may proffer in support of a factor it considers probative of infringement under the doctrine. The trial judge, however, has a duty to decide whether the proffered evidence is relevant. This duty to assess relevance is no different in a doctrine of equivalents case than in any other type of case. Relevance will be self-evident to the judge in a case tried to the bench. In a jury trial, however, the judge must admit only relevant evidence, and instruct the jury to consider only the admitted evidence in reaching its decision.

In answer to the second question posed by this court en banc, infringement under the doctrine of equivalents is an issue of fact to be submitted to the jury in a jury trial with proper instructions, and to be decided by the judge in a bench trial. The answer to the third question posed by this court en banc necessarily flows from the answer to the second question. The trial judge does not have discretion to choose whether to apply the doctrine of equivalents when the record shows no literal infringement.

V

This court reviews a jury verdict on the fact question of infringement under the doctrine of equivalents for prejudicial error in the jury instructions, *Biodex Corp. v. Loredan Biomedical, Inc.*, 946 F.2d 850, 854, 20 U.S.P.Q.2d 1252, 1254 (Fed. Cir. 1991), *cert. denied*, 504 U.S. 980, 112 S. Ct. 2957, 119 L. Ed. 2d 579 (1992), and lack of substantial evidence supporting the verdict, *see Genentech*, 29 F.3d at 1565.

The sufficiency of jury instructions is not tested in a vacuum. "It is well established that [each] instruction 'may not be judged in artificial isolation,' but must be considered in the context of the ... trial record." *Estelle v. McGuire*, 502 U.S. 62, 72, 112 S. Ct. 475, 482, 116 L. Ed. 2d 385 (1991) (quoting *Cupp v. Naughten*, 414 U.S. 141, 147, 94 S. Ct. 396, 400, 38 L. Ed. 2d 368 (1973)); *see also Biodex*, 946 F.2d at 862. The words of the instructions take on meaning from the context of what happened at trial, including how the parties tried the case and their arguments to the jury. Accordingly, we must examine the trial context in which the jury instructions were given by the trial court.

Hilton Davis offered evidence of and argued function, way, and result in asserting the doctrine of equivalents. Warner-Jenkinson responded in kind. Warner-Jenkinson also offered evidence of independent development, contending repeatedly that its lack of knowledge of the '746 patent when it developed its ultrafiltration process excused it from infringement under the doctrine. In its appeal brief, Warner-Jenkinson summarized its interpretation of the doctrine of equivalents:

> [The doctrine of equivalents] is an equitable remedy available only upon a suitable showing of the equities. To demonstrate that the equities favor application of the doctrine, the patentee must put forth proof of the equities, and the trial court must find the type of conduct which triggers its application. *London v. Carson Pirie Scott & Co.*, [946 F.2d 1534, 1538, 20 U.S.P.Q.2d 1456, 1458 (Fed. Cir. 1991)]; *Charles Greiner & Co. v. Mari-Med Mfg., Inc.*, 962 F.2d 1031, 1035-36, 22 [U.S.P.Q.2d] 1526, 1529 (Fed. Cir. 1992). As an equitable remedy, the doctrine is an issue of law for the court, not the jury. Here, no equitable basis exists for the application of the doctrine. Warner-Jenkinson's processes were developed in cooperation with knowledgeable and experienced vendors in the field including Osmonics....

There was no copying or piracy. As noted, however, the doctrine of equivalents is not an equitable remedy available only on a showing of the equities. Lack of awareness of the patent or its disclosure does not excuse infringement. *Parker v. Hulme*, 18 F. Cas. at 1143. Accordingly, Warner-Jenkinson could not succeed in erecting an equitable defense to infringement.

In this context, the trial court instructed the jury about the doctrine of equivalents in terms of function, way, and result: You *may* find infringement under the doctrine of equivalents when the accused process and the claimed invention perform substantially the same function in substantially the same way to yield substantially the same result even though the processes differ in name, form or shape. (Emphasis added.) This formulation correctly stated that the jury "may" rely on the function-way-result test, recognizing that this test is often enough to show infringement under the doctrine. In particular, the trial court tailored its function-way-result instruction to the parties' reliance on evidence of function, way, and result in this case.

Moreover, the trial court's instructions correctly resisted Warner-Jenkinson's effort to erect an equitable threshold for application of the doctrine of equivalents. The doctrine of equivalents has no equitable or subjective component. The cases Warner-Jenkinson cites to the contrary — *London*, 946 F.2d at 1538, and *Charles Greiner*, 962 F.2d at 1035-36 — reaffirm that the *Graver Tank* objective criteria, as limited by prosecution history and prior art, confine the range of equivalents. These cases do not condition effective patent protection on proof of bad faith. Accidental or "innocent" infringement is still infringement. Intent becomes a requirement only if and when the patent owner seeks enhanced damages or attorney fees for willful infringement under 35 U.S.C. §§ 284-285. In this case, for example, the jury took Warner-Jenkinson's lack of intent into account when it found that Warner-Jenkinson did not willfully infringe. Therefore, under the trial court's instructions, Warner-Jenkinson's evidence of independent development played its proper role: it shielded Warner-Jenkinson from an enhanced damages award, but did not provide a basis for avoiding application of the doctrine. The evidence of independent development in this case, directed as it is only to the issue of whether the accused infringer acted with knowledge of the patent, is irrelevant to showing substantial differences. This court cannot fault the absence of any reference to such evidence in the jury instructions.

Under these circumstances, the trial court's function-way-result instruction correctly guided the jury to consider the relevant evidence. In a perfect world, the trial court might have provided further guidance — by instructing the jury, for instance, that Warner-Jenkinson's independent development was not an excuse to infringement. Nonetheless, the trial court's function-way-result instruction directed the jury to consider, in assessing infringement, the only evidence relevant to the substantiality of the differences that was offered at trial. Significantly, Warner-Jenkinson did not object to this instruction. Rather, Warner-Jenkinson objected to sending the doctrine of equivalents question to the jury at all, contending that independent development excused it from infringing.

The trial context left the jury to consider the evidence of function, way, and result presented by both parties, the only available evidence going to the substantiality of the differences. In the context of this trial, the instructions properly focused the jury on the evidence relevant to the doctrine of equivalents.

When a jury makes a finding on infringement under the doctrine of equivalents, this court will uphold that finding if supported by substantial evidence. *Genentech*, 29 F.3d at 1565. "It is not for this Court to even essay an independent evaluation of this evidence. This is the function of the trial court." *Graver Tank*, 339 U.S. at 611, 70 S. Ct. at 857. Thus, the next question is the sufficiency of the evidence to support the jury verdict.

The '746 claims recite a pH "from approximately 6.0 to 9.0." Warner-Jenkinson at times used a lower pH of 5.0. The claims also recite a pressure of "approximately 200 to 400 p.s.i.g." Warner-Jenkinson used a pressure somewhere in a range of 200 to nearly 500 p.s.i.g.

Substantial evidence supports the jury finding that Warner-Jenkinson's pH variation from the claimed approximate range was insubstantial. The claimed pH limitation prevents damage to the membrane and produces a neutral final dye product. Dr. Cook, one of the inventors, testified that a pH of 5 would have the same effect as a pH of 6, as would any pH above 2. Even Warner-Jenkinson's expert agreed that Hilton Davis' process would operate at a pH of 5. The record contains substantial evidence that one of skill in the art would know that performing ultrafiltration at a pH of 5 would allow the membrane to perform the same function, in an equivalent way, to achieve the same result as at a pH of approximately 6 to 9.

Substantial evidence also supports the jury finding that Warner-Jenkinson's pressure for some of its membranes was in the claimed range of approximately 200 to 400 p.s.i.g. Warner-Jenkinson argues for pressure measurement at the high pressure pump instead of at the membrane. Warner-Jenkinson's pressure at the high pressure pump may have been as high as nearly 500 p.s.i.g. The specification, however, defines the pressure as "applied to the upstream side of the membrane." The '746 patent, col. 6, lines 20-21. In any event, the record contains substantial evidence that Warner-Jenkinson's pressure performed the same function — forcing the solution through the membrane — in an equivalent way, to achieve the same result.

As for pore size, the trial record details the difficulty of measuring a membrane's exact pore size in light of variations in fluid and pressure conditions. The record contains considerable evidence, however, about the pore size necessary to separate dye molecules from smaller molecular impurities. The record thus includes substantial evidence that Warner-Jenkinson necessarily used membranes of the claimed "nominal pore diameter of 5 to 15 Angstroms" to accomplish ultrafiltration.

Nor does prosecution history estoppel preclude application of the doctrine of equivalents in this case. "Whenever prosecution history estoppel is invoked as a limitation to infringement under the doctrine of equivalents, 'a close examination must be made as to, not only what was surrendered, but also the reason for such a surrender.'" *Insta-Foam Prods., Inc. v. Universal Foam Sys., Inc.*, 906 F.2d 698, 703, 15 U.S.P.Q.2d 1295, 1298 (Fed. Cir. 1990) (quoting *Bayer AG v. Duphar Int'l Research B.V.*, 738 F.2d 1237, 1243, 222 U.S.P.Q. 649, 653 (Fed. Cir. 1984)). The inventors amended the '746 claims to recite "a pH from approximately 6.0 to 9.0" to avoid the disclosure in the Booth patent of an ultrafiltration process operating at a pH higher than 9. This amendment surrendered pHs above 9, but does not bar Hilton Davis from asserting equivalency to processes such as Warner-Jenkinson's operating sometimes at a pH below 6.

Warner-Jenkinson performed the process disclosed in the '746 patent — purifying dye by collecting relatively large dye molecules on the concentrate side of a membrane. Warner-Jenkinson did not use precisely the claimed process parameters, but the jury found the differences between Warner-Jenkinson's and the claimed processes insubstantial. The record contains substantial evidence support-ing this finding of infringement under the doctrine of equivalents.

VI

While agreeing that the substantiality of the differences between the claimed and accused products or processes is the ultimate question under the doctrine of equivalents, one dissent contends that "[t]he authority to exercise the unique remedy which is the doctrine of equivalents lies exclusively in courts of equity." This dissent argues that, because the Patent Act of 1952 does not expressly provide a general remedy for infringement under the doctrine of equivalents, the doctrine must be, like other judge-created extensions of inadequate legal reme-dies, purely equitable. This reasoning, however, is a sharp departure from a cen-tury of Supreme Court decisions issued under a stable statutory regime.

The Supreme Court has long held that the question of infringement, whether literal or by equivalents, is a question of fact for the jury if properly demanded. For example, in *Coupe v. Royer*, 155 U.S. 565, 15 S. Ct. 199, 39 L. Ed. 263 (1895), the Court faced an accused infringer's contention that the trial court had improperly instructed the jury to the plaintiff's advantage regarding the question of infringement under the doctrine of equivalents. Remanding the case for a new trial, the Court held that, despite the lack of a genuine issue of fact regarding either the proper construction of the patent claim or the nature of the accused device, the question of infringement under the doctrine presented a question requiring trial to the jury. *Id.* at 579-80, 15 S. Ct. at 205. In so holding, the Court merely followed its decision in *Winans v. Denmead*: "whether, in point of fact, the defendant's [devices] did copy the plaintiff's invention, in the sense above explained [i.e., by an equivalent], is a question for the jury." *Winans v. Denmead*, 56 U.S. (15 How.) at 344, 14 L. Ed. 717. Citations for this principle can, of course, be multiplied. *See, e.g., Royer v. Schultz Belting Co.*, 135 U.S. 319, 325, 10 S. Ct. 833, 835, 34 L. Ed. 214 (1890); *Tyler v. Boston*, 74 U.S. (7 Wall.) 327, 330-31, 19 L. Ed. 93 (1869)....

The dissent also suggests that Congress could have, but has not, included the doctrine of equivalents in the Patent Act of 1952, 35 U.S.C. §§ 1-376 (1988 & Supp. V 1993). According to this dissent, "[i]f Congress wanted to provide for [infringement by] equivalents to what is claimed, it knew how to do it." This argument suffers at least three fatal flaws. First, the statutory definition of infringement, which appears in 35 U.S.C. § 271(a), makes no reference to claims at all. Thus, the definition of infringement is at best equivocal on the question of infringement under the doctrine of equivalents. Second, the Supreme Court itself has noted that "§ 271(a) of the new Patent Code [of 1952], which defines 'infringement,' left intact the *entire* body of case law on direct infringement." *Aro Mfg. Co. v. Convertible Top Replacement Co.*, 365 U.S. 336, 342, 81 S. Ct. 599, 602, 5 L. Ed. 2d 592 (1961) (emphasis added). Thus, contrary to the dissent's inference that the Patent Act of 1952's silence repealed *Graver Tank* and its forebears, the Supreme Court in *Aro* states that section 271(a) left intact the doctrine of equivalents.

Third, and perhaps most importantly, infringement was defined and understood long before 1952. According to section 4 of the Patent Act of 1790, anyone who without authority "devise[d], ma[d]e, construct[ed], use[d], employ[ed], or vend[ed]" a patented invention was liable to the patentee for "such damages as shall be assessed by a jury." Patent Act of 1790, § 4, 1 Stat. at 111. Similarly, according to section 5 of the Patent Act of 1793, anyone who "ma[d]e, devise[d], and use[d], or s[old]" a patented invention was liable to the patentee for a sum "at least equal to three times the price, for which the patentee has usually sold or licensed to other persons, the use of said invention," a liability to be adjudicated in a legal, not equitable, "action on the case." Patent Act of 1793, ch. 11, § 5, 1 Stat. 318, 322. Section 14 of the Patent Act of 1836 simply provided for a legal "action for damages for making, using, or selling" a patented invention without authority. Patent Act of 1836, § 14, 5 Stat. at 123. Finally, section 59 of the Patent Act of 1870 simply provided "that damages for the infringement of any patent may be recovered by action on the case." Patent Act of 1870, § 59, 16 Stat. at 207. Against this stable backdrop of statutory definitions of infringement, definitions which are virtually indistinguishable from the current 35 U.S.C. § 271(a), the Supreme Court has recognized actions at law for recovery for infringement under the doctrine of equivalents since its *Winans v. Denmead* decision in 1854. In light of this authority, this court detects no basis to hold that the doctrine of equivalents was rendered extrastatutory and thus equitable by virtue of the silent repeal that the dissent finds in the Patent Act of 1952.

A separate dissent concurs in our conclusion that the function-way-result test is not "the" test for equivalents. This dissent, however, would prefer to treat the substantiality of the differences as "only one of the factors according to *Graver*, arguably the most important factor, which a court should consider in deciding whether to apply" the doctrine of equivalents. The Supreme Court, in our view, made the fundamental question "whether under the circumstances the change [in the accused product or process] was so insubstantial that ... invocation of the doctrine of equivalents [is] justified." *Graver Tank*, 339 U.S. at 610, 70 S. Ct. at 857.

A third dissent contends that "because we know what the claim means and we know what process parameters Warner-Jenkinson uses, the issue of infringement under the doctrine [of equivalents] ... resolves itself into one of law," reviewable de novo on appeal. The Supreme Court squarely renounced arrogation of the fact-finding function in *Graver Tank*, however, recognizing that an appellate court is not best qualified to assess the facts in a doctrine of equivalents case: A finding of equivalence is one of fact.... Like any other issue of fact, final determination requires a balancing of credibility, persuasiveness and weight of evidence. It is to be decided by the trial court [in a bench trial] and that court's decision, under general principles of appellate review, should not be disturbed unless clearly erroneous. *Particularly is this so in a field where so much depends upon familiar-*

ity with specific scientific problems and principles not usually contained in the general storehouse of knowledge and experience. Graver Tank, 339 U.S. at 609-10, 70 S. Ct. at 857 (emphasis added). In short, the Supreme Court settled the question of the standard of review in doctrine of equivalents cases, foreclosing the dissent's contention.

This dissent also argues for adoption of a new "legal limitation" on the doctrine of equivalents prohibiting "*enlargement of the claim.*" The rule against enlargement of claim scope during claim construction is well settled. *See, e.g., Keystone Bridge Co. v. Phoenix Iron Co.,* 95 U.S. 274, 278-79, 24 L. Ed. 344 (1877). This dissent errs, however, in arguing that application of the doctrine of equivalents enlarges the claim scope. Instead the doctrine of equivalents provides the same protection to the substance of the claim scope provided by the doctrine of literal infringement. As explained in *Graver Tank,* when there are no substantial differences between the claimed and accused products or processes, "they are the same" in the eyes of the patent law. *Graver Tank,* 339 U.S. at 608, 70 S. Ct. at 856 (quoting *Machine Co. v. Murphy,* 97 U.S. at 125, 24 L. Ed. 935). The rule against enlargement, although an essential tenet of claim construction, thus contributes nothing to the inquiry into infringement under the doctrine.

This dissent also purports to discern in some of the Supreme Court's decisions a second "legal limitation" on the doctrine of equivalents limiting "the range of infringing substitutions to those in which components were substituted which were known to be equivalents" when the patent issued. The dissent's analysis is flawed, however. The Court has recognized that post-issuance improvements can infringe under the doctrine. *See Sanitary Refrigerator,* 280 U.S. at 40-43, 50 S. Ct. at 12-13. Our cases have followed the same course. *See, e.g., Moleculon,* 872 F.2d at 409; *Hughes Aircraft Co. v. United States,* 717 F.2d 1351, 1365, 219 U.S.P.Q. 473, 483 (Fed. Cir. 1983). In *Graver Tank,* furthermore, the Court recognized the ingenuity of would-be pirates, who may always be expected to find new ways to avoid the literal scope of a patent claim:

> One who seeks to pirate an invention, like one who seeks to pirate a copyrighted book or play, may be expected to introduce minor variations to conceal and shelter the piracy. Outright and forthright duplication is a dull and very rare form of infringement.

Graver Tank, 339 U.S. at 607, 70 S. Ct. at 856. The doctrine "evolved in response to this experience," *id.* at 608, 70 S. Ct. at 856, and stands as a bulwark against such "insubstantial changes," *id.* at 607, 70 S. Ct. at 856. Limiting the range of potentially infringing substitutions to those known at the time of the patent's issuance would undermine the doctrine, denying patent owners protection of the substance of their inventions against new forms of infringement.

Finally, this third dissent takes issue with the jury's evaluation of the evidence and this court's refusal to apply prosecution history estoppel. *Graver Tank* bound this court only to review the jury's fact findings and not to rely on our indepen-

dent views. As has been demonstrated, each of the jury's fact findings is supported by substantial evidence. Therefore this court must affirm the jury's fact findings, regardless of what result this court might have reached had it been entrusted
with fact finding at trial. *See Lavender v. Kurn*, 327 U.S. 645, 653, 66 S. Ct.
740, 744, 90 L. Ed. 916 (1946).

As for prosecution history estoppel, as explained, this doctrine turns on the
reasons for claim amendments during prosecution. *Insta-Foam*, 906 F.2d at 703.
That the '746 inventors amended the claims to recite "a pH from approximately
6.0 to 9.0" to avoid the prior art disclosure of a process operating at a pH higher
than 9 does not bar Hilton Davis from asserting equivalency to Warner-Jenkinson's process sometimes operating at a pH below 6.

CONCLUSION

Substantial evidence supports the jury verdict of infringement under the
doctrine of equivalents. The judgment of the district court is affirmed.

PAULINE NEWMAN, CIRCUIT JUDGE, concurring.

The doctrine of equivalents has neither greatly excited the centers of legal
scholarship, nor seriously stirred action-oriented industry. Indeed, there remains
a telling silence on the part of the technology community, for or against. Despite
the controversial changes proposed in opinions of this court, there has been little
objective policy exploration, economic analysis, legislative proposal, or even a
search for consensus. There has, of course, been a good deal of speculation flowing from the inconsistency of our decisions.

The court today holds that no change is appropriate in the common law of
equivalency as developed by the Supreme Court. I join in that holding, for our
conclusion is in accord with precedent, and this en banc decision provides needed
repose: the proposed new test of a threshold "equity" determination has been laid
to rest, and the criteria of *Graver Tank* have been reaffirmed. Indeed, any change
in the legal and factual fundamentals so explicitly laid out by the Supreme Court
is beyond our judicial authority. I have, however, come to doubt that the doctrine
of equivalents is the best way to achieve the result for which it arose, and I
encourage the technology-user community to consider whether new procedures,
through the legislative process, may better serve the national interest.

Our decision, like every decision of patent principle, affects the national
interest in technologic innovation. I have sought to understand how that effect is
manifested in the doctrine of equivalents. In so doing I have taken an analytic
path not discussed by the court, albeit a path that I believe underlies the common
law of equivalency. This path has led me into the thicket of the sociology and
economics of patent law, for I have attempted to place the basic question — the
role and application of the doctrine of equivalents — into the practical context of
the purposes and workings of the patent system, as informed by modern scholarship.

Patent Claims

The juridical approach to equivalency began before patents contained "claims" in the detail in which they are now written, and did not change as claim style evolved. The Patent Act of 1836 required all patentees to state what was "claimed," a practice that was already the custom. *See* U.S. Patent Office, Information to Persons Having Business to Transact at the Patent Office (1836), reproduced in Karl Lutz, *Evolution of the Claims of U.S. Patents*, 20 J. Pat. Off. Soc'y 457, 464 (1938). The development of claim style[3] was guided by growing cadres of professional patent examiners and registered patent attorneys, along with the growth of prior art and competing technologies. Indeed, the increasing specificity in claim style probably made it easier for the "unscrupulous copyist," the words of *Graver Tank*, to appropriate the substance of the invention while evading the letter of the claims.

The public notice aspect of what the patentee "claims," upon interaction with the patent examiner and on consideration of the prior art, is a powerful argument for strict literal reading of claims, even if the result is injustice in particular cases. However, the patent system is of ever-increasing importance, due to the dependence of industry on technology, the reduced opportunity to rely on trade secrecy because of today's enlarged analytical capability, the ease and speed of imitation and modification once the innovator has shown the way, the harshness of modern competition, and the ever-present need for industrial incentives. These factors weigh on the side of the innovator, and thus favor a rule that tempers the rigor of literalness. *See Patlex Corp. v. Mossinghoff*, 758 F.2d 594, 599, 225 U.S.P.Q. 243, 247 (Fed. Cir.) ("encouragement of investment-based risk is the fundamental purpose of the patent grant"), *modified*, 771 F.2d 480, 226 U.S.P.Q. 985 (Fed. Cir. 1985).

The principle of equivalency thus serves a commercial purpose, as it adjusts the relationship between the originator and the second-comer who bore neither the burden of creation nor the risk of failure. However, there is also the major consideration of the progress of technology. How does the existence of a "doctrine" that transcends the statutory purpose of legal notice of the patent's scope affect that progress? Does the doctrine of equivalents affect the research, development, investment, and commercialization decisions of today's technologic industry, in a way that concerns the national interest?

And if not, what's all the fuss about?

Innovation and Equivalency

Despite our national dependence on technologic advance, there is a sparseness of practical study of whether and how the doctrine of equivalents affects modern industrial progress and the public welfare. However, a helpful debate is develop-

---

[3] The evolution from so-called "central" to "peripheral" claiming was gradual ....

ing among scholars, centered upon the optimum scope of patent claims. For example, Robert P. Merges and Richard R. Nelson, *On the Complex Economics of [Patent] Scope*, 90 Colum. L. Rev. 839 (1990), suggest that the optimum claim scope is that which will promote "competition in research"; while Edmund W. Kitch, *The Nature and Function of the Patent System*, 20 J.L. & Econ. 265, 275-80 (1977), suggests that since competition in research is inefficient, broad claims to the originator would provide optimum incentives and serve the larger social welfare. These analyses have drawn thoughtful commentary and further development. For example, touching on the complexity of the issue of equivalency in *Patent Law and Rent Dissipation*, 78 Va. L. Rev. 305, 348 (1992), Mark F. Grady and Jay I. Alexander write that the "doctrine of equivalents is really the method through which the extent of an invention's technological signal is established." These and other controversial theories aid our understanding, although practical implementation seems to be quite elusive, for determination of the national interest is as complex as the many forms of technology and the varied research and industrial strategies of their development....

Competition in research and development is important to the nation. There are important distinctions between competition in the research (inventing) stage and in commercial activity. Competition in research, however inefficient its economics, serves the advancement of knowledge in myriad ways. It is often observed that investment in commercialization tends to be more risk-sensitive than investment in research, apparently since the costs of product development and capital plant often dwarf the cost of making the invention. Yet industrial innovation is served by the patent system when the commercial investment is made. To the extent that the doctrine of equivalents enlarges the value of the patent to the innovator it also increases the net social value, as well as serving as a risk-reducing factor in commercial investment. The relevant economic theories on these points are varied, and the analyses are interesting. *See, e.g.*, Janusz A. Ordover, *Economic Foundations and Considerations in Protecting Industrial and Intellectual Property*, 53 Antitrust L.J. 503, 506-07 (1985) (discussing the effects on innovative efforts of competition in research and development).

The complexities of these relationships far exceed the highlights I have touched. On the present state of the law I have concluded that the doctrine of equivalents, on balance, serves the interest of justice and the public interest in the advancement of technology, by supporting the creativity of originators while requiring appropriators to adopt more than insubstantial technologic change.

Equivalency and Risk

Patent law provides rules of exclusion, priority, and competition that are understood by today's industrial enterprises. Whether from the viewpoint of the originator of technology or the appropriator, the impact of the doctrine of equivalents is as only one of many commercial uncertainties and possibilities. I doubt if much, or any, reliance is placed by originators on the doctrine of equivalents when specific investment decisions are made; at least not by those who have studied precedent. The effect of the doctrine of equivalents as an innovation incentive is more generalized, more subtle.

I believe that the major contribution of the doctrine of equivalents is now, and always has been, to the idea of a fairer, less technocratic, more practical patent system; one that is oriented toward encouraging technologic innovation and discouraging free riding; one that is not at the "mercy of verbalism," in the words of *Graver Tank*. In this way the doctrine of equivalents can contribute a degree of added investment confidence to the inherently risky environment of new technology. However, it will not serve that function if its application is so unpredictable that it cannot be relied upon. Indeed, the determination of technologic equivalency should be reasonably predictable by not only the innovator but also the competitor. When applied to a particular patented invention, it should be reasonably predictable whether a specific device will be found "equivalent." ...

Rethinking the Doctrine

....

Our decision today, while rejecting the proposed equitable considerations that would have added further uncertainty, does not answer the difficult question of improving the predictability and reducing the uncertainty of technologic decision-making. For this reason, I have wondered whether it may be possible to devise a better way to meet the needs now served by the doctrine of equivalents.

For example, the patent law places strong pressure on filing the patent application early in the development of the technology, often before the commercial embodiment is developed or all of the boundaries fully explored. Since the patentee is barred from enlarging the claims after two years from the date of issuance, later developments are excluded from the patent system unless they independently meet the criteria of patentability. From the originator's viewpoint, the inability to protect such developments may be a factor in recourse to the doctrine of equivalents. And from the viewpoint of the potential competitor, there is no opportunity to test possible encumbrances on later developments.

Most legal documents can be reformed, or amended, or supplemented. However, the available mechanisms for patent documents are extremely limited, for neither the reissue nor reexamination procedure permits adding to the disclosure. Thus some technologic variants can be reached only through litigation invoking the doctrine of equivalents. I invite creative thinking by the bar and technology communities, for if there were statutory procedures whereby patentees could protect their continuing work, there might be justification for limiting infringement to the literal scope of claims thus obtained.[4] A statutory system that could

---

[4] For example, some countries have handled the issue of continuing developments through a statutory form called a "patent of addition," a mechanism whereby a patentee can add additional disclosure and claims to a patent after it has issued.

accommodate the major factual scenarios of technologic equivalency could provide added certainty both to patentees and to those seeking to build on the subject matter of the patent. I commend the various suggestions already made in recent literature, for they start us on the path to a more useful mechanism for resolution of the question of technologic equivalency.

Summary

The patent law is directed to the public purposes of fostering technological progress, investment in research and development, capital formation, entrepreneurship, innovation, national strength, and international competitiveness. Our review of the doctrine of equivalents takes place in this context, not as an abstraction insulated from commercial reality. The questions before us are not simple. However, until the technology community provides a better answer, I know of no improvement upon the Court's holding that the doctrine of equivalents may be invoked when needed to "temper unsparing logic and prevent an infringer from stealing the benefit of an invention." *Graver Tank*, 339 U.S. at 608, 70 S. Ct. at 856, 85 U.S.P.Q. at 330 (quoting *Royal Typewriter Co. v. Remington Rand*, 168 F.2d 691, 692, 77 U.S.P.Q. 517, 518 (1948)).

PLAGER, CIRCUIT JUDGE, with whom CHIEF JUDGE ARCHER and CIRCUIT JUDGES RICH and LOURIE join, dissenting.

1

The court today tells us some important things about the doctrine of equivalents. We are told that application of the doctrine turns on one primary test: the substantiality of the differences between the claimed and accused products. The function-way-result test, so often recited since *Graver Tank* as the controlling test, is not "the" test. Rather, in assessing substantiality, other objective indicia may be considered, such as the known interchangeability of the accused and claimed elements by persons reasonably skilled in the art; whether there is evidence of intentional copying; and whether there is evidence of an attempt to design around the patented matter.

Function-way-result still plays a part, although exactly what that part is may seem obscure to some. That test, it is explained, arose in days of relatively simple mechanical technology. More sophisticated and innovative products may require more sophisticated analysis and thus different evidence, although it would appear that this depends as much on the lawyer and the judge as on the product: the trial judge will decide whether the additional evidence, if any, offered by the patentee is "relevant" to the case. Straight function-way-result turned out to be sufficient for the ultrafiltration through osmosis technology involved in this case.

The court also tells us that the burden is on the patentee to produce the necessary evidence of insubstantiality, and that these evidentiary questions are questions of fact.

Taken singly, most of these propositions are familiar. Packaged as they are, they may come as a revelation to many in the bar, as they no doubt do to the parties in this case. The court's statement that "[t]his case presents an opportunity to restate — not to revise — the test for infringement under the doctrine of equivalents" is difficult to take literally. What the court has given us is a recipe in which familiar ingredients are to be mixed in a different way, to produce what must be presumed to be a better product. But there is no reason to suppose that the new product will in fact be better. The mixing is still to be done in the dark, by the multiple hands of a jury under minimal instruction. When that product, an announced "yes, it infringes" or "no, it does not" arrives at this court, we will remain as blinded as we are now in our ability to pierce the doctrinal veil.

If we are to know where we are going with the doctrine of equivalents, we must know whence it came. The court denies that the doctrine has its roots in a court's traditional equity powers, but provides no substitute explanation for its origin. As a result, we are left with two major problems that are not satisfactorily resolved: what are the controlling bounds of the doctrine, and what are the proper respective roles of judge and jury....

By today's opinion, the majority essentially blesses the continued unfettered use of the doctrine of equivalents, at the discretion of a jury, noting that in some cases at least the ritual chant will be quite sufficient justification for a rewriting of the claimed limitations. This ignores the fact that, after 1870, claims, not their equivalents, are the determinants of the scope of protection granted by the patent. Claiming practice today serves a purpose which the earlier practice did not, namely providing competitors with notice of the precise invention that they may not make, use, or sell.

Another problem with the doctrine is that appellate review of many of these doctrine of equivalents cases is largely pro forma. Federal district judges, perhaps understandably, by and large make little pretense of liking these patent infringement cases, and are quite content to give them, and all the issues in them, to juries to decide. The cases typically come to us on appeal with nothing more than a general verdict finding infringement. There is no explanation by the jury of the rationale behind their verdict, if any exists. This case is a good example.

....

The legal rights established by a patent are defined by the claims. Competitors and other members of the public are entitled to rely on the scope of the claims set out in a patent, as the statute requires, and to design around the patentee's statutorily-protected rights. *Hoganas AB v. Dresser Indus., Inc.*, 9 F.3d 948, 951, 28 U.S.P.Q.2d 1936, 1939 (Fed. Cir. 1993) ("It would not be appropriate for us now to interpret the claim differently just to cure a drafting error.... That would unduly interfere with the function of claims in putting competitors on notice of the scope of the claimed invention."). In the famous nose of wax analogy, the Supreme Court in *White v. Dunbar*, 119 U.S. 47, 51-52, 7 S. Ct. 72, 74-75, 30 L. Ed. 303 (1886), said:

Some persons seem to suppose that a claim in a patent is like a nose of wax, which may be turned and twisted in any direction, by merely referring to the specification, so as to make it include something more than, or something different from, what its words express.... The claim is a statutory requirement, prescribed for the very purpose of making the patentee define precisely what his invention is; and it is unjust to the public, as well as an evasion of the law, to construe it in a manner different from the plain import of its terms. This has been so often expressed in the opinions of this court that it is unnecessary to pursue the subject further.

In most cases, if the claims do not literally apply to the allegedly infringing product, that should end the matter. But, when there is a wrong for which there is no adequate remedy at law, equity courts have traditionally gone beyond the law to impose a just and equitable result. Thus in those special cases in which the competitor's product is literally different but the difference is so insubstantial as to constitute a "fraud on the patent," a court in the exercise of its extraordinary equity power may extend the remedy of infringement in order to protect the rights of the patentee granted by law.

The power of courts of equity to deviate from the strict requirements of law is not without limits. Even in the interests of justice, courts of equity are not free to make unfettered and unreviewable decisions. They are as much subject to rules of law as are the law courts. Thomas Jefferson, arguing against giving federal courts broad equitable powers, said, "Relieve the judges from the rigour of text law, and permit them, with pretorian discretion, to wander into it's equity, and the whole legal system becomes incertain." 9 Papers of Thomas Jefferson 71 (J. Boyd ed. 1954).

....

There are several ways to address the anomalous situation of having had juries involved previously in the application of the doctrine of equivalents. We might acknowledge the existence of the past practice of giving the issue of the doctrine of equivalents to juries; declare that practice to be antithetical to the jurisprudential roots of the doctrine; and end the practice. As a follow-up, we could give useful guidance to trial judges on how to assess when a situation called for the special imposition of equity into the otherwise statutorily-defined infringement context. This guidance necessarily would emphasize the importance of keeping such matters as copying, independent discovery, and wrongful intent conceptually separate and distinct. Further experience with determining when and in what circumstances the doctrine is appropriately applied would no doubt refine and extend our understanding of these matters.

This would be a bold and clean solution to the matter. Though bold, it would not be radical, its roots being squarely in the great traditions of our courts going back centuries to the office of the King's Chancellor. It would overturn no established law, and would clarify much confusion emanating from the old cases. And it cannot be denied that it would make a major contribution to bringing rationality to this area of patent law.

A second though less bold alternative might be to share the responsibility for the doctrine between judge and jury. Trial judges would be instructed that it is their responsibility to determine when the differences between the patent claims and the allegedly infringing product are so insubstantial, and the circumstances so sufficiently special, as to warrant making the remedy afforded by the doctrine of equivalents available to a patentee. This determination would be independent of the question of whether the doctrine entitles the patentee to relief. That latter question, and the actual application of the doctrine using the function-way-result formula, would be left to the jury. Again, guidance could be given to trial judges on determining when those circumstances exist. This approach to the problem of judge and jury would have the effect of acknowledging the equitable basis for the doctrine, while preserving the historical practice of giving the function-way-result decision to the jury.

Under this alternative, the trial judge could make the determination at the beginning of the trial process, for example in response to a motion for partial summary judgment regarding the patentee's count alleging infringement under the doctrine of equivalents. Or, in an appropriate case, the trial judge could await presentation of the evidence so as to better understand the extent of the differences between the accused product and the claims, and then rule in response to a motion for judgment on that count. In either event, this court could require that on appeal there would be detailed findings of fact and conclusions of law to review, regardless of what the jury did under the function-way-result test.

[From the dissent by JUDGE NIES, in which CHIEF JUDGE ARCHER joined in parts, which chiefly advocates treating equivalents as a matter of law for the judge to decide:]

Nothing in *Graver II* [*supra*] warrants the finding of infringement in this case. The accused process does not substitute equivalents for each claim element. Hilton Davis set the range of equivalent pH and pressure values by the claim language "approximately 6.0 to 9.0" and "approximately 200 to 400 p.s.i.g." It was not proved that 5.0 is the equivalent to one of skill in the art of approximately 6.0 to 9.0 pH or 500 p.s.i.g. is similarly equivalent to approximately 200-400 p.s.i.g. Hilton Davis had no claiming difficulties as in *Graver*. There is no indication in the specification that the invention was broader than claimed. In any event, the patentee merely had to set wider ranges during prosecution (or within two years from issuance) if the claim language did not reflect his invention. The claim would then have been examined for patentability on that basis. Whether such a claim would have been allowed, we do not know and cannot speculate. Hilton Davis is bound by the ranges it specified.

Under controlling Supreme Court precedent, the standard for infringement under the doctrine includes the legal limitation that a claim may not be enlarged beyond what was allowed by the Patent Office....

As Warner-Jenkinson argues, it has been held liable without any possibility of notice that its process fell within the claims of the '746 patent. Claims must tell the public not only what it cannot do but also what it can do. *Permutit Co.*, 284 U.S. at 60, 52 S. Ct. at 55.

I would reverse the judgment of infringement.

NOTE

Administrative Solutions? The suggestion in Judge Newman's concurrence — that claims be modified only in an administrative proceeding — is attractive. Greater certainty of process and outcome might be expected. But note that unless notice of such a modification procedure were given immediately, competitors would still be at a loss to know that the claims of a patent might be changed by a legal tribunal.

CORNING GLASS WORKS v. SUMITOMO ELECTRIC U.S.A., INC.

868 F.2d 1251, 9 U.S.P.Q.2d 1962 (Fed. Cir. 1989)

NIES, CIRCUIT JUDGE.

Sumitomo Electric U.S.A., Inc. (SEUSA), Sumitomo Electric Industries, Ltd. (SEI), and Sumitomo Electric Research Triangle, Inc. (SERT), (collectively Sumitomo) appeal from the judgment of the United States District Court for the Southern District of New York (Connor, J.), holding Sumitomo liable for infringement of claims 1 and 2 of United States Patent No. 3,659,915 ('915) and claim 1 of United States Patent No. 3,884,550 ('550), all directed to the structure of optical waveguide fibers. On appeal, Sumitomo challenges the validity of both patents and the finding of infringement of the '915 patent by one of its accused products. We affirm the judgment in all respects.

General Technology

The inventions involved in this case relate to optical waveguide fibers of the type now widely used for telecommunications, such as long-distance telephone transmissions. Such fibers were developed as a medium for guiding the coherent light of a laser a distance suitable for optical communications.

It had long been known that light could be guided through a transparent medium that was surrounded by another medium having a lower refractive index (RI). A glass fiber surrounded by air, for example, will function as a conduit for light waves, because air has a lower RI than glass. To prevent scratches, imperfections, or foreign materials on the fiber surface from scattering light away from the fiber, glass fibers were cladded [i.e., wrapped, enclosed] with a glass layer having a lower RI. Before 1970, however, these glass-clad, glass-core fibers, referred to generally as "fiber optics," were capable of transmitting light of practical intensity only for very short distances due to high attenuation of the glass fibers then available. While suitable for illumination or for imaging systems, as in endoscopic probes, they could not be used for optical communications.

Another impediment to the use of conventional fiber optics for optical communications was the need that the fiber limit the transmitted light to preselected rays or "modes." In contrast, conventional fibers were designed to pass the maximum amount of incident light. The relatively large core diameter of conventional fibers permitted modes of light to enter the core over a fairly wide range of angles which, provided they entered at less than the critical angle, would be propagated along the fiber. Upon entering a fiber core, the light modes travel to the cladding and then back into the core, thus "bouncing" back and forth in a zig-zag path along the length of the fiber. The shallower the angle at which the modes enter the core, the less they will "bounce" and the sooner they will reach the receiving end of the fiber. When the number of modes are restricted, intelligibility of the information transmitted increases. The optimum restriction is achieved when only a single mode is transmitted, and by limiting the core diameter, that purpose is accomplished.

By the mid-1960's, worldwide efforts were ongoing to develop long-distance lightwave transmission capability. In particular, the British Post Office sought an optical waveguide with an attenuation of 20 db/km, the approximate transmission efficiency of the copper wire commonly used in telephone communications.

The '915 Invention

Corning's work on optical waveguides began in 1966, when it was contacted by the British Post Office. Drs. Robert D. Maurer and Peter C. Schultz, working at Corning, developed the world's first 20 db/km optical waveguide fiber by early 1970. That achievement was due, in part, to the development of a fiber with a pure fused silica cladding and a fused silica core containing approximately three percent by weight of titania as the dopant in the core. [Dopants are chemicals added to another material (here, fused silica) to alter one or more of its properties (here, the RI). The effect of the titania was to increase the RI of the core.] It was also due to the careful selection of the core diameter and the RI differential between the core and the cladding.

[The] announcement [of the invention] created enormous interest and was the subject of many articles in both technical and general publications. The inventors' advancement in technology won them accolades from various societies and institutes, for which they were presented with many prestigious awards and honors. In addition, the invention of the '915 patent has achieved impressive commercial success on a worldwide basis. The district court determined that "[t]he 915 patent clearly covers a basic, pioneering invention."

The '915 patent discloses a fused silica optical waveguide fiber capable of limiting the transmitted light to preselected modes for use in optical communication systems. Specifically, such a fiber is disclosed as having a doped fused silica core and a fused silica cladding (doping optional), wherein the RI of the core is greater than that of the cladding. Prior to the filing date of the application for the '915 patent, the inventors had experimented with dopants which increased the RI of fused silica, e.g. titania, and the '915 specification mentions only such positive dopant materials. At the time the application was filed, the inventors did not know of specific dopants that would decrease the RI of fused silica, although it had been known in the art since 1954 that the introduction of fluorine decreases the RI of certain multicomponent glasses.

The '550 Invention

Corning's titania-doped fibers required heat treatment to reduce attenuation to an acceptable level. An undesirable result of that treatment was a lowering of the mechanical strength of the fibers. Consequently, Corning sought to develop a low attenuation fiber which did not require heat treatment. In 1972, Drs. Maurer and Schultz found a solution in doping a fused silica core with germania, which also had the advantage of transmitting more light than using titania.

The '454 Invention

Corning recognized that when optical waveguide fibers were produced by flame hydrolysis, they contained hydroxyl ions. The residual hydroxyl ions absorbed light at certain wavelengths used in optical communications and, if they remained, would increase the attenuation of the fiber at those wavelengths. Working at Corning, Dr. Robert D. DeLuca invented a process to overcome this inherent problem by introducing a chlorine-containing drying atmosphere into the furnace during the [making of the fiber].

The infringement issue on appeal involves only Sumitomo's S-3 fibers which were found to infringe under the doctrine of equivalents.

The district court found that [the *Graver*] test for infringement was met, stating:

> Although fiber S-3 is not within the literal language of either claim 1 or 2 of the '915 patent, it performs substantially the same function in substantially the same way to obtain the same result as the optical waveguide fiber described in those claims of the '915 patent.

In the instant case, there is no dispute that the accused S-3 fiber performs substantially the same overall function to obtain the same overall result as the claimed invention. The question then is whether it does so in "substantially the same way." As stated in *Perkin Elmer Corp. v. Westinghouse Electric Corp.*:

> Perkin-Elmer's repeated assertions that the claimed and accused devices perform substantially the same function and achieve substantially the same end result are not helpful. That circumstance is commonplace when the devices are sold in competition. That a claimed invention and an accused

device may perform substantially the same function and may achieve the same result will not make the latter an infringement under the doctrine of equivalents where it performs the function and achieves the result in a substantially different way.

The accused S-3 fibers are optical waveguides as defined in the claims at issue in that the fibers have the differential in RI between core and cladding and the structural dimensions necessary for the preselection of particular modes of light waves. Thus, these limitations of claim 1 which are required by the preamble are met in the accused S-3 fibers. Also, there is no dispute over a literal reading of [the claim] on these fibers. Corning concedes, however, that all of the limitations of [the claim] do not literally read on the accused fibers. Although each claim limitation may not literally be found in the accused structure, the "substantially the same way" prong of the *Graver Tank* test is met if an equivalent of a recited limitation has been substituted in the accused device. Applying these principles, the district court found that the accused S-3 fibers infringed the '915 claims. In so ruling, the district court recognized that the claim limitation calling for addition of a dopant to the core was not literally met in the accused S-3 fibers. Nevertheless, the court found that the substitution of "fluorine ... dopant which negatively alters the index of refraction of fused silica [ ] in the cladding" equivalently met the limitation requiring the addition to the core of "a dopant which positively alters the index of refraction of fused silica."

Sumitomo alleges clear error in the court's finding of equivalency. Per Sumitomo, nothing was substituted in the core of the S-3 fiber for a dopant which performed the function of increasing the core's refractive index, and, therefore, "an element" required by the claim, namely, a doped core, is entirely missing. Sumitomo asserts, that where an element of a claim is entirely missing, there is no infringement. The premise on which Sumitomo relies, known as the "All Elements" rule, correctly states the law of this circuit adopted in banc in *Pennwalt. See Pennwalt* (infringement requires that each element of a claim or its substantial equivalent be found in the accused device). However, we do not agree that an "element" of the claim is entirely "missing" from the S-3 fibers.

Sumitomo's analysis illustrates the confusion sometimes encountered because of misunderstanding or misleading uses of the term "element" in discussing claims. "Element" may be used to mean a single limitation, but it has also been used to mean a series of limitations which, taken together, make up a component of the claimed invention. In the All Elements rule, "element" is used in the sense of a limitation of a claim. Sumitomo's analysis is faulty in that it would require equivalency in components, that is, the substitution of something in the core for the absent dopant. However, the determination of equivalency is not subject to such a rigid formula. An equivalent must be found for every limitation of the claim somewhere in an accused device, but not necessarily in a corresponding component, although that is generally the case.

Corning urges that the question of equivalency here is a narrow one: Is the substitution of a negative dopant in the cladding equivalent to a positive dopant in the core? When the limitations of [the claim] are analyzed individually, the accused S-3 fibers literally meet the limitation that the fiber be composed of a core of fused silica as well as the limitation that "the index of refraction [of the core] is of a value greater than the index of refraction of said cladding layer." The question of equivalency then does center on the part of the claim following the word "core," namely, "to which a dopant material ... has been added to a degree in excess of that of the cladding layer." If those limiting words are met equivalently, no "element," i.e., limitation, of the claim is missing.

This court has not set out in its precedent a definitive formula for determining equivalency between a required limitation or combination of limitations and what has been allegedly substituted therefor in the accused device. Nor do we propose to adopt one here. We note that the district court resolved the question by comparison of the function/way/result of the substitution with the function/way/result of the limitation in the context of the invention; that is, the court made a subsidiary analysis comparable to the overall function/way/result analysis mandated for determining infringement of the claim under the doctrine of equivalents. In particular, after explaining how the negative dopant of the S-3 fiber worked, it found:

> The use of fluorine as a [negative] dopant in the cladding thus performs substantially the same function in substantially the same way as the use of a [positive] dopant in the core to produce the same result of creating the refractive index differential between the core and cladding of the fiber which is necessary for the fiber to function as an optical waveguide.

The district court's "function/way/result" equivalency analysis with respect to a claim limitation appears to be a helpful way to approach the problem and entirely in accord with the analysis actually made in *Graver Tank*.

Finally, Sumitomo asserts that because the prior art, namely, United States Patent No. 3,320,114 (the Litton patent) teaches that a differential in the RI can be achieved between core and cladding in a fiber optic by negative doping of the cladding, Corning cannot assert equivalency between positive dopant in the core and negative dopant in the cladding. To do so, per Sumitomo, would "expan[d] the claim to encompass what was already in the public domain, i.e., a fiber with a pure undoped core." Contrary to Sumitomo's argument, the substitution of an ingredient known to be an equivalent to that required by the claim presents a classic example for a finding of infringement under the doctrine of equivalents. *Graver Tank*, 339 U.S. at 609 (important factor [in determining equivalency] is whether persons reasonably skilled in the art would have known of the interchangeability). Nothing is taken from the "public domain" when the issue of equivalency is directed to a limitation only, in contrast to the entirety of the claimed invention. This is such a case. The Litton patent teaches nothing about

optical waveguides. Thus, the finding of equivalency in the substitution of a
negative dopant in the cladding takes nothing from the "public domain."

We are unpersuaded the finding of equivalence is clearly erroneous. [Affirmed.]

NOTES

1. An Analogy. To understand the difference between the claimed invention
and the accused product, consider this example: a patent includes as an element
"the addition to boiling water of enough ice to bring the temperature of the
resulting mixture to just below boiling." Would an accused infringer who instead
heats water until just below the boiling point infringe — would the heated water
be "equivalent" to the boiling water cooled by ice?

2. What Is an Element (II)? *Pennwalt* reinforced the "All Elements Rule,"
and opened a controversy over the meaning of an element. (See notes following
Pennwalt for three views on the meaning of an element.) *Sumitomo* appears to
weigh in with a major modification of the strict All Elements Rule announced by
the *Pennwalt* majority — or at least that is how most observers view it.

To see why, recall this passage from the opinion:

> "Element" may be used to mean a single limitation, but it has also been
> used to mean a series of limitations which, taken together, make up a com-
> ponent of the claimed invention. In the All Elements rule, "element" is used
> in the sense of a limitation of a claim.... An equivalent must be found for
> every limitation of the claim somewhere in an accused device, but not
> necessarily in a corresponding component, although that is generally the
> case.

3. "Nested" Function/Way/Result Test. *Sumitomo* is also significant for its
addition to the function/way/result test. (Actually, as the court notes, it was
merely approving the approach taken by Judge Connor of the Southern District
of New York, a judge with long experience in patent cases.) The trial court
applied the *Graver Tank* test to the key element of the claimed invention — the
doped core of the fiber optic strand. In deciding whether the accused product's
positive doping of the cladding was equivalent to the claim element calling for
negative doping of the core, the district court employed what the Federal Circuit
called a "subsidiary" function/way/result test to an *individual element* or limitation — the doped fiber optic strand core. Thus, as one part of its overall analysis,
the district court asked whether the doping of the accused product's cladding
performed the same function to achieve the same result in the same way as the
negative doping of the claimed invention.

An interesting critique of this aspect of *Sumitomo* appears in Player, *Elemental
Equivalence: Interpreting "Substantially the Same Way" Under Pennwalt after*

Corning Glass, 71 J. PAT. & TRADEMARK OFF. SOC'Y 546, 552, 553 (1989).
Player argues:

> The District Court's reasoning confused function with result and led to a conclusion that merely begged the question, i.e., the District Court reasoned as follows:
>
> > (1) the same result was obtained, but it was necessary to determine if the result was obtained "in the same way";
> >
> > (2) to determine if the result was obtained "in the same way," it was necessary to determine if the substituted element was the equivalent of the claim element;
> >
> > (3) the element substituted for the claim element was an equivalent because the result obtained was the same.
>
> Since the function of the negative dopant was the opposite of the positive dopant it is hard to understand how the negative dopant in the S-3 fiber could have been considered to perform "substantially the same function" as the positive dopant in the claimed invention, although the end result achieved was the same.

4. *Background Reading.* For background on the business context of Corning's patent litigation, see *Corning to Get $25 Million in Suit*, N.Y. TIMES, Dec. 6, 1989, p. D5, col. 1; Pechter, *Corning Boosts Fiber Output Capacity and Designs Tougher Fiberoptic Cable*, WALL ST. J., Mar. 20, 1990, p. A4, cols. 1-2.

5. *Comparative Equivalence.* Foreign patent systems have concepts similar to our doctrine of equivalents. *See, e.g., Handle Cord for Battery* case, German Fed. Sup. Ct., Oct. 3, 1989, *reprinted at* 22 INT'L REV. INDUS. PROP. & COPYRIGHT L. 104, 106, 107 (1991) (Under European Patent Convention article 69, judge must balance, in "equivalents" case, reasonable reward to inventor against certainty to others in the field; even if accused device is outside literal scope of patentee's claims, embodiment infringes if one skilled in the art could identify equivalent means "as being equally effective in the solution of the problem underlying the invention" — akin to *Graver Tank* interchangeability standard). But some have criticized the effectiveness of patents in foreign systems, in part because of weak infringement doctrines. *See* Hideo Ozaki, *How Can a Patent Be Successfully Enforced in Japan?*, PAT. WORLD, Mar. 1991, at 36 (although many infringement cases brought in Japan, there were only 21 reported decisions from district courts in 1989; "Out of the 21 aforementioned cases, infringement was found in only four; in the remaining 17, the court decided that there was no infringement. This is suggestive of a general climate of patent litigation in Japan where enforcement of patent through a court is not an easy task.").

1. THE EFFECT OF PRIOR ART

WILSON SPORTING GOODS CO. v. DAVID GEOFFREY & ASSOCIATES

904 F.2d 677, 14 U.S.P.Q.2d 1942 (Fed. Cir. 1990),
cert. denied, 111 S. Ct. 537 (1990)

RICH, CIRCUIT JUDGE.

These appeals, consolidated by agreement, are from two actions brought by Wilson Sporting Goods Co. (Wilson) [against defendants David Geoffrey & Associates, Dunlop, et al., collectively called "Dunlop"] for infringement of United States Patent 4,560,168 ('168), entitled "Golf Ball." Trial was before a United States Magistrate by consent[, who, with the aid of a jury, found the patent infringed]. We reverse in part and vacate in part each judgment.

Wilson is a full-line sporting goods company and is one of about six major competitors in the golf ball business. Among its well-known balls are the Pro-Staff and Ultra. Dunlop is also a major player in the golf ball business. It competes head-to-head with Wilson by selling the Maxfli Tour Limited and Slazenger balls.

Wilson accused Dunlop of infringing claims 1, 7, 15-16, and 19-22 of its '168 patent.

For more than a century, golfers have been searching for a "longer" ball. As one of the parties put it, "distance sells." Inventors have experimented with numerous aspects of ball design over the years, but as United States Golf Association (U.S.G.A.) rules began to strictly control ball size, weight, and other parameters, inventors focused their efforts on the "dimples" in the ball's surface. According to one witness, new dimple designs provide the only real opportunity for increasing distance within the confines of U.S.G.A. rules.

Dimples create surface turbulence around a flying ball, lessening drag and increasing lift. In lay terms, they make the ball fly higher and farther. While this much is clear, "dimple science" is otherwise quite complicated and inexact: dimples can be numerous or few, and can vary as to shape, width, depth, location, and more.

Wilson's '168 patent claims a certain configuration of dimples on a golf ball cover. The shape and width of the dimples in the '168 patent is for the most part immaterial. What is critical is their location on the ball. The goal is to create a more symmetrical distribution of dimples.

Generally speaking, the dimples in the patent are arranged by dividing the cover of a spherical golf ball into 80 imaginary spherical triangles and then placing the dimples (typically several hundred) into strategic locations in the triangles. The triangles are constructed as follows. First, the ball is divided into an imaginary "icosahedron," as shown in Figure [8-3, top left]. An icosahedral golf ball is completely covered by 20 imaginary equilateral triangles, 5 of which cover each pole of the ball and ten of which surround its equator. Second, the midpoints of each of the sides of each of the 20 icosahedral triangles are located, as shown in Figure [8-3, top middle]. Third, the midpoints are joined, thus subdividing each icosahedral triangle into four smaller triangles. [From footnote: The central sub-triangles are referred to in the patent claims as "central triangles" (we have labeled one "A" [in Figure 8-3, top right]), whereas the three sub-triangles surrounding each central triangle are referred to as "apical triangles." The latter are so named because each of them contains an apex or tip of the larger icosahedral triangle.]

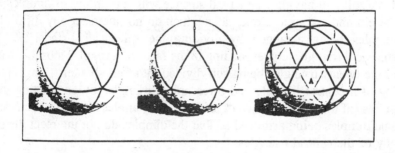

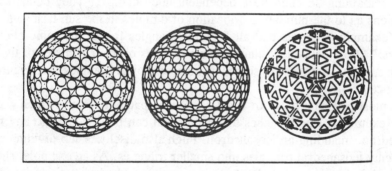

Figure 8-3

The resulting 80 imaginary triangles are shown in Figure [8-3, top right]. Critically important are the light lines which join the midpoints. As can be seen from Figure 3, they form the arcs of circles which pass completely around the widest part of the ball. There are six such circles, referred to in the patent as "great circles."

All of the claims of the '168 patent require this basic golf ball having eighty sub-triangles and six great circles. Particular claims require variations on the placement of dimples in the triangles, with one common theme — the dimples must be arranged on the surface of the ball so that no dimple intersects any great circle. Equivalently stated, the dimples must be arranged on the surface of the ball so that no dimple intersects the side of any central triangle. See Figure [8-3, bottom left], below. When the dimples are arranged in this manner, the ball has six axes of symmetry, compared to prior balls which had only one axis of symmetry.

Wilson employee Steven Aoyama filed his patent application on April 27, 1984. Twenty seven claims were presented. All were allowed on the first action without comment by the examiner. The patent issued on December 24, 1985, to Wilson as assignee of Aoyama.

Claim 1, the only independent claim, reads:

> 1. A golf ball having a spherical surface with a plurality of dimples formed therein and six great circle paths which do not intersect any di[m]ples, the dimples being arranged by dividing the spherical surface into twenty spherical triangles corresponding to the faces of a regular icosahedron, each of the twenty triangles being sub-divided into four smaller triangles consisting of a central triangle and three apical triangles by connecting the midpoints [of the sides] of each of said twenty triangles along great circle paths, said dimples being arranged so that the dimples do not intersect the sides of any of the central triangles.

[Bracketed insertions ours.]

The remaining 26 claims are dependent upon claim 1. They contain further limitations as to the number and location of dimples in the sub-triangles. Claim 7, for example, requires that all "central triangles [have] the same number of dimples." Other dependent claims locate dimples on the perimeter of the apical triangles, so that dimples are shared by adjacent apical triangles. See Figure [8-3, bottom center].

The most pertinent prior art is a 1932 British patent to Pugh, which was cited by the examiner. Pugh teaches that a golf ball can be divided into any regular polyhedron, including an icosahedron. Pugh also discloses sub-dividing each of the twenty icosahedral triangles into smaller triangles. As an example, shown in Figure [8-3, bottom right], Pugh divides each icosahedral triangle into sixteen sub-triangles, in contrast to the four sub-triangles required by the '168 patent. (The dimples in Pugh are triangular.)

Nonetheless, Pugh's sixteen sub-triangles are merely further divisions of four larger sub-triangles. Claim 3 of Pugh explains his invention (our emphasis):

> 3. A method of distributing a pattern with substantial uniformity over the surface of a sphere, such as a golf ball, which consists in ... form[ing] equilateral triangles in the case of the ... *icosahedron* ..., dividing the sides of the triangles so found into the same number of equal or substantially equal parts and finally *joining corresponding points in each pair of sides of each triangle by a series of arcs of great circles*, substantially as described.

The prior art also includes several patents to Uniroyal and a Uniroyal golf ball sold in the 1970's. The Uniroyal ball is an icosahedral ball having six great circles with 30 or more dimples intersecting the great circles by about 12-15 thousandths of an inch. We discuss it extensively below.

There are four accused products, all of which the jury found to infringe.

The accused balls (collectively "Dunlop's balls") have dimples which are arranged in an icosahedral pattern having six great circles, but the six great circles are not dimple-free as the claims literally require.

The only theory of liability presented to the jury by Wilson was infringement under the doctrine of equivalents. Dunlop's argument for reversal is straightforward. It contends that there is no principled difference between the balls which the jury found to infringe and the prior art Uniroyal ball; thus to allow the patent to reach Dunlop's balls under the doctrine of equivalents would improperly ensnare the prior art Uniroyal ball as well.

Infringement may be found under the doctrine of equivalents if an accused product "performs substantially the same overall function or work, in substantially the same way, to obtain substantially the same overall result as the claimed invention." *Pennwalt.* Even if this test is met, however, there can be no infringement if the asserted scope of equivalency of what is literally claimed would encompass the prior art. *Id.*; *Senmed, Inc. v. Richard-Allan Medical Indus.*, 888 F.2d 815, 821, 12 U.S.P.Q.2d 1508, 1513 (Fed. Cir. 1989). This issue — whether an asserted range of equivalents would cover what is already in the public domain — is one of law, which we review de novo, but we presume that the jury resolved underlying evidentiary conflicts in Wilson's favor.

This court on occasion has characterized claims as being "expanded" or "broadened" under the doctrine of equivalents. Precisely speaking, these characterizations are inaccurate. To say that the doctrine of equivalents extends or expands the claims is a contradiction in terms. The claims — i.e., the scope of patent protection as defined by the claims — remain the same and application of the doctrine expands the right to exclude to "equivalents" of what is claimed.

The doctrine of equivalents, by definition, involves going beyond any permissible interpretation of the claim language; i.e., it involves determining whether the accused product is "equivalent" to what is described by the claim language.

This distinction raises an interesting question: If the doctrine of equivalents does not involve expanding the claims, why should the prior art be a limitation on the range of permissible equivalents? It is not because we construe claims narrowly if necessary to sustain their validity. As we have said, the doctrine of equivalents does not involve expansion of the claims. Nor is it because to hold otherwise would allow the patentee to preempt a product that was in the public domain prior to the invention. The accused products here, as in most infringement cases, were never "in the public domain." They were developed long after the invention and differ in several respects from the prior art.

The answer is that a patentee should not be able to obtain, under the doctrine of equivalents, coverage which he could not lawfully have obtained from the PTO by literal claims. The doctrine of equivalents exists to prevent a fraud on a patent, *Graver Tank & Mfg. Co.*, not to give a patentee something which he could not lawfully have obtained from the PTO had he tried. Thus, since prior art always limits what an inventor could have claimed, it limits the range of permissible equivalents of a claim.

Whether prior art restricts the range of equivalents of what is literally claimed can be a difficult question to answer. To simplify analysis and bring the issue onto familiar turf, it may be helpful to conceptualize the limitation on the scope of equivalents by visualizing a hypothetical patent claim, sufficient in scope to literally cover the accused product. The pertinent question then becomes whether that hypothetical claim could have been allowed by the PTO over the prior art. If not, then it would be improper to permit the patentee to obtain that coverage in an infringement suit under the doctrine of equivalents. If the hypothetical claim could have been allowed, then prior art is not a bar to infringement under the doctrine of equivalents.

Viewing the issue in this manner allows use of traditional patentability rules and permits a more precise analysis than determining whether an accused product (which has no claim limitations on which to focus) would have been obvious in view of the prior art. In fact, the utility of this hypothetical broader claim may explain why "expanded claim" phraseology, which we now abandon, had crept into our jurisprudence. Finally, it reminds us that Wilson is seeking patent coverage beyond the limits considered by the PTO examiner.

In this context it is important to remember that the burden is on Wilson to prove that the range of equivalents which it seeks would not ensnare the prior art Uniroyal ball. The patent owner has always borne the burden of proving infringement, and there is no logical reason why that burden should shift to the accused infringer simply because infringement in this context might require an inquiry into the patentability of a hypothetical claim. Any other approach would ignore the realities of what happens in the PTO and violate established patent law. Leaving this burden on Wilson does not, of course, in any way undermine the presumed validity of Wilson's actual patent claims. In the present situation, Wilson's claims will remain valid whether or not Wilson persuades us that it is entitled to the range of equivalents sought here.

The specific question before us, then, is whether Wilson has proved that a hypothetical claim, similar to claim 1 but broad enough to literally cover Dunlop's balls, could have been patentable. As we have explained above, Dunlop's balls are icosahedral balls with six great circles, five of which are intersected by dimples. The balls contain 432 to 480 dimples, 60 of which intersect great circles in amounts from 4 to 9 thousandths of an inch. In order for a hypothetical claim to cover Dunlop's balls, its limitations must permit 60 dimples to intersect the great circles by at least 9 thousandths of an inch. Thus, the issue is whether a hypothetical claim directed to an icosahedral ball having six great circles intersected by 60 dimples in amounts up to 9 thousandths of an inch could have been patentable in view of the prior art Uniroyal ball.

On the Uniroyal ball, the extent to which the dimples intersect the great circles is from 12 to 15 thousandths of an inch. Stated as a percentage of dimple radius, the intersection permitted in the hypothetical claim is 13% or less, and the dimples on the Uniroyal ball intersect by 17% to 21%. The number of dimples which intersect the great circles is also similar for the hypothetical claim and the prior art Uniroyal ball. The pertinent hypothetical claim limitation reads on any ball having 60 or less intersecting dimples. This limitation reads on the prior art Uniroyal ball, which has 30 intersecting dimples. If viewed in relative terms, the hypothetical claim limitation reads on any ball which has less than 14% of its dimples intersecting great circles. Roughly 12% of the dimples on the Uniroyal ball intersect great circles.

We hold that these differences are so slight and relatively minor that the hypothetical claim — which permits twice as many intersecting dimples, but with slightly smaller intersections — viewed as a whole would have been obvious in view of the Uniroyal ball. As Dunlop puts it, there is simply "no principled difference" between the hypothetical claim and the prior art Uniroyal ball. Accordingly, Wilson's claim 1 cannot be given a range of equivalents broad enough to encompass the accused Dunlop balls.

Before separately analyzing the asserted dependent claims, we should first explain why we are bothering to do so. This court has stated: "It is axiomatic that dependent claims cannot be found infringed unless the claims from which they depend have been found to have been infringed." While this proposition is no doubt generally correct, it does not apply in the circumstances of this case.

Here, we have reversed the judgment of infringement of independent claim 1 solely because the asserted range of equivalents of the claim limitations would encompass the prior art Uniroyal ball. The dependent claims, of course, are *narrower* than claim 1; therefore, it does not automatically follow that the ranges of equivalents of these narrower claims would encompass the prior art, because of their added limitations. We have considered each asserted dependent claim and conclude that none could be given a range of equivalents broad enough to encompass Dunlop's balls because that would extend Wilson's patent protection beyond hypothetical claims it could lawfully have obtained from the PTO. [Reversed in part, vacated in part.]

NOTES

1. *Applying the Test.* The *Wilson Sporting Goods* "hypothetical claim" test has now been applied in several cases. In *Key Mfg. Group, Inc. v. Microdot, Inc.*, 925 F.2d 1444, 17 U.S.P.Q.2d (BNA) 1806 (Fed. Cir. 1991), Judge Rader wrote for the court:

Microdot's structure is described in the prior art, specifically in [several] patents. While not obligatory in every doctrine of equivalents determination, the hypothetical claim rationale of *Wilson Sporting Goods Co.* helps define the limits imposed by prior art on the range of equivalents. The Wilson hypothetical claim analysis does not envision application of a full-blown patentability analysis to a hypothetical claim. Wilson simply acknowledges that prior art limits the coverage available under the doctrine of equivalents.

A range of equivalents may not embrace inventions already disclosed by prior art. A hypothetical claim drawn to cover literally the Microdot nut would not be patentable over the prior art. The [prior art] patents would make the [claimed] Microdot nut obvious. Contrary to Key's assertion, no single prior art reference need include each element of the hypothetical claim. The question under Wilson is whether the hypothetical claim "could have been allowed by the PTO over the prior art." Because the Microdot nuts and, thus the hypothetical claim, are obvious in light of these three prior art references, the doctrine of equivalents does not reach the accused nuts.

In *We Care, Inc. v. Ultramark Int'l Corp.*, 930 F.2d 1567, 18 U.S.P.Q.2d (BNA) 1562 (Fed. Cir. 1991), the Federal Circuit stated:

Although We Care could not show literal infringement, the court determined that We Care would likely be able to prove that the SHOCK BLOCK device infringed the '916 patent under the doctrine of equivalents. In applying this doctrine, however, we are convinced that the district court erred in not adequately considering whether the range of equivalents sought by We Care for the '916 patent would "ensnare the prior art." *Wilson Sporting Goods Co*. Ultra-Mark contended in the district court that the '916 patent claims could not obtain a range of equivalents covering Ultra-Mark's device without also covering one or more prior art devices. As a result, the court considered whether claims of the '916 patent, "extend[ed]" by the doctrine of equivalents broadly enough to read on the [accused] device, would have been anticipated by the prior art. This analysis was performed in connection with the court's validity analysis. The district court concluded that every element of independent claim 1 of the '916 patent, as "extend[ed]" by the doctrine of equivalents, was not identically disclosed by any one of the eight relevant prior art patents for electrical outlet covers. [But] [t]he district court's analysis did not go far enough. The court failed to consider whether the teachings of [the prior art] would have made obvious the range of equivalents afforded the '916 claims. On the record before us, we cannot determine what the eight cited prior art patents teach or whether, based on those teachings, claims broad enough to encompass the [accused] device would have been obvious. Accordingly, we vacate the preliminary injunction and remand the case to the district court to determine whether the range of equivalents sought by We Care encroaches upon the prior art.

2. Reaction to Wilson. Like any new test, the one proposed by Judge Rich in *Wilson* has been subjected to scrutiny, as well as a certain degree of criticism. *See, e.g.*, Parker, *Doctrine of Equivalents Analysis after Wilson Sporting Goods: The Hypothetical Claim Hydra*, 18 AM. INTELL. PROP. L. ASS'N Q.J. 262 (1990) (arguing that presentation to jury of "hypothetical claim" during infringement stage will complicate matters and confuse the jury because of the subsequent presentation regarding the actual claim during the validity stage of the trial). *Cf.* [Judge] Rich, *Interpretation of Claims and Extent of Protection — American Perspectives*, 21 INT'L REV. IND. PROP. & COPYRIGHT L. 497 (1990) (describing *Wilson* test).

2. PROSECUTION HISTORY ESTOPPEL

EXHIBIT SUPPLY CO. v. ACE PATENTS CORP.
315 U.S. 126 (1942)

Respondent began the present litigation against the respective petitioners for infringement of the Nelson Patent No. 2,109,678 of March 1, 1938, for a "contact switch for ball rolling games." The defenses [included] non-infringement and a file wrapper estoppel. [T]he Seventh Circuit held Claim 4 of the patent valid and infringed.

We granted certiorari on a petition which challenged only the decree of infringement below, on the ground that it enlarged the scope of the patent as defined by the claim, by resort to the doctrine of equivalents, and that Nelson, the patentee, by the amendment of his claims in the Patent Office, had surrendered Claim 4 so far as it would otherwise read upon the alleged infringing devices.

The patent relates to the structure of a resilient switch or circuit closer, so disposed on the board of a game table as to serve as a target which, when struck by a freely rolling ball, will momentarily close an electrical circuit. [See Figure 8-4.] Specifications and drawings disclose a target or switch comprising a conductor standard [Figure 8-4, element 11] mounted in the table and carrying a coil spring [18] having a leg [19] pendantly disposed in a conductor ring [i.e., the cup-shaped hole, 23] located in the table and slightly offset from the standard. The standard and ring are wired in a circuit with a relay coil and a source of electrical energy. When a ball rolling on the table bumps the coil spring from any direction, the leg of the spring is deflected momentarily bringing it into contact with the ring [i.e., 19 hits 23], so as to close the circuit for operating the relay coil and any connected auxiliary game device. Any desired number of targets may be placed on the board in a suitably spaced relationship; in pin ball games a single ball may successively bump and close a number of the switch devices.

The prior art as disclosed by the record shows no device in which the coil spring serves both as a target and a switch. The advantages of the device are said to be that the combination is peculiarly adapted to use in pin ball games; that the coil spring structure is so organized as to form both a switch for operating auxiliary recording or signalling devices and a target which is accessible from any direction.

Claim 4 claims as the elements of the invention the conductor standard anchored in the table, the coil spring surrounding the standard which carries the spring pendantly from its top, with the spring spaced from the standard to enable the

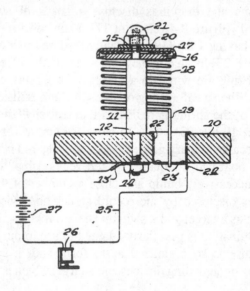

Figure 8-4

spring to be resiliently flexed, "and conductor means in said circuit and embedded in the table at a point spaced from the standard and engageable by a portion of the spring when it is flexed to close the aforementioned circuit."

The six devices alleged to infringe the patent differ from the particular claim of the invention described in the specifications, only in the specific form and method of supporting the "conductor means" which is "engageable by a portion of the spring when it is flexed." [The Court goes on to state that the accused devices generally have conductors which are suspended *above* the pinball table.]

Comparison of the several accused devices shows that in all but [two] the conductor means complementary to the coil spring is not embedded in the table, but is supported by an insulated plate resting on the table or an insulating core held in position by the standard.

Petitioners insist that respondent is estopped to assert infringement by the file wrapper record in the Patent Office and in any event that estoppel can be avoided and infringement established only by resort to the doctrine of equivalents, which they assert is incompatible with the statutory requirements for the grant of a patent and with the doctrine that the patent claims measure the patented invention.

The file wrapper history, so far as now relevant, relates to Claim 4 now in issue. The original Claim with its amendments is set forth as follows: (Matter added by amendment in parenthesis; matter stricken in italics and underscored.)

(4). In a ball rolling game having a substantially horizontal table over which balls are rollable, the combination with said table of a substantially vertical standard anchored in said table with its lower end carrying on the underside of the table a lead for an electric circuit and its upper end extending a substantial distance above the top surface of the table, a coil spring surrounding the standard, means carrying said spring pendantly from the upper portion of the standard (ABOVE THE TABLE) with the coils of the spring spaced from the standard *and the lower end of the coil spring terminating at a distance above the top surface of the table* to enable the spring to be resiliently flexed when bumped by a ball rolling on the table, said spring being in the aforementioned circuit and constituting a conductor, and *other* conductor means (IN SAID CIRCUIT AND EMBEDDED IN) *carried by* the table at a point spaced from the standard and engageable by a portion of the spring when it is flexed to close the aforementioned circuit.

The original application contained six claims, all of which the examiner rejected because he thought no patentable significance had been shown. The inventor submitted certain amendments, and two new claims, and induced the examiner to reconsider the patentability of the invention. Four of the claims were then allowed, but the examiner rejected Claim [4] as failing to claim the invention. He said:

It is old in the art to make an electrical contact by flexing a coil spring as shown by the art already cited in the case. In order to distinguish over the references therefor, the applicant's particular type of contact structure, comprising an extension to the coil spring adapted to engage an annular [i.e., ring-shaped] contact embedded in the table, must appear in the claims....

Applicant rejected the examiner's suggestion that the "contact structure" be adapted to engage "an annular contact embedded in the table." Instead he cancelled "other" from the claim and substituted for "carried by" the phrase, "in said circuit and enbedded in," saying Claim [4] has been "significantly amended" "to define the complementary conductor contact as being embedded in the table." He added that "it is too far to go to state that the specific leg 19 must be defined," and "the allowed claims can it seems, be very simply avoided by taking the leg 19, separating it from the spring 18 and embedding it as a pin in the table so that the spring when flexed would contact the pin.... Claim 7 covers such alternative form and ... in justice to applicant ... should be allowed."

The examiner in reply recognized as "true" applicant's suggestion that if the leg pendant from the spring "were removed from the spring and embedded in the table an operative device would result," but pointed out that the device claimed by the amendment "would be inoperative as the coil spring could not both terminate at a distance above the table and extend into a ferrule embedded therein." Thereupon the applicant added to the claim the words "above the table" and cancelled the phrase, "and the lower end of the coil spring terminating at a distance above the top surface of the table." The claim as amended was then allowed as Claim 4.

The claim before amendment plainly read on [two of] plaintiff's [products] in which the nail or pin conductor is driven into the table, since the nail or pin is a "conductor means carried by the table" "engageable by a portion of the spring when flexed." The claim thus read is for an operative device since the nail or pin projects above the table and may be engaged by the coil spring similarly located. The claim, as amended and allowed as Claim 4, likewise reads on [two of] plaintiff's [embodiments] if the nail or pin conductor which is driven into the table is "embedded in the table."

Petitioners do not seriously assert here that it is not so embedded. [T]he patentee by amending the claim so as to define the conductor means as embedded in the table did not exclude from the amended claim devices [of this sort] and they must be deemed to be infringements.

There remains the question whether respondent may rely upon the doctrine of equivalents to establish infringement by the four other accused devices. Respondent concedes that the conductor means in the four devices are not literally "embedded in the table," but insists that the changes in structure which they exhibit over that of plaintiffs' [devices] are but the mechanical equivalents of the "conductor means embedded in the table" called for by the amended claim, and so are entitled to the protection afforded by the doctrine of equivalents. Petitioners do not seriously urge that the conductor means in the four accused devices are not mechanical equivalents of the conductor means embedded in the table which the patent claims. Instead they argue that the doctrine should be discarded because it does not satisfy the demands of the statute that the patent shall describe the invention. R.S. § 4888, 35 U.S.C. § 33.

We do not find it necessary to resolve these contentions here. Whatever may be the appropriate scope and application of the doctrine of equivalents, where a claim is allowed without a restrictive amendment, it has long been settled that recourse may not be had to that doctrine to recapture claims which the patentee has surrendered by amendment.

Assuming that the patentee would have been entitled to equivalents embracing the accused devices had he originally claimed a "conductor means embedded in the table," a very different issue is presented when the applicant in order to meet objections in the Patent Office, based on references to the prior art, adopted the phrase as a substitute for the broader one "carried by the table." Had Claim [4] been allowed in its original form it would have read upon all the accused devices since all the conductor means complementary to the coil spring are "carried by the table." By striking that phrase from the claim and substituting for it "embedded in the table" the applicant restricted his claim to those combinations in which the conductor means, though carried on the table, is also embedded in it. By the amendment he recognized and emphasized the difference between the two phrases and proclaimed his abandonment of all that is embraced in that difference. The difference which he thus disclaimed must be regarded as material, and since the amendment operates as a disclaimer of that difference it must be strictly construed against him.

It follows that what the patentee, by a strict construction of the claim, has disclaimed — conductors which are carried by the table but not embedded in it — cannot now be regained by recourse to the doctrine of equivalents, which at most operates, by liberal construction, to secure to the inventor the full benefits, not disclaimed, of the claims allowed.

DIXIE USA, INC. v. INFAB CORP.

927 F.2d 584, 17 U.S.P.Q.2d (BNA) 1969 (Fed. Cir. 1991)

Dixie USA, Inc. and Buchboard Patient Shifters, Inc. appeal the judgment of the district court granting summary judgment of non-infringement of U.S. Patent 4,067,079. [W]e affirm.

On April 5, 1976, Ernest C. Buchman filed an application for a United States patent for an apparatus to transport hospital patients. There were ten claims in the application: claim 1 was an apparatus claim and claims 2-6 were dependent therefrom; claim 7 was a method claim and claims 8-10 depended from that claim.

Claim 1 read:

A patient shifting aid comprising:

a plastic slab forming a support surface upon which a patient is adapted to be placed and having sufficient thickness to support the weight of a patient placed thereon; and

a plurality of openings in said slab and disposed adjacent the periphery of said support surface providing means for gripping the plastic slab to effect sliding movement of the plastic slab and the patient support thereon.

Figure [8-5] illustrate[s] Buchman's device.

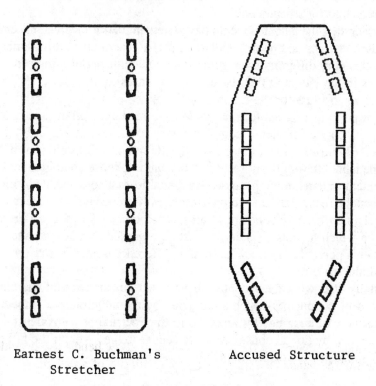

Earnest C. Buchman's   Accused Structure
Stretcher

Figure 8-5

Casual inspection readily reveals a plurality of handhold openings consisting of rectangular and round holes. The claims, when filed, did not limit the nature of the holes.

The Patent and Trademark Office (PTO) rejected all the claims under 35 U.S.C. § 103 on the ground that their subject matter would have been obvious. Applicant responded by cancelling claims 6-10, amending claim 1 in a manner not relevant here, and adding claim 11, which included a limitation requiring that the plurality of openings be rectangular and round. He stated that none of the cited patents discloses rectangular and round openings and that that feature distinguished claim 11 from the prior art. The PTO again rejected all the claims in the application.

The applicant responded by cancelling claims 1-5, which did not require that the openings be rectangular and round, and amending claim 11 (renumbering it as claim 1) to include a limitation that the device be translucent, i.e., enable the taking of x-rays through the plastic slab. The PTO then issued the patent with claim 1 as the sole claim which reads:

A patient shifting aid comprising:

a plastic slab having rounded corners forming a rectangular support surface upon which a patient is adapted to be placed and having sufficient thickness to support the weight of a patient placed thereon while enabling the obtaining of x-rays through the plastic slab to determine the extent of patient injury without the necessity of additional shifting of the patient;

a plurality of openings in said slab and disposed adjacent the periphery of said support surface providing means for gripping the plastic slab to effect sliding movement of the plastic slab and the patient support [sic, supported] thereon;

said plurality of openings comprising *generally rectangular openings* having rounded corners and *rounded openings* for grasping the slab for moving a patient;

said openings being disposed inwardly from the periphery of the slab a greater distance than the thickness of the slab;

said slab having a sliding surface opposite said support surface which frictionally engages the support for the patient shifting and said sliding surface and said support surface being formed smoothly to minimize frictional resistance to sliding movement;

and said slab having sufficient flexibility to allow bending to provide clearance for the hands of a person effecting shifting of a patient.

(Emphasis added).

The owner of this patent is Buchboard Patient Shifters, Inc., and Dixie USA, Inc. has been exclusive licensee since January 1, 1979. They jointly filed a patent infringement suit against appellees on January 21, 1989. Appellees subsequently moved for summary judgment on the ground of non-infringement. The district court granted the motion and this appeal followed.

[W]e conclude that there is no genuine issue as to any material fact and that the district court did not err on that point. We next determine whether the court erred in concluding that appellees were entitled to judgment as a matter of law.

The accused device is conceded to have the following structure [shown in Figure 8-5, on the right].

One should note that the handhold openings are all rectangular, not rectangular and round. Appellants concede that the apparatus does not literally infringe the patent.

The district court determined that appellees' devices do not infringe under the doctrine of equivalents because appellants are estopped by prosecution history from recapturing what they surrendered in prosecution in order to obtain allowance of the patent. Appellants argue that the facts of this case require that the doctrine of equivalents be given considerable weight when balancing it with the competing doctrine of prosecution history estoppel; that the content and timing of the sole amendment to the proposed claim language describing the openings as rectangular and round creates a genuinely disputed issue concerning application of prosecution history estoppel; and that the defense of prosecution history estoppel, even if applicable, does not necessarily preclude a factual finding of infringement by equivalence.

To prevail under the doctrine of equivalents, a patentee must show that the accused device "performs substantially the same function in substantially the same way to obtain the same result." *Graver Tank*. However, when a patentee, during the prosecution of his application, adds a limitation to rectangular and round openings in response to a rejection based on prior art references describing rectangular openings, in an effort to overcome that rejection, the patentee cannot later successfully argue that an accused device that lacks the rectangular and round limitation infringes the patent.

In this case, Buchman, during the prosecution of the patent application, stated to the PTO that what distinguished his invention from the relevant prior art was the presence of both round and rectangular openings. He specifically stated, "[r]egarding claim 11, none of the cited patents disclose[s] the specific shape and location of the claimed rectangular *and* round openings." (Emphasis in original).

The PTO still did not issue the patent. Applicant then added the element of translucence and cancelled all the remaining claims that lacked the requirement that the openings be rectangular and round. With those changes, the patent was granted. The applicant thus surrendered the right to have a device that does not have both rectangular and round openings found to be equivalent to a claimed invention that does.

Appellants argue that they should be able to obtain some degree of equivalence even in the face of prosecution history estoppel, and that a total preclusion of equivalence should not apply. As a general proposition, that principle is correct, but the district court did not apply total preclusion in this case. The court considered the nature of the prior art and the amendments and arguments made during the prosecution and concluded that the scope of equivalence being urged by appellants is precisely that which is forbidden to them by their own prior conduct.

Appellants also argue that it was not the addition of the "rectangular and round" limitation that caused the examiner to allow the patent, but the later-added translucence limitation. We disagree. While the allowance did follow the addition of the translucence limitation, the amendment that made that addition also cancelled claims 1-5, which lacked the "rectangular and round" limitation. Without this latter cancellation, we believe that no reasonable fact-finder could have found that the patent would have been issued. We have considered appellants' other arguments and are not persuaded by them that the district court erred.

Affirmed.

NOTES

1. *Clarifying Amendments.* In *Moeller v. Ionetics, Inc.*, 794 F.2d 653, 229 U.S.P.Q. (BNA) 992 (Fed. Cir. 1986), patentee Moeller claimed a cation-sensing electrode, which used cation-trapping antibiotics and a sensing electrode, separated from the solution to be tested by a membrane. His claim contained the element "means including an electrode body for supporting the membrane, and an electrode disposed within said body," which the prosecution history showed was added in response to an examiner's rejection on the basis of prior art showing (1) antibiotic cation trapping in biological systems, and (2) incorporation of these substances to form a membrane in an electrode system. The accused product contained an electrode that, unlike Moeller's, protruded from its casing, which defendant argued brought it outside the scope of equivalents. The issue turned on the significance of the "electrode *disposed within said body*" limitation in the claim.

According to the court, "[t]he purpose of the examiner's amendment, expressly stated, was to 'more particularly point out the invention.'" 794 F.2d at 659. The court continued:

> *Loctite* [*Corp. v. Ultraseal*, 781 F.2d 861, 871, 228 U.S.P.Q. (BNA) 90, 96 (Fed. Cir. 1985) [stated]:
>
> > Amendment of claims is a common practice in prosecution of patent applications. No reason or warrant exists for limiting application of the doctrine of equivalents to those comparatively few claims allowed exactly as originally filed and never amended. Amendments may be of different types and may serve different functions. Depending on the nature and purpose of an amendment, it may have a limiting effect within a spectrum ranging from great to small to zero.
>
> The court went on to add that:
>
> > [W]henever the doctrine is evoked, "a close examination must be made as to, not only what was surrendered, but also the reason for such a surrender"; the fact that claims were narrowed "does not always mean

that the doctrine of file history estoppel completely prohibits a patentee from recapturing some of what was originally claimed."

Id., 781 F.2d at 871, 228 U.S.P.Q. at 96.

794 F.2d at 659.

On the basis of the examiner's rationale for the amendment, the court concluded that Moeller had not limited his claim to electrodes wholly surrounded by a casing; it vacated the district court's summary judgement ruling in favor of defendant and remanded.

Several cases have followed suit. For example, in *LaBounty Mfg., Inc. v. United States Int'l Trade Com'n*, 867 F.2d 1572, 1576, 9 U.S.P.Q.2d (BNA) 1995 (Fed. Cir. 1989), the court remanded a case for reconsideration of whether the accused product fell within the range of equivalents of the patentee's claim. The accused infringer had argued that the claims, covering a heavy metal shearing device (i.e., "industrial strength scissors"), included a limitation specifying the distance between the cutting shear and the support for holding the end of the metal piece that was cut, and that this limitation had been added in response to an examiner's rejection over prior art. The accused device did not literally meet the limitation. The court rejected defendant's assertion that prosecution history estoppel barred use of the doctrine of equivalents: "Our precedent does not preclude an analysis of the prior art pertinent to a limitation which was added to overcome a rejection based on that art." And: "The effect may or may not be fatal to application of a range of equivalents broad enough to encompass a particular accused product. It is not fatal to application of the doctrine itself."

See also Jonsson v. Stanley Works, 14 U.S.P.Q.2d (BNA) 1863 (CAFC 1990) (prosecution history estoppel applies to continuation-in-part application).

2. Estoppel Versus Interpretation. Keep in mind that prosecution history estoppel is resorted to only when the doctrine of equivalents is asserted as the basis of infringement. And remember that the use of the file wrapper as "legislative history" even for *literal infringement* has been condoned by most courts. *See, e.g., Dental Vulcanite Co. v. Davis*, 102 U.S. (12 Otto) 222, 26 L. Ed. 149 (1880); *Crawford v. Heysinger*, 123 U.S. 589, 8 S. Ct. 399, 31 L. Ed. 269 (1887).

3. Related Reading. A Note, *Patent Claims and Prosecution History Estoppel in the Supreme Court*, 53 Mo. L. Rev. 497 (1988), contrasts what the author sees as two distinct strains of estoppel in the Federal Circuit cases: the "broad estoppel" of *Kinzenbaw v. Deere & Co.*, 741 F.2d 383, 222 U.S.P.Q. (BNA) 929 (Fed. Cir. 1984), and progeny; and the "narrow estoppel" of *Hughes Aircraft Co. v. United States*, 717 F.2d 1351, 219 U.S.P.Q. 473 (Fed. Cir. 1983), and cases which follow it. The author points out that estoppel is a poor basis for the doctrine since a critical element in normal legal estoppel, reliance (e.g., by the public or accused infringer), need not be present. The note concludes by calling for application of the narrow brand of estoppel represented by *Hughes*. *See* *generally* Rich, *Infringement Under Section 271 of the Patent Act of 1952*, 21 GEO. WASH. L. REV. 521 (1953).

3. HISTORY AND ECONOMIC FUNCTION OF THE DOCTRINE OF EQUIVALENTS

The doctrine of equivalents developed in the early nineteenth century as an equitable remedy through jury charges by members of the Supreme Court while sitting as Circuit Justices. Early cases from each court are *Odiorne v. Winkley*, 18 F. Cas. 581, 2 Gall. 51 (C.C.D. Mass. 1814) (No. 10,432) (Story, Circuit Justice) ("Mere colorable differences, or slight improvements, cannot shake the right of the original inventor...."); and *Park v. Little*, 18 F. Cas. 1107, 3 Wash. C.C. 196 (C.C.D. Pa. 1813) (No. 10,715) (Washington, J.). By 1849, the doctrine of equivalents had become well established, as manifested by the detailed treatment of the doctrine in CURTIS, LAW OF PATENTS (1849). *Compare Winans v. Denmead*, 56 U.S. (15 How.) 330, 14 L. Ed. 717 (1853).

The early cases stressed the equitable expansion of the scope of protection for limited situations, particularly those where an accused infringer had copied and added only a "colorable" variation. An infringing device that incorporated a significant difference could be captured under the doctrine of equivalents only in the case of a pioneer patent.

In 1849, in the first edition of his treatise, George Tickenor Curtis (who incidentally later defended Dred Scott in the *Dred Scott* case) synthesized the caselaw of the day into a "doctrine" of equivalents.

The requirement for only "substantial" identity — made famous by the statement of the Court in *Graver Tank* — may be traced at least to a jury charge by Justice Washington in 1817 where he used the term "substantially [the same] in order to exclude all formal difference; and when I speak of the same result, I must be understood as meaning the same kind of result although it may be different in extent." *Gray v. James*, 10 F. Cas. 1015, 1 Peters, C.C. 394, 397-98, 1 Robb Patent Cases 120, 124 (C.C.D. Pa. 1817) (No. 1015) (Washington, Circuit Judge).

Thus contrary to the Court's statement in *Graver Tank*, the doctrine was well established prior to *Winans v. Denmead*. In any event, the post-*Winans* cases show the application of the doctrine in a wide variety of settings. *See Charles Greiner & Co. Inc. v. Mari-Med Mfg. Inc.*, 22 U.S.P.Q.2d (BNA) 1526, 1529 (Fed. Cir. 1992) (holding that infringement under doctrine is exception, not rule, according to older "equitable equivalents" cases).

An important series of nineteenth century equivalents cases, which presaged a critical passage in *Graver Tank*, centered around whether the accused product used an element that was known to be "interchangeable" at the time the patentee filed his application. In general, the Court held that substituting an interchangeable part whose features were known when the patent application was filed constituted infringement. On the other hand, no infringement was found where, at the time of filing, no one knew of the interchangeability. In *Carver v. Hyde*, 41 U.S. 513, 519 (1842), Justice Taney wrote that "if the defendant had ... made an improvement which more effectually secured the object intended to be accomplished by the plaintiff's patent, it would be difficult to maintain, that it could not be lawfully used, because it produced the same result with the plaintiff's invention." In *Seymour v. Osborne*, 78 U.S. 516, 555-56 (1870), the Court elaborated:

> Actual inventors of a combination of two or more ingredients in a machine, secured by letters patent in due form, are entitled, even though the ingredients are old, if the combination produces a new and useful result, to treat every one as an infringer who makes and uses or vends the machine to others to be used without their authority or license. They cannot suppress subsequent improvements which are substantially different, whether the new improvements consist in a new combination of the same ingredients, or of the substitution of some newly-discovered ingredient, or of some old one, performing some new function not known at the date of the letters patent, as a proper substitute for the ingredient withdrawn from the combination constituting their invention.

See also Gould v. Rees, 82 U.S. 187, 194 (1872) ("an alteration in a patented combination which merely substitutes another old ingredient for one of the ingredients in the patented combination is an infringement of the patent, if the substitute performs the same function and was well known at the date of the patent as a proper substitute for the omitted ingredient, but the rule is otherwise if the ingredient substituted was a new one, or performs a substantially different function, or was not known at the date of the plaintiff's patent as a proper substitute").

With this historical overview in mind, we turn now to the economic function of the doctrine of equivalents. (The following section is adapted and modified from Merges & Nelson, *On the Complex Economics of Patent Scope*, 90 COLUM. L. REV. 839 (1990)).

An Economic Rationale

Courts have determined how broadly they see "equivalents" based on the degree of advance over the art the original patent represents. When the patent is on a "mere improvement," the courts tend not to consider as "equivalent" a product or process that is even a modest distance beyond the literal terms of the claims. *Brill v. Washington Elec. & Ry. Co.*, 215 U.S. 527 (1910); *Kinzenbaw v. Deere & Co.*, 741 F.2d 383, 222 U.S.P.Q. (BNA) 929 (Fed. Cir. 1984). On the other hand, a patent representing a "pioneer invention" — which the Supreme Court has defined as "a patent concerning a function never before performed, a wholly novel device, or one of such novelty and importance as to make a distinct step in the progress in the art," *Boyden Power-Brake Co. v. Westinghouse*, 170 U.S. 537, 569 (1898) — is "entitled to a broad range of equivalents." 4 D.

CHISUM, PATENTS § 18.04[2] (1978 & rev. 1992). That is, when a pioneer patent is involved, a court will stretch to find infringement even by a product whose characteristics lie considerably outside the boundaries of the literal claims. For an ecomomic argument in favor of broad claims for some pioneering inventions, see Howard Chang, *Patent Scope, Antitrust Policy, and Cumulative Innovation*, 26 RAND J. ECON. 34 (1995).

Of course the question of infringement also turns on the precise characteristics of the allegedly infringing device. Following the test laid down by the Supreme Court in *Graver Tank*, courts confronted with a device accused of infringing inquire whether it performs the same function and achieves the same result as the invention in the claims, and whether it does so in the same way. Where the accused device shows only minor or "insubstantial" variations in one of these elements — such as the small movement of one part or a minor change in structure — infringement will be found even if the patentee's invention is a "mere improvement." *See, e.g., Tigrett Indus. v. Standard Indus.*, 162 U.S.P.Q. (BNA) 32, 36 (W.D. Tenn. 1967), *aff'd*, 411 F.2d 1218, 162 U.S.P.Q. (BNA) 13 (6th Cir. 1969), *aff'd by an equally divided court*, 397 U.S. 586 (1970) (claim for playpen calling for "a pair of spaced openings" for two converging drawstrings to adjust side webbing infringed by device with one hole for drawstrings). And even a pioneer patent is not infringed by a device that achieves a different result, or achieves it in a different way. *See, e.g., Mead Digital Sys. v. A.B. Dick Co.*, 723 F.2d 455, 464, 221 U.S.P.Q. (BNA) 1035 (6th Cir. 1983) (finding that ink-jet printer patent, though a "quantum leap" in the art, was not infringed by a product that itself operated in a very different way).

One important set of cases under this doctrine has grappled with the question of whether new technologies, unforeseen at the time the patent was issued, can constitute equivalents. This issue arises when a subsequent device that uses new technology is accused of infringing the original patent. The early cases were split, but the prevailing view now is that new technology can be equivalent. *Compare Graver Tank & Mfg. Co. v. Linde Air Prods. Co.*, 339 U.S. 605, 608 (1950) ("An important factor [in determining equivalency] is whether persons reasonably skilled in the art would have known of the interchangeability of an ingredient not contained in the patent with one that was.") *and Gould v. Rees*, 82 U.S. (15 Wall.) 187, 194 (1872) (no infringement where accused infringer "substitutes another [ingredient] in the place of the one omitted, which was new or performs a substantially different function, or [which] ... is old, but was not known at the date of the plaintiff's invention as a proper substitute ...") *with Texas Instruments, Inc. v. United States Int'l Trade Comm'n*, 805 F.2d 1558, 1563, 231 U.S.P.Q. (BNA) 833, 835 (Fed. Cir. 1986) ("It is not required that those skilled in the art knew, at the time the patent application was filed, of the asserted equivalent means of performing the claimed functions; that equivalent is determined as of the time infringement takes place.") *and Pennwalt Corp. v. Durand-Wayland, Inc.*, 833 F.2d 931, 4 U.S.P.Q.2d 1737, 1745 n.4 (Fed. Cir. 1987) ("It is clear that an equivalent can be found in technology known at the time of the invention, as well as in subsequently developed technology.") (Bennett, J., dissenting). *See generally Micro Motion, Inc. v. Exac Corp.*, 741 F. Supp. 1426, 1434, 16 U.S.P.Q.2d (BNA) 1001 (N.D. Cal. 1990) (adopting Federal Circuit view because of "the special expertise of the Federal Circuit in patent cases, the relative recency of the Federal Circuit opinions on this issue, and the sound rationale asserted by the Federal Circuit for using the date of alleged infringement to determine equivalence.").

This is true despite the statement in *Graver Tank* that an important determinant in the equivalents inquiry is whether "persons reasonably skilled in the art would have known of the interchangeability of an ingredient not contained in the patent with one that was." *Cf.* Adelman & Francione, *The Doctrine of Equivalents in Patent Law: Questions Pennwalt Did Not Answer*, 137 U. PA. L. REV. 673, 696 n.103, 697 (1989) (arguing that "this factor [interchangeability] should be used to reject rather than support the application of the doctrine of equivalents," because it signifies that a patentee could have, but mistakenly or intentionally did not, included these interchangeable features in her original claims (footnote omitted)).

Notwithstanding the "interchangeability" language in the leading Supreme Court case on the subject, a device performing the same function and achieving the same result in the same way as a patented invention can be found to infringe even if it uses technology developed after the patent was issued. This is subject to two caveats: 1) new technologies can constitute equivalents only so long as they do not perform a different function or cause the device to operate in a substantially different way; and 2) a truly meritorious improvement can escape even *literal* infringement under the "reverse" doctrine of equivalents discussed below.

That these distinctions may not always be easy to make is demonstrated by the case of *Hughes Aircraft Co. v. United States*, 717 F.2d 1351, 219 U.S.P.Q. (BNA) 473 (Fed. Cir. 1983). Hughes Aircraft had a patent, developed by employee Williams, on a means of controlling the attitude (i.e., adjusting the vertical angle) of a communications satellite. The claims called for receiving and directly executing control signals from a ground station on earth. After the patent was issued, advances in semiconductor technologies permitted satellites to use on-board microprocessors to process and execute control signals without communicating with the ground. "Advanced computers and digital communications techniques developed since [the] Williams [patent]," said the Federal Circuit, "permit doing on-board a *part* of what Williams taught as done on the ground." The court concluded: "[P]artial variation in technique, an embellishment made possible by post-Williams technology, does not allow the accused spacecraft to escape the 'web of infringement.'" *Id.* at 1365 (emphasis in original) (citation omitted). Another case found a patented method for laying pipe, calling for a beam of light to align pipe segments, infringed by the use of later-developed laser beam technology. *Laser Alignment, Inc. v. Woodruff & Sons*, 491 F.2d 866, 180 U.S.P.Q. (BNA) 609 (7th Cir. 1974).

A recent case involving Texas Instruments' pioneering patent on the hand-held calculator shows the court applying the doctrine of equivalents in a way that is sensitive to the need to encourage improvements on a basic technology. The Federal Circuit held that major improvements in all the essential elements of hand-held calculators rendered the improved devices non-infringing. *Texas Instruments, supra*, 805 F.2d at 1570, 231 U.S.P.Q. (BNA) at 840:

> It is not appropriate in this case, where all of the claimed functions are performed in the accused devices by subsequently developed or improved means, to view each such change as if it were the only change from the disclosed embodiment of the invention. It is the entirety of the technology embodied in the accused devices that must be compared with the patent disclosure ....

The specification supporting Texas Instruments' pioneer patent, for instance, described the use of integrated circuits containing bipolar transistors. The improvements all used integrated circuits having metal oxide semiconductor (MOS) transistors. This is an example of improvements in *materials*.

The improved calculators receive input via a device that scans the "matrix" under the keyboard at frequent intervals, whereas the original design had a conductive strip underneath the keypad. This is an example of an improvement that *reduced the number of components* in the invention. Also, the original Texas Instruments display was shown in its specification as a small thermal printer that printed dots on a tape in response to output signals from the processor. The accused devices all use liquid crystal displays (LCDs), the familiar lighted display that does not produce a paper copy, an example of an improvement that *increases the efficiency of an individual component*.

Finally, the internal processing elements of the original calculator were manufactured as discrete components, which were electrically interconnected in the final design. The newer calculators, in contrast, have all their logic on one integrated circuit, eliminating the necessity for many electrical interconnections. This is an example of enhanced *overall design*.

The court concluded "that the total of the technological changes beyond what the inventors disclosed transcends ... equitable limits ... and propels the accused devices beyond a just scope for the [Texas Instrument] patent." 805 F.2d at 1571. Although the mode of analysis used in *Texas Instruments* — described as the "as a whole" test for equivalents — was apparently criticized in *Pennwalt*,[1] it has

---

[1] The Federal Circuit, sitting en banc, appeared to adopt the alternative "element-by-element" test in *Pennwalt Corp. v. Durand-Wayland, Inc.*, 833 F.2d 931, 936, 4 U.S.P.Q.2d (BNA) 1737, 1741 (Fed. Cir. 1987) ("[I]f ... even a single function required by a claim or an equivalent function is not performed by [an accused device], ... [a] finding of no infringement must be upheld."). Judge Pauline Newman, who wrote the *Texas Instruments* opinion, dissented along with five of twelve judges, and wrote separately: "One-to-one correspondence between every element of a claim and an accused device is the standard formula for inquiry into literal infringement. But this formula

surfaced again in more recent cases, and so apparently still lives.[2] In any event this opinion is instructive for its focus on the merits of the accused device. *But see* Bretschneider, *How to Craft and Interpret Means Plus Function Claims in Light of the* Pennwalt *and* Texas Instruments *Cases*, 6 AM. INTELL. PROP. L. ASS'N SELECTED LEGAL PAPERS 68, 73 (1988) ("the degree of uncertainty created by this 'invention as a whole' test is nearly intolerable").

This opinion — especially its emphasis on changes in materials, number and simplicity of components, and increased overall efficiency — should serve as a model for applying the doctrine of equivalents. It suggests an important addition to conventional equivalency analysis. Once a court completes its assessment of the significance of the patented device, it should consider in addition the importance of the advance represented in the *accused* device. This was in essence the approach taken by the court in the *Texas Instruments* case. The Federal Circuit denied infringement where the accused calculators showed significant improvements in many respects over the patentee's design. Especially instructive was the court's strict attention to the *specification* of the pioneer patent in that case. The equivalents inquiry, even for a pioneer patent, should be centered around whether the improved structures of the accused device show major differences from the structures disclosed in the original specification. Specifically, the court should look for differences in the following areas:

- Materials
- Changes in the number of components
- Greatly improved efficiency in individual components
- Increased efficiency in the way components work together, i.e., overall design improvements

This does not mean that the accused device should be found non-infringing if it is nonobvious with respect to the patentee's invention. A device can be both patentable and an infringement of an earlier patent — the common case of blocking patents. *See Atlas Powder Co. v. E.I. du Pont de Nemours & Co.*, 750 F.2d 1569, 1580-81, 224 U.S.P.Q. 409 (Fed. Cir. 1984).

---

is an incorrect application of the doctrine of equivalents .... The doctrine can not, by its nature, be reduced to rigid rules."

[2] *Sun Studs, Inc. v. ATA Equip. Leasing, Inc.*, 872 F.2d 978, 989, 10 U.S.P.Q.2d (BNA) 1338, 1347 (Fed. Cir. 1989) ("An apparatus claim describing a combination of components does not require that the function of each be performed by a separate structure in the apparatus. The claimed and accused devices must be viewed and evaluated as a whole."); *Corning Glass Works v. Sumitomo Elec. U.S.A., Inc.*, 868 F.2d 1251, 1259, 9 U.S.P.Q.2d 1962, 1968 (Fed. Cir. 1989). ("An equivalent must be found for every limitation of the claim somewhere in an accused device, but not necessarily in a corresponding component, although that is generally the case .... [T]he determination of equivalency is not subject to ... a rigid formula.").

But *at some point* the characteristics of the accused device ought to be considered, and its merits ought to be a factor of importance in the equivalents determination. The *Graver Tank* formulation of the doctrine supports this. *See Graver Tank & Mfg. Co. v. Linde Air Prods. Co.*, 339 U.S. 605, 610 (1950) (only "insubstantial" changes are encompassed by the doctrine of equivalents).

In the *Texas Instruments* case, the accused devices incorporated improvements in the many respects discussed. What makes *Texas Instruments* worthy of emulation is its focus on the degree to which the accused device represents an advance over the patented device. In a way, this simply brings some symmetry to the equivalency issue. Just as a court looks to the degree of advance over the prior art in deciding whether the patented device is a pioneer or only a minor improvement, so too should the courts be encouraged to examine the accused device. If it represents a significant advance, this is a factor that should weigh in its favor when the issue of infringement by equivalency is decided. Analysis along these lines might have reduced the blocking effect of pioneer patents in some fields. *See* Merges & Nelson, *supra*.

An effective doctrine of equivalents will contribute to more rapid technical advance. As Emerson said, "Invention breeds invention." Multiple and competitive sources of invention are socially preferable to a structure where there is only one or a few sources. Public policy, including patent law, ought to encourage inventive rivalry, and not hinder it. As some economic models (discussed in Merges & Nelson, *supra*) show, a rivalrous structure surely has its inefficiencies. But such a structure does tend to generate rapid technical progress and seems a much better social bet than a regime where only one or a few organizations control the development of any given technology.

While there are exceptions, where only a few organizations controlled the development of a technology, technical advance appeared sluggish. The company with the inside track has often failed to move aggressively; the Edison lightbulb patent is perhaps the best example. (See Merges & Nelson, *supra*, for elaboration of these historical cases.) At the same time, the history of many industries — beginning with the steam engine — shows that outsiders with promising approaches have been held back. There are many cases in which the product in question was a multi-component system, and broad patents on components led to blockages. These were resolved, in effect, by the development of more or less automatic (if elaborate) cross-licensing schemes. These should not be understood as mechanisms to achieve orderly development of the basic technology, but rather as mechanisms to cancel out the blocking effects of broad patents. While sometimes these have come about privately, in other cases patent logjams have been broken only with the powerful force of government intervention. These episodes testify to the blocking power of broad patents as well as social creativity in working around them; they do not argue for the social efficacy of broad patents in every case.

NOTES

1. *Related Cases.* In *Genentech, Inc. v. Wellcome Found., Inc.*, 14 U.S.P.Q.2d (BNA) 1363 (D. Del. 1990), the court held that biotechnological advances subsequent to the patentee's filing date do not remove the accused product from the scope of the patent's equivalents, thus extending the general principle to biotechnology cases, where rapid advances have occurred and can be expected to continue. A jury later found that the patent at issue was infringed but awarded zero damages. *See* 39 PAT. TRADEMARK & COPYRIGHT J. (BNA) 503 (Apr. 1990).

2. *Interchangeability and the* **Wilson** *Test.* One court has touched on the relationship between *Graver*'s "interchangeability" and the doctrine of equivalents analysis in *Wilson Sporting Goods* (*supra* this chapter).

> To support its infringement finding, the trial court erroneously relied on the interchangeability of Microdot's and Key's nuts. While neither party disputes the interchangeability of Microdot's and Key's nuts, an interchangeable device is not necessarily an equivalent device. Key failed to meet the burden of showing the accused Microdot nuts contain a substantial equivalent of every element or limitation of the '961 claims.

Key Mfg. Group, Inc. v. Microdot, Inc., 925 F.2d 1444, 1449, 17 U.S.P.Q.2d (BNA) 1806 (Fed. Cir. 1991). The court went on to hold that a "hypothetical claim" according to *Wilson* would not be patentable because of prior art. Hence an addition to the *Graver* analysis is suggested: interchangeability must be supplemented by evidence that the interchangeable equivalent is *not* too close to the prior art.

Note generally the symmetry between concepts introduced in various aspects of equivalents analysis. *Graver* suggests that obvious substitutions — i.e., straightforward interchangeability — ought to be deemed infringing. The economic analysis above suggests that highly original improvements — i.e., very creative interchangeability — ought to be deemed non-infringing. And *Wilson* suggests that substitutions that are a straightforward extension of the *prior art* ought to be deemed non-infringing. All three concepts rely on notions of nonobviousness at some level (although the economic analysis suggests a kind of "super-nonobviousness" as a test). But while the first two compare the accused device with the claimed invention, the last (*Wilson*) compares the accused device with the prior art. Such is the adaptability and interconnected nature of patent doctrines. *Cf.* Chisum, *Comment: Anticipation, Enablement, and Obviousness: An Eternal Golden Braid*, 15 AM. INTELL. PROP. L. ASS'N Q.J. 57 (1987).

4. EQUIVALENTS FOR MEANS-PLUS-FUNCTION CLAIMS: § 112 ¶ 6

Section 112, ¶ 6 of the Patent Act reads as follows:

> An element in a claim for a combination may be expressed as a means or step for performing a specified function without the recital of structure, material, or acts in support thereof, and such claim shall be construed to cover the corresponding structure, material, or acts described in the specification and equivalents thereof.

35 U.S.C. § 112 (1986 & Supp. VI 1991).

As pointed out in Commentary written by one of the chief drafters of the 1952 Patent Act:

> The last paragraph of [35 U.S.C. §] 112 relating to so-called functional claims is new. It provides that an element of a claim for a combination ... may be expressed as a means or step for performing a specified function, without the recital of structure, material or acts in support thereof. It is unquestionable that some measure of greater liberality in the use of functional expressions in combination claims is authorized than had been permitted by some court decisions, and that decisions such as that in *Halliburton Oil Well Cementing Co. v. Walker*, 329 U.S. 1 (1946), are modified or rendered obsolete, but the exact limits of the enlargement remain to be determined.... The paragraph ends by stating that such a claim shall be construed to cover the corresponding structure, material, or acts described in the specification and equivalents thereof. This relates primarily to the construction of such claims for the purpose of determining when the claim is infringed (note the use of the word "cover"), and would not appear to have much, if any, applicability in determining the patentability of such claims over the prior art, that is, the Patent Office is not authorized to allow a claim which "reads on" the prior art.

P.J. Federico, *Commentary on the New Patent Act*, 35 U.S.C.A. 1, 24-25 (1954).

As the following cases show, the courts have had mixed success in delineating "the exact limits of the enlargement" represented by § 112 ¶ 6.

LAITRAM CORP. v. REXNORD, INC.

939 F.2d 1533, 19 U.S.P.Q.2d (BNA) 1367 (Fed. Cir. 1991)

NIES, CHIEF JUDGE.

Rexnord, Inc., appeals the judgment of the United States District Court for the Eastern District of Wisconsin that claims 21 and 22 of U.S. Patent No. 4,051,949 ('949), assigned to Laitram Corp., were infringed by Rexnord. Laitram brought suit charging, inter alia, that Rexnord's 4707 conveyor product infringed the '949 patent. Rexnord defended on the grounds that its accused product did not infringe any claims of the '949 patent. The district court ruled that Rexnord's 4707 conveyor product infringed claims 21 and 22 of the '949 patent. [We reverse.]

The invention claimed in the '949 patent is directed to a conveyor belt which addresses the problem of tippage of containers being conveyed.

The claimed invention generally consists of a modular plastic conveyor belt of raised rib construction, which allows smooth transfer of containers to and from the head and tail ends of a conveyor via a transfer comb. The conveyor belt is composed of a plurality of plastic modules which are pivotally connected at their link ends. [See Figure 8-6. Note that the invention overall is analogized to a chain; thus each module is analogized to a "link" in the chain and referred to as a "link-like element." Figure 8-6 shows three complete links and part of a fourth (at left).]

U.S. Patent   Oct. 4, 1977   Sheet 2 of 3   **4,051,949**

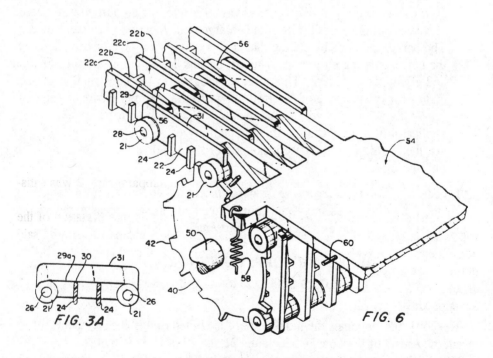

Figure 8-6

To establish infringement, every limitation set forth in a patent claim must be found in an accused product or process exactly or by a substantial equivalent.

Corning Glass. The patentee bears the burden of proving infringement by a preponderance of the evidence.

At issue herein is claim 21 of the '949 patent, the only independent claim charged to be infringed.

[This claim reads:]

> 21. A linked belt adapted to move through a circular arc for use in conjunction with a conveyor comb having a plurality of spaced-apart parallel teeth, said belt comprising: [1] a plurality of like modules, each of said modules including a first and second like pluralities of link ends of substantially identical width, each such end being formed to circumscribe a pivotal hole through said width; [2] means for joining said pluralities to one another so that the axes of said holes of said first plurality are arranged coaxially, the axes of said holes of said second plurality are arranged coaxially and the axes of respective holes of both pluralities of link ends are substantially parallel; [3] a plurality of spaced apart elongated upstanding vanes mounted on said modules so as to extend in a substantially parallel direction to one another in a direction transversely to the axes of said holes of said both pluralities and protrude substantially perpendicularly from said module; [4] said link ends being dimensioned and spaced apart by a distance slightly greater than said width; [5] said link ends of each of said modules being releasably engaged between the link ends of an adjacent module except for individual link ends disposed at the extreme sides of said belt; [6] means for pivotally connecting said modules at engaged link ends; [7] said elongated vanes of each of said modules being arranged in staggered relation with respect to the vanes of adjacent modules, said vanes of each module being spaced from one another sufficiently to form a multiplicity of channels lying beneath the upper most surface of said belt when staggered, said channels being adapted to receive said teeth.

We are persuaded that Laitram failed to prove that subparagraph 2 was satisfied either literally or by an equivalent.

Rexnord asserts that the district court legally erred in its interpretation of the following language of subparagraph 2 of claim 21: "[2] means for joining said pluralities [of link ends] to one another so that the axes of said holes of said first plurality are arranged coaxially, the axes of said holes of said second plurality are arranged coaxially and the axes of respective holes of both pluralities of link ends are substantially parallel; ...." [Hereinafter subparagraph 2.] Rexnord argues, as it did below, that this claim language must be interpreted in accordance with 35 U.S.C. § 112, paragraph 6 (1988) (hereinafter "section 112(6)").

Absent section 112(6), claim language which requires only a means for performing a function might be indefinite. While the use of means-plus-function language in a claim is clearly permissible by reason of section 112(6), a means clause does not cover every means for performing the specified function. Rather, [section 112(6)] means exactly what it says:

To determine whether a claim limitation is met literally, where expressed as a means for performing a stated function, the court must compare the accused structure with the disclosed structure, and must find equivalent structure as well as identity of claimed function for that structure.

Pennwalt.

Thus, section 112(6) "rules out the possibility that any and every means which performs the function specified in the claim literally satisfies that limitation. While encompassing equivalents of those means disclosed in the specification, the provision, nevertheless, acts as a restriction on the literal satisfaction of a claim limitation." *Id.* The district court, therefore, erred, as a matter of law in holding that this limitation was met merely because there was some means in the accused device that performed the stated function. The means-plus-function language must not only read on the accused device, but also, if the accused structure is different from that described in the patent, the patentee must prove, for literal infringement, that the means in the accused device is structurally equivalent to the means described in the specification.

Looking to '949's specification, the means for joining a plurality of link ends is described as follows:

> Each of the link-like elements is formed of a pair of like link end sections 21 joined by at least one intermediate or connecting section 22 having a generally rectangular cross section with a greater depth (or height) than width. [These form the "slats" on the link.] Thus all link-like elements have substantially identical lengths (i.e. the distance between the extremities of each pair of joined link ends). All of the link-like elements of a module are joined as a unit by at least one and preferably a pair of spaced cross-members 24 formed integrally with connecting sections 22 to form a rigid structure.
>
> ....
>
> Cross members 24 function to maintain the link-like elements in parallel relation so that the surfaces of end sections 21 are kept parallel and pivot holes 26 aligned, thereby minimizing bending stresses across pivot pin 28. Thus, the link ends are first connected by elongated bars to form link elements, and these link elements are connected by cross members. This combination of structure joins the pluralities of link ends.

As illustrated in [Figure 8-7, top] the structure forms a grid, which Laitram refers to as an H-shape arrangement. [In Figure 8-7, you are looking down on a link module; when in operation, it would move from left to right.]

Laitram asserted and the district court found that the structure [in Figure 8-7, bottom] met the means limitation of subparagraph 2.

The above structure is an accused 4707 conveyor belt module without its top plate. The top plate normally overlies the top of the reach bars and is molded to or with such bars. Samples of the V-shaped molded plastic structure shown above

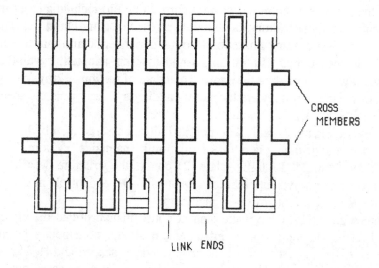

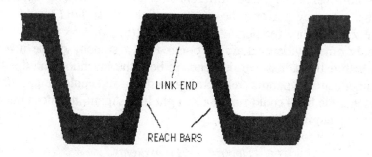

Figure 8-7

were submitted to the court by Laitram. This is the only structure which Laitram asserts satisfies subparagraph 2.

There is no dispute that the V-shaped structure of the accused device is not the same means for joining a plurality of link ends which is set out in '949's specification. The 4707 device does not have structure joining link ends into link elements and structure joining these link elements by one or more cross members into a rigid grid.

Laitram argues that an interpretation of claim 21 which reads the structural limitation of a cross member into claim 21 is impermissible despite section 112(6), because claim 24 of the patent (a claim which depends from claim 21, but which is not in suit) specifically requires a cross member. Laitram explains that claim 21 cannot also require a cross member because to so hold would emasculate the doctrine of claim differentiation. Several fallacies are readily apparent in this argument.

First, the interpretation of the "means for joining" to include a cross member comes from the specification via section 112(6), not from claim 24. Thus, the prohibition against reading limitations from a dependent claim into the independent claim is not violated. If Laitram's argument were adopted, it would provide a convenient way of avoiding the express mandate of section 112(6). We hold that one cannot escape that mandate by merely adding a claim or claims specifically reciting such structure or structures.

In any event, claims 21 and 24 do not, as Laitram asserts, thereby have exactly the same scope and, thus, claim differentiation is maintained. Claim 21 remains broader than claim 24. Literally, claim 21 covers the structure described in the specification and equivalents thereof. *Pennwalt*. Dependent claim 24 does not literally cover equivalents of cross members.

Laitram argues that, even if the district court misinterpreted the claim under section 112(6), the judgment of infringement should nonetheless be affirmed because the district court's error is harmless. The V-shaped and H-shaped structures, per Laitram, are the "same" because they perform the same function. As indicated however, even if true, different structures are not ipso facto equivalent merely because they perform the same function. To so hold would effectively eliminate the statutory restriction of section 112(6). *Id.*

The only other evidence Laitram points to is testimony of the inventor and others which explains that the link ends in both the invention and the 4707 belt were maintained in a parallel relationship so that a rod could be put through the link ends and the belts could run in a straight line. Again, that does not establish the necessary equivalency.

Doctrine of Equivalents

This inquiry of equivalency to the joining means under the doctrine may not be as limited as under section 112(6). *Pennwalt*, 833 F.2d at 934, 4 U.S.P.Q.2d at 1739. However, at most, Laitram makes conclusory assertions of infringement under the doctrine and again asserts that the function of the joining means reads on the reach bars. On the basis of the evidence of record presented to us, we can find no basis for remand for a factual determination that the joining means was met equivalently for purposes of infringement under the doctrine. [Reversed.]

NOTES

1. *"Means-Plus-Function" Claim Elements.* Recall the claim element at issue in the preceding case:

> means for joining said pluralities [of link ends] to one another so that the axes of said holes of said first plurality are arranged coaxially, the axes of said holes of said second plurality are arranged coaxially and the axes of respective holes of both pluralities of link ends are substantially parallel ....

Look at Figure 8-7, bottom. Does this device (the "4707 device") have "means for joining" modules together? The court said: "The 4707 device does not have structure joining link ends into link elements and *structure joining these link elements by one or more cross members* into a rigid grid." (Emphasis added.) Does the quoted claim language literally call for cross members? If not, how can the absence of cross members allow a device to escape from infringement?

Is a cross member piece necessary to align the holes used to join link elements together? If so, perhaps the portion of the above-quoted claim (subparagraph [2]) calling for means for joining "so that the axes of said holes of said first plurality are arranged coaxially, the axes of said holes of said second plurality are arranged coaxially and the axes of respective holes of both pluralities of link ends are substantially parallel" could be read as requiring a cross member. Could the "reach bars" in the accused 4707 device be construed as cross members? If not, would the 4707 device necessarily escape infringement?

De GRAFFENRIED v. UNITED STATES

20 Cl. Ct. 458, 16 U.S.P.Q.2d (BNA) 1321 (Cl. Ct. 1990)

[Plaintiff held several patents on a machine used in boring large guns, e.g. cannons. Specifically, he devised a way to control the tendency of the boring head to get off center in the gun barrel as it was boring — a problem known in the art as "runout." The patentee's solution to the runout problem involved using an accelerometer which sensed when the boring head was going off-center. Specifically, the claims recited "means for generating a runout signal." In his specification, the patentee disclosed an accelerometer made from a sphere suspended between two electrodes. The accused device, used at a federal arsenal (and referred to as "the Arsenal accelerometer" in the opinion), employed a coil suspended in an electric field created by multiple electrodes.]

The central structural difference between the Arsenal accelerometer and the capacitive displacement accelerometer described in the patent [at issue] is that the indicator patent accelerometer suspends a sphere between the electrodes while the Arsenal device employs a forcer coil. In both cases, a suspended mass is placed in an electric field formed by a number of electrodes, and acceleration forces caused by runout move the suspended mass closer to and farther from a given supporting electrode. Since these two structures are sufficiently close to be deemed equivalents in physical structure, the Arsenal device would literally infringe [this] element of Claim 1 under defendant's proposed interpretation of Section 112.

In any event, however, the term "equivalent" in Section 112 should not be interpreted as being limited to structures that are "equivalent" to the physical structure of the "means" disclosed in a patent. The literal wording of Section 112 contains no such requirement. The statute merely refers to structures "described in the specification and equivalents thereof." It does not state that the only possible "equivalents" to the structures described in the specification are devices with equivalent physical structures, i.e., it does not provide structures "described in the specification and structural equivalents thereof." The concept of equivalence has meaning in patent law outside of Section 112 and the concept has not been limited to equivalent physical structures. As noted above, a device that does not literally infringe a patent claim may nevertheless be found to infringe the claim under the doctrine of equivalence. [I]n *Graver Tank*, [t]he Court noted that "[a]n important factor [in the determination of equivalence] is whether persons reasonably skilled in the art would have known of the interchangeability of an ingredient not contained in the patent with one that was." *Id.* at 609. Thus, under the *Graver Tank* standards, a finding could be made that two devices are Section 112 "equivalents" and, hence, that infringement exists even when the two devices are different "in name, form or shape," *id.* at 608, i.e., even if there was no equivalence in the physical structures.

It is appreciated that applying the doctrine of equivalence is distinct from determining literal infringement of a claim using means plus function language under 35 U.S.C. § 112. But in using the term "equivalents" in Section 112, Congress intended to reference the *Graver Tank* concepts of equivalence. As explained in *Palumbo* [v. *Don-Joy*, 762 F.2d 969, 226 U.S.P.Q. (BNA) 5 (Fed. Cir. 1985)], at 975 n.4, 226 U.S.P.Q. at 8-9 n.4:

> Although, as we pointed out in *D.M.I., Inc. v. Deere & Co.*, [755 F.2d 1570, 225 U.S.P.Q. 236 (Fed. Cir. 1985)], there is a difference between a doctrine-of-equivalents analysis and a literal infringement analysis involving "equivalents" under § 112, *Graver Tank* concepts of equivalents are relevant in any "equivalents" determination. The fact that *Graver Tank* preceded the 1952 Patent Act by two years and the last paragraph of § 112 was new, suggests that the underlying principles of equivalents in *Graver Tank* could be used in a § 112 literal infringement analysis. Limiting Section 112 "equivalents" to objects that are structurally equivalent to those objects described in a patent specification would undermine Congress' intent in 1952 in adding the third paragraph of Section 112.

By specifically authorizing the use of "means plus function" terminology, Congress apparently recognized that such terminology can be a highly efficient way to draft a patent claim, i.e., to define the metes and bounds of the patentee's invention. However, limiting literal infringement of "means plus function" claims to objects that have physical structures equivalent to those objects specifically described in the patent specification could seriously undermine the usefulness of such claims. For example, if a claim calls for a means for detecting acceleration, to be assured of broad "literal" coverage a patentee would have to list virtually every known accelerometer structure that could function in the patented device. All structures that perform a particular function described in a claim fall within the literal terms of that claim element, expressed simply as a "means" for performing that function. Equivalence of physical structure may be an appropriate part of the analysis but it is not a sine qua non for a finding of Section 112 "equivalents."

Applying the *Graver Tank* concepts, the Arsenal's capacitive displacement accelerometer and related circuitry would be "equivalent" to each of the three accelerometers disclosed in the patent. Based on the totality of the evidence submitted at trial, the court concludes that persons reasonably skilled in the art knew at the time the patent was issued that, after appropriate and obvious modification, the Arsenal accelerometer and related circuitry would be interchangeable with any of the three accelerometers referenced in the controller patent. Moreover, the Arsenal device qualifies as a Section 112 equivalent under the tripartite function-way-result test of *Graver Tank*. Whether viewed in isolation or viewed as a part of a runout controller, the Arsenal's capacitive displacement accelerometer performs the same function in substantially the same way and accomplishes the same result as the accelerometers referenced in the controller patent. They all function to detect acceleration and thereby detect runout, and the result of their use is a signal indicative of the direction and magnitude of runout. Clearly, there are some differences in the way the accelerometers operate, but, when all facts are considered, they operate in substantially the same way. Each device converts movement of a mass into a sinusoidal electrical signal which contains information pertaining to both the direction and magnitude of runout. Thus, the Arsenal device literally infringes element 3 of Claim 1.

NOTES

1. *Comparing Doctrine of Equivalents and § 112 ¶ 6.* The Federal Circuit speaks with at least a slightly forked tongue on the relationship between the doctrine of equivalents and § 112 ¶ 6:

> [T]he word "equivalent" in § 112 should not be confused, as it apparently was here, with the "doctrine of equivalents." In applying the doctrine of equivalents, the fact finder must determine the range of equivalents to which the claimed invention is entitled, in light of the prosecution history, the pioneer-non-pioneer status of the invention, and the prior art. It must then be determined whether the entirety of the accused device or process is so "substantially the same thing, used in substantially the same way, to achieve substantially the same result" as to fall within that range. *Graver Tank*. In applying the "means plus function" paragraph of § 112, however, the sole question is whether the single means in the accused device which performs the function stated in the claim is the same as or an equivalent of the corresponding structure described in the patentee's specification as performing that function.

D.M.I., Inc. v. Deere & Co., 755 F.2d 1570, 225 U.S.P.Q. (BNA) 236 (Fed. Cir. 1985). Next:

Although, as we pointed out in *D.M.I., Inc. v. Deere & Co.*, there is a difference between a doctrine-of-equivalents analysis and a literal infringement analysis involving "equivalents" under § 112, *Graver Tank* concepts of equivalents are relevant in any "equivalents" determination. The fact that *Graver Tank* preceded the 1952 Patent Act by two years and the last paragraph of § 112 was new, suggests that the underlying principles of equivalents in *Graver Tank* could be used in a § 112 literal infringement analysis.

Palumbo v. Don-Joy Co., 762 F.2d 969, 975 n.4, 226 U.S.P.Q. (BNA) 5 (Fed. Cir. 1985). *See also Data Line Corp. v. Micro Techs., Inc.*, 813 F.2d 1196, 1201, 1 U.S.P.Q.2d (BNA) 2052, 2055 (Fed. Cir. 1987) ("Where a claim sets forth a means for performing a specific function, without reciting any specific structure for performing that function, the structure disclosed in the specification must be considered, and the patent claim construed to cover both the disclosed structure and equivalents thereof."); *Intellicall, Inc. v. Phonometrics, Inc.*, 952 F.2d 1384, 21 U.S.P.Q.2d 1383 (Fed. Cir. 1992) (to satisfy means-plus-function limitation literally, so as to establish infringement, accused device must perform the identical function required by the limitation and must incorporate the structure disclosed in the specification, or its substantial structural equivalent, as the means for performing that function). Frequent citation of *Pennwalt* and *Texas Instruments*, both discussed earlier this chapter, in both § 112 ¶ 6 and normal equivalency cases adds to the impression that there is substantial overlap between the two types of analysis.

   2. Policy Points. *Using "Regular" Equivalents Analysis in ¶ 6 Cases.* It might be argued that even if it were possible to use two different standards for "regular" equivalents analysis and § 112 ¶ 6 analysis, it is confusing and serves no useful purpose. In response to the suggestion that this obviates the section itself, and thus violates the canon of statutory construction saying that the legislature must have meant something in each section of a statute, it can be said that the *main* function of ¶ 6 is to specifically approve of "means-plus-function" claims.

   Using ¶ 6 Equivalents Analysis in "Regular" Cases. One appealing feature of ¶ 6 is that it roots equivalents analysis in something concrete — the structure recited in the patentee's specification. Perhaps this approach should carry over to regular doctrine of equivalents cases, where it often seems as if there is very little conceptual firm footing. Certainly referring to the specification would be more substantive than the "function/way/result" test of *Graver Tank*. This is in keeping with the suggestions made earlier within Section B.3, *An Economic Rationale*, for the doctrine of equivalents; the specification would be helpful in deciding just how much of an advance the accused infringer has made over the patentee's work.

C. THE REVERSE DOCTRINE OF EQUIVALENTS

BOYDEN POWER-BRAKE CO. v. WESTINGHOUSE
170 U.S. 537 (1897)

The history of arresting the speed of railway trains by the application of compressed air is one (to which the records of the patent office bear frequent witness) of a gradual progress from rude and imperfect beginnings, step by step, to a final consummation, which, in respect to this invention, had not been reached when the patent in suit was taken out, and which, it is quite possible, has not been reached to this day. It is not disputed that the most important steps in this direction have been taken by Westinghouse himself.

The original substitution of the air brake for the old hand brake was itself almost a revolution; but the main difficulty seems to have arisen in the subsequent extension of that system to long trains of freight cars, in securing a simultaneous application of brakes to each of perhaps 40 or 50 cars in such a train, and finally in bringing about the instantaneous as well as simultaneous application of such brakes in cases of emergency, when the speediest possible stoppage of the train is desired to avoid a catastrophe.

[The Court describes the development of the air brake. The "straight air brake," introduced in the late 1860s, used the steam engine of the train to compress air and distribute it (by means of a valve controlled by the engineer) in a single long series of tubes to each car. This was more powerful than the old hand brake but still took a long time to work, a serious problem on a train of any size. Next came the "automatic brake," which had an auxiliary reservoir beneath each car to store compressed air from the main reservoir, and a "triple valve," a set of three interrelated valves: (1) the "feeding-in valve," from the train pipe, i.e., the main pipe running from the engine, to the auxiliary reservoir, allowing the auxiliary reservoir to fill so as to be ready when the brakes were applied; (2) a valve from the auxiliary reservoir to the brake cylinder, which allowed a flow of compressed air to apply the brakes, called the "main valve"; (3) and a "release valve" from the brake cylinder to the open air. The brake worked via the "backpressure" from the air in the reservoir, rather than from direct pressure from the main air supply. Because of this, Westinghouse devised an improvement on the basic design: if a car broke away from the train, the air in the reservoir would automatically apply the brakes. A further improvement was the basis for the patent involved in this case, an extra set of air pipes directly connecting the main air pipe with each brake cylinder, so as to supply an extra boost of pressure in emergencies. This was carried out by making the piston in the brake cylinder respond to full force application by opening the extra valve from the main pipe — a so-called "second traverse" of the piston. [Figure 8-8, next page, bottom row illustrates the Westinghouse brake; the drawing on the bottom right shows the valve configuration for an emergency stop, or "quick action."]

BOYDEN

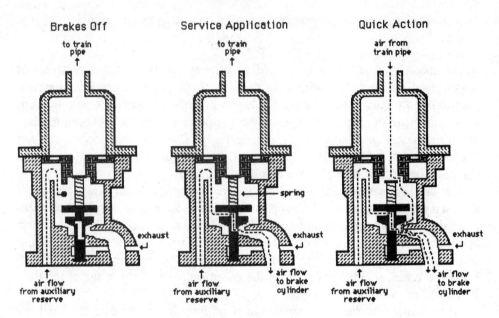

WESTINGHOUSE

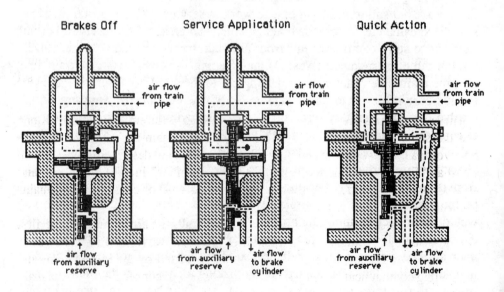

Figure 8-8

[The] patent [in suit], although it introduced a novel feature into the art, does not seem to have been entirely successful in its practical operation, since in October of the same year an improvement was patented (No. 376,837), with the object of still further increasing the rapidity of action.

We are now in position to take up the several claims of the patent in suit, and their defenses thereto. It may be stated generally that the position of complainants in this connection is that the novel feature of this patent, in respect to which they are entitled to be protected, is the opening of a passage directly from the train pipe to the brake cylinder, without passing through the auxiliary reservoir, and without reference to the means by which such passageway is controlled.

Complainants' case must rest either upon the theory that the admission of compressed air directly from the train pipe to the brake cylinder is patentable as a function, or that the means employed by the defendants for that purpose are a mechanical equivalent for the auxiliary valve described in the patent.

The first and fourth claims of this patent are as follows:

(1) In a brake mechanism, the combination of a main air pipe, an auxiliary reservoir, a brake cylinder, a triple valve, and an auxiliary valve device, actuated by the piston of the triple valve, and independent of the main valve thereof, for admitting air in the application of the brake directly from the main air pipe to the brake cylinder, substantially as set forth.

(4) The combination, in a triple-valve device, of a case or chest, a piston fixed upon a stem, and working in a chamber therein, a valve moving with the piston stem, and governing ports and passages in the case leading to connections with an auxiliary reservoir and a brake cylinder and to the atmosphere, respectively, and an auxiliary valve actuated by the piston stem, and controlling communication between passages leading to connections with a main air pipe and with the brake cylinder, respectively, substantially as set forth.

These two claims are practically little more than different expressions of one and the same invention. In both of them there is a main air pipe, an auxiliary reservoir, a brake cylinder, a triple valve and piston, described in the fourth claim as "fixed upon a stem and working in a chamber" in a case or chest, and an auxiliary valve; and in the fourth claim, also, a case or chest, which contains the whole device, and is immaterial.

In both of these claims an auxiliary valve is named as an element. In the first it is described as "actuated by the piston of the triple valve, and independent of the main valve thereof," and in the fourth as "actuated by the piston stem, and controlling communication between passages leading to connections with the main air pipe and with the brake cylinder."

To what liberality of construction these claims are entitled depends, to a certain extent, upon the character of the invention, and whether it is what is termed, in ordinary parlance, a "pioneer." This word, although used somewhat loosely, is commonly understood to denote a patent covering a function never before performed, a wholly novel device, or one of such novelty and importance as to mark a distinct step in the progress of the art, as distinguished from a mere improvement or perfection of what had gone before. Most conspicuous examples of such patents are the one to Howe, of the sewing machine; to Morse, of the electrical telegraph; and to Bell, of the telephone. The record in this case would indicate that the same honorable appellation might be safely bestowed upon the original air brake of Westinghouse, and perhaps, also, upon his automatic brake. In view of the fact that the invention in this case was never put into successful operation, and was to a limited extent anticipated by the Boyden patent of 1883, it is perhaps an unwarrantable extension of the term to speak of it as a "pioneer," although the principle involved subsequently, and through improvements upon this invention, became one of great value to the public. The fact that this invention was first in the line of those which resulted in placing it within the power of an engineer, running a long train, to stop in about half the time and half the distance within which any similar train had stopped, is certainly deserving of recognition, and entitles the patent to a liberality of construction which would not be accorded to an ordinary improvement upon prior devices. At the same time, as hereinafter observed, this liberality must be exercised in subordination to the general principle above stated, — that the function of a machine cannot be patented, and hence that the fact that the defendants' machine performs the same function is not conclusive that it is an infringement.

The device made use of by the defendants is exhibited in patents No. 481,134 and No. 481,135, both dated August 16, 1892, and both of which were granted after the commencement of this suit. There are two forms of this patent, one of which, illustrated in patent No. 481,135, is here given in its three positions [in Figure 8-8, top row], — of release, service application and quick action.

In this device there is found a main air pipe, an auxiliary reservoir, a brake cylinder, a triple (or, rather, a quadruple) valve and piston with three ports — First, for the admission of air from the train pipe to the brake cylinder through the feeding-in valve, 26; second, for the passage of air from the auxiliary reservoir to the brake cylinder through the apertures, i, j, k, in the stem slide valve; and, third, for the release of air from the brake cylinder to the exhaust port by means of [a] valve. Whether this device has an auxiliary valve, or not, is one of the main questions in the case; complainants' theory being that [the] poppet valve [i.e., the valve with the spring, shown most clearly in the center illustration on the top row of Figure 8-8], is an auxiliary valve, while defendants' claim is that it is in reality the main valve. [The Court concludes it is an auxiliary valve as that term is used in the claims at issue.]

But, even if it be conceded that the Boyden device corresponds with the letter of the Westinghouse claims, that does not settle conclusively the question of infringement. We have repeatedly held that a charge of infringement is sometimes made out, though the letter of the claims be avoided. The converse is equally true. The patentee may bring the defendant within the letter of his claims, but if the latter has so far changed the principle of the device that the claims of the patent, literally construed, have ceased to represent his actual invention, he is as little subject to be adjudged an infringer as one who has violated the letter of a statute has to be convicted, when he has done nothing in conflict with its spirit and intent.

We have no desire to qualify the repeated expressions of this court to the effect that, where the invention is functional, and the defendant's device differs from that of the patentee only in form, or in a rearrangement of the same elements of a combination, he would be adjudged an infringer, even if, in certain particulars, his device be an improvement upon that of the patentee. But, after all, even if the patent for a machine be a pioneer, the alleged infringer must have done something more than reach the same result. He must have reached it by substantially the same or similar means, or the rule that the function of a machine cannot be patented is of no practical value. To say that the patentee of a pioneer invention for a new mechanism is entitled to every mechanical device which produces the same result is to hold, in other language, that he is entitled to patent his function. Mere variations of form may be disregarded, but the substance of the invention must be there.

We are induced to look with more favor upon this device, not only because it is a novel one, and a manifest departure from the principle of the Westinghouse patent, but because it solved at once, in the simplest manner, the problem of quick action, whereas the Westinghouse patent did not prove to be a success until certain additional members had been incorporated into it. The underlying distinction between the two devices is that in one a separate valve and separate by-passage are provided for the train-pipe air, while in the other [Boyden] has taken the old triple (or quadruple) valve, and by a slight change in the functions of two of its valves, and the incorporation of a new element, has made a more perfect brake than the one described in the Westinghouse patent. If credit be due to Mr. Westinghouse for having invented the function, Mr. Boyden has certainly exhibited great ingenuity in the discovery of a new and more perfect method of performing such function. If his [invention] be compared with the later Westinghouse patent, No. 376,837, which appears to have been the first completely successful one, the difference between the two, both in form and principle, becomes still more apparent, and the greater simplicity of the Boyden [device] certainly entitles it to a favorable consideration. If the method pursued by the patentee for the performance of the function discovered by him would naturally have suggested the device adopted by the defendants, that is in itself evidence of an intended infringement; but, although Mr. Boyden may have intended to accomplish the same results, the Westinghouse patent, if he had had it before him, would scarcely have suggested the method he adopted to accomplish these results. Under such circumstances, the law entitles him to the rights of an independent inventor.

Upon a careful consideration of the testimony, we have come to the conclusion that the Boyden device is not an infringement of the complainants' patent, and the decree of the circuit court of appeals is therefore affirmed.

NOTES

1. *Relationship Between Reverse Doctrine and § 112 ¶ 6.* Some cases have pointed out a similarity between the reverse doctrine of equivalents and the equivalency standard of § 112 ¶ 6:

> [This] section has no effect on the function specified — it does not extend the element to equivalent functions. *Pennwalt.* Properly understood section 112 ¶ 6 operates more like the reverse doctrine of equivalents than the doctrine of equivalents because it restricts the scope of the literal claim language. [F]or a means-plus-function limitation to read on an accused device, the accused device must incorporate the means for performing the function disclosed in the specification or a structural equivalent of that means, plus it must perform the identical function. Section 112 ¶ 6 can never provide a basis for finding that a means-plus-function claim element is met literally where the function part of the element is not literally met in an accused device.

Johnston v. IVAC Corp., 885 F.2d 1574, 1580, 12 U.S.P.Q.2d (BNA) 1382 (Fed. Cir. 1989).

2. *Federal Circuit Recognizes Doctrine.* In *SRI Int'l v. Matsushita Elec. Corp. of Am.*, 775 F.2d 1107, 227 U.S.P.Q. (BNA) 577 (Fed. Cir. 1985) (en banc), the Federal Circuit reaffirmed the availability of the reverse doctrine of equivalents as a defense to literal infringement. The case involved a patent on a filter used to encode color information in a color television camera. The patent claimed a filter with two sets of parallel stripes of equal width "relatively angularly superimposed" over one another. The image to be televised is placed behind the filter. When a scanning beam passes over the image the stripes on the filter encode three distinct output signals corresponding to the three-primary-color content of the image. *SRI Int'l v. Matsushita Elec. Corp. of Am.*, 591 F. Supp. 464, 465-69, 224 U.S.P.Q. 70 (N.D. Cal. 1984), *rev'd in part and remanded*, 775 F.2d 1107, 227 U.S.P.Q. (BNA) 577 (Fed. Cir. 1985). The stripes must be aligned at different angles with respect to the vertical for the filter to work. The accused device used a similar design to achieve the same result, but the stripes in its filters must be at forty-five degree angles to one another. The resulting pattern of overlapping stripes causes a different type of signal to be encoded by the scanning beam. By using a different device to decode these signals, the defendant's camera filter ultimately achieves the same output signal as the patentee's.

The court unanimously recognized the validity of a reverse equivalents defense:

> The law ... acknowledges that one may only appear to have appropriated the patented contribution, when a product precisely described in a patent claim is in fact "*so far* changed in principle" that it performs in a "*substantially*

different way" and is not therefore an appropriation (reverse doctrine of equivalents).

775 F.2d at 1123, 227 U.S.P.Q. (BNA) 577 at 580 (emphasis in original) (lead opinion, five judges joining); *id.*, at 1132 (Davis, J., concurring); *id.*, at 1132, 1133 (Kashiwa, J., dissenting, five judges joining). But the court divided sharply on the issue of whether the defendant's camera filter was "so far changed in principle" that it was excused from infringement without more factual proof. *Compare* 775 F.2d at 1125 (genuine issues of material fact still unresolved) (lead opinion, five judges joining); *with id.*, at 1132 (reverse equivalents is always a matter of fact, not law) (Davis, J., concurring) *and id.*, at 1132, 1133 (no genuine factual issues left to resolve; one of two alternative legal findings is that reverse equivalents defense is valid here as a matter of law) (Kashiwa, J., dissenting, five judges joining). *See* 4 D. CHISUM, PATENTS § 18.03[1] (Rev. 1988). It remanded the case with explicit instructions for the trial court to consider the accused infringer's reverse equivalents defense.

3. *Relationship to Nonobviousness?* The *Boyden* Court makes two provocative statements:

> [A]lthough Mr. Boyden may have intended to accomplish the same results, the Westinghouse patent, if he had had it before him, would scarcely have suggested the method he adopted to accomplish these results.

And:

> We are induced to look with more favor upon this device, not only because it is a novel one, and a manifest departure from the principle of the Westinghouse patent, but because it solved at once, in the simplest manner, the problem of quick action, whereas the Westinghouse patent did not prove to be a success until certain additional members had been incorporated into it.

Is the Court suggesting that any nonobvious invention will be deemed free of infringement? Would such a rule make sense? What about blocking patents — would this rule eliminate them? Would that be beneficial? Some of these points are touched on in the following section.

4. *Brake Background.* For some background on the development of the air brake, see A. Martin, *Railroads Triumphant: The Growth, Rejection and Rebirth of a Vital American Force* (1991).

1. REVERSE EQUIVALENTS IN BIOTECHNOLOGY

A fascinating reverse equivalents issue was raised in *Scripps Clinic & Research Found. v. Genentech, Inc.*, 927 F.2d 1565, 18 U.S.P.Q.2d (BNA) 1001, 18 U.S.P.Q.2d (BNA) 1896 (Fed. Cir. 1991), a case typical of an early wave of biotechnology patent actions. Genentech invented and patented the recombinant DNA form of the blood protein Factor VIII:C, a blood clotting agent made by the body and useful in treating patients with clotting disorders. Scripps, meanwhile, had obtained a patent on purified Factor VIII:C, which it made by isolating and purifying the protein from raw human blood. Scripps sued Genentech for infringement of its product patent, citing the conventional rule that a product patent covers the product no matter how it is made. After attempting to distinguish its recombinant version from Scripps' purified natural protein, Genentech ultimately relied on a pragmatic defense: that the recombinant version was by far cheaper to make, and therefore ought not to be deemed an infringement. Reversing the district court, the Federal Circuit held that Scripps had not committed inequitable conduct in procuring its patent, and had not suppressed the best mode for carrying out its invention. But the court remanded for a determination of whether the reverse doctrine of equivalents applied in these circumstances:

> The so-called "reverse doctrine of equivalents" is an equitable doctrine invoked in applying properly construed claims to an accused device. Just as the purpose of the "doctrine of equivalents" is to prevent "pirating" of the patentee's invention, *Graver Tank*, 339 U.S. 605, 607, 608, (1950), so the purpose of the "reverse" doctrine is to prevent unwarranted extension of the claims beyond a fair scope of the patentee's invention.

> The reverse doctrine of equivalents flows from the Supreme Court's statement in *Graver Tank* that an accused article may avoid infringement, even if it is within the literal words of the claim, if it is "so far changed in principle from a patented article that it performs the same or a similar function in a substantially different way." 339 U.S. at 608-09. Application of the doctrine requires that facts specific to the accused device be determined and weighed against the equitable scope of the claims, which in turn is determined in light of the specification, the prosecution history, and the prior art.

> The record contained evidence of the properties of plasma-derived and recombinantly produced VIII:C, which was presented primarily by Scripps in connection with its proofs of infringement. There was deposition testimony that there were differences between VIII:C from plasma and VIII:C obtained by recombinant techniques; a Scripps' witness described the products as "apples and oranges," referring specifically to stability and formulations. The parties disputed, in connection with the summary judgment motions, the capabilities of the respective processes in terms of the purity and specific activities that were enabled for the respective products. The record on this point is extensive.

> Genentech argues that its product is equitably seen as changed "in principle," particularly when viewed in the context of the prior art. Genentech asserts that the specific activities and purity that are obtainable by recombinant technology exceed those available by the Scripps process; an assertion disputed by Scripps, but which if found to be correct could provide — depending on the specific facts of similarities and differences — sufficient ground for invoking the reverse doctrine. These aspects were not discussed by the district court.

The principles of patent law must be applied in accordance with the statutory purpose, and the issues raised by new technologies require considered analysis. Genentech has raised questions of scientific and evidentiary fact that are material to the issue of infringement. Consideration of extrinsic evidence is required, and summary judgment is inappropriate. The grant of summary judgment of infringement of [the product] claims is reversed. The issue requires trial.

927 F.2d at 1581.

2. AN ECONOMIC APPROACH TO THE *SCRIPPS* PROBLEM

The following discussion is adapted from Merges & Nelson, *On the Complex Economics of Patent Scope*, 90 COLUM. L. REV. 839 (1990).

The Supreme Court in *Boyden v. Westinghouse* announced the reverse doctrine of equivalents, and the Federal Circuit has alluded to it several times in recent years. But little has been said about the rationale behind it. This section attempts a defense of the doctrine, an economic justification for it, and a discussion of occasions when it might usefully be applied.

To understand what role the reverse doctrine can play, it must be set in context. In truth, it is an extreme form of a related group of doctrinal tools in patent law. The goal of these tools is to accommodate two sets of property rights: those of a pioneer, or first inventor who opens up a new set of technological opportunities, and those of improvers, who follow with refinements, applications, and extensions of the pioneer's basic work. When the pioneer clashes with the improver over property rights, patent law responds with one of several solutions.

Most commonly, the improver will seek an improvement patent. This explicitly recognizes that the pioneer has a dominant position. It is of course preferable for an inventor to have her own patent free and clear of anyone else's claims. An inventor will therefore not often voluntarily characterize her invention as subservient. One example of patents that are so characterized is an improvement patent whose claims are drafted in a special format called "Jepson claims." *See, e.g., Pentec, Inc. v. Graphic Controls Corp.*, 776 F.2d 309, 227 U.S.P.Q. 766 (Fed. Cir. 1985). *See generally* R. ELLIS, PATENT CLAIMS § 197 (1949). Improvement patents are specifically provided for in the Patent Act, see 35 U.S.C § 101 (1988). A Jepson claim has the same effect as a judicial finding that a patented invention is "dominated" by another invention. Strictly speaking, only a patent drafted in Jepson format is an improvement patent.

Alternatively, when the pioneer sues an infringer who holds a patent (which may or may not take the form of an improvement patent per se), a court may hold the improver's patent is valid but subservient to the pioneer's patent. These outcomes are common. *See United States Steel Corp. v. Phillips Petr. Co.*, 865 F.2d 1247, 9 U.S.P.Q.2d 1461 (Fed. Cir. 1989) ("'Dominating' patents are not uncommon."). According to traditional doctrine, significant technical improvements in a device accused of infringement do not excuse the infringement. *See*, *e.g.*, *Herman v. Youngstown Car Mfg. Co.*, 191 F. 579, 584-85 (6th Cir. 1911); *Bendix Corp. v. United States*, 199 U.S.P.Q. 203 (Ct. Cl. Trial Div. 1978), *aff'd*, 600 F.2d 1364, 204 U.S.P.Q. (BNA) 617 (Ct. Cl. 1979) ("Improvement in plaintiff's invention by defendant's modifications, while possibly affording a basis for a separate patent on the improvement, does not constitute a defense of noninfringement."). *See also Atlas Powder Co. v. E.I. duPont de Nemours & Co.*, 750 F.2d 1569, 224 U.S.P.Q. 409 (BNA) 409 (Fed. Cir. 1984) (issuance of patent to accused infringer is irrelevant to question of infringement under the doctrine of equivalents). In such a case, a court will find that the accused infringer holds a valid but subservient patent — in effect an improvement patent.

Under either scenario, the end result is that the pioneer patent and the improver will hold blocking patents. Two patents are said to block each other when one patentee has a broad patent on an invention and another has a narrower patent on some improved feature of that invention. The broad patent is said to "dominate" the narrower one. In such a situation, the holder of the narrower ("subservient") patent cannot practice her invention without a license from the holder of the dominant patent. At the same time, the holder of the dominant patent cannot practice the particular improved feature claimed in the narrower patent without a license.

Two aspects of this situation may seem counterintuitive: that the narrower (subservient) patent could ever be issued by the Patent Office, given the existence of the broad patent in the prior art; and that once the subservient patent were issued, the holder of the dominant patent would be prevented from practicing an invention that clearly falls within the scope of her claims. Subservient patents may be issued, however, when they disclose an improved feature which meets the statutory tests of novelty and nonobviousness. *See, e.g.*, *Atlas Powder Co. v. E.I. duPont de Nemours & Co.*, 750 F.2d 1569, 224 U.S.P.Q. 409 (Fed. Cir. 1984) (the fact that the subservient patentee has invented a nonobvious variant of a device covered by a broad patent does not mean that the broad patent is invalid for lack of enabling disclosure under 35 U.S.C. § 112); *B.G. Corp. v. Walter Kidde & Co.*, 79 F.2d 20, 22 (2d Cir. 1935) (L. Hand, J.) ("It is true that [the inventor of the spark plug] did not foresee the particular adaptability of his plug to the airplane .... Nevertheless, he did not shoot in the dark; he laid down with perfect certainty what he wished to accomplish and how .... He is not charged with a prophetic understanding of the entire field of its usefulness."); *Amerace Corp. v. Ferro Corp.*, 532 F. Supp. 1188, 1202, 213 U.S.P.Q. 1099, 1202 (D. Tex. 1982)). And a subservient patent can prevent a dominant patent holder from practicing the particular improved feature claimed in the subservient patent. This stems from the fact that the patent grant is a right to *exclude*, not an affirmative right to practice an invention. *See* 35 U.S.C. § 154. Thus the dominant patentee can exclude the subservient patentee from practicing her invention at all; and the subservient patentee can exclude the dominant patentee from practicing her specific improved feature. *See Atlas Powder, supra; Ziegler v. Phillips Petr. Co.*, 483 F.2d 858, 177 U.S.P.Q. 481 (5th Cir. 1973). *Cf. Cochrane v. Deener*, 94

U.S. 780, 787 (1856); *Cantrell v. Wallick*, 117 U.S. 689, 694 (1886). *See* Chapter 6, Section B.3.a, *Enablement and the Temporal Paradox.*

Even where a court finds a patent subservient to another — thus creating blocking patents — the holder of the subservient patent is still better off than if she had never filed a patent at all, for two reasons. First, she can exclude the holder of the broad patent from practicing her improvement. Although the improver may literally infringe the broad patent, she may gain some bargaining leverage by obtaining the subservient patent. Second, because of this, she may be able to reduce the dominant patentee's damages in an infringement action; the dominant patentee would not have replaced all the infringer's sales, presumably, because the infringer's sales were based at least in part on her improved feature. *See Water Techs. Corp. v. Calco, Ltd.*, 850 F.2d 660, 7 U.S.P.Q.2d (BNA) 1097 (Fed. Cir. 1988). *See* 5 D. CHISUM, PATENTS § 20.03[3] (1989), at 20-135 through 20-136 ("In a case of blocking industrial property rights, the reasonable royalty would have to reflect an appropriate apportionment of the expected economic benefits.")

In the face of very substantial technological improvements, however, blocking patents may not be an effective accommodation of the rights of the parties. This is where the reverse doctrine of equivalents can — and sometimes has — come into play.

Although the doctrine is rarely used (*see Ethyl Molded Prods. Co. v. Betts Package, Inc.*, 9 U.S.P.Q.2d 1001, 1026 (E.D. Ky. 1988) ("The reverse doctrine of equivalents, although frequently argued by infringers, has never been applied by the Federal Circuit.")), it holds great potential for resolving certain cases where a literal infringement is made out but seems unfair or likely to lead to bad results. These cases involve improvements that represent very significant advances over the basic pioneering invention.

At first blush, the technical merits of the allegedly infringing device might seem to be irrelevant where literal infringement is concerned. After all, a patent is the right to exclude; an astoundingly meritorious improvement, while no doubt deserving a patent of its own, ought not escape infringement. The improver can patent the improvement, but this should not affect the original patentee's rights.

This is an appealing argument. An economic rationale for improvement patents would stress their tendency to encourage bargaining between improvers and original patentees. To the extent the improver has a very significant cost-saving technology, it would be in the interest of the original patentee to cross-license with the improver, to gain access to the improved technology.

Unfortunately, the original patentee may use her patent as a "holdup" right, in an attempt to garner as much of the value of the improvement as possible. The "holdup" problem was originally applied to situations where one buyer needs to acquire complementary assets from a number of sellers; some of the sellers may raise their prices to capture some of the value the buyer attributes to holding all the assets. *See, e.g.*, Calabresi & Malamed, *Property Rules, Liability Rules, and Inalienability: One View of the Cathedral*, 85 HARV. L. REV. 1089, 1106-07

(1972) (example of sale of small parcels of land to buyer who needs all parcels, e.g., to build a highway; used as illustration of the necessity for a "liability rule" such as eminent domain, as opposed to an absolute or "property rule"). It has been extended to two-party contracts, see Klein, Crawford & Alchian, *Vertical Integration, Appropriable Rents, and the Competitive Contracting Process*, 21 J.L. & ECON. 21 (1978); Klein, *Transaction Cost Determinants of "Unfair" Contractual Arrangements*, 70 AM. ECON. REV. PAP. & PROC. 356 (1980), reprinted in READINGS IN THE ECONOMICS OF CONTRACT LAW 139 (V. Goldberg ed., 1988) (describing post-contract formation opportunities to assert holdup rights). The paper by Klein, Crawford and Alchian presents the best analogy to the improver-original patentee bargaining situation. This paper describes the opportunities for exerting holdup rights where one firm, after investing in an asset with a low salvage value and a rent stream that is highly dependent on an asset owned by another firm, can be held up by the other firm's attempt to capture a large proportion of the rent stream of the combined assets. The owner of an improvement that contributes a very significant part of the value of the "original patent plus improvement" combination — i.e., an improvement that represents a major technical advance — is subject to the same sort of "holdup" by the original patent holder.

The chances of the pioneer's holdup right being successful depend on the relative contributions of the original patented invention and the improvement to the "original plus improvement" combination. Where the original invention contributes most of the value, or where the original and improvement inventions contribute roughly equal value, issuing an improvement patent may be a reasonable solution. But where the original patent contributes very little value compared to the improvement, the holdup problem may be significant. That is, the holder of the original patent may use it to extract much of the value of the "original plus improvement" combination from the improver.

To see why this would be bad from society's point of view, consider this example. An original patent has a value of $100; an improvement, also worth $100, is invented, and its inventor wishes to obtain the right to use it by bargaining with the holder of the original patent. Here the parties may well reach a bargain whereby the original patentee gains $50 of the value of the improvement, and the improver keeps $50 of this gain, for a total allocation of $150 for the original patentee and $50 for the improver. (Of course, the gain may be greater if the original patentee is especially "strategic"; or it may be lower if she is exceptionally "fair"; or the parties might not reach any agreement at all, and the improvement will have to wait until the original patent expires; but the 50-50 allocation is a good approximation, based on empirical findings. *See* H. RAIFFA, THE ART AND SCIENCE OF NEGOTIATION 48 (1982) (describing experiments where the best predictor of final agreement price was the midway point between the opening offers of sellers and buyers).) While this may tend to reduce the incentives to invent improvements below the optimal level — since the improver keeps only $50 of the $100 in extra value generated by the improvement — it is a reasonable result in this case given the strong policy in favor of preserving the reward for the original patentee, and thus incentives for future original patentees. And of course it recognizes that part of the value of the improvement stems from the pioneering invention — which is (in the language of torts) a "but for" cause of the improvement.

But where the improvement adds value of $900 compared to the original patent's value of $100, the holdup problem becomes acute. Here if the parties bargain for an equal allocation of the improvement's value, the improver keeps only $450 of the total value of the improvement, $900. The reduced incentives to invent such substantial improvements are obvious from this example; not even the strong policy favoring incentives for the original patentee to invent can justify such a "windfall" to the original patentee at the expense of the improver. Note also that the social cost in those cases where the parties cannot agree, and where the very significant improvement therefore sits on the shelf for the life of the original patent, is by definition great. Note too that such "deadlocks" do occur, and in fact a certain number of them are predictable, even where the bargaining parties are acting rationally. *See* Cooter, Marks & Mnookin, *Bargaining in the Shadow of the Law: A Testable Model of Strategic Behavior*, 11 J. LEGAL STUD. 225, 226 (1982) (even optimal bargaining strategies imply a positive probability of deadlock).

The reverse doctrine of equivalents solves the problem, by in effect excusing the improver from infringement liability — and therefore removing the original patentee's holdup right. Reverse equivalents, of course, did not evolve in explicit recognition of this problem. In fact, the most efficient way to deal with the problem would probably be a system of compulsory licensing, whereby the improver would pay a "fair" royalty to the original patentee. This is not part of U.S. patent law, however. Current patent law in fact leaves us with two "second-best" alternatives, finding infringement or finding no infringement. Thus the account of the reverse doctrine of equivalents given here is meant to be an explanation of how to work with our admittedly second-best system.

But the fear of the inefficient use of holdup power does provide a rational account of the doctrine, and might even assist courts in applying it. Assertion of a holdup right may be inefficient for three reasons: first, it may prevent the improvement from being introduced until the original patent expires; second, it may cause a delay shorter than the full patent term, e.g., because of litigation or bargaining time; and third, it may lead to higher cost to the consumer. In this connection, it is worth noting that many studies find that the social returns to particular innovations far exceed the private returns; thus society as a whole may well bear the greatest efficiency loss. *See* Griliches, *Research Expenditures, Education and the Aggregate Agricultural Production Function*, 44 AM. ECON. REV. 961 (1964) (social rate of return on agricultural research is at least 150% greater than the private rate of return to the researchers); Mansfield et al., *Social and Private Rates of Return from Industrial Innovations*, 91 Q.J. ECON. 221 (1977) (concluding that social rate of return on 17 major product innovations was between 77% and 150% greater than the private rate of return); Bresnahan, *Measuring the Spillovers from Technical Advance: Mainframe Computers in Financial Services*, 76 AM. ECON. REV. 742, 753 (1986) (very large social gain from mainframe computers, 1.5 to 2.0 orders of magnitude above cost of inventing them).

Note too that the same rationale could be applied to analysis of infringement under the doctrine of equivalents; the more significant the technological advance represented by the allegedly infringing device, the less willing the courts should be to find it an equivalent of the patentee's device. Perhaps it is even more useful in that context. Because reverse equivalents applies only where there is *literal* infringement, the improvement at issue has to be very significant to qualify for infringement immunity under the reverse doctrine of equivalents. If literal infringement were often excused, the original patentee would not have much faith in the value of her patent; this might significantly reduce her incentive to invent in the first place. But where the improvement allegedly infringes only under the doctrine of equivalents — a less certain area of the original patentee's scope — there will likely be less of an impact on the original inventor's incentives.

So doctrine can be more sensitive to the degree of advance represented by the improvement where it allegedly infringes under the doctrine of equivalents. In terms of the model discussed in this section, the doctrine of equivalents — as opposed to reverse equivalents — can be used to remedy a greater number of potentially inefficient "holdups" by original patentees.

To see when reverse equivalents might make sense, consider the problem of broad claims encompassing embodiments that can be made only after significant additional research is performed. The *Westinghouse* case is an example; Boyden's brake involved a triple-valve, and was therefore within the boundaries of the Westinghouse patent. The Court nevertheless refused to find infringement, since Boyden's invention was "a manifest departure from the principle of the patent ...." *Westinghouse, supra*, 170 U.S. 537, 572. Judge Newman of the Federal Circuit has acknowledged that the reverse equivalents doctrine "is invoked when claims are written more broadly than the disclosure warrants." *Texas Instruments, Inc. v. United States Int'l Trade Comm'n*, 846 F.2d 1369, 1372 (Fed. Cir. 1986), *denying rehearing of* 805 F.2d 1558, 231 U.S.P.Q. (BNA) 833, 835 (Fed. Cir. 1986).

The "Harvard mouse" patent on transgenic mice may someday give rise to a similar situation. Doctors Phillip Leder and Timothy Stewart of the Harvard Medical School received a patent for their successful work involving transgenic mice. They isolated a gene which is associated with cancer in mammals (including humans) and then injected the gene into a fertilized mouse egg, which yielded transgenic mice that are extremely sensitive to carcinogens. *See* U.S. Patent No. 4,736,866, issued April 12, 1988. This makes the mice excellent animal "models" for studying cancer drugs. Leder and Stewart claimed not only the technique they had used, or the particular transgenic mice variety they had created, but rather all "non-human transgenic mammals" produced by their technique. If subsequently-developed technology falling within its claims requires very substantial additional research, the reverse doctrine of equivalents might be relevant. If, for instance, a latter-day Boyden comes along and invents a recombinant cow after very substantial research well beyond that of Leder and Stewart, a court should find that technique non-infringing. *See* Bozicevic, *The "Reverse Doctrine of Equivalents" in the World of Reverse Transcriptase*, 71 J. PAT. & TRADEMARK OFF. SOC'Y 353, 360-69 (1989) (arguing that the Leder and Stewart patent ought to be narrowed under reverse equivalents if, for example, a subsequent inventor discloses a "substantially different" method of introducing foreign genetic material into a mammal's genome). Despite the Federal Circuit's unwillingness to use the reverse doctrine of equivalents so far, there is nothing in its statement of the doctrine that would preclude its application in such a case. *See, e.g.,* *United States Steel Corp. v. Phillips Petr. Co.*, 865 F.2d 1247, 9 U.S.P.Q.2d (BNA) 1461, 1466 n.9 (Fed. Cir. 1989) (approving of trial court's treatment of reverse equivalents as question of whether "the 'principle' of the contribution made by the inventor [is] ... unchanged in the accused product").

In any event, *some* content must be given to the reverse doctrine of equivalents, since the Supreme Court has indicated that this doctrine does form part of patent law. This section simply attempts to find one rational account for the doctrine.

NOTES

1. *Applying the Economic Approach to Biotechnology.*

In the *Scripps* case, the trial court might consider the "value-added" of the accused recombinant protein as compared to that of the patentee's natural, purified protein. This would be consistent with Judge Newman's directions to "weigh[ ]" the "facts specific to the accused device" against "the equitable scope of the claims ...," and might even be seen as an appropriate method to carry out those directions.

Merges, *A Brief Note on Blocking Patents and the Reverse Doctrine of Equivalents in Biotechnology Cases*, 72 J. PAT. & TRADEMARK OFF. SOC'Y 870 (1991).

2. *Shortchanging the Pioneer?* The preceding discussion assumes that in some cases the "value added" by the improvement exceeds the contribution of the original pioneering invention. How can this be, it might be asked, when without the original contribution there would be nothing to add value to? Isn't all the value of the original-plus-improvement combination in some sense attributable to the pioneer?

In some sense this objection cannot be countered, except by an appeal to pragmatic considerations. In general, if cause A is a "but for" cause of some event C, then the fact that contributing cause B is also required cannot undercut the claim that A is "the cause" of event C. A, in other words, is a necessary condition for event C; so how can one say A is "unimportant," or "less important than B" in bringing about C?

The answer is that in some cases one *must* say so to avoid absurd results. In the field of torts, for instance, courts scrutinize a "but for" cause of some catastrophic event to determine further whether it is the (or at least a) *proximate cause* of the event. The conventional justification is that the liability of one who brings about a "but for" cause must be cut off at some point, or else the long series of events following her behavior — over which she has no control — will wind up costing her a great deal of money. Unfairly, the reasoning goes.

The same thinking may be applied to a pioneer inventor. True, she is a necessary cause of all improvements which follow — by definition. (It is useless to quibble about when someone else would have come up with the pioneering advance, and whether that someone would have been one of the improvers.) But she is not a *sufficient* cause of the improvement. Other causal strands are required to bring this about. Because of this, the original pioneer cannot justly lay claim to all improvements that flow from her basic work. Although absurd examples are easy to contrive — Newton claiming "credit" for the Apollo spacecraft, van Neumann for a supercomputer — more pedestrian examples prove the same point. Westinghouse's air brake, for example, was substantially improved upon by Boyden's (according to the Court); so too with the accused calculators in the *Texas Instruments* case. In both cases, courts refused to say that the "cause-in-fact" (the pioneering inventions) were truly the proximate cause of the improvements. Enough substantial effort *over and above* the pioneering work was required to make the improvements that the courts felt it was necessary to limit the scope of the pioneer patent so as to exclude the improvements.

Perhaps reasoning similar to that of the cause-in-fact/proximate cause variety is in order here. Just as the distinction between causal types is socially useful, in that it limits the scope of liability for one's actions, a distinction between creation of pioneer inventions and claims to very significant improvements is in order. The fear of responsibility for a never-ending cascade of events flowing from an original cause-in-fact would render any action fraught with risk, and hence deter no doubt useful actions. By the same token, the promise of infringement liability for any improvement, no matter how significant, might well deter some improvers — or at least, in light of the holdup bargaining problem described above, might deter the improvements from reaching the market. Thus there is the need for a socially useful distinction here too. In other words, the law is justified in saying in certain cases that an improver, such as Boyden, is the *main* reason the pioneer-plus-improvement combination is a technical success. Although "but for" the pioneer, the improvement is not possible, the improvement might still be considered the "proximate cause" of the pioneer-plus-improvement's success. Just as in the case of tort law, *legal* causation may be different from *actual* causation where sound policy demands.

3. For a general treatment of the bargaining problem between a pioneer and an improver, see Robert P. Merges, *Intellectual Property Rights and Bargaining Breakdown: The Case of Blocking Patents*, 62 TENN. L. REV. 75 (1994) (arguing that reverse doctrine of equivalents can be used to influence reluctant pioneers

looking to exert "holdup rights" on radical improvers). *See also* Suzanne Scotchmer & Jerrry Green, *On the Division of Profit in Sequential Innovation*, 26 RAND J. ECON. 20 (1995) (describing empirically rare case where pioneer can bargain in advance with improver).

D. INDIRECT INFRINGEMENT

In this chapter so far we have focused on acts of direct infringement — cases where the defendant in an infringement case made, used or sold something said to be covered by the patentee's property right. What if the accused infringer simply sells a key part of the overall device covered by the patent? What if the infringer merely participates with others in a course of conduct that leads to infringement? These cases of so-called "indirect infringement," covered by Patent Act §§ 271(b) and (c), are the subject of this section.

§ 271. Infringement

(b) Whoever actively induces infringement of a patent shall be liable as an infringer.

(c) Whoever sells a component of a patented machine, manufacture, combination or composition, or a material or apparatus for use in practicing a patented process, constituting a material part of the invention, knowing the same to be especially made or especially adapted for use in an infringement of such patent, and not a staple article or commodity of commerce suitable for substantial noninfringing use, shall be liable as a contributory infringer.

The following case, an important Supreme Court opinion on contributory infringement, is the ideal starting point. But note: intertwined in the § 271(c) issue is a complex issue involving "patent misuse" — the inequitable "leveraging" of a patent, discussed at length in Chapter 11. As you read the case, be aware that a "non-staple" item under the statute is an item made to work with a patented device that has no "substantial noninfringing use" — i.e., is basically useful *only* in conjunction with the patented device.

DAWSON CHEMICAL CO. v. ROHM & HAAS CO.
448 U.S. 176, 206 U.S.P.Q. (BNA) 385 (1980)

This case presents an important question of statutory interpretation arising under the patent laws. The issue before us is whether the owner of a patent on a chemical process is guilty of patent misuse, and therefore is barred from seeking relief against contributory infringement of its patent rights, if it exploits the patent only in conjunction with the sale of an unpatented article that constitutes a material part of the invention and is not suited for commercial use outside the scope of the patent claims. The answer will determine whether respondent, the owner of a process patent on a chemical herbicide, may maintain an action for contributory infringement against other manufacturers of the chemical used in the process. To resolve this issue, we must construe the various provisions of 35 U.S.C. § 271, which Congress enacted in 1952 to codify certain aspects of the doctrines of contributory infringement and patent misuse that previously had been developed by the judiciary.

The doctrines of contributory infringement and patent misuse have long and interrelated histories. The idea that a patentee should be able to obtain relief against those whose acts facilitate infringement by others has been part of our law since *Wallace v. Holmes*, 29 F. Cas. 74 (No. 17,100) (C.C. Conn. 1871). The idea that a patentee should be denied relief against infringers if he has attempted illegally to extend the scope of his patent monopoly is of somewhat more recent origin, but it goes back at least as far as *Motion Picture Patents Co. v. Universal Film Mfg. Co.*, 243 U.S. 502 (1917). The two concepts, contributory infringement and patent misuse, often are juxtaposed, because both concern the relationship between a patented invention and unpatented articles or elements that are needed for the invention to be practiced.

The catalyst for this litigation is a chemical compound known to scientists as "3, 4-dichloropropionanilide" and referred to in the chemical industry as "propanil." In the late 1950's, it was discovered that this compound had properties that made it useful as a selective, "post-emergence" herbicide particularly well suited for the cultivation of rice.

Efforts to obtain patent rights to propanil or its use as a herbicide have been continuous since the herbicidal qualities of the chemical first came to light. The initial contender for a patent monopoly for this chemical compound was the Monsanto Company. In 1957, Monsanto filed the first of three successive applications for a patent on propanil itself. After lengthy proceedings in the United States Patent Office, a patent, No. 3,382,280, finally was issued in 1968. It was declared invalid, however, when Monsanto sought to enforce it by suing Rohm and Haas Company (Rohm & Haas), a competing manufacturer, for direct infringement.

Invalidation of the Monsanto patent cleared the way for Rohm & Haas, respondent here, to obtain a patent on the method or process for applying propanil. This is the patent on which the present lawsuit is founded. [O]n June 11, 1974, the United States Patent Office issued Patent No. 3,816,092 (the Wilson patent) to Harold F. Wilson and Dougal H. McRay.

Petitioners, too, are chemical manufacturers. They have manufactured and sold propanil for application to rice crops since before Rohm & Haas received its patent. They market the chemical in containers on which are printed directions for application in accordance with the method claimed in the Wilson patent. Petitioners did not cease manufacture and sale of propanil after that patent issued, despite knowledge that farmers purchasing their products would infringe on the patented method by applying the propanil to their crops. Accordingly, Rohm & Haas filed this suit. The complaint alleged not only that petitioners contributed to infringement by farmers who purchased and used petitioners' propanil, but also that they actually induced such infringement by instructing farmers how to apply the herbicide. When Rohm & Haas refused to grant licenses [to petitioner Dawson], petitioners raised a defense of patent misuse and counterclaimed for alleged antitrust violations by respondent. [The district court ruled for Dawson, finding that Rohm & Haas had practiced "patent misuse" under § 271(d), covered at length in Chapter 11. The Fifth Circuit reversed.]

The parties agree that Rohm & Haas makes and sells propanil; that it has refused to license petitioners or any others to do the same; that it has not granted express licenses either to retailers or to end users of the product; and that farmers who buy propanil from Rohm & Haas may use it, without fear of being sued for direct infringement, by virtue of an "implied license" they obtain when Rohm & Haas relinquishes its monopoly by selling the propanil.

Petitioners assert that there has been misuse because respondent has "tied" the sale of patent rights to the purchase of propanil, an unpatented and indeed unpatentable article, and because it has refused to grant licenses to other producers of the chemical compound. [*See* Chapter 11.]

[T]he doctrine of contributory infringement had its genesis in an era of simpler and less subtle technology. Its basic elements are perhaps best explained with a classic example drawn from that era. In *Wallace v. Holmes*, 29 F. Cas. 74 (No. 17,100) (C.C. Conn. 1871), the patentee had invented a new burner for an oil lamp. In compliance with the technical rules of patent claiming, this invention was patented in a combination that also included the standard fuel reservoir, wick tube, and chimney necessary for a properly functioning lamp. After the patent issued, a competitor began to market a rival product including the novel burner but not the chimney. Under the sometimes scholastic law of patents, this conduct did not amount to direct infringement, because the competitor had not replicated every single element of the patentee's claimed combination. Yet the court held that there had been "palpable interference" with the patentee's legal rights, because purchasers would be certain to complete the combination, and hence the infringement, by adding the glass chimney. The court permitted the patentee to enforce his rights against the competitor who brought about the infringement, rather than requiring the patentee to undertake the almost insuperable task of finding and suing all the innocent purchasers who technically were responsible for completing the infringement.

The *Wallace* case demonstrates, in a readily comprehensible setting, the reason for the contributory infringement doctrine. It exists to protect patent rights from subversion by those who, without directly infringing the patent themselves, engage in acts designed to facilitate infringement by others. This protection is of particular importance in situations, like the oil lamp case itself, where enforcement against direct infringers would be difficult, and where the technicalities of patent law make it relatively easy to profit from another's invention without risking a charge of direct infringement.

The judicial history of contributory infringement may be said to be marked by a period of ascendancy, in which the doctrine was expanded to the point where it became subject to abuse, followed by a somewhat longer period of decline, in which the concept of patent misuse was developed as an increasingly stringent antidote to the perceived excesses of the earlier period.

The contributory infringement doctrine achieved its high-water mark with the decision in *Henry v. A. B. Dick Co.*, 224 U.S. 1 (1912). In that case a divided Court extended contributory infringement principles to permit a conditional licensing arrangement whereby a manufacturer of a patented printing machine could require purchasers to obtain all supplies used in connection with the invention, including such staple items as paper and ink, exclusively from the patentee. The Court reasoned that the market for these supplies was created by the invention, and that sale of a license to use the patented product, like sale of other species of property, could be limited by whatever conditions the property owner wished to impose.

[The Court then reviews the "inevitable" reaction to this case and its progeny, a series of cases wherein suits for contributory infringement were unsuccessful, and patentees' efforts to commercialize inventions under certain restrictive licensing agreements led to the invalidation of the patents under the doctrine of patent misuse; *see* Chapter 11.]

[I]n *Mercoid Corp. v. Mid-Continent Investment Co.*, 320 U.S. 661 (1944) (*Mercoid I*), and *Mercoid Corp. v. Minneapolis-Honeywell Regulator Co.*, 320 U.S. 680 (1944) (*Mercoid II*), the Court definitely held that any attempt to control the market for unpatented goods would constitute patent misuse, even if those goods had no use outside a patented invention.

The critical inquiry in this case is how the enactment of § 271 affected the doctrines of contributory infringement and patent misuse. Viewed against the backdrop of judicial precedent, we believe that the language and structure of the statute lend significant support to Rohm & Haas' contention that, because § 271(d) immunizes its conduct from the charge of patent misuse, it should not be barred from seeking relief. The approach that Congress took toward the codification of contributory infringement and patent misuse reveals a compromise between those two doctrines and their competing policies that permits patentees to exercise control over nonstaple articles used in their inventions.

Section 271(c) identifies the basic dividing line between contributory infringement and patent misuse. It adopts a restrictive definition of contributory infringement that distinguishes between staple and nonstaple articles of commerce. It also defines the class of nonstaple items narrowly.

The limitations on contributory infringement written into § 271(c) are counterbalanced by limitations on patent misuse in § 271(d). In our view, the provisions of § 271(d) effectively confer upon the patentee, as a lawful adjunct of his patent rights, a limited power to exclude others from competition in nonstaple goods. A patentee may sell a nonstaple article himself while enjoining others from marketing that same good without his authorization. By doing so, he is able to eliminate competitors and thereby to control the market for that product. Moreover, his power to demand royalties from others for the privilege of selling the nonstaple item itself implies that the patentee may control the market for the nonstaple good; otherwise, his "right" to sell licenses for the marketing of the nonstaple good would be meaningless, since no one would be willing to pay him for a superfluous authorization.

Rohm & Haas' conduct is not dissimilar in either nature or effect from the conduct that is thus clearly embraced within § 271(d). It sells propanil; it authorizes others to use propanil; and it sues contributory infringers. These are all protected activities. Rohm & Haas does not license others to sell propanil, but nothing on the face of the statute requires it to do so. To be sure, the sum effect of Rohm & Haas' actions is to suppress competition in the market for an unpatented commodity. But as we have observed, in this its conduct is no different from that which the statute expressly protects. The one aspect of Rohm & Haas' behavior that is not expressly covered by § 271(d) is its linkage of two protected activities — sale of propanil and authorization to practice the patented process — together in a single transaction. We find nothing in this legislative history to support the assertion that respondent's behavior falls outside the scope of § 271(d). To the contrary, respondent has done nothing that would extend its right of control over unpatented goods beyond the line that Congress drew. Respondent, to be sure, has licensed use of its patented process only in connection with purchases of propanil. But propanil is a nonstaple product, and its herbicidal property is the heart of respondent's invention. Respondent's method of doing business is thus essentially the same as the method condemned in the *Mercoid* decisions, and the legislative history reveals that § 271(d) was designed to retreat from *Mercoid* in this regard.

The policy of free competition runs deep in our law. It underlies both the doctrine of patent misuse and the general principle that the boundary of a patent monopoly is to be limited by the literal scope of the patent claims. But the policy of stimulating invention that underlies the entire patent system runs no less deep. And the doctrine of contributory infringement, which has been called "an expression both of law and morals," *Mercoid I*, 320 U.S., at 677 (Frankfurter, J., dissenting), can be of crucial importance in ensuring that the endeavors and investments of the inventor do not go unrewarded.

NOTE

The Aro Cases: Repair/Reconstruction and Contributory Infringement. In *Aro Mfg. Co. v. Convertible Top Co.*, 365 U.S. 336, 81 S. Ct. 599, 5 L. Ed. 2d 592 (1961) (*Aro I*), and *Aro Mfg. Co. v. Convertible Top Co.*, 377 U.S. 476, 84 S. Ct. 1526, 12 L. Ed. 2d 457 (1964) (*Aro II*), the Court made some involved but important statements on the issue of contributory infringement. These decisions emerged from a single case involving an action for contributory infringement based on the manufacture and sale of a specially cut fabric designed for use in a patented automobile convertible top combination. In *Aro I*, the Court held that purchasers of the specially cut fabric used it for "repair" rather than "reconstruction" of the patented combination; accordingly, under the patent law they were not guilty of infringement. 365 U.S. at 340.

In *Aro II*, the Court held that supplying replacement fabrics specially cut for use in the infringing repair constituted contributory infringement under § 271(c). The Court held that the specially cut fabrics, when installed in infringing equipment, qualified as nonstaple items within the language of § 271(c), and that supply of similar materials for infringing repair had been treated as contributory infringement under the judicial law that § 271(c) was designed to codify. 377 U.S. at 485-88. It also held that § 271(c) requires a showing that an alleged contributory infringer know that the combination for which his component was especially designed was both patented and infringing. 377 U.S. at 488-91.

For more recent cases on the "repair/reconstruction" doctrine, see *Dana Corp. v. American Precision Co.*, 827 F.2d 755, 758 (Fed. Cir. 1987) (repair/reconstruction a matter of law); *Porter v. Farmers Supply Serv.*, 617 F. Supp. 1175, 1185 n.6 (D. Del. 1985), *aff'd*, 790 F.2d 882 (Fed. Cir. 1986) (same); *Met-Coil Sys. v. Korners Unltd.*, 803 F.2d 684, 687, 231 U.S.P.Q. 474, 477 (Fed. Cir. 1986) (finding of contributory infringement requires finding of direct infringement by someone); *Standard Oil Co. v. Nippon Shokubai Kagaku Kogyo Co.*, 754 F.2d 345, 348-49, 224 U.S.P.Q. 863, 865-66 (Fed. Cir. 1985) (same).

C.R. BARD, INC. v. ADVANCED CARDIOVASCULAR SYSTEMS

911 F.2d 670, 15 U.S.P.Q.2d (BNA) 1540 (Fed. Cir. 1990)

PLAGER, CIRCUIT JUDGE.

This is a case of claimed infringement of a method patent for a medical treatment. Defendant-Appellant Advanced Cardiovascular Systems, Inc. (ACS) was marketing [a] perfusion catheter for use in coronary angioplasty [, a surgical procedure whereby clogged arteries in the heart are re-opened by inserting a balloon and inflating it slightly]. Plaintiff-Appellee C.R. Bard, Inc. (Bard) sued ACS for alleged infringement of U.S. Patent No. 4,581,017 ('017), which Bard had purchased all rights to as of December 31, 1986. The '017 patent relates to a method for using a catheter in coronary angioplasty. The district court granted plaintiff Bard summary judgment against ACS, finding infringement of claim 1 of the '017 patent. We reverse the grant of summary judgment and remand the case for further proceedings.

Plaintiff Bard alleges that the ACS catheter is especially adapted for use by a surgeon in the course of administering a coronary angioplasty in a manner that infringes claim 1 of the '017 patent, that therefore ACS is a contributory infringer, and that ACS actively induces infringement. Of course, a finding of induced or contributory infringement must be predicated on a direct infringement of claim 1 by the users of the ACS catheter. For purposes of this case, the statute requires that ACS sell a catheter for use in practicing the '017 process, which use constitutes a material part of the invention, knowing that the catheter is especially made or adapted for use in infringing the patent, and that the catheter is not a staple article or commodity of commerce suitable for substantial noninfringing use. In asserting ACS's contributory infringement of claim 1, Bard seeks to establish the requisite direct infringement by arguing that there is no evidence that any angioplasty procedures using the ACS catheter would be noninfringing. Testing this assertion requires a two step analysis. First is a determination of the scope of the claim at issue. Second is an examination of the evidence before the court to ascertain whether, under § 271(c), use of the ACS catheter would infringe the claim as interpreted.

Bard argues that [a] prior art patent teaches the use of the catheter with the inlets (side openings) where the blood enters the tube placed only in the aorta, whereas the '017 method in suit involves insertion of the catheter into the coronary artery in such a manner that the openings "immediately adjacent [the] balloon fluidly connect locations within [the] coronary artery surrounding [the] proximal and distal portions of [the] tube." Thus, Bard argues, a surgeon, inserting the ACS catheter into a coronary artery to a point where an inlet at the catheter's proximal end draws blood from the artery, infringes the '017 patent.

[I]t is important to note that the ACS catheter has a series of ten openings in the tube near, and at the proximal end of, the balloon. The first of these openings — the one closest to the balloon — is approximately six millimeters (less than ¼ inch) from the edge of the proximal end of the balloon. The remainder are located along the main lumen at intervals, the furthest from the balloon being 6.3 centimeters (approximately 2½ inches) away.

It would appear that three possible fact patterns may arise in the course of using the ACS catheter. The first pattern involves positioning the catheter such that all of its side openings are located only in the aorta. This is clearly contemplated by the prior art '725 patent cited by the examiner. In the second of the possible fact patterns, all of the side openings are located within the coronary artery. This situation appears to have been contemplated by the '017 patent, the method patent at issue. In the third fact pattern, some of the side openings are located in the aorta and some are located in the artery.

There is evidence in the record that 40 to 60 percent of the stenoses that require angioplasty are located less than three centimeters from the entrance to the coronary artery. ACS argues that therefore the ACS catheter may be used in such a way that all of the openings are located in the aorta. Even assuming that the trial judge's conclusion is correct that claim 1 is applicable to the third of the fact patterns, it remains true that on this record a reasonable jury could find that, pursuant to the procedure described in the first of the fact patterns (a noninfringing procedure), there are substantial noninfringing uses for the ACS catheter.

Whether the ACS catheter "has no use except through practice of the patented method," *Dawson Chemical Co. v. Rohm & Haas Co.*, is thus a critical issue to be decided in this case. As the Supreme Court recently noted, "[w]hen a charge of contributory infringement is predicated entirely on the sale of an article of commerce that is used by the purchaser [allegedly] to infringe a patent, the public interest in access to that article of commerce is necessarily implicated." *Sony Corp. v. Universal City Studios, Inc.*, 464 U.S. 417, 440 (1983) [declining to find contributory copyright infringement in sale of video cassette recorders].

Viewing the evidence in this case in a light most favorable to the nonmoving party, and resolving reasonable inferences in ACS's favor, it cannot be said that Bard is entitled to judgment as a matter of law. The grant of summary judgment finding ACS a contributory infringer under § 271(c) is not appropriate.

A person induces infringement under § 271(b) by actively and knowingly aiding and abetting another's direct infringement. Bard argues that ACS induced infringement under § 271(b) by: 1) providing detailed instructions and other literature on how to use its catheter in a manner which would infringe claim 1; and 2) having positioned the inlets near the balloon's proximal end so as to allow a user of the ACS catheter to infringe claim 1. Because a genuine issue of material fact exists, a grant of summary judgment finding ACS induced infringement is also not appropriate.

NOTES

1. Knowledge Requirement: § 271(c). The Federal Circuit has held that Patent Act § 271(c) requires a showing that the alleged contributory infringer knew that the combination for which her component was especially designed was both patented and infringing. *Trell v. Marlee Elecs. Corp.*, 912 F.2d 1443, 16 U.S.P.Q.2d (BNA) 1059 (Fed. Cir. 1990).

2. Inducing Infringement. The concepts of contributory infringement and inducement evolved to address infringing activity that somehow lacked the element of a direct making, using or selling of the patented invention. As we have seen, contributory infringement sweeps into the net of infringement the making, use or sale of *less than* the entire patented device. Inducement, on the other hand, involves behavior which omits any making, using or selling but which nevertheless amounts to an attempt to appropriate the value of an invention. It is often described as activity that "aids and abets" infringement.

A good example of inducement at work is *Water Techs. Corp. v. Calco, Ltd.*, 850 F.2d 660, 669, 7 U.S.P.Q.2d (BNA) 1097, 1103 (Fed. Cir.), *cert. denied*, 488 U.S. 968 (1988). In this case Gartner, one of the defendants, was hired as a consultant by Calco to design a portable water purification system to compete with that sold by the plaintiff/patentee. (The patentee's system involved an advanced purification resin.) Gartner complied by supplying plans for an infringing device. The court called it a classic case of inducement.

> Gartner gave the patented Aqua-Chem resin formula to Calco in August or September of 1980 in connection with licensing Calco to make Gartner's water purifying straw, a product containing less than 100 cc of resin. By September 1980, Calco was also aware of the patents but, with Gartner's assistance, on November 4, 1980, manufactured a first batch of the ... resin which it put into straws marketed under the trademark POCKET PURIFIER owned by Gartner. Gartner tested the straws, helped Calco obtain EPA approval, and wrote the directions for use of the product by consumers. Calco sold 400-500 units of devices made with the first batch of resin.

Although section 271(b) does not use the word "knowing," the case law and legislative history uniformly assert such a requirement. Gartner argues that no proof of a specific, knowing intent to induce infringement exists. While proof of intent is necessary, direct evidence is not required; rather, circumstantial evidence may suffice. The requisite intent to induce infringement may be inferred from all of the circumstances. Gartner's activities provide sufficient circumstantial evidence for this court to affirm the district court's finding that he intentionally induced Calco's and the public's direct infringement. Under the facts here, although Gartner's liability as a direct infringer may be de minimis, we see no reason to hold him liable for less than all damages attributable to Calco's infringing sales on the basis of his inducement of direct infringement.

850 F.2d at 668-69.

On the use of circumstantial evidence to show intent to induce, see *Moleculon Research Corp. v. CBS, Inc.*, 793 F.2d 1261, 1272, 229 U.S.P.Q. (BNA) 805, 813 (Fed. Cir. 1986), *cert. denied*, 479 U.S. 1030 (1987) (sale of puzzle amounted to inducement to infringe puzzle solution patent). On what may constitute inducement, see, e.g., 4 D. CHISUM, PATENTS § 17.04[2], [3], [4] (1978 & Supp. 1991) (and cases cited therein) (licensing, design, and advertising of infringing product may constitute active inducement). On remedies, see *id.*, at § 20.03[7][b][iv] (appropriate relief against one inducing infringement may be same as that against direct infringer). *See generally* Miller, *Some Views on the Law of Patent Infringement by Inducement*, 53 J. PAT. OFF. SOC'Y 86 (1971).

3. *A Hypothetical.* If one were to make copies of a patent specification and distribute it along with a component used in the claimed invention, would this be contributory infringement? What if you made copies of the specification and distributed it to all the competitors of the patentee; would this be inducement?

4. *A Comparative Look.* Although of course the European Patent Convention does not affect infringement — being concerned only with matters of the patent *grant* — individual European countries have doctrines broadly similar to those embodied in § 271(b) and (c). *See, e.g.*, United Kingdom Patent Act of 1977, § 60, discussed in 1 M. VITORIA ET AL., ENCYCLOPEDIA OF UNITED KINGDOM AND EUROPEAN PATENT LAW § 4-204 (1977 & Supp. 1991). And the Community Patent Convention will cover such acts of infringement when it takes effect. *See* Community Patent Convention, Article 30 (it is infringement to sell something which it is "obvious" will lead to infringement).

In Japan, contributory infringement is an accepted part of the law. *See* T. TANABE & H. WEGNER, JAPANESE PATENT PRACTICE 83-85 (1986). But note that under Article 101 of the Japanese patent statute, contributory infringement is present only when one makes or sells an article useable *exclusively* with the patented device. This has been interpreted very narrowly; even a hypothetical alternative use is enough to escape infringement. This is obviously much harder on the patentee than the nonstaple article of commerce standard of Patent Act § 271(c).

E. INFRINGEMENT AND FOREIGN ACTIVITY

Recently, patent infringement was broadened to include supplying components in or from the United States for an invention assembled outside the United States. *See* Patent Act § 271(f). This section overruled *Deepsouth Packing Co. v. Laitram Corp.*, 406 U.S. 518, 173 U.S.P.Q. (BNA) 769 (1972), which had held that exporting components of a patented combination for quick assembly overseas was not infringement. Section 271(f) reads:

> (f)(1) Whoever without authority supplies or causes to be supplied in or from the United States all or a substantial portion of the components of a patented invention, where such components are uncombined in whole or in part, in such manner as to actively induce the combination of such components outside of the United States in a manner that would infringe the patent if such combination occurred within the United States, shall be liable as an infringer.
>
> (2) Whoever without authority supplies or causes to be supplied in or from the United States any component of a patented invention that is especially made or especially adapted for use in the invention and not a staple article or commodity of commerce suitable for substantial noninfringing use, where such component is uncombined in whole or in part, knowing that such component is so made or adapted and intending that such component will be combined outside of the United States in a manner that would infringe the patent if such combination occurred within the United States, shall be liable as an infringer.

A recent bit of legislation affects another prickly area of patent infringement: the rights of a U.S. process patent holder to gain redress for importation into the U.S. of products made by infringing her process patent. Current § 271(g) reads in part:

> Whoever without authority imports into the United States or sells or uses within the United States a product which is made by a process patented in the United States shall be liable as an infringer, if the importation, sale, or use of the product occurs during the term of such process patent.

This changes long-standing law, which insulated importers of products made by infringing a valid U.S. patent abroad. *See generally* Comment, *The Process Patent Amendments Act of 1988: Solving an Old Problem, But Creating New Ones*, 1989 B.Y.U. L. REV. 567 (1989) (criticizing details of provisions in Process Patent Amendments that require patentee to give notice that a process patent is being infringed; suggesting these be narrowly interpreted so that most importers could be held liable for infringement).

NOTES

1. *"Making" an Infringement.* The Federal Circuit has indicated a strong willingness to spread the net of infringement to include acts that might have escaped in the past. In *Paper Converting Mach. Co. v. Magna-Graphics Corp.*, 745 F.2d 11, 19-20 (Fed. Cir. 1984), for instance, the court found infringement when the accused infringer had not actually constructed an infringing device, but had tested "significant, unpatented assemblies of elements ... enabling the infringer to deliver the patented combination in parts to the buyer, without testing the entire combination...." This new, more flexible approach to what constitutes a "making" under § 271(a) has been criticized. *See* Note, *Patent Infringement: Redefining the "Making" Standard to Include Partial Assemblies*, 60 WASH. L. REV. 889 (1985) (arguing that *Paper Converting* improperly rejected the traditional "operable assembly" standard for determining a "making," and that the result will be that pre-patent expiration testing will constitute infringement, contrary to congressional intent). *See generally* Note, *Liability Under the Process Patent Amendment Act of 1988 for Use of a Patented Process Outside the United States*, 60 GEORGE WASH. L. REV. 268 (1991).

2. *International Trade Commission Forum.* Partly in response to early decisions holding that importing a product made from a patented process overseas is not infringement, Congress passed legislation allowing a patentee to exclude such imports via a proceeding before the International Trade Commission. *See* 19 U.S.C. § 1337a (1988); Krosin & Koslowski, *Patent-Based Suits at the International Trade Commission Following the 1988 Amendments to Section 337*, 17 AM. INTELL. PROP. L. ASS'N Q.J. 47 (1989). However, one recent case held that a product patent which essentially covers a technique of manufacture is not a "process" within the meaning of this statute. *See Amgen, Inc. v. U.S. Int'l Trade Comm'n*, 902 F.2d 1532, 1538, 14 U.S.P.Q.2d (BNA) 1734, 1739 (Fed. Cir. 1990) (patent on biological "host cell" is not a patent on a process within the meaning of § 337).

3. *Patents in Space.* For background on the patenting of inventions derived from outer space activities, and infringing activity taking place in outer space, see G. REYNOLDS & R. MERGES, OUTER SPACE: PROBLEMS OF LAW AND POLICY (1988); Reynolds, *Patents in Space: Hearings before the Subcomm. on Courts, Intellectual Property and the Administration of Justice, House Comm. on the Judiciary*, 101st Cong., 1st Sess. 50 (1989) (statement of Professor Glenn H. Reynolds, space expert and raconteur); Burk, *Application of United States Patent Law to Commercial Activity in Outer Space*, 6 COMP. & HIGH TECH. L.J. 295 (1991).

NOTE ON INFRINGEMENT UNDER THE PROCESS PATENT AMENDMENTS ACT OF 1988

In 1988, Congress changed the longstanding rule that importation of the product of an infringing process did not constitute infringement. The 1988 amendments added section 271(g) to the Patent Act:

§ 271. Infringement of patent

(g) Whoever without authority imports into the United States or offers to sell, sells, or uses within the United States a product which is made by a process patented in the United States shall be liable as an infringer, if the importation, offer to sell, sale, or use of the product occurs during the term of such process patent. In an action for infringement of a process patent, no remedy may be granted for infringement on account of the noncommercial use or retail sale of a product unless there is no adequate remedy under this title for infringement on account of the importation or other use, offer to sell, or sale of that product. A product which is made by a patented process will, for purposes of this title, not be considered to be so made after —

(1) it is materially changed by subsequent processes; or
(2) it becomes a trivial and nonessential component of another product.

Process Patent Amendments Act of 1988, Pub. L. No. 100-418, §§ 9001-07, codified at 35 U.S.C. § 102(g) (1996).

A recent series of cases engages various important issues raised by the 1988 amendments. In *Eli Lilly & Co. v. American Cyanamid Co.*, 82 F.3d 1568, 38 U.S.P.Q.2d 1705 (Fed. Cir. 1996), for example, the Federal Circuit established the standard for determining when an infringing product has been "materially changed" prior to importation. This important defense, which limits the scope of § 271(g), applies whenever there is "a significant change in the compound's structure and properties." The materiality of a change, in other words, will be measured in terms of the physical structure of the claimed and accused (imported) products.

To understand the new test, consider the *Eli Lilly* case itself. Lilly held various patents on methods for manufacturing a pharmaceutical product, specifically a broad-spectrum antibiotic known as "cefaclor." Cefaclor is a member of the class of cephalosporin antibiotics, all of which are based on a common cephem nucleus. Although there are many different cephem compounds, only a few are effective as antibiotics. Each of the known commercial methods for producing cefaclor requires the production of an intermediate cephem compound known as an enol. Once the desired enol cephem intermediate is obtained, it is then subjected to several processing steps in order to produce cefaclor.

In 1995, Lilly purchased the patent at issue in the case, U.S. Patent No. 4,160,085. Claim 5 of that patent defines a method of producing enol cephem compounds, including what is called "compound 6," an enol cephem similar to the one Lilly uses in its process for manufacturing cefaclor. According to the court,

> [c]ompound 6 differs from cefaclor in three respects. Although both compound 6 and cefaclor are based on the cephem nucleus, compound 6 has a hydroxy group at the 3-position on the cephem nucleus, a para-nitrobenzyl carboxylate ester at the 4-position, and a phenylacetyl group at the 7-position. Cefaclor has different groups at each of those positions: it has a chlorine atom at the 3-position, a free carboxyl group at the 4-position, and a phenylglycyl group at the 7-position. Each of those differences between compound 6 and cefaclor contributes to the effectiveness of cefaclor as an orally administered antibiotic drug. The free carboxyl group at the 4-position is believed important for antibacterial activity; the chlorine increases cefaclor's antibiotic potency; and the phenylglycyl group enables cefaclor to be effective when taken orally.
>
> To produce cefaclor from compound 6 requires four distinct steps. First, the hydroxy group is removed from the 3-position and is replaced by a chlorine atom, which results in the creation of "compound 7." Second, compound 7 is subjected to a reaction that removes the phenylacetyl group at the 7-position, which results in the creation of "compound 8." Third, a phenylglycyl group is added at the 7-position, which results in the creation of "compound 9." Fourth, the para-nitrobenzyl carboxylate ester is removed from the 4-position, which results in the creation of cefaclor.

82 F.3d 1568, 1570.

The district court found that compound 6 and cefaclor differ significantly in their structure and properties, including their biological activity, and hence that there had been a "material change" in the imported compound which brought it outside the scope of Lilly's patent under § 271(g).

The Federal Circuit agreed, after considering the rationale behind the "materially changed" provision:

> A concern raised during Congress's consideration of the process patent legislation was whether and to what extent the new legislation would affect products other than the direct and unaltered products of patented processes — that is, whether the new statute would apply when a product was produced abroad by a patented process but then modified or incorporated into other products before being imported into this country.
>
> Lilly argues that the "materially changed" clause of section 271(g) must be construed in light of its underlying purpose, which is to protect the economic value of U.S. process patents to their owners. Prior to the enactment of the Process Patent Amendments Act, the value of a U.S. process patent could be undermined by a manufacturer who used the process abroad and then imported the product into this country. Because the purpose of the process patent legislation was to protect against such subversion of protected

economic rights, Lilly argues that the statute should be read to apply to any such scheme that undercuts the commercial value of a U.S. process patent. In Lilly's view, the product of a patented process therefore should not be considered "materially changed" if the principal commercial use of that product lies in its conversion into the product that is the subject of the infringement charge. Because cefaclor is the only product of compound 6 that is sold in the United States market, Lilly argues, the change in compound 6 that results in cefaclor — no matter how significant as a matter of chemical properties or molecular structure — is not a "material change" for purposes of section 271(g).

Although we are not prepared to embrace Lilly's argument, we acknowledge that it has considerable appeal. Congress was concerned with the problem of the overseas use of patented processes followed by the importation of the products of those processes, and a grudging construction of the statute could significantly limit the statute's effectiveness in addressing the problem Congress targeted. That is especially true with respect to chemical products, as to which simple, routine reactions can often produce dramatic changes in the products' structure and properties.

Nonetheless, while the general purpose of the statute informs the construction of the language Congress chose, purpose cannot displace language, and we cannot stretch the term "materially changed" as far as Lilly's argument would require. The problem is that the language of the statute refers to changes in the product; the statute permits the importation of an item that is derived from a product made by a patented process as long as that product is "materially changed" in the course of its conversion into the imported item. The reference to a "changed" product is very hard to square with Lilly's proposed test, which turns on the quite different question of whether the use or sale of the imported item impairs the economic value of the process patent.

The facts of this case demonstrate how far Lilly's test strays from the statutory text. While Lilly notes that there are only four steps between compound 6 and cefaclor, and that all four steps involve relatively routine chemical reactions, Lilly does not suggest any limiting principle based on the structure of the intermediate product or the nature of the steps necessary to produce the imported product. Thus, even if there were ten complex chemical reactions that separated compound 6 from cefaclor, Lilly's test would characterize the two compounds as not "materially" different as long as the primary commercial use of compound 6 in this country was to produce cefaclor.

Besides not responding to the natural meaning of the term "changed," Lilly's construction of the "materially changed" clause would create a curious anomaly. Lilly's value-based construction of the clause turns in large measure on Lilly's contention that the only commercial use for compound 6 in this country is to produce cefaclor; that is, Lilly views compound 6 and cefaclor as essentially the same product because compound 6 has no commercial use in the U.S. market except to produce cefaclor. Under that approach, however, the question whether compound 6 was "materially changed" in the course of its conversion to cefaclor would depend on whether and to what extent other derivative products of compound 6 are marketed in this country. Thus, under Lilly's theory compound 6 would become materially different from cefaclor if and when compound 6 came to have other commercial uses in the United States, even though the respective structures and properties of the two compounds remained unchanged.

That is asking the statutory language to do too much work. We cannot accept the argument that the question whether one compound is "materially changed" in the course of its conversion into another depends on whether there are other products of the first compound that have economic value. We therefore do not adopt Lilly's proposed construction of section 271(g). We look instead to the substantiality of the change between the product of the patented process and the product that is being imported. In the chemical context, a "material" change in a compound is most naturally viewed as a significant change in the compound's structure and properties. Without attempting to define with precision what classes of changes would be material and what would not, we share the district court's view that a change in chemical structure and properties as significant as the change between compound 6 and cefaclor cannot lightly be dismissed as immaterial. Although compound 6 and cefaclor share the basic cephem nucleus, which is the ultimate source of the antibiotic potential of all cephalosporins, the cephem nucleus is common to thousands of compounds, many of which have antibiotic activity, and many of which are dramatically different from others within the cephem family. Beyond the cephem nucleus that they have in common, compound 6 and cefaclor are different in four important structural respects, corresponding to the four discrete chemical steps between the two compounds. While the addition or removal of a protective group, standing alone, might not be sufficient to constitute a "material change" between two compounds (even though it could dramatically affect certain of their properties), the conversion process between compound 6 and cefaclor involves considerably more than the removal of a protective group. We therefore conclude that the statutory text of section 271(g) does not support Lilly's contention that it is likely to prevail on the merits of its infringement claim.

82 F.3d 1572-73. *See also Bio-Tech. Gen. Corp. v. Genentech, Inc.*, 80 F.3d 1553, 1559, 38 U.S.P.Q.2d 1321 (Fed. Cir. 1996) (imported product which literally infringes claim cannot be considered "materially changed").

F. THE EXPERIMENTAL USE "EXCEPTION" TO INFRINGEMENT

Despite the absolute language of § 271, there is a well-recognized, judicially created exception to infringement, commonly known as the "experimental use" exception. The exception allows for the unlicensed construction and use of a patented invention under certain circumstances. Experimental use had its origins in Justice Story's opinion in *Whittemore v. Cutter*, 29 F. Cas. 1120 (C.C.D. Mass. 1813) (No. 17,600). In this case, the defendant appealed a jury instruction, to the effect that the "making of a machine ... with a design to use it for profit" constituted infringement. Justice Story upheld the trial judge's instruction, and stated that

> it could never have been the intention of the legislature to punish a man, who constructed such a machine merely for philosophical experiments, or for the purpose of ascertaining the sufficiency of the machine to produce its described effects.

29 F. Cas. at 555. Other cases followed, generally limiting the exception to these quite narrow grounds. *See* Note, *Experimental Use as Patent Infringement: The Impropriety of a Broad Exception*, 100 YALE L.J. 2169, 2169 (1991) (stating that the experimental use exception "should be applied as it has been in the past: in a very restrictive manner, consistent with the purpose and function of the patent system.").

In *Roche Prods., Inc. v. Bolar Pharmaceuticals, Inc.*, 733 F.2d 858, 221 U.S.P.Q. (BNA) 937 (Fed. Cir.), *cert. denied*, 469 U.S. 856 (1984), the Federal Circuit considered the experimental use defense for the first time. Here the defendant, Bolar, engaged in infringing acts prior to expiration of plaintiff's patent in order to facilitate FDA testing so as to be ready to market the drug as soon as the patent expired. The Federal Circuit overruled the district court's finding of non-infringement, holding the experimental use exception did not include "the limited use of a patented drug for testing and investigation strictly related to FDA drug approval requirements ...." 733 F.2d at 861.

> Bolar's intended "experimental" use is solely for business reasons and not for amusement, to satisfy idle curiosity, or for strictly philosophical inquiry.... Bolar may intend to perform "experiments," but unlicensed experiments conducted with a view to the adaption of the patented invention to the experimenter's business is a violation of the rights of the patentee to exclude others from using his patented invention.

733 F.2d at 863.

The following excerpt reflects a good deal of thought about the basis for and proper scope of the experimental use exception.

EISENBERG, PATENTS AND THE PROGRESS OF SCIENCE: EXCLUSIVE RIGHTS AND EXPERIMENTAL USE, 56 U. Chi. L. Rev. 1017 (1989)*

....

If basic research cannot be insulated from the patent system entirely, it might still be possible to reconcile a system of exclusive patent rights in prior discoveries with the interest of the scientific community in allowing subsequent researchers to enjoy free access to such discoveries by exempting the use of patented inventions in research from infringement liability. While the United States patent statute does not provide such an exemption, the courts have long recognized, at least in principle, that a purely "experimental use" of a patented invention, with no commercial purpose, should be exempt from infringement liability. But since the use of patented inventions in noncommercial research rarely provokes a lawsuit, most of the judicial decisions considering the scope of the experimental use exemption have involved disputes between commercial competitors. Within this universe of cases the experimental use defense has been frequently raised but rarely sustained. For the most part, the courts have held that the experimental use defense does not apply to the facts of the particular cases before them. As a consequence, the purpose and scope of the experimental use defense are not well defined. As the use of patented inventions becomes increasingly important to the progress of research science and increasingly threatening to the interests of patent holders, this vaguely defined doctrine is becoming less satisfactory. The issue has begun to command the attention of the bar, commentators, and Congress.

In this article I analyze the proper scope of an experimental use exemption from patent infringement liability by comparing the rationales behind promoting technological progress through granting exclusive patent rights in inventions with competing arguments for promoting scientific progress by allowing all investigators to enjoy free access to the discoveries of other scientists.

....

If one assumes that the level of incentives provided by an unqualified seventeen year patent monopoly is either optimal or too low, then it arguably follows that the use of a patented invention in research should only be exempt from infringement liability when it has no adverse impact on the patent holder's profits. A broader exemption would reduce the value of the patent monopoly and thereby reduce incentives to make and disclose new inventions. Without articulating this rationale, some courts seem to have taken approximately this position on the proper scope of the experimental use defense.

....

The 1890 Robinson patent treatise, which the courts have continued to cite in experimental use cases into the 1980's, offers a slightly more refined version of the no-harm standard, asserting that the use of an invention should not constitute

---

*Reprinted with permission of Rebecca S. Eisenberg.

infringement unless it is "hostile to the interest of the patentee ... represented by the emoluments which he does or might receive from the practice of the invention by himself or others." [WILLIAM C. ROBINSON, THE LAW OF PATENTS FOR USEFUL INVENTIONS § 898 at 55-56 (Boston, 1890).] According to this view of "experimental use," where the use of an invention in research produces "no pecuniary result" the patent holder has not lost any of her "emoluments" and her interests are not antagonized. On the other hand, if the user conducts experiments with a view to adapting the invention to a business purpose, the use constitutes infringement, and "even experimental uses will be sometimes enjoined though no injury may have resulted." Consistent with this approach, the courts have generally refused to recognize an experimental use exemption for research performed by commercial firms.

This definition of experimental use refines the no-harm standard by drawing a distinction between commercial and noncommercial research. While this distinction might appear to be an appropriate place to draw the line between research uses that should trigger infringement liability and those that should be protected from liability by an experimental use exemption, the difference between commercial and noncommercial research in fact often has little to do with the financial interests of patent holders.

An isolated use of a patented invention in purely academic research with no commercial implications might have little impact on the profitability of the patent, assuming that in the absence of an exemption the researcher would forego use of the invention rather than obtaining a license. But for inventions with significant markets among researchers, such as patented laboratory techniques and other research tools, exempting even purely academic researchers from the patent monopoly could deprive patent holders of a portion of the monopoly profits they might otherwise expect to earn and thereby reduce incentives to make and disclose such inventions in the future. Research users are ordinary consumers of such an invention. To exempt such users from infringement liability would plainly undermine the interest of the patent holder in "the emoluments which he might receive from the practice of the invention by others." In this context the incentives justification for patents [developed earlier in this article] suggests that researchers, like other consumers, should be required to pay royalties to the developers of inventions that are useful to them in order to maintain a level of incentives that is adequate to justify developing such inventions.

An incentives analysis also argues against an exemption for research users who are potential competitors of the patent holder rather than potential customers. For example, consider the case of a researcher who is using a patented invention to develop alternative means of solving the same problem. A research exemption in this context would not only deprive the patent holder of the royalties that this particular user might otherwise pay, but also threatens ultimately to cut short the effective duration of the patent holder's monopoly if the user succeeds in developing a competing technology that can be used without infringing the patent claims. Such research is plainly hostile to the financial interests of the patent holder and reduces the expected profitability of the patent, suggesting that an exemption from infringement liability in this context would reduce patent incentives.

[Professor Eisenberg then turns to the other side of the issue, scientists' need for free access to prior research.] In addition to permitting scrutiny of research claims, free access promotes scientific progress by permitting other scientists to use prior discoveries in subsequent research....

The interests of the subsequent researcher (and of the scientific community as a whole) are less clearly at odds with the interests of the earlier researcher in the case of subsequent efforts to extend prior research than they are in the case of subsequent efforts to scrutinize prior research claims. Although prior researchers still stand to lose professional status if subsequent research calls into question the validity of their claims, they also stand to gain further recognition and status if their prior discoveries prove important to future discoveries. One might therefore expect scientists to be eager to extend licenses to those who would use their discoveries in subsequent research.

Nonetheless, there are a number of reasons why access to prior discoveries that is contingent on obtaining a license from the original discoverer might be a less satisfactory means of promoting scientific progress than free access to such discoveries.

The most obvious reason is that it is cheaper and easier to obtain free access to prior discoveries than it is to obtain licenses from prior researchers. Even assuming that most prior researchers would be willing, once consulted, to allow subsequent researchers to use their discoveries free of charge, it would be costly and burdensome for scientists to negotiate for licenses with each of the prior researchers whose work contributes to their own. Moreover, since research often leads down unexpected paths, it may be difficult to foresee just which prior discoveries will prove useful in a research project. Interrupting an ongoing research project to obtain a license to use a prior discovery that has unexpectedly proved relevant to the inquiry could cause wasteful delays. These transaction costs alone could add up to a significant burden for researchers.

Free access also spares subsequent researchers the cost of paying royalties to their predecessors for the use of their discoveries. To the extent that prior researchers might otherwise charge such royalties, free access in effect provides a subsidy for subsequent research. Research subsidies may be especially appropriate for basic research that generates substantial public benefits yet cannot pay its own way in the market. Research is a costly and uncertain enterprise, and it often yields unexpected benefits to those who have not paid for it. The argument for subsidy may be less compelling when extended to research sponsored by private companies in the expectation of earning a profit, or to applied research the results of which may be effectively monopolized through patent protection or secrecy. But even if a subsidy is appropriate, it does not necessarily follow that prior researchers should bear the burden of this subsidy rather than society as a whole. It might be fairer and more efficient (ignoring the transaction costs outlined above) for the government to subsidize research in amounts sufficient to allow researchers to pay for access to the prior discoveries they need to use in their research. On the other hand, considerations of fairness might argue for placing this burden on prior researchers, given that in all likelihood they themselves benefitted from the free availability of earlier research results in making their own discoveries. Researchers who themselves benefitted from access to the discoveries of scientists who came before them might fairly be called upon to make similar contributions to the efforts of scientists who come after them.

Free access may also be necessary in order to override the interest of prior researchers in keeping their discoveries away from research competitors. Scientists may want to carve out a domain of exclusivity in subsequent research for themselves and their collaborators in order to improve their odds of being first to make future discoveries. They may see other researchers working on similar problems as competitors who threaten to divert future recognition, research grants, and even commercial intellectual property rights in the output of research using the prior discovery.

Recommendations

The case of an experimental use exemption is strongest when the subsequent researcher is using a patented invention to check the validity of the patent holder's claims. Free access to patented inventions for the limited purpose of permitting scrutiny of new research claims serves the policies underlying the patent law as well as the interests of research science. Indeed, patent law promotes scrutiny of the research claims embodied in patented inventions through its requirement that patent holders make enabling disclosures of their inventions freely available to the public....

Depending on the scope of the patent claims and the results of the subsequent research, it may not be necessary to give patent holders any remedy at all for the use of their inventions in research in order to protect their interests. For example, if a subsequent researcher develops an improvement that falls within the scope of the claims of the earlier patent, the financial interests of the patent holder may be adequately protected by allowing enforcement of the patent after the research is completed when the improvement is ready for commercial exploitation. So long as the subsequent researcher may not exploit the improvement commercially without a license from the patent holder, an experimental use exemption from infringement liability during the research stage would not deprive the patent holder of an opportunity to recover a fair share of the value of the improvement, and the exemption therefore should not undermine patent incentives. On the other hand, if the subsequent researcher is able to develop a substitute technology that does not infringe the patent claims, denying the patent holder a remedy for the research use could prevent the patent holder from earning an adequate return on the initial investment in developing the earlier patented invention.

It is often impossible to tell in advance whether a subsequent researcher's use of a patented invention will lead to an improvement falling within the scope of the claims of the prior patent or to a substitute technology falling outside the patent claims. The uncertainty arises in part because it is difficult to predict the course and outcome of research projects, and in part because it is difficult to determine the validity and scope of patent claims until these matters are resolved in litigation.

These difficulties argue against giving patent holders an injunctive remedy to prevent subsequent researchers from using their inventions to make further advances in the same field. Such a remedy would compel subsequent researchers to negotiate with their rivals for a license before they could use patented inventions in their research. Given the problems outlined above in negotiating for a license under these circumstances, it is likely that in many cases the parties would be unable to reach an agreement even though the subsequent research might offer significant social benefits.

Nonetheless, in some cases it may be appropriate for a court to require the researcher to pay a reasonable royalty to the patent holder after the fact in order to be sure that the patent holder is adequately compensated for the use of the patented invention. Damages for the research use may be unnecessary if the original patent is broad enough in scope to cover the improved technology developed by the researcher. In this situation, the patent holder's interests will be adequately protected by enforcement of the patent when the improved technology is ready for commercial exploitation. On the other hand, if the subsequent researcher uses the patented invention to invent around the patent, developing a new technology that may be exploited without infringing the patent claims, the patent holder will have no means of extracting payment from the researcher at the commercial exploitation stage. In these circumstances, denying the patent holder a damage remedy for the research use would undermine the value of the patent monopoly and lead to unjust enrichment of the researcher.

Determination of reasonable royalties is never an easy task. When a patented invention is only one input in the development of a subsequent invention, the courts should be careful not to set damages at a level that deprives subsequent researchers of the rewards of their own superior insights or that makes it unprofitable to exploit the new technology....

In sum, I make the following recommendations concerning the proper scope of an experimental use exemption from patent infringement liability:

(1) Research use of a patented invention to check the adequacy of the specification and the validity of the patent holder's claims about the invention should be exempt from infringement liability.

(2) Research use of a patented invention with a primary or significant market among research users should not be exempt from infringement liability when the research user is an ordinary consumer of the patented invention.

(3) A patent holder should not be entitled to enjoin the use of a patented invention in subsequent research in the field of the invention, which could

potentially lead to improvements in the patented technology or to the development of alternative means of achieving the same purpose. However, it might be appropriate in some cases to award a reasonable royalty after the fact to be sure that the patent holder receives an adequate return on the initial investment in developing the patented invention.

NOTES

1. *Patent Transactions*. For more on the "transaction costs" approach to this and other problems, see Robert P. Merges, *Of Property Rules, Coase, and Intellectual Property*, 94 COLUM. L. REV. 2655 (1994).

2. *Comparative Notes*. European Community Patent Convention Art. 31 (b) provides that patent protection shall not extend to "acts done for experimental purposes relating to the subject-matter of the patented invention." Germany, France, the United Kingdom, Italy, the Netherlands, Belgium, Luxembourg, Ireland, Greece and Spain have either amended their national patent laws to conform with Article 31(b) of the Community Patent Convention or have legislation pending to achieve this effect. See also Japanese Patent Law of 1978 Art. 69(1) (to same effect).

3. *More on the* Bolar *Case*. One holding in the *Bolar* case was almost immediately overruled through legislation; see 35 U.S.C. § 271(e)(1), enacting a drug regulatory testing exemption from infringement, which permits pre-expiration regulatory testing of a patented drug. This provision was introduced as part of the Drug Price Competition Act, Public Law 98-417 (1984), and amended in 1988 for veterinary drugs. (The trade-off for this exemption was patent term restoration for pharmaceutical patents, which allows patentees to obtain extensions of their patents to partly offset the regulatory review period.) The scope of exempt subject matter under § 271(e) has been interpreted to cover medical devices. *See Eli Lilly & Co. v. Medtronic, Inc.*, 872 F.2d 402, 10 U.S.P.Q.2d (BNA) 1304 (Fed. Cir. 1989) (Nies, J.), *aff'd*, 110 S. Ct. 2683, 15 U.S.P.Q.2d (BNA) 1121 (1990).

Chapter 9

REMEDIES

Once a patent has been found valid and infringed, the court must fashion a remedy for the patentee. Patent remedies are governed primarily by §§ 283 and 284 of the Patent Act:

§ 283. Injunctive relief.

The several courts having jurisdiction of cases under this title may grant injunctions in accordance with the principles of equity to prevent the violation of any right secured by patent, on such terms as the court deems reasonable.

§ 284. Damages.

Upon finding for the claimant the court shall award the claimant damages adequate to compensate for the infringement, but in no event less than a reasonable royalty for the use made of the invention by the infringer, together with interest and costs as fixed by the court. The court may receive expert testimony as an aid to the determination of damages or of what royalty would be reasonable under the circumstances.

A. INJUNCTIVE RELIEF

As we shall see, a great deal of litigation time is expended on the complex issue of damages. And no doubt compensation for past infringement in the form of damages is an important component of the patentee's relief. But perhaps a more important remedy from the patentee's point of view is the right to enjoin the defendant-infringer from continuing infringing activities. The basis for this right was well stated by Judge Markey, sitting by designation in a 1978 case before the Sixth Circuit:

> Patents must by law be given "the attributes of personal property." 35 U.S.C. § 261. The right to exclude others is the essence of the human right called "property." The right to exclude others from free use of an invention protected by a valid patent does not differ from the right to exclude others from free use of one's automobile, crops, or other items of personal property. Every human right, including that in an invention, is subject to challenge under appropriate circumstances. That one human property right may be challenged by trespass, another by theft, and another by infringement, does not affect the fundamental indicium of all "property," i.e., the right to exclude others.

Panduit Corp. v. Stahlin Bros. Fibre Works, Inc., 575 F.2d 1152, 1158 n.5, 197 U.S.P.Q. (BNA) 726 (6th Cir. 1978) (Markey, J., by designation).

The foregoing provides a clear rationale for the issuance of a permanent injunction after a patent is found valid and infringed. This is the general practice, to which there are only very limited exceptions (see *Vitamin Technologists* and notes, below). Of more practical concern in most cases is whether a *preliminary* injunction will issue prior to the full adjudication of the infringement case on the merits.

1. PRELIMINARY INJUNCTIONS

Standards for the granting of preliminary injunctions have changed significantly in recent years. But the purpose remains the same: to stop the wrongdoing (infringement) as soon as possible. *See, e.g., Teledyne Indus. v. Windmere Prods., Inc.*, 433 F. Supp. 710, 741 (S.D. Fla. 1977) (to permit infringement during pendency of suit would be to grant a license valid as long as the infringer could contest the suit and encourage others to infringe as well).

Because of the significance of preliminary injunctions, we begin by surveying the requirements for obtaining this important remedy.

ORR v. LITTLEFIELD

18 F. Cas. 837 (C.C.D.N.H. 1845)

This was a bill in equity. It alleged, that before the 20th of January, 1836, Isaac Orr was the inventor of a new improvement in stoves, called the air-tight stove, and on that day obtained a patent therefor. The bill contained further averments that the respondents [James Littlefield and others] had not respected the patent, but made and sold stoves like those described in his specification; and hence the bill prayed, among other things, for an injunction to restrain the respondents from making or selling any more air-tight stoves, during the residue of the time the patent has to run. [Orr introduced evidence of prior successful adjudication and a series of profitable licenses.]

This motion for an injunction is in accordance with a special prayer in the bill. The subject-matter of the bill is, also, one in which it is usual and fit for the court to interpose by this remedy, and on a proper state of facts before a final decision is had on the merits; because every stove sold is an injury if the patent is valid, and without such a remedy, — the supposed offence being constantly repeated, — the causes of action and the multiplicity of suits would probably become much extended, and relief, in that way, prove very defective. An injunction, in such a case, proves to be useful as a bill of peace. On the contrary, however, such injunctions are a check on the business of respondents; and interferences subjecting others to a loss before a full trial between the same parties, are not always to be justified. In what cases, then, should injunctions issue? It is not enough that a party has taken out a patent, and thus obtained a public grant, and the sanction or opinion of the patent office in favor of his right, though that opinion, since the laws were passed requiring some examination into the originality and utility of inventions, possesses more weight. But the complainant must furnish some further evidence of a probable right; and though it need not be conclusive evidence, — else additional hearing on the bill would thus be anticipated and superseded, — yet it must be something stronger than the mere issue, however careful and public, of the patent, conferring an exclusive right; as, in doing that, there is no opposing party, no notice, no long public use, no trial with any one of his rights. The kind of additional evidence is this. If the patentee, after the procurement of his patent, conferring an exclusive right, proceeds to put that right into exercise or use for some years, without its being disturbed, that circumstance strengthens much the probability that the patent is good, and renders it so likely, as alone often to justify the issue of an injunction in aid of it. After that it becomes a question of public policy no less than private justice, whether such a grant of a right, exercised and in possession so long, ought not to be protected, until avoided by a full hearing and trial.

In this case, the evidence is plenary and uncontradicted as to the use and sale of this patent by the inventor and his representative for several years, publicly and without dispute. Computing from the original grant, the time is over nine years, and since the re-issue of the letters patent it is nearly three. [T]he time to be regarded under this view is what has elapsed since the original issue or grant. In *Hill v. Thompson*, 3 Mer[ivale's Chancery Rep]. 622 [Great Britain (1817)], the time was only three years from the first grant. In *Ogle v. Ege* [18 F. Cas. 619 (No. 10,462) (C.C.D. Pa. 1826)], it was but six years. And though in some cases reported, it had been thirteen, and in others twenty years, yet it is believed, that seldom has a court refused an injunction in applications like this, on account of the shortness of time after the grant, however brief, if long enough to permit articles or machines to be constructed by the patentee in conformity to his claim, and to be sold publicly and repeatedly, and they have been so sold and used under the patent without dispute. Here the sales were extensive and profitable from 1836 downwards, and the right as well as the possession does not appear to have been contested till 1842. In *Hill v. Thompson*, [*supra*, at] 624, it is true that the court dissolved an injunction, when only about one year had elapsed since any work had been completed under the patent, and only two years since the specification was filed, the chancellor calling it a patent "but of yesterday;" but, he added, that he would not dissolve it, if an "exclusive possession of some duration" had followed; though an answer had been put in denying all equity, and doubts existed as to the validity of the patent; and no sales under it were proved in that case. So though the patent had been issued thirteen years, and the evidence is doubtful as to acquiescence in the possession or use, an injunction may be refused. But in the present case, the acquiescence appears to have been for several years universal.

Another species of evidence, beside the issue of the patent itself, and long use and possession under it, so as to render it probable the patent is good, and to justify an injunction, is the fact, that if the patent becomes disputed, the patentee prosecutes for a violation of his rights, and recovers. Same authorities. This goes upon the ground, that he does not sleep over his claims or interests, so as to mislead others, and that, whenever the validity of his claim has been tried, he has sustained it as if good. But such a recovery is not regarded as binding the final rights of the parties in the bill, because the action was not between them; though when the judgment is rendered without collusion or fraud, it furnishes to the world some strong as well as public assurance, that the patent is a good one. In view of the evidence of this character in the present action, it is not contradicted, nor impaired at all, by the judgments having been given on verdicts and defaults under agreements. Such judgments, when, as is admitted here, not collusive, are as strong, if not strong[er] evidence of the patentee's rights, than they would have been, if the claim was so doubtful as to be sent to a jury for decision, rather than to be so little doubtful as to be admitted or agreed to after being legally examined. Both of these circumstances, therefore, possession and judgments, unite in support of an injunction in the present case.

But if this injunction leads to serious injury in suspending works, the court can require security, if desired, of the complainant, to indemnify for it, if the patent is avoided.

NOTES

1. Something More. Although patents have the attributes of property, they are a strange species of it for two reasons: they are temporary, and they can be invalidated (more easily than title to real property). Because of this, proof of "something more" than simply good title is demanded of the patentee before a preliminary injunction will issue. The following case explores the modern requirements in this regard.

2. Bonds. An omitted part of the preceding case refers to the possibility that the patentee can put up a bond before the injunction issues to compensate the accused infringer for the disruption of her activities in the event the patent is found invalid or not infringed. The practice continues today, in patent cases and all others, under Federal Rule of Civil Procedure 65(c). *See, e.g., Amicus, Inc. v. Post-Tension of Texas*, 5 U.S.P.Q.2d (BNA) 1731, 1736 (S.D. Tex. 1987) (bond of $350,000 required of patentee, "which the [c]ourt deems proper for payment of such costs or damages as may be incurred by any party who is found to have been wrongfully enjoined or restrained"); *Rohm & Haas Co. v. Cumberland Chem. Corp.*, 220 U.S.P.Q. (BNA) 978 (S.D. Tex. 1983) (no bond required in light of plaintiff's ability to pay for any wrongdoing caused by improper injunction).

A Georgia court made creative use of the bonding option in the case of *Flo-Con Sys., Inc. v. Leco Corp.*, 845 F. Supp. 1576, 1583, 29 U.S.P.Q.2d 1443 (S.D. Ga. 1993):

Although Flo-Con is entitled to relief under 35 U.S.C. § 283 for the reasons stated above, at this juncture its request that Leco be enjoined from manufacture, use, promotion, and sale of the allegedly infringing products overreaches necessity. Flo-Con and Leco are in direct competition, and, while the market may not be evenly split, each enjoys a substantial market share. As alluded to by Leco, even a temporary prohibition against Leco's allegedly infringing products would give Flo-Con a substantial competitive advantage extending beyond simply the enjoined products. Such an injunction also would adversely affect Leco's standing in the market and, most significantly, deprive consumers of the benefits that flow from healthy competition.

A more workable solution than the blanket prohibition requested by Flo-Con is to require that Leco remit monthly payments to the registry of the Court similar to those it would make under a license agreement. Requiring the submission of such monthly payments assures compensation to Flo-Con if it prevails on the merits but avoids the problems associated with a blanket injunction — that is, it allows Leco to continue its presence in the marketplace and preserves the benefits of competition.

For this relief plan to serve its intended function, however, it must not distort the market. The plan's most likely source of market distortion arises from Leco's natural inclination to encourage the use of products that substitute for those subject to the payment requirements imposed by this Order. To prevent such actions, Leco's authority to manipulate the prices of and offer sales incentives for its tundish slide gates and slide gate accessories is restricted. As requested by Leco, however, Flo-Con is similarly restricted to prevent it from taking unfair advantage of Leco's lost marketing flexibility.

H.H. ROBERTSON CO. v. UNITED STEEL DECK, INC.

820 F.2d 384, 2 U.S.P.Q.2d (BNA) 1926 (Fed. Cir. 1987)

PAULINE NEWMAN, CIRCUIT JUDGE.

United Steel Deck, Inc. (USD) and Nicholas J. Bouras, Inc., (Bouras) appeal the Order of Preliminary Injunction of the United States District Court for the District of New Jersey in favor of the H.H. Robertson Company (Robertson). USD and Bouras were enjoined *pendente lite* from making, using, and selling certain structures which were found to infringe United States Patent No. 3,721,051 (the '051 or Fork patent). We affirm.

Background

Robertson is the owner of the '051 patent, invention of Frank W. Fork, issued on March 20, 1973 and entitled "Bottomless Sub-Assembly for Producing an Underfloor Electrical Cable Trench." The invention is a concrete deck structure sub-assembly for distributing electrical wiring. Robertson charged Bouras and its affiliated manufacturing company USD with infringement.

In moving for preliminary injunction Robertson alleged that "there is a reasonable probability of eventual success on the patent infringement claim"; that "the Fork patent was held valid, infringed, contributorily infringed and enforceable by the United States District Court for the Northern District of Ohio in ... *Bargar* [an earlier case]"; that the "accused structures of USD and Bouras are the same or substantially the same as those held ... to infringe in *Bargar*"; that "[w]here, as here, the patent has been held valid and infringed, irreparable harm is presumed ... and the harm ... cannot be fully compensated by money damages"; and that the "balance of equities heavily weighs in favor of Robertson."

The district court held a four-day hearing on the motion, during which witnesses including experts testified on the issues of patent validity and infringement. The legal and equitable issues were briefed and argued. The court concluded that Robertson had "established a basis for the relief it seeks," and granted the preliminary injunction.

Analysis

The standards applied to the grant of a preliminary injunction are no more nor·less stringent in patent cases than in other areas of the law. The court in *Smith International* [, *Inc. v. Hughes Tool Co.*, 718 F.2d 1573, 1577-79, 219 U.S.P.Q. (BNA) 686, 689-90 (Fed. Cir.), *cert. denied*, 464 U.S. 996 (1983)] discussed the so-called "more severe" rule that has at times weighed against the grant of preliminary injunctions in patent cases, stating:

> The basis for the more severe rule appears to be both a distrust of and unfamiliarity with patent issues and a belief that the ex parte examination by the Patent and Trademark Office is inherently unreliable.

Id. at 1578, 219 U.S.P.Q. at 690. *See also Atlas Powder Co. v. Ireco Chemicals*, 773 F.2d 1230, 1233, 227 U.S.P.Q. 289, 292 (Fed. Cir. 1985) ("burden upon the movant should be no different in a patent case than for other kinds of intellectual property"). The existing standards for relief *pendente lite*, fairly applied, can accommodate any special circumstances that may arise.

The grant or denial of a preliminary injunction is within the discretionary authority of the trial court. Appellate review is on the basis of whether the court "abused its discretion, committed an error of law, or seriously misjudged the evidence." *Smith International*, 718 F.2d at 1579, 219 U.S.P.Q. at 691.

The district court applied to Robertson's motion the Third Circuit standard:

> An applicant for a preliminary injunction against patent infringement must show: ... (1) a reasonable probability of eventual success in the litigation and (2) that the movant will be irreparably injured pendente lite if relief is not granted.... Moreover, while the burden rests upon the moving party to make these two requisite showings, the district court "should take into account, when they are relevant, (3) the possibility of harm to other interested persons from the grant or denial of the injunction, and (4) the public interest."

This is substantially the same standard enunciated by this court. See, for example, *Roper Corp. v. Litton Systems, Inc.*, 757 F.2d 1266, 1270-73, 225 U.S.P.Q. 345, 347-50 (Fed. Cir. 1985), and *Atlas Powder*, 773 F.2d at 1231-34, 227 U.S.P.Q. at 290-93.

The first question before the district court was whether the movant Robertson had demonstrated a reasonable likelihood that USD and Bouras would fail to meet their burden at trial of proving, by clear and convincing evidence, that the Fork patent claims were invalid.

The burden of proving invalidity is with the party attacking validity. The evidence adduced in connection with a motion for preliminary relief must be considered in this light. Robertson retained the burden of showing a reasonable likelihood that the attack on its patent's validity would fail.

[T]he burden is always on the movant to demonstrate entitlement to preliminary relief.

Before the district court, USD and Bouras argued that all of the Fork patent claims at issue were invalid for obviousness in terms of 35 U.S.C. § 103, and that claim 2 was invalid in terms of 35 U.S.C. § 112. The asserted invalidity for obviousness was based on references that had been before the Ohio court in [the prior case]. The district court in its opinion referred to the detailed analysis by the court [in the prior case] and to its decision that the accused infringers in that case had failed to establish the invalidity of the claims. The district court stated that the "finding of validity of the Fork '051 patent in [this case] is persuasive evidence of validity" with respect to the references before that court. Even the "severe rule" against the grant of preliminary injunctions in patent cases was tempered when a patent had been upheld in other forums or its validity had been acquiesced in by others. A prior adjudication upholding patent validity after a fully litigated trial, including similar issues of fact and law, contributes strong support to the grant of a preliminary injunction.

On the record before us, the court's conclusion is based on factual findings that have not been shown to be clearly erroneous.

The grant of a preliminary injunction does not require that infringement be proved beyond all question, or that there be no evidence supporting the viewpoint of the accused infringer. The grant turns on the likelihood that Robertson will meet its burden at trial of proving infringement. We sustain the district court's conclusion that "there is a reasonable probability that Robertson will eventually establish that Bouras and USD induced infringement of the Fork '051 patent."

Equitable Considerations

The movant for preliminary injunction must show not only a reasonable likelihood of success on the merits, but also the lack of adequate remedy at law or other irreparable harm.

In matters involving patent rights, irreparable harm has been presumed when a clear showing has been made of patent validity and infringement. *Smith Interna-*

tional, 718 F.2d at 1581, 219 U.S.P.Q. at 692. This presumption derives in part from the finite term of the patent grant, for patent expiration is not suspended during litigation, and the passage of time can work irremediable harm. The opportunity to practice an invention during the notoriously lengthy course of patent litigation may itself tempt infringers.

The nature of the patent grant thus weighs against holding that monetary damages will always suffice to make the patentee whole, for the principal value of a patent is its statutory right to exclude. The presumption of irreparable harm in patent cases is analogous to that applicable to other forms of intellectual property, as discussed in *Roper Corp.*, 757 F.2d at 1271-72, 225 U.S.P.Q. at 348.

The district court held that irreparable injury was presumed because Robertson had established a "strong likelihood of success in establishing validity and infringement." Such presumption of injury was not, however, irrebuttable. During oral argument, in response to an inquiry from the bench, USD and Bouras urged that money damages are an adequate remedy. In response, Robertson emphasized the few remaining years of patent life.

Even when irreparable injury is presumed and not rebutted, it is still necessary to consider the balance of hardships. The magnitude of the threatened injury to the patent owner is weighed, in the light of the strength of the showing of likelihood of success on the merits, against the injury to the accused infringer if the preliminary decision is in error. Results of other litigation involving the same patent may be taken into account, and the public interest is considered. No one element controls the result.

When the movant has shown the likelihood that the acts complained of are unlawful, the preliminary injunction "preserves the status quo if it prevents future trespasses but does not undertake to assess the pecuniary or other consequences of past trespasses." *Atlas Powder Co.*, 773 F.2d at 1232, 227 U.S.P.Q. at 291. The court in *Atlas Powder* thus distinguished between remedies for past infringement, where there is no possibility of other than monetary relief, and prospective infringement, "which may have market effects never fully compensable in money." *Id.* The cautionary corollary is that a preliminary injunction improvidently granted may impart undeserved value to an unworthy patent.

Thus substantial deference is due the district court's equitable judgment. The district court in its opinion referred to the USD/Bouras portrayal of disruption, loss of business, and loss of jobs, and to Robertson's business needs and patent rights. Observing that "[t]his patent does not have many more years to run," the court held "the equities weigh heavily against the wrongdoer." *Id.* The court stated that the "protection of patents furthers a strong public policy ... advanced by granting preliminary injunctive relief when it appears that, absent such relief, patent rights will be flagrantly violated."

The grant of a preliminary injunction, if not based on legal error or a serious misjudgment of the evidence, is reviewable only to ascertain whether the grant was within a reasonable range of discretion. We have considered all of the arguments of the parties, and the record before us. The district court's conclusion reflects a reasonable consideration and balance of the pertinent factors, evaluated in accordance with the established jurisprudence, and does not exceed the court's discretionary authority.

Affirmed.

NOTES

1. *Presuming Irreparable Injury. Smith Int'l, Inc. v. Hughes Tool Co.*, cited in the preceding case, was an important early opinion in the Federal Circuit that laid the groundwork for the expanded availability of injunctive relief that has been a hallmark of the court.

> Without this injunctive power of the courts, the right to exclude granted by the patent would be diminished, and the express purpose of the Constitution and Congress, to promote the progress of the useful arts, would be seriously undermined. The patent owner would lack much of the "leverage," afforded by the right to exclude, to enjoy the full value of his invention in the market place. Without the right to obtain an injunction, the right to exclude granted to the patentee would have only a fraction of the value it was intended to have, and would no longer be as great an incentive to engage in the toils of scientific and technological research.... However, courts have over the years developed a reluctance to resort to preliminary injunctions in patent infringement cases, and have constructed a rather strict standard for the granting of this form of equitable relief.... The usual requirement of a showing of probability of success on the merits before a preliminary injunction will issue has historically been even stronger in a patent case. Besides having to prove title to the patent, it has been stated as a general proposition that the movant must show that the patent is beyond question valid and infringed.... The very nature of the patent right is the right to exclude others. Once the patentee's patents have been held to be valid and infringed, he should be entitled to the full enjoyment and protection of his patent rights. The infringer should not be allowed to continue his infringement in the face of such a holding. A court should not be reluctant to use its equity powers once a party has so clearly established his patent rights. We hold that where validity and continuing infringement have been clearly established, as in this case, immediate irreparable harm is presumed. To hold otherwise would be contrary to the public policy underlying the patent laws.

Smith International, 718 F.2d at 1577-78, 1581. *See generally* Steven E. Shapiro, *Preliminary Injunction Motions in Patent Litigation*, 33 IDEA: J.L. & TECH. 323, 325 (1993) ("Since its institution, the Federal Circuit has taken great steps to lessen the burden of patentees seeking preliminary injunctions.... Of the approximately fifty (50) trial court patent preliminary injunction decisions reported in the

United States Patent Quarterly (Second), more than sixty (60%) percent have granted injunctions.").

2. Cutting Back. The *per se* rule announced in *Smith International* has been cut back somewhat in subsequent cases, including *H.H. Robertson*. In *We Care, Inc. v. Ultramark Int'l Corp.*, 930 F.2d 1567, 18 U.S.P.Q.2d (BNA) 1562 (Fed. Cir. 1991), the Federal Circuit stated:

> Although We Care could not show literal infringement, the court determined that We Care would likely be able to prove that the SHOCK BLOCK device infringed the '916 patent under the doctrine of equivalents. In applying this doctrine, however, we are convinced that the district court erred in not adequately considering whether the range of equivalents sought by We Care for the '916 patent would "ensnare the prior art." *Wilson Sporting Goods Co....* On the record before us, we cannot determine what the eight cited prior art patents teach or whether, based on those teachings, claims broad enough to encompass the [accused] device would have been obvious. Accordingly, we vacate the preliminary injunction and remand the case to the district court to determine whether the range of equivalents sought by We Care encroaches upon the prior art.

See also Eli Lilly & Co. v. American Cyanamid Co., 82 F.3d 1568, 38 U.S.P.Q.2d 1705, 1713 (Fed. Cir. 1996):

> If a claim of lost opportunity to conduct research were sufficient to compel a finding of irreparable harm, it is hard to imagine any manufacturer with a research and development program that could not make the same claim and thus be equally entitled to preliminary injunctive relief. Such a rule would convert the "extraordinary" relief of a preliminary injunction into a standard remedy, available whenever the plaintiff has shown a likelihood of success on the merits. For that reason, adopting the principle that Lilly proposes would "disserve the patent system."

But see Bio-Tech. Gen. Corp. v. Genentech, Inc., 80 F.3d 1553, 38 U.S.P.Q.2d 1321, 1331 (Fed. Cir. 1996):

> [T]he district court determined that Genentech would be harmed if [appellant] BTG were allowed to enter the market because Genentech would lose revenues and goodwill, and would be required to reduce its research and development activities. BTG has not demonstrated that these findings are clearly erroneous.

The current Federal Circuit approach — which is best described as "case by case," and perhaps even "unstable" — is also evident in the following two excerpts, the first from *PPG Indus., Inc. v. Guardian Indus. Corp.*, 75 F.3d 1558, 37 U.S.P.Q.2d 1618, 1625-26 (Fed. Cir. 1996):

Guardian places heavy reliance on this court's decision in *High Tech Medical Instrumentation, Inc. v. New Image Indus., Inc.*, 49 F.3d 1551, 33 U.S.P.Q.2d 2005 (Fed. Cir. 1995), where the court reversed a preliminary injunction .... In this case, by contrast, we have upheld the district court's conclusion that ... PPG's showing ... was sufficiently strong to invoke the presumption of irreparable harm. Because we agree with the district court that Guardian failed to rebut that presumption, we sustain the court's ruling that PPG met its burden of showing that it would suffer irreparable harm in the absence of an order granting preliminary injunctive relief.

Guardian argues that the balance of hardships and the public interest both counsel in favor of denying the injunction. The district court, however, considered both factors and reached the contrary conclusion, and we are not prepared to overturn that determination. The district court concluded that PPG would suffer significant harm from the denial of an injunction, while an injunction would be less burdensome for Guardian, as it would require only a temporary interruption in Guardian's production and sale of its SMG glass.

With regard to the public interest, the court acknowledged that an injunction would deprive the public of one of the suppliers of solar control glass. The court, however, balanced that interest against the strong public policy favoring the enforcement of patent rights. Because the court found it unlikely that the injunction would result in a shortage of solar control glass, the court found that, on balance, the public interest favored PPG.

Guardian argues that PPG will be unable to satisfy the requirements of Guardian's customers, particularly the large automobile manufacturers, for solar control glass. To address that objection, however, the district court gave Guardian the right to return to court for relief from the preliminary injunction if Guardian were unable to fulfill its current contracts with automobile manufacturers, either with noninfringing compositions or by purchase from PPG on reasonable terms. Guardian made an initial request for temporary relief from the injunction, which was granted. The record does not reflect that Guardian has made any further requests, although the district court has made clear that it would be prepared to entertain any such requests if they should be made. In the absence of a showing that the district court has been unresponsive to Guardian's interest in fulfilling its current contract obligations, or to the public's interest in obtaining an adequate supply of solar control glass, we cannot conclude that the district court abused its discretion in finding that both the balance of hardships and the public interest favor PPG.

Next consider *High Tech Med. Instrumentation, Inc. v. New Image Indus., Inc.*, 49 F.3d 1551, 1556-57, 33 U.S.P.Q.2d 2005 (Fed. Cir. 1995) (Bryson, J.):

The district court based its finding of irreparable harm not on any affirmative showing of prospective harm to [plaintiff] HTMI, but on a presumption of irreparable harm stemming from the strength of HTMI's showing on the merits. HTMI follows the same tack: it does not identify any specific injury it would suffer from the denial of a preliminary injunction, but instead relies entirely on the presumption of irreparable harm.

Reasoning by analogy from decisions involving other forms of intellectual property, this court has held that a presumption of irreparable harm arises when a patentee makes a clear showing that a patent is valid and that it is infringed. The presumption of irreparable harm is unavailable here, however, because, as we have discussed, the record does not support HTMI's claim that it is likely to succeed in proving [infringement] .... Aside from the presumption, the district court pointed to no evidence that would support a finding of irreparable injury, and we find none.

HTMI does not make or sell dental endoscopes and does not license their manufacture and sale under the '001 patent. Although a patentee's failure to practice an invention does not necessarily defeat the patentee's claim of irreparable harm, the lack of commercial activity by the patentee is a significant factor in the calculus. Because it does not compete with New Image or have licensees who could be injured by competition from New Image, HTMI does not run the risk of losses of sales or goodwill in the market; nor has HTMI suggested that New Image's activities have precluded it from licensing its patent or entering the market. There also is no indication in the record that HTMI needs an injunction to protect its right to refuse to exploit its invention commercially or to prevent others from doing so. To the contrary, the evidence shows that HTMI offered a license to New Image, so it is clear that HTMI is willing to forgo its patent rights for compensation. That evidence suggests that any injury suffered by HTMI would be compensable in damages assessed as part of the final judgment in the case.

Neither in its brief nor in oral argument has HTMI contended that New Image would be unable to respond in damages for any infringement that may be found at trial. To be sure, "the nature of the patent grant weighs against holding that monetary damages will always suffice to make the patentee whole." *Hybritech Inc. v. Abbott Lab.*, 849 F.2d at 1456-57, 7 U.S.P.Q.2d at 1200; see also *H.H. Robertson* .... Nonetheless, "there is no presumption that money damages will be inadequate in connection with a motion for an injunction pendente lite." *Nutrition 21 v. United States*, 930 F.2d 867, 872, 18 U.S.P.Q.2d 1347, 1351 (Fed. Cir. 1991).

Cf. Reebok, Int'l v. J. Baker, Inc., 32 F.3d 1552, 31 U.S.P.Q.2d 1781 (Fed. Cir. 1994) (preliminary injunction denied where plaintiff/patentee no longer produces shoe covered by design patent, and plaintiff's reputation will not be materially harmed by sale of relatively small number of defendant's shoes, and where plaintiff could therefore be fully compensated by money damages).

3. ***Status Quo and Adequacy of Money Damages.*** The "status quo" to be preserved by a preliminary injunction is not the competitive situation facing the parties on the day the infringement suit is filed, the Federal Circuit has held. In *Atlas Powder Co. v. Ireco Chems.*, 773 F.2d 1230, 227 U.S.P.Q. (BNA) 289 (Fed. Cir. 1985), the defendant appealed a trial court decision to issue a preliminary injunction, on the ground that it altered the status quo, i.e., defendant's substantial business in infringing merchandise:

> If Ireco has allowed itself to become excessively dependent upon infringing sales, the status quo catchword does not necessarily allow it to continue such dependence, apart from other factors. The concept is not inconsistent with stopping trespasses "cold turkey." This does not, of course, mean that the alleged injury done by the injunction to Ireco is not to be carefully considered, only that "status quo" is not a talisman to dispose of the question by itself.

773 F.2d at 1232. The court went on to address the defendant's contention that money damages would adequately compensate the patentee:

> Ireco's arguments that infringement and related damages are fully compensible in money downplay the nature of the statutory right to exclude others from making, using, or selling the patented invention throughout the United States. While monetary relief is often the sole remedy for past infringement, it does not follow that a money award is also the sole remedy against future infringement. The patent statute further provides injunctive relief to preserve the legal interests of the parties against future infringement which may have market effects never fully compensable in money. If monetary relief were the sole relief afforded by the patent statute then injunctions would be unnecessary and infringers could become compulsory licensees for as long as the litigation lasts.

773 F.2d at 1233. But see the following pre-Federal Circuit cases, where courts refuse to find irreparable injury to the patentee because the alleged infringer is solvent and money will adequately compensate the injury. *Nuclear-Chicago Corp. v. Nuclear Data, Inc.*, 465 F.2d 428 (7th Cir. 1972); *Rohm & Haas Co. v. Mobil Oil Corp.*, 525 F. Supp. 1298, 1307 (D. Del. 1981); *Jenn-Air Corp. v. Modern Maid Co.*, 499 F. Supp. 320, 333 (D. Del.), *aff'd*, 659 F.2d 1068 (3d Cir. 1981).

These cases have been eclipsed by recent Federal Circuit opinions, however. And the cases show that the district courts are getting the message. One court, faced with an infringer's argument that the patentee could not be suffering irreparable injury because it was not practicing the invention, responded:

> We find that it is consistent with intellectual property law principles that a patent holder need not practice his invention in order to prevent others from practicing what he invented.... [An earlier case in this district] noted that the

infringer's contention that the patentee was not marketing a comparable product, and therefore could not lose market share on the specific product in question, was not as persuasive as the patentee's argument that it was suffering irreparable injury because the infringer was gaining in general market share of related products and because the patentee's reputation might be harmed by the continuing sales of the infringing product.

E.I. duPont de Nemours & Co. v. Polaroid Graphics Imaging, Inc., 706 F. Supp. 1135, 1144-45, 10 U.S.P.Q.2d (BNA) 1579 (D. Del. 1989).

4. *Shooting from the Hip?* A recent law review note criticizes the Federal Circuit's liberalization of preliminary injunction doctrine:

> The CAFC has been quick to preliminarily enjoin defendants from continuing activities aimed at developing technologies patented by others without first completing the comprehensive determinations of validity and infringement that would occur during a trial. This tendency of the court to "shoot first and ask questions later" creates a hardship for business. Furthermore, rather than supporting research and development efforts, this tendency has discouraged investment in the development of the technologies involved.

Note, *The Impact of the Creation of the Court of Appeals for the Federal Circuit on the Availability of Preliminary Injunctive Relief Against Patent Infringement*, 23 IND. L. REV. 169 (1990). This note found that the post-Federal Circuit success rate for preliminary injunction motions was 52%, which it found was statistically significantly higher than the 36% rate from the preceding twenty-nine years.

5. *Taking Better Aim?* Recent opinions have pulled back from the almost *per se* granting of preliminary injunctions in the immediate post-*Smith International* era. For instance, in *Rosemount, Inc. v. United States Int'l Trade Comm'n*, 910 F.2d 819, 821, 15 U.S.P.Q.2d (BNA) 1569 (Fed. Cir. 1990), the Federal Circuit upheld the International Trade Commission's reversal of an administrative law judge's grant of a preliminary injunction. After observing that the Commission applies the same standard as a district court, Judge Nies of the Federal Circuit commented on the propriety of the Commission's decision on the facts before it:

> [T]he Commission found that the presumption of irreparable harm had been rebutted by evidence of Rosemount's delay in bringing this action, its grant of two licenses, its large market share as compared to the minuscule share of [the accused infringer], the presence of twelve major noninfringing competitors in the U.S. market, and the availability of a damage remedy in district court. The Commission further found that Rosemount's U.S. market share had experienced a growth rate in sales for the two previous fiscal years and was expected to increase its share over the next four to five years, whereas [the infringer's] very small U.S. market share was unlikely to increase during the pendency of this investigation. It further rejected Rose-

mount's argument that a presumption of irreparable harm could be overcome only by evidence that the accused infringer had stopped importation. With respect to the factor of harm to the movant, this court has recognized that, in appropriate circumstances, a presumption of irreparable harm may be afforded a patent owner where that party has made a strong preliminary showing of patent validity and continued infringement in connection with its request for relief *pendente lite*. However, like any other presumption of fact, a presumption of irreparable harm to a patent owner does not override the evidence of record.

See also American Home Prods. Corp. v. Johnson & Johnson Corp., 22 U.S.P.Q.2d 1561, 1567 (E.D. Pa. 1991) (dictum: size of infringer's presence in industry is relevant in injunction decision).

2. PERMANENT INJUNCTIONS

VITAMIN TECHNOLOGISTS, INC. v. WISCONSIN ALUMNI RESEARCH FOUNDATION

146 F.2d 941 (9th Cir. 1944)

Appellee Wisconsin Alumni Research Foundation brought its complaint below alleging that appellant Vitamin Technologists, Inc., [was] making an infringing use of a process of producing vitamin D by activating ergosterol and yeast, claimed to be organic substances of dietary value, with the ultraviolet rays of the spectrum, produced by a mercury vapor lamp, a use of the rays claimed to be in violation of one or another of three patents, Nos. 1,680,818, 1,871,136 and 2,057,399. These patents were secured by Dr. Steenbock of the faculty of the University of Wisconsin and assigned to appellee. They are hereafter referred to as the first, second and third patents in the order of their dates of patenting. The second patent is claimed to be an extension in part of the first patent and the third patent such a continuation [i.e., extension] of the second. Infringements of product claims of the patents were also alleged.

Appellant answered claiming unclean hands, laches, invalidity of the claims on their face, and anticipation. The district court found the challenged claims valid and adjudged infringements by appellant both as to the process and its products and the court's interlocutory judgment ordered a perpetual injunction. This appeal followed.

The Success of the Monopoly of the Aid to or Cure of the Rachitic

Appellee contends that all the claims obtain support from the commercial success of the monopoly granted. It describes the great number of children suffering from malformation of their bodies due to the defective bone metabolism. The record contains pathetic pictures of such malformations and statistics of the large numbers of such unfortunates. Other maturer sufferers are described, all proving the great numbers of afflicted who, *ex necessitate* if they are to use such a boon to humanity, have been customers of the licensees of appellee. From the appellee's business manager it appears that it was largely from need of the poor that the business was supported. He testified

> Q. In what classes of people do you find, according to your information, that rickets is more prevalent?
> A. It is my understanding that rickets is found to a great extent in the so-called poorer class of people.

We take notice of the future continuance of the poor and of others afflicted and that such customers are excluded by the patents, if valid, from any unlicensed source of the remedy of foods so irradiated to contain vitamin D.

Dr. Steenbock's continuing interest in the management of appellee's business is apparent from his testimony regarding the refusal of licensing of the irradiation of oleomargarine, one of the foods of the poor, with the antirachitic vitamin D. His testimony in this regard is relevant to the issue, later considered, of an inequitable misuse of the monopoly of the patent as warranting the denial of equitable relief. *Cf. Morton Salt Co. v. G.S. Suppiger Co.*, 314 U.S. 488, 492 [1942].

Part of the income [from the patents] is used for advertising to expand the business and profits and part of the remainder for research in natural science of an undisclosed character by the University of Wisconsin, a state of powerful vested interests in dairy enterprises, to which no profits from the declined oleomargarine irradiation afford support. An undisclosed part of Dr. Steenbock's share is used in scientific research.

The record contains several of the license agreements of the Wisconsin corporation which appellant claims have extended the monopoly of the patent over material not covered by the patent as in *United States v. Masonite Co. and Mercoid Corp. v. Mid-Continent Co.*, [316 U.S. 265 (1942)]. In the latter case the relief of injunction was refused a patentee because the owner of the patent, the Mid-Continent Co., required its licensee to pay royalties on an unpatented article which was an element in the patented article. [See Chapter 11.]

"Courts of equity may, and frequently do, go much farther both to give and withhold relief in furtherance of the public interest than they are accustomed to go when only private interests are involved." *Virginian R. Co. v. System Federation*, 300 U.S. 515, 552, 57 S. Ct. 592, 601, 81 L. Ed. 789. "Where an important public interest would be prejudiced," the reasons for denying injunctive relief "may be compelling."

This raises the question, not argued, whether the effect on the public health of refusing to the users of oleomargarine, the butter of the poor, the right to have such a food irradiated by the patented process is against the public interest. As seen, the general business manager of the Wisconsin corporation testified that it is the poor people suffering with rickets who constitute the principal market for appellee's monopolized processes and products. The evidence and appellee's briefs are replete with well verified statements of the great boon to humanity of Dr. Steenbock's scientific discoveries for the prevention and cure of rickets. The truth of such statements make the stronger the contention that it is a public offense to withhold such processes from any of the principal foods of the rachitic poor, or, indeed, from those of any such sufferers.

We judicially notice the legislation in Wisconsin and other states of large vested interests in dairying imposing heavy restrictions upon the competition of oleomargarine with butter. Various devices are used such as taxation of oleomargarine itself, on its sale, in license fees of its vendors and the like penalties for violation of the restrictions. We take it, however, that such restrictive legislation does not require us to disregard its value as a food, so attractive and so satisfying to the human palate. Indeed, in these days of war-restricted diet, oleomargarine has become the butter of the well-to-do and the rich.

Suppression of the use of the property in a patent has often been held the right of the holder of the patent monopoly, but the question has not been raised in connection with the public interest in restoring the health of the afflicted. An early case, reviewing many others, on the question of suppressing the use of a patent against the public interest is *Continental Paper Bag Co. v. Eastern Paper Bag Co.*, 210 U.S. 405 [(1908)]. There it is held that the suppression of the use of a patent for paper bags was not against the public interest, but the Court's opinion, 210 U.S.at page 430, concludes with this statement.

> Whether, however, a case cannot arise where, regarding the situation of the parties in view of the public interest, a court of equity might be justified in withholding relief by injunction, we do not decide.

In the last decade, in the many cases cited above and in others, the relief of a court of equity has been denied because of the conduct of the patentee with reference to his monopoly property, against the public interest. We know of no case in the Supreme Court since the *Paper Bag* case, *supra*, which has considered the patentee's refusal to license the use of its patent to protect the health of great numbers of the public such as are here shown to be suffering with rickets. It is strongly arguable that such a suppression of the patent's use is vastly more against the public interest than its use for a mere control of prices, *Masonite*, *supra*, or the tieing of unpatented with patented material in *Mercoid Corp.*, *supra*.

[These matters are suggested to the Attorney General for investigation.] Since our consideration of the record convinces us that the patents are invalid, we have concluded that equity will best be served by disposing of the case on that ground. [The court finds the patents anticipated; e.g., "It thus appears that the claimed process of preparing food materials and exposing them to irradiation by ultraviolet rays from all sources has been anticipated from time immemorial by the farmer in hay curing in the sun and the coconut grower sun-drying the cut meat of the coconut. We hold that claims 1, 2, 3 and 8 of the first patent are invalid because of such anticipation."]

[The following is an excerpt from appellee's motion for rehearing in 1945:]

We now have before us from the Wisconsin corporation what, if the case be resubmitted, it will prove as excusing the refusal of the irradiation of oleomargarine. Upon consideration of the proffered evidence all three judges now conclude the refusal unwarranted and against the public interest and deny the motion to remand for proof of these facts. We further hold that such refusal to permit such irradiation warrants the refusal of the equitable injunctive and accounting relief sought by the corporation, though we hold the public interest is served better by our decision that the patents are invalid.

NOTES

1. *A Rare Exception.* To the extent that the court holds in the preceding case that the enforcement of the patent would be against the public interest because of health concerns, it is an extreme outlier in the history of injunctive relief for patentees. For more background on the circumstances of this case, with such details as the fact that Steenbock did patent irradiation techniques partly out of a desire to keep them out of the hands of the margarine industry, see Apple, *Patenting University Research: Henry Steenbock and the Wisconsin Alumni Research Foundation*, 80 Isis 375 (1989). However, few cases refuse to enforce patents for broad public policy reasons. *But see Milwaukee v. Activated Sludge*, 69 F.2d 577 (7th Cir.), *cert. denied*, 293 U.S. 576 (1934) (patentee of sewage treatment process denied an injunction against the City of Milwaukee because it would have forced the municipality to dump raw sewage into Lake Michigan); *Nerney v. New York*, 83 F.2d 409, 411 (2d Cir. 1936) (denying an injunction to the holder of a patent for railroad brakes where the defendant railroad company had fifteen thousand cars equipped with the infringing brakes, and thus a public hardship would ensue; stating broadly that injunctive relief should be denied "where it was not absolutely essential to the patentee and caused the infringing defendant irreparable damages."). *See generally*, Note, *Patents for Critical Pharmaceuticals: The AZT Case*, 17 AM. J.L. & MED. 145 (1991) (summarizing cases where injunctions have been denied; concluding that Congress should compensate holder of AZT patent for compulsory licensing of third-party manufacturers to address AIDS epidemic).

Much more common are statements such as the following, which is drawn from a discussion of an infringer's argument regarding the "public interest" prong of the conventional preliminary injunction standard discussed in *H.H. Robertson, supra*:

> While the public interest is unquestionably advanced through the marketing of potentially lifesaving devices ..., Congress has determined it better for the nation in the long run to afford the inventors of novel, useful and nonobvious products short-term exclusivity on such products rather than to permit free competition in the goods. Congress has not seen fit to differenti-

ate between what might be referred to as lifesaving devices and those of a more trivial or less important nature.

Eli Lilly & Co. v. Medtronic, Inc., 7 U.S.P.Q.2d (BNA) 1439, 1445 (E.D. Pa. 1988), *rev'd and remanded*, 872 F.2d 402, 10 U.S.P.Q.2d 1304 (Fed. Cir.), *reh'g denied*, 879 F.2d 849, 11 U.S.P.Q.2d (BNA) 1649 (Fed. Cir. 1989).

To the same effect is the recent case of *Polaroid v. Kodak*, where the court was asked to consider the "public interest" in deciding whether to grant a stay of an injunction. The response:

> Not only will an injunction injure Kodak customers and goodwill, it will also, according to Kodak, cause a "major disruption" of business. If and when Kodak is forced to shut down its instant camera production, 800 full-time and 3700 part-time employees will lose their jobs, and the company will lose its $200 million investment in plant and equipment.
>
> I am not unmindful of the hardship an injunction will cause — particularly to Kodak customers and employees. It is worth noting, however, that the harm Kodak will suffer simply mirrors the success it has enjoyed in the field of instant photography. To the extent Kodak has purchased that success at Polaroid's expense, it has taken a "calculated risk" that it might infringe existing patents....
>
> Kodak's characterization of the public interest ... misconstrues the very concept of public benefit. The public policy at issue in patent cases is the "protection of rights secured by valid patents." Courts grant — or refuse to stay — injunctions in order to safeguard that policy, even if those injunctions discommode business and the consuming public.

Polaroid Corp. v. Eastman Kodak Co., Civil Action No. 76-1634-Z, D. Mass., Oct. 11, 1985, Slip Op. at 3, 4. *But see Atari Corp. v. Sega of Am., Inc.*, 869 F. Supp. 783, 32 U.S.P.Q.2d 1237, 1244 (N.D. Cal. 1994) (denying preliminary injunction for patentee, in part because "[defendant] employs 1200 permanent and 100 temporary employees... and [it] ... would immediately terminate 85% of [them] if the injunction were to issue, and [it] would file for bankruptcy," and also because "there are 65 independent software developers and 10 independent peripheral manufacturers that design and sell software and peripherals compatible with Sega game units, 35 of which derive 50% or more of their income from sale of Sega-compatible products, that would be economically harmed by the issuance of an injunction against [it].").

2. *Other Denials of a Permanent Injunction.* In *Foster v. American Mach. & Foundry Co.*, 492 F.2d 1317, 182 U.S.P.Q. (BNA) 1 (2d Cir. 1974), the court upheld what amounted to a compulsory license: a reasonable royalty damage award (described later in the chapter), but no injunction. The appellate court opinion is concise on this point:

> We do not find any difficulty in agreeing that an injunction would be an inappropriate remedy in this case. An injunction to protect a patent against

infringement, like any other injunction, is an equitable remedy to be determined by the circumstances. It is not intended as a club to be wielded by a patentee to enhance his negotiating stance. Here, as the District Court noted, the appellee manufactures a product; the appellant does not. In the assessment of relative equities, the court could properly conclude that to impose irreparable hardship on the infringer by injunction, without any concomitant benefit to the patentee, would be inequitable.

Instead, the District Court avoided ordering a cessation of business to the benefit of neither party by compensating appellant in the form of a compulsory license with royalties. This Court has approved such a "flexible approach" in patent litigation. Here the compulsory license is a benefit to the patentee who has been unable to prevail in his quest for injunctive relief. To grant him a compulsory royalty is to give him half a loaf. In the circumstance of his utter failure to exploit the patent on his own, that seems fair.

492 F.2d at 1324. *See also E.I. duPont de Nemours & Co. v. Phillips Petr. Co.*, 835 F.2d 277, 278, 5 U.S.P.Q.2d (BNA) 1109 (Fed. Cir. 1987) (upholding grant of stay of preliminary injunction where patentee duPont (1) had licensed all who desired entry into the polyethylene business, the subject of the patent, and (2) planned to exit the market; "harm to duPont here is of a different nature than harm to a patentee who is practicing its invention and fully excluding others").

3. *Eminent Domain*. Under 28 U.S.C. § 1498(a), a patentee's only remedy in suits against the U.S. government is "reasonable and entire compensation." Thus, in the context of government procurement, the patentee has no right to enjoin the government from continued making or using of the patented invention. It has been held that this provision merely implements the government's eminent domain power. *See Crozier v. Fried Krupp Aktiengesellschaft*, 224 U.S. 290 (1912) (suit under predecessor to 28 U.S.C. § 1498(a) answers all requirements as to compensation necessary to sustain the statute as an exercise of the power of eminent domain).

Note that under current law, a patentee has no right of recovery at all against *state* governments because of recent interpretations of the Constitution's Eleventh Amendment grant of sovereign immunity; *see Chew v. California*, 893 F.2d 331, 13 U.S.P.Q.2d (BNA) 1393 (Fed. Cir. 1990). Consequently, cases like *Milwaukee v. Activated Sludge*, cited *supra*, would no longer require denial of an injunction; the state agency user would be immune from an infringement suit. Legislation is pending to change this, as the copyright law was recently changed.

For discussion of the rule in Great Britain, where a general infringement exemption for the Crown was abrogated in 1977, and where the government must now pay a reasonable compensation for infringement, see W.R. CORNISH, INTELLECTUAL PROPERTY: PATENTS, COPYRIGHT TRADE MARKS AND ALLIED RIGHTS § 7-055 (2d ed. 1989).

In addition, other cases have refused to enforce the patentee's right to exclude for the same reason as the *Vitamin Technologies* court above: patent misuse. As we shall see in Chapter 11, this can be a potent defense in an infringement suit. In general, unlike *Vitamin Technologists*, these cases usually turn on allegations of antitrust-related misuse: tie-ins, improper extension of the patent term by private agreement, etc. Once a court finds that the patentee has misused her patent, two results follow: the patentee's remedy (a permanent injunction) is denied, and the infringer may be explicitly permitted to use the patented technology royalty-free. The patentee, however, may "purge" her misuse and (presumably) reinstate her property right. For a study of the impact of compulsory licenses ordered on related grounds under the antitrust laws, see STAFF REPORT OF THE SUBCOMM. ON PATENTS, TRADEMARKS, AND COPYRIGHTS OF THE SENATE COMM. ON THE JUDICIARY, 86TH CONG., 2D SESS., COMPULSORY LICENSING OF ANTITRUST JUDGMENTS 13 (1960) (written by Marcus A. Hollabaugh and Robert L. Wright, summarizing results of compulsory licenses). Arguments pro and con are surveyed in STAFF REPORT OF THE SUBCOMM. ON PATENTS, TRADEMARKS, AND COPYRIGHTS OF THE SENATE COMM. ON THE JUDICIARY, 86TH CONG., 2D SESS., COMPULSORY LICENSING OF ANTITRUST JUDGMENTS 13 (1958) (written by Catherine S. Corry). A good overview of the issue is provided by F. SCHERER, INDUSTRIAL MARKET STRUCTURE AND ECONOMIC PERFORMANCE 457 (2d ed. 1980) ("All in all, the substantial amount of evidence now available suggests that compulsory patent licensing, judiciously confined to cases in which patent-based monopoly power has been abused ... would have little or no adverse impact on the rate of technological progress ....").

4. More on Compulsory Licensing. For background on compulsory licensing, see the following sources. B. BUGBY, THE GENESIS OF THE AMERICAN PATENT AND COPYRIGHT SYSTEM (1967), at 143 (the Senate proposed a compulsory licensing provision in the first Patent Act of 1790, modelled on similar provisions in state copyright acts, but it was rejected by the House); V. BUSH, SOME PROPOSALS FOR IMPROVING THE PATENT SYSTEM, STUDY NO. 1, SUBCOMM. ON PATENTS, TRADEMARKS & COPYRIGHTS, SENATE COMM. ON THE JUDICIARY, DEC. 20, 1956 (proposing minimum "working" requirement and compulsory license as remedy); Feit, *Biotechnology Research and the Experimental Use Exception to Patent Infringement*, 71 J. PAT. & TRADEMARK OFF. SOC'Y 819 (1989) (proposing compulsory license for patent infringed during experimentation to improve the patented technology); Stern, *Tales from the Algorithm War: Benson to Iwahashi, It's Deja Vu All Over Again*, 18 AM. INTELL. PROP. L. ASS'N Q.J. 371 (1991) (proposing non-injunction remedy for software algorithms); Tandon, *Optimal Patents with Compulsory Licensing*, 90 J. POL. ECON. 470 (1982); Schecter, *Would Compulsory Licensing of Patents Be Unconstitutional?*, 22 VA. L. REV. 287 (1936) (arguing that such licenses would be constitutionally permitted). For background on compulsory licensing in the copyright field, see Ross, *The Compulsory License: How Did We Get There and How Does It Work?*, COMMUN. & L., June 12, 1989, at 1. *Cf.* Gordon, *Fair Use as Market Failure: A Structural and Economic Analysis of the Betamax Case and Its Predecessors*, 82 COLUM. L. REV. 1600 (1982).

5. *Liability Rules*. The denial of a permanent injunction would leave a patentee with only one remedy: money damages. This, in effect, would convert a patent from a property right — the right to exclude — into an entitlement for compensation, or a "liability rule." The following section, *Patent Remedies, Property Rules and Liability Rules*, explores the implications of such a change and constructs a defense of traditional property rule thinking in the face of assertions that a compulsory licensing scheme would better serve the public interest and economic development. Note in this regard that compulsory licensing is an integral and accepted part of many foreign intellectual property systems. *See, e.g.*, Comment, *Compulsory Patent Licensing in the United States: An Idea Whose Time Has Come*, 8 Nw. J. INT'L L. & BUS. 666 (1988); Rogers, *The Revised Canadian Patent Act, the Free Trade Agreement, and Pharmaceutical Patents: An Overview of Pharmaceutical Compulsory Licensing in Canada*, 10 EUR. INTELL. PROP. REV. 351 (1990) (describing changes to the Canadian Patent Act in 1986-87, which revised the compulsory licensing provisions of the 1969 Act to make it more difficult to obtain a compulsory license to manufacture pharmaceutical products in Canada).

3. PATENT REMEDIES, PROPERTY RULES AND LIABILITY RULES

The economic literature emphasizing property rights, transactions, and institutions — loosely referred to as the New Institutional Economics — has blossomed in recent years. Institutions as disparate as the individual contract, the firm, the employment relationship, and even the cartel have been swept under the umbrella of this new mode of economic analysis. Yet, curiously, intellectual property rights have been ignored. Those, like the present author, who have perpetrated economically-oriented studies of intellectual property, have emphasized the tradeoff between incentives to produce new technologies and the desire to see them diffused. As a consequence, this literature is concerned primarily with doctrines touching on patent validity, infringement, and scope. *But see* Robert P. Merges, *Of Property Rules, Coase, and Intellectual Property*, 94 COLUM. L. REV. 2655 (1994) (making arguments similar to those described here).

While theorists emphasize the *creation* of technology to be covered by property rights, the active market for the *exchange* of these properties is ignored. This section addresses this omission. In particular, its goals are (1) to locate the rules governing patent transactions on the Coasian landscape, i.e., characterize them in terms of the literature on property rights and transaction costs; (2) to examine how those rules influence transactions; and (3) suggest some minor adjustments in the rules to better facilitate bargaining in certain sticky cases.

As might be imagined, the consequence of this change in orientation is a greater emphasis on remedies in patent cases. Remedies doctrines, after all, define what rights the property holder has in the face of an infringement and thus constitute the framework for the bargain (if any) between the parties. We will have occasion to mention infringement doctrine in connection with a certain type of transaction, that between a pioneer inventor and the inventor of a radical improvement to the pioneering technology. But it will be seen that even in this instance there is an underlying remedial impetus that gives shape to the doctrine.

The Coase Theorem and Intellectual Property Rights

The cornerstone of thinking about property transactions is the Coase Theorem. The "strong form" of the theorem says that in a world with zero transaction costs, the initial legal allocation of rights is unimportant; they will be transferred to their highest-value use through private bargains. Coase, *The Problem of Social Cost*, 3 J. L. & ECON. 1 (1960). Where transaction costs are positive, this cannot be assumed; the theorem implies that we must pay attention to transaction costs in assigning initial rights.

Applying the "strong form" to patent law involves a few preliminary steps, but yields the conventional result. The theorem envisions rivals whose economic activities interfere with each other. Two classic examples describe the conflict: the railway-versus-farmer problem, where the railway creates sparks that may damage the farmer's field, and the factory-versus-laundry problem, where the factory creates smoke that interferes with the laundry's ability to clean clothes. To apply the theorem to patent law, we must focus on the problem of rival economic activities. The clearest example is the conflict between a patentee and a competitor accused of infringement.

The strong form of the theorem states that whether the patentee's patent is held valid and infringed by the accused infringer is unimportant. The patentee's technology will wind up in the hands of the one best able to exploit it. If the patent is held valid and infringed, and the accused infringer has the best use for it, she will purchase it from the patentee. If the patentee is the highest-value user, she will either retain the right (if the patent is enforced) or buy out the infringer (if it is not).

In the positive transaction costs case, we would need to make two more inquiries before deciding how the initial rights ought to be allocated. If the technology were difficult to value, we would give the initial right to the patentee and let her bargain with the infringer. If transaction costs were high, on the other hand, we would adopt a "liability rule," which would permit the infringer to use the technology covered by the patentee's right, but require the infringer to fully compensate the patentee.

Features of Intellectual Property as Coasian Rights

The quick sketch given above should be troubling; all sorts of issues are assumed away or swept up into catch-all phrases. But of the many complications which are simplified, one stands out: the nature of the asset being fought over.

The basic Coasian analysis assumes rival economic agents exploiting fixed resources. The factory is already in place, as is the laundry; the question is how to allocate rights over the use of air. The asset being fought over is the right to use the air, which by definition is fixed. (If it weren't, private bargains would not be the parties' only option; they could invest resources in producing more air, which would undoubtedly change the calculus.)

Technology is sometimes different. Where a patentee and accused infringer are fighting over the right to use a certain technological principle, they may closely resemble the factory owner and the laundry owner. If the infringer is bidding to enter the patentee's market, then the infringer's use of the resource (the technology) would negatively affect the patentee. Likewise, if the patentee can exclude her from her only viable market, the infringer will be harmed too. Although the patentee and infringer are *direct* competitors — and thus may engage in strategic behavior more often than the factory owner and laundry owner — the basic structure of competing uses of a resource follows the pattern of Coase Theorem discussions.

But in other cases the two parties may not be facing a zero-sum game. Sometimes *both* can use the technology at the same time without harming the other. One example: where the infringer appropriates (or builds on) the technology to exploit a market quite distinct from the patentee's (e.g., remote in a business sense or geographically). In this case (under certain assumptions) no bargain is necessary to accommodate the activities of the parties. They could both enjoy positive net profits. Thus the imposition of property rights in this case cannot be justified in the normal Coasian terms. The rationale for such rights must not be to facilitate bargains that would take place anyway, but to *force parties to bargain* in the first place. Here the distributional concerns (i.e., who gets how much of the resource) of intellectual property law show through most clearly. This is at odds with the Coase Theorem's basic focus on efficiency, rather than distribution.

Some Coasian Examples

Before turning to the interesting case of an inchoate interference, we will first survey several brief examples of the more conventional Coasian situation in the context of intellectual property rights.

The Zero-Sum Infringement

Assume an infringer simply copies an inventor's technology and begins selling into the inventor's market. Assume further that this infringer has no cost advantage over the inventor; that is, putting aside the R&D cost which the infringer saved by copying the invention, the infringer's production cost is the same as that of the inventor. Finally, assume that the infringer has not improved on the technology in any way.

Under these circumstances, since the market size is fixed and the infringer brings nothing new to it, the joint profits of the infringer and the inventor will always equal the same amount. (This is the definition of a zero-sum situation.) Thus, since the goal of the Coasian analysis is to maximize joint profits, we will be indifferent as to which of the two makes the sales.

To see why, assume the inventor is selling two units at $50 apiece. When the R&D costs are deducted from the $100 total profits, the inventor is left with $80. Then the infringer enters the scene. If the infringer sells 1 unit for $50, and the inventor sells the other unit for $50, the joint profits will still be $80 (the infringer's $50 plus the inventor's $30, which again follows from the fact that the inventor's $50 in gross profits is reduced by the $20 R&D cost). Likewise, if the infringer sells 2 units and the inventor sells none, the infringer's $100 profit is partially offset by the inventor's loss of $20; the joint profits are still $80. No "side deals" between the parties will change this. As a result, there is no need to allocate any sort of legal right; from the point of view of overall efficiency, society comes out the same regardless of whether the inventor or the infringer sells the units, or they each sell one.

Of course, there would be precious little incentive to invent if the infringer were permitted to sell both units and the inventor were left with a $20 loss for her troubles. But in elementary Coasian analysis, this is not important; the distribution of profits does not matter, only the joint profits of the two parties. (We discuss below the intellectual property system's strong concern with this distributional issue.)

The Efficient Infringer

Assume there is an inventor who has invested considerable resources to develop a particular technology. The technology is embodied in a product. She is currently the lone seller of the product and earns profits of $10. Along comes an infringer. The infringer can make higher profits selling into the same market because she is a more efficient producer. Her revenue schedule (assuming only she and the inventor occupy the market) is as follows: if she sells 1 unit of the product, she earns $100; if she sells 2 units, $150; 3 units, $125; and downward from there. The infringer's entry harms the inventor directly, because there is fixed demand in this market, so each sale by the infringer means one less sale by the inventor. But the infringer also harms the inventor indirectly, for example by eroding its brand name, taking away sales in ancillary markets, and the like. (These sorts of damages are very common in patent infringement cases.) Table I describes the outcomes that result for both parties when the infringer sells various numbers of units.

Table I: Profits for Each Unit of Infringer's Sales

	Infringer's Sales			
	0	1	2	3
Infringer's Gross	0	100	150	125
Indirect Damage	0	-60	-120	
Damage to Inventor in This Market	0	-60	-120	
Inventor's Profits in This Market	10	-50	-110	

Table II: Joint Profits

	Joint Profits Infringer's Sales		
	0	1	2
Inventor Action			
Stay in Market	10	-10	-80
Leave Market	0	40	30

From the standpoint of overall efficiency, we are most interested in maximizing the joint profits of the two parties. There are several joint profit scenarios, depending on how many units the infringer decides to sell and whether the inventor decides to stay in this market or get out.

Assuming no cooperation between the two, they will decide on their course of action based on whether any rights have been assigned. If the inventor has no right to exclude the infringer or otherwise receive compensation, the infringer will sell 2 units, which maximizes her profits (i.e., $150). Meanwhile the inventor will lose money, either $120 if she does not continue to sell into this market, or $230 if she does.

However, if the parties can bargain, they can reach an agreement that will make them both better off. Specifically, they can agree on some "middle ground" between the inventor's optimal (infringer sells no units) and infringer's optimal (she sells 2). If the inventor pays the infringer to sell fewer units, the inventor will be better off; if the payment is high enough, the infringer will be better off than she would be if she sold the extra unit. This is precisely what would happen: the inventor would pay the infringer $55 to sell only one unit. That way the inventor loses less than if the infringer sold two units ($115 instead of $120; see Table I). The inventor's $115 loss after the payment is a combination of her loss from the infringer's sale of 1 unit ($60) plus the payment of the $55. The infringer makes more — $155, her profit of $100 for selling 1 unit plus the $55 payment — than she would if she sold two units ($150). Everyone is, if not happy, at least better off. This bargain is a consequence of the fact that the parties' joint profit is maximized when the infringer sells 1 unit and the inventor gets out of the market, as shown in Table II. In technical terms, the parties have "split the surplus from cooperation" which is $10, the difference between the highest joint profit ($40) and the joint profit that would result if they did not cooperate ($30, the southeast corner of Table II). (The split gives the infringer $5 more than the $150 she would have had, or $155, and allows the inventor to save $5 by losing only $115, less than the $120 she would have lost if the infringer sold 2 units.)

All of this assumes that the inventor has no legal right to exclude the infringer from the market, or otherwise receive compensation from the infringer. Change this assumption; assume some form of right has been given to the inventor (whom we will now call the patentee, in recognition of this grant). The Coase Theorem says that if there are no transaction costs the outcome will not change with the granting of the patent. The distribution of resources between the two parties may (and in this case will) change, but the outcome that is overall most efficient will still prevail.

Before the infringer's entry, the patentee is making $10 selling the product. The patent gives the patentee the right to exclude the infringer from the market. This means that after the infringer's (attempted) entry, the infringer will sell 0 units and the patentee will continue to make $10.

Our analysis above indicated that when parties can bargain, they will reach an agreement that maximizes their joint profits. Even though the patentee now has the right to exclude, joint profits are still maximized if the patentee leaves the market and the infringer sells 1 unit. This is indeed the bargain we would expect, despite the existence of the patent. The infringer would pay the patentee $15, the patentee would leave the market, and the infringer would sell 1 unit. The outcome, in other words, would be the same. The only difference would be that after the dust settled on this bargain, the patentee would be left with $15 and the infringer would have $25. Contrast this with the outcome where there was no patent: the patentee lost $115 and the infringer made $155. Thus although from the standpoint of overall efficiency there is no difference (we still see the infringer selling 1 unit and the patentee leaving the market), when we grant the patent the patentee (inventor) gets a much bigger share of the total profits to be made from the technology. This, in a nutshell, provides a fine justification for the patent system. Since society receives the same benefits (i.e., infringer selling 1 unit) whether or not we grant the patent, it only makes sense to tailor the distribution of benefits to favor the inventor/patentee. This way we will receive more inventions over time. And this allocation of property rights balances to some extent the contributions of the two parties: the inventor, who created the technology, and the infringer, who is a more efficient producer of the product embodying the technology.

Inchoate Interferences: Dynamic and Distributional Concerns

The preceding example of a Coasian bargain over technology assumed that the infringer caused immediate damage to the inventor/patentee's market. As in other conventional Coasian situations, the interference between economic activities comes first, and the bargain comes second. Without transaction costs, the original location of the right is irrelevant; only the bargain matters. When transaction costs are introduced (as they will be below), the right is assigned to solve the interference problem in light of the bargaining situation the parties face. Here the interference comes first, then the right, then the bargain. Many cases related to inventions and new technology fit this pattern. Again, the infringer's activities impact the inventor in much the same way that sparks from the locomotive affect the farmer or the smoke from the factory affects the laundry.

But earlier we saw that the interference between an inventor and an infringer may sometimes be so inchoate that no immediate allocation of rights is necessary to achieve an efficient solution. This is the case where there is no present interference, in other words, only hypothetical smoke or sparks. Another way to state this emphasizes the relationship between the externality and the right. In these cases involving intellectual property, *the right creates the interference*. There is nothing akin to the smoke produced by the factory or the sparks shooting out from the locomotive. The infringer can carry on her activities without directly and immediately affecting the patentee. Perhaps she is selling to a market unrelated to the patentee's. Perhaps she has added a feature that the patentee has not thought of, and this feature creates a separate market sector from that of the patentee. In such cases, there is no direct and immediate effect on the patentee. Thus, no bargains are necessary to accommodate the activities of the two parties. From the perspective of the Coase Theorem, this implies that no rights are necessary either. In fact, it might be thought to carry a stronger implication: the imposition of rights in such a situation is downright bad from the point of view of efficiency.

To analogize this situation to a conventional Coasian one, imagine that the factory produces trace amounts of smoke. This smoke has no direct, immediate effect on the laundry. In Coasian terms, there is no interference, and no need for a bargain, and therefore no need for a smoke-related right. In such a situation, giving the laundry a right to be free of such smoke creates the potential for a windfall, especially if it is a property right. (In this case, as discussed below, it would serve as a "holdup" right and permit the laundry to extort a good deal of the value of the factory's operations.)

The analogy is incomplete, however, since it fails to take into account a feature of major concern to those who study the economics of technology: dynamics. (In fact, the entire Coasian picture seems particularly static, so the objection might well apply outside the realm of technology.) Conditions might — indeed, can be expected to — change. The absence of direct, immediate harm is a temporary feature of the situation. The patentee might expand into the market carved out by the infringer. The patentee might develop an improvement along the lines explored by the infringer. In either case, direct, immediate harm akin to the smoke from the factory or the sparks from the locomotive is in the cards. It is only a matter of time and changing conditions.

To extend the factory/laundry analogy, assume the laundry might someday expand into the ultra-sanitary cleaning market for surgical gowns, lab coats, etc. In this business area, even trace amounts of smoke cannot be tolerated. Under this assumption, the trace amounts of smoke produced by the factory create an *inchoate* interference between the activities of the parties. In the Disney World of perfect information, of course, both parties understand each other's future expansion paths, and both know their profits in future lines of business. So in this world there is no difference between the inchoate interference caused by the trace amount of smoke and the actual interference caused by large amounts of smoke.

They will bargain to the efficient solution as if the activity were already occurring.

Outside of Disney World, however, the parties will not enter into such a bargain until the interference presents itself, or perhaps just shortly before. The laundry may not even be aware of the trace amounts of smoke until it is considering entering the sanitary laundry market. The future profits from this market — essential to rational bargaining over the extent of smoke that can be tolerated — will also be unclear. Should rights be defined now to smooth this future bargaining? In other words, should rights be assigned so as to *create* the interference that will lead to a Coasian bargain?

In straight Coasian terms, it is difficult to imagine when such rights would make sense. In its preliminary "pure" form, the Coase Theorem says that parties will bargain around the rights to the efficient solution, regardless of the locus of the rights. But, as discussed, there is no need for an efficient solution until there is actual interference between the parties' economic activities.

As mentioned, one reason the Coasian analysis might still apply is that the parties can envision a future interference, which might make a prospective transaction worthwhile. As discussed above and in the following section, however, this is unlikely given the great uncertainty attending new technology and its economic prospects. A more tenable rationale for the early assignment of rights might be found in a sometimes neglected corner of Coasian analysis: distributional effects.

In the farmer and railroad example, the allocation of rights has no effect on efficiency, but significant impact on the distribution of resources. Giving the right to farmers makes farming more lucrative, relative to railway work. Because of this, at the margin more people will go into farming than railway work. In the patent example, giving strong patent protection to the patentee will encourage future inventors to pursue their ideas, and might discourage infringers from using them or improving on them.

Traditionally, this distributional feature of the allocation of rights is *the* central justification for patents: we want to reward inventors, so we give them a property right good against infringers. Note how this contrasts with the typical discussion of the Coase Theorem, which puts distributional issues second, if it considers them at all. The patent system's emphasis on "just rewards" for the inventor, and thus incentives for future inventors, puts distributional questions first. More explicitly, the patent system constantly recognizes that today's distribution of rights has a major impact on tomorrow's invention investment decisions. In this way, an emphasis on current distribution reveals an underlying concern with future behavior — i.e., dynamics.

To summarize, we began by considering whether the Coase Theorem could be applied to transactions over intellectual property rights. We saw some features of these transactions that differed from the conventional Coasian analysis: that some uses of technology do not present a zero-sum bargaining situation; and that in some cases there is currently no interference between the economic activities of the parties that requires an immediate Coasian bargain. Despite these special features, we described some intellectual property-related disputes that resembled the conventional Coasian situation. Several of these illustrated that, unlike conventional Coasian situations, distributional concerns (and the dynamic effects of distribution) were essential to the rationale for intellectual property rights.

A Catalogue of Transaction Costs in Technology Exchanges

Information Costs

Earlier we rejected the notion that a prospective Coasian bargain would be desirable before interference developed between an inventor and others wishing to use her technology. Implicit in this is the notion that such a bargain would require expensive investments in information about the future. These investments might usefully be viewed as transaction costs. (They might alternatively be thought of as preliminary expenses necessary to even determine whether a bargain is necessary (what might be termed Coasian set-up costs)).

Even when two parties are bargaining over the *current* transfer of rights to some technology, a great deal of information is needed. From the licensor's side, she would like to know exactly how valuable her own technology is. This could be a function of the size of the potential market(s) for it or an end product in which it is a component. Value may also be determined by cost savings, either to producers (especially if process technology is being licensed) or consumers. Just as importantly, the licensor would like to know how valuable the technology would be to the licensee. This entails several other pieces of knowledge concerning the details of the licensee's cost function, marketing strength in various market segments, and even information about the licensee's proprietary research efforts, which would tell whether the licensor's technology had complementarities with the licensee's, or whether it was redundant. Add to these the normal informational requirements regarding the licensee's past performance under similar contracts, general financial health, etc.

From the licensee's side, even more information would seem to be desirable. Primarily, the potential licensee wants to know about the details of the technology: exactly how does it work? Has it been tried using parameters that approximate the licensee's? What problems and limitations has the licensor found regarding the technology? How much "tacit" know-how is required to really make it work effectively? Why is the licensor willing to license it? In addition, the licensee would like information about the licensor's threat point: the licensor's cost of inventing the technology, whether the licensor has discovered a fundamental new technology that will supersede the old one, etc. Add to these the normal desiderata — licensor's reputation, target rate of return, etc. — and one is faced with a large menu of required information.

As an aside, it should be mentioned that on one view the information required by the licensee serves as an interesting rationale for the entire patent system. As

Arrow has pointed out, without a property right, the licensor is in a pickle: if in trying to strike a deal she discloses the technology, she has nothing left to sell, but if she does not the buyer has no idea what is for sale. Patents (and to a lesser extent trade secrets) protect the licensor's property so she can confidently offer it for sale.[1]

Strategic Bargaining Costs

Technology transactions give rise to a great deal of strategic bargaining. Technology is a unique asset; by definition, patentable technology is unique in the sense that it goes beyond what the prior art has taught. There are no price lists for Grade A technology; there is no ready market for a medium-grade invention. Thus there is vast occasion for differing valuations, or differing bargaining strategies ostensibly based on differing valuations. The result of the potentially huge variance in valuation is a potentially complex bargaining game. Evidence abounds that this potential is often realized.

In some ways, technology fits closely the paradigm described by Cooter in his article *The Cost of Coase*, 11 J. LEG. STUD. 1 (1982). Bilateral monopolies dominate in the licensing arena, as licensors (by definition monopolists, at least in a limited sense, with respect to patented technology) deal with licensees trying to augment their proprietary technological portfolio. The result may be a deadlock: no deal is made, and the right is not assigned to its highest-value use.

Opportunism and Monitoring Costs

Technology licenses are notoriously difficult to enforce, and parties to them have major incentives to cheat. The result is another set of costs that must be considered when technology transfers are contemplated.

From the licensor's point of view, a host of opportunism/enforcement issues arise. Primarily, she is concerned that the licensee might cheat by incorporating the patented technology into more products than she reports, or selling more units than she reports. In addition, there is always the possibility that the licensee is only entering into the deal to acquire the technology; she may sell a few units, terminate the agreement, and then either introduce a product incorporating non-infringing technology or simply challenge the licensor to enforce her rights.

From the licensee's point of view, the major threat is that the technology simply will not work. This is especially dangerous where a large lump-sum "downpayment" must be made at the outset of the licensing arrangement.

---

[1] K. Arrow, *Economic Welfare and the Allocation of Resources for Invention*, in THE RATE AND DIRECTION OF INVENTIVE ACTIVITY 609 (1962). Compare this to an offhand remark by Douglass North, to the effect that "patent laws and trade secret laws are designed to raise the costs of those kinds of exchange deemed to inhibit innovation." D. NORTH, INSTITUTIONS, INSTITUTIONAL CHANGE, AND ECONOMIC PERFORMANCE 47-48 (1990). Both points may be accurate; for present purposes what matters is that both focus on the transactional role of intellectual property rights.

Obviously, contractual forms have emerged to address these concerns. Equally obvious, however, is the fact that these are expensive to negotiate, and even when they are in place they are not always sufficient to fully protect the parties from these risks.

To summarize, a number of major transaction costs face those who would enter into technology contracts. There is an abundance of empirical evidence — ranging from the anecdotal to the statistically comprehensive — that proves this point.

Property Rules Versus Liability Rules

If Coase built the columns supporting transaction cost analysis, Calabresi and Malemed (C & M) filled out the walls with their description of property rules and liability rules. Calabresi & Melamed, *Property Rules, Liability Rules and Inalienability: One View of the Cathedral*, 85 HARV. L. REV. 1089 (1972). According to C & M, the extent and nature of transaction costs in a particular case dictates whether one of the parties to the Coasian bargain ought to have an absolute property right or simply the right to collect damages caused by the other party's encroachment. C & M assert that several factors point toward a property rule: few parties, difficult valuation problems, and otherwise low transaction costs. Other factors indicate that a liability rule might better effectuate the bargain: many parties (especially where any one has the power to "hold up" the whole enterprise), likelihood of strategic bargaining, and otherwise high transaction costs.

Property Rules: The Baseline

It is not too difficult to fit intellectual property rights exchanges into C & M's cathedral, although, as we shall see, they may require a few minor architectural changes to be comfortable. As a first approximation, many of the rights exchanges we are interested in imply the need for a property rule. Most technology licenses involve only two parties. Valuation problems are very tricky and expensive to resolve. And courts are, if anything, in a worse position than the parties to determine the value of the rights to be exchanged, making the feasibility of a liability rule all the more dubious.

Patent law explicitly acknowledges these facts. The basic remedy in a patent infringement case is the injunction; although damages for past infringement are always available, courts very seldom substitute ongoing damages for the injunction. Under the patent statute, as courts are wont to point out, a patent is defined as "the right to exclude others"; and frequent reference is made to the provisions of the statute that speak of patents as a form of property. The bottom line for infringers is that they will be excluded from the patentee's market for starters; damages (sometimes quite significant ones) follow.

Liability Rules: The Exception

Liability rules are not unknown to patent law, however. They come in two forms, temporary and (rarely) permanent. The temporary liability rule comes into play when an accused infringer makes, sells or uses a product that, while not covered by the precise literal scope of the patentee's patent, falls within the general shadow of the patent. In these cases the infringement is said to be under the "doctrine of equivalents." The liability rule aspect stems from the fact that the infringer in such a case will not usually be temporarily enjoined during the trial. If she loses, however, a permanent injunction will almost surely follow. See the note following *H.H. Robertson, supra.* A transaction cost account of this rule is possible. Such an account would stress that where the doctrine of equivalents is involved, the high cost of establishing the boundaries of the property right, and the extra uncertainty regarding the right, make a property rule less desirable at least until the rights are clarified.

Permanent liability rules are less common. They generally arise because the patentee is not currently selling into the market served by the infringer, and this market is deemed to be important to the public. Where this is the case, it usually follows that the patentee is behaving strategically, i.e., excluding the infringer for reasons other than protecting an important market. Since such strategic motives often lead to higher transaction costs, a liability rule may be justified. In addition, other disparate public interest factors sometimes justify a liability rule. And in one case of interest, *Wisconsin Alumni Research Foundation* (earlier in this chapter), the court simply refused to enforce the patent at all on public interest grounds.

Finally, one other measure is hypothetically capable of producing a liability rule: the eminent domain power. Although it has almost never been used, it could be asserted to force a patentee into a transaction she wanted to avoid. (*See* notes following *Wisconsin Alumni Research Found., supra.*) In fairness, public interest concerns, and not party-to-party transaction costs, seem to account for these cases.

The eminent domain power is more important as a threat than an operative tool. In several cases where technology useful to the military was not being developed because of a logjam of conflicting property rights, the U.S. government has broken the logjam by forcing the parties to cross-license or otherwise integrate the technology. No doubt the lurking threat of the eminent domain power contributed to the potency of the government's appeal. In at least one case, a long-term industry patent pool was formed in the wake of the government's forced licensing; this pool itself embodied an interesting governance structure built on an industry-wide liability rule. *See* Merges & Nelson, *On the Complex Economics of Patent Scope*, 90 COLUM. L. REV. 839 (1990).

Indeed, all patent pools legitimately designed to foster technology exchanges function according to liability rules. Typically firms are required to license in all technology of use in the industry. In exchange, they are permitted to use any of the other members' technology after paying licensing fees. These fees are calibrated to reflect the significance of the technology being licensed; for administrative convenience, the technology in the pool is usually divided into several broad classes. The licensing pools in the airframe and automobile industries operate under these sorts of rules, as have those of many other industries. *Id.*

Informal exchange norms can also serve to institute a liability rule exchange system on industry. In the semiconductor, consumer electronics, and chemical industries, patents were thought of as bargaining chips. They were used to facilitate technology trades, or at least to fend off infringement suits in a convenient way. Cross-licensing was (and to some extent still is) the norm in these industries. Thus, in an operational sense, a liability rule exchange system prevailed; the legal right to exclude was rarely enforced fully. Whether this norm emerged because of economic forces in the industry such as rapid development and mutually interdependent research efforts, or because of historical forces unrelated to increased efficiency, is an interesting question that is left open here. I simply wish to point out occasions where the dominant property rule of patent law has led to results consistent with a liability rule — yielding in these instances what might be termed a private liability rule.

To summarize: economic theory, beginning with the Coase Theorem and including the literature on transaction costs, provides a solid rationale both for the general availability of injunctions (i.e., basic property rule) in patent law, and the exceptions to that rule where only damages are available to a patentee (i.e., a liability rule).

B. DAMAGES

REASONABLE ROYALTY

PANDUIT CORP. v. STAHLIN BROS. FIBRE WORKS, INC.

575 F.2d 1152, 197 U.S.P.Q. (BNA) 726 (6th Cir. 1978)

MARKEY, CHIEF JUDGE [of the C.C.P.A., sitting by designation]

Appeal from a judgment of the district court, adopting the report of the special master awarding plaintiff, as damages for patent infringement, a reasonable royalty of 2.5%. We reverse and remand.

In 1964 plaintiff Panduit Corp. (Panduit) sued defendant Stahlin Bros. Fibre Works, Inc. (Stahlin) for infringement of Panduit's Walch patent No. 3,024,301, covering duct for wiring of electrical control systems. In 1969, the district court found claim 5 valid and infringed by the "Lok-Slot" and "Web-Slot" ducts made and sold by Stahlin, enjoined Stahlin from further infringement, and ordered an accounting. That judgment was affirmed on appeal.

Thereafter, the district court adjudged Stahlin in contempt of the court's injunction, because of Stahlin's making and selling the "Tear Drop" duct, a colorable imitation of the infringing "Lok-Slot." That judgment was also affirmed on appeal.

In 1971, the district court appointed a master to determine Panduit's damages pursuant to 35 U.S.C. § 284, to take evidence, and render a report on the issues of treble damages, interest, costs, and attorney fees. The district court, in adopting in toto the master's report, considered the master's findings of fact not clearly erroneous, and stated that "the Master had correctly applied the law to the circumstances of this case." The report recommended $44,709.60 in damages, based on a royalty of 2.5% of gross sales price, the percentage being calculated on Stahlin's testimony that its normal profit on all of its products was 4.04% and the concept that a "reasonable royalty" entailed some level of profit to the "licensee." *Horvath v. McCord Radiator and Mfg. Co.*, 100 F.2d 326 at 335, 40 U.S.P.Q. 394 at 403 (6th Cir. 1938), *cert. denied*, 308 U.S. 581, 60 S. Ct. 101, 84 L. Ed. 486, 43 U.S.P.Q. 520 (1939).

The duct manufactured by Panduit was invented by its president, Jack Caveney. Panduit began to make and sell the duct in 1955, and Caveney applied for a patent in 1956. In an interference proceeding in the Patent Office, it was determined that Walch, an employee of General Electric, was the first inventor of the duct. A patent issued to General Electric, as Walch's assignee, on March 6, 1962. Panduit then acquired the Walch patent from General Electric and established a firm policy of exercising its right to that patent property, i.e., of the right to exclude others from making and selling the patented duct.

Stahlin began to manufacture and sell the "Lok-Slot" and "Web-Slot" ducts in 1957, and continued to do so after issuance of the Walch patent and its sale to Panduit in 1962. On January 1, 1963, Stahlin introduced a price cut of approximately 30% on its "Lok-Slot" and "Web-Slot" ducts.

Panduit seeks $808,003 as damages for lost profits on lost sales over the period March 6, 1962, the date of first infringement, to August 7, 1970, the effective date of the initial injunction; or, alternatively, a 35% reasonable royalty rate yielding $625,940. In addition, Panduit seeks $4,069,000 in profits lost on Panduit's own sales because of Stahlin's price cut.

The dispositive issue is whether the master's determination of a reasonable royalty was in error.

OPINION

The statute requires that the patent owner receive from the infringer "damages adequate to compensate for the infringement." In *Aro Mfg. Co. v. Convertible Top Replacement Co.*, 377 U.S. 476 at 507 (1964), the Supreme Court stated:

> But the present statutory rule is that only "damages" may be recovered. These have been defined by this Court as "compensation for the pecuniary loss he (the patentee) has suffered from the infringement, without regard to the question whether the defendant has gained or lost by his unlawful acts." They have been said to constitute "the difference between his pecuniary

condition after the infringement, and what his condition would have been if the infringement had not occurred." *Yale Lock Mfg. Co. v. Sargent*, 117 U.S. 536, 552 [1886]. The question to be asked in determining damages is "how much had the Patent Holder and Licensee suffered by the infringement. And that question (is) primarily: had the Infringer not infringed, what would Patent Holder-Licensee have made?"

Panduit argues that the district court erred (1) in denying Panduit its lost profits due to lost sales, or, in the alternative, a 35% reasonable royalty; and (2) in denying Panduit its lost profits from its own actual sales due to Stahlin's price cut.

Lost Profits Due to Lost Sales

To obtain as damages the profits on sales he would have made absent the infringement, i.e., the sales made by the infringer, a patent owner must prove: (1) demand for the patented product, (2) absence of acceptable noninfringing substitutes, (3) his manufacturing and marketing capability to exploit the demand, and (4) the amount of the profit he would have made.

It is not disputed that Panduit established elements (1) and (3). Regarding (2), the master found that: "The evidence clearly shows the existence of acceptable non-infringing substitute ducts which would have permitted the defendant to retain its customers." That finding, as discussed below, was in error. However, Panduit is not entitled to its lost profits on lost sales in this case because of its failure to establish element (4).

The district court upheld as not clearly erroneous the master's finding that "there was insufficient evidence from which a fair determination could be made as to the amount of profit plaintiff would have made on such sales."

Panduit's Achilles heel on element (4) is a lack of evidence on its fixed costs. Panduit alleges that its omission is overcome by other evidence. [But] Stahlin did dispute Panduit's accounting theory, presenting its own expert witnesses to contradict it. Under [prior cases], the accuracy of the patent owner's accounting method is "a matter to be decided on the basis of testimony in the hearing before the Master." The master here found, on the basis of the evidence before him, and the district court agreed, that Panduit's accounting theory was deficient.

On the issue of Panduit's lost profits on lost sales, we affirm the district court.

Reasonable Royalty

When actual damages, e.g., lost profits, cannot be proved, the patent owner is entitled to a reasonable royalty. A reasonable royalty is an amount "which a person, desiring to manufacture and sell a patented article, as a business proposition, would be willing to pay as a royalty and yet be able to make and sell the patented article, in the market, at a reasonable profit." *Goodyear Tire and Rubber Co. v. Overman Cushion Tire Co.*, 95 F.2d 978 at 984, 37 U.S.P.Q. 479 at 484

(6th Cir. 1937) (citing *Rockwood v. General Fire Extinguisher Co.*, 37 F.2d 62 at 66, 4 U.S.P.Q. 299 at 303 (2d Cir. 1930)), *appeal dismissed*, 306 U.S. 665 (1938).

The key element in setting a reasonable royalty after determination of validity and infringement is the necessity for return to the date when the infringement began. In the present case, that date is March 6, 1962. On that date, Panduit possessed the particular property right found to have been infringed by Stahlin. On that date, Panduit had a particular profit margin, and the property right to exclude others from making, using, or selling the patented product. 35 U.S.C. § 271. At that point Stahlin chose to continue the making and selling of the patented product.

As a result of Stahlin's election to infringe its property right, Panduit has suffered substantially. Though unable to prove the actual amount of lost profits or to establish a damage figure resulting from Stahlin's price cut, Panduit was clearly damaged by having been forced, against its will, to share sales of the patented product with Stahlin. Further, Panduit has been forced into thirteen years of expensive litigation, involving $400,000 in attorney fees, a trial, a contempt proceeding to enforce the court's injunction, a hearing on damages, and three appeals. For all this, the "damages adequate to compensate for the infringement," 35 U.S.C. § 284, have thus far been found to total $44,709.60.

Having elected to continue the manufacture and sale of the patented duct after the patent issued, and having elected to manufacture and sell a second infringing product in the face of the court's injunction, Stahlin was able to make infringing sales, as found by the master, totalling $1,788,384.

The setting of a reasonable royalty after infringement cannot be treated, as it was here, as the equivalent of ordinary royalty negotiations among truly "willing" patent owners and licensees. That view would constitute a pretense that the infringement never happened. It would also make an election to infringe a handy means for competitors to impose a "compulsory license" policy upon every patent owner.

Except for the limited risk that the patent owner, over years of litigation, might meet the heavy burden of proving the four elements required for recovery of lost profits, the infringer would have nothing to lose, and everything to gain if he could count on paying only the normal, routine royalty non-infringers might have paid. As said by this court in another context, the infringer would be in a "heads-I-win, tails-you-lose" position.

On the date a patent issues, a competitor which made no investment in research and development of the invention, has four options: (1) it can make and sell a non-infringing substitute product, and refrain from making, using, or selling a product incorporating the patented invention; (2) it can make and sell the patented product, if the patent owner be willing, negotiating a license and paying a reasonable (negotiated) royalty; (3) it can simply take the invention, running the risk that litigation will ensue and that the patent will be found valid and infringed, or (4) it can take a license under option (2) and thereafter repudiate its contract, challenging the validity of the patent. Determination of a reasonable royalty, after election of option (3), cannot, without injustice, be treated as though the infringer had elected option (2) in the first place.

Determination of a "reasonable royalty" after infringement, like many devices in the law, rests on a legal fiction. Created in an effort to "compensate" when profits are not provable, the "reasonable royalty" device conjures a "willing" licensor and licensee, who like Ghosts of Christmas Past, are dimly seen as "negotiating" a "license." There is, of course, no actual willingness on either side, and no license to do anything, the infringer being normally enjoined, as is Stahlin, from further manufacture, use, or sale of the patented product.

The amount of a reasonable royalty after infringement turns on the facts of each case, as best they may be determined. Among the relevant facts are: "what plaintiff's property was, to what extent defendant has taken it, its usefulness and commercial value as shown by its advantages over other things and by the extent of its use."

In determining that a reasonable royalty rate here was 2.5%, the master found: (1) there were present in the market on the date of first infringement acceptable noninfringing substitutes and competing duct producers, (2) Panduit could not have maintained a high price differential in the face of competition from the substitute ducts, (3) on the hypothetical negotiation date, both Panduit and Stahlin would have been aware of the competitive state of the market, and of the probability of future price cuts, including Stahlin's, (4) the testimony of Stahlin's patent law expert, Scofield, was "more credible and persuasive and more in line with the factual realities of this case" than the testimony of Panduit's patent law expert, and (5) Stahlin's profit on gross sales of all its products for the relevant period was 4.04%, and there was "no evidence to indicate that the profit on its duct sales was significantly higher than the profit on its total sales generally." The district court held those findings not clearly erroneous. We disagree.

In adopting the master's report, the district court stated:

> The Master based his finding that noninfringing substitutes were available principally upon the additional finding that defendant was markedly successful in switching its customers to noninfringing products when that became necessary. The latter finding is not clearly erroneous, and although defendant was not actually selling the principal noninfringing substitute ... during the relevant time period, it is not erroneous to conclude that the substitute was available.

The district court also found the master correct in defining an acceptable noninfringing substitute as "a product which customers are willing to buy in place of the infringing product."

There can be no doubt that, as found by the District Court, the substantial value of the patent was recognized by the infringer in its catalogues and other advertisements. The advantages proclaimed in these advertisements carry more forceful recognition of the value of the patent infringed than belated denial of its value rejects. Also pertinent are the comments of the court in *Georgia-Pacific Corp. v. U.S. Plywood-Champion Papers*, 318 F. Supp. 1116 at 1123, 166 U.S.P.Q. 235 at 241 (S.D.N.Y. 1970), *aff'd*, 446 F.2d 295, 170 U.S.P.Q. 369 (2d Cir. 1971), *cert. denied*, 404 U.S. 870, 92 S. Ct. 105, 30 L. Ed. 2d 114 (1971):

> Noteworthy is the fact that, despite the allegedly fierce competition between the Weldtex (the patented goods) and other decorative plywoods, GP (plaintiff-infringer) deliberately decided to duplicate Weldtex notwithstanding the caveat of GP's own counsel that an expensive infringement suit was inevitable. GP's calculated infringement of Weldtex is an admission by conduct that it regarded Weldtex as occupying a uniquely favorable position in the market.

In the present case, the master's finding that Panduit had competitors was not erroneous, but the implication drawn therefrom was. At the time the patent issued, there were four competitors, but they were recognized as making and selling not substitutes but infringing ducts. Competition between those selling infringing ducts was admittedly fierce. Infringer Stahlin, however, cannot expect to pay a lesser royalty, as compensation for its infringement, on the ground that it was not the only infringer.

Illustrative of the absence of acceptable substitutes is Stahlin's inability to avoid infringement, even if it had ever wanted to. Having begun manufacture of the duct in 1957, Stahlin continued after the patent issued in 1962, after Panduit instituted its infringement suit in 1964, and after the district court's injunction in 1969.

At the time of the first injunction, virtually all of Stahlin's sales of electrical duct were of the infringing type. Stahlin's early-but-grudging recognition of the unique advantages of Panduit's patented duct was evidenced by an intra-company memo. Dated June 21, 1957, it was issued in the earliest stages of Stahlin's manufacture of the "Lok-Slot":

> It seems that some of our customers have preferred a full-slotted channel; one that permits slipping the wire in place rather than threading the end through an opening. It's [sic] advantages are questionable but we always try to give our customers even more than they want. Thus, we have developed the Lok-Slot construction. Lok-Slot construction is evident in the name. Like any slot, Lok-Slot permits easy entry of wires. Unlike any other slot, Lok-Slot keeps the wires from readily popping up all over the place while connections are being made. The reason is Lok-Slot's slim throat construction which allows single wires in and out easily enough but "chokes up" on "mass exits." Using Panel Channel with Lok-Slot construction, wires don't have to be threaded through the channel openings.... The Lok-Slot construction is not a cure-all. Frankly, it is not quite as easy to remove and put on the covers with this construction. In any event, there are some customers

who prefer the full-slotted construction ... and Lok-Slot is the best design approach yet to this form of channel. In other words, don't push this construction ... but if there is customer preference in this direction, you have the best design to offer.

The district court opinion following the infringement trial recognized the same advantages over non-infringing ducts:

General Electric produced a steel grille which had perforated round roles through which wires were threaded. This device was patented in the 1930's. Another product in use in the early 1950's was a U-shaped wiring duct which incorporated multiple openings in the side walls through which wires were threaded and then connected to the electrical components. However, ducts with holes also had shortcomings. When these ducts were filled with wires, the wires were rather inaccessible and it was difficult to trace individual wires or to revise the wiring. For example, to remove any wire from the duct, it was necessary to disconnect the wire and thread it back through the hole. If the wire was not near the top of the duct, it was frequently necessary to remove a number of wires to gain access to the wire being traced or rerouted. Mr. Walch, in 1953 as a senior advance engineer at General Electric, was given a broad assignment to improve wiring practices, including the improvement of wiring duct design. Four desirable functions or results were stressed by Mr. Walch in his work on the design of an improved wiring duct: (1) Easy insertion of wires in the duct; (2) Prevention of accidental removal of wires from the duct; (3) Provision of maximum useful space for leading wires out of the duct; and (4) Facilitation of intentional removal of wires from the duct.

That evaluation was affirmed on appeal by this court.

Proof of the absence of noninfringing substitutes:

(I)nvolves some of the same evidence as that which was introduced in support of the validity of the patent. The patent owner who had proved a long-felt need for a particular invention has a lighter burden in establishing that his customers, as well as the infringer's customers, were in fact seeking to obtain the patented solution to such need or problem. The other side of the coin involves a strong showing by the infringer that although the patent may have embodied some trifling improvement which was patentable to a narrow extent, such improvement did not create any preference for the patented product rather than a noninfringing substitute.

The prior district and appellate court opinions leave no doubt that the patented product filled a waiting need and met with commercial success due to its merits. Stahlin's own intra-company memo, and its $1,788,384 sales of infringing ducts during the period when allegedly acceptable noninfringing substitutes are now said to have been available, leave no doubt that the patented improvement created a substantial customer preference. A product lacking the advantages of that patented can hardly be termed a substitute "acceptable" to the customer who wants those advantages. The post-hoc circumstance that Stahlin, when finally forced to obey the court's injunction, was successful in "switching" customers to a noninfringing product, does not destroy the advantage-recognition attributable to the patent over the prior 15 years. Those preferred advantages were recognized by Stahlin itself, by other infringers, by customers, by the district court, and by this court. That Stahlin's customers, no longer able to buy the patented product from Stahlin, were willing to buy something else from Stahlin, does not establish that there was on the market during the period of infringement a product which customers in general were, in the master's words, "willing to buy in place of the infringing product." Moreover, Stahlin's "switching" occurred years after the date on which the determination of available substitutes must focus, i.e., the date of first infringement.

[From footnote 9:] The "acceptable substitute" element, though it is to be considered, must be viewed of limited influence where the infringer knowingly made and sold the patented product for years while ignoring the "substitute." There are substitute products for virtually every patented product; the availability of railroads and box cameras should not of itself diminish royalties payable for infringement of the right to exclude others from making and selling the Wright airplane or the Polaroid camera.

Hence, the 2.5% royalty rate recommended by the master and adopted by the district court is clearly erroneous on its face, the master's recommendation having been based in large part on erroneous finding (1), that there were "acceptable" noninfringing substitutes during the relevant period.

The master's finding (2), that Panduit could not have maintained its high price differential (allegedly 30%) because of competition from substitutes, and his finding (3) that in March 1962 the parties were aware of the probability of a future price cut, must also fall. Evidence is lacking, as we have said, that acceptable substitutes were on the market on the focus-date of first infringement. For some five years after Stahlin began manufacture of its "Lok-Slot" duct, purchasers of the patented product were willing to pay a substantial differential. It was not until January 1, 1963, some nine months after the hypothetically "willing" licensor and licensee are supposed to have negotiated a royalty, that Stahlin made its price cut. We find no evidence in the record to support the master's supposition that the parties would have had that future price cut in mind in March 1962. On the contrary, the hypothesis is that Stahlin was a royalty-paying licensee on January 1, 1963, and nothing of record indicates an expectation that a licensee would cut its price or that any particular room existed to accommodate both a price cut and royalty payments.

Section 284 of the statute authorizes the use of experts in determining a reasonable royalty. However, the master's reliance on Scofield's testimony, and the district court's acceptance thereof, were clearly erroneous. That testimony was in substantial conflict with case law established in this circuit and elsewhere.

Scofield testified that a reasonable royalty could be equated to the average value of all negotiated royalties, which in his experience was "between 1 and 5 per cent of the net selling price of the products," and concluded that a reasonable royalty in this case would be 2.5%. He specifically testified that his experience was in the negotiation of licenses generally, and that he had no experience in the determination of a reasonable royalty after infringement under § 284. Scofield specifically assumed, for purposes of his testimony, that there existed in the present case acceptable noninfringing substitutes. He further ignored evidentiary facts considered relevant by this and other circuits. The analysis of this court in [a prior case] is instructive:

> In fixing a reasonable royalty, the primary inquiry, often complicated by secondary ones, is what the parties would have agreed upon, if both were reasonably trying to reach an agreement. This must be modified by the commercial situation, and when the result is to interfere with a patent monopoly, which the patentee was in position to and desired to keep, by retaining the entire market himself, his compensation for parting against his will with that opportunity must take due account of the loss to him of anticipated profits on the business which the licensees will thus get away from him. It is a step further, and we think a necessary one, to say that, when the patentee's business scheme involves a reasonable expectation of making future profits by the continuing sale to the purchaser of the patented machine, of supplies to be furnished by the patentee, which future business he will lose by licensing a competitor to make the machine, this expectant loss is an element to be considered in retroactively determining a reasonable royalty; and this is so even though the expectation of such future business was not the result of any system of contract obligations, but was only expectation reasonably based on established business methods and customs.

Attorney Scofield may well have been "persuasive," but his testimony was based on general experience and invalid assumptions. There was clear error therefore in finding (4), that Scofield's testimony was "in line with the factual realities of this case."

Finding (5) was erroneously based on Stahlin's actual overall profit in all its products and on absence of proof of Stahlin's actual profit on its infringing sales. The infringer's profit element, in the post-judgment "reasonable royalty" equation, is not related to the infringer's actual profit; nor is it designed to insure the anomalous result of guaranteeing an actual profit to an infringer (or the profit it would have made if there had been no infringement). The licensee-profit element is but one of the measures applicable in March 1962, and should be based on the customary profit allowed licensees in the industry at that time. Whether, as events unfurled thereafter, Stahlin would have made an actual profit, while paying the royalty determined as of March 1962, is irrelevant. If there had been no infringement, and if Stahlin had actually agreed to pay a royalty in March 1962, and if that royalty rate had then proven onerous, Stahlin might have renegotiated the royalty rate or canceled the license. But those options are no longer available to Stahlin, and their consideration in a formula for setting the royalty rate which would have been reasonable in March 1962 was error.

Conclusion

Elements necessary to the determination of a reasonable royalty in the present case [including] Panduit's actual profit margin in March 1962, and the customary profit allowed licensees in the electrical duct industry, were not determined by the master in his report and cannot be discerned from the record. They therefore must be determined on remand. On remand, the following factors must also be considered: (1) the lack of acceptable noninfringing substitutes, (2) Panduit's unvarying policy of not licensing the Walch patent, (3) the future business and attendant profit Panduit would expect to lose by licensing a competitor, and (4) that the infringed patent gave the entire marketable value to the infringed duct.

NOTES

1. *Cornerstone Case*. *Panduit* is the cornerstone case on the law of lost profits (*see, e.g., Gyromat Corp. v. Champion Spark Plug Co.*, 735 F.2d 549, 222 U.S.P.Q. 4 (Fed. Cir. 1984)), although the Federal Circuit has stated that it is not the "exclusive" standard.

2. *Fantasy Contract*. The reasonable royalty measure of damages requires a "hypothetical negotiation" between the patentee and infringer. A recent Federal Circuit case comments on the anomalous nature of a doctrine that requires a court to reconstruct such a nonexistent bargain:

> Like all methodologies based on a hypothetical, there will be an element of uncertainty; yet, a court is not at liberty, in conducting the methodology, to abandon entirely the statutory standard of damages "adequate to compensate" for the infringement. The royalty arrived at must be "reasonable" under all the circumstances; i.e., it must be at least a close approximation of what would be "adequate to compensate" for the "use made of the invention by the infringer." 35 U.S.C. § 284.
>
> The methodology encompasses fantasy and flexibility; fantasy because it requires a court to imagine what warring parties would have agreed to as willing negotiators; flexibility because it speaks of negotiations as of the time infringement began, yet permits and often requires a court to look to events and facts that occurred thereafter and that could not have been known to or predicted by the hypothesized negotiators.
>
> Forced to erect a hypothetical, it is easy to forget a basic reality — a license is fundamentally an agreement by the patent owner not to sue the licensee. In a normal negotiation, the potential licensee has three basic choices: forego all use of the invention; pay an agreed royalty; infringe the

patent and risk litigation. The methodology presumes that the licensee has made the second choice, when in fact it made the third.

Whatever royalty may result from employment of the methodology, the law is not without means for recognizing that an infringer is unlike a true "willing" licensee; nor is the law without means for placing the injured patentee "in the situation he would have occupied if the wrong had not been committed."

Fromson v. Western Litho Plate & Supply Co., 853 F.2d 1568, 1575-76, 7 U.S.P.Q.2d 1606 (Fed. Cir. 1988). The hypothetical negotiation called for here is reminiscent of restitution analysis, where a court is called on to construct the *ex post* bargain it believes the parties would have struck if they had in fact bargained. *See, e.g.*, Note, *A Theory of Hypothetical Contract*, 94 YALE L.J. 415 (1985) (arguing that a hypothetical bargain should be found in the law of restitution whenever high transaction costs prevented an actual bargain and the court can construct a deal which makes both parties better off, i.e., that is Pareto superior). The application of this Note's methodology in the context of a hypothetical reasonable royalty negotiation would be difficult (because of the valuation problem identified earlier in this chapter). But if it were applied, it would in some cases yield results quite different from those obtained with the current approach. Specifically, it might produce results more in line with pre-*Panduit* cases such as *Rockwood v. General Fire Extinguisher Co.*, 37 F.2d 62, 66 (2d Cir. 1930) (setting royalty rate at amount the parties would have actually agreed on before time of infringement).

3. A Doctrine at War With Itself? In some respects the approach taken in *Panduit* suggests that the notion of a "reasonable" royalty is absurd as a measure of damages. Having infringed, the court seems to suggest, the infringer is not entitled to full representation in the hypothetical "reasonable royalty" negotiations. Note especially the court's statements about the infringer's profits as a factor to consider in assessing the amount of the royalty the parties would have set *ex ante* (i.e., before the infringement). In effect, the court is saying that although these profits are an "element" of the analysis, a court should not bend over backwards to insure that a profit is actually made. Compare this with the court's attitude regarding the validity of the patent and its infringement by the other party to the license: these are taken as accepted facts at the time of the negotiation, even though of course they could not be known then. Thus, while the court declines to take account of one *ex post* fact — the actual profit of the parties — it is eager to assume into the earlier negotiations the facts that the patent is valid and infringed by the accused products.

What policy reason would the court give for attributing this "selective foresight" to the parties? Do you agree? Is there any societal interest in holding down the infringer's damages in a case such as this?

4. Punitive Effect. The court in *Panduit* takes pains to justify factors leading to a relatively high "reasonable royalty" figure. The most important one is that remedies doctrine should not put the infringer back into the position of a true licensee when it has been established that instead of licensing, she infringed. The court raises the fear that such a rule creates precious little disincentive to a party contemplating infringing in place of licensing.

Is it true that a rule of damages which awarded the patentee the actual market-value "reasonable royalty" would tend to make the infringer indifferent as between an *ex post* damages award and an *ex ante* license agreement? Remember that in the case of the damage award, the patentee will also enjoin the infringer from further sales of the product. Does this mean that the infringer is always worse off to infringe as opposed to licensing? Some factors to consider: the sunk costs of the infringer's productive capacity and the length of time remaining on the patent. Where very large costs are required to set up operations, and a long time is left on the patentee's patent term, a rational infringer is probably not indifferent between *ex ante* licensing and *ex post* damages plus an injunction; the value of the injunction, in other words, may make a big difference. If this is so, the infringer is certainly not "encouraged" to infringe merely because the damage award is the same as the *ex ante* licensing fee would have been. Note that the infringer's financial stake in these set-up costs amounts to a "reliance interest" in the use of the patentee's technology, akin to the reliance interest identified and discussed in the famous contracts article by Fuller & Perdue, *The Reliance Interest in Contract Damages* (pts. 1-2), 46 YALE L.J. 52, 373 (1936-1937).

In light of the discussion of strategic bargaining earlier in this chapter (Section A.3), one might in fact construct a defense of a damages measure which tried to be neutral as between the patentee and the infringer. On this view, an infringer who decided to forgo the bargaining expense necessary to convince a patentee of the infringer's valuation of the patented technology could use the courts as a "fallback" forum in which to make its case. That is, where an infringer decided that the risk of an infringement proceeding was worth it, she should be permitted to make her case for the valuation of the patentee's technology in court. This *might* have the effect of making patentees more reasonable in future licensing negotiations.

5. Second Best. On the other hand, the approach in *Panduit* emphasizes that the true goal of § 284 is full compensation for the infringement. Just because the patentee cannot meet the difficult burden required to actually establish lost profits does not mean that goal should be ignored. Again, the reliance analogy comes to mind. In the article by Fuller & Perdue, *supra*, the authors state that expectation damages will often have the effect of (indirectly) protecting a party's reliance interest in the contract. In fact, the authors state, "To encourage reliance we must therefore dispense with its proof." Fuller & Perdue, *supra*, at 62. By the same token, it might be argued that the best way to protect lost profits is to "dispense with their proof — by awarding a stiff "reasonable" royalty. This has the added advantage of stating a coherent approach to an otherwise almost-meaningless term, "reasonable."

Thus, in practice, a reasonable royalty based on the hypothetical willing licensor and willing licensee is often higher than the reasonable royalty which a noninfringer would have paid. As the Federal Circuit explained in *Stickle v. Heublein, Inc.*, 716 F.2d 1550, 1563, 219 U.S.P.Q. 377, 387 (Fed. Cir. 1983):

> [T]he trial court may award an amount of damages greater than a reasonable royalty so that the award is "adequate to compensate for the infringement."
> ... Such an increase, which may be stated by the trial court either as a reasonable royalty for an infringer (as in *Panduit*) or as an increase in the reasonable royalty determined by the court, is left to its sound discretion.

And yet, excessive enhancement under the *Panduit* banner will not fly either. For example, in *Mahurkar v. C.R. Bard*, 79 F.3d 1572, 1580, 38 U.S.P.Q.2d 1288 (Fed. Cir. 1996), the trial court had fixed the total reasonable royalty rate at 34.88%, which it broke into two components: (1) a 25.88% base rate, and (2) a 9% "kicker." The Federal Circuit (per Judge Rader) reversed on the grounds that this was not acceptable under § 284:

> When engaging in its judicially-sanctioned speculation as to the results of a hypothetical negotiation, the trial court appears to have considered evidence of Bard's actual net profit, the profit margin Bard would have been able to negotiate, and Bard's research and development savings. The court specifically found Bard was entitled to a 10% profit margin. It also determined that Bard realized a net profit of 29.16% on its sales of the Hickman catheters and saved 6.72% in research and development costs....
>
> ... Although one method for proving damages, the *Panduit* methodology does not include a "kicker" to account for litigation expenses or for any other expenses.
>
> ... In this case, the district court invoked *Panduit* out of context. This case did not feature a lost profits award at all, but instead reasonable royalties. To apply the *Panduit* test, the trial court would have needed to ascertain whether Bard's and Mahurkar's products competed for the same customers, whether the market included acceptable noninfringing substitutes, and whether Dr. Mahurkar had the capacity to exploit the demand. Without such evidence in this record, the trial court invoked *Panduit* out of context.
>
> More important, *Panduit* does not authorize additional damages or a "kicker" on top of a reasonable royalty because of heavy litigation or other expenses. In sections 284 and 285, the Patent Act sets forth statutory requirements for awards of enhanced damages and attorney fees. The statute bases these awards on clear and convincing proof of willfulness and exceptionality. *Panduit* at no point suggested enhancement of a compensatory damage award as a substitute for the strict requirements for these statutory provisions. The district court's "kicker," on the other hand, enhances a damages award, apparently to compensate for litigation expenses, without

meeting the statutory standards for enhancement and fees. Therefore, the district court abused its discretion in awarding a 9% "*Panduit* kicker."

But cf. King Instruments Corp. v. Perego, 65 F.3d 941, 951 n.6 (Fed. Cir. 1995) (seemingly approving, in dictum, of "discretionary increases" when "plaintiffs cannot prove direct and foreseeable damages in the form of lost profits.").

GEORGIA-PACIFIC CORP. v. UNITED STATES PLYWOOD CORP.

318 F. Supp. 1116, 166 U.S.P.Q. (BNA) 235 (S.D.N.Y. 1970),
modified, 446 F.2d 295, 170 U.S.P.Q. 369 (2d Cir.),
cert. denied, 404 U.S. 870 (1971)

Following the decision of the Court of Appeals [finding Claim 1 of United States Plywood's (USP) Deskey Patent No. 2,286,068 covering "Weldtex" striated fir plywood valid and infringed by Georgia-Pacific (GP)], the case was referred to a special master to determine the amount of damages to be awarded to USP under 35 U.S.C. 284. The master, computing damages upon the basis of GP's profits derived from the sale of the infringing article, awarded $685,837.00 to USP.

While the parties agree upon the doctrinal criteria of a reasonable royalty, they differ sharply in their application of those principles to the hard specifics of the evidence. The extreme divergence of the parties is reflected in the difference between GP's submission that the reasonable royalty herein should be fixed at a figure somewhere between a dollar and one-half to three dollars per thousand square feet and USP's claim that the minimum reasonable royalty should be the rate of fifty dollars per thousand square feet.

A comprehensive list of evidentiary facts relevant, in general, to the determination of the amount of a reasonable royalty for a patent license may be drawn from a conspectus of the leading cases. The following are some of the factors *mutatis mutandis* seemingly more pertinent to the issue herein:

1. The royalties received by the patentee for the licensing of the patent in suit, proving or tending to prove an established royalty.

2. The rates paid by the licensee for the use of other patents comparable to the patent in suit.

3. The nature and scope of the license, as exclusive or non-exclusive; or as restricted or non-restricted in terms of territory or with respect to whom the manufactured product may be sold.

4. The licensor's established policy and marketing program to maintain his patent monopoly by not licensing others to use the invention or by granting licenses under special conditions designed to preserve that monopoly.

5. The commercial relationship between the licensor and licensee, such as, whether they are competitors in the same territory in the same line of business; or whether they are inventor and promotor.

6. The effect of selling the patented specialty in promoting sales of other products of the licensee; the existing value of the invention to the licensor as a generator of sales of his non-patented items; and the extent of such derivative or convoyed sales.

7. The duration of the patent and the term of the license.

8. The established profitability of the product made under the patent; its commercial success; and its current popularity.

9. The utility and advantages of the patent property over the old modes or devices, if any, that had been used for working out similar results.

10. The nature of the patented invention; the character of the commercial embodiment of it as owned and produced by the licensor; and the benefits to those who have used the invention.

11. The extent to which the infringer has made use of the invention; and any evidence probative of the value of that use.

12. The portion of the profit or of the selling price that may be customary in the particular business or in comparable businesses to allow for the use of the invention or analogous inventions.

13. The portion of the realizable profit that should be credited to the invention as distinguished from non-patented elements, the manufacturing process, business risks, or significant features or improvements added by the infringer.

14. The opinion testimony of qualified experts.

15. The amount that a licensor (such as the patentee) and a licensee (such as the infringer) would have agreed upon (at the time the infringement began) if both had been reasonably and voluntarily trying to reach an agreement; that is, the amount which a prudent licensee — who desired, as a business proposition, to obtain a license to manufacture and sell a particular article embodying the patented invention — would have been willing to pay as a royalty and yet be able to make a reasonable profit and which amount would have been acceptable by a prudent patentee who was willing to grant a license.

In the present case there is no formula by which these factors can be rated precisely in the order of their relative importance or by which their economic significance can be automatically transduced into their pecuniary equivalent.

"The primary inquiry, often complicated by secondary ones, is what the parties would have agreed upon, if both were reasonably trying to reach an agreement." [*Faulkner v. Gibbs*, 199 F.2d 635, 639 (9th Cir. 1952).]

The rule is more a statement of approach than a tool of analysis. It requires consideration not only of the amount that a willing licensee would have paid for the patent license but also of the amount that a willing licensor would have accepted. What a willing licensor and a willing licensee would have agreed upon in a supposititious negotiation for a reasonable royalty would entail consideration of the specific factors previously mentioned, to the extent of their relevance. Where a willing licensor and a willing licensee are negotiating for a royalty, the hypothetical negotiations would not occur in a vacuum of pure logic. They would involve a marketplace confrontation of the parties, the outcome of which would depend upon such factors as their relative bargaining strength; the anticipated amount of profits that the prospective licensor reasonably thinks he would lose as a result of licensing the patent as compared to the anticipated royalty income; the anticipated amount of net profits that the prospective licensee reasonably thinks he will make; the commercial past performance of the invention in terms of public acceptance and profits; the market to be tapped; and any other economic factor that normally prudent businessmen would, under similar circumstances, take into consideration in negotiating the hypothetical license.

As pointed out in an earlier decision herein by this Court, the very definition of a reasonable royalty assumes that, after payment, "the infringer will be left with a profit."

The "willing seller" rule contemplate[s] a marshaling of all of the pertinent facts which, like cards dealt face up, are for all to see. And it then contemplates the supposititious meaning of buyer and seller, who are able, on the basis of the overall roundup of information, to become "willing" buyers and sellers, at a royalty which will enable the buyer to make and sell at a reasonable profit.

The Court, having considered GP's critique, finds that USP's presentation is, in decisive respects, rooted in reality. For the most part, where facts have been hypothesized by USP, they are premised on record evidence, direct and circumstantial. This is particularly true with respect to such elements as reasonably anticipated rates of profit, probable volume of sales, normal economic motivations, and the prevailing business outlook, all as of the time of the supposititious negotiations.

Moreover, the Court has taken into account the modifying effect of the facts developed subsequent to 1955 and has assessed them together with all other probative evidence so far as they bear upon the reasonableness of the assumptions and expectations of the parties in their hypothetical negotiations in 1955.

There is some confusion in GP's analysis arising out of the circumstance that USP was unable to prove before the master the amount of its lost profits as damages. GP argues that the same deficiencies of proof similarly vitiate USP's present effort to use, as one of the primary factors for evaluating a reasonable royalty, the profits that it would have reasonably anticipated it would make at the time when a royalty would have been negotiated hypothetically with GP. Similarly, GP is in error when it argues that, because this Court rejected the master's use of GP's infringing profits as the legal measure of damages, evidence of GP's reasonably anticipated profits as of 1955 is irrelevant to the present inquiry.

Certain basic statistics are not in dispute. GP's sales of the infringing striated plywood totalled 15,899,000 square feet and amounted to sales proceeds to GP of $2,547,393. The period of the infringement was March 1955 through September 1958.

The manufacturing part of the infringement began in February 1955. The hypothetical negotiations are, therefore, timeplaced in February 1955 and the relevant factors are viewed in that frame of time-reference.

USP's undeviating policy was to maintain its patent monopoly on sales of striated fir plywood in the United States. Its exploitation of the Deskey patent through the sale of Weldtex was extremely successful and profitable. The Court of Appeals characterized the commercial success of Weldtex as a factor of "very great significance."

USP manufactured and sold Weldtex in substantial quantities since 1946. From April 30, 1951 to January 31, 1955, the annual average sales of Weldtex [were] approximately $6,000,000. During the last six quarter-annual periods before the infringement, extending up to January 31, 1955, sales of Weldtex totalled $9,325,022, the quarterly average being $1,554,170, compared with quarterly average sales of $1,456,605 during the period from April 30, 1951 to January 31, 1955. During the quarter ending April 30, 1955, the Weldtex sales amounted to $1,601,814.

In February 1955, USP had no reason to anticipate that there would be a significant decline in the demand for Weldtex in the foreseeable future. In fact, no such decline took place for two years subsequent to February 1955.

The commodity most relevant to the subject of USP's monopoly was striated fir plywood. GP argues that the relevant commodity is "decorative plywood" as a class, of which striated fir plywood (exemplified by USP's Weldtex) was only one of many; that USP's monopoly was diluted by the competition of other decorative plywoods with Weldtex; and that this competition in February 1955 was a factor that significantly tended to reduce the royalty for Weldtex that would have been negotiated hypothetically at that time. In fact, GP contends that the competition that Weldtex faced was so keen that only a minimal royalty can be justified.

Noteworthy is the fact that, despite the allegedly fierce competition between Weldtex and other decorative plywoods, GP deliberately decided to duplicate Weldtex notwithstanding the caveat of GP's own counsel that an expensive infringement suit was inevitable. GP's calculated infringement of Weldtex is an admission by conduct that it regarded Weldtex as occupying a uniquely favorable position in the market.

In this connection, it is also important to consider that, without a license from USP, GP could not legitimately manufacture striated fir plywood and, on the other hand, the granting of a license by USP to GP would place GP in direct and active competition with USP in the United States with respect to striated fir plywood. Obviously, only an adequate royalty would make this proposition palatable to USP.

The separate question — whether there were other competing decorative plywood panels — poses an inquiry into the extent of that competition and its ultimate bearing upon the determination of the amount of a reasonable royalty.

During the period February 1955 to 1958, Weldtex was not confronted with significant competition except that created by GP's infringing striated.

The evidence that, in February 1955, Weldtex was without keen competition is corroborated by admissions from GP's own files relating to times both before and after the hypothetical negotiations. For example, GP's attorney, in a letter dated July 23, 1953, said that Weldtex "has been without any substantial competition."

While in a generalized sense Weldtex was only one of a number of decorative wall panels that were competitive, the Court accepts Mr. Heilpern's testimony that, to determine whether and to what extent various plywood and similar products were competitive with each other, it is necessary to know their respective price ranges and the respective markets that had been developed for them. The Court is convinced that, in February 1955, the commercial value of Weldtex was not undermined by competition.

It follows that, in February 1955, the time of the hypothetical negotiations, the determination of a reasonable royalty would have been strongly influenced by the then dominant market position of Weldtex. While this element cannot be converted into commensurable arithmetical terms, it is a highly significant fact in the mix of factors.

The evidence referred to must be considered in conjunction with USP's policy not to license anyone to sell Weldtex in the United States or in any other area where USP was capable of making its own sales. In the licenses that USP did grant for the manufacture of Weldtex in the United States, USP stipulated that the licensee could sell only to USP or USP's designee.

The master found that USP had the financial and physical capacity to market an additional amount of striated fir plywood equaling 80% of the amount infringingly sold by GP. While the master and the Court found that USP had possessed that capacity, the master found, and the Court approved the finding, that the proof was insufficient to establish that USP would have in fact manufactured and sold any measurable quantity of Weldtex between February 1955 and September 1958, in addition to the quantities of Weldtex which they did actually manufacture and sell during that period.

What is pertinent for present purposes is that, at the time of the hypothetical negotiations, USP did have the physical and financial capacity to market an additional 12,784,000 square feet of Weldtex between March 1955 and September 1958 and that, when it would have entered into the hypothetical licensing agreement with GP, it was not doing so because it could not have produced additional Weldtex itself.

Next to be considered is the matter of the market demand for Weldtex in or about February 1955 and the then reasonable anticipation as to the continuance of that customer popularity. GP argues that Weldtex had passed its apogee just before GP began its infringing sales of striated plywood. Citing sales statistics, GP claims that Weldtex lost standing in each succeeding year since early 1955.

The more persuasive fact is that, in February 1955, there was no reason to anticipate any significant decline in the foreseeable future in the demand for the striated fir plywood on which USP had a legal monopoly. USP executives in fact anticipated no such decline.

The circumstance that the Deskey patent (which had issued on June 9, 1942) had only a little over four years to run from February 1955 until it expired on June 9, 1959 and the argument of GP that the reasonable royalty should therefore be minimal (as testified to by GP's witness L. G. Buckley), are neutralized by certain practical business considerations: (1) because striated fir plywood was a product of demonstrated great commercial success, GP did not assume any risk in this respect; (2) a royalty calculated as a percentage of footage actually sold or volume of actual sales, as distinguished from a license fee expressed in advance as a flat amount of dollars, would mean that GP did not assume any fixed financial obligation; (3) the opportunity to engage in the sale of a patented product even several years before the patent's expiration would constitute a definite advantage to GP who intended to market the product after the expiration of the patent; and (4) GP could get into the profitable production of striated fir plywood with only the modest investment required for a striating machine, amounting to approximately $12,000 to $15,000.

The amount of profits that USP was making and could (in February 1955) reasonably expect to continue to make on its sales of Weldtex by licensing no one to sell Weldtex in the United States is of major relevance to the determination of the amount of royalty that USP would accept from GP and that GP would offer. USP was enjoying the profits of a readily salable product. USP was in a position to retain the entire market on striated fir plywood for itself. The result of GP's infringement was to interfere with that monopoly and, as planned, to put GP in direct competition with USP's Weldtex throughout the period of infringement. The hypothetical license would have been one whereby GP would have been permitted to market striated fir plywood throughout the United States (as GP infringingly did).

In the hypothetical negotiations, USP would have been reasonable in taking the position that it would not accept a royalty significantly less than the profit it was making by its policy of licensing no one to sell striated fir plywood in the United States.

Computed by the absorption method, USP's average rate of profit on its Weldtex sales was $48.64 per thousand square feet at the time of the infringement.

Another element emphasized by USP as one that it would have taken into account in the hypothetical negotiations to fix a reasonable royalty was the profits it was making on collateral or convoyed sales of other USP products that were generated by Weldtex sales.

Both the special master and the Court have found that USP had failed to prove that it would have earned a measurable or specific amount of additional profits on collateral sales in the absence of GP's infringement; and thus USP had failed to sustain a recovery of damages in any assessable amount under the heading of such lost profits.

There is logic to USP's present argument distinguishing between the profits derivable from collateral or convoyed sales as one of the elements relevant to the fixation of a reasonable royalty (the current issue) and, on the other hand, the loss of profits from such sales as part of actually sustained damages (the issue previously litigated before the master). The fact of the existence and the substantiality of such profits and the fact of the loss of some of those profits in the event that GP were licensed to sell striated fir plywood were established by USP. And such facts have some bearing upon the determination of a reasonable royalty.

It would have been reasonable on USP's part in February 1955 to have expected to make future profits through collateral or convoyed sales, which USP would have anticipated losing at least in part by licensing GP to make striated fir plywood.

The profitability of the collateral or convoyed sales was significant not only from the viewpoint of USP's bargaining position but also in terms of GP's own expectations of an economic advantage, obvious both to USP and GP. GP's reasonable expectation of collateral profits from convoyed sales of products sold along with its striated fir plywood is a factor in the hypothetical negotiations. In point of fact, GP sales of striated fir plywood did generate collateral sales.

The record therefore leads to the finding that consideration of the collateral sales factor by both parties would have tended to increase significantly the amount of the reasonable royalty hypothetically negotiated between them; and the Court so finds. The record, however, does not enable the Court to quantify the monetary amount of that economic significance in terms of a dollar and cents figure although the factor of profits on collateral sales did possess the economic significance already pointed out.

GP would not have been at a significant competitive disadvantage in marketing striated plywood because (1) GP's striated plywood was exactly the same product as Weldtex for which USP had developed the market; (2) GP had contacts with all of USP's customers; and (3) GP's striated plywood would have been welcomed by the trade as an additional source of supply that would make the market competitive.

GP was willing to assume substantial risks and costs in order to make and sell striated fir plywood without authority from USP. The Court finds that GP would have been willing to pay a substantial royalty to USP in order to obtain reasonably anticipated large profits without the risk of infringement liability.

The Court has considered the evidence in order to quantify the amount of profits that GP would reasonably have expected, at the time of the hypothetical negotiations, to earn on its production and sale of striated fir plywood. This is a different question from the amount of infringing profits that GP actually did make — $685,837, according to the special master.

GP took, as its own guide for the purpose of profit expectations, the profit that USP was then making on its Weldtex sales. The evidence supports the inference that GP was able to estimate, fairly accurately, the amount of USP's costs on Weldtex; and that GP knew that its own costs would not be significantly higher.

In any event, since the Court has found that USP's average rate of profit on its Weldtex sales was $48.64 per thousand square feet at the time of the infringement, the Court also finds that GP would reasonably have expected to earn on its manufacture and sale of striated fir plywood profits at least approximately the same rate.

Moreover, this figure of $48.64 per thousand square feet must be amplified by virtue of the collateral sales factor insofar as that factor would have reasonably entered into GP's thinking at the time of the hypothetical royalty negotiations.

The Court finds that, at the time of the hypothetical negotiations, GP would reasonably have expected to derive substantial additional profits from collateral sales of other [products] (particularly non-specialty items) sold along with its striated fir plywood, a specialty item. This is a significant factor to be considered by the Court in determining the reasonable royalty because it has the logical tendency, as a matter of simple economics, to increase the amount of the reasonable royalty.

In view of the foregoing, the figure of $48.64 per thousand square feet of striated fir plywood sold, representing GP's probable expectation of profit on that item alone, would not reflect the factor of GP's expectation of profits on collateral sales generated by the sale of striated plywood.

The evidence does not permit an inference as to the quantum, even approximately, of the profits derivable from collateral sales by GP. To assess this factor separately and monetarily by assigning a dollar and cents valuation to it would involve impermissible conjecture and speculation. In the circumstances, therefore, the indisputable fact that such profits would be generated in a significant amount by the sale of striated fir plywood is treated by the Court as a factor strengthening USP's bargaining position and supporting the reasonableness of the figure of the profit rate on the sale of striated fir plywood.

THE AMOUNT OF THE REASONABLE ROYALTY

a) *GP's argument that the value of striated fir plywood was substantially attributable to elements other than the Deskey patent*

This case does not permit application of the principle of apportionment inasmuch as the Deskey patent was not one for an improvement on an article nor was GP's infringement of a patented feature sold together with unpatented parts. Decisions illustrating the rule applicable to patented improvements or to patented parts of articles also embodying unpatented parts are not apposite for the reason that the Deskey patent covered and Weldtex represented a marketable article — a panel of striated fir plywood — as an entirety.

The Deskey patent, though using the prior art to a degree, gives substantially the entire value to the structure represented by the infringing article.

GP attempts to attenuate the significance and value of the Deskey patent by arguing that approximately 50 per cent of the value of striated fir plywood was not essentially attributable to the Deskey patent, but rather was allocable to the method employed on the three-ply panel to "balance" the striation of the face ply and to its decorative effect. [The court reviews the various prior art techniques for dealing with balancing, and concludes that more effective balancing did not account for either the patentee's or the infringer's sales.]

There is no basis for GP's argument that the value of striated fir plywood is significantly attributable to elements other than the Deskey patent. Such a proposition is as illogical as a claim that, because an automobile needs wheels to run, an automobile motorized by a patented electronic device owes its substantial value to the wheels.

b) *The significance of the decorative appearance of Weldtex and GP striated in relation to the question of the amount of a reasonable royalty*

The decorative appearance of Weldtex was not per se a patented element of the Deskey invention. Upon that circumstance as a foundation fact, GP erects the argument that whatever value of Weldtex may be attributable to its decorative appearance must be disregarded in determining the amount of a reasonable royalty for the use of the Deskey patent because "decorative appearance" is a feature beyond the scope of that patent.

The face of GP's infringing striated fir plywood was, from the viewpoint of deep striations and appearance, structurally and esthetically a replica of USP's Weldtex. This was the inevitable result of the infringement because the decorative effect or appearance of Weldtex and GP striated is an inherent, indivisible, and inextricable characteristic of Deskey's deep and random striations.

c) *Absence of a prevailing royalty or royalties in generally comparable circumstances*

GP claims that the amount of a reasonable royalty is strongly evidenced by the proofs concerning (1) the financial arrangements between USP and Deskey; (2) the royalties payable under the five licenses granted by USP to its contract or "captive" mills; (3) the royalties payable under the three licenses granted by USP outside the United States; (4) eight or more miscellaneous other licenses cited by GP; and (5) the opinion testimony of GP's experts.

Accepting GP's proofs as possessing sufficient probative value to render them admissible, the Court finds that that evidence does not significantly tend to indicate the amount of a reasonable royalty in the present situation. In each instance, the royalty or other payment cited by GP was made under circumstances that are sharply and fundamentally different from the congeries of controlling facts presently before the Court. [Specifically, the court finds that the license from the inventor Deskey was drawn up before the invention was proven a success, and that five licenses with "captive mills" were inapposite because the licensees were not competitors but captive producers.]

[As to foreign licenses:] The significance of these royalties is largely neutralized by the credible evidence that these licenses were granted by USP outside the United States, in areas where USP itself had no established sales facilities. As to the Australian and New Zealand licenses, USP had no idea what kind of a market could be established there for Weldtex, which was a new product in those remote countries; and, therefore, USP fixed a minimum royalty. USP's purpose in granting the licenses was not so much to obtain royalty income as to establish relationships with the licensees.

CONCLUSION

The Court finds and concludes that $50.00 per thousand square feet of the patented product, striated fir plywood, made and sold by GP, represents a fair reasonable royalty that should be paid by GP. This amounts to $800,000, which is hereby awarded to USP, together with interest on the said award computed from the date of the last infringement, September 1, 1958, to the date of payment of the award.

NOTE

A Benchmark. The detailed, considered analysis in the preceding case is often said to be a benchmark against which a district court's treatment of reasonable royalty issues will be measured. *See, e.g., SmithKline Diagnostics, Inc. v. Helena Labs. Corp.*, 926 F.2d 1161, 1168, 17 U.S.P.Q.2d (BNA) 1922 (Fed. Cir. 1991) ("The district court correctly considered the factors enumerated in *Panduit* and *Georgia-Pacific Corp. v. United States Plywood Corp.* in finding what it considered a reasonable royalty ...." (citations omitted)).

HANSON v. ALPINE VALLEY SKI AREA, INC.

718 F.2d 1075, 219 U.S.P.Q. (BNA) 679 (Fed. Cir. 1983)

The patent involved in this case was issued to the appellee Hanson in 1961. It covers a method and apparatus for making snow used in winter sports. Prior to Hanson's invention, snow was made by mixing water and compressed air, and ejecting the combination under high pressure from a nozzle. The water froze and, by combining with water in the air, produced snow crystals. This method required a considerable amount of energy to compress the air, and the nozzles frequently froze.

Hanson's patent disclosed a new method of making snow. As the magistrate explained, rather than relying on compressed air,

> [t]he Hanson process discharges water into a hub mounted in the center of a spinning propeller. The water is then fragmented into droplets by the propeller blades generating spontaneous ice nuclei.... The efficiency of the

[Hanson] snowmaking system [as opposed to the prior art method] is based upon the turbulence of the air created by the airstream which increased cooling capacity.

The magistrate found that "the airless snowmaking method of the Hanson patent is at least five to seven times as energy efficient as the prior art compressed air method...."

In 1969, Hanson licensed his patent to Snow Machines International, which subsequently assigned the license to Snow Machines Incorporated (both referred to as "SMI"), for a royalty of 2.5 percent of sales and 2.5 percent of the stock of SMI. Since 1969, about 1,500 SMI machines have been manufactured and sold, and SMI paid total royalties of approximately $26,000. The magistrate found that "[w]ithin the short span of twelve years, the airless snowmaking process has developed substantially and presently accounts for almost one half of all artificially produced snow." The Hanson patent expired in 1978.

Hanson filed the present suit in February 1973. He alleged that appellant Alpine Valley Ski Area, Inc. ("Alpine") had infringed his patent through the use of three snow-making machines manufactured by Hedco, Inc. Hedco defended the suit for Alpine.

After a trial without a jury, the district court held that the Hanson patent was valid, that Alpine had infringed the patent by its use of the Hedco machines, and that Hanson was entitled to an accounting for damages. The court found that Alpine "has used the Hedco H-2d, Mark II and Mark III machines to produce snow." The court of appeals affirmed the determinations of validity and infringement.

The district court referred the issue of damages to the United States Magistrate as a special master. After a trial, the magistrate recommended that Hanson be awarded damages of $12,250 for the infringement. The court concluded that "the Magistrate correctly decided this matter."

The magistrate found that Alpine had used the three Hedco machines to produce snow and that Alpine had operated one of the machines during the 1972-73 and 1973-74 seasons and the two other machines during one season. He held that the evidence did not provide any basis for determining either the profits Alpine made or the profits Hanson lost through the infringement, and that damages therefore had to be determined on the basis of a reasonable royalty for the patent. In making that determination, the magistrate applied the "willing licensee-willing licensor rule. That is, at what royalty rate would a licensee accept a license and a licensor grant a license if both parties genuinely wish to execute a license in an arm's length transaction."

The magistrate accepted the testimony of Hanson's witness, Sidney Alpert, whom he characterized as "a highly regarded expert in the field of negotiating patent licenses," that "the royalty rate and licenses granted under the Hanson patent must be uniform."

Applying the pertinent factors for determining a reasonable royalty set forth in *Georgia-Pacific Corp.*, the magistrate concluded that the reasonable royalty in this case must be based upon a portion of the annual cost savings attributable to use of the Hanson patent. Expert testimony on this record indicates that one-third of the cost savings would be deemed acceptable to both parties in an arm's length license negotiation. Furthermore, based upon energy costs at the time of infringement in 1972-73, the airless snowmaking method of the Hanson patent generates a dollar savings of $75.00 per gallon (of water used to make snow) per minute. That is, under the Hanson method, the cost of producing snow using one gallon of water for one minute is $75.00 less than the cost of producing snow under the compressed air method using one gallon of water for one minute. Thus the cost savings for the Hanson method is a function of any machine's capacity to make snow.

The magistrate concluded that a reasonable royalty would be one-third of the $75 savings per gallon of water that the Hanson method produced over the earlier compressed air method. Multiplying the $75 per gallon by the snowmaking capacity of the three Hedco machines Alpine used and the four years of use involved, the magistrate determined that Hanson was entitled to royalties of $3,000, $1,750, and $7,500 for each of the Hedco machines used, or a total of $12,250.

The magistrate held that [t]he proofs offered in the case at hand do not suggest any basis for establishing profits experienced by the infringing Defendant in the use of the process patent nor do they establish a loss of income or loss of profit suffered by the patentee on any tangible basis by virtue of the nature of the interest the patentee has. We have no basis for rejecting that factual determination.

[The court affirms the magistrate's finding that existing licenses were not comparable to that which would have been entered into by the parties.] Finally, we cannot say that the magistrate erred in refusing to consider certain offers to license the Hanson patent at a 2.5 percent royalty as showing an established rate. The magistrate excluded evidence of those proposals because they were offers in compromise made in contemplation of infringement litigation and therefore inadmissible under Rule 408 of the Federal Rules of Evidence.

The fact that licenses were offered at a particular rate does not show that that rate was the "established" rate, since the latter requires actual licenses, not mere offers to license. (We discuss below the exclusionary ruling insofar as the excluded evidence related to the magistrate's determination of a reasonable royalty under the willing licensor-willing licensee rule.) Moreover, since the offers were made after the infringement had begun and litigation was threatened or probable, their terms "should not be considered evidence of an 'established royalty,'" since "[l]icense fees negotiated in the face of a threat of high litigation costs 'may be strongly influenced by a desire to avoid full litigation....'" *Panduit*, 575 F.2d at 1164, n.11, 197 U.S.P.Q. at 736, n.11.

Since there was no established royalty for licensing the Hanson patent, the magistrate necessarily had to use "a willing-buyer/willing-seller concept." The infringement in the present case began in 1972.

[Defendant's expert] stated that the licensor would have insisted on a uniform license based on the gallons-per-minute rated capacity of the Hanson-method machines, and would have refused to grant a license based on actual use or other criteria relating to the situation of the particular licensee. The magistrate's acceptance of [this] analysis and approach was fully justified by the record before him.

Alpine challenges the magistrate's determination of a reasonable royalty on a number of grounds.

Alpine contends that because it acquired the Hedco machines for experimental purposes and did not use them much, the royalty should have been based upon actual use rather than upon estimated savings reflecting the snowmaking capacity of the machines.

Apart from the fact that this theory is inconsistent with the magistrate's determination that Hanson would have granted licenses only at a uniform rate and not based on actual use, the record contains substantial evidence that actual use of the snowmaking machinery would not have been the basis upon which a willing licensor and a willing licensee would have established the royalty. As [Hanson's expert] noted, it would have been extremely difficult to monitor actual use. Apparently no complete or accurate records were kept of the actual use of the Hedco machines at Alpine's resort.

Equally or more important, a royalty based upon actual use would have been inconsistent with the function snowmaking equipment serves at a ski resort and the reasonable needs and expectations of both the licensor and the licensee. A resort has snowmaking machinery to enable it to function at times when there is no or insufficient natural snow. As the magistrate stated, the resort hopes that "natural snow will always be sufficient and that artificial snow will never be needed." He noted that the "machines insure the business can function without natural snow" and that Hanson's "expert likened the machine to an insurance policy." The magistrate justifiably concluded that in these circumstances "[t]he number of hours a machine is used is irrelevant; the desire is never to use the machine. The machine's utility simply does not depend upon its hours of operation."

A royalty based on actual use would produce unsatisfactory results here for both the licensor and the licensee. If there were extensive snow during the season, there would be little use of the machine and the patentee would receive an inadequate return for the value of his invention. On the other hand, if there were little or no snow, the licensee would have to pay exceptionally large royalties.

We have no basis for rejecting the magistrate's factual conclusion that in the circumstances the parties to the licensing negotiations would have agreed upon a royalty rate that would insure a fair and reasonable return to the patentee and avoid the payment of excessive royalties by the licensee, without regard to the size of the snowfall. The royalty rate the magistrate used, based upon the expert evidence, would have accomplished that objective.

The magistrate based his determination of a reasonable royalty upon the estimated cost savings resulting from Alpine's use of the infringing Hedco machines. Reliance upon estimated cost savings from use of the infringing product is a well settled method of determining a reasonable royalty. The method is appropriate where other approaches (such as established royalty or lost profits) would be "difficult."

In determining Alpine's savings from use of the Hedco machines, [Hanson's expert] based his calculations on the use of the machines for 800 hours a year. He explained that this constituted an average season's use of snowmaking systems for resorts in the area where Alpine is located. Although Alpine challenges a number of the assumptions and calculations upon which Dilworth based his determinations, we cannot say that the magistrate's conclusions, based upon expert testimony, are clearly erroneous.

Alpine argues that the royalty the magistrate set is unreasonable because it would not have allowed it to make a profit.

Since the royalty the magistrate set was based upon one-third of Alpine's estimated savings through use of the infringing Hedco machines, it is difficult to understand the basis of Alpine's contention that the royalty would not have allowed it to make a profit. The issue of the infringer's profit is to be determined not on the basis of a hindsight evaluation of what actually happened, but on the basis of what the parties to the hypothetical license negotiations would have considered at the time of the negotiations. "Whether, as events unfurled thereafter, [Alpine Valley] would have made an actual profit, while paying the royalty determined as of [1972], is irrelevant." *Panduit*. Alpine has not shown that the royalty the magistrate set would not have allowed it a reasonable profit.

Alpine further contends that no willing licensee would accept the "high" royalty awarded. But as [one court] noted:

> [W]hether ... [the] defendant ... [was] never willing to pay a reasonable royalty[ ] is irrelevant.... The willing-buyer/willing-seller concept is ... employed by the court as a means of arriving at reasonable compensation and its validity does not depend on the actual willingness of the parties to the lawsuit to engage in such negotiations.... There is, of course, no actual willingness on either side...."

Panduit.

Alpine could have avoided infringement, and paying royalties therefor, by purchasing non-infringing machines from SMI. It chose, however, to purchase and use Hedco's infringing machines. Having followed that course, it cannot invalidate an otherwise reasonable royalty on the claim that by hindsight it would have been better off if it had purchased the non-infringing SMI machines.

Affirmed.

NOTES

1. *Methods for Determining Royalties.* If the overall approach of *Georgia-Pacific* is the dominant one, there are still variations in the way it is applied. *Hanson* is an example: note the emphasis on cost savings as the *basis* for the hypothetical negotiations between the parties. Other grounds for negotiations, and other factors affecting such negotiations, have been considered in various cases. *See, e.g., Studiengesellschaft Kohle, mbH v. Dart Indus.*, 862 F.2d 1564, 9 U.S.P.Q.2d (BNA) 1273 (Fed. Cir. 1988) (reasonable royalty based on a sliding scale of 4-3-2% plus up-front payments; district court found that the patentee would not have licensed the subject patent for less owing to most favored licensee clauses contained in licenses with other licensees); *Stickle v. Heublein, Inc.*, 716 F.2d 1550, 219 U.S.P.Q. 377 (Fed. Cir. 1983) (case remanded because district court had no proper foundation for its finding that royalty would be based on sales volume of tacos made with patented machine; industry licensing agreements very rarely calculated royalties on this basis).

2. *An Alternative Approach.* Some cases base a finding of reasonable royalty on the infringer's own pre-infringement projection of the profits that would result from infringement. This has been referred to as the "analytical method" for determining reasonable royalty damages. *See* Skenyon & Porcelli, *Patent Damages*, 70 J. PAT. & TRADEMARK OFF. SOC'Y 762, 765 (1988). For example, in *TWM Mfg. Co. v. Dura Corp.*, 789 F.2d 895, 229 U.S.P.Q. (BNA) 525 (Fed. Cir. 1986), the Federal Circuit affirmed the district court's 30% reasonable royalty determination, based upon the findings of a special master employing this method. According to the master, top management of Dura, the infringer, wrote a memorandum before infringement began projecting a gross profit average of 52.7% from infringing sales of a wheeled vehicle suspension. The special master subtracted overhead expenses from this figure to arrive at a total anticipated net profit in the range of 37% to 42%. The industry standard net profit, which had been demonstrated as 6.56% to 12.5%, was then subtracted from the total anticipated net profit, resulting in an anticipated net profit realized from sales of infringing devices, and thus the 30% that was applied as the reasonable royalty.

On the other hand, in *Hughes Tool Co. v. Dresser Indus.*, 816 F.2d 1549, 2 U.S.P.Q.2d (BNA) 1396 (Fed. Cir.), *cert. denied*, 484 U.S. 914 (1987), the Federal Circuit vacated and remanded the district court's determination of a reasonable royalty based on the "analytical" or "infringer's projection" method. The district court's award of damages to Hughes, calculated as a royalty of 25% of the dollar amount of Dresser's total sales of infringing drill bits, was based upon pre-infringement projected total profits of 60% of sales. On appeal, Dresser attacked not the royalty method used by the district court but rather its factual underpinnings, i.e., the projected profits figure. The Federal Circuit agreed. There was evidence demonstrating that Dresser had projected a 60% return on *additional* investment required to make the drill bits, i.e., that expected profit on incremental sales would yield a 60% return on this extra investment. This, the court said, was not to be confused with a projected profit on sales of the overall product. The article by Skenyon and Porcelli, *supra*, notes that this is possibly the "only defense to a reasonable royalty case based on the analytical method. The infringer's potentially fatal profit projection must itself be directly attacked ...." *Id.*, at 767.

3. Earlier Offers to License. The court in *Hanson* dismisses the importance of license terms offered prior to the finding of validity and infringement. If the true goal of the hypothetical negotiation approach were to duplicate the deal the parties would have struck prior to infringement, this evidence would have to be given greater weight. *See Deere & Co. v. International Harvester Co.*, 710 F.2d 1551, 1557, 218 U.S.P.Q. (BNA) 481, 486 (Fed. Cir. 1983) (the district court "could properly discount the probative value of [a] license" with 1% royalty rate, and award a 15% royalty instead, because that license "was negotiated against a backdrop of continuing litigation and I[nternational] H[arvester] infringement of the patent"); *Bio-Rad Labs. v. Nicolet Instrument Corp.*, 739 F.2d 604, 617, 222 U.S.P.Q. (BNA) 654 (Fed. Cir.), *cert. denied*, 469 U.S. 1036 (1984) (affirming reasonable royalty of 33% while royalty rates in industry were normally between 3% and 10%). *But cf. Trell v. Marlee Elecs. Corp.*, 912 F.2d 1443, 1446, 16 U.S.P.Q.2d (BNA) 1059 (Fed. Cir. 1990) (remanding to district court which had found that single license agreement between patentee and third party at 6% established reasonable royalty; suggesting that since this agreement covered products other than the patented one, and since patented invention was only minor feature of infringing product, reasonable royalty in this case might well be *less* than this 6% figure). *See generally Rude v. Westcott*, 130 U.S. 152 (1889) ("In order that a royalty may be accepted as a measure of damages against an infringer, who is a stranger to the license establishing it, it must be paid or secured before the infringement complained of; it must be paid by such a number of persons as to indicate a general acquiescence in its reasonableness by those who have occasion to use the invention; and it must be uniform at the places where the licenses are issued."). In the *Rude* case, the Supreme Court rejected a trial court finding that a prior agreement between the patentee and a third party established the proper royalty rate as between the infringer and the patentee. The tone of the case suggests that the Court found the asserted royalty rate quite high under the circumstances.

In *Studiengesellschaft Kohle, mbH v. Dart Indus.*, 862 F.2d 1564, 1570-71, 9 U.S.P.Q.2d 1273 (Fed. Cir. 1988), the Federal Circuit affirmed a district court reasonable royalty determination that relied heavily on a royalty figure proposed *after* a patent had been found valid and infringed. The Federal Circuit opinion quoted the following passage by the district court, in which that court discussed the prior case of *Ziegler v. Phillips Petr. Co.*, 483 F.2d 858, 177 U.S.P.Q. (BNA) 481 (5th Cir.), *cert. denied*, 414 U.S. 1079 (1973):

> The settlement in *Phillips* transpired after the Fifth Circuit had reversed the District Court's finding of no infringement. At the time of the *Phillips*

negotiations, then, Ziegler had the same strength that is ascribed to him in a hypothetical negotiation — an unquestionably valid patent. Ziegler and Phillips agreed to a lump sum settlement of 5 million [dollars] and a future running royalty of 1.5%. Taken together, as the Master properly held they should be, the effective rate of the *Phillips* agreement was 2.15%. [T]his settlement is highly probative evidence.... *Phillips* involved a licensing patentee who had a post-infringement determination of his patent's validity and proceeded to agree to a rate of compensation for the patent. This brand of post-infringement evidence is distinct from other post-infringement evidence because both Phillips and Ziegler knew that the next step in the process was the exact type of accounting exercise that is being undertaken in this case.

4. Collateral Sales. The hypothetical negotiations between the parties are expected to include provision for "convoyed" or "tag along" sales. These are sales of unpatented items, perhaps used with the patented item, which are enhanced by the licensee's ability to sell the patented item. *See, e.g., Trans-World Mfg. Corp. v. Al Nyman & Sons*, 750 F.2d 1552, 1568, 224 U.S.P.Q. 259, 269 (Fed. Cir. 1984) (exclusion of evidence regarding enhancement of eyeglasses sales as a result of patented display was reversible error; effect of using the patented product in promoting sales of other products of the licensee is a factor to be considered in determining a reasonable royalty); *TWM Mfg. Co. v. Dura Corp.*, 789 F.2d 895, 901, 229 U.S.P.Q. (BNA) 525 (Fed. Cir. 1986) (upholding 30% royalty finding by trial court; "Where a hypothetical licensee would have anticipated an increase in sales of collateral unpatented items because of the patented device, the patentee should be compensated accordingly."). *Cf. Deere & Co. v. International Harvester Co.*, 710 F.2d 1551, 1561, 218 U.S.P.Q. (BNA) 481 (Fed. Cir. 1983) (Davis, J., dissenting) (refusing to sanction "tag-along" sales as part of the royalty, because this was "an improper tying relationship" and therefore a form of patent misuse).

5. A Question of Fact. In *Smithkline Diagnostics, Inc. v. Helena Labs. Corp.*, 926 F.2d 1161, 1164, 17 U.S.P.Q.2d (BNA) 1922 (Fed. Cir. 1991), the court stated the standard of review for cases regarding damages:

[T]he amount of a prevailing party's damages is a finding of fact on which the plaintiff bears the burden of proof by a preponderance of the evidence. Thus, where the amount is fixed by the court, review is in accordance with the clearly erroneous standard of Fed. R. Civ. P. 52(a).

6. Trial Court's Discretion. In the same case, the Federal Circuit made clear that a trial court need not accept the figures presented by one or the other of the parties when deciding on the reasonable royalty:

With respect to Helena's contention that the 25% royalty rate cannot be upheld because that figure was not specifically advocated by either party, we agree with the district court's ultimate conclusion that it was not restricted to selecting either the 48% or 3% figures advanced respectively by SKD and Helena. A district court is not limited to selecting one or the other of the specific royalty figures urged by counsel as reasonable.... On the contrary, the determination of a reasonable royalty must be based upon the entirety of the evidence and the court is free to, indeed, must reject the royalty figures proffered by the litigants, as the district court did in this case, where the record as a whole leads the court to a different figure. Accordingly, unless we are convinced that the district court clearly erred in the inference it drew from all of the evidence, the 25% royalty must be affirmed as reasonable.

926 F.2d at 1168.

C. LOST PROFITS

YALE LOCK MANUFACTURING CO. v. SARGENT
117 U.S. 536 (1886)

This is a suit by James Sargent against the Yale Lock Manufacturing Company, to recover for the infringement of reissued letters patent No. 4,696, granted to Sargent for an "improvement in locks."

[A]n interlocutory decree was entered finding the reissued patent to be valid and to have been infringed, and awarding a perpetual injunction and an account of profits and damages. The master reported $7,771 damages in favor of the plaintiff. The defendant has appealed to this court.

[After holding that the patent is valid and infringed, the Court turns to damages.] On the question of damages, the defendant contends that there was no sufficient or legal proof that the plaintiff suffered the damages reported and adjudged, or any other damages.

This is a case where the patentee granted no licenses, and had no established license fee, but supplied the demand for his lock himself, and was able to supply that demand. The market for the lock was limited to safe-makers. No one but a safe-maker wanted or would buy such a lock. The master was unable to determine, from the proofs, what profits, if any, the defendant had made from the use of the turning bolt. He disallowed all items of damage from the loss to the plaintiff of the sale of infringing locks sold by the defendant, and confined his award to the enforced reduction of price on the locks which the plaintiff sold, caused by the infringement. That this is a proper item of damages, if proved, is clear. It is a pecuniary injury caused by the infringement, and is the subject of an award of damages, although the defendant may have made no profits and the plaintiff may have had no established license fee. As the plaintiff, at the time of the infringement, availed himself of his exclusive right by keeping his patent a monopoly, and granting no licenses, the difference between his pecuniary condition after the infringement, and what his condition would have been if the infringement had not occurred, is to be measur[e]d, so far as his own sales of locks are concerned, by the difference between the money he would have realized from such sales if the infringement had not interfered with such monopoly, and the money he did realize from such sales. If such difference can be ascertained by proper and satisfactory evidence, it is a proper measure of damages. The damages to be recovered (Rev. St. §§ 4919, 4921) are "actual damages;" and they may properly include such losses to the plaintiff as were allowed in this case. The turning bolt was the essential feature of the Sargent lock. The defendant adopted Sargent's arrangement, and then reduced the price of the lock, forcing Sargent to do the same, in order to hold his trade. The evidence shows that the reduction of prices by Sargent was solely due to the defendant's infringement. The only competitor with Sargent in the use of his turning-bolt arrangement, during the period covered by the accounting, was the defendant. We think the master made proper allowances for all other causes which could have affected the plaintiff's prices; that the proper deduction was made for the use of the Rosner device in the defendant's lock; and that the damages awarded are no greater than the testimony warranted. The decision that the plaintiff, as owner of the patent, was entitled to recover the damages, was correct.

NOTES

1. *Older Cases.* Some caution must be used when reading the older cases on damages. Before 1946, when the current statutory rules on damages took form, a patentee had two primary theories of recovery. In equity, in addition to an injunction, the patentee could seek an "accounting" of the *infringer's* profits. This was permitted on the theory that the infringer held these profits in a "constructive trust" for the patentee; the "trust" was imposed to prevent the infringer from profiting from wrongdoing. *See, e.g., W.L. Gore & Assocs. v. Carlisle Corp.,* 198 U.S.P.Q. 353, 364 (D. Del. 1978) (in pre-1946 cases, "The action for profits was akin to the equitable action for a constructive trust"). In actions at law, the patentee's damages were measured by his or her own loss. As a consequence, older cases discussing an "accounting" of damages must not be confused with contemporary cases on "lost profits," as the latter are centered around one means of measuring the amount of loss the patentee suffered as a consequence of the infringement. Confusion is at times compounded by contemporary references to "an accounting" — by which is meant an accounting of the *patentee's* lost profits.

Even today, however, the infringer's profits are sometimes taken into account in determining damages under the "reasonable royalty" approach discussed in the preceding section of this chapter. *See, e.g.,* Conley, *An Economic Approach to Patent Damages,* 15 AM. INTELL. PROP. L. ASS'N Q.J. 354 (1987) ("The analytical approach is a return to awarding to the patent owner the infringer's profits from the use of the invention, without the problem of apportionment which made that basis for relief so difficult to prove that Congress abolished it in favor of a reasonable royalty, to be sure that the patent owner received something for the infringement."). *Cf. Kori Corp. v. Wilco Marsh Buggies & Draglines, Inc.*, 761 F.2d 649, 653-56, 225 U.S.P.Q. 985, 987-89 (Fed. Cir. 1985) (*infringer's* profits used as measure of patentee's lost profits damages).

2. *"But For" Standard.* The key to a finding of lost profits is that the patentee would have made more sales (or more money on the sales it made) *but for* the infringer's presence in the market. *State Indus. v. Mor-Flo Indus.*, 883 F.2d 1573, 1577, 12 U.S.P.Q.2d 1026 (Fed. Cir. 1989) ("To get lost profits as actual damages, the patent owner must demonstrate that there was a reasonable probability that, but for the infringement, it would have made the infringer's sales.").

RITE-HITE CORP. v. KELLEY CO.

56 F.3d 1538, 35 U.S.P.Q.2d 1065 (Fed. Cir. 1995) (en banc)

LOURIE, CIRCUIT JUDGE.

Kelley Company appeals from a decision of the United States District Court for the Eastern District of Wisconsin, awarding damages for the infringement of U.S. Patent 4,373,847, owned by Rite-Hite Corporation. *Rite-Hite Corp. v. Kelley Co.*, 774 F. Supp. 1514, 21 U.S.P.Q.2d 1801 (E.D. Wis. 1991). The district court determined, *inter alia*, that Rite-Hite was entitled to lost profits for lost sales of its devices that were in direct competition with the infringing devices, but which themselves were not covered by the patent in suit. The appeal has been taken in banc to determine whether such damages are legally compensable under 35 U.S.C. § 284. We affirm in part, vacate in part, and remand.

BACKGROUND

On March 22, 1983, Rite-Hite sued Kelley, alleging that Kelley's "Truk Stop" vehicle restraint infringed Rite-Hite's U.S. Patent 4,373,847 ("the '847 patent").[1] The '847 patent, issued February 15, 1983, is directed to a device for

---

[1]Claim 1 of the patent reads:

A releasable locking device for securing a parked vehicle to an adjacent relatively stationary upright structure, said device comprising

a first means mountable on an exposed surface of the structure,

a second means mounted on said first means for substantially vertical movement relative thereto between operative and inoperative modes,

the location of said second means when in an inoperative mode being a predetermined distance beneath the location of said second means when in an operative mode and in non-contacting relation with the vehicle,

and third means for releasably retaining said second means in an operative mode;

said second means including a first section projecting outwardly a predetermined distance from said first means and the exposed surface of the structure,

one end of said first section being mounted on said first means for selective independent movement relative thereto along a predetermined substantially vertical path,

and a second section extending angularly upwardly from said first section and being spaced outwardly a substantially fixed distance from said first means and the exposed securing a vehicle to a loading dock to prevent the vehicle from separating from the dock during loading or unloading. Any such separation would create a gap between the vehicle and dock and create a danger for a forklift operator.

Rite-Hite distributed all its products through its wholly-owned and operated sales organizations and through independent sales organizations (ISOs). During the period of infringement, the Rite-Hite sales organizations accounted for approximately 30 percent of the retail dollar sales of Rite-Hite products, and the ISOs accounted for the remaining 70 percent. Rite-Hite sued for its lost profits at the wholesale level and for the lost retail profits of its own sales organizations. Shortly after this action was filed, several ISOs moved to intervene, contending that they were "exclusive licensees" of the '847 patent by virtue of [various agreements] between themselves and Rite-Hite. The court determined that the ISOs were exclusive licensees and accordingly, on August 31, 1984, permitted them to intervene. The ISOs sued for their lost retail profits.

The district court bifurcated the liability and damage phases of the trial and, on March 5, 1986, held the '847 patent to be not invalid and to be infringed by the manufacture, use, and sale of Kelley's Truk Stop device. The court enjoined further infringement. *Rite-Hite Corp. v. Kelley Co.*, 629 F. Supp. 1042, 231 U.S.P.Q. 161 (E.D. Wis. 1986). The judgment of liability was affirmed by this court[, see] 819 F.2d 1120, 2 U.S.P.Q.2d 1915 (Fed. Cir. 1987).

On remand, the damage issues were tried to the court. Rite-Hite sought damages calculated as lost profits for two types of vehicle restraints that it made and sold: the "Manual Dok-Lok" model 55 (MDL-55), which incorporated the invention covered by the '847 patent, and the "Automatic Dok-Lok" model 100 (ADL-100), which was not covered by the patent in suit. The ADL-100 was the first vehicle restraint Rite-Hite put on the market and it was covered by one or more patents other than the patent in suit. The Kelley Truk Stop restraint was designed to compete primarily with Rite-Hite's ADL-100. Both employed an electric motor and functioned automatically, and each sold for $1,000-$1,500 at the wholesale level, in contrast to the MDL-55, which sold for one-third to one-half the price of the motorized devices. Rite-Hite does not assert that Kelley's Truk Stop restraint infringed the patents covering the ADL-100.

Of the 3,825 infringing Truk Stop devices sold by Kelley, the district court found that, "but for" Kelley's infringement, Rite-Hite would have made 80 more sales of its MDL-55; 3,243 more sales of its ADL-100; and 1,692 more sales of dock levelers, a bridging platform sold with the restraints and used to bridge the edges of a vehicle and dock. The court awarded Rite-Hite as a manufacturer the

---

surface of the structure,

said second means, when in an operative mode, being adapted to interlockingly engage a portion of the parked vehicle disposed intermediate the second section and said first means;

said second means, when in an inoperative mode, being adapted to be in a lowered nonlocking relation with the parked vehicle.

wholesale profits that it lost on lost sales of the ADL-100 restraints, MDL-55 restraints, and restraint-leveler packages. It also awarded to Rite-Hite as a retailer and to the ISOs reasonable royalty damages on lost ADL-100, MDL-55, and restraint-leveler sales caused by Kelley's infringing sales. Finally, prejudgment interest, calculated without compounding, was awarded. Kelley's infringement was found to be not willful.

On appeal, Kelley contends that the district court erred as a matter of law in its determination of damages. Kelley does not contest the award of damages for lost sales of the MDL-55 restraints; however, Kelley argues that (1) the patent statute does not provide for damages based on Rite-Hite's lost profits on ADL-100 restraints because the ADL-100s are not covered by the patent in suit; (2) lost profits on unpatented dock levelers are not attributable to demand for the '847 invention and, therefore, are not recoverable losses; (3) the ISOs have no standing to sue for patent infringement damages; and (4) the court erred in calculating a reasonable royalty based as a percentage of ADL-100 and dock leveler profits. Rite-Hite and the ISOs challenge the district court's refusal to award lost retail profits and its award of prejudgment interest at a simple, rather than a compound, rate.

We affirm the damage award with respect to Rite-Hite's lost profits as a manufacturer on its ADL-100 restraint sales, affirm the court's computation of a reasonable royalty rate, vacate the damage award based on the dock levelers, and vacate the damage award with respect to the ISOs because they lack standing. We remand for dismissal of the ISOs' claims and for a redetermination of damages consistent with this opinion.

DISCUSSION

In order to prevail on appeal on an issue of damages, an appellant must convince us that the determination was based on an erroneous conclusion of law, clearly erroneous factual findings, or a clear error of judgment amounting to an abuse of discretion.

A

Kelley's Appeal

I. *Lost Profits on the ADL-100 Restraints*

The district court's decision to award lost profits damages pursuant to 35 U.S.C. § 284 turned primarily upon the quality of Rite-Hite's proof of actual lost profits. The court found that, "but for" Kelley's infringing Truk Stop competition, Rite-Hite would have sold 3,243 additional ADL-100 restraints and 80 additional MDL-55 restraints. The court reasoned that awarding lost profits fulfilled the patent statute's goal of affording complete compensation for infringement and compensated Rite-Hite for the ADL-100 sales that Kelley "anticipated taking from Rite-Hite when it marketed the Truk Stop against the ADL-100."

Kelley maintains that Rite-Hite's lost sales of the ADL-100 restraints do not constitute an injury that is legally compensable by means of lost profits. It has uniformly been the law, Kelley argues, that to recover damages in the form of lost profits a patentee must prove that, "but for" the infringement, it would have sold a product covered by the patent in suit to the customers who bought from the infringer. Under the circumstances of this case, in Kelley's view, the patent statute provides only for damages calculated as a reasonable royalty. Rite-Hite, on the other hand, argues that the only restriction on an award of actual lost profits damages for patent infringement is proof of causation-in-fact. A patentee, in its view, is entitled to all the profits it would have made on any of its products "but for" the infringement. Each party argues that a judgment in favor of the other would frustrate the purposes of the patent statute. Whether the lost profits at issue are legally compensable is a question of law, which we review de novo.

Our analysis of this question necessarily begins with the patent statute. [Section 284 of the Patent Act] mandates that a claimant receive damages "adequate" to compensate for infringement. Section 284 further instructs that a damage award shall be "in no event less than a reasonable royalty"; the purpose of this alternative is not to direct the form of compensation, but to set a floor below which damage awards may not fall. Thus, the language of the statute is expansive rather than limiting. It affirmatively states that damages must be adequate, while providing only a lower limit and no other limitation.

The Supreme Court spoke to the question of patent damages in *General Motors*, stating that, in enacting § 284, Congress sought to "ensure that the patent owner would in fact receive full compensation for 'any damages' [the patentee] suffered as a result of the infringement." *General Motors* [*v. Devex Corp.*, 461 U.S. 648, 653-54 (1983)], 461 U.S. at 654 ... ; *see also* H.R. Rep. No. 1587, 79th Cong., 2d Sess., 1 (1946) (the Bill was intended to allow recovery of "any damages the complainant can prove"); S. Rep. No. 1503, 79th Cong., 2d Sess., 2 (1946), (same). Thus, while the statutory text states tersely that the patentee receive "adequate" damages, the Supreme Court has interpreted this to mean that "adequate" damages should approximate those damages that will fully compensate the patentee for infringement. Further, the Court has cautioned against imposing limitations on patent infringement damages, stating: "When Congress wished to limit an element of recovery in a patent infringement action, it said so explicitly." *General Motors*, 461 U.S. at 653, (refusing to impose limitation on court's authority to award interest).

In *Aro Mfg. Co. v. Convertible Top Replacement Co.*, 377 U.S. 476 (1964), the Court discussed the statutory standard for measuring patent infringement damages, explaining:

> The question to be asked in determining damages is "how much had the Patent Holder and Licensee suffered by the infringement. And that question [is] primarily: had the Infringer not infringed, what would the Patentee Holder-Licensee have made?"

377 U.S. at 507 (plurality opinion) (citations omitted). This surely states a "but for" test. In accordance with the Court's guidance, we have held that the general rule for determining actual damages to a patentee that is itself producing the patented item is to determine the sales and profits lost to the patentee because of the infringement.

Preliminarily, we wish to affirm that the "test" for compensability of damages under § 284 is not solely a "but for" test in the sense that an infringer must compensate a patentee for any and all damages that proceed from the act of patent infringement. Notwithstanding the broad language of § 284, judicial relief cannot redress every conceivable harm that can be traced to an alleged wrongdoing. For example, remote consequences, such as a heart attack of the inventor or loss in value of shares of common stock of a patentee corporation caused indirectly by infringement are not compensable. Thus, along with establishing that a particular injury suffered by a patentee is a "but for" consequence of infringement, there may also be a background question whether the asserted injury is of the type for which the patentee may be compensated.

Judicial limitations on damages, either for certain classes of plaintiffs or for certain types of injuries have been imposed in terms of "proximate cause" or "foreseeability." Such labels have been judicial tools used to limit legal responsibility for the consequences of one's conduct that are too remote to justify compensation. The general principles expressed in the common law tell us that the question of legal compensability is one "to be determined on the facts of each case upon mixed considerations of logic, common sense, justice, policy and precedent." See 1 Street, Foundations of Legal Liability 110 (1906) (quoted in W. Page Keeton et al., Prosser & Keeton on the Law of Torts § 42, at 279 (5th ed. 1984)).

We believe that under § 284 of the patent statute, the balance between full compensation, which is the meaning that the Supreme Court has attributed to the statute, and the reasonable limits of liability encompassed by general principles of law can best be viewed in terms of reasonable, objective foreseeability. If a particular injury was or should have been reasonably foreseeable by an infringing competitor in the relevant market, broadly defined, that injury is generally compensable absent a persuasive reason to the contrary. Here, the court determined that Rite-Hite's lost sales of the ADL-100, a product that directly competed with the infringing product, were reasonably foreseeable. We agree with that conclusion. Being responsible for lost sales of a competitive product is surely foreseeable; such losses constitute the full compensation set forth by Congress, as interpreted by the Supreme Court, while staying well within the traditional meaning of proximate cause. Such lost sales should therefore clearly be compensable.

Recovery for lost sales of a device not covered by the patent in suit is not of course expressly provided for by the patent statute. Express language is not required, however. Statutes speak in general terms rather than specifically expressing every detail. Under the patent statute, damages should be awarded "where necessary to afford the plaintiff full compensation for the infringement." *General Motors*, 461 U.S. at 654, 103 S. Ct. at 2062. Thus, to refuse to award reasonably foreseeable damages necessary to make Rite-Hite whole would be inconsistent with the meaning of § 284.

Kelley asserts that to allow recovery for the ADL-100 would contravene the policy reason for which patents are granted: "[T]o promote the progress of ... the useful arts." U.S. Const., art. I, § 8, cl. 8. Because an inventor is only entitled to exclusivity to the extent he or she has invented and disclosed a novel, nonobvious, and useful device, Kelley argues, a patent may never be used to restrict competition in the sale of products not covered by the patent in suit. In support, Kelley cites antitrust case law condemning the use of a patent as a means to obtain a "monopoly" on unpatented material.

These cases are inapposite to the issue raised here. The present case does not involve expanding the limits of the patent grant in violation of the antitrust laws; it simply asks, once infringement of a valid patent is found, what compensable injuries result from that infringement, i.e., how may the patentee be made whole. Rite-Hite is not attempting to exclude its competitors from making, using, or selling a product not within the scope of its patent. The Truk Stop restraint was found to infringe the '847 patent, and Rite-Hite is simply seeking adequate compensation for that infringement; this is not an antitrust issue. Allowing compensation for such damage will "promote the Progress of ... the useful Arts" by providing a stimulus to the development of new products and industries.

Kelley further asserts that, as a policy matter, inventors should be encouraged by the law to practice their inventions. This is not a meaningful or persuasive argument, at least in this context. A patent is granted in exchange for a patentee's disclosure of an invention, not for the patentee's use of the invention. There is no requirement in this country that a patentee make, use, or sell its patented invention. If a patentee's failure to practice a patented invention frustrates an important public need for the invention, a court need not enjoin infringement of the patent. *See* 35 U.S.C. § 283 (1988) (courts may grant injunctions in accordance with the principles of equity). Accordingly, courts have in rare instances exercised their discretion to deny injunctive relief in order to protect the public interest. *See, e.g., Hybritech, Inc. v. Abbott Lab.*, 4 U.S.P.Q.2d 1001 (C.D. Cal. 1987) (public interest required that injunction not stop supply of medical test kits that the patentee itself was not marketing), *aff'd*, 849 F.2d 1446, 7 U.S.P.Q.2d 1191 (Fed. Cir. 1988); *Vitamin Technologists, Inc. v. Wisconsin Alumni Research Found.*, 64 U.S.P.Q. 285 (9th Cir. 1945) (public interest warranted refusal of injunction on irradiation of oleomargarine); *City of Milwaukee v. Activated Sludge, Inc.*, 21 U.S.P.Q. 69 (7th Cir. 1934) (injunction refused against city operation of sewage disposal plant because of public health danger). Whether a patentee sells its patented invention is not crucial in determining lost profits damages. Normally, if the patentee is not selling a product, by definition there can be no lost profits. However, in this case, Rite-Hite did sell its own patented products, the MDL-55 and the ADL-100 restraints.

[T]he only *Panduit* factor that arguably was not met in the present fact situation is the second one, absence of acceptable non-infringing substitutes. Establishment of this factor tends to prove that the patentee would not have lost the sales to a non-infringing third party rather than to the infringer. That, however, goes only to the question of proof. Here, the only substitute for the patented device was the ADL-100, another of the patentee's devices. Such a substitute was not an "acceptable, non-infringing substitute" within the meaning of *Panduit* because, being patented by Rite-Hite, it was not available to customers except from Rite-Hite. *Cf. State Indus.*, 883 F.2d at 1578, 12 U.S.P.Q.2d at 1030-31. Rite-Hite therefore would not have lost the sales to a third party. The second *Panduit* factor thus has been met. If, on the other hand, the ADL-100 had not been patented and was found to be an acceptable substitute, that would have been a different story, and Rite-Hite would have had to prove that its customers would not have obtained the ADL-100 from a third party in order to prove the second factor of *Panduit*.

Kelley's conclusion that the lost sales must be of the patented invention thus is not supported. Kelley's concern that lost profits must relate to the "intrinsic value of the patent" is subsumed in the "but for" analysis; if the patent infringement had nothing to do with the lost sales, "but for" causation would not have been proven. However, "but for" causation is conceded here. The motive, or motivation, for the infringement is irrelevant if it is proved that the infringement in fact caused the loss. We see no basis for Kelley's conclusion that the lost sales must be of products covered by the infringed patent....

Affirmed in part, vacated in part, and remanded.

NIES, J., dissenting in part, joined by CHIEF JUDGE ARCHER, SENIOR CIRCUIT JUDGE SMITH, and CIRCUIT JUDGE MAYER.

The majority uses the provision in 35 U.S.C. § 284 for "damages" as a tool to expand the property rights granted by a patent. I dissent.

The majority divorces "actual damages" from injury to patent rights. The majority holds that a patentee is entitled to recover its lost profits caused by the infringer's competition with the patentee's business in ADL restraints, products not incorporating the invention of the patent in suit but assertedly protected by other unlitigated patents. Indeed, the majority states a broader rule for the award of lost profits on any goods of the patentee with which the infringing device competes, even products in the public domain.

I would hold that the diversion of ADL-100 sales is not an injury to patentee's property rights granted by the '847 patent. To constitute legal injury for which lost profits may be awarded, the infringer must interfere with the patentee's property right to an exclusive market in goods embodying the invention of the patent in suit. The patentee's property rights do not extend to its market in other goods unprotected by the litigated patent. Rite-Hite was compensated for the lost profits for 80 sales associated with the MDL-55, the only product it sells embodying the '847 invention. That is the totality of any possible entitlement to lost profits. Under 35 U.S.C. § 284, therefore, Rite-Hite is entitled to "damages" calculated as a reasonable royalty on the remainder of Kelley's infringing restraints.

As a preliminary matter, I wish to state my reasons for rejecting the arguments made by appellee Rite-Hite in support of the district court's judgment. The district court held, and Rite-Hite argues on appeal, supported by the amici, that the only restriction on the award of "actual damages" for patent infringement is proof of causation in fact, that is, satisfaction of a "but-for" test. Under that test, it would follow that Rite-Hite is entitled to any profits it lost due to the infringer's competition, whether it lost sales of restraints embodying the invention in suit, or those protected by other patents, or even products in the public domain, i.e., never patented or the subject of expired patents. The district court applied a "but-for" standard to award lost profits on dock levelers as well.

....

A "but-for" test tells us nothing about whether the injury is legally one which is compensable. As above stated, the lack of proximate causation will preclude recovery for certain losses even though a "but-for" standard of injury in fact is satisfied.... [P]recedent before 1946 unequivocally established that compensable lost profits were restricted to those the patentee would have made from commercializing the invention. Further, Congress reenacted the provision for "damages" with that understanding.

An examination of pre-1946 Supreme Court precedent discloses that the legal scope of actual damages for patent infringement was limited to the extent of the defendant's interference with the patentee's market in goods embodying the invention of the patent in suit. This limitation reflects the underlying public policy of the patent statute to promote commerce in new products for the public's benefit. More importantly, it protects the only property rights of a patentee which are protectable, namely those granted by the patent.

An injunction preserves the patentee's exclusive right to market embodiments of the patented invention.

These clearly established principles, however, do not lead to the conclusion that the patentee's failure to commercialize plays no role in determining damages.... The patent system was not designed merely to build up a library of information by disclosure, valuable though that is, but to get new products into the marketplace during the period of exclusivity so that the public receives full benefits from the grant. The Congress of the fledgling country did not act so quickly in enacting the Patent Act of 1790 merely to further intellectual pursuits.

[I]t is anomalous to hold that Congress, by providing an incentive for the patentee to enter the market, intended the patentee to be rewarded the same for letting his property lay fallow during the term of the patent as for making the investment necessary to commercializing a new product or licensing others to do so, in order that the public benefits from the invention. The status quo may serve the patentee's interest, but that is not the only consideration. The patent grant "was never designed for [an inventor's] exclusive profit or advantage." *Kendall v. Winsor*, 62 U.S. (21 How.) 322, 328, 16 L. Ed. 165 (1858)....

An attempt to recover actual damages for lost sales of a competitive unprotected product was made in *Metallic Rubber Tire Co. v. Hartford Rubber Works Co.*, 275 F. 315, 323-24 (2d Cir.), *cert. denied*, 257 U.S. 650, 42 S. Ct. 57, 66 L. Ed. 416 (1921). The Second Circuit held there could be no award of lost profits where the patentee, a maker of competitive tires, never manufactured and sold a tire containing the invention of the patent in suit. Similarly, in *Carter*, 5 F. Cas. at 201-02, the court instructed the jury that a patentee's loss by reason of its inability to sell plows other than those embodying the patent infringed were "[r]emote consequential damages" and not recoverable. As further explained in *Carter* [*v. Baker*, 5 F. Cas. 195, 201-02 (No. 2,472) (C.C.D. Cal. 1871)], 5 F. Cas. at 202, the award of lost profits must be the "direct and legitimate fruits of that patent. They may have sustained damages from [loss of sales of a competing unprotected device], but they are too remote." In *Standard Mailing Machines Co. v. Postage Meter Co.*, 31 F.2d 459 (D. Mass. 1929), the court limited the patentee to a reasonable royalty award because the patentee, although marketing a competitive product, was not "in the market during the infringing period, prepared to sell machines embodying the patented invention." *Id.* at 462. In *McComb v. Brodie*, 15 F. Cas. 1290, 1295 (No. 8,708) (C.C.D. La. 1872), the court instructed the jury to award lost profits only if the patentee was ready to supply the market with patented goods and the infringer diverted those sales.

The majority agrees that the types of compensable injury for patent infringement are not unlimited. The majority draws the line against recovery for an inventor's heart attack or for the decrease in the value of stock of a corporate patentee....

In the majority's view, the consideration of patent rights ends upon a finding of infringement. The separate question of damages under its test does not depend on patent rights but only on foreseeable competitive injury. This position cannot be squared with the premise that compensation is due only for injury to patent rights. Thus, the majority's foreseeability standard contains a false premise, namely, that the "relevant market" can be "broadly defined" to include all competitive truck restraints made by the patentee. The relevant market for determining damages is confined to the market for the invention in which the patentee holds exclusive property rights.

This reasoning awards patent infringement damages as if for a kind of unfair competition with the patentee's business. However, infringement of a patent is not a species of common law unfair competition; it is a distinct and independent federal statutory claim. Moreover, the clear purpose of the patent system is to stimulate a patentee to put new products into the marketplace during the patent term, not to compensate the patentee "fully" while the public benefit from the invention is delayed until the invention falls into the public domain. Compensation in the form of lost profits for injury to the exclusive market in patented goods has provided the incentive to achieve that objective.

If damages are awardable based on lost sales of a patentee's business in established products not protected by the patent in suit, the patentee not only has an easier case as a matter of proof, but also would receive greater benefits in the form of lost profits on its established products than if the patentee had made the investment necessary to launch a new product. That lost profits on an established line are likely to be greater than on a new device cannot be gainsaid. This result is not in accordance with the purpose of the patent statute. Actual damages are meant to compensate a patentee for losing the reward of the marketplace which the patentee's use of the invention would otherwise reap. Without such loss, Congress has mandated compensation in the form of a reasonable royalty.

The old rule stimulated a patentee's commerce in patented goods. The new rule makes it more profitable to the patentee to protect the status quo. The status quo is not "progress in the arts." Article I, sec. 8. I conclude the majority's rule is a wrong interpretation of the statute; indeed, it may exceed the constitutional power to provide inventors with the exclusive right to their discoveries.

[A] key factor in the majority's decision awarding damages for lost sales of the ADL-100 is that the "device" is "patented." The majority does not, nor did the parties, discuss what inventions the one or more patents on the ADL-100 cover. Nevertheless, the majority declares the ADL-100 provides the only alternative technology. While it is inappropriate for an appellate court to make findings, the finding by the majority is erroneous if one examines the record independently. There are other mechanisms for securing trucks to loading docks. Indeed, the Patent Office considered Kelley's Truk-Stop sufficiently different from the prior '847 patent to grant Kelley its own patent. Unfortunately for Kelley, this court earlier upheld the finding that its different structure was sufficiently similar to the '847 patent to constitute infringement. 819 F.2d 1120, 2 U.S.P.Q.2d 1915 (Fed. Cir. 1987). But there were other alternatives which could be substituted. In any event, the one or more patents on technology used in the ADL-100 were never asserted against Kelley, and the validity of those patents is untested. If those patents are invalid, the majority's analysis collapses. Given that Kelley has had no legal basis for bringing a declaratory judgment action challenging the unlitigated patents (never having been charged with their infringement), the majority imposes liability and overlooks the unfairness in its theory. If the unlitigated patents are significant to damages, Kelley deserves an opportunity to defend against them. A clearer denial of due process is rarely seen. The award of damages for competition with Rite-Hite's market for ADL-100s is no more supportable than an injunction against infringement of the ADL-100 patents.

If nothing else, the patent term limit provision of 35 U.S.C. § 154 is skewed by protecting the profits on goods made under one patent for infringement of another. Under the majority's decision, the 17-year terms of the ADL-100 patents are meaningless. Rite-Hite is entitled to the add-on years provided by the later '847 patent after the terms of the ADL-100 patents expire.

No one argues that Rite-Hite is violating the antitrust laws. However, an award of damages for infringement of one patent based on losses of sales of a product not within the protected market violates antitrust policies. Under those policies,

Rite-Hite is not entitled to tribute for infringement of one patent for losses in connection with a competitive product protected, if at all, only by other patents.

[Newman, J., joined by Rader, J., concurred in the holding regarding the "but for" standard for lost sales, but dissented as to other issues discussed in note 3 below].

NOTES

1. *Products, Patents and Markets.* To understand the case, one needs to know how Kelley could sell a product that infringed Rite Hite's patent, while Rite Hite's competing product was not covered by its patent. The following chart and the diagrams on the following pages help to explain the situation. (Price information is for retail sales (in contrast to the prices quoted early in the preceding opinion) and is taken from the Federal Circuit opinion and the district court opinion, 774 F. Supp. 1514, 1526.)

Product and patent	Main features	How is it positioned?	Vertical movement mechanism	Price (est.)
Rite Hite MDL-55 product/ '847 patent in suit	Vertical moving hook	Manual operation	Ratchet and pawl mechanism	$900 to $1375
Rite Hite ADL-100 product/ 4,264,259 patent	Vertical, rotating hook, mounted on a spring-loaded carriage	Electric motor	Sprocket and chain	$2500 to $3000
Kelley product (Kelley's 4,488,325 patent)	U-shaped hook/bar	Electric motor	Rack and pinion mechanism	$2300 to $2800

The chart clarifies that Kelley's infringing product had features similar to and competed with Rite Hite's ADL-100 product. Note also the price column: it suggests that Kelley's strategy was to compete on major features with the ADL-100, while undercutting it slightly on price. Indeed, it might be argued that Kelley's success was due to the fact that it understood which features of the ADL-100 were the truly popular ones, and it cut out some of the more elaborate features of the ADL-100, thus cutting the price. As an alternative, it is tempting to argue that the price differential between the ADL-100 and the Kelley product represents the extra cost to Rite Hite of its extensive R&D program. However, it is clear that Kelley too was trying to innovate (note its own '325 patent).

U.S. Patent   Feb. 15, 1983   Sheet 1 of 3   4,373,847

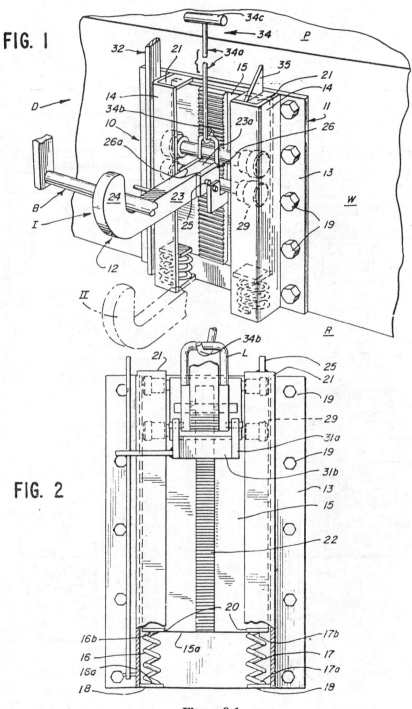

Figure 9-1

Figure 9-2

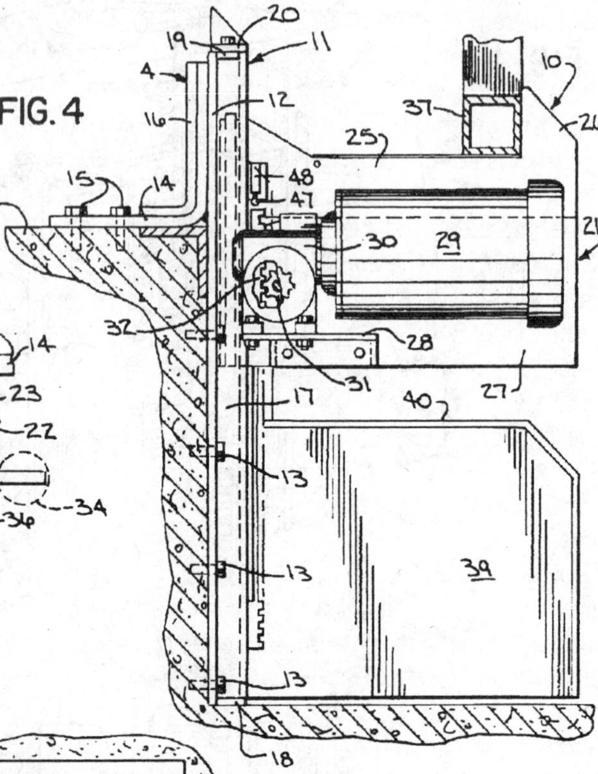

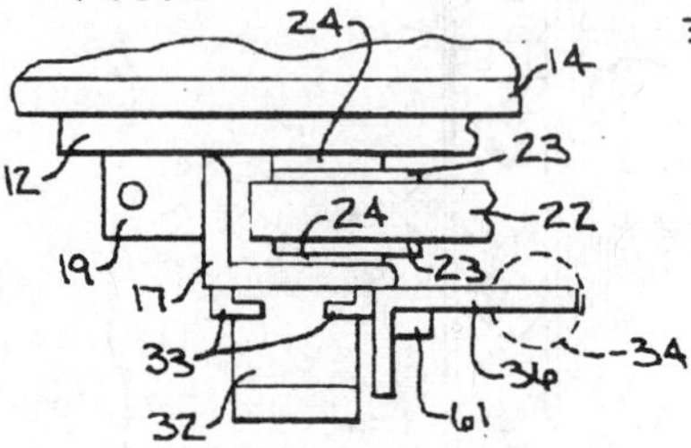

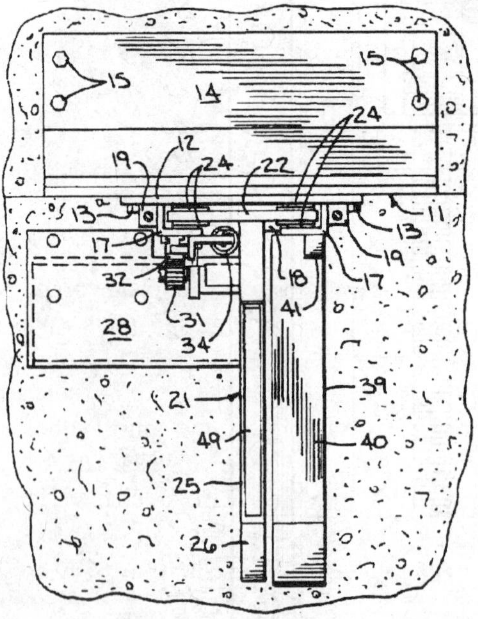

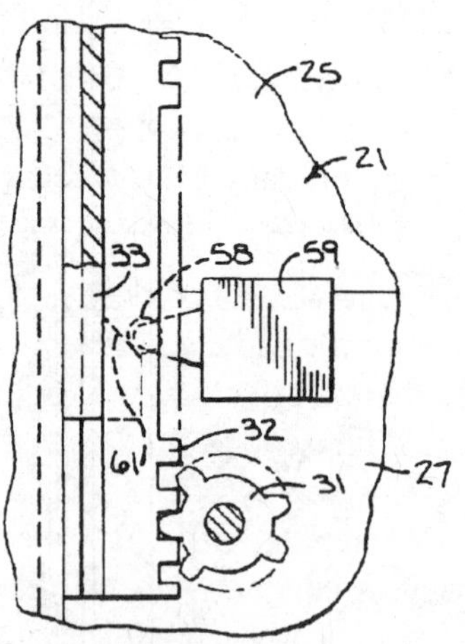

2. The Introduction to this book, Chapter 1, takes pains to point out that markets are not coextensive with patents, nor even in many cases with single inventions. The *Kelley* case is, among other things, a prolonged set of musings on this theme. The majority is at pains to address the ex post nature of the compensation for infringement which it sees at the heart of the case. Thus, the fact that infringing Kelley products compete *in the same market* that Rite-Hite is selling in is all that matters. The fact that Rite-Hite's actual product offering in that market is not covered by the patent in suit is irrelevant. The infringer is competing in the patentee's market; it was foreseeable that this infringement would cost the patentee; and that is the end of the matter. The majority position may thus be summarized as: reward patentees ex post with *market* exclusivity to enhance ex ante incentives to invent. (Note, however, that the dissent does not take the opposite position, in the sense of advocating no compensation to the patentee; the issue is only the *extent* of compensation.) Reasonable royalties are still the floor.

The dissent by the remarkable late Judge Nies takes aim directly at the majority's central thesis. To paraphrase: it is improper to extend a property right over a set of claimed embodiments into a mechanism of market exclusivity. Unless the patentee is selling something that falls within the claims of the patent, lost profits are beyond question not available. This is because to grant them in such a situation in effect *extends the scope of the patent* to cover subject matter not within its claims. The patent right, in other words, defines the boundaries of the legally cognizable domain protected against direct harm by the infringer. (Again, this does not imply no compensation, but only that a reasonable royalty should be awarded rather than lost profits.)

An omitted footnote in the majority opinion accuses the dissent of confusion on this point:

> The partial dissent of Judge Nies appears to confuse exclusion under a patent of a product that comes within the scope of the claims with the determination of damages to redress injury caused by patent infringement once infringement has been found.

What point was Judge Nies trying to make by criticizing the extension of the zone of lost profit damages beyond the scope of the patent claims at issue? Was she right that, in effect, allowing compensation for loss of non-covered product sales extends the scope of the patent right to include those non-covered products?

3. *The Rest of the Story.* In other parts of the opinion, the court (1) held that the "entire market value rule" did not apply to the infringer's sale of non-infringing but complementary "dock levellers" (see below in this chapter); (2) the independent sales organizations (ISO's) who had joined the suit must be dismissed, since they had insufficient ownership interest in the patents to sue for direct infringement; and (3) the trial judge had not abused its discretion in setting the reasonable royalty rate for sales of infringing products that did not cause lost sales on the part of the patentee.

4. *Liability Rule Entitlement?* The dissent argues that the measure of the lost profits remedy must be the claims of the patent at issue. The majority sees no conceptual barrier to protecting that claimed invention by allowing lost profits for closely related but unclaimed products. As the dissent points out, this in effect extends the economic reach of the patent to include unclaimed products. The majority, however, sees nothing wrong in this extension, so long as (1) it serves the goal of compensating the patentee for foreseeable harm to the patent, and (2) it is strictly limited to ex post compensation, i.e., no injunction is available. This latter point relates to the discussion, earlier in this chapter, of patents as strong property rule-type entitlements. The majority says, in effect, that so long as the unclaimed subject matter is not brought within the strong property rule entitlement — i.e., as long as a court does not enjoin sales of unclaimed products — there is no distortion of the patent right:

> The present case does not involve expanding the limits of the patent grant in violation of the antitrust laws; it simply asks, once infringement of a valid patent is found, what compensable injuries result from that infringement, i.e., how may the patentee be made whole. Rite-Hite is not attempting to exclude its competitors from making, using, or selling a product not within the scope of its patent.

While it is true that granting ex post damages for lost sales of unclaimed products is not the same as an injunction preventing the sale of noninfringing products by the "infringer," it is also true that the majority's damages rule does in effect extend the scope of the patentee's entitlement. In those cases where the patentee can prove that *Kelley*-type lost profits are legitimate, a limited liability rule regime covering the patentee's unclaimed products will be in effect. Subject to these limitations, the patentee is entitled to ex post compensation for economic harm in the market for unclaimed products. Prospective infringers will unquestionably anticipate that they must pay these damages if they intrude into the patentee's market. In some cases, this will make it uneconomical for the infringer to enter. (Only where higher lost profits damages deter entry will the *Kelley* rule change anything, since even before *Kelley* the patentee was entitled to reasonable royalties for these infringing but non-competing sales.) Thus we may conclude that the effective economic power held by the patentee has indeed been expanded. It only confuses matters to cling to the property rule/liability rule distinction; whatever the nature of the entitlement, it has economic consequences. Whether they are good ones, as the majority contends, or illegitimate ones, as Nies argues in her dissent, is a different matter.

Note, however, in favor of the majority, that an ex ante injunction prohibiting infringing sales will *in effect* protect the patentee's market in unclaimed goods in situations such as *Kelley*; hence, arguably, the *Kelley* rule leaves the patentee no better off than if an injunction had issued before a single infringing sale had taken place.

The scope of the implicit liability rule entitlement can be measured by the limitations on *Kelley*-type damages, which are substantial. Ex post compensation will only be available where the patentee can prove:

- That it is selling unclaimed products,
- That sale of infringing products has caused a loss in sales of the patentee's unclaimed products, and
- That it was reasonably foreseeable on the part of the infringer that sales of these infringing products would cause the patentee to lose sales of unclaimed products.

Subject to these restrictions, after *Kelley* a patentee does have an entitlement that covers unclaimed products. In that sense Judge Nies was correct that *Kelley* extends the patentee's entitlement. At the same time, these limitations may be significant in many cases. If so, then the extension is a modest one. Where, as would often seem the case, the patentee's sales are limited to products that are covered by the patent, *Kelley* changes nothing. Where no loss in the patentee's sales can be shown, *Kelley* changes nothing. And most important, where it is difficult to predict the effect of infringing sales on the market for the patentee's related but unclaimed product(s), *Kelley* presumably changes nothing.

5. *Protecting a Stream of New Products*. One interesting feature of the *Kelley* case is the lurking presence of other Rite Hite patents not directly at issue in the case. These patents, which directly cover the ADL-100, are important for at least two reasons: (1) they provide support for the majority's conclusion that, notwithstanding the fact that the patentee is selling products that are not covered by the patent in suit, there are no "*acceptable* non-infringing substitutes" for the patented product, so the *Panduit* standard is met; and (2) they demonstrate that the patent in suit is only one of many patents owned by Rite Hite, and that Rite Hite is engaged in a long-term project of R&D related to truck loading and docking systems.

The first point is challenged by Judge Nies in her dissent; *Panduit* is satisfied only if these other patents are valid, a conclusion that cannot be assumed under our patent system.

The second point goes to the equities of the case, as the court saw them, and also illustrates an interesting perspective on the role of individual patents in protecting a stream of R&D results. The majority opinion reflects a belief that it is important to take into account Rite-Hite's overall research project. The patented product is only one of a series. Rite Hite is going about improving the field of truck docking in many different ways. The court seems to imply that to limit Rite Hite's lost profit damages to infringing sales that took away sales only of products covered by the patent in suit would somehow fail to give Rite Hite full credit for its overall research program. In some ways, this undercurrent in the case reflects a wholesome perspective: that there are severe limits to recognizing only the individual patent as the single unit of analysis in patent policy.

In a related vein, consider the issue of contributory infringement for the sale of unpatented products that are useful only in conjunction with the patented product. Under a contributory infringement theory, a patentee can in effect prevent sale of related but uncovered items. This issue, discussed in some detail in Chapter 11, shows that in cases other than the *Kelley* situation a patent can lawfully be used to control an ancillary market not defined strictly by the bounds of the patent. These cases go beyond *Kelley* in one respect, however: since a court may issue an injunction to prevent future contributory infringement, the patentee's unclaimed but complementary products are in effect protected by a *property rule*, rather than the weaker liability rule created by *Kelley*.

On the other hand, as the dissent implies, the traditional reasonable royalty measure of damages also compensates the patentee, while respecting the patent itself as the limit of the patentee's lost profit entitlement. The dissent's real complaint, ultimately, is that the liability rule entitlement for unclaimed products ought to be less valuable than the majority thinks. Recall that the dissent cites as a rationale for its position the fact that under the majority rule the patentee reaps a high reward even though it is not making and selling the patented invention.

KING INSTRUMENTS, INC. v. PEREGO

65 F.3d 941 (Fed. Cir. 1995)

RADER, J.

[Video tape cassettes are sold in bulk without any magnetic tape. Each closed cassette contains only a leader tape connected to its two winding hubs. Tape manufacturers add magnetic tape later by splicing the tape into the middle of the leader tape and winding it into the cassette. Patentee King and infringer/competitors Perego and Tapematic, Inc. market competing machines that automatically splice and wind magnetic tape into otherwise completed video cassettes. King's U.S. patent 3,637,153 discloses a partially automated machine for loading magnetic tape into a cassette. As an optional accessory to its tape loader, Tapematic provides a reel changer that automatically switches to and splices a second reel of magnetic audio or video tape when the first reel runs out. The court determined that certain claims of the '153 patent, though drafted to cover the magnetic-to-leader tape splicing of a tape loader, were infringed by the magnetic-to-magnetic splicing mechanism in Tapematic's reel changer. King did not sell a reel changer for its own tape loader, however. The excerpts from the opinions that follow are taken from the portions of the majority opinion and dissent that address the *Kelley* issue, viz., whether King can collect lost profits damages for foregone sales of its tape loader occasioned by Perego's infringement.]

Congress has not amended the Patent Act, nor has the Supreme Court interpreted the term "damages" to require exploitation of the invention as a prerequisite to recovery of lost profits. Moreover, such a prerequisite runs contrary to the language and enactment history of section 284.

The long history of the Patent Act shows that its language does not require a patentee to make the patented invention to qualify for damages....

A patentee is awarded a patent for disclosure of a patentable invention "[t]o promote the Progress of ... useful Arts." U.S. Const. art. I, § 8, cl. 8. A patentee need not make, use, or sell an invention to gain patent protection. Upon proper disclosure of a protectable invention, a patentee acquires the right to exclude others from making, using, or selling the invention.

[T]he Patent Act creates an incentive for innovation. The economic rewards during the period of exclusivity are the carrot. The patent owner expends resources in expectation of receiving this reward. Upon grant of the patent, the only limitation on the size of the carrot should be the dictates of the marketplace. Section 284 attempts to ensure this result by deterring infringers and recouping market value lost when deterrence fails.

Providing lost profits compensation in this case preserves those constitutional incentives. Moreover, construing section 284 in harmony with the breadth of its language allows the market, rather than courts, to dictate the incentives. This court should not presume to determine how a patentee should maximize its reward for investing in innovation. Yet denying the patentee its provable lost profits in this or any case where the patentee chooses to market a competing non-patented product would have this result.

The market may well dictate that the best use of a patent is to exclude infringing products, rather than market the invention. A patentee, perhaps burdened with costs of development, may not produce the patented invention as efficiently as an infringer. Indeed, the infringer's presence in the market may preclude a patentee from beginning or continuing manufacture of the patented product. Thus, as apparent in this case, the patentee may acquire better returns on its innovation investment by attempting to exclude infringers from competing with the patent holder's nonpatented substitute.

Under this situation, the Patent Act is working well. The patentee is deriving proper economic return on its investment in acquiring a patent right. The public benefits from the disclosure of the invention and the ability to exploit it when the patent term expires....

Requiring exploitation would force patent owners to accept a reasonable royalty in cases where a reasonable royalty is inadequate compensation. Infringers would in effect receive the windfall of a retroactive compulsory license from the patent owner.

A hypothetical example shows how an infringer could profit from such a rule. A hypothetical patentee could market a product covered by a patent and efficiently supply all demand for the product. A competitor seeking a license under the patent would not succeed. The patentee profits more by supplying the demand itself than by granting a license on terms which would allow the competitor to reasonably operate. In this situation, no reasonable royalty exists. Willing negotiators, assuming they both act in their own best interests, would not agree to any royalty. The value of exercising the right to exclude is greater than the value of any economically feasible royalty. If the competitor infringes in this situation and the patentee can recover only a "reasonable royalty," the patentee does not receive "adequate compensation" as the statute requires. The same reasoning applies anytime the patent owner benefits more by excluding others than by licensing.

In such situations, if lost profits are not available simply because the patent holder does not market a product pursuant to its patent, infringement may actually be profitable. If licensing (rather than excluding) competitors would have proven more rewarding to the patentee, the patentee would have licensed. Instead, the market dictated that exclusion was the best way to recover innovation investments. Limiting the patentee's recovery to a reasonable royalty, however, would give the infringer what the market denied — a license. Fortunately the Patent Act does not create such incentives to infringe. Rather, it guarantees damages adequate to compensate for infringement — which include provable lost profits.

Requiring a patentee to exploit the infringed claims as a prerequisite for lost profits damages would also create two significant practical problems. First, the remedy for infringement would depend partly on the type and number of claims selected by the inventor, rather than on their scope. Second, infringement trials would become more cumbersome and complex because a patentee would have to prove that the claims cover both its competitor's product and its own.

A hypothetical again illustrates this problem. An inventor originates a useful, nonobvious device composed of the elements A, B, C, and Q_1. A device consisting of ABC is well known. The addition of Q_1 is a significant advance. The inventor or someone on the research team knows, however, that element Q_2 or element Q_3 could function in the device in place of Q_1. Because of the different characteristics of the elements Q_1, Q_2, and Q_3, and the different language necessary to describe these elements, the three embodiments are not readily comprehended in a single claim. Thus, in order to cover the subject matter of the three independent claims, $ABCQ_1$, $ABCQ_2$, and $ABCQ_3$, three separate patents could issue, perhaps with differing inventive entities.

The inventor then markets a device covered by claim $ABCQ_1$. Competitors — unable to acquire a license — deliberately market devices which literally infringe claims $ABCQ_2$ and $ABCQ_3$. According to the dissenting opinion, the inventor cannot recover his lost profits for this infringement. The inventor instead must, in effect, grant a compulsory license to willful infringers. Moreover, the infringers have an incentive to infringe to acquire what the market does not supply, a mandatory license.

The potential for increasing the complexity of patent litigation is especially disturbing. The inventor would have to prove that its own product falls under the patent. Infringers would escape lost profits and acquire a mandatory license by showing the inventor's product is not within the claims. The length, cost, and complexity of an infringement trial would conceivably double. The damages phase of a trial would feature an entire new issue of "reverse infringement." The inventor would have to show that the patent's claims read on the inventor's own product, while the infringer would try to show they do not. Once again, as a precondition for lost profits, the parties would parse the claims and call on experts to apply the claim language to an unaccused device.

The language of the 1952 Act did not contemplate creation of an entire new issue of "reverse infringement." The language of the Patent Act recognizes that the value of a claim to the patentee, and the extent of harm from infringement, do not depend on whether the patentee markets the claimed device. To adequately compensate for infringement of the right to exclude, as section 284 requires, "damages" includes lost profits on competing products not covered by the infringed claims.

NIES, CIRCUIT JUDGE, dissenting in part.

In *Rite-Hite v. Kelley Co.*, 56 F.3d 1538, 35 U.S.P.Q.2d 1065 (Fed. Cir. 1995) (in banc), this court divorced lost profit damages from injury to the patentee's business in goods protected by the infringed patent. A patentee was held entitled to damages based on lost trade in its goods protected under an unlitigated patent which competed with the infringing goods. In this case, the panel majority eliminates the *Rite-Hite* requirement for the patentee to put out, at least, a competitive counterpart for the infringing product. Under this decision, any economic loss to a patentee's business is held legally compensable as damages for patent infringement....

[In discussing the requirement that a patented invention be commercialized,] [t]he panel majority cites [an] equity case which held that a patent could not be refused on the ground it might be used only to protect another patented invention of which it was a part. *Special Equipment Co. v. Coe, Comm'r of Patents*, 324 U.S. 370, 65 S. Ct. 741, 89 L. Ed. 1006 (1945). A majority of the court believes it follows that disclosure of an invention is, in itself, sufficient for damages to a patentee's business in unpatented goods. However, an injunction is directed to the equity power of the court and may be denied. *Rite-Hite*, 56 F.3d at 1547-48. Damages are provided by a rule of law respecting what constitutes legal injury and may not be refused as a matter of the court's discretion. The majority compares apples and oranges....

Congress made the policy choice that the "carrot" of an exclusive market for the patented goods would encourage patentees to commercialize the protected inventions so that the public would enjoy the benefits of the new technology during the patent term in exchange for granting a limited patent monopoly.

If the patentee did not commercialize the invention directly or by license, until now the patentee could not prove actual damages but, nevertheless, was entitled to the remedies of damages calculated as a reasonable royalty and an injunction. Now the patentee is rewarded the same as, indeed, more than, if it had made the investment to bring the goods into the market. [From footnote 12: King's profit margin was determined on an incremental basis on an established line where fixed costs had been recouped. The majority speaks of damages to recoup development costs of the invention. The record here is devoid of evidence respecting such costs.] However, no legislation has ever been proposed to compensate a patentee for losses to its unpatented business in order to correct the inadequacies the majority sees in the legal scope of damages which have heretofore been awardable. This court has simply judicially legislated an expansion of patent rights from protection of an exclusive market in patented goods to protection of the patentee's unpatented business as well. The court does away with the "carrot" Congress determined would get new products into the economy.

NOTES

1. *Property Rule Apples and Liability Rule Oranges.* The dissent paints a hypothetical where a patentee determines that it will maximize profit by maintaining a monopoly on production, as opposed to licensing a competitor and thereby establishing a duopoly. In the terminology of the majority, this demonstrates that in some cases there is no hypothetical "reasonable royalty" that will place the patentee back in his or her pre-infringement condition. In such a case, the majority argues, "[t]he value of exercising the right to exclude is greater than the value of any economically feasible royalty." It thus follows that forcing a reasonable royalty on the patentee makes him or her worse off than before the infringement.

There are three problems with this analysis. First, where the profit to be gained by excluding competitors exceeds the profit from licensing, the patentee will indeed exclude. But he or she will also, as the majority notes, "supply the entire market." Thus, lost profits will be available *a fortiori*.

Second, the majority speaks as if the dissent had advocated an ongoing reasonable royalty for the life of the patent. It forgets that the relevant period under discussion begins when the infringement begins and ends when a final injunction is issued — which virtually always happens in patent cases (and should, see Robert P. Merges, *Of Property Rules, Coase, and Intellectual Property*, 94 COLUM. L. REV. 2655 (1994)). The dissent is not arguing that the patentee must give up its "right to exclude." Damages are always assessed ex post, and virtually always *in addition to* upholding the patentee's "right to exclude" by issuing an injunction. For this reason it is also wrong to accuse the dissent of advocating a "retroactive compulsory license from the patent owner." Since by definition patent infringement has already occurred at the time damages are assessed, a court is *always* assessing such a license. But it is temporary, not ongoing. The "apples and oranges" analogy in the dissent goes directly to this issue, which is also discussed earlier in the notes following *Kelley*. Just as in *Kelley*, both sides are arguing over the extent of ex post damages to be awarded to the patentee — i.e., over the value of a liability rule entitlement.

Next, the majority extends its analysis to explicitly cover the case where the patentee is not selling a product covered by its patent. In such a case, where no license was issued we can assume, according to the majority, that "the market dictated that exclusion was the best way to recover innovation investments." In this case, "[l]imiting the patentee's recovery to a reasonable royalty ... would give the infringer what the market denied — a license."

This assumes a lot. Quite frequently, an independent inventor, later deemed an infringer, invents the same subject matter as the patentee and begins to market a product based on it while the patentee is still prosecuting his or her patent. In such a case, it is wrong to infer that the lack of a license stemmed from a profit-maximizing decision on the part of the patentee. Likewise, patentees are not omniscient; they have been known to turn down licensing requests that would in fact have been profitable. Often information asymmetries between licensor and licensee keep each party from a full, comprehensive assessment of the joint profits from a potential license. *Cf.* Robert P. Merges & Richard R. Nelson, *On the Complex Economics of Patent Scope*, 90 COLUM. L. REV. 839 (1990). And even fully informed, rational parties sometimes experience "bargaining break-down" due to strategic behavior in the licensing process. *See* Robert P. Merges, *Intellectual Property Rights and Bargaining Breakdown: The Case of Improvement Inventions and Blocking Patents*, 62 TENN. L. REV. 75 (1994).

Finally, be aware of the implicit "baseline" in the majority's analysis. It assumes that almost the sole goal of patent damages doctrine is to put the patentee back into the pre-infringement position. This assumes that otherwise the infringer will have an incentive to infringe. The problem with this is that it confuses the patentee's damage recovery with the infringer's loss from infringement. The two are not the same. In many — perhaps most — cases, the infringer will lose more than simply the damages it pays out to the patentee. When an injunction is issued, for example, the infringer's investment in assets designed specifically to produce the infringing item will likely lose a great deal of value. The same goes for investments in distribution channels, marketing, and the like. These losses may well be enough *on their own* to dissuade an infringer from entering a market. Even when they are not sufficient in themselves, they may well be when combined with even a "modest" reasonable royalty award.

Clearly, we need not look solely to the patentee's recovery as the measure of the infringer's loss. Consequently, we need not be so concerned with eliminating incentives to infringe. Instead, we might keep in mind that high damage awards encourage other perverse and sometimes wasteful investments — on the part of patentees. The acquisition of patents solely to later collect damages; the expenditure of large sums on consultants charged with the task of creating ever more exotic damages theories; and the disincentive for competitors to compete vigorously, perhaps by coming close to the line of infringement, are all worth considering in this connection.

On the other hand, as pointed out in the notes following *Kelley*, the majority's argument can be forcefully restated as: compensate the patentee for all losses that an injunction would have prevented.

2. *Dissecting the Hypothetical.* The majority creates an instructive hypothetical to demonstrate why the rule advocated by the dissent would create perverse incentives. In the hypothetical, a research project yields three related patents, each reciting elements A,B, and C in combination with (respectively) elements Q_1, Q_2, and Q_3. The patentee sells a product covered by the $ABCQ_1$ patent, and the infringer sells a competing product covered by the $ABCQ_2$ or $ABCQ_3$ patent.

The majority implies that the patentee in this situation would be deprived of a full, robust return on its investment if it were denied lost profits damages.

Consider these issues: first, was this the situation in *King Instrument* — was the infringer's product a patented variant of the patentee's marketed product?; (2) might the patentee respond by selling nominal quantities of products covered by the second and third patents, and if so, is that one of the perverse results the majority implies will follow from the dissent's rule?; and (3) is there a policy justification for giving lower damages for the infringer's sale of products covered by patents that do not cover the originator's commercial product (e.g., anti-patent stockpiling notions)?

Note that as to question (2), patentees who responded to the dissent's rule by rushing to market a device covered by the patent would be mimicking the behavior of firms trying to secure trademark rights by making actual commercial use of the trademark in commerce. *Cf.* ROBERT P. MERGES, PETER MENELL, MARK LEMLEY & THOMAS JORDE, INTELLECTUAL PROPERTY IN THE NEW TECHNOLOGICAL AGE (1997), at Chapter 5: Trademarks (describing this as a "race to appropriate" situation).

1. NONINFRINGING SUBSTITUTES

RADIO STEEL & MANUFACTURING CO. v. MTD PRODUCTS, INC.
788 F.2d 1554, 229 U.S.P.Q. (BNA) 431 (Fed. Cir. 1986)

The infringer contends that the damages [awarded in the accounting phase of the trial below] were excessive. We affirm.

The case involves U.S. Patent No. 3,282,600, owned by Radio Steel & Mfg. Co. (Radio Steel). The patent covers an improved wheelbarrow. The complaint alleged that MTD Products, Inc. (MTD), had manufactured and sold wheelbarrows that infringed the patent. Following a trial in the accounting phase of the case, the district court awarded Radio Steel damages of $588,719.93 plus post-judgment interest and costs. The court found that "[t]he overwhelming majority of MTD's sales of the infringing wheelbarrows was to three retail store chains: White Stores, Montgomery Ward, and K-Mart." It determined that Radio Steel was entitled to recover lost profits on MTD's sales to K-Mart and the White Stores, which it calculated at $296,937.21. On MTD's sales to stores other than those two, the court ruled that Radio Steel was entitled to a reasonable royalty of ten percent, which amounted to $155,634.81. The court held that MTD's infringement was not willful and therefore declined to enhance the damages or to award attorney fees. [See Section D below.]

In awarding lost profits, the district court applied the standard announced in *Panduit Corp. v. Stahlin Bros. Fibre Works, Inc.* Under *Panduit*, to receive lost profits a patent owner must prove: (1) demand for the patented product, (2) absence of acceptable noninfringing substitutes, (3) his manufacturing and marketing capability to exploit the demand, and (4) the amount of the profit he would have made. The district court found that Radio Steel had proved the four elements of Panduit with respect to sales MTD made to K-Mart and the White Stores.

On appeal, MTD challenges only the district court's finding that there were no acceptable noninfringing substitutes. That was a finding of fact that we can reverse only if it is clearly erroneous. MTD has not shown that the finding has that fatal flaw.

The district court found that the patented wheelbarrow has several attributes which demonstrate an absence of substitutes.

> The patented wheelbarrow could be shipped unassembled, thereby allowing more compact shipping with lower shipping costs. The wheelbarrows could be easily assembled at the stores.... The absence of the "shin scraper" brace along the rear of the legs, which was necessary in other wheelbarrows to achieve structural regidity [sic], also added to the popularity of the patented wheelbarrow.... Although other noninfringing contractor-type wheelbarrows exist in the market, such wheelbarrows are not acceptable substitutes for the patented product.

MTD contends, however, that wheelbarrows for many years past

> ... perform the same function of transporting a load contained in a bowl or tray on one wheel propelled by an operator holding the handles on which the bowl or tray is mounted and propelling the assembly on the single wheel. All wheelbarrows which have been on the market produce this result and are available acceptable substitutes. Some of these wheelbarrows ... have two-piece handles which facilitate packaging of the parts of the wheelbarrow, and these too are available acceptable non-infringing wheelbarrows.

This argument is another formulation of the contention, rejected twice by the district court and once by this court, that the patent simply was a combination of old elements. It ignores the district court's earlier ruling in the liability phase that "[i]t is the totality of all the elements and their interaction with each other which is the inventor's contribution to the art of wheelbarrow making." It also ignores the statement in our prior opinion that "as the district court held, the '600 patent 'descri[bed] ... a new and improved complete wheelbarrow.'" The various wheelbarrows to which MTD refers incorporate only some, but not all, of the elements of the patent. They do not establish that the district court's finding that these were not acceptable noninfringing substitutes is clearly erroneous.

NOTES

1. *Other Cases.* Other cases repeat the emphasis on the patentee's unique features in deciding whether there are any noninfringing substitutes. In *Yarway Corp. v. Eur-Control USA, Inc.*, 775 F.2d 268, 276, 227 U.S.P.Q. (BNA) 352 (Fed. Cir. 1985), the court said:

With regard to [*Panduit*] factor (3) [sic; (2)], the absence of noninfringing substitutes, we need only point to the testimony of Mr. Woodfield. The testimony indicates that devices covered by the '592 patent account for 25 percent of the total desuperheater market, but that there exists within this total market a "special niche" or a mini-market for desuperheaters covered by the '592 patent. Only Eur-Control and Yarway sell to that market. Devices sold outside the 25 percent will desuperheat steam, but are not equal or equivalent to [Yarway's] Gustafsson invention. Thus, this mini-market is the relevant market for purposes of determining lost profits. Appellants' argument that a mere 25 percent market share precludes a finding of no acceptable substitutes is clearly unsupported in light of this mini-market. Instead, the evidence supports the court's finding that there is no noninfringing acceptable substitute to meet the specific needs of this relevant market. The court's reduction of the award from 100 to 85 percent, also supported by the testimony, is a reflection of the judge's determination that some buyers of desuperheaters might not be aware of Yarway and thus not purchase from it. This is a reasonable inference from the evidence as a whole.

In addition to defining relevant markets narrowly, courts have favored the patentee in other ways. In *Kaufman Co. v. Lantech, Inc.*, 926 F.2d 1136, 17 U.S.P.Q.2d 1828 (Fed. Cir. 1991), for example, after noting that "[a]ny doubts regarding the calculatory precision of the damage amount must be resolved against the infringer," 926 F.2d at 1141, the Federal Circuit dismissed the trial court's finding that the infringer made many of its sales because of its ability to customize the patented machine, a stretch-wrapping device for wrapping large loads on shipping pallets. "This 'ability to customize,'" said the court, "is irrelevant to the availability of acceptable noninfringing substitutes." 926 F.2d at 1142. The court went on to note:

> The reputation for performing customized work, and the ability to competitively price and manufacture film-driven machines signifies that Kaufman may have been more accommodating to prospective customers than Lantech. However, this customer preference for Kaufman service does not tend to show that Lantech would not have made the sale had Kaufman not infringed. Had Kaufman not infringed on Lantech's patent rights, there would be no other supplier of film-driven prestretch machines that customers could prefer over Lantech.

926 F.2d at 1143. *Cf. Modine Mfg. Co. v. Allen Group, Inc.*, 14 U.S.P.Q.2d 1210, 1218-20 (N.D. Cal. 1989), *aff'd*, 917 F.2d 538 (Fed. Cir. 1990) (supporting plaintiff's contention that it could have sold its radiators, and 95% of infringer's, with 21.9% price increase, despite defendant's evidence that many of its customers had no previous business relationship with plaintiff, and concluding that "the demand for [the patented radiator] reached near inelastic levels.").

2. An Easy Case. Frequently, the patent owner and infringer are the only suppliers in the market, and the owner is seeking to recover profits lost through every sale made by the infringer. *See Water Techs. Corp. v. Calco, Ltd.*, 850 F.2d 660, 672, 7 U.S.P.Q.2d (BNA) 1097, 1106 (Fed. Cir. 1988); *Amstar Corp. v. Envirotech Corp.*, 823 F.2d 1538, 1543, 3 U.S.P.Q.2d (BNA) 1412, 1415 (Fed. Cir. 1987); *Lam, Inc. v. Johns-Manville Corp.*, 718 F.2d 1056, 1065, 219 U.S.P.Q. (BNA) 670, 675 (Fed. Cir. 1983). In the two-supplier market, it is reasonable to assume, provided the patent owner has the manufacturing and marketing capabilities, that it would have made the infringer's sales. *Del Mar Avionics, Inc. v. Quinton Instrument Co.*, 836 F.2d 1320, 1327, 5 U.S.P.Q.2d (BNA) 1255, 1260 (Fed. Cir. 1987). In these instances, the *Panduit* test is usually straightforward and dispositive. *Cf. Water Techs.*, 850 F.2d at 671-72, 7 U.S.P.Q.2d at 1106 ("[w]here a patent owner maintains that it lost sales equal in quantity to the infringing sales, our precedent has approved generally the [*Panduit* test]....").

3. Attacking the "Nexus" Concept. The notion that an infringer's sales were primarily a function of the features of the infringing product covered in the patentee's patent is closely related to the notion that the commercial success of a patented product is a function of its patented features. In both cases, courts assume a causal connection between the patented features and the appeal to consumers. For a critique of this reasoning, and a call for increased emphasis on the failure of other competitors to invent the patented features, see Merges, *Economic Perspectives on Innovation: Commercial Success and Patent Standards*, 76 CAL. L. REV. 803 (1988). Applying the reasoning in this article to the problem of the *Panduit* factors, perhaps it would be sensible to credit proof that the infringer's product did *not* do well absent the patented feature. What other factors might account for an infringer's success? (*Cf.* the discussion of the *Lantech* case, above.) What harm occurs when an accused infringer whose product includes valuable features, or whose reputation for customer service is superior, is excluded from the market?

Antitrust Learning on Market Definition: A Critique of "No Substitute" Cases

As we have seen the Federal Circuit has not been overly precise in its analysis of what constitutes a noninfringing substitute under factor (2) of the *Panduit* test. Cases such as *Radio Steel* and *Yarway* in fact narrow the definition of the patentee's product category almost to the limit; at the extreme, they can be read as stating a *per se* rule that a patentable invention by definition has no substitutes. Thus an infringing product has *per se* taken sales from the patentee. In effect, a duopoly is assumed where a legal monopoly should have existed.

Aside from the unfairness this approach works on the infringer, it has a major conceptual problem. Patentees have argued strenuously in connection with accused infringers' antitrust-related claims that a patent does not in and of itself confer market power on the patentee. For example, in *A.I. Root Co. v. Computer/Dynamics, Inc.*, 806 F.2d 673, 676 (6th Cir. 1986), the court declared prior Supreme Court statements on the subject to be "overbroad and inapposite" and rejected the presumption of market power based on the "cogent reasoning" of Note, *The Presumption of Economic Power for Patented and Copyrighted Products in Tying Arrangements*, 85 COLUM. L. REV. 1140, 1141 (1985) ("the presumption does not serve as an adequate proxy for evidence of actual economic power ... and should be rejected."). *See also USM Corp. v. SPS Techs., Inc.*, 694 F.2d 505 (7th Cir. 1982), *cert. denied*, 462 U.S. 1107 (1983). *But see Jefferson Parish Hosp. Dist. No. 2 v. Hyde*, 466 U.S. 2, 16 (1984) (reiterating that patent creates presumption of market power). *See generally* Lemley, *The Economic Irrationality of the Patent Misuse Doctrine*, 78 CAL. L. REV. 1599 (1990); Chapter 11, *infra*.

For our purposes, this discussion is relevant because it points to the patent system's inconsistency regarding a patent's uniqueness and economic leverage. In the antitrust and misuse context, patentees argue that their patent does *not* in fact confer much economic power. Yet when it comes to arguing for lost profits, patentees turn around and argue strenuously the "absence of non-infringing substitutes," i.e., a high degree of product uniqueness or (in other words) market power. This justifies, among other things, elaborate calculations of price increases the patentee had to forego because of the infringement. (In many cases, these are based on economic models, designed by expert economic consultants, that very explicitly assume monopoly power by the patentee.) When are patentees to be believed?

One view has it that the antitrust/misuse approach to market definition must be imported into the law of damages as well. Under this "more rigorous" approach, courts

> would ... assess the existence of acceptable noninfringing substitutes using well recognized economic principles applied in antitrust cases. Two such approaches exist, both of which are applied routinely in antitrust cases. The first is to estimate statistically the cross-elasticity of demand between the patent and possible noninfringing substitutes, where cross-elasticity is defined as "the responsiveness of the sales of one product to price changes of the other." The second is specified in the Merger Guidelines of the Department of Justice, which is used to identify mergers that may substantially lessen competition. Under the Guidelines, substitutes are identified by assuming a hypothetically small but significant (5%) non-transitory price increase for the subject product. If an economically significant group of consumers would switch their purchases from the subject product to another product, the other product is deemed a substitute.

Krosin & Kozlowski, *Patent Damages*, in PATENT LITIGATION 1990 (Patents, Copyrights, Trademarks, and Literary Property Course Handbook No. 300

PLI/Pat. 53) (1990). *See also* Culbertson & Weinstein, *Product Substitutes and the Calculation of Patent Damages*, 70 J. PAT. & TRADEMARK OFF. SOC'Y 749 (1988) (arguing for adoption of same standard).

Then there are those who advocate the opposite: import the more tractable approach taken in patent damage actions into the misuse standard. *See* Burchfiel, *Patent Misuse and Antitrust Reform: "Blessed Be the Tie"?*, 4 HARV. J.L. & TECH. 1 (1991) ("[I]t is far preferable to adopt an interpretation of the patent misuse market power standard that would avoid economic factors such as market share or the existence of substitutes, in favor of indicia ... such as the tying product's uniqueness, desirability to consumers, or distinctiveness in the often very narrow market for the patented product."; in cases on patent damages, "an extremely narrow relevant product market [is] defined to include only the patented and accused machines, which constituted a 'special niche' or 'mini-market' as the 'relevant market' for determining lost profits. These cases clarify the appropriate rule for determining substitutes in markets for patented technology."). *Cf. Patent Licensing Reform Act of 1988: Hearing before the Subcomm. on Courts, Civil Liberties and the Administration of Justice of the Comm. on the Judiciary of the House of Representatives on H.R. 4086*, 100th Cong., 2d Sess. 183 (1988) (statement of Prof. Merges) (testimony in connection with patent misuse-related legislation; stating that markets for specific technologies are often very "thin," with few direct substitutes available for particular inventions or components). *See generally*, Webb & Locke, *Intellectual Property Misuse: Developments in the Misuse Doctrine*, 4 HARV. J.L. & TECH. 257 (1991); Merges, *Reflections on Current Legislation Affecting Patent Misuse*, 70 J. PAT. & TRADE-MARK OFF. SOC'Y 793 (1988).

It should be noted that there is no statutory imperative that the law of damages be consistent with patent misuse doctrine. However, logical consistency dictates that if one is purporting to use the same test to achieve different ends, the test ought not be changed simply to accommodate the different ends. Still, perhaps a reconciliation can be achieved.

Even if the "narrow" definition of substitutes in *Radio Steel, Yar-Way* and other cases is followed, there is still room for the antitrust-based conceptions of product substitutes to affect the *amount* of lost profits. An excellent example comes from the damages portion of a recent mega-case on Polaroid's instant photography patents, *Polaroid Corp. v. Eastman Kodak Co.*, 16 U.S.P.Q.2d (BNA) 1481 (D. Mass. 1990), where the court ultimately assessed total damages of $873,158,971 (corrected from the original figure of $909,457,567.00, see 17 U.S.P.Q.2d (BNA) 1711 (D. Mass. 1991)).

> At various times during the trial Polaroid seemed to argue that all evidence about conventional photography should be excluded because conventional photography was not an acceptable substitute for instant photography.

Kodak argued that conventional photography was an "economic substitute" for instant. Kodak did not attempt to quantify the number of Kodak instant purchasers who would have turned to conventional products in Kodak's absence; Kodak simply urged that the relative price of instant and conventional photography was a significant variable in the demand formula for instant products and therefore must be considered in any assessment of the market. Instant photography occupied a unique niche in the overall photography market during the infringement period. Consumers sought the emotional "instant experience" of having a picture develop immediately, usually in the presence of the subject. Although instant photography was unique, it did not exist in a vacuum; it also competed with conventional photography for the consumer's photographic dollar. Those who purchased infringing Kodak instant products at Kodak prices would not have considered conventional products as an acceptable substitute at the time of purchase, but the relationship between the relative advantages of conventional and instant photography was an integral part of each consumer's decision. If Polaroid were simply claiming that it could have made Kodak's sales at the same time at similar prices, there would be no question in my mind that consumers would have made the same choice vis-à-vis conventional photography. However, Polaroid's claim is not so simple.

Polaroid's experts spun a scenario in which the prices Polaroid would have charged were substantially higher and in which, through a complicated massaging of the demand curve, the great bulk of sales would have occurred later than they did historically. In this "but for" scenario, the effect of conventional photography on the instant photography market must be considered. The evidence of competition between instant and conventional products is overwhelming. Even Polaroid's econometric expert attempted to include the effect of competition from conventional photography in his computation. The relative values of instant and conventional changed throughout the period of infringement. On the facts before me, I must consider that relationship when deciding whether Polaroid's scenario, which differs so substantially from the historical world, is feasible. *Contrary to Polaroid's urging, the law does not require this Court to ignore the effect of competitive forces on the market for patented goods just because there are no noninfringing alternatives. Indeed, the law requires a careful assessment of all market influences when determining lost profit or reasonable royalty damages.* I find that conventional photography was not an acceptable substitute for instant photography during the period of infringement. Competition between conventional and instant photograph (which changed throughout the ten years of infringement) did, however, affect the price that consumers were willing to pay for instant photography. Therefore, I have assessed what effect the competition would have had on Polaroid's ability to charge more for its instant products and on the profitability of delaying the introduction of certain lower-priced products. [In another section of the opinion, the court concludes that in fact this competition had no effect on Polaroid's profit margins or product introduction-related profits.]

(Emphasis added.)

The *Polaroid* approach steers its way between the liberal "no adequate substitutes" analysis under Federal Circuit lost profits cases and the "no market power" view now espoused for patent-related antitrust cases. The court in effect concedes that there are no substitutes in the market for patented products. But it then goes on to consider the effect of *economically significant* but non-substitute products on the profit the patentee would have made absent infringement. It admits, in other words, that the patented product is unique; but it refuses to equate uniqueness with total insulation from market forces. In a word, there may be no exact substitutes, but there are economic substitutes. These exert price discipline on the patentee's pricing.

One way to state this in terms of conventional antitrust analysis is to say that although the cross elasticities of demand for the patented item and related items are not high enough to call them identical products, the availability of some (perhaps imperfect) substitutes, coupled with at least some price elasticity in the demand for the patented good, means that the patentee would have faced some price discipline even if she could have made the infringer's sales. One can even imagine a scenario where, if the infringer had not been in the patentee's market, she would have moved into a parallel market from which she could have exerted greater price discipline on the patentee.

NOTES

1. *Market Definition: New Learning.* Some recent scholarship in the area of antitrust market definition is of special relevance to a consideration of the noninfringing substitute element of the *Panduit* test. In a paper by R. Hatman, D. Teece, W. Mitchell & T. Jorde, *Product Market Definition in the Context of Innovation*, University of California at Berkeley Center for Research in Management, Consortium on Competitiveness and Cooperation, Working Paper No. 90-7 (1990), the authors argue that traditional market definition techniques are seriously flawed when applied to markets for highly innovative and technology-intensive products. Specifically, they point out that current Department of Justice guidelines assume a much too static view, which "biases market definition downwards in industries experiencing rapid technological change, where competition often takes place on performance attributes, and not price." "The more innovative the new product or process," the authors argue, "the greater the conventional market power will appear, because price changes will have little or no influence on demand for a truly innovative product." *Id.* at 6-7. The authors propose an approach whereby product attributes are included in the assessment of demand and supply.

2. *Surveying the Damage(s).* One recent article advocates a direct questionnaire to purchasers of the infringer's product, with an eye toward establishing that they perhaps purchased infringing items because of the infringer's marketing approach, brand name, service reputation, or the like. *See* Skenyon and Porcelli, *Patent Damages*, 70 J. PAT. & TRADEMARK OFF. SOC'Y 762, 782 (1988). Such a survey was in fact performed in connection with the *Polaroid* case, *supra*. The district court commented:

> Of course, there would be problems with this data; consumers might not remember, may be unable to recognize how they were influenced, or may be biased from subsequent events. Kodak attempts to support its claim that a significant number of Kodak purchasers would not have bought Polaroid by offering a survey done at the time Kodak was ordered from the market. The survey asked Kodak purchasers whether they would like to receive a Polaroid camera or a conventional Kodak camera in place of their Kodak instant camera. Many preferred to receive a conventional camera.... The survey did not ask the respondents whether, without Kodak, they would have forgone the purchase of instant at the time they bought it; the survey asked what type of camera customers would like at that moment, after however many years of instant camera ownership and given all the changes in the photographic market. The results, therefore, do not support Kodak's claim [that cameras were purchased for reasons other than the patented features.]

Id., at footnotes 13 and 14.

3. *Other Panduit Factors.* We have discussed in detail an important component of the *Panduit* test for lost profits, the availability of noninfringing substitutes. But this is only the second of four factors to consider. Recall the others: (1) demand for the patented product, (3) the patentee's manufacturing and marketing capability to exploit the demand, and (4) the amount of the profit the patentee would have made. Of these, (1) tends to be relatively straightforward; courts tend to assume that the presence of a substantial infringer alone establishes demand for the patented product. *See, e.g., Gyromat Corp. v. Champion Spark Plug Co.*, 735 F.2d 549, 222 U.S.P.Q. (BNA) 4 (Fed. Cir. 1984) ("[t]he substantial number of sales by Champion of infringing products containing the patented features itself is compelling evidence of the demand for the [patented] product," since such sales "necessarily meant that there were buyers who wanted the product and were willing to pay Champion's price.").

Factor (3) can sometimes stand in the way of relief, as in the case of Robert Kearns, an independent inventor who was barred from recovering lost profits damages from Ford Motor Company on his invention, the intermittent car windshield wiper, because he would have been unable to build a factory and supply the world's carmakers. *See* Ed Andrews, *Ford Loses Patent Suit on Wipers*, N.Y. TIMES, Jan. 31, 1990, at D1 col. 3; *and* J. White, *Jury Finds Ford Violated Patent for Wipers*, WALL ST. J., Jan. 31, 1990, at A6 col. 3. To the same effect is *Datascope Corp. v. SMEC, Inc.*, 879 F.2d 820, 11 U.S.P.Q.2d (BNA) 1321 (Fed. Cir. 1989), where the court said that "[t]he demand which a patentee must have the capacity to meet is measured by the total sales, by the patentee and the infringer, of the patented product." The court upheld the district court's finding that the patent owner did not meet its burden of proving manufacturing and marketing capability with respect to foreign sales because the evidence showed that none of the patent owner's sales representatives were assigned to foreign customers and no attempt was ever made to make foreign sales.

On the other hand, where the patentee has even minimal resources, the "ability to meet demand" factor (factor (3)) is often not an obstacle. The patent owner may satisfy the requisite demand not only through its own internal manufacturing and marketing capabilities, but also by licensing and subcontracting. In *Yarway Corp. v. Eur-Control USA, Inc.*, 775 F.2d 268, 276, 227 U.S.P.Q. (BNA) 352 (Fed. Cir. 1985), for example, the Federal Circuit upheld a finding that plaintiff had the ability to meet market demand where plaintiff purchased the patented products from defendant's sister company, based upon testimony that defendant and the sister company operated as separate profit centers which were interested in maintaining their respective profits and operating activities. In *Gyromat Corp. v. Champion Spark Plug Co., supra*, the third *Panduit* element was established by testimony that plaintiff could have handled the increased production by itself and, in addition, could have subcontracted substantial portions of the work without serious adverse affect on its overall profit margin.

Element (4), the amount of the profit the patentee would have made, is intermingled with element (2), absence of noninfringing substitutes. In addition, this element leads to consideration of a number of other issues. An example is the effect of closely similar products on the profit margins the patentee would have made on those infringing sales it would have made. The excerpt from *Polaroid* above shows how courts handle this issue. Other examples, such as the possibility that the patentee would have made "tag-along" or "convoyed" sales, are considered in the context of reasonable royalty calculations earlier in this chapter and to some extent in the materials that follow. For an example of a very detailed treatment of these issues — a veritable one volume treatise on damages, with working examples — consult the district court opinion on damages in the *Polaroid* case, *Polaroid Corp. v. Eastman Kodak Co.*, 16 U.S.P.Q.2d (BNA) 1481 (D. Mass. 1990), *modified*, 17 U.S.P.Q.2d (BNA) 1711 (D. Mass. 1991).

Price Erosion: The Proper Methodology

It is quite common now for patentees to argue that entry by the infringer not only took unit sales away but also reduced the price the patentee could charge for its product. Judge Frank Easterbrook of the Seventh Circuit, sitting by designation, made some useful observations on the proper analysis of this "price erosion" issue (albeit in a context where reasonable royalty and lost profits tend to blur) in *In re Mahurkar Patent Litig.*, 831 F. Supp. 1354, 1383-85, 1389, 1391-92, 28 U.S.P.Q.2d 1801 (N.D. Ill. 1993):

A patent owner who does not manufacture the invention expects to make money principally if not exclusively from the royalty. Then it is necessary to enter into the complex counterfactual process of approximating the royalty that would have been agreed on by parties that did not agree on anything at all. See *Panduit* .... But when the patent's owner (or, here, his exclusive licensee) also makes the patented article, the profitability of the owner's manufacture and sale also determines the royalty that would be charged. To see this, consider a simple example. Firm #1 can make a patented article for $7, a cost that includes goods, machinery, labor, sales, and the competitive return on invested capital. If there were no competition, the profit-maximizing price would be, let us suppose, $10. At a higher price, so many sales would be lost to less effective, but cheaper, competing products, that total profits would decline. The $3 difference between cost and profit-maximizing price is a return to the patent, an implicit royalty. I state the royalty in dollars rather than a percentage of the price, but the two are equivalent. Here, where the price is $10, it would be easy to restate the $3 return as a 30% royalty.

How much would Firm #1 charge to allow some other manufacturer into the business? Not less than $3, because it can earn that much by making the article itself. Whether it can get more depends on the costs someone else would incur in making the article. Suppose Firm #2 would incur costs of $8 in manufacturing and selling the patented article. Firm #2 would not pay more than $2 in royalty for the privilege, and Firm #1 would not take less than $3. If Firm #2 would incur costs of $7 in manufacture and sale, it would pay a royalty up to $3, but not more. (It is important to remember that the "cost" of $7 includes the competitive rate of return on the capital invested in the process. An accountant would call this a profit. Thus Firm #2 "makes a profit" on this transaction even with a royalty of $3 per item, but no more of a profit than it would earn from some other use of its time and resources.) Finally, suppose Firm #2 would incur costs of only $6 in making and selling the article, indicating that Firm #2 is more efficient than Firm #1. Now what royalty would be charged? Firm #2 would be willing to pay as much as $4 per item; Firm #1 would accept as little as $3; how they divide the difference will depend on their bargaining strategies and the elasticity of demand. Lower costs of production reduce the profit-maximizing price, and the two firms would share the higher profits associated with the greater output. The royalty per item might even fall, although Firm #1's total return would rise. The point here is that Firm #1 (which I am treating as the patentee and manufacturer combined) would be able to collect a royalty exceeding the difference between its cost and the market price only if Firm #2 has lower costs. This is a standard conclusion of the economic literature, which the parties have given me no reason to doubt. See Roger D. Blair & David L. Kaserman, Law and Economics of Vertical Integration and Control 58-68 (1983).

None of the evidence introduced in this case suggests that [infringer] IMPRA was more efficient than [patent licensee] Quinton. The technology of making the Mahurkar catheter is well established. Evidence during the damages phase of the trial shows that both IMPRA and Quinton could expand their output without increasing unit costs. Each firm also has an established sales force that visits most if not all potential users of hemodialysis catheters, so that an increase in output does not lead to a marked increase in selling expenses per unit (or to any difference between the firms in the rate of increase). That is to say, the marginal cost of each firm appears to be flat in the relevant range of production. Either could double its output by adding a second production line, and so on. Because Quinton and IMPRA have stable average and variable costs of production, and because Quinton appears to be the more efficient producer, Quinton would not be able to collect from IMPRA, as a royalty, any sum greater than the difference between its cost and the price customers are willing to pay.

Although the royalty cannot be greater than compensatory damages in a case such as this, compensatory damages easily can exceed the reasonable royalty. An infringer's activities do more than divert sales to the infringer. They also depress the price. Competition drives price toward marginal cost. In a fully competitive market, the item in my hypothetical would be available for $7. Consumers, although willing to pay more, need not do so; customers willing to pay $10 would enjoy the extra $3 as a consumer surplus, and customers willing to pay less than $10 but more than $7 would begin to buy, and they too would reap some consumer surplus. Thus the loss to Firm #1 in the hypothetical could be as large as $3 multiplied by the entire volume it could sell at a price of $10. Damages thus exceed the reasonable royalty, which would be measured by $3 multiplied by Firm #2's sales. Notice, however, that the damages are not as large as $3 times the actual sales of Firm #1 and Firm #2 put together. Customers will buy more at a price of $7 than they will at a price of $10. The correct way to compensate Firm #1 is to award it $3 times the number of units it would have sold had there been no infringement — or, to put it differently, the monopoly output times the monopoly profit, a profit made lawful by the patent. The patent holder does not receive the monopoly price times the competitive output. See generally John W. Schlicher, Patent Law: Legal and Economic Principles § 9.05 (1992).

Although it is easy to conclude that compensatory damages are the proper measure in this case, it is not at all easy to decide what those damages are. For markets cannot be dropped into bins marked "competition" and "monopoly." There are degrees of competition. It is easy to award Mahurkar and Quinton damages on the number of units IMPRA actually sold. Just multiply IMPRA's sales by Quinton's profits per sale — being careful to subtract that portion of the accountant's understanding of "profit" that reflects only the competitive rate of return on Quinton's investment. But

IMPRA's sales drove down the price of all catheters using the Mahurkar design. How much could Quinton have charged had there been no competition from IMPRA? From all infringers combined? We need to know how fast price falls with an increase in output attributable to infringers' sales. To use the technical term, what is the elasticity of demand facing a sole manufacturer of hemodialysis catheters using the '968 design? The record does not point to an inevitable conclusion on this question. It is a counterfactual.

During the entire time Quinton has made and sold the Quinton-Mahurkar catheter, it has faced competition from firms that have copied its product — most of which have now conceded infringement and stopped....

The best one can do in the absence of a sophisticated (or any!) study of elasticities is to ask whether modest changes in the price of catheters with the Mahurkar design would have led to substantial declines in output, enough to make the increase unprofitable. Modest changes for this purpose are 10% per year so that the price of the Quinton-Mahurkar catheter would have progressed in increments from $32.81 in 1986 to $52.84 in 1991, instead of the $35.89 it actually reached in that year. Some rough estimation is involved here, but it is not "speculation" by any means. Getting to $50 is quite plausible; [Defendant's expert] Prof. [F.M.] Scherer noted that it does not require any dramatic inelasticity in the market demand for the product. See also, e.g., Dennis W. Carlton & Jeffrey Perloff, Modern Industrial Organization 332 — 42 (1990); William M. Landes & Richard A. Posner, *Market Power in Antitrust Cases*, 94 Harv. L. Rev. 937, 939-52 (1981); *Landes and Posner on Market Power: Four Responses*, 95 Harv. L. Rev. 1787-1874 (1982), for descriptions of the relation among elasticity of demand, market share, marginal cost, and price.

The figure of $52 for a Quinton-Mahurkar product is one that IMPRA's witness Mounia, who for years worked in the dialysis section of a leading hospital, testified would not send buyers scampering to alternatives.

How much would the total sales of catheters of Mahurkar's design have fallen at a price of $53? An elasticity of demand expresses a percentage change in sales for a given percentage change in price. What Perri calls a "10% increase" in price is not in fact that large an increase, because Perri was speaking in nominal dollars. An average change of 10% per year would have exceeded only slightly the average change in the cost of medical care. Adjusting instead for general changes in the value of money would deduct between 3.09% and 4.34% per year during 1986 to 1991. Statistical Abstract Table 753. Thus what Perri called a 10% increase would be a small price increase using the price of medical care as a benchmark, or a 5.6% to 7% annual increase using the price level in the whole economy as a benchmark. The economy as a whole is the preferable benchmark for this purpose because price changes in medical care are linked to labor in addition to inputs of supplies. Next we need to know the elasticity. I determined above that Quinton was experiencing a roughly stable variable cost of $13 for catheters. Professor Scherer provides this standard formula relating price, marginal cost, and elasticity at the profit-maximizing price:

$$[(P\text{-}MC)/P]=[1/\in]$$

In this equation P is price, MC is marginal cost, and epsilon is the elasticity of demand. This simplification may appear to ignore the role of fringe suppliers such as Cook, but their influence is reflected in the elasticity derived from actual prices in the industry. If P = $53, MC = $13, then $\in$ = 1.33. For every 1% increase in price, total sales fall by 1.33%.

This still does not entirely capture quantity effects. The formula gives the elasticity at the monopoly price. A monopolist continues to increase price past the point where its gross revenues begin to fall (this is what it means to say that the elasticity exceeds 1). Its profits continue to increase for some time after revenue begins to fall because it saves money by producing fewer units. Perri thought that $52 or so was the monopoly price and proposed 10% annual increases to get there only because Quinton did not want to aggravate its customers, on whose goodwill it depends to sell other products. I cannot treat the movement from $32 to $52 as if the elasticity were 1.33 in the entire area. For much of this range the elasticity is apt to be less than 1. The best I can do is to assume that the average elasticity, throughout the range of potential movement, is 1 — which turns out to be a working assumption of many economists.

For current purposes, recall, we are assuming that Quinton has cornered the market in devices covered by the '968 patent. So to determine what Quinton's sales would be in a given year, it is necessary to take the actual total sales of Mahurkar catheters — that is, sales of Quinton, Vas-Cath, Kendall, IMPRA, and other infringers combined — and reduce them by 1% times the amount by which the imputed monopoly price exceeds the actual selling price in that year. This is a question on which the parties should submit their calculations under the procedure established in Part VII of this opinion.

This should not be difficult. Here is an example. According to Kone's data, the net price of Quinton's catheters increased from $32.81 in 1986 to $33.15 in 1987, a change of approximately 1%. The 10% figure I have accepted implies an increase to $36.09. The value of the dollar fell by 3% in 1987, so the "real" increase Quinton would have achieved had it been freed of the infringers, net of the actual change and the change in the value of money, was 6%. That implies a reduction in unit sales of 6% compared with what Quinton and the infringers, put together, actually delivered in 1987. To arrive at lost profits for catheters in 1987, then, it is necessary to multiply that number of units by $36.09 (because, had there been no competition from the infringers, Quinton would have sold them all) and subtract the variable cost of $13 per catheter. It is also necessary to subtract Quinton's profit of $32.81-13=$19.81 on the units it actually sold. The resulting number is lost profits.

The procedure should be much the same for kits and trays, except that the record does not support a conclusion that the price of kits and trays would have gone up at 10% per year. Much of the price of these items reflects the cost of staple products plus labor. To determine Quinton's lost profits on kits and trays, it is necessary to use the actual selling price for the year, increased by the change in the catheter's price. For example, in 1991 Quinton actually sold catheters for $35.89 and trays for $74.19. I have concluded that, but for the infringers' competition, Quinton could have sold the Mahurkar catheter in that year for $52.84, a difference of $16.95. Quinton would have had market power in catheters but not the other components of kits and trays. Thus to determine the price for which trays would have sold in 1991, it is necessary to add $74.19 and $16.95, for a total of $91.14. A similar process yields the adjusted price of kits and trays for the other years and permits a computation of lost profit per kit and tray.

Before we move on, one final reality check. IMPRA says that these numbers are off the wall because they exceed by a great deal what it views as a "reasonable royalty" for the Mahurkar catheter. A few percent of the selling price, according to Mr. Green, is all he would pay; yet 10% per year compounded for five or six years is a significant multiplier. IMPRA's unwillingness to pay significant royalties might well be justified — in competition.

With competition reduced to that offered by femoral, alternating-flow, and ... dual-lumen catheters such as Cook's, however, the value of Mahurkar's intellectual property would increase. Even during a time of rampant infringement Quinton has been paying Mahurkar a hefty royalty. As of January 1, 1988, Quinton was paying Mahurkar a royalty of 9% on its sales of all products containing his catheters. This is a lot more than 9% on the value of the catheter itself. Trays sold for more than twice the price of the catheter, so a 9% royalty on a tray is more like a 20% royalty on the catheter it contains. If Mahurkar's contribution was worth this much even while Quinton faced competition from firms that were selling his invention without paying for his contribution, it is a very valuable piece of intellectual property indeed. And of course Quinton's own contribution, including development of a workable product and entrepreneurial risk-taking, is significant. The price implied by the method I have used is not out of line with this recognition.

2. THE MARKET SHARE RULE

STATE INDUSTRIES v. MOR-FLO INDUSTRIES

883 F.2d 1573, 12 U.S.P.Q.2d (BNA) 1026 (Fed. Cir. 1989)

Mor-Flo Industries, Inc. and its subsidiary, American Appliance Manufacturing Corporation (Mor-Flo), infringed State Industries, Inc's. (State) Patent No. 4,447,377, covering a method of insulating water heaters with foam. After the damages trial, the district court awarded State lost profits on approximately 40% of Mor-Flo's infringing sales and a royalty of 3% on the remaining 60%. It concluded that Mor-Flo's infringement was not willful and denied enhanced damages and attorney's fees. We affirm the judgment insofar as it awards lost profits and a 3% royalty.

Background

The '377 patent claims a method of insulating the tank of a water heater by using polyurethane foam. The method includes wrapping the tank with a plastic sheet shaped as an envelope, installing a surrounding jacket and cover, pouring foam through an opening in the cover into the envelope, and then plugging the opening. The envelope contains the liquid foam while it rises and prevents it from invading areas, such as the electrical components and combustion chamber, which must be kept free of foam.

Mor-Flo's method found to be infringing used a cylindrical piece of plastic that was pulled over the top of the tank with fiberglass positioned around the combustion chamber at the bottom of the tank. The "sleeve" was taped below the top of the fiberglass. A jacket was then installed over the tank and sleeve, a top was installed, and foam was shot into the sleeve through an opening in the top.

The water heater industry is intensely competitive and marked by small profit margins. The invention is pertinent to all water heaters, but the infringement at issue here is restricted to residential gas water heaters, in particular those deemed "energy efficient" by the American Society of Heating, Refrigeration and Air Conditioning Engineers. Foam provides greater insulating capacity than the other alternative, fiberglass; therefore, foam-insulated heaters have cost advantages in terms of material, packaging and freight. The greater insulating capacity enables foam-insulated heaters to meet the energy code requirements imposed by many states by using less space than fiberglass-insulated heaters. The density of foam also strengthens the outer jacket of the water heater and makes it more resistant to denting.

In deciding the damages question, the district court faced three issues: lost profits, reasonable royalty and willful infringement. Infringement occurred between May 8, 1984, when the patent issued, and June 9, 1986, when Mor-Flo switched to the noninfringing method of fiberglass foam stops, which eliminates need for the envelope taught by the patent in suit yet keeps foam from invading the combustion chamber. State produced evidence of lost sales, and took the position that it should recover lost profits for its market share of Mor-Flo's infringing sales and a reasonable royalty for the remainder. It also asked increased damages for willful infringement and attorney fees.

The district court agreed with State in the award of lost profits for part of its damages and a royalty for the rest. The court found there was a growing demand for foam-insulated water heaters, the '377 patent was the first method developed to meet this demand, and there were no other methods available during the pertinent period that were either noninfringing or acceptable as substitutes. Specifically, the court found "that, during the period of infringement, all but one of State's competitors in the United States sold foam insulated water heaters made using State's patented method, or one of a strikingly similar configuration, and/or Patent No. 4,527,543 [also assigned to State] — namely Mor-Flo/American; Hoyt Heater Company; Rheem Manufacturing Company; and Bradford-White."

A.O. Smith Corporation, the only clearly noninfringing competitor used the less preferable fiberglass insulation. Hoyt also sold only fiberglass-insulated heaters until 1985 when it added a foam-insulated heater to its inventory. The court found that fiberglass was not an acceptable substitute for foam because of foam's advantages in reducing the size of water heaters, increasing resistance to denting, and meeting governmental energy standards.

The court also found that State was capable of producing during the relevant period, and had sales and distribution capacity to ship and sell, sufficient foam-insulated water heaters to exploit its market share of Mor-Flo's sales. Finding that State has approximately 40% of the gas water heater market nationwide, the court awarded State the profits it lost on 40% of the sales of 754,181 infringing Mor-Flo water heaters.

For the remaining 60% of Mor-Flo's sales, State asked for a royalty of 8 to 10%. Mor-Flo presented no evidence of what it would have paid for a license, but argued that in no event should the royalty rate be above its net profit margin which, for the seventeen months preceding the date infringement began, was 2.1%. The district court awarded a royalty of 3% on the remaining 60% of infringing sales. Finally, the court concluded the infringement was not willful because Mor-Flo relied in good faith on advice of outside counsel that its process was not infringing.

Mor-Flo appeals both the award of actual damages and the reasonableness of the royalty. State cross-appeals the reasonableness of the royalty and the court's failure to hold Mor-Flo's infringement willful and to award increased damages and attorney's fees.

Discussion

The measure of damages is an amount which will compensate the patent owner for the pecuniary loss sustained because of the infringement. But the floor for a damage award is no less than a reasonable royalty, and the award may be split between lost profits as actual damages to the extent they are proven and a reasonable royalty for the remainder.

To get lost profits as actual damages, the patent owner must demonstrate that there was a reasonable probability that, but for the infringement, it would have made the infringer's sales. But "[t]he patent holder does not need to negate all possibilities that a purchaser might have bought a different product or might have foregone the purchase altogether."

With only slight modification we think [the *Panduit* test] fits here and confirms the district court's judgment.

Absence of Substitutes and Market Share

This is the first time we have considered whether lost profits can be based on market share. Other courts of appeals that have faced the question have found it unnecessary to answer it.

Here we have multiple competitors and the patent owner contends that all the competitors infringed or sold a far less preferable alternative — fiberglass. The district court made the absence of acceptable substitutes, *Panduit* item (2), a neutral factor by crediting all the other competitors with their market shares as State requested. If the court is correct in its finding that the other competitors were likely infringers of one or the other of State's patents, State would have been entitled to their shares of the market on top of its own, and a correspondingly greater share of Mor-Flo's sales. If it is wrong in whole or in part, State would have been entitled to its current share or to a lesser increase in share. We need not decide which it is because it would make no difference to the outcome. State would get at least what it asked for, because as discussed further below the district court found, and we agree, that State's share of the market was proven.

But Mor-Flo should not complain because if anything it received a windfall from this approach. To the extent infringing competitors got credit for sales that should have gone to State, the share of the market against which Mor-Flo's damages might be assessed is reduced. So we think that in these circumstances the presence or absence of acceptable noninfringing alternatives does not matter. The question then becomes whether an established market share combined with the other *Panduit* factors is sufficient to show State's loss to a reasonable probability.

The finding that State has a 40% national market share is unassailable, and Mor-Flo does not seriously contend otherwise, or that State did not have the capacity to produce enough heaters to satisfy at least 40% of Mor-Flo's sales. It says rather that the majority of the infringing sales occurred in California where State shared with Rheem and A.O. Smith 10% of the market, while Mor-Flo had 70% and Hoyt had 20%. From this Mor-Flo argues that it is unrealistic to think State could achieve 40% of the West Coast market, especially where Hoyt, which manufactured noninfringing fiberglass-insulated heaters along with foam-insulated heaters, was Mor-Flo's next largest competitor.

State tells us there is no evidence to support this "Western Region" theory and our search of the record shows it was at best an incidental argument. Nevertheless, the district court made findings that State had the capacity to absorb its share of the market and we are shown no reason why they are wrong. From the evidence, there was demand for heaters made by the patented method, and State and Mor-Flo were head-to-head competitors. State was a nationally recognized leader in the industry, and it produced specific evidence that it had lost sales to Mor-Flo's infringing heaters on both coasts. For example, a retailer of State's heaters in California testified that he lost sales to a developer for 3,000 heaters annually to Mor-Flo. Another retailer testified that he lost sales to Mor-Flo in Connecticut. There is nothing speculative about these losses. After finding that State had sufficient marketing and manufacturing capabilities to meet its market share of the demand it is eminently reasonable for the district court to infer that State could have sold its market share of Mor-Flo's infringing sales wherever the opportunity occurred. We accordingly agree with the court that it is probable, at least, that State could have met the demand.

Amount of Profit

The district court awarded State its incremental profit on foam-insulated gas water heaters reflecting the percentage of sales revenue State lost because of Mor-Flo's infringement that would have been its profit. This approach is well established and appropriate for determining damages for patent infringement. There is some testimony that fixed costs might have varied slightly, but the district court did not abuse its discretion in concluding that any increase in fixed costs was minimal and that award of incremental profits was appropriate. No greater precision is required.

In our view, the foregoing discussion compels the conclusion that the district court acted well within its discretion when it awarded damages for Mor-Flo's infringing activity based on State's share of the market.

Affirmed.

NOTES

1. *Correct Arithmetic?* Why should the patentee's market share figure be based on the continued presence of the infringer? If the infringer's sales were eliminated from the picture entirely, the remaining market share for the patentee would of course be higher. Perhaps the correct approach would be to split the infringer's market share between the patentee and the remaining noninfringing substitutes.

Then again, why assume that the patentee and remaining noninfringing substitutes would split the patentee's sales equally? Perhaps the patentee would have taken the lion's share of them. Or, if their prices are lower, perhaps the noninfringing sellers would have. It seems artificial to suppose that in a dynamic market situation changing one variable (the presence of the infringer) would produce predictable results. But then again, perhaps the main goal of the exercise is to compensate the patentee, not to reach accurate conclusions on the effect of hypothetical market events.

2. District Court Discretion. The Federal Circuit has made clear that, as with other damages issues, the district court has a good deal of discretion in deciding whether to apply the "market share rule."

> In *State Industries*, we held that the grant of lost profits based on market share was not an abuse of discretion. However, that holding does not mean that the contrary is true, i.e., that the failure to award lost profits based on market share would constitute an abuse of discretion. We hold that such a failure to award lost profits in the present case was not an abuse of discretion.

Slimfold Mfg. Co. v. Kinkead Indus., 932 F.2d 1453, 1458, 18 U.S.P.Q.2d (BNA) 1842 (Fed. Cir. 1991).

3. Fixed Versus Variable Costs. The incremental income approach used in *State Industries* recognizes that typically, the cost of producing additional units of the patented product is not as great as the cost of producing the first. *Paper Converting Mach. Co. v. Magna-Graphics Corp.*, 745 F.2d 11, 22, 223 U.S.P.Q. (BNA) 591, 599 (Fed. Cir. 1984). This approach separates the costs the patent owner historically incurred into fixed and variable components. Generally, the patent owner would incur the variable costs in producing additional volume but, unless new investment is required, would not incur those costs which are fixed and already paid. Incremental costs are subtracted from incremental revenue in order to determine lost profits. The incremental income method for determining the cost of making the infringer's sales has been widely used in determining patent infringement damages. Detailed accounting issues are often involved in this determination. *See, e.g., Polaroid, supra* (discussion of whether research and development, overhead, and certain labor costs were variable or fixed; finding that Polaroid's incremental cost to manufacture the volume of cameras it would have sold without Kodak's infringement is $27.64).

Judge Frank Easterbrook of the Seventh Circuit, sitting by designation, gave the following example in discussing the *Mor-Flo* rule:

> Full compensation is possible only if each infringer pays damages computed by multiplying the total lost profit by each infringer's share of the infringing sales. For example, suppose the patent holder's lost profit (including price erosion) is $10 million and that there are four infringers. Infringer A sold 50,000 units, B sold 100,000 units, C sold 150,000 units, and D sold 200,000 units, for total infringing sales of 500,000 units. A's share of the infringing products is 10%, B's is 20%, C's is 30%, and D's is 40%. At the close of trial, A should be required to pay $1 million, and so on. This

procedure fully compensates the patent holder. It is the mirror image of the damages model used in antitrust cases, appropriate for the same reasons: It compensates victims fully while giving each offender the correct incentives. Suppose A, B, C, and D form a cartel, increasing the price of widgets. When customer X files suit, A will not be permitted to defend by saying that, had it not joined the cartel, B, C, and D still would have raised prices, so that X still would have paid too much. A, as a member of the cartel, is liable for the whole overcharge — but any given customer recovers only for its actual purchases, so a member of the cartel is liable only on the units it sold. In the patent case each infringer is liable for the whole price erosion, but only in proportion to the units it actually sold.

In re Mahurkar Patent Litig., 831 F. Supp. 1354, 1392, 28 U.S.P.Q.2d 1801 (N.D. Ill. 1993).

4. *Lack of Symmetry?* Patent doctrine allows the aggrieved patentee to be quite creative about what would have happened in the absence of the infringement. This is necessary, it is thought, to effectuate the law's policy of fully compensating the patentee. For the sake of symmetry, however, it might be supposed that the infringer should have a chance to argue what he or she might have done in the absence of infringement. Obviously, if the defendant is not permitted to present evidence of this ilk, the analysis is quite skewed: only the patentee's "best case" scenario is presented, rather than a more realistic scenario. In some ways, this oversight resembles the simplistic analysis of rules in terms of straightforward "first order" incentives and effects. This analysis fails to take account of the "second order" responses to the rules. Consider for example analysis of the effects of a higher tax rate in a certain jurisdiction. The first order effect is higher revenue; in the short run, we can expect revenue to stay pretty much the same, so the higher rate yields more tax revenues. Over time, however, firms may move out of the jurisdiction, or shift activities to low-tax industries, or even spend more on evasion.

The trend in patent law damages since the 1980s has been to allow patentees more and more latitude to describe the second order effects of the infringer's entry and presence in the market for the patented good. Each step in the liberalization of patent damages has been carried out under the banner of full compensation: (1) liberal market substitution analysis (i.e., easy proof of "no non-infringing substitutes"; (2) evidence of price erosion; (3) market share analysis under *State Industries, supra*; and (4) lost profits for unpatented goods, both (a) components ("convoyed sales," subject to the "complete market value" rule), and (b) lost profits for unpatented substitutes sold by the patentee (à la *Rite-Hite*). Almost all of these damages require the patentee to spin a narrative entitled "what life would have been like without the infringer."

By the same token, it would seem self-evident that courts should invite evidence of second order responses *by infringers* under the (increasingly ornate) hypothetical scenarios being spun by patentees. That is, we would want to know what a reasonable infringer would have done in response to price hikes by the patentee, significant sales of unpatented components and unpatented substitutes, and the like.

Take the lost profits scenario in a *Kelley*-type case, for example. Assume that the unpatented substitute was not the subject of a separate patent as it was in fact in that case, but instead was a public domain substitute for the patented good. Isn't it reasonable to assume that the infringers, once excluded from the market for patented embodiments, would quickly shift production to the same public domain product being sold by the patentee? Likewise, even under the facts of *Kelley*, we might ask whether the products not covered by the patent in suit, but separately patented by the patentee, could have been imitated without infringing the separate patents. This seems odd, of course, but it is logically compelled by the Federal Circuit's reasoning in the case.

Have courts in fact invited evidence of how the infringer would likely have responded to being excluded from the market for the patented item? Unfortunately, no. Consider the following excerpt from *Zygo Corp. v. Wyko Corp.*, 79 F.3d 1563, 1571, 38 U.S.P.Q.2d 1281 (Fed. Cir. 1996):

> The central damages issue on appeal is whether the [trial] court erred in concluding that Wyko's SIRIS interferometer was not an acceptable non-infringing alternative to the Zygo interferometers. The record indicates that Wyko stopped marketing the SIRIS interferometer when it began marketing the [infringing] Wyko 6000 interferometer. Wyko argues that the award of lost profits was error on the theory that they would have continued making and selling the SIRIS had they not made and sold the Wyko 6000 interferometers.
>
> It is axiomatic, however, that if a device is not available for purchase, a defendant cannot argue that the device is an acceptable noninfringing alternative for the purposes of avoiding a lost profits award. A lost profits award reflects the realities of sales actually lost, not the possibilities of a hypothetical market which the infringer might have created. Thus, whether or not the SIRIS was an acceptable noninfringing alternative is relevant only for the period of time that the SIRIS interferometer was being marketed by Wyko.

This reasoning, if it continues, does not bode well for symmetry in patent damages doctrine.

3. THE "WHOLE MARKET" RULE AND "TAG-ALONG SALES"

In an omitted passage in *State Industries*, *supra*, the court states:

> The [district] court based the award on the profit margin of the heater as a unit in accord with the entire market value rule, which permits recovery of damages based on the value of the entire apparatus containing several features, where the patent related feature is the basis for customer demand.

See *TWM* [*v. Dura Corp.*], 789 F.2d [895 (Fed. Cir. 1986)] at 901, 229 U.S.P.Q. [(BNA) 525] at 528. In the face of the district court's finding to the contrary, Mor-Flo now argues that foam insulation was not the basis for consumer demand and several unidentified nonpatented components were key. But it did not identify or present evidence of the value of these non-patented components. In any event, no components can be used separately, except as spare and repair parts for which State does not claim damages. See *Kori Corp. v. Wilco Marsh Buggies & Draglines, Inc.*, 761 F.2d 649, 656, 225 U.S.P.Q. 985, 989 (Fed. Cir. 1985) (the entire market rule is properly applied when the nonpatented devices cannot be sold without the patented feature). There is no merit to this argument and we leave undisturbed the district court's adoption of the entire market rule.

See also TWM Mfg. Co. v. Dura Corp., 789 F.2d 895, 901, 229 U.S.P.Q. (BNA) 525 (Fed. Cir. 1986) ("The entire market value rule allows for the recovery of damages based on the value of an entire apparatus containing several features, when the feature patented constitutes the basis for customer demand."); *King Instrument Corp. v. Otari Corp.*, 767 F.2d 853, 865, 226 U.S.P.Q. (BNA) 402, 410-11 (Fed. Cir. 1985), *cert. denied*, 475 U.S. 1016, 106 S. Ct. 1197 (1986); *Paper Converting Mach. Co. v. Magna-Graphics Corp.*, 745 F.2d 11, 22, 223 U.S.P.Q. (BNA) 591, 599 (Fed. Cir. 1984); *Kori Corp. v. Wilco Marsh Buggies & Draglines, Inc.*, 761 F.2d 649, 656, 225 U.S.P.Q. (BNA) 985, 989 (Fed. Cir.), *cert. denied*, 474 U.S. 902, 106 S. Ct. 230 (1985) (it is the "'financial and marketing dependence on the patented item under standard marketing procedures' which determines whether the non-patented features of a machine should be included in calculating compensation for infringement."); *Tektronix, Inc. v. United States*, 552 F.2d 343, 351 193 U.S.P.Q. (BNA) 385, 393 (1977), *cert. denied*, 439 U.S. 1048 (1978) ("in establishing lost profits, the deciding factor ... is whether '[n]ormally the patentee (or its licensee) can anticipate sale of such unpatented components as well as of the patented' ones."); *Hughes Tool Co. v. G.W. Murphy Indus.*, 491 F.2d 923, 928, 180 U.S.P.Q. (BNA) 353, 356 (5th Cir. 1973) (relevant inquiry is what patentee would have made, which might include lost sales of unpatented but related items; "Whether or not the article would have some commercial usefulness without the patented feature is irrelevant where it is clear the patentee would have made the sale of the article had not the defendant infringed.").

Compare this with the following statement from *Seymour v. McCormick*, 57 U.S. (16 How.) 480, 490-91 (1853):

> If the measure of damages be the same whether a patent be for an entire machine or for some improvement in some part of it, then it follows that each one who has patented an improvement in any portion of a steam engine or other complex machines may recover the whole profits arising from the skill, labor, material, and capital employed in making the whole machine,

and the unfortunate mechanic may be compelled to pay treble his whole profits to each of a dozen or more several inventors of some small improvement in the engine he has built. By this doctrine even the smallest part is made equal to the whole, and "actual damages" to the plaintiff may be converted into an unlimited series of penalties on the defendant.

We think, therefore, that it is a very grave error to instruct a jury "that as to the measure of damages the same rule is to govern, whether the patent covers an entire machine or an improvement on a machine."

It appears, from the evidence in this case, that McCormick sold licenses to use his original patent of 1834 for twenty dollars each. He sold licenses to the defendants to make and vend machines containing all his improvements to any extent for thirty dollars for each machine, or at an average of ten dollars for each of his three patents. The defendants made and sold many hundred machines, and paid that price and no more. They refused to pay for the last three hundred machines under a belief that the plaintiff was not the original inventor of this last improvement, whereby a seat for the raker was provided on the machine, so that he could ride, and not be compelled to walk as before. Beyond the refusal to pay the usual license price, the plaintiff showed no actual damage. The jury gave a verdict for nearly double the amount demanded for the use of three several patents, in a suit where the defendant was charged with violating one only, and that for an improvement of small importance when compared with the whole machine. This enormous and ruinous verdict is but a corollary or necessary consequence from the instructions given in that portion of the charge of the court on which we have been commenting, and of the doctrines therein asserted, and to which this court cannot give their assent or concurrence.

Is it possible for the "improvement" spoken of in *McCormick* to be a separate "component" from the point of view of the "entire market value" rule discussed in *State Industries*? Is there any room in the *State Industries* approach for a consideration of the point raised by the Supreme Court — that an infringer may have to pay multiple damages, all based on the "entire market value" of the item, to each of a series of patentees who hold patents on a component of the item? Is the Supreme Court here too solicitous of the infringer?

Note that, as in the context of reasonable royalty determinations, sales of "tag-along" items can be included in the patentee's lost profit award. One court has held that sales of unpatented accessories, even though not made at the same time as the sale of the patented item, can be included in the patentee's lost profits. *See Kalman v. Berlin Corp.*, 9 U.S.P.Q.2d (BNA) 1191, 1197 (D. Mass. 1988) (lost profits on patented filter device should include lost sales on screens and accessories). In another case — starting at first glance — the Federal Circuit held the patentee entitled to lost profits damages even though it did not sell a product including the patented feature. *See Scripto-Tokai Corp. v. Gillette Co.*, 22 U.S.P.Q.2d (BNA) 1678 (Fed. Cir. 1992).

NOTES

1. *"Lost Growth."* The court in *Lam, Inc. v. Johns-Manville Corp.*, 718 F.2d 1056, 1065, 219 U.S.P.Q. (BNA) 670, 675 (Fed. Cir. 1983), approved an award of the patent owner's lost profits on other, unpatented products because the burden of the infringement suit had interfered with the patent owner's ability to grow — a new branch on the speculative tree of damages. Cases such as *Lam* illustrate the high damage awards that may be obtained under the rubric of lost profits. In that case, the Federal Circuit found that Lam would have made a profit of $89,309 on the infringing products, at the existing price, but the final judgment approved by the Federal Circuit was $1,639,824, including treble damages and attorney's fees. These issues are discussed in the next section.

2. *Sufficient Evidence Required.* To obtain lost profit damages for tag-along items, sufficient evidence is required to show that the asserted sales really do tend to "tag along." Consider this statement from *Kaufman Co. v. Lantech, Inc.*, 926 F.2d 1136, 17 U.S.P.Q.2d 1828 (Fed. Cir. 1991):

> The district court awarded Lantech lost profits on spare parts that are typically concomitant with the sale of a patented film-driven prestretch machine. This award is not at issue in this appeal. Lantech does assert that the district court clearly erred by not awarding profits from lost plastic wrap sales. The trial court decided that the award would be speculative because Lantech did not present any evidence of profits gained from plastic wrap sales during the period of infringement.
>
> In determining whether a patentee should be awarded lost profits on unpatented accessory sales, the deciding factor is whether the patentee could normally anticipate the sale of unpatented items as well as the patented ones. There must be a reasonable probability that the patentee would have made the sale of the plastic wrap had the defendant not made the infringing sale. The *Panduit* test is applicable to this issue.
>
> Lantech did not present sufficient evidence to show that plastic film sales typically accompany the sale of a plastic stretch wrapping machine. Therefore, Lantech did not prove that there was a demand for Lantech's accessories. Furthermore, the district court found that Lantech provided no data concerning the amount of film sold to its customers who did purchase the patented machine. Therefore, Lantech failed to show the amount of profit the patentee would have made if the patentee had made the infringing sales. Consequently, Lantech failed to establish the first and fourth components of the *Panduit* test. The finding of the district court was not clearly erroneous.

926 F.2d at 1143. *See also Paper Converting Mach. Co. v. Magna-Graphics Corp.*, 745 F.2d 11, 23, 223 U.S.P.Q. (BNA) 591, 599 (Fed. Cir. 1984); *Gyromat Corp. v. Champion Spark Plug Co.*, 735 F.2d 549, 554, 222 U.S.P.Q. (BNA) 4, 7 (Fed. Cir. 1984).

D. WILLFUL INFRINGEMENT AND ATTORNEY FEES

Patent Act § 284 says simply: "[T]he court may award increased damages up to three times the amount found or assessed." This power is reserved for cases of so-called willful infringement. The following excerpt from *Polaroid Corp v. Eastman Kodak Co.* summarizes the law on this topic. Note the emphasis throughout on attorney opinion letters as a determining factor. And keep in mind that if the damages had been trebled in this case, they would have totalled almost $2.7 *billion*.

POLAROID CORP. v. EASTMAN KODAK CO.

16 U.S.P.Q.2d (BNA) 1481 (D. Mass. 1990), *modified*,
17 U.S.P.Q.2d (BNA) 1711 (D. Mass. 1991)

VIII. *Willfulness*

The willfulness inquiry is, by necessity, a fact-sensitive one. Conduct clearly evidencing good faith and reasonableness in one context may fall far short in another; identical factors may be assigned substantially different weight depending on the totality of the circumstances. *Radio Steel & Mfg. Co. v. MTD Products, Inc.*, 788 F.2d 1554, 1559 [229 U.S.P.Q. (BNA) 431] (Fed. Cir. 1986). One important factor courts consider is whether the infringer timely obtained, and took into account, the opinion of qualified patent counsel before taking the actions eventually found infringing. *Rite-Hite Corp. v. Kelley Co.*, 819 F.2d 1120, 1125 [2 U.S.P.Q.2d 1915] (Fed. Cir. 1987). Simply obtaining an opinion of counsel, however, will not insulate the infringer. Reliance on counsel's opinion must be reasonable in the circumstances.

In order to recover punitive damages, the patentee shoulders a considerable burden. It must prove willful infringement by clear and convincing evidence. *E.I. DuPont de Nemours & Co. v. Phillips Petroleum Co.*, 849 F.2d 1430, 1439-40 [7 U.S.P.Q.2d (BNA) 1129] (Fed. Cir.), *cert. denied*, 109 S. Ct. 542 (1988). Ordinary patent suits can be hard-fought and involve close or novel questions about which reasonable minds, in good faith, may disagree. What distinguishes willfulness is evidence that the infringer deliberately disregarded the patent or flagrantly disregarded the patent laws and had no reasonable basis for believing it had the right to act as it did. *Stickle v. Heublein, Inc.*, 716 F.2d 1550, 1556 [219 U.S.P.Q. 377] (Fed. Cir. 1983).

The theme for Polaroid's willfulness charge is based on a single assertion. According to Polaroid, no skilled attorney would have advised Kodak that the patents in suit were invalid or not infringed by Kodak's instant film and cameras. In its turn, Kodak states that, as it developed its integral instant photography system, it repeatedly obtained validity and infringement opinions from Francis T. Carr, a leading national expert in patent clearance and unabashedly praised by Polaroid's counsel throughout the damages portion of the trial. Since Mr. Carr's advice to Kodak was so at odds with the advice Polaroid contends any skilled attorney would have rendered, Polaroid asks the Court to believe that Kodak somehow either manipulated Mr. Carr, or the information Carr received, in order to reach a result desired by Kodak, namely, various opinions of counsel that ratified and masked Kodak's willful infringement of Polaroid's patents. That dog will not hunt. Polaroid has failed to produce a single shred of evidence that supports this claim, as the following review of the record demonstrates.

Findings of Fact

Kodak retained Mr. Carr and his firm, Kenyon & Kenyon, at the inception of its instant integral photography program, seven years before producing its first commercial product. During the lengthy and detailed patent clearance process he performed for Kodak, Mr. Carr considered over 250 Polaroid and non-Polaroid patents and rendered 67 written and countless oral opinions on both the film and camera patents. [An example of the court's detailed analysis of some of these opinions follows.]

Probe though it did at trial, Polaroid could uncover no irregularities in Kodak's actions in obtaining Mr. Carr's opinion on [the] '821 [patent], or in Mr. Carr's actions in formulating the advice he gave Kodak. Mr. Carr compared '821 to the prior art, reviewed the file wrapper and prosecution history, discussed the Kodak technology with Kodak engineers, and gave his considered advice, well before Kodak began manufacturing the film unit. That advice simply turned out to be wrong.

The Totality of the Circumstances

Throughout the damages phase of the trial, Polaroid's counsel and Professor [Robert] Adelman [Polaroid's expert] praised Mr. Carr, acknowledged his pre-eminence and expertise in the field of patent clearance, and never questioned his good faith in rendering the opinions and advice he gave Kodak over the years. Throughout Professor Adelman's testimony, however, two different themes have emerged. First, Professor Adelman stated, repeatedly and without qualification as to each of the patents in suit, that any "skilled attorney" would have recognized that the Polaroid patents were valid and that Kodak's products infringed. Second, Polaroid suggests that Mr. Carr's opinions were flawed because Kodak simply used him to ratify their knowing and willful infringement. The record clearly contradicts the first claim, as it shows a patent clearance process that could serve as a model for what the law requires. On the second claim, Polaroid has produced not a shred of evidence. The willfulness claim therefore fails.

The legal standard is clear. "When a potential infringer has actual notice of another's patent rights, he has an affirmative duty to exercise due care to determine whether or not he is infringing ... Such affirmative duty includes, inter alia, the duty to seek and obtain competent legal advice from counsel before the initiation of any possible infringing activity...." *Underwater Devices, Inc. v. Morrison-Knudsen Co.*, 717 F.2d 1380, 1389-90 [219 U.S.P.Q. (BNA) 569]

(Fed. Cir. 1983) (emphasis omitted). The Federal Circuit has recognized that opinions of counsel can be manipulated and concluded that there can be "no per se rule that an opinion letter from patent counsel will necessarily preclude a finding of willful infringement, ... nor is there a per se rule that the lack of such a letter necessarily requires a finding of willfulness." *Rite-Hite Corp. v. Kelley Co., Inc.*, 819 F.2d 1120, 1125 [2 U.S.P.Q.2d (BNA) 1915] (Fed. Cir. 1987).

Not all opinions of counsel are created equal, certainly, and reliance on the opinion must be reasonable in the circumstances. Thus, in *Underwater Devices, Inc.*, above, the Court determined that the infringer was not justified in relying on the opinion of in-house counsel when counsel did not "take the steps normally considered necessary and proper in preparing an opinion," such as reviewing the file history of the patent, and the opinion itself contained "only bald, conclusory and unsupported remarks regarding validity and infringement." 717 F.2d at 1390. Similarly, in *Bott v. Four Star Corp.*, 807 F.2d 1567, 1572 [1 U.S.P.Q.2d 1210] (Fed. Cir. 1986), the Court found willfulness when the defendant had a long history of ignoring plaintiff's patents and counsel's oral opinion was entirely conclusory. In *Radio Steel & Mfg. Co. v. MTD Products, Inc.*, 788 F.2d 1554, 1559 [229 U.S.P.Q. 431] (Fed. Cir. 1986), however, the Court found no willful infringement in the totality of the circumstances even though patent counsel did not review the file wrapper or prior art before advising the defendant, orally, that the patent was invalid.

A defendant does not escape liability simply by obtaining the opinion of patent counsel. Courts have found willfulness when the infringer ignored advice of counsel and did not seek an updated opinion, *Central Soya Co. v. George A. Hormel & Co.*, 723 F.2d 1573, 1577 [220 U.S.P.Q. (BNA) 490] (Fed. Cir. 1983), or when, inter alia, an opinion letter, conclusory in nature, was provided just two days before the defendant issued its first invoice for the infringing device. *Dickey-John Corp. v. International Tapetronics Corp.*, 710 F.2d 329, 332-33 [219 U.S.P.Q. (BNA) 402] (7th Cir. 1983). In the totality of the circumstances surrounding the infringement in *Datascope Corp.*, 879 F.2d at 828, the Court found defendant's reliance on counsel's conclusory opinion unreasonable when the opinion did not address the validity of plaintiff's patents or the doctrine of equivalents, and counsel did not consult the prosecution history of the patent.

The uncontroverted facts demonstrate that Kodak consulted Mr. Carr eagerly and often as it developed its instant integral photography system. Mr. Carr examined Kodak's products, sometimes even requesting additional tests in order to understand how the technology worked, and carefully studied any related Polaroid patents. The patent clearance process involved review of the file wrapper, the prosecution history, and the prior art. Of the ten patents and thirty-four different claims eventually considered by Judge Zobel [in the district court infringement phase of this case], seven patents were found valid and claims infringed. Altogether, Mr. Carr reviewed over 250 Polaroid and non-Polaroid patents (containing literally hundreds of claims) and rendered countless oral and 67 written opinions on the entire range of products Kodak developed as part of its instant photography program. In the totality of these circumstances, Mr. Carr's advice simply turned out to be incorrect concerning the relatively few patents eventually found infringed.

Polaroid would have the Court believe that Mr. Carr's advice was mistaken on these patents because Kodak manipulated the information he received in order to have a handy file of opinions which would protect the company from later charges of willful infringement. Nothing in the record supports this claim. This is hardly the case of "damn the torpedoes, full speed ahead," where the infringer's decisions were firmly settled before consulting patent counsel. *H.B. Fuller Co. v. National Starch & Chem. Corp.*, 689 F. Supp. 923, 952 n.20 [7 U.S.P.Q.2d (BNA) 1753] (D. Minn. 1988), nor was Kodak facing enormous "market pressure and urgency" that may have made reliance on counsel's inadequate opinion unreasonable. *Datascope Corp.*, 879 F.2d at 828. Mr. Carr monitored the field for years, had access to Kodak records, reports, and personnel, and was placed under no financial constraints by Kodak. His opinions, "although later shown to be incorrect, contained significant, scientifically based objective factors to justify [defendant's] conclusion of no infringement." *Studiengesellschaft Kohle m.b.H. v. Dart Industries, Inc.*, 862 F.2d 1564, 1579 [9 U.S.P.Q.2d (BNA) 1273] (Fed. Cir. 1988) (emphasis deleted).

The theme is put succinctly in *Stickle*, 716 F.2d at 1560 n. 7:

> Counterbalancing this consideration is that one who legitimately challenges the validity of a patent should not be overly penalized. Thus, a tension arises between these competing interests.

[Conclusion: no willful infringement.]

NOTES

1. Related Cases. In *TWM Mfg. Co. v. Dura Corp.*, 789 F.2d 895, 229 U.S.P.Q. (BNA) 525 (Fed. Cir. 1986), the court commented on the relation between "bad faith" and willful infringement.

> Dura concedes that the district court's finding of willful infringement is the law of the case. Dura contends, however, that absence of a finding of its "bad faith" precludes an award of enhanced damages for that willful infringement.
>
> This court reviews an award of enhanced damages under an abuse of discretion standard and has repeatedly affirmed enhanced awards based on findings of willful infringement. See cases cited in *S.C. Johnson & Son, Inc. v. Carter-Wallace, Inc.*, 781 F.2d 198, 200, 228 U.S.P.Q. 367, 368 (Fed. Cir. 1986). Dura cites no law requiring a finding of "bad faith" before awarding increased damages for willful infringement. Nor has Dura shown

an abuse of discretion in the district court's response to Dura's "bad faith" arguments after the remand. The treble damage award must be affirmed.

Datascope Corp. v. SMEC, Inc., 879 F.2d 820, 823, 828-29, 11 U.S.P.Q.2d (BNA) 1321 (Fed. Cir. 1989), like *Polaroid* and many other cases on willfulness, centered around the effect of an attorney opinion letter:

> The district court found SMEC's infringement nonwillful. It credited SMEC's obtaining of an opinion of counsel [concerning validity and infringement] of Datascope patents "at a time when Schiff was still attempting to develop his noninfringing prewrapped prototype," and concluded that "an honest doubt existed as to the validity and infringement of Datascope's patents." It particularly noted that a panel of this court, "in affirming the judgment of liability was not unanimous." Based on its finding of nonwillfulness, the district court denied increased damages under 35 U.S.C. § 284 and attorney fees under 35 U.S.C. § 285.
>
> Datascope says the court's finding of good faith is clearly erroneous and "based upon a misconception of governing law." We agree.
>
> In analyzing the "totality of the circumstances," the district court pointed to the opinion of counsel SMEC sought, saying that opinion "concern[ed] the validity and possible infringements of patents held by Datascope." That was a clearly erroneous evaluation by the district court. That opinion said nothing whatever about the validity of the '339 patent or any Datascope patent, and the opinion's reference to infringement is not only conclusory, but ignores entirely the question of infringement under the doctrine of equivalents. Further, an opinion on equivalents in this case would have been impossible, SMEC's attorneys having never ordered, let alone consulted, the '339's prosecution history before rendering their opinion.
>
> Our review of the record convinces us that the district court seriously underestimated Schiff's skepticism regarding the advice of counsel and similarly underestimated the court's own findings about the market pressure and urgency faced by SMEC.
>
> The district court's reference to this court's 2-1 decision affirming the judgment of liability was inappropriate in this case. The dissent was ... based on the view that infringement under the doctrine of equivalents was precluded by prosecution history estoppel. If SMEC had relied on or even consulted the prosecution history during the period relevant to consideration of willfulness reference to estoppel in the dissent might have relevance. In this case SMEC did not consult the prosecution history. [Reversed and remanded for findings of willful damages under § 284 and attorney fees under § 285.]

2. *Punitive Damages/Cautionary Effect.* Clearly no infringer can ignore the possibility of willful infringement damages. Assuming a "close call" on the decision to introduce a possibly infringing product, this may be the decisive element in forcing an infringer to abandon its plans. Of course, the degree of extra caution it brings forth will depend mightily on the infringer's assessment of (1) the probability and (2) the likely amount of increased damages for willful infringement. Note that in other contexts, commentators have argued that supra-compensatory damages can bring with them excessive incentives to litigate. *See, e.g.*, BREIT & ELZINGA, ANTITRUST PENALTY REFORM: AN ECONOMIC ANALYSIS (1986). *Cf.* Cooter & Rubinfeld, *Economic Analysis of Legal Disputes and Their Resolution*, 27 J. ECON. LIT. 1067, 1081 (1989) (summarizing empirical work regarding effect of increasing compensatory damage levels on amount of litigation; in antitrust cases, "where reputational effects are important, and where the parties tend to be pessimistic, ... treble damages lead to a decrease in the proportion of cases resolved by trial and an increase in the number of settlements. ").

3. *Designing Around.* From *Ziggity Sys. v. Val Watering Sys.*, 769 F. Supp. 752, 775 (E.D. Pa. 1990):

> Based on the totality of the circumstances, I find that defendants acted in good faith in attempting to design around the patents-in-suit and had a reasonable basis for believing that their new trigger pins were flat and, thus, not infringing the patents-in-suit. Consequently, I further find that defendants' infringement of the patents-in-suit was not willful.

ATTORNEY FEES

Section 285 of the patent statute provides: "The court in exceptional cases may award reasonable attorney fees to the prevailing party."

MATHIS v. SPEARS

857 F.2d 749, 8 U.S.P.Q.2d (BNA) 1551 (Fed. Cir. 1988)

Appeals and cross-appeals from a judgment of the United States District Court for the Central District of California setting the quantum of previously granted awards of attorney fees and expenses. Cleo D. Mathis and Vico Products Manufacturing Co., Inc. (Mathis) challenge the amount and bases of the awards. Bill Spears, Hydrabaths, [etc.] (collectively Hydro) challenge the denial of prejudgment interest on the award. We affirm [except for the prejudgment interest issue] the judgment in all respects and impose a sanction.

BACKGROUND

Mathis dragged the seven appellees into court in three suits, each filed against a different grouping of the appellees and each charging infringement of three United States utility patents, Nos. 3,890,655 ('655), 3,890,656 ('656), and 3,946,449 ('449), all entitled "Whirlpool Jet For Bathtubs," and Design Patent No. 244,462, entitled "Whirlpool Jet Nozzle For Bathtubs and the Like." The district court consolidated the actions.

During discovery, Hydro sought all Mathis documents showing sales of the claimed jets before November 24, 1975, the filing date of the design patent application. Mathis produced only nine invoices, none showing any invalidating activity. Obtaining, over Mathis' objection, a court order for access to Mathis' files, Hydro discovered 295 undisclosed invoices for jet sales predating November 24, 1975; two showing sales of the jet claimed in the design patent more than one year before its filing date; three showing sales of jets more than one year before the filing date of the '449 application.

With truth thus discovered, Mathis dedicated the design patent (but not the '449 patent) to the public and moved to withdraw it. The district court granted the motion but allowed Hydro to use evidence relating to the design patent to show unenforceability of the utility patents and to establish the case as exceptional under 35 U.S.C. § 285.

Following an eight-day bench trial on patent validity and enforceability, the district court issued an opinion holding that all claims of the three utility patents were invalid under at least one of 35 U.S.C. §§ 102, 103, and 112, and unenforceable for inequitable conduct.

Citing Mathis' inequitable conduct before the Patent and Trademark Office (PTO), its discovery abuses, its continuation of the suits on the utility patents when aware of prior art that "clearly rendered them invalid," and its misleading "simulation" at trial of a prior art device, the district court said Mathis' "course of conduct demonstrates a recklessness with regard to the truth, which justifies an award of attorneys' fees under the 'exceptional case' provision of 35 U.S.C. § 285."

On March 21, 1986, the district court entered judgment. In the face of the irrefutable evidence of invalidity and unenforceability described above, and with not even a seeming semblance of a sense of shame, Mathis appealed.

Quantum of the Award

While Mathis' appeal from the March 21, 1986 judgment was pending in this court, the district court conducted proceedings to establish the quantum of attorney fees and expenses, and, on June 27, 1986, issued detailed findings and conclusions. The court awarded attorney fees totalling $580,183.50 and expenses totalling $83,421.91, with post-judgment interest calculated from March 21, 1986, the date of the judgment by which Hydro became entitled to the fees. [The judge] denied Hydro's request for pre-judgment interest, saying she lacked authority to grant that request.

Mathis appealed the award, challenging each basis as improper and each amount as unreasonable. Hydro cross-appeals the denial of its request for prejudgment interest on the award.

ISSUES

Whether the district court abused its discretion in setting the amount of the award.

Whether the district court erred in denying pre-judgment interest on the award. Whether this consolidated appeal is frivolous.

OPINION

This case illustrates the truism that abuses of the patent system and the judicial process are not limited to infringers. Blatantly misleading the PTO, Mathis obtained four patents it had to know were invalid. Mathis then wasted the resources of the trial and appellate courts and those of seven defendants in a charade in which Mathis attempted to employ the courts as handmaidens to its iniquity.

Quantum of the Award

Confusing (or obfuscating) the purpose of Section 285, Mathis attacks the award as though it is made to Hydro's attorneys.

The purpose of Section 285 is to reimburse a party injured when forced to undergo an "exceptional" case.

In the present case, a wrong has been done. Mathis has severely injured Hydro, having forced it to defend, at monstrous expense, its right freely to compete, subjecting Hydro to a totally unwarranted suit and two unwarranted appeals. Provisions for increased damages under 35 U.S.C. § 284 and attorney fees under 35 U.S.C. § 285 are available as deterrents to blatant, blind, willful infringement of valid patents. The only deterrent to the equally improper bringing of clearly unwarranted suits on obviously invalid or unenforceable patents is Section 285. No award under Section 285 can fully compensate a defendant subjected to bad faith litigation, e.g., for loss of executives' time and missed business opportunities. In determining the compensatory quantum of an award under Section 285 in such an egregious case, therefore, courts should not be, and have not been, limited to ordinary reimbursement of only those amounts paid by the injured party for purely legal services of lawyers, or precluded from ordinary reimbursement of legitimate expenses defendant was unfairly forced to pay. See *Central Soya Co. v. Geo. A. Hormel & Co.*, 723 F.2d 1573, 1578, 220 U.S.P.Q. 490, 493 (Fed. Cir. 1983).

Moreover, when confronted with litigation brought in bad faith, a court's exercise of its inherent power to rectify, at least in part, the injustice done the defendant serves additionally to defend the court and the judicial process against abuse.

We do not, of course, here suggest that all successful defendants are entitled to attorney fees or to attorney fees and expenses. The requirement in Section 285 of establishing an "exceptional case" remains a formidable and adequate barrier to unwarranted awards. Similarly, Section 285's requirement that the fees awarded be "reasonable" is a safeguard against excessive reimbursement. Because of the variety of acts that may render a case "exceptional," we do not hold that all awards under Section 285 may or must include expenses, or expenses of any particular type or amount. The district court's inherent equitable power and informed discretion remain available in determining the level of exceptionality rising out of the offender's particular conduct, and in then determining, in light of that conduct, the compensatory quantum of the award, including the amount of attorney fees, what if any expenses shall be included, and the rate of prejudgment interest, if any, on the award.

Citing *Central Soya*, Mathis says, incredibly, that this court requires that only prevailing patent owners be made whole with an award of all fees and expenses, and that Hydro is not entitled to such an award because it was accused of willful infringement. That argument ignores the language of Section 285, which authorizes an award "to the *prevailing* party" (emphasis added), whether patentee or accused infringer. See S. Rep. No. 1503, 79th Cong., 2d Sess. (1946), reprinted in 1946 U.S. Code Cong. Serv. 1386, 1387 (predecessor to Section 285 "made general so as to enable the court to prevent a gross injustice to an alleged infringer"). That argument also ignores the language in the case Mathis cites. In *Central Soya* this court said the "purpose of § 285 is, in a proper case and in the discretion of the trial judge, to compensate the prevailing party for its monetary outlays in the prosecution or defense of the suit." 723 F.2d at 1578, 220 U.S.P.Q. at 493.

The record reflects, as the court found, Hydro's "complete documentation relating to the amount of fees incurred in connection with the patent issues of this litigation, including invoices, time entries, and summaries detailing the time expended, billing rates, and disbursements incurred," and that "there was no duplication of effort."

[The district court properly considered surveys of average patent fees published by the American Intellectual Property Law Association.]

In *Central Soya* this court affirmed an award of expenses as properly within the scope of Section 285, saying "[w]e interpret attorney fees [under 35 U.S.C. § 285] to include those sums that the prevailing party incurs in the preparation for and performance of legal services related to the suit."

Congress enacted Section 285 to codify in patent cases the "bad faith" equitable exception to the American Rule. Recognizing the good faith/bad faith distinction, Congress expressly limited such awards to "exceptional cases" to discourage conduct which fell within the scope of "exceptional," by requiring the party acting exceptionally to bear the expenses of the opposing party. It would be inconsistent with the intent of § 285 to limit the prevailing party to something less.

Similarly, we conclude in this case that it would be inconsistent with the intent of Section 285 to limit prevailing-party Hydro to something less than the fees and expenses to which it was subjected by Mathis in this "very exceptional" case of "gross injustice."

[The court goes on to award (1) expert witness fees, (2) lodging expenses for Hydro's attorneys, and (3) "overhead" expenses such as salaries for paralegals; it then remands the case for determination of a proper amount for a sanction under Rule 38 of the F.R.C.P., to compensate Hydro for the costs of the frivolous appeal.]

NOTES

1. *Grounds for Granting Attorney Fees.*

Among the types of conduct which can form a basis for finding a case exceptional are willful infringement, inequitable conduct before the P.T.O., misconduct during litigation, vexatious or unjustified litigation, and frivolous suit. *Standard Oil Co. v. American Cyanamid Co.*, 774 F.2d 448, 455, 227 U.S.P.Q. 293, 298 (Fed. Cir. 1985). Such conduct must be supported by clear and convincing evidence. *Reactive Metals [& Alloys Corp. v. ESM, Inc.*, 769 F.2d 1578, 1582, 226 U.S.P.Q. 821, 824 (Fed. Cir. 1985).]

Beckman Instruments, Inc. v. LKB Produkter AB, 892 F.2d 1547, 1551, 13 U.S.P.Q.2d (BNA) 1301 (Fed. Cir. 1989) (affirming trial court's grant of attorney fees for defendant's "vexatious strategy" in litigating the case, which included arguing spurious antitrust counterclaims and other defenses, and violation of an injunction; but ordering reduction in amount from full fees of almost $2,000,000 to "the portion of [the] attorney fees which related to the vexatious litigation strategy and other misconduct.").

E. PATENT MARKING: STATUTORY NOTICE

Patent Act § 287 reads:

Patentees, and persons making or selling any patented article for or under them, may give notice to the public that the same is patented, either by fixing thereon the word "patent" or the abbreviation "pat.," together with the number of the patent, or when, from the character of the article, this can not be done, by fixing to it, or to the package wherein one or more of them is contained, a label containing a like notice. In the event of failure so to mark, no damages shall be recovered by the patentee in any action for infringement, except on proof that the infringer was notified of the infringement and continued to infringe thereafter, in which event damages may be recovered only for infringement occurring after such notice. Filing of an action for infringement shall constitute such notice.

DEVICES FOR MEDICINE, INC. v. BOEHL

822 F.2d 1062, 3 U.S.P.Q.2d 1288 (Fed. Cir. 1987)

Appeal from a judgment of dismissal entered in response to a jury verdict that Devices For Medicine, Inc. (DFM) was entitled to no damages because it failed to give to John Boehl, Cardiovascular Instruments, Inc., and Orlando Regional

Medical Center, Inc. [(BOEHL)] the notice required by 35 U.S.C. § 287. We affirm.

Background

DFM, as exclusive licensee of inventor P.O. Littleford, sued BOEHL for infringement of U.S. Patents No. 4,166,469, 4,243,050, and 4,345,606. The patents disclose and claim apparatus ("introducers") and methods of using the introducers to insert medical devices in the human body. To limit the trial at hand to the sole question of whether DFM was entitled to any damages, BOEHL stipulated that it would not contest infringement or validity.

In a two-day trial, DFM presented its case. BOEHL submitted no evidence and presented no witnesses, but simply moved for a directed verdict and rested when its motion was denied. The jury found that DFM was not entitled to any damages. The district court then entered judgment dismissing the complaint.

Issues

Did the district court abuse its discretion in denying a new trial sought on the basis of error alleged in its instruction on the § 287 notice requirement?

[From footnote:] The jury returned this unanimous verdict:
JURY QUESTION # 1: What monetary amount, if any, do you award to Plaintiff for the infringements by Defendants BOEHL and CII? $0.00 (Answer question 2 without regard to your previous answer). JURY QUESTION # 2: What monetary amount, if any, do you award to Plaintiff for the infringements by [the other defendants in the case]? $0.00.

The district court committed no abuse of discretion in denying DFM's motion for entry of a judgment that the patents were infringed and not invalid, and properly entered an order of dismissal on the jury verdict in this case.

The district court gave this instruction on the section 287 notice requirement:

> Before you make any finding that the plaintiff is entitled to any damages you must first determine [that] the plaintiff's licensees have marked the licensed introducer with the proper patent notice. In the event you find there was a failure to mark a proper patent notice in the licensed introducer by any of the plaintiff's licensees the plaintiff cannot recover damages unless the plaintiff can show that the defendants were notified and were aware that the method was an infringement. Notice is not required on the method claims as to an infringement but must be marked on an appliance.

DFM made no further objection, but argues on appeal that the stipulation of infringement [entered into by the parties] made notice unnecessary, that John Boehl admitted "knowledge of the patents," and that notice is not required when the patent contains method claims, citing *Bandag, Inc. v. Gerrard Tire Co.*, 704 F.2d 1578, 1581, 217 U.S.P.Q. 977, 979 (Fed. Cir. 1983), and *Hanson v. Alpine*

Valley Ski Area, Inc., 718 F.2d 1075, 1083, 219 U.S.P.Q. 679, 685 (Fed. Cir. 1983).

Absent notice, Boehl's "knowledge of the patents" is irrelevant. Section 287 requires "proof that the infringer was notified of the infringement." In *Bandag*, and in *Hanson*, this court specifically noted a distinction between cases in which only method claims are asserted to have been infringed and cases like the present case, where DFM alleged infringement of all its apparatus and method claims.

In sum, the record of the trial makes clear that DFM had a full and fair opportunity to present its case to the jury. In doing so, it failed to carry its burden of convincing the jury that it had performed affirmative acts in compliance with § 287. DFM's licenses did not require its licensees to mark the introducer product and there was no evidence that any product ever bore a patent marking. The claimed method is the use of the product. Having sold the product unmarked, DFM could hardly maintain entitlement to damages for its use by a purchaser uninformed that such use would violate DFM's method patent. Because DFM did not present to the jury an adequate evidentiary basis on which it could have based a contrary verdict, any error in the instruction given, if error there were, was necessarily harmless. As this trial was, trials must be fair, not perfect. The district court did not abuse its discretion in denying the motion for new trial DFM filed on the basis of alleged error in the instruction.

Moreover, DFM simply ignores the rule of law that implies a license to practice its claimed method to anyone who purchases one of its claimed introducers. See *Met-Coil Systems Corp. v. Korners Unlimited, Inc.*, 803 F.2d 684, 231 U.S.P.Q. 474 (Fed. Cir. 1986). It is undisputed that DFM's licensees pay a royalty of $2.25 on each introducer they sell, that all three defendants, immediately on receipt of notice of infringement, ceased purchasing introducers from anyone not licensed by DFM, and that, if the jury had found that any damages were due DFM, and if the judgment were for DFM after a full trial on infringement and validity, the total payable by all three defendants would total $285.75. BOEHL cites that trivial amount as the basis for the stipulation to attempt resolution of the dispute in a trial on the damages issue, a basis far less burdensome to the litigants. [This warrants a sanction under Rule 38 of the F.R.C.P.]

Affirmed.

NOTES

1. *Marking: Strategic Considerations*. In general, if one's product contains a feature that is patented, or that is the subject of a currently pending patent application, it makes sense to so mark the item. This is especially true in the case of the pending patent. To see why, consider the competitor's dilemma when she sees notice of a pending patent. She has actual notice at this point that infringement might result in damages. Yet she has no idea which feature of the product is the subject of the patent application. Nor indeed does she know what kind of patent is being sought — a process patent on the method of making the product, a method-of-use patent or a full blown product patent on one or more features of it. Combined with the possibility of long pendency times under our patent system, this has the potential to create a good deal of doubt in the mind of the competitor. Of course, competitors can always keep a close eye on the publication of European and Japanese patent applications, and on the issuance of patents in those countries. This will often provide some "early warning" regarding the likely content of the U.S. patent application. Note incidentally that this provides yet another argument for switching to the European/Japanese approach of publishing applications: less uncertainty concerning possible infringements.

Another strategic concern is that sometimes notice is *not* desirable. Some practitioners advise their clients to suppress notice in certain cases because they do not consider the benefit of damages worth the cost of notifying competitor's of the patent. Sometimes this is used to plan a "sneak attack" on competitors; once they have invested in plant and equipment, an action is brought seeking an injunction, which after all is the primary threat in many cases, and which of course is available even when no notice is given. Second, there are times when a patent may be relatively easy to invent around. In such cases, it is thought prudent not to direct one's competitors to the specifics of one's invention. The less they know, and the harder it is for them to find out, the better. One would think that a hard-headed competitor would always be on the lookout for patents that will reveal details of the competition's approach; but it is thought by at least some practitioners that this is not always the case.

2. *False Marking*. Because marking a product with notice of a patent can have (indeed, is intended to have) a serious cautionary effect on one's competitors, there may be a temptation to mark when it is not warranted. This is why the Patent Act contains a provision on false marking. It reads as follows:

§ 292. False marking

(a) Whoever, without the consent of the patentee, marks upon, or affixes to, or uses in advertising in connection with anything made, used, or sold by him, the name or any imitation of the name of the patentee, the patent number, or the words "patent," "patentee," or the like, with the intent of counterfeiting or imitating the mark of the patentee, or of deceiving the public and inducing them to believe that the thing was made or sold by or with the consent of the patentee; or Whoever marks upon, or affixes to, or uses in advertising in connection with any unpatented article, the word "patent" or any word or number importing that the same is patented, for the purpose of deceiving the public; or Whoever marks upon, or affixes to, or uses in advertising in connection with any article, the words "patent applied for," "patent pending," or any word importing that an application for patent has been made, when no application for patent has been made, or if made, is not pending, for the purpose of deceiving the public —

Shall be fined not more than $500 for every such offense.

(b) Any person may sue for the penalty, in which event one-half shall go to the person suing and the other to the use of the United States.

In general, the key phrases are "with the intent of" or "for the purpose of" "deceiving the public." *See, e.g., Boyd v. Schildkraut Giftware Corp.*, 936 F.2d 76 (2d Cir. 1991) (evidence that compact manufacturer, which had been instructed to delete reference in labels to patent holder's patent number, misunderstood instructions and accidentally shipped compacts with holder's number supported finding that mismarking was accidental and unintentional and for brief period); *Arcadia Mach. & Tool Inc. v. Sturm, Ruger & Co.*, 786 F.2d 1124 (Fed. Cir. 1986) (label which read that contents of package "may be manufactured under" one or more of listed patents or pending applications was not deceptive in violation of false patent marking statute when box was used for various models).

Courts have consistently held that if the item in question arguably reads on the claims of the asserted patent, it is not "mismarked" under § 292 even if it is later determined that the embodiment in question does not in fact contain the patented features. *See, e.g., United States ex rel. Scharmer v. Carrollton Mfg. Co.*, 377 F. Supp. 218 (D. Ohio 1974) (controlling standard with respect to whether this section prohibiting false marking of patent has been violated is not whether patent incontrovertibly covers product to which patent number has been affixed but whether it "reads" on the products so that a person could hold an honest belief that it applied).

In addition, in a case where false marking was asserted against a company that stated in a letter that the ship it planned to build would embody a certain patent, it was noted that

> Anyone may bring an action under section 292 for falsely marking as "patented" any unpatented "article." Like section 271, section 292 requires that the article mismarked actually exist. In other words, the article must be completed before section 292 will allow a claim to continue.

Lang v. Pacific Marine & Supply Co., 895 F.2d 761, 765, 13 U.S.P.Q.2d 1820 (Fed. Cir. 1990) (denying false marking claim).

One last consideration: one who marks an item falsely is estopped from claiming that the item in question does not infringe the patent whose number it was marked with. This is the doctrine of "mismarker estoppel." *See, e.g., Boyd v. Schildkraut Giftware Corp.*, 936 F.2d 76 (2d Cir. 1991) (act of impermissibly placing patent number on product, if limited in time and quantity, does not bar mismarker from establishing that his product does not use patent, but deliberate mismarking of even limited nature or inadvertent mismarking over prolonged period would justify estoppel).

Chapter 10

REISSUE AND REEXAMINATION

From very early on the Patent Office and the courts recognized that some procedure was necessary to adjust the contents of patents after they had been issued. *See, e.g., Grant v. Raymond*, 31 U.S. (6 Pet.) 218 (1832) (Marshall, C.J.) (affirming reissue "[i]f, by an innocent mistake, the instrument introduced to secure this [patent] privilege fails in its object," i.e., has a defective specification). To this end the reissue procedure slowly coalesced out of a series of doctrines and Patent Office practices. *See generally* 4 D. CHISUM, PATENTS § 15.02 (1978 & Supp. 1992). Today the basic requirements for obtaining a reissue are set out in § 251 of the Patent Act:

§ 251. Reissue of defective patents

Whenever any patent is, through error without any deceptive intention, deemed wholly or partly inoperative or invalid, by reason of a defective specification or drawing, or by reason of the patentee claiming more or less than he had a right to claim in the patent, the Commissioner shall, on the surrender of such patent and the payment of the fee required by law, reissue the patent for the invention disclosed in the original patent, and in accordance with a new and amended application, for the unexpired part of the term of the original patent. No new matter shall be introduced into the application for reissue.

The Commissioner may issue several reissued patents for distinct and separate parts of the thing patented, upon demand of the applicant, and upon payment of the required fee for a reissue for each of such reissued patents.

The provisions of this title relating to applications for patent shall be applicable to applications for reissue of a patent, except that application for reissue may be made and sworn to by the assignee of the entire interest if the application does not seek to enlarge the scope of the claims of the original patent.

No reissued patent shall be granted enlarging the scope of the claims of the original patent unless applied for within two years from the grant of the original patent.

Reissue can be a very useful tool in preparing a patent for litigation. Reissue permits a patentee to alter language in patent claims which, with hindsight, might cause problems during litigation. And, should potentially invalidating references be discovered before trial, the reissue proceeding can be used to narrow the claim scope and avoid the references. By the same token, where the accused infringer's product appears to narrowly avoid literal infringement, a broadening reissue may be useful. Intervening rights — discussed below — may come into play in this situation.

Although a host of issues surround the reissue procedure, this chapter touches on only the two most important ones: (1) when a reissue is available, and (2) the rights of third parties who commence activities after the issuance of a patent but before reissue of the same patent — i.e., the question of "intervening rights."

A. CONDITIONS FOR REISSUE

MENTOR CORP. v. COLOPLAST INC.

998 F.2d 992, 27 U.S.P.Q.2d 1521 (Fed. Cir. 1993)

LOURIE, J.

Following a March 1992 jury verdict, judgment was entered against Coloplast, Inc., holding, inter alia, that all the original and reissued claims of Mentor Corporation's U.S. Patent Re. 33,206 were willfully infringed [and] not invalid. Coloplast appeals on the issues of validity and infringement.

In July 1989, Mentor sued Coloplast for infringement of U.S. Patent 4,475,910, entitled "Male Condom Catheter Having Adhesive on Rolled Portion." While the lawsuit was pending, it was reissued as the '206 patent.

The claimed invention relates to a condom catheter which is used on male patients suffering from incontinence. Claims 1-4 of the '206 patent recite a catheter having a pressure sensitive adhesive on a non-stick (release) layer located on the outer surface of a condom sheath prior to it being rolled up, such that on rolling the sheath outwardly, the adhesive on the outer surface comes into contact with and sticks to the inner surface. When unrolled, the adhesive which was initially applied to the release layer on the outer surface is thereby transferred to the inner surface.

Coloplast argues that claims 6-9 of the reissue patent are invalid because they are not based on "error" within the meaning of 35 U.S.C. Section 251 (1988). Coloplast argues that Mentor deliberately and intentionally amended its claims in response to a prior art rejection and that such conduct is not reissuable error. Thus, it asserts, the [district] court erred as a matter of law [in ruling for Mentor on this issue]. We agree.

Reissue "error" is generally liberally construed, and we have recognized that "[a]n attorney's failure to appreciate the full scope of the invention" is not an uncommon defect in claiming an invention. *In re Wilder*, 736 F.2d 1516, 222 U.S.P.Q. 369 (Fed. Cir. 1984), *cert. denied*, 469 U.S. 1209, 105 S. Ct. 1173, 84 L. Ed. 2d 323 (1985). However, the reissue procedure does not give the patentee "a second opportunity to prosecute de novo his original application."

The deliberate cancellation of a claim of an original application in order to secure a patent cannot ordinarily be said to be an "error" and will in most cases prevent the applicant from obtaining the canceled claim by reissue. The extent to which it may also prevent him from obtaining other claims differing in form or substance from that canceled necessarily depends upon the facts in each case and particularly on the reasons for the cancellation.

If a patentee tries to recapture what he or she previously surrendered in order to obtain allowance of original patent claims, that "deliberate withdrawal or amendment ... cannot be said to involve the inadvertence or mistake contemplated by 35 U.S.C. Section 251, and is not an error of the kind which will justify the granting of a reissue patent which includes the matter withdrawn." "The recapture rule bars the patentee from acquiring, through reissue, claims that are of the same or of broader scope than those claims that were canceled from the original application." *Ball Corp.* [*infra*].

Reissue claims that are broader in certain respects and narrower in others may avoid the effect of the recapture rule. If a reissue claim is broader in a way that does not attempt to reclaim what was surrendered earlier, the recapture rule may not apply. However, in this case, the reissue claims are broader than the original patent claims in a manner directly pertinent to the subject matter surrendered during prosecution. Mentor thus attempted to reclaim what it earlier gave up. Moreover, the added limitations do not narrow the claims in any material respect compared with their broadening.

The limitation in claim 6 that the catheter material be "flexible" did not materially narrow the claims, which already recited that the material be "resilient." Likewise, the limitation that the catheter be rolled outward to form a "single" roll did not materially limit the claims; the catheter can only be rolled and applied from a single end to form a single roll when the other end is connected to a urine collection means. Further, the addition of the words "thereon," referring to the location of the adhesive release layer on the outer surface prior to unrolling, and "only," referring to the adhering of the adhesive to the inner surface after unrolling, did not materially narrow the claims.

Thus, since none of reissue claims 6-9 meets the legal requirements for reissue, the court erred in denying the motion for judgment of invalidity as a matter of law. We therefore reverse that part of the court's judgment.

HEWLETT-PACKARD CO. v. BAUSCH & LOMB INC.

882 F.2d 1556, 11 U.S.P.Q.2d 1750 (Fed. Cir. 1989)

NIES, CIRCUIT JUDGE.

Bausch and Lomb Incorporated (B & L) appeals from a final judgment, in favor of Hewlett-Packard Company (HP), entered by the United States District Court for the Northern District of California in a patent infringement suit. The judgment is based on the district court's holdings that B & L's United States Patent No. Re. 31,684 ('684) is unenforceable and partially invalid. We affirm-in-part, vacate-in-part, and remand.

The court held claims 10-12, which were added during reissue, invalid because B & L filed blatantly inaccurate affidavits to support reissue. Absent the affidavits, the court held, B & L failed to comply with the requirements of the oath specified in 35 U.S.C. § 251 (1982) and 37 C.F.R. § 1.175 (1988).

We affirm the court's holding that claims 10-12, but not claims 1-9, are invalid because the reissue application was defective. [W]e vacate that part of the judgment [finding inequitable conduct] and remand for reconsideration.

ISSUES

Is a failure to include narrower or dependent claims in a patent sufficient in itself to establish error warranting reissue under 35 U.S.C. § 251? Where a reissue patent issues from a defective application, are all claims invalid or are only the claims added or amended during reissue invalid?

BACKGROUND

John Yeiser invented an "X-Y Plotter," described in United States Patent No. 3,761,950 ('950), in which chart paper moves under a marking pen. Yeiser's patent issued in 1973 with nine claims. Following a series of assignments, the Milton Roy Company (MRC) acquired the '950 patent. The invention claimed in that patent was commercialized only briefly. MRC had been out of the plotter business for some time when, in late 1980 or early 1981, HP introduced its first moving-paper X-Y plotter, with great success.

B & L, a competitor of HP, discovered the '950 patent during an investigation of HP's patent protection on its plotter. In 1982, B & L bought the '950 patent from MRC for $30,000, admittedly for the purpose of gaining leverage in negotiations — hoping to obtain a cross license from HP — and possible litigation. The record indicates that B & L was concerned, however, that claim 1, which arguably covers HP's plotter and is the only independent claim asserted, was overly broad. To obtain narrower claims which would incorporate details of the HP plotter specifically, B & L filed a reissue application containing three new claims, 10-12. The original nine claims of the '950 patent were included in the reissue application without substantive change.

The PTO rejected the application, *inter alia*, on the grounds that B & L failed to specify either an error warranting reissue or how the error occurred. B & L successfully overcame the PTO rejections by supplementing the initial declaration with two affidavits signed by the patent agent, Lawrence Fleming, who had prosecuted the original patent. The facts surrounding those affidavits and the effect they had on the reissue will be discussed below in detail in connection with addressing the issues of the validity and enforceability of the '684 patent, which are the central issues of this appeal.

With issuance of the '684 patent imminent, B & L charged HP with infringement. HP countered with a petition for reexamination of claims 1, 2, and 10-12 over certain prior art. The PTO found that HP's petition raised a substantial new question of patentability, but ultimately upheld the validity of all claims. HP then filed a declaratory judgment action in October 1984, asserting invalidity of all claims under 35 U.S.C. §§ 102, 103, 112, and 251 (1982), and later added an allegation of unenforceability for inequitable conduct in B & L's prosecution of the reissue application. B & L counterclaimed, charging HP with infringement of claims 1 and 2, which were original claims, and claims 10-12 added by reissue.

On a summary judgment motion, the district court held claims 10-12, but not claims 1-9, invalid. More specifically, the court found that the oath (declaration) in the application for reissue was defective. B & L contends that, as a matter of law, the oath was not defective. On the other hand, HP urges that, because the oath was defective, the district court should have held original claims 1-9 also invalid.

FACTS CONCERNING THE REISSUE AFFIDAVITS

The facts surrounding the two Fleming affidavits submitted by B & L to support the reissue application are central to the issues of validity and enforceability. Accordingly, those facts must be set forth in detail.

Upon acquisition of the '950 patent, B & L immediately began steps to secure its reissue. The matter was handled by Bernard Bogdon, B & L's in-house counsel, and William Hyer, outside patent counsel. Hyer delegated the task to an associate of his firm, Jonathan Jobe. It was Jobe's first experience with drafting a reissue application.

Working from the '950 patent file and the specifics Hyer gave him on the HP plotter, Jobe drafted the reissue application, adding three dependent claims to Claim 1 to cover specific features of the HP plotter. Jobe drafted the declaration, later signed by B & L's vice president, George More, to state that the '950 patent was "partly or wholly inoperative ... by reason of the patentee claiming less than he had a right to claim in that he had a right to claim [his invention] more specifically," and that the omission of the dependent claims was caused "because of oversight and without deceptive intent on the part of said John O. Yeiser or his attorney." No one had at that time consulted with Lawrence Fleming, the patent agent (by then retired) who had prosecuted the '950 patent.

Although he signed the declaration, More knew nothing about the alleged "error," either personally or based on others' investigations. Indeed, he was told that he was better off not asking any questions. Jobe testified that he included the reference to an "oversight" because "it is required by the statute" and because he could not "imagine any deceptive reason for not including those claims."

Filed in due course, the reissue application was rejected on the ground:

> The declaration is insufficient because it does not specify an error. The addition of narrower claims, by itself, is not an error. Note that there is no allegation that base claim 1 is inoperative or invalid. Why are claims of narrower scope necessary? The declaration is further insufficient because it does not specify how the error arose or occurred. The statement that the alleged errors occurred or arose because of oversight on the part of the

inventor or his attorney does not specify in detail how and why such an oversight occurred. A declaration from the original attorney may be in order.

Following the examiner's rejection, Jobe made his first contact with Fleming, by telephone, informing him generally of the nature of the reissue application and of the PTO rejection and asking how Fleming's alleged "oversight" occurred. In essence, per the district court, Jobe asked Fleming how he could have made the "tremendous blunder" of omitting claims specifically encompassing features of the pinch roller assembly [element of the accused devices]. Fleming attempted to justify his action with the explanation, later confirmed by letter, that he was unable to get much information from [the inventor] Yeiser. [This turned out not be true; thus the inequitable conduct charge against B & L.]

The PTO maintained its rejection of B & L's reissue application despite the first Fleming affidavit, reiterating the same grounds as in its initial rejection. Specifically, the PTO found that the More declaration and the Fleming affidavit failed to specify an error or how, when, and why the alleged error arose. Particularly addressing Fleming's affidavit, the examiner stated:

> The Fleming affidavit states that the contacts and ability to communicate with the inventor by the agent who prepared the application were significantly limited. It is acceptable on this point. It is not acceptable however as to how and by whom the scope of the subject matter claimed was determined and why.

At this point, house counsel Howard Robbins took over prosecution of the reissue. After speaking with Fleming, Robbins drafted the second Fleming affidavit. In that affidavit, Fleming averred that he had been given a "crude model of the invention" to review on only one occasion for about two hours; that the scope of the claims was determined solely by him based on this brief disclosure; that he had no discussions with Yeiser concerning the scope of the claims; and that Yeiser had sold his plotter business and was not focusing on such matters. Robbins' accompanying argument to the PTO reiterated these "facts" and that Fleming's action was "without full cognizance of what was significant in view of the art." The PTO reconsidered the original declaration, together with the two Fleming affidavits, and found them sufficient under 37 C.F.R. § 1.175. Accordingly, the PTO allowed claims 1-12 in reissue patent '684.

VALIDITY
Reissue Claims 10-12 Are Invalid

Even before specific provisions were included in the patent statute for correcting defective patents, Chief Justice Marshall, in *Grant v. Raymond*, 31 U.S. (6 Pet.) 218 (1832), articulated the principle that a defective patent was an inadequate exchange for the patentee's disclosure of an invention and that a new patent should be issued, in appropriate circumstances, which secures to the patentee the benefits which the law intended. The circumstances under which reissue is permissible are now set forth in 35 U.S.C. § 251.

B & L argues that an "error" is present, within the meaning of section 251, if it can be discerned from the patent specification, claims, and prosecution history that the patentee could have included a narrower claim, unless there is evidence that such "omission" was intentional. The omission of narrower claims 10-12, per B & L, also falls within the statutory language that the patentee claimed "less than he had a right to claim." The district court found that the facts in the Fleming affidavits were essential to reissue and that without those facts, which turned out to be "grossly inaccurate," there was no error warranting reissue. Conversely, B & L asserts that More's original declaration established "reissuable error" and that the Fleming affidavits were both unnecessary and wrong only in immaterial details. Our precedent rejects B & L's simplistic interpretation of the reissue statute with respect to what constitutes error under section 251.

As explained in *In re Wilder* [*supra*]:

> There are two distinct statutory requirements that a reissue oath or declaration must satisfy. First, it must state that the patent is defective or partly inoperative or invalid because of defects in the specification or drawing, or because the patentee has claimed more or less than he is entitled to. Second, the applicant must allege that the defective, inoperative, or invalid patent arose through error without deceptive intent. *Id.* at 1518, 222 U.S.P.Q. at 370.

In sum, the statutorily required "error" of section 251 has two parts: (1) error in the patent, and (2) error in conduct.

On the first part, the precedent of this court is that the expression "less than he had a right to claim" generally refers to the scope of a claim. Thus, that provision covers the situation where the claims in the patent are narrower than the prior art would have required the patentee to claim and the patentee seeks broader claims. Conversely, the alternative that the patentee claimed "more ... than he had a right to claim" comes into play where a claim is too broad in scope in view of the prior art or the specification and the patentee seeks narrower claims.

In this case, B & L averred that the inventor claimed "less" than he had a right to claim, which ordinarily would mean that B & L sought broader claims by reissue. But B & L did not seek broader claims; instead, B & L sought to add several dependent claims in hopes that it could assert the patent should independent claim 1 be held invalid. Otherwise, the dependent claims add nothing to the patent's protection against infringements. Any device that infringes new claims 10-12 ipso facto infringes carry-over claim 1, which B & L maintains is valid. Thus, in fact, B & L is not asserting that the claims in the '684 patent are inoperative (i.e., ineffective to protect the invention) by reason of the patentee claiming either too much or too little in scope, but because he included, in a sense, too few claims.

Although neither "more" nor "less" in the sense of scope of the claims, the practice of allowing reissue for the purpose of including narrower claims as a hedge against the possible invalidation of a broad claim has been tacitly approved, at least in dicta, in our precedent. For purposes of this case, we will assume that that practice is in accordance with the remedial purpose of the statute, although B & L clearly did not allege an "error" in the patent which meets the literal language of the statute. We need not decide here whether omission of narrow claims which more specifically cover a broadly claimed invention meets the first prong of the requirement for error, that is, error in the patent, because B & L clearly did not establish the second prong, namely, inadvertent error in conduct. Contrary to B & L's position, a reissue applicant does not make a prima facie case of error in conduct merely by submitting a sworn statement which parrots the statutory language.

The language of the current statute, "error without deceptive intent," replaced, but did not substantively change, the language of the prior statute, section 4916 of the Revised Statutes, 35 U.S.C. § 64 (1946), "error ... by inadvertence, accident, or mistake, and without fraudulent or deceptive intent." The term "error" encompasses "inadvertence, accident or mistake," and those words were eliminated as redundant.

The 1952 revision of the patent laws made no substantive change in the definition of error under section 251. "Error" is interpreted in the same manner as under section 64 of the old law, i.e., accident, inadvertence, or mistake. The statutory provision has been implemented and expanded by the PTO regulations of 37 C.F.R. § 1.175, which require an oath or declaration with respect to both aspects of error under section 251 and further require an explanation as to how and when the error in conduct arose and how and when it was discovered. B & L asserts the theory that, whenever it is apparent that narrower claims could have been obtained, error warranting reissue exists. Under B & L's theory, the dual error inquiry collapses into one because the omission of additional narrow claims not only makes the patent "defective," but also gives rise to an inference of "oversight." Were that theory correct, it is difficult to conceive of any extant patent for which a right of reissue would not exist, a view which this court has unequivocally [sic] and repeatedly rejected. For example, as explained in *In re Weiler*, 790 F.2d 1576, 229 U.S.P.Q. 673 (Fed. Cir. 1986), reissue is not intended to give the patentee simply a second chance to prosecute the patent application:

> The reissue statute was not enacted as a panacea for all patent prosecution problems, nor as a grant to the patentee of a second opportunity to prosecute de novo his original application.

Id. at 1582, 229 U.S.P.Q. at 677. *Weiler* further advises:

[T]he grant of reissues [is not required] on anything and everything mentioned in a disclosure.... [Section] 251 does not authorize a patentee to represent his application. Insight resulting from hindsight on the part of new counsel does not, in every case, establish error.

Id. at 1583 n.4, 229 U.S.P.Q. at 677-78 n.4.

B & L seeks to avoid the admonitions of *Weiler* with an argument, in effect, that an error in conduct must be presumed, absent affirmative evidence that the defect in the patent which is asserted in the reissue application was intentional. For this premise, B & L relies on language in *Ball* [*Corp. v. United States*, 729 F.2d 1429, 221 U.S.P.Q. (BNA) 289 (Fed. Cir. 1984)] stating that reissue was there appropriate because "there is no evidence that the [patentee] intentionally omitted or abandoned the claimed subject matter." 729 F.2d at 1435-36, 221 U.S.P.Q. at 294. In *Ball*, that analysis was apropos; it is not germane here. The patentee in *Ball* was seeking broader claims and an inquiry [into whether similar claims had been abandoned during the original prosecution] was necessary under the facts presented. B & L does not suggest circumstances which would constitute abandonment of the subject matter of the dependent claims while not, at the same time, abandoning the subject matter of the independent claim. Thus, B & L's proposed restriction on reissue where narrower claims are sought is, in truth, no restriction at all.

Returning to the district court's holdings, we discern no legal error in its conclusion that the original More declaration in itself was inadequate to establish error and that the supplemental Fleming affidavits were necessary. The Fleming affidavits were critical to provide the required explanation of what his error was and how and why it occurred.

The evidence of record establishes beyond doubt that Fleming's affidavits, in explaining why narrow claims were not included, were factually untrue. We need not repeat those errors, which are set out above and are substantially undisputed. B & L argues that the misstatements were innocent and should be ignored. Assuming that they were due only to Fleming's faulty memory, the misstatements are not thereby corrected to provide a valid assertion of error. Accordingly, the district court properly held that the factual inaccuracy of the affidavits eliminated the basis for reissue and rendered the '684 patent invalid, albeit only as to claims 10-12. [The "carry-over" claims from the original patent were held valid, and the case remanded for findings on inequitable conduct.]

NOTES

1. *Related Regulations.* The regulations require the applicant to file a reissue oath as follows:

> (3) When it is claimed that such patent is inoperative or invalid "by reason of the patentee claiming more or less than he had the right to claim in the patent," distinctly specifying the excess or insufficiency in the claims.

....

(5) Particularly specifying the errors relied upon, and how they arose or occurred.

37 C.F.R. § 1.175(a)(3), (5) (1991). The term "error" has been interpreted to refer to both errors of fact and errors of law. A typical error of fact would be an incorrect assertion of fact in an application, with a resulting error in a claim. An error of law might concern the nature of claim drafting based upon a good faith application of judicial decisions. These issues are explored further in the cases and notes that follow.

2. "Intent." It is sometimes claimed, based on language in some cases, that the patentee must have intended to claim in the original application the subject matter sought by reissue. *In re Hounsfield*, 699 F.2d 1320, 216 U.S.P.Q. (BNA) 1045 (Fed. Cir. 1983), put this notion to rest with its holding that there is no requirement in the statute that an "intent to claim" be shown in the original application. Nonetheless, the court did state that evidence of an "intent to claim" is one factor to consider in determining whether the reissue application meets the statutory "error without any deceptive intention" test, and/or whether the reissue application claims the "same invention" as that disclosed in the original patent.

3. Defects in Specification or Claims; "New Matter." Generally, as the court in the preceding case points out, reissue is appropriate to correct some "error" in the specification or claims of a patent. When the error concerns the claims, the reissue can either expand the claims (to correct an "underclaiming" error) or contract them (to correct an "overclaiming" error). More on this in subsequent sections of this chapter. But what kind of defect in the specification gives a right to a reissue?

A typical example of remediable error is found in *In re Oda*, 443 F.2d 1200, 170 U.S.P.Q. (BNA) 268 (C.C.P.A. 1970), where an applicant's translation error from the original Japanese patent which substituted "nitrous" instead of "nitric" was held not to involve "new matter" within the meaning of Patent Act § 251.

In *Brenner v. Israel*, 400 F.2d 789, 158 U.S.P.Q. (BNA) 584 (D.C. Cir. 1968), the court had to square the "new matter" prohibition of § 251 with the requirement of § 119 that a "certified copy of the original foreign application" be filed "before the patent is granted," if the applicant wishes to avail himself of the priority date of a prior foreign application. In *Brenner*, the defect the applicant wished to correct via reissue was his omission of the certified copy of the prior foreign filing with his original U.S. application. In the course of its opinion, the court commented on the propriety of seeking reissue in such a case:

> [T]o ascertain the will of Congress in this very narrow context, care must be taken before concluding that it really intended that a trivial clerical error, such as the one which occurred here, should operate forever to deprive a patent applicant of a priority right to which he would otherwise be entitled.

We do not think it did. In fact, Congress placed in the Patent Act another provision, Section 251, which in our view controls the disposition of this case.... The patent issued was partly inoperative (insofar as it did not include the priority right), and the patentee (by failing to file the certified copy, although it did inform the Patent Office of its intention to claim the priority right and the existence of the foreign patent appears on the face of its application) did claim less than he had a right to claim. In any event, the purpose of this section is to allow patentees to correct inadvertent errors without penalty other than the payment of a small fee. This was such a case.

400 F.2d at 790-91. *See also In re Peters*, 723 F.2d 891, 221 U.S.P.Q. (BNA) 952 (Fed. Cir. 1983) (it was error to restrict the appellants to claims containing a particular structural limitation which was not critical to the patentability of the invention and where the overall disclosure reasonably conveyed to one of skill in the art that the inventor had possession of the broad invention at the time the original application was filed).

   4. *History of Reissue Law.* An interesting historical account describes the growth of the reissue as an abusive tool in the mid-nineteenth century, and the eventual elimination of most abuses with the passage of the precursor to today's reissue statute. Dood, *Pursuing the Essence of Inventions: Reissuing Patents in the Nineteenth Century*, 32 TECH. & CULT. 999, 1007 (1991) (graph of reissues sought as percentage of outstanding patents peaks in late 1870s at approximately 1.2% before settling into modern level of less than .1 percent).

SCRIPPS CLINIC & RESEARCH FOUNDATION, INC. v. GENENTECH, INC.

927 F.2d 1565, 18 U.S.P.Q.2d 1896 (Fed. Cir. 1991)

[Scripps'] R'011 patent is a reissue of Patent No. 4,361,509 ("the '509 patent"), granted on November 20, 1982. Genentech challenged the adequacy of the patentee's reason for seeking reissue, stating that this reason was insufficient in terms of 35 U.S.C. § 251. On this ground the district court granted Genentech's motion for partial summary judgment of invalidity of claims 17, 18, 24-29, and 34.

However, the district court erred in its conclusion of law.

The principal error that the inventors sought to cure was the claiming of "less than [they] had a right to claim in the patent" due to the omission of product claims. The '509 patent contained only process and product-by-process claims. In the reissue application inventors Zimmerman and Fulcher declared that they had always viewed the Factor VIII:C product as their invention, pointing out that the '509 specification stated that it was an object of their invention to produce highly purified Factor VIII:C. [From footnote:] Broadened claims by reissue must be applied for within two years of grant of the original patent. This requirement was met.

An error of law is not excluded from the class of error subject to correction in accordance with the reissue statute. Although attorney error is not an open invitation to reissue in every case in which it may appear, see *In re Weiler*, the purpose of the reissue statute is to avoid forfeiture of substantive rights due to error made without intent to deceive.

When the statutory requirements are met, reissuance of the patent is not discretionary with the Commissioner; it is mandatory ("shall"). See *In re Handel*, 312 F.2d 943, 948, 136 U.S.P.Q. 460, 464 (C.C.P.A. 1963) ("the whole purpose of the statute, so far as claims are concerned, is to permit limitations to be added to claims that are too broad or to be taken from claims that are too narrow").

Genentech does not dispute that error was made, and does not challenge the principle of the availability of product claims to the purified Factor VIII:C. Further, Genentech does not assert that the attorneys' initial view of the unavailability of product claims involved any deceptive intention. The district court, holding that there was insufficient reason for reissue, appeared to interpret § 251 as requiring a showing that the error in claiming the product could not have been avoided, in order to be eligible for cure. This is not the framework of the reissue statute.

The law does not require that no competent attorney or alert inventor could have avoided the error sought to be corrected by reissue. Failure of the attorney to claim the invention sufficiently broadly is "one of the most common sources of defects."

> An attorney's failure to appreciate the full scope of the invention is one of the most common sources of defects in patents. The fact that the error could have been discovered at the time of prosecution with a more thorough patentability search or with improved communication between the inventors and the attorney does not, by itself, preclude a patent owner from correcting defects through reissue.

[*In re Wilder*, 736 F.2d 1516, 1519 222 U.S.P.Q. (BNA) 369, 371 (Fed. Cir. 1984), *cert. denied*, 469 U.S. 1209 (1985).]

Subjective intent is not determinative of whether the applicants erred in claiming less than they had a right to claim. "Intent to claim" is not the criterion for reissue, and has been well described as "but judicial shorthand, signifying a means of measuring whether the statutorily required error is present." *In re Weiler*.

On undisputed facts, the inventors established that they had claimed less than they had a right to claim, that they had done so in error, and that there was not deceptive intention. The application for reissue fully complied with the statutory and regulatory requirements. As a matter of law, reissue claims 17, 18, 24-29, and 34 are not invalid on this ground. The grant of partial summary judgment is reversed. On remand, partial summary judgment shall be entered for Scripps on this ground. [The court goes on to remand the case for trial to determine whether the reissue claims were enabled by the specification as amended upon reissue.]

NOTES

1. *What About Weiler?* The court several times cites *In re Weiler*, 790 F.2d 1576, 229 U.S.P.Q. (BNA) 673 (Fed. Cir. 1986). In that case, the Federal Circuit affirmed a Board of Appeals denial of a request for reissue. After the examiner had found that the applicant's initial application actually claimed three distinct inventions, the applicant (Weiler) acquiesced in the restriction requirement and elected one set of claims. Later, upon learning that the elected claims had issued without any divisional applications having been filed, Weiler sought (via new counsel) a reissue of the patent to include subject matter similar to that which had been eliminated from the original application by the restriction requirement. The disallowance of this request was proper, the Federal Circuit said, because

> Weiler's reliance on allegations of the inventors' ignorance of drafting and claiming technique and counsel's ignorance of the invention is unavailing. Those allegations could be frequently made, and, if accepted as establishing error, would require the grant of reissues on anything and everything mentioned in a disclosure. Weiler supplies no facts indicating how the ignorance relied on caused any error as the basis of his failure to claim the subject matter of [the claims sought to be introduced by reissue]. [Section] 251 does not authorize a patentee to re-present his application. Insight resulting from hindsight on the part of new counsel does not, in every case, establish error.

790 F.2d at 1583 n.4.

THE RECAPTURE RULE

An important refinement on the rule that only genuine error justifies a reissue is the recapture rule, actually a species of prosecution history estoppel (see Chapter 8). This prevents an applicant from seeking claims on reissue that were abandoned in the original application.

BALL CORP. v. UNITED STATES

729 F.2d 1429, 221 U.S.P.Q. (BNA) 289 (Fed. Cir. 1984)

This case presents the question whether a patentee is barred by the recapture rule from securing, through reissue, claims to subject matter previously canceled from the original application. Plaintiff-appellee, Ball Corporation (Ball), brought suit against the Government for unauthorized use of the invention claimed in U.S. patent No. Re. 29,296 (July 5, 1977) to Krutsinger, et al. (the Krutsinger patent). The Government moved for summary judgment and Ball filed a cross-motion for summary judgment. Both motions were denied. We conclude that the trial judge properly denied the Government's motion for summary judgment, and we remand the case for trial.

BACKGROUND

The invention covered by the Krutsinger patent relates to a dual slot antenna assembly intended for use on missiles. The antenna consists of two thin cylindrical concentric conductors assembled so that they are radially spaced slightly apart to form a cavity. The cavity may be void or may be filled with a dielectric material. The axial length of the conductors is substantially equal to one-half wavelength at the anticipated operating frequency of the antenna.

In the preferred embodiment of the invention, the connection of the inner and outer cylindrical concentric conductive elements to the source is accomplished by means of a single coaxial transmission feedline. It is this feedline element around which the present controversy revolves. In particular, this case involves the number of feedlines to the outer conductor that may be properly claimed in the Krutsinger reissue patent in light of the prosecution history of the original patent application.

The Canceled Claims

Dependent claims 8 and 9 are the only claims of the original application critical to this appeal. Claim 8 includes the single feedline, whereas claim 9 does not. Claim 8 calls for "at least one" conductive lead to be connected to the edge of one of the conductors. Claim 9 requires that "a plurality of leads" be connected to the edge of one of the conductors at circumferentially spaced intervals.

In the first office action on the original application the examiner rejected claims 1-8 and indicated that claims 9 and 10 should be limited to a plurality of feedlines. The claims were amended and, on July 14, 1972, the examiner made his second rejection final. The examiner again suggested the allowability of the plurality of feedlines claims if presented in independent form. The remaining claims were rejected over the newly cited reference, Cork, U.S. patent No. 2,234,234. The Cork patent discloses a single feedline and is similar in all other material respects to Krutsinger's antenna.

Following the second office action, Ball added limitations to the claims requiring that a plurality of leads be connected to an edge of the outer conductor. These leads were recited to be spaced-apart at intervals substantially equal to one wavelength at the anticipated operating frequency of the antenna. Ball also canceled claim 7 and dependent claim 8 (the canceled claims), of the original application.

Subsequently, Ball decided that it was entitled to claims broad enough to include the single feedline. On July 16, 1975, within the 2-year statutory period for broadened reissue provided in 35 U.S.C. § 251, Ball filed a reissue application. Claims 1-4 of the reissue application comprised the four claims of the original patent. New claims 5-7 were added to the reissue application. Only the new claims, 5-7, directed to the single feedline embodiment, are in issue in this proceeding.

The Alleged Error

In support of its reissue application Ball stated that the original patent was partially inoperative because it claimed less than Ball had a right to claim. Ball identified as error the undue limitation of the claims of the original patent to a plurality of feedlines:

> [T]he unwarranted limited scope of our original patent claims were errors [sic] that arose without any deceptive intention as a result of inadequate and/or ineffective communication with our former patent attorney, ... and/or as a result of an inadequate understanding on our part of the potential effect of recitations in the original patent claim language under United States laws; ....

U.S. patent No. Re. 29,296 issued on July 5, 1977, on the basis of the reissue application.

The Reissue Claims

Ball filed an administrative claim with the United States Navy on January 18, 1978, seeking damages and compensation for unauthorized use of, inter alia, the invention covered by claims 5, 6, and 7 of U.S. patent No. Re. 29,296.

Issues

Two issues are raised in this appeal: (1) whether the error alleged by Ball is sufficient as a matter of law under 35 U.S.C. § 251 (1976) to support reissue; and (2) whether Ball is estopped from securing, through reissue, claims covering the single feedline feature.

The Government contends that Ball's deliberate cancellation of the single feedline claims was not error. That act was taken to avoid a prior art rejection and, in the Government's view, the recapture rule bars Ball from securing similar claims through reissue. The Government also contends that the deliberate nature of Ball's acts estops Ball from securing similar claims through reissue.

The Recapture Rule

The Government asserts that the nature of error that will justify reissue is narrowly circumscribed to ensure that reissue remains the exception and not the rule.

The 1952 revision of the patent laws made no substantive change in the definition of error under section 251. While deliberate cancellation of a claim cannot ordinarily be considered error, the CCPA has repeatedly held that the deliberate cancellation of claims may constitute error, if it occurs without deceptive intent. [T]he CCPA has construed the term error under section 251 broadly.

The Ninth Circuit employed a more rigid standard in *Riley v. Broadway-Hale Stores, Inc.* [217 F.2d 530, 531 n.1, 103 U.S.P.Q. (BNA) 414, 415 n.1 (9th Cir. 1954)] stating: "when the chief element added by reissue has been abandoned while seeking the original patent, the reissue is void." The trial judge sought to determine whether Ball had made a deliberate judgment that claims of substantially the same scope as the new reissue claims would have been unpatentable. The Government, arguing from *Riley*, submits that the trial judge's approach loses sight of the feature given up by a patentee in order to secure the original patent. We decline to adopt the rigid standard applied in *Riley*, in favor of the more liberal approach taken by the CCPA.

[T]he Government argues that we need not reach the issue of claim scope because the sufficiency of error is a threshold issue. While claim scope is no oracle on intent, the Government fails to apprehend its role. Rarely is evidence of the patentee's intent in canceling a claim presented. Thus, the court may draw inferences from changes in claim scope when other reliable evidence of the patentee's intent is not available. Claim scope is not the lodestar of reissue. Rather, the court's reliance on that indicator in the case law appears to be born of practical necessity as the only available reliable evidence.

The Government relies heavily on *Haliczer v. United States*, [356 F.2d 541, 148 U.S.P.Q. (BNA) 565 (Ct. Cl. 1966)]. The Court of Claims in that case held the reissue claims invalid because the patentee sought to acquire through reissue the same claims that had earlier been canceled from the original application. The recapture rule bars the patentee from acquiring, through reissue, claims that are of the same or of broader scope than those claims that were canceled from the original application. On the other hand, the patentee is free to acquire, through reissue, claims that are narrower in scope than the canceled claims. If the reissue claims are narrower than the canceled claims, yet broader than the original patent claims, reissue must be sought within 2 years after grant of the original patent.

Ball's Reissue Claims

The trial judge required the Government to establish that the applicant has made a deliberate decision that the canceled claims are unpatentable. The Government argues that that standard is not correct because it loses sight of the feature that the patentee gave up during prosecution of the original application. We find the Government's argument entirely unpersuasive. The proper focus is on the scope of the claims, not on the individual feature or element purportedly given up during prosecution of the original application. The trial judge quite properly focused on the scope of the claims and we find no error in this respect. He determined that the reissue claims were intermediate in scope — broader than the claims of the original patent yet narrower than the canceled claims.

The alleged inadequacy of Ball's proffered error is not as clear as the Government contends. The error supporting reissue submitted by Ball comports with the statute and regulations.

The canceled claims, claims 7 and 8, define the invention quite broadly. Canceled claim 8 requires feed means including at least one conductive lead. The reissue claims, in contrast, include limitations not present in the canceled claims: the cavity is filled with a dielectric material; and an electrical signal feed assembly replaces the feed means of the canceled claims. The electrical signal feed assembly is a network of leads with a single coaxial feedline to that network. The network consists of a plurality of thin ribbon-like conductive leads.

The reissue claims are, however, broader in one respect. The canceled claims are limited to an antenna of cylindrical configuration, whereas the reissue claims are not so limited. We are aware of the principle that a claim that is broader in any respect is considered to be broader than the original claims even though it may be narrower in other respects. That rule will not bar Ball from securing the reissue claims here on appeal.

Pursuant to section 251, broadened reissue must be sought within 2 years after issuance of the original patent. The CCPA, in *In re Rogoff* [261 F.2d 601, 603-04, 120 U.S.P.Q. (BNA) 185, 186 (C.C.P.A. 1958)], noted that section 251

> contains no exceptions or qualifications as to time or extent of enlargement. The sole issue, therefore, is whether the claims on appeal enlarge, i.e., broaden, the patent claim. It is well settled that a claim is broadened, so far as the question of right to reissue is concerned, if it is so changed as to bring within its scope any structure which was not within the scope of the original claim. In other words, a claim is broadened if it is broader in any respect than the original claim, even though it may be narrowed in other respects....

Thus, the principle that a claim is broadened if it is broader in any respect than the original claim serves to effect the bar of section 251 against reissue filed later than 2 years after issuance of the original patent. In this case, Ball filed its application for reissue within the 2-year period for broadened reissue specified in section 251.

We know of no authority applying the above rule to reissue claims relative to the scope of canceled claims within the 2-year period for broadened reissue. Nor do we perceive the wisdom of such extension in this case. The rule is rigid and properly so in that it effects an express statutory limitation on broadened reissue. The recapture rule, however, is based on equitable principles. The rigidity of the broader-in-any-respect rule makes it inappropriate in the estoppel situation presented in this appeal.

B. INTERVENING RIGHTS

The requirements of novelty and nonobviousness in effect protect the public's reliance interest in prior art: inventors can seize on anything that is publicly available, and no patentee can threaten this reliance interest by patenting what is already in the public domain. But the public also has a reliance interest in the scope of issued patents. Competitors may come to rely on the precise wording of a claim in designing around the patented device or selling a non-infringing substitute for it. Because a patentee is permitted, via reissue, to revise her claims (and even broaden them within two years of the issuance of her patent), the public's reliance interest in the scope of the claims may be threatened. Section 252 attempts to accommodate the rights of the relying public with those of the inventor seeking revised claims on reissue. It reads:

§ 252. Effect of reissue

The surrender of the original patent shall take effect upon the issue of the reissued patent, and every reissued patent shall have the same effect and operation in law, on the trial of actions for causes thereafter arising, as if the same had been originally granted in such amended form, but in so far as the claims of the original and reissued patents are identical, such surrender shall not affect any action then pending nor abate any cause of action then existing, and the reissued patent, to the extent that its claims are identical with the original patent, shall constitute a continuation thereof and have effect continuously from the date of the original patent.

No reissued patent shall abridge or affect the right of any person or his successors in business who made, purchased or used prior to the grant of a reissue anything patented by the reissued patent, to continue the use of, or to sell to others to be used or sold, the specific thing so made, purchased or used, unless the making, using or selling of such thing infringes a valid claim of the reissued patent which was in the original patent. The court before which such matter is in question may provide for the continued manufacture, use or sale of the thing made, purchased or used as specified, or for the manufacture, use or sale of which substantial preparation was made before the grant of the reissue, and it may also provide for the continued practice of any process patented by the reissue, practiced, or for the practice of which substantial preparation was made, prior to the grant of the reissue, to the extent and under such terms as the court deems equitable for the protection of investments made or business commenced before the grant of the reissue.

SEATTLE BOX CO. v. INDUSTRIAL CRATING & PACKING, INC.

756 F.2d 1574, 225 U.S.P.Q. 357 (Fed. Cir. 1985)

This appeal is from a decision, on remand from this court, of the United States District Court for the Western District of Washington, which declined to accord appellants any intervening rights under 35 U.S.C. § 252 as to certain infringing products. We affirm in part and reverse in part.

BACKGROUND

Seattle Box Company (Seattle Box) and Industrial Crating and Packing, Inc. (Industrial) both provide oil pipe bundling services to oil companies. Seattle Box initiated the present action against Industrial on July 2, 1980, alleging the infringement of U.S. Patent No. 4,099,617 ('617) entitled "Shipping Bundle for Numerous Pipe Lengths." On August 19, 1980, Seattle Box was granted reissue of the '617 patent in U.S. Patent No. Re 30,373 (Re '373). Consequently, on October 10, 1980, Seattle Box amended its complaint, alleging infringement of the Re '373 patent.

Briefly, the patented invention defines a system of stacking ("bundling") tiers of pipes across parallel horizontal beams or sleepers. To ensure that adjacent pipes remain separated, double-concave wooden spacer blocks are used. Figure [10-1] below, illustrating one such tier, depicts [a] pipe[ ] which lie[s] across wooden sleepers [i.e., beams], and spacers [or wood supports] which separate the pipes. (Stacking these tiers results in a pipe "bundle.") The weight of the overhead load (a product of the upper tiers of pipe which are not shown) is absorbed by the spacer blocks [or wood supports]. Claim 1 of the '617 patent required that a spacer block have a height "greater than the diameter of the pipe." However, in the Re '373 patent, claim 1 was amended to specify a spacer block "of a height *substantially equal to or* greater than the thickness of the tier of pipe length." (Emphasis in the claim.)

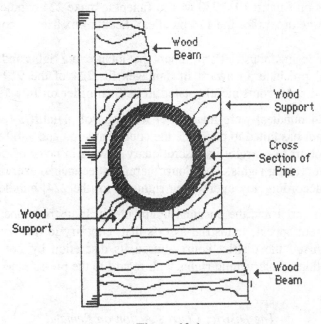

Figure 10-1

On the issues of validity and infringement, the district court held in favor of Seattle Box, and after an accounting for lost profits, entered judgment. Industrial appealed to this court, arguing invalidity and non-infringement. Speaking for this court, Judge Nichols stated that the district court correctly held that the Re '373 patent was not invalid. But the district court's finding of liability for pipe bundling activities Industrial performed before the Re '373 patent issued was reversed because under the first paragraph of 35 U.S.C. § 252 the reissue claims were not "identical" to the original claims, and therefore infringement could only be asserted for the Re '373 patent and not the '617 patent. [We also] vacated the district court's award of post-reissue damages for infringement of the Re '373 patent, holding that the defense of intervening rights under the second paragraph of 35 U.S.C. § 252 was properly raised. Since the district court had not made any findings under § 252, we remanded the case for the district court's consideration of "whether to use its broad equity powers to fashion an appropriate remedy." We declared that such a remedy is discretionary, and suggested a range of options available to the district court.

Supporting its assertion that the doctrine of intervening rights applies to the post-reissue bundles (there are 919 bundles in issue), Industrial presented the affidavit testimony of Vernon Zier, Industrial's in-house accountant, who summarized Industrial's business records. Zier averred that on August 19, 1980 (the date of the Re '373 patent), there were orders for 114 bundles which were subsequently completed after that date. In addition, Industrial's inventory of spacer blocks on August 19, 1980 was sufficient to make 224 bundles (this figure incorporates the orders for the 114 bundles). Seattle Box has not contested these facts.

After considering Industrial's argument that intervening rights under 35 U.S.C. § 252 should preclude an award of damages for 224 of the 919 post-reissue bundles, the district court merely stated in its final order on July 19, 1982 that:

> [The 224 bundles] were made after the grant of plaintiff's reissue patent. Defendant has failed to persuade the court that good and valid reasons exist for the court to exercise its discretionary powers in favor of the Defendant as to intervening rights. The Court therefore declines to exercise its discretion in according any intervening rights as to [the 224] bundles.

It is from this order and the ensuing judgment that Industrial appeals.

In the current appeal, Industrial asserts that, contrary to this court's instructions, on remand the district court abused its discretion by not making any findings relating to intervening rights with regard to the pre-reissue spacer block inventory.

The District Court's Action on Remand

We hold (for the reasons expressed below) that the cursory ruling by the district court disregards our prior opinion, and constitutes an abuse of discretion.

[The court says why, and goes on to state that it can resolve the issue without need for a further remand.]

Intervening Rights

[S]ection 252 provides that when certain conditions are present a reissue shall not abridge or affect certain rights of those who acted before the reissue was granted. See Federico, *Commentary on the New Patent Act*, 35 U.S.C.A. 1, 46 (1954). Because of such pre-reissue activity, an infringer might enjoy a "personal intervening right" to continue what would otherwise be infringing activity after reissue. The underlying rationale for intervening rights is that the public has the right to use what is not specifically claimed in the original patent. *Sontag Chain Stores Co. v. National Nut Co.*, 310 U.S. 281, 290 (1940). Recapture through a reissue patent of what is dedicated to the public by omission in the original patent is permissible under specific conditions, but not at the expense of innocent parties. *Id.* at 293 (the defendant, who had built and begun to operate its machines in a form not covered by the original patent, was allowed to continue the post-reissue activity which infringed the reissue patent). Therefore, one may be able to continue to infringe a reissue patent if the court decides that equity dictates such a result.

[From footnote:] Industrial, as it states in the section of its brief entitled "Relief Sought by Industrial Before the District Court," neither sought a continued right to bundle pipe in a manner infringing the reissue patent, nor contended that it should not pay compensation for any of its post-reissue bundling activities. Instead, it urged only that damages should not be awarded for the 224 bundles made from pre-reissue inventory. We limit our inquiry to whether damages may be avoided for these 224 and make no determination as to whether the doctrine of intervening rights would have precluded damages for the remaining 695 bundles (919 less 224) had Industrial set forth adequate equitable factors supporting an application of intervening rights as to all post-reissue activities.

As we said in our first opinion, once the doctrine of intervening rights is properly raised, the court must consider whether to use its broad equity powers to fashion an appropriate remedy. We also held that § 252 was to be applied in this case in accordance with equity. Accordingly, the district court should have considered the relevant facts as applied to the portion of the statute which questions whether "substantial preparation was made [by the infringer] before the grant of the reissue." Specifically, the district court's inquiry should have been — and it is now our burden to decide — whether the post-reissue use of the 224 bundles which were made from pre-reissue spacer blocks constituted "substantial preparation" to merit the protection afforded by intervening rights, so as to protect "investments made ... before the grant of reissue." We stress that all those spacer blocks were on hand when the reissue patent issued.

Two sets of the district court's factual findings weigh heavily in the present equitable determination of the application of intervening rights. First, in the district court's initial findings in its first decision, it was established that, prior to the Re '373 patent, Industrial and its patent attorney were fully aware of the '617 patent. Second, the district court found that Industrial continued manufacturing after reissue on the advice of its patent counsel. This advice-of-counsel was given to Industrial in April 1980, while the '617 patent was still extant, some 3 months before the Re '373 patent issued (August 17, 1980), and over two months before Industrial's patent counsel was even informed by Seattle Box's patent counsel (July 9, 1980) of the reissue patent claims which had been allowed by the examiner. This pre-reissue advice, followed by Industrial, was to hold the concave block height to about $^1/_{16}$ of an inch shorter than the pipe diameter. From these facts, it is apparent that Industrial was attempting to design its spacer blocks (including those it held on the date of the reissue patent) "around" the original '617 patent claims which called for a spacer block with a height "*greater* than the diameter of the pipe" (emphasis added). It turned out that these blocks infringed the reissue patent (Re '373), but they plainly did *not* literally infringe the original '617 patent (and probably did not infringe that patent under the doctrine of equivalents).

To enable Seattle Box now to recapture (in the form of damages for post-reissue use of the 224 bundles made from pre-reissue spacer blocks) matter which Seattle Box had already dedicated to the public in the original patent, at the expense of Industrial which knew of the precise claims of that '617 patent, could open the door to a "gross injustice." *Sontag Stores Co.*, 310 U.S. at 293-94. In these circumstances, the new reissue claims in this case present a compelling case for the application of the doctrine of intervening rights because a person should be able to make business decisions secure in the knowledge that those actions which fall outside the original patent claims are protected. Here, the spacer blocks involved were made or acquired, before the reissue, so as not to infringe the then existing '617 patent.

Another fact which weighs heavily is that at the time of reissue Industrial had existing orders for 114 bundles. As we have noted, the remedy of intervening rights is calculated to protect an infringer's preexisting investments and business. Prior business commitments, such as previously placed orders and contracts, are one such example.

Another important factor courts have considered is whether non-infringing goods can be manufactured from the inventory used to manufacture the infringing product. The cost and ease of converting infringing items to non-infringing items is an important equitable consideration because the "infringer" can then avoid a total loss of his good faith investment. In this case, the district court did not make any finding of the cost of conversion or of possible non-infringing uses. Instead, as previously discussed, a finding was made in its initial order as to non-infringing uses, but then it was retracted. In addition, Industrial has not asked for the continued use (without liability) of goods on hand at the time of ultimate judgment.

After weighing the facts and factors, we conclude that Industrial should clearly have been allowed to dispose of old inventory remaining on hand at the time of reissue, without liability to Seattle Box. The district court's conclusion to the contrary was an abuse of discretion. We therefore reverse the determination that intervening rights do not protect Industrial from owing damages as to the 224 bundles. [The court goes on to hold that the district court did not clearly err in assessing, as to the remainder of the 919 bundles, lost profits and not reasonable royalty damages.]

NOTES

1. *Remedial Options Under § 252.* In its original opinion on appeal, the Federal Circuit gave the trial court several options:

> The trial court is given the discretion to fashion a remedy from a wide range of options available to it. The court may, for example, (1) confine Industrial to the use of those double-concave blocks already in existence, (2) permit Industrial to continue in business under conditions which limit the amount, type, or geographical location of its activities, or (3) permit Industrial to continue in business unconditionally.

Seattle Box Co., Inc. v. Industrial Crating & Packing, Inc., 731 F.2d 818, 830, 221 U.S.P.Q. (BNA) 568 (Fed. Cir. 1984) (*"Seattle Box I"*).

2. *Some History: Effect of Reissue.* In *Seattle Box I*, the Federal Circuit gave some valuable background on older reissue cases:

> An original patent cannot be infringed once a reissue patent has issued, for the original patent is surrendered. At one point in the history of the American patent law, this surrender precluded any action for infringement for acts done prior to the surrender. Courts would not allow a patentee to bring an action in response to acts done before the reissue patent issued since no patent existed upon which one could allege infringement. Courts, moreover, would dismiss for a failure to state a cause of action any action filed before the patent was surrendered since the patent sued on no longer existed. Courts acted, in other words, as if the original patent never was. See Federico, *Intervening Rights in Patent Reissues*, 30 GEO. WASH. L. REV. 603, 605 (1962).

731 F.2d at 837. Note that § 252 changed this result by providing that claims which are "carried over" from the original patent have their original effective date, and so can be defended against pre-reissue infringement. *Id.*

3. *Recent History: Reissue "Opposition" Procedures.* Reissue proceedings under old rules in effect from 1977 to 1982 provided that the PTO could render "advisory opinions" regarding patentability over prior art. These were based on so-called "no defect" oaths under the "Dann Amendments," which did not require the patent owner to make an oath or declaration regarding the presence of

an error. They were in effect reissues prompted by third party concerns or activities. *See In re Dien*, 680 F.2d 151, 214 U.S.P.Q. (BNA) 10 (C.C.P.A. 1982). *In re Keil*, 808 F.2d 830, 1 U.S.P.Q.2d 1427 (Fed. Cir. 1987), involved an appeal from the PTO Board of Patent Appeals and Interferences affirming denial of a reissue application which had no changes to its text. The CAFC held that a reissue application under the Dann amendments, 37 C.F.R. § 1.175(a)(4), repealed effective July 1, 1982, is merely a request for an advisory opinion and thus the appeal was to be dismissed for lack of jurisdiction. Statutory reexamination under Patent Act §§ 301-307 has replaced these "advisory opinions."

4. *Test for Intervening Rights*. The court states in omitted footnote 6 in *Seattle Box II*:

> In the first *Seattle Box* opinion we set forth a single straightforward test, derived from § 252, for determining when the doctrine of intervening rights might protect an alleged infringer: whether the claims of the original patent repeated in the reissue patent are infringed. Because no claim from the original patent was repeated in the reissue patent, we held that the defense of intervening rights was properly raised. 731 F.2d at 830, 221 U.S.P.Q. at 576.

The implication is that if a claim of the reissue was repeated from the original patent, no defense of intervening rights would be available as to that claim. *See also Tillotson, Ltd. v. Walbro Corp.*, 831 F.2d 1033, 4 U.S.P.Q.2d (BNA) 1450 (Fed. Cir. 1987) (a reissue claim is broader in scope than the original claims if it contains within its scope any conceivable apparatus or process which would not have infringed the original patent claims).

Also, cases such as *Bic Leisure Prods., Inc. v. Windsurfing Int' l, Inc.*, 1 F.3d 1214, 1222, 27 U.S.P.Q.2d 1671 (Fed. Cir. 1993), distinguish between two types of intervening rights in § 252: absolute and equitable. Under this terminology, *Seattle Box* presents an issue of equitable intervening rights. In the *BIC* case, however, the infringer argued that although it had some units in inventory and under sales contract that were covered by the reissued claims, it was entitled to absolute intervening rights because these products did not infringe the original claims.

> BIC had 5,245 [sail] boards in inventory as of the reissue date. The district court found that BIC had another 5,625 boards on order. Specifically, the district court found that the telex purchase order, dated February 10, 1983, between BIC and an affiliated supplier, BIC Marine, bound BIC to purchase the sailboards. This court discerns no error in the trial court's determination that these sailboards were purchased within the meaning of section 252 before the [patent reissue] date of March 8, 1983. Because BIC purchased the boards before the reissue date, the district court properly excluded the post-reissue sale of the 10,870 sailboards from the computation of damages.

5. *"Parallel Prosecution."* Notice that in the main case, Seattle Box amended its initial complaint to include a count for infringement of the reissued claims, which had reissued after the initial complaint was filed. This is one example of the use of reissue and reexamination in "parallel" with litigation, a growing trend. See the fine article by Re, *"Parallel Prosecution": Effect of Patent Prosecution on Current Litigation*, 73 J. Pat. Trademark Off. Soc'y 965 (1991). *Cf. In re Amos*, 21 U.S.P.Q.2d (BNA) 1271 (Fed. Cir. 1991) (lack of objective intent to claim subject matter does not preclude reissue for matter disclosed but not claimed in original application).

5. Several courts have grappled with the question of when claims in an original and reissue patent are "identical" under § 252. *See, e.g., Westvaco Corp. v. International Paper Co.*, 991 F.2d 735, 741-742, 26 U.S.P.Q.2d 1353 (Fed. Cir. 1993). In *Westvaco*, the patentee sought damages for sale of infringing products prior to the date the reissue patent was granted. The court refused, on the grounds that certain limitations in the reissued claims of the patent meant that they were no longer identical to the claims in the original:

> Westvaco argues that the scope of reissue claim 5 is significantly broader than that of original claim 5 because of the change in claim terminology. We agree. First, the original claim defined the layers of low density poly-ethylene polymer as being "coated on" the paperboard substrate and the tie material, and the ethylene vinyl alcohol copolymer as being "coextruded on" the paperboard substrate. The reissue claim does not include such limitations. The language of original claim 5 is limiting because it defines the type of structure which results from the coating and coextruding, i.e., "coated" layers and a "coextruded" layer. Second, the reissue claim terms, "exterior to" and "interior to," broaden the claim so that it could encompass a laminate with layers disposed between those layers explicitly recited. The original claim is not so broad. Our conclusion applies with equal force to claim 6 since that claim is dependent on claim 5.

See also Boyett v. St. Martin's Press, 884 F. Supp. 479 (M.D. Fla. 1995) (claim changes in reissue patents which merely clarify language already in claims cannot be construed as substantive changes).

C. REEXAMINATION

In 1980 Congress sought "to strengthen investor confidence in the certainty of patent rights by establishing a system of administrative reexamination of doubtful patents," and to do so "without recourse to expensive and lengthy infringement litigation." H.R. Rep. No. 96-1307, 96th Cong., 2d Sess. 3-4, *reprinted in* 1980 U.S.C.C.A.N. 6460, 6462-63. *See* Act to Amend the Patent and Trademark Laws, Pub. L. No. 96-517, 94 Stat. 3015 (1980), codified at 35 U.S.C. §§ 301-307 (1988 & Supp. 1991). Thus was born the reexamination system. Reexamination usually arises in anticipation of, or as a consequence of, infringement litigation.

Anyone, including the patentee, can request reexamination (for a fee). But the legislative history of the reexamination statute makes clear that reexamination should be granted only upon a showing of a "substantial new question of patentability," based *only* upon printed publications and patents. H.R. REP. at 7, U.S.C.C.A.N. at 6466. The procedure was limited so as to protect the patentee from having to revisit issues raised and overcome in the original prosecution. And one case interpreting the statute and Patent Office regulations implementing it held that one who requests reexamination has very limited rights; she is entitled to (1) receive notice of the Office's decision regarding reexamination, (2) receive a copy of the patentee's response to the request, and (3) file rejoinder to that response, but nothing more. *Syntex (U.S.A.) Inc. v. U.S. Patent & Trademark Office*, 882 F.2d 1570, 11 U.S.P.Q.2d (BNA) 1866 (Fed. Cir. 1989). *See generally* 35 U.S.C. § 304 (1982); 37 C.F.R. § 1.530 (1991); 37 C.F.R. § 1.535 (1988).

Within three months after the request is filed, the Patent Office will determine whether the request raises "a substantial new question of patentability affecting any claim of the patent...." 35 U.S.C. § 303(a) (1988); 37 C.F.R. § 1.515(a) (1991). Based upon that determination, the PTO will issue an order granting or denying reexamination. An order denying reexamination can be reviewed if the requester files a petition. 37 C.F.R. § 1.515(c) (1991).

In deciding whether a "substantial new question of patentability" is raised, the PTO uses a "materiality" criterion. A substantial new question regarding patentability can be present "even if the examiner would not necessarily reject the claim as either fully anticipated by, or obvious in view of, the prior patents or printed publications." Speranza & Goldman, *Reexamination — The Patent Challenger's View*, 15 AM. INTELL. PROP. L. ASS'N Q.J. 85 (1987) (citing various provisions of the MANUAL OF PATENT EXAMINING PROCEDURES).

A reexamined patent has much the same effect as one that has been reissued. For instance, in *Kaufman Co. v. Lantech, Inc.*, 807 F.2d 970, 1 U.S.P.Q.2d (BNA) 1202 (Fed. Cir. 1986), the court held that amendments made during reexamination affected the patentee's ability to assert pre-reexamination infringement in exactly the same fashion as amendments made during *reissue*: if the amended claims are "without substantive change" from the original claims, the amended claims can be asserted over a defendant for pre-reexamination infringement. *See Seattle Box Co. v. Industrial Crating & Packing, Inc.*, 731 F.2d 818, 828, 221 U.S.P.Q. (BNA) 568, 575 (Fed. Cir. 1984) (adopting "without substantial change" rule for reissued claims). This holding came despite an argument by defendant (Lantech) that *any* amendment made during reexamination must necessarily be a "substantial change"; the court noted that "[t]he substantial new question standard [for determining whether a reexamination is warranted] was incorporated to prevent abuse and harassment of patentees, not to manifest a Congressional intent that any amendment in the reexamination proceedings must be deemed substantial and therefore trigger an intervening right." *Kaufman Co.*, 807 F.2d at 978. *See also Laitram Corp. v. NEC Corp.*, 21 U.S.P.Q.2d 1276 (Fed. Cir. 1991) (amendments made to patent claims during reexamination are not per se substantive when the amendments are made following rejection based on prior art; to determine whether claim change is substantive, it is necessary to analyze claims of original and reexamined patents in light of particular facts, including prior art, prosecution history, other claims and any other pertinent information).

Once litigation has started, a court has discretion to order a defendant to conduct a patentability search and to order a plaintiff to request reexamination based on the results of the search. Or, if a party to the litigation voluntarily requests reexamination, the court may (but need not) stay the litigation until reexamination has been completed. If litigation is settled, a general provision in a settlement agreement not to file any suit in a "court" challenging the validity of the patent does not encompass a reexamination request. *Joy Mfg. Co. v. National Mine Serv. Co.*, 810 F.2d 1127, 1 U.S.P.Q.2d (BNA) 1627 (Fed. Cir. 1987).

In general, reexamination gives a number of advantages to the accused infringer. These include: (1) elimination of the statutory presumption of patent validity (see below); (2) "isolation" of the patent validity issue from other issues, e.g., infringement; and (3) ability to "fire the first shot" in the dispute. Speranza & Goldman, *Reexamination — The Patent Challenger's View*, 15 AM. INTELL. PROP. L. ASS'N Q.J. 85 (1987). In addition, reexaminations are quicker on average than full-blown infringement or declaratory judgement litigation. *See* Cumulative Reexamination Statistics, 1986 (available upon request from the United States Patent and Trademark Office), *cited in* Conger, *Patent Reexamination Reexamined*, 1986 DET. C.L. REV. 523 (1986) *supra*, at note 157 (of the total of 962 requests had been filed as of February 28, 1986, reexamination pendency averaged 16.6 months). Yet this speed does not come at the expense of thoroughness; if a reference can be cited to the Office, a full consideration will be made. *See, e.g., In re Baxter Travenol Labs.*, 21 U.S.P.Q.2d (BNA) 1281 (Fed. Cir. 1991) (testimony from author of prior art reference, and other evidence, cited by examiner invalidating patent on reexamination).

On the negative side, the challenger should realize these disadvantages: (1) the same examiner who allowed the patent will review it on reexamination; (2) reexamined patents, though technically not res judicata in a future infringement action, are accorded a great deal of respect by courts, and hence a reexamination can bolster the "strength" of the patentee's patent, see *Kaufman Co. v. Lantech, Inc.*, 807 F.2d 970, 1 U.S.P.Q.2d (BNA) 1202 (Fed. Cir. 1986) (where a patent has been reissued or a reexamination certificate has been issued after consideration of the same prior art relied upon in litigation to show invalidity, the challenger's burden of proof in that litigation, as an evidentiary matter, is usually more difficult to sustain); and (3) as mentioned above, there are limited opportunities to take an active part in the process once it is set in motion. *Id. See generally* Shear & Galliani, *Patent Practice: Strategies for Submitting Newly Discovered Prior Art After Allowance of an Application*, 7 COMP. & HIGH TECH. L.J. 1 (1991); Adamo, *Reexamination — To What Avail? An Overview*, 63 J. PAT. OFF. SOC'Y 616 (1981); Burnett, *The "Nuts and Bolts" of Patent Reexamination*, 9 AM. PAT. L. ASS'N Q.J. 183 (1981). Furthermore, for the patentee considering initiating a reexamination herself, there is the extra consideration that a reexamination puts the entire patent "at risk," whereas a reissue application, at worst, results in the rejection of the reissue but leaves the original patent intact.

Indeed, future reforms in the reexamination system should include (1) broadening the types of prior art that can be cited in order to initiate a reexamination, and (2) increasing the participation of third party reexamination initiators.

These proposals have proceeded quite far along the legislative path at various times, and it is likely that they will finally make it over the top sometime soon. A representative bill, from a recent session of Congress, was called The Patent Reexamination Reform Act of 1995, H.R. 1732/S. 1070 (1995).

The bill was aimed at the perceived shortcomings of the current reexamination system, which have yielded a very disappointing volume of reexamination requests. Its most significant proposal called for limited, yet meaningful, participation by a third-party requester throughout the reexamination proceeding. Under the bill, third parties could provide written comments during each round of prosecution in the reexamination proceeding. A third-party requester, for example, would be permitted to provide written comments on statements made by the patent owner in response to an Office action. The bill also expanded the grounds upon which reexamination could be initiated to include enablement and related issues under Patent Act § 112, except for the best mode requirement. Finally, the bill allowed a third-party requester to appeal a final decision of the PTO in favor of the patent owner. To balance these expanded rights of third-party requesters, the bill included limitations on whether and when a request for reexamination could be filed. In addition — and most importantly — the bill stripped third-party requesters of the right to further litigate validity issues when they appealed the Patent Office's final decision. This is an important limitation in itself, to be sure; but more, it points the way toward more comprehensive integration of the administrative and judicial functions in relation to patent validity issues. Efforts in this direction are most welcome in light of the exploding frequency and cost of patent litigation. *See* N. Thane Bauz, *Reanimating U.S. Patent Reexamination: Recommendations for Change Based Upon a Comparative Study of German Law*, 27 CREIGHTON L. REV. 945 (1994).

For a discussion of some newsworthy reexaminations ordered by the Commissioner of Patents, see Terri Suzette Hughes, *Patent Reexamination and the PTO: Compton's Patent Invalidated at the Commissioner's Request*, 14 J. MARSHALL J. COMPUTER & INFO. L. 379 (1996) (invalidation of notorious if short-lived patent on multimedia technology).

QUANTUM CORP. v. RODIME, PLC

65 F.3d 1577 (Fed. Cir. 1995)

PLAGER, J.

The question in this declaratory judgment action is whether amendments made during a prior reexamination proceeding impermissibly broadened the scope of the patent claims at issue in violation of 35 U.S.C. § 305 (1988), and, if so, the legal effect thereof. Defendant patentee Rodime PLC (Rodime) appeals the decision of the United States District Court for the District of Minnesota. In its decision, the district court granted Quantum Corporation's (Quantum) motion for summary judgment that [certain] claims of U.S. Patent No. B1 4,638,383 (the reexamined '383 patent) are invalid because they were impermissibly broadened during reexamination. We affirm.

Rodime is the owner of the reexamined '383 patent, which issued on November 29, 1988. The reexamined '383 patent is directed to a micro hard-disk drive system (3.5 inch drive) suitable for use in portable computers with performance parameters comparable to those available in 5.25 inch disk drive systems. Quantum, the plaintiff in this declaratory judgment action, is the manufacturer of disk drives which, Rodime alleges in its counterclaim, infringe its patent.

The claim limitation at issue in this appeal relates to the storage capability of the hard-disk. The storage capability of a hard-disk is a function of the track density; the greater the track density, the more data that can be stored in a given area of the disk. Track density may be defined in terms of "tracks per inch" (tpi), calculated based on the number of concentric tracks present within an inch along the radius of the hard-disk.

On November 19, 1985 ..., two engineers at Rodime filed a patent application for the invention [at issue]. Claim 1 of this application recited, *inter alia*, a track density of "approximately 600" tpi. The examiner, in a first office action, rejected all the claims as obvious [in light of prior art pertaining to 5.25 inch disks, including track densities].

In a response dated May 23, 1986, applicants canceled the original claims and inserted new claims some of which recited a track density of "at least 600" tpi. The examiner subsequently allowed these new claims, and the patent issued on January 20, 1987, as U.S. Patent No. 4,638,383 (the original '383 patent). Claims 4, 6, 7, 9, and 14 of the original '383 patent all recited a track density of "at least 600 concentric tracks per inch."

On September 28, 1987, Rodime, the owner of the original '383 patent pursuant to an assignment from the inventors, requested reexamination of its patent. Finding a substantial new question of patentability, see 35 U.S.C. § 303, the United States Patent and Trademark Office (PTO) granted Rodime's request for reexamination of all 16 claims in the original '383 patent. In an office action dated April 19, 1988, the examiner rejected all but two of the original claims. Rodime responded by canceling certain claims, amending others, and adding [some] dependent claims. With respect to the claims at issue in this appeal,

Rodime made substantial amendments including changing the track density limitation from "at least 600" tpi to "at least approximately 600" tpi. These claims were allowed, as amended, and the '383 reexamined patent issued on November 29, 1988, as U.S. Patent No. B1 4,638,383.

Quantum filed a motion for summary judgment that Claims 4, 6, 7, 9, 14, and 19-27 of the reexamined '383 patent are invalid under 35 U.S.C. § 305 for being impermissibly broadened by Rodime during reexamination. According to Quantum, Rodime's amendment during reexamination of the track density limitation from "at least 600" tpi to "at least approximately 600" tpi broadened the scope of the claims to cover certain disk drives with approximately but less than 600 tpi that were not covered by the original '383 patent claims, and therefore these claims are invalid under 35 U.S.C. § 305. [The district court agreed with Quantum and granted summary judgment.]

35 U.S.C. § 305 states, in relevant part, that "[n]o proposed amended or new claim enlarging the scope of a claim of the patent will be permitted in a reexamination proceeding." An amended or new claim has been enlarged if it includes within its scope any subject matter that would not have infringed the original patent.

Accordingly, the claims at issue have been improperly broadened in violation of 35 U.S.C. § 305 if the track density limitation in the claims of the reexamined '383 patent — "at least approximately 600 tpi" — is broader than the track density limitation in the claims of the original '383 patent — "at least 600 tpi."

Rodime's principle argument on appeal is that the addition of the word "approximately" to the track density limitation only made explicit what was already implicitly included in the claim, and therefore did not expand the scope of the claims at issue.

The major flaw in Rodime's argument is that it focuses solely on the term "600 tpi" instead of the claim limitation as a whole, in context. Rodime offered no evidence to show that one skilled in the art understood "at least 600 tpi" to be the same as "at least approximately 600 tpi" or that the patentee defined it as such in the patent or during prosecution.

Absent such a definition or evidence that the claim limitation as a whole has a special meaning to one of skill in the art, we see no error in the district court's use of dictionary definitions to ascertain the ordinary meaning of the relevant claim limitation. The addition of "approximately" which means "reasonably close to," eliminates the precise lower limit of that range, and, in so doing extends the scope of the range. The term "at least approximately 600 tpi" therefore defines an open-ended range starting slightly below 600.

Since the amended limitation includes subject matter not covered by the original claims, i.e. track densities below 600 tpi, we conclude that Rodime expanded the scope of their claims during reexamination in violation of 35 U.S.C. § 305.

[T]he Patent Act is silent regarding the proper remedy to be employed by a district court in a patent infringement suit when it determines that claims were improperly broadened during reexamination in violation of 35 U.S.C. § 305. Neither the express words in section 305 nor its legislative history provide any guidance in this situation; they merely recite the prohibition against broadening during reexamination.

Despite the absence of specific statutory language or precedent of this court in support of the district court's judgment that the claims at issue are invalid, we conclude that, as a matter of law, the district court arrived at the correct result. The purpose of the reexamination process is to provide a mechanism for reaffirming or correcting the PTO's action in issuing a patent by reexamining patents thought to be of doubtful validity. Consistent with this overall purpose, Congress enacted section 305 which, while allowing an applicant to amend his claims or add new claims to distinguish his invention over cited prior art, explicitly prohibits any broadening of claims during reexamination. If an applicant fails to claim as broadly as he or she could have, the proper recourse, if within two years of issuance of the patent, is to file a reissue application, see 35 U.S.C. § 251, not to remedy this problem in a reexamination proceeding.

As with violations of other statutes in the Patent Act, claims that do not comply with section 305 cannot stand. Rodime agrees, but maintains that the proper recourse is for this court to exercise its inherent equitable powers by restricting the scope of the claims to their original terms, avoiding a holding of infringement against any devices that would not have been covered by any of the original claims as they existed prior to reexamination. We disagree. Although we construe claims, if possible, so as to sustain their validity, it is well settled that no matter how great the temptations of fairness or policy making, courts do not redraft claims. Moreover, even if we could consider equities, they do not favor Rodime; they broadened their claims during reexamination despite the explicit prohibition against doing so in section 305.

Likewise, the district court cannot remand the case to the PTO to have the broadening language deleted from the claims. *Cf. Green v. Rich Iron Co.*, 944 F.2d 852, 20 U.S.P.Q.2d 1075 (Fed. Cir. 1991) (holding that a district court could not compel a patentee to seek reissue of his patent). To conclude otherwise would discourage instead of encourage compliance with section 305. If the only penalty for violating section 305 is a remand to the PTO to have the reexamined claims narrowed to be commensurate in scope with what the applicant was only entitled to in the first place, then applicants will have an incentive to attempt to broaden their claims during reexamination, and, if successful, be able to enforce these broadened claims against their competitors. This result essentially renders the prohibition in section 305 meaningless.

NOTE

Is it true that, no matter what the temptations of fairness, courts do not redraft a patentee's claims? Consider the doctrine of equivalents, and especially the branch of equivalents cases extolling the appeal of "equitable" equivalents. Despite what the court says — it always insists that the doctrine does not broaden claims — the practical effect of a decision finding infringement under the doctrine of equivalents is to prevent others from making, using or selling the embodiment found to infringe. (Put it this way: what lawyer would advise a client to put on the market an embodiment identical to that of a competitor just found by the court to infringe under the doctrine of equivalents?)

In general, the interaction between courts and Patent Office sometimes appears less smooth than it could be. (Compare the European Patent Office, which, at least as to issues of validity, combines the administrative and judicial functions rather completely.) Should this be remedied? Can you think of an argument why not? What values under the heading "separation of powers" might be implicated by closer interaction?

1. ISSUES OF CONSTITUTIONALITY AND FAIRNESS

A constitutional challenge to the reexamination statute was raised by the plaintiff in *Patlex Corp. v. Mossinghoff*, 758 F.2d 594, 225 U.S.P.Q. (BNA) 243 (Fed. Cir.), *modified*, 771 F.2d 480, 226 U.S.P.Q. (BNA) 985 (Fed. Cir. 1985). The Federal Circuit upheld the reexamination statute in the face of a challenge under the due process clause of the Fifth Amendment to the Constitution. The patentee had argued the unconstitutionality of retroactively applying the reexamination procedure to his patent, which was issued before the reexamination procedure became part of the law. The court rejected this argument, and also held that a patentee is not deprived of a property right when the statutory presumption of validity (Patent Act § 282) is not applied to his patent during reexamination; the "right" to this presumption, said the court, is not a property right subject to the protection of the Constitution.

Other cases have reiterated that the reexamination statute does not give the patentee the benefit of the statutory presumption of validity during reexamination. In *In re Etter*, 756 F.2d 852, 225 U.S.P.Q. (BNA) 1 (Fed. Cir. 1985), the Federal Circuit specifically held that the presumption of validity does not apply to claims involved in reexamination proceedings. The majority opinion in *Etter* indicated that the presumption was a trial court procedural rule and that claim examination in a reexamination was essentially a return to the initial examination, so that trial-related presumptions do not apply. A vocal three-judge dissent stated that "the Court has made reexamination into a proceeding which affords advantages to an infringer over his position in Court." It was indicated that to an infringer of greater economic power than the patent owner, delay is an advantage. In addition, the lack of res judicata effect against the infringer from a reexamination proceeding gives the infringer two opportunities to attack the patent. 756 F.2d at 862. *Cf. In re Yamamoto*, 740 F.2d 1569, 1571, 222 U.S.P.Q. (BNA) 934, 936 (Fed. Cir. 1984) (claims subject to reexamination will "be given their broadest reasonable interpretation consistent with the specification, and limitations appearing in the specification are not to be read into the claims," just as in the original prosecution of an application).

For some commentators, this smacks of blatant unfairness. *See, e.g.*, Conger, *Patent Reexamination Reexamined*, 1986 DET. C.L. REV. 523 (1986) ("[T]he advent of statutory reexamination now allows infringers to make an end run around the presumption of validity, bypassing both the burden of proof and the standard of proof in the process. Should the patent bar more fully use reexamination, it is evident that patents will become little more than publications which create ill-defined and evanescent rights. Rather than increase public confidence in patents, patents will enjoy less respect and certainty than before."); Note, *Examining the Federal Circuit's Position on the Presumption of Validity During Patent Reexamination*, 32 WAYNE L. REV. 1405 (1986) ("Congress intended the statutory presumption of validity to continue to attach to an issued patent — even during administrative reexamination. Furthermore, because a third party can force a patentee to undergo reexamination and because the presumption of validity is not applied, the patentee is deprived of property rights. This violates the fundamental fairness requirement of procedural due process [under the Constitution].").

2. FOREIGN OPPOSITION PROCEEDINGS

Reexamination is the closest the U.S. system comes to a major feature of foreign patent systems: the opposition. Opposition procedures are common in many European patent systems, and opposition is specifically provided for in the European Patent Convention, Articles 99-105. *See* 1 CHARTERED INSTITUTE OF PATENT AGENTS, EUROPEAN PATENTS HANDBOOK Ch. 25 (M. Atchley gen. ed., 1988 & Supp. 1991) (EUROPEAN HANDBOOK). These procedures are *inter partes* and allow for the introduction of physical evidence, testimony of inventors, and testimony of experts in the field of art to administratively or judicially determine patentability. *See, e.g.*, EUROPEAN HANDBOOK, §§ 25.10, 25.13, 25.14. *See generally* Benson, *The New Reexamination Law — A Legislative History*, 9 AM. PAT. L. ASS'N Q.J. 227, 228 (1981).

A related procedure allows third parties limited participation in the *prosecution* of the patent application; thus under this procedure, unlike an opposition, the patent need not be granted for third parties to begin their attack on the patent. *See* European Patent Convention § 115(1). The publication of patent applications 18 months after filing makes this procedure possible. Publication of patent applications began in Germany in 1968 (patterned after the 1964 Dutch practice), and has now been adopted by the European Patent Office and in Japan. Publication at 18 months permits any person to closely monitor a competitor's patent application.

The European Patent Convention limits the filing of an opposition to nine months after the patent is granted. *See* European Patent Convention ("EPC") Art. 99(1). The nine month period is long enough to evaluate patents and short enough so that the patentee gains reasonable certainty concerning his grant early enough for commercial investments.

In the European system, opposition may be based on one of several grounds: nonpatentable subject matter; lack of novelty; lack of inventive step; and inadequate disclosure. *See* EPC Arts. 52-57. Once the opposition has been filed, it may be continued even after the opponent withdraws. Rules of the European Patent Convention, Rule 60(1). In a concession favoring opponents, the rules on European oppositions permit opposition in any of the official languages of the Convention (English, French and German). Thus an opponent may file in a different language from the one used by the patentee during prosecution. In addition, where several oppositions have been filed, they will be communicated to each of the opponents; this permits a "coordinated attack" on a patent by those who would be adversely affected by it. *Id.*, Rule 57(2). Moreover, despite the strict nine-month limit, anyone who is accused of infringement may join an ongoing opposition even after the end of the nine month period. *See* EPC Art. 105(1). This is known as "intervention" in an opposition. *See* EUROPEAN HANDBOOK, § 25.3.2.

As might be expected, one important function of the opposition is to bring to light certain categories of obscure prior art not likely to be accessible to an examiner acting alone:

> Questions of novelty and obviousness founded upon publication through prior use or obscure dissemination are more likely to be raised at this stage than in the pre-grant examination. In resolving difficult issues of this kind it is not clear how far Opposition Divisions [within the EPO] will resort to notions of onus or standard of proof.

M. VITORIA, W.R. CORNISH ET AL., 1 ENCYCLOPEDIA OF UNITED KINGDOM AND EUROPEAN PATENT LAW § 13-305 (1977 & Supp. 1991). *See also* EUROPEAN HANDBOOK, § 25.7.3.

This is only one of several reasons why competitors of a patentee may prefer an opposition to a full-blown infringement case. The others are: (1) the expertise of the EPO, which makes it cheaper to address validity issues because there is less need to educate the decisionmakers regarding the technology; (2) removal of the validity issues from the litigation forum where they may naturally "spill over" into considerations of infringement, relative merits of the inventor versus the accused infringer, etc.; and (3) lower cost, partly a function of (1) and (2). (Note that the cross-communication between opponents helps lower the cost of major, multi-party oppositions). In addition, society in general would appear to benefit from early resolution of validity issues. If the patent is deemed valid, investment can proceed apace in the technology; and if it is found invalid, or reduced in scope, on account of the opposition, non-infringing competitors will be encouraged to commercialize their products more quickly without the lingering threat of an infringement suit.

In Japan, oppositions share many of the features just described. After initial publication (at 18 months from filing), but before final issuance of the patent, the Japanese Patent Office "lays open" the application for opposition. If the application is not opposed, or the opposition(s) is (are) met successfully, the patent issues. There is a "preliminary" property right in an application that has been subjected to the second publication or "laying open": the patentee, if the patent issues, can receive compensation for infringements occurring during the laid open period. Also in Japan the patentee is not given notice of the grounds of opposition unless and until the examiner rejects the application. *See* T. TANABE & H. WEGNER, JAPANESE PATENT LAW § 043.1 (1979). Post-issuance oppositions are available in Japan; this only makes sense since courts in infringement cases cannot consider the validity of patents. *See id.*

On the other hand, Japanese oppositions also reveal the negative effects of the opposition procedure. The greatest negative in the eyes of most patentees is the potential for an opposition to delay issuance of a patent for a very substantial period of time. Because competitors file oppositions, rather than patent examiners per se, patentees claim that these competitors can intentionally turn these proceedings into a quagmire. On this view, the strategic uses of oppositions — primarily to tie up an applicant, and wear him or her down — make them by far a net negative proposition for patentees. According to Tanabe and Wegner:

> In Japan, it is not unusual for a company to file a large number of oppositions against its competitors each year.... [I]f success is measured in terms of [defeating the application entirely] *or* having a chance to create estoppels and otherwise *limit* the interpretation of the claims which are published as the patent grant, then the Japanese companies filing such multiple oppositions are quite successful. This is particularly the case where the applicant is a large company.

TANABE & WEGNER § 043. The recent experiences of American companies demonstrate how true this is. *See, e.g.,* D. Spero, *Patent Protection or Piracy — A CEO Views Japan*, HARV. BUS. REV., Sept./Oct. 1990, at 58 (article by President of Fusion Systems, Inc., a small U.S. company which claims that (1) its Japanese patent application was "picket fenced" (i.e., surrounded by hundreds of competing patent applications), and (2) subjected to protracted opposition). *But cf.* B. Gomes-Casseres, *Fusion Systems*, HARVARD BUS. SCHOOL CASE STUDY (1990) (concluding that Fusion lost its Japanese rights by not taking advantage of the Japanese patent system and allowing competitors to overwhelm it). *See generally Japanese Patent Policy: Hearings Before the Subcomm. on Foreign Commerce and Tourism, Comm. on Commerce, Science, and Transportation,* U.S. Senate, Feb. 28, 1989 (inquiry into unfair aspects of Japanese patent system).

In some European countries, a relatively inexpensive nullity proceeding is available in addition to an opposition. These proceedings have some features in common with a third-party request for reexamination, but they generally allow more participation by the requester. *See* EUROPEAN HANDBOOK Ch. 26.

Note that in addition to being an early non-litigation forum for determining validity, the opposition procedures create a powerful incentive to fully disclose all relevant prior art — obviating the need, for the most part, for stringent "inequitable conduct" standards. If the applicant does not disclose relevant art, a competitor surely will when filing an opposition.

Chapter 11

PATENT TRANSACTIONS: RULES AND RESTRICTIONS

While most patent cases, as well as most of the academic literature on patents, emphasize the *creation* of technology to be covered by property rights (i.e., validity) and the impact of those rights on *competition* (i.e., infringement), the active market for the *exchange* of these properties is sometimes ignored. In practice, enabling and facilitating these transactions is arguably the most significant economic function of the patent system. Thus to view patent licenses and assignments as peripheral aspects of the patent system is to miss a key point: arguably these transactions are at the center of the system. This chapter attempts to set forth the rules governing patent transactions and to explore briefly how those rules influence actual exchanges.

It has been argued that transactional rules are growing in importance along with the growth in the volume of intellectual property-based transactions:

> [I]ntellectual property rights make more feasible various organizational structures that firms and individuals are increasingly using to produce goods and services. Since these organizations are at least partially based on contracts, they provide a growing source of commercial transactions that necessarily include an intellectual property component.
>
> Intellectual property rights appear to enhance and, in some cases, to enable these contract-based organizations — which run the gamut from consulting arrangements to "out-sourcing" agreements in which firms purchase components formerly manufactured by themselves. In general, intellectual property rights make such transactions less risky, and hence feasible in more instances, because they make it easier for the licensor — often the supplier of a productive input — to police the activities of the licensee. The strong policy favoring injunctions is one example of how licensors can use intellectual property rights to police licensee activities; another example is courts' strict adherence to the field-of-use limitations that many licensing agreements contain. In these and other ways, intellectual property rights give the input supplier greater control over the activities of the licensee, which makes the external production of inputs and the concomitant transfer by contract more feasible. To put it another way, intellectual property rights reduce the licensee's opportunistic possibilities and thereby lower transaction costs.

Robert P. Merges, *Intellectual Property and the Costs of Commercial Exchange: A Review Essay*, 93 MICH. L. REV. 1570, 1573-74 (1995) (footnotes omitted).

In light of the fast-moving changes in commercial practices, one word of caution is in order at the outset of this chapter: many of the cases on patent transactions are outdated. They spring from an era when patents were associated with illegal monopolies, and hence were thought to be tantamount to inchoate antitrust violations. This view, especially prominent in the Supreme Court cases from the 1930s until the 1960s, has been eclipsed in recent years. One must be cautious in assessing the continuing force of older cases condemning various licensing terms and strategies, partly because of the founding of the Federal Circuit in 1982, and partly as a consequence of the academic "law and economics" revolution whose impact was felt strongly beginning in the 1970s. Although some of these older cases have been explicitly criticized in more recent jurisprudence (e.g., the *SPS* case majority opinion by Judge Posner), many have never been officially modified. Where this is so, an attempt is made in the notes following the case to point out suggested modifications in recent academic literature. This is a reflection of the fact that in this area at least, academic commentary has preceded judicial action.

The context for licensing and assignment transactions is of course set by the Patent Act. The following provisions are most relevant.

§ 261. Ownership; assignment

Subject to the provisions of this title, patents shall have the attributes of personal property.

Applications for patent, patents, or any interest therein, shall be assignable in law by an instrument in writing. The applicant, patentee, or his assigns or legal representatives may in like manner grant and convey an exclusive right under his application for patent, or patents, to the whole or any specified part of the United States.

A certificate of acknowledgment under the hand and official seal of a person authorized to administer oaths within the United States, or, in a foreign country, of a diplomatic or consular officer of the United States or an officer authorized to administer oaths ... shall be prima facie evidence of the execution of an assignment, grant or conveyance of a patent or application for patent.

An assignment, grant or conveyance shall be void as against any subsequent purchaser or mortgagee for a valuable consideration, without notice, unless it is recorded in the Patent and Trademark Office within three months from its date or prior to the date of such subsequent purchase or mortgage.

§ 262. Joint owners

In the absence of any agreement to the contrary, each of the joint owners of a patent may make, use or sell the patented invention without the consent of and without accounting to the other owners.

A. ANTITRUST AND PATENT MISUSE

1. ILLEGAL TIE-INS

MORTON SALT CO. v. G.S. SUPPINGER CO.
314 U.S. 488 (1942)

Respondent brought this suit in the district court for an injunction and an accounting for infringement of its Patent No. 2,060,645, of November 10, 1936, on a machine for depositing salt tablets, a device said to be useful in the canning industry for adding predetermined amounts of salt in tablet form to the contents of the cans.

[T]he trial court, without passing on the issues of validity and infringement, granted summary judgment dismissing the complaint. It took the ground that respondent was making use of the patent to restrain the sale of salt tablets in competition with its own sale of unpatented tablets, by requiring licensees to use with the patented machines only tablets sold by respondent. The Court of Appeals for the Seventh Circuit reversed, because it thought that respondent's use of the patent was not shown to violate § 3 of the Clayton Act, 15 U.S.C. § 14, as it did not appear that the use of its patent substantially lessened competition or tended to create a monopoly in salt tablets. We granted certiorari because of the public importance of the question presented and of an alleged conflict of the decision below with [two other cases] and with the principles underlying the decisions in [certain older Supreme Court cases].

The Clayton Act authorizes those injured by violations tending to monopoly to maintain suit for treble damages and for an injunction in appropriate cases. But the present suit is for infringement of a patent. The question we must decide is not necessarily whether respondent has violated the Clayton Act, but whether a court of equity will lend its aid to protect the patent monopoly when respondent is using it as the effective means of restraining competition with its sale of an unpatented article.

Both respondent's wholly owned subsidiary and the petitioner manufacture and sell salt tablets used and useful in the canning trade. The tablets have a particular configuration rendering them capable of convenient use in respondent's patented machines. Petitioner makes and leases to canners unpatented salt deposition machines, charged to infringe respondent's patent. For reasons we indicate later, nothing turns on the fact that petitioner also competes with respondent in the sale of the tablets, and we may assume for purposes of this case that petitioner is doing no more than making and leasing the alleged infringing machines. The principal business of respondent's subsidiary, from which its profits are derived, is the sale of salt tablets. In connection with this business, and as an adjunct to it, respondent leases its patented machines to commercial canners, some two hundred in all, under licenses to use the machines upon condition and with the agreement of the licensees that only the subsidiary's salt tablets be used with the leased machines.

It thus appears that respondent is making use of its patent monopoly to restrain competition in the marketing of unpatented articles, salt tablets, for use with the patented machines, and is aiding in the creation of a limited monopoly in the tablets not within that granted by the patent. A patent operates to create and grant to the patentee an exclusive right to make, use and vend the particular device described and claimed in the patent. But a patent affords no immunity for a monopoly not within the grant, and the use of it to suppress competition in the sale of an unpatented article may deprive the patentee of the aid of a court of equity to restrain an alleged infringement by one who is a competitor. It is the established rule that a patentee who has granted a license on condition that the patented invention be used by the licensee only with unpatented materials furnished by the licensor, may not restrain as a contributory infringer one who sells to the licensee like materials for like use. *Motion Picture Patents Co. v. Universal Film Mfg. Co.*, 243 U.S. 502, 510 [1917].

The grant to the inventor of the special privilege of a patent monopoly carries out a public policy adopted by the Constitution and laws of the United States. But the public policy which includes inventions within the granted monopoly excludes from it all that is not embraced in the invention. It equally forbids the use of the patent to secure an exclusive right or limited monopoly not granted by the Patent Office and which it is contrary to public policy to grant.

It is a principle of general application that courts, and especially courts of equity, may appropriately withhold their aid where the plaintiff is using the right asserted contrary to the public interest. Respondent argues that this doctrine is limited in its application to those cases where the patentee seeks to restrain contributory infringement by the sale to licensees of competing unpatented articles, while here respondent seeks to restrain petitioner from a direct infringement, the manufacture and sale of the salt tablet depositor. It is said that the equitable maxim that a party seeking the aid of a court of equity must come into court with clean hands applies only to the plaintiff's wrongful conduct in the particular act or transaction which raises the equity, enforcement of which is sought; that where, as here, the patentee seeks to restrain the manufacture or use of the patented device, his conduct in using the patent to restrict competition in the sale of salt tablets does not foreclose him from seeking relief limited to an injunction against the manufacture and sale of the infringing machine alone.

Undoubtedly "equity does not demand that its suitors shall have led blameless lives"; but additional considerations must be taken into account where maintenance of the suit concerns the public interest as well as the private interests of suitors. Where the patent is used as a means of restraining competition with the patentee's sale of an unpatented product, the successful prosecution of an infringement suit even against one who is not a competitor in such sale is a powerful aid to the maintenance of the attempted monopoly of the unpatented article, and is thus a contributing factor in thwarting the public policy underlying the grant of the patent. Maintenance and enlargement of the attempted monopoly of the unpatented article are dependent to some extent upon persuading the public of the validity of the patent, which the infringement suit is intended to establish. Equity may rightly withhold its assistance from such a use of the patent by declining to entertain a suit for infringement, and should do so at least until it is made to appear that the improper practice has been abandoned and that the consequences of the misuse of the patent have been dissipated.

The reasons for barring the prosecution of such a suit against one who is not a competitor with the patentee in the sale of the unpatented product are fundamentally the same as those which preclude an infringement suit against a licensee who has violated a condition of the license by using with the licensed machine a competing unpatented article, *Motion Picture Patents Co. v. Universal Film Mfg. Co., supra*, or against a vendee of a patented or copyrighted article for violation of a condition for the maintenance of resale prices. It is the adverse effect upon the public interest of a successful infringement suit in conjunction with the patentee's course of conduct which disqualifies him to maintain the suit, regardless of whether the particular defendant has suffered from the misuse of the patent. The patentee, like these other holders of an exclusive privilege granted in the furtherance of a public policy, may not claim protection of his grant by the courts where it is being used to subvert that policy.

It is unnecessary to decide whether respondent has violated the Clayton Act, for we conclude that in any event the maintenance of the present suit to restrain petitioner's manufacture or sale of the alleged infringing machines is contrary to public policy and that the district court rightly dismissed the complaint for want of equity.

Reversed.

NOTES

1. *Effect on Licensors.* Whatever the theory behind *Morton Salt*, what is important for our purposes is its effect on licensors. This case restricts a patentee/licensor from "tying" the sale of unpatented products to the sale of a patented product. The basic idea is that it is wrong to "leverage" a patent monopoly, or "extend" it, by requiring that a licensee buy something *in addition* to the patented item itself. Note the remedy for such an attempt: the accused infringer will escape liability because of the court's equitable power to simply not enforce the patent. Note further that (1) the misuse, the inequitable "tying," need *not* rise to the level of an antitrust violation for the infringer to have this remedy; and (2) the misuse may occur in licensing agreements having nothing at all to do with the accused infringer, who may never have licensed the technology from the patentee. (In other words, the injury giving rise to a "misuse" defense is one that the public suffers, not necessarily the infringer herself.)

From the point of view of a patentee/licensor, this doctrine has the effect of eliminating or at least severely restricting the use of licensing terms which may have a quite legitimate purpose. Many have noted, for instance, that in some instances the best way to determine how much a licensee is using a patented item is to keep track of her purchases of some unpatented *input* item. (It would be as if you asked a friend to keep track of the amount of gasoline she used when borrowing your car to determine the extent of her use.) This is known as "metering." In *Morton Salt*, the theory is that Morton used a licensee's purchases of unpatented salt tablets as a way to determine how much she was using the patented salt-adding canning machine. *See, e.g.*, Bowman, *Tying Arrangements and the Leverage Problem*, 67 YALE L.J. 19 (1957); W. BOWMAN, PATENT AND ANTITRUST LAW (1973). *But see* Kaplow, *Extension of Monopoly Through Leverage*, 85 COLUM. L. REV. 515, 541 (1985) (critiquing metering rationale).

As we will see, in almost every instance where the Court has found, in these slightly dated cases, a patent misuse, recent scholarship suggests a legitimate reason for the licensing term that led to the finding of misuse. The question then is, in light of this new learning, do these older cases retain their force? As we will see below, the question has to a limited extent been answered already by recent legislation concerning misuse — the 1988 amendments to § 271 of the Patent Act. (See Section A.9, below.)

2. Resale Price Maintenance. In the case of *United States v. General Elec. Co.*, 272 U.S. 476, 485 (1926), the Court had held that it was permissible for a patentee to specify in a license agreement the resale price of the patented item (or an item made with the patented item). But this holding was questioned and limited in a subsequent case, *United States v. Line Materials Co.*, 333 U.S. 287 (1948):

> [T]he ultimate question for our decision on this appeal may be stated, succinctly and abstractly, to be as to whether in the light of the prohibition of § 1 of the Sherman Act, ... two or more patentees in the same patent field may legally combine their valid patent monopolies to secure mutual benefits for themselves through contractual agreements between themselves and other licensees, for control of the sale price of the patented devices....
>
> [T]hough the sublicenses in terms followed the pattern of *General Electric* in fixing prices only on Line's own patents, the additional right given to Line by ... Southern ..., to be the exclusive licensor of the dominant Lemmon patent [owned by Southern], made its price fixing of [Line's] own Schultz devices effective over devices embodying also the necessary Lemmon patent. By the patentees' agreement the dominant Lemmon and the subservient Schultz patents were combined to fix prices. In the absence of patent or other statutory authorization, a contract to fix or maintain prices in interstate commerce has long been recognized as illegal per se under the Sherman Act. This is true whether the fixed price is reasonable or unreasonable.

333 U.S. at 305, 307-08. *See* FINAL REPORT, TEMPORARY NATIONAL ECONOMIC COMM., S. DOC. NO. 35, 77th Cong., 1st Sess. 36, 37 (1941).

3. "Purging" the Misuse. Patent misuse is an equitable doctrine. If the patentee can show she has abandoned or "purged" her misuse and that the consequences of the misuse have been dissipated, the patent can become enforceable again. *See, e.g., B.B. Chem. Co. v. Ellis*, 314 U.S. 495, 498 (1942) ("[I]t will be appropriate to consider petitioner's right to relief when it is able to show that it has fully abandoned its present method of restraining competition in the sale of unpatented articles and that the consequences of that practice have been fully dissipated."). In some cases, it is impossible to purge the misuse, for instance, where the patentee has obtained her patent via intentional fraud on the Patent Office. *Kearney & Trecker Corp. v. Giddings & Lewis, Inc.*, 452 F.2d 579 (7th Cir. 1971). In the remaining cases, after effective elimination of an illegal provision in a license agreement or upon cessation of other improper practices, and after dissipation of the consequences of the misuse, the patent owner may again enforce the patent. *United States Gypsum Co. v. National Gypsum Co.*, 352 U.S. 457 (1957). Of course, the patentee can only seek a remedy for acts of infringement occurring after the misuse was purged. *McCullough Tool Co. v. Well Surveys, Inc.*, 343 F.2d 381, 410 (10th Cir. 1965); *Eastern Venetian Blind Co. v. Acme Steel Co.*, 188 F.2d 247, 254 (4th Cir., 1951); *Sylvania Indus. Corp. v. Visking Corp.*, 132 F.2d 947, 959 (4th Cir. 1943). Likewise, a patentee cannot collect royalties that accrue while an illegal license agreement is in effect. *United States Gypsum Co. v. National Gypsum Co., supra.* Courts have split over whether nonenforcement of an offending provision is enough to establish that it has been purged. *Compare Metals Disintegrating Co. v. Reynolds Metal Co.*, 228 F.2d 885, 889 (3d Cir. 1956) (no misuse where illegal provisions in a license agreement were not enforced); *Westinghouse Elec. Corp. v. Bulldog Elec. Prods. Co.*, 179 F.2d 139, 145 (4th Cir. 1950) (misuse purged by abandoning all efforts to enforce unlawful price control provisions), *with Berlenbach v. Anderson & Thompson Ski Co.*, 329 F.2d 782 (9th Cir. 1964) (declaring intention not to enforce an offending clause did not purge the misuse, since the clause remained in effect); *Ansul Co. v. Uniroyal, Inc.*, 445 F.2d 872, 881-82 (2d Cir. 1971), *cert. denied*, 404 U.S. 1018 (1972) (relaxation of resale price policy activities, without firmer steps to convince distributors of their actual freedom to establish their own prices, held not to constitute purge of misuse).

4. *Misuse: Still Worth Its Salt?* Recent developments have clouded the prospects of patent misuse as a defense to infringement. Chief among these is the 1988 legislation that changed the treatment of tie-ins and the like (discussed below).

2. PATENT TERM EXTENSION BY PRIVATE AGREEMENT

BRULOTTE v. THYS CO.

379 U.S. 29, 143 U.S.P.Q. (BNA) 264 (1964)

MR. JUSTICE DOUGLAS delivered the opinion of the Court.

Respondent, owner of various patents for hop-picking, sold a machine to each of the petitioners for a flat sum and issued a license for its use. Under that license there is payable a minimum royalty of $500 for each hop-picking season or $3.33 $^1/_3$ per 200 pounds of dried hops harvested by the machine, whichever is greater. The licenses by their terms may not be assigned nor may the machines be removed from Yakima County [, Washington State]. The licenses issued to petitioners listed 12 patents relating to hop-picking machines; but only seven were incorporated into the machines sold to and licensed for use by petitioners. Of those seven all expired [in] or before 1957. But the licenses issued by respondent to them continued for terms beyond that date.

Petitioners refused to make royalty payments accruing both before and after the expiration of the patents. This suit followed. One defense was misuse of the patents through extension of the license agreements beyond the expiration date of the patents. The trial court rendered judgment for respondent and the Supreme Court of Washington affirmed.

We conclude that the judgment below must be reversed insofar as it allows royalties to be collected which accrued after the last of the patents incorporated into the machines had expired.

The Constitution by Art. I, § 8 authorizes Congress to secure "for limited times" to inventors "the exclusive right" to their discoveries. Congress exercised that power by 35 U.S.C. § 154 which provides in part as follows:

> Every patent shall contain a short title of the invention and a grant to the patentee, his heirs or assigns, for the term of seventeen years, of the right to exclude others from making, using, or selling the invention throughout the United States, referring to the specification for the particulars thereof.

The right to make, the right to sell, and the right to use "may be granted or conferred separately by the patentee." *Adams v. Burke*, [84 U.S.] 17 Wall. 453, 456 [1873]. But these rights become public property once the 17-year period expires.

The Supreme Court of Washington held that in the present case the period during which royalties were required was only "a reasonable amount of time over which to spread the payments for the use of the patent." But there is intrinsic evidence that the agreements were not designed with that limited view. As we have seen, the purchase price in each case was a flat sum, the annual payments not being part of the purchase price but royalties for use of the machine during that year. The royalty payments due for the post-expiration period are by their terms for use during that period, and are not deferred payments for use during the pre-expiration period. Nor is the case like the hypothetical ones put to us where non-patented articles are marketed at prices based on use. The machines in issue here were patented articles and the royalties exacted were the same for the post-expiration period as they were for the period of the patent. That is peculiarly significant in this case in view of other provisions of the license agreements. The license agreements prevent assignment of the machines or their removal from Yakima County after, as well as before, the expiration of the patents.

Those restrictions are apt and pertinent to protection of the patent monopoly; and their applicability to the post-expiration period is a telltale sign that the licensor was using the licenses to project its monopoly beyond the patent period. They forcefully negate the suggestion that we have here a bare arrangement for a sale or a lease at an undetermined price based on use. The sale or lease of unpatented machines on long-term payments based on a deferred purchase price or on use would present wholly different considerations. Those arrangements seldom rise to the level of a federal question. But patents are in the federal domain; and "whatever the legal device employed" a projection of the patent monopoly after the patent expires is not enforceable. The present licenses draw no line between the term of the patent and the post-expiration period. The same provisions as respects both use and royalties are applicable to each. The contracts are, therefore, on their face a bald attempt to exact the same terms and conditions for the period after the patents have expired as they do for the monopoly period. We are, therefore, unable to conjecture what the bargaining position of the parties might have been and what resultant arrangement might have emerged had the provision for post-expiration royalties been divorced from the patent and nowise subject to its leverage.

In light of those considerations, we conclude that a patentee's use of a royalty agreement that projects beyond the expiration date of the patent is unlawful per se. If that device were available to patentees, the free market visualized for the post-expiration period would be subject to monopoly influences that have no proper place there.

Automatic Radio Co. v. Hazeltine, 339 U.S. 827 [1950] is not in point. While some of the patents under that license apparently had expired, the royalties claimed were not for a period when all of them had expired. That license covered several hundred patents and the royalty was based on the licensee's sales, even when no patents were used. The Court held that the computation of royalty payments by that formula was a convenient and reasonable device. We decline the invitation to extend it so as to project the patent monopoly beyond the 17-year period.

A patent empowers the owner to exact royalties as high as he can negotiate with the leverage of that monopoly. But to use that leverage to project those royalty payments beyond the life of the patent is analogous to an effort to enlarge the monopoly of the patent by tieing the sale or use of the patented article to the purchase or use of unpatented ones.

Reversed.

NOTES

1. *From the Dissent.* After arguing that Thys was actually charging his licensees for two separate things — use of his idea, and use of a particular machine — the dissent poses a hypothetical:

Assume that a Thys contract called for neither an initial flat-sum payment nor any annual minimum royalties; Thys' sole recompense for giving up ownership of its machine was a royalty payment extending beyond the patent term based on use, without any requirement either to use the machine or not to use a competitor's. A moment's thought reveals that, despite the clear restriction on use both before and after the expiration of the patent term, the arrangement would involve no misuse of patent leverage. Unless the Court's opinion rests on technicalities of contract draftsmanship and not on the economic substance of the transaction, the distinction between the hypothetical and the actual case lies only in the cumulative investment consisting of the initial and minimum payments independent of use, which the purchaser obligated himself to make to Thys. I fail to see why this distinguishing feature should be critical. If anything the investment will encourage the purchaser to use his machine in order to amortize the machine's fixed cost over as large a production base as possible. Yet the gravamen of the majority opinion is restriction, not encouragement, of use.

379 U.S. at 35-36.

2. Updates. In *Meehan v. PPG Indus.*, 802 F.2d 881, 886 (7th Cir. 1986), *cert. denied*, 479 U.S. 1091 (1987), the court held that when royalty payments extend unchanged beyond the life of a patent, the patent has been abused and the agreement is unlawful per se. Similarly, *Boggild v. Kenner Prods.*, 776 F.2d 1315, 1320-21 (6th Cir. 1985), *cert. denied*, 477 U.S. 908 (1986), held that where pre-expiration and post-expiration royalties are the same, the agreement is per se unlawful.

3. Another Dissent. A recent commentary takes issue with the premises on which *Brulotte* is based. See Caprio, *The Trouble with Brulotte: The Patent Royalty Term and Patent Monopoly Extension*, 1990 UTAH L. REV. 813 (1990). The authors claim that *Brulotte* was based on the notion that the patent application was licensed for especially good terms based on the prospect that a patent would issue, and the royalty rate called for if no patent issued was too high given the ease of entry into the industry. This is not true in many cases, according to the authors, and the rule "would invalidate a multitude of economically beneficial licensing agreements" as a consequence. *Id.* An additional flaw in the case, they say, is that it presumes the patentee and licensee are competitors, but in most cases they are not. *Id.* at 848.

4. First Sale Doctrine. *Adams v. Burke*, 84 U.S. (17 Wall.) 453 (1873), cited in the preceding case, is an important case forbidding post-sale restrictions. The Court upheld the right of a funeral parlor in Natick, Massachusetts to use a patented coffin lid purchased in Boston from a seller holding an exclusive territorial license from the patentee. The right of the patentee to limit sales ends, the Court stated, when the patented item is sold. This is an important doctrine, for it insulates purchasers further down the distribution chain from a charge of infringement growing out of a transaction further up the chain. A similar doctrine operates in Europe; this has caused some confusion in light of Community-wide rules decreeing the free exchange of goods, since the seller of an item may have a valid patent in country *A* but not country *B*, and may wish to prevent the transport of the item from country *A* to country *B*, where it could be copied free of infringement liability. *See, e.g.*, Waite & Jones, *Biotechnological Patents in Europe — The Draft Directive*, 5 EUR. INTELL. PROP. REP. 145 (1989) (describing operation of European "first sale" or "exhaustion of rights" doctrine).

5. Tie-Outs. The practice of requiring a licensee *not* to deal with competitors as a condition of a license has been held to be a violation of the antitrust laws. *See Dubuit v. Harwell Enters.*, 336 F. Supp. 1184, 171 U.S.P.Q. (BNA) 550, 1972 Trade Cases (CCH) ¶ 73,959 (D.N.C. 1971) (patent holder, by entry into an exclusive distributorship contract prohibiting distributor from manufacturing and distributing any equipment which would compete with patentee's goods, whether or not such equipment was covered by a valid patent, engaged in patent misuse and holder's patent could not be enforced against a third party even if patent holder had not tried to enforce "tie-out" provision of the contract).

6. Package Licenses. Closely related to the tie-in is the package license, where a licensor refuses to license individual patents separately but instead requires that they be licensed in a bundle. This has been held per se illegal by the Supreme Court under some circumstances. *See Automatic Radio Mfg. Co. v. Hazeltine Research, Inc.*, 339 U.S. 827 (1950). The rule against conditioning announced in *Automatic Radio* was tempered when the Court held that a package provision inserted for the convenience of the parties, rather than being forced or "conditioned" by the patent owner, did not result in misuse. *Zenith Radio Corp. v. Hazeltine Research, Inc.*, 395 U.S. 100, 138 (1969). *Compare American Sec. Co. v. Shatterproof Glass Corp.*, 268 F.2d 769, 777 (3d Cir.), *cert. denied*, 361 U.S. 902 (1959) (condemning forced mandatory package licensing under a leverage theory), *with Carpet Seaming Tape Licensing Corp.*, *infra* this chapter; *Glen Mfg., Inc. v. Perfect Fit Indus.*, 420 F.2d 319, 321 (2d Cir.), *cert. denied*, 397 U.S. 1042 (1970); *International Mfg. Co. v. Landon, Inc.*, 336 F.2d 723, 729 (9th Cir. 1964), *cert. denied*, 379 U.S. 988 (1965) (permitting forced package licensing of "blocking" patents). *See also Hensley Equip. Co. v. Esco Corp.*, 383 F.2d 55, 61 (5th Cir. 1967); *Beckman Instruments, Inc. v. Technical Dev. Corp.*, 433 F.2d 55, 61 (7th Cir. 1970) (upholding package license agreement with fixed royalty rate that expired when the last patent covered by the agreement expired), *cert. denied*, 401 U.S. 976 (1971); *McCullough Tool Co. v. Well Surveys, Inc.*, 343 F.2d 381 (10th Cir. 1965) (same); *Leesona Corp. v. Varta Batteries, Inc.*, 522 F. Supp. 1304 (S.D.N.Y. 1981) (same). *See generally* Note, *An Economic Analysis of Royalty Terms in Patent Licenses*, 67 MINN. L. REV. 1198, 1219 (1983); *USM Corp. v. SPS Techs., Inc.*, 694 F.2d 505, 511 (7th Cir. 1982) (Posner, J.), *cert. denied*, 462 U.S. 1107 (1983) (suggesting that where package is actually a "single product" package licenses and post-expiration royalties may be permissible).

This issue has been explored extensively with respect to the "block booking" of motion pictures. *See United States v. Loew's Inc.*, 371 U.S. 38 (1962) (where the seller has some market power over both components, as with a collection of copyrighted motion pictures, block booking of the motion pictures is an illegal tying arrangement). The literature suggests that a package sale may enable the seller to charge a higher price than the sum of the prices he could obtain if the products were sold separately. *See* Stigler, *United States v. Loew's Inc., A Note on Block Booking*, 1963 SUP. CT. REV. 152, 153. *See also* Kenney & Klein, *The Economics of Block Booking*, 26 J.L. & ECON. 497 (1983). *See generally* Hall, *Renting Ideas*, 64 J. BUS. 21 (1991) (explains royalty terms conventional theory cannot account for, in terms of efficient tax and performance bond; enforcement by rightsholder encouraged by arrangement tying royalties to licensee's sales).

ARONSON v. QUICK POINT PENCIL CO.
440 U.S. 257, 201 U.S.P.Q. (BNA) 1 (1979)

We granted certiorari to consider whether federal patent law pre-empts state contract law so as to preclude enforcement of a contract to pay royalties to a patent applicant, on sales of articles embodying the putative invention, for so long as the contracting party sells them, if a patent is not granted.

(1)

In October 1955 the petitioner, Mrs. Jane Aronson, filed an application for a patent on a new form of keyholder. Although ingenious, the design was so simple that it readily could be copied unless it was protected by patent. In June 1956, while the patent application was pending, Mrs. Aronson negotiated a contract with the respondent, Quick Point Pencil Co., for the manufacture and sale of the keyholder.

The contract was embodied in two documents. In the first, a letter from Quick Point to Mrs. Aronson, Quick Point agreed to pay Mrs. Aronson a royalty of 5% of the selling price in return for "the exclusive right to make and sell keyholders of the type shown in your application." The letter further provided that the parties would consult one another concerning the steps to be taken "[i]n the event of any infringement."

The contract did not require Quick Point to manufacture the keyholder. Mrs. Aronson received a $750 advance on royalties and was entitled to rescind the exclusive license if Quick Point did not sell a million keyholders by the end of 1957. Quick Point retained the right to cancel the agreement whenever "the volume of sales does not meet our expectations." The duration of the agreement was not otherwise prescribed.

A contemporaneous document provided that if Mrs. Aronson's patent application was "not allowed within five (5) years, Quick Point Pencil Co. [would] pay ... two and one half percent (2½%) of sales ... so long as you [Quick Point] continue to sell same."

In June 1961, when Mrs. Aronson had failed to obtain a patent on the keyholder within the five years specified in the agreement, Quick Point asserted its contractual right to reduce royalty payments to 2½% of sales. In September of that year the Board of Patent Appeals issued a final rejection of the application on the ground that the keyholder was not patentable, and Mrs. Aronson did not appeal. Quick Point continued to pay reduced royalties to her for 14 years thereafter.

The market was more receptive to the keyholder's novelty and utility than the Patent Office. By September 1975 Quick Point had made sales in excess of $7 million and paid Mrs. Aronson royalties totaling $203,963.84; sales were continuing to rise. However, while Quick Point was able to pre-empt the market in the earlier years and was long the only manufacturer of the Aronson keyholder, copies began to appear in the late 1960's. Quick Point's competitors, of course, were not required to pay royalties for their use of the design. Quick Point's share of the Aronson keyholder market has declined during the past decade.

(2)

In November 1975 Quick Point commenced an action in the United States District Court for a declaratory judgment that the royalty agreement was unenforceable. Quick Point asserted that state law which might otherwise make the contract enforceable was preempted by federal patent law. This is the only issue presented to us for decision.

Both parties moved for summary judgment on affidavits, exhibits, and stipulations of fact. The District Court concluded that the "language of the agreement is plain, clear and unequivocal and has no relation as to whether or not a patent is ever granted." Accordingly, it held that the agreement was valid, and that Quick Point was obliged to pay the agreed royalties pursuant to the contract for so long as it manufactured the keyholder.

The Court of Appeals reversed, one judge dissenting. It held that since the parties contracted with reference to a pending patent application, Mrs. Aronson was estopped from denying that patent law principles governed her contract with Quick Point. Although acknowledging that this Court had never decided the precise issue, the Court of Appeals held that our prior decisions regarding patent licenses compelled the conclusion that Quick Point's contract with Mrs. Aronson became unenforceable once she failed to obtain a patent. The court held that a continuing obligation to pay royalties would be contrary to "the strong federal policy favoring the full and free use of ideas in the public domain," *Lear, Inc. v. Adkins*, 395 U.S. 653, 674 (1969). The court also observed that if Mrs. Aronson actually had obtained a patent, Quick Point would have escaped its royalty obligations either if the patent were held to be invalid, or upon its expiration after 17 years, see *Brulotte v. Thys Co.* Accordingly, it concluded that a licensee should be relieved of royalty obligations when the licensor's efforts to obtain a contemplated patent prove unsuccessful.

(3)

On this record it is clear that the parties contracted with full awareness of both the pendency of a patent application and the possibility that a patent might not issue. The clause de-escalating the royalty by half in the event no patent issued within five years makes that crystal clear. Quick Point apparently placed a significant value on exploiting the basic novelty of the device, even if no patent issued; its success demonstrates that this judgment was well founded. Assuming, arguendo, that the initial letter and the commitment to pay a 5% royalty was subject to federal patent law, the provision relating to the 2½% royalty was explicitly independent of federal law. The cases and principles relied on by the Court of Appeals and Quick Point do not bear on a contract that does not rely on a patent, particularly where, as here, the contracting parties agreed expressly as to alternative obligations if no patent should issue.

Commercial agreements traditionally are the domain of state law. State law is not displaced merely because the contract relates to intellectual property which may or may not be patentable; the states are free to regulate the use of such intellectual property in any manner not inconsistent with federal law. *Kewanee Oil Co. v. Bicron Corp.*, 416 U.S. 470, 479, 94 S. Ct. 1879, 1885, 40 L. Ed. 2d 315 (1974). In this as in other fields, the question of whether federal law preempts state law "involves a consideration of whether that law 'stands as an obstacle to the accomplishment and execution of the full purposes and objectives of Congress.'" If it does not, state law governs.

In *Kewanee Oil Co.*, we reviewed the purposes of the federal patent system. First, patent law seeks to foster and reward invention; second, it promotes disclosure of inventions, to stimulate further innovation and to permit the public to practice the invention once the patent expires; third, the stringent requirements for patent protection seek to assure that ideas in the public domain remain there for the free use of the public.

Enforcement of Quick Point's agreement with Mrs. Aronson is not inconsistent with any of these aims. Permitting inventors to make enforceable agreements licensing the use of their inventions in return for royalties provides an additional incentive to invention. Similarly, encouraging Mrs. Aronson to make arrangements for the manufacture of her keyholder furthers the federal policy of disclosure of inventions; these simple devices display the novel idea which they embody wherever they are seen.

Quick Point argues that enforcement of such contracts conflicts with the federal policy against withdrawing ideas from the public domain and discourages recourse to the federal patent system by allowing states to extend "perpetual protection to articles too lacking in novelty to merit any patent at all under federal constitutional standards."

We find no merit in this contention. Enforcement of the agreement does not withdraw any idea from the public domain. The design for the keyholder was not in the public domain before Quick Point obtained its license to manufacture it. In negotiating the agreement, Mrs. Aronson disclosed the design in confidence. Had Quick Point tried to exploit the design in breach of that confidence, it would have risked legal liability. It is equally clear that the design entered the public domain as a result of the manufacture and sale of the keyholders under the contract.

Requiring Quick Point to bear the burden of royalties for the use of the design is no more inconsistent with federal patent law than any of the other costs involved in being the first to introduce a new product to the market, such as outlays for research and development, and marketing and promotional expenses. For reasons which Quick Point's experience with the Aronson keyholder demonstrate, innovative entrepreneurs have usually found such costs to be well worth paying.

Finally, enforcement of this agreement does not discourage anyone from seeking a patent. Mrs. Aronson attempted to obtain a patent for over five years. It is quite true that had she succeeded, she would have received a 5% royalty only on keyholders sold during the 17-year life of the patent. Offsetting the limited terms of royalty payments, she would have received twice as much per dollar of Quick Point's sales, and both she and Quick Point could have licensed any others who produced the same keyholder. Which course would have produced the greater yield to the contracting parties is a matter of speculation; the parties resolved the uncertainties by their bargain.

(4)

No decision of this Court relating to patents justifies relieving Quick Point of its contract obligations. We have held that a state may not forbid the copying of an idea in the public domain which does not meet the requirements for federal patent protection. Enforcement of Quick Point's agreement, however, does not prevent anyone from copying the keyholder. It merely requires Quick Point to pay the consideration which it promised in return for the use of a novel device which enabled it to pre-empt the market.

In *Lear, Inc. v. Adkins*, 395 U.S. 653 (1969), we held that a person licensed to use a patent may challenge the validity of the patent, and that a licensee who establishes that the patent is invalid need not pay the royalties accrued under the licensing agreement subsequent to the issuance of the patent. Both holdings relied on the desirability of encouraging licensees to challenge the validity of patents, to further the strong federal policy that only inventions which meet the rigorous requirements of patentability shall be withdrawn from the public domain. Accordingly, neither the holding nor the rationale of *Lear* controls when no patent has issued, and no ideas have been withdrawn from public use.

Enforcement of the royalty agreement here is also consistent with the principles treated in *Brulotte v. Thys Co.* There, we held that the obligation to pay royalties in return for the use of a patented device may not extend beyond the life of the patent. The principle underlying that holding was simply that the monopoly granted under a patent cannot lawfully be used to "negotiate with the leverage of that monopoly." The Court emphasized that to "use that leverage to project those royalty payments beyond the life of the patent is analogous to an effort to enlarge the monopoly of the patent...." Here the reduced royalty which is challenged, far from being negotiated "with the leverage" of a patent, rested on the contingency that no patent would issue within five years.

No doubt a pending patent application gives the applicant some additional bargaining power for purposes of negotiating a royalty agreement. The pending application allows the inventor to hold out the hope of an exclusive right to exploit the idea, as well as the threat that the other party will be prevented from using the idea for 17 years. However, the amount of leverage arising from a patent application depends on how likely the parties consider it to be that a valid patent will issue. Here, where no patent ever issued, the record is entirely clear that the parties assigned a substantial likelihood to that contingency, since they specifically provided for a reduced royalty in the event no patent issued within five years.

This case does not require us to draw the line between what constitutes abuse of a pending application and what does not. It is clear that whatever role the pending application played in the negotiation of the 5% royalty, it played no part in the contract to pay the 2½% royalty indefinitely.

Our holding in *Kewanee Oil Co.* puts to rest the contention that federal law pre-empts and renders unenforceable the contract made by these parties. There we held that state law forbidding the misappropriation of trade secrets was not pre-empted by federal patent law. We observed: "Certainly the patent policy of encouraging invention is not disturbed by the existence of another form of incentive to invention. In this respect the two systems [patent and trade secret law] are not and never would be in conflict."

Enforcement of this royalty agreement is even less offensive to federal patent policies than state law protecting trade secrets. The most commonly accepted definition of trade secrets is restricted to confidential information which is not disclosed in the normal process of exploitation. See Restatement of Torts § 757, Comment b, p. 5 (1939). Accordingly, the exploitation of trade secrets under state law may not satisfy the federal policy in favor of disclosure, whereas disclosure is inescapable in exploiting a device like the Aronson keyholder.

Enforcement of these contractual obligations, freely undertaken in arm's-length negotiation and with no fixed reliance on a patent or a probable patent grant, will "encourage invention in areas where patent law does not reach, and will prompt the independent innovator to proceed with the discovery and exploitation of his invention. Competition is fostered and the public is not deprived of the use of valuable, if not quite patentable, invention."

The device which is the subject of this contract ceased to have any secrecy as soon as it was first marketed, yet when the contract was negotiated the inventiveness and novelty were sufficiently apparent to induce an experienced novelty manufacturer to agree to pay for the opportunity to be first in the market. Federal patent law is not a barrier to such a contract.

Reversed.

NOTES

1. *Blackmun's Concurrence.* The concurring opinion by Blackmun shows that he has a much harder time distinguishing the facts of the case before him from those in *Brulotte*:

> For me, the hard question is whether this case can meaningfully be distinguished from *Brulotte*. There the Court held that a patent licensor could not use the leverage of its patent to obtain a royalty contract that extended beyond the patent's 17-year term. Here Mrs. Aronson has used the leverage of her patent application to negotiate a royalty contract which continues to be binding even though the patent application was long ago denied.
>
> The Court asserts that her leverage played "no part" with respect to the contingent agreement to pay a reduced royalty if no patent issued within five years. Yet it may well be that Quick Point agreed to that contingency in order to obtain its other rights that depended on the success of the patent application. The parties did not apportion consideration in the neat fashion the Court adopts.
>
> In my view, the holding in *Brulotte* reflects hostility toward extension of a patent monopoly whose term is fixed by statute. Such hostility has no place here. A patent application which is later denied temporarily discourages unlicensed imitators. Its benefits and hazards are of a different magnitude from those of a granted patent that prohibits all competition for 17 years. Nothing justifies estopping a patent-application licensor from entering into a contract whose term does not end if the application fails.

440 U.S. at 266-67.

2. *Differential Royalties.* There is authority for the proposition that licenses granted to competing licensees at about the same time, or with no significant intervening change in surrounding economic conditions, where they call for royalties sufficiently different to impair the ability of the disfavored licensee(s) to complete, may constitute both a misuse of the licensed industrial property and an unfair method of competition violating § 5 of the Federal Trade Commission (FTC) Act. *See LaPeyre v. FTC*, 366 F.2d 117 (5th Cir. 1966); *Laitram Corp. v. King Crab*, 244 F. Supp. 9 (D. Alaska 1965), *modified*, 245 F. Supp. 1019 (D. Alaska 1966); *Peelers Co. v. Wendt*, 260 F. Supp. 193 (D. Wash. 1966).

3. *Territorial and Field-of-Use Limitations*. Patent Act § 261 says: "The applicant, patentee, or his assigns or legal representatives may ... grant and convey an exclusive right under his application for patent, or patents, to the whole *or any specified part* of the United States." Territorial limitations, such as the one imposed by the patentee in *Adams v. Burke*, 84 U.S. (17 Wall.) 453 (1873) (described in a Note to a case earlier in this chapter) are therefore authorized. What about limitations to a particular field of use, e.g., a license to use a chemical compound as a topical dermatological treatment except for the removal of skin wrinkles? *See General Talking Pictures v. Western Elec.*, 305 U.S. 124 (1938) (field of use license upheld). *See also Ansul Co. v. Uniroyal, Inc.*, 306 F. Supp. 541, 163 U.S.P.Q. (BNA) 517 (S.D.N.Y. 1969) (same), *aff'd in part, rev'd in part and remanded*, 448 F.2d 872, 169 U.S.P.Q. (BNA) 759 (2d Cir. 1971), *cert. denied*, 404 U.S. 1018 (1972); *Benger Labs. v. R.K. Laros*, 209 F. Supp. 639 (E.D. Pa. 1962), *aff'd per curiam*, 317 F. 2d 455 (3d Cir. 1963), *cert. denied*, 375 U.S. 833 (1963) (separate licenses, one exclusively for the veterinary field and the other exclusively for the human field, sustained); *Chemagro v. Universal Chem.*, 244 F. Supp. 486 (E.D. Tex. 1965) (upholding legality of license prohibiting reformulation for use in the home gardening field, but permitting use in the commercial field). This makes sense, since different end uses by different licensees may make the licensed technology of greater value to one licensee than it is to another; this will in general justify any differential in royalties among licensees.

From an economic point of view, permitting differential royalty rates for various end uses simply allows the patentee to practice "price discrimination" — i.e., charge each group of users the maximum it is willing to pay for the technology. It is thought that there is seldom any harm in permitting this. *See* Besen & Raskind, *An Introduction to the Law and Economics of Intellectual Property*, 5 J. ECON. PERSP. 3, 5 (1991) (explaining first sale doctrine as way to prevent patentee from exercising "excessive" price discrimination). *Cf.* Staaf, *International Price Discrimination and the Gray Market*, 4 INTELL. PROP. J. 301 (1989) (describing gray market for "parallel imports" as attempt to circumvent U.S. manufacturers' price discrimination policies; drawing analogy to Robinson-Patman Act in defense of these attempts to defeat price discrimination).

3. FRAUDULENT PATENT ACQUISITIONS AS AN ANTITRUST DEFENSE: BACK INTO THE SHADOWS

In *Walker Process Equip., Inc. v. Food Mach. & Chem. Corp.*, 382 U.S. 172, 176 (1965), the Supreme Court announced that fraudulent acquisition of a patent could rise to the level of an antitrust violation under certain circumstances. For the next thirty years or so, this was a viable defense, much-loved by infringement defendants as a way to get some counter-leverage in the strategic litigation wars.

See James B. Kobak, Jr., *Professional Real Estate Investors and the Future of Patent-Antitrust Litigation:* Walker Process *and* Handgards *Meet* Noerr-Pennington, 63 ANTITRUST L.J. 185 (1994).

In numerous cases courts applied *Walker Process* vigorously. In an important case the Ninth Circuit, for example, found that a jury had had sufficient evidence to show that a patentee had "attempt[ed] to enforce a government granted monopoly to which the patent holder knows he has no right," and had engaged in bad-faith prosecution of the infringement suit. *Handgards, Inc. v. Ethicon, Inc.*, 743 F.2d 1282 (9th Cir. 1984), *cert. denied*, 469 U.S. 1190 (1985). Since Handgards had proved "(1) by clear and convincing evidence that Ethicon prosecuted the ... patent in bad faith, (2) that Ethicon had a specific intent to monopolize the relevant market, and (3) that a dangerous probability of success existed," the Ninth Circuit affirmed Ethicon's antitrust liability. *Id.* at 1289.

Almost thirty years after *Walker Process*, however, the tables turned dramatically. In *Professional Real Estate Investors, Inc. v. Columbia Pictures Indus., Inc.*, 508 U.S. 49, 113 S. Ct. 1920 (1993), the Supreme Court once again confronted a charge that a patentee had procured a patent by fraud, and therefore that the ensuing litigation to enforce it had been a "sham." (Such a showing is required under the so-called *Noerr-Pennington* doctrine of antitrust law, which generally exempts appeals to the governmental process from antitrust liability.) The *Professional Real Estate* Court found that an objectively reasonable effort to litigate cannot be "sham," within the meaning of the *Noerr* doctrine, regardless of the plaintiff's subjective intent. As a consequence, after *Professional Real Estate*, it has become quite difficult to prevail on a claim that a plaintiff suing for infringement of a patent or copyright was attempting to monopolize in violation of the antitrust laws. *See* James B. Kobak, Jr., *Professional Real Estate Investors and the Future of Patent-Antitrust Litigation:* Walker Process *and* Handgards *Meet* Noerr-Pennington, 63 ANTITRUST L.J. 185 (1994). *See, e.g., Novo Nordisk of N. Am., Inc. v. Genentech Inc.*, 885 F. Supp. 522, 35 U.S.P.Q.2d 1058 (S.D.N.Y. 1995) (defendant has immunity, under *Noerr-Pennington* doctrine, from plaintiffs' claim for antitrust injury allegedly suffered in defending attempt to enforce invalid patents before U.S. International Trade Commission); *FilmTec Corp. v. Hydranautics*, 67 F.3d 931, 36 U.S.P.Q.2d 1410 (Fed. Cir. 1995) (patent infringement action was not objectively baseless litigation subject to suit under antitrust laws, even though plaintiff was held, on appeal, to lack valid title to patent in suit). Interestingly, in *Hydranautics v. FilmTec Corp.*, 70 F.3d 533, 36 U.S.P.Q.2d 1773 (9th Cir. 1995) (refusing to dismiss fraudulent procurement-type antitrust claim because plaintiff asserted facts in its complaint that, if true, would prove that defendant obtained patent by fraud), a contrary opinion in the same case was issued by the Ninth Circuit. These cases stem from the ownership dispute that is at the heart of the other *FilmTec* opinions in this chapter.

NOTE

On the general topic of acquiring patents and competition policy, a recent paper has this to say:

> [U]nder contemporary conditions, the dominance of the large, vertically integrated R&D firm is giving way to an industrial structure featuring more diverse organizational forms. The emergence of "strategic partnering," joint ventures, and the like is changing the landscape of many industries. One effect is that large, all-encompassing firms, vertically integrated into R&D, are less common than they were before. This makes it less likely that "killer patent portfolios," of the type made famous in the *United Shoe* case, will dominate whole industries. Indeed, I have argued elsewhere that stronger intellectual property rights may lower transaction costs, thus encouraging dis-integration via contract-intensive organizations. On the other hand, stronger patent rights bring new problems. In particular, there is now a greater incentive to perfect "creative" patent acquisition practices not widely employed previously, which may open new avenues of anticompetitive behavior. For example, some firms now acquire third party patents which are then re-submitted to the Patent Office and broadened to cover competitor's products. This practice of intentional acquisitions to block competitors raises difficult and potentially serious questions of patent policy, and highlights the need to adapt both patent and antitrust doctrine to new patent acquisition practices.

Robert P. Merges, "Antitrust Review of Patent Acquisitions: Property Rights, Firm Boundaries, and Organization," paper presented at the Conference on Intellectual Property and Competition Policy, sponsored by the Bureau of Competition, Industry Canada, Aylmer, Quebec, May, 1996.

4. A BRIEF NOTE ON JUSTICE HOLMES AND THE LOGIC OF PARTIAL EXCLUSION

Justice Holmes disposed of the problem of restrictions in patent license agreements with an impressive flourish in his dissent in *Motion Picture Patents Co. v. Universal Film Mfg. Co.*, 243 U.S. 502, 510 (1917):

> I suppose that a patentee has no less property in his patented machine than any other owner, and that, in addition to keeping the machine to himself, the patent gives him the further right to forbid the rest of the world from making others like it. In short, for whatever motive, he may keep his device wholly out of use. *Continental Paper Bag Co. v. Eastern Paper Bag Co.* 210 U.S. 405 [1908]. So much being undisputed, I cannot understand why he may not keep it out of use unless the licensee, or, for the matter of that, the buyer, will use some unpatented thing in connection with it. Generally speaking, the measure of a condition is the consequence of a breach, and if

that consequence is one that the owner may impose unconditionally, he may impose it conditionally upon a certain event. *Non debit cui plus licet, quod minus est non licere.* D. 50, 17, 21 [Ulpian].

No doubt this principle might be limited or excluded in cases where the condition tends to bring about a state of things that there is a predominant public interest to prevent. But there is no predominant public interest to prevent a patented teapot or film feeder from being kept from the public, because, as I have said, the patentee may keep them tied up at will while his [monopoly] lasts. Neither is there any such interest to prevent the purchase of the tea or films that is made the condition of the use of the machine. The supposed contravention of public interest sometimes is stated as an attempt to extend the patent law to unpatented articles, which of course it is not, and more accurately as a possible domination to be established by such means. But the domination is one only to the extent of the desire for the teapot or film feeder, and if the owner prefers to keep the pot or the feeder unless you will buy his tea or films, I cannot see, in allowing him the right to do so, anything more than an ordinary incident of ownership, or, at most, a consequence of the *Paper Bag* Case, on which, as it seems to me, this case ought to turn.

243 U.S. at 519-20.

This view was explicitly addressed in *United States v. Masonite Corp.*, 316 U.S. 265, 277-78 (1942):

> But it will not do to say that since the patentee has the power to refuse a license, he has the lesser power to license on his own conditions. There are strict limitations on the power of the patentee to attach conditions to the use of the patented article. As Chief Justice Taney said in *Bloomer v. Mc-Quewan*, [55 U.S.] 14 How. 539, 549 [1852], when the patented product *"passes to the hands of the purchaser, it* is no longer within the limits of the monopoly. It passes outside of it, and is no longer under the protection of the act of Congress."

The quote from *Bloomer* emphasizes that so long as the patented item is within the patentee's control, she can attach conditions to its use — and therefore the courts can place "strict limitations" on these conditions to guard against abuse.

The Latin phrase cited by Holmes, which is taken from a Roman Digest entry attributed to the great jurist Ulpian, translates roughly as "He to whom the greater is lawful ought not to be debarred from the less as unlawful." It is thus one form of the general maxim, "the greater includes the lesser." Its application in this context lends a great deal of logical appeal to Holmes' position, which seems to be that a patentee can attach any condition she wants to the use of her patent, since she has the right to exclude others from using it entirely.

There are several problems with this form of reasoning. First, it contains a possible fallacy: that the greater power *logically and necessarily* implies each and every lesser power. Holmes looks to the statute and finds that a patent gives its holder the complete power to exclude. (That is the ultimate conclusion in the *Paper Bag* case, which upheld the patentee's absolute right to an injunction.) But is this initial grant really so complete, or is it accompanied by restrictions (express or implied) on the ways it may be used? There are two ways the grant of a right to exclude could fall short of the absolute power Holmes assumes it is: (1) as an empirical matter, the right to restrict the use of an invention may be worth more to its holder than an absolute right to exclude, perhaps in the long run anyway; and (2) the government's *initial grant* of the right to exclude might contain limitations (express or implied) that render it something less than an absolute power. In either case, the right to exclude might not in fact be the greater power, or it might be greater in general but yet still exclude certain lesser powers.

As to (1) above, if you assume that the right to exclude is really the "greater power," the "lesser powers" to restrict follow; the question is whether this assumption is legitimate. That is, in the syllogism (A) Greater includes lesser; (B) Right to exclude greater than right to restrict use; (C) Therefore right to exclude includes right to restrict use, the conclusion (C) might logically follow, but premise (B) may not be valid. Admittedly, this is difficult (although not impossible) to envision in our case. Instead of imagining scenarios where the inventor extorts all sorts of advantage via restrictions on the use of an invention, perhaps it is more worthwhile to focus on the issue of how we should measure the "greater" and "lesser" powers. From the point of view of licensees in dire need of an invention, the power of the patentee to keep it from them entirely may (in the short run anyway) be a greater power than the right to restrict their behavior in exchange for the use of the invention. But the story may be otherwise from *society's* point of view. Although the reduction in output from an industry in dire need of an invention may be large, it is not impossible to imagine that the long-term reduction in output stemming from a successful and far-reaching monopoly in an entire industry may lead to a greater reduction in output. Since it is conceivable that the holder of a key patent could obtain this result through restrictions on its use, it follows that the (long-term) "power" flowing from the right to restrict may in fact be greater than the power to exclude competitors entirely. Again, the key is that the patentee's power is asserted not only over its licensees, but also, although indirectly, over society at large. *Cf.* Turner, *Legal Restrictions on Exploitation of the Patent Monopoly: An Economic Analysis*, 76 YALE L.J. 267, 276 (1966) ("sound answers to the problems the [tie-in] cases posed cannot be reached by ... metaphysical assertions that the right to exclude totally necessarily embraces the right to exclude partially" (citations omitted)).

The second, and perhaps more important, counterargument turns the "greater/lesser" logic employed by Holmes against him. Instead of conceiving the patentee's absolute right to exclude as the starting point of the analysis, and then looking for lesser powers that flow from this, take an earlier starting point: before the patent issues, or before a patent system is even put in place. At this point, the patentee has no rights whatsoever. Without a statute to confer it, she has no power, greater or lesser. The legislature, contemplating the need for and specifics of a patent system, holds all the power. One might say that they have the power to declare a very pro-patentee system, a very anti-patentee (i.e., weak protection) system, or indeed no patent system at all. The latter, in a sense, is their greatest power over the inventor/prospective patentee. And of course all the "lesser" powers — to create various patent systems, giving protections weak and strong — flow from this greater power. As a consequence, one cannot question the legislature's right to restrict the patentee to certain licensing practices, even in light of a patent's general power to exclude; for if the legislature can deny a patent altogether (exercise greater power), surely it can issue one with restrictions (exercise lesser powers). And so we see that at least with respect to legislation, Holmes' argumentation strategy can just as easily support the opposite view. *See generally* Meyers & Lewis, *The Patent "Franchise" and the Antitrust Laws, Part I*, 30 GEO. L.J. 117 (1941) (contrasting "private property" view of patents with "public franchise" view, and suggesting latter is more appropriate).

Note that in his dissent in *Motion Picture Patents* Holmes goes on to argue that the majority diverges from longstanding precedent, and therefore disturbs the settled expectations of patentees, an argument which holds less force today now that restrictions on licensing are an accepted part of the patent/antitrust relationship.

The appeal of the Holmesian construct has not been lost on modern observers. The "Chicago School" position on license restrictions is an example. (For this view, see, e.g., Bowman, *Tying Arrangements and the Leverage Problem*, 67 YALE L.J. 19 (1957)). Under this approach a tie-in, for example, should only very rarely constitute patent misuse, since the maximum value the patentee can obtain from a license is the full monopoly rent from the invention, and it makes no difference whether this rent is collected directly or via a tie-in of some kind. In other words, there is a fixed quantum of value stemming from the invention; we should be indifferent as to how the patentee collects it. Note the affinity with Holmes' reasoning: the "greater power" (full monopoly rent) includes all the lesser powers (licensing restrictions) needed to realize that greater power (or rent).

The "Chicago School" view is explained nicely — and dissected — by Kaplow, who argues first that there is no workable distinction between maximizing the value of current monopoly power and extending that power into new markets (which even Chicago School theorists condemn). Second, Kaplow makes the common-sensical point that it very often *does* matter how a given quantum of power is used; he cites the example of a terrorist on the loose with a stick of dynamite, a case where we certainly do care where this fixed degree of power is brought to bear. Although Kaplow remains somewhat agnostic about the patentee's ability to leverage in a variety of situations, he successfully undermines the simplistic assumptions of the "fixed quantum" view of tie-ins and the like. Kaplow, *Extension of Monopoly Through Leverage*, 85 COLUM. L. REV. 515

(1985). *See also* Slawson, *Excluding Competition Without Monopoly Power: The Use of Tying Arrangements to Exploit Market Failure*, 36 ANT. BULL. 457 (1991). *Cf.* Klitzke, *Patent Licensing: Concerted Action by Licensees*, 13 DEL. J. CORP. L. 459 (1988) ("nonexclusive licenses granted to more than one competitor at the same level of product distribution may be anticompetitive if the licenses contain the same restraints and the restraints either reduce competition between the licensees or unreasonably exclude nonlicensees from the market. Where the purpose of price restrictions in licenses to competing sellers is to establish horizontal price fixing or horizontal allocation of markets, section one of the Sherman Act may be violated. Indeed, the violation may be illegal per se."); Panel Discussion (Katsch, Brown & Scherer), *The Value of Patents and Other Legally Protected Commercial Rights*, 52 ANT. L.J. 542 (1984) (criticizing Chicago School view). *See generally* Turner, *Legal Restrictions on Exploitation of the Patent Monopoly: An Economic Analysis*, 76 YALE L.J. 267, 300-06 (1966) (critical of tie-ins in certain circumstances).

NOTES

    1. *Poking Holes in the Paper Bag Case.* Justice Douglas directed one of his typically stinging patent case dissents at the "absolute" property rule position of the *Paper Bag* case, cited by Holmes in the preceding section:

> [A] patentee's "title is exclusive, and so clearly within the constitutional provisions in respect of private property that he is neither bound to use his discovery himself, no permit others to use it." That theory was adopted by this Court in *Continental Paper Bag Co. v. Eastern Paper Bag Co....* I think it is time to be rid of that rule.... It is a mistake ... to conceive of a patent as but another form of private property. The patent is a privilege "conditioned by a public purpose." The public purpose is "to promote the Progress of Science and useful Arts." The exclusive right of the inventor is but the means to that end.... But the *Paper Bag* case marked a radical departure from that theory. It treated the "exclusive" right of the inventor as something akin to an "absolute" right. It subordinated the public purpose of the grant to the self-interest of the patentee. The result is that suppression of patents has become commonplace. Patents are multiplied to protect an economic barony or empire, not to put new discoveries to use for the common good.... The use of a new patent is suppressed so as to preclude experimentation which might result in further invention by competitors. A whole technology is blocked off. The result is a clog to our economic machine and a barrier to an economy of abundance.

Special Equip. Co. v. Coe, 324 U.S. 370, 381-83 (1945). Another case from the same general era comments on the right of a patentee not to practice his or her invention, in the context of wide-ranging remarks on the private and public aspects of patents:

It is surely questionable, then, whether the control of our industrial development, so far as it is exercised through patents, should be left solely to
patentees; as the public interest is deeply involved, it would seem wise that
representatives of the public should at least participate in decisions of any
such matters. For patents are governmentally created monopolies. The Supreme Court has called them "public franchises," granted by the government,
acting on behalf of the public. It is, accordingly, appropriate to ask whether
the holder of such a public franchise should be permitted, without any
governmental control whatever, to decide that no public use should be made
of the franchise during its life or only such public use as the franchise-
holder, in its utterly unregulated discretion, deems wise, and at such prices
as it sees fit to exact. We accord no such powers to the holder of a public
franchise to run a bus line or to sell electric power. To bring patents into
line with the constitutional provision relating to patents, it is worth considering whether they should not, by statute, be assimilated, to some extent, to
certificates of convenience and necessity.

Picard v. United Aircraft Corp., 128 F.2d 632, 645 (2d Cir. 1942) (Frank, J.,
concurring).

5. LICENSEE AND ASSIGNOR ESTOPPEL

LEAR, INC. v. ADKINS
395 U.S. 653, 162 U.S.P.Q. (BNA) 1 (1969)

MR. JUSTICE HARLAN delivered the opinion of the Court.

In January of 1952, John Adkins, an inventor and mechanical engineer, was
hired by Lear, Incorporated, for the purpose of solving a vexing problem the
company had encountered in its efforts to develop a gyroscope which would meet
the increasingly demanding requirements of the aviation industry. The gyroscope
is an essential component of the navigational system in all aircraft, enabling the
pilot to learn the direction and altitude of his airplane. With the development of
the faster airplanes of the 1950's, more accurate gyroscopes were needed, and
the gyro industry consequently was casting about for new techniques which
would satisfy this need in an economical fashion. Shortly after Adkins was hired,
he developed a method of construction at the company's California facilities
which improved gyroscope accuracy at a low cost. Lear almost immediately
incorporated Adkins' improvements into its production process to its substantial
advantage.

The question that remains unsettled in this case, after eight years of litigation
in the California courts, is whether Adkins will receive compensation for Lear's
use of those improvements which the inventor has subsequently patented. At
every stage of this lawsuit, Lear has sought to prove that, despite the grant of a
patent by the Patent Office, none of Adkins' improvements were sufficiently
novel to warrant the award of a monopoly under the standards delineated in the

governing federal statutes. Moreover, the company has sought to prove that Adkins obtained his patent by means of a fraud on the Patent Office. In response, the inventor has argued that since Lear had entered into a licensing agreement with Adkins, it was obliged to pay the agreed royalties regardless of the validity of the underlying patent.

The Supreme Court of California unanimously vindicated the inventor's position. While the court recognized that generally a manufacturer is free to challenge the validity of an inventor's patent, it held that "one of the oldest doctrines in the field of patent law establishes that so long as a licensee is operating under a license agreement he is estopped to deny the validity of his licensor's patent in a suit for royalties under the agreement. The theory underlying this doctrine is that a licensee should not be permitted to enjoy the benefit afforded by the agreement while simultaneously urging that the patent which forms the basis of the agreement is void."

Almost 20 years ago, in its last consideration of the doctrine, this Court also invoked an estoppel to deny a licensee the right to prove that his licensor was demanding royalties for the use of an idea which was in reality a part of the public domain. *Automatic Radio Manufacturing Co. v. Hazeltine Research, Inc.*, 339 U.S. 827, 836 (1950). We granted certiorari in the present case to reconsider the validity of the *Hazeltine* rule in the light of our recent decisions emphasizing the strong federal policy favoring free competition in ideas which do not merit patent protection.

At the very beginning of the parties' relationship, Lear and Adkins entered into a rudimentary one-page agreement which provided that although "(a)ll new ideas, discoveries, inventions, etc., related to ... vertical gyros become the property of Mr. John S. Adkins," the inventor promised to grant Lear a license as to all ideas he might develop "on a mutually satisfactory royalty basis." As soon as Adkins' labors yielded tangible results, it quickly became apparent to the inventor that further steps should be taken to place his rights to his ideas on a firmer basis. On February 4, 1954, Adkins filed an application with the Patent Office in an effort to gain federal protection for his improvements. At about the same time, he entered into a lengthy period of negotiations with Lear [that eventually resulted in an agreement on September 15, 1955], when the parties approved a complex 17-page contract which carefully delineated the conditions upon which Lear promised to pay royalties for Adkins' improvements.

The parties agreed that if "the U.S. Patent Office refuses to issue a patent on the substantial claims (contained in Adkins' original patent application) or if such a patent so issued is subsequently held invalid, then in any of such events Lear at its option shall have the right forthwith to terminate the specific license so affected or to terminate this entire Agreement...." As the contractual language indicates, Adkins had not obtained a final Patent Office decision as to the patentability of his invention at the time the licensing agreement was concluded. Indeed, he was not to receive a patent until January 5, 1960. This long delay has its source in the special character of Patent Office procedures [i.e., the rejection and amendment procedure of prosecution].

Adkins narrowed his claim drastically to assert only that the design of the apparatus used to achieve gyroscope accuracy was novel. In response, the Office issued its 1960 patent, granting a 17-year monopoly on this more modest claim.

During the long period in which Adkins was attempting to convince the Patent Office of the novelty of his ideas, however, Lear had become convinced that Adkins would never receive a patent on his invention and that it should not continue to pay substantial royalties on ideas which had not contributed substantially to the development of the art of gyroscopy. In 1957, after Adkins' patent application had been rejected twice, Lear announced that it had searched the Patent Office's files and had found a patent which it believed had fully anticipated Adkins' discovery. As a result, the company stated that it would no longer pay royalties on the large number of gyroscopes it was producing at its plant in Grand Rapids, Michigan (the Michigan gyros). Payments were continued on the smaller number of gyros produced at the company's California plant (the California gyros) for two more years until they too were terminated on April 8, 1959.

As soon as Adkins obtained his patent in 1960, he brought this lawsuit in the California Superior Court. He argued to a jury that both the Michigan and the California gyros incorporated his patented apparatus and that Lear's failure to pay royalties on these gyros was a breach both of the 1955 contract and of Lear's quasi-contractual obligations. Although Lear sought to raise patent invalidity as a defense, the trial judge directed a verdict of $16,351.93 for Adkins on the California gyros, holding that Lear was estopped by its licensing agreement from questioning the inventor's patent. [The trial judge eventually held (on confusing grounds) that no royalties were owed on the Michigan gyros since they were more akin to the prior art devices. The California Supreme Court affirmed on the licensee estoppel issue, but awarded a royalty for the Michigan gyros, on the theory that they were not in fact built solely with the aid of prior art technology.]

The doctrine of estoppel has been considered by this Court in a line of cases reaching back into the middle of the 19th century. Before deciding what the role of estoppel should be in the present case and in the future, it is, then, desirable to consider the role it has played in the past.

A

While the roots of the doctrine have often been celebrated in tradition, we have found only one 19th century case in this Court that invoked estoppel in a considered manner. And that case was decided before the Sherman Act made it clear that the grant of monopoly power to a patent owner constituted a limited exception to the general federal policy favoring free competition. *Kinsman v. Parkhurst*, [59 U.S.] 18 How. 289 (1856).

[Subsequently] this Court found the doctrine of patent estoppel so inequitable that it refused to grant an injunction to enforce a licensee's promise never to contest the validity of the underlying patent. "It is as important to the public that competition should not be repressed by worthless patents, as that the patentee of a really valuable invention should be protected in his monopoly ...." *Pope Manufacturing Co. v. Gormully*, 144 U.S. 224, 234 (1892).

Although this Court invoked an estoppel in 1905 without citing or considering *Pope's* powerful argument, *United States v. Harvey Steel Co.*, 196 U.S. 310 [1905], the doctrine was not to be applied again in this Court until it was revived in *Automatic Radio Manufacturing Co. v. Hazeltine Research, Inc.*, which declared, without prolonged analysis, that licensee estoppel was "the general rule."

In so holding, the majority ignored the teachings of a series of decisions this Court had rendered during the 45 years since *Harvey* had been decided. During this period, each time a patentee sought to rely upon his estoppel privilege before this Court, the majority created a new exception to permit judicial scrutiny into the validity of the Patent Office's grant. Long before *Hazeltine* was decided, the estoppel doctrine had been so eroded that it could no longer be considered the "general rule," but was only to be invoked in an ever narrowing set of circumstances.

The lower courts, both state and federal, have also hedged the impact of estoppel by creating exceptions which have indicated a recognition of the broader policies pointing to a contrary approach. It is generally the rule that licensees may avoid further royalty payments, regardless of the provisions of their contract, once a third party proves that the patent is invalid. *See, e.g., Drackett Chemical Co. v. Chamberlain Co.*, 63 F.2d 853 (6th Cir. 1933). Some courts have gone further to hold that a licensee may notify the patent owner that he is repudiating his agreement, regardless of its terms, and may subsequently defend any action for royalties by proving patent invalidity. Note, *The Doctrine of Licensee Repudiation in Patent Law*, 63 YALE L.J. 125 (1953).

The uncertain status of licensee estoppel in the case law is a product of judicial efforts to accommodate the competing demands of the common law of contracts and the federal law of patents. On the one hand, the law of contracts forbids a purchaser to repudiate his promises simply because he later becomes dissatisfied with the bargain he has made. On the other hand, federal law requires, that all ideas in general circulation be dedicated to the common good unless they are protected by a valid patent. *Sears, Roebuck v. Stiffel Co.*, [376 U.S. 225 (1964)]; *Compco Corp. v. Day-Brite Lighting, Inc.*, [376 U.S. 234 (1964)]. When faced with this basic conflict in policy, both this Court and courts throughout the land have naturally sought to develop an intermediate position which somehow would remain responsive to the radically different concerns of the two different worlds of contract and patent. The result has been a failure. Rather than creative compromise, there has been a chaos of conflicting case law, proceeding on inconsistent premises. Before renewing the search for an acceptable middle ground, we must reconsider on their own merits the arguments which may properly be advanced on both sides of the estoppel question.

It will simplify matters greatly if we first consider the most typical situation in which patent licenses are negotiated. In contrast to the present case, most manufacturers obtain a license after a patent has issued. Since the Patent Office makes an inventor's ideas public when it issues its grant of a limited monopoly, a potential licensee has access to the inventor's ideas even if he does not enter into an agreement with the patent owner. Consequently, a manufacturer gains only two benefits if he chooses to enter a licensing agreement after the patent has issued. First, by accepting a license and paying royalties for a time, the licensee may have avoided the necessity of defending an expensive infringement action during the period when he may be least able to afford one. Second, the existence of an unchallenged patent may deter others from attempting to compete with the licensee.

Under ordinary contract principles the mere fact that some benefit is received is enough to require the enforcement of the contract, regardless of the validity of the underlying patent. Nevertheless, if one tests this result by the standard of good-faith commercial dealing, it seems far from satisfactory. For the simple contract approach entirely ignores the position of the licensor who is seeking to invoke the court's assistance on his behalf. Consider, for example, the equities of the licensor who has obtained his patent through a fraud on the Patent Office. It is difficult to perceive why good faith requires that courts should permit him to recover royalties despite his licensee's attempts to show that the patent is invalid. *Compare Walker Process Equipment, Inc. v. Food Machinery & Chemical Corp.* [382 U.S. 172, 176 (1965)].

Even in the more typical cases, not involving conscious wrongdoing, the licensor's equities are far from compelling. A patent, in the last analysis, simply represents a legal conclusion reached by the Patent Office. Moreover, the legal conclusion is predicated on factors as to which reasonable men can differ widely. Yet the Patent Office is often obliged to reach its decision in an ex parte proceeding, without the aid of the arguments which could be advanced by parties interested in proving patent invalidity. Consequently, it does not seem to us to be unfair to require a patentee to defend the Patent Office's judgment when his licensee places the question in issue, especially since the licensor's case is buttressed by the presumption of validity which attaches to his patent. Thus, although licensee estoppel may be consistent with the letter of contractual doctrine, we cannot say that it is compelled by the spirit of contract law, which seeks to balance the claims of promisor and promisee in accord with the requirements of good faith.

Surely the equities of the licensor do not weigh very heavily when they are balanced against the important public interest in permitting full and free competition in the use of ideas which are in reality a part of the public domain. Licensees may often be the only individuals with enough economic incentive to challenge the patentability of an inventor's discovery. If they are muzzled, the public may continually be required to pay tribute to would-be monopolists without need or justification. We think it plain that the technical requirements of contract doctrine must give way before the demands of the public interest in the typical situation involving the negotiation of a license after a patent has issued.

We are satisfied that *Hazeltine Research, Inc.*, *supra*, itself the product of a clouded history, should no longer be regarded as sound law with respect to its "estoppel" holding, and that holding is now overruled.

B

The case before us, however, presents a far more complicated estoppel problem than the one which arises in the most common licensing context. The problem arises out of the fact that Lear obtained its license in 1955, more than four years before Adkins received his 1960 patent. Indeed, from the very outset of the relationship, Lear obtained special access to Adkins' ideas in return for its promise to pay satisfactory compensation.

Thus, during the lengthy period in which Adkins was attempting to obtain a patent, Lear gained an important benefit not generally obtained by the typical licensee. For until a patent issues, a potential licensee may not learn his licensor's ideas simply by requesting the information from the Patent Office. During the time the inventor is seeking patent protection, the governing federal statute requires the Patent Office to hold an inventor's patent application in confidence. If a potential licensee hopes to use the ideas contained in a secret patent application, he must deal with the inventor himself, unless the inventor chooses to publicize his ideas to the world at large. By promising to pay Adkins royalties from the very outset of their relationship, Lear gained immediate access to ideas which it may well not have learned until the Patent Office published the details of Adkins' invention in 1960. At the core of this case, then, is the difficult question whether federal patent policy bars a State from enforcing a contract regulating access to an unpatented secret idea.

Adkins takes an extreme position on this question. The inventor does not merely argue that since Lear obtained privileged access to his ideas before 1960, the company should be required to pay royalties accruing before 1960 regardless of the validity of the patent which ultimately issued. He also argues that since Lear obtained special benefits before 1960, it should also pay royalties during the entire patent period (1960-1977), without regard to the validity of the Patent Office's grant. We cannot accept so broad an argument.

Adkins' position would permit inventors to negotiate all important licenses during the lengthy period while their applications were still pending at the Patent Office, thereby disabling entirely all those who have the strongest incentive to show that a patent is worthless. While the equities supporting Adkins' position are somewhat more appealing than those supporting the typical licensor, we cannot say that there is enough of a difference to justify such a substantial impairment of overriding federal policy.

Nor can we accept a second argument which may be advanced to support Adkins' claim to at least a portion of his post-patent royalties, regardless of the validity of the Patent Office grant. The terms of the 1955 agreement provide that royalties are to be paid until such time as the "patent ... is held invalid," § 6, and the fact remains that the question of patent validity has not been finally determined in this case. Thus, it may be suggested that although Lear must be allowed to raise the question of patent validity in the present lawsuit, it must also be required to comply with its contract and continue to pay royalties until its claim is finally vindicated in the courts.

The parties' contract, however, is no more controlling on this issue than is the State's doctrine of estoppel, which is also rooted in contract principles. The decisive question is whether overriding federal policies would be significantly frustrated if licensees could be required to continue to pay royalties during the time they are challenging patent validity in the courts.

It seems to us that such a requirement would be inconsistent with the aims of federal patent policy. Enforcing this contractual provision would give the licensor an additional economic incentive to devise every conceivable dilatory tactic in an effort to postpone the day of final judicial reckoning. We can perceive no reason to encourage dilatory court tactics in this way. Moreover, the cost of prosecuting slow-moving trial proceedings and defending an inevitable appeal might well deter many licensees from attempting to prove patent invalidity in the courts. The deterrent effect would be particularly severe in the many scientific fields in which invention is proceeding at a rapid rate. In these areas, a patent may well become obsolete long before its 17-year term has expired. If a licensee has reason to believe that he will replace a patented idea with a new one in the near future, he will have little incentive to initiate lengthy court proceedings, unless he is freed from liability at least from the time he refuses to pay the contractual royalties. Lastly, enforcing this contractual provision would undermine the strong federal policy favoring the full and free use of ideas in the public domain. For all these reasons, we hold that Lear must be permitted to avoid the payment of all royalties accruing after Adkins' 1960 patent issued if Lear can prove patent invalidity.

Adkins' claim to contractual royalties accruing before the 1960 patent issued is, however, a much more difficult one, since it squarely raises the question whether, and to what extent, the States may protect the owners of unpatented inventions who are willing to disclose their ideas to manufacturers only upon payment of royalties. [The court remands this question to the California Supreme Court.]

Vacated and remanded.

NOTES

1. *The Inevitable Dissent.* In dissent, Chief Justice Warren and Justice Black joined Justice Douglas in suggesting that state trade secret law be declared invalid insofar as it applied to trade secret licensing agreements. For a taste of the economic devastation that this proposal would have caused, see R. SHERWOOD, INTELLECTUAL PROPERTY AND ECONOMIC DEVELOPMENT 113 (1990) (interview data from South American countries detailing the costs of a system where no employee may be restrained from transferring trade secret information to competitors, and hence where what the author calls "predatory hiring" is commonplace).

2. Criticism. The *Lear* case has been criticized on a number of grounds. *See, e.g.*, Dreyfuss, *Dethroning Lear: Licensee Estoppel and the Incentive to Innovate*, 72 VA. L. REV. 677 (1986) (arguing that *Lear* rule hurts licensees, especially small companies, because of the licensor's risk that a patent will be invalidated); Schlicher, *A Lear v. Adkins Allegory*, 68 J. PAT. OFF. SOC'Y 427 (1986) (*Lear* does not make economic sense). *But cf.* Note, *The Doctrine of Licensee Repudiation in Patent Law*, 63 YALE L.J. 125 (1953) (arguing that the basic policy of *Lear* is correct).

3. Federal Circuit Refuses to Extend. In *Foster v. Hallco Mfg. Co.*, 947 F.2d 469, 20 U.S.P.Q.2d (BNA) 1241 (Fed. Cir. 1991), the Federal Circuit held that a consent decree respecting validity may bar future litigation of that issue, despite the argument that a challenge to such a consent decree is on the same footing as a challenge to a licensor's patent as in *Lear*.

> The Supreme Court in *Lear* did not consider the policy concerns evoked when preserving the finality of a judgment, but only the policies involved in resolving the right of a patent licensee to challenge the validity of the licensed patent in a suit for royalties under the contract....
>
> [W]e cannot conclude that the public policy expressed in *Lear* is so overriding that challenges to validity must be allowed when under normal principles of res judicata applicable to a consent judgment, such challenge would be precluded. Accordingly, we reverse the district court's ruling on this issue. [Remanded for detailed consideration of res judicata issue.]

On several other occasions, the Federal Circuit has made clear that it intends to limit *Lear* to its facts. *See Sun Studs, Inc. v. ATA Equip. Leasing, Inc.*, 872 F.2d 978, 991-93, 10 U.S.P.Q.2d (BNA) 1338, 1349-50 (Fed. Cir. 1989) (patent policy expressed in *Lear* does not bar enforcement of contract promise to share royalties); *Hemstreet v. Spiegel, Inc.*, 851 F.2d 348, 350-51, 7 U.S.P.Q.2d (BNA) 1502, 1504-45 (Fed. Cir. 1988) (*Lear* does not bar enforcement of term in settlement agreement consenting to pay royalties even if patent later held invalid).

4. Estoppel and Oppositions. One rationale for the decision in *Lear* is that the licensee often has a superior position from which to challenge the licensed patent. This is a function of the licensee's role as a competitor, as well as of its access to details of the invention. In this sense, the Court sees licensee challenges to validity as almost a form of opposition. See Chapter 10. Does reexamination, the

U.S. version of oppositions now available to licensees (or anyone), remove one argument against licensee estoppel?

DIAMOND SCIENTIFIC CO. v. AMBICO, INC.

848 F.2d 1220, 6 U.S.P.Q.2d (BNA) 2028 (Fed. Cir.),
cert. dismissed, 487 U.S. 1265 (1988)

This appeal from an order of the District Court granting plaintiff's motion to strike three affirmative defenses is before us to decide whether the doctrine of assignor estoppel prevents this assignor-inventor and his company, who are sued for infringement, from challenging the validity of the patents previously assigned by him to the assignee.

Appellee Diamond Scientific Co. (Diamond) employed Dr. Clarence Welter from 1959 until 1974. During that time, Dr. Welter invented a vaccine against gastroenteritis in swine, and filed a patent application for "Transmissible Gastroenteritis Vaccines and Methods of Producing the Same." While making this patent application, Dr. Welter assigned all of the rights in the patents to Diamond Laboratories, Inc. (the predecessor of Diamond). Eventually, Diamond's predecessor was awarded the following patents from this application: No. 3,479,430; No. 3,585,108; and No. 3,704,203.

In 1974 Dr. Welter left Diamond, where he had become a vice-president, and formed his own company, appellant Ambico, Inc. (Ambico). Ambico began manufacturing and selling a gastroenteritis vaccine for swine. Diamond began this patent infringement suit against Ambico and Dr. Welter, claiming infringement of the three patents that Dr. Welter had assigned to Diamond. The defendants' answer raised, among other defenses, three grounds for patent invalidity: [§§ 112, 102, and 103.] Diamond's motion to strike these three defenses asserted the doctrine of assignor estoppel. The district court granted Diamond's motion, and this appeal followed.

The central issue to be decided is whether in this case the assignor-inventor of the patents (or a company in privity with him) can defend the infringement suit brought by the assignee by challenging the validity of the patents previously assigned, or whether the equitable doctrine of assignor estoppel prevents the assignor from claiming that the patents are invalid.

This is the first opportunity presented to this court to examine the doctrine of assignor estoppel. Although the Supreme Court has examined this doctrine or a related doctrine — licensee estoppel — several times this century, its opinions have hardly been definite or definitive. [After reviewing the older cases, the court turns to *Lear*.]

[I]n *Lear*, the Court addressed the somewhat analogous doctrine of licensee estoppel. Reasoning that "the equities of the licensor do not weigh very heavily when they are balanced against the important public interest in permitting full and free competition in the use of ideas which are in reality a part of the public domain[,]" the Court explicitly abolished licensee estoppel. Although *Lear* involved the licensing, rather than the assignment, of a patent, the opinion reviewed the history of "patent estoppel" in general, and indicated that the Court's previous decisions had sapped much of the vitality, if not the logic, from the assignment estoppel doctrine as well.

Lear resolved the issue of licensee estoppel by writing its obituary; but for courts wrestling with assignor estoppel it was less clear whether *Lear* had also sounded the death knell for that doctrine. Certainly, there was nothing in its holding that eliminated the doctrine. Beyond the questioning dicta in *Lear*, the Court has left assignment estoppel untouched for the past nineteen years.

The federal court cases, decided either shortly before *Lear* or since then, that discuss the doctrine of assignor estoppel reveal some uncertainty about the continued vitality of the doctrine. At least two courts have acknowledged the doctrine, although rejecting on the facts its application to the cases before them. At least five other courts have indicated their belief that assignor estoppel is no longer the prevailing rule of law. None of these courts provided much analysis of the doctrine or the reasons supporting its application in the specific circumstances, preferring instead to view the general rationale as rejecting any further use of assignor estoppel. Two other courts have held that an assignee may be estopped from challenging the validity of the assigned patent. However, the distinction between an assignor and an assignee of a patent gives those cases a distinctly different, but equally apparent, reason for application of estoppel. If an assignee of a patent were allowed to challenge the patent, it could be placed in the legally awkward position of simultaneously attacking and defending the validity of the same patent.

In examining *Lear*, one important distinction between assignors and licensees becomes apparent — a distinction that cautions against the automatic application to assignment cases of the rationale underlying *Lear* and licensees. The public policy favoring allowing a licensee to contest the validity of the patent is not present in the assignment situation. Unlike the licensee, who, without *Lear* might be forced to continue to pay for a potentially invalid patent, the assignor who would challenge the patent has already been fully paid for the patent rights.

Assignor estoppel is an equitable doctrine that prevents one who has assigned the rights to a patent (or patent application) from later contending that what was assigned is a nullity. The estoppel also operates to bar other parties in privity with the assignor, such as a corporation founded by the assignor. The estoppel historically has applied to invalidity challenges based on "novelty, utility, patentable invention, anticipatory matter, and the state of the art."

The four most frequently mentioned justifications for applying assignor estoppel are the following: "(1) to prevent unfairness and injustice; (2) to prevent one [from] benefiting from his own wrong; (3) by analogy to estoppel by deed in real estate; and (4) by analogy to a landlord-tenant relationship." Cooper, *Estoppel to Challenge Patent Validity: The Case of Private Good Faith vs. Public Policy*, 18 Case W. Res. 1122 (1967). Although each rationale may have some utility depending on the facts presented by the particular case, our concern here is primarily with the first one.

Courts that have expressed the estoppel doctrine in terms of unfairness and injustice have reasoned that an assignor should not be permitted to sell something and later to assert that what was sold is worthless, all to the detriment of the assignee.

[I]t is the implicit representation by the assignor that the patent rights that he is assigning (presumably for value) are not worthless that sets the assignor apart from the rest of the world and can deprive him of the ability to challenge later the validity of the patent. To allow the assignor to make that representation at the time of the assignment (to his advantage) and later to repudiate it (again to his advantage) could work an injustice against the assignee.

Our holding is that this is a case in which public policy calls for the application of assignor estoppel. We are, of course, not unmindful of the general public policy disfavoring the repression of competition by the enforcement of worthless patents. Yet despite the public policy encouraging people to challenge potentially invalid patents, there are still circumstances in which the equities of the contractual relationships between the parties should deprive one party (as well as others in privity with it) of the right to bring that challenge.

We note first that Dr. Welter assigned the rights to his inventions to Diamond in exchange for valuable consideration (one dollar plus other unspecified consideration — presumably his salary over many years and other employment benefits). Dr. Welter also executed an inventor's oath, which stated his belief, *inter alia*, that he was the first and sole inventor, that the invention was never known or used before his invention and that it was not previously patented or described in any publication in any country. Furthermore, Dr. Welter apparently participated actively in the patent application process, including drafting the initial version of the claims and consulting on their revision.

Appellants would now defend against accusations of infringement by trying to show that the three patents in issue are invalid because the inventions either were inadequately disclosed by the specifications, lacked novelty, or would have been obvious to one of ordinary skill at the time the inventions were made. If appellants are permitted to raise these defenses and are successful in their proof, Dr. Welter will have profited both by his initial assignment of the patent applications and by his later attack on the value of the very subjects of his earlier assignment. In comparison, Diamond will have given value for the rights to Dr. Welter's inventions only to have him later deprive Diamond of the worth of those assigned rights.

We agree with the district court that the equities weigh heavily in favor of Diamond. Although the doctrine of assignor estoppel may no longer be a broad equitable device susceptible of automatic application, the case before us is appropriate for its use. When the inventor-assignor has signed the Oath, Power of Attorney and Petition, which attests to his belief in the validity of the patents, and has assigned the patent rights to another for valuable consideration, he should be estopped from defending patent infringement claims by proving that what he assigned was worthless. That is an implicit component of the assignment by Welter to Diamond which is immune from contradiction. The inventor's active participation in the prosecution and preparation of the patent applications, as is alleged here, would tilt the equities even more heavily in favor of the assignee, but consideration of this factor is not necessary to the result.

It is also irrelevant that, at the time of the assignment, Dr. Welter's patent applications were still pending and the Patent Office had not yet granted the patents. What Dr. Welter assigned were the rights to his inventions. That Diamond may have later amended the claims in the application process (a very common occurrence in patent prosecutions), with or without Dr. Welter's assistance, does not give appellants' arguments against estoppel any greater force. Our concern must be the balance of the equities. The fact is that Dr. Welter assigned the rights to his invention, irrespective of the particular language in the claims describing the inventions when the patents were ultimately granted. In *Westinghouse [Elec. & Mfg. Co. v. Formica Insulation Co.*, 266 U.S. 342 (1924)], the Court observed that the scope of the right conveyed in the assignment of patent rights before the granting of the patent "is much less certainly defined than that of a granted patent, and the question of the extent of the estoppel against the assignor of such an inchoate right is more difficult to determine than in the case of the patent assigned after its granting." 266 U.S. at 352-53. However, the Court merely suggested that "[t]his difference might justify the view that the range of relevant and competent evidence in fixing the limits of the subsequent estoppel should be more liberal than in the case of an assignment of a granted patent[,]" and found it unnecessary to decide the question. *Id*. at 353.

Nevertheless, *Westinghouse* does allow for an accommodation in such circumstances. To the extent that Diamond may have broadened the claims in the patent applications (after the assignments) beyond what could be validly claimed in light of the prior art, *Westinghouse* may allow appellants to introduce evidence of prior art to narrow the scope of the claims of the patents, which may bring their accused devices outside the scope of the claims of the patents in suit. *Id*. at 350. This exception to assignor estoppel also shows that estopping appellants from raising invalidity defenses does not necessarily prevent them from successfully defending against Diamond's infringement claims.

Affirmed.

NOTES

1. *Concurrence.* From the concurrence by Judge Newman:

> I write separately to state my belief that it is time to reaffirm the principle of assignor estoppel; that is, to reinstate assignor estoppel as the general rule rather than the exception. Such rule would place on the assignor/challenger the burden of proving that an apparently valid deed of assignment should not

be enforced in accordance with the applicable laws of contracts and property transfers, rather than placing on the assignee the burden of proving that equity is on its side.

848 F.2d at 1227 (Newman, J., concurring). *But see* Note, *The Doctrine of Estoppel in Patent Litigation*, 55 YALE L.J. 842 (1946) (stating that problem of invalid patents is pervasive, and limited remedy such as abolishing assignor estoppel is not enough to solve the problem).

2. Related Case. In *Diamond Scientific*, the court stated that "[t]he estoppel also operates to bar other parties in privity with the assignor, such as a corporation founded by the assignor." In a subsequent case, *Shamrock Techs., Inc. v. Medical Sterilization, Inc.*, 903 F.2d 789, 14 U.S.P.Q.2d (BNA) 1728 (Fed. Cir. 1990), the court returned to the privity theme:

> What constitutes "privity" varies, depending on the purpose for which privity is asserted. Privity, like the doctrine of assignor estoppel itself, is determined upon a balance of the equities. If an inventor assigns his invention to his employer company *A* and leaves to join company *B*, whether company *B* is in privity and thus bound by the doctrine will depend on the equities dictated by the relationship between the inventor and company *B* in light of the act of infringement. The closer that relationship, the more the equities will favor applying the doctrine to company *B*.... The district court correctly determined that, considering the balance of equities and the relationship of [assignor and ex-employee] Luniewski and [Medical Sterilization, Inc., or MSI, the company assignor Luniewski joined after leaving plaintiff's employ] no genuine issue of material fact exists regarding privity in this case. The undisputed facts are: (1) in July 1983 Luniewski left Shamrock to join MSI as Vice-President in charge of Operations; (2) Luniewski owns 50,000 shares of MSI stock; (3) MSI was formed in 1982 to sterilize surgical instruments and manufacture other medical goods; yet as soon as Luniewski was hired in 1983, MSI built facilities for processing PTFE with radiation; (4) Luniewski oversaw the design and construction of those facilities; (5) Luniewski was hired in part to start up MSI's infringing operations; (6) the decision to begin processing PTFE with radiation was made jointly by Luniewski and the president of MSI; (7) MSI began manufacturing PTFE with radiation in 1985; and (8) Luniewski was in charge of MSI's PTFE operation. MSI attempts to distinguish *Diamond Scientific*, citing *National Cash Register Co. v. Remington Arms Co.*, 283 F. 196, 202 (D. Del. 1922), *aff'd*, 286 F. 367 (3d Cir. 1923), ... for the proposition that there is no privity between a corporation and a mere employee thereof. However, as above indicated, Luniewski was far more than a mere employee of MSI and the undisputed facts establish MSI's direct involvement of Luniewski [sic] in MSI's infringing operations. MSI clearly availed itself of Luniewski's "knowledge and assistance" to conduct

infringement. The district court committed no error in finding MSI in privity.

903 F.2d at 793-94.

3. *Logic Versus Policy*. One premise of *Lear* is that licensee is in a superior position to challenge the licensed patents. Isn't this also true — in fact, more so — when the inventor herself wishes to challenge the packet? Also, note that *Lear* allowed the licensee to challenge the patent after the licensee had received the benefit of using the invention for more than four years. Here the inventor is not permitted to challenge the patent despite receiving a benefit of only $1.00 (plus other unspecified consideration). Is there any doubt how the Federal Circuit would decide *Lear* if it were presented as a matter of first impression today?

4. *Related Articles*. A pair of student commentators from the Lone Star state have squared off in a shootout over the merits of assignor estoppel. *See* Note, *Life After Death for Assignor Estoppel: Per Se Application to Protect Incentives to Innovate*, 68 TEX. L. REV. 251 (1989) (assignor estoppel best thing since sliced bread); Note, Diamond Scientific Co. v. Ambico: *Enforcing Patent Assignor Estoppel*, 26 HOUS. L. REV. 761 (1989) ("Instead of truly balancing equities, the court's analysis ignores those equitable factors most relevant to a patent validity challenge. [T]his note criticizes the *Diamond* court's application of assignor estoppel — an abrupt departure from the case law trend encouraging patent challenges.").

6. A BRIEF NOTE ON CONTRACTING AROUND THE PATENT ACT

It is perhaps surprising that only recently has a literature appeared to probe in detail the issue of "contracting around" rules governing transactions. As Ayres and Gertner point out, however, the traditional account of so-called "default rules" (i.e., rules that apply if parties don't change them by agreement) was premised on transaction costs. The simple notion was that we had the default rules we did because these are the ones most parties would agree on most of the time if they had spent the time to consider the issues they address. *See* Ayres & Gertner, *Filling Gaps in Incomplete Contracts: An Economic Theory of Default Rules*, 99 YALE L.J. 87 (1989). The matter is a bit more complex than that, however; and it is complex in a way that has great relevance to many of the problems considered in this chapter on patent licensing.

Ayres and Gertner use the concepts of "default rules" and "immutable rules" to describe the legal background to most negotiations. Default rules can be changed by agreement, as mentioned; immutable rules cannot. They go on to develop a theory of default rules which differs from the traditional account in several ways. Most importantly, they change the focus from lowering transaction costs, or approximating what most parties would do if they took the time to do it, to creating incentives for socially desirable information disclosure. *Id.* at 92-95. This latter goal is to be achieved, they say, by the use of so-called "penalty defaults," which are explicitly designed to punish a party who withholds information from the other contracting party whose disclosure would have made for a better or fairer deal. *Id.* at 97. Ayres and Gertner also argue that penalty defaults could provide incentives for parties to specify contractual terms where it would be less costly for the parties to do so than for courts to fill gaps ex post with the terms the parties would have wanted. *Id.* at 93, 97.

What is most relevant to the question of licensing is when the patent law should state a default rule, i.e., allow parties to bargain around a rule, and when the law should contain an immutable rule that cannot be altered by agreement. Two examples in patent law spring to mind: altering the basic statutory patent term by agreement, and agreeing not to challenge a licensed or assigned patent. How does the Ayres/Gertner framework apply to these problems?

Ayres and Gertner assert that "[i]mmutability is justified only if unregulated contracting would be socially deleterious because parties internal or external to the contract cannot adequately protect themselves." *Id.* at 88. One example of social harm from unregulated contracting is said to arise in the case of certain contract modifications where one party to the contract must incur significant sunk costs before the other party begins performance. The party who has not yet begun performing may be able to exact additional payment by threatening not to perform unless the contract is renegotiated on more favorable terms. Mandatory rules may prevent such opportunistic efforts to modify contracts.

The question in the case of private patent term extensions and no-challenge clauses is whether parties "external to the contract" need to be protected. In general, it would seem to depend on a number of factors: (1) the market power of the licensor; (2) the strategic significance of the patented item; (3) the identity of the licensee; and (4) the overall structure of the industry, among others.

One can imagine scenarios where these factors suggest the need for a mandatory (or immutable) rule. For example, where a licensor controls a key technology in an industry dominated by it and a licensee, an enforceable no-challenge agreement could essentially guarantee patent validity. To the extent the no-challenge clause is "purchased" by implicit price concessions and/or market division, this would obviously have negative effects on the industry. In a sense, it would permit patentees in highly concentrated industries to purchase "invalidity insurance." This assumes two things: (1) entry by new firms into the industry is difficult — in the lingo of industrial organization, that the market is not "contestable"; and (2) patent challengers unable to afford the $350,000 or so needed to prosecute the average patent infringement case could not obtain outside financing for that purpose, e.g., under a deal to give the financier a portion of the extra profits arising from invalidating the patent. (This is perhaps realistic, in light of the "free rider" problem: those who did *not* finance the suit would be able to exploit the invalidated patent too, without having spent the money to invalidate it, and hence with a cost advantage right off the bat.) Under these circumstances, but perhaps not others, it makes sense to adopt an immutable *Lear v. Adkins* rule making no-challenge clauses unenforceable.

It also seems possible (but more difficult) to imagine a scenario where private patent term extension has negative effects on an industry. Assuming the same industry structure as in the preceding example, the smaller, unlicensed competitors could avoid the effects of the licensor-licensee private extension simply by remaining unlicensed. This might put them to a difficult choice — take a license and stay alive (though burdened with royalty obligations for more than the patent term), or try to survive and prosper in the post-expiration period. In some circumstances, this might be too harsh a choice to place on licensees, such as where the licensor promises to annihilate competitors who do not take out a license. (This would presumably raise other antitrust issues, however.) In other situations, a license term in excess of the statutory term might be linked to other licensing restrictions — grantbacks, exclusive dealing, etc. — in such a way that it forms part of an overall scheme of domination. *See generally* J. TIROLE, THE THEORY OF INDUSTRIAL ORGANIZATION 221 (1988) (reciting standard Cournot model, where monopolist has incentive to share duopoly with potential entrant, rather than co-exist as duopolists; implies possibility of using licensing as opportunity for monopoly-splitting agreement); Hylton, *Economic Rents and Essential Facilities*, 1991 B.Y.U. L. REV. 1243, 1252-57 (1991) (describing "essential facilities doctrine" in antitrust law, which mandates sharing of key asset needed by competitors but held by a single firm; noting that mandatory sharing of the asset will not benefit consumers if sharing is accompanied by collusion). *Cf.* Adelman & Jaeger, *Patent-Antitrust: Patent Dynamics and Field-of-Use Licensing*, 50 N.Y.U. L. REV. 273, 295-99, 306-8 (1975) (possibility of trading field-of-use licenses for entry into oligopolistic industry; suggesting per se rules of illegality where such licenses are offered to selected competitors, or are offered to two or more competitors). *But cf.* Meyers, *Field-of-Use Restrictions as Procompetitive Elements in Know-How Licensing Agreements in the United States and the European Communities*, 12 NW. J. INT'L L. & BUS. 364 (1991). But certainly there are many other situations, often discussed in the literature critical of *Lear*, where parties legitimately wish to extend their relationship beyond the admittedly arbitrary statutory period.

Of course, an entirely different argument, though still in the Ayres/Gertner spirit, can be made against patent extensions. Congress has set the patent term as one foundational element in the "contract" between society and the inventor. Thus any private extensions the inventor negotiates with licensees can be said to violate *this* contract. And unless the Patent Office — acting on behalf of society at large — is allowed into the licensor-licensee deal to renegotiate the terms of the original patent grant, a critical party to the original patent grant "contract" is not represented — the public. Of course, this view assumes that the interests of the Patent Office might somehow differ from those of the *licensee*; it might be thought that the licensee, as a member of the public, is simply negotiating away her right (given by the Patent Office) to use the technology after the inventor's patent term expires. On this view, an immutable statutory term has the curious effect of taking a bargaining chip away from the *licensee*!

Even if this is true, two defenses are possible: First, like the law of good faith and unconscionability, the law of patent terms must be immutable to protect parties from their own foolhardy actions, or at least actions that are forced by extortionate bargaining behavior. Paternalism might play a role, even in the hard-hearted commercial world of patent law. On this view, the best way to protect against patent extensions due to unfair bargaining is to outlaw such extensions entirely. (Note that refinements on the *Brulotte* rule, suggested in *Aronson*, permit the licensing parties to allocate the technology into patented and unpatented trade secret components, with the potential for post-expiration royalties on the latter.) Second, even if it is in an individual's interest to sell (or waive) her right to practice a patented invention after the term expires, society in general may have good reasons not to permit it. Not everything, after all, is negotiable. One cannot sell oneself into slavery, for example, no matter how favorable the terms. Perhaps Congress has considered access to public domain technology an immutable right over the years, not out of a blind policy against autonomy in this one area of the law, but out of a faith that there are seldom good reasons to give up this right. *Cf.* Coase, *The 1987 McCorkle Lecture: Blackmail*, 74 VA. L. REV. 655 (1988) (blackmail is illegal because these transactions are never desirable).

Ultimately, the default versus immutable rule framework cannot resolve this question; that depends on more understanding concerning the potential for and extent of "third-party" harm from patent extensions and no-challenge clauses. But at least there is a useful vocabulary for discussing the issues.

7. GRANT-BACK CLAUSES

TRANSPARENT-WRAP MACHINE CORP. v. STOKES & SMITH CO.

329 U.S. 637 (1947)

MR. JUSTICE DOUGLAS delivered the opinion of the Court.

This is a suit for a declaratory judgment and an injunction, instituted by respondent for the determination of the legality and enforceability of a provision of a patent license agreement. The District Court entered judgment for petitioner, holding the provision valid. The Circuit Court of Appeals reversed by a divided vote, being of the opinion that the provision in question was illegal under the line of decisions represented by *Mercoid Corporation v. Mid-Continent Co.*, 320 U.S. 661 [1944]. The case is here on a petition for a writ of certiorari which we granted because of the public importance of the question presented.

Petitioner, organized in 1934, has patents on a machine which bears the trade-mark "Transwrap." This machine makes transparent packages, simultaneously fills them with such articles as candy, and seals them. In 1937 petitioner sold and respondent acquired the Transwrap business in the United States, Canada, and Mexico, the right to use the trade-mark "Transwrap," and an exclusive license to manufacture and sell the Transwrap machine under the patents petitioner then owned or might acquire. The agreement contained a formula by which royalties were to be computed and paid. The term of the agreement was ten years with an option in respondent to renew it thereafter for five year periods during the life of the patents covered by the agreement. The agreement could be terminated by petitioner on notice for specified defaults on respondent's part. The provision of the agreement around which the present controversy turns is a covenant by respondent to assign to petitioner improvement patents applicable to the machine and suitable for use in connection with it.

[From footnote 1:] The relevant portions of this provision read as follows:

> If the Licensee shall discover or invent an improvement which is applicable to the Transwrap Packaging Machine and suitable for use in connection therewith and applicable to the making and closing of the package, but not to the filling nor to the contents of the package, it shall submit the same to the Licensor, which may, at its option, apply for Letters Patent covering the same. In the event of the failure of the licensor so to apply for Letters Patent covering such additional improvements, inventions or patentable ideas, the Licensee may apply for the same. In the event that such additional Letters Patent are applied for and are granted to the Licensor, they shall be deemed covered by the terms of this License Agreement and may be used by the Licensee hereunder without any further consideration, license fee or royalty as above provided. In the event that any such additional improvements are patented by the Licensee for use in connection with Transwrap Packaging Machines, (after the refusal or failure of the Licensor to apply for Patents thereon), the Licensor may, nevertheless, have the use but not the exclusive use of the same outside of the several territories covered by this License Agreement. The expenses of obtaining any such Patents shall be paid by the party applying therefor.

The parties had operated under the agreement for several years when petitioner ascertained that respondent had taken out certain patents on improvements in the machine. Petitioner notified respondent that its failure to disclose and assign these improvements constituted a breach of the agreement and called on respondent to remedy the default. When that did not occur petitioner notified respondent that the agreement would be terminated on a day certain. Thereupon respondent instituted this action asking that the provisions respecting the improvement patents be declared illegal and unenforceable and that petitioner be enjoined from terminating the agreement.

In a long and consistent line of cases the Court has held that an owner of a patent may not condition a license so as to tie to the use of the patent the use of other materials, processes or devices which lie outside of the monopoly of the patent. *Motion Picture Patents Co. v. Universal Film Mfg. Co., Morton Salt Co. v. S.S. Suppiger Co.,* [etc.]. If such practices were tolerated, ownership of a patent would give the patentee control over unpatented articles which but for the patent he would not possess. The requirement that a licensee under a patent use an unpatented material or device with the patent might violate the antitrust laws but for the attempted protection of the patent. The condemnation of the practice, however, does not depend on such a showing. Though control of the unpatented article or device falls short of a prohibited restraint of trade or monopoly, it will not be sanctioned. *Morton Salt Co.* For it is the tendency in that direction which condemns the practice and which, if approved by a court either through enjoining infringement or enforcing the covenant, would receive a powerful impetus.

The Circuit Court of Appeals was of the view that the principle of those cases was applicable here and rendered illegal and unenforceable the covenant to assign the improvement patents to petitioner. It stated,

> The owner of all property, by withholding it upon any other terms, may, if he can, force others to buy from him; land is the best example and every parcel of land is a monopoly. But it is precisely in this that a patent is not like other property; the patentee may not use it to force others to buy of him things outside its four corners. If the defendant gets the plaintiff's patents, it will have put itself in that position, in part at any rate, by virtue of the compulsion of its own patents.

It went on to note that since all improvement patents would not expire until after expiration of petitioner's patents on the machine, the arrangement put respondent at a competitive disadvantage, for respondent would lose the negative command over the art which ownership of the improvement patents would have given it. Moreover, respondent, though able to renew the license on conditions stated in the agreement, would be irretrievably tied to it so as to be "Forced, either to cease all efforts to patent improvements, or to keep renewing the contract in order to escape the consequences of its own ingenuity."

First. The first difficulty we have with the position of the Circuit Court of Appeals is that Congress has made all patents assignable and has granted the assignee the same exclusive rights as the patentee. The statute does not limit the consideration which may be paid for the assignment to any species or kind of property. At least so far as the terms of the statute are concerned, we see no difference whether the consideration is services, or cash, or the right to use another patent.

An improvement patent may, like a patent on a step in a process, have great strategic value. For it may, on expiration of the basic patent, be the key to a whole technology. One who holds it may therefore have a considerable competitive advantage. And one who assigns it and thereby loses negative command of the art may by reason of his assignment have suffered a real competitive handicap. For thereafter he will have to pay toll to the assignee, if he practices the invention. But the competitive handicap or disadvantage which he suffers is no greater and no less whether the consideration for the assignment be the right to use the basic patent or something else of value. That is to say, the freedom of one who assigns a patent is restricted to the same degree whether the assignment is made pursuant to a license agreement or otherwise.

Second. What we have said is not, of course, a complete answer to the position of the Circuit Court of Appeals. For the question remains whether here, as in *Mercoid Corporation v. Mid-Continent Co.*, *supra*, and its predecessors, the condition in the license agreement violates some other principle of law or public policy. The fact that a patentee has the power to refuse a license does not mean that he has the power to grant a license on such conditions as he may choose.

As we have noted, such a power, if conceded, would enable the patentee not only to exploit the invention but to use it to acquire a monopoly not embraced in the patent. Thus, if he could require all licensees to use his unpatented materials with the patent, he would have, or stand in a strategic position to acquire, a monopoly in the unpatented materials themselves. Beyond the "limited monopoly" granted by the patent, the methods by which a patent is exploited are "subject to the general law." Protection from competition in the sale of unpatented materials is not granted by either the patent law or the general law. He who uses his patent to obtain protection from competition in the sale of unpatented materials extends by contract his patent monopoly to articles as respects which the law sanctions neither monopolies nor restraints of trade.

It is at precisely this point that our second difficulty with the view of the Circuit Court of Appeals is found. An improvement patent, like the basic patent to which it relates, is a legalized monopoly for a limited period. The law permits both to be bought and sold. One who uses one patent to acquire another is not extending his patent monopoly to articles governed by the general law and as respects which neither monopolies nor restraints of trade are sanctioned. He is indeed using one legalized monopoly to acquire another legalized monopoly.

Mercoid Corporation v. Mid-Continent Co., *supra*, and its predecessors, by limiting a patentee to the monopoly found within the four corners of the grant, outlawed business practices which the patent law unaided by restrictive agreements did not protect. Take the case of the owner of an unpatented machine who leases it or otherwise licenses its use on condition that all improvements which the lessee or licensee patents should be assigned. He is using his property to acquire a monopoly. But the monopoly, being a patent, is a lawful one. The general law would no more make that acquisition of a patent unlawful than it would the assignment of a patent for cash. Yet a patent is a species of property; and if the owner of an unpatented machine could exact that condition, why may not the owner of a patented machine?

It is true that for some purposes the owner of a patent is under disabilities with which owners of other property are not burdened. The difficulty is that Congress has not made illegal the acquisition of improvement patents by the owner of a basic patent. [T]he end result is the same whether the owner of a basic patent uses a license to obtain improvement patents or uses the wealth which he accumulates by exploiting his basic patent for that purpose. In sum, a patent license may not be used coercively to exact a condition contrary to public policy. But what falls within the terms of the assignment statute is plainly not per se against the public interest.

It is, of course, true that the monopoly which the licensor obtains when he acquires the improvement patents extends beyond the term of his basic patent. But as we have said, that is not creating by agreement a monopoly which the law otherwise would not sanction. The grant of the improvement patent itself creates the monopoly. On the facts of the present case the effect on the public interest would seem to be the same whether the licensee or the licensor owns the improvement patents.

There is a suggestion that the enforcement of the condition gives the licensee less incentive to make inventions when he is bound to turn over to the licensor the products of his inventive genius. Since the primary aim of the patent laws is to promote the progress of science and the useful arts, an arrangement which diminishes the incentive is said to be against the public interest. Whatever force that argument might have in other situations, it is not persuasive here. Respondent pays no additional royalty on any improvement patents which are used. By reason of the agreement any improvement patent can be put to immediate use and exploited for the account of the licensee. And that benefit continues so long as the agreement is renewed. The agreement thus serves a function of supplying a market for the improvement patents. Whether that opportunity to exploit the improvement patents would be increased but for the agreement depends on vicissitudes of business too conjectural on this record to appraise.

Third. We are quite aware of the possibilities of abuse in the practice of licensing a patent on condition that the licensee assign all improvement patents to the licensor. Conceivably the device could be employed with the purpose or effect of violating the anti-trust laws. He who acquires two patents acquires a double monopoly. As patents are added to patents a whole industry may be regimented. The owner of a basic patent might thus perpetuate his control over an industry long after the basic patent expired. Competitors might be eliminated and an industrial monopoly perfected and maintained. Through the use of patents pools or multiple licensing agreements the fruits of invention of an entire industry might be systematically funneled into the hands of the original patentee.

A patent may be so used as to violate the anti-trust laws. Such violations may arise through conditions in the license whereby the licensor seeks to control the conduct of the licensee by the fixing of prices or by other restrictive practices. Congress, however, has made no specific prohibition against conditioning a patent license on the assignment by the licensee of improvement patents. But that does not mean that the practice we have here has immunity under the anti-trust laws. Indeed, the recent case of *Hartford-Empire Co. v. United States*, 323 U.S. 386, 324 U.S. 570 [1945] dramatically illustrates how the use of a condition or covenant in a patent license that the licensee will assign improvement patents may give rise to violations of the anti-trust laws.

The District Court found no violation of the anti-trust laws in the present case. The Circuit Court of Appeals did not reach that question. Hence it, as well as any other questions which may have been preserved, are open on our remand of the cause to the Circuit Court of Appeals.

We only hold that the inclusion in the license of the condition requiring the licensee to assign improvement patents is not per se illegal and unenforceable.

Reversed.

NOTES

1. *Questions.* Review the agreement between the parties in the case. Would the Patent Act permit enforcement of agreements that essentially allocate the right to claim inventorship, as this agreement appears to? Can parties decide by contract who is an "inventor" under the Patent Act? Or should this be interpreted as a provision allocating the right to prosecute a patent application and compel an assignment of it, i.e., a provision regarding ownership rather than inventor status? Note the Court's point that the licensee retains the nonexclusive right to use improvements it invents. Does it follow from this that they are not harmed by the assignment of improvements provision? Is a nonexclusive right to use as valuable as the statutory right to exclude? (See Section A.12, *Licensing of Government Inventions*, below.) If not, does this lessened right — contrary to the Court's view — reduce the incentives for the licensee to invent improvements? If so, should we care; does it matter which *party* does the inventing, or is it the overall "volume" of inventing that counts? *Cf.* Merges & Nelson, *On the Complex Economics of Patent Scope*, 90 COLUM. L. REV. 839 (1990) (arguing that multiple and rivalrous sources of invention are preferred). Finally, consider the Court's argument that the grant-back clause in the agreement at issue is fundamentally different from a tie-in provision, because the invention "added on" to the original patent is itself covered by a patent, unlike the normal tie-in case where the tied item is unpatented. Why does this matter? If the distinction is to be relied on, what will keep licensors from patenting tied items and defending tie-in clauses on this ground?

2. *No Per Se Legality Rule.* Exclusive grantbacks may be challenged if they threaten to substantially lessen competition and extend beyond the reasonable purview of the original patent(s). *See, e.g., Hartford-Empire Co. v. United States*, 323 U.S. 386, 324 U.S. 570 (1945) (the use of a condition or covenant in a patent license that the licensee will assign improvement patents may give rise to violations of the anti-trust laws); *United States v. National Lead Co.*, 63 F. Supp. 513, 524 (S.D.N.Y. 1945) (unlawful grantback on inventions not yet conceived), *aff'd*, 332 U.S. 319 (1947); *United States v. General Elec. Co.*, 82 F. Supp. 753, 815-16 (D.N.J. 1949). *Cf. Santa Fe-Pomeroy, Inc. v. P & Z Co.*, 569 F.2d 1084, 1101 (9th Cir. 1978) (technology did not occupy relevant market, and grantback was properly limited in time and subject matter); *Shinzu Nippon Koki Co. v. Irvin Indus.*, 1975-1 Trade Cas. (CCH) ¶ 60,347 at 66,443 (N.Y. Sup. Ct. 1975) (reciprocal exchanges of patents and know-how on developments or improvements of licensed know-how were permissible). Recent antitrust guidelines from the U.S. Justice Department state that non-exclusive grantback provisions generally will eliminate antitrust risks in this area. See ANTITRUST DIVI-

SION, U.S. DEP'T OF JUSTICE, ANTITRUST GUIDE FOR INTERNATIONAL OPERATIONS (1977) at Case I.

3. *Comparative Rules.* The grantback law in the EEC and Japan is different from U.S. law. Non-exclusive grant-backs are lawful so long as the licensor undertakes a similar obligation. The idea is that so long as neither licensor nor licensee has exclusive rights over improvements, no anticompetitive effect will ensue. This rule has been criticized. *See* Schlicher, *The Law and Economics of Licensing Biotechnology Patent and Related Property Rights in the U.S.*, in TECHNOLOGY LICENSING 1987 (Practicing Law Institute, Patents, Copyrights, Trademarks, and Literary Property Course Handbook Series, 235 PLI/Pat. 333) at n.37 ("If the concern is that grant-backs deter the licensee from engaging in further research, a provision which does so becomes lawful if the licensor agrees to deter himself from engaging in additional research. Two wrongs add up to a right. That law ought to be properly exploited by profit-maximizing licensors and licensees in concentrated industries.").

8. REMEDIES IN PATENT-RELATED ANTITRUST CASES

Compulsory licensing was a popular remedy in patent-related antitrust cases in the 1940s and 1950s.

> While it has been contended that ... the District Court was not free in the present case to require the issuance of royalty-free licenses, we feel that, without reaching the question whether royalty-free licensing or a perpetual injunction against the enforcement of a patent is permissible as a matter of law in any case, the present decree represents an exercise of sound judicial discretion.

United States v. National Lead Co., 332 U.S. 319, 338 (1947). In this case, the Supreme Court affirmed a judgement by the District Court which dissolved an international agreement between companies in the titanium alloy business. The members of the agreement, which was alleged to constitute a cartel, agreed to (1) cross-assign patents; (2) divide world markets geographically; and (3) keep each other apprised of technical developments. 332 U.S. at 341-42. The Court went on to authorize the District Court's compulsory licensing remedy in the case:

> The findings show vigorous and apparently profitable competition on the part of each of the four producers, including an intimation that the smaller companies are gaining ground rather than losing it. Keen competition has existed both before and after the elimination, by the 1933 agreement and understanding, of certain patent advantages from among the weapons of competition. The competition between National Lead and du Pont has been carried into this Court where today National Lead supports the Government's proposal for royalty-free licenses, while du Pont argues strongly for a complete dismissal of the proceedings and contends that, in any event, if

there are to be compulsory licenses they at least should require payment of uniform, reasonable royalties as provided in the present decree.

Further assurance against continued illegal restraints upon interstate and foreign commerce through misuse of these patent rights is provided through the compulsory granting to any applicant therefor of licenses at uniform, reasonable royalties under any or all patents defined in the decree. On the facts before us, neither the issuance of such licenses on a royalty-free basis nor the issuance of a permanent injunction prohibiting the patentees and licensees from enforcing those patents has been shown to be necessary in order to enforce effectively the Anti-Trust Act. In the absence of a showing to the contrary, it is obvious that some patents should entitle their owners to receive higher royalties than others. Also, it is clear that several patents, each of equal value, ordinarily should entitle their owners to a larger total return in royalties than would one of them alone. It follows that to reduce all royalties automatically ... regardless of their nature and regardless of their number, appears, on its face, to be inequitable without special proof to support such a conclusion. On the other hand, it may well be that uniform, reasonable royalties computed on some patents will be found to be but nominal in value. Such royalties might be set at zero or at a nominal rate. The conclusion, however, would depend on the facts of each case.

Recognizing the difficulty of computing a reasonable royalty, nevertheless, that conception is one that already has been recognized both by Congress and by this Court. The term frequently has been employed in Sherman Antitrust case consent decrees. In the present case, the royalties charged to and paid by [certain licensees] provide enough guidance to indicate that the reasonableness of future royalties may be determined in this case with less difficulty than often might confront a court faced with such a task.

We hold, therefore, that paragraphs 4 and 7 of the [District Court] decree should not be modified either so as to provide for compulsory royalty-free licenses or so as to enjoin the patentees or licensees from enforcing the terms of the patents involved.

332 U.S. at 348-50. *See also* Note, *Compulsory Licensing by Antitrust Decree*, 56 YALE L.J. 77 (1946) (detailed description of administrative procedure set up to license bottle industry patents in the wake of *Hartford-Empire Co. v. United States*, 323 U.S. 386, 324 U.S. 570 (1945); reprints portion of final district court consent decree in appendix).

In some cases, courts were not so generous to the patentees; compulsory royalty-free licenses were ordered by consent judgement. *See* STAFF OF THE SUBCOMM. ON PATENTS, TRADEMARKS, AND COPYRIGHTS OF THE SENATE COMM. ON THE JUDICIARY, 86TH CONG., 2D SESS., COMPULSORY LICENSING UNDER ANTITRUST JUDGMENTS 1 (Comm. Print 1960) (written by Marcus A. Hollabaugh and Robert L. Wright) (studying impact of compulsory licenses on subsequent industry structure; concluding that overall these consent judgments created more competitive industry while permitting patentee/antitrust violator to survive). *See also* F.M. SCHERER, INDUSTRIAL MARKET STRUCTURE AND ECONOMIC PERFOR-MANCE 456-57 (2d ed. 1980) ("All in all, the substantial amount of evidence now available suggests that compulsory patent licensing, judiciously confined to cases in which patent-based monopoly power has been abused ... would have little or no adverse impact on the rate of technological progress...."). *See generally* STAFF OF THE SUBCOMM. ON PATENTS, TRADEMARKS, AND COPYRIGHTS OF THE SENATE COMM. ON THE JUDICIARY, 86TH CONG., 2D SESS., COMPULSORY LICENSING OF PATENTS — A LEGISLATIVE HISTORY (Comm. Print 1958) (written by Catherine S. Corry) (collecting case histories of proposed bills to order compulsory patent licensing).

Even now, a lone voice or two can be heard singing the praises of the compulsory license. *See* Comment, *Compulsory Patent Licensing in the United States: An Idea Whose Time Has Come*, 8 Nw. J. INT'L L. & BUS. 666 (1988); Tandon, *Optimal Patents With Compulsory Licensing*, 90 J. POL. ECON. 470 (1982) (theoretical model).

9. ANTITRUST VERSUS PATENT-RELATED "MISUSE" STANDARDS: RECENT LEGISLATIVE TRENDS

As courts, led by academic commentators, have become more sophisticated in their thinking about antitrust issues, they have begun in recent years to question the need for a distinct doctrine of patent misuse. Judge Posner, writing for the Seventh Circuit in *USM Corp. v. SPS Techs., Inc.*, 694 F.2d 505, 511 (7th Cir. 1982), asked head-on "whether the patent-misuse doctrine ... constitutes a general code of patent licensing distinct from antitrust law." He stated:

The doctrine arose before there was any significant body of federal antitrust law, and reached maturity long before that law (a product largely of free interpretation of unclear statutory language) attained its present broad scope. Since the antitrust laws as currently interpreted reach every practice that could impair competition substantially, it is not easy to define a separate role for a doctrine also designed to prevent an anti-competitive practice — the abuse of a patent monopoly. One possibility is that the doctrine of patent misuse, unlike antitrust law, condemns any patent licensing practice that is even trivially anti-competitive, at least if it has no socially beneficial effects....

[T]here is increasing convergence of patent-misuse analysis with standard antitrust analysis.... One still finds plenty of statements in judicial opinions that less evidence of anti-competitive effect is required in a misuse case than in an antitrust case.... But apart from the conventional applications of the doctrine we have found no cases where standards different from those of antitrust law were actually applied to yield different results.... If misuse claims are not tested by conventional antitrust principles, by what principles shall they be tested? Our law is not rich in alternative concepts of monopolistic abuse; and it is rather late in the day to try to develop one without in the process subjecting the rights of patent holders to debilitating uncertainty.

694 F.2d at 512.

In its earliest opinion in this area, *Windsurfing Int'l v. AMF, Inc.*, 782 F.2d 995, 1001 (Fed. Cir. 1986), the Federal Circuit seemed to be in agreement with Posner. "To sustain a misuse defense involving a licensing arrangement not held to have been per se anticompetitive by the Supreme Court," the court wrote,

> a factual determination must reveal that the overall effect of the license tends to restrain competition unlawfully in an appropriately defined relevant market. And that "the patentee has impermissibly broadened" the "physical or temporal scope" of the patent grant "with anti-competitive effect."
>
> Recent economic analysis questions the rationale behind holding any licensing practice per se anti-competitive.

782 F.2d at 1001-2.

However, later the same year, in *Senza-Gel Corp. v. Seiffhart*, 803 F.2d 661, 665 n.5 (Fed. Cir. 1986), the same court retreated from this position.

> Commentators and courts have questioned the rationale appearing in Supreme Court opinions dealing with misuse in view of recent economic theory and Supreme Court decisions in non-misuse contexts. See *Windsurfing Int'l v. AMF, Inc.*... We are bound, however, to adhere to existing Supreme Court guidance in the area until otherwise directed by Congress or by the Supreme Court.

803 F.2d at 670-71.

The *Senza-Gel* court found patent misuse in a tie-in context by applying patent misuse cases, rather than antitrust tie-in decisions:

> [Defendant's] effort to equate the determination of product separability for misuse purposes with product separability for antitrust purposes must fail in light of Ninth Circuit and Supreme Court law, which requires that "consumer behavior" (market demand) be examined to determine the separability of products in determining whether there is a tying arrangement for antitrust purposes. Thus there is no conflict in the district court's holding that there are two products sufficient to sustain a defense of patent misuse, and its determination that a genuine issue of material fact exists on whether there are two products for antitrust purposes. The law of patent misuse in licensing need not look to consumer demand (which may be non-existent) but need look only to the nature of the claimed invention as the basis for determining whether a product is a necessary concomitant of the invention or an entirely separate product. The law of antitrust violation, tailored for situations that may or may not involve a patent, looks to a consumer demand test for determining product separability.

803 F.2d at 670-71, 670 n.14.

Commentators have been equally divided in their views. *Compare* Merges, *Reflections on Current Legislation Affecting Patent Misuse*, 70 J. PAT. & TRADE-MARK OFF. SOC'Y 793 (1988) (defending a separate doctrine of patent misuse); Burchfiel, *Patent Misuse and Antitrust Reform: "Blessed Be the Tie,"* 4 HARV. J. L. & TECH. 1 (1991) (same, on basis that antitrust standard is difficult and expensive); *with* Note, *The Economic Irrationality of the Patent Misuse Doctrine*, 78 CAL. L. REV. 1599 (1990); Note, *Standard Antitrust Analysis and the Doctrine of Patent Misuse: A Unification Under the Rule of Reason*, 46 U. PITT. L. REV. 209 (1984). *See generally* Kaplow, *The Patent-Antitrust Intersection: A Reappraisal*, 97 HARV. L. REV. 1813 (1984).

The critics of misuse, aided by practitioners whose clients were tired of defending against spurious misuse counterclaims in infringement suits, proposed amendments to the portion of the patent statute that specifies certain exceptions to the general patent misuse principle — § 271(d). As finally adopted in 1988, the newly amended version of this section reads as follows (note that subsections (4) and (5) are new):

§ 271. Infringement of patent

....

(d) No patent owner otherwise entitled to relief for infringement or contributory infringement of a patent shall be denied relief or deemed guilty of misuse or illegal extension of the patent right by reason of having done one or more of the following: (1) derived revenue from acts which if performed by another without his consent would constitute contributory infringement of the patent; (2) licensed or authorized another to perform acts which if performed without his consent would constitute contributory infringement of the patent; (3) sought to enforce his patent rights against infringement or contributory infringement; (4) refused to license or use any rights to the patent; or (5) conditioned the license of any rights to the patent or the sale of the patented product on the acquisition of a license to rights in another patent or purchase of a separate product, unless, in view of the circumstances, the patent owner has market power in the relevant market for the patent or patented product on which the license or sale is conditioned.

35 U.S.C. § 271(d) (1986 & Supp. VI 1991); subsections (4) and (5) added by H.R. 4972, P.L. 100-73 (102 Stat. 4674), 100th Cong. 2d Sess. 1988.

Before the effects of the new subsections in § 271(d) can be discussed, a brief word is in order about the relationship between contributory infringement and patent misuse.

As described in Chapter 8, contributory infringement allows a patentee to stop clever infringers from chipping away at a patent. Since direct infringement requires making, using or selling a device with all the limitations of the patentee's claim, infringers would naturally seek to sell something lacking a claimed element, but which can easily be "finished" or adapted by the purchaser to form a complete patented device. The contributory infringement section of the Patent Act, § 271(c), was created to prevent just such an injustice. This section grew out of early patent decisions creating an exception in equity to the harsh and mechanistic rule requiring patentees to show that an alleged infringer was selling a product that incorporated each and every element of the patentee's product. *See* Oddi, *Contributory Infringement/Patent Misuse: Metaphysics and Metamorphosis*, 44 U. PITT. L. REV. 73 (1982) (hereafter, Oddi, *Metaphysics*).

As discussed in depth in Oddi, *Metaphysics*, contributory infringement and patent misuse have always existed in a kind of reciprocal tension. As contributory infringement is expanded — that is, as more acts done by others are found to violate a patent despite the absence of literal infringement — the patentee's right expands. But as more acts are found to constitute patent misuse, the patentee's rights contract. The linkage between the concepts is that they both involve activities that are *ancillary* to the patent. For instance, the Supreme Court held in *Dawson Chem. Co. v. Rohm & Haas Co.* (Chapter 8, Section D) that it was contributory infringement for the defendant to sell a patented product that had no substantial use other than in conjunction with the patentee's process patent for applying that product. This is an extension of the patentee's process patent to cover an ancillary activity — sale of a related (non-staple) item for use in the process. Compare this with the patentee's activities in *Morton Salt, supra*; the Court there held that the tying of the ancillary product (salt) to the purchase of the patented item was illegal patent misuse. In both cases, the central issue was an ancillary activity not directly covered by the patent. Contributory infringement extends the patentee's rights to prohibit third-party activities ancillary to the patent, and patent misuse limits the patentee's right to contractually control ancillary activity.

This is the basis for the language in § 271(d)(1) and (2) describing alleged misuse activities "which if performed by another without [the patentee's] consent would constitute contributory infringement of the patent." This states the relationship between contributory infringement and misuse explicitly, if not quite clearly: the *patentee* may do something that would be contributory infringement if done by someone else. The logic proceeds from the fact that both contributory infringement and patent misuse are concerned with *ancillary* activities, activities done at the periphery of the patent grant. If some act is so closely related to the patent that it would be contributory infringement if done by someone else, that act, when done by the patentee, must be acceptable — i.e., it must *not* be misuse. (Note that much of the confusion in interpreting this section stems from its *negative* definition of misuse.) In other words, closely related activities can be contributory infringement; the same activities — precisely *because* they are so closely related — are not illegitimate attempts to extend the patent monopoly if made by the patentee. They are not, that is to say, patent misuse.

Subsections (3) through (5) of § 271(d) elaborate on this theme. They are specific instances of acceptable patentee behavior. Thus the patentee may (i.e., it is not misuse if the patentee does): enforce her patent; refuse to license it; or condition a license on the purchase of non-patented items (i.e., create a tie-in) under certain circumstances.

a. Applying Amended § 271

Several recent cases shed some light on the practical effect of the 1988 amendments to § 271.

From *In re Recombinant DNA Technology Patent & Contract Litigation*, 850 F. Supp. 769, 774, 30 U.S.P.Q.2d 1881, 1895-97 (S.D. Ind. 1994):

> Lilly argues that the holdings in *Morton Salt, United Shoe* and *National Lockwasher*, among others, illustrate that a finding of per se patent misuse is appropriate in this case. Lilly alleges that provisions in two license agreements entered by Genentech support such a finding. The provision in the Insulin Agreement that Lilly challenges as patent misuse provides:
>
> > 8.12 Lilly Use of Non-Genentech Recombinant Microorganism. Genentech may, at its option, terminate Lilly's rights hereunder with respect to one or more countries or terminate this Agreement in its entirety in the event Lilly shall sell Recombinant Insulin which is produced or derived from the product of any Recombinant Microorganism for whose use no royalty is due to Genentech hereunder, unless Lilly is obliged by circumstances essentially beyond its control to make such Insulin sales involving such other Recombinant Microorganism, [sic]. Lilly shall advise Genentech on each occasion on which it files for government approval for the sale of any such product and again on any such approval.
>
> A similar provision in [another licensing] Agreement stipulates:
>
> > 9.08 Genentech may, at its option, terminate KabiGen's rights hereunder with respect to one or more countries or terminate this Agreement in its entirety in the event KabiGen or an affiliate-licensee hereunder of KabiGen or AB Kabi shall sell for human purposes a product containing human growth hormone, and any analog thereof having substantially the same or improved efficacy, which is produced by or derived from the product of any microorganism or other non-pituitary source and for whose use no royalty is due to Genentech hereunder. KabiGen shall advise Genentech on each occasion on which it or the affiliate-licensee hereunder files for governmental approval for the sale of any such product and again upon the grant of any such approval.
>
> Lilly's patent misuse charge focuses on Genentech's retention of a right to terminate the agreement should Lilly or Kabi sell recombinant insulin or hGH, respectively, produced or derived without using either Genentech microorganisms or Genentech patented technology. Lilly argues that this right to terminate presents a continual, inchoate threat. Specifically, if Lilly

should use materials and services of others for the production of human insulin or develop its own rather than use those of Genentech, Genentech can terminate Lilly's right both to Genentech's materials and patented technology. This threat, Lilly contends, counters the public interest by stifling both competition and innovation. Thus, Lilly argues, the provisions are Genentech's attempt by means other than that of free competition to extend the bounds of its lawful monopoly such that Lilly and Kabi are forced to use solely "... Genentech patented technology and/or Genentech materials in their production of insulin and hGH, respectively." Lilly Memo. at 3.

Were it not for the 1988 Patent Misuse Reform Act, we believe precedent would dictate a finding in Lilly's favor. Although the Insulin and hGH Agreements grant Lilly and Kabi, respectively, both unpatented materials and patented technology, we do not believe this sufficiently distinguishes the instant case from others in which per se patent misuse historically has been found. It is clear that Genentech's contractual right to terminate the agreements should the licensees sell recombinant insulin or hGH for which Genentech receives no royalty includes the right to cancel the patent license of the licensee. The retention of such a right appears to use the patent as leverage to insure that the licensee will not use the microorganisms and the technology of competitors. This type of tying arrangement previously has been condemned as per se patent misuse. Moreover, the fact that the provisions are rights to terminate rather than explicit prohibitions on the licensees' use of competitors' products does not lessen their impact. As noted earlier in this Entry, the Supreme Court has found that such a tying method is as effective as an express covenant not to use competitor's products or technology. *See United Shoe*, 258 U.S. at 458.

However, the 1988 Patent Misuse Reform Act has placed limitations on the finding of patent misuse in tying arrangements. The Act eliminates per se findings of patent misuse in such situations. When the Act governs, a finding of patent misuse is prohibited unless the patentee is shown to have market power in the relevant market for the patent involved in the tying arrangement.

Lilly argues that the Act is inapplicable ... because the language of the Act does not include the type of tying arrangement here in issue.

This issue is a difficult one to resolve. The difficulty arises in interpreting the relevant section of the 1988 Patent Misuse Reform Act in light of the history of the doctrine of patent misuse. Through the years, courts have found per se patent misuse in varying forms of tying arrangements. In some cases, the patentee is conditioning the license of his patent on the licensee agreeing to use some specific unpatented product. *See, e.g., Morton Salt*. In other cases, the patentee is conditioning the license of his patent on the licensee agreeing not to use the products or devices of a competitor. *See, e.g., National Lockwasher*, 137 F.2d 255.

Courts have recognized that the two situations involve slightly different factual situations, but generally refer to both situations as tying arrangements. We cannot find an instance in which a court has indicated that the two tying arrangements should be treated differently. Some commentators, however, have referred to the former situations as "tie-ins" and the latter as "tie-outs." This is important to Lilly's argument in that Lilly insists that the above-quoted language of the Act refers only to "tie-in" arrangements. The tying arrangements challenged in the instant actions, Lilly contends, are "tie-outs" and, thus, unaffected by the Act.

We believe the statutory provision in issue reasonably could be read to encompass situations like the instant one, where the patentee has conditioned the license to the patent rights on the licensee's implicit agreement not to purchase certain, separate products. Because we believe that the statutory language is unclear, we turn to the legislative history for guidance.

An examination of the legislative history of the Act leads us to conclude that the language of the Act is meant to encompass both types of tying situations. For example, the Congressional Record of the Senate regarding the Act indicates that Congress' intention was to deal with "… a small piece of the patent misuse problem — tying arrangements — and leaves the rest for us to address in the future." 134 Cong. Rec. S17146-02 (daily ed. Oct. 21, 1988) (statement of Sen. DeConcini). Certainly, this passage does not suggest that some tying arrangements were not included in the statutory language. Moreover, the Congressional Record of the Senate reads: "Reform of patent misuse will ensure that the harsh misuse sanction of unenforceability is imposed only against those engaging in truly anticompetitive conduct." *Id.* (statement of Sen. Leahy). We are convinced that Congress would not have fashioned a "rule-of-reason type" approach for one form of tying arrangement and excluded from that approach another intimately related tying situation, especially in light of its clear purpose of permitting a misuse defense only when the patentee has acted anticompetitively. Contrary to Lilly's argument, we do not believe that Congress recognizes a difference between "tie-ins" and "tie-outs."

From *LifeScan Inc. v. Polymer Technology International Corp.*, 35 U.S.P.Q.2d 1225, 1237-38 (W.D. Wash. 1995):

[Patentee] LifeScan [owner of a patent on a blood glucose meter] has moved for summary judgment on the issue of whether or not there was misuse of the three patents at issue in this case, the '468, the '346 and the '487. Polymer has asserted misuse of the patents as a defense to liability.

The Supreme Court interpreted Sec. 271(d) in *Dawson [supra]*. In *Dawson* the court held that "the provisions of Sec. 271(d) effectively confer upon the patentee, as a lawful adjunct of his patent rights, a limited power to exclude others from competition in nonstaple goods. A patentee may sell a nonstaple article himself while enjoining others from marketing the same good without his authorization." *Id.* at 201. A nonstaple article is "one which was designed to carry out the patented process and has little or no utility outside of the patented process." Polymer has presented no evidence disputing LifeScan's claim that the test strips designed for use with Life-Scan's One Touch meters are nonstaple items. The court finds that the blood glucose test strips are nonstaple items.

The court notes that in *Dawson* the patentee was permitted to limit competition in the sale of an unpatented staple item, whereas here the strip itself is patented, thus making this an even stronger case in favor of a finding of no misuse.

The court is not persuaded by Polymer's arguments that the holding in *Dawson* has been restricted by the enactment of the Patent Misuse Reform Act of 1988, codified at 35 U.S.C. 271(d)(4)(5). It is clear from the legislative history that Congress intended to extend, not limit, the protection provided by *Dawson*. See 134 Cong. Rec. S17146-48 (Oct. 21, 1988) (Amendments enacted to "support [the] enhancement of intellectual property rights" and to "deter misuse claims that unnecessarily burden infringement litigation"). Since the 1988 amendments courts have continued to interpret *Dawson* as this court does here.

As the court has found that blood glucose test strips are nonstaple items, the court holds that LifeScan has not misused the patents at issue. Therefore, the court hereby GRANTS LifeScan's motion for summary judgment of no misuse of the '468, the '346 and the '487 patents.

b. Tying Into the Academic Literature

Subsection (5) of § 271(d), added in 1988, has occasioned the greatest debate in the literature, perhaps because tie-ins are a popular licensing device. (We discuss reasons why this is so in a moment.) To understand this subsection, however, two preliminary points must be addressed. We must first revisit *Dawson Chem. Co. v. Rohm & Haas Co.*, 448 U.S. 176 (1980), the Supreme Court case construing § 271(d) (and (c)) which influenced the 1988 revisions to § 271(d). Second, we must review the literature calling for elimination of patent misuse as a separate defense, distinct from antitrust violations, as this literature is directly responsible for § 271(d)(5)'s partial retraction of the traditional tie-in rule in misuse cases.

To summarize *Dawson* (excerpted and discussed in Chapter 8), recall that the Supreme Court upheld the plaintiff's contributory infringement charge against the defendant, who was found to have sold propanil, an unpatented chemical compound, specifically for a use (i.e., as an herbicide) protected by plaintiff's method-of-use patent. Recall further that the case hinged on the fact that propanil was a "non-staple" article of commerce — i.e., its only real use was as an herbicidal, which use was covered by plaintiff's "method of using propanil as an herbicide" patent. (Sale of non-staples, i.e., products with no substantial nonin-fringing use, is specifically defined as contributory infringement under Patent Act § 271(c).) The following cogent comments from a thorough treatment of the issues in the case summarize the Court's reasoning:

> Three premises affording patent protection to "essential nonstaples" seem to underlie the result in *Dawson*. First, there is a fundamental difference between staples and nonstaples (in particular, "essential nonstaples"), requir-ing different treatment under the doctrines of contributory infringement and patent misuse; second, "essential nonstaples" would be protected but for the metaphysics of patent law; and third, the power to license nonstaples free from patent misuse (section 271(d)(2)) implies the power to refuse to license competitors to sell nonstaples.

Oddi, *Metaphysics* (relying on the Court's statement that "by enacting §§ 271(c) and (d), Congress granted to patent holders a statutory right to control nonstaple goods that are capable only of infringing use in a patented invention, *and that are essential to that invention's advance over prior art*," 448 U.S. at 213 (emphasis added)).

This holding, which permits a patentee to tie an unpatented but nonstaple item to the sale of a patented item, provides a good platform for reviewing criticisms of patent misuse. In articles such as Note, *The Economic Irrationality of the Patent Misuse Doctrine*, 78 CAL. L. REV. 1599 (1990), and Note, *Standard Antitrust Analysis and the Doctrine of Patent Misuse: A Unification Under the Rule of Reason*, 46 U. PITT. L. REV. 209 (1984), the authors, following the lead of Judge Posner in the *USM* case, *supra*, question the wisdom of a separate patent misuse defense. The thinking is that antitrust has evolved a "precise" methodology for ascertaining when improper market leverage is being used by a patentee (or anyone, for that matter), and that the relatively imprecise "equita-ble" doctrine of misuse only adds confusion and uncertainty to the scene. This is especially so, according to the *Irrationality* note, because the remedy for misuse is so sweeping (total unenforceability of the patent) and potentially so unrelated to the patentee's activities vis-à-vis the infringer (i.e., license terms in the patentee's agreements with third parties can form the foundation of the infringer's misuse counterclaim).

While these criticisms have some force (especially the latter one, which sug-gests the need for a modification of misuse principles), the *Dawson* situation represents a good example of the case that can be made for continuation of the misuse doctrine in some guise or other. As was said in testimony leading up to the amendments to § 271(d),

> [S]ince the markets for specific technologies are often very "thin," with few direct substitutes available for particular inventions or components, the consumer-demand test of *Jefferson Parish* is of very limited use in this context. [*See* Caves, Crookell & Killing, *The Imperfect Market for Technol-*

ogy Licenses, 45 OXFORD BULL. ECON. & STATS. 249 (1983).] Second, because of these "thin" markets, product separability will often be difficult to determine. It will turn on the specific technology involved — spelled out in the claims of the patent in suit. Thus only a court intimately familiar with patent claim construction will be in a position to make this delicate determination.

Licensing Reform Act of 1988: Hearing before the Subcomm. on Courts, Civil Liberties and the Administration of Justice of the Comm. on the Judiciary of the House of Representatives on H.R. 4086, 100th Cong., 2d Sess. 183 (1988) (statement of Professor R. Merges), *reprinted as* Merges, *Reflections on Current Legislation Affecting Patent Misuse*, 70 J. PAT. & TRADEMARK OFF. SOC'Y 793 (1988).

The claim here is not so much that the antitrust-based test of an illegal tie-in — i.e., that the patentee/licensor has "market power" in the market for the tied product — is wrong, but that it is difficult to implement in the context of markets for goods sold for use with a patented item. To take the *Dawson* case as an example, perhaps the antitrust test would produce the same result: if the patentee did not have market power in the market for herbicides, tying the sale of propanil to the use of the patented product would not be misuse. But rather than fight over questions of market definition — for instance, was the market all herbicides, as Dawson would argue, or those which worked on the same weeds as propanil, or those which so worked and are administered in the same way, as Rohm & Haas would argue — it seems more straightforward to dispose of questions of market power. *See* Burchfiel, *Patent Misuse and Antitrust Reform: "Blessed Be the Tie,"* 4 HARV. J.L. & TECH. 1 (1991) (pointing out administrative difficulty of working with antitrust standards, and therefore desirability of retaining separate misuse doctrine).

Unfortunately, the amendments to § 271(d) resolve this problem for us by making an antitrust-like inquiry mandatory in tie-in cases under § 271(d)(5). Note, however, that there is legislative history which points out that the amendments to § 271(d) do not totally eliminate a separate patent misuse doctrine. Representative Robert Kastenmeier, who introduced H.R. 4086, the bill that added the amendments, stated:

> The proposed amendment requires that the person who engages in tying conduct must possess "market power in the relevant market." The term "market power" is used in this context in order to permit the courts to reasonably assess the potential for anticompetitive effect of a particular practice. We have chosen not to explicitly guide the courts as to the level of "market power" required for a finding of misuse.... Courts should evaluate the question of "market power" in the context of the patent, where a patent license is involved, the product and the market in which the tie-in occurs. This type of fact specific contextual analysis should make the fact-finding process more sensitive to the realities of the market-place.

134 CONG. REC. H10,648 (daily ed. Oct. 20, 1988) (remarks of Rep. Kasten-meier; citations omitted). *But cf.* Sussman, *Tying, Refusals to License, and Copyright Misuse: The Patent Misuse Model*, 36 J. COPYRIGHT OFF. SOC'Y U.S.A. 300, 319-20 (1989) (collecting legislative history supporting position that antitrust rule was meant to be adopted when § 271(d) was amended).

Arguably, in this context market power is not really what we are interested in; the real question is whether the patent ought to extend to the activities carried on by the patentee. In light of *Dawson*, § 271(d)'s negative definitions of patent misuse have been transmuted into affirmative rights against accused infringers (see Oddi, *Metaphysics*, *supra*). This means that, rather than inquiring solely into whether a certain practice is misuse, we must recognize that if there is no misuse under § 271(d), an affirmative grant of additional rights to the patentee has been created. Thus, curiously, a finding of "no market power" under the new § 271(d)(5) could well permit a patentee not only to tie a certain product to its patented product, but also to sue others selling the tied product for contributory infringement.

In the legislative hearings on what became § 271(d)'s recent amendments, it was stated that there is a peculiar place for misuse *in patent law*, as distinct from antitrust law. Statement of Prof. R. Merges, *supra*. The rationale for this is that we must, after *Dawson*, view § 271(d), and its "negative" misuse rules, as a source of additional rights for the patentee. Curiously, then, patent misuse is actually a matter of patent scope! This is ultimately the best reason to keep it as a separate doctrine. (Judge Rich has made the same point with respect to contributory infringement. *See* Rich, *Interpretation of Claims and Extent of Protection — American Perspectives*, 21 INT'L REV. IND. PROP. & COPYRIGHT L. 497 (1990)). Patent scope, after all, ought to be a matter of patent law.

The point cannot be taken too far, however. It is impossible to claim, for instance, that the recent amendments to § 271(d)(5) make competing sellers of staple articles liable for contributory infringement where a patentee also sells the staple article along with a patented item. This is because of two other sections of the Patent Act: the general statement in § 271(d) that contributory infringement provides the benchmark for determining misuse; and § 271(c), which excludes sale of staple articles from the definition of contributory infringement. On this view, the revisions to § 271(d) simply break the logical connection between misuse and contributory infringement in the context of tie-ins. Thus it is the market power of the patentee in the market for the patented product that now counts for misuse purposes, rather than the staple or nonstaple characteristics of the tied-in article. Surely a defense exists for such a rule, most notably one centered on either (1) the "metering" argument (i.e., that sales of the tied-in unpatented item are used to determine the extent of use of the patented item), or (2) the "appropriability" argument, which suggests that a tie-in may be needed for the patentee to obtain the full benefit of its invention. On (1), see Note, *Economic Irrationality* and sources cited therein; on (2), see Teece, *Profiting from*

Technological Innovation: Implications for Integration, Collaboration, and Public Policy, 15 RES. POL'Y 285 (1986); J. DIRLAM & A. KAHN, FAIR COMPETITION: THE LAW AND ECONOMICS OF ANTITRUST POLICY 190-92 (1954) (arguing that dividing product into tying and tied components can be arbitrary, and "tying" necessary; that product should be looked at as a package; and that true test of antitrust violation should be whether customers can choose the product on its merits).

On the other hand, under some circumstances the metering argument can be used as a ruse to cover a coerced tie-in. Louis Kaplow has noted, for instance, that it is not necessary that the patentee supply the staple item for it to serve the metering function; it is a matter of accounting for the staple input, whatever the source. Kaplow, *Extension of Monopoly Through Leverage*, 85 COLUM. L. REV. 515, 541 (1985). Likewise, it would seem that a *required* tie-in of a *staple* item might go beyond a necessary "appropriability" mechanism, and extend into the range of "over-appropriation." Teece himself emphasizes that what he calls "co-specific assets" are normally used as the mechanism of appropriation; a close look at the definition of "co-specific" reveals that this is merely a synonym for nonstaple items. Thus while the patentee might make the staple item available for metering purposes, and while the patentee might be permitted to sell some nonpatented items to appropriate the full value of an invention, neither rationale completely undercuts the traditional staple/nonstaple distinction. Put in terms of § 271(d)(5) and its legislative history, there may still be room left for a consideration of the staple/nonstaple nature of the tied item in a determination of patent misuse. This only makes sense in light of the close relationship between contributory infringement (§ 271(c)) and patent misuse (§ 271(d)), and of the transmutation of § 271(d)'s negative rules into affirmative rights after *Dawson*.

The appropriation theme is picked up, though not under that terminology, in a helpful article summarizing the law and analytics of tie-ins co-authored by antitrust titan William Baxter. William F. Baxter and Daniel P. Kessler, "The Law and Economics of Tying Arrangements: Lessons for Competition Policy Treatment of Intellectual Property," paper presented at the Conference on Intellectual Property and Competition Policy, sponsored by the Bureau of Competition, Industry Canada, in Aylmer, Quebec, May 1996. In addition to the incentive effects, the paper identifies two other "supply-side" effects of tying: provision of a commitment device (by virtue of the metering effects of a tie-in: linking the inventor's compensation to the manufacturer's output prevents the inventor from selling the same or a similar concept to a competing manufacturer); and, of course, foreclosure of ancillary product markets. Chief effects on the demand side are said to center on the increased opportunities for price discrimination. Where "bundling" the two products together increases the total base of consumers using the product, this is beneficial; where it reduces total usage, it is not.

Ultimately, contributions such as this should facilitate further reform of the patent misuse doctrine. Sensible suggestions include (from Note, *Irrationality*):

(1) restrict misuse to cases where the accused infringer herself is harmed by it; (2) restrict the remedy in each case, e.g., by making patent extensions invalid only as to the portion of the license term greater than the patent term; and (from Oddi, *Metaphysics*) (3) inquire into overall welfare effects before imposing liability; and perhaps (4) permit competitors to sell nonstaple items, but require them to pay a royalty to the patentee.

NOTES

1. From Note, *Vertical Territorial Restrictions as Patent Misuse*, 61 S. CAL. L. REV. 215 (1987):

> [W]hile patent misuse based on VTRs [Vertical Territorial Restrictions] is dependent on antitrust law for its basic theories of anticompetitive effect, the policy foundations justifying the antitrust Rule of Reason do not apply in the patent misuse context. Consequently, the approach courts take when analyzing whether VTRs constitute patent misuse should differ from the approach taken in deciding if such restrictions violate antitrust laws. This Note demonstrates that under certain circumstances, a per se patent misuse rule for VTRs is appropriate.

2. From K. Heyer, An Economic Analysis of Patent Licensing Restrictions, Ph.D. Thesis, UCLA (Economics) (1983), summarized in Vol. 44/05-A DISSERTATION ABSTRACTS INT'L 1525:

> [Restrictions in licensing agreements] can also serve to enhance economic efficiency, such as when they help overcome free-rider problems that destroy the incentives of licensees to provide special pre-sale services, or when they provide an economic incentive for licensees to maintain final product quality and preserve the reputation of a valuable patent. These considerations indicate that neither the form nor the fact of competition-limiting provisions can alone provide an unambiguous guide to deciding individual cases on efficiency grounds. This study develops an efficiency criterion for evaluating patent licensing restrictions. The basic argument is that since the patent grant already bestows upon an inventor a legal monopoly over the patented product or process being licensed, licensing restrictions should not be considered efficiency harming unless they limit competition between the patent and its substitutes, or between sellers in a product market not defined by or owing its existence to the patent.
>
> This efficiency criterion is then applied to two antitrust cases: *U.S. v. Ethyl Gasoline* (1940), and *U.S. v. General Electric* (1926). In each case the traditional view that patent licensing restrictions were used to cartelize a market is tested against alternative, efficiency-enhancing explanations. In the *Ethyl* case the cartel explanation is rejected and a quality-guaranteeing explanation is found to be plausible. In the *GE* case the cartel explanation is

found to be weaker than generally believed, and a number of plausible efficiency-enhancing reasons for the licensing practices are examined.

Compare Priest, *Cartels and Patent License Arrangements*, 20 J. L. & ECON. 309, 331-32 (1977) (critiquing Supreme Court decision in *E. Bement & Sons v. National Harrow Co.*, 186 U.S. 70 (1902), where Court validated firm's practice of assigning patents to a holding company to which its competitors had assigned their patents, under arrangement where holding company set price licensee firms must charge; author finds that royalty was administrative fee; that no firm practiced patents of other firms; "The mutual concessions of validity led to no integration of patented processes, which suggests either that no patent was superior but all were redundant, or that the motive for the assignment was not to transfer rights to the use of the processes, but to transfer the legal right to set licensee prices. Under either interpretation, the arrangement restrains trade."). *Cf.* Rockett, *Choosing the Competition and Patent Licensing*, 21 RAND J. ECON. 161 (1990) (model showing that patent licensor chooses weak competitors to keep good competition out); Meurer, *The Settlement of Patent Litigation*, 20 RAND J. ECON. 1 (1989) ("Th[e] incentive for licensing is diminished, however, by antitrust rules that impair the ability of parties to the license to maintain monopoly output restrictions. As a result, settlement might not be an efficient bargaining outcome, even when potential litigants have common information about the outcome of a trial."); J. Schlicher, *The Law and Economics of Licensing Biotechnology Patent and Related Property Rights in the United States*, in PRACTICING LAW INSTITUTE, PATENTS, COPYRIGHTS, TRADEMARKS, AND LITERARY PROPERTY COURSE HANDBOOK SERIES, TECHNOLOGY LICENSING 1987, 235 PLI/PAT. 333 (1987) (providing economic rationale for many common licensing terms); Gallini & Wright, *Technology Transfer Under Asymmetric Information*, 21 RAND J. ECON. 147 (1990) (explains common provisions in licensing arrangements in terms of transaction cost theory).

4. The state of the art treatment of patent licensing under antitrust law is contained in the U.S. Justice Department's "Antitrust Guidelines for the Licensing of Intellectual Property," issued April 6, 1995. The Guidelines were drafted with significant input from the noted economist Richard Gilbert of the University of California, Berkeley. The Guidelines mark the introduction of the notion of an "innovation market" in antitrust analysis — a highly useful addition to antitrust analysis, from the point of view of intellectual property lawyers. An innovation market is the total set of conditions that affect the investment in and reception of new technological advances in an industry. As such, innovation markets reflect a concern with the effects of firm behavior on the future prospects for innovation in an industry. Intellectual property law is of course one important source of incentives that greatly affect the innovation dynamic. Hence analysis of innovation markets will undoubtedly further the cause of explicating the intellectual property/antitrust interface.

10. PATENT POOLS

CARPET SEAMING TAPE LICENSING CORP.
v. BEST SEAM INC.

616 F.2d 1133, 206 U.S.P.Q. 213, 1980-2 Trade Cases (CCH)
¶ 63,290 (9th Cir. 1980)

In this case involving the validity and enforceability of a number of patents on products and processes used in seaming carpets, at the close of the plaintiff's case the trial judge [declared one patent invalid for inequitable conduct or "fraud on the Patent Office and] declare[d] invalid three patents on grounds of patent misuse. In finding misuse, the trial judge failed to apply the appropriate standards for assessing the antitrust violations found, and specifically applied an erroneous standard to the question of whether the patents accumulated by the appellant were blocking patents. For these reasons, we reverse the judgment in favor of appellees and remand the case to the trial court for further proceedings.

Appellant, Carpet Seaming Tape Licensing Corporation ("Carpet Seaming"), a Texas corporation holding the patents here involved, brought these actions against appellees, Best Seam Incorporated ("Best Seam"), a California corporation making and selling hot-melt adhesive carpet seaming tape, [and] Vectron Industries, Inc. ("Vectron"), another California corporation also making and selling hot-melt adhesive carpet seaming tape.

The method for seaming carpets most accepted today is a face-seaming process using a hot-melt adhesive tape. Carpet sections are positioned pile-side-up on the floor, and the edges to be joined are rolled back just far enough to allow placement of the tape beneath the seam. The adhesive which is in solid form on the tape is then melted, and the carpet edges pressed down upon it for bonding as the adhesive resolidifies. This system has largely supplanted sewing as well as back-seaming (a process in which carpet sections are turned pile-side-down, and the seaming work is performed on the back of the carpet) since it allows the work to be done quickly and without the need for moving cumbersome sections of carpet once they have been positioned as the installer desires.

The tape utilized in this process is composed of three elements. The uppermost element is a layer of hot-melt adhesive. Hot-melt adhesive is solid and nonadhesive at room temperature. When heated, it becomes molten and forms a bond which it retains when cooled and resolidified. During the manufacturing of the tape, the adhesive layer is bonded to the second element of the tape, a layer of synthetic mesh which lends the tape strength. The seaming process actually involves the bonding of two pieces of carpet to this single strip of mesh. The final element of the tape is a paper barrier which prevents the adhesive layer from bonding to whatever lies beneath it when it is heated. As a further refinement, the adhesive layer is embossed into parallel ridges which melt into a single smooth layer of adhesive at the appropriate heat for bonding. The embossing feature provides the worker using the tape with a quick visual index for gauging adequate heating of the adhesive.

Of the four patents directly at issue before the district court, three were originally obtained by Charles D. Burgess. Burgess "038" covers the three-element tape described above without the added feature of embossed ridges. Burgess "876" covers the seaming process described above using the "038" tape. Burgess "830" describes the process for manufacturing the "038" tape. The fourth patent (the "Winkler patent") was obtained by Alexander Winkler and covered tape using embossed ridges. Two other patents also involved were Burgess "703," a predecessor of the Burgess patents outlined above, which describes a process for seaming carpets using a two-element tape like the "038" tape but without the paper barrier, and a patent issued to Michael L. Clymin (the "Clymin patent") covering a three-element tape in which the adhesive is deposited in unconnected parallel bands on the tape rather than as ridges upon a smooth layer of adhesive as in the Winkler patent.

Charles Burgess in March, 1966, produced a two-element tape and process which could be used successfully to seam carpets, but which required placing newspaper as a barrier beneath the tape to prevent the adhesive from sticking to the floor or padding below the tape. It was only on concrete floors that this step of placing newspapers beneath the two-element tape was not required, since the adhesive used by Burgess would not adhere to concrete. [I]n his application [for what became the "703" patent] Burgess [did not] disclose the step of placing newspapers beneath the tape, although he regularly used this step in practicing and demonstrating his process. The trial court found that the use of such a barrier was known in the art of carpet seaming for many years prior to March, 1966 and that omission of this step, which it found necessary to the practice of the two-element process, constituted fraud by Burgess on the Patent Office invalidating not only the "703" patent, but the other three Burgess patents as well.

In May, 1966, Burgess added a paper barrier web as an element of his tape, and on December 6, 1966, he filed a second patent application, a continuation-in-part to his March 18 application, for patents on the three-element tape described above and the processes for making and using it. After further Patent Office action, the December 6 application resulted in the issuance of the "038" patent on September 3, 1968, the "876" patent on October 13, 1970, and the "830" patent on February 16, 1971. In January, 1968, Burgess sold his business and the pending applications to Giffen Industries, Inc. ("Giffen"), which subsequently transferred them to appellant [Carpet Seaming Tape Licensing Corp.].

Besides obtaining exclusive licenses for the Burgess patents, appellant also obtained exclusive licenses for the Clymin patent and the Winkler patent. [The licensor of the Clymin patent, Consolidated Foods Corporation (CFC), retained a nonexclusive right to practice that invention. The licensor of the valuable Winkler embossed ribbed tape patent, Bruck Industries, Inc. (Bruck) received a two-and-a-half percent reduction in the royalty rate for licenses which were granted to it by appellant in accordance with appellant's standard nonexclusive license arrangement, and agreed to pay $75,000 liquidated past royalties upon condition that other major infringers either be licensed or sued for infringement.]

The Burgess, Winkler, and Clymin patents have been available for licensing at a four percent royalty rate for flat tape and a five percent rate for embossed and ribbed tape. However, the trial court found that these royalty rates were anticompetitive in that they would cause competitors licensed to use the patents to either go out of business or raise their prices to a point at which they would be at a severe competitive disadvantage compared to Laminated Plastics, Inc., the manufacturing subsidiary of Giffen and the parent of Carpet Seaming.

Granting appellee's motion to dismiss at the conclusion of appellant's case-in-chief was not appropriate for the following reasons. First, the record was not developed fully enough to adequately determine the points of law upon which the judgment rested. Second, the district court erred in the standard it applied for assessing the presence of fraud in connection with the Burgess "703" patent.

[T]he trial court [also] labored under a misapprehension as to the relationship between two or more patents which can give rise to a blocking situation. The trial court found it necessary only to conclude that the Winkler and Clymin patents did not block the Burgess patents or each other. Not considered was the possibility that the Burgess patents might block the Winkler or Clymin patents, despite the fact that the case law establishes that basic patents may often block improvement patents on a basic product or process. This omission was significant, since a finding that the Burgess patents did block either Clymin or Winkler would have an impact on the inference to be drawn from the appellant's conduct in pooling those patents.

Finally, the trial court failed to articulate or apply appropriate standards in assessing the antitrust violations found at trial.

Next, the trial court ruled the four patents in suit unenforceable because appellant Carpet Seaming violated Section 2 of the Sherman Act by unlawfully attempting to monopolize and conspiring to monopolize the manufacture and sale of hot-melt thermoplastic carpet seaming tapes, as follows:

> (F)irst, through the unlawful accumulation on the part of Giffen Industries, Inc. and its subsidiaries, of the Burgess and Clymin patents and exclusive license rights under the Winkler patent; secondly, in the knowingly wrongful assertion of the Clymin patent as covering ribbed tape against defendant Best Seam, Incorporated and others; and, thirdly, in the unlawful combination of the Giffen Companies through plaintiff with Bruck Industries, Inc. for the enforcement of the Burgess, Clymin and Winkler patents against competitors of Bruck Industries, Inc. and Laminated Plastics.

These conclusions as to misuse and antitrust violations when viewed in conjunction with the trial court's findings of fact demonstrate that the law applied at the trial deviated from the correct legal standards governing the offenses recounted. The trial court's legal conclusions are so summary that it is virtually impossible to ascertain what legal standards were in fact applied.

In this circuit, a prima facie case of attempt to monopolize requires proof of three elements: (1) specific intent to control prices or destroy competition with respect to a part of commerce; (2) predatory or anticompetitive conduct directed to accomplishing the unlawful purpose; and (3) a dangerous probability of success. [I]n its findings of fact, the trial court repeated several times that the purpose of both appellant and the other parties to the pooling agreement was to license the entire carpet seaming industry. Standing alone, this amounts to no more than an intent to legally exploit the power inherent in the patent grant, which a patent holder is entitled to do. To show misuse, a patentee must have the purpose of exercising anticompetitive power outside the lawful scope of that granted by the patent.

The accumulation of patents is not per se illegal. A patent pool may, however, be rendered unlawful if accompanied by an illegitimate purpose or anticompetitive consequences beyond those inherent in the grants of the patents in question. The trial judge made no findings of specific adverse impact on the market for hot-melt carpet seaming tapes. Consequently, we are forced to conclude that he relied on illicit purpose as rendering illegal the pooling of the Burgess, Winkler, and Clymin patents.

A well-recognized legitimate purpose for a pooling agreement is exchange of blocking patents. *Standard Oil Co. v. United States*, 283 U.S. 163 (1931). As the Supreme Court stated in *Standard Oil*, 283 U.S. at 172, n.5:

> This is often the case where patents covering improvements of a basic process, owned by one manufacturer, are granted to another. A patent may be rendered quite useless, or "blocked," by another unexpired patent which covers a vitally related feature of the manufacturing process. Unless some agreement can be reached, the parties are hampered and exposed to litigation. And, frequently, the cost of litigation to a patentee is greater than the value of a patent for a minor improvement.

A reversal of the trial court's conclusion on blocking is thus required, as well as reversal of its conclusion as to misuse, since the blocking issue bears directly on the question of illicit purpose of the pooling agreement even though the Winkler patent was found invalid on other grounds not appealed.

Finally, we must consider the wrongful assertion and enforcement of the pooled patents as a ground for violation of the antitrust laws and misuse. Once again, the trial court's treatment of the question makes it difficult to determine what standard was applied at trial in assessing the violation. Attempted enforcement of a patent does not amount to a violation of the antitrust laws. To amount to an antitrust violation or patent misuse, such attempted enforcement must be in bad faith. Moreover, infringement suits are presumed to be in good faith. The trial court did not mention, much less give adequate consideration, to the requisite element of bad faith, the presumption of good faith, or the appropriate high burden of proof on this issue. Upon remand, appellant should be granted the

opportunity to prove that any misuse has been abandoned and that the consequences have been dissipated. [Reversed and remanded.]

NOTES

1. *When Pools Are Anticompetitive.* In some cases particular patent pools are
condemned as advancing an anticompetitive scheme. *See United States v. Singer
Mfg. Co.*, 374 U.S. 174 (1963) (assignment of patent rights for primary purpose
of restraining import competition); *Duplan Corp. v. Deering Milliken, Inc.*, 540
F.2d 1215 (4th Cir. 1976), *on remand*, 444 F. Supp. 648 (D.S.C. 1977) (improper motive to dominate unlicensed competitors), *aff'd in part and rev'd in part*,
594 F.2d 979 (4th Cir. 1979), *cert. denied*, 444 U.S. 1015 (1980); *United States
v. Vehicular Parking, Ltd.*, 54 F. Supp. 828 (D. Del. 1944) (patent pool organized among members controlling 95% of industry, and which featured resale
price maintenance and restrictions on amount of free service members could provide, and other business matters, was illegal under the Sherman Act). In Priest,
Cartels and Patent License Arrangements, 20 J.L. & ECON. 309 (1977), evidence
is presented that patent pools can serve as a way to divide sales in an industry
and coordinate prices, and therefore can assist greatly in establishing a cartel. *See
also* Andewelt, *Analysis of Patent Pools Under the Antitrust Laws*, 53 ANTITRUST
L.J. 611 (1984); McGee, *Patent Exploitation: Some Economic and Legal
Problems*, 9 J.L. & ECON. 135 (1966). Note, *Compulsory Licensing and the
Patent Pool Problem*, 46 YALE L.J. 1402 (1937).

2. *Kinder, Gentler Treatment for Pools.* Several cases hold that pooling
agreements can have a tendency to diminish the incentives for individual members
to compete on a technological basis and will be closely scrutinized where the
market structure raises competitive concerns (i.e., where the pool members
belong to a concentrated industry and account for a substantial share of that
industry's sales or output, where entry barriers are high, etc.). In *United States
v. Manufacturers Aircraft Ass'n*, 1976-1 Trade Cas. (CCH) ¶60,810 (S.D.N.Y.
1975) (consent decree), for instance, a long-standing patent pool among aircraft
manufacturers was broken up. The workings of this patent pool are described and
defended, and the antitrust action criticized, in Bittlingmayer, *Property Rights,
Progress, and the Aircraft Patent Agreement*, 31 J.L. & ECON. 227 (1988). *See
also* Dykman, *Patent Licensing Within the Manufacturer's Aircraft Association
(MAA)*, 46 J. PAT. OFF. SOC'Y 646, 647 (1964) (describing formation of industry
licensing pool, at behest of government, because, "[n]o one would license the
other under anything like a reasonable basis."). *See generally* Merges & Nelson,
On the Complex Economics of Patent Scope, 90 COLUM. L. REV. 839 (1990)
(describing this and other "forced" pools). *See also United States v. Automobile
Mfrs. Ass'n*, 307 F. Supp. 617 (C.D. Cal. 1969) (major U.S. automobile
manufacturers were charged with impermissibly delaying technological advancement), *aff'd in part and appeal dismissed in part sub nom. Grossman v. Automobile Mfrs. Ass'n*, 397 U.S. 248 (1970), *modified*, 1982-83 Trade Cas. (CCH)

¶ 65,088 (C.D. Cal. 1982); ANTITRUST DIVISION, U.S. DEP'T OF JUSTICE, ANTI-TRUST GUIDE CONCERNING RESEARCH JOINT VENTURES (1980) at 16, Cases A and H (describing similar pools).

3. Nonexclusive Pools Fare Better. If the fear is that a patent pool will facilitate industry coordination, if not outright cartelization, an "open entry policy," whereby any new firm may license the pooled technology, will alleviate these concerns. *See, e.g., Cutter Labs. v. Lyophile-Cryochem Corp.*, 179 F.2d 80, 92 (9th Cir. 1949); *King v. Anthony Pools, Inc.*, 202 F. Supp. 426 (S.D. Cal. 1962) ("The pooling of patents and cross-licensing which are open equally to the public on the same terms do not fall within the interdiction [of the patent misuse doctrine].").

4. Transaction Cost Rationale for Pools and Joint Ventures. Patent pools regularize technology transactions. Hence they can significantly reduce the transaction costs of exchanging technology when compared to a series of one-shot licensing deals. In fact, a pool can be thought of as a single overriding institutional arrangement that specifies the general parameters of technology exchanges but leaves certain details open to further negotiations. *See* Robert P. Merges, *Contracting into Liability Rules: Intellectual Property and Collective Rights Organizations*, 84 CAL. L. REV. __ (forthcoming 1996). *See generally* Jorde & Teece, *Innovation, Cooperation and Antitrust: Striking the Right Balance*, 4 HIGH TECH. L.J. 1 (1989) (discussing antitrust aspects of joint ventures in detail).

Likewise, joint ventures can be explained in terms of transaction costs. Although information exchange between joint venturers is often limited by the antitrust authorities (see, e.g., *United States v. Alcan Alum. Ltd.*, 1985-1 Trade Cas. (CCH) ¶ 66,427 (W.D. Ky. 1985), it is generally permissible for the parties to an R&D joint venture to share information relating to the technology to be developed. *See In re General Motors Corp.*, 103 F.T.C. 374 (1984). This makes sense, because a joint venture can be thought of as a pre-negotiated pool. From this perspective, not only should most pools be tolerated (see Bittlingmayer, above) but joint ventures should be encouraged as well. To see why, consider that the transaction costs of negotiating a pooling agreement will often be steep, due to (1) differing assessments of the technological merits of the contributions of the members of the pool; (2) private information held by each member concerning the precise characteristics of the technology and the details of the patent position (all relevant prior art, etc.); and (3) strategic bargaining possibilities created by the negotiations over the potentially large "pooling surplus" that may result from the creation of the pool. *See* Scotchmer, *Standing on the Shoulders of Giants: Cumulative Research and the Patent Law*, 5 J. ECON. PERSPS. 29 (1991); Folster, *Firms' Choice of R&D Intensity in the Presence of Aggregate Increasing Returns to Scale*, 13 J. ECON. BEHAV. & ORG. 387 (1990). *See generally* O. WILLIAMSON, MARKETS AND HIERARCHIES: ANALYSIS AND ANTITRUST IMPLICATIONS 21-37 (1975). Because of these factors, it may make sense for those planning to enter a field expected to be characterized by crossing and conflicting property rights claims to "pre-contract" for technology exchange before any technology is in fact developed. It may be easier to strike a deal before costs are sunk and egos are on the line. For a very helpful general account of the differing dynamics of ex ante and ex post contracting for complementary technologies, see Suzanne Scotchmer, Joint Ventures and Other Cooperative Arrangements (U.C. Berkeley Dep't of Economics working paper 1996).

11. LICENSING IN THE EEC

Members of the European Economic Community have acceded to the Treaty of Rome, which among other things sets up regulations regarding the licensing of technology. Under the Treaty, the European Commission reserves the right to review the terms of licensing agreements for possible anticompetitive effects. For U.S.-based licensors, this means that licensing agreements must either be reviewed by the Commission or fit into one of the exemptions to the Treaty's requirements. See Marks, *Patent Licensing and Antitrust in the United States and the European Economic Community*, 35 AM. U.L. REV. 963 (1986). The European Commission has adopted a "white list" and "black list" approach, whereby acceptable and unacceptable practices are set forth. These licensing regulations of the European Economic Community, promulgated under Article 85(3) of the Treaty of Rome, are listed in the *Official Journal of the European Communities*, August 16, 1984, at p. L-219.

One Commission decision under these regulations struck down as anticompetitive a series of licensing agreements for the commercialization of a new strain of seed. At least two terms of the agreements violated Article 85, according to the Commission: the "tying-out" of competitors (i.e., licensee agreements not to buy competing products), and a ban on "parallel imports," or purchases of the licensed product from another licensee instead of the licensor. See *Maize Seed* decision summarized at 14 INT'L REV. IND. PROP. & COPYRIGHT L. 256 (1983). Similar restrictions were struck down in licensing agreements for windsurfers. See Venit, *In the Wake of Windsurfing: Patent Licensing in the Common Market*, 18 INT'L REV. IND. PROP. & COPYRIGHT L. 1 (1987) (describing decision condemning (1) restrictions on licensee sales and manufacturing in territories where licensor had no parallel patents, and (2) clause prohibiting licensee from challenging licensor's patent). See generally ORG. FOR ECON. COOP. & DEVELOPMENT, COMPETITION POLICY AND INTELLECTUAL PROPERTY RIGHTS (1989) (describing pro- and anti-competitive effects of individual licensing terms). But cf. *Kai Ottung v. Klee & Weilbach A/S*, reported at 22 INT'L REV. IND. PROP. & COPYRIGHT L. 61, 65 (1991) (not a violation of art 85(1) of the Treaty of Rome in and of itself to call for payment of royalties for indefinite term, possibly extending beyond expiration of patent, at least where licensee has right to terminate agreement at any time; "commercial assessment of value" may dictate this kind of payment structure); Korah, *Do's and Don't's for Technology Licensing Into the European Economic Community*, 2 INTELL. PROP. J. 3 (1991). For comparisons with Japan, see Taylor et al., *A Comparison of International Intellectual*

Property Licensing in the United States and Japan, 9 UCLA PAC. BAS. L.J. 104 (1991); Nicholson, *Japanese Fair Trade Commission Guidelines for Licensing Agreements: An Overview and a Critique*, 21 GA. J. INT'L & COMP. L. 1 (1991).

12. LICENSING OF GOVERNMENT INVENTIONS

In 1980, in response to objections that government-financed inventions were languishing, Congress ended the longstanding federal policy permitting individual federal agencies to set their own licensing policies. In its stead, Congress enacted a policy meant to be uniform (though exceptions are allowed): patent rights may be owned by the *researchers*, the grant recipients, rather than by the government. In addition, where the government does retain ownership, exclusive licenses are permitted and encouraged. *See* P.L. 96-517, Dec. 12, 1980, 94 Stat. 3019, *codified at* 35 U.S.C. §§ 201-211 (1986). (Note that the policy applies to non-profits — i.e., universities and research institutes — *and* to small businesses as well; but large companies have been included in the new treatment by Executive Order and general acquiescence. And note that the policy was extended to inventions made in federally funded laboratories at government agencies by the Federal Technology Transfer Act of 1986, P.L. 99-502, Oct. 20, 1986, 100 Stat. 1785) Along with the creation of the Federal Circuit in 1982, this has been hailed as a revolutionary change in patent policy in the U.S. *Cf.* Ku, *Licensing DNA Cloning Technology*, 23 LES NOUVELLES 112 (June 1983) (describing use of new federal ownership policy to secure patent protection for widely licensed Cohen-Boyer genetic engineering patent).

This new policy dovetails with the policy at some universities to retain title to all inventions resulting from industry-sponsored research and then grant either an exclusive or nonexclusive license to the sponsor. The rationale for retaining title is that it ensures that research results will be used for the benefit of the public. *See* N. WADE, THE SCIENCE BUSINESS: REPORT OF THE TWENTIETH CENTURY FUND TASK FORCE ON THE COMMERCIALIZATION OF SCIENTIFIC RESEARCH 57 (1984). In this way, the invention or process will definitely be developed rather than merely patented by a sponsor in an attempt to suppress an area of technology possibly valuable to its competitors.

This new policy has created a wide array of issues. For brevity's sake, only two will be considered here: the use (or non-use) of federal "march-in" rights, and the growing "market" among university research labs for licenses (formal and informal) of intellectual property rights during ongoing research. The larger issues such as the overall success of the new policy must await some historical data and experience to be usefully debated.

Field of Use Restrictions and March-in Rights

University licensing personnel are faced with a difficult problem: how to attract interested licensees for patented technology whose interests coincide with the university's. One example of a divergence between the interests of the university-licensor and the licensee occurs when the university holds a patent that might be useful for a variety of applications. If the applications are different enough, no single licensee may be interested in developing all of them. This is a problem for the university; maximum royalties and — equally important in many cases — maximum social benefits depend on the development of all the applications.

One solution to the potential conflict is the "field of use" restriction in a licensing agreement. This device allows the licensee to practice the licensed invention only in specified fields, i.e., for particular applications. The university-licensor is then free to license the technology to other licensees for other fields of use.

This permits the university to allocate the individual inventions generated by the sponsored research to those companies that can utilize them best, rather than granting all of the rights to a company that may only be able or willing to develop a small portion of the work. Finally, as part of a multiple field of use licensing strategy, the university retains title to the patent which allows it to research related issues in the future without having to risk infringement, or having to purchase licenses to patents developed by its own researchers, in order to perform further research in the field.

Field of use restrictions are generally legal under the Patent Act and U.S. antitrust law. The Patent Act does not expressly authorize field of use limitations in patent licenses. However, the Supreme Court has held such limitations valid and enforceable where they relate to utilization of licensed industrial property and where they are imposed upon a manufacturing licensee. *See General Talking Pictures v. Western Elec.*, 305 U.S. 124 (1938). Likewise, different end uses by different licensees may make the licensed technology of greater value to one licensee than it is to another; this will in general justify any differential in royalties among licensees, *Carter-Wallace, Inc. v. United States*, 449 F.2d 1374 (Ct. Cl. 1971), a situation that has in some cases given rise to antitrust-related objections. *See LaPeyre v. FTC*, 366 F.2d 117 (5th Cir. 1966). Note however, that if such licensing practices result from a combination of the licensor and one or more "favored" licensee(s), they may also amount to a conspiracy to monopolize under § 2 of the Sherman Act.

The field of use restriction is understandable in light of the economic forces facing the licensor and licensee. The uncertainty facing the licensee centers on which applications it will find feasible. Because of this, licensees will in general prefer complete exclusivity. This means, of course, that there are likely to be many applications which go undeveloped.

A similar licensee tactic is to include a "march-in" rights provision. March-in rights allow the licensor to monitor the diligence of the licensee and re-take possession of the technology. March-in rights may be retained in private licensing agreements, as between a university and private firm. In contrast, march-in rights are retained *by statute* where a patent is obtained on the results of research funded by the federal government. Since this relatively little known statutory provision applies to many important inventions, and since it is the basis for many private agreements, it is worth setting out:

> (1) With respect to any subject invention in which a small business firm or nonprofit organization has acquired title under this chapter, the Federal agency under whose funding agreement the subject invention was made shall have the right, in accordance with such procedures as are provided in regulations promulgated hereunder to require *the contractor, an assignee or exclusive licensee of a subject invention* to grant a nonexclusive, partially exclusive, or exclusive license in any field of use to a responsible applicant or applicants, upon terms that are reasonable under the circumstances, and if the contractor, assignee, or exclusive licensee refuses such request, to grant such a license itself, if the Federal agency determines that such —

>> (a) action is necessary because the contractor or assignee has not taken, or is not expected to take within a reasonable time, *effective steps to achieve practical application of the subject invention in such field of use;* (b) action is necessary to alleviate health or safety needs which are not reasonably satisfied by the contractor, assignee, or their licensees; (c) action is necessary to meet requirements for public use specified by Federal regulations* and such requirements are not reasonably satisfied by the contractor, assignee, or licensees; ...

> (2) ... [A]ny contractor, inventor, assignee, or exclusive licensee adversely affected by a determination under this section may, at any time within sixty days after the determination is issued, file a petition in the United States Claims Court, which shall have jurisdiction to determine the appeal on the record and to affirm, reverse, remand or modify, as appropriate, the determination of the Federal agency.

35 U.S.C. § 203 (1989) (emphasis added). *See also* 37 C.F.R. § 4016 (1989) regulations detailing how march-in rights must be exercised).

There are a number of unanswered questions raised by this provision. First, may a federal agency "march-in" and begin making a patented product, or using a patented process, or must it license a third-party to do so (i.e., can the government be an "applicant" under this provision)? The march-in right would become a very potent tool indeed if the government — which is not constrained by market forces — were to interpret this right as allowing it to seize control of a technology and begin production on its own. Obviously, the availability of such a potent "self help" remedy might affect the willingness of a government licensee, or of a licensee who takes a license from an institution holding patent rights subject to this section (e.g., a university), to take out a license in the first place.

Another issue centers on the second highlighted passage in the excerpt from the statute reproduced above, concerning the conditions under which the march-in right may be exercised: where action is required because the licensee has not taken "effective steps to achieve practical application of the subject invention in such field of use," or where "action is necessary to alleviate health or safety needs which are not reasonably satisfied by the contractor, assignee, or their licensees," or where "action is necessary to meet requirements for public use specified by Federal regulations ...." These are vague and potentially troublesome standards; it is more than interesting to contemplate how they might be used by an activist government unit in a perceived crisis. As one example, consider a scenario where the manufacturer of a pharmaceutical used in AIDS therapy comes under public fire for its pricing of the drug. And consider further what effect the exercise of march-in rights in such a situation might have on future licensing transactions.

A third issue concerns compensation, if any, which must be paid to a licensee for its expenses incurred prior to exercise of the march-in right.

Restrictions Accompanying the Transfer of Biological Materials

Although a novel strategy when first proposed, it has now become commonplace for scientists to send requested biological materials to another lab under a cover letter setting forth conditions on the use of the materials. Typical conditions include: (1) that the sender will have a royalty-free license to practice the results of the receiver's research; (2) that the receiver must acknowledge the sender's contribution, and pay the sender royalties for the share of any inventions the receiver may make that incorporates the sent materials; and (3) that the receiver may not publish any information regarding the sent material without the prior consent of the sender.

In a situation where the lab requesting the material does use it in its research, there is no doubt that any resulting invention "depends" in some sense on the contribution of those materials. The problem is in agreeing on a valuation of that contribution.

This is of course a problem in any licensing negotiation. But it is exacerbated in the case of transfer restrictions because these must be agreed upon *before* any invention is made. If it is difficult to value an *existing* technology, it seems also quite difficult to value a technology *that does not yet exist. See* E. MANSFIELD, A. ROMEO, D. TEECE, S. WAGNER & P. BRACH, TECHNOLOGY TRANSFER, PRODUCTIVITY, AND ECONOMIC POLICY (1982).

A related problem is that where the restrictions provide that the parties must agree on some compensation the sender of the materials — the self-styled "licensor" — is in the driver's seat. *After* the invention is made, there may be at least some rough idea of its value. Where this is true, the sender of the material knows approximately the dimensions of the profit likely to be made by the "licensee" (i.e., receiving lab). The sender thus knows roughly how much he or she can ask for. If the agreement on compensation had been made before the materials were sent, both parties would have been ignorant of the prospects for the as-yet nonexistent technology. This would undoubtedly affect how much the sender could ask for. *See* F. BIDAULT, TECHNOLOGY PRICING: FROM PRINCIPLES TO STRATEGY (B. Page & P. Sherwood trans., 1989) (a very useful book in general as a source for technology pricing strategies).

This is one example of how the unsettled state of the law makes bargaining more difficult regarding biotechnology products developed by university research scientists. Until courts announce — or parties agree to — some rules for valuing the components in a biotechnology invention, there will be room for a great deal of one-sided bargaining in situations like this.

It is interesting to note, however, that the economic literature on transaction costs makes predictions about the eventual structure of an industry where such costs are a factor. In particular, if it turns out that the opportunities for "strategic bargaining" (i.e., bargaining solely for as much as one can get) are many, firms will evolve so as to make such transactions unnecessary, primarily by acquiring a firm or hiring people who perform the function that was formerly contracted for. *See* R. Coase, *The Nature of the Firm*, 4 ECONOMICA 386 (1937). In the case of universities, this would simply mean bringing the basic research function in-house. Of course, this entails many costs itself; after all, the university environment offers many attractions for the best researchers. As a result, "internalizing" the basic research function will likely become common only if contracting becomes extremely costly.

B. ASSIGNMENT AND OWNERSHIP

WATERMAN v. MACKENZIE

138 U.S. 252 (1891)

[Plaintiff Lewis Waterman sued defendant for infringing his patent on a fountain pen. Defendant asserted that plaintiff was not the owner of the patent at issue, since he had assigned it to his wife who had then assigned it to the firm of Asa Shipman. Mrs. Waterman later granted her husband a license under the patent, and before the suit she also attempted to assign it back to him. Defendant sought to have the infringement suit dismissed on the grounds that Shipman, the assignee of the patent, was the only person who could file the infringement suit.]

Every patent issued under the laws of the United States for an invention or discovery contains "a grant to the patentee, his heirs and assigns, for the term of seventeen years, of the exclusive right to make, use, and vend the invention or discovery throughout the United States and the territories thereof." The monopoly thus granted is one entire thing, and cannot be divided into parts, except as authorized by those laws. The patentee or his assigns may, by instrument in writing, assign, grant, and convey, either (1) the whole patent, comprising the exclusive right to make, use, and vend the invention throughout the United States; or (2) an undivided part or share of that exclusive right; or (3) the exclusive right under the patent within and throughout a specified part of the United States. A transfer of either of these three [sic] kinds of interests is an assignment, properly speaking, and vests in the assignee a title in so much of the patent itself, with a right to sue infringers. In the second case, jointly with the assignor. In the first and third cases, in the name of the assignee alone. Any assignment or transfer, short of one of these, is a mere license, giving the licensee no title in the patent, and no right to sue at law in his own name for an infringement. In equity, as at law, when the transfer amounts to a license only, the title remains in the owner of the patent; and suit must be brought in his name, and never in the name of the licensee alone unless that is necessary to prevent an absolute failure of justice, as where the patentee is the infringer, and cannot sue himself. Any rights of the licensee must be enforced through or in the name of the owner of the patent, and perhaps, if necessary to protect the rights of all parties, joining the licensee with him as a plaintiff.

Whether a transfer of a particular right or interest under a patent is an assignment or a license does not depend upon the name by which it calls itself, but upon the legal effect of its provisions. For instance, a grant of an exclusive right to make, use, and vend two patented machines within a certain district is an assignment, and gives the grantee the right to sue in his own name for an infringement within the district, because the right, although limited to making, using, and vending two machines, excludes all other persons, even the patentee, from making, using, or vending like machines within the district. On the other hand, the grant of an exclusive right under the patent within a certain district, which does not include the right to make, and the right to use, and the right to sell, is not a grant of a title in the whole patent-right within the district, and is therefore only a license. Such, for instance, is a grant of "the full and exclusive right to make and vend" within a certain district, reserving to the grantor the right to make within the district, to be sold outside of it. So is a grant of "the exclusive right to make and use," but not to sell, patented machines within a certain district. So is an instrument granting "the sole right and privilege of manufacturing and selling" patented articles, and not expressly authorizing their use, because, though this might carry by implication the right to use articles made under the patent by the licensee, it certainly would not authorize him to use such articles made by others. An assignment of the entire patent, or of an undivided part thereof, or of the exclusive right under the patent for a limited territory, may be either absolute or by way of mortgage, and liable to be defeated by non-performance of a condition subsequent, as clearly appears in the provision of the statute, that "an assignment, grant, or conveyance shall be void as against any subsequent purchaser or mortgagee for a valuable consideration without notice, unless it is recorded in the patent-office within three months from the date thereof." Rev. St. § 4898.

Before proceeding to consider the nature and effect of the various instruments given in evidence at the hearing in the circuit court, it is fit to observe that, (as was assumed in the argument for the plaintiff,) by the law of the state of New York, where all the instruments were made and all the parties to them resided, husband and wife are authorized to make conveyances and contracts of and concerning personal property to and with each other, in the same manner and to the same effect as if they were strangers.

By the deed of assignment of February 13, 1884, the plaintiff assigned to Mrs. Waterman the entire patent-right. That assignment vested in her the whole title in the patent, and the exclusive right to sue, either at law or in equity, for its subsequent infringement.

The next instrument in order of date is the "license agreement" between them of November 20, 1884, by which she granted to him "the sole and exclusive right and license to manufacture and sell fountain pen-holders containing the said patented improvement throughout the United States." This did not include the right to use such pen-holders, at least if manufactured by third persons, and was therefore a mere license, and not an assignment of any title, and did not give the licensee the right to sue alone, at law or in equity, for an infringement of the patent. The plaintiff not having amended his bill, pursuant to the leave granted by the circuit court, by joining the licensor as a plaintiff, this point requires no further notice.

The remaining question in the case, distinctly presented by the plea, and adjudged by the circuit court, is of the effect of the deed of November 25, 1884, by which Mrs. Waterman assigned to the firm of Asa L. Shipman's Sons all her right, title and interest in the invention and the patent, with an express provision that the assignment should be null and void if she and her husband, or either of them, should pay at maturity a certain promissory note of the same date made by them, and payable to the grantees. This instrument, being a conveyance made to secure the payment of a debt, upon condition that it should be avoided by the subsequent payment of that debt at a time fixed, was a mortgage, in apt terms, and in legal effect. On the same day, the mortgagees assigned by deed to Asa L. Shipman all their title under the mortgage, and the promissory note thereby secured. Both assignments were recorded in the patent office within three months after their date, and the title thereby acquired by Shipman was outstanding in him at the times of the subsequent assignment of the patent-right by Mrs. Waterman to the plaintiff, and of the filing of this bill. This last assignment was therefore subject to the mortgage, though not in terms so expressed. By a mortgage of personal property, differing in this respect from a pledge, it is not merely the possession or a special property that passes; but, both at law and in equity, the whole title is transferred to the mortgagee, as security for the debt, subject only to be defeated by performance of the condition, or by redemption on bill in equity within a reasonable time, and the right of possession, when there is no express stipulation to the contrary, goes with the right of property.

[After contrasting the cases on mortgages of real and personal property, the Court concludes that the right of a personal property mortgagee to obtain an injunction and otherwise exercise ownership depends on whether a right of possession passed with the mortgage.] When it is provided by statute that a mortgage of personal property shall not be valid against third persons, unless the mortgage is recorded, a recording of the mortgage is a substitute for, and (unless in case of actual fraud) equivalent to, a delivery of possession, and makes the title and the possession of the mortgagee good against all the world. A patent-right is incorporeal property, not susceptible of actual delivery or possession; and the recording of a mortgage thereof in the patent-office, in accordance with the act of congress, is equivalent to a delivery of possession, and makes the title of the mortgagee complete towards all other persons, as well as against the mortgagor. The right conferred by letters patent for an invention is limited to a term of years, and a large part of its value consists in the profits derived from royalties and license fees. In analogy to the rules governing mortgages of lands and of chattels, and with even stronger reason, the assignee of a patent by a mortgage duly recorded, whose security is constantly wasting by the lapse of time, must be held (unless otherwise provided in the mortgage) entitled to grant licenses, to receive license fees and royalties, and to have an account of profits or an award of damages against infringers. There can be no doubt that he is "the party interested, either as patentee, assignee, or grantee," and as such entitled to maintain an action at law to recover damages for an infringement; and it cannot have been the intention of congress that a suit in equity against an infringer to obtain an injunction and an account of profits, in which the court is authorized to award damages, when necessary to fully compensate the plaintiff, and has the same power to treble the damages as in an action at law, should not be brought by the same person. The necessary conclusion appears to us to be that Shipman, being the present owner of the whole title in the patent under a mortgage duly executed and recorded, was the person, and the only person, entitled to maintain such a bill as this; and that the [defendant's] plea, therefore, was rightly adjudged good.

Decree affirmed.

NOTES

1. *Exclusive Licensee Standing.* It is a generally accepted principle that an exclusive licensee has the right to bring an action for infringement. *See, e.g., Littlefield v. Perry*, 88 U.S. (21 Wall.) 205, 223 (1875); *Kenyon v. Automatic Instrument Co.*, 160 F.2d 878, 73 U.S.P.Q. (BNA) 21 (6th Cir. 1947); *Black & Decker Inc. v. Hoover Serv. Center, Inc.*, 20 U.S.P.Q.2d 1612 (D. Conn. 1991).

2. *When to Begin Standing.* In *Arachnid, Inc. v. Merit Indus., Inc.*, 19 U.S.P.Q.2d (BNA) 1513 (Fed. Cir. 1991), the court held that the obligee of an agreement to assign cannot sue until assignment takes place.

1. SECTION 261: PATENT RECORDING STATUTE

FILMTEC CORP. v. ALLIED-SIGNAL INC.

939 F.2d 1568, 19 U.S.P.Q.2d (BNA) 1508 (Fed. Cir. 1991)

PLAGER, CIRCUIT JUDGE.

Allied-Signal Inc. and UOP Inc. (Allied), defendants-appellants, appeal from the preliminary injunction issued by the district court. The trial court enjoined Allied from "making, using or selling, and actively inducing others to make use or sell TFCL membrane in the United States, and from otherwise infringing claim 7 of United States Patent No. 4,277,344 ['344]." Because of serious doubts on the record before us as to who has title to the invention and the ensuing patent, we vacate the grant of the injunction and remand for further proceedings.

Background

The application which ultimately issued as the '344 patent was filed by John E. Cadotte on February 22, 1979. The patent claims a reverse osmosis membrane and a method for using the membrane to reduce the concentration of solute molecules and ions in solution. [This may be useful in desalinizing ocean water.] Cadotte assigned his rights in the application and any subsequently issuing patent to plaintiff-appellee FilmTec Corp. (FilmTec). This assignment was duly recorded in the United States Patent and Trademark Office. Defendant-appellant Allied manufactured a reverse osmosis membrane and FilmTec sued Allied for infringing certain claims of the '344 patent.

[From footnote 1:] Prior to founding FilmTec, Cadotte and the other founders were employed in various responsible positions at the North Star Division of Midwest Research Institute (MRI), a not-for-profit research organization. MRI was principally engaged in contract research, much of it for the United States (Government), and much of it involving work in the field of reverse osmosis membranes. The evidence indicates that the work at MRI in which Cadotte and the other founders were engaged was being carried out under contract (the contract) to the Government "to provide research on In Situ-Formed Condensation Polymers for Reverse Osmosis Membranes." The contract provided that "MRI agrees to grant and does hereby grant to the Government the full and entire domestic right, title and interest in [any invention, discovery, improvement or development (whether or not patentable) made in the course of or under this contract or any subcontract (of any tier) thereunder]."

It appears that sometime between the time FilmTec came into being in 1977 (there is evidence that it was organized in the summer of 1977, and incorporated in September of that year) and the time Cadotte submitted his patent application in February of 1979, he made the invention that led to the '344 patent. As we will explain, just when in that period the invention was made is critical.

Cadotte left MRI in January of 1978. Cadotte testified that he conceived his invention the month after he left MRI. Allied disputes this, and alleges that

Cadotte conceived his invention and formed the reverse osmosis membrane of the '344 patent earlier — in July of 1977 or at least by November of 1977 when he allegedly produced an improved membrane. Allied bases this on certain entries in the notebooks which Cadotte kept during this period. The trial judge found that "Cadotte's 1977 North Star notebook entries establish that he did [while still at MRI] combine the two chemicals which are claimed in the '344 patent."

However, because of its view of the issues, the trial court concluded it did not need to decide whether that combination resulted in the claimed invention. This was because in granting the preliminary injunction, the trial court concluded that as a matter of law even if the invention was made while Cadotte was employed at MRI, under the contract the Government could have no more than equitable title to the patent, which title cannot be raised as a defense by Allied. The district court stated that the

> government's rights in an invention discovered by an employee while under contract are equitable, and are not available as a defense by the alleged infringer against the legal titleholder.

Cited for this proposition was *Sigma Eng'g Serv., Inc. v. Halm Instrument Co., Inc.*, 33 F.R.D. 129, 138 U.S.P.Q. 297 (E.D.N.Y. 1963). [The district court then issued an injunction.]

Issues on Appeal

On appeal from the grant of the preliminary injunction, Allied argues that the trial court committed reversible error on each of five substantive issues. In Allied's view, the contract vested legal title to the invention in the Government and, therefore, FilmTec lacks standing to bring suit; Cadotte misled the patent examiner as to the Government's possible rights in the invention and the '344 patent is unenforceable; the '344 patent is invalid because the invention claimed would have been obvious; when the claims are properly read, the Allied membrane does not infringe the '344 patent; and finally, the district court misapplied the test for issuance of a preliminary injunction.

Discussion

We address first the question of title to the '344 patent. It is important to keep in mind that the issue before us is not who should ultimately be held to have title to the patent, but whether, in view of the state of the title, it can be said that FilmTec has a reasonable likelihood of success on the merits of that issue, sufficient to warrant the grant of the preliminary injunction.

Allied alleges that the evidence establishes that the contract between MRI and the Government grants to the Government "all discoveries and inventions made within the scope of their [i.e., MRI's employees] employment," and that the invention claimed in the '344 patent was made by Cadotte while employed by MRI. From this Allied reasons that rights in the invention must be with the

Government and therefore Cadotte had no rights to assign to FilmTec. If FilmTec lacks title to the patent, FilmTec has no standing to bring an infringement action under the '344 patent. FilmTec counters by arguing that the trial court was correct in concluding that the most the Government would have acquired was an equitable title to the '344 patent, which title would have been made void under 35 U.S.C. § 261 (1988) by the subsequent assignment to FilmTec from Cadotte. [The relevant portion of § 261 reads: "An assignment, grant or conveyance shall be void as against any subsequent purchaser or mortgagee for a valuable consideration, without notice, unless it is recorded in the Patent and Trademark Office within three months from its date or prior to the date of such subsequent purchase or mortgage."]

The parties agree that Cadotte was employed by MRI and that the contract between MRI and the Government contains a grant of rights to inventions made pursuant to the contract. However, the record does not reflect whether the employment agreement between Cadotte and MRI either granted or required Cadotte to grant to MRI the rights to inventions made by Cadotte. Allied argues that Cadotte's inventions were assigned nevertheless to MRI. Allied points to the provision in the contract between MRI and the Government in which MRI warrants that it will obligate inventors to assign their rights to MRI.

While this is not conclusive evidence of a grant of or a requirement to grant rights by Cadotte, it raises a serious question about the nature of the title, if any, in FilmTec. FilmTec apparently did not address this issue at the trial, and there is no indication in the opinion of the district court that this gap in the chain of ownership rights was considered by the court.

Since property rights in an invention itself could not, under any conventional meaning of the term, be considered real property, they are by definition personal property. While early cases have pointed to the myriad ways in which patent rights — that is, property in patents — are closer in analogy to real than to personal property, the statutes establish as a matter of law that patents today have the attributes of personal property. And 35 U.S.C. § 261 makes clear that an application for patent as well as the patent itself may be assigned. Further, it is settled law that between the time of an invention and the issuance of a patent, rights in an invention may be assigned and legal title to the ensuing patent will pass to the assignee upon grant of the patent. *Gayler v. Wilder*, 51 U.S. (10 How.) 477, 493, 13 L. Ed. 504 (1850).

If an assignment of rights in an invention is made prior to the existence of the invention, this may be viewed as an assignment of an expectant interest. An assignment of an expectant interest can be a valid assignment. *[S]ee generally Contract Rights as Commercial Security: Present and Future Intangibles*, 67 Yale L.J. 847, 854 n.27 (1958). In such a situation, the assignee holds at most an equitable title.

Once the invention is made and an application for patent is filed, however, legal title to the rights accruing thereunder would be in the assignee (subject to the rights of a subsequent purchaser under § 261), and the assignor-inventor would have nothing remaining to assign. In this case, if Cadotte granted MRI rights in inventions made during his employ, and if the subject matter of the '344 patent was invented by Cadotte during his employ with MRI, then Cadotte had nothing to give to FilmTec and his purported assignment to FilmTec is a nullity. Thus, FilmTec would lack both title to the '344 patent and standing to bring the present action. See 28 U.S.C. § 1498 (1988).

The question of FilmTec's right to maintain the action against Allied should not be confused with the question of whether Allied could defend by arguing that title to the patent was in a third party — the Government — and therefore Allied has a good defense against any infringement suit. [T]he issue here is not whether title lies in the Government or some other third party; it is rather whether FilmTec has made a sufficient showing to establish reasonable likelihood of success on the merits, which includes a showing that title to the patent and the rights thereunder are in FilmTec.

As noted, the district court was of the view that if the Government was the assignee from Cadotte through MRI, the Government would have acquired at most an equitable title, and that legal title would remain in Cadotte. (The legal title would then have passed to FilmTec by virtue of the later assignment, pursuant to § 261 of the statutes.) [Its authority was the *Sigma Engineering* case, *supra*; Judge Plager recounts the facts as follows: the defendant there sought to dismiss the complaint as not brought by the real party in interest, since plaintiff took its rights from an ex-employee who had a duty to assign inventions to the ex-employer; but the employee never transferred any rights to the ex-employer, so the ex-employer had at most an equitable claim and was not an indispensable party to the suit.]

In our case, the contract between MRI and the Government did not merely obligate MRI to grant future rights, but expressly granted to the Government MRI's rights in any future invention. Ordinarily, no further act would be required once an invention came into being; the transfer of title would occur by operation of law. If a similar contract provision existed between Cadotte and MRI, as MRI's contract with the Government required, and if the invention was made before Cadotte left MRI's employ, as the trial judge seems to suggest, Cadotte would have no rights in the invention or any ensuing patent to assign to FilmTec.

It is well established that when a legal title holder of a patent transfers his or her title to a third party purchaser for value without notice of an outstanding equitable claim or title, the purchaser takes the entire ownership of the patent, free of any prior equitable encumbrance. *Hendrie v. Sayles*, 98 U.S. 546, 549 (1879). This is an application of the common law bona fide purchaser for value rule.

Section 261 of Title 35 goes a step further. It adopts the principle of the real property recording acts, and provides that the bona fide purchaser for value cuts off the rights of a prior assignee who has failed to record the prior assignment in the Patent and Trademark Office by the dates specified in the statute. Although the statute does not expressly so say, it is clear that the statute is intended to cut off prior legal interests, which the common law rule did not.

Both the common law rule and the statute contemplate that the subsequent purchaser be exactly that — a transferee who pays valuable consideration, and is without notice of the prior transfer. The trial judge, with reference to FilmTec's rights as a subsequent purchaser, stated simply that "FilmTec is a subsequent purchaser from Cadotte for independent consideration. There is no evidence presented to imply that FilmTec was on notice of any previous assignment." The court concluded that, even if the MRI contract automatically transferred title to the government, such assignment is not enforceable at law as it was never recorded.

Since this matter will be before the trial court on remand, it may be useful for us to clarify what is required before FilmTec can properly be considered a subsequent purchaser entitled to the protections of § 261. In the first place, FilmTec must be in fact a purchaser for a valuable consideration. This requirement is different from the classic notion of a purchaser under a deed of grant, where the requirement of consideration was a formality, and the proverbial peppercorn would suffice to have the deed operate under the statute of uses. Here the requirement is that the subsequent purchaser, in order to cut off the rights of the prior purchaser, must be more than a donee or other gratuitous transferee. There must be in fact valuable consideration paid so that the subsequent purchaser can, as a matter of law, claim record reliance as a premise upon which the purchase was made. That, of course, is a matter of proof.

In addition, the subsequent transferee/assignee — FilmTec in our case — must be without notice of any such prior assignment. If Cadotte's contract with MRI contained a provision assigning any inventions made during the course of employment either to MRI or directly to the Government, Cadotte would clearly be on notice of the provisions of his own contract. Since Cadotte was one of the four founders of FilmTec, and the other founders and officers were also involved at MRI, FilmTec may well be deemed to have had actual notice of an assignment. Given the key roles that Cadotte and the others played both at MRI and later at FilmTec, at a minimum FilmTec might be said to be on inquiry notice of any possible rights in MRI or the Government as a result of Cadotte's work at MRI. Thus once again, the key to FilmTec's ability to show a likelihood of success on the merits lies in the relationship between Cadotte and MRI.

In our view of the title issue, it cannot be said on this record that FilmTec has established a reasonable likelihood of success on the merits. It is thus unnecessary for us to consider the other issues raised on appeal concerning the propriety of the injunction. The grant of the preliminary injunction is vacated and the case remanded to the district court.

NOTES

1. *Fine Distinctions.* The preceding case turns on a fine distinction: the difference between an obligation to assign in the future, as in *Sigma Engineering* (cited in the case), and the current assignment of an expectancy. The latter, as Judge Plager explains it, is a *complete* assignment of inchoate rights. The former, on the other hand, is an *inchoate* assignment of inchoate rights. To relieve an inventor of title to an invention, according to the case, the assignment must be complete even if the invention assigned is not yet realized. Thus the crucial questions for the district court to reconsider are whether the inventor, Cadotte, had "pre-assigned" his rights in any MRI-related inventions to MRI, and of course whether the disputed invention was made during his employment at MRI. Lastly, the question of FilmTec's actual notice of Cadotte's prior assignment must be addressed. On the importance of prospective versus retrospective applicability of an agreement to assign, see *Georgia-Pacific Corp. v. Lieberam*, 22 U.S.P.Q.2d (BNA) 1383 (11th Cir. 1992).

2. *Applying the Statute.* The court states: "In this case, if Cadotte granted MRI rights in inventions made during his employ, and if the subject matter of the '344 patent was invented by Cadotte during his employ with MRI, then Cadotte had nothing to give to FilmTec and his purported assignment to FilmTec is a nullity." But § 261 is more complex than this implies, as the court makes clear later in the opinion. Specifically, if MRI never recorded its assignment from Cadotte, or if the government never recorded its assignments from MRI, § 261 might come into play. Under its terms, a subsequent bona fide purchaser for value takes title free of any prior assignments *if* any of those assignments are not recorded within three months of their execution. In other words, such an assignment is not "a nullity" unless the prior assignment was recorded. It is generally agreed that in such a case, the employer, can specifically enforce the agreement to assign; but it is likewise true that the assignment may not be reworded until a patent application is filed, at the earliest. See R. ELLIS, PATENT ASSIGNMENTS AND LICENSES § 39 (1936); *In re Chillingsworth*, 1897 Comm'rs Dec. 72; 80 OFFIC. GAZ. PAT. OFF. 1892 (1897). Note that in the preceding case the court states that Film-Tec, Cadotte's subsequent assignee, is probably not a bona fide purchaser, since it has notice (via Cadotte) of the prior assignment.

Kahn v. General Motors Corp., 33 U.S.P.Q.2d 2011 (S.D.N.Y. 1995), showcases an interesting assignment issue. Leonard Kahn had assigned rights to a certain patent application during the course of employment at a research lab. The written assignment, to Kahn Research Laboratories, Inc. ("KRLI"), of Serial No. 251,947 ("Grandparent Application"), included rights to all patents issuing "by continuation or continuation-in-part" ("CIP") from the assigned application. The lab later went bankrupt, and Kahn re-acquired his invention rights at auction. On April 19, 1977, U.S. Patent 4,018,994 was issued to Kahn on a CIP application from two parent applications which were, in turn, CIPs of the Grandparent Application (251,947) Kahn had originally assigned. The court stated:

GM argues that Kahn's failure to produce a written instrument assigning KRLI's patent rights to him at auction per se defeats the assignment. I disagree. [S]ection [261] does not preclude the acquisition of equitable interests under oral contracts. *Westinghouse Elec. & Mfg. Co. v. Formica Insulation Co.*, 288 F. 330 (6th Cir. 1923). At the 1974 auction, Kahn could not have acquired legal title to the '994 Patent, in any case, since neither the patent nor its application existed. An oral agreement at Kahn's auction could, in theory, have transferred equitable title to a future patent.

Kahn's acquisition of KRLI's future equitable rights at the auction presents a question of fact. Did he prove an assignment from KRLI at the auction? GM argues that in the back and forth between Kahn and KRLI the rights to a future CIP application for the '994 Patent were left in limbo without an owner after KRLI dissolved. This position conforms with the law and the facts of this case. Kahn did not adduce sufficient evidence that he reacquired KRLI's equitable rights in the future '994 patent. Kahn has no personal knowledge of what transpired at the auction. He made no showing of what he purchased through his lawyer at the auction other than claiming that he bought whatever assets KRLI had. The documents Kahn introduced to support his claim about the auction are far from conclusive. Kahn did not explain on what authority he arranged for the auction. Kahn claimed that he paid $14,901 for KRLI's patent rights. Subsequently, he contradicted himself by testifying that he had never paid anything at any auction for the '994 patent rights. (Tr. 34). Kahn has simply failed to prove by a preponderance of the credible evidence that he reacquired the rights to the '994 patent. However, this conclusion does not settle the matter.

Kahn finally argues that as an alleged infringer, GM may not defend on the ground that a third party has equitable title. Kahn relies on *Mercantile Bank v. Howmet Corp.*, 524 F.2d 1031, 1034 [188 U.S.P.Q. 353] (7th Cir. 1975), and on *VDI Tech. v. Price*, 90 Civ. 341-M, 1994 WL 485778, at *5 n.9 (D.N.H. Aug. 31, 1994) ("in 'patent litigation between private parties the equitable rights of ownership of strangers to the suit cannot be raised as defenses against the legal titleholder of a patent'"). This principle makes a lot of sense. Kahn proved prima facie his legal title to the patent. GM's only defense states that before the '994 patent issued, Kahn assigned equitable future rights in his invention to his research laboratory, and that those equitable rights got lost when KRLI dissolved. It would be unfair to allow GM to hide behind the putative rights of a nonparty, especially where, as here, neither side contends that such a party exists.

The law favors ownership of patents, and while that ownership may be gossamer as in the case at bar, it has not devolved, as GM says, on an unidentified third party.

33 U.S.P.Q.2d 2011, at 2013-14.

3. *Some Quirks*. If *A* assigns to *B* on January 1, and then to *C* on January 2, *C* will not know definitively whether it has taken good title until it checks the Patent Office recordation files on March 2. Note also that only *B*'s assignment matters as between *B* and *C*; *C* need never record to obtain good title against *B*. *See* Patent Act § 261. (But if *A* conveys a third time, to *D*, *C* had better record within three months!).

4. *Instruments to Record*. Patent Act § 261 says "[a]n assignment, grant or conveyance" must be recorded to defeat the claims of a subsequent bona fide purchaser. Can an exclusive license be a grant or conveyance? It might seem as though it can, if it amounts to a conveyance, i.e., excludes the patentee herself from practicing the invention, lasts for the duration of the patent term, etc. But in general, an exclusive license does not operate as a grant or conveyance under § 261. A non-exclusive license is definitely not a grant or conveyance, however, which makes sense since by the nature of the license a nonexclusive licensee should expect that the licensor will make (or already has made) other licenses. Because title never changes hands under a nonexclusive license, the patentee, and not the nonexclusive licensee, must bring any infringement suits to enforce the patent. *See Blair v. Lippincott Glass Co.*, 52 F. 226 (D. Ind. 1892) (going further, holding that nonexclusive licensee may not be a party to an infringement suit). *Cf. Independent Wireless Tel. Co. v. Radio Corp. of Am.*, 269 U.S. 459, 468 (1926) (nonexclusive licensee can join patentee/titleholder as defendant, and court will re-assign him or her to plaintiff's side).

The fact that the Patent Office records need only show prior assignments to protect the rights of prior assignees opens the door to a significant opportunity for malfeasance by a patentee. She could grant a license, or a series of licenses, and then assign her patent — and the assignee would take title *subject to* the licenses she had granted. (The "constructive notice" of § 261 does not apply to prior licenses, in other words.) *See, e.g., Keystone Type Foundry v. Fastpress Co.*, 272 F. 242 (2d Cir. 1921) ("when defendant took its assignment, it had long passed into the text-books that such assignee acquired title subject to prior licenses of which the assignee must inform himself as best he can, and at his own risk."); *Sanofi, S.A. v. Med-Tech Veterinarian Prods., Inc.*, 565 F. Supp. 931, 939, 220 U.S.P.Q. (BNA) 416 (D.N.J. 1983). This is mitigated to some extent, however, by two factors: (1) the assignee takes subject to the license, but also takes the right to receive royalties flowing from the pre-assignment licenses, unless the assignor explicitly reserves the right to such royalties (in which case the assignee will know about the prior licenses), see R. ELLIS, PATENT ASSIGNMENTS AND LICENSES § 83, at 95 (1936); and (2) as a practical matter, most licenses are recorded despite the fact that recording them within three months does not automatically cut off the rights of subsequent assignees. The recording of documents other than assignments is expressly approved of in the Patent Office Rules of Practice. *See* 37 C.F.R. § 1.331(a) (1991) ("other documents affecting title" and "licenses" may be recorded). According to one commentator, because of this, and "[i]n view of the almost universal habit of attorneys to search the title of patents which their clients are considering purchasing, there is in almost all cases actual notice of everything on record prior to the time the assignment is made." R. ELLIS, PATENT ASSIGNMENTS AND LICENSES § 166, at 180 (1936).

5. *Remedies of a Defrauded Assignee/Licensor.* In our unhappy scenarios, *C*, the (unwitting) second assignee, often loses title to the patent. But of course, *C* has other remedies for *A*'s dishonest conduct. Where *C* owes money to *A* under the contract embodying *A*'s second assignment, *C* can rescind for misrepresentation. (This is true even where *A* does not intentionally misrepresent her ownership of the patent, e.g., where, unbeknownst to her, a prior employment relationship vests title to an invention in a third party such as the former employer; see A. FARNSWORTH, CONTRACTS § 4-12, at 243 (1982).) A purchaser has a right to rely on the record title, in other words, for purposes of contract law. *Heywood-Wakefield Co. v. Small*, 96 F.2d 496, 37 U.S.P.Q. (BNA) 363 (1st Cir. 1938). Moreover, a warranty of good title (but *not* a warranty of validity or an indemnification for costs of infringement suits) is implied in an assignment (or a license, or any contract covered by the Uniform Commercial Code, for that matter). *See* U.C.C. § 2-312(a) (implied warranty that "the title conveyed shall be good").

6. *Challenging Federal and University Licenses.* An important, if obscure, case holds that aggrieved third parties have no standing to challenge a patent license growing out of federally funded research. *See Southern Research Inst. v. Griffin Corp.*, 938 F.2d 1249, 19 U.S.P.Q.2d 1761 (11th Cir. 1991) (construing 35 U.S.C. § 202 et seq., in light of Administrative Procedures Act (APA)). Note that in this case, however, the allegedly aggrieved third party, who had lost out on the license to another firm, did have actual notice of the government's intent to grant the license, which vitiated (the court held) the defendants' duty to publicize the proposed license. *See also University Patents, Inc. v. Kligman*, 762 F. Supp. 1212, 20 U.S.P.Q.2d 1401 (E.D. Pa. 1991) (refusing to dismiss university's action against tenured professor for alleged breach of employment contract in failing to assign to university patent rights in preparation for invention relating to photoaged skin, even though university's standard "patent agreement," contained in its research investigators' handbook, was never executed by professor, since reasonable jury could find that implied contract to assign patent was formed between professor and university, in view of evidence, although scant, showing that professor was aware of patent policy and manifested intent to be bound by it, showing that university resources were used to invent photoaging process, and showing that placement of these resources at professor's disposal constituted consideration).

2. RIGHTS OF THE EMPLOYED INVENTOR

UNITED STATES v. DUBILIER CONDENSER CORP.

289 U.S. 178 (1933)

Three suits were brought in the District Court for Delaware against the respondent as exclusive licensee under three separate patents issued to Francis W. Dunmore and Percival D. Lowell. The bills recite that the inventions were made while the patentees were employed in the radio laboratories of the Bureau of Standards, and are therefore, in equity, the property of the United States. The prayers are for a declaration that the respondent is a trustee for the government, and, as such, required to assign to the United States all its right, title, and interest in the patents, for an accounting of all moneys received as licensee, and for general relief. The District Court consolidated the cases for trial, and after a hearing dismissed the bills. The Court of Appeals for the Third Circuit affirmed the decree.

The courts below concurred in findings which are not challenged and, in summary, are:

The Bureau of Standards is a subdivision of the Department of Commerce. Its functions consist in the custody of standards. In 1915 the Bureau was charged by Congress with the duty of investigation and standardization of methods and instruments employed in radio communication, for which special appropriations were made. In recent years it has been engaged in research and testing work of various kinds for the benefit of private industries, other departments of the government, and the general public. One section of the electrical division [of the Bureau] is the radio section. Dunmore and Lowell were employed in the radio section and engaged in research and testing in the laboratory. In the outlines of laboratory work the subject of "airplane radio" was assigned to the group of which Dunmore was chief and Lowell a member. The subject of "radio receiving sets" was assigned to a group of which J. L. Preston was chief, but to which neither Lowell nor Dunmore belonged.

In May, 1921, the Air Corps of the Army and the Bureau of Standards entered into an arrangement whereby the latter undertook the prosecution of forty-four research projects for the benefit of the Air Corps. Project No. 38 was styled "visual indicator for radio signals," and suggested the construction of a modification of what was known as an "Eckhart recorder." Project No. 42 was styled "airship bomb control and marine torpedo control." Both were problems of design merely.

In the summer of 1921 Dunmore, as chief of the group to which "airplane radio" problems had been assigned, without further instructions from his superiors, picked out for himself one of these navy problems, that of operating a relay for remote control of bombs on airships and torpedoes in the sea, "as one of particular interest and having perhaps a rather easy solution, and worked on it." In September he solved it.

In the midst of aircraft investigations and numerous routine problems of the section, Dunmore was wrestling in his own mind, impelled thereto solely by his own scientific curiosity, with the subject of substituting house-lighting alternating current for direct battery current in radio apparatus. He obtained a relay for operating a telegraph instrument which was in no way related to the remote control relay devised for aircraft use. The conception of the application of alternating current concerned particularly broadcast reception. This idea was conceived by Dunmore August 3, 1921, and he reduced the invention to practice December 16, 1921. Early in 1922 he advise his superior of his invention and spent additional time in perfecting the details. February 27, 1922, he filed an application for a patent.

In the fall of 1921 both Dunmore and Lowell were considering the problem of applying alternating current to broadcast receiving sets. This project was not involved in or suggested by the problems with which the radio section was then dealing and was not assigned by any superior as a task to be solved by either of these employees. It was independent of their work and voluntarily assumed.

While performing their regular tasks they experimented at the laboratory in devising apparatus for operating a radio receiving set by alternating current with the hum incident thereto eliminated. The invention was completed on December 10, 1921. Before its completion no instructions were received from and no conversations relative to the invention were held by these employees with the head of the radio section, or with any superior.

They also conceived the idea of energizing a dynamic type of loud speaker from an alternating current house-lighting circuit and reduced the invention to practice on January 25, 1922. March 21, 1922, they filed an application for a "power amplifier." The conception embodied in this patent was devised by the patentees without suggestion, instruction, or assignment from any superior. Dunmore and Lowell were permitted by their chief, after the discoveries had been brought to his attention, to pursue their work in the laboratory and to perfect the devices embodying their inventions. No one advised them prior to the filing of applications for patents that they would be expected to assign the patents to the United States or to grant the government exclusive rights thereunder.

The respondent concedes that the United States may practice the inventions without payment of royalty, but asserts that all others are excluded, during the life of the patents, from using them without the respondent's consent. The petitioner insists that the circumstances require a declaration either that the government has sole and exclusive property in the inventions or that they have been dedicated to the public so that anyone may use them.

A patent is property, and title to it can pass only by assignment. If not yet issued, an agreement to assign when issued, if valid as a contract, will be specifically enforced. The respective rights and obligations of employer and employee, touching an invention conceived by the latter, spring from the contract of employment.

One employed to make an invention, who succeeds, during his term of service, in accomplishing that task, is bound to assign to his employer any patent obtained. The reason is that he has only produced that which he was employed to invent. His invention is the precise subject of the contract of employment. A term of the agreement necessarily is that what he is paid to produce belongs to his paymaster. On the other hand, if the employment be general, albeit it covers a field of labor and effort in the performance of which the employee conceived the invention for which he obtained a patent, the contract is not so broadly construed as to require an assignment of the patent.

The reluctance of courts to imply or infer an agreement by the employee to assign his patent is due to a recognition of the peculiar nature of the act of invention, which consists neither in finding out the laws of nature, nor in fruitful research as to the operation of natural laws, but in discovering how those laws may be utilized or applied for some beneficial purpose, by a process, a device, or a machine. It is the result of an inventive act.

Though the mental concept is embodied or realized in a mechanism or a physical or chemical aggregate, the embodiment is not the invention and is not the subject of a patent. This distinction between the idea and its application in practice is the basis of the rule that employment merely to design or to construct or to devise methods of manufacture is not the same as employment to invent. Recognition of the nature of the act of invention also defines the limits of the so-called shop right, which, shortly stated, is that, where a servant, during his hours of employment, working with his master's materials and appliances, conceives and perfects an invention for which he obtains a patent, he must accord his master a nonexclusive right to practice the invention. *McClurg v. Kingsland*, [42 U.S.] 1 How. 202 [1843], *Solomons v. United States*, 137 U.S. 342 [1890]. This is an application of equitable principles. Since the servant uses his master's time, facilities, and materials to attain a concrete result, the latter is in equity entitled to use that which embodies his own property and to duplicate it as often as he may find occasion to employ similar appliances in his business. But the employer in such a case has no equity to demand a conveyance of the invention, which is the original conception of the employee alone, in which the employer had no part. This remains the property of him who conceived it, together with the right conferred by the patent, to exclude all others than the employer from the accruing benefits. These principles are settled as respects private employment.

Does the character of the service call for different rules as to the relative rights of the United States and its employees? The title of a patentee is subject to no superior right of the government. The grant of letters patent is not, as in England, a matter of grace or favor, so that conditions may be annexed at the pleasure of the executive.

No servant of the United States has by statute been disqualified from applying for and receiving a patent for his invention, save officers and employees of the Patent Office during the period for which they hold their appointments. This being so, this court has applied the rules enforced as between private employers and their servants to the relation between the government and its officers and employees.

In *Solomons v. United States*, [*supra*, 137 U.S. at 346] it was said:

> The government has no more power to appropriate a man's property invested in a patent than it has to take his property invested in real estate; nor does the mere fact that an inventor is, at the time of his invention, in the employ of the government transfer to it any title to or interest therein. An employee, performing all the duties assigned to him in his department of service, may exercise his inventive faculties in any direction he chooses, with the assurance that whatever invention he may thus conceive, and perfect is his individual property. There is no difference between the government and any other employer in this respect.

The distinction between an employment to make an invention and a general employment in the course of which the servant conceives an invention has been recognized by the executive department of the government. A lieutenant in the Navy patented an anchor while he was on duty in the Bureau of Equipment and Recruiting, which was charged with the duty of furnishing anchors for the Navy; he was not while attached to the Bureau specially employed to make experiments with a view to suggesting improvements to anchors or assigned the duty of making or improving. The Attorney General advised that, as the invention did not relate to a matter as to which the lieutenant was specially directed to experiment with a view to suggesting improvements, he was entitled to compensation from the government for the use of his invention in addition to his salary or pay as a navy officer. [Citing 19 Op. Attys. Gen. 407.]

The United States is entitled, in the same way and to the same extent as a private employer, to shop rights, that is, the free and nonexclusive use of a patent which results from efforts of its employee in his working hours and with material belonging to the government. *Solomons*, *supra*, [137 U.S. at] 346, 347.

When the United States filed its bills, it recognized the law as heretofore declared; realized that it must like any other employer, if it desired an assignment of the respondent's rights, prove a contractual obligation on the part of Lowell and Dunmore to assign the patents to the government. The averments clearly disclose this.

Thus the government understood that respondent could be deprived of rights under the patents only by proof that Dunmore and Lowell were employed to devise the inventions. The findings of the courts below show how far the proofs fell short of sustaining these averments.

The government is consequently driven to the contention that, though the employees were not specifically assigned the task of making the inventions still, as the discoveries were "within the general field of their research and inventive work" the United States is entitled to an assignment of the patents. The courts below expressly found that Dunmore and Lowell did not agree to exercise their inventive faculties in their work and that invention was not within its scope. In this connection it is to be remembered that the written evidence of their employment does not mention research, much less invention; that never was there a word said to either of them, prior to their discoveries, concerning invention or patents or their duties or obligations respecting these matters; that, as shown by the records of the Patent Office, employees of the Bureau of Standards and other departments had while so employed received numerous patents and enjoyed the exclusive rights obtained as against all private persons without let or hindrance from the government. In no proper sense may it be said that the contract of employment contemplated invention. The circumstances preclude the implication of any agreement to assign their inventions or patents.

The record affords even less basis for inferring a contract on the part of the inventors to refrain from patenting their discoveries than for finding an agreement to assign them.

The bills aver that the inventions and patents are held in trust for the United States, and that the court should so declare. It is claimed that, as the work of the Bureau, including all that Dunmore and Lowell did, was in the public interest, these public servants had dedicated the offspring of their brains to the public, and so held their patents in trust for the common weal, represented here in a corporate capacity by the United States. The patentees, we are told, should surrender the patents for cancellation, and the respondent must also give up its rights under the patents.

The trust cannot be express. Every fact in the case negatives the existence of one. Nor can it arise ex maleficio. The employees' conduct was not fraudulent in any respect. They promptly disclosed their inventions. Their superiors encouraged them to proceed in perfecting and applying the discoveries. Their notebooks and reports disclosed the work they were doing, and there is not a syllable to suggest their use of time or material was clandestine or improper. No word was spoken regarding any claim of title by the government until after applications for patents were filed. And, as we have seen, no such trust has been spelled out of the relation of master and servant, even in the cases where the employee has perfected his invention by the use of his employer's time and materials. The cases recognizing the doctrine of shop rights may be said to fix a trust upon the employee in favor of his master as respects the use of the invention by the latter, but they do not affect the title to the patent and the exclusive rights conferred by it against the public.

The decrees are affirmed.

NOTES

1. From the dissent by Justice Stone:

It seems clear that, in thus exercising their inventive powers in the pursuit of ideas reaching beyond their specific assignments, the inventors were discharging the duties expected of scientists employed in the laboratory;

Dunmore, as well as his supervisors, testified that such was their conception of the nature of the work. The conclusion is irresistible that their scientific curiosity was precisely what gave the inventors value as research workers; the government employed it and gave it free rein in performing the broad duty of the Bureau of advancing the radio art by discovery and invention.

289 U.S. at 212.

2. The "Shop Right" and the Implied License. A shop right is a personal right and does not pass by mere assignment, nevertheless it does pass where there is a complete succession to the entire business and good will of the previous shop right holder. *Neon Signal Devices, Inc. v. Alph-Claude Neon Corp.*, 54 F.2d 793, 12 U.S.P.Q. (BNA) 339 (W.D. Pa. 1931). Also, the holder of a shop right cannot license another to exercise this right. *See Ushakoff v. United States*, 327 F.2d 669 (Ct. Cl. 1964). In the earlier shop right cases, the inventor often appeared to acquiesce in the employer's use of the invention, giving the arrangement the air of an implied license. But the implied license element, if it was ever required, is no longer essential to the right.

In general, if an accused infringer can prove that she is operating within the scope of a license — implied or express — granted by the patentee, she will have a complete defense. *De Forest Radio Tel. Co. v. United States*, 273 U.S. 236 (1926), provides a good example. De Forest Radio filed suit in the Court of Claims against the United States, seeking to recover for an alleged unlawful use by the government of certain patented vacuum tubes used in radio communication. De Forest had invented the famous "audion" tube, and assigned it to Western Electric Company, which had in turn assigned it to American Telegraph & Telephone (AT&T). During World War I, the U.S. Government requested the right to make audions, and AT&T replied by saying that it would take no steps to stop the Government, but did not waive any of its rights under the patent. AT&T then actively helped the Government make the audions. Later, AT&T executed a "release" of any claims it might have against the government or its subcontractors. The Government defended De Forest's subsequent suit on the basis of AT&T's war-time license. The Court held that

> [t]he agreement by the Telephone Company that it would not do anything to interfere with the immediate making of the audions for the United States, interpreted in the light of its subsequent action in assisting the United States ..., [and] in furnishing the needed information and drawings and blueprints for such manufacture ... made such conduct clearly a consent to their manufacture and use, and a license, and this without any regard to the effect of the subsequent release by [AT&T] of compensation for such manufacture and use.

273 U.S. at 241.

The Court went on to state:

No formal granting of a license is necessary in order to give it effect. Any language used by the owner of the patent or any conduct on his part exhibited to another, from which that other may properly infer that the owner consents to his use of the patent in making or using it, or selling it, upon which the other acts, constitutes a license, and a defense to an action for a tort. Whether this constitutes a gratuitous license, or one for a reasonable compensation, must, of course, depend upon the circumstances; but the relation between the parties thereafter in respect of any suit brought must be held to be contractual, and not an unlawful invasion of the rights of the owner. Concede that, if the owner had said, "If you go on and infringe my patent, I shall not attempt to enjoin you, but I shall subsequently sue you for infringement," the tort would not be waived; that is not this case. Here the circumstances show clearly that what the company was doing was not only fully consenting to the making and using by the United States of the patent, but was aiding such making and using, and in doing so was licensing it, only postponing to subsequent settlement what reasonable compensation, if any, it might claim for its license.

273 U.S. at 241-42. The defense of an implied license is closely related to another strategy popular today, especially in the electronics industry: taking a sublicense from a firm which had entered into a broad cross license with the owner of the desired technology. *See, e.g., Intel Corp. v. ULSI System Tech., Inc.*, 21 U.S.P.Q.2d (BNA) 1922 (D. Or. 1991) (defendant unsuccessfully tried to defensively sublicense from Hewlett-Packard, which had entered into prior broad cross license with plaintiff).

3. *A Disastrous Implied License*. Richard Rosenbloom and Karen Freeze tell the story of a disastrous — and inadvertent — "license" that may have cost the U.S. dominance in the video cassette recorder (VCR) market. Richard Rosenbloom & Karen Freeze, *Ampex Corporation and Video Innovation*, 2 RESEARCH ON TECH. INNOV., MGT. & POL'Y (1985) (reprinted Harv. Bus. Sch. Reprint Series) (ambiguous letter from U.S.-based Ampex Corp. to Sony inadvertently gave away a license over basic video recorder technology). *See generally* Rosenbloom & Cusumano, *Technological Pioneering and Competitive Advantage: The Birth of the VCR Industry*, 29 CAL. MGT. REV. 51 (1987); J. LARDNER, FAST FORWARD: HOLLYWOOD, THE JAPANESE AND THE VCR WARS (1987).

4. *Implied Duties*. Note that a specific contractual provision may not be the only basis for a duty to assign rights in inventions. *See* 5 E. LIPSCOMB, WALKER ON PATENTS § 19:13 (3d ed. 1986). Thus a duty to assign may be implied in place of a shop right where an employee is hired to solve a particular problem. *See, e.g., Magnetic Mfg. Co. v. Dings Magnetic Separator Co.*, 16 F.2d 739 (7th Cir. 1927); *Goodyear Tire & Rubber Co. v. Miller*, 22 F.2d 353, 356 (9th Cir. 1927); *Houghton v. United States*, 23 F.2d 386 (4th Cir. 1928).

5. *Relief for the Employed Inventor*. Dratler, *Incentives for People: The Forgotten Purpose of the Patent System*, 16 HARV. J. ON LEGIS. 129 (1979), critiques the current system of nearly automatic assignment of patents obtained by employed inventors. This article discusses the more pro-employee stance taken in some foreign countries. To the same effect is Baker & Brunel, *Restructuring the Judicial Evaluation of Employed Inventors' Rights*, 35 ST. LOUIS U. L. REV. 399 (1991) (arguing for overhaul of current semi-automatic assignment system, in favor of small employed inventors). For those who believe the employed inventor needs no help from the law, consider this: many employers require employees to assign rights to inventions made a year or more *after* leaving the company! *See Georgia-Pacific Corp. v. Lieberam*, 22 U.S.P.Q.2d (BNA) 1383 (11th Cir. 1992) (considering such an agreement to assign).

3. CO-OWNERSHIP OF PATENTS

R. MERGES & L. LOCKE, CO-OWNERSHIP OF PATENTS: A COMPARATIVE AND ECONOMIC VIEW, 72 J. Pat. & Trademark Off. Soc'y 586 (1990)

There are three questions that arise with co-ownership of patents: (1) can each co-owner independently work the patent without being obligated to compensate the other co-owners for any profits derived from it?; (2) can a co-owner's share be transferred to a third party without the consent of the other co-owners?; and (3) can a co-owner's share be subdivided by transferring *portions* of it to third parties?

(1) We favor keeping the U.S. rule permitting co-owners to work patents without compensating other co-owners; (2) contrary to the current U.S. rule, a co-owner's share should not be transferrable to a third party without the consent of the other co-owners; and (3) also contrary to the current rule, no co-owner should be permitted to subdivide his or her interest by transferring portions of it to third parties.

Joint inventors, generally speaking, must apply for a patent jointly. 35 U.S.C. § 116. (For information on the 1984 amendments to § 116, see Carstens, *Joint Inventorship Under 35 U.S.C. § 116*, 73 J. PAT. & TRADEMARK OFF. SOC'Y 616 (1991).) The grant of a joint patent makes each joint patentee (also called a joint owner, co-owner or tenant-in-common) an owner of an undivided one-half interest in the patent. *Drake v. Hall*, 220 F. 905, 906 (7th Cir. 1915); *Bendix Aviation Corp. v. Kury*, 88 F. Supp. 243, 248 (E.D.N.Y. 1950); 5 E. LIPSCOMB'S WALKER ON PATENTS § 19:39 at 462. (Of course, if there were three joint inventors, each would own a one-third undivided interest, and so on.)

Patent rights are different from any other form of property, so that rules adopted with respect to co-owners of ordinary chattels cannot safely be followed. *Talbot v. Quaker-State Oil Refining*, 104 F.2d 967, 968 (3d Cir. 1939). For example, co-owners are said to be at the mercy of one another, as described in *Walker on Patents*; in the absence of a special agreement to the contrary:

One tenant in common of a patent right, however small his or her undivided interest in a patent, may exercise that right to any extent he or she pleases, without the consent of any co-tenant. The tenant in common may make, use and sell specimens of the patented invention to any extent, and may license others to do so, and neither the tenant nor the tenant's licensees can be enjoined from a continuance in so doing. Nor can any recovery of profits or damages be had against such licensee at the suit of any co-tenant of any such licensor. And no recovery of profits or damages can be had against one co-tenant who, without the consent of the others, has made, used or sold specimens of the patented thing. The same rules apply as between two or more joint licensees or patentees, so that one joint patentee cannot restrain use of the patent, or require an accounting of profits, by the assignee of the other joint patentee under an unimpeached assignment.

5 E. LIPSCOMB'S WALKER ON PATENTS § 19:39 at 464-65, and cases cited therein (footnotes omitted). Other sources for these general rules include: *Willingham v. Star Cutter Co.*, 555 F.2d 1340, 1344 (6th Cir. 1977); *Talbot v. Quaker-State Oil Refining*, 104 F.2d at 968; R. ELLIS, PATENT ASSIGNMENTS § 397 (3d ed. 1955).

These common law rules are partially codified at 35 U.S.C.A. § 262, which states:

> In the absence of any agreement to the contrary, each of the joint owners of a patent may make, use or sell the patented invention without the consent of and without accounting to the other owners.

Exceptions to these general rules have been found and an accounting of profits required in certain cases involving fraud, such as where a co-owner's interest was procured by fraud, or where a co-owner has led a licensee to believe that he was the sole owner. *Haserot v. Keller*, 228 P. 383 (Cal. App.), *hearing denied* (Ca. 1924) (interest procured by fraud); *Seidensticker v. Bean*, 300 P. 366 (Colo. 1931) (co-owner represented as sole owner to licensee). In addition, with respect to licenses, there is some (albeit scant and early) authority for the proposition that co-owners should divide royalties pro rata, but the weight of authority "is overwhelmingly *contra.*" R. ELLIS, PATENT ASSIGNMENTS § 397. *Talbot v. Quaker-State Oil Refining*, 104 F.2d 967; *Kabbes v. Philip Carey Mfg. Co.*, 63 F.2d 255 (6th Cir. 1933); *Blackledge v. Weir & Craig Mfg. Co.*, 108 F. 71 (7th Cir. 1901).

The Consequences of Assigning an Undivided Partial Interest

Under the express terms of the patent law, every patent application, patent or patent interest is assignable, without restriction. 35 U.S.C.S. § 261; *Transparent-Wrap Mach. Corp. v. Stokes & Smith Co.*, 329 U.S. 637 (1947). The results of an assignment of an undivided partial interest in an invention can be extraordinary.

Any co-owner is free to assign his interests in whole or in undivided part to another party, again in the absence of agreements to the contrary. The effect of an assignment of an undivided interest by a sole owner of a patent is clear:

> Tenancy in common in a patent right will arise whenever the sole owner of such a right in all or part of the territory of the United States conveys to another an undivided interest in the whole or part of what he or she owns.... The ordinary incidents of tenancy in common therefore appertain to such ownership and each owner becomes entitled to use the invention without accounting to the other.

5 E. LIPSCOMB'S WALKER ON PATENTS § 19:39 at 461.

Note that an assignment can create this situation even where the assignor does not realize it. A remarkable case is where one of two or more co-owners assigns a partial undivided interest. An example follows: If there were two co-inventors or co-owners, for example *A* and *B*, and *A* sold a 25 percent undivided interest to *C*, then what *A* sold to *C* is a 25 percent undivided interest in what *A* owned. *A* owned an undivided interest in the entire invention. Strictly speaking, such an assignment would make assignee *C* a co-owner of *A*'s interest in the invention. What the assignment does in effect, though, is to create a third co-owner sharing the rights of the original co-owners. Assignee *C* in the above case would own an undivided interest in the entire invention through owning an undivided 25 percent of *A*'s undivided interest in the entire invention. *C* would be able to license the entire invention to another party without having to account to either *A* or *B* for profits. *Talbot v. Quaker-State Oil Refining*, 104 F.2d 967. *See also* R. ELLIS, PATENT ASSIGNMENTS § 391.

As the quote above from *Walker on Patents* indicates, the general rules regarding co-owners apply however small the size of a co-owner's undivided interest. *Rainbow Rubber Co. v. Holtite Mfg. Co.*, 20 F. Supp. 913 (D. Md. 1937); *see also* dicta in favor of general rules being applied to 1 percent undivided interests in *Eickmeyer v. U.S.*, 231 U.S.P.Q. 821, 822 (Ct. Cl. 1986). This apparently means that, in the absence of special agreements to the contrary, anyone assigned an undivided partial interest, by all or any of the co-owners, and regardless of the percentage owned, has essentially the same rights as other co-owners and can make, use, sell and license the invention. This would be true whether an undivided 1 percent interest or an undivided 99 percent interest in one or all of the co-owners' rights was assigned. Even if a 1 percent undivided interest was assigned, a license to the entire invention could be sold by the party owning the 1 percent undivided interest and there would be no duty to account for profits. This would be true even if there were one or a very few potential customers.

The rules create obvious problems. But these are in turn exacerbated by two additional rules. First, all co-owners must join in a patent infringement suit. A "primary interest" protected by this requirement is "the interest of a co-owner in being able to license third parties under his or her patent without harassing suits by other co-owners." *Willingham v. Star Cutter Co.*, 555 F.2d at 1344. *See* Note, *Indispensability of an Absent Co-Patentee in an Infringement Suit*, 47 YALE L.J. 1224 (1938). Thus a co-owner with a 1% interest can block an infringement suit by the other co-owner who holds the 99% interest. Relatedly, a license from one co-owner is as good as if given by all the co-owners; such a license is a "complete defense to an infringement suit" by other co-owners. *Talbot v. Quaker-State Oil Refining*, 104 F.2d at 967-68.

The actual percentage share of a co-owner becomes important only when infringement damages are at issue. It becomes important then because, as just noted, there is some authority that all co-owners must join in such a lawsuit, yet any recovery will be divided in proportion to the respective interests of the co-owners. *Herring v. Gas Consumers' Ass'n*, 9 F. 556, 557 (E.D. Mo. 1878).

For certain purposes, therefore, there is arguably no effective difference between an assignment of a 1 percent undivided interest and an assignment of a 99 percent undivided interest as far as certain important rights of the assignee/co-owner are concerned. Assignments of undivided partial interests can pose a substantial trap for the unwary, and therefore special protective agreements are significant.

A Comparative View

The U.S. rule on assignability and transfer of whole or part interests is out of step with that of other countries. The continental countries and Japan require consent among co-owners of a patent when any of them disposes of their rights in it.

In addition, some continental patent laws require co-owners to compensate the other co-owners when they derive profit from working the patent individually. For example, the relevant section of the Patent Law of France reads as follows:

> (1) Joint ownership of the patent application or of the patent shall be governed by the following provisions:
>
> (a) Each joint owner may work the invention for his own benefit subject to equitably compensating the other joint owners who do not personally work the invention or who have not granted a license. Failing agreement between the parties, such compensation shall be fixed by the District Court; ...
>
> (c) Each joint owner may grant to a third party a nonexclusive license for his own benefit subject to making equitable compensation to the other joint owners who do not personally work the invention or who have not granted a license. Failing agreement between the parties, such compensation shall be fixed by the District Court.
>
> However, the draft licensing contract shall be notified to [sic] the other joint owners with an offer to transfer the share at a specified price.

Within three months of such notification, any of the other joint owners may oppose the granting of a license on condition that he acquires the share of the joint owner wishing to grant the license.

Failing agreement within the time limit laid down in the above paragraph, the price shall be fixed by the District Court;

(d) An exclusive license may only be granted with the agreement of all the joint owners or by the authorization of the court;

(e) Each joint owner may, at any moment, assign his share.

The joint owners shall have a right of pre-emption for a period of three months from the notification of the intended assignment. Failing agreement on the price, such price shall be fixed by the District Court....

(4) In the absence of provisions to the contrary, the provisions of this Section shall apply. The joint owners may derogate from this Section at any time by means of a joint ownership agreement.

Patent Law of France, Law No. 68-1 of January 2, 1968, as amended, *reprinted in* 3 INDUSTRIAL PROPERTY LAWS AND TREATIES — Text 2-001, pp. 001-015 (1978 & Supp. 1989), Article 42, Text 2-001 at 009.

The law in the Federal Republic of Germany is similar, in application if not on its face. Even though there are no detailed provisions on co-ownership in the German patent code, German law is quick to assume that two or more persons engaged in a joint venture of any kind, including most co-inventors, have formed a partnership. *See* Bernhard Geissler, *Book Review* (Review of Kurt Bartenbach, Zwischenbetriebliche Forschungs- und Entwicklungskooperation und das Recht der Arbeitnehmererfinding (1985), 19 INT'L REV. IND. PROP. & COPYRIGHT L. 416 (1988). *See also* A. Szakowski, *Legal Regulation of Joint Inventions in Poland*, in 3 INT'L PROTECTION OF IND. PROP. 7 at 9-10 (S. Soltysinski ed., 1983) ("A similar interpretation [to the French rule] has been arrived at in the theory and case law of West Germany" (citation omitted)). Where co-owners are deemed partners, they are prohibited from unilaterally selling their share in individual pieces of partnership property. *Id.*

The laws in Japan and Great Britain share some of the characteristics of the continental rules, but also contain some elements present in the U.S. rule.

Japanese and British co-owners have the right to work the patent without being liable to other co-owners for infringement, Patents Act of 1977 (United Kingdom), § 36, entered into force June 1, 1978, *reprinted in* 7 INDUSTRIAL PROPERTY LAWS AND TREATIES — Text 2-001, pp. 001-113 (1978 & Supp. 1989); Japanese Patent Act of 1968, Article 73(2), *cited in* R. RUSSELL, PATENTS AND TRADEMARKS IN JAPAN 118 (3d ed. 1974), but no co-owner may transfer his or her interest "without the consent of the other or others." Patents Act of 1977 (United Kingdom), § 36(3); Japanese Patent Law of 1968, as amended, Article 73(1), *cited in* T. DOI, THE INTELLECTUAL PROPERTY LAW OF JAPAN (1980) at 54. *See also* A. KUKIMOTO, SUMMARY OF JAPANESE PATENT LAW 160 (1971). In both countries, these rules can be varied by agreement. *See* T. WHITE, PATENTS FOR

INVENTIONS at §§ 9-201 through 9-202 (4th ed. 1974) (Great Britain); R. RUSSELL, PATENTS AND TRADEMARKS IN JAPAN 118 (3d ed. 1974). (White adds an interesting aside: "Where sale or licensing is not contemplated, the amount of a 'share' in a patent can have no significance, since all one co-patentee can do without the others is work the patent for his own benefit, and what fraction of it he is supposed to be working is clearly immaterial. But the custom of assigning peculiar fractions of patents is well documented from the reports...." *Id.*, § 9-201 at 347.) Under the British cases distinguishing permissible working from impermissible assignment without consent, a co-owner may appoint an agent to work the invention, but may not form a company to work it nor give the right to work it to an independent contractor operating for its own profit. *Id.*, § 9-202 at 348.

An Economic Perspective

An economic view of the common ownership problem highlights the fact that co-owners have incentives to behave "opportunistically" with respect to one another — i.e., to cheat on each other. One view of the problem would see the patent as a common property resource, where those with access to the resource have an incentive to overuse it. The classic example of such a situation is the "tragedy of the commons," where common pasture land is overexploited since each individual owner of animals using the pasture maximizes earnings by using the land beyond the point where it is cost effective. There is an extensive economic literature on this problem. *See, e.g.*, G. Hardin, *The Tragedy of the Commons*, 162 SCI. 1243 (1968). *See also* P. DASGUPTA & G. HEAL, ECONOMIC THEORY AND EXHAUSTIBLE RESOURCES (1979).

While it would be nice to assert that we are the first to apply the "tragedy of the commons" concept to co-ownership of patents, it would be wrong. The first such treatment appeared 100 years ago in William C. Robinson's classic treatise on patent law. Section 796 of the treatise states:

> Although no exact similitude exists between a patent privilege and any other property, yet the resemblance which it bears to a common of pasture is sufficient to suggest a possible solution of the present question. Both the patent privilege and the common of pasture are to be exercised within definite territory by specified means of enjoyment, and with a limited and determinable amount of profit. In both, the appropriation to himself, by one owner, of more than his just share of such profit is an unjust invasion of the rights of the others, whether, in the one case, by the introduction of an excessive number of commonable beasts, or, in the other, by distributing the patent privilege to an increased number of proprietors or licensees. Any assignment of either right which does not impose a greater burden on the common property, and any use of either by the owner which does not curtail its proper use by his co-owners, is fair and equitable although the ultimate result to him may far exceed any advantage which his co-owners may actually obtain. Now the law finds no difficulty in regulating the rights and

duties of commoners of pasture. It recognizes the fact that the profit is limited in amount and, therefore, prevents its distribution among a greater number of cattle than the owners have the right to introduce. But it does not measure the keenness of their appetites, nor the capacity of their stomachs, nor the benefit derived by one owner over another on account of his choicer breed of animals or the higher value to him of the food obtained.

2 W. ROBINSON, ROBINSON ON PATENTS § 796 at 571 n.2 (1890).

Robinson then notes that common ownership situations outside patent law are governed by interlocking duties among those who share the common resource. This allows the "commoners" to restrict each other from overuse. Robinson proposes to apply this treatment to co-owners of patents:

[D]oes not this suggest that the joint-owners of a patent privilege enjoy all the rights to which they are entitled, as against each other, when each is allowed to practice the invention without accountability to his co-owners for any benefit which his superior skill or larger capital may enable him to realize, and to assign his interest to one other person, natural or artificial, for what price he pleases, with the same power to use and assign; but that, as in the case of a commoner, he should not be allowed to introduce into the common property a greater number of those agencies by which its profits are to be absorbed, to the inevitable diminution of the advantage which his co-owners would otherwise have rightfully enjoyed?

Id.

By this Robinson means to adapt the law of common pasturage to the co-ownership of patents. Thus a co-owner need not share the proceeds of his own exploitation of the patent with the other co-owners; this would create a disincentive to maximize the value of one's share in the common resource. There would be a reduced reward for outperforming the other co-owners, for example as a result of "superior skill or larger capital," because the additional profit would have to be split among all the co-owners. (Another way of seeing this is to view the proceeds flowing from the outperforming co-owner to the other co-owners as a windfall to these other co-owners; they could in effect free-ride on the investment of time, energy, capital, etc. of the ambitious co-owner.)

But neither should a co-owner be permitted to transfer his interest as many times as he can get away with; this would be tantamount to a commoner continually introducing new animals to the common pasturage. Additional profit in this case would come out of the pockets of the other co-owners, who are left to compete with the greedy co-owner's multiple assignees and licensees. In short, as Robinson rightly describes things, where profits are derived from superior use of the co-owner's interest, they should not be split with the others; but where a co-owner attempts to opportunistically profit *at the direct expense of the other owners* (e.g., by transferring his or her interest repeatedly, thereby creating a series of new competitors), the law should prohibit the activity.

At the same time, Robinson overlooked an important consideration when he pressed the position that co-owners should be free to assign their interests a single time to anyone of their choosing. Robinson's view does have the merit of promoting competition when an invention is being commercialized; the alternative rule — which we favor — does permit co-owners to withhold their consent to a transfer, thus perhaps giving them a tool to restrict competition by preventing a co-owner from transferring his or her interest to an efficient competitor. But the alternative to the Robinson position on this point is on balance more desirable. First, Robinson's rule would reduce the disincentives to engage in joint invention — because there is no possibility that the other joint inventors/co-owners can transfer their interests to a co-owner with whom the other co-owners will not be able to cooperate, e.g., because the new co-owner has very different plans for the commercialization of the technology. Second, and most important, adopting a rule whereby the consent of co-owners is required for *any* transfer of a co-owner's rights would bring the U.S. into conformity with the international norm on this point. This is an important consideration in this era of patent law harmonization.

But Robinson's basic insight is nonetheless correct. Consider once again the distinction he makes between profits derived from the individual initiative of a co-inventor and those achieved at the expense of the other co-owners. This distinction can be defended a number of ways. Conceptually, the co-inventor rightfully claims an undivided share in an invention, and thus has the right to use that invention. Any profit derived from use should, therefore, not give rise to a claim for compensation by other co-owners; the co-owner using the invention is simply exercising his or her rights, and without the right to do so those rights would mean little. But where a co-owner appropriates some of the value rightfully belonging to the other co-owners, then the law should step in. Consequently, multiple assignments and licenses of purportedly "different" shares of a co-owner's interest in the invention mean that the co-owner is, in effect, consuming some of the value of the invention that rightfully belongs to the other co-owners.

The U.S. rule would be better if it tracked Robinson's reasoning on individual initiative and multiple assignments, which at heart reduces to an analysis of incentives. The current rule, where the law permits multiple assignments and licenses by each co-owner without consent of the others, could lead to exploitation by a greedy co-owner. Such a co-owner may have an incentive to consume some of the value of the other co-owner's interests in the invention. At a minimum, there is no rule to *prevent* such a greedy co-owner from taking advantage of the others. This counsels strongly for adoption of the continental rule, whereby co-inventors may not transfer their interest or any "share" in it without consent of the other co-owners.

At the same time, the current U.S. rule permitting a co-owner to *work* an invention without compensating the other co-owners should be retained. As Robinson correctly pointed out, the opposite rule results in unfairness, since non-working (or even lazy) co-owners could sit back and reap an equal share of the ambitious co-owner's profits. This free-rider effect might be strong enough in some cases to actually make it foolish for a co-owner to work the invention.

[A game theory model of the effects of the American rules can be found in the original version of this article in 72 J. PAT. & TRADEMARK OFF. SOC'Y 586.]

Some Practical Suggestions

As discussed at length above, the need for special protective agreements should, therefore, be addressed in every case of joint invention. Such agreements should address, among other issues, accounting between the joint patentees, co-operation against infringers and limitations on rights in the invention generally.

The need for special protective agreements should also be addressed in every case of an assignment of an undivided partial interest. Such assignments should contain covenants regarding issues such as accounting between the co-owners and restrictions on sales of interests in the patent without consent of the other co-owner(s).

One final caveat: Ellis points out that agreements between joint inventors are not assignments and might not be binding on assignees who take without notice. (*See FilmTec, supra.*) In such a situation, the only remedy would be by suit against the original joint inventor. Ellis suggests the following method to cover this situation: Each joint patentee assigns his interest to the other, includes desired covenants in the assignment, and then records the assignment. Besides providing record notice to third parties, an effect of this procedure would be to place desired limits on what each co-owner *owns* and so can assign to third parties.

Chapter 12

TRADE SECRETS AND FEDERAL PREEMPTION

State trade secret law exists as a backdrop to the federal patent statute. Even without the protection of the patent statute, an inventor has certain rights under state trade secret law. In the first part of this chapter we outline those rights; in the second, we examine the interface between state intellectual property law and the federal system, i.e., the extent to which federal patent law preempts various forms of state protection.

A. TRADE SECRETS

Since trade secrets are protected by state law, there are in reality 50 trade secret regimes in the U.S., a mix of statute and common law. However, the state-based nature of trade secret protection has always been mitigated to some extent by the presence of recurrent principles, often stated in important cases, which give some consistency to the treatment of trade secret issues in the courts of the various states. This was reflected in the Restatement of Torts, § 757 comment b, which for years served as the basic definition of a trade secret. In fact, a majority of the states have adopted the Restatement's definition of trade secret. The Restatement acknowledges that "[a]n exact definition of a trade secret is not possible," but sets forth the following definition:

> [A trade secret is] [a]ny formula, pattern, device or compilation of information which is used in one's business, and which gives him an opportunity to obtain an advantage over competitors who do not know or use it.

It also lists six factors "to be considered in determining whether given information is [a person's] trade secret":

> (1) the extent to which the information is known outside of his business; (2) the extent to which it is known by employees and others involved in his business; (3) the extent of measures taken by him to guard the secrecy of the information; (4) the value of the information to him and to his competitors; (5) the amount of efforts or money expended by him in developing the information; (6) the ease or difficulty with which the information could be properly acquired or duplicated by others.

RESTATEMENT OF TORTS § 757 cmt. b (1939). This is "[t]he most [often] cited listing of the objective criteria for determining the existence of a trade secret." M. JAGER, TRADE SECRETS LAW § 5.05 (1985). *See also* 1 R. MILGRIM, TRADE SECRETS § 2.01 n.2 (1988); *FMC Corp. v. Taiwan Tainan Giant Indus. Co.*, 730

F.2d 61, 63 (2d Cir. 1954). This definition is still used in spite of the decision of the authors of the Restatement (Second) of Torts to omit any discussion of trade secret. *See* 4 RESTATEMENT (SECOND) OF TORTS at 1-2 (1979).

In recent years, an even greater source of consistency in trade secret law has emerged: the Uniform Trade Secret Act. Promulgated on the same model as the Uniform Commercial Code (U.C.C.), the UTSA (as it is called) has now been adopted (sometimes with modifications) in some 41 states. Because this Act states the most up-to-date restatement of trade secret principles, and because its influence is expected to grow, this chapter will be organized around the principles of the Uniform Trade Secret Act. We will make note of some important cases decided outside the framework of the Act, and of certain continuing deviations from it, but for the most part it will help us organize our thinking on trade secret issues.

Here is a schematic outline of the basic UTSA principles:

> "Trade Secret" means information, including a formula, pattern, compila-tion, program, devise, method, technique, or process, that:
>
> (i) Derives independent economic value, actual or potential from
>
>> [a] not being generally known [to persons who can use and obtain econ-omic value from its disclosure or use], AND
>>
>> [b] not being readily ascertainable by proper means by other persons who can use and obtain economic value from its disclosure or use, AND
>
> (ii) is the subject of efforts that are reasonable under the circumstances to maintain its secrecy.

UTSA § 1(4), 14 U.L.A. 537 (1980). Finally, in 1995, the American Law Institute published the Restatement (Third) of Unfair Competition, which closely tracks many of the concepts (and even the language) of the UTSA. For example, § 39 of the Restatement 3d defines a trade secret as "any information that can be used in the operation of a business or other enterprise and that is sufficiently valuable and secret to afford an actual or potential economic advantage over others." RESTATEMENT (THIRD) OF UNFAIR COMPETITION § 39 (1993).

Despite the fact that trade secret law springs from multiple sources, there are common elements that give this body of law some basic consistency. We explore each of these elements in the sections that follow. In addition to these basic definitional elements, an important component of trade secrets disputes is the issue of remedies. Accordingly, we discuss remedies issues at the end of Section A.

1. "... NOT GENERALLY KNOWN...."

AMERICAN CREDIT INDEMNITY CO. v. SACKS

213 Cal. App. 3d 622, 262 Cal. Rptr. 92 (Cal. Ct. App. 1989)

Plaintiff and appellant American Credit Indemnity Company (ACI) appeals an order of the trial court denying its application for a preliminary injunction against defendant and respondent, its former employee, Lola N. Sacks (Sacks), now doing business as LNS Insurance Services.

The issue presented is whether, under the Uniform Trade Secrets Act (UTSA) ([Cal.] Civ. Code, § 3426 et seq.), Sacks may solicit ACI policyholders she serviced during her employment, or whether she must limit the use of ACI's customer list to an announcement of new affiliation.

We hold the UTSA protects ACI's customer list as a trade secret, and Sacks's solicitation of ACI's clients constituted a misappropriation within the meaning of the UTSA, and should have been enjoined by the trial court.

Background

ACI is a national underwriter of credit insurance. This esoteric insurance is sold to manufacturers, wholesalers and certain service organizations which sell on credit terms to other businesses, and is designed to protect an insured against excessive bad debts. As far as can be discerned from the record, only three firms write this type of insurance. ACI is a leader in the field, and in 1987 it had 42 offices which generated gross premiums in excess of $56 million.

ACI estimates that although any company in the described category of potential customers with annual revenues in excess of $2 million might insure its accounts receivable, only 6.5 percent actually do. ACI claims it has captured more than half of this market.

Sacks became an ACI agent on February 5, 1979. She formerly had worked in the toy industry and had been an ACI policyholder. By 1987, Sacks had become a top ACI agent. She personally serviced 43 of the 136 Los Angeles office policies. Although some of these policies had been "inherited" by Sacks when other ACI agents left the office, she had been the responsible salesperson on the majority. Some of the leads which resulted in policies written by Sacks had been provided by ACI; others Sacks had developed.

On March 4, 1988, Sacks resigned from ACI. She sent a letter dated March 7, 1988, to each of the approximately 50 ACI policyholders she personally had serviced. It stated: "After almost fifteen years as both an agent and policyholder, I have left [ACI] and am very pleased to announce the formation of an independent insurance agency. [para.] I shall continue to specialize in Credit Insurance but will now primarily be representing Fidelity and Deposit Company of Maryland [F&D], who [sic] is offering companies a very interesting alternative to the types of policies being written by [ACI]. If you would like to learn more about the [F&D] policy, I will be happy to discuss it in detail with you when you are ready to review your ongoing credit insurance needs at renewal time. [para.] In the meantime, ACI will assign a new agent to your policy. If I can be of assistance to you during the transition period or answer any questions for you at any time, please do not hesitate to call me. [para.] I have really enjoyed our past association and hope we don't lose touch!"

On March 23, 1988, ACI filed a verified complaint against Sacks seeking injunctive relief which alleged Sacks had used ACI's " 'Trade Secrets' " to solicit ACI's clients. The complaint defined as " 'Trade Secrets' " its client list, the expiration dates of ACI policies, lists of all leads for potential business, claims histories, and other information concerning the special needs of clients. ACI alleged it required its employees to sign confidentiality agreements with respect to this information.

The complaint further alleged that in the course of discovery in another lawsuit (the Wixom action), Sacks had received log books containing the names of approximately 3,000 ACI leads and clients maintained by ACI from 1985 through October 1986. In that case, Sacks had stipulated to a protective order as to the log books. ACI characterized the Wixom action as a suit for defamation brought by Sacks against a former ACI secretary.

The parties had agreed certain "proprietary and confidential information belonging" to ACI "consisting of log books of leads from August, 1983 through the present, [would] be used only for the legitimate purposes of this [the Wixom] litigation [and] [t]hat said material will not be disclosed, discussed, copied, published, or made available in any manner whatsoever to persons other than the parties, their attorneys, and those with a legitimate need to know in order to assist in the prosecution or defense of this action and cross-action."

Based upon the allegations of the complaint, the trial court issued a TRO which directed Sacks not to divulge, make known or make any use of ACI's trade secrets and not to solicit business from any person or entity which had been an existing ACI client during the time Sacks had been employed by ACI or any potential ACI client Sacks had become aware of as a result of her ACI employment.

After issuance of the TRO, the parties conducted expedited discovery which disclosed the following facts: Sacks first contemplated leaving ACI in approximately April 1987. She began discussions with F&D in October 1987, and attended meetings at F&D's Baltimore headquarters in late January 1988. Sacks told F&D her ACI policyholders represented approximately $800,000 in annual premiums and "perhaps half of [those] policyholders might be interested in writing business with" F&D.

In February 1988, Sacks signed a lease and installed phone service at her new office but averred "until the last day as an agent with ACI (March 4, 1988) I properly serviced all ACI policyholders including but not limited to submitting policy renewal applications and obtaining new business. Indeed, between January, 1988 and March 4, 1988, I obtained 18 renewal applications for ACI and obtained three new applications for ACI, ..." (Italics deleted.)

Sacks told several ACI clients of her possible association with F&D at the time she met with them for the purpose of renewal of their policies. Of these clients, she advised at least two to stay with ACI even though the clients wanted to follow her, and the great majority of these policyholders renewed with ACI.

Sacks claimed the March 7th letter had been "carefully drafted ... to refute any charge of wrongdoing that might be brought by ACI." Sacks pointed out the letter specifically suggested waiting until renewal time before making any change in coverage and assured the client that ACI would continue to service the policy.

Although Sacks also telephoned each client to which she had sent the March 7th letter in order to convey a personal communication of her departure, she denied soliciting business or discouraging continuation of coverage with ACI during those calls.

One major policyholder with which Sacks had discussed her new affiliation decided to change carriers to F&D. This policy, which expired on March 31, 1988, accounted for approximately $230,000 in annual premiums or almost 30 percent of the premiums Sacks generated. [A]pproximately one week after Sacks told this client she intended definitely to join F&D, the client told Sacks it would not renew the ACI policy but would place its business with F&D.

Sacks admitted it is easier to renew a policy than to sell it in the first instance because a prospective client must be sold on the concept of credit insurance. Sacks renewed policies at a rate that ranged between 65 and 75 percent.

Sacks believed the sales leads produced by ACI belonged to ACI, but the sales leads she had developed belonged to her.

At the first oral hearing, the trial court had stated the March 7, 1988, letter constituted a solicitation, but the trial court's written order concluded Sacks had a right to solicit the clients of her former employer with which she personally had become acquainted during the course of her employment.

The trial court also found the evidence did not support ACI's allegation of misappropriation of trade secrets. To the extent ACI's unfair competition claim had merit, the trial court held money damages provided an adequate remedy.

ACI contends its customers list, policy expiration dates and related information constitute trade secrets. ACI asserts Sacks used these trade secrets to negotiate with F&D and to divert ACI business to F&D.

The ACI customer list constitutes a trade secret

a. *UTSA*

The Legislature enacted the UTSA in 1984 and it became effective on January 1, 1985. In the event of a conflict between prior case law and the statute, the UTSA controls.

The stated purpose of the UTSA is to provide "unitary definitions of trade secret and trade secret misappropriation, and a single statute of limitations for the various property, quasi-contractual, and violation of fiduciary relationship theories of noncontractual liability utilized at common law. The Uniform Act also codifies the results of the better reasoned cases concerning the remedies for trade secret misappropriation." (Comrs. Prefatory Note to Uniform Trade Secrets Act, 14 West's U. Laws Ann. (1980) Trade Secrets 537, 538.)

The UTSA defines a trade secret as "information, including a formula, pattern, compilation, program, device, method, technique, or process, that: (1) Derives independent economic value, actual or potential, from not being generally known to the public or to other persons who can obtain economic value from its disclosure or use; and (2) Is the subject of efforts that are reasonable under the circumstances to maintain its secrecy." (Civ. Code, § 3426.1, subd. (d).)

If the two-prong UTSA test is applied to the present situation, it must be concluded the ACI customer list is "information" which has potential economic value because it allows a competitor to direct sales efforts to the elite 6.5 percent of those potential customers which already have evinced a predisposition to purchase credit insurance.

Although a large number of firms could purchase credit insurance to protect their accounts receivable, most do not. Sacks admitted in her deposition a prospective client first had to be sold on the concept of credit insurance before an agent could attempt to sell a policy, and that 65 to 75 percent of policyholders renew.

Further, ACI took reasonable steps to insure the secrecy of this information as required by the UTSA. Sacks stipulated in the Wixom action that certain confidential information consisting of the subpoenaed log books with leads from August 1983 forward would be subject to a protective order. Also, ACI required its employees to sign confidentiality agreements respecting its client list, expiration date of policies, lists of business leads, claims histories, and related client information. Thus, under the UTSA, the ACI customer list constitutes a trade secret.

Identical result under pre-UTSA case law

California courts protected retail delivery routes of customers as against a former employee for many years before enactment of the UTSA.

This protection expanded to include customer lists of other types of businesses. (E.g., *Scavengers P. Assn. v. Serv-U-Garbage Co.* (1933) 218 Cal. 568 [24 P.2d 489] [the salvage business]; *Cal. Intelligence Bureau v. Cunningham* (1948) 83 Cal. App. 2d 197 [188 P.2d 303] [the unique service of investigating charities to protect subscribers from fraudulent or unworthy solicitation]; *Klamath-Orleans Lumber, Inc. v. Miller* (1978) 87 Cal. App. 3d 45 [151 Cal. Rptr. 1188 [the manufacture of load binders].)

In *State Farm Mut. etc. Ins. Co. v. Dempster* (1959) 174 Cal. App. 2d 418 [344 P.2d 821], customer information nearly identical to that found here received protection. There, an insurance company sought to enjoin its former agents from interfering with policyholders the agents had serviced. The former agents had contacted policyholders at automobile insurance renewal time and had advised them not to renew with State Farm.

State Farm asserted trade secret status as to various information including " 'the names, addresses and telephone numbers of policyholders, the amounts and types of insurance ..., due dates of premiums and amounts thereof, ..., and particularly the renewal and expiration dates of policies in force.' " (*State Farm Mut. etc. Ins. Co. v. Dempster, supra*, 174 Cal. App. 2d at p. 422.)

The *State Farm* court found "the very recital of the nature of the information acquired by the salesman and the unique interest of the company in the information, places it in the category of the trade secret ...." (*State Farm Mut. etc. Ins. Co., supra*, 174 Cal. App. 2d at p. 426.)

We perceive no substantial difference between the information at issue in *State Farm* and this case. In fact, the list of ACI policyholders constitutes a more elite compilation than the automobile policyholders involved in *State Farm* and therefore is more deserving of protection.

Under either the UTSA or at common law, the ACI customer list is a trade secret.

Sacks contends her conduct merely invited business inquiry by announcing new business affiliation and that this activity is not prohibited by the UTSA definition of misappropriation because such conduct falls within the common law right to compete fairly. The UTSA defines misappropriation as: "(1) Acquisition of a trade secret of another by a person who knows or has reason to know that the trade secret was acquired by improper means; or (2) Disclosure or use of a trade secret of another without express or implied consent by a person who: (A) Used improper means to acquire knowledge of the trade secret; or (B) At the time of disclosure or use, knew or had reason to know that his or her knowledge of the trade secret was: (i) Derived from or through a person who had utilized improper means to acquire it; (ii) Acquired under circumstances giving rise to a duty to maintain its secrecy or limit its use; or (iii) Derived from or through a person who owed a duty to the person seeking relief to maintain its secrecy or limit its use; ...." (Civ. Code, § 3426.1, subd. (b).)

The portion of the definition which applies here proscribes "disclosure or use" of a trade secret, without express or implied consent, by a person who acquired knowledge of the trade secret under circumstances giving rise to a duty to maintain its secrecy or limit its use. Clearly, in the broadest construction of this definition, Sacks's letter to ACI policyholders constituted a "use" of the ACI customer list.

Restated in the terms of the UTSA definition of misappropriation, Sacks contends the UTSA cannot so limit the use of the ACI customer list as to usurp her right to announce a new business affiliation. We conclude the common law right to compete fairly and the right to announce a new business affiliation have survived enactment of the UTSA. However, Sacks's March 7 letter went beyond an appropriate professional announcement and constituted a solicitation of the ACI customer list.

A seminal and frequently quoted case in this area is *Avocado Sales Co. v. Wyse* (1932) 122 Cal. App. 627 [10 P.2d 485]. There, an avocado salesman could not be enjoined from "canvassing and soliciting" (*id.*, at p. 628) the fruit stands, markets, cafes and hotels he had called upon on behalf of his former employer because a list of retail avocado sellers could not be viewed as confidential. The court asked: "Could not any [avocado] salesman see at a glance where to attempt to sell his wares?" (*Id.*, at p. 634.) That is, in the absence of any secret, there could be no trade secret.

Similarly, our Supreme Court has declined to protect the customers of a floor wax manufacturer or a janitorial service because "the names and addresses of persons, firms and corporations using the type of products sold by plaintiff are commonly known to the trade, and ... they are called upon by salesmen for various companies." (*Continental Car-Na-Var Corp. v. Moseley*, (1944) 24 Cal. 2d 104, 108-109 [148 P.2d 9].)

Obviously, in the absence of a protectable trade secret, the right to compete fairly outweighs the employer's right to protect clients against competition from former employees. Also, even when a trade secret customer list exists, the common law cases acknowledged a right to announce a new affiliation as contrasted with a solicitation for patronage.

At common law, the boundary separating fair and unfair competition in the context of a protected customer list has been drawn at the distinction between an announcement and a solicitation. [T]he [Supreme] court observed that "[m]erely informing customers of one's former employer of a change of employment, without more, is not solicitation."

[T]he right to announce a new affiliation, even to trade secret clients of a former employer, is basic to an individual's right to engage in fair competition. Therefore, the acquisition of trade secrets under circumstances giving rise to a duty to limit their use, as is the case here, clearly allows for such an announcement. To hold otherwise unnecessarily would contravene widely accepted and well-established business practices.

Sacks claims the March 7 letter merely announced a change of employment. Although the letter begins as an announcement of her departure from ACI and affiliation with F&D, it soon assumes a different tone. Sacks informs ACI's customers of the interesting competitive alternative F&D offers as compared to ACI's policies. She invites their inquiry about the F&D policy and indicates she would be happy to discuss it in detail when they are ready to renew. She personally petitions, importunes and entreats ACI's customers to call her at any time for information about the better policies F&D can provide and for assistance during the agent transition period.

Sacks is endeavoring to obtain their business. Sacks, in a word, solicited. Therefore, as a matter of law, Sacks's letter of March 7, 1988, constituted a solicitation.

Money damages inadequate

Determination of the solicitation issue in favor of ACI does not necessitate the further conclusion the trial court should have issued the preliminary injunction, especially after Sacks already had mailed the letter. However, we conclude Sacks's conduct, considered in the aggregate, merited such judicial intervention.

The UTSA provides that "actual or threatened misappropriation may be enjoined." (Civ. Code, § 3426.2, subd. (a).) Given the aggressive manner in which Sacks chose to terminate her employment, ACI likely will sustain continuing interim harm in the absence of an injunction. Further, based on our ruling that ACI's customer list is a trade secret, and that Sacks's letter amounted to a solicitation, ACI is likely to prevail on the merits at trial.

Therefore, the matter is remanded to the trial court to enable it to form injunctive relief consistent with the views expressed herein.

NOTES

1. *Contract, Property, Tort.* Trade secrets are an interesting legal hybrid, as the preceding case makes clear. They are, as the court states, a property right; in the preceding case, Sacks was found to infringe that right, which properly belonged to her ex-employer, ACI. But the solicitation also has elements of a breach of contract; the "wrong" of soliciting was a wrong precisely because of the (contractual) employment relationship between Sacks and ACI. Finally, notice the tort element: the solicitation was a violation of Sacks' duty of care to her employer. These elements are each developed in various cases that follow.

2. *Inventions as Trade Secrets.* The definition of "trade secret" in the UTSA is "information, including a formula, pattern, compilation, program, device, method, technique, or process ...." Obviously, this includes much more than a customer list, as in the preceding case. As we shall see, the misappropriation of an ex-employer's technical information or even invention is also covered by the UTSA. How does this broad definition of trade secret compare with the definition of patentable subject matter in § 101 of the Patent Act?

3. *Proprietary Data Is a Trade Secret.* The Supreme Court has held that an applicant for registration of pesticides has a trade secret property interest in its health, safety, and environmental data which is protected by the "takings" clause of the Fifth Amendment of the Constitution. *Ruckelshaus v. Monsanto Co.*, 467 U.S. 986 (1984). The intangible nature of the right does not preclude a finding that there has been a taking. *Id.*, at 987. *See generally* Comment, *The Taking of Trade Secrets: What Constitutes Just Compensation?*, 48 U. PITT. L. REV. 247 (1986). Further evidence that trade secrets are a property right is found in the fact that they are regularly licensed. *See, e.g.*, Jager & Anderson, *Trade Secret Licensing*, in TECHNOLOGY LICENSING 1989 (Practicing Law Institute Publication 265 PLI/Pat. 211 1989); MacDonald, *Know-How Licensing and the Antitrust Laws*, 62 MICH. L. REV. 351 (1964). For a discussion of the expansive definition given to the concept of "trade secrets" in recent years, and a proposal to restrict it somewhat, see Note, *Inevitable Disclosure Trade Secret Disputes: Dissolutions of Concurrent Property Interests*, 40 STAN. L. REV. 519 (1988). In a related vein, one interesting comment calls for pre-identification of trade secrets prior to commencement of employment. Comment, *The Specifically-Defined Trade Secret: An Approach to Protection*, 27 SANTA CLARA L. REV. 537 (1987). *See also* Robinson, *The Confidence Game: An Approach to the Law About Trade Secrets*, 25 ARIZ. L. REV. 347 (1984); Weisner & Cava, *Stealing Trade Secrets Ethically*, 47 MD. L. REV. 1076 (1988).

4. *Trade Secrets and Employee Mobility.* Frequently, allegations of misappropriation of trade secrets follow when an employee leaves to compete with an ex-employer, as in the preceding case. This brings into tension the policies behind intellectual property law (i.e., investment protection) and employment law (i.e., employee mobility). One court, commenting on the difficulties that arise when a former employee is enjoined from using information about customers of the former employer, put it thus:

> [S]uch information comprises general skills and knowledge acquired in the course of employment. Those are things an employee is free to take and to use in later pursuits, especially if they do not take the form of written records, compilations or analyses. Any other rule would force a departing employee to perform a prefrontal lobotomy on himself or herself. It would disserve the free market goal of maximizing available resources to foster competition.... [I]t would not strike a proper balance between the purposes of trade secrets law and the strong policy in favor of fair and vigorous business competition. All this does not render helpless an employer worried that the skills and knowledge an employee acquires during the course of employment will give him or her an undue competitive advantage. Nothing prevents such an employer from guarding its interests by a restrictive covenant. But it would really be unfair competition to allow the employer without such a covenant to obtain trade secret status for the fruits of ordinary experience in the business, thus compelling former employees to reinvent the wheel as the price for entering the competitive market.

Fleming Sales Co. v. Bailey, 611 F. Supp. 507, 514-15 (N.D. Ill. 1985). *See also Colson Co. v. Wittel*, 569 N.E.2d 1082, 210 Ill. App. 3d 1030, 155 Ill. Dec. 471 (Ill. Ct. App.), *appeal denied*, 580 N.E.2d 110 (Table) (Sup. Ct. Ill. 1991) (pre-employment nondisclosure/noncompete agreement necessary to restrict employee's use of customer lists developed during employment).

5. *Importance of Pre-Employment Agreements.* As the *Fleming Sales* case described in note 4 indicates, obtaining agreements not to disclose trade secrets and/or not to compete with the employer for a reasonable period of time after leaving are important contractual devices for limiting the deleterious effects of employee mobility. Note that generally the consideration requirement in contract law makes it advisable to execute these agreements just prior to commencement of employment.

California prohibits restrictive covenants by statute. *See* CAL. BUS. & PROF. CODE §§ 16600 (West 1984). The Ninth Circuit has construed section 16600 to provide that "the employer will be able to restrain by contract only that conduct of the former employee that would have been subject to judicial restraint under the law of unfair competition, absent the contract." *Hollingsworth Solderless Terminal Co. v. Turley*, 622 F.2d 1324, 1338 (9th Cir. 1980) (citation omitted). In California, a former employee commits the tort of unfair competition when he uses in competition against his former employer "trade or business secrets or confidential information, or the like, not readily accessible to others." *Id.* at 1330. "The fundamental test is whether ... the knowledge gained by an employee is secret and confidential." *Id.* at 1331. *See Cambridge Filter Corp. v. International Filter Co.*, 548 F. Supp. 1301, 1305 (D. Nev. 1982) (applying California law; § 16600 allows restrictive covenants to protect against disclosure of trade secrets "if the former employee reveals or uses confidential information so that his sales activities constitute unfair competition," so "[t]herefore, the covenants not to compete and concerning trade secrets contained in the employment agreement are not illegal per se.").

6. *Recent Developments.* In a string of recent cases, courts have held that certain information acquired in the course of employment was protectable as a trade secret despite the fact that it is very difficult to disentangle this "information" from the general skills and knowledge the employee built up during employment. *See, e.g.*, *Pepsico, Inc. v. Redmond*, 54 F.3d 1262 (7th Cir. 1995) (general merchandising strategies protectable). *See also* Note, Johanna L. Edelstein, *Intellectual Slavery? The Doctrine of Inevitable Disclosure of Trade Secrets*, 26 GOLDEN GATE U. L. REV. 717 (1996).

2. "... NOT READILY ASCERTAINABLE BY PROPER MEANS...."

S.O.S., INC. v. PAYDAY, INC.

886 F.2d 1081, 12 U.S.P.Q.2d (BNA) 1241 (9th Cir. 1989)

This appeal from grants of summary judgment turns on the interpretation of a computer software agreement and presents issues of copyright law as well as pendent state law claims arising under trade secret, contract, and tort law. We affirm in part, reverse in part, and remand.

S.O.S., Inc. specializes in furnishing computer hardware and software to companies that process payrolls, ledgers, and accounts receivable. Payday, Inc. is a company which provides payroll and financial services to the entertainment industry.

In October 1978, S.O.S. acquired from Hagen Systems (not a party to this action) a non-exclusive license to unpublished business software called "Brown Tank." Under the license, S.O.S. could sublicense Brown Tank to end users provided Hagen Systems' proprietary and confidential rights in the software were protected. S.O.S. also had the right to prepare derivative works [i.e., modifications] based on Brown Tank.

In November or December 1983, Payday's outside accountant, Mike Waldrip, told S.O.S.'s president, Bob Oliver, that Payday wanted to computerize in order to attract an important client. The initial understanding between Oliver and Waldrip was that Payday would use software furnished by S.O.S. on Waldrip's computer instead of installing a computer in its own office.

On December 14, 1983, Oliver sent Payday a draft contract, which [included] a software agreement.

The software agreement provides, in full:

> A software agreement covering the software outlined in the documentation furnished PAYDAY by SOS. The total purchase price of this software is $5,325 including sales tax. SOS agrees to modify the system to produce a text file capable of transfer in ASCII string code to magnetic tape at 800BPI for transfer of information to EDP (Service Bureau). *This series of programs is the property of SOS, and PAYDAY is acquiring the right of use, SOS retains all rights of ownership.* The payment schedule covering the software is $1,325 upon execution of this agreement and $1,000 on the 14th day of each month until a total of $5,325 has been paid. Changes and modifications other than those mentioned above, will be on a time and material basis at the rate of $50 per hour.

(Emphasis added.)

The contract does not use the terms "copyright" or "trade secrets." The parties did not discuss the meaning of the highlighted language referring to rights of "ownership" and "use."

Most of the programming of the payroll software was done by two employees of S.O.S., Eiichi Koyama and Bacchus Chu. Two hundred thirty-six separate programs comprise the total package prepared for Payday. Of these, approximately 89 were derived or adapted from Brown Tank. Payday's controller, Sharon Goodman, was the liaison to the programming team. She described Payday's needs to S.O.S. but did not participate in the coding process.

The system (software and hardware) that S.O.S. provided was adequate for Payday's new client but not for Payday's entire business. In March 1984, S.O.S. and Payday modified portions of the contract. Under the modified agreement, Payday was to use S.O.S.'s computer for a monthly fee of $1,500; also, Payday agreed to pay monthly an additional $1,500 against accumulated programming charges. S.O.S. continued developing programs for Payday.

In late February 1985, Chu and Koyama left S.O.S. to form an independent consulting service, but continued to render services for S.O.S. They continued to work on modifications to the payroll programs, for which they billed S.O.S. $28.00 an hour. They were also entrusted with systems backup, the routine copying of S.O.S.'s programs to protect against accidental loss. In April 1985, Chu and Koyama proposed to Goodman that Payday purchase an in-house computer system equipped with a broad array of software to provide financial services to the entertainment industry. Payday would make this software available to its customers on a timesharing basis. Chu and Koyama would perform programming services for Payday directly, at less than the $50.00 an hour Payday was currently paying S.O.S. for these services.

Notes taken by Goodman indicate concern over the cost of securing a copy of the payroll programs. She noted that Chu and Koyama could "make [a] copy and put [it] somewhere." Chu and Koyama told her they could change the programs 20%, and that this would make them new programs, no longer the property of

S.O.S. They planned to copy the payroll programs into Payday's computer and then convert them into a different computer language called "BITS BASIC." Payday intended to send a letter to S.O.S. in July 1985, telling S.O.S. that Payday needed a copy of the payroll programs, but this letter was never sent. Instead, Payday solicited a competing bid from S.O.S. to provide an in-house computer system.

Chu and Koyama met with Oliver on July 6, 1985. They told Oliver that Payday would pay its account balance with S.O.S. if S.O.S. would give Payday an unprotected copy of the payroll programs. Oliver rejected this proposal.

On July 7, 1985, Koyama went to the S.O.S. office and made at least one copy of the payroll software, which he gave to Payday. Oliver began monitoring S.O.S.'s computers for unauthorized entry, and changed the passwords. A day or two later, Chu or Koyama made an unauthorized entry into S.O.S.'s computer system by circumventing the password program.

Payday installed its new computer on July 14, 1985. The next day, Chu and Koyama put into Payday's computer the payroll software and various other programs taken from S.O.S.'s computer. During the next few days, Chu and Koyama converted the payroll programs from their original language into a format called "ASCII," which was in turn translated into the BITS BASIC computer language.

S.O.S. sued for infringement of copyright and pendent state law claims for breach of contract, misappropriation of trade secrets, and account stated. Payday counterclaimed under various state law theories. The district court granted summary judgment in favor of Payday on S.O.S.'s copyright infringement, breach of contract, and misappropriation claims, and in favor of S.O.S. on its account stated claim and on Payday's counterclaims.

Trade Secrets

S.O.S. appeals the district court's grant of summary judgment in favor of Payday on S.O.S.'s trade secrets count under the Uniform Trade Secrets Act, Cal. Civ. Code §§ 3426 et seq. The facts S.O.S. alleges are essentially the same as in its copyright count, with particular reliance on the way in which Payday obtained its copy of the software. S.O.S. has produced evidence that Payday requested a copy of the software from S.O.S., which S.O.S. refused to provide unless Payday agreed to pay for modifications to block access to the source code, and that Payday responded with self-help, obtaining a copy through Chu and Koyama, who had acquired a copy from the S.O.S. computer.

[From footnote:] Section 3426.1(b) provides:

"Misappropriation" means:

(1) Acquisition of a trade secret of another by a person who knows or has reason to know that the trade secret was acquired by improper means ...

Section 3426.1(a) provides:

"Improper means" includes ... breach or inducement of a breach of a duty to maintain secrecy, or espionage through electronic or other means. Reverse engineering or independent derivation alone shall not be considered improper means."

The district court relied on its copyright license analysis to reject S.O.S.'s claim:

> As a licensee, PAYDAY has the contractual right to use the computer software, and to copy its content for its own purposes. PAYDAY cannot be held liable for misappropriation of trade secrets because it has a license to use the computer software free from contractual limitations or restrictions. A licensee of a trade secret is not an infringer.

The district court should have focused on how Payday acquired its copy. There is a genuine issue of fact as to whether the contract gave Payday a right to possess only a protected copy of the software if it elected to process its customers' work on its own computer, or whether Payday was entitled to possess an unprotected copy.

The district court relied on *Aktiebolaget Bofors v. United States*, 194 F.2d 145, 148 (D.C. Cir. 1951), to support its conclusion that a licensee of a trade secret cannot be an infringer. That case, however, holds only that one who lawfully acquires a trade secret, not just tangible property based on a trade secret, can use that trade secret in any manner not otherwise prohibited by contract or other body of law. It is precisely the lawfulness of Payday's acquisition of the trade secret, in the form of the unprotected source code, that is at issue here.

Summary judgment in favor of Payday on this issue was error. S.O.S. has produced evidence rendering the contract susceptible to the interpretation that Payday did not have the right to possess an unprotected copy of the program. S.O.S. also presented evidence sufficient to create genuine issues of material fact as to whether Payday knew or had reason to know that the source code was acquired by improper means, and whether the source code was subject to reasonable efforts by S.O.S. to maintain its secrecy.

We reverse the district court's grant of summary judgment in favor of Payday on the issue of copyright infringement, and remand for further proceedings consistent with this opinion. We also reverse and remand on S.O.S.'s breach of contract and trade secrets counts.

NOTES

1. Is reverse engineering a proper means of obtaining access to what otherwise would be a trade secret? *See Acuson Corp. v. Aloka Co.*, below.

2. *High-Flying Trade Secrets?* A famous case involving the use of "improper means" to discover a trade secret is *E.I. DuPont de Nemours & Co. v. Christopher*, 431 F.2d 1012, 166 U.S.P.Q. (BNA) 421, 167 U.S.P.Q. (BNA) 1 (5th Cir. 1970), *cert. denied*, 400 U.S. 1024 (1971). The Christophers had been caught taking aerial photos of DuPont's new methanol production plant. They defended against DuPont's trade secret misappropriation claim on the ground that

it was not illegal to overfly the area. The Fifth Circuit held that under Texas law this activity was an improper means of discovering the trade secret, despite the fact that it did not by itself violate any law:

> In the instant case the Christophers deliberately flew over the DuPont plant to get pictures of a process which DuPont had attempted to keep secret. The Christophers delivered their pictures to a third party who was certainly aware of the means by which they had been acquired and who may be planning to use the information contained therein to manufacture methanol by the DuPont process. The third party has a right to use this process only if he obtains this knowledge through his own research efforts, but thus far all information indicates that the third party has gained this knowledge solely by taking it from DuPont at a time when DuPont was making reasonable efforts to preserve its secrecy. In such a situation DuPont has a valid cause of action to prohibit the Christophers from improperly discovering its trade secret and to prohibit the undisclosed third party from using the improperly obtained information.

431 F.2d 1012, 1016. Regarding the topic of the next section, reasonable precautions, the court stated: "Reasonable precautions against predatory eyes we may require, but an impenetrable fortress is an unreasonable requirement." 431 F.2d at 1017. *Cf. Procter & Gamble Co. v. Nabisco Brands, Inc.*, 111 F.R.D. 326, 229 U.S.P.Q. (BNA) 689 (D. Del. 1986) (defendant in the course of a patent infringement suit over "soft cookies" sought to identify as proprietary some secret photographs of plaintiff's manufacturing facilities and internal memoranda containing information from industrial espionage informants; plaintiff requested the photographs during the course of discovery; court rejected defendant's contention that the photos, or the fact that they were taken, constituted trade secrets, and ordered that they be turned over). *See generally* Note, *Trade Secrets in Discovery: From First Amendment Disclosure to Fifth Amendment Protection*, 104 HARV. L. REV. 1330 (1991).

3. *Prior Disclosure as a Defense.* The flip side of information "not readily available by proper means" is information which has been disclosed. When information is "derived wholly from public sources," an action for breach of confidence or misappropriation cannot be maintained. *Lehman v. Dow Jones & Co.*, 606 F. Supp. 1152, 1160-61 (S.D.N.Y. 1985). *See also Miller v. Owens-Illinois, Inc.*, 187 U.S.P.Q. (BNA) 47, 48 (D. Md. 1975) (holding that compensation is not warranted if the accused misappropriator had prior knowledge of facts before they were disclosed to him in confidence). *Kewanee Oil Co. v. Bicron Corp.*, 416 U.S. 470, 476 (1974) stated the same theme:

> Novelty, in the patent law sense, is not required for a trade secret.... However, some novelty will be required if merely because that which does not possess novelty is usually known; secrecy, in the context of trade secrets, thus implies at least minimal novelty.

See also Roboserve, Ltd. v. Tom's Foods, Inc., 940 F.2d 1441, 20 U.S.P.Q.2d (BNA) 1321 (11th Cir. 1991) (Georgia law of trade secrets could not protect unpatented part or combination of parts in vending machine after machine was sold, since seller of machine could not demonstrate that access to alleged trade secret has been strictly limited; thus sale destroyed any reasonable expectation of secrecy by placing machines in public domain); *Sheridan v. Mallinckrodt, Inc.*, 568 F. Supp. 1347, 1352 (N.D.N.Y. 1953).

4. *Is Large-Scale Licensing Disclosure?* An interesting case pushing the limits of trade secrecy is *Data General Corp. v. Digital Computer Controls, Inc.*, 357 A.2d 105 (Del. Ch. 1975). That case involved 6,000 copies of a manual that had been distributed, but the measures taken to preserve confidentiality were significant. The court held that the large-scale distribution of the manual under fairly stringent nondisclosure terms did not constitute prior disclosure insulating defendant from a trade secret suit.

The limits of this logic may be seen in the "package licenses" often accompanying mass-marketed software. As you may have read yourself, the "licensor" of software puts a notice on the outside of the package setting forth "conditions of use." Among these is often a prohibition on reverse engineering of the software. Would this very large-scale licensing qualify as a public disclosure of the information? Would the restrictions accompanying this very widescale prohibition be seen as "reasonable means" to maintain secrecy under the circumstances? *See, e.g., Kemp, Mass Marketed Software: The Legality of the Form License Agreement*, 48 LA. L. REV. 87 (1987); Note, *The Enforceability of State "Shrink-Wrap" License Statutes in Light of Vault Corp. v. Quaid Software, Ltd.*, 74 CORNELL L. REV. 222 (1988). The latter note refers to an important preemption case in which a federal court invalidated a Louisiana state statute expressly authorizing enforcement of "package licenses." See Section B of this chapter, below.

5. *Idea Submissions.* Do "improper means" include taking an idea submitted by an outsider? There are a host of cases on this topic, which involves elements of contract law (specifically restitution or implied in fact contract) as well as trade secrets. *See generally* Kent, The Protection of Idea Submissions, 203 N.Y. L.J. 3, col. 1 (May 25, 1990); Note, *Agreements With Authors Regarding Idea Submissions Should Be Specific*, 4 LOY. ENTERTAINMENT L.J. 183 (1984). *Cf. Werlin v. Readers' Digest Ass'n*, 528 F. Supp. 451 (S.D.N.Y. 1981); *Desny v. Wilder*, 46 Cal. 2d 715, 739, 299 P.2d 257 (1956).

A recent case proves that not only the "little person" has ideas taken by large organizations. *See Contracts: Liability For Use of Buchwald Movie Idea Does Not Require Substantial Similarity*, 39 PAT. TRADEMARK & COPYRIGHT J. (BNA) 205 (Jan. 18, 1990) (describing *Buchwald v. Paramount Pictures Corp.*, Calif. Super. Ct., No. C 706083 (Jan. 8, 1990), where contract to compensate humorist Art Buchwald in exchange for the right to make a movie "based upon" his story idea was held not to require that the resulting movie be substantially similar to the story idea; holding Paramount Pictures Corp. liable for breaching its "idea submission" contract with Buchwald in connection with its movie *Coming to America*).

Note the presence of a contract in *Buchwald*; in general, courts have held that one submitting an idea does not have a property right in the idea *unless* she can establish that the disclosed idea or information was: (1) disclosed to the defendant in a confidential relationship; (2) novel or original; and (3) actually used or adopted by defendant. *Noble v. Columbia Broadcasting Sys.*, 270 F.2d 938 (D.C. Cir. 1959); *Thermo Trim, Inc. v. Mobil Oil Corp.*, 194 U.S.P.Q. 450, 455 (W.D.N.Y. 1977). Implicit in the finding that an idea is disclosed in a confidential relationship is that it would not be used without compensation. *Perry v. Apex Smelting Co.*, 173 U.S.P.Q. 826 (N.D. Ohio 1972), *modified*, 477 F.2d 137 (6th Cir. 1973). *See also Whitfield v. Lear*, 751 F.2d 90, 92 (2d Cir. 1984) (applying California law) ("[I]f a producer accepts a submitted idea with full knowledge that the offeror expects payment in the event of use, California courts impose liability under a theory of implied-in-fact contract"). *Cf. Desny v. Wilder*, 46 Cal. 2d 715, 299 P.2d 257, 270 (1956) ("The idea man who blurts out his idea without having first made his bargain has no one but himself to blame for the loss of his bargaining power.")

Some idea submission cases contain an element of employee mobility, as in *S.O.S.* above. *See, e.g., Ralph Andrews Prods., Inc. v. Paramount Pictures Corp.*, 222 Cal. App. 3d 676, 271 Cal. Rptr. 797 (Cal. Ct. App. 1990) (reversing trial court holding that defendant was insulated from misappropriation liability by lack of knowledge that person submitting idea for game show called "Anything for Money" had an employment/agency relationship with plaintiff; facts show that defendant may have been chargeable with constructive knowledge of this relationship).

6. Transaction Costs and Idea Submissions. Because of the possibility that an unrelated product modification or introduction, or unrelated movie or the like, will appear after a similar idea has been submitted, it has become common practice for companies to return such letters with a form letter. The form usually states that the sender must acknowledge that she will be satisfied with whatever compensation, if any, the company deems appropriate for the idea, and that she will not be able to file a suit for theft of the idea. *See* 1 R. MILGRIM, TRADE SECRETS § 8.03[2] (1988); *Davis v. General Foods Corp.*, 21 F. Supp. 445 (S.D.N.Y. 1937) (plaintiff's unsolicited recipe returned with form letter).

Obviously, many idea submitters will not like the possibility of going uncompensated for their trouble. As a consequence, many an idea will die in the files of creative people. Recall that one rationale for the patent system, which applied also to trade secrets, is "Arrow's Disclosure Paradox" (named for economist Kenneth Arrow): that information can be valued only after disclosure to another party, but then its value is lost because the other party already has it. As we have seen, this is one way patents encourage transactions: by protecting the invention against unauthorized use, a patent gives an inventor confidence to approach a potential licensee without fear that the idea will be stolen.

Of course, as the idea submission cases show, there is a flip side to this. The patent gives a certain amount of protection to the potential licensee as well. It defines precisely what the invention is, thus making it clear which embodiments will constitute an infringement. Contrast this with the idea submission cases where the "idea" is often only vaguely specified. This creates the fear that an unrelated but perhaps roughly similar product introduction, film, etc., will be labeled as a "theft" of the idea. If the idea could be specified in more detail, and the contract governing the relationship could be drawn so as to precisely describe what will and will not constitute "infringement" of the idea, perhaps more of these transactions would take place. On the other hand, if the costs of negotiating these contracts was higher than the expected value of the gain from trading the idea, parties might not bother with them. Perhaps the answer then is to have the legislature — either Congress or the states — draft the contract instead. Pass a statute, in other words, regulating these cases. This might encourage more such transactions. Note incidentally that on one view, a "transactions-oriented" view, the patent law is an elaborate version of such a pre-written (i.e., legislated) "contract."

The Writer's Guild, an organization of entertainment industry writers, has already taken a step along the road to reducing transaction costs in this regard. The Guild runs a "submission registry," to which submitters send a copy of their script, idea, etc. Then if a dispute breaks out later, the registry serves as good evidence of the existence and date of the idea. *See* J. Horowitz, *Whose Idea Is It, Anyway?*, N.Y. TIMES, Mar. 15, 1992, sec. 2, at 1, col. 1-4.

3. "... SUBJECT OF REASONABLE EFFORTS TO MAINTAIN SECRECY...."

SHEETS v. YAMAHA MOTORS CORP., U.S.A.

849 F.2d 179, 7 U.S.P.Q.2d (BNA) 1461 (5th Cir. 1988)

Appellant, Wilbert J. Sheets, appeals the district court's dismissal of his lawsuit which asserted causes of action against appellees under the Louisiana Uniform Trade Secrets Act and the equitable doctrine of unjust enrichment. We affirm the dismissal.

Wilbert J. Sheets is a 66 year old resident of Gonzales, Louisiana. He retired in 1973 from his job as a machinist at Exxon. His two sons, Wayne and Tommy, opened a motorcycle dealership in 1974 in Gonzales called Cycle Country U.S.A. Cycle Country became a Yamaha dealership in March 1976. Wayne and Tommy were the sole partners in the dealership; Wayne handled sales and Tommy handled maintenance and repairs. Wilbert worked with his sons at Cycle Country, helping with maintenance and acting as a mechanic and troubleshooter. Wilbert, however, was not a salaried employee of Cycle Country and did not receive any compensation for the services he provided the dealership.

In December 1979, Cycle Country received an initial shipment of two model number 125 Yamaha tri-motorcycles. This was the first tri-motorcycle manufactured by Yamaha. Its intended purposes included recreational use in water, mud, dust, snow, and other elements. It was advertised as being an "all-terrain vehicle" suitable for hunting, fishing, farming, professional racing, "swampratting," and desert and mountain travel. Cycle Country sold one of these tri-motorcycles to a customer and used the other as a demonstrator.

In February 1980, Cycle Country received a shipment of 50 additional model 125's. Members of the Sheets family bought a number of these tri-motorcycles and raced them. Tommy, Wayne, and Wilbert all personally experienced problems with the engine stalling or drowning on the 125. Cycle Country received similar complaints from other customers to whom the dealership had sold 125's. Similar complaints were also being received by other Yamaha dealers in the area. Evidently the placement of the air intake system at the back of the machine between the two rear wheels allowed water, dust, and other foreign matter to be drawn into the carburetor, causing the vehicle to stall or drown out. The debris was also causing premature wearing of internal engine parts. Tommy and Wayne asked their father to see if he could fix this problem with the 125's engine.

In March 1980, Wilbert Sheets modified the engine of Cycle Country's demonstrator model by running an air hose from the air intake box between the rear wheels to the front of the tri-motorcycle under the seat. The hose acted as a snorkel for the air intake system, bringing in air from the front of the vehicle at a higher level than before. Wilbert plugged up the air intake pipe located within the air intake box. Wilbert also experimented with different sizes of fuel jets to find the size effective with the air box improvements in ensuring the proper air/fuel mixture. Overall, Wilbert Sheets claims these modifications effectively solved the stalling problems and enabled the tri-motorcycle to perform as advertised.

With the exception of the fuel jet modification, the entire device could be seen either by removing the seat of the tri-motorcycle, which did not require tools, or by turning the machine on its side. Customers of Cycle Country were permitted to drive the modified demonstrator model. Appellant also modified a number of the tri-motorcycles owned by friends and relatives who belonged to the Cycle Country tri-motorcycle racing team. Neither Cycle Country nor appellant, however, sold a tri-motorcycle with the air snorkel device, nor did appellant ever sell an air snorkel device. Wilbert Sheets continued to fine tune his modification on the tri-motorcycles owned by family and friends over the next few months.

Appellant claims to have told those individuals not to make his invention known to others. He claims he felt these people would not divulge his invention because by doing so they would lose their competitive edge in racing. Neither Tommy nor Wayne nor Wilbert, however, placed any restrictions upon the resale of these modified tri-motorcycles. Some of the modified tri-motorcycles were in fact resold the following year.

In mid-March 1980, Wayne Sheets showed and explained the air snorkel device to Bob Aaron, a Yamaha U.S.A. district sales manager, during Aaron's regular bimonthly visit to Cycle Country. Apparently Wayne Sheets did not show Aaron the entire modification but did tell him that his father had devised a modification to the engine which would solve the problems the machine was experiencing. Appellant claims Aaron returned two weeks later with two Yamaha representatives from Japan who examined and photographed the modified tri-motorcycle. Appellant claims he arrived at Cycle Country just as Aaron and the Yamaha representatives were leaving and remembers one of the representatives holding a camera. Aaron did not make out a dealer report documenting this second visit to Cycle Country, contrary to his usual habit. At trial he denied remembering this second visit and the names of the two Yamaha representatives. Tommy and Wayne Sheets had been present during this visit and their testimony supported their father's claims.

Two weeks later, appellant claims Aaron returned to Cycle Country with two more representatives from Yamaha. Only Wayne Sheets was present at the shop during this visit, and he did not recall if anyone had photographed or examined the modified tri-motorcycle during this visit. Again, no dealer report was made of this visit by Aaron.

Aaron visited the shop again in August 1980 and, according to Tommy Sheets, asked Tommy to bring a modified tri-motorcycle to a Yamaha service seminar in New Orleans later in the month. Tommy complied with this request. This seminar was limited to Yamaha employees and dealers. Wilbert Sheets' modification evidently was discussed at the seminar as a solution to the shifting and drowning problems the 125 was experiencing.

In April 1981, Tommy and Wayne Sheets sold their interests in Cycle Country, including the modified demonstrator, to a third party, and entered into a release with Yamaha U.S.A. Wilbert Sheets was not a party to this release.

In November 1981, Wilbert Sheets saw a Yamaha advertisement in Outdoor Life magazine, publicizing the company's new tri-motorcycle model number 175 which contained an air intake device very similar to his modification on the 125. Wilbert Sheets immediately sought legal advice and eventually filed suit in federal district court against Yamaha Motors Corp., U.S.A. on October 5, 1982. His suit claimed damages for the alleged advantages and benefits realized by Yamaha as a result of Yamaha's alleged misappropriation of his invention and its incorporation by Yamaha into the model 175 tri-motorcycle. His claims were based in part upon the Louisiana Uniform Trade Secrets Act for misappropriation of a trade secret and upon unjust enrichment principles in Louisiana law.

On March 21, 1983, Wilbert Sheets applied for a United States patent on his air intake device. After abandonment of this patent application, Wilbert Sheets filed a second patent application on February 19, 1985. His patent counsel was notified on June 11, 1985, by the United States Patent and Trademark Office that most of his claims were unpatentable because of a previous patent issued on January 29, 1985, to Ko Tanaka of Shizuoka, Japan, and assigned to Yamaha Japan.

Trial on the merits of appellant's suit against Yamaha U.S.A. and Yamaha Japan was held before the district court without a jury on August 25 and 26 and

December 29, 1986. Following the presentation of appellant's case, appellees moved for involuntary dismissal under Fed. R. Civ. P. 41(b). On April 3, 1987, the district count dismissed the entire case under Rule 41(b) after finding that Wilbert Sheets had failed adequately to maintain the secrecy of his invention and thus could not recover under the Trade Secrets Act or for unjust enrichment. The court, however, awarded Wilbert Sheets sanctions under Fed. R. Civ. P. 11 and 37 of $25,000 against Yamaha U.S.A. and Yamaha Japan for failure of the Yamaha firms to carry out pretrial discovery in good faith and for needlessly increasing the costs of the litigation.

Appellant appeals the district court's finding that he failed to make reasonable efforts to maintain the secrecy of his invention as required under the Trade Secrets Act and the court's finding that he had no cause of action for unjust enrichment.

In this diversity jurisdiction lawsuit, we look to the law of the state of Louisiana to determine the substantive rights of the parties under both of appellant's claims. As to the trade secrets claim, Louisiana has adopted a version of the Uniform Trade Secrets Act, La. Rev. Stat. Ann. § 51:1431 et seq. Under this act, a "trade secret" is defined in § 51:1431(4) as:

> information [etc....], that: (a) derives independent economic value, actual or potential, from not being generally known [...] and (b) is the subject of efforts that are reasonable under the circumstances to maintain its secrecy.

Comment (f) under this provision provides:

> Reasonable efforts to maintain secrecy have been held to include advising employees of the existence of a trade secret, limiting access to a trade secret on a "need to know basis," and controlling plant access. On the other hand, public disclosure of information through display, trade journal publications, advertising, or other carelessness can preclude protection.

Comment (f) shows that Louisiana has adopted the concept of "relative secrecy" as opposed to "absolute secrecy" in its trade secrets act. "The efforts required to maintain secrecy are those reasonable under the circumstances, and courts do not require extreme and unduly expensive procedures be taken to protect trade secrets." *Tubular Threading, Inc. v. Scandaliato*, 443 So.2d 712, 714 (La. Ct. App. 1983). *See also E.I. DuPont de Nemours & Co. v. Christopher*, 431 F.2d 1012 (5th Cir. 1970), *cert. denied*, 400 U.S. 1024 (1971) (explaining relative secrecy under Texas law).

The district court found that Wilbert Sheets had failed to use reasonable efforts under the circumstances to maintain the secrecy of his modification to the Yamaha tri-motorcycle and thus was not entitled to recover damages for the alleged misappropriation of the modification under the Uniform Trade Secrets Act. The determination of whether relative secrecy exists in a particular case is a question of fact reviewable by this Court under the clearly erroneous standard of review.

Upon our review of the record, we must conclude that the district court's finding that appellant failed to take reasonable efforts under the circumstance to maintain the secrecy of his invention is not clearly erroneous. As the district court noted, appellant allowed one of the modified tri-motorcycles to be shown at a Yamaha service seminar in August 1980. He also let Cycle Country, a company in which he had no proprietary interest, use a modified tri-motorcycle as a demonstrator, apparently without restriction. Further, he installed his modification on the tri-motorcycles of at least nine other individuals and gave them, at most, only minimal instructions not to reveal the modification to others. These limited attempts at secrecy appear to have had more to do with maintaining the Cycle Country racing team's competitive edge in racing and less to do with maintaining the secrecy of the modification itself.

Apparently, appellant also allowed several Yamaha representatives to enter Cycle Country and examine and photograph his modification without taking any efforts at maintaining the secrecy of the modification. There had been no need for appellees to resort to subterfuge or other improper means in order to obtain information pertaining to the modification. A disclosure of a trade secret to others who have no obligation of confidentiality extinguishes the property right in the trade secret. *Ruckelshaus v. Monsanto Co.*, 467 U.S. 986, 1002 (1984).

Wilbert Sheets also asserts a cause of action under general equitable principles of unjust enrichment, or an *actio de in rem verso*, under Louisiana law. Following French jurisprudence, the Louisiana Supreme Court has adopted five prerequisites to this type of action:

> (1) [T]here must be an enrichment, (2) there must be an impoverishment, (3) there must be a connection between the enrichment and resulting impoverishment, (4) there must be an absence of "justification" or "cause" for the enrichment and impoverishment, and finally (5) the action will only be allowed when there is no other remedy at law, i.e., the action is subsidiary or corrective in nature.

The district court gave several reasons for holding that Wilbert Sheets did not have a cause of action under the doctrine of unjust enrichment. We address only one of these rationales, as we find it dispositive. The district court was concerned that the application of the unjust enrichment doctrine in this case would contravene the more particularized requirements of the Louisiana Uniform Trade Secrets Act. We share the district court's concern and hold that the fourth and fifth prerequisites to the application of this equitable doctrine were not met in this case.

Louisiana enacted an express statutory scheme to protect individuals and entities in the position of Wilbert Sheets when it adopted the Uniform Trade Secrets Act. Under Louisiana law, Wilbert Sheets is not entitled to fall back on the equitable doctrine of unjust enrichment after failing to establish a trade secret due to his failure to make reasonable efforts to maintain secrecy. Thus, in a very real sense the enrichment by Yamaha was brought about by Wilbert Sheets' own failure to maintain the secrecy of his invention.

Louisiana law makes clear that when an adequate remedy at law is available, the court may not resort to principles of equity. An action for unjust enrichment must not be allowed to defeat the purpose of a rule of law directed to the matter at issue. Wilbert Sheets had a remedy under the Trade Secrets Act by which he could have recovered for the alleged misappropriation of his modification to the Yamaha tri-motorcycle. He failed to gain the protection of this act by his carelessness. Under Louisiana law he cannot now invoke principles of equity to recover for the benefits he alleges appellees enjoyed at his expense.

NOTES

1. *Related Patent Issues.* Could Wilbert Sheets have received a patent for his air intake modification to the motorcycle? Is it dispositive of this issue that he abandoned his patent application?

If the Japanese patent has a U.S. counterpart (which is likely, considering the large U.S. market for this product), what defense would Sheets (or anyone, for that matter) have against a charge of infringement? In an argument that the person named in the Japanese patent (and its U.S. counterpart) "did not himself invent" it under § 102(f), does it matter that the act of deriving the invention from Sheets (if that is what really happened) occurred in Japan rather than the U.S.? If Sheets had not abandoned his U.S. application, how would the case have been different? Would the outcome be different if the U.S. adopted a "first to file" patent system?

2. *"All We Have Is Memories .... "* In the preceding case, assuming Sheets had taken sufficient steps to protect his invention as a trade secret, would it matter in the case if the Japanese visitors had not taken photographs, but instead memorized the configuration of Sheets' air intake design? *See Rohm & Haas Co. v. Adco Chem. Co.*, 689 F.2d 424 (3d Cir. 1982) (former employee misappropriates a trade secret when he discloses a secret process from memory). *See also McKay v. Communispond, Inc.*, 581 F. Supp. 801, 808 (S.D.N.Y. 1983).

3. *More on Reasonable Efforts.* Reasonable precautions to protect secrecy "need not be absolute or 100 percent perfect." *General Aniline & Film Corp. v. Frantz*, 50 Misc. 2d 994, 272 N.Y.S.2d 600, 606 (N.Y. Sup. Ct.), *modified*, 52 Misc. 2d 197, 274 N.Y.S.2d 634 (1966). *See also DuPont v. Christopher, supra.*

Reasonable precautions take a number of forms: confidentiality agreements with employees, e.g., *Syntex Ophthalmics v. Novicky*, 591 F. Supp. 28 (N.D. Ill. 1983); employee guidance on confidentiality, *Johns-Manville Corp. v. Guardian Indus. Corp.*, 221 U.S.P.Q. 319 (E.D. Mich. 1983), *modified*, 223 U.S.P.Q. 974 (E.D. Mich. 1984); written employee confidentiality policies, *CPG Prods. Corp. v. Mego Corp.*, 214 U.S.P.Q. 206 (S.D. Ohio 1961); publication screening to prevent disclosure of trade secrets by employees, *Johns-Manville*, 221 U.S.P.Q. at 349-50; tight physical security precautions, *id.*; restrictions on visitors,

Anaconda Co. v. Metric Tool & Die Co., 485 F. Supp. 410 (E.D. Pa. 1980); secret ingredients, *Minnesota Mining & Mfg. Co. v. Technical Tape Corp.*, 192 N.Y.S.2d 102 (N.Y. Sup. Ct. 1959), *aff'd*, 235 N.Y.S.2d 830 (2d Dept. 1962); separation of departments, *USM Corp. v. Marson Fastener Corp.*, 379 Mass. 90, 393 N.E.2d 895 (1979); separate locked areas for secret documents and drawings, *id.*; and the like. *Cf. In the Matter of Innovative Constr. Sys.*, 793 F.2d 875, 883-84 (7th Cir. 1986) (reasonable security measures found even though process formula posted in area accessible by all employees).

Prior disclosure, to be a defense, must be sufficient for the claimed trade secret to be ascertained. *See A.H. Emery Co. v. Marcan Prods. Corp.*, 389 F.2d 11, 15-16 (2d Cir.), *cert. denied*, 393 U.S. 835, 89 S. Ct. 109, 21 L. Ed. 2d 106 (1968) (even though parts drawings may on occasion have been shown to a limited number of outsiders for a particular purpose, this did not in itself necessarily destroy the secrecy which protected them before they were so disclosed; and sale of scale destroyed any trade secret in scale design, but this was not the case as to "tolerance data, on the other hand, [which] could not be obtained through observation or analysis of the cell itself, and sales of the product did not constitute a release of plaintiff's claim to secrecy in that regard."). Where a product was sold for the limited purpose of negotiating a license, it is not considered available to the general public. *Biodynamic Techs., Inc. v. Chattanooga Corp.*, 644 F. Supp. 607, 612 (S.D. Fla. 1986).

4. An Egbert Analogy. The court said Wilbert Sheets had no proprietary interest in Cycle Country, but the store was owned by his two sons as sole partners. Additionally, the cycles he modified were owned by friends and family on the Cycle Country racing team. Recall *Egbert v. Lippmann*, the "corset case" from Chapter 4. Would asking these people to keep the modification a secret be like Mr. Barnes asking his wife not to let anyone see her corset steels? How is this different? If Sheet were to apply for a patent, under *Egbert*, when would he have to apply?

INTEGRATED CASH MANAGEMENT SERVICES v. DIGITAL TRANSACTIONS, INC.

920 F.2d 171, 17 U.S.P.Q.2d (BNA) 1054 (2d Cir. 1990)

The central question presented by this appeal is whether trade secret protection extends to the manner in which several non-secret utility programs are arranged to create a computer software product. Defendants-appellants Digital Transactions, Inc. ("DTI"), Nicholas C. Mitsos, Alfred Sims Newlin, and Behrouz Vafa appeal from a judgment, entered in the United States District Court for the Southern District of New York (Robert J. Ward, Judge), enjoining their use and distribution of this software product. On this appeal, DTI and the individual defendants contend that the district court erred in extending trade secret protection to the combination of utility programs comprising the product. For the reasons set forth below, we affirm.

Plaintiffs-appellees Integrated Cash Management Services, Inc. and Cash Management Corporation (collectively, "ICM") design and develop computer software. ICM's programs are marketed to banks which, in turn, market the programs to the financial and treasury departments of various corporations. ICM develops generic programs which are readily customized to suit a particular client's specifications. It invests millions of dollars in the research and development of these generic programs and in structuring these programs to create its software product. The ICM programs at issue in the present case are: SEUNIMNT, a generic universal database management system; Telefon, a generic communications program; Menu System/Driver, a treasury work station program; and Report Writer, a financial report customizing program. ICM claims to employ a "winning combination" of these generic programs which, it argues, deserves protection as a trade secret.

Individual defendants Mitsos, Newlin, and Vafa each worked for ICM. Mitsos left ICM in September 1986. Alfred Sims Newlin was employed by ICM as a computer programmer between September 1984 and March 1987. Both Newlin and Vafa signed nondisclosure agreements with ICM in which they agreed not to disclose or use any confidential or proprietary information of ICM upon leaving the company's employ.

Newlin and Vafa left ICM on March 13, 1987 and began working at DTI three days later. Before leaving ICM, Newlin copied certain ICM files onto a personal diskette. He took that diskette with him without informing ICM. Vafa also left ICM with a copy of source code he had written for ICM. He later destroyed that file, however. Within two weeks of the individual defendants' commencement of work at DTI, it had created a prototype database manager program. This program, and other generic programs subsequently produced for DTI by Newlin and Vafa, were found by the district court to "operate in substantially the same manner as comparable ICM generic programs." The products developed by DTI were similar to those produced by ICM in both the design of component utilities and in overall structure or "architecture."

A plaintiff claiming misappropriation of a trade secret must prove: "(1) it possessed a trade secret, and (2) defendant is using that trade secret in breach of an agreement, confidence, or duty, or as a result of discovery by improper means." On this appeal, DTI and the individual defendants do not challenge the district court's determination that any trade secret misappropriation would constitute a breach of confidence. Indeed, such a challenge would have been fruitless given the nondisclosure agreements signed by Newlin and Vafa. However, DTI and the individual defendants contend that the district court erred in finding that the "architecture" of ICM's system was a protectable trade secret. We disagree.

Applying [the Restatement § 757 comment b] factors to the software program at issue in this case, it is evident that ICM retains a protectable trade secret in its product. The manner in which ICM's generic utility programs interact, which is the key to the product's success, is not generally known outside of ICM. Contrary to defendants' suggestion, the non-secret nature of the individual utility programs which comprise ICM's product does not alter this conclusion. "[A] trade secret can exist in a combination of characteristics and components, each of which, by itself, is in the public domain, but the unified process, design and operation of which, in unique combination, affords a competitive advantage and is a protectable secret." *Imperial Chem. Indus. Ltd. v. National Distillers and Chem. Corp.*, 342 F.2d 737, 742 (2d Cir. 1965). As the district court found, the architecture of ICM's product, or the "way in which [ICM's] various components fit together as building blocks in order to form the unique whole" [constitutes a trade secret].

Moreover, ICM's combination of programs was not disclosed in ICM's promotional literature, which contains merely a user-oriented description of the advantages of ICM's product. The defendants have not shown that the limited information available in the promotional literature contains sufficient technical detail to constitute disclosure of the product's architecture.

The remaining factors to be considered in ascertaining the existence of a trade secret, are also satisfied in this case. ICM has taken measures to protect the secrecy of its product architecture. The doors to the premises were kept locked. Employees, including Newlin and Vafa, were required to sign nondisclosure agreements which provided that "[w]hen employment is terminated, the [former employee] agrees not to use, copy or disclose any of ICM's secrets, software products, software tools or any type of information and software which belongs to ICM." The large investment in research and development of ICM's product has not been challenged by the defendants. Finally, the expert testimony reveals that the ICM product's architecture could not be readily duplicated without the secret information acquired by ICM through years of research. The architecture of the ICM system was not "readily ascertainable," other than by the improper disclosure and use by Newlin and Vafa.

Defendants-appellants contend that two aspects of the district court's injunction against them are improper. First, they challenge the court's six-month injunction prohibiting Newlin and Vafa from becoming involved in the development of programs similar to ICM's product. They argue that this injunction unfairly precluded Newlin and Vafa from utilizing their training and general experience in the field of computer programming. We believe that the court crafted this aspect of its injunction with a careful eye toward the balance between the right of a former employer to protect trade secrets and the right of a former employee to utilize his skills and experience.

Second, the defendants-appellants challenge the district court's perpetual injunction against their distribution of any version of ICM's four generic utility programs in existence as of October 26, 1989, the date decision was rendered. They contend that this perpetual injunction gives ICM an undeserved windfall by extending the restriction beyond the six-month period which the court considered necessary "to neutralize the 'head start' gained by DTI from the improper use of ICM's trade secrets." We disagree.

In contrast to the district court's six-month injunction against the defendants' use of ICM's programs, the court's perpetual injunction is aimed at preventing defendants' distribution of those programs as they existed on October 26, 1989. Defendants are thereby prevented from simply shelving the misappropriated information for six months, and then distributing the ICM product as their own. Following the six-month period, defendants may internally use ICM's four generic programs and may alter or modify them as they choose. However, defendants may not distribute any unmodified ICM programs either during or after the six-month period. The district court's injunction, when considered *in toto*, is a reasonable and wise exercise of discretion.

Affirmed.

NOTES

If DTI had obtained samples of an unpatented ITM product by buying them on the open market, and if no patent ever issued on the product, would ITM have a trade secret claim? Is this what the UTSA means by "reverse engineering," which, "alone," cannot constitute "improper means"? These issues are explored in the following case.

ACUSON CORP. v. ALOKA CO.

209 Cal. App. 3d 425, 257 Cal. Rptr. 368, 10 U.S.P.Q.2d (BNA)
1814 (Cal. Ct. App. 1989) (review denied and ordered "not
published" by California Supreme Court)

Plaintiff Acuson Corp. (Acuson) sued its competitor, defendant Aloka Co., Ltd. (Aloka) for misappropriation of alleged trade secrets. Aloka had purchased and studied an example of Acuson's product. Despite uncontroverted evidence that hundreds of the product had already been sold on the open market, the trial court granted broad injunctive relief to prevent Aloka from using any information learned through its examination of Acuson's product. Since it is fundamental that things publicly disclosed cannot be trade secrets, we reverse.

Acuson and Aloka both manufacture ultrasonic imaging equipment, a widely used medical diagnostic tool. That device uses sound waves to produce moving images of the inside of a patient's body. It works much like sonar: A transducer emits and directs inaudible, high frequency sound waves. Tissues in the body reflect the sound. The transducer detects the echoes, and a computer processes them into an image. Finally, a video monitor displays the image.

While Aloka has been manufacturing ultrasonic imaging equipment much longer than Acuson, neither is a newcomer to the business. Aloka, a Japanese company, was formed in 1950 and has been manufacturing ultrasonic equipment since 1960. Acuson, a Delaware corporation, was formed in 1981 and first sold ultrasonic equipment in 1983.

Acuson's product is the Acuson 128, apparently so named because it simultaneously uses 128 ultrasonic channels. Aloka makes different models. One of these, the SSD-650, also uses 128 channels but in staggered bursts of 32 channels at a time. The parties seem to agree that the Acuson 128 provides finer resolution. But the Aloka SSD-650 is less expensive.

In November 1985 Aloka decided to buy an Acuson 128. The parties disagree on Aloka's motives. Aloka compared the Acuson 128 with its own product and claims that comparison was its reason for the purchase. According to Acuson, Aloka also planned to copy Acuson's product.

Acuson attaches much significance to the way in which Aloka obtained an Acuson 128. Aloka, of course, had no reason to expect that Acuson would want to assist its competitor by selling it an Acuson 128 directly. And Aloka did not bother to ask. Instead it asked its American distributor, Johnson & Johnson Ultrasound (Johnson & Johnson), to purchase the unit. Johnson & Johnson arranged to buy one through Northeastern Medical Equipment Co. (Northeastern).

Northeastern's representative, Bruce Gallit, ordered the machine from Acuson. He also asked for service manuals and a crate suitable for export. Gallit explained that the equipment was going overseas and could not be serviced by Acuson's technicians. Acuson delivered the unit to Northeastern as requested on May 5, 1986. Aloka received it on May 12, 1986, and paid Johnson & Johnson's invoice in full. Johnson & Johnson paid Northeastern.

At Aloka's plant in Tokyo, Aloka's engineers operated the Acuson 128 and compared it with their own product. Although the engineers partially dismantled the Acuson unit, they did not read the machine's software. The engineers recorded their observations in notebooks. The parties do not say how long Aloka's engineers spent examining the Acuson 128, but the evidence suggests that they spent only 11 days on the entire project.

[After a dispute with the distributor, Acuson found out that Aloka had been the true purchaser. Acuson demanded return of the machine; Aloka refused.]

Acuson filed this action against Aloka on October 6, 1987, claiming that Aloka had misappropriated its trade secrets. Six months later Acuson moved for a preliminary injunction, and the court issued an injunction in the form proposed by Acuson.

Aloka's main contention is that the Acuson 128 cannot contain trade secrets since hundreds of the machine have been sold. The argument rests on two well-established principles. First, a trade secret loses its secrecy, and thus its protection under state law, after being disclosed to the public. (Civ. Code, § 3426.1, subd. (d)(1).) Second, state law may not prohibit the copying of objects in the public domain.

The concept of public disclosure is embodied in the statutory definition of "trade secret." While the point may be obvious, it bears emphasis that the term "secret" has a literal meaning in the context of trade secret law. "The character of the secret if important to the business is not material but it must, as the term implies, be kept secret by the one who claims it." In particular, information and goods publicly disclosed cannot be trade secrets.

The other important principle that affects this case derives from federal law. Patent and copyright law provide the exclusive means of obtaining a monopoly on a product that has been disclosed to the public. In contrast, "ownership of a trade secret does not give the owner a monopoly in its use, but merely a proprietary right which equity protects against usurpation by unfair means." If federal law leaves an object in the public domain, state law may not prohibit its copying. [See cases later in this chapter.]

These principles, applied to the uncontradicted facts of this case, compel the conclusion that Aloka is free to examine and even to copy the Acuson 128 to the extent it lacks protection under federal patent or copyright law.

Uncontradicted evidence shows that the Acuson 128 has been disclosed to the public. At least hundreds of the product have been sold since it was introduced in 1983. If the term "hundreds" is vague, it is because the record demonstrates an understandable reluctance on Acuson's part to disclose actual sales figures. The company has admitted, however, that virtually all of its revenues derive from sales of the Acuson 128, and one can divide sales revenue by unit price to obtain an approximate figure. Acuson does not contest Aloka's assertion that it sold about 400 units in 1984 in the United States alone.

[The court then turns to Acuson's alleged efforts to protect its trade secrets.] A software license represents the first of Acuson's claimed efforts to maintain secrecy. The software covered by the license is required to operate the Acuson 128. The license consists of a single paragraph in a one-page document entitled "Terms and Conditions," a form contract which purports to set out the standard terms of sale for an Acuson 128. The relevant paragraph provides as follows:

> Buyer agrees that the Equipment [the Acuson 128] contains software which is proprietary to the Seller. Buyer is granted a license to use Seller [sic] proprietary software in connection with this Equipment only in the matter and in the form originally delivered by Seller. Any other use or disclosure to others of the software is prohibited. Buyer is granted a right to transfer this license to any subsequent purchaser of the Equipment who agrees to be bound by these terms in the same manner as the Buyer.

The practical effect of the software license is to make commercial duplication of the Acuson 128 difficult for someone who has agreed to the "Terms and Conditions." Having replicated the machine one would still need software to operate it, and the licensing provision would bar the software's copying and "disclosure to others."

[From footnote:] Of course, Aloka never signed a document containing the software license agreement. Instead, Acuson alleged that Aloka had notice of license because Gallit, the president of Northeastern, had signed a two-page "Quotation" which included the "Terms and Conditions." Northeastern, however, claimed that the "Quotation" was not authentic. This factual dispute does not affect the disposition of this appeal since, as discussed below, the preliminary injunction is not predicated upon a finding that the software license was ever breached.

Digressing from its defense of the injunction under trade secret law, Acuson argues that the injunction can also be justified as a remedy for a breach of the software license. But we reject this argument since the trial court did not find that Aloka breached or participated in a breach of the software licensing agreement and since the preliminary injunction, which does not even refer to software, is not predicated upon such a breach. Thus, we infer no such finding.

Accordingly, in evaluating the software license's impact on this case we are concerned only with its effectiveness as a method to maintain the confidentiality of any trade secrets that might exist in the Acuson 128's hardware. The narrow question we face is this: Assuming for the sake of argument that any alleged trade secrets contained in the Acuson 128 had survived the machine's public sales, would the software license represent a reasonable effort to protect any such secrets? The answer can only be no, since the license does not purport to prevent a buyer from operating the machine, disassembling its hardware, studying its functions, and comparing it with other machines. As we have already discussed, nothing that such an examination reveals can be a trade secret.

The Acuson 128 contains padlocks which make it more difficult to examine certain parts. Aloka's engineers broke two of them in order to study the machine. While "breaking padlocks" has a dishonest sound, one must bear in mind that a buyer buys the locks along with the machine and is free to cut them. The "Terms and Conditions" of sale do not mention the locks, and Acuson does not claim that buyers have any obligation to leave them intact.

Because the locks belong to the person who buys the machine, they cannot maintain the machine's secrecy. Indeed, they probably are not even intended to do so. Aloka plausibly speculates that the locks' intended function is to show Acuson that unauthorized personnel have provided maintenance service. Acuson's maintenance personnel have the keys to the locks, and a warranty provision in the "Terms and Conditions" provides that "[a]djustments will be contingent upon Seller's examination disclosing that defects have not been caused by ... incorrect repair or servicing not performed or authorized by Seller."

But even if Acuson's explanation of the locks were correct, the locks still would not convert lawful reverse engineering into a tort. Unless a buyer has made an enforceable promise not to examine the machine, a lock protects trade secrets about as effectively as a sign reading "Please don't look inside."

In summary, the Acuson 128 lost any trade secrets it may have contained when sold in large numbers to buyers who were free to resell to whomever they chose. Neither Acuson's software license, its confidentiality agreements with employees and distributors, nor its internal padlocks actually serve to protect the secrecy of a machine that has been disclosed to the public. Accordingly, nothing that an examination of the machine discloses can be a trade secret.

The order granting a preliminary injunction is reversed. Appellant Aloka shall recover its costs on appeal.

NOTES

1. *Does Public Sale Always Destroy Trade Secrets?* In *Sinclair v. Aquarius Elecs., Inc.*, 42 Cal. App. 3d 216, 226, 116 Cal. Rptr. 654 (Cal. Ct. App. 1974), the plaintiff inventor sold to the defendant manufacturer the idea of making portable brain wave monitors. The manufacturer bargained for the right to exploit the idea in exchange for the obligation to pay royalties to the inventor. The product was successful. When the manufacturer failed to pay royalties, the inventor sued. The court enforced the agreement. Although the product had, because of the manufacturer's marketing efforts, passed into the public domain and become available for copying, that did not void the obligation to pay royalties. The manufacturer had validly bargained for a jump on the market.

Kubic, Inc. v. Hull, 56 Mich. App. 335, 224 N.W.2d 80 (Mich. Ct. App. 1974) presents a similar situation. An employee took confidential drawings used in a product's manufacture. Although the employee might have duplicated the product through reverse engineering, the stolen drawings saved time. The court held that the prior sale of 22 of the products did not constitute public disclosure because the product was not easy to examine, because it would be difficult to obtain an example of the product from the customer, and because reverse engineering would take much time. Despite its belief that trade secrets might survive public disclosure, the court nevertheless recognized that competitors could lawfully duplicate the product. *Id.* at 95. Moreover, the court vacated an injunction that prevented the former employee's duplication efforts, on the theory that the ex-employee should be able to do what others had the right to do. *Cf. Data General Corp. v. Digital Computer Controls, Inc.*, 357 A.2d 105 (Del. Ch. 1975) (distribution of 6,000 copies of manual under nondisclosure agreement does not amount to public dissemination, so trade secret status maintained).

2. *Fair and Honest Means.* The legislative history to the California version of the UTSA states: "The acquisition of the known product must of course, also be by a fair and honest means, such as purchase of the item on the open market for reverse engineering to be lawful ...." (Legis. Com. comments to CIV. CODE § 3426.1.) "[F]air and honest means" are the converse of "improper means" the statutory term that the Uniform Act's drafters chose to encompass an unforeseeably broad range of ethically objectionable behavior. As the drafters noted, "[o]ne of the broadly stated policies behind trade secret law is 'the maintenance of standards of commercial ethics'" and "[a] complete catalogue of improper means is not possible.'" (Legis. Com. com. to CIV. CODE § 3426.1.) To be sure, the concept of "improper means" has always been very broad. A comment to the earlier restatement observed that "means may be improper ... even though they do not cause any other harm than that to the interest in the trade secret." (RESTATEMENT (SECOND) OF TORTS § 757, cmt. f).

But unless a defendant has harmed the plaintiff's interest in a trade secret, there is no basis for liability under trade secret law. It is this principle that makes sense of the Uniform Act's comment that lawful reverse engineering is predicated upon acquisition of a product by "fair and honest means." As the court in the *Acuson* case noted:

> Someone who, for example, knowingly uses the stolen design for a yet-unreleased product will be liable under trade secret law even though the product is later sold to the public. There is liability because the product was still secret at the time; actual trade secrets were compromised by unethical behavior. (E.g., *Forro Precision, Inc. v. Intern. Business Machines* (9th Cir. 1982) 673 F.2d 1045; *Dior v. Milton* (1956) 155 N.Y.S.2d 443.)

257 Cal. Rptr. at 381.

3. *An Economic Rationale for "Improper Means."* "Every producer of information desires, ex ante ..., access to his competitors' information as well as protection of his own. The law strikes a balance between these inconsistent desires by prohibiting only the most costly means of unmasking commercial secrets. They are costly in major part because of the defensive maneuvers they incite.... Where on the contrary the social costs of enforcing secrecy through the legal system would be high, the benefits of shared information are likely to exceed the net benefits of legal protection. There are gains when manufacturers are permitted to reverse engineer each other's products .... Withholding legal protection is not all social loss, therefore, and in addition it economizes on what would be high costs of legal protection." Friedman, Landes & Posner, *Some Economics of Trade Secret Law*, 5 J. ECON. PERSPS. 61, 67 (1991).

4. TRADE SECRET REMEDIES: THE "HEAD START" CONCEPT

LAMB-WESTON, INC. v. McCAIN FOODS, LTD.
941 F.2d 970, 19 U.S.P.Q.2d (BNA) 1775 (9th Cir. 1991)

Lamb-Weston's attempt to spiral ahead of its competitors was allegedly thwarted by the misappropriation by McCain of Lamb-Weston's trade secrets for manufacturing curlicue french fries. To keep Lamb-Weston from being left to twist in the wind before the trial on the merits, an eight-month preliminary injunction was imposed, barring McCain from producing or selling products made with the technology in question. McCain appeals and we affirm.

Lamb-Weston, a potato processor, began in 1986 to develop the technology for producing curlicue french fries. The unique process involved a helical blade and water-feed system. McCain, a competitor, began work on a manufacturing process for curlicue fries in 1989.

In January 1990, McCain approached several Lamb-Weston employees to help its development. At that time, Richard Livermore, who had helped create the Lamb-Weston blade and process, allegedly gave McCain a copy of Lamb-Weston's confidential patent application. Livermore later went to work for McCain. Subsequently, Jerry Ross, the independent contractor who fabricated the Lamb-Weston blade, was hired by McCain to craft a helical blade for it. McCain left the decisions about the specifications, materials and manufacturing process to Ross, knowing he was still working on Lamb-Weston's blades. Lamb-Weston was issued two patents for its blade system on May 22, 1990. In August, after discovering Ross was working for McCain, Lamb-Weston had him sign a confidentiality agreement. Contemporaneously, it sent a letter to McCain asserting concern that McCain was misappropriating its trade secrets. In October, Lamb-Weston insisted Ross sign an exclusivity agreement. McCain then requested and received from Ross all the information he had on the McCain blade.

According to Lamb-Weston, with the help of Ross and Livermore, McCain built a prototype before the patents issued in May 1990. By June, McCain had the blades hooked up to a prototype water-feed system and by December was producing curlicue fries.

During the following month, Lamb-Weston sued for misappropriation of trade secrets. The parties consented to proceedings before a magistrate judge, who entered an eight-month preliminary injunction against McCain in March 1991. [The court decides that some form of relief was appropriate, since McCain had reason to know that Ross was transferring Lamb-Weston's trade secrets.]

McCain argues that the court abused its discretion by imposing a geographically overbroad injunction. The court enjoined it from selling curlicue french fries worldwide even though Lamb-Weston's foreign market is limited. Arguing that Lamb-Weston cannot be harmed in countries where it is not selling, McCain urges this court to limit the injunction to those countries where Lamb-Weston actually sells its product.

McCain argues that the court erred by failing to make specific findings about the length of its alleged head start. McCain also contends the injunction was an abuse of discretion because it is too long.

The court made no explicit findings about how long it would have taken McCain to develop independently its helical blade. It simply imposed an eight-month injunction for McCain's head start without explaining its method of calculation. McCain asserts that this violates Federal Rule of Civil Procedure 52(a), which requires that the court specify its findings of fact and conclusions of law. The court indicated that the eight-month duration corresponded to McCain's head start. Although we encourage district courts to make more specific findings of fact, we conclude that the statement here was sufficient for the purposes of Rule 52(a).

"[T]he appropriate duration for the injunction should be the period of time it would have taken [the defendant], either by reverse engineering or by independent development, to develop [the product] legitimately without use of [plaintiff's] trade secrets." *K2 Ski Co. v. Head Ski Co.*, 506 F.2d 471, 474 (9th Cir. 1974).

McCain argues that April 19, 1990 is the only date for which there is evidence of misappropriation and that at most it had a one-year advantage beginning on that date. It asserts that with a one-year head start, the injunction imposed on March 27, 1991, should have ended on April 19, 1991, one year from the misappropriation date.

If we were to accept McCain's argument that the misappropriation was April 19 and the head start should be calculated from that date, the injunction imposed was not an abuse of discretion simply because it ended a year and seven months after that date. Lamb-Weston presented testimony that its development time for the materials, dimensions and fabricating process for the blade was about a year and a half. Additional testimony was given about Lamb-Weston's reputation for ingenuity and its development time for the blade design.

[From footnote 4:] McCain's reliance on the comments to section 2 of the Uniform Trade Secrets Act [in force in Oregon, the law applicable to this case] is misplaced. The comments indicate that an injunction would be inappropriate where the misappropriator has not taken advantage of the head start or a good-faith competitor has already caught up with the misappropriator. Nothing suggests either is true here.

We reject McCain's argument that if the misappropriation through Ross occurred on April 19, it had only a 33-day head start because Lamb-Weston's patents were issued May 22. Although the shape of the blade and the slicing process was public on May 22, the specifications, materials and manufacturing process for making the blade were still trade secrets because they were not included in the patent applications.

Oregon law affords broad protection to trade secrets so public disclosure of the blade shape did not exonerate McCain from previous illegal use of that trade secret or the subsequent illegal use of the remaining trade secrets. Although a defendant may ask the court to vacate an injunction after the trade secret is public, "the injunction may be continued for an additional reasonable period of time in order to eliminate commercial advantage that otherwise would be derived from the misappropriation." 1989 Or. Laws 646.463(1). The eight-month injunction was not an abuse of discretion.

Affirmed.

NOTES

1. *Patents and "Head Starts."* If Lamb-Weston received a patent, what possible reverse engineering could McCain engage in legally? Is it a violation of the best mode requirement under § 112 of the Patent Act for Lamb-Weston to omit from its disclosure "specifications, materials and [information about the] manufacturing process for making the blade"? If not, what does this say about the adequacy of disclosure in a patent specification? At the least, it highlights the reason why most licensees demand trade secret and "know-how" information in addition to a license to use the patented product or process.

2. *Confidentiality Agreements and Head Starts.* In *Kewanee Oil Co. v. Bicron Corp.*, 416 U.S. 470 (1974), the former employees had signed confidentiality agreements. *Id.* at 473. The Court upheld the district court's granting of a permanent injunction against the disclosure or use by respondents of 20 of the 40 claimed trade secrets until such time as the trade secrets had been released to the

public, had otherwise generally become available to the public, or had been obtained by respondents from sources having the legal right to convey the information. *Id.* at 473-74. *Accord, Henry Hope X-Ray Prods., Inc. v. Marron Carrel, Inc.*, 674 F.2d 1336, 1342 (9th Cir. 1982) (the limitation to confidential information contains the implicit temporal limitation that information may be disclosed when it ceases to be confidential); *Sigma Chem. Co. v. Harris*, 586 F. Supp. 704, 710 (E.D. Mo. 1984) (injunctive relief to enforce a confidentiality agreement of unlimited duration, "because an employee has an absolute, temporally unlimited duty not to disclose his/her employer's trade secrets and thus the absence of a time limit, is not a defect."); *Sigma Chem. Co. v. Harris*, 605 F. Supp. 1253, 1264 (E.D. Mo. 1985) (confidentiality agreement unlimited in time enforceable for "so long as [the] trade secret information remains secret."). *But see Howard Schultz & Assoc. v. Broniec*, 239 Ga. 181, 236 S.E.2d 265, 270 (1977) ("The nondisclosure covenant here contains no time limitation and hence it is unenforceable"); *Gary Van Zeeland Talent, Inc. v. Sandas*, 54 Wis. 2d 202, 267 N.W.2d 242, 250 (1978) (unlimited duration of agreement not to disclose trade-secret customer list makes the agreement per se void).

B. FEDERAL PREEMPTION OF STATE LAW

KEWANEE OIL CO. v. BICRON CORP.
416 U.S. 470, 181 U.S.P.Q. (BNA) 673 (1974)

We granted certiorari to resolve a question on which there is a conflict in the courts of appeals: whether state trade secret protection is pre-empted by operation of the federal patent law. Harshaw Chemical Co., an unincorporated division of petitioner, is a leading manufacturer of a type of synthetic crystal which is useful in the detection of ionizing radiation. In 1949 Harshaw commenced research into the growth of this type crystal and was able to produce one less than two inches in diameter. By 1966, as the result of expenditures in excess of $1 million, Harshaw was able to grow a 17-inch crystal, something no one else had done previously. Harshaw had developed many processes, procedures, and manufacturing techniques in the purification of raw materials and the growth and encapsulation of the crystals which enabled it to accomplish this feat. Some of these processes Harshaw considers to be trade secrets. The individual respondents are former employees of Harshaw who formed or later joined respondent Bicron. While at Harshaw the individual respondents executed, as a condition of employment, at least one agreement each, requiring them not to disclose confidential information or trade secrets obtained as employees of Harshaw. Bicron was formed in August 1969 to compete with Harshaw in the production of the crystals, and by April 1970, had grown a 17-inch crystal.

[T]he Court of Appeals reversed the District Court, finding Ohio's trade secret law to be in conflict with the patent laws of the United States. We hold that

Ohio's law of trade secrets is not preempted by the patent laws of the United States, and, accordingly, we reverse.

The subject of a trade secret must be secret, and must not be of public knowledge or of a general knowledge in the trade or business. This necessary element of secrecy is not lost, however, if the holder of the trade secret reveals the trade secret to another "in confidence, and under an implied obligation not to use or disclose it." These others may include those of the holder's "employees to whom it is necessary to confide it, in order to apply it to the uses for which it is intended." Often the recipient of confidential knowledge of the subject of a trade secret is a licensee of its holder. The protection accorded the trade secret holder is against the disclosure or unauthorized use of the trade secret by those to whom the secret has been confided under the express or implied restriction of nondisclosure or nonuse. The law also protects the holder of a trade secret against disclosure or use when the knowledge is gained, not by the owner's volition, but by some "improper means," Restatement of Torts § 757(a), which may include theft, wiretapping, or even aerial reconnaissance. A trade secret law, however, does not offer protection against discovery by fair and honest means, such as by independent invention, accidental disclosure, or by so-called reverse engineering, that is by starting with the known product and working backward to divine the process which aided in its development or manufacture. Novelty, in the patent law sense, is not required for a trade secret. However, some novelty will be required if merely because that which does not possess novelty is usually known; secrecy, in the context of trade secrets, thus implies at least minimal novelty.

The subject matter of a patent is limited to a "process, machine, manufacture, or composition of matter, or ... improvement thereof," 35 U.S.C. § 101, which fulfills the three conditions of novelty and utility as articulated and defined in 35 U.S.C. §§ 101 and 102, and nonobviousness, as set out in 35 U.S.C. § 103. If an invention meets the rigorous statutory tests for the issuance of a patent, the patent is granted, for a period of 17 years, giving what has been described as the "right of exclusion." This protection goes not only to copying the subject matter, which is forbidden under the Copyright Act, but also to independent creation.

The first issue we deal with is whether the States are forbidden to act at all in the area of protection of the kinds of intellectual property which may make up the subject matter of trade secrets.

Article I, § 8, cl. 8, of the Constitution grants to the Congress the power "(t)o promote the Progress of Science and useful Arts, by securing for limited Times to Authors and Inventors the exclusive Right to their respective Writings and Discoveries ..." In the 1972 Term, in *Goldstein v. California*, 412 U.S. 546 (1973), we held that the cl. 8 grant of power to Congress was not exclusive and that, at least in the case of writings, the States were not prohibited from encouraging and protecting the efforts of those within their borders by appropriate legislation. The States could, therefore, protect against the unauthorized rerecording for sale of performances fixed on records or tapes, even though those performances qualified as "writings" in the constitutional sense and Congress was empowered to legislate regarding such performances and could pre-empt the area if it chose to do so. This determination was premised on the great diversity of interests in our Nation — the essentially non-uniform character of the appreciation of intellectual achievements in the various States. Evidence for this came from patents granted by the States in the 18th century. 412 U.S., at 557.

Just as the States may exercise regulatory power over writings so may the States regulate with respect to discoveries. States may hold diverse viewpoints in protecting intellectual property to invention as they do in protecting the intellectual property relating to the subject matter of copyright. The only limitation on the States is that in regulating the area of patents and copyrights they do not conflict with the operation of the laws in this area passed by Congress, and it is to that more difficult question we now turn.

The question of whether the trade secret law of Ohio is void under the Supremacy Clause involves a consideration of whether that law "stands as an obstacle to the accomplishment and execution of the full purposes and objectives of Congress." We stated in *Sears, Roebuck & Co. v. Stiffel Co.*, 376 U.S. 225, 229 (1964), that when state law touches upon the area of federal statutes enacted pursuant to constitutional authority, "it is 'familiar doctrine' that the federal policy 'may not be set at naught, or its benefits denied' by the state law. This is true, of course, even if the state law is enacted in the exercise of otherwise undoubted state power."

The patent law does not explicitly endorse or forbid the operation of trade secret law. However, as we have noted, if the scheme of protection developed by Ohio respecting trade secrets "clashes with the objectives of the federal patent laws," then the state law must fall. To determine whether the Ohio law "clashes" with the federal law it is helpful to examine the objectives of both the patent and trade secret laws.

The patent laws promote progress by offering a right of exclusion for a limited period as an incentive to inventors to risk the often enormous costs in terms of time, research, and development. The productive effort thereby fostered will have a positive effect on society through the introduction of new products and processes of manufacture into the economy, and the emanations by way of increased employment and better lives for our citizens. In return for the right of exclusion — this "reward for inventions" — the patent laws impose upon the inventor a requirement of disclosure. When a patent is granted and the information contained in it is circulated to the general public and those especially skilled in the trade, such additions to the general store of knowledge are of such importance to the public weal that the Federal Government is willing to pay the high price of 17 years of exclusive use for its disclosure, which disclosure, it is assumed, will stimulate ideas and the eventual development of further significant advances in the art. The Court has also articulated another policy of the patent law: that which is in the public domain cannot be removed therefrom by action of the States.

The maintenance of standards of commercial ethics and the encouragement of invention are the broadly stated policies behind trade secret law. "The necessity of good faith and honest, fair dealing, is the very life and spirit of the commercial world." *National Tube Co. v. Eastern Tube Co.*, 3 Ohio Cir. Cr. R., N.S. at 462.

As we noted earlier, trade secret law protects items which would not be proper subjects for consideration for patent protection under 35 U.S.C. § 101. As in the case of the recordings in *Goldstein v. California*, Congress, with respect to nonpatentable subject matter, "has drawn no balance; rather, it has left the area unattended, and no reason exists why the State should not be free to act."

Since no patent is available for a discovery unless it falls within one of the express categories of patentable subject matter of 35 U.S.C. § 101, the holder of such a discovery would have no reason to apply for a patent whether trade secret protection existed or not. Abolition of trade secret protection would, therefore, not result in increased disclosure to the public of discoveries in the area of nonpatentable subject matter. Also, it is hard to see how the public would be benefitted by disclosure of customer lists or advertising campaigns; in fact, keeping such items secret encourages businesses to initiate new and individualized plans of operation, and constructive competition results. This, in turn, leads to a greater variety of business methods than would otherwise be the case if privately developed marketing and other data were passed illicitly among firms involved in the same enterprise.

The question remains whether those items which are proper subjects for consideration for a patent may also have available the alternative protection accorded by trade secret law. Certainly the patent policy of encouraging invention is not disturbed by the existence of another form of incentive to invention. In this respect the two systems are not and never would be in conflict. Similarly, the policy that matter once in the public domain must remain in the public domain is not incompatible with the existence of trade secret protection. By definition a trade secret has not been placed in the public domain.

The more difficult objective of the patent law to reconcile with trade secret law is that of disclosure, the quid pro quo of the right to exclude. We are helped in this stage of the analysis by Judge Henry Friendly's opinion in *Painton & Co. v. Bourns, Inc.*, 442 F.2d 216 (CA2 1971). There the Court of Appeals thought it useful, in determining whether inventors will refrain because of the existence of trade secret law from applying for patents, thereby depriving the public from learning of the invention, to distinguish between three categories of trade secrets:

> (1) the trade secret believed by its owner to constitute a validly patentable invention; (2) the trade secret known to its owner not to be so patentable; and (3) the trade secret whose valid patentability is considered dubious.

Id. at 224. Trade secret protection in each of these categories would run against breaches of confidence — the employee and licensee situations — and theft and other forms of industrial espionage.

As to the trade secret known not to meet the standards of patentability, very little in the way of disclosure would be accomplished by abolishing trade secret protection. With trade secrets of nonpatentable subject matter, the patent alternative would not reasonably be available to the inventor. "There can be no public interest in stimulating developers of such (unpatentable) knowhow to flood an overburdened Patent Office with applications (for) what they do not consider patentable." *Ibid.* The mere filing of applications doomed to be turned down by the Patent Office will bring forth no new public knowledge or enlightenment, since under federal statute and regulation patent applications and abandoned patent applications are held by the Patent Office in confidence and are not open to public inspection.

Even as the extension of trade secret protection to patentable subject matter that the owner knows will not meet the standards of patentability will not conflict with the patent policy of disclosure, it will have a decidedly beneficial effect on society. Trade secret law will encourage invention in areas where patent law does not reach, and will prompt the independent innovator to proceed with the discovery and exploitation of his invention. Competition is fostered and the public is not deprived of the use of valuable, if not quite patentable, invention.

Even if trade secret protection against the faithless employee were abolished, inventive and exploitive effort in the area of patentable subject matter that did not meet the standards of patentability would continue, although at a reduced level. Alternatively with the effort that remained, however, would come an increase in the amount of self-help that innovative companies would employ. Knowledge would be widely dispersed among the employees of those still active in research. Security precautions necessarily would be increased, and salaries and fringe benefits of those few officers or employees who had to know the whole of the secret invention would be fixed in an amount thought sufficient to assure their loyalty. Smaller companies would be placed at a distinct economic disadvantage, since the costs of this kind of self-help could be great, and the cost to the public of the use of this invention would be increased. The innovative entrepreneur with limited resources would tend to confine his research efforts to himself and those few he felt he could trust without the ultimate assurance of legal protection against breaches of confidence. As a result, organized scientific and technological research could become fragmented, and society, as a whole, would suffer.

Another problem that would arise if state trade secret protection were precluded is in the area of licensing others to exploit secret processes. The holder of a trade secret would not likely share his secret with a manufacturer who cannot be placed under binding legal obligation to pay a license fee or to protect the secret. The result would be to hoard rather than disseminate knowledge. Instead, then, of licensing others to use his invention and making the most efficient use of existing manufacturing and marketing structures within the industry, the trade secret holder would tend either to limit his utilization of the invention, thereby depriving the public of the maximum benefit of its use, or engage in the time-consuming and economically wasteful enterprise of constructing duplicative manu-facturing and marketing mechanisms for the exploitation of the invention. The detrimental misallocation of resources and economic waste that would thus take place if trade secret protection were abolished with respect to employees or licensees cannot be justified by reference to any policy that the federal patent law seeks to advance.

Nothing in the patent law requires that States refrain from action to prevent industrial espionage. In addition to the increased costs for protection from burg-lary, wire-tapping, bribery, and the other means used to misappropriate trade secrets, there is the inevitable cost to the basic decency of society when one firm steals from another. A most fundamental human right, that of privacy, is threat-ened when industrial espionage is condoned or is made profitable; the state interest in denying profit to such illegal ventures is unchallengeable.

The next category of patentable subject matter to deal with is the invention whose holder has a legitimate doubt as to its patentability. The risk of eventual patent invalidity by the courts and the costs associated with that risk may well impel some with a good-faith doubt as to patentability not to take the trouble to seek to obtain and defend patent protection for their discoveries, regardless of the existence of trade secret protection. Trade secret protection would assist those inventors in the more efficient exploitation of their discoveries and not conflict with the patent law. In most cases of genuine doubt as to patent validity the potential rewards of patent protection are so far superior to those accruing to holders of trade secrets, that the holders of such inventions will seek patent pro-tection, ignoring the trade secret route. For those inventors "on the line" as to whether to seek patent protection, the abolition of trade secret protection might encourage some to apply for a patent who otherwise would not have done so. For some of those so encouraged, no patent will be granted and the result "will have been an unnecessary postponement in the divulging of the trade secret to persons willing to pay for it. If (the patent does issue), it may well be invalid, yet many will prefer to pay a modest royalty than to contest it, even though *Lear* allows them to accept a license and pursue the contest without paying royalties while the fight goes on. The result in such a case would be unjustified royalty payments from many who would prefer not to pay them rather than agreed fees from one or a few who are entirely willing to do so." *Painton & Co. v. Bourns, Inc.*, 442 F.2d, at 225. The point is that those who might be encouraged to file for patents by the absence of trade secret law will include inventors possessing the chaff as well as the wheat.

Eliminating trade secret law for the doubtfully patentable invention is thus likely to have deleterious effects on society and patent policy which we cannot say are balanced out by the speculative gain which might result from the en-couragement of some inventors with doubtfully patentable inventions which deserve patent protection to come forward and apply for patents. There is no conflict, then, between trade secret law and the patent law policy of disclosure, at least insofar as the first two categories of patentable subject matter are concerned.

The final category of patentable subject matter to deal with is the clearly patentable invention, i.e., that invention which the owner believes to meet the standards of patentability. It is here that the federal interest in disclosure is at its peak; these inventions, novel, useful and nonobvious, are "the things which are worth to the public the embarrassment of an exclusive patent." The interest of the public is that the bargain of 17 years of exclusive use in return for disclosure be accepted. If a State, through a system of protection, were to cause a substantial risk that holders of patentable inventions would not seek patents, but rather would rely on the state protection, we would be compelled to hold that such a system could not constitutionally continue to exist. In the case of trade secret law no reasonable risk of deterrence from patent application by those who can reasonably expect to be granted patents exists. Trade secret law provides far weaker protection in many respects than the patent law. While trade secret law does not forbid the discovery of the trade secret by fair and honest means, e.g., independent creation or reverse engineering, patent law operates "against the world," forbidding any use of the invention for whatever purpose for a significant length of time. The holder of a trade secret also takes a substantial risk that the secret will be passed on to his competitors, by theft or by breach of a confidential relationship, in a manner not easily susceptible of discovery or proof. Where patent law acts as a barrier, trade secret law functions relatively as a sieve. The possibility that an inventor who believes his invention meets the standards of patentability will sit back, rely on trade secret law, and after one year of use forfeit any right to patent protection, 35 U.S.C. § 102(b), is remote indeed.

Nor does society face much risk that scientific or technological progress will be impeded by the rare inventor with a patentable invention who chooses trade secret protection over patent protection. The ripeness-of-time concept of invention, developed from the study of the many independent multiple discoveries in history, predicts that if a particular individual had not made a particular discovery others would have, and in probably a relatively short period of time. If something is to be discovered at all very likely it will be discovered by more than one person. Even were an inventor to keep his discovery completely to himself, something that neither the patent nor trade secret laws forbid, there is a high probability that it will be soon independently developed. If the invention, though still a trade secret, is put into public use, the competition is alerted to the existence of the inventor's solution to the problem and may be encouraged to make an extra effort to independently find the solution thus known to be possible. The inventor faces pressures not only from private industry, but from the skilled scientists who work in our universities and our other great publicly supported centers of learning and research.

We conclude that the extension of trade secret protection to clearly patentable inventions does not conflict with the patent policy of disclosure. Perhaps because trade secret law does not produce any positive effects in the area of clearly patentable inventions, as opposed to the beneficial effects resulting from trade secret protection in the areas of the doubtfully patentable and the clearly unpatentable inventions, it has been suggested that partial pre-emption may be appropriate, and that courts should refuse to apply trade secret protection to inventions which the holder should have patented, and which would have been, thereby, disclosed. However, since there is no real possibility that trade secret law will conflict with the federal policy favoring disclosure of clearly patentable inventions partial pre-emption is inappropriate. Neither complete nor partial pre-emption of state trade secret law is justified.

NOTES

1. *Loss of Patent Right.* The majority opinion states that one who "elects" to use trade secret protection, instead of a patent, may forfeit the right to a patent, citing Patent Act § 102(b). Recall that some element of "publicness" is required to call into play the statutory bar provisions of this section. What about the non-public use of a trade secret? *See* § 102(g); query whether conscious election to rely on trade secret protection is an abandonment, suppression or concealment of an invention under this section.

2. *Skimming the Literature.* Several useful articles are cited in the original version of the preceding opinion: Doerfer, *The Limits on Trade Street Law Imposed by Federal Patent and Antitrust Supremacy*, 80 HARV. L. REV. 1432, 1454 (1967); Wydick, *Trade Secrets: Federal Preemption in Light of Goldstein and Kewanee (Part II — Conclusion)*, 56 J. PAT. OFF. SOC'Y 4, 23 (1974); Note, *Patent Preemption of Trade Secret Protection of Inventions Meeting Judicial Standards of Patentability*, 87 HARV. L. REV. 807, 828 (1974).

BONITO BOATS, INC. v. THUNDER CRAFT BOATS, INC.

489 U.S. 141, 9 U.S.P.Q.2d (BNA) 1847 (1989)

We must decide today what limits the operation of the federal patent system places on the States' ability to offer substantial protection to utilitarian and design ideas which the patent laws leave otherwise unprotected. In *Interpart Corp. v. Italia*, 777 F.2d 678 (1985), the Court of Appeals for the Federal Circuit concluded that a California law prohibiting the use of the "direct molding process" to duplicate unpatented articles posed no threat to the policies behind the federal patent laws. In this case, the Florida Supreme Court came to a contrary conclusion. It struck down a Florida statute which prohibits the use of the direct molding process to duplicate unpatented boat hulls, finding that the protection offered by the Florida law conflicted with the balance struck by Congress in the federal patent statute between the encouragement of invention and free competition in unpatented ideas. We granted certiorari to resolve the conflict, and we now affirm the judgment of the Florida Supreme Court.

In September 1976, petitioner Bonito Boats, Inc. (Bonito), a Florida corporation, developed a hull design for a fiberglass recreational boat which it marketed under the trade name Bonito Boat Model 5VBR. Designing the boat hull required substantial effort on the part of Bonito. The 5VBR was placed on the market sometime in September 1976. There is no indication in the record that a patent application was ever filed for protection of the utilitarian or design aspects of the hull, or for the process by which the hull was manufactured. The 5VBR was favorably received by the boating public, and "a broad interstate market" developed for its sale.

In May 1983, after the Bonito 5VBR had been available to the public for over six years, the Florida Legislature enacted Fla. Stat. § 559.94 (1987). The statute makes "[i]t ... unlawful for any person to use the direct molding process to duplicate for the purpose of sale any manufactured vessel hull or component part of a vessel made by another without the written permission of that other person."

On December 21, 1984, Bonito filed this action in the Circuit Court of Orange County, Florida. The complaint alleged that respondent here, Thunder Craft Boats, Inc. (Thunder Craft), a Tennessee corporation, had violated the Florida statute by using the direct molding process to duplicate the Bonito 5VBR fiberglass hull, and had knowingly sold such duplicates in violation of the Florida statute. Bonito sought "a temporary and permanent injunction." Respondent filed a motion to dismiss the complaint, arguing that under this Court's decisions in *Sears, Roebuck & Co. v. Stiffel Co.*, 376 U.S. 225 (1964), and *Compco Corp. v. Day-Brite Lighting, Inc.*, 376 U.S. 234 (1964), the Florida statute conflicted with federal patent law and was therefore invalid under the Supremacy Clause of the Federal Constitution. On appeal, a sharply divided Florida Supreme Court agreed with the lower courts' conclusion that the Florida law impermissibly interfered with the scheme established by the federal patent laws.

From their inception, the federal patent laws have embodied a careful balance between the need to promote innovation and the recognition that imitation and refinement through imitation are both necessary to invention itself and the very lifeblood of a competitive economy.

Taken together, the novelty and nonobviousness requirements [of the current patent act] express a congressional determination that the purposes behind the Patent Clause are best served by free competition and exploitation of that which is either already available to the public, or that which may be readily discerned from publicly available material. The federal patent system thus embodies a carefully crafted bargain for encouraging the creation and disclosure of new, useful, and nonobvious advances in technology and design in return for the exclusive right to practice the invention for a period of years.

The attractiveness of such a bargain, and its effectiveness in inducing creative effort and disclosure of the results of that effort, depend almost entirely on a backdrop of free competition in the exploitation of unpatented designs and innovations. The novelty and nonobviousness requirements of patentability embody a congressional understanding, implicit in the Patent Clause itself, that free exploitation of ideas will be the rule, to which the protection of a federal patent is the exception. Moreover, the ultimate goal of the patent system is to bring new designs and technologies into the public domain through disclosure. State law protection for techniques and designs whose disclosure has already been induced by market rewards may conflict with the very purpose of the patent laws by decreasing the range of ideas available as the building blocks of further innovation. The offer of federal protection from competitive exploitation of intellectual property would be rendered meaningless in a world where substantially similar state law protections were readily available. To a limited extent, the federal patent laws must determine not only what is protected, but also what is free for all to use.

Thus our past decisions have made clear that state regulation of intellectual property must yield to the extent that it clashes with the balance struck by Congress in our patent laws. The tension between the desire to freely exploit the full potential of our inventive resources and the need to create an incentive to deploy those resources is constant. Where it is clear how the patent laws strike that balance in a particular circumstance, that is not a judgment the States may second-guess. We have long held that after the expiration of a federal patent, the subject matter of the patent passes to the free use of the public as a matter of federal law. Where the public has paid the congressionally mandated price for disclosure, the States may not render the exchange fruitless by offering patent-like protection to the subject matter of the expired patent.

In our decisions in *Sears* and *Compco* we found that publicly known design and utilitarian ideas which were unprotected by patent occupied much the same position as the subject matter of an expired patent. The *Sears* case involved a pole lamp originally designed by the plaintiff Stiffel, who had secured both design and mechanical patents on the lamp. The District Court found that Stiffel's patents were invalid due to anticipation in the prior art, but nonetheless enjoined Sears from further sales of the duplicate lamps based on a finding of consumer confusion under the Illinois law of unfair competition. The Court of Appeals affirmed. This Court reversed, finding that the unlimited protection against copying which the Illinois law accorded an unpatentable item whose design had been fully disclosed through public sales conflicted with the federal policy embodied in the patent laws. A similar conclusion was reached in *Compco*, where the District Court had extended the protection of Illinois' unfair competition law to the functional aspects of an unpatented fluorescent lighting system.

The pre-emptive sweep of our decisions in *Sears* and *Compco* has been the subject of heated scholarly and judicial debate. Read at their highest level of generality, the two decisions could be taken to stand for the proposition that the States are completely disabled from offering any form of protection to articles or processes which fall within the broad scope of patentable subject matter. [T]he broadest reading of *Sears* would prohibit the States from regulating the deceptive simulation of trade dress or the tortious appropriation of private information.

That the extrapolation of such a broad pre-emptive principle from *Sears* is inappropriate is clear from the balance struck in *Sears* itself. The *Sears* Court made it plain that the States "may protect businesses in the use of their trademarks, labels, or distinctive dress in the packaging of goods so as to prevent others, by imitating such markings, from misleading purchasers as to the source of the goods." Thus, while *Sears* speaks in absolutist terms, its conclusion that the States may place some conditions on the use of trade dress indicates an implicit recognition that all state regulation of potentially patentable but unpatented subject matter is not ipso facto pre-empted by the federal patent laws.

At the heart of *Sears* and *Compco* is the conclusion that the efficient operation of the federal patent system depends upon substantially free trade in publicly known, unpatented design and utilitarian conceptions. In *Sears*, the state law offered "the equivalent of a patent monopoly," in the functional aspects of a product which had been placed in public commerce absent the protection of a valid patent. While our decisions since *Sears* have taken a decidedly less rigid view of the scope of federal pre-emption under the patent laws, e.g., *Kewanee*, we believe that the *Sears* Court correctly concluded that the States may not offer patent-like protection to intellectual creations which would otherwise remain unprotected as a matter of federal law. Both the novelty and the nonobviousness requirements of federal patent law are grounded in the notion that concepts within the public grasp, or those so obvious that they readily could be, are the tools of creation available to all. They provide the baseline of free competition upon which the patent system's incentive to creative effort depends. A state law that substantially interferes with the enjoyment of an unpatented utilitarian or design conception which has been freely disclosed by its author to the public at large impermissibly contravenes the ultimate goal of public disclosure and use which is the centerpiece of federal patent policy. Moreover, through the creation of patent-like rights, the States could essentially redirect inventive efforts away from the careful criteria of patentability developed by Congress over the last 200 years. We understand this to be the reasoning at the core of our decisions in *Sears* and *Compco*, and we reaffirm that reasoning today.

We believe that the Florida statute at issue in this case so substantially impedes the public use of the otherwise unprotected design and utilitarian ideas embodied in unpatented boat hulls as to run afoul of the teaching of our decisions.

In contrast to the operation of unfair competition law, the Florida statute is aimed directly at preventing the exploitation of the design and utilitarian conceptions embodied in the product itself. The sparse legislative history surrounding its enactment indicates that it was intended to create an inducement for the improvement of boat hull designs. To accomplish this goal, the Florida statute endows the original boat hull manufacturer with rights against the world, similar in scope and operation to the rights accorded a federal patentee. Like the patentee, the beneficiary of the Florida statute may prevent a competitor from "making" the product in what is evidently the most efficient manner available and from "selling" the product when it is produced in that fashion.

In this case, the Bonito 5VBR fiberglass hull has been freely exposed to the public for a period in excess of six years. For purposes of federal law, it stands in the same stead as an item for which a patent has expired or been denied: it is unpatented and unpatentable. Whether because of a determination of unpatentability or other commercial concerns, petitioner chose to expose its hull design to the public in the marketplace, eschewing the bargain held out by the federal patent system of disclosure in exchange for exclusive use. Yet, the Florida statute allows petitioner to reassert a substantial property right in the idea, thereby constricting the spectrum of useful public knowledge. Moreover, it does so without the careful protections of high standards of innovation and limited monopoly contained in the federal scheme.

That the Florida statute does not remove all means of reproduction and sale does not eliminate the conflict with the federal scheme. In essence, the Florida law prohibits the entire public from engaging in a form of reverse engineering of a product in the public domain. This is clearly one of the rights vested in the federal patent holder, but has never been a part of state protection under the law of unfair competition or trade secrets. The duplication of boat hulls and their component parts may be an essential part of innovation in the field of hydrodynamic design. Variations as to size and combination of various elements may lead to significant advances in the field. Reverse engineering of chemical and mechanical articles in the public domain often leads to significant advances in technology. If Florida may prohibit this particular method of study and recomposition of an unpatented article, we fail to see the principle that would prohibit a State from banning the use of chromatography in the reconstitution of unpatented chemical compounds, or the use of robotics in the duplication of machinery in the public domain.

Moreover, as we noted in *Kewanee*, the competitive reality of reverse engineering may act as a spur to the inventor, creating an incentive to develop inventions that meet the rigorous requirements of patentability. The Florida statute substantially reduces this competitive incentive, thus eroding the general rule of free competition upon which the attractiveness of the federal patent bargain depends. The protections of state trade secret law are most effective at the developmental stage, before a product has been marketed and the threat of reverse engineering becomes real. During this period, patentability will often be an uncertain prospect, and to a certain extent, the protection offered by trade secret law may "dovetail" with the incentives created by the federal patent monopoly. See Goldstein, *Kewanee Oil Co. v. Bicron Corp.: Notes on a Closing Circle*, 1974 Sup. Ct. Rev. 81, 92.

Finally, allowing the States to create patent-like rights in various products in public circulation would lead to administrative problems of no small dimension. The federal patent scheme provides a basis for the public to ascertain the status of the intellectual property embodied in any article in general circulation.

The Florida scheme blurs this clear federal demarcation between public and private property. One of the fundamental purposes behind the Patent and Copyright Clauses of the Constitution was to promote national uniformity in the realm of intellectual property. See The Federalist No. 43, p. 309 (B. Wright ed. 1961). Since the Patent Act of 1800, Congress has lodged exclusive jurisdiction of actions "arising under" the patent laws in the federal courts, thus allowing for the development of a uniform body of law in resolving the constant tension between private right and public access. See 28 U.S.C. § 1338. This purpose is frustrated by the Florida scheme, which renders the status of the design and utilitarian "ideas" embodied in the boat hulls it protects uncertain. Given the inherently ephemeral nature of property in ideas, and the great power such property has to cause harm to the competitive policies which underlay the federal patent laws, the demarcation of broad zones of public and private right is "the type of regulation that demands a uniform national rule." Absent such a federal rule, each State could afford patent-like protection to particularly favored home industries, effectively insulating them from competition from outside the State.

Petitioner and its supporting amici place great weight on the contrary decision of the Court of Appeals for the Federal Circuit in *Interpart Corp. v. Italia*. In upholding the application of the California "antidirect molding" statute to the duplication of unpatented automobile mirrors, the Federal Circuit stated: "The statute prevents unscrupulous competitors from obtaining a product and using it as the 'plug' for making a mold. The statute does not prohibit copying the design of the product in any other way; the latter if in the public domain, is free for anyone to make, use or sell." 777 F.2d, at 685. The court went on to indicate that "the patent laws 'say nothing about the right to copy or the right to use, they speak only in terms of the right to exclude.'" *Ibid.*, quoting *Mine Safety Appliances Co. v. Electric Storage Battery Co.*, 56 C.C.P.A. (Pat.) 863, 864, n.2, 405 F.2d 901, 902, n.2 (1969).

We find this reasoning defective in several respects. The Federal Circuit apparently viewed the direct molding statute at issue in *Interpart* as a mere regulation of the use of chattels. Yet, the very purpose of antidirect molding statutes is to "reward" the "inventor" by offering substantial protection against public exploitation of his or her idea embodied in the product. Such statutes would be an exercise in futility if they did not have precisely the effect of substantially limiting the ability of the public to exploit an otherwise unprotected idea.

The States are simply not free in this regard to offer equivalent protections to ideas which Congress has determined should belong to all. For almost 100 years it has been well established that in the case of an expired patent, the federal patent laws do create a federal right to "copy and to use." Affirmed.

NOTES

1. For more on the *Sears-Compco* doctrine, see Symposium, *Product Simulation: A Right or a Wrong?*, 64 COLUM. L. REV. 1178 (1964).

2. *Empirical Premises Questioned.* A recent article criticizes the opinion in *Bonito* on the grounds that it assumes, without any real information, that the Florida statute will "divert" inventors away from the patent system and toward reliance on state protection. *See* Wiley, *Bonito Boats: Uninformed But Mandatory*

Innovation Policy, 1989 SUP. CT. REV. 283 (1989). *But see* Shipley, *Refusing to Rock the Boat: The Sears/Compco Preemption Doctrine Applied to Bonito Boats v. Thunder Craft*, 25 WAKE FOREST L. REV. 385 (1990) (defending decision as consistent application of *Sears-Compco*).

1. A NOTE ON THE "CROWDING OUT RATIONALE" FOR PREEMPTION

The Court gave several justifications for its holdings. The discussion here will focus on only one rationale, which will be referred to as the "crowding out" theory.

According to the Supreme Court, state laws that protect the same subject matter as is protected by federal patent law have the potential to re-direct inventive efforts away from potentially patentable research. Presumably this might "distort" research in directions contrary to those desired by Congress when it passed the Patent Act. As a consequence, it is implicit in the scheme of the federal patent system that state protection not get "too close," because this might divert research that would have been directed toward potentially patentable inventions.

The problem with this thinking is that it assumes that when researchers make decisions about where to invest, they choose between two mutually exclusive types of research: potentially patentable, and non-patentable. The Supreme Court envisions a world where inventors might "slack off," stopping their research efforts short of what is needed to achieve a patent, if they can get "equivalent" protection for less ambitious research. If such protection is available, they will invest in less ambitious, presumably "safer," projects; this will reduce the amount of "patent-oriented" research and cut into the volume of patents as well. (This view of things also assumes that Congress has determined that the extra effort required to make something patentable makes that thing more valuable as well.)

Are any of these assumptions true? Only the last one, perhaps; Congress does ask something significant of an inventor who would obtain a patent, whereas state protection schemes often require something more modest, as in *Bonito Boats*. As to the other assumptions, it appears that most researchers do research first, and then consider various legal options for protecting it. One reason they do this is clear: *it is impossible in most cases to tell whether a particular project or project type is of the "patentable" variety or not.* Only when the researcher has the initial experimental results in hand does she turn to the patent attorney for guidance. Only at this point does she know whether she has something patentable or not. Although many researchers take patents into account in deciding which projects to pursue, it is not a major factor. Nor can it be, since patents are granted for results, not plans.

Seen in this light, state intellectual property laws are not a threat for the reasons identified by the Court. In fact, state protection might actually increase the amount of research firms take on — and ultimately the number of patents too!

This is because state intellectual property laws may increase the overall incentives faced by the firm trying to decide whether to engage in a research project or not. If the incentive is greater, more research will be undertaken. And if more research is undertaken, more *patentable* research will result.

The preceding point can be restated as follows. The Supreme Court pictures an inventor faced with two urns, one marked "potentially patentable" and the other marked "state protection." The Court's point is that increasing the value of a ball picked from the second urn will decrease the number of balls chosen from the first urn. My point is that in some cases, and perhaps most cases, the inventor *does not know* which type of urn she is facing; in fact, it is as though she were presented with one large urn, in which some of the balls are marked "patentable" and the others "state protection." Because she does not know at the outset of the game which type of ball she will pick, an increase in the value of *either type* of ball will increase her expected return and thus increase the number of balls she is willing to pick.

This is a more accurate representation of the choices facing many inventors. Consequently one must recognize that state intellectual property laws may have an effect *opposite* of that stated by the Court: they may increase the number of "draws" from the undifferentiated urn marked "potential inventions," therefore increasing the number of patentable as well as state-protectable inventions.

This is not to say that the Court was wrong in its holding in *Bonito Boats*. On the contrary, there will often be federalism-based concerns that are implicated by a system of state intellectual property laws. But the "crowding out" theory used by the Court may be wrong, at least in some cases, and therefore should not be used to justify a strong patent pre-emption position.

2. FEDERALISM AND PREEMPTION

A larger economic perspective might illuminate this case in a number of ways. For example, one way to conceptualize what the Florida legislature did is as follows. It might have reached the conclusion that the boat industry was facing ever-higher design costs in an otherwise competitive industry. The California legislature, for instance, apparently concluded that it cost a producer $40,000 to design a mold, but competitors could make direct-copy molds for as little as $1,000. *See* Sganga, *Direct Molding Statutes: Potent Weapons, But Are They Constitutional?*, 71 J. PAT. & TRADEMARK OFF. SOC'Y 70, 71-72 (1989). The problem, from this point of view, would be how to get boat companies to make new hulls under such circumstances. The absence of patent protection for designs, as well as the fact that the process itself is old and thus unpatentable, make federal law unavailing. The options are then (1) a direct subsidy, or (2) a state intellectual property right.

The legislature might well conclude that the second option is better, because it does not cost the state government any money directly. It can be expected to raise the price of boats sold by companies that would have copied the design if that had been legal. But, since those companies can still "reverse engineer" the original hull design — only the direct molding process is prohibited, not exacting duplication by other means — their design costs may yet be lower than those of the firm that designed the hull. For argument's sake, say the costs with non-direct molding reverse engineering duplication are $20,000.

Under these facts, the statute will raise the average cost of this design from $20,500 ($40,000 plus $1,000 divided by the two firms) to $30,000 ($40,000 plus $20,000 divided by two). The increase of $9,500 in the average cost will be largely taken from consumers, who will pay more for boats sold by the copyist/reverse engineering firm. The legislature will have decided, in effect, that this expense was worthwhile to get more boat hull designs.

This sounds like the kind of decision legislatures make all the time. Why should we question it in this context?

The answer lies in an area touched on by the *Bonito* court: "Absent ... a federal rule, each State could afford patent-like protection to particularly favored home industries, effectively insulating them from competition from outside the State." In the example given above, the danger is that the original design firms may all be in-state, and the copyists (and most consumers) may be out of state. The effect of the statute in this circumstance would be to raise the average design cost — and thus the price of boats — in states other than those where the legislature sits.

In an era when states are taking the initiative in promoting a number of industries seen as important, the rationale just elaborated could be invoked in a wide range of situations. For example, some economists have investigated the extent to which intellectual property protection and direct subsidies are interchangeable. *See* Wright, *The Economics of Invention Incentives: Patents, Prizes, and Research Contracts*, 73 AM. ECON. REV. 691 (1983). Would the Court question a direct subsidy to boat hull designers in the amount of $20,000 for making a new design? If not, how could the impact of such a subsidy be distinguished from that of the statute at issue in *Bonito*? (Hint: the subsidy would presumably be financed by taxes on instate activities, while under the facts presented the state intellectual property right would raise the loss of *out-of-staters*. These are just some of the interesting questions which the Court's rationale suggests.

This federalism aspect of the case thus seems most important. Even before the drafting of the Constitution, the need for a *uniform* national agency was no doubt felt. This was due in no small part to the controversy over steamboat patents raging at the time. In the 1770s and '80s, two rival inventors, James Fitch and Charles Rumney, each claimed they had invented a workable steamboat. As was the custom in colonial times, they sought protection for their inventions at the state level. The result was that, as each presented his case to a new state legislature, conflicting and overlapping monopolies were granted. To clarify their rights, each then sought special legislation from the federal government, then operating under the Articles of Confederation.

The situation was quite confused, and the factors surrounding each inventor's claim were hotly disputed. The battle for credit as to priority of invention was fought in individual meetings with each federal representative, as well as by the publication of pamphlets advocating the "true" story of the steamboat's invention. Even George Washington was involved, first as a backer of Rumsey then as an informal arbitrator in the dispute. But because the status of federal grants at this time was unclear, not much progress was made. Nevertheless, the steamboat case, with its complex facts pleaded to legislators, was said to be a major impetus behind the call for a uniform national patent system in the Constitution and then in the first Congress. And the 1790 Patent Act was among the first orders of business taken up in the new federal legislature.

The need for an inherently *federal* patent system was thus recognized from very early on. It was, in fact, part of a larger felt need for national standards to govern interstate commerce. *See* R. MORRIS, THE FORGING OF THE UNION: 1781-1789 (1987). Indeed, one of the foundational cases giving broad compass to the commerce clause of the Constitution grew out of the conflict over state monopolies granted to the rival steamboat inventors discussed above. *See Gibbons v. Ogden*, 22 U.S. (9 Wheat.) 1 (1824). Arguably, *Bonito Boats* simply updates this theme — recall the Court's reference to "administrative problems of no small dimension" — and provides a necessary tonic to the subtle state encroachment on important national turf.

OVERVIEW OF DESIGN PATENTS*

Due to a lengthy processing time, high application cost, strict and wavering standards, and a long history of judicial hostility, the design patent system has been criticized as ineffective and in need of reform. J.H. Reichman, *Design Protection and the New Technologies: The United States Experience in a Transnational Perspective*, 19 U. BALT. L. REV. 6, 23 (1991). As the courts have recently become more receptive to design patents, interest has been renewed in this form of intellectual property protection. This section provides a basic introduction to the design patent system.

A design may consist of surface ornamentation, configuration, or both. The Design Patent Act was codified under the Patent Act of 1954 in 35 U.S.C. § 171, which allows a design patent to be obtained for "any new, original and ornamental design for an article of manufacture ..." and provides that all provisions relating to patents for inventions also apply to design patents. Design patents are issued for a fourteen-year term.

I. Requirements for Patentability

A design is patentable if it meets the usual requirements for patentability (novelty, nonobviousness, etc.) and, in addition, is ornamental and not dictated by functional considerations. The Patent and Trademark Office defines a design as "the visual characteristics or aspects displayed by the object. It is the appearance presented by the object which creates a visual impact upon the mind of the observer." U.S. Patent and Trademark Office, *Manual of Patent Examining Procedure* § 1502 (5th ed. rev. 8, 1988).

The statute provides that the design must appear on an "article of manufacture." This includes silverware, *Gorham Mfg. Co. v. White*, 81 U.S. (14 Wall.) 511 (1871); cement mixers, *In re Koehring*, 37 F.2d 241 (C.C.P.A. 1930); furniture, *In re Rosen*, 673 F.2d 388 (C.C.P.A. 1982); and containers for liquids, *Unette Corp. v. Unit Pack Co.*, 785 F.2d 1026 (Fed. Cir. 1986).

A. Novelty

Novelty is established if no prior art shows exactly the same design. A design is novel if the "ordinary observer," viewing the new design as a whole, would consider it to be different from, rather than a modification of, an already existing

---

*With Janine McGrath.

design. *See, e.g., Clark Equip. Co. v. Keller*, 570 F.2d 778, 799 (8th Cir. 1978). Although the § 102(b) statutory bars apply, i.e., there is a one-year grace period, there is no "experimental use" exception for design patents. *See Tone Bros. v. Sysco*, 23 U.S.P.Q. (BNA) 1184 (S.D. Iowa 1992).

B. Nonobviousness

Because Section 171 provides that the provisions of Title 35 relating to utility patents also apply to design patents, a design must be nonobvious, which requires the "exercise of the inventive or originative faculty." *Smith v. Whitman*, 148 U.S. 674, 679 (1893).

Prior to the adoption of a uniform standard to determine nonobviousness in design patents, the courts were in conflict over whether to use an "ordinary designer" standard or that of an "ordinary intelligent man" when applying the *Graham* test. *See In re Laverne*, 356 F.2d 1003 (C.C.P.A. 1966). Determining the nonobviousness of a design patent, as opposed to a utility patent, is unpredictable, as it is an inherently subjective inquiry, depending largely on personal taste. In evaluating nonobviousness of utility patents, judges can measure the distance between the prior art and a new invention on the basis of uniform scientific criteria and technical data, while the evaluation of the distance between an appearance design and its predecessors necessarily involves "value judgments that are hard to quantify and unreliable at best." Reichman, *supra*, at 33 n.164. *See In re Bartlett*, 300 F.2d 942, 944 (C.C.P.A. 1962) (noting that the determination of patentability in design cases depends on the subjective conclusion of each judge). The requirement of nonobviousness has been cited as a primary factor in limiting the availability of design protection in the United States from the 1920's on. Reichman, *supra*, at 24. The Federal Circuit's liberalization of the nonobviousness requirement has lowered the invalidation rate of design patents from seventy-five to one hundred percent only a few years ago, to thirty-eight percent today. *Id*. at 37.

In 1981, the Court of Customs and Patent Appeals held that the *Graham* test applies to design patents, and that nonobviousness should be measured in terms of a "designer of ordinary capability who designs articles of the type presented in the application." *In re Nalbandian*, 661 F.2d 1214, 1216 (C.C.P.A. 1981). The new standard allows for objective evidence of expert testimony from designers in the field to be used to prove nonobviousness. *Id*. at 1217. The Federal Circuit subsequently adopted this standard. While this approach appears more evenhanded and has led to more patents being upheld as valid, it may not solve the problem of unpredictability, because the opinions of different designers can vary considerably. William T. Fryer, III, *Industrial Design Protection in the United States of America — Present Situation and Plans for Revision*, 70 J. PAT. & TRADEMARK OFF. SOC'Y 821, 829 (1988).

The Federal Circuit emphasized the presumptive validity of a design patent and placed the burden on the challenger to come forward with clear and convincing proof of nonobviousness. *See, e.g., Trans-World Mfg. Corp. v. Al Nyman & Sons*, 750 F.2d 1552, 1559-60 (Fed. Cir. 1984); *Avia Group Int'l v. L.A. Gear Cal.*, 853 F.2d 1557, 1562 (Fed. Cir. 1988). The court also upheld the notion that, to find obviousness, reference must be made to prior art with the same over-all appearance of the patented design rather than referring to a combination of features from several references. *Litton Sys., Inc. v. Whirlpool Corp.*, 728 F.2d 1423, 1443 (Fed. Cir. 1984). Most significantly, the Federal Circuit held that objective secondary considerations, such as commercial success and copying, which apply to utility patents, are relevant to determining nonobviousness of design patents. *See, e.g., Litton*, 728 F.2d at 1441; *Avia*, 853 F.2d at 1564. The theory supporting the consideration of commercial success is that the purpose of a design patent is to increase salability, so if a design has been a success it "must have been sufficiently novel and superior to attract attention." *Robert W. Brown & Co. v. De Bell*, 243 F.2d 200, 202 (9th Cir. 1957); *see also* 1 DONALD S. CHISUM, PATENTS § 1.04[2][f], at 1-208 (1992). Evidence of commercial success must be related to the patented design rather than to factors such as functional improvement or advertising. *See, e.g., Litton*, 728 F.2d at 1443; *Avia*, 853 F.2d at 1564.

C. Ornamentality

A patentable design must be ornamental — it must create a pleasing appear-ance. To satisfy the requirement of ornamentality, a design "must be the product of aesthetic skill and artistic conception." *Blisscraft of Hollywood v. United Plastics Co.*, 294 F.2d 694, 696 (2d Cir. 1964). This requirement has been met by articles which are outside the realm of traditional "art." *See In re Koehring*, 37 F.2d 421, 422 (C.C.P.A. 1930) (determining a design for a cement mixer to be ornamental because it "possessed more grace and pleasing appearance" than prior art). A number of cases have denied patentability to designs which are concealed during the normal use of an object on the basis that ornamentality requires the design to be visible while the object is in its normal and intended use. *See* CHISUM, *supra,* § 1.04[2][c], at 1-190-91.

D. Functionality

If a design is "primarily functional rather than ornamental," or is "dictated by functional considerations," it is not patentable. *Power Controls Corp. v. Hybri-netics, Inc.*, 806 F.2d 234, 238 (Fed. Cir. 1986). The functionality rule furthers the purpose of the design patent statute, which is to promote the decorative arts. In addition, the rule prevents granting in essence a monopoly to functional features that do not meet the requirements of a utility patent. Recognizing that strict application of the functionality rule would invalidate the majority of modern designs, the Federal Circuit validated designs with a higher functionality factor than had been tolerated by the courts previously. Reichman, *supra*, at 40. This is evidenced in cases upholding design patents for an eyeglass display rack, *Trans-World Mfg. Corp. v. Al Nyman & Sons*, 750 F.2d 1552 (Fed. Cir. 1984); fiberglass camper shells, *Fiberglass in Motion, Inc. v. Hindelang*, No. 83-1266 (Fed. Cir., Apr. 19, 1984) (LEXIS, Genfed library, USApp file); and containers for dispensing liquids, *Unette Corp. v. Unit Pack Co.*, 785 F.2d 1026 (Fed. Cir. 1986). The Federal Circuit has held that a design may have functional components as long as the design does not embody a function that is necessary to compete in the market. *Avia*, 853 F.2d at 1563. If the functional aspect of a design may be achieved by other design techniques, then it is not primarily functional. *Id*. This more flexible approach reflects a recognition by the court that the majority of valuable industrial designs that should be granted protection in order to stimulate economic growth are a combination of functional and aesthetic features.

II. Claim Requirements and Procedure

Two major criticisms of the design patent system in the United States are that it is too expensive and that protection takes too long to obtain. *See* Fryer, *supra*, at 834; Reichman, *supra*, at 24 (procedural requirements make design protection in the United States much "slower and costlier to obtain" than in other countries); Perry J. Saidman, *Design Patents — The Whipping Boy Bites Back*, 73 J. PAT. & TRADEMARK OFF. SOC'Y 859 (1991) (defending these criticisms).

In 1988, the cost of a design patent application was estimated at $1,000. Fryer, *supra*, at 835. A large part of this cost is the expense of preparing the drawings which constitute the claim. The drawings "must contain a sufficient number of views to constitute a complete disclosure of the appearance of the article." 37 C.F.R. § 1.152. All that is required in writing is a very brief description of the drawings. The adequate disclosure and definiteness of the claim required by Section 112 are accomplished by the drawings. No more than one claim may be included in a design application. An application may illustrate more than one embodiment of a design only if the embodiments involve a "single inventive concept" and can be protected by a single claim. *In re Rubenfield*, 270 F.2d 391, 396 (C.C.P.A. 1959).

Design patents normally issue two to three years after filing. Saidman, *supra*, at 861. This leaves a design patent applicant without any protection from copiers during this long waiting period, as opposed to copyright protection which requires no initial procedural requirement and takes only a few months for registration to be issued. Fryer, *supra*, at 840, 835. It has been noted that the current system is "unsuited to the fast-moving but short-lived product cycle characteristic of today's market for mass-produced consumer goods." Reichman, *supra*, at 24. While there is general agreement that a new form of protection for industrial design is needed, Congress has yet to adopt any of the proposed legislation. An example of proposed legislation that would afford better protection for designs is Design Copyright Protection, which employs a modified copyright form of protection as an alternative to the design patent. *See* Fryer, *supra*, at 839-46. Alternatively, proposed legislation would protect functional industrial designs, including those that are neither aesthetically nor technically innovative. Reichman, *supra*, at 121-22.

III. Infringement

The standard for finding infringement of a design patent was defined in *Gorham Mfg. Co. v. White*, where the Supreme Court held that "if in the eye of an ordinary observer, giving such attention as a purchaser usually gives, two designs are substantially the same, if the resemblance is such as to deceive such an observer, inducing him to purchase one supposing it to be the other, the first one patented is infringed by the other." 81 U.S. (14 Wall.) 511, 528 (1872).

The "eye of the ordinary observer" standard continues to be the rule. *See Oakley, Inc. v. International Tropic-Cal, Inc.*, 923 F.2d 167, 169 (Fed. Cir. 1991). The ordinary observer is one who has "reasonable familiarity" with the object in question and is capable of making a comparison to other objects which have preceded it. *Applied Arts Corp. v. Grand Rapids Metalcraft Corp.*, 67 F.2d 428, 430 (6th Cir. 1933). The key factor is similarity, rather than consumer confusion. *Unette*, 785 F.2d at 1029 (holding that "likelihood of confusion as to the source of goods is not a necessary or appropriate factor for determining infringement of a design patent.").

The second prong of the infringement analysis is the "point of novelty" test, which is distinct from the issue of similarity. Under the "point of novelty" test, the similarity found by the ordinary observer must be attributable to the novel elements of the patented design which distinguish it from prior art. *Litton*, 728 F.2d at 1444; *Avia*, 853 F.2d at 1565; *FMC Corp. v. Hennessy Indus., Inc.*, 836 F.2d 521, 527 (Fed. Cir. 1987). Unless the accused design appropriates the novel features of the patented design, there has been no infringement. *Avia*, 853 F.2d at 1565. The scope of the patented claim, and its points of novelty, are determined by examining the field of the prior art. *See Litton*, 728 F.2d at 1444 (holding that where the field of prior art is "crowded," the scope of a claim will be construed narrowly).

After determining the scope of the patented claim, the infringement inquiry focuses only on the protectable aesthetic components of a patented design. *See Lee v. Dayton-Hudson Corp.*, 838 F.2d 1186, 1188 (Fed. Cir. 1988) (holding that "it is the non-functional, design aspects that are pertinent to determinations of infringement"). Thus, this test permits strong similarities to be excused if the defendant can prove that she borrowed "only commonplace or generic ideas, functional features, or other nonprotectable matter" while adding sufficient variation to protectable elements of the design. Reichman, *supra*, at 44.

Whether a design is infringed when it is used on an entirely different type of article than the patented one has not been settled. CHISUM, *supra*, § 1.04[4], at 1-225. In *Avia Group Int'l v. L.A. Gear Cal.*, where the patented design was for an adult athletic shoe and the accused design was for a children's shoe, the court found infringement, and held that even in a situation where the patent holder has not put out a product, or where the patented design is embodied in a product that does not compete with the patent holder's product, a finding of infringement is not precluded. 853 F.2d at 1565. This decision indicates that the Federal Circuit is willing to extend design patent protection beyond "literal infringement" and protect the design concept itself. Reichman, *supra,* at 53.

Table of Cases

References are to page numbers. Principal cases and the pages
where they appear are set out in italics.

Index

A

B

E

F

FALSE MARKING OF PATENT, pp. 1097, 1098.

FEDERAL PREEMPTION OF STATE LAW.
Trade secrets, pp. 1271 to 1287.

FIELD-OF-USE LIMITATIONS, p. 1152.
Licensing of government inventions, pp. 1204 to 1208.

FILE WRAPPER.
Infringement claims, pp. 826, 827.

FINANCIAL SERVICES INDUSTRY.
Business methods, pp. 139 to 157.
Economic patent rationales, pp. 154 to 157.
Potential impact of patents, pp. 152, 153.
Traditional patent prohibition, p. 154.

FIRST SALE DOCTRINE.
Right of patentee to limit sales, pp. 1144, 1145.

FIRST TO FILE, pp. 37, 38.
Double patenting, order of filing, pp. 798 to 807.

FIRST TO INVENT, pp. 37, 38.

FOREIGN FILING LICENSES, pp. 458, 459.

FOREIGN PRIORITY.
See INTERNATIONAL PRIORITY.

FOUR CORNERS TEST, p. 237.

FRAUD.
Antitrust violations.
    Fraudulent acquisition as antitrust defense, pp. 1152 to 1154.
    Fraudulent procurement as antitrust violation, p. 763.
Fraudulent use inventions, pp. 210 to 213.
Inequitable conduct generally.
    See INEQUITABLE CONDUCT.

FUNCTIONALITY.
Overview of design patents, Appx. I(D).

FUNCTIONAL LANGUAGE.
Claims, pp. 721 to 723.

G

GENERAL AGREEMENT ON TARIFFS AND TRADE (GATT).
Double patenting, pp. 806, 807.
Patentable subject matter, pp. 110, 157, 158.
Summary of changes to United States law, p. 41.
Trade related aspects of intellectual property (TRIPs).
    Effect on patent terms, pp. 41, 42.
    Negotiations, pp. 39, 40.

GENERAL UTILITY, p. 189.

GENUS/SPECIES ISSUES.
Chemical cases, pp. 634 to 636.
Double patenting, p. 803.

GOVERNMENT INVENTIONS.
Licensing.
    Antitrust and patent misuse, pp. 1204 to 1208.

J

K

L

M

U

V

W

WRITTEN DESCRIPTION.
Printed matter rule, p. 76.
Requirement, pp. 702 to 714.

DATE DUE